THE NIXON TAPES: 1973

THE NIXON TAPES

1973

Edited and annotated by

Douglas Brinkley *and* Luke A. Nichter

Houghton Mifflin Harcourt

BOSTON   NEW YORK

2015

For information about permission to reproduce selections from this book,
write to Permissions, Houghton Mifflin Harcourt Publishing Company,
215 Park Avenue South, New York, New York 10003.

www.hmhco.com

Library of Congress Cataloging-in-Publication Data is available.
ISBN 978-0-544-61053-8

Printed in the United States of America
DOC 10 9 8 7 6 5 4 3 2 1

For two special daughters,
Benton Brinkley and Ava Anne Nichter

CONTENTS

INTRODUCTION

On January 20, 1973, Richard Nixon was inaugurated for his second term as U.S. president. Speaking in front of twenty thousand spectators and tens of millions of TV viewers, the sixty-year-old Nixon was on top of the world. There was something for everybody in the inaugural speech. For anti–Vietnam War liberals, Nixon spoke about being on the "threshold of a new era of peace." Conservatives were treated to a line that anticipated the Reagan Revolution: "Government must learn to take less from people so that people can do more for themselves." Nixon, having trounced George McGovern in the 1972 election by a margin of 520 electoral votes to 17, even brazenly appropriated the most celebrated phrase from President John F. Kennedy's 1961 address and made it his own. "In our own lives, let each of us ask not just what will government do for me," Nixon said, "but what can I do for myself?"

Although the euphoric Nixon was hatless on his inauguration day and the temperature was in the low forties, storm clouds were gathering in the distance. Just twelve days earlier the trial of the five burglars arrested at the Watergate offices of the Democratic National Committee, as well as two accomplices, had begun. All of Nixon's men were under legal duress. Howard Hunt pleaded guilty on January 11. Only four days later Bernard Barker, Frank Sturgis, Eugenio Martinez, and Virgilio Gonzalez did the same. That was the beginning of the end for the Nixon administration; the investigation would intensify further over the next eighteen months, consuming everything in its path. As *The Nixon Tapes: 1973* demonstrates, the president, before his second term ever began, was hostage to the Watergate crisis.

Nixon's fall from grace has been referred to as a Shakespearean tragedy. Because Gerald Ford pardoned Nixon, we may never learn the full truth of Watergate. Yet it is unlikely that Nixon could have gone to trial, whether in the Senate or as a result of a later criminal or civil case. Classified information would have had to be made public, which would have been unacceptable to the CIA, FBI, NSA, and other government agencies. Nixon had to be pardoned.

A Nixon show trial would also have been damaging to the presidency as an institution. After Harry Truman's death in December 1972 and Lyndon Johnson's a month later, Nixon went through Watergate alone. While Nixon's predecessors would not have defended abuses of power, they could have launched a bipartisan defense of the presidency, executive privilege, and Nixon's secret tapes. After all, Nixon's predecessors had also secretly taped, and their tapes remained their personal property, just as Nixon had expected his tapes to remain when his system was installed.

But because of Ford's act there was no trial. Instead, there was a series of proxy trials for the rest of the 1970s, the most significant being the Church Committee and *U.S. v. Gray, Felt, Miller.* These proceedings — during which virtually every living high-ranking figure testified — focused on a quarter-century of abuses of governmental power, including assassinations of foreign leaders, wiretapping, domestic surveillance, and illegal invasions of Americans' privacy. As of this publication, despite numerous Freedom of Information Act requests, the Church Committee records remain sealed.

When listening to the Nixon tapes of 1973, it is impossible not to hear growing paranoia in the president's voice. Nixon's greatest downfall, in fact, was his lack of trust in subordinates. If he had had a more trustworthy staff, he wouldn't have created the White House Plumbers Unit, which set him apart from the opposition research teams of Kennedy and Johnson. If Nixon had simply used the FBI, CIA, and NSA the ways his predecessors had, his tally of law-breaking offenses wouldn't have been so substantial. Indeed, his lack of trust in those three national security agencies led directly to the creation of the Plumbers on his authority, derived from the Huston Plan (which had been created by the leaders of the FBI, CIA, and NSA in coordination with the White House).

Even with the publication of this volume many mysteries regarding Watergate remain unsolved more than forty years later. Who ordered the break-in? What were the burglars looking for? Why did so many have FBI or CIA backgrounds? Ideally in the coming years, a large number of the remaining Nixon tapes, as well as other records currently restricted from public access, will finally become available. Judge John Sirica tried to get answers to some of these questions, getting to motive, but in one case the testimony of the government's star witness, Al Baldwin, remains sealed. "The question will arise, undoubtedly," Sirica said, "what was the motive for doing what you people say you did."

One of the great tragedies revealed in this book is the refusal of Dean Mitchell, Haldeman, and Ehrlichman to level honestly with Nixon following the break-in when the crisis was still manageable. The White House staff's instinct was to keep details from Nixon in order to protect him, but they ended up fatally wounding his presidency. Nixon should have put his advisors in a White House conference room and told them to reveal the complete story of the Watergate break-in. Instead, as is made clear in this book, the first time Nixon did this was March 22, 1973, and by then everyone was turning on each other. By April, every major White House figure had a defense attorney, and many were cooperating with the prosecutors.

From the final batch of Nixon tapes released by the National Archives in August 2013, featured in this book, it is abundantly clear that the Watergate break-in was part of a much larger coordinated effort related to domestic intelligence. This effort was based on the Huston Plan, a forty-three-page report that was cobbled together by an ad hoc committee formed from the intelligence agencies and chaired by J. Edgar Hoover. Thanks to Edward Snowden, we know more about NSA abuses of power today than in the Nixon era. The Huston Plan and related correspondence remain classified as "Top Secret."

An overall impression this book offers is that Nixon didn't really care about Watergate, since he wasn't directly involved in the break-in or the planning of it. But he cared an awful lot about what Watergate might uncover — and almost did: the seventeen Kissinger/Haig wiretaps beginning in 1969 designed to stop leaks related to U.S.-Soviet arms talks; the Huston Plan; and the military spy ring overseen by Joint Chiefs of Staff chairman Thomas Moorer, which uncovered a pattern of thefts of highly classified documents from Henry Kissinger's briefcase. The full details of these remain classified today and involve the most top-secret levels of the intelligence community. Nixon alluded to their importance in his 1975 grand jury testimony, which was made public only in November 2011.

In 1973 historian Arthur M. Schlesinger Jr. published his classic *The Imperial Presidency*, warning of an Executive Branch run amok, willing to shred the Constitution in order to acquire power. What Nixon most worried about being uncovered during the Watergate crisis of 1973 was not his high crimes and misdemeanors, or even the "imperial presidency" itself, but a kind of shadow government — similar to President Dwight D. Eisenhower's "military-industrial complex" — a partnership between the White House and intelligence agencies that had been growing since the beginning of the Cold War, nurtured by leaders of both political parties.

During the spring of 1973, one of Nixon's last hopes was that William Sullivan — the former FBI chief of domestic intelligence who was in line to replace J. Edgar Hoover until they had a falling-out during the fall of 1971 — would protect his presidency. Sullivan knew all about the seventeen Kissinger/Haig wiretaps, the Huston Plan, and the military spy ring. Therefore, Nixon, a gambler, bet that making Sullivan the head of the FBI in 1973, to replace L. Patrick Gray, would protect him, his secrets, and the presidency. Sullivan's name has popped up over the years, but never with proper historical context. What Nixon didn't realize was that Sullivan — the only high-ranking liberal Democrat at the FBI — had turned on the White House by May 1973. Since he died in a hunting accident in 1977, Sullivan could not be called to testify and tell his side of the story during *U.S. v. Gray, Felt, Miller*.

The last thirteen months of Nixon's presidency were never taped. We have no real-time record of Vice President Spiro Agnew's resignation, the Yom Kippur War, the Washington Energy Conference, House Republican leader Gerald Ford becoming vice president, or Nixon's historic trip to NATO and the Middle East during the summer of 1974. Yet, there are plenty of interesting foreign policy moments on the tapes from January to July 1973 that are included in this volume. The 1973 Superpower Summit in Washington, DC, when Nixon hosted Leonid Brezhnev on American soil for the first time, was a historic breakthrough in the realm of détente. The Soviet leader loved the time he spent one-on-one with Nixon in the Oval Office, at Camp David, and in a mock cabinet meeting. To use Nixon's phrase, Brezhnev "slobbered all over" him. On the People's Republic of China (PRC) front the appointment of liaison officers — the precursor to ambassadors — in 1973 was a major diplomatic breakthrough. The PRC appointed Huang Zhen and Nixon went with veteran troubleshooter David K. E. Bruce. This volume illuminates how U.S.-China relations matured following Nixon's dramatic 1972 trip. Had Nixon not resigned in disgrace in August 1974, the establishment of full diplomatic relations probably would have occurred earlier than it did (though the deaths of Mao Zedong and Zhou Enlai, both in 1976, could have slowed those efforts).

Nixon's economic policy is also showcased in 1973. With George Shultz as secretary of the treasury, the gold standard was ended for good in the spring. People had two years to trade in dollars for the equivalent in gold. Since then, our currency — the world's currency — has been backed by nothing except the paper it is printed on (and the reputation of the United States). Nixon set this new financial paradigm in motion — the creation of the modern financial system.

· · ·

The vast majority of people recorded on the Nixon taping system did not know they were being recorded. The existence of the taping system was disclosed on July 16, 1973, by Alexander Butterfield during testimony before the Senate Select Committee on Presidential Campaign Activities, as part of the Watergate investigation. "Mr. Butterfield, are you aware of the installation of any listening devices in the Oval Office of the president?" thirty-year-old Republican counsel Fred Thompson asked. It was an unexpected question. Under oath, Butterfield had no choice but to answer honestly. "I was aware of the listening devices. Yes, sir," he answered. The testimony changed the course of the Nixon presidency and American history. As Senator Howard Baker said, the purpose of the Senate investigation into the June 17, 1972, Watergate break-in and subsequent White House cover-up was to find out "what the president knew and when he knew it." The tapes provided a way to answer those questions accurately, but they needed to be intact. On the reel for June 20, 1972, the recording was erased at a crucial point, an action for which Nixon's secretary, Rose Mary Woods, largely took responsibility.

When taping began, the system was always supposed to be Nixon's strength, his ultimate trump card. Only he knew the full score — the complete record of what was said in his presence. When the Watergate investigation reached Nixon's inner circle, his tapes could be used to refute the charges against Bob Haldeman and John Ehrlichman. But what Nixon didn't expect is that his tapes went from a strength to being his ultimate downfall. The problem was, once White House counsel John Dean made accusations regarding what Nixon said during one-on-one meetings, the only way to challenge Dean's exhaustive testimony before the Ervin Committee was to dig deep into the tapes. As Nixon did so, he concluded that while the tapes highlighted weaknesses in some of Dean's facts, they were far more damaging to Nixon than they were to his accusers.

"Would you rather have a competent scoundrel or an honest boob in office?" Nixon's Watergate counsel, J. Fred Buzhardt, asked. "You can make a strong argument that for a president in this day and time you don't want a babe in the woods. He's got to deal with some pretty rough-and-tumble people."

The American people had chosen Richard Nixon twice, in 1968 and 1972, even though both times they would be surprised by the pragmatic opportunist they got. For better or for worse, more than four decades later, Nixon continues to defy easy categorization. We honor him for his shrewd diplomacy with China, on the one hand, and loathe him for the Watergate debacle, on the other. He occupies a complicated place in our national public consciousness. To borrow a line from Nixon himself, we will always "have Nixon to kick around."

CAST OF CHARACTERS

Abrams, Creighton Commander, Military Assistance Command, Vietnam (MACV)
Abzug, Bella Member of the U.S. House of Representatives (D-NY)
Agnew, Spiro Vice President of the United States
Aiken, George U.S. Senator (R-VT)
Aleksandrov, Andrei Assistant to Soviet General Secretary Leonid Brezhnev
Alsop, Joseph Syndicated columnist, *Washington Post*
Anderson, Jack Syndicated columnist, "Washington Merry-Go-Round"
Annenberg, Walter U.S. Ambassador to Great Britain
Arends, Leslie Member of the U.S. House of Representatives (R-IL)
Ash, Roy Assistant to the President for Executive Management and Director of the Office of Management and Budget
Bailey, F. Lee Attorney for James McCord
Baker, Howard U.S. Senator (R-TN)
Baker, Robert "Bobby" Former political advisor to Lyndon Johnson
Barker, Bernard Former CIA contractor; Watergate burglar
Baroody, William Special Assistant to the President
Bayh, Birch U.S. Senator (D-IN)
Bennett, Donald Former DIA Director
Bernstein, Carl Reporter, *Washington Post*
Bittman, William Attorney for Howard Hunt
Brandt, Willy Chancellor of West Germany
Brezhnev, Leonid General Secretary of the Soviet Union
Brock, William U.S. Senator (R-TN)
Brown, Clarence "Bud" Member of the U.S. House of Representatives (R-OH)
Bruce, David K. E. Chief of the U.S. delegation to the Paris Peace Talks; Chief of the U.S. Liaison Office in Beijing
Buchanan, Patrick Special Consultant to the President for Media Analysis and Speech Writing
Buckley, William F. Editor in Chief, *National Review*
Bugayev, Boris Pavlovich Soviet Minister of Civil Aviation
Bull, Stephen Special Assistant to the President
Bunker, Ellsworth U.S. Ambassador to South Vietnam

Burger, Warren Chief Justice of the U.S. Supreme Court

Burns, Arthur Chairman of the Federal Reserve Board

Bush, George H. W. U.S. Ambassador to the United Nations; Chairman of the Republican National Committee

Butterfield, Alexander Deputy Assistant to the President

Butz, Earl Secretary of Agriculture

Buzhardt, J. Fred Special Counsel for Watergate Matters

Byrd, Robert U.S. Senator (D-WV)

Byrne, William Judge of the U.S. District Court for the Central District of California

Caulfield, John Staff assistant, White House counsel's office

Chancellor, John Anchor, *NBC Nightly News*

Chapin, Dwight Deputy Assistant to the President

Chennault, Anna Republican and informal advisor to Richard Nixon

Chiang Kai-shek President of the Republic of China (Taiwan)

Clawson, Kenneth White House Deputy Director of Communications

Cole, Kenneth Executive Director of the Domestic Council

Colson, Charles Special Counsel to the President

Connally, John Former Secretary of the Treasury

Cox, Archibald Watergate Special Prosecutor

Cromer, Earl of (Rowland Baring) British Ambassador to the United States

Curtis, Carl U.S. Senator (R-NE)

Cushman, Robert Former Deputy Director of Central Intelligence

Dash, Samuel Chief Counsel to the Ervin Committee

Dean, John Counsel to the President

DeLoach, Cartha "Deke" Former Assistant Director of the FBI

De Poix, Vincent DIA Director

Diem, Ngo Dinh Former President of South Vietnam (assassinated in 1963)

Dobrynin, Anatoly Soviet Ambassador to the United States

Eastland, James U.S. Senator (D-MS)

Ehrlichman, John Assistant to the President for Domestic Affairs

Eisenhower, Dwight 34th President of the United States (1953–61)

Ellsberg, Daniel Former RAND analyst, coauthor of the Pentagon Papers

Ervin, Sam U.S. Senator (D-NC)

Felt, Mark Associate Director of the FBI

Fensterwald, Bernard Attorney for James McCord

Fielding, Fred Associate Counsel to the President

Fielding, Lewis Psychiatrist to Daniel Ellsberg

Flanigan, Peter Assistant to the President and Executive Director of the Council on International Economic Policy

Ford, Gerald Minority Leader of the U.S. House of Representatives (R-MI)

Fortas, Abe Former Associate Justice of the U.S. Supreme Court; former advisor to Lyndon Johnson

Fulbright, J. William U.S. Senator (D-AR); Chairman of the Foreign Relations Committee

Garment, Leonard Acting Counsel to the President

Gayler, Noel Director of the NSA

Glanzer, Seymour Assistant U.S. Attorney

Goldwater, Barry U.S. Senator (R-AZ); 1964 presidential candidate

Gray, L. Patrick Interim Director of the FBI

Gromyko, Andrei Soviet Foreign Minister

Gurney, Edward U.S. Senator (R-FL)

Haig, Alexander Deputy National Security Advisor; Vice Chief of Staff of the U.S. Army; White House Chief of Staff

Haldeman, H. R. "Bob" White House Chief of Staff

Halperin, Morton Former National Security Council staff member

Harlow, Bryce Counselor to the President

Hart, Gary Manager of Senator George McGovern's 1972 campaign

Heath, Edward Prime Minister of the United Kingdom

Helms, Richard Director of the CIA; U.S. Ambassador to Iran

Higby, Larry Deputy Assistant to the President

Hoffa, Jimmy Labor union leader

Holdridge, John National Security Council staff member

Hoover, J. Edgar Director of the FBI

Hruska, Roman U.S. Senator (R-NE)

Huang Zhen Chief of the PRC Liaison Office in Washington

Hughes, Howard Businessman and philanthropist

Hughes, James Donald Deputy Commander of the U.S. Air Force

Humphrey, Hubert Former Vice President

Hunt, E. Howard Former CIA officer; member of the White House "Plumbers"

Huston, Tom Former Associate Counsel and Staff Assistant to the President

Jackson, Henry "Scoop" U.S. Senator (D-WA)

Jenkins, Al National Security Council staff member

Jenkins, Walter Former assistant to Lyndon Johnson

Johnson, Lyndon B. 36th President of the United States (1963–69)

Johnson, Wallace Special Assistant to the President for Legislative Affairs; Assistant Attorney General of the Land and Natural Resources Division

Kalmbach, Herbert Personal attorney for Richard Nixon

Kendall, Don CEO of PepsiCo

Kennedy, Edward U.S. Senator (D-MA)

Kennedy, John 35th President of the United States (1961–63)

Kennedy, Robert Former Attorney General

Kissinger, Henry National Security Advisor

Klein, Herbert White House Director of Communications

Kleindienst, Richard Attorney General

Knowland, William Former U.S. Senator (R-CA)

Korologos, Thomas Deputy Assistant to the President for Congressional Relations

Kraft, Joseph Columnist, Field Newspapers Syndicate

Krogh, Egil "Bud" Co-Director of the White House "Plumbers"; Under Secretary of Transportation

Laird, Melvin Secretary of Defense; Counselor to the President

Lake, Anthony Former National Security Council staff member

LaRue, Fred CRP advisor to John Mitchell

Le Duc Tho Special Advisor to the North Vietnamese delegation to the Paris Peace Talks

Liddy, G. Gordon Member of the White House "Plumbers"; CRP General Counsel, Finance Committee

Lon Nol Prime Minister of Cambodia

MacGregor, Clark Counsel to the President for Congressional Relations

Magruder, Jeb CRP Deputy Director

Mansfield, Michael Majority Leader, U.S. Senate (D-MT)

Mao Zedong Chairman of the People's Republic of China

Mardian, Robert Assistant Attorney General of Internal Security Division

Maroulis, Peter Attorney for G. Gordon Liddy

Mathias, Charles "Mac" U.S. Senator (R-MD)

McCloskey, Peter Member of the U.S. House of Representatives (R-CA)

McCord, James Former CIA Director of Security; former CRP security consultant; Watergate burglar

McGovern, George U.S. Senator (D-SD); 1972 Democratic presidential nominee

McNamara, Robert Former Secretary of Defense; President of the World Bank

Meir, Golda Prime Minister of Israel

Mitchell, John Former Attorney General

Mitchell, Martha Wife of John Mitchell

Mollenhoff, Clark Journalist and former special counsel to Richard Nixon

Moore, George Deputy Chief of Mission of the U.S. Embassy in Sudan

Moore, Richard Special Counsel to the President

Moorer, Thomas Chairman of the Joint Chiefs of Staff

Muskie, Edmund U.S. Senator (D-ME); 1972 Democratic presidential candidate

Nguyen Van Thieu President of South Vietnam

Nichols, Louis Former Assistant Director of the FBI

Nixon, Richard 37th President of the United States (1969–74)

O'Brien, Lawrence Former Chairman of the Democratic National Committee

Oliver, R. Spencer DNC Executive Director of the Association of State Democratic Chairmen

Packwood, Robert U.S. Senator (R-OR)

Parkinson, Kenneth CRP Counsel

Patolichev, Nikolai Soviet Minister of Foreign Trade

Petersen, Henry Assistant Attorney General of the Criminal Division

Pompidou, Georges President of France

Porter, Herbert CRP staff member

Rabin, Yitzhak Israeli Ambassador to the United States

Rather, Dan White House correspondent, CBS News

Rebozo, Charles "Bebe" Banker and personal friend of Richard Nixon

Reisner, Robert CRP Appointments Secretary

Reitz, Kenneth Director of CRP Young Voters for the President

Reston, James "Scotty" Vice President, *New York Times*

Richardson, Elliot Secretary of Health, Education, and Welfare; Secretary of Defense; Attorney General

Rockefeller, Nelson Governor of New York (R)

Rogers, William Secretary of State

Rooney, John Member of the U.S. House of Representatives (D-NY)

Rothblatt, Henry Attorney for Watergate burglars Bernard Barker, Frank Sturgis, Virgilio Gonzalez, Eugenio Martinez

Ruckelshaus, William Administrator of the EPA; Deputy Attorney General

Safire, William Columnist, *New York Times;* former White House speechwriter

Scali, John Special Counsel to the President

Schlesinger, James Director of Central Intelligence

Schmidt, Helmut Finance Minister of West Germany

Scott, Hugh U.S. Senator (R-PA); Minority Leader

Scowcroft, Brent Deputy Assistant to the President for National Security Affairs

Segretti, Donald CRP consultant

Shaffer, Charles Attorney of John Dean

Shepard, Geoff Associate Director of the Domestic Council

Shultz, George Director of the Office of Management and Budget; Secretary of the Treasury

Silbert, Earl Principal U.S. Attorney for the District of Columbia

Sirica, John Chief Judge of the U.S. District Court for the District of Columbia

Sisco, Joseph Assistant Secretary of State for Near Eastern and South Asian Affairs

Sloan, Hugh CRP Treasurer

Smathers, George Former U.S. Senator (R-FL)

Sonnenfeldt, Helmut National Security Council senior staff member

Stans, Maurice Former Secretary of Commerce; CRP Finance Committee Chair

Stennis, John U.S. Senator (D-MS); Chairman of the Committee on Armed Services

Strachan, Gordon Staff assistant to Bob Haldeman

Sullivan, William C. Former Assistant Director of Domestic Intelligence, FBI

Sullivan, William H. Deputy Assistant Secretary of State for East Asian and Pacific Affairs

Symington, Stuart U.S. Senator (D-MO)

Tanaka, Kakuei Prime Minister of Japan

Thieu, Nguyen Van See Nguyen Van Thieu

Thompson, Fred Minority Counsel to the Earvin Committee

Thompson, Sir Robert British military officer and counterinsurgency expert

Timmons, William Assistant to the President for Legislative Affairs

Tolson, Clyde Former Associate Director of the FBI

Tordella, Louis Deputy Director of the NSA

Tran Kim Phuong South Vietnamese Ambassador to the United States

Tran Van Lam South Vietnamese Foreign Minister

Trend, Sir Burke British Cabinet Secretary

Trudeau, Pierre Prime Minister of Canada

Tuck, Dick Democratic political consultant

Tunney, John U.S. Senator (D-CA)

Ulasewicz, Anthony New York Police Department detective; White House security consultant

Vesco, Robert Financier; donor to CRP

Wallace, George Governor of Alabama (D)

Walters, Johnnie Commissioner of the IRS

Walters, Vernon Deputy Director of Central Intelligence

Warren, Gerald Deputy White House Press Secretary

Watson, Marvin Former White House Appointments Secretary to Lyndon Johnson

Weicker, Lowell U.S. Senator (R-CT)

Weinberger, Caspar Director of the Office of Management and Budget; Counselor to the President; Secretary of Health, Education and Welfare

Wells, Bernard Former Assistant to FBI official William C. Sullivan; Executive Director of the Intelligence Evaluation Committee

Widnall, William Member of the U.S. House of Representatives (R-NJ)

Williams, Edward Bennett Attorney for the DNC

Woods, Rose Mary Personal Secretary to the President

Woodward, Bob Reporter, *Washington Post*

Young, David National Security Council staff member; Co-Director of the White House "Plumbers"

Zhou Enlai Premier of the People's Republic of China

Ziegler, Ronald White House Press Secretary

ABBREVIATIONS AND TERMS

AID Agency for International Development
AP Associated Press
ARVN Army of the Republic of Vietnam (South Vietnam)
Central Committee Soviet high-ranking policy committee
CIA Central Intelligence Agency
CRP Committee to Re-elect the President (popularly known as "CREEP")
DIA Defense Intelligence Agency
DMZ Demilitarized zone
DNC Democratic National Committee
DRV Democratic Republic of Vietnam (North Vietnam)
EOB Executive Office Building
EPA Environmental Protection Agency
FBI Federal Bureau of Investigation
FBS Forward Base Systems
GAO U.S. Government Accountability Office
GVN Government of Vietnam (South Vietnam)
HUD Department of Housing and Urban Development
ICCS International Commission on Control and Supervision
IRS Internal Revenue Service
ITT International Telephone & Telegraph Corporation
MBFR Mutual and Balanced Force Reductions
Memcon Memorandum of conversation
MFN Most favored nation
MIA Missing in action
MIRV Multiple independently targetable reentry vehicle (ballistic missile)
NATO North Atlantic Treaty Organization
NSA National Security Agency
NSC National Security Council
NSSM National Security Study Memorandum
OEP White House Office of Emergency Preparedness
OPEC Organization of the Petroleum Exporting Countries
PIO Public Information Officer

PLO Palestine Liberation Organization
Polaris/Poseidon American sea-based ballistic missile systems
Politburo Soviet executive committee composed of top Central Committee members
POW Prisoner of war
PRC People's Republic of China
PRG Provisional Revolutionary Government (Communist government in waiting)
ROC Republic of China (Taiwan)
SAC Special Agent in Charge (FBI)
SALT Strategic Arms Limitation Treaty (SALT I)
SDS Students for a Democratic Society
Skybolt American air-launched ballistic missile system
UN United Nations
UPI United Press International
USIA United States Information Agency
VC Viet Cong
WSAG Washington Special Actions Group (subcommittee of NSC)

JANUARY-FEBRUARY

Bombing for peace

January 1, 1973, 9:40 a.m.
Richard Nixon and Charles Colson
OVAL OFFICE

"I saw him aging right before my eyes,"* *Charles Colson, special counsel to the president, wrote of Richard Nixon as he appeared at the end of 1972. The year had promised in November to end on a high note for the White House. Not only had Nixon won reelection by a historic margin, but Henry Kissinger, national security advisor, had managed to negotiate a preliminary accord in the Vietnam War peace talks in Paris. At the time, Kissinger leaked news of the breakthrough to Max Frankel, senior editor at the* New York Times, *much to Nixon's dismay. When the accord fell apart a month later, Nixon felt the added pressure of public opinion to force the enemy to return to the talks, and he ordered massive bombing of North Vietnam to begin on December 18. Critics feared that the war had begun all over again, but when the North Vietnamese capitulated at the very end of the month, Nixon had the satisfaction of ending the so-called December bombing. Still exhausted from the pressure of the previous weeks, the president was in his office on New Year's morning, discussing with Colson the imminent departure of one of his more potent aides, Alexander Haig, soon to be named army vice chief of staff.*

• • •

NIXON: Well, all in all, the New Year starts though — you know I was just thinking through the years — not that we wanted to go through the agony of these last — I mean, it was not easy, the Christmas bombing, so forth and so on. But in a way, perhaps it was a good thing. You know what I mean? To the benefit of everything.

COLSON: I think on this one, Mr. President, I watched the toll that it took on you, and it was tough.

NIXON: Oh, I am fine.

COLSON: No, I can tell. I can tell looking at your face, when the strain was as great as it was, but in the end, if Henry [Kissinger] works out the settlement now, it will clearly be your settlement. And it was not headed that way. It was just as well that we have had this little bit of slip. There has been a difference between the two. And, it was too much — Henry was getting too much — public —

NIXON: Yeah. There is another thing too that is happening. That happens, looking at

---

* Charles W. Colson, *Born Again* (Chosen Books, 1976), p. 86; John Herbers, "Nixon Increases Scope of Duties for 3 in Cabinet," *New York Times*, January 6, 1973, p. 13.

it from another standpoint. The end of the war is on any basis now, that is halfway reasonable, our credibility in the world is enormously increased by this.

COLSON: Yes.

NIXON: They can squeal all they want, but boy, I'll tell you, when they squeal it just gives you a hell of a lot more respect among others.

COLSON: That's right.

NIXON: So we've done that. We haven't backed into it. We haven't been political about it. They realize they are dealing with a tough man, a strong man.

COLSON: When they accept that it goes a long way.

NIXON: Here is this country, it allowed the Left, the McGovernites, to force them instead of sort of sucking back, to get out on a limb again. And I think you can saw it off.

COLSON: I do, too.

NIXON: [unclear] intend to saw it off.

COLSON: I think there are some more other advantages. One, if the South Vietnamese squawk they will have less credibility now.

NIXON: That's right.

COLSON: Because everybody knows we did everything humanly possible and really put the North Vietnamese to the wall. And secondly, I think you have taken a hell of a toll on the North Vietnamese. [unclear] NBC, it was very interesting. I watched the network news last night and it is obvious what they had intended to do to us this weekend—

NIXON: Mm-hmm.

COLSON: —was just murder—

NIXON: [unclear] on the bombing. Sure.

COLSON: —and they had seven or eight minutes of Hanoi prisoner film footage, taken by a Japanese film company and distributed by the North Vietnamese—I mean propaganda film.

NIXON: Sure.

COLSON: But Jesus—

NIXON: And they ran it?

COLSON: Just leveled Hanoi. That was pretty devastating itself. They were showing civilian coffins.

NIXON: [unclear]?

COLSON: No, sir.

NIXON: You don't?

COLSON: No, not now that it is over. I think—

NIXON: [unclear]?

COLSON: I think they were just building up to it. I think the bastards were building up a nice crescendo to the return of the Congress and they would have—

NIXON: [unclear]

COLSON: No, no. I think there was a beautifully orchestrated buildup coming, that *New York Times* piece yesterday, both NBC and CBS were playing it the same day.

NIXON: [unclear] maybe they were frustrated and upset by what happened. Don't you think so?

COLSON: I think you pulled the rug out from under them, totally. I think when they — I don't think they expected it. [unclear] take them by surprise.

NIXON: I think they expected a [bombing] pause, but they didn't expect — Haig expected they would stop. They didn't expect the North Vietnamese frankly to capitulate.

A call from the chief justice
January 2, 1973, 8:56 a.m.
Richard Nixon and Warren Burger
WHITE HOUSE TELEPHONE

Warren Burger, Nixon's surprise choice as chief justice of the Supreme Court in 1969, was in many ways a kindred spirit. Both men were born to families that struggled to remain in the middle class, Burger in Minnesota and Nixon in Southern California. Neither was the product of the Ivy League schooling that produced many presidents of their era and nearly all Supreme Court justices. Prospering even without personal popularity, both Nixon and Burger, conservative, highly ambitious Republicans, arrived in Washington during the World War II era. As 1973 began, Burger was considering one of the cases that would mark his court, Miller v. California, *which simultaneously considered the definition and legality of pornography.*

• • •

NIXON: Hello?

BURGER: Good morning, Mr. President.

NIXON: Well, I understood you called yesterday on the New Year and I should have called you.

BURGER: Well, not at all. Did we — I just wanted to —

NIXON: How are you feeling?

BURGER: Oh, just fine.

NIXON: Yeah.

BURGER: You certainly look fit.

NIXON: Yeah, well, we got the — my gosh, did you go to the game by chance?

BURGER: No, no. I have been to the —

NIXON: I never go to those games. Because, I tell you why I don't is that whenever they are sellouts — I went to one, Oklahoma and — I mean, Texas and Arkansas about three years ago — and the problem was that it really causes such commotion because over a hundred people have to go when I go. Sixty press and forty Secret Service, well, that just takes a hundred seats away from people that just die —

BURGER: That takes some of the fun out of it.

NIXON: — and if you could see it on television. I went up to Camp David and I just saw it up there. I was working up there anyway.

BURGER: With the instant replay it is much better.

NIXON: It is the only way to see a game. Of course there is something to the excitement of hearing the audience.

BURGER: Well, I haven't gone to one for years. I spent yesterday just the way you did. I was down here at nine o'clock and worked all day.

NIXON: That's right.

BURGER: I even missed the game.

NIXON: This is the time to — actually in these periods like this when people are all gone, I am just — been in the office today and yesterday, and you can get a lot of the paperwork done that you just put aside and say, "I will do that when I get a few minutes." You know?

BURGER: I wanted to start the year with a clean empty box.

NIXON: I do it every time. My box is just as clean as it can be.

BURGER: I unfortunately didn't get out all my opinions, but I got all the little stuff out of the way. So now the decks are cleared for another session.

NIXON: Yeah, now you can — you get your mind clear so that you can make the big decisions.

BURGER: We will have one coming out pretty soon, too.

NIXON: Oh boy.

BURGER: I am struggling with this pornography thing. I don't know whether, I don't know how we are coming out. I am coming out hard on it.

NIXON: Good, good.

BURGER: Whether I get the support or not.

NIXON: You're right. Well, I feel terrible. Of course I am a square. I'm like Alan, I am a square on that. I mean a square in the sense that I read those cases when I did the Hill versus *Time* thing [*Time, Inc. v. Hill*, a 1967 freedom of the press case before the U.S. Supreme Court, for which Nixon argued the Hill side].

BURGER: Yeah.

NIXON: And you know because it related to the whole freedom of the press thing, and let's face it, it's just gone overboard, that's all. It is always a question of balance. I mean, maybe you can — they go back to this sixteenth-century stuff and say, "What's wrong with that, that was great art?" Well, the stuff today is not great art. The stuff today, its purpose — what is that term that they have — you —

BURGER: Redeeming social purpose.

NIXON: Yeah, good God.

BURGER: One of the biggest frauds —

NIXON: Oh, that was a [Associate Justice William J.] Brennan opinion, wasn't it?

BURGER: I think so.

NIXON: Yeah, yeah.

BURGER: That was a phrase that emanated from some of the campuses in this period.

NIXON: Redeeming social purposes. [laughs]

BURGER: It is, you know, all this means is that if they have one of the outrageous orgies then if they mention Vietnam, or the condition of the ghettos, it redeems the whole thing.

NIXON: Yeah, oh boy. Well, isn't that something. What else do you have? Do you have other decisions? Is the busing thing coming out?

BURGER: No, that is way down the road.

NIXON: That's good. The longer the better.

BURGER: The longer the better is right.

NIXON: Right. Maybe we can get some legislation passed and get that out of the way.

BURGER: We have got to — I think things are coming. I get impatient, but they are coming. And by the way, this young fellow, he is young now for you and me — by twelve years, [Associate Justice William] Rehnquist, he is a real star.

NIXON: Isn't that great?

BURGER: He has got guts.

NIXON: Well, we will try to give you, one day, if we ever get a chance, to try and get another one.

BURGER: Get another fellow.

NIXON: I don't — I have no ideas. I understand that they — you remember General MacArthur's famous statement when he spoke to the Congress? I would put it a little differently for Supreme Court justices. Supreme Court justices never die and they never fade away. Right? [laughs]

BURGER: [laughs] You got to get some young fellows up here, and not any more sixties. Like —

NIXON: You guys are all right. My guys in their sixties are great. The Burger, [Harry] Blackmun, [Lewis F.] Powell triumvirate, but I tell you — let me say, I agree. I think one of the problems in the Congress — I was looking over a list here of our Republicans and good God! I mean we have got people over seventy that I hadn't realized. I mean Les Arends, Bill Widnall, and so forth. They are too old. They are too old. You know what I mean?

BURGER: You can't keep —

NIXON: Not because — understand, up until — I think you could, frankly — in a court, you could serve till seventy-five, because there it is a different kind of thing.

BURGER: The pace is different.

NIXON: But at the Congress I think in the House and the Senate you should be out of there by seventy. You know, that's a murderous thing down there.

BURGER: That is the big reform that needs to be had over there. It is just getting some vigorous young guys in their forties.

NIXON: Nobody should run for the House if he's over forty, because he can't amount to anything. Run for the first time I mean, and nobody should run for the Senate if he is over fifty, for the first time.

BURGER: Yeah.

NIXON: You see because you have to be in so you can serve for twenty years. I have been trying to preach this. George Bush is going to help a lot in that respect. He is a great choice for chairman.

BURGER: Well, he will be an attractive guy to attract candidates, the young —

NIXON: Yeah, you see we have Bush on that point. And [Bill] Brock is going to be the Senate campaign committee man. He is a young, vigorous fellow, and Bill — Bud Brown, you know, the son of —

BURGER: Clarence?

NIXON: Clarence's son. Who is just bright as a tack. He is going to do the House job. He is — well, he is a big, smart, not nearly as abrasive as Clarence and almost as smart. So I think we will have a fine team getting candidates this time.

BURGER: Well, it is mighty nice of you to take the trouble to call back. We just wanted to leave our greetings —

NIXON: Well, we will see you on the inauguration. I mean, you are the guy who has to swear me in, you know?

BURGER: Yes, the vice president I talked to the other day. I guess that tradition has varied with the vice president.

NIXON: Yeah.

BURGER: But he called me and asked me if I would do it, and I said yes and I will do two for the price of one!

NIXON: That's right. That's right.

BURGER: Well —

NIXON: Well, actually what happens is that in — the vice president actually normally does pick somebody else. I had [William F.] Knowland swear me in in '56. I don't know who did it the other time. I've forgotten. Knowland did it in '56, but it doesn't make — it's a matter of — it varies, and I think it is really neater to have you do both.

BURGER: Yes, it reduces one more body on the platform.

NIXON: That's right. That's right. [laughs] I hadn't thought of that, hadn't thought of that.

BURGER: Space is going to be a premium.

NIXON: That's right. Well, we will look forward to seeing you.

BURGER: We are looking forward to seeing you, too.

NIXON: One of the beauties of my oath, you know, it is very short. His is quite long. His is the same as the — you know the difference. Did you know there was a difference?

BURGER: Yeah, yes.

NIXON: His is that long one that you give to senators, but mine is very short. I just swear to uphold and defend the Constitution of the United States.

BURGER: About seven lines long.

NIXON: Yeah. Even I can remember that. Okay.

BURGER: Good to talk to you.

NIXON: Bye.

"As long as that court proceeding is on, the Congress
should keep its goddamn hands off."
January 8, 1973, 4:05 p.m.
Richard Nixon and Charles Colson
EXECUTIVE OFFICE BUILDING

*On Monday, January 8, 1973, the Watergate scandal arrived in the most prominent venue
to consider it up to that time. The U.S. District Court in Washington, Judge John J. Sirica
presiding, heard the case of the five men arrested for breaking into the Democratic National Committee headquarters the previous June, along with two White House aides
suspected of complicity: G. Gordon Liddy and E. Howard Hunt. Sirica, a longtime Republican, didn't intimidate Nixon, however. He was far more concerned with plans then ac-
celerating in Congress to broaden its initial, somewhat sporadic Watergate investigation,
spearheaded by Senator Edward Kennedy (D-MA). As Nixon and his advisor Colson
sorted through the powerful Washingtonians then reacting to the scandal, they focused
on Martha Mitchell, wife of Attorney General John Mitchell and an infamous operator in
her own right. They also discussed the lawyer Edward Bennett Williams, counsel to the
Democratic National Committee and owner of the Washington Redskins football team.
Nixon and Colson seemed confident in early January that the scandal could be contained,
discounting the dogged determination of others to find out, as Sirica put it just before the
trial began, "What did these men go into the headquarters for? What was their purpose?
Who hired them to go in there?"*

• • •

NIXON: Incidentally, Haldeman was telling — told me that apparently that Hunt is going
to [unclear] now — very definitely. I think it's the right thing for him to do, Chuck.
COLSON: He's doing it on my urging.
NIXON: Well, I understand that Haldeman is after some kid they've got that — whether
he was — quit because he wanted him to bug Gary Hart.
COLSON: Yeah, that's true. Yeah, he was the one that bugged McGovern headquarters.
Yeah, I suspect so.
NIXON: But how could that be, for this reason: Watergate came before McGovern got
off the ground and I didn't know why the hell we were bugging McGovern.
COLSON: Well, remember that was after the California primary.
NIXON: Watergate was?
COLSON: Yeah.
NIXON: Oh.
COLSON: We knew, I mean, at that time [unclear].
NIXON: Hmm, Christ. I hope he didn't tell McGovern.
COLSON: [laughs] Well —
NIXON: Well, suppose — I told Haldeman, I said, well, "Suppose those in the — Con-

---

* Walter Rugaber, "7 Go to Trial Tomorrow," *New York Times*, January 7, 1973, p. 26.

gress does call him [Hunt]." He said, "He didn't do it." You know, nothing. That's the thing about all of this. We didn't get a goddamn thing from any of it that I can see.

COLSON: Well, apparently we did, of course, at Watergate — mainly [Howard] Hughes, and we knew.

NIXON: I don't know. Well, don't let it get you down.

COLSON: Oh, hell no —

NIXON: I know it's tough for all of you — Bob [Haldeman], John [Ehrlichman], and the rest. We're just not going to let it get us down. This is a battle. It's a fight. It's war and we just fight with a little, you know — remember, we'll cut them down one of these days. Don't you agree?

COLSON: I do. The only thing I hope is that the trial — apparently Liddy is going to go the trial.

NIXON: Not now.

COLSON: That's probably a good thing because the only one who's in a — is in a very desperate —

NIXON: Sensitive position is Hunt.

COLSON: — and the others will just tell the truth and prove their case. But there is one advantage to it. There will be a hell of a lot of stuff that's come out.

NIXON: Yeah.

COLSON: And there will be some counts that will not be, that will be dropped, I think, against Hunt at this point, and there will be appeals pending in the other cases. Now that has got to be [unclear]. That makes it very, very —

NIXON: As long as this trial is going on, the Congress will keep its goddamn cotton-pickin' hands off that trial —

COLSON: Well, it could be because obviously they will prejudice the defendants in this connection. You could get a — it — a lot of this only comes out, this will delay the Congress getting to the point where they could even immunize the witnesses. A question of prosecuting because of lack of rules of evidence and that kind of specifics, et cetera. And the only question we have hanging from it at all is the fact that [unclear] no government reports, providing these guys did what they — Ehrlichman.

NIXON: Well, first of all, they're going to make the government prove its case, but none of them are going to testify, isn't that correct?

COLSON: Correct.

NIXON: Are they?

COLSON: That's another subject — McCord [unclear] hanging on to [unclear].

NIXON: [unclear] appeal for all these guys.

COLSON: [unclear]

NIXON: But you know, Chuck, it's something they all undertook knowing the risks. Right? What do they think?

COLSON: I [unclear].

NIXON: Did they think they'd get caught?

COLSON: No, I don't think that at all. I think they thought that, well, practically—

NIXON: The Democrats would drop it after the election? No?

COLSON: I think they figured that these were all guys who—CIA.

NIXON: Yeah.

COLSON: And—

NIXON: Yeah.

COLSON: —they all were taking orders from people like [unclear] acting on behalf of John Mitchell and others [unclear].

NIXON: Mitchell would take care of them [unclear]. How could he?

COLSON: Yeah.

NIXON: No way.

COLSON: That's what they were—Hunt's lawyer, he said he thought he, Hunt, objected to it violently because of the way Liddy handled the job. He said Liddy ordered him into Watergate. [unclear] He said he didn't want any part of it. So we won't have to. But, he and Hunt may recognize—

NIXON: Well, I'm glad that you [unclear]. [unclear] because basically I—question of clemency—Hunt's is a simple case. I mean, after all, the man's wife is dead, was killed. He's got one child that has—

COLSON: Brain damage from an automobile accident.

NIXON: That's right.

COLSON: [unclear] one of his kids.

NIXON: We'll build that son of a bitch up like nobody's business. We'll have Buckley write a column and say, you know, that he should have clemency, if you've given eighteen years of service.

COLSON: [unclear] We'll write one.

NIXON: That's what we'll do.

COLSON: He served under Hunt in CIA, of course. [unclear]

NIXON: We'll call him after. That's it. It's on the merits. I would have difficulty with some of the others.

COLSON: Oh, yeah.

NIXON: You know what I mean?

COLSON: Well, the others aren't going to get the same—aren't—the vulnerabilities are different with the others also.

NIXON: Are they?

COLSON: Yeah.

NIXON: Why?

COLSON: Well, because Hunt and Liddy did the work. The others didn't know anything direct that is [unclear]. [unclear] bankrupt today.

NIXON: Well, I think I agree, but you know—

COLSON: See, I don't give a damn if they [laughs] spend five years in jail in the interim.

NIXON: Oh, no.

COLSON: What I want of course—they took that attitude—

NIXON: They took that attitude because —

COLSON: I mean they can't hurt us. Hunt and Liddy were direct guardians of the meetings. Discussions are very incriminating for us. More important that they —

NIXON: Liddy is pretty tough.

COLSON: Yeah, he is. Apparently one of these guys who's a masochist. He enjoys punishing himself. That's okay as long as he remains stable. I think he's tough.

NIXON: Yeah.

COLSON: He's an ideologue, not the kind who [unclear].

NIXON: [unclear] Let's not hope by God —

COLSON: Yeah.

NIXON: Jesus.

COLSON: [unclear] Good [unclear] they right wing —

NIXON: [unclear] Well, it's the last day I'm fifty-nine. [unclear]

• • •

NIXON: I wrote a little note to Ed Williams — his offer — about his offer to go to the game, and that sort of thing, a nice little note.

COLSON: What the hell does he want?

NIXON: Would you be bugged if I see him?

COLSON: No, the guys won't see him. He hasn't set the [unclear].

NIXON: Now, I assume, Chuck —

COLSON: Yeah, he is coming.

NIXON: Yeah.

COLSON: He wanted to come in at three thirty today —

NIXON: That's right. I thought it would be good.

COLSON: And I just don't know [unclear]. [unclear] said that he got drunk because he was —

NIXON: He does look like [unclear] of the Irish, remember?

COLSON: Yeah, and he was lamenting the fact that he ever took the Watergate case out with him because he said he missed that. It ruined his chances of getting appointed to the Supreme Court.

NIXON: Well, maybe he has a good chance for it. Now, you know what I mean?

COLSON: That's what he wants.

NIXON: Well, you could point out, you know, the fact that if they make some mental notes [unclear] what the hell [unclear]. When you get to — presidents have always — Bobby Baker, say you want the facts. [unclear] Let's face it, the Johnson [unclear]. Democratic Party — and all that, and frankly that, the president is sort of puzzled that they seem to take the Watergate as a vendetta. It's not — I'm not angry, you understand, because you've got to represent the client. Just was puzzled by it. And they got word that they got out before [unclear] much really happened. Good — get the point?

COLSON: That — I think that I —

NIXON: [unclear]

COLSON: The thing I'm sure he recognized is that the Watergate matter was completely out of his control. That's his [unclear].

NIXON: Yeah.

COLSON: He only gets to the civil side. He can't — there's nothing now that he can do with the Watergate.

NIXON: Yeah.

COLSON: And he realizes we've had wild publicity adverse to what the jury [unclear] they could indict him. Right? [unclear]

NIXON: [unclear] but let him feel there's no hard feelings. We don't have hard feelings, but that's the — we can handle people. I'm a great believer in just being, you know —

COLSON: He wants to [unclear].

NIXON: How is he?

COLSON: [unclear]

NIXON: Anyway the point is that you want to see him for other — that you never know, we've got to play every string we've got here. Don't you agree?

COLSON: Absolutely.

NIXON: Think he's worth seeing?

COLSON: [unclear] definitely see him. No problem with that.

NIXON: He is a friend of the soothsayer — [Martha] Mitchell.

COLSON: Mitchell.

NIXON: She signed his letter, you know. That's how we got the letter, and it's obvious that he's trying to at least make a — hold out some sort of a [unclear].

COLSON: Oh, absolutely. Absolutely. Because the way that really came about is he called me and asked if she could run it over and give it to him. Send it over — I told him, I said, "Forget it." I said [unclear], "I don't know what you've got." I'm glad I gave it to him. But, I did call him back and I said, you know, "Be glad to have you drop by and say hello to people." He just said, "Set a time." He couldn't believe that George [unclear].

NIXON: Well, we've got to figure it, Chuck [unclear]. This could go on and on and on [unclear] it would be one witness after another.

COLSON: I don't think that's important at this time. I'm not worried about the court proceeding —

NIXON: Well, as long as the court proceeding is going on [unclear] by God, Mansfield, the opposition has clearly — [unclear] great, great danger for the Congress to get [unclear]. They cannot — it — Jesus Christ, suppose it's for the Communists [unclear] everybody else would be jumping down the throats of the Congress for interfering with the rights of the — the quote charged but not yet proven guilty individuals.

COLSON: Look at Ellsberg.

NIXON: Look at the [murderer Charles] Manson case. You remember what I said about that? Christ, that's a — now what the hell is this? Where is the single standard here, Chuck?

COLSON: Well, this is the classic case of the double standard. There hasn't been, except for Bill Buckley, one single iota of sympathy for these fellows. None at all.

NIXON: Well, the point is, too, it isn't just the sympathy. The point is there hasn't been any outrage about whether they're guilty or not, no cry of outrage raised about the Congress meddling in their civil rights. Goddamn it, the Congress goes forward with an investigation while they are still in — I think that's why the court proceeding has its advantage. As long as that court proceeding is on, the Congress should keep its goddamn hands off.

COLSON: Well —

NIXON: I think some of our guys up there have got to do that. They've got to say that.

COLSON: [unclear]

NIXON: Or will they?

COLSON: No, I think they will. I think they have been relatively silent on this and that's just as well because at this point let's not throw —

NIXON: Democrats.

COLSON: — Democrats into the wash here.

NIXON: Yeah, but Mansfield's not optimum on this.

COLSON: Yeah, but that was Watergate written quite some time ago. [unclear]

NIXON: Oh, was it? Is that so?

COLSON: He wrote that letter back in November. Just released it. I think the reason he released it frankly was to —

NIXON: Take Teddy [Kennedy] off the hook.

COLSON: Yeah, take Teddy off the hook. And also, it was kind of a warning that you'd better have an open trial. And I think the timing of that was more designed not to let us think we could get away with being able to suppress, without complications, suppress [unclear] because throughout the [unclear].

NIXON: [unclear] sweetheart. Yeah.

COLSON: That's right.

NIXON: [laughs] Unfortunately. Unfortunately. We're not that way. Can you imagine the way Johnson would have handled it?

COLSON: Yeah. I can.

NIXON: Yeah.

COLSON: The U.S. attorney would get off his fanny like that or [unclear]. Just take a little tip. [unclear]

NIXON: [unclear] Well, I don't know. We can't control that show. I don't — we can't get away [unclear].

COLSON: I don't think so.

NIXON: No.

COLSON: No, the stake will be sort of a stalemate.

NIXON: That's what it amounts to basically. That's all Watergate. And incidentally we'll survive it.

COLSON: Oh, sure.

NIXON: I just don't believe that as time goes on. I think people can tire of it too. The Watergate thing can hang around like ITT and I think you get tired of ITT.

COLSON: Terribly. Terribly.

NIXON: You think so?

COLSON: Yes, I do. I think they'll develop the Watergate probe on this, unless they get a big name. If they do that it's a different story — so be it.

NIXON: What do you think, if they get big names, the big name denies it but, that's what happened in Africa, but you really must be [unclear] to fix somebody. That must be very basically a hearsay proposition all, all up and down the line from what I — well, now you told me that. I just sensed it, what the hell — at least Mitchell was that smart. He was close to it but not in it directly.

COLSON: No.

NIXON: No, they can't —

COLSON: This is perjury.

NIXON: Perjury that's a damn hard rap to prove. [unclear]

COLSON: [unclear]

NIXON: We did it with [Alger] Hiss. Well, I'll tell you, it ain't easy. You gotta get it. They haven't got that kind of evidence on Mitchell, [unclear], or anybody else. Have they?

COLSON: No, I don't think that — I don't know who the hell — I keep finding that difficult to build a case on this [unclear].

NIXON: You fight from [unclear]. I don't know what to fight.

COLSON: No, well, I think if they get to the stage where they are volunteering and the Senate gets really serious, really concerned about putting them on television. Complicates the justice. That's one of the things I get most concerned with him and that was last week was the [unclear] agreeing to drop certain counts of Hunt's indictment in exchange for a guilty plea on three counts.

NIXON: They can do that?

COLSON: Yes, but you see, that precludes him from taking jeopardy on two different counts. Therefore, he couldn't refuse to accept congressional immunity [unclear] even though it may be given, but the Fifth Amendment says I can't be forced to testify against myself [unclear]. I am not questioning the way duty is [unclear].

NIXON: Oh, you fight that right through?

COLSON: Yeah.

NIXON: And, if necessary you say, "I want to — "

COLSON: I mean, Bittman's admitting he can take that one to the Supreme Court.

NIXON: You don't want — a hell of a [unclear].

COLSON: [unclear] will probably pass enough time, so that by then he will have served his sentence.

NIXON: I don't think that's — I don't know [unclear].

COLSON: Teddy's in an awkward position. The way it looks, we can't [unclear] him. It's hard to figure about this.

NIXON: Oh, did he?

COLSON: Yes, sir. Yesterday, in the *Washington Post* [unclear] to go through the [unclear], just takes a jackhammer to attract.

NIXON: [unclear] I've read that one chapter —

COLSON: Yeah. Fantastic. I was going to tell you to take that [unclear] right now. This gal was under that portrait in the Barbados report.

NIXON: He may be destroyed before he gets off the ground, Chuck.

COLSON: Yeah, I think so. I think Ted Kennedy may be [unclear] —

NIXON: Because you see, come in in the first chapter is [unclear].

COLSON: [unclear] run into it.

NIXON: Well, that's what you're doing.

• • •

NIXON: Let me tell you one thing, that your president is working on [unclear] looks good now. The Watergate thing goes too far and we start getting investigated for it. We will have to get out and get everybody's [unclear] on it. The Johnson bugging of the president, for example. Now you talk about bugging the Democratic Committee and failing that, for example, and bugging a candidate for president the last two weeks of the campaign —

COLSON: Or close to it.

NIXON: — by the FBI.

COLSON: Yeah.

NIXON: By the FBI. Deke DeLoach did it. Johnson ordered him. Deke DeLoach has told Mitchell — Hoover had told Mitchell that it was done. The question is whether or not Mitchell will say that and whether he believed Deke DeLoach [unclear] job. Liddy is a former FBI man and he [unclear] like that and said, "I was ready to do it," you see, under oath. Would he mind doing it?

COLSON: He works for [PepsiCo Chief Executive Officer] Don Kendall.

NIXON: Well, I don't want to, but I just say [unclear]. But say that "I heard they're going to play for keeps."

COLSON: Well, there's another thing that has to be brought out too, and that is if we get really in thick, and if the going gets rough in Congress — I don't know whether it will, you know. The court proceeding is going to run its course, and that's beyond our control — the country's control. Then I think we've got to prepare — whether or not we use it, or not — [unclear] floating around. Birch Bayh [unclear] security money [unclear].

NIXON: [unclear] can we [unclear]. Well, I just don't know. I just don't know. If we did, why have we done it before?

COLSON: Well, because Clark Mollenhoff ran a whole series on Birch Bayh's funding. I think they kind of look the other way. The Justice Department — but those were [unclear].

NIXON: Statute of limitations problem. [unclear] I don't know. But anyway we've got that on the [unclear]. I don't know how [unclear]. How do we get such stuff out [unclear]?

COLSON: With Kennedy, when Kennedy said [unclear].

NIXON: That I don't know about. But that's one story.

COLSON: The point is that the only way that those guys [unclear] they really [unclear].

NIXON: But the point is — but let me say, having that in mind, would you not agree, though, that, that the Johnson thing would indicate to you that the president of the United States [unclear] would — I would frankly hope and wish we could add that half of the problem. I would like for it to happen. Although maybe it was better that it not happen. Because Johnson cannot deny that it happened.

COLSON: Just knowing Johnson, I wonder if he actually saw the need to call up Marvin Watson and say, "Marvin, you get DeLoach's ass over here and tell him what you want done." [unclear] Regardless, it doesn't matter whether it was someone close to Johnson or Johnson.

NIXON: Of course he says he did it because of Vietnam and — all that. But nevertheless, he [unclear] to great deal McGovern [unclear] — his talks with the North Vietnamese, the [unclear] and all that.

COLSON: [Former press secretary to presidents Kennedy and Johnson] Pierre Salinger or [unclear]. Handed it to the president.

NIXON: Close to the election, close to the election but [unclear] a hell of a lot though.

COLSON: Yeah.

NIXON: That's the whole point.

COLSON: I was thinking if it came to it that that could be something [unclear].

NIXON: With what kind of an effect — it would have some effect on [unclear].

COLSON: I [unclear].

NIXON: They would certainly say now [unclear]. Look here, what the hell are we talking about here? [unclear] We would deny on a stack of Bibles that he didn't know anything about it. And now who the hell is going to believe it?

COLSON: Nobody.

NIXON: Well, we would say it was done for political purposes —

COLSON: It would be like the January 25 announcement when you talked about a whole series of issues and went on — everybody after that including some where a list of questions [unclear]. Mansfield said, "Well, that's what we've been urging it on the president all the time [unclear]" he says it is [unclear]. And your answer would be, "I'll let the court proceeding go ahead [unclear] and now that, now that you're not satisfied with justice [unclear] and meet with — "

NIXON: Right.

COLSON: Let's call a spade a spade. Somebody had to deal with it. Deke would do it. He would do anything.

The end of American aggression in Vietnam

January 20, 1973, 1:04 a.m.

Richard Nixon and Charles Colson

WHITE HOUSE TELEPHONE

On January 15, President Nixon momentously ordered the end of all U.S. bombing, shelling, and mining in North Vietnam. Among the many who voiced approval was the Senate minority leader, Hugh Scott of Pennsylvania. Scott was a staunch Nixon loyalist — a feeling that was never fully mutual. The president's move to end the bombing was patently intended to draw a signature from Hanoi's representatives on the long-delayed peace agreement. That part of the strategy seemed to work, but another key party to the peace accord, the South Vietnamese president, Nguyen Van Thieu, proved jittery and elusive — even more than usual — sorely trying Nixon's patience.

• • •

NIXON: Whatever people thought of the bombing last week, which is the result of a media thing. Good God! With this development now — you know, if they can, and that is why you mustn't say it too soon till we sign the agreement. And we still have got the problem of that son of a bitch Thieu — we'll get the word on him tomorrow, but he'll go. He'll go before committing suicide, but put yourself in the position of the opposition. How the hell do you think we got it? When Henry [Kissinger], after ten days — you remember the cables? —

COLSON: Oh, yes.

NIXON: — he gave up. We would have been in the war for three or four more months!

COLSON: That's right.

NIXON: And hundreds of Americans would have been killed. What do they want?

COLSON: That's right. That's exactly right. Now, I think the war issue, Mr. President, I think it's going to take a big bounce when it really is locked up and people know it is locked up and they get a — you know, it is going to take — they are going to be from Missouri — they are going to take two or three days to say "show me," but then it is going to turn on the critics. I think they are going to have one very tough time for a few months. I really do. Hugh Scott took a whack at them yesterday. He was on television last night.

NIXON: For a change? Good God, his first statement was terrible.

COLSON: Yeah, he was horrible, but he said the critics cut off threats that lengthened the Vietnam War and that the —

NIXON: He — what?

COLSON: He said it lengthened the war. It was ill advised.

NIXON: Good.

COLSON: The only thing that could upset peace is the possibility that Hanoi is misled by the critics of the [U.S.] government.

NIXON: Good.

COLSON: It is starting. Well, you see, all that reflects is that Hugh Scott, who smells the political winds.

NIXON: Right.

---

* Michael B. Coakley, "Hugh Scott, a Giant in Pa. and Congress, Dies at 93," *Philadelphia Inquirer,* July 23, 1994.

COLSON: He knows that we have got an issue now that he's been on the right side of. No, I think you're going to find a very —

NIXON: Now listen, Chuck, as I told Haldeman, your job is to see that by God we put it to them. I mean assuming it works out.

COLSON: I want it —

NIXON: It is going to work out one way or the other. If Thieu doesn't go that's going to — that isn't too bad either.

COLSON: Nope, it isn't.

NIXON: We go ahead and make our deal —

COLSON: Sure.

NIXON: — and we sink Thieu and everybody says, "Thank God he was a tough son of a bitch on both sides." To hell with him.

COLSON: That's right. Well, we accomplished our objectives. We gave the people in South Vietnam an opportunity [to survive], and if Thieu wants to hang himself that's his business. No, I think if we get our prisoners back and you have a cease-fire —

NIXON: But if we do more than that — get the prisoners back, a cease-fire, and you know —

COLSON: Survival of the Thieu government, and — oh, hell, there will be —

NIXON: Peace with honor when they would have bugged out, and then we just pour it right to them.

COLSON: And we really can, Mr. President. I think at that point we really will. We're beginning to hurt them.

"There are times when abortions are necessary."
January 23, 1973, 6:22 p.m.
Richard Nixon and Charles Colson
EXECUTIVE OFFICE BUILDING

On January 22, 1973, the landmark case Roe v. Wade *was decided by the U.S. Supreme Court. In this excerpt of a conversation that covered a variety of topics, Nixon and Colson discuss the case's impact on expanding abortion rights. While the audio quality is especially poor, Nixon seems to suggest that he understands why some people might want an abortion, such as in the case of an interracial pregnancy.*

• • •

NIXON: What is the situation, incidentally, with regard to the Supreme Court decision on abortion [unclear]?

COLSON: [unclear] two dissenting [unclear].

NIXON: Who?

COLSON: [unclear]

NIXON: Well, it doesn't make any difference.

COLSON: It doesn't make a difference at all. I wanted to look and see [unclear].

[Unclear exchange]

NIXON: A girl and a boy, and the girl gets knocked up, and then the couple, of course, doesn't worry about the pill. She goes down to her doctor to get an abortion. [unclear] three-month rule. Shit! And the doctor says, "I thought it was three."

COLSON: The ruling though, Mr. President, I'm not a Catholic, but I'm —

NIXON: I know, I know. And I admit, I mean there are times when abortions are necessary. I know that. You know, [unclear] between a black and a white. [unclear]

COLSON: Or rape.

NIXON: Or rape. [unclear] You know what I mean. There are times.

COLSON: The reason I oppose it — I have a fourteen-year-old daughter.

NIXON: Yeah.

COLSON: It encourages permissiveness.

NIXON: That's right. It breaks the dam.

"This will be a very brief meeting."

January 23, 1973, 8:38 p.m.

Richard Nixon and cabinet (Spiro Agnew, William Rogers, George Shultz, Elliot Richardson, Richard Kleindienst, Rogers Morton, Earl Butz, Frederick Dent, Peter Brennan, Caspar Weinberger, James Lynn, Claude Brinegar, Roy Ash, John Scali, Anne Armstrong, Bob Haldeman, John Ehrlichman, Henry Kissinger, Peter Flanigan, William Timmons, Ronald Ziegler, Raymond Price, Herbert Stein, Kenneth Cole, and George H. W. Bush)

CABINET ROOM

Nixon was never one for long or substantive cabinet meetings. He never put anything important to a binding vote of his cabinet. He was the president, which in his mind meant he was to make the decisions and inform his cabinet of his actions. Here, Nixon briefs his cabinet on the terms of the Paris Peace Accords, which had been initialed by Henry Kissinger and Le Duc Tho only two hours earlier in the French capital. Nixon reviewed the televised address that he planned to make that evening, the official announcement that the nation's longest war was finally over.

• • •

NIXON: This will be a very brief meeting. The purpose is, frankly, is to be sure that the cabinet is in the eyes of the world and the eyes of the nation [unclear] before the announcement is made. Let me tell you why the announcement must be very brief and why our discussion must be brief about the announcement today and why the, for example, the briefing — the legislative briefing will only be pro forma like this, is that we're going to have a legislative briefing again tomorrow which will be quite substantial. Well, let me start by saying that I will announce at ten o'clock a very brief talk on television that we've completed an agreement today to end the war [unclear] peace with honor [unclear]. I will read a joint statement that is being issued at ten o'clock. That's one of the reasons why this has to be tight until then even though I can inform you. I will read the statement to you here now, and I will explain briefly why it meets our goals. "At twelve thirty today Paris time, January 23, the agreement on ending the war and preserving peace for Vietnam was initialed by Dr. Henry Kissinger on behalf of the United States, and Special Adviser Le Duc Tho on behalf of the Democratic Republic of Vietnam. This agreement will be formally signed by the parties participating in the Paris Conference on Vietnam on January 27, 1973, at the International Conference Center in Paris. The cease-fire will take effect at twenty-four hundred Greenwich Mean Time, January 27, 1973." I will explain that in a minute. "The United States and the Democratic Republic of Vietnam express the hope that this agreement will ensure stable peace in Vietnam and contribute to the preservation of lasting peace in Indochina and Southeast Asia." That is the announcement to be made in Hanoi and Washington, and done at ten o'clock tonight. Now, what this agreement does, and what the protocols which are tortuous and fairly important, to the extent that the protocols in the agreement ensure anything, is to accomplish all of the goals that I laid down in the January 25 [1972 speech]. You remember there were four. I said first, that there had to be a return of all of our prisoners of war, and an account for all of those missing in action. I said that there had to be an internationally supervised cease-fire. I said there should be a withdrawal of all American forces, and there should be a right of the people of South Vietnam to determine their own future, outside [unclear]. All of those conditions have been met. As far as the implementation is concerned, as it affects the prisoners, is in sixty days from Saturday all prisoners will have been returned and all missing in action will be accounted for. Sixty days from Saturday all American forces in Vietnam are to have been withdrawn, and in terms of the internationally supervised cease-fire, the cease-fire [unclear] at seven o'clock Washington time [unclear]. In terms of what it means for Cambodia and Laos, and so forth, I think it is — let me say this, at this point that this is a subject that will come up with the [congressional] leaders meeting — in other words, we will probably have to answer it. I think it will be for Henry to take just a moment on Cambodia and Laos, because the Vietnam thing is all that I am really going to talk about tonight. It is very significant that this covers Vietnam and has an understanding with regard to Cambodia and Laos. Now, do you understand that Cambodia and Laos are not all that specific, but they are vitally important — go ahead, Henry, take over on that.

KISSINGER: The major thing is that it is essential not to talk about that.

NIXON: That's right. We'll all wait until tomorrow when the agreement comes out.

KISSINGER: Well, but that won't —

NIXON: Even then —

KISSINGER: — that won't be the agreement either.

NIXON: That's right.

KISSINGER: We have strong reason to believe that there will be a cease-fire in Laos within fifteen days of the agreement in Vietnam, so by around February 10. The two parties there are already negotiating, and we have as I said a strong reason to believe, which can be jeopardized only by [unclear] of talk here. Secondly, with respect to Cambodia, the situation is more complex because there are factions there that are not all in control of the parties involved, but we believe that a de facto cease-fire will emerge there which will be a little bit messier than the one in Laos over a comparable period of time after the agreement is signed by the secretary of state on Saturday. But the degree of formality with respect to the Laos cease-fire is greater than the degree of formality of the Cambodian cease-fire, but we have understandings with respect to both.

NIXON: These are understandings that you will not see in the agreement so when I use the term "Indochina" that is what we are basing it on. And of course they are going to enforce the [unclear] with Laos and Cambodia have been a sanctuary for — oh, a couple of other points should be made. After a great deal of pulling [unclear], the government of South Vietnam's general and present views in particular are totally onboard and they will issue a statement, I presume a — practically issued already —

KISSINGER: Thieu is going on television half an hour after you, Mr. President.

NIXON: I will make a statement in here that he totally supports this and that is because he has told us that he does.

KISSINGER: That is correct and he will express that publicly within half an hour of your speech.

NIXON: So he — now, as far as the problems are concerned we have to be aware that between now and the cease-fire that there will be fighting. Both sides will be trying to grab as much as they can. When I say there will be, I assume that because that happens in all cease-fires. After the cease-fire, that there will be inevitably — in this kind of guerrilla warfare where you do not have a line, there will be violations, and that is why the supervisory body is so important. Which is, what is it, eleven —

KISSINGER: Eleven [hundred and] sixty [members], Mr. President.

NIXON: I wouldn't want to be one of them.

KISSINGER: Well, actually it is eleven sixty in the international body, and in addition to that there is, for a while, a commission on which we serve which has thirty-three hundred members of which we supply a fourth, and after we drop out of it, there will be a supervisory force composed of the two Vietnamese bodies that has about sixteen hundred. So the total supervisory mechanism will range from thirty-three hundred to forty-six hundred, and it is being distributed over the country in a very effective way. Now whatever limitations these supervisory bodies have had in the past, these international forces are four times larger than any that has operated there before. The two-party commission never existed at all, and the machinery by which they operate, including provisions for minority [unclear], it sets a better stance to get something done that the treaty —

NIXON: One little note of interest is this, [unclear] the question is always "When did you believe that it was going to break?" Well, as I informed the leaders on the tenth of January at their first meeting, after a tortuous ten days of negotiations in December, the negotiations reached a total deadlock, not simply on details but totally. The North Vietnamese were stonewalling. It was obvious that they were going to continue to stonewall. [unclear] it was then we resumed the main policy and then on the thirtieth of December they, at our invitations to return to the conference table, started pushing. The technical talks began on the second. Henry arrived on the eighth of January and began talks. You might indicate, Henry, what happened on the eighth or the ninth. Obviously he was there for more than that. He was there for four or five days.

KISSINGER: My talks — the talks on the agreement itself resumed on the eighth.

NIXON: Let's say on Monday.

KISSINGER: That was Monday. The first day was brutal in every respect.

NIXON: As Bill [Rogers] knows, Henry's message the first day made us all think, "Here we go again." The first day was no hope.

KISSINGER: It was a total absolute deadlock. So, at the president's instruction, I told them — I sent them a message that I would have to leave on Wednesday night. Then, on the next day, which happened to be the president's birthday, we made a very major advance on the two outstanding issues in the agreement and they began to work with great energy on the technical agreement and up to then they had an unbelievable [unclear] in charge of the technical agreement. They put their vice minister in charge, and I asked the fellow to discuss the technical thing, so that started moving on the ninth, and that happened to be the president's birthday and I sent him a cable saying they had broken our hearts before but if this is maintained another day or two we would have a breakthrough. He said, "Well, let's not get too optimistic, but if it is it would be the finest birthday present I have ever had and — "

NIXON: The cable [unclear]. [laughs]

KISSINGER: Then it continued so, and by the end of that week we had — nearly we had settled almost the entire agreement and that is when we exchanged messages with all the principals with respect to the protocols. Then, having a set of the principles, details had to be worked out that occasionally logistics and arrangements for the [unclear] last week. So when I arrived last night there were, in respect to the agreement itself, only three things to be done which we settled very quickly this morning — I mean with respect to the protocols, three things to be done. Then a great deal of the surrounding problems, the international conference and so forth, was one of the most — they were determined to settle today by twelve thirty.

NIXON: Well, for example, they had — another interesting side note is that today — I thought that because of President Johnson's death that that might give the [unclear] an opportunity to take a little more time, they would take it. So I sent a message over to Henry and just pointed out that obviously, but also I thought it might help a little to clear up with the South Vietnamese. Henry fired back, he said that they are so determined to settle that we better go. So that didn't shake them a bit. When they were ready they were ready. They didn't want to be put in the —

KISSINGER: It kept them from settling today.

NIXON: Right, yeah. [laughs]

KISSINGER: But their confidence that — we had decided that after four years of negotiations [unclear] that last night that we finished the English and Vietnamese texts they
took the English text home with them and locked it in a safe lest we take a page out
and slip in another one. [laughs]

NIXON: Let me just summarize the Saigon leadership by saying, it is quite interesting to note while Mel [Laird] is here that without the success of the Vietnamization program there could have been no settlement because the South Vietnamese
would not have settled unless they were confident they could defend themselves
and the North Vietnamese would not have the incentive to settle if they thought
the South Vietnamese were all easy to knock over. So Vietnamization played a part.
Our own military actions of course played a very decisive part because without our
cunning, which means without our quick doing something that they didn't want
us to do — they had very little incentive. I would say also that I would have to say
that the settlement was not made easier by the totally irresponsible actions of the
Congress. I do not refer to the whole Congress, over and over again over the past
four years — the Congress particularly the Senate and even in this session when they
knew we were going back to the conference table passed resolutions which called
basically for a settlement which was far less than they were willing to settle for, and
far less than we got. Just so some of them would worry, I say it one sentence in my
speech tonight, actually three [unclear], I'm speaking to many people of this so-
called Mansfield resolution — prisoners for withdrawal. Isn't that a good deal? We
get our POWs back after we withdraw. Isn't that a good deal? Well, I'll tell you the
people that understand that probably better than anyone else, and better than most
senators and congressmen of that persuasion, are the wives of the prisoners of war
who said our people, our men, did not become prisoners and they did not suffer
and they did not wait, and we did not fight this war just to get them back. And their
colleagues did not die just for the purpose of getting our prisoners of war back. The
difficulty with the POW for withdrawal proposal, which is the proposal — the most
responsible proposal of all the irresponsible ones, this is the least irresponsible I
would say. The difficulty is it would end the war for us, but the war for fifty million
people in Indochina would continue. The agreement we have is a cease-fire for Vietnam, and with the possibility of a cease-fire for Laos and Cambodia. And so what we
have done, by insisting on "peace with honor," we not only have our prisoners back
for our withdrawal in return for a supervised cease-fire stopping the war for the In-
dochinese, and also we have the right for the South Vietnamese to determine their
own future under proper supervised [unclear] something which also we would not
have had with the prisoners for withdrawal. What I am trying to say is it has been
rather long, it's been rather painful, it's been very difficult on you, I know. You wondered, "Why we didn't get out? This was Johnson's war anyway. Why didn't we blame
it on the Democrats and get out and so forth and so on?" The reason is this isn't

Johnson's war, or Kennedy's war. I mean, I [unclear] what I think irresponsible — it happened that it started under Kennedy's administration and it continued in Johnson's administration and in my view it was very badly handled and they much knew they made mistakes. But the point is whatever happened, the United States was involved. We have now withdrawn our forces down to the minimal group that is there. We have now achieved an agreement which achieves our goals of peace for Vietnam that has had war for practically twenty-five years, and the right of the people of South Vietnam to determine their future without having a Communist government imposed upon them against their will. And in my view the fact that we [unclear] we as a country, it will mean a lot certainly to the seventeen million in South Vietnam. But the fact that the United States was responsible will have, in my view, a decisive effect on what is going on in the world. We hear it said that the United States by engaging in Vietnam [unclear] in the world, I assure you that if the United States did not prove to be responsible in Vietnam, did get an end to this war with defeat, with surrender, prisoners for withdrawal, the Chinese wouldn't consider us worth talking to. The Russians wouldn't consider us worth talking to. The Europeans with all their bitching would not consider us to be reliable allies and so what is involved here which most of the members in the Senate and the House eventually will understand, which all of us around this table must understand, is the United States must play a role to keep the peace. And as the only one that can save the free world we have to be responsible, and that is what this peace is all about. [applause]

"The American people are hoping that this mess in South Vietnam is over."

January 24, 1973, 8:36 a.m.
Richard Nixon, Henry Kissinger, and congressional leaders (Michael Mansfield, Robert Byrd, John Stennis, John McClellan, J. William Fulbright, Henry Jackson, Gale McGee, Hugh Scott, Robert Griffin, Strom Thurmond, Milton Young, George Aiken, John Tower, Barry Goldwater, John McFall, Gerald Ford, George Mahon, Thomas Morgan, Samuel Stratton, Joe Waggonner, Leslie Arends, William Bray, Elford Cederberg, William Maillard, Samuel Devine, and Jack Kemp)
CABINET ROOM

The morning after his televised announcement, Nixon gave a wider briefing for bipartisan congressional leaders. This followed the typical pattern of briefings for any major White House announcement: Republican leaders, congressional leaders, and the cabinet. While Nixon drew on history to defend his Vietnam policy — like Eisenhower, he said, major bombing at the very end of negotiations was needed to "prick the boil" and achieve a breakthrough — he faced a much more skeptical crowd in this meeting than he had with his cabinet the night before. The fault lines seen here were a prelude to White House–congressional disagreement to come once the Paris Peace Accords started to fail only a few months later.

• • •

NIXON: The Korean cease-fire, and I was in this room when we talked about it, President Eisenhower had to order as I recall — he ordered devastating bombing and, deliberately, in the case of civilian areas of North Korea, and that pricked the boil and was done. But, we still haven't got peace in Korea, as you know. That's why we deal with it [unclear] we're working on it. As far as this is concerned, we would have to agree, there are problems. You have raised some of the problems. But, I would say that it would be extremely helpful if the members of the House — the Congress — Democrat and Republican, to the extent as leaders that you can, that instead of consoling our fears on this one — don't be, of course, going out and saying well, everything's done, it's going to be all that. Be quite honest, and you've got to be honest, but also don't — I think it's very important for us not to, after getting this agreement, to send messages to Hanoi and messages to Saigon that well, we don't think it's going to last, and all that sort of thing. If you talk that way, the way [unclear]. It's going to happen. Now we've got to talk to — I would like if you can, you can simply say what I said last night. It's a good agreement. It's peace with honor. It not only ends the war for us, which of course the prisoners-for-withdrawal deal, which many members of the House and Senate, just the week after we announced the agreement, had voted for. The prisoners for withdrawal, assuming the other side would have given it, which I think was very doubtful — well, I know it was doubtful — would have ended the war for us, and the war would have continued with a thousand casualties a week for fifty million people, in South [unclear], and Indochina, and in Vietnam. So what we have here is, we've got our prisoners. We have more than that. We've got peace, not only for America, but peace at least, as fragile as it may be, for all of the people of Indochina, and certainly for Vietnam, for a while.

• • •

KISSINGER: There is no specific provision for the replacement of North Vietnamese forces. There is a provision requiring the demobilization and reduction of forces. Essentially, there is a provision that prohibits the introduction of new personnel, of new military personnel. There is a prohibition against the use of Cambodian and Laotian base areas. There's a prohibition against the use of infiltration routes through Cambodia and Laos, and there is a prohibition against the movement of military units across the demilitarized zone.

• • •

NIXON: The point is — the point I'm going to say is, that we're not going to indicate that it's all going to be peaches and cream, that there aren't going to be any violations of the cease-fire. The Russians [unclear] going to go along. Le Duc Tho will make a statement today which will be very conciliatory, and so forth and so on. After what Thieu said last night, Le Duc Tho's got to come out and say something. If Thieu talks too much about victory, he'll talk about victory. And the response of the Russians, and the Chinese, their public statements may say one thing, and they may do something else. What I am saying is that the United States, your government, this administration, I can assure you, will use every influence we have to bear to get the

Russians and the Chinese — each of whom wants something from us, and we want something from them — to cooperate with us and see that this part of the world, which for twenty-five years has been cursed by war, the Japanese, civil war, and so forth, finally has a period of peace. And that's what it's really all about.

· · ·

AIKEN: Now Mr. President, I just think we ought to face up to the hard facts of life. The American people are hoping that this mess in South Vietnam is over, and that the costs of the war will be over, and that the defense budget can be drastically cut. And the bitter medicine in this whole thing, and I think it's inevitable, I'm not saying that, the bitter medicine is that you've got to come out with billions of dollars to support both South Vietnam and with billions of dollars to support North Vietnam. I believe even LBJ earlier, and I think he on a previous occasion has said we've got to spend a billion on war rehabilitation on South and North Vietnam. And then, this is going to present an awful matter, total, in view of the fiscal situation in this country. And the American people are going to be upset at the end of the war about how can you go on giving billions of dollars over a long period to South Vietnam, and then the aid to the North Vietnamese. And that's a bitter situation, and then when we put that in the defense budget, it's going to be bad. I think we can put it in the foreign aid bill, and the foreign aid bill is the most unpopular bill we have but Defense is in such trouble that I don't think we better put it in Defense, and the uprising among the rank-and-file man on Main Street against rebuilding North Vietnam and Hanoi is going to be bad. It's going to be a hell of a situation. I think they're happy today, but they'll be [unclear] as hell [in a few weeks] when they find out the facts of life.

NIXON: Well, I remember, George, when you and I were on the Herter Committee. We knew it was going to be damn unpopular, soon after that war, to pour those billions of dollars into Europe. But we had to come back and sell it, because it was a darn good investment in peace. Let me also say, however, it's a question of doubts. The question is here, in comparison, yes, there will be some expenditures for economic and other purposes in this part of the world. But, it's going to be one hell of a lot less than the expenditures of continuing this war. That's the point.

· · ·

JACKSON: Mr. President, I thought maybe you could answer, maybe you're going to cover it, I don't know, I shouldn't ask it —

NIXON: No, no, you can get this out of the way, right now.

JACKSON: The first thing we'll all be hit with is: When will the list come out, and other details regarding the supervision and the investigation of all prisoners and their names? We're just going to be deluged on that one point, I would think.

KISSINGER: The provisions for supervision are being published today, together with the other supervisory details. The list of prisoners will be handed over on the day of signing, which is to say on Saturday —

NIXON: Saturday.

JACKSON: They will be made public at that point.

KISSINGER: Then, they should be made public Saturday or Sunday. The investigation of the missing in action and the visit to graves, a procedure has been established for exchanging information and for investigative teams to look into disputed cases.

• • •

NIXON: I'm not suggesting this peace is perfect. No peace that is negotiated is perfect. The only one that is perhaps perfect in many things is unconditional surrender. And I may say, that has serious shortcomings, too, in Vietnam. But I do say, this *is* a peace that *can* work and give the people of Viet — Southeast Asia a chance to determine their own future. And I can only say thank God for those who stood by. I have great respect, as I say, for those who had a different view. Thank God for, also, a lot of brave men, who went out there, and didn't want to go to war any more than any of us wanted to go to World War II and the rest, brave as we all taught them. They gave their lives, some of them became prisoners, and we ought to be damn proud.

"The all-volunteer army means not having them drafted"

January 26, 1973, 8:37 a.m.
Richard Nixon and Republican congressional leaders (Spiro Agnew, Hugh Scott, Robert Griffin, Norris Cotton, Wallace Bennett, John Tower, William Brock, Gerald Ford, Leslie Arends, John Rhodes, Barber Conable, Robert Wilson, George H. W. Bush, Roy Ash, John Ehrlichman, William Timmons, Richard Cook, Thomas Korologos, Kenneth Cole, Frederic Malek, Ronald Ziegler, Richard Kleindienst, George Shultz, and Caspar Weinberger)
CABINET ROOM

Today few people remember that following the signing of the Paris Peace Accords that ended the Vietnam War, Nixon ended the military draft and established what was then termed the all-volunteer army. The draft had been universally hated, yet it was difficult to end the practice as long as continued war required fresh deployments. "The draft survives principally as a device by which we use compulsion to get young men to serve at less than the market rate of pay," the economist J. Kenneth Galbraith said.

Nixon vowed to end the draft as early as his 1960 bid for the presidency. He repeated the pledge during his 1968 campaign, saying, "It is not so much the way they are selected that is wrong, it is the fact of selection." Here, Director of the Office of Management and Budget Caspar Weinberger briefs Nixon on the expected cost increases of establishing all-volunteer armed forces. "Mr. President," House Republican leader Gerald Ford said, "the American people wanted the all-volunteer army, so they have to pay for it."

• • •

WEINBERGER: This is the rather familiar story now to everyone except the press, and that is that the priorities have changed very drastically. The human resources expenditures, this is in dollars over here, have gone from about sixty billion up to close to a hundred and thirty-one billion by the end of '75. This is projected out through 1975. Defense stays just about level in dollars, very little change at all, and in percentage,

Defense is going way down. It's under thirty percent now. And human resources are about forty-seven percent of the total budget. So, the change there is very dramatic, a complete reversal, and it is illustrative of the different priorities that we now have. This is a little further explanation of the Defense outlays, seventy-five, seventy-six, seventy-four point eight [billion dollars], these are almost level figures. And they will jump in 1974 about four billion dollars, but all of that is pay and price increases. All of that is the amount associated with the all-volunteer armed force and the other pay increases that have been had in the military, plus the additional pension fund. There is no increase in activity at all, here represented there. As a matter of fact, there is a rather substantial decrease in the number of men that will be in Defense, and you can see that here. Here, with 1968 there were three and a half million military personnel. This year, in 1974, the president is requesting funds for two point two million, now, in a very steady decline. But this line shows the average pay and allowances for each person in the military, uniformed personnel. And that's gone from fifty-five hundred average to ten thousand dollars a year average, and that's where the increase has come, in the costs of military personnel. We have another chart that isn't blown up but will be in the chart book.

ARENDS: Could I ask a question? Is that approximate amount of money spent for Defense still approximately fifty-eight percent for personnel, personnel cost out of the total budget of the military?

WEINBERGER: That's right. Yes, sir. The payroll costs in the military now run just about fifty-eight percent, and the interesting figure you have here, it's in the chart book, I didn't have it blown up. How much will a billion dollars pay for? In 1964, a billion dollars would pay for two hundred nineteen thousand men. In 1974, a billion dollars gets a hundred thousand men. And, actually, that's the difference that has occurred on this question, and that's why although there are sharp reductions in Defense, we stay just about level rather than having this big peace dividend that everyone [unclear] —

NIXON: The point, Les, let me make a point that you and John [Stennis] and the Armed Services Committee fellows should be aware of — are aware of I am sure — is this. That is why any comparison basically in dollars or rubles, whichever way you want to explain it, of the amount we spend or percentage of GNP or whatever you have, between ourselves and the Soviet Union, is totally irrelevant, because when they put, say, seventy billion dollars, shall we say, equivalent, in defense, if they put seventy billion dollars in defense, my guess is the amount of their personnel costs is much less, because — and their hardware is much more. They're buying more hardware; we're buying more men. We pay more for the men. In other words, their men come cheaper. Now, as a matter of fact, they have a bigger — because of their great emphasis on land forces, they have [unclear], but their costs for men are infinitely less than ours [unclear]. So, this poses — let me tell you about this defense thing, and this is where I am going to argue that the other side [unclear]. God knows we'd like to keep it as low as we can, but you have to have enough. You have to have enough in order to bargain, as we go into the second round of SALT talks, and the rest, and MBFR, et cetera. But we also have to have enough for our own defense. And at the present time, we see that number, fifty-eight percent, all the costs going into personnel, you aren't buying a hell of a lot of hardware. You're buying a lot, but not as much. Roy, of course, one of the things even though he is going to be now on the budget side of State, that's Roy Ash, is acutely aware of this subject, right, Roy? It's a real problem.

ASH: Certainly vis-à-vis what the Soviets are doing, actually it's very critical —

NIXON: Yes. Yes, sir. The main reasons with these comparisons, as we go down the line, and say how much, if you look at our new stock, how much we've got, and so forth and so on. We've got a huge outlay of men and women and so forth in the army, of course what you're not getting [unclear].

UNKNOWN: Mr. President, I think we have to accept this is the price we have to pay for an all-volunteer army.

NIXON: Because it is. And of course, let me say, I would hope when you fellows go to campuses and so forth this year, if the all-volunteer army means not having them drafted, that's not a bad point to emphasize. I think it should have some appeal, shouldn't it, Jerry?

FORD: Mr. President, the American people wanted the all-volunteer army, so they have to pay for it.

After the war

January 31, 1973, 10:10 a.m.
Richard Nixon and Henry Kissinger
WHITE HOUSE TELEPHONE

On January 27, 1973, each of the factions involved in the Vietnam War accepted the Paris Peace Accords, ending the war — or at least getting the United States out of it. Four days later, Nixon was scheduled to appear at his first news conference since the previous October. In the morning, he and Kissinger discussed the day's agenda and the practical ways by which the United States would ensure that the peace accords remained in effect. As a start, Kissinger was to travel to Hanoi during a mid-February tour that also included Beijing and Tokyo.

• • •

NIXON: What about — oh, I see some leak to the effect that — that Thieu and I will meet in Hawaii.

KISSINGER: Well, that must have been —

NIXON: Well —

KISSINGER: — either Vietnamese —

NIXON: Yeah.

KISSINGER: — or from the Agnew party.

NIXON: Yeah. Well, I'll simply say that I hope at some time to meet with him. Don't you think so?

KISSINGER: That's right.

NIXON: Say it publicly. One other point: with regard to the resupply of North Vietnamese and VC in South Vietnam, how do they do it? I mean, if Cambodia is closed, and Laos is closed, and the DMZ —

KISSINGER: They will —

NIXON: — allows only civilian modalities —

KISSINGER: Well —

NIXON: What — what's the deal?

KISSINGER: They will get — this is something: the legal entry points have yet to be determined, but —

NIXON: Right.

KISSINGER: — there will probably be two seaports and one point at the DMZ.

NIXON: And, as I understand it then, that, on the basis of the agreement, that they can supply people over those seaports. Is that right?

KISSINGER: Well, all they can do is to re — is to —

NIXON: I know.

KISSINGER: — replace weapons.

NIXON: But, replace weapons that are —

KISSINGER: They cannot —

NIXON: — worn out, used, et cetera, et cetera. Right?

KISSINGER: They have no legal right to bring in anything else.

NIXON: Anything new. I know, I know. I know. [laughs]

KISSINGER: Nor — nor, for that matter, have they got a right to bring in uniforms and things like that, technically speaking.

NIXON: Yeah. I know, I know. The — we all know that if the agreement is kept — and there's nothing wrong with the agreement; it's just a question of whether they keep it.

KISSINGER: That's right.

NIXON: You could add fifteen thousand clauses; it wouldn't mean a thing.

KISSINGER: Exactly.

NIXON: This agreement is just — is, is a totally airtight agreement if it's kept.

KISSINGER: Exactly —

NIXON: No question about it.

KISSINGER: Exactly —

NIXON: No question. I just wanted to know that. These are questions Ron [Ziegler] thought might come up, and I want to —

KISSINGER: Right. I wouldn't, incidentally — I sent you a note yesterday — volunteer anything about their murdering activities there, in the context of their — of attacking Hanoi, if it's done in the context of replying to people who are accusing us of — of carpet bombing.

NIXON: Well, that's the only way I was going to use it.

KISSINGER: Right.

NIXON: Big no —

KISSINGER: Because they'll —

NIXON: — because if they say that we're — if they say we're killing civilians, we'll say, "Well, now, there are a lot of civilians killed in the South."

KISSINGER: That's right.

NIXON: Which we've got to do. We can't be —

KISSINGER: So, in that context, it can be done. And, I think if one volunteers too harsh an attack on them, it —

NIXON: I don't intend to, but I've got to answer that in case they —

KISSINGER: Oh, yes.

NIXON: — say that we've killed people in the North.

KISSINGER: Absolutely.

NIXON: Because, we've been — I mean, we have to realize here that, shit, we have to be rather gingerly, but they haven't been too [laughs] — I mean, they've gone from —

KISSINGER: They've been pretty restrained in their public comments about us —

NIXON: Restrained — restrained. Right, right. But, I mean, on the — in terms of the — I've been very restrained in terms of the — what is achieved, and all that sort of thing. But, be that as it may, we shall see. Well, those are the only things I have. You have anything else on that? Anything else you think — ?

KISSINGER: On the military activities, now —

NIXON: They've receded, I see.

KISSINGER: They've receded. The biggest fight is now going on in an area where the South Vietnamese tried to grab some territory [Sa Huynh, Binh Dinh Province, Republic of Vietnam] right after the cease — right at the cease-fire. They tried to seize a naval base —

NIXON: Yeah.

KISSINGER: — along the shore — along the coast, north of the Cua Viet River. And the North Vietnamese are trying to retake that. That's the only big fight that's now going on.

NIXON: But, it's really going quite well, isn't it?

KISSINGER: Well, the South Vietnamese —

NIXON: Even —

KISSINGER: — have fought extremely well.

NIXON: Even — but what — no, not on that. But, I meant — I meant the cease-fire is going quite well.

KISSINGER: That's right.

NIXON: I mean, the very thing —

KISSINGER: It's the activity inside of —

NIXON: — the very thing that we said, that it would recede —

KISSINGER: Yes.

NIXON: — even the press —

KISSINGER: Every day is getting —

NIXON: — reluctantly [laughs] concludes that it's going down.

KISSINGER: Exactly right.

NIXON: They're going to have one hell of a time with this thing. They're going to have one hell of a time. I mean, you know, assuming that some of this does recede.

•   •   •

NIXON: Now, with regard to the Cambodian unilateral cease-fire, is that in force and still in force? And we, according to the — looking at the news — the summary this morning from the intelligence, we are not bombing in Cambodia because of that. Is that correct?

KISSINGER: That is correct.

NIXON: And, that's seventy-two hours, and the enemy is respecting it up to this point?

KISSINGER: Up to this point, yeah.

NIXON: In Cambodia. But — so, it might be extended another seventy-two. I just have —

KISSINGER: Oh, no. This will, this will be extended indefinitely. Lon Nol's is indefinite. We just stood down for seventy-two hours, to see —

NIXON: Yeah.

KISSINGER: — how it would work.

NIXON: No. And if it's —

KISSINGER: And, as long as it holds, we will observe it.

NIXON: Mm-hmm. And, as far as Lao — Laos is concerned, we can just say, "We have reason to believe there will be a negotiated cease-fire on a — "

KISSINGER: "In a reasonable time — in a reasonably short time."

NIXON: Yeah, that's right. Okay.

KISSINGER: Right.

"This energy crisis is much deeper . . . much more severe than anybody in this country realizes."
January 31, 1973, 4:52 p.m.
Richard Nixon and John Connally
OVAL OFFICE

By 1973, John Connally was a Republican in everything but party affiliation. A loyal aide to Lyndon Johnson and former governor of Texas, nonetheless he served as Nixon's secretary of the treasury and organized Democrats for Nixon in 1972. He grew close to Nixon, who eventually considered Connally his preferred successor in 1976. A change in party affiliation was inevitable, but — out of respect for Johnson — Connally refused to make it while LBJ was still alive. Here, only a week after Johnson died, Connally discusses his plans to switch parties but first warns Nixon of a looming energy crisis.

•   •   •

CONNALLY: I think, Mr. President, you've got — you have two major problems. If I may be presumptuous enough to suggest two of the problems that you're going to face —

NIXON: [laughs] You ought to know!

CONNALLY: — right away. One, and I — you and I have talked about this many times, and I'll just mention these and then leave them alone — but, I mentioned both of them to George Shultz this morning — I'm going to tell you that he and I had breakfast this morning — I think this energy crisis is much deeper, much broader, much more severe than anybody in this country realizes. And I think it's going to require a great deal of your personal understanding and attention. You could well see gasoline rationing in the United States this summer. You got fuel rationing now — fuel oil. You got gas rationing right now.

NIXON: Really?

CONNALLY: And it's going to get worse next year than it is this summer — at this point. We don't have the refinery capacity. And as our demand increases. And this — even in this last cold spell, universities were shut down. The University of Texas, for instance, in Austin, Texas, delayed its open — reopening for one week because it had no heat. The San Marcos State Teachers College, where President Johnson went, could not reopen. Many industrial concerns shut down their production completely, because they had no fuel. The gas companies are rationing their industrial customers anytime there's a cold spell. Now, most of these customers can use fuel oil. Like the utilities, they can burn fuel oil to generate electricity. But, it's more expensive for 'em, so they like gas. Plus, the environmentalists raise hell when they burn fuel oil. So, they don't like to do it. Fuel oil, now, is being laid down on the East Coast for six — over six dollars a barrel. I will not be at all surprised to see crude oil laid down — if you can get it — on the East Coast of the United States, this year, at five dollars a barrel. The idea that domestic crude is going to kick the lid significantly is not going to happen. Foreign crude is really going to happen — or, the price increase is going to happen for domestic crude. Because this is one of the things that the Arabs — OPEC nations, the Arab nations are doing — they are, in fact, taking over control of the oil itself to market. They are marketing it to the highest bidder. And the highest bidder, it could be Japan, Germany, Italy, and so forth. And the United States is going to have to posture itself, very quickly, to get into this issue, where, as a nation, we can compete with other nations in buying oil, because the oil companies can't do it. And I would predict that in this year, if not more than eighteen months, you're going to see a complete revolution of the manner of production and sale of oil, and pricing of crude products around the world. It's going to have a hell of an impact on this country.

• • •

CONNALLY: I've done a lot of thinking about it. Nellie [Connally] and I have talked about it. Frankly I have talked to some of my very closest friends [from the Johnson White House]. [Former press secretary] George Christian, [former special counsel] Larry Temple, some of those that I have been politically associated with over the years. They all think that really there's no — that I don't have any choice, and I don't think I really have a choice. In my lifetime I don't think the Democratic Party will ever come back to mean what I stand for. I don't think that I could ever be, in my lifetime, even comfortable with the Democratic Party. I don't think there's any question about it. From the standpoint of principle, all future political aspirations aside, just on the basis on what you stand for, what you like to see preserved and protected and promoted in this country, I have to leave the Democratic Party. Now, becoming an independent is no answer. So the only—it's a two-party country, so the only answer to me, not that I agree with the Republican Party per se at all times. I subscribe to your policies I think a hell of a lot more than I do—in any event that your policies are the Republican policies. So I have no real problems with that, and I am prepared to do it. I don't want to do it. I want—I have thought about doing it in a low-key way. I talked to Dick Kleindienst yesterday, and Dick talked about it [unclear].

NIXON: Oh yeah? Good.

CONNALLY: He brought it up. I've been talking to him.

NIXON: He's a good politician.

CONNALLY: Yes he is. He suggested that the way to do it, and it may not be a bad one, is to just do it on [unclear].

NIXON: [unclear]

CONNALLY: And I thought about talking to Chuck [Colson] about the possibility of just announcing it maybe tomorrow morning on the *Today* show. I think it ought not to be a studied—

NIXON: Yeah.

CONNALLY: —sort of thing that almost has to come out casually. Just a fairly casual thing, and I admit I don't know that I will do it tomorrow because I really need to talk to—

NIXON: You need to sort of let some people know.

CONNALLY: I really need to let some people know it. And I think it is premature to do it tomorrow, but [unclear].

NIXON: That might be the best thing. [unclear]

CONNALLY: I think you pick a time—it is a very delicate thing. And it's [unclear] with Johnson passing away.

NIXON: Makes it a lot easier.

Nixon in China again
February 1, 1973, 9:45 a.m.
Richard Nixon and Henry Kissinger
OVAL OFFICE

With the struggle to end the Vietnam War over, Nixon turned his attention to a topic of great interest to him: U.S. relations with China and the USSR. He and Kissinger discussed the possibilities for further realignment in a post-Vietnam era. While Kissinger was heading for his extensive post–Vietnam War tour through eastern Asia, Nixon dreamed of another visit to China for himself—a trip that was not to be.

• • •

NIXON: I also think when you're in Beijing you should explore the possibility of my taking another trip there. I don't know whether we should or not, but let me say — of course, if I go we have to put Japan on.

KISSINGER: But that might not be bad.

NIXON: Japan is always a problem because of the radicals. But at the present time, I saw something — a Japanese poll indicating that sixty percent thought that the emperor should visit us, and seventy-eight percent wanted the president to go to Japan. So we have a lot of friends in Japan, you know. The Japanese are not all that dumb.

KISSINGER: But if you want that option we have to invite the [unclear] emperor over here.

NIXON: Have the emperor first?

KISSINGER: Yeah.

NIXON: I don't mind having the emperor.

KISSINGER: I mean, if we could put him on the schedule —

NIXON: That will be the only other visit this year, Henry. It can't be the Zulus or anything else.

KISSINGER: But if you have him here then after that you have the option of going there.

NIXON: I would like to go to China, you see, at a time, again, there might be a better time of year [as opposed to February, when Nixon first visited] when it's more pleasant. We might get a better reception too with the Chinese at that time.

KISSINGER: Oh, no question.

NIXON: And I just don't see him again, you know what I mean? Zhou Enlai?

KISSINGER: Oh, you certainly would get a popular reception next time.

NIXON: Yeah. And that could be helpful.

KISSINGER: Yeah.

NIXON: See?

KISSINGER: I'll get this [unclear] set with Zhou.

NIXON: Well, just tell him I'd like to do it. There are great important things that I feel that — that I have got to turn this country around. You can tell him things like that. But I did not want to do it, but tell him that we have to meet with the Russians on the other thing. But I want to keep talking to them.

KISSINGER: Well, then I'll tell him that —

NIXON: That I would like to do it.

KISSINGER: Well, also that we expect if the Russians attack them it's very useful to have [unclear].

NIXON: Yeah. Yeah. Another point we have to have in mind is what the hell we do on Taiwan. Now, as you know, I think they might call in our chip on that. You think they will?

KISSINGER: They will, yes. Well, what I thought —

NIXON: Our chip there is not too much anyway. All we promised is that we'd —

KISSINGER: Pull out our forces.

NIXON: Cut down our sources—forces, right? Vietnam-related forces come out anyway. That would be—

KISSINGER: The Vietnam-related forces come out immediately. And the other ones would be reduced gradually.

NIXON: So do it.

KISSINGER: I thought I should preempt it by telling them when I get there that we will pull out the Vietnam-related forces and give them a schedule.

NIXON: Right.

KISSINGER: That way they can't raise the other forces.

NIXON: Yeah. But you see, what the Chinese have done to work out, Henry, is this. And I don't know whether this is in their—I mean, it wouldn't be possible with the jackasses from North Vietnam. You see what I mean? The Chinese may be subtle enough to understand. Taiwan is such a bustling, productive, et cetera, community, they ought to work out some kind of a federation, you know what I mean?

KISSINGER: I think they're willing to do that.

NIXON: What I call—like basically, Puerto Rico. And I mean let both flowers bloom. See my point?

KISSINGER: What I think they will come to, what they will gradually accept—

NIXON: Otherwise it's war. You know what I mean?

KISSINGER: No, they won't use force. That you can count on.

NIXON: Well, not with us. But how else are they going to get the Taiwanese, for example? I mean [unclear]. But I don't see—the Taiwanese are doing so well economically, Henry, they're never going to let, never going to say, "All right, we're now going to become part of the PRC." Never.

KISSINGER: No, it's not going to happen that way. I think what they will want from us is—well, first, that we pull out some of our forces. That will get us through this year.

NIXON: Yeah.

KISSINGER: For the time being, what they really want from us is protection against Russia. Taiwan is subsidiary. Eventually, we may have to come to a position similar to Japan's, which is that we maintain consular relations in Taiwan and diplomatic relations in Beijing, in return for a promise by them they wouldn't use force against Taiwan, but we hope that Chiang Kai-shek will have died before then.

NIXON: Japan has consular relations with Taiwan?

KISSINGER: Yeah.

NIXON: It'd be a bitch for us.

KISSINGER: It'd be a bastard.

NIXON: Well, the thing to do is to have it build up—

KISSINGER: But this wouldn't be, I don't see that—

NIXON: The thing to do is have it build up in American public opinion before then. We just got to do it.

KISSINGER: It can't happen much before '75.

NIXON: The later the better. I still think Zhou Enlai should consider — reconsider — not Washington, but San Clemente. You see my point?

KISSINGER: Let me talk to him about it.

NIXON: You see my point?

KISSINGER: What he could do is go to the UN.

NIXON: He could go to the UN; we've talked about that. And then we'd meet up there, you mean?

KISSINGER: No. In connection to that, stop in San Clemente.

NIXON: Oh, I see. I will not in four years go to the UN. I'm never going there again.

KISSINGER: But of course, it hurts you. If he goes to the UN, he's going to give a tough —

NIXON: Sure.

KISSINGER: — talk. Now the disadvantage of having Brezhnev in October is that he'll certainly go to the UN.

NIXON: Oh, well, Henry, that's part of it. What the hell do we care?

KISSINGER: We shouldn't care.

NIXON: Look, we always worry about them huffing and puffing. There are worse things.

KISSINGER: I think, Mr. President, from our point of view, assuming we could find a formulation on that nuclear treaty that doesn't drive the Chinese up a wall. The Russians are sufficiently eager to have it, so that if we could keep it out there in front of them until October it would buy us good Russian behavior for the rest of year.

"The charges against our Democrat friends"

February 3, 1973, 11:05 a.m.

Richard Nixon and Charles Colson

OVAL OFFICE

Five days after his U.S. District Court convicted two men associated with the Watergate break-in — the other five pleaded guilty — Judge John Sirica boldly asserted that another court should expand upon the case. Sirica was more outspoken both on the bench and outside the court than he had ever been before, and certainly more so than most federal judges. Nixon was aghast, and he was no less frustrated with the fast-moving situation in Congress. When he turned his attention to the impending investigation in the Senate, he suggested that his staff, including Counsel to the President John Dean, go on the offensive. Specifically, he told Colson that he wanted Dean to dig more deeply into long-standing (and ultimately disproven) charges that Democratic senator Daniel Brewster of Maryland had accepted bribes from the Spiegel catalog company.

• • •

NIXON: What the hell is the strategy going to be here now? We just have to — all we're doing is just to sort of letting him — you know, here's the judge now saying — his goddamn conduct is shocking as a judge.

COLSON: It is.

NIXON: He's not being — I mean I suppose he's on the other side. What's he bucking for? Is he looking — is he young enough to look for an appointment from a Democrat in four years?

COLSON: No, no, no. I don't think — Sirica is a tough, hard-boiled, law-and-order judge, who —

NIXON: You can't blame him — I'm not blaming him. I just wonder why he's going far beyond.

COLSON: No, he's a Republican. I know him pretty well.

NIXON: Yeah.

COLSON: I have been with him at various events — social events —

NIXON: Right.

COLSON: Very decent guy. Dedicated to you, and to Eisenhower. I can't understand what happened to him. He's been ill. The only thing I can figure is that he didn't — this case just got under his craw for some reason. He's a hotheaded Italian and he blew it. He's handled himself terribly, awful — refusing to accept the plea. And of course the odd thing about this is, Mr. President — the U.S. attorney who has been prosecuting this case —

NIXON: Silbert.

COLSON: — is not our guy. He's — I would imagine he is a Democrat — has been there since 1964 at the U.S. attorney's office, but I think Sirica could easily be doing what he is being told to do.

NIXON: I mean, I don't know — now what happens? He is trying to keep the Senate from conducting a big investigation. And I thank God it's Ervin. I mean when you really come down to it, Ervin — at least — he's now going to be hoist on his own petard because he's the great constitutionalist, and if they talk about hearsay and all the rest, if I were [unclear].

COLSON: I don't know that Ervin has decided what to do. I've talked to him once. He is very reasonable. He says you know this fight over separation of powers has gone on for two hundred years. It will go on for two hundred more years. He said it is just one of those things that Congress and the Executive will always be debating.

• • •

NIXON: Getting back to this once again. I noticed Jackson said he didn't take it [chairmanship of what would become the Ervin Committee] because maybe his own campaign was involved. He means that — he thinks we were spying on him. Huh?

COLSON: No, I think Jackson knows that we were feeding him a lot of stuff in the campaign — not we, but we were arranging for stuff to be fed to him.

NIXON: Mm-hmm.

COLSON: And I think he wants to stay out of it.

NIXON: Well, what if anything there is being done or can be done on the counterattacks? Are any of charges against our Democrat friends being investigated? Have they been, and will they be?

COLSON: Yeah.

NIXON: I just don't know.

COLSON: There isn't anything that balances —

NIXON: [unclear]

COLSON: No.

NIXON: Well, let me ask one other thing. This [former senator Daniel] Brewster [scandal related to his acceptance of an illegal gratuity] thing is, according to Bobby B[aker] — he says runs a hell of a lot deeper and runs to a number of Democratic senators, and maybe a Republican or so. Now, what are we doing about having an investigation, calling in Spiegel, putting him under oath, the FBI, and say what other senators — go right down the list. What are we doing about that?

COLSON: That's a good point. I don't know what we are doing.

NIXON: I think it should be done. I think there should be — now, understand — the ability to [unclear]. I think you ought to discuss this — with who?

COLSON: John [Dean].

NIXON: John Dean. And say — and it should get over to Kleindienst. And say, after all, "Brewster has made very a serious charge on television this morning and that there are a lot of senators involved. This charge must now be investigated. And therefore, I think that the attorney general ought to order the FBI to call in Spiegel and various people and conduct an investigation." You see my point?

COLSON: Reopen the grand jury.

NIXON: Yes.

A "cool detachment" from the United Nations

February 3, 1973, 12:12 p.m.

Richard Nixon and Henry Kissinger

OVAL OFFICE

Nixon's choice to replace George H. W. Bush as ambassador to the United Nations was a former television reporter, John Scali. During his years as diplomatic correspondent at ABC News, Scali had not only reported on Cold War developments, he'd even become involved in some of them, notably the Cuban Missile Crisis, when he was a liaison who was trusted by both Soviet and American officials. Though a longtime Democrat, Scali impressed Nixon and left broadcasting in 1971 to serve for two years as his special advisor on foreign policy. In December 1972, Nixon announced Scali's UN appointment, which was set to take effect in mid-February. Nixon's antipathy toward the UN had been present since the international body was founded, but it was unmistakable in 1973.

But first, Nixon discussed his admiration for Great Britain's place in international relations. Nixon's enthusiasm extended to the British prime minister, Edward Heath, who had been in office since 1970. Heath had been the head of Britain's Conservative Party for five years before that. Nixon, who could be astute regarding other nations, seemed naive regarding the complexity of Heath's attitude toward the United States. In fact, the prime minister distrusted the so-called special relationship between the two nations, regarding it as a form of domination by the United States. It was a trap he avoided in person with

Nixon, as well as in British-American affairs. Instead, Heath was focused on making Europe Britain's priority for the future. The problems that would challenge the special relationship later in 1973 had a basis in Nixon's simplistic, even nostalgic concept of Great Britain.*

• • •

NIXON: You know, I am so glad that we got Heath over here —

KISSINGER: Oh, that was a good meeting —

NIXON: — because we've got to have a friend in Europe —

KISSINGER: That helps.

NIXON: — and he's the only solid one we've got.

KISSINGER: Yeah.

NIXON: And, by golly, let's play them.

KISSINGER: Definitely —

NIXON: I mean, you've got a good relationship with him. I mean, as you know, when I need to talk to him, and I think that we —

KISSINGER: You have a superb relationship with Heath.

NIXON: With Heath now we'll want to play to get him and we've got to play with him. See, what I think he appreciates, Henry, is that we didn't bug him on Northern Ireland.

KISSINGER: No way.

NIXON: He knows that. He appreciates the fact that we didn't bug him on Rhodesia. He appreciates the fact that we didn't bug him on other things —

KISSINGER: But then you did it in such a delicate way when you said, "All right, now, we've talked about Northern Ireland."

NIXON: Yeah. We're — God, now, and — but now, therefore, on a much bigger thing he didn't give us hell, and as a matter of fact made all the right noises. But I really feel — the thing I want to say to you is that I know we've got some studies going on in view of the role of NATO and so forth and so on. What I was trying to do in talking to you was to push the British —

KISSINGER: But they're doing it now.

NIXON: — into thinking about this.

KISSINGER: No, no.

NIXON: And I actually think that our guys — I have the feeling about this being about the British. You may disagree. They're no longer a world power, but the British are bright and they think strategically. And I think the right British guy is better than the right guy in the State Department.

KISSINGER: No question.

NIXON: Now, what I want you to do —

KISSINGER: They're better trained.

---

* Luke A. Nichter, *Richard Nixon and Europe: The Reshaping of the Postwar Atlantic World* (Cambridge University Press, 2015), p. 115.

NIXON: — what I want you to do — take a fellow like Thompson. We haven't got anybody in our government that is as good as Thompson on that field. Take a fellow
like that guy, that [British defense expert] Alastair Buchan. I don't find many people
around here in the State Department that think as, you know, in the broad terms as
you do. I don't know if you agree with me, but what I think — I would like for you
to take the best British brains and the best American brains and put them together
in — combine. The only question I ask is whether we are missing out on a good
Frenchman. The French civil service, according to what I hear, and I think certainly
on the economic side, is as good as any in the world —

KISSINGER: No question —

NIXON: On the foreign policy side are we missing some people? Now, you know, for
example, we've got two or three French newsmen that you rate as well as the British.
Right?

KISSINGER: But the French are different. The French, in terms of intellect and maybe
even education, may be even superior to the British, but they don't have the — they
don't — they are too doctrinaire.

NIXON: Yeah.

KISSINGER: And they don't have the tradition of thinking in global terms. The French
have always thought largely in European terms. But, I think it'd be too dangerous
to do —

NIXON: Okay. All right. Fine.

KISSINGER: — before March.

NIXON: Very well. What about — ?

KISSINGER: After the election we should try.

NIXON: Oh, we will. Of course, of course. Nothing now. I was thinking of then, after
the elections —

KISSINGER: I think —

NIXON: — not the German one. Let me ask about that. Do you have anybody among
the Germans that [unclear]? They say the defense minister's a pretty good man —

KISSINGER: No, the old defense minister, Helmut Schmidt.

NIXON: They threw him out, huh?

KISSINGER: No —

NIXON: Promote him?

KISSINGER: They made him finance minister. They had a crisis with their finance minister leaving. Then, in order to — it was a complicated maneuver. In order to appoint
a new minister they would have had to convene Parliament. They were afraid that if
they convened Parliament, they might get a vote of no confidence, so they shifted —

NIXON: Yeah?

KISSINGER: They played around with the ministers that were already in office and then
they didn't have to be confirmed by Parliament. This shifted Schmidt from Defense
to Finance, which he wanted because Defense — Schmidt wants to become chancellor. It's awfully tough to go from Defense to become chancellor.

NIXON: What is the situation on Brandt's throat?

KISSINGER: Unfortunately, it's not malignant. Now that's a terrible thing to say—

NIXON: I know what you mean.

KISSINGER: What I mean—

NIXON: You mean, unfortunately, he's in very good health.

KISSINGER: Unfortunately, he's likely to hang on in there, yeah.

NIXON: He is a dolt.

KISSINGER: He is a dolt—

NIXON: He is a dolt—

KISSINGER: —and he's dangerous.

NIXON: Well, I'm afraid he's dangerous. I really have to agree with you. I agree. God, you know, isn't it a shame, though, with the—? I was thinking of the German minds, of, well, basically, of the late nineteenth century. And frankly there were some pretty good—well, I guess the Germans have had their problems, but the Germans, in terms of producing global thinkers—there's no Italians—

KISSINGER: There was a curious—

NIXON: I had a curi—I had a very interesting talk with Heath in the car, you know. He was—we were talking about—there were lots of—I said, "Tell me, what men in Europe have you got?" As I said, we were talking about World War II and afterwards. I said, "What leaders in Europe have you got?" [unclear] And you know his beautiful understanding, he said, "Well," he said, "I'm afraid I find it rather difficult to think about that at the moment." He said, "Pompidou." And he—Pompidou, this is my point, I said, "Pompidou has the brains and so forth to do it, but his interests are basically inward and parochial, and not outward and global."

KISSINGER: No.

NIXON: He said, "Exactly." He said he had had the same experience with him. When he talked to Pompidou, they're always talking about tactical things for tomorrow, or economic things and so forth. Brandt he considers to be—he didn't say it quite as bluntly—he just considers to be dumb.

KISSINGER: Well—

NIXON: And—but interestingly enough he picked the one guy—he likes the Italians that I have met. [Prime Minister Giulio] Andreotti—

KISSINGER: Very good. Andreotti is very good—

NIXON: Yeah, but he picked the one—I said, "Now, look at the small countries. Who have you got?" He says, "None, yet there is one fellow that is quite good: [Austrian chancellor Bruno] Kreisky." He knew exactly where I was hitting. Down in that damn little country of Austria you've got one bright guy.

KISSINGER: Yes.

NIXON: Kreisky.

KISSINGER: Kreisky, he was impressive when you saw him—

NIXON: Remember?

KISSINGER: —in some—

NIXON: Well, the point about Kreisky is that. You see, I look back and I think what you and I've got to do is to think in terms of how we get the best brains in the world to work on some of these matters. And maybe we've just got to do it ourselves [unclear].

KISSINGER: No, we can certainly do —

NIXON: But I — do you remember after World War II, do you agree? I mean, not — well, after World War I you had [Paris Peace Conference negotiator Jan] Smuts and people like that on the scene. After World War II, you can pick five or six leaders of Europe who were worth talking to. The Dutchman was very good. Do you remember his name? After World War II the — when he went to the World Court, you know, all that sort of thing? The Dutchman. There was a good Dane there. I remember, the — but at the present time, whether it's the diplomatic corps —

KISSINGER: You see at that time the Europeans — take Holland. It had an empire many times larger than itself, so it had to think in big terms —

NIXON: Yeah.

KISSINGER: The Europeans have become provincial, and one thing you're doing by letting the British in on these things is you're really doing them a favor —

NIXON: Oh [unclear] —

KISSINGER: — by enabling them to continue to think in big terms.

NIXON: Yeah. Did you notice, no interesting thing that, you know, we had all those briefing papers on the economics and the rest, and I did spend an hour and a half with Shultz in which we ran it through, but the interesting thing was to me that Heath, instead of getting down — he got in serious on this side — but did you notice he wanted — he, himself, really wanted to talk about the big picture?

KISSINGER: Oh, yeah.

NIXON: In other words, Heath has changed enormously since 1970. Remember our first meeting? He was talking in more minute terms —

KISSINGER: Yeah.

NIXON: — and more immediate terms, but now Heath is thinking globally and the rest. And that's the reason why I wanted to talk to him yesterday to give him sort of — so he could start with —

KISSINGER: Well, I thought —

NIXON: — his view of the world, and then to come in on this. And then —

KISSINGER: Well, I thought —

NIXON: — he didn't say much, but he got —

KISSINGER: Well —

NIXON: — the point.

KISSINGER: Well, I thought — well, partly because even he cannot think in these big terms anymore. If you haven't got the power, then you haven't really got the incentive to think in those —

NIXON: Yeah, I know.

KISSINGER: — terms.

NIXON: I know.

KISSINGER: And — but I thought, as you were talking, that there's really no leader in the non-Communist world today who could make such a survey without notes. We didn't give you any talking points.

NIXON: No. We always don't. I've — actually, the one guy that enjoyed it was Burke Trend.

KISSINGER: Oh, yeah. Oh, he was — he's very impressed by you.

NIXON: He's just a great guy, too.

KISSINGER: Yeah.

NIXON: It's a shame he's leaving, though, isn't it? What is it — his age?

KISSINGER: Sixty. He's reaching retirement age, which is compulsory in Britain.

NIXON: Well, we do a lot of business [unclear]. What I have in mind is that the British could block for us in the [European Economic] Community.

KISSINGER: That's right.

NIXON: Now, they won't want to waste it, but now that they're in, they can make the Community turn [unclear] —

KISSINGER: And I think we should have —

NIXON: — and the British can also, in the NATO thing, force the Europeans to think a little more, you know, as to what their obligations are. They can help us. They can help reassure NATO, no doubt. [unclear] Heath and Trend both asked a very perceptive question. They said, "How much of this can you tell to NATO?" Now, the point is you can tell them goddamn little.

KISSINGER: That's right.

NIXON: But on the other hand, the British can, knowing what our thinking is, it occurs to me that Heath — add to it, and it occurs to them as well — can sort of lead the Europeans and reassure them, so that as we do — but, I'm keenly aware of the fact that as far as that FBS is a concern, like you talk in your briefing papers, it's a goddamn good tradeoff. But, as you know, we'll scare them to death.

KISSINGER: Yeah.

NIXON: So, therefore, the thing to do is to prepare it so that they can see that the tradeoff is in their interest. I also realize that in terms of conventional forces and the rest that how much more we can do remains — is problematical. And yet, we've got to — we've got to prepare the Europeans for the fact that they're living now in a world so different from what it was when NATO was set up that we've just got to rethink it. What you said about seven thousand tactical weapons, now is — and that we found uses for a hundred in the last exercise. Now, what in the name of God have we got them there for, and why can't we use nuclear tradeoffs? They're getting [unclear] —

KISSINGER: Exactly, Mr. President. This is a key point.

NIXON: [unclear] But what — we don't hear any of this. It's like when we have NSC meetings. You know, they sit there and you ask and then the Chiefs give their views, and Laird gives his — I think Richardson will be much better —

KISSINGER: Much better.

NIXON: Don't you think so?

KISSINGER: Much better. I spent two hours with him —

NIXON: If we force him to think about it —

KISSINGER: — this morning.

NIXON: Force him to think about it —

KISSINGER: I spent two hours with him, and I said — I told him, "Look, Elliot, I give you two weeks. I won't send out a directive for two weeks to you. Get some directive to the Chiefs along the lines of what the president has said to you. Establish yourself as the president's man in the Pentagon." Because I think it's better anyway if he takes on the Chiefs.

NIXON: Yeah. But coming into this, coming around to this, my view is that when you get back from China — first, you ought to take off two or three days. Second —

• • •

NIXON: When do you — When will you meet again with the Russians over there in connection with [unclear]?

KISSINGER: About the first of March.

NIXON: And then you're going to have to have some positions? Well, that would be fair. You've always been able to handle the agreements —

KISSINGER: Well, we don't have to have a position on the Middle East, although it would help. We do have to have a position on that nuclear treaty.

NIXON: That's right. We've got to have something to give them.

KISSINGER: Yeah.

NIXON: Right?

KISSINGER: Right. And we may have to go a little further than the British want us to go.

NIXON: That doesn't bother you?

KISSINGER: But we may be able to use it —

NIXON: You've got to realize that in this instance, even though we reassure the British and the Europeans all the time that the game is between the Russians and ourselves. You know it, I know it —

KISSINGER: And we may use this Poseidon deal to keep the British quiet, and to keep the Russians quiet we just weasel the odds if we do the Poseidon deal.

NIXON: Keep the Russians quiet?

KISSINGER: Well, supposing we tell the Russians —

NIXON: Announce the Poseidon deal then?

KISSINGER: Suppose — well, because if we tell the Russians, "Look, we'll go halfway towards you on this nuclear treaty but in order to keep our allies quiet we have to do — "

NIXON: Mm-hmm.

KISSINGER: Then they have to choose. Because I think it is in our interest to keep the British in the nuclear business. The pressure on us will become too great if we are the only nuclear power.

NIXON: Absolutely. Well, I am rather surprised that Heath is willing to state it. Aren't you?

KISSINGER: He realizes they'll be a nothing country if they're not in it.

NIXON: Is that it?

KISSINGER: They've got no grounds for it. They haven't got the domestic structure for large armed forces.

NIXON: They've still got a fleet.

KISSINGER: Yeah, but not —

NIXON: Not much?

KISSINGER: Not much.

NIXON: Poseidon would really give them a psychological lift, wouldn't it?

KISSINGER: Yeah. It'd give them another ten years' lease on life. Of course, it's now clear that if we had given them the Skybolt, their airplanes would still be useful.

NIXON: That was a terrible mistake, Henry.

KISSINGER: It was a disaster.

NIXON: What did he do that for?

KISSINGER: Because we wanted to get the British out of the nuclear prison. Then he didn't have the guts to go through with it.

NIXON: Well, it was the McNamara decision, wasn't it — ?

KISSINGER: Yes.

NIXON: Wasn't that the McNamara period?

KISSINGER: Yep. And then Kennedy, as always, having taken the first step, then when he met [Prime Minister Harold] Macmillan he caved and gave him Polarises. And they figured they'd screw them on the Polarises later.

NIXON: But Skybolt would really have — what it would have done would have kept in being a very good British air force. Right?

KISSINGER: It would have kept in being a hundred and fifty British airplanes, which would stand. [unclear] The first Skybolt only had a three-hundred-mile range, but if you had extended it, they could still be — they'd still be a major factor.

NIXON: Yeah. Yeah.

KISSINGER: It was a disastrous decision.

NIXON: God, what we've done to the British in this is unconscionable. What we did to them in '56 [during the Suez crisis] was terrible.

KISSINGER: It was a disaster.

NIXON: What we've did and done to them since then, unbelievable what we've done. And when you think of what the British have done for the world, you know? Goddamn it, without the British, Hitler would have Europe today.

KISSINGER: No question.

NIXON: Hitler would have them.

KISSINGER: Own them.

NIXON: The son of a bitch would still be living.

KISSINGER: No question.

NIXON: Right?

KISSINGER: No question.

NIXON: Without the British—they were the only ones that had kept the line. We say it over and over again, but we talk about our sacrifice—

KISSINGER: Of course.

NIXON: —and, sure, we did a hell of a lot, but the British stood there alone, they held the tide back, and, also, the psychological, too.

KISSINGER: [British historian Hugh] Trevor-Roper thinks we were a little too effective in World War II.

NIXON: Why?

KISSINGER: That if we had made a partial settlement—

NIXON: With the Germans?

KISSINGER: —with the Germans.

NIXON: I agree. Oh, I always felt that.

KISSINGER: But he doesn't think—he said the tragedy was—we were speculating what would have happened—

NIXON: That's right.

KISSINGER: —if one of these plots on Hitler had succeeded.

NIXON: Yeah.

KISSINGER: And he felt then we should have made peace quickly—

NIXON: Absolutely—

KISSINGER: —but he felt that we shouldn't have.

NIXON: Absolutely. The unconditional surrender thing was wrong. I mean, I know how we all felt at that time, but we were totally wrong. And what would have happened, and it would have happened without a question, is that the Germans then would have been there as a—

KISSINGER: As a barrier—

NIXON: —shield against the damn Russians.

KISSINGER: That's right.

NIXON: And, also, the tragedy is—the tragedy is that we threw it all away at a time that we were looking down the Russian throats. That's what burns me up.

KISSINGER: That's right.

NIXON: Henry, for God's sakes, the United States had ground forces, we had a monopoly on the bomb, the British were still there—

KISSINGER: Well, Mr. President—

NIXON: —we were looking down their throats and damn it, and the fact that Roosevelt was sick, probably, everything else, we just gave them everything.

KISSINGER: Well, considering what you have done—

NIXON: That's right.

KISSINGER: Uh—

NIXON: You wonder now, the point that I made to Heath and I really feel, I don't know if—I don't know whether we can make it. We now have parity. The only reason I don't think we can—we may be—there's a considerable doubt if we can make it—is because of the will of Europe, the will of America, and also—now, the other side of the coin is—the other side is that the Russians have some problems, too.

KISSINGER: Yeah.

NIXON: And that—that's why the theory that you expressed yesterday of assuming that they are—that some evil genius is directing all this, that may be true, but it could also be true that there is not an evil genius, that they're trying to—that it isn't a planned thing, that it's just a bureaucracy moving along, moving along—

KISSINGER: That could be. That could be. That could very well be. But we have one practical matter on the SALT delegation.

• • •

NIXON: Well, let's put in the back of our minds that I am going to offer Mrs. [Lyndon] Johnson the UN thing, you know, the Shirley Temple position.

KISSINGER: Oh, yes. That would be good.

NIXON: She would probably—

KISSINGER: She would be spectacular.

NIXON: —but I am going to offer that to her.

KISSINGER: Scali would be [unclear]. [laughs]

NIXON: I was so amused when I was talking to [unclear] at the dinner. I said, "By any chance will you be coming over to speak at the UN anytime soon?" [unclear] He said, "I abhor the place so much. I just can't bring myself to go there." Goddamn it, the British are sick of the UN. What has turned them off on it so much?

KISSINGER: Well, it's all these racial problems, all the African problems, then the Suez. It is always the double standards.

NIXON: Just remember I will never go before them again.

KISSINGER: No.

NIXON: I am not going to do it. Even if it is Scali there, and all the rest, I won't go meet with Bush. I don't care who is there. The UN, now that is the job of the secretary of state.

KISSINGER: And actually you were there twice and they treated you—

NIXON: I was there several times. Basically not only by the membership of the UN but also, let's face it, by the damn Secretariat. By his staff—

KISSINGER: Well, it was—

NIXON: —[unclear] waving their arms around.

KISSINGER: —said he couldn't meet you at the door because he was at a dinner of the Pakistan ambassador. It was an outrage. And then this idea that we don't know where [unclear] sit on the floor listening to [unclear] speak. I mean that is ridiculous.

NIXON: Sitting there, nobody got up when he came in. I think with the UN just a cool detachment is what is required. I even gave a twenty-fifth-anniversary dinner for the poor bastards. We have done everything. I have gone the extra mile.

KISSINGER: Oh, yeah.

NIXON: I want you to have, incidentally, a talk with Scali soon, before he gets up there, and tell him, "Now, look, John, there is one thing to be understood. Under no circumstances — your job is [unclear]. The president is not going to be available. Not in this term. We have done it twice now." You know what I mean? [unclear] Henry, with the UN, I think the American public now is getting pissed off. I think the straw that broke the camel's back was the [Popular Front for the Liberation of Palestine] hijacking thing.

KISSINGER: Yeah.

NIXON: They let it go on. They didn't support us on it. The right of liberation I think is also their favorite [unclear] —

KISSINGER: Well, also the way they jumped up and down when Nationalist China was evicted.

NIXON: That was horrible.

KISSINGER: That was revolting.

NIXON: Remember how they danced?

KISSINGER: Revolting.

NIXON: Like a bunch of apes. Well, have a good time in New York.

A new face on the FBI

February 13, 1973, 9:48 a.m.
Richard Nixon and Charles Colson
OVAL OFFICE

The death of J. Edgar Hoover in May 1972 rocked the Federal Bureau of Investigation, which Hoover had headed since its inception forty-seven years before. Nixon appointed L. Patrick Gray as acting director in the void that followed. A longtime navy officer, Gray had served in Nixon's Justice Department since 1969, but he was a newcomer to the bureau. As a result, he depended heavily on Hoover's seasoned associate director, Mark Felt, who was later identified as Bob Woodward and Carl Bernstein's secret source "Deep Throat." One month later, news broke of the event that would affect both men dramatically, the Watergate break-in. Quietly and very efficiently, FBI agents undertook the first and perhaps the most thorough of all of the investigations of the Watergate scandal. At the same time, Gray, Felt, and at least one other veteran FBI administrator, William Sullivan, were maneuvering to nab the permanent directorship. That process wouldn't end even after Nixon formally nominated Gray for the job on February 15. As Nixon traded ideas about the FBI, Colson remembered him "leaning back in his chair, crossed legs resting comfortably on his massive carved mahogany desk." When Nixon's thoughts turned to Watergate, Colson expressed his opinion that the White House should find out who ordered the break-in. Nixon "dropped his feet to the floor and came straight up in his chair," Colson recalled, "'Who do you think did this? Mitchell? Magruder?' He was staring intently into my eyes, face flushed, anger in his voice."

• • •

---

* Colson, *Born Again*, p. 98.

NIXON: Well, you need a man. Would you keep Gray?

COLSON: Yes, sir. I would now.

NIXON: Now, you mean send him to the Senate for confirmation?

COLSON: Yep, I would.

NIXON: Why?

COLSON: Well, because first of all, I would back him up with a very strong deputy. Because I think if you took Gray out now, with all of the turmoil in the bureau, I mean — there's a — everything that's going on in that bureau is being leaked out.

NIXON: Yeah. Well, how could we stop it?

COLSON: By creating certainty. You see, I'm afraid one of the problems over there is that there isn't anybody who knows they're in charge. Now —

NIXON: Who's the deputy you have in mind?

COLSON: Well, I've suggested a fellow by the name of Bill Sullivan who's a —

NIXON: They say he's the first one [unclear] out of a lot of them —

COLSON: Oh, he is.

NIXON: — because he was not a Hoover man.

COLSON: Well, he was our man. That's —

NIXON: I know.

COLSON: Al Haig called me yesterday and said, Jesus, you know, get Sullivan back in there. Haig is very high on Sullivan. I don't know Sullivan, but I know of so many people who do think highly of him, and that those are all the people I —

NIXON: What about putting [unclear] in that job. Do you think that would be a good idea?

COLSON: No, sir. I don't think so.

NIXON: Did you think also it might be a reflection on Gray, too, I suppose, about his investigation of the Watergate hearing?

COLSON: Yeah. I think in a way it is. And you might want to move Gray at the end of the year, but I'd get through this year without rocking that boat and I would try to get him — confirm Gray. He's, after all — Gray's loyalty to you —

NIXON: Totally.

COLSON: Totally. So give him the strength and back him up with some tough people and make sure he understands what he has to do. I mean there — the most important thing over there is to be goddamn sure that that department and that bureau understand that we've got enough troubles with the Hill without creating any more for ourselves.

NIXON: Right.

COLSON: And this is a partisan game. This is no longer law enforcement or investigation. This is part of —

NIXON: Sure. What'd you mean, Watergate?

COLSON: Watergate.

NIXON: Oh, hell, yes.

COLSON: And I read this —

NIXON: The partisan press builds up Ervin now as Mister Civil Liberties. Shit! Ervin is a goddamn racist. [unclear] everything!

COLSON: [laughs] Hysterical. But they're going to make a — they'll have a political circus. But it is —

NIXON: Remember how they built up that poor jackass [Senator] Ralph Flanders?

COLSON: Yeah.

NIXON: I mean [unclear] — built him up as the greatest thing. Poor bastard — well, he was an idiot!

COLSON: Well —

NIXON: He's a sweet guy — Ralph Flanders.

COLSON: Well, no — he was nothing.

NIXON: But he took [Senator Joseph] McCarthy out.

COLSON: McCarthy's great comment about bring the butterfly net [unclear]. [laughs]

NIXON: Oh, God, I wish we had more of Pat Grays. Well, anyway, that's that. [unclear] In my view, there's a couple of good guys who work around here. Everyone around here forgets the goddamn thing in the White House. [unclear] You just figure you're going to have some leaks in the television, the press, and just say that's going to be that way. How are you doing on it? Is there anything else you could do?

COLSON: Well, the only thing you can do, Mr. President —

NIXON: I mean if you can't — you've got to get for example Magruder's operation, Haldeman, and Ehrlichman and the rest — Dean.

COLSON: Yes.

NIXON: If they all get into this, they're going to go through the ITT thing in spades.

COLSON: Well, of course, that's what they want to do to us, you know? That's the whole point of that exercise.

NIXON: To burn some others?

COLSON: Correct. Correct.

NIXON: Now don't you agree we should stay away?

COLSON: I think we have to — I don't think there's any choice but to go up there and tough it through. And I do think we have to be very, very hard-nose with that committee. And if they want Haldeman, Ehrlichman, me — I'm sure they will — we have to limit the areas that they're going to go into, and I mean —

NIXON: Well, I'm not sure. The best thing there — we can work it out — is to — you can let them have lower people like Chapin and Strachan and the rest. Hell, I never talked to Chapin and Strachan and the rest. Let them have them, and — but in terms of the people that are direct advisors to the president you can say they can do it by written interrogatories, by having Ervin leading in the majority, the two counsel, majority and minority leaders do it — written interrogatories. But don't go up there on television.

COLSON: Mm-hmm.

NIXON: How does that sound to you as a possible compromise?

COLSON: I think it's a good compromise. There's a risk, you know, but —

NIXON: They may not. They may not accept it. But I don't think — I had thought that maybe we ought to just hard-nose and say nobody can go. I'm afraid that that gives an appearance of total cover-up, which would bother me a bit — you know, I should just say no. You can't have Chapin. You can't have Strachan. You can't have, you know — and since the White House won't allow anybody, you might give them some others. I don't know. I mean maybe we could think about it. I can't get him to talk about it just to testify. That'll break it down to Kissinger — break it down to Haldeman and Ehrlichman. Can't do that. And of course that's why you can't go. The people that are — who have direct access to the president can't go.

COLSON: Well, you know the difficulty with it, Mr. President? I've been thinking about this over the weekend. I tried to talk it through with one of my perceptive law partners, who's a brilliant trial lawyer. And his point was — which I thought was a goddamn good one — he said you can't go at all. He says there's nothing in the facts of the Watergate — the Segretti — that you had any involvement in at all. But they're going to start asking you other questions, and —

NIXON: That you were involved in also.

COLSON: And they're going to come — well, something that I may not even be thinking about right now. But —

NIXON: In the campaign.

COLSON: In the campaign, sure. Or in the precampaign period, and things that have not a damn thing to do with Watergate, or Segretti, but —

NIXON: Well, their license, apparently, is to go into everything in the campaign.

COLSON: Yeah, that's right.

NIXON: That's the problem.

COLSON: But why should one — you know, that's an area where you don't know where to draw the line. You can't be a little bit pregnant and —

NIXON: Well, we'll decide, of course, [unclear] cross that bridge till we get to it.

COLSON: Now, I think you're right in terms of trying to limit those who have had direct access to you because that creates a problem and —

NIXON: I'm sure — absolutely.

COLSON: I would —

NIXON: But even there, I mean, [unclear]. I don't think you can [unclear] as a certainty at the Chapin and Strachan level. I don't think I would go that low.

COLSON: No, and I don't think you need to.

NIXON: I'd say no, [unclear].

COLSON: Sure. That doesn't make any difference. Let them do it. And let them take the whole damn committee apparatus. Of course, the other point which I'm going to mention to Haldeman before I take off is that if — whoever did order Watergate, if it's going to come out in the hearings, for God's sakes, let it out.

NIXON: Step out now.

COLSON: Let's get rid of it now. Take our losses.

NIXON: Well, who the hell do you think did this? Mitchell? He can't do it. He'll perjure himself so he won't admit it. Now that's the problem. Magruder?

COLSON: I know Magruder has.

NIXON: Well, then he's perjured himself, hasn't he?

COLSON: Probably.

NIXON: All right. What'd you say then? Let's take our losses. Who the hell's going to step forward and say it? See my point? You've got it set — Liddy, of course, is — he directed Watergate. But who do you have in mind? I mean I'm afraid that we can't risk it, Chuck, unless you have somebody in mind.

COLSON: No! I — well —

NIXON: My advice — would you suggest Mitchell go in and say, "Why" — well, he'd say, "Well, I — this must've occurred. I did not realize it at the time, but — "

COLSON: Yeah.

NIXON: Mitchell seems to have stonewalled it up to this point. I can't figure out what he said.

COLSON: Well, he's — you know, John has got one of those marvelous memories that "I don't know. I don't remember what was said."

NIXON: "I was busy at the time."

COLSON: Yeah.

NIXON: Do you think it's going to come out?

COLSON: I don't know.

NIXON: That's the point.

COLSON: I haven't seen anything yet related to this whole incident that has not come out one way or another. And it's just that slow painful process of pulling it out piece by piece.

NIXON: Of course, I don't want you to blatantly [unclear] his memory [unclear].

COLSON: Oh, hell!

NIXON: When I'm thinking about Watergate, though, that's the whole point — they went through this tremendous investigation [unclear]. Unless one of the seven begins to talk. That's the problem.

COLSON: That you never know. You never know.

NIXON: Well, then the question is as far as the seven, that the only ones that really know — Hunt knows, I would imagine. I imagine Liddy would know. McCord?

COLSON: Probably.

NIXON: All right. Those are the three.

COLSON: Well, what my prospective [law] partner — who knows Sirica very, very well and has tried many cases in front of Sirica — what he thinks Sirica will do, at the critical moment, is call in one of them and say, "Okay, you don't go to jail if you tell me everything you know." And —

NIXON: Make a deal for his immunity?

COLSON: Make a deal with them before he sentences them.

NIXON: Would they accept this?

COLSON: Would they accept it? I don't think Hunt would.

NIXON: You don't?

COLSON: No. No, I really don't. No. I mean I think he's a —

NIXON: Extremist?

COLSON: Yeah. He's too much of a believer. On the other hand, who knows, you know? He's lost his wife, which was a great source of strength to him. He's got four kids.

NIXON: Trouble in Hunt's case, which is that he has contact with you and Ehrlichman on other matters.

COLSON: Sure.

NIXON: That's the problem.

COLSON: Sure. But it — but they're not matters that I'm really concerned about. So he went and interviewed someone on ITT, but that's perfectly logical as hell. That's what you have a fellow like that available for.

NIXON: Yeah.

COLSON: But the — you know, the whole — the unfortunate part of it is, and you're — it's imperative that people here not get bogged down in it.

NIXON: Yes. That's right.

COLSON: The unfortunate part of it is that it is a diversion. There's no limit to what they can do with it if they wanted. And the reason you have to hard-line it with certain people —

NIXON: Mm-hmm.

COLSON: — is that there is no limit to what they can do to it in terms of, well — hell, you know — even arranging the Democrats for Nixon ads. Yeah, we had some technical violations of the statute. A few mailings that were done by different committees outside of here. Yeah. Those were technical violations of the statute.

NIXON: Sure.

COLSON: Nobody evaded the statute. [unclear] can't. But you know, if you wanted to make them into capital cases, you can.

NIXON: Weren't there technical violations on the other side?

COLSON: Sure. Sure, but —

NIXON: [unclear] reasons for them.

COLSON: But the — certainly, but the problem is that they're just going to get the — if they could get Ehrlichman, Haldeman, or me, to say under oath that we were aware of anything that was a violation of a statute, then they've got a circus on their hands.

NIXON: Mm-hmm.

COLSON: And either you have to have a John Mitchell–type memory or [laughs] or not appear.

NIXON: Well, that — your view would be to let Strachan go, or Chapin go.

COLSON: My view has along, always been, Mr. President, that in the case of Haldeman, Ehrlichman, and I, the only three you can probably do this with — that they should be either written interrogatories or appointive-type things where they list out some highly specific areas. And that's it and not beyond that. And if they try to get beyond that, you just — you hard — you stonewall it or you just don't remember something when you have to.

NIXON: Right. Right.

"I don't want to give the indication that we're afraid of anything."

February 14, 1973, 10:13 a.m.
Richard Nixon and Charles Colson
OVAL OFFICE

When Colson made known his plans to resign from the White House as of March 1973 in order to work at a Washington law firm, Nixon gave him a final assignment, and an attractive one, to tour Europe for three weeks on various errands. In a final talk, the two men analyzed the options for concealing the extent of activity surrounding Watergate among members of the White House staff. The need for a united front and consistent information reminded Nixon of a previous cause célèbre, the Alger Hiss case of 1948–50. When Hiss, a New Dealer and diplomat, was accused of spying for the Soviet Union, he denied the charge and it seemed likely to fade. At that juncture, Nixon, who was then serving in Congress, aggressively pursued the case. In fact, he staked his career on it, and he persisted, despite what he considered a concerted effort at stonewalling by the Truman administration. Hiss was eventually imprisoned, but not for espionage. With Nixon pressing every point — including some still considered dubious — Hiss was convicted of committing perjury in some of the early remarks he made in his own defense. Nixon and Colson discussed the myriad men and institutions — including the FBI — that would have to be controlled in order to contain the scandal of Nixon's presidency. The Hiss case haunted Nixon throughout his maneuverings during the Watergate scandal. Though the two episodes were far more different than alike, they shared one thing of importance: Richard Nixon, in a state of desperation, all of his own making.

• • •

NIXON: Well, are you on your way?

COLSON: Yes, sir. I think — I've just been packing and getting briefed —

NIXON: Yeah. Yeah.

COLSON: — by the State Department.

NIXON: Yeah.

COLSON: I've finished up my office work.

NIXON: Well, I think when you're there — now, the thing to do is to try to put out of your mind all of the problems in which I — you've got to fish these things out. We always do. We [unclear] around here. Watergate and all that sort of thing is going to be there. It's going to be [unclear] for what it is. And I think that you've got to take periods like this. You're off at least two weeks — three weeks.

COLSON: I'll be off and it'll be about three weeks.

NIXON: Good. Just get out there and don't read any papers, and —

COLSON: Well —

NIXON: Take the *New York Herald*.

COLSON: It's—

NIXON: It's the only paper left, which is basically the *Washington Post* [unclear]. It's worse than the *Washington Post*.

COLSON: Right.

NIXON: [unclear] the *Post*—the *Times*—the *New York Times*.

COLSON: Yeah, they take the worst of each. It's—

NIXON: Awful.

COLSON: Terrible.

NIXON: For political people in Europe, it's [unclear] up the wall. All right.

COLSON: Well, I very much appreciate your—

NIXON: Yeah. What is your last-minute assessment of the Watergate thing and so forth? What's going to happen on the—

COLSON: Well, I had a long talk—

NIXON: —sentences this week?

COLSON: I had a long talk with Bob [Haldeman] about it yesterday, Mr. President.

NIXON: [unclear]

COLSON: After we talked—and then I met last evening for a couple of hours with [Colson's attorney and law partner] Dave Shapiro. He's a—apart from being a splendid trial lawyer and smart—and he gave me a rationale which he's writing up for John Dean for invoking executive privilege for all but certain defined areas where individual wrongdoing might be involved. He believes we're on very solid ground if that's the course we want to take.

NIXON: Mm-hmm.

COLSON: His analysis of it is that if you can't have a confidential—the president cannot have immediate advisors and a confidential relationship unless he is assured that that confidentiality can be preserved, like a law clerk with a judge or congressional aide, and—

NIXON: Mm-hmm.

COLSON: It makes a very, very good case, and expresses it very articulately. I talked to [Fred] Fielding, who is Dean's assistant, this morning and told him that Shapiro would come in and work with him next week if he is—this week if you want to. I think it's the only course to take. I mean it—you—

NIXON: Start breaking over and [unclear]. The problem is that, I guess [unclear] the precedents are so important—is the break over on Flanigan and [executive privilege] justified that.

COLSON: Well, no, Flanigan we did just that. We said that it was a privileged relationship—separation of powers we argued. However, we would voluntarily make it available for a restricted area negotiated in advance. And—

NIXON: Well, I expect some additional area—

COLSON: That's what we do this thing with. And—

NIXON: Oh, yeah.

COLSON: And, uh —

NIXON: Do you mean you'd have Haldeman testify?

COLSON: Well, I told Bob yesterday I thought perhaps Bob should not at all —

NIXON: Yeah.

COLSON: Ehrlichman, MacGregor, and myself, Timmons — only as the clearly defined areas in which — where we waive the privilege, basically.

NIXON: Yeah.

COLSON: On any matters that have already — we've already been questioned by the FBI.

NIXON: The point that I think, is this — the point that I'm concerned about is you've got to figure which is worse — to waive the privilege in this town, or just — and people say, "Well, they stonewalled it." I knew this — that the charge of cover-up and innuendo of charges that we've done — it's all of — are worse than what comes out. You know, I think you've got to realize that I've got — I always go back of course to my own experience in the Hiss case. The Hiss case, of course, the administration was doubly guilty. First, he was guilty. But second, what really creamed him was that — the charge that the administration was trying to cover it up. [unclear] Justice Department didn't have the wisdom to drop the case after they — after we got the facts on him. But you only have to use the red herring — not knowing all these facts, of course — and we killed him. It was the cover-up that hurt, not the fact that Hiss was guilty. Get my point?

COLSON: It's — of course, this instance is distinguishable in that you have had a very exhaustive investigation. No one can really uncover —

NIXON: True. But —

COLSON: What — what — ?

NIXON: When they say the investigation — you see that, Chuck, the line is the investigation was not followed through; it was covered up. No, I don't think we have a choice. That's my point. That's why I don't want to give the indication that we're afraid of anything — that's my point. I think it should be extremely limited though. I don't want to see you down there, whether [unclear] you know, they get you into other things —

COLSON: That's got nothing to do with this. That's the point Shapiro made that I thought was most perceptive. He said, "Where you have already testified to a grand jury or to the FBI — "

NIXON: Yeah.

COLSON: " — in that area you have already exercised a waiver — beyond that, no." Now, if you do that that's fine, of course then they can do it, hell. If I had me on the witness stand and I wanted to create a headline a day, I could ask about when one of the milk producers first came into —

NIXON: Yeah, I know —

[Unclear exchange]

COLSON: Nothing to do with Watergate — nothing to do with Segretti. I never heard of him, but you could go on a fishing expedition.

NIXON: The thing is the — that they're going to want to get you based on Hunt.

COLSON: Yeah.

NIXON: They just — that's something we just can't get into.

COLSON: Well, you're —

NIXON: The thing is, for example, too, like a story "Colson this morning commented that Liddy had the FBI internal security taps." But I can't believe that's true. I mean, I don't know what they're talking about.

COLSON: I — that could have been true. They had that [White House "Plumbers"] security unit set up in the basement of the EOB which Bud Krogh ran.

NIXON: Oh, I see. They were, at that time, in the country —

COLSON: Oh, sure. And they were — that was perfectly legitimate. I mean that's the kind of thing they were hired to do —

NIXON: Mm-hmm.

COLSON: Investigating the authenticity of —

NIXON: [unclear]

COLSON: — of the [ITT lobbyist] Dita Beard letter [describing a pledge of campaign funds in exchange for an antitrust settlement by the Department of Justice] was a perfectly legitimate thing. And, I told the FBI about that. There wasn't anything to hide. The thing you can't do is you can't get partway pregnant. You can't start talking about one aspect of a relationship —

NIXON: Yeah.

COLSON: — with a White House employee and not another —

NIXON: What is — what does Shapiro think Mitchell should do?

COLSON: Shapiro believes that if Mitchell was indeed responsible that he should step forward now and take the heat, and —

NIXON: Not go to jail! He can't do that.

COLSON: Well, his point is he's going to anyway. Shapiro's point is if he was guilty and if it's going to come out in the hearings, then don't let it come out in the hearings. Take our own losses ourselves.

NIXON: Well, that's very nice but let's come back again to [unclear].

COLSON: It depends on what John knew. I don't know what he knew —

NIXON: Well —

COLSON: — firsthand.

NIXON: Right. They claim that he knew he was aware of — talked to Hunt and all that sort of thing. Is that correct? Is that what's going to come out? That hasn't yet.

COLSON: That hasn't yet. That's right. But you see, John doesn't have any privilege. John doesn't have any —

NIXON: Yeah.

COLSON: — immediate relationship to you. He was a —

NIXON: No.

COLSON: — cabinet officer and he had — did have —

NIXON: I was talking about the campaign.

COLSON: So, he doesn't—

NIXON: Nothing about his—the campaign. I stayed miles away from it.

COLSON: Shapiro's only analysis, just as a cold-blooded analytical lawyer—if you're going to have a big explosion on national television and let goddamn Magruder—

NIXON: Magruder—those are the two, I guess, that are really a problem.

COLSON: You'd have the same problem, of course, if he knew about it.

NIXON: Oh, he did—

COLSON: I'm sure he did.

NIXON: He had to know about it.

COLSON: I know he did.

NIXON: How about Mitchell? Do you think he did?

COLSON: John is—John has the most marvelous—

NIXON: Great stone face.

COLSON: Yeah. And convenient memory. I mean, he can—

NIXON: Yeah, yeah. But the point is memory or not—you mean that this concern about Hunt cracking which you expressed—correct? I suppose if the judge calls him in—do you think that Hunt might just say, "Well, I'll tell my whole story." My view is that he won't tell the whole story. My view is that he'd say, "All right, I will tell what it is." But, the—I think what he would do frankly is to tell on Mitchell. Do you think that's what he would tell them?

COLSON: Yes, sir.

NIXON: Or Magruder.

COLSON: Well, I don't—

NIXON: My view is that he would limit the losses. He wouldn't go all the way.

COLSON: No. He would limit the losses.

NIXON: I don't think he would come in and say, "Well, I worked here for Colson on the Dita Beard thing and I worked on this, that, and the other thing." Or would he?

COLSON: No. Because there isn't anything that—

NIXON: But they didn't—the judge doesn't need to get into that.

COLSON: There's nothing to do with Watergate.

NIXON: But he'd say, "I will tell you about Watergate [unclear]."

COLSON: He might do that—I don't think so. But, normally I wouldn't question Howard Hunt. Normally—

NIXON: No. I know, because of his emotional problem.

COLSON: But he's just too—

NIXON: He thinks he's killed his wife, and so forth.

COLSON: Yeah. It's a tough one. It's a really tough one.

NIXON: Mm-hmm.

COLSON: I don't think he'll crack. But I—but who knows? I mean, how do you know what goes through the minds of anybody in a situation like this?

NIXON: Right.

COLSON: God only knows.

NIXON: [unclear] it's very tough. You see these blacks, for example, go in [and burglarize]. None of these guys [Watergate burglars] had weapons, did they?

COLSON: No.

NIXON: Gee —

COLSON: You know that's the — of course that's the —

NIXON: Burglary without weapons!

COLSON: That's the travesty of the whole damn thing, Mr. President. No one was hurt. It was a stupid thing — dumb. But, my God, it isn't like the Hiss trial. It isn't like the [unclear]. There's no —

NIXON: [unclear] I know that.

COLSON: In terms of the —

NIXON: I just —

COLSON: — consequences publicly it's just preposterous —

NIXON: My point isn't that Hiss was a traitor — it was the cover-up.

COLSON: Yeah.

NIXON: The cover-up is the [unclear].

COLSON: That's the problem —

NIXON: That's where really we've got to cut our losses. My losses have to be cut. The president's losses have got to be cut on the cover-up deal.

COLSON: Right.

NIXON: Not the merits of the thing, Christ. I pled the merits all the way up. I said, "Well, they did it and it was wrong." Period.

COLSON: Mm-hmm.

NIXON: But as far as this here we're not covering up a damn thing.

COLSON: Hell! We're not covering up any —

NIXON: The problem with Magruder is that basically he's so close to Bob. Do you think that's what it is? I suppose they figure if Magruder it'll be into Haldeman. Correct? Is that where you think that one trail leads?

COLSON: That's what they would assume, but — I mean, that's what some people would assume, but I don't — I think he was divorced publicly well enough in advance of all of this stuff that —

NIXON: Well, he's not — Bob had no contact with Hunt. Did he — ?

COLSON: No.

NIXON: Or McCord?

COLSON: No.

NIXON: Or Liddy?

COLSON: No. I don't believe so. Oh, hell no. I don't think that's —

NIXON: His contact was with Magruder, correct?

COLSON: Yeah. Or through Gordon Strachan, which was the other link that —

NIXON: Well —

COLSON: — that they would draw. But Bob is in a different position. Bob is so much an extension of you. I mean, his everyday — his day's work —

NIXON: I'm not talking about his privilege. I'm talking about what could come out on him and—

COLSON: The only thing that could come out is probably that they, you know, they—those people over there were crazy with memoranda. They wrote everything down.

NIXON: Every time Bob called in somebody would write it down.

COLSON: Sure. Or people would use his name. I mean, that happens to me. That happens to Ehrlichman.

NIXON: Yeah.

COLSON: And that's another problem. You can't control who says, "Well—"

NIXON: "Colson wants this done."

COLSON: "—Colson wants this done." And either that—I just—somebody just—

NIXON: Well, they [unclear]. They even use the—they say, "The president wants this or that done." Or, you know, "The boss wants this or that done" and so forth. And of course [unclear] most people [unclear].

COLSON: Yeah. I never did that deliberately. But that's—but a lot of people do do that, of course.

NIXON: Well, fortunately, I didn't see any of them, you know? As far as my situation here—is extremely good. I never talked to—I divorced myself from the tactics of the campaign.

COLSON: Yeah. Very good.

NIXON: [unclear] my own schedule.

COLSON: Very wise.

NIXON: I wouldn't let people come in and talk politics. Mitchell didn't. [unclear] never saw Magruder until after [unclear]. Never saw him. Ehrlichman one day went over there and met all those guys [unclear]. MacGregor told me [unclear]. That's good, too.

COLSON: Oh, no. I think I—I think the only pitfall, Mr. President, and this is the one that I've—I think I've got everybody—I think everybody's thinking on the right line. The only pitfall is the moment you open up the Pandora's box in the White House you can lead into nineteen other totally irrelevant trails—the ones that would cause daily embarrassment. My feeling is hard-line it in terms of what you are willing—

NIXON: Right.

COLSON: —to talk about.

NIXON: You know the thing about it of course is that you have this enormous difficult double standard in the press, for instance. You can take this story about today about the—that they had access to the confidential memoranda. Now, who the hell is that coming from, I would ask? See, they've got this and they're dripping it out little by little. Who—where are they getting these stories, Chuck?

COLSON: The bureau.

NIXON: The FBI?

COLSON: Yes, sir.

NIXON: Did they question the FBI [unclear]. How did the FBI know?

COLSON: Well, the FBI would have been in a — would have been sending that information over to Liddy and Hunt.

NIXON: Mm-hmm.

COLSON: And every leak we've had, Mr. President, has been out of the bureau. That's one of the reasons that when you asked me my opinion yesterday, I don't know whether —

NIXON: About Gray.

COLSON: I don't know whether Gray's the best man or not, but I —

NIXON: [unclear]

COLSON: Yes, certainly. Let him go in and fire some of the bastards that he thinks have [unclear].

NIXON: Yeah.

COLSON: The whole damn —

NIXON: You fire them, on the other hand, they go out and talk more. What then?

COLSON: Well, the hell — they're talking now. If — there isn't anything that I ever told the bureau that I haven't seen come out in print. And, it does — it really does raise questions about the integrity of the bureau's process. You have to be a little careful what you —

NIXON: [unclear]. Well, when Hoover was there it didn't leak.

COLSON: It didn't happen.

NIXON: Did not happen.

COLSON: Oh, hell no! They were scared stiff.

NIXON: I could talk to Hoover about all sorts of things and I talked to him very freely over the years and it never, never came out.

COLSON: Well, because they knew that if anybody talked —

NIXON: To the press.

COLSON: — to them. And —

NIXON: You take the [unclear]. I'd seen the thing this morning. They make a big thing out of some contribution we received that would sort of [unclear] more than a five-thousand-dollar contribution. You know that wasn't really a blunder. Was it? Good God! Our people spent thirty-four million dollars. Where the hell [unclear]?

COLSON: No, that thing — he wrote off all the loans, which was a direct avoidance of the statute and we —

NIXON: Not an evasion.

COLSON: Sir?

NIXON: Not an evasion.

COLSON: Not an evasion.

NIXON: Not a violation, therefore.

COLSON: No, but my God, I mean if you're going to write it on something — so the Seafarers gave us — Paul Hall gave us a hundred thousand dollars. Well, that's — they've written about that now four days in a row. But [major donor to George McGovern's campaign Henry] Kimmelman writes off a half a million and — which was an avoidance —

NIXON: You mean he loaned that much [unclear]? Oh, for Christ's sake, that's a — are our people are going to make anything out of it?

COLSON: Oh, we screamed about it. We screamed about it during the campaign. But —

NIXON: So it's a contribution?

COLSON: Sure. They carried it as a loan all through the campaign because they didn't want to show this big sum of money coming from these people.

NIXON: Oh.

COLSON: After the election they'd write off the loan. So it becomes a contribution absolute.

NIXON: Wouldn't our counsel get into that hearing?

COLSON: Oh, absolutely. Absolutely.

NIXON: Paul [O'Brien, CRP attorney] ought to be hanging on that.

COLSON: That's the kind of thing that — where you know, if our fundraising and money is being held up to inspection, his should be the same way.

NIXON: Get Kimmelman right in and say, "Did you do this? Did you do this?"

COLSON: Oh, I'd call on every one of those guys. You can have a parade. If that's the way they want to play the game, then they've got to know — the people on the Hill have got to know that's the way our guys are going to play the game, which I think they would. But the bottom line, Mr. President, of all of this, really, is that I just don't think the public gives a damn. Now they — everybody enjoys a sideshow and this town gets all excited over the — that kind of circus.

NIXON: I agree, too.

COLSON: But I think you just have to go up there and say the matter of principle that — and be very hard about it, and then say, "What the hell, if the country — "

NIXON: Right.

COLSON: You're going to get the Left all exercised. Because it's something they can talk about.

NIXON: Right.

COLSON: I just don't think the man in the street cares.

NIXON: Right, right, right.

COLSON: The people that I have talked to the last forty-eight hours have — just have one overwhelming sentiment and that is my God, how proud they are to be Americans — how proud they are of you. Everybody — it's been an interesting phenomenon. Everyone I've talked to has said, "Congratulate the president on the prisoners." And that just — the impact of that is the equivalent of a thousand Watergates. He just —

NIXON: You know, even though it's a symbolic thing when I ordered that they take the [POW] flag up.

COLSON: Wonderful. Beautiful statement.

NIXON: They [the press] buried the thing. The networks should have given [unclear].

COLSON: No. The *Washington Post* buried it [unclear].

NIXON: They did because they just — they knew it was very effective. But you think the average person got something?

COLSON: Oh, absolutely. Absolutely. No, I —

NIXON: [unclear] just stuck it right in the groin. [unclear]

COLSON: Yeah, your statement was marvelous. It's the time to fly the flag high. I talked to [labor leader Frank] Fitzsimmons who of course was so thrilled. He's staying with me Monday. Last night, my God, he would do anything. He said, "That man — I just love that man." He said, "I am just so proud." He said, "Think of the courage. Think of bringing those boys home. He brought them home. He brought them home." But people are saying that. I mean that's the way that —

NIXON: Here's one place where our media friends have misjudged.

COLSON: Yes, sir.

NIXON: They thought the coming home of the POWs would be a time for national remorse and that sort of shit. All of a sudden it turns out that people are just delighted that POWs are brave and heroes —

• • •

COLSON: Mr. President, I thank you for allowing me to go on this trip.

NIXON: Oh, that's fine. You go ahead.

COLSON: Without —

NIXON: Have a good time.

COLSON: I'll be winding up when I get back. I don't want to be maudlin but it was kind of ironic with the prisoners coming back.

NIXON: Well, I said that to Ziegler — forgive me for Helms being sent to Ghana.

COLSON: All right, sir. [unclear] Proudest thing I've ever done in my life, sir.

NIXON: Well, that's — you're not leaving. You're just going across the street.

COLSON: [unclear] a block away — I, uh —

NIXON: Right. A block away, huh?

COLSON: Half a block away. I — at your service for anything, anytime —

NIXON: Right.

COLSON: — anyway.

NIXON: Well, I appreciate it. You went beyond the call of duty. Fine. Get a little rest. You go on.

"This envelope full of stuff"
February 14, 1973, 5:34 p.m.
Richard Nixon and John Ehrlichman
OVAL OFFICE

John Ehrlichman, assistant to the president for domestic affairs, was at the core of the president's inner circle. Formerly a successful lawyer in Seattle, he had moved to the capital in

1969 to join the Nixon administration, and over the years he handled a wide array of issues, most of them regarding everyday government business within the United States. Ehrlichman also, however, involved himself enthusiastically in political activities that ranged from the simply zealous to the starkly illegal. Discussing upcoming confirmation hearings for Patrick Gray as director of the FBI, Nixon and Ehrlichman focused on the potential risks his testimony posed to an administration that shielded so much. Nixon was increasingly concerned about the many leaks that he perceived as emanating from the FBI, most of them concerning the widening Watergate scandal. In discussing the acting director, Ehrlichman described an envelope full of material especially damning to the White House that he and John Dean had given personally to Gray, for safekeeping. To both Nixon and Ehrlichman, Gray was essential, yet neither knew him well enough to know just how far he would or could go to protect their secrets. All the while, Nixon spoke of clearing the air and avoiding any type of cover-up.

• • •

NIXON: What about Gray's process?

EHRLICHMAN: All right. If you'd like to get into that —

NIXON: I think this — I really don't feel myself that — I've thought about it — these and some other things. I've been doing a lot of thinking about it. I think we had better take a known quantity with weaknesses that we're aware of in this particular area than to try to take somebody else. Gray is loyal. I realize he's weak in some areas. I realize there'll be some confirmation problem, but let's look at that for just a moment. Maybe it's just as well to have Gray get up there and have them beat him over the head about Watergate, and have him say what the hell he's done.

EHRLICHMAN: Well, he's prepared to do that. I've been over this today with John Dean to see —

NIXON: Mm-hmm.

EHRLICHMAN: — what he says the problems will be. He says it will be a very long, very tough confirmation, and will be an opportunity for a different set of senators to get into the Watergate than the Ervin group.

NIXON: Yeah.

EHRLICHMAN: It will be the Tunneys and Kennedys.

NIXON: Right.

EHRLICHMAN: And the Bayhs and so on. But recognizing that — Gray tells a very good story.

NIXON: Mm-hmm.

EHRLICHMAN: And he could be expected —

NIXON: He tells basically the story that I think ought to be done. But the main problems with Watergate are not the facts. Sure, the facts — the this, that, and the other thing — the main problem is the cover-up thing.

EHRLICHMAN: Yeah.

NIXON: Now damn it, we just can't have an appearance of cover-up. And I think we can simply say that, yes, the — we want — and let him get up there. You see, if you don't, if you kick him upstairs to the circuit court, they'll say that we're afraid. There's no way we'll get around it. It'll look like a cover-up. It does get a different set. It gets Kennedy, and Tunney, and the rest. So that they'll get after Gray. Gray, it seems to me, makes a rather good impression. I don't know — I haven't seen him on television. Does he?

EHRLICHMAN: Reasonably good. He's very earnest.

NIXON: Yeah. Mm-hmm.

EHRLICHMAN: He's very square corners.

NIXON: Yeah.

EHRLICHMAN: You know, kind of the retired navy captain. He's vulnerable according to John's analysis. He's vulnerable on two counts. One is whether or not he handled Watergate adequately and John says, "I think he'll acquit himself very nicely there."

NIXON: He does?

EHRLICHMAN: The other is his stewardship of the bureau over the period of the last eight months.

NIXON: Yeah.

EHRLICHMAN: There, John says, the established bureaucracy of the bureau will be feeding all kinds of garbage —

NIXON: Yeah.

EHRLICHMAN: — to the committee —

NIXON: Yeah.

EHRLICHMAN: — and Gray will be on the defense.

NIXON: Mm-hmm.

EHRLICHMAN: So he says we're liable to be in for a few surprises, on other cases or the handling of other matters or things of that kind that are incalculable right now. But he said he doesn't think that he is in serious jeopardy, and on balance, he thinks Gray is — as you say, is a known quantity. He is a guy we can tell to do things and he will do them. Now he's been a little weak on that.

NIXON: I know.

EHRLICHMAN: Because of this.

NIXON: Yeah.

EHRLICHMAN: He's been afraid of what he'd have to face at the time of confirmation.

NIXON: Yeah.

EHRLICHMAN: John says —

NIXON: Once he's confirmed —

EHRLICHMAN: He thinks if —

NIXON: He'd be tough.

EHRLICHMAN: — if, but only if you call Gray over and you read him chapter and verse. And you say, "Pat — "

NIXON: I have agreed to do it.

EHRLICHMAN: He says you. Now I can do this, but he said you.

NIXON: Right.

EHRLICHMAN: You would say, "Pat, I had an arrangement with J. Edgar Hoover that up until now I have not had with you and I missed it. Once you're confirmed, I want it understood that we go back to a personal relationship."

NIXON: Without the attorney general.

EHRLICHMAN: "That when I call, you respond."

NIXON: Mm-hmm.

EHRLICHMAN: And that "we have to have an absolutely tight relationship."

NIXON: Well, how can we get it so that not only I call but if you call?

EHRLICHMAN: Well, then you could delegate that and go from there. As it is now, John says we made a mistake in the inception in not tying him down tight enough. But we did it for a number of reasons. He was contingent, and we had this thing hanging up, and he's tracked reasonably well. Now, he has some guilty knowledge in connection with the Watergate that only Dean and I know about that has to do with Hunt. We turned some stuff over to Gray to get it out of here. That'll never come out. He'll never testify to that. There isn't any way that he could testify to that.

NIXON: What if he —

EHRLICHMAN: Well, it just isn't necessary. There's no way for anybody to know. And that he understands that that set of circumstances never happened and it's never, never appeared — never came out.

NIXON: Where are the files?

EHRLICHMAN: I don't know where he's got them, but he's got them. We felt that we want to be in a position to say we had turned everything over to the FBI, so I called him up to my office one day, and we said, "Pat, here's a big fat envelope."

NIXON: What is this — stuff that Hunt did on that case in California?

EHRLICHMAN: Well, no, it's other stuff, and Dean's never told me what was in the envelope.

NIXON: I don't know what Hunt dealt in myself.

EHRLICHMAN: Well, he must have dealt in a hell of a lot of stuff.

NIXON: [unclear] doing some things.

EHRLICHMAN: He did some things for Chuck, apparently, that he made a record of.

NIXON: Was that in this envelope?

EHRLICHMAN: Yeah.

NIXON: That Chuck make a record of it?

EHRLICHMAN: No, but Hunt did.

NIXON: How did you get Hunt's stuff?

EHRLICHMAN: Well, we opened his safe. See, Dean took everything out of his safe, and we turned everything over to FBI agents who came for it, except this envelope full of stuff. And, then I called Gray to my office. Dean came in. I said, "Pat, here's an envelope. We want to be in a position to say we've turned everything over to the FBI, so we're giving it to you. I don't care what you do with it as long as it never appears."

NIXON: Suppose that they ask him about other activities, with Hunt and so forth — what does he say about — ?

EHRLICHMAN: Presumably he says, "I honestly don't know of any because" — maybe he never opened the envelope. If he was smart, he didn't.

NIXON: I don't want to get into that with him — the envelope.

EHRLICHMAN: I understand.

NIXON: Can I avoid that?

EHRLICHMAN: But I want you to know about it. The — at some point in time, if you haven't already, Bob or I or John Dean or somebody ought to give you the rundown on how this Ervin hearing is going to go — the kinds of things that are liable to come smoking up so you're not surprised. But we think that there's a reasonably good possibility of coming through it very much like we've come through the trial with a certain amount of day-to-day flak.

NIXON: Oh, sure.

EHRLICHMAN: And evening television stuff, but no lasting results.

NIXON: Well, I suppose this is all dependent — I talked to Bob a little bit about that case — given me some feel — but I suppose, John, it depends. See, [unclear] came back from California and I had a two-day meeting.

EHRLICHMAN: Right. Right.

NIXON: But really the problem is that one of these guys could crack.

EHRLICHMAN: Sure.

NIXON: One of them could. The one that could crack that it would really hurt would be Hunt.

EHRLICHMAN: Yeah, Magruder could really hurt in a different direction.

NIXON: Well, Magruder, if he cracks, he goes to prison.

EHRLICHMAN: Yes.

NIXON: Well, I — unless he takes immunity. Is that what he would do?

EHRLICHMAN: Possibly. Possibly.

NIXON: What do you think?

EHRLICHMAN: There are several of these guys that we're relying on. Sloan is not a problem.

NIXON: He doesn't know anything.

EHRLICHMAN: But Magruder is a problem of —

NIXON: Magruder knows a hell of a lot.

EHRLICHMAN: Yeah.

NIXON: [unclear] bring them in. Let's face it. Didn't Magruder perjure himself?

EHRLICHMAN: Yep.

NIXON: Or did he? I don't know.

EHRLICHMAN: Sure did.

NIXON: But I think he did. From what I've heard he must have.

EHRLICHMAN: Sure did.

NIXON: He said he was not involved — he didn't have the knowledge and he did. Is that right?

EHRLICHMAN: Basically, that's it.

NIXON: Yeah. But beyond that—I mean beyond Magruder—who the hell else perjured himself? Did Mitchell?

EHRLICHMAN: I assume so without knowing.

NIXON: Well, who else have we got?

EHRLICHMAN: The thing has a very good chance if it's handled right. We cut our losses here, cut our losses there, try and shore up Howard Baker here and there.

NIXON: [unclear]

EHRLICHMAN: Bill Safire [unclear].

NIXON: From what I had heard, I thought your [unclear]. I'm not going to be taken by surprise by anything.

EHRLICHMAN: Okay, well—

NIXON: When I say that I mean the only real problems that I see basically are whether if—to the extent that it ties into the White House staff—you know, I was just thinking it's fortunate all that lip service and everything else we've done—at least I've never met any of these people.

EHRLICHMAN: That's right.

NIXON: Except for Magruder. I don't ever—I don't—I never met Hunt. Never talked to—and haven't discussed these things, fortunately.

EHRLICHMAN: Yep. I've met Hunt once. Never—

NIXON: I knew something—I mean the Segretti operation must have been—or that—or no—or Colson in areas other than Watergate, but purely political stuff.

EHRLICHMAN: Yeah.

NIXON: Which was perfectly legal.

EHRLICHMAN: Yeah.

NIXON: Nothing wrong with it.

EHRLICHMAN: Yeah.

NIXON: I think they did some work on Teddy Kennedy or something. That's in the paper already.

EHRLICHMAN: Did some investigating.

NIXON: Yeah.

EHRLICHMAN: The other issue I—

NIXON: [unclear]—

EHRLICHMAN: —raise at this point—

NIXON: Yeah.

EHRLICHMAN: —is because the handling of Gray in other hands—Eastland and his group could go in an unpredictable direction. I just don't know. And so that's the one lingering hazard. Now, the other prime candidate is Henry Petersen.

NIXON: Mm-hmm.

EHRLICHMAN: The criminal deputy and he's in just as bad shape.

NIXON: Oh, Christ. Yes.

EHRLICHMAN: You know—and without the ties that Gray has.

NIXON: He wouldn't care what happened to us.

EHRLICHMAN: Oh, Ruckelshaus is a possibility. There's one other fellow named Vernon Acree who's the head of Customs who's a possibility.

NIXON: No.

EHRLICHMAN: But that's about the—

NIXON: On the Gray thing—

EHRLICHMAN: —about the spread.

NIXON: —for instance, I see your point. It's two Watergate hearings.

EHRLICHMAN: That's right.

NIXON: Would Gray—would not be called before the Ervin Committee?

EHRLICHMAN: No. Well, he could be, but probably wouldn't be. So sort of double indemnity—what is—double—

NIXON: Double jeopardy.

EHRLICHMAN: —jeopardy.

NIXON: [unclear] come down on him.

EHRLICHMAN: Uh—

NIXON: It's a tough [unclear]—

EHRLICHMAN: I—it really is.

NIXON: We just don't have a good, strong man—a loyalist.

EHRLICHMAN: Well—

NIXON: [unclear]

EHRLICHMAN: Yeah, that's it. We combed, you know, about as well as we can. Let me come at it from another side. We had the idea of nominating Maury Stans for a confirmable place.

NIXON: I heard about that.

EHRLICHMAN: The thought there is to pull out some of the poison—to air it in another proceeding. Maury's pretty clean—tells a good story. He's righteously indignant. So nominate him. Get him up before the Senate Foreign Relations Committee, or some other committee. Let them ask him about campaign financing. Let him tell his story and be vindicated in that process. Pretty good collateral action. I'm inclined to think that there's some of that in Gray—and the case could be made that the Gray thing would do the same thing. You'd have papers say, "Gee, now that he's told the whole story, that was a hell of an investigation. And the administration really did turn over every rock."

NIXON: Well, for example, they'll ask, "Did you investigate—did you get it straight from Haldeman?" They didn't.

EHRLICHMAN: No, the FB—the bureau never did it. At least not that I know of.

NIXON: But did they get one from you?

EHRLICHMAN: Oh, they got two from me.

NIXON: Colson?

EHRLICHMAN: Sure.

NIXON: Why not Haldeman?

EHRLICHMAN: They—it just never led to him. If they'd wanted to, he was available.

NIXON: And that's what he would say.

EHRLICHMAN: Yeah.

NIXON: Yeah.

EHRLICHMAN: Sure.

NIXON: Could I [unclear]?

EHRLICHMAN: No problem.

NIXON: [unclear]

EHRLICHMAN: Yeah.

NIXON: I think I'd send him up. I'd simply send him up.

EHRLICHMAN: Okay. Okay.

NIXON: [unclear] You know, we constantly get this story repeated, John, which [unclear]. The Nixon administration's program of investigating domestic subversive groups, as you know—that goddamn thing started—you know what I mean? On this—in the Watergate story this morning, that thing started as you know, years ago.

EHRLICHMAN: Sure.

NIXON: And reached its peak under Bobby Kennedy.

EHRLICHMAN: Oh, the taps and stuff. Yeah. Sure, sure.

NIXON: And that those became available to Hunt.

EHRLICHMAN: Yeah.

NIXON: I don't know how the hell they became available to Hunt.

EHRLICHMAN: They didn't. They didn't.

NIXON: Huh?

EHRLICHMAN: They didn't.

NIXON: You sure?

EHRLICHMAN: Yes, sir.

NIXON: Those were available to you as I recall.

EHRLICHMAN: But there was never any connection between Dave Young's leak operation.

NIXON: Oh, that's Dave Young.

EHRLICHMAN: Yeah. See, and that's where he tied in and now we had Hunt working for Dave Young for a brief period of time.

NIXON: Oh, I see.

EHRLICHMAN: And what he was doing down there was simply a job of analysis. He was taking all those leaks and matching them up—

NIXON: Yeah.

EHRLICHMAN: —to see where a commonality among them was—

NIXON: Yeah.

EHRLICHMAN: —to try and determine which documents they came from.

NIXON: But we had to check that?

EHRLICHMAN: Oh, why of course. But he never got tap materials—

NIXON: Yeah.

EHRLICHMAN: —from anything.

NIXON: Did Dave Young get it?

EHRLICHMAN: Oh, Dave Young never got any of this domestic tap stuff.

NIXON: Who the hell did?

EHRLICHMAN: Well, I got some of it. Bob got a lot of it. Bob got most of it, I think. I'm not aware that anybody else ever did.

• • •

NIXON: The point is if you're ever asked in the Domestic Council about it, I would show some outrage.

EHRLICHMAN: Why sure.

NIXON: That this, the Nixon administration — what the hell. We cut them back!

EHRLICHMAN: That's right, way back. We cut the army clear out — see, they had the army doing all this.

NIXON: [unclear]

EHRLICHMAN: We cut all that out.

NIXON: The army out of it and we had the number of domestic taps has been cut down to the barest necessary to protect the national security.

EHRLICHMAN: We'll, we finally took them off. We took all of them off except the national security taps.

NIXON: But they're done domestically as well as —

EHRLICHMAN: They're done domestically but they're done, you know, pursuant to that statute and the number is way, way down.

NIXON: I'm inclined to think that we just better [unclear] because I think at the present time we have the worst of both worlds. We can't leave it uncertain. Now how do you handle Kleindienst on this? I've got to run.

EHRLICHMAN: Oh, I'll just inform him. He'll be happy as a clam.

NIXON: Yeah. That I've got to see him alone. I —

EHRLICHMAN: Right. I would not tell Kleindienst until after you've talked to Gray.

NIXON: Okay. Should we meet Gray more privately tomorrow?

EHRLICHMAN: Yeah. Yeah.

NIXON: All right.

EHRLICHMAN: Okay.

NIXON: I'm going to the Pentagon at one o'clock and I could be back by, let's say four o'clock.

EHRLICHMAN: Four o'clock.

NIXON: Because I don't know how long it'll take.

EHRLICHMAN: Okay, fine.

NIXON: You and I will see him together.

EHRLICHMAN: All right. All right.

NIXON: We'll decide that damn thing.

EHRLICHMAN: I think just —

NIXON: Just you give me a very brief talking paper.

EHRLICHMAN: Yeah, all right.

NIXON: You can just say that "the president wants to have a candid talk with you about this." [unclear] "Pat, we haven't made up our minds. He wants to talk to you first."

EHRLICHMAN: All right.

NIXON: That'll keep him.

EHRLICHMAN: All right. Good. Okay, I've got other stuff, but I'll —

NIXON: Tell him all the damn heat he is going to be through.

EHRLICHMAN: Yep, we've got to do that.

NIXON: You could bring it in in the morning if you want. I have nothing to — in fact, he could have come in this morning. Wait a minute. Tomorrow's Thursday. No, I've put a cabinet meeting on Friday. Thought I'd let George [Shultz] send [unclear].

EHRLICHMAN: Good.

NIXON: [unclear] which is good and let — Agnew's [unclear] a report [unclear].

EHRLICHMAN: Good. Well, I'll get him in tomorrow afternoon. We won't put it on your schedule. I'll get a talker in before that.

NIXON: Okay.

Testing the mettle of Acting Director Gray

February 16, 1973, 9:08 a.m.
Richard Nixon, Patrick Gray, and John Ehrlichman
OVAL OFFICE

Two days after discussing Pat Gray in depth, Nixon and Ehrlichman met with him and had a long talk. They discussed leaks, loyalty, and the role of the FBI in serving the president and the nation — in that order. The underlying topic was Gray's ability to deal with the press and two different congressional hearings, without compromising any secrets. Nixon's part of the conversation, which developed into a paean to J. Edgar Hoover, was more lecturing than probing, with the result that Gray probably learned more about Nixon than the president did about Gray.

• • •

NIXON: Hi. How are you?

GRAY: Mr. President. How are you, sir?

NIXON: How are you? Nice to see you.

GRAY: You look great.

NIXON: Fine. How're you feeling?

GRAY: Good.

NIXON: Fine.

GRAY: Mean — nasty. [laughs] That's right. [unclear] a bit happy —

EHRLICHMAN: That's because I got you up early this morning?

GRAY: A little bit early.

NIXON: Let me ask you. How is your health —

GRAY: Good.

NIXON: — since you had your operation?

GRAY: Good, Mr. President. I called that thing Sunday morning when we were waiting to go to Mass. I told Bea, I said, "That damn obstruction is back." And that's exactly what it was. There was no evidence of tumors, no cancer.

NIXON: Mm-hmm.

GRAY: There's just a simple adhesion down there.

NIXON: In other words, as far as your ability to work and everything, why there's no question that you're ready to put in the long hours.

GRAY: No — still doing it. Did it right in the hospital the day after the operation. I had my executive assistant up and started right away.

NIXON: Let me ask a couple of other things having to do with whether we decide here. As you probably are aware — what this — if you were to be nominated — and I think, of course I've talked to John Mitchell about Tolson. You obviously open up before a different committee than the Ervin Committee — the whole Watergate thing. Now the question is whether you feel that you can handle it — whether that's a good thing, bad thing, and so forth. What I mean is the Watergate Committee, you know, has its — Ervin and three or four jackasses on it and so forth. It will be bad enough there. Your committee would have Kennedy and Tunney on it.

GRAY: Right. And Bayh.

NIXON: They'd like to make quite a deal about the thing. What I'm getting at is this — I'm not concerned about the substance — about the facts coming out. I am — all I'm thinking is whether it's to the interest of everybody concerned to have the man who is to be nominated for director of the bureau be badgered and so forth on whether it's good for us to have that story told twice before two committees, et cetera. So why don't you give me your judgment on that? You must have thought about it.

GRAY: Oh, yes.

NIXON: You must have thought also of the kind of a story you'd have to tell when you'd be examined on it. It would not be limited to Watergate. They would probably ask you about such things as, "Do you know about any other things that the bureau's done — have you got into this domestic wiretapping," where incidentally, parenthetically, whatever you're hearing, it's time to start getting out the truth there — which is heighten the evidence that is on hand. It's the Robert Kennedy administration — Justice Department, when there were over a hundred a year. It's been cut down to a very small amount. Then I would be a bit goddamn defensive about it. I'd say, "Yes, we have to do it, because this involves the possibility of violent groups that we've got" — this, what happened to Wallace, [unclear] judicial judgment. [unclear]

EHRLICHMAN: He can tell a strong story.

NIXON: Yeah, say, "Look, what do you want us to do about this? Do you want to let people get shot?"

• • •

NIXON: It has to do with national security. There're a hell of a lot of people, these violent groups, who would threaten these — the Jews and all the others that run around — the Arabs.

GRAY: Mm-hmm.

NIXON: Either side now. There's this violent [American] Jewish Committee that wants to kill the Arabs and the Arabs want to kill the Jews and Christ, they're—

EHRLICHMAN: Terrorism is a tragic problem.

NIXON: Terrorism—hijacking is another thing. And you've got to get into that. Right? Some of that requires wiretapping. Higher—and your authority—your responsibility in hijacking—your responsibility for this. I think that you've got to get—and I want, John and me for next time. [unclear] I'm already hitting them. I don't believe we should be defensive. First of all, we're doing less. Second, it's extremely necessary. We must not be denied the right to use the weapon. The idea that we're wiretapping a lot of political groups is bullshit.

GRAY: That's right and that's simply not—

NIXON: Let's get back to the fundamental part of it.

GRAY: It's the other—

NIXON: You know the mood of the Congress. As you know, they're panicked—depressed by Watergate, and so forth. What should we do? Would it hurt or help for you to go up there and be bashed about that?

GRAY: I think, probably, Mr. President, I'm the man that's in the best position to handle that thing.

NIXON: Why?

GRAY: Because I've consistently handled it from the outset, before Judge Sirica's order came to play [*United States v. U.S. District Court*], when we were talking only procedure not substance, and I handled all kinds of questions from all kinds of press people and then when Sirica shut the valve, why I had to shut up, even on things procedural. I've been intimately connected with it. I've been responsible for quite a bit of the decision making insofar as the Federal Bureau of Investigation is concerned. I feel that I would have taken a greater beating had not the Ervin Committee been established and this is always a possibility there that you're not going to get too much flak before Judiciary. I think you'd—I think I'm going to take the expected heat from Kennedy, Bayh, Hart, Tunney—that group. But I don't think it's going to be nearly as severe as it would have been had not the Ervin Committee been established. I think that's where it's all going to hang out and I'm not ashamed for it to hang out because I think the administration has done a hell of a fine job in going after this thing and I think we're prepared to present it in just that light. Now if you bring somebody else in, you can be attacked as ducking the issue, trying to put a new boy in so he can go up there and say, "I didn't have anything to do with this. This happened on Gray's watch. Get him back here and let him talk about it." I think it's a thing we ought to meet head-on, on every front.

NIXON: In other words, you'd be—let me say, what kind of story could you tell—and say that you just go in and, "We had a very intensive investigation. We ran down all leads." Who'd you talk to? "Yes, we questioned at very great length—took sworn statements." Did you swear in statements?

GRAY: Yes, we did.

NIXON: And that members of the White House staff— "Why didn't you question Haldeman?" What do you say to that?

GRAY: Perfectly good reason we didn't question Mr. Haldeman. Because no agent, even the case agent right at the lowest level, felt that any trail led to Mr. Haldeman. He did not recommend that a lead be set out to interview Mr. Haldeman. The field supervisor did not. The circulation charts did not. The bureau supervisor did not—

NIXON: It did—leads did lead to others?

GRAY: It did lead to others.

NIXON: Colson and so forth.

GRAY: And we went after them. This is one I had—

NIXON: What about Mitchell? You questioned Mitchell.

GRAY: Sir? Yes, sir.

NIXON: Yeah, Mitchell was questioned.

[WAITER enters.]

GRAY: Oh, thank you.

[WAITER leaves.]

NIXON: You questioned Stans and so forth.

GRAY: Yes, we— Stans three times— Mitchell once. Bob Haldeman not at all. I'm not really afraid of that thing because I called those agents in at the end of that first week and just gave them unshirted hell and told them to go and go with all the vim and vigor possible. I furthermore called Larry O'Brien that Saturday morning and I said, "Mr. O'Brien, I hear there're some rumors around this town that the FBI is not pursuing this with vigor." And, he said, "No, no," he said. "Let me assure you we're very happy with what you're doing." So, I'm going to lay that on their backs and other things like that. I don't fear that investigation at all, Mr. President.

NIXON: What else do you think they will raise? Morale in the bureau, and so forth and so on?

GRAY: Well, I think they'll do that but I think we can shoot that down easily because I've got all kinds of letters from the field that I wouldn't let come to you. I stopped them. They tried to respond to this criticism that morale is bad. It's actually higher than it's ever been in the bureau.

NIXON: What is the situation, for example — you see, you haven't been able to do anything or have you, up to this point, about the leaks — you know are all coming from the bureau. That the whole story, we've found, is coming from the bureau.

GRAY: Well, I'm not completely ready to buy that, Mr. President. We have done something. I've been wiping people out of there, you know, like the Assyrian [army] on the foe. I wiped out a whole division.

NIXON: Do we have any question about the leaks — those leaks coming from the bureau?

GRAY: Well—

EHRLICHMAN: Yeah, Pat and I talked about this issue and then—

NIXON: [unclear] wish he would come forth.

EHRLICHMAN: — there have been [unclear].

NIXON: That isn't what our *Time* magazine guy says. He's got a direct channel to the bureau.

EHRLICHMAN: That's right.

GRAY: Well, he probably has. [*Time* magazine reporter] Sandy Smith used to talk to a lot of guys in the bureau and I won't talk to the SOB anymore because if he lays the cards down —

NIXON: This is very high.

GRAY: No. We laid the cards on the table and that's low — three times, right. Laid them right out there. Gave the same cards to *Newsweek* and each one wrote differently and I just said no more to this clown and I won't deal with him.

NIXON: Well —

EHRLICHMAN: [unclear] there is no two ways about it —

NIXON: Smith has written stuff that is true, right out of the bureau —

EHRLICHMAN: There is no —

NIXON: Right out of the bureau?

EHRLICHMAN: — question, about their getting —

NIXON: Yeah.

EHRLICHMAN: — the information —

NIXON: Yeah.

EHRLICHMAN: — off the 703s or whatever those forms are —

NIXON: Yeah.

EHRLICHMAN: — the investigation summary forms.

NIXON: So they —

GRAY: 302s?

NIXON: Yeah.

EHRLICHMAN: And —

NIXON: Because, I would say if they were false, then I would just say it was time to —

GRAY: There are some things —

NIXON: — bring those things to an end. But this is a case where they have true information and I say well, damn it, that's somebody from the bureau. Do you think Petersen's office puts it out?

GRAY: Mr. President, you have to realize that other people than we get the 302s and I have put some pretty strong controls on our dissemination and our accounting. And, I don't say that it's not possible it can come from the bureau. It is possible.

NIXON: Well, let me ask you this, for example. Did you follow through on the directive which I understand was given that everybody in the bureau was to take a lie detector test as to whether — what part they played in the wiretapping of my plane in 1968? Has that been done?

GRAY: No, that directive was not given out.

NIXON: Well, it's given now.

GRAY: Yes, sir.

NIXON: Yeah. Now, what happened there? Who dropped the ball on that?

EHRLICHMAN: I don't know of it, Mr. President.

GRAY: Do—

NIXON: Yeah. There—that charge has been around. Whether it's true or not, I don't know. But that is to be—that has to be—the *Washington Star* has the straight story. Johnson killed it in the *Star*, but it has to be checked out just for the integrity of the bureau.

GRAY: I checked out some of the allegations that John Dean gave me on [Johnson National Security Council staff member] Bromley Smith I guess the bloke's name is, and what they were doing on [Republican] Anna Chennault [who was wiretapped on Johnson's orders during the 1968 presidential election due to her contacts with the Nixon campaign and the South Vietnamese government] and how they tried to—

NIXON: But there was a wiretap. There was a phone wiretap for sure and there was an allegation that—

GRAY: On your plane, sir?

NIXON: Hoover told me—

GRAY: Mm-hmm.

NIXON: —that the bureau tapped my plane—

GRAY: Mm-hmm.

NIXON: —in 1968 and he told Mitchell the same thing.

GRAY: Mm-hmm.

NIXON: Now I want everybody in the bureau who has anything to do with wiretapping at that time questioned and given a lie detector test.

GRAY: Mm-hmm.

NIXON: Not because I'm telling you this but because the allegation's been made and the *Star*'s been running the story—

GRAY: Right.

NIXON: —and we want to knock it down. Don't you believe you should?

GRAY: Oh, sure. But I haven't—

NIXON: You see my point?

GRAY: I didn't have any directive like that. I had some questions from John Dean about Bromley Smith, Anna Chennault, and company.

NIXON: I understand. I'm not making charges, but I do know that that has come up. All we do is to play it very—

GRAY: I wouldn't put it past them to do it.

NIXON: I wouldn't put it past Johnson.

GRAY: No.

NIXON: It's not trying to do him in but it is very important that it be known in the *Star* and I think the *Star* is working with one magazine—I don't know which one—that it be known, that that's been investigated. So that we just don't say, "Well, the bureau didn't do it." I know the bureau's sensitivity on that, but are the same people that do wiretapping for the bureau now, are they the same ones you had in '68?

GRAY: We think, Mr. President, that if such an order came, it came to Deke DeLoach from Lyndon Johnson and that it —

NIXON: Well, then DeLoach must be brought in and put on a —

GRAY: Yeah, if Deke got it, he gave it.

NIXON: All right, he used to have it. He's going to lie detector also.

GRAY: Mm-hmm.

NIXON: He's out, I know, but he's still got to take one. I mean, this has gotten — I want this — don't you agree, John? We've got to get to the bottom of the damn thing.

GRAY: Well, I want to, you know —

NIXON: I'm not going to be in here denying it from here unless the director of the FBI tells me that it's been checked.

GRAY: Right.

NIXON: The FBI cannot be above the law on this thing.

GRAY: Oh, I know it. No, if this was done we've got to look into it and if — even if the allegation is there we've got to look into it.

EHRLICHMAN: Was Felt there in those days?

GRAY: No. He was not at — he may have been in the bureau. I shouldn't answer that too quickly.

NIXON: Who would you put — who do you think would be the fellow who would be the second man over there?

GRAY: I think, Mr. Nixon, that my recommendation to you now would be to continue Felt, but I think what I've got to do is and which I'm in the process of doing, is come up with an overall plan to submit to you and you and I should discuss that plan.

NIXON: The only problem you have on Felt is that the lines lead very directly to him, and I can't believe it, but they lead right there and —

EHRLICHMAN: Well, you know we've tried to trap him —

GRAY: I don't believe —

EHRLICHMAN: The trap is — set traps around to see if we can turn something up and —

NIXON: Well, why don't you get in the fellow that's made the charge then.

EHRLICHMAN: Well, maybe that's the step to take.

NIXON: Of course he's not a newsman, on the other hand.

EHRLICHMAN: No.

NIXON: He's a lawyer —

EHRLICHMAN: That's right.

NIXON: — for *Time*.

GRAY: I know who he is, Mr. President.

NIXON: And, well —

GRAY: I knew the reason. I knew the allegations existed, and I think one thing, Mr. President, I would like to say to you, because I believe I must say it to you. Those people over there are like little old ladies in tennis shoes and they've got some of the most vicious vendettas going on and their gossip mill is —

NIXON: You mean in the administration?

GRAY: In the FBI.

NIXON: In the FBI.

GRAY: Sure, it's the damnedest —

NIXON: [unclear] hating everybody else.

GRAY: That's right.

NIXON: I have been hearing — what about this fellow Sullivan? Good, bad, or indifferent? Would you bring him back? Would that [unclear]?

GRAY: I wouldn't bring him back at all. I wouldn't touch him at all.

NIXON: Why not?

GRAY: His first words when he came back to Washington, in response to questions from some of the people in the Domestic Intelligence Division as to why he was here — in two words, "For revenge." Bill Sullivan was a very disappointed man when Hoover put Deke DeLoach in the position as assistant to the director.

NIXON: He fired him — I mean — yeah.

EHRLICHMAN: Hoover didn't like him.

GRAY: Didn't like him and he began attacking Hoover. The guy is too nervous. He's not articulate at all.

NIXON: Fine. Well, coming back though to Felt. It would be very, very difficult to have Felt in that position without having that charge cleared up.

GRAY: I —

NIXON: And, incidentally, let me say this — this is also a directive. He's to take a lie detector test on it.

GRAY: [unclear]

NIXON: Put it right to him now.

GRAY: Do you want him to do — ?

NIXON: You're willing for him to take a lie detector test, aren't you?

GRAY: Sure. Why shouldn't he? I've taken — hell, I've —

NIXON: All right, has he ever taken one?

GRAY: I don't know.

NIXON: Have him take one. Now, that charge has been made. John, you prepare the questions — you know, that have been made. Has he talked to *Time* magazine? This and that and the other thing. And he's to do it or he isn't going to get the job. That's the way it has to be. You see, the thing is that there's a lack of discipline over there at the present time. And we've — that's part of the problem — the morale. That's part of the problem with leaks.

GRAY: In the FBI, Mr. President?

NIXON: This is absurd. This stuff didn't leak when Hoover was there. I've never known of a leak when Hoover was there. I could talk to him in this office about everything.

And the reason is that — it wasn't because they loved him, but they feared him. And they've got to fear the man at the top and that's why I'd get it again — and Hoover would lie-detect those guys. I know that he even did it to Lou Nichols once because of charges made he leaked. You've got to play it exactly that way. You've got to be brutal, tough, and respected, because the — we can't have any kind of a relationship with the bureau — which is necessary, you know, here. We can't have any kind of a relationship unless we can trust it and I've —

GRAY: That's right.

NIXON: I used to have, and I would expect with the director in the future to have a relationship — with Hoover, he'd come in about every month. He'd be there at breakfast or he'd come in here. He'd come in alone, not with the attorney general. I'd talk about things. I used to have him — my contact with him, it wasn't, you know — he'd always said that he didn't want me to designate one person he called on things and raising hell about Helms and the agency — CIA, and the State Department, and so forth. Much of it was extremely valuable, but — and it never leaked out of here. You know that he was giving me the stuff that he had. And he talked — Ehrlichman was my contact. Ehrlichman will be in the future. You've got to have one man —

GRAY: Mm-hmm.

NIXON: — that will not talk.

GRAY: Mm-hmm.

NIXON: I wouldn't think of having it to go to anybody else. I could use Dean but he's too busy on other things so I'd rather it be with John. The point is — I digress — the reason, Pat, that the relationship of the director — to the director and the president — is like the relationship between the president and the commander — and the chairman of the Joint Chiefs.

GRAY: Right. I understand.

NIXON: I — as you know, Mel Laird was very tough on that, but he didn't — he always wanted to be in with the Chiefs. And just yesterday, two days ago, I brought Moorer over, didn't let anybody from the NSC staff come in, didn't let them know. There wasn't a hell of a lot we wanted to talk about that they couldn't have heard, but I didn't tell them. The reason was that I found this summer, for example, at a time when right after we had the May 8 bombing, that I had put out several directives to continually step up the bombing because I knew that this — that was the time to put the pressure on to bring about the negotiation. And Moorer told me that he sent over at least twelve recommendations that never reached my desk because Laird didn't want to go forward on it. Now, goddamn it, this is not going to happen. Now, with the bureau, it's the president's director, not that you have the attorney general's director. Now having said that, though, we can't do it — we cannot do it unless there's total communication and total discipline in that bureau. And, hell, I think if we pick up *Time* magazine and see that something's leaked out, either out of the bureau — I understand leaking out of the CIA, those goddamn cookie pushers — but if it leaks out of the bureau, then the whole damn place ought to be fired. Really it should, until — just move them all out to the field. I think you've got to do it like they did in the war. You say — whenever, you know — you remember in World War II. The Germans, if they went through these towns and then one of their soldiers, a sniper, hit one of them, they'd line up the whole goddamn town and say, "Until you talk you're all getting shot." I really think that's what has to be done. I mean I don't think you can be Mr. Nice Guy over there.

GRAY: I haven't been. I think, Mr. President —

NIXON: The leaks are occurring — from someplace.

GRAY: That's right, from someplace. But as to discipline, I have done things with regard to discipline that Mr. Hoover didn't dare to do. I took on [unclear] and I met him face-to-face, and I threw him right out of the Federal Bureau of Investigation.

NIXON: Good.

GRAY: These guys know they can't lie —

NIXON: [unclear] —

GRAY: — to me like they used to lie to Hoover.

NIXON: — [unclear]. I'm not really referring to that kind of stuff.

GRAY: Mm-hmm.

NIXON: Frankly, I am referring to discipline of the highest sensitivity involving what may be political matters.

GRAY: Oh, I know.

NIXON: Partisan political matters. But I've got to know, for example, what's going on that — even now, on occasion, let's suppose something on the Pentagon Papers leaks out. Let us suppose there's a leak to a certain member of the press. I've got to have a relationship here where you go out and do something and deny on a stack of Bibles.

GRAY: Right.

NIXON: Okay.

GRAY: Right. Well, I understand.

NIXON: You've got to get that because I don't have anybody else. I can't hire some asshole from the outside.

GRAY: No. No.

EHRLICHMAN: The relationship is a self-starting one in a sense —

GRAY: Mm-hmm.

EHRLICHMAN: — and Hoover used to call —

NIXON: Assert —

EHRLICHMAN: — and say, "We've picked up something here."

• • •

NIXON: Hoover, of course, was a great cops-and-armed-robbers guy in through the whole area. He was overly suspicious, actually. But that helped a bit, because as a result, he got us information, which is extremely helpful. Because you see, these past four years have not been an easy — we've had almost the entire bureaucracy, including many in Defense, who were opposed to what we were doing in Vietnam, opposed to Cambodia, opposed to Laos, opposed to [the] May 8 [bombing of Hanoi and mining of Haiphong harbor]. It worked, and of course went up the wall when I ordered the December bombing. We — and incidentally, most of the White House staff was against it. They didn't go out and yap about it but they were against it. I understand that. My point is that with the media against you, with the bureaucracy against you, with the professors, with the church people and the rest — let alone the Congress — it's a hard damn fight. Now, at the present time we've come through with that big issue — come through rather well. And we have some allies from dif — unexpected sources driving the goddamn media right up the wall. These POWs turned out so well.

GRAY: Mm-hmm.

NIXON: Let me tell you, there were times — and Lyndon Johnson told me this same thing — when I felt that the only person in this goddamn government who was standing with me was Edgar Hoover. He was the only one.

GRAY: Well, I was sure standing there with you all the way through it.

NIXON: But I was sure of it. I was sure of it. Now what did I mean? I don't mean just coming in and saying, "Now look, Mr. President, you're doing great."

GRAY: No. No.

NIXON: He would often do that. But the point was that he would break his ass if he saw something that was wrong being done — if somebody was pissing on us — I mean leaks.

GRAY: Mm-hmm.

NIXON: That sort of thing — not interfering with the rights of the press — not interfering with the, you know, all that crap.

GRAY: Right. Sure.

NIXON: The thing is that in your case — you see, the difficulty with having someone who is basically — as you are — a Nixon loyalist, and a friend — first of all they're going to raise hell because you're that.

GRAY: Sure — oh, I know it.

NIXON: Second, a Nixon loyalist and a friend feels generally, and I've found this to be true of half the cabinet — he's got to go or bend over backwards to prove that he's neutral.

GRAY: Mm-hmm.

NIXON: We can't have that. Publicly you must do that. Publicly. But privately what you've got to do is to do like Hoover. Now, the reason Hoover's relationship with me was so close, even closer than with Johnson, even though he saw Johnson more often, was that we started working on the Hiss case. He knew that he could trust me. I knew I could trust him. And as a result, he told me things that — like this wiretap he told me about. He didn't know there was any. Understand? My purpose in checking this wiretap business is not to put it out. I don't intend to put it out. But I damn well want to know who did it. See what I mean? I want to know who the bureau used and I want it known, should we — see, then you may find that whoever is the guilty one will put out the story —

GRAY: Mm-hmm.

NIXON: — and that he did that — and that will be useful. We've got to know such things. That's the whole point.

EHRLICHMAN: Knowledge —

NIXON: Of course, Johnson should not have done that.

GRAY: No question about it.

NIXON: Johnson should not have wiretapped or — either the plane or the phones. The phones were done for sure. We — even DeLoach has admitted that. But the planes he denies now. Hoover told me the plane — the cabin on my plane for the last two weeks of the campaign — they put it on the basis of Madame Chennault or some goddamn thing — were tapped. What the hell do you think happened then? Every damn thing we had — we didn't have any discussions about — we didn't have political discussions — went to Johnson and you know what the hell he did with them? Gave them to Humphrey.

GRAY: Humphrey. Sure.

NIXON: That kind of a game is a hell of a game.

GRAY: We could get positive evidence of that. We could nail Deke on that because I'm sure, from what checking I've done on this other thing, that it came through Deke.

NIXON: I just want to be sure that I know who did it. Well, let me say this, the main thing — the main point is that, as I said, the — I think it's going to be a bloody confirmation.

GRAY: Oh, I do, too.

NIXON: I think — all right, I think we just wanted you to know that if you do go through it, you've got to be prepared to take the heat and get bloodied up. But if you do go through a bloody one — you do go through a bloody confirmation — let's remember that you're probably going to be in probably for just four years.

GRAY: That's right.

NIXON: And they're going to throw you out and then let's do some good for the country. As you know, I would never ask the director of the bureau to do anything wrong. I mean — but I am certainly going to have to ask the director of the bureau at times to do things that are going to protect the security of this country —

GRAY: No problem.

NIXON: — this country — this bureaucracy. Pat, you know this [U.S. Navy yeoman Charles] Radford one [who leaked classified material to journalist Jack Anderson], too. It's crawling with, Pat, at best unloyal people and at worst treasonable people.

GRAY: Treasonable people.

NIXON: We have got to get them — break them.

GRAY: Right. I know that. I agree.

NIXON: The way to get them is through you. See?

GRAY: I agree. I have no problems with that.

NIXON: We have to pick up people — some people. That's the price of it.

GRAY: I would like to. I wish the one [federal charge for removing records from the

Bureau of Indian Affairs] on [*Washington Post* journalist Les] Whitten would have stuck — the informant.

NIXON: Whitten — oh, Christ. That — I'm not concerned.

GRAY: Small potatoes.

NIXON: It isn't the press that bothers me. It's the people within the bureaucracy that bother me. Those are the ones that there's no excuse for leaks, right? So, we — I think, under the circumstances, that it seems to me just — I've asked these questions only to be the devil's advocate for a moment. I think that you've got to make the decision — if you've got the health — if you've got the desire, and also if you can — if you feel that you can have a — the kind of a relationship that we had with Hoover — which, of course, we can't — we shouldn't have had up to this point.

GRAY: No.

NIXON: And you can't have it before your conf — well, there we've said it. From the moment you're nominated, I think you've got to start cracking the whip, having in mind the fact that always — that you don't want to crack any whips that are going to force some bastard to go out and testify against your nomination.

GRAY: That's right. That's the thing.

NIXON: So you've got to be careful. But the moment you're confirmed then I think we've got to have the kind of relationship we had with Hoover. We had — I, on the other hand — we had — we knew everything because I knew everybody and they were supporting me. But then I think we've got to do that. You've got to watch everything around the world in your own shop. Watch the papers and see [unclear] and if you think something's not right, for example — for Christ's sake, you can tail people, you know, from time to time.

GRAY: Sure. Sure.

NIXON: Suppose we've got some jackass in the State Department, some assistant to the secretary as we know is a little off — so you tail him.

• • •

NIXON: That's the way Hoover did it.

GRAY: Sure, and those things can be done easily and — can be done perfectly on the record, just like this thing was done here on —

NIXON: Well, we think of — I think I've talked — we've had the court keep this very closely held. We think you're the best man for the job. We know that the bloody — I — one of the reasons I'd say, as far as the Watergate, I'd rather put it all out there and not be defensive. The other side of the coin if we don't quite do this thing — they're going to call you in on it.

GRAY: That's right. Sure.

NIXON: It's personal — hotter and hotter temperature — the Ervin Committee will call you in.

GRAY: Sure.

NIXON: So that's the feeling we have. Now the question is to, I guess, you and John will work that out as far as how the announcement should be made.

EHRLICHMAN: Yeah.

NIXON: How are your relations with Eastland?

GRAY: Very good. And was —

NIXON: Is he for you?

GRAY: Very good. Yes, I'm positive of that.

NIXON: Yeah. That's very important. Should — who else should be informed? Hruska, at least? Hruska?

EHRLICHMAN: Well, we've haven't told the attorney general yet. [laughs]

NIXON: Well, hell, the attorney general will support that.

EHRLICHMAN: There's no question about that. Yes.

NIXON: Well, let us talk to him.

EHRLICHMAN: We — I think we can get most of the clearances. I don't know where Eastland is at the moment.

NIXON: Do you want me to tell him, Pat? Do you want me to tell the attorney general?

EHRLICHMAN: I think that'd be good.

NIXON: I'll tell him today.

GRAY: All right.

NIXON: So then what — when will we announce though? I want to get it done — what do you mean clearances?

EHRLICHMAN: Well, just this idea of contacting Eastland and Hruska — and I don't know who else gets, well I imagine they'd be the only two.

GRAY: That'd be [unclear].

EHRLICHMAN: [unclear] the Appropriations Subcommittee —

GRAY: Probably John Rooney's people on the Senate side, too.

NIXON: Well, why don't you — Kleindienst will be coming to the cabinet meeting. Could you and Pat meet now and work out that thing?

EHRLICHMAN: Sure.

NIXON: Because I want — time is of the essence. I'd like to get this done like by today. All right. Yeah. We've got to move. It'll leak — this damn Gray's a leaker! [laughs]

GRAY: Yes, I am, Mr. President.

NIXON: [laughs] [unclear]

GRAY: A Nixon loyalist. I tell you you're goddamn right I am!

Using aid to support peace in the two Vietnams
February 20, 1973, 7:30 p.m.
Richard Nixon and Henry Kissinger
WHITE HOUSE TELEPHONE

On the same day that Kissinger returned from his Asian trip, Nixon was flying back to Washington from a vacation in Florida. On landing, the president was described as "smiling and in obvious good spirits." Though the two men arrived at Andrews Air Force Base within twenty minutes of one another, they traveled separately to the White House for an *evening meeting. Kissinger immediately expressed suspicion that the North Vietnamese would be difficult, if not impossible, to control within the commitments of the Peace Accords. Nixon was even more suspicious of those involved in the peace movement in the United States, and as the two men warmed to the topic, they agreed that in the first stage of peace, it was the liberals in the United States who were the enemy.**

• • •

NIXON: The way I would get at it is to, frankly, take them on, one by one, and say, "Now, damn it, let us — let's be cold turkey with you." You can't say this, but we've got to have some leverage. If these clowns start something, we can cut it off. That's really what it gets down to.

KISSINGER: Exactly.

NIXON: I mean, suppose, for example, that they do not withdraw their forces from — as — you know, like my wire to you when you were over there; if they do not withdraw their forces from Cambodia and Laos, they get no aid. Right?

KISSINGER: Exactly.

NIXON: What other — what other leverage have we got? The purpose of this is the leverage to get them the hell out. I think that's a very strong point to make to them on a confidential basis. Don't you think so?

KISSINGER: Well, I think that — I think — I'm not so worried about selling the right-wingers, but the — the conservatives — ah, the liberals are, of course, totally —

NIXON: [laughs]

KISSINGER: — corrupt, morally.

NIXON: I know, but what are you going to say to them? Are —

KISSINGER: I'll put it on human — I'll say — I'll put it on human — humanitarian grounds to them. I mean, I'll just — I don't say that's our reason, but I'll tell them that —

NIXON: Well, it's also a — I think with them, too, I'd be a little more pragmatic. I think we'd say, "Look, this is the only way that we can have any leverage to keep the peace in the area." That's what they want. They should. Or, may — then, maybe, they'll vote against it, huh?

KISSINGER: Well —

NIXON: [laughs]

KISSINGER: — that's one of the problems with these people.

NIXON: [laughs] They don't want the peace, do they? They don't want it to keep; they just want it to fail. Is that — is that the thing?

KISSINGER: They, basically, want it to fail. That's my reluctant conclusion —

NIXON: Well —

KISSINGER: But think we can put it on a basis, to be honest —

NIXON: But, on the other hand, I think —

KISSINGER: — and not humanitarian, necessarily. We could say —

---

* "Kissinger Reports to Nixon on Talks," UPI, February 21, 1973.

NIXON: If you say "humanitarian," it'll look like reparations, and that sort of thing—

KISSINGER: No, I mean, what we could say is, "We have to find something to work with the North Vietnamese on to—"

NIXON: That's right.

KISSINGER: —[unclear]—

NIXON: Give 'em a stake in the peace. I'd just simply—that what we're looking—what we want to do is to give the Viet—Viet—the North Vietnamese and the South Vietnamese a stake in the peace.

KISSINGER: And we can't do that.

NIXON: We can't do that if we have no communication and no participation.

KISSINGER: Exactly.

NIXON: I think that's the thing.

David K. E. Bruce: Mr. Ambassador

February 21, 1973, 11:33 a.m.
Richard Nixon and Henry Kissinger
OVAL OFFICE

As Nixon and Kissinger continued their analysis of Kissinger's Asian tour, they addressed the crucial—and very exciting—prospect of filling newly created diplomatic posts in Beijing. Both hit on the same person for the preeminent position of emissary. David K. E. Bruce, Maryland-born, was a man of savoir faire and cunning intelligence. Starting after World War II, he served presidents of both parties and was sent as ambassador to France, West Germany, and Great Britain, in succession, with other posts in between, including a stint as assistant secretary of state. Bruce had so much irresistible charm that Nixon, who wholly distrusted the State Department, stubbornly refused to regard him as a department employee—or "career man."*

• • •

NIXON: Let me ask you one other thing about the China position. I like the two names you suggest, but here is something if you well realize, where we have Bruce—

KISSINGER: Yeah.

NIXON: I wonder if we couldn't offer it to Bruce.

KISSINGER: I'll have to check it with the Chinese whether they want someone quite that visible. But I—

NIXON: See my point?

KISSINGER: But our minds have really been working very similarly.

• • •

KISSINGER: Our minds have been working on exactly the same wavelength. I was thinking after I left China why not let in Bruce, and—

NIXON: Well, I think we do want to [unclear]. And maybe they may not like that.

---

* "Oral History Interview with David Bruce," March 1, 1972, Harry S. Truman Library website.

KISSINGER: And we could still have Holdridge —

NIXON: Holdridge — look, Holdridge [unclear] it will work, but Bruce has such class. And he would know, and he has such judgment. And it would be a hell of a bipartisan stroke.

KISSINGER: And, of course, they love old men.

NIXON: Well, listen. You understand another thing, it's a bipartisan stroke; he's a Democrat. You know? He's the only establishment Democrat I know that supported us. Do you know any other?

KISSINGER: No. And we could have the two others. If we had Bruce, [Al] Jenkins, and Holdridge we would have one powerhouse team.

NIXON: Yeah.

KISSINGER: I'd like Holdridge because I'd like to get rid of him. That's no reflection on him. He'd be good there but I need a somewhat more intellectual type here now.

NIXON: But you see, we want to keep it — Bruce will play our game; he'll keep it out of the State Department channels. Everybody of course would want to go. But we must not let this go to a career man. We must not.

KISSINGER: Mr. President, if you send a career man there, you might as well — you're better off not having it.

NIXON: But they won't understand the game.

• • •

NIXON: I think the program of working with the Chinese can have great possibilities.

KISSINGER: But that really has to be done by you and me.

NIXON: Alone!

KISSINGER: Alone.

NIXON: Alone. Alone.

KISSINGER: This is too dangerous.

NIXON: You know I was thinking that —

KISSINGER: But you know, it's amazing, I thought exactly the same thing about David Bruce as you did.

"He's on our side. No question about that."
February 23, 1973, 9:35 a.m.
Richard Nixon and John Ehrlichman
OVAL OFFICE

On February 22, Senator Howard Baker (R-TN) appeared at the White House for what he termed a "secret" meeting with the president. Baker was co-chair of the recently launched Senate Select Committee on Presidential Campaign Activities, better known as the Watergate Committee. A longtime friend of Nixon, he felt some obligation to hear him out in advance of the investigative work of the committee. Through Baker, Nixon tried unsuccessfully to arrange for the committee to interrogate Haldeman and Ehrlichman in private. He also did his best to leave the impression that former attorney general John

Mitchell was responsible for all of the illegal activities associated with Watergate. The following day, Nixon discussed Baker's visit and the developing situation with Ehrlichman. Since their strategy at that juncture was to pin the ultimate blame on Mitchell, their focus was on Richard Kleindienst, the attorney general. That discussion led to an assertion that a "cover-up is worse than whatever comes out," followed immediately by a survey of whom they could trust to keep their secrets.*

. . .

NIXON: Now on Kleindienst, I want to talk with you later perhaps. I might decide myself [unclear] at this meeting tomorrow. But—see what I mean? [unclear] Baker's line is about what you'd expect. His—I went through all the [unclear]. He says that he would like to have his contact be Kleindienst. That he and Ervin met with Kleindienst. Kleindienst has great stroke with Ervin [unclear]. I, of course, threw Dean at him [unclear] on that he didn't say anything against him. But he did say that he [unclear] then, of course, Wally Johnson and—the other point that he made is that—

EHRLICHMAN: Mm-hmm.

NIXON: —which leads me to believe—and I just want to be sure that I get Kleindienst on our line—our tug. And then let him be the settler. Now does that bother you or not?

EHRLICHMAN: Doesn't bother me if he'll do it. He—and here's the way to get him to do it, I think.

NIXON: It's going to be goddamn tough. Or don't you agree?

EHRLICHMAN: Kleindienst has a kind of a metaphysical attachment to John Mitchell.

NIXON: I don't want to scare him to death. I said, incidentally—I scared him. I put it very hard. I put it very hard. And I'll talk to you a little about this tomorrow because I put it very hard to Baker about Mitchell.

EHRLICHMAN: Good.

NIXON: Because Baker's, you know, hinting about the White House staff and all that. And I said, well, I checked them all over and I said unless somebody's lying, I said my main concern, however—he said, "What do you [unclear] someone of these seven or somebody that's around there at a lower level [unclear] guy who's not even going to get a pension [unclear] maybe I should talk to him." I said, "Yeah, you should have a private talk." So I've got to get Mitchell in by this coming Monday. Now, that may be, frankly, not quite true. I mean, you come down to it, as we know—the Magruder thing and the thing I'm concerned about the Magruder thing is that there's Bob [Haldeman].

EHRLICHMAN: Yeah.

NIXON: And that Magruder is just awfully close to Bob. And I don't think Magruder would say something. But he might.

EHRLICHMAN: If he did, he would implicate Mitchell. He would protect Bob, I suspect. I think that's the way now.

---

* John Dean, *The Nixon Defense: What He Knew and When He Knew It* (Viking, 2014).

NIXON: Now, all right—now, on the other one, no problem with you, as I see it. The other one, of course, is Colson.

EHRLICHMAN: Yeah.

NIXON: Now, the one that could do him in is Hunt.

EHRLICHMAN: Yep.

NIXON: And the likelihood of that, I think, is not so great.

EHRLICHMAN: And Magruder.

NIXON: And Magruder? How does—did Magruder work with Colson?

EHRLICHMAN: Magruder claims to Dean—and Magruder's playing a game—he's telling different people different things apparently and I've not talked to him. But the impression I have is that Magruder's peddling the line that Colson is the guy who put the unmitigated pressure on him.

NIXON: To change the bug.

EHRLICHMAN: To do this.

NIXON: To bug?

EHRLICHMAN: Yep.

NIXON: Well, you see, Colson denies that completely. Thank God.

EHRLICHMAN: I know it. I know it.

NIXON: I've asked both Bob and Colson.

EHRLICHMAN: Well—

NIXON: Well, I don't know. I can't, you see—one thing that we'll talk about tomorrow—I have really got to know whether or not, because—mainly because I've got to go—then I'll deny that I ever heard it.

EHRLICHMAN: Sure.

NIXON: I've got to know if Bob knew about it. I've got to know whether Colson knew about it.

EHRLICHMAN: Yep.

NIXON: If they both—if they did, then they're going to play our games—

EHRLICHMAN: That's right.

NIXON: —because this is how we're going to—that's where executive privilege comes in. Now executive privilege I got very—hardly anyplace on this idea [unclear]. Here's his plan which would be a very good one if we did do it. It's not bad. But he's on our side. No question about that. He has—he isn't going to go on the business of what the Democrats did to us, however, unless he says, "Now let's play it this way." He says what he'd like to do is go to it with the Watergate, which is—

EHRLICHMAN: Yep.

NIXON: And I said to him—and I gave him a good lecture about how the Hiss case was handled, a successful investigation [unclear]. We ruled out hearsay. We ruled out guilt by association and innuendo and so forth. I said you ought to really insist on that. I'm going to keep hitting that line all the time—

EHRLICHMAN: Good. That's good.

NIXON: He wanted me to make—issue a statement to the effect that we would cooperate with the committee. I said, "Well, I'm going to have a press conference one of these days," and I'll also say I've always stated that, I mean, I'm not going to put out any written statement to the effect. Somebody's going to ask me and I'll say that it's—Justice Department. Now, he then says, however, that the way he feels the way the thing will work bad, and I think he's correct in his strategy here, would be to call a lot of pipsqueak witnesses—little shitasses—over periods of weeks to build it up. And then build up the pressure to call—now you've got to call Colson—

EHRLICHMAN: Yeah.

NIXON: —you've got to call Haldeman—

EHRLICHMAN: Yeah.

NIXON: —you've got to call Ehrlichman and Chapin—whoever the hell. Sorry, they'll have Chapin anyway. He says that he believes—his strategy is this: he thinks they're—they should conduct their own private investigation now and then he's going to confront Ervin. "Look, there's seven guys over here"—the big fish. "What's all this shuffling about?" The question is whether or not it goes higher. And so let's—what he believes that they should try to call the big men right away. Prick the boil and then from then on everybody's going to be bored to death. Now that is good strategy provided you can call. I said, well, now we can't do this because of executive privilege. I said you can't deny this.

EHRLICHMAN: Yeah.

NIXON: He said, well, what he's talking about—he's—he has sounded Ervin and limits it to—total limitation as to the subjects and Ervin will rule out all other questions and so forth. He said this could have one hell of a dramatic impact. I said yeah and I said you're going to have these people dragged up. Now the real question, John, and you've got to address yourself to it and I think you're better to address yourself to it than either Bob or Colson. Who, really, are we afraid of to come out there on executive privilege? It's really Bob—Colson's another. I don't think you have a problem.

EHRLICHMAN: I don't have the problem.

NIXON: You didn't work with Hunt.

EHRLICHMAN: I don't have the problem.

NIXON: [unclear]

EHRLICHMAN: But—

NIXON: The point is that I don't want to get Bob or Colson, frankly, in the position of being up in the public domain and going for perjury.

EHRLICHMAN: Well—

NIXON: Of course, written interrogatories involve perjury, too.

EHRLICHMAN: All right, you've got three. You, really—well, including Stans you've got four big fish.

NIXON: Yeah. Oh, incidentally, that was Ervin's thing. Evidently he didn't say that he thought that—he said that he thought that Stans was the one that probably put them on it and I said, "That is utterly ridiculous" because I can tell that of all the people involved here Stans doesn't know a goddamn thing. He's outraged. He's meticulous and the rest. So you see people are getting to him about stuff.

EHRLICHMAN: Yeah, yeah.

NIXON: It's wrong. So I —

EHRLICHMAN: The money end of this is a troublesome end.

NIXON: Yeah.

EHRLICHMAN: Mitchell and Stans are involved in that.

NIXON: Yeah, Mitchell and Stans and Kalmbach.

EHRLICHMAN: And Kalmbach, right.

NIXON: Right.

EHRLICHMAN: Right.

NIXON: None of whom we can keep out of testifying.

EHRLICHMAN: And those chips are going to have to pretty much fall where they may, as I see it.

NIXON: What are they going to say?

EHRLICHMAN: Well —

NIXON: They raised the money?

EHRLICHMAN: There's a hell of a lot of money and it floated around and there weren't receipts and there was funny bookkeeping and there was a lot of hanky-panky and money went to Mexico and back and there were just a hell of a lot of odds and ends of stuff over there. Now, Stans says he's clean and I suspect he is. I think he can tell a damn good story.

NIXON: Knowing Stans, yes.

EHRLICHMAN: So Mitchell was going to end up being the fall guy in that.

NIXON: What'll Mitchell say?

EHRLICHMAN: I don't know what he'll say. I just don't know what he'll say. He's been puffing his pipe and looking at the ceiling and saying, "You guys got a problem" and — we're beginning to get to him a little bit. Dean's been hammering away on him to impress on him that he's got a problem here.

NIXON: Well, what does he — the money — I don't know what can he say except to say, "Well, I just frankly didn't keep as close enough control — "

EHRLICHMAN: Well, I think that's the best —

NIXON: " — over the disbursement of this money."

EHRLICHMAN: — that's his best defense.

NIXON: "I didn't control it."

EHRLICHMAN: That's his best defense.

NIXON: It's his only defense. And it may be correct.

EHRLICHMAN: "I was at the Justice Department" and so on and so forth. Well —

NIXON: It may be correct. And it may not be correct.

EHRLICHMAN: I doubt it. I doubt it.

NIXON: You think he knew?

EHRLICHMAN: I think he knew and I think LaRue was sort of his agent, and kept him posted, per —

NIXON: LaRue?

EHRLICHMAN: Oh, yeah. LaRue's in this thing up to his ass.

NIXON: Has he been called?

EHRLICHMAN: LaRue's a mysterious shadowy figure that hasn't been called and he —

NIXON: But he was into it?

EHRLICHMAN: Oh, yeah. Yeah. Now, Bob had what we call constructive knowledge.

NIXON: How could that be?

EHRLICHMAN: Through a fellow named Gordon Strachan.

NIXON: Yeah.

EHRLICHMAN: Gordon Strachan's job here was Bob's liaison with the campaign.

NIXON: Right.

EHRLICHMAN: Gordon Strachan kept the most meticulous attention to the details.

NIXON: Yeah.

EHRLICHMAN: But very little of it was actually imparted to Bob. What Strachan was, was a sort of a data bank so that if Bob needed to know something he'd pick up the phone and say, "Gordon, what about this or that?" And he knew.

NIXON: My point is — did Bob know that information was coming from tapped sources?

EHRLICHMAN: No, but I suspect Strachan did. And it was a situation where Bob —

NIXON: Strachan just mixes it.

EHRLICHMAN: Well, Strachan probably never comes into it — probably never does. Because Strachan's job was not to direct anybody to do anything. He was just to keep informed.

NIXON: Information changer.

EHRLICHMAN: Right.

NIXON: Okay.

EHRLICHMAN: Now, on Colson, you have two diametrically opposite stories.

NIXON: You have his —

EHRLICHMAN: You have his and you have Dean's conclusions born of a lot of odds and ends of circumstantial evidence that he's putting together. Dean tells me privately that he thinks that Colson was in fact in meetings and that Colson probably was the efficient cause of Magruder doing this tap work. Now that's John's — that's his conclusion based on circumstantial evidence.

NIXON: I don't believe it. I don't think Colson — I believe Colson's totally capable of it. But I would doubt if Colson would be that unintelligent, that's all.

EHRLICHMAN: I just — I —

NIXON: A lot of people would love it.

EHRLICHMAN: Well, let me tell you —

NIXON: But I don't —

EHRLICHMAN: — the Hunt trip to Dita Beard was a bonehead play.

NIXON: Oh, it was. Silliest thing I ever heard of.

EHRLICHMAN: And that was a Colson operation —

NIXON: I know.

EHRLICHMAN: — from beginning to end. So I have to assume that Hunt was kind of intrigued with —

NIXON: Well, maybe Colson was very possibly behind this whole thing —

EHRLICHMAN: I think he was. I think he was because Hunt's a cops-and-robber type. Now, I'm not going to tell you with any degree of assurance that Chuck's involved —

NIXON: I know.

EHRLICHMAN: — but what's important to know about this is that there are circumstances which —

NIXON: Yeah.

EHRLICHMAN: — diligent counsel could put together —

NIXON: Yeah. Yeah. Fine.

EHRLICHMAN: — in the same way as John did.

NIXON: Now, the point is then we come to the executive privilege thing —

EHRLICHMAN: Yeah.

NIXON: This is going to be the first thing that we've got to decide.

EHRLICHMAN: Right.

NIXON: And Kleindienst, what — I'm going to tell Kleindienst today about executive privilege, that he should — if he insists on written interrogatories, then he can negotiate —

EHRLICHMAN: Well —

NIXON: — from that. I think — or should they say, all right, go see what they'll work out with regard to a — limited questions, knowing in advance what they're going to be, period?

EHRLICHMAN: Here's —

NIXON: You understand, John, I'm for the written interrogatories.

EHRLICHMAN: Sure.

NIXON: And I'm for nothing. And I [unclear] written interrogatories, but if you go beyond that then if — we've got to realize that if the committee is eventually going to come down unanimous — or are you going to talk?

EHRLICHMAN: Yeah, yeah.

NIXON: — and I say no, I can't let them talk. We're then in a bind that is impossible.

EHRLICHMAN: I understand.

NIXON: I'm not —

EHRLICHMAN: I understand.

NIXON: — complaining about the heat. To the last, take the heat.

EHRLICHMAN: All right, here's another way. Ziegler's point is that — we were talking about this yesterday — that the damage that you take is as a result of somebody like me or Bob or somebody walking up the Capitol steps through the gauntlet of television cameras —

NIXON: Yeah.

EHRLICHMAN: — regardless of what's said inside.

NIXON: Right.

EHRLICHMAN: All right. Supposing you were to say to Ervin and Baker, "Look, you and your two counsel — "

NIXON: I told him that and he wouldn't buy it.

EHRLICHMAN: " — come on down here and talk to — "

NIXON: Uh —

EHRLICHMAN: " — anybody you want"?

NIXON: I went through that with them. I tried that on them. I said, "You can come down. You can examine — you and Ervin and so forth." Now it may be that I should put that then to — I should put that to them —

EHRLICHMAN: Yeah.

NIXON: — as our concession, that we'll — that we can — that he — the two counsel — he, Ervin, and the two counsel — and they can come down and have a deposition.

EHRLICHMAN: Kleindienst could carry this.

NIXON: Yeah.

EHRLICHMAN: He could say we're afraid of this becoming a circus.

NIXON: Yeah, yeah.

EHRLICHMAN: Oh, is there some way of protecting the — ?

NIXON: Now, the point is, though — did you realize that does not protect us — Colson? That's not going to protect him from — they can go right into Colson and get the same thing.

EHRLICHMAN: Colson will handle himself beautifully.

NIXON: Yeah.

EHRLICHMAN: He's righteously indignant. He's been on the Elizabeth Drew show.

NIXON: Yeah.

EHRLICHMAN: He's taken the *Today* show questions and he says, "Hell, I haven't anything to hide and I'm fine. I'm clean" and all the rest of it.

NIXON: Right, right, right. Except he'll perjure himself.

EHRLICHMAN: I don't know. I can't tell you that's perjury. All I can tell you —

NIXON: The only point about perjury is this — having proved it in the Hiss case — we had the son of a bitch in the first hearing. And I did not, with regard to —

EHRLICHMAN: Yeah.

NIXON: — the other side of it — whether it's against Mitchell or Colson, it's a hell of a hard rap to prove.

EHRLICHMAN: Oh, sure. And —

NIXON: Don't you agree? As a trial lawyer?

EHRLICHMAN: That's right. And this would be a circumstantial case.

NIXON: [unclear] and if I — I would need to prove perjury. I don't believe you can convict a person on circumstantial evidence on perjury. I don't believe it can be done.

EHRLICHMAN: Well —

NIXON: You can under the law.

EHRLICHMAN: Yeah.

NIXON: But with Hiss —

EHRLICHMAN: PR.

NIXON: You know how we did it? Oh, you mean PR-wise?

EHRLICHMAN: Well, that's what I say. It's very hard to do PR-wise.

NIXON: I guess. But I just, frankly, want to keep out —

EHRLICHMAN: You have — you had confrontation. You had one man. You had the dramatic —

NIXON: I'm not thinking — and also we got the typewriter.

EHRLICHMAN: Yeah. Sure.

NIXON: We proved it out there. That's hard evidence.

EHRLICHMAN: Yep.

NIXON: But the confrontation proved it in the public mind. And in this thing, the public mind, they're probably going to be convinced. They're going to believe the worst. They're going to believe the worst probably of me, about Bob, and maybe about Colson.

EHRLICHMAN: I —

NIXON: It's too bad.

EHRLICHMAN: I don't think so. I don't think so. Ron argues that you're convicted the minute you walk up the Capitol steps.

NIXON: I see.

EHRLICHMAN: And that just being dragged out of the White House — dragged across town — dragged up those steps —

NIXON: I would guess, of course — I didn't tell you, but — and as I — I don't mean that Baker won't carry the load for us — he said, "If you decide it we'll do it."

EHRLICHMAN: Is that so?

NIXON: You know, if you decide, he said.

EHRLICHMAN: Yeah.

NIXON: But he says, "This is what I want you to know — "

EHRLICHMAN: Let's take the other —

NIXON: [unclear]

EHRLICHMAN: Let's take the other case now. Let's suppose we said as a matter of long-standing policy back seven generations, the president's immediate staff does not testify, regardless of what the matter is.

NIXON: Right.

EHRLICHMAN: And so in effect we take the Fifth Amendment and we sit here and we just sit it out. Is that worse?

NIXON: Yeah, it's a cover-up. It's a cover-up. I think that's worse than what'll come out, in my opinion.

EHRLICHMAN: Well, I think so, too.

NIXON: I'm afraid, John, I've — I'd like to do that —

EHRLICHMAN: I think so, too.

NIXON: —from a personal standpoint. But believe me, I've been through this. The cover-up is worse than whatever comes out. It really is.

EHRLICHMAN: Uh—

NIXON: Unless somebody is going to go to jail. I'm not going to let anybody go to jail. That I promise you. That is the worst.

EHRLICHMAN: The—all right.

NIXON: Cover-up is worse, believe me, than all the walking up the Capitol steps. It's worse than walking up those Capitol steps.

EHRLICHMAN: Let's suppose Kleindienst negotiated quietly with Ervin to try and get depositions or informal interrogations, or whatever—

NIXON: Yeah.

EHRLICHMAN: —you want to call it here, and comes back and says, "I can't get them." Then it seems to me the strong position for you to take is totally openhanded. Let it all hang out. Let—you know, let the breath of freedom blow.

NIXON: Right. And everybody go up.

EHRLICHMAN: And everybody goes up and we saturate them.

NIXON: Right. Right at the outset.

EHRLICHMAN: Yeah.

NIXON: Well—that's the Baker intent?

EHRLICHMAN: Yeah.

NIXON: Well, let me say that I'll start with written interrogatories from the beginning. I mean—with Kleindienst. And then I'll tell him the backup position. But you can go to the business of their—of a—depositions by the two chairmen and so forth but not under television.

EHRLICHMAN: Now that would be the other possibility to go to the committee chambers not in a televised proceeding.

NIXON: But [unclear]. Well—no, if you go to the committee chambers you're still going to have the still pictures and television up there.

EHRLICHMAN: In and out, the sketches and all that. Yeah.

NIXON: Yeah.

EHRLICHMAN: Yeah.

NIXON: Well, I think the written interrogatories are a good thing. The written's the best. But I mean—I really think the compromise position, which is an honest and decent compromise is Ervin, the two senior men, plus the two counsel coming down.

EHRLICHMAN: Uh—

NIXON: Or we can say that the four could come down.

EHRLICHMAN: Well, or then you can leave it this way, that if you fellows really turn up something in the course of this and I'm confident you won't.

NIXON: We'll look again.

EHRLICHMAN: Then come on in and talk to me about it.

NIXON: Yeah, yeah, yeah, yeah.

EHRLICHMAN: And I'm not [unclear] —

NIXON: Okay. Now, what do I need to know about these with regard to how he feels about [unclear]? Obviously, it's — Baker, incidentally does — he wasn't there [unclear] smooth over this or that but Baker said it was a great mistake when Korologos called and it was. I didn't know that anybody had Korologos call him and suggest that [George] Webster [director of Attorneys for Nixon in 1972] be the counsel. You see, I mean — that's what blew that.

EHRLICHMAN: That's silly.

NIXON: Who did that? Who suggested that?

EHRLICHMAN: I don't know.

NIXON: You see, we were working on Timmons. Timmons isn't the most clever fellow at times. Harlow would not have made such a mistake. But Korologos telephoned him and he says he likes Tom and the rest. But when I had mentioned this idea of Webster's name, it may be that Bob in cases like this is a little bit too direct.

EHRLICHMAN: That's too bad.

NIXON: You know, that's —

EHRLICHMAN: We had better channels on Howard than that.

NIXON: Well, I thought so. But I want you to check that out.

EHRLICHMAN: I sure will.

NIXON: You better check that out.

EHRLICHMAN: I sure will.

NIXON: To rule out such a boo-boo. I think some of our relations with the Congress are complicated by the fact that we departmentalize everything. Bob will tell Higby to go tell to Timmons, and Timmons will say, "Korologos, get to see Webster."

EHRLICHMAN: Yeah, yeah. That's too bad.

NIXON: That blew that. That's what blew it.

EHRLICHMAN: Well, okay —

NIXON: He was nice about it, but I could see he was very bugged. He just thought it was stupid.

EHRLICHMAN: That — well, I do, too. Dean would be the ideal contact, but Dean —

NIXON: Suspect?

EHRLICHMAN: Well, he's really not.

NIXON: Who likes him? No, no, no. Not on this case. But how is he with Kleindienst?

EHRLICHMAN: Fine. Should be fine with Kleindienst.

NIXON: Right, good.

The loyalty of Kleindienst

February 23, 1973, 10:08 a.m.
Richard Nixon and Richard Kleindienst
OVAL OFFICE

Minutes after speaking with Ehrlichman about the importance of positioning Kleindienst *as a buttress against Senate investigators, Nixon spoke to him personally and very force-fully. Kleindienst, an Arizonan who had been educated at Harvard and its law school, was a staunch Republican, especially tough on crime. He joined the Nixon administration at its outset as deputy attorney general and then stepped up to the main post after Mitchell resigned in June 1972 to manage the president's reelection campaign. Kleindienst, how-ever, resented the way that interlopers from Nixon's inner circle at the White House made personnel decisions at Justice. He was never close to Nixon or that inner circle, and so it was that when Nixon approached him about using the implied power of executive privi-lege to hold the Senate Watergate Committee at bay, Kleindienst couldn't give the presi-dent the easy answer that he wanted. He would leave the administration within months, but even before Kleindienst made his plans known to the White House, Nixon helped him to make the decision to leave sooner rather than later.**

• • •

NIXON: Hello, Dick. How are you?

KLEINDIENST: How are you feeling?

NIXON: Good to see you.

KLEINDIENST: Nice seeing you.

NIXON: Fine, how are you?

KLEINDIENST: I feel fine. Mm-hmm. Well, if I may —

NIXON: Don't let Connally go. No, my only suggestion to be sure you're [unclear].

KLEINDIENST: It's a shame to have to have you do something —

NIXON: [unclear]

KLEINDIENST: I'm ashamed to have to have you comment on them.

NIXON: Let's see if I have to sign this appointment. I always — I have these things to sign. There you go. I had a talk with Connally yesterday morning. Personal thing out of the way. I want you to know there was [unclear]. He told me about his talks with you and was also talking about Diggs — or I don't know what other — but in terms of the law relationship we're to go that route. [unclear] three routes.

KLEINDIENST: Where's that?

NIXON: First, you should not go with Mitchell. You must not do that. I've told Kevin that. Second, you should not go with [George] Smathers because it's [unclear].

KLEINDIENST: [unclear]

NIXON: You'll make a lot of money with Smathers, but you'd have to deal with a lot of Jews and other people. Smathers is in with some bad people. Third, Connally's a decent man and I've had business with his firm. Since he'd make you one of the managers of the firm — it's a big firm — you'd have your voice in things. And since he would not be pushing you to get in business — you see, you wouldn't have to sell your soul. Very few get business. Well, you'd be tremendously valuable to him. You like Connally and he likes you. Now, he's the guy that's going to run that firm. You'd make a hell of a lot of money. You'd live in Washington, and if you want to go the law

---

* "Richard Kleindienst, Attorney General in Nixon Cabinet, Dies," *L.A. Times,* February 4, 2000.

way, that's infinitely better than New York firms. New York firms are selfish, horrible bastards. Texas would be selfish, too, but they're at least decent about it, and Connally would be good. Connally also is going to be in on a lot of good international stuff and you could have a lot of fun with that. You can join him around the world and so forth. You'd be a very good asset to him, which I told him, and you could add—and, you have something to bring to him that you can't bring to Mitchell, and you don't want to bring to Smathers. The other possibility you have in law is to go in for yourself. The difficulty with that is that, then everybody's going to be coming to you, frankly, for influence peddling. See, the Connally firm is big, established. They've got clients already and they wouldn't say, well, they came because of that—the main thing I found when I went into a firm in New York—they were very nice about it—but they did kind of—I felt an obligation to get out and try to hustle some business for them. And, of course, people did come to us, sometimes for the wrong reason. It was embarrassing. You should never be out feeling that you've got a rod in your back to get out and, you know, to hustle business. You'll do that. You'll do it anyway, but you must always be in a position, Dick, to be able to turn down something that doesn't smell good. There it is. How does it sound? Now, you just think about it.

KLEINDIENST: That's why I came out to see him. My goodness.

NIXON: Connally is so decent about it and [unclear].

KLEINDIENST: [unclear]

NIXON: Well, I had a good talk with him and I think it may have helped to start your [unclear] because he already compiled [unclear] ideal. Your age is right. See, you're under fifty. And you see, most senior partners—you'd have to be sixty or old—five or sixty-five. Most of them are senile. So you are at the right age. You might want to consider even—you might even go to Houston, at some point. You know, you might go to—it's a hell of a firm. It's one of the big firms.

KLEINDIENST: It's actually bigger than any firm in New York now. It's two hundred lawyers.

NIXON: Two hundred lawyers. Christ, it's bigger than Mitchell's. Mitchell's is one hundred thirty or forty, I think.

KLEINDIENST: [unclear] —

NIXON: But the bigness is not—

KLEINDIENST: —[unclear] of the law that dictates that I can't negotiate about something like that.

NIXON: Yeah.

KLEINDIENST: —while I'm in the department, I think.

NIXON: Right. You shouldn't.

KLEINDIENST: I'm not having any further conversations—

NIXON: Yeah.

KLEINDIENST: —about the job.

NIXON: Right.

KLEINDIENST: I think you and I—

NIXON: Right, right.

KLEINDIENST: —had a general attitude about—

NIXON: I think what you should do is to tell them you can't negotiate. You shouldn't—matter of fact, you should never get out that you're talking to them. But my own view is that if you were to—of course some other thing you could do would be to take over as the head of a corporation, but—

KLEINDIENST: I don't want to do that.

NIXON: Pain in the ass. My view is—

KLEINDIENST: [unclear]—

NIXON: —it would be better to have—you're a lawyer. You like to be—you like the law, and if I were you—if I were to advise you I'd sort of, gee, tell John about people now. I told John that if you were to go [unclear] here, which he, of course, appreciates. He's got to [unclear], too. But, he doesn't have to [unclear]. Now the other thing I wanted to get into, obviously, is Watergate, and—want to talk to you candidly about it. And this affects your plans. You were talking about staying on through July or August or something like that. I had thought—

KLEINDIENST: I'll stay on as long as you want.

NIXON: —as—I would like for you to stay—I'd like to ask you to stay and I want you to tell Connally this—through—until their reports. I never assumed that you should be here. I think it's another reason for that. From your own standpoint, if you could really come to think about it, I mean—because you know, I felt you should stay at least through the [congressional] session, but my view is that if you'd should stay through the year—if you leave earlier, you have a new attorney general in there who's got to go through all this. You've really got to be the guy who's in there leading the department. I think, also, either the department—you've got to say you have no plans to leave. You—at this point and you can say you want to stay through the year. And I think that's what you should do and I think—and I know this is—it is going to cost you half a year. You will lose a hundred thousand dollars. Let's face it. But if you would stay through the year, I would appreciate it.

KLEINDIENST: I want to stay there as long as you want me, Mr. President.

NIXON: Yeah. Now, understand, when I say through the year, I mean their damn report's supposed to come out in February. And I mean, you ought to be there so you can control it. And then I'd get out if I were you. Before we get into the election year, so as—another thing I told Connally, I mean—you should—this is just [unclear] I don't know what his political plans are. We're trying, of course, to have him not leave. [unclear]—

KLEINDIENST: He'll never tell you about politics even [unclear] switch.

NIXON: But, I said—you know, I—John, as far as your options are concerned, if you should decide to move on their side I said you couldn't have a better moment than [unclear]. Incidentally, there [unclear] delegate [unclear] and—which I—and I think you're—but I think you ought to stay here. I think, too, if you were to move out earlier, at this point—I didn't realize Watergate wouldn't be over, you know, in six months. But they're going to—Christ, they're going to take years to screw around with the goddamn thing and I think that—you had nothing to do with Watergate, as you know, not a goddamn thing. Mitchell did, and so consequently if you were to go to talk to [unclear].

KLEINDIENST: Another reason why I was thinking about it earlier—when I went up to Camp David, in my initial conversation with Haldeman and Ehrlichman, they both indicated to me that they knew that I was [unclear].

NIXON: Yeah.

KLEINDIENST: Yeah.

NIXON: Well, they were thinking at that time that that would be over—you see, at that time, that that would be over. But now it isn't. And if you'd stay through the year, a year's a good time anyway.

KLEINDIENST: I suppose the problem is kids in school.

NIXON: Oh, you're going to stay then?

KLEINDIENST: I am going to stay here.

NIXON: Great.

KLEINDIENST: [unclear]

NIXON: All right. Now let me come to the point.

KLEINDIENST: Well, Mr. President, I want to stay there. [unclear] as my wife.

NIXON: How's [Deputy Attorney General Joseph] Sneed doing, my old friend?

KLEINDIENST: He's doing all right. He's coming into an entirely different—you know.

NIXON: It's hard for him to learn. He's a fine man.

KLEINDIENST: Sure. He's a very fine man.

NIXON: Loyal—

KLEINDIENST: Sure. He's got—

NIXON: [unclear]

KLEINDIENST: He's a fine man. He's just got a little training course to go through, and he and I get along great.

NIXON: Finally, there's the other thing—is a type—this is very closely held because [unclear] deny any—Howard Baker dropped down. I had a reception for a couple of senators, congressmen, and so forth [unclear]. So Howard dropped down a little bit earlier and chatted with me. So, just—greatest confidence about this thing, because I naturally haven't talked to anybody about this thing. I wanted, frankly—I didn't want to know about any of our people. I didn't want to know about whether they're interested in Mitchell—the critical question—

KLEINDIENST: [unclear]

NIXON: Yeah. Now, I have through Dean—I've gotten the—I mean, what I think is—

KLEINDIENST: Through who?

NIXON: Dean.

KLEINDIENST: Dean.

NIXON: John Dean.

KLEINDIENST: Oh, John Dean.

NIXON: John Dean who's in charge of the hearings. He's got all the [unclear].

KLEINDIENST: Very bright young fellow.

NIXON: Yeah. You have confidence in him, now, don't you? What I would like on that, if you would — I would like for you to use him exclusively on Watergate. Now, I don't want you to talk to anybody else. I don't want you to talk to Ehrlichman. I don't want you to talk to Haldeman. I don't want you to talk to Colson, or anybody else — just Dean. Fair enough?

KLEINDIENST: Sure. That's what I would —

NIXON: Yeah.

KLEINDIENST: I'd do it anyway.

NIXON: Now, Howard came down for the purpose of telling me what are his plans for the hearings, briefly speaking. [unclear] what he's planning to do — what he's going to do is to — that to — try to make the hearings — make it appear the Republicans are cooperating. The hearings are honest and the administration's cooperating. So I assure you we're [unclear] small ones.

KLEINDIENST: That was the strategy we've had, I think.

NIXON: Huh?

KLEINDIENST: I think that's — what are the strategies —

NIXON: If — I said, provided this didn't become a circus [unclear]. But, secondly, I said his treatment — he would like, he said, to meet Ervin, and I said I strongly would like to use — to have you — they want to talk to you. And I said fine. He said Ervin likes you and that you have his confidence and that — and of course Baker — of course wants you. I said fine. I said, as far as I'm concerned, everything's through Kleindienst. I suggested that Dean could be available for things, too. He's concerned about that. He didn't say so, but I could sense it. So my view is —

KLEINDIENST: Howard shouldn't have ever talked to John Dean.

NIXON: Yeah, yeah. My feeling is that I want you to be the man. But in being the man I want you to be basically our man on it all the way — that you would naturally be.

KLEINDIENST: That's what I'm there for.

NIXON: I want to tell you, before I think of all — another thing is that we get into other tactics. Howard said, well, he felt that the — he sort of had the impression that Haldeman did [unclear] what happens with Stans. It's a bad trip. Stans — you know Maury. He is so straight-laced and all that sort of thing. Well, unsophisticated and naive — that if he ever helped such a caper he'd resign that day. He had no knowledge whatever of a [unclear]. And I know this is true. He's totally outraged about it now. Now, however, it is getting to the point whether that will come out. There was this — there were funds which were raised [unclear] raised a couple hundred thousand dollars cash. And that sort of thing and so forth, which were used by the security group for their earliest activities.

KLEINDIENST: Yeah.

NIXON: Therefore, Maury, as the finance chairman, is ostensibly responsible for that because he started it. Now that brings us, however, to the fellow that I really think the greatest possibility, and that's — is Mitchell. Now on Mitchell — Mitchell has laid the line, you know — anyway, something about — I forget. I've forgotten, so let me tell you what I understand. I remember in the Hiss case — perjury, the hardest rap to prove. We convicted Hiss [unclear] line through the confrontation of [unclear]. However, it took two years to convict him in the courts, and then we had go to [unclear] comprehend. Look — now, John, I don't know this, but I can't help but believe — assume that John must have known about these activities.

KLEINDIENST: I think he must have found out about them.

NIXON: Yeah. And he must have had someone other than —

KLEINDIENST: I think, if I recall —

NIXON: The point is that John has denied it categorically and so what I'm concerned about is the perjury.

KLEINDIENST: So am I.

NIXON: But, now, with that in mind, I told — and I've — and Baker loves Mitchell.

KLEINDIENST: So do I.

NIXON: I said to him — I said now Howard — nothing wrong with that — and I told Baker why. I said, now John, the way I put it to him, I did not let up on John. [unclear] I said John has a horrible domestic problem. I said Martha, you know, is very sick. And John wasn't paying any attention and these kids ran away with it. Now that's the line I've taken and that's the one I want you to take. John Mitchell is a pure, bright guy who would never have done such a thing. The kids ran away with it. And if John did lie, it was simply because he'd forgotten. Now whether that will wash or not I don't know, but if that's — that I just want you to know that I consider the Mitchell problem the main one. I don't want John — I don't think John will care if there's [unclear]. He'll sort of grin and say that's okay, and he'll survive. But I don't want John — I can't have John run the possibility of a charge of perjury. You know what I mean? Period.

KLEINDIENST: I couldn't have said it any better. That should get him out of it.

NIXON: Yeah.

KLEINDIENST: Because it's the same viewpoint —

NIXON: Yeah. All right. Now, to come to the White House staff, I think you should know about it. Dean is conducting an investigation. I figure — and Gray is conducting an investigation and so forth. And I think putting Gray's name up — one of the reasons I didn't was simply to say well, goddamn it, we had a hell of an investigation here. If you want to ask about Watergate, he can say with righteous indignation he conducted a hell of an investigation. The guys are guilty.

KLEINDIENST: That's the positive side of the coin.

NIXON: That's what he's doing. Now —

KLEINDIENST: And he'll do it quite good.

NIXON: Now the other thing is you come to White House staff. Ehrlichman didn't know a goddamn thing, that's for sure. He had — you know what I mean, he was working in other fields. However, that — see, Hunt worked with him on drugs, on the —

KLEINDIENST: The Pentagon Papers. I think that was with respect to [unclear].

NIXON: What?

KLEINDIENST: I said there could —

NIXON: [unclear] No question. He'll have to be called. Now, Colson is the other possibility — Colson's close friendship. See, they served in the Marine Corps together. With Hunt the fact that Colson has worked with Hunt on the ITT, which he did, would lead certainly to strong innuendo that Colson was in this. Colson totally denies it. He may be lying.

KLEINDIENST: He can take care of himself.

NIXON: Yeah. But I don't know. Now the other is Haldeman. The problem with Haldeman's case, frankly, is Magruder. Magruder did work for Haldeman. Magruder was over there. Magruder —

KLEINDIENST: Magruder's got the same problem Mitchell has to [unclear] —

NIXON: I got — don't you think — ?

KLEINDIENST: Huh?

NIXON: Yeah.

KLEINDIENST: I don't know.

NIXON: Well, I —

KLEINDIENST: It's possible that he and Mitchell both might have known.

NIXON: I think we — well, that's what people assume. Now with Magruder, you've got the problem that if you go to him, he's not a very strong personality. And Magruder, I don't know.

KLEINDIENST: I think he —

NIXON: Magruder will probably turn on Mitchell rather than Haldeman. That's my guess. He's Haldeman's man.

KLEINDIENST: I don't think he'll turn on anybody.

NIXON: You don't?

KLEINDIENST: No, I think he's got [unclear].

NIXON: [unclear], huh?

KLEINDIENST: I really do.

NIXON: Now we come down to this.

KLEINDIENST: [unclear] jeopardize, if he does.

NIXON: I don't know. I hope so. I mean — look, let's face it. You take a guy like Jeb and Chapin. All these guys — for Christ's sakes, I mean, you and I know that this is a very silly operation, and so forth and so on. See? But it's a campaign and that — and also you are aware of the fact that, you know the — that Hoover told Mitchell separately and me separately that the FBI bugged our plane in 1968 for the last three weeks.

KLEINDIENST: Oh, yeah, that.

NIXON: You were aware of that?

KLEINDIENST: Yes.

NIXON: It was a fact. You know what I mean? And that fellow [Deke DeLoach] who works for Coca-Cola—Pepsi-Cola—now sort of backs off a little. He says we [the FBI] only bugged the telephones.

KLEINDIENST: It's pretty bad, too. Wasn't it? [unclear] alone.

NIXON: Huh? See my point? But the FBI [unclear] bugging the candidates—distinguished from the goddamn committee. And the FBI and the government doing it. What the Christ do you think of that? Ervin said no they're certain [unclear]. He won't, of course. That's the reason that they fought not to have it extended to other campaigns. But now—let's come back—

KLEINDIENST: Well, Mr. President, let me comment on that right here. I don't know tact—

NIXON: I don't want to smear Johnson.

KLEINDIENST: I don't know tactically right now, in my own mind, whether [unclear] is to have that now. It might be the thing that'll save us.

NIXON: I don't want to hurt Johnson. I don't want to get into smearing a dead man.

KLEINDIENST: Well—

NIXON: And it looks like, you see, say they're [unclear] did that to me. And that's why we did it, because they bugged us. What do you—?

KLEINDIENST: No, I—and I've thought a great deal about this before I had [unclear]. It all depends on the course that this investigation takes. If it turns itself into a wild charge—

NIXON: Charge. Right.

KLEINDIENST: —then maybe you want to consider that. If Ervin could be made aware of this fact, it might be a restraining—it'd be—influence, you know, because if they could be made aware of the fact that [unclear]—

NIXON: Yeah.

KLEINDIENST: —campaign. You know?

NIXON: Yeah.

KLEINDIENST: Beginning of the next campaign.

NIXON: That's right.

KLEINDIENST: Then we're going to really turn it into something. You know, they might not want to do that because what Johnson did—what the FBI did—goes so far beyond this implication [unclear] the Watergate thing. They just don't compare. In fact, that really is what we—

NIXON: But we got—this didn't accomplish anything for us. Our [unclear]—

KLEINDIENST: The thing is that everything is so stupid. Ludicrous. Segretti, Watergate, and everything.

NIXON: What the Christ worked?

KLEINDIENST: Yeah.

NIXON: Theirs worked. Shit, they busted up the windows of the headquarters in Phoenix and burned the goddamn thing. They destroyed — did twenty-five thousand dollars' worth of property in San Francisco.

KLEINDIENST: Right.

NIXON: They ran a riot in Los Angeles right out of McGovern headquarters.

KLEINDIENST: Right.

NIXON: Now, when Ervin and [unclear] all come down and see you, the key point is executive privilege. Now here, I've got to ask you to take a very hard line. Now here's what I — here's Baker's point. Baker's point and Ervin's line — see, Ervin is hung up on executive privilege. He isn't hung up just for this. He wants to break it down totally. He wants Kissinger — everybody else, because he's wrong about this. He's wrong about this. You know, executive privilege can be broken down to its [unclear]. Now, so I — what his point is — what he's got a good one in one sense. His view is that after their — when they start the hear — [unclear]. Bring out all the big guys right away. Get it over with.

KLEINDIENST: [unclear]

NIXON: And let those assholes go on there and people will be tired. I think that's rather smart. In other words, rather than having them build up — drip, drip, drip, drip, drip. Call Haldeman, call Mitchell, call the rest — good strategy, don't you think? You talk about strategy. That's Hiss.

KLEINDIENST: Howard and I are good friends and I'll have no difficulty [unclear] with him.

NIXON: Now, but the strategy is his problem and yours. The second point, however, is that Ervin and he will want to talk to you about your cooperation. Now, one is FBI files. Now I — and I want you to tell Ervin this. That you examined the record of this and you found that the only other hearing that was really like this was the Hiss case. Just like this. That at that time, the then Congressman Nixon [unclear] in effect that Hiss was [unclear]. I had a couple friends hear that Truman categorically refused to allow the FBI to cooperate with the committee. They gave us absolutely not a goddamn thing. In fact, they thought that [unclear]. Okay.

KLEINDIENST: In 1948?

NIXON: Sure.

KLEINDIENST: Is that a fact?

NIXON: [unclear] because there they were trying to protect themselves politically. Just bugging — the point is the FBI did not cooperate with the committee. Now what Ervin or Baker are going to ask for this is — they're going to ask for the raw data to be given to him and the two counsel and so forth. You've got to determine that — my own view is that it probably goes too far. But, I don't know whether you give them FBI raw data and allow them to investigate.

KLEINDIENST: Well, here's what I had suggested. We had conversations about it, you know, with the strategy that we'd do. Number one, I could, not on the grounds of any executive privilege, but just policy, say I'm not going to turn over, you know, FBI files to anybody. It's our policy. We don't do that. But anyway, that, I think will prob-ably get to the bottom of it. But I think it might do more harm than good because of the political situation.

NIXON: So what would you do?

KLEINDIENST: My recommendation would be this: several people have been thinking about this with me and I think are inclined to agree that we will give them a sum-mary of the information of witnesses in the FBI files and we'll summarize.

NIXON: I wonder, Dick, on that. Let's — why don't you, so that I get into that sort of thing. Why don't you talk to — tell Dean to discuss this?

KLEINDIENST: I've discussed this with him and he agrees with me.

NIXON: [unclear] all right.

KLEINDIENST: Let me add a footnote on that —

NIXON: Yeah.

KLEINDIENST: — Mr. President. I would say to them, "Okay, we're not going to let you see these raw files, just to protect innocent people, et cetera. We'll summarize them for you." In the event the full committee feels that our summaries have been inaccurate we will devise a procedure that an officer of the FBI be present where the minority and majority counsel can come down and look at them, at action —

NIXON: Yeah.

KLEINDIENST: — investigative reports just to satisfy themselves that we were —

NIXON: Whatever you do, the more important point — the FBI files concern raw data and so forth — and because you well know, if you ever read an FBI file [unclear]. Now, the other point though is more firm. Now, the executive privilege — what I want to avoid, Dick, is not their testifying [unclear] but what I want to avoid is haul-ing the Haldemans and the Ehrlichmans, for example, up there, television lights and so forth and being grilled by a Senate committee — the president's two assistants. That I don't want. Now, how do you get around it? Baker's position is he and Ervin will develop a very narrow line of inquiry and limit it to that. That isn't the problem. It isn't the narrow line of inquiry. It isn't the questions — how they would answer. It's putting it on television — putting it on their circus, which is what they want. The damage is done by that. The damage is not done by what they say. I'm not concerned about what they will testify to, and I'm not concerned about the questions, and I'm not concerned about it being under oath. I am concerned about them being called up there, because then it'll mean they'll haul Kissinger up and say, "What now did the president really do when he decided to mine — bomb Hanoi." Now goddamn it, we're just not going to have that. That's my point. Now, the other angle, which I've already approached, would be to have written interrogatories. Written inter-rogatories they wouldn't buy. Now, there's a middle ground. That's what should be your starting position. [unclear] people. The other ground, which I think could be a very good compromise — satisfactory to me — would be that for anybody in an — to an executive privilege sign — that rather than appearing before the committee, that they will agree to — and then the senior member, Ervin on the Democratic side,

Baker on the Republican side, and the two counsel can interrogate them under oath, like a deposition and cover all questions, but that it be on that basis.

KLEINDIENST: In a nonpublic—

NIXON: A nonpublic forum.

KLEINDIENST: —executive—

NIXON: That's right.

KLEINDIENST: How about another—?

NIXON: And it would be down here.

KLEINDIENST: How about another fallback position? I think that would be a good proposal, but how about as a final fallback position in that you produce Haldeman and Ehrlichman in the Senate? It would be in an executive session—a closed session of the full committee.

NIXON: That's bullshit.

KLEINDIENST: It would, I think, produce the same results, and the same information.

NIXON: Except they haul them up there. You see, I suppose, going up to the Capitol and coming out, committee members coming out and saying, and so forth. Well, it's better. It's—

KLEINDIENST: It'd be better to take—it'd be better if we can get by them.

NIXON: Huh?

KLEINDIENST: If you could get by that.

NIXON: But, let me say, I think to start with written interrogatories, you know, in which they will—and then my view, Dick, very strongly, is that I think—is that the best thing to do is, from our standpoint, thinking of Kissinger in the future in particular, he's the one I'm really most concerned about here—the best thing, really, would be the business of the minority and the majority counsel. Now, what the hell? That really covers it. What the hell is the content involved—other members of the committee won't get to harangue them?

KLEINDIENST: Well, it also provides for them the basic information they're seeking.

NIXON: But they want information. Then the question is do they want information or publicity?

KLEINDIENST: Yeah.

NIXON: That's the point. If they want information, they'll take—they can do it.

KLEINDIENST: I think they want both of them.

NIXON: Yeah. Oh, sure.

KLEINDIENST: Well, you know Sam Ervin's got quite a posture—

NIXON: Yeah.

KLEINDIENST: —traditionally in the government as being very jealous.

NIXON: [unclear]

KLEINDIENST: Individual rights, you know?

NIXON: Oh, yes. Yeah.

KLEINDIENST: Actually, we couldn't get a better fellow. He's a very righteously—

NIXON: Yeah.

KLEINDIENST: — indignant man, but he's also a very good man.

NIXON: Yeah. Yeah.

KLEINDIENST: He's not a bad man.

NIXON: Yeah. We could say this, that we — the president said this has never been done, but I wanted you to point out that the Hiss case thing — the president went through this, and they refused, and I broke the goddamn case by — and doing it with my own investigators. The FBI did not cooperate. The Justice Department tried to drop the case and this and that — even, and I — and therefore I want cooperation. You could point this out. You can say this: that I've often talked to you about this in another vein. You could say, when planning the thing came up — you could say I had a talk about this [unclear] and when you say when we talked about the planning at that time and that's the president's view. We want to cooperate as best we can, but I do not want — I cannot break down executive privilege to that point. I'm not — let me make this — I'm not going to make this kind of a thing. I want you to be very hard-lined on that.

KLEINDIENST: Who can you think of now that has your recollection and knowledge of what happened in the Hiss case, so that I could talk to him, just so I don't have to trouble you about it? Who was involved in it with you?

NIXON: [unclear] All the committee members aren't —

KLEINDIENST: To the extent that it's convenient for you, I want you to think about that. Maybe you can think of some person who might still be alive.

NIXON: Well, [unclear] to say [unclear] but I hit Howard Baker on it. I said the reason — I said the Un-American Activities Committee was basically a cataclysmic failure — had a bad reputation except on that case, which I personally handled. And the reason that case even got grudging respect from those who were totally on Hiss's side was its conduct. And I went after this. I said I conducted it like a court. I said there was no hearsay. There was no innuendo. There was no guilt by association. And I said there was no hearsay present. But the point is I want you to hammer that hard to Ervin, the impression is this — there should be no hearsay except this damn judge has allowed hearsay and everything else down here in this other case. Hearsay, innuendo, et cetera, et cetera. Don't you think so?

KLEINDIENST: Yes, I do. We can't keep it profession [unclear]. Ninety days I spent around last year when I was in the hospital.

NIXON: Right.

KLEINDIENST: Those —

NIXON: Read the Six — read the first chapter of Six Crises. That tells the story of the Hiss case.

KLEINDIENST: Does it?

NIXON: Yeah. Do you have the book?

KLEINDIENST: Yes, sir, I do and I haven't read it for a long time, but —

NIXON: Read the first chapter of Six Crises. It tells the story of what we're trying to do. And that'll give you a good feeling. It doesn't say that the FBI — well, pretty well implied — that the FBI utterly refused. Hoover was on my side, but he utterly refused to get it. I'll tell you what I did do. I'm sure you know, Dick, that somewhere in the FBI there was a priest by the name of Father Cullen around then who knew one of the Catholic FBI agents and he really stuck up for the FBI, too. That's all [unclear] about it. Nothing else.

KLEINDIENST: Why do you think Hoover permitted himself to be used by Johnson in the '68 campaign?

NIXON: Deke DeLoach did it. He was ordered to.

KLEINDIENST: Hoover didn't know about it?

NIXON: [unclear]

KLEINDIENST: Somehow I thought he knew about it.

NIXON: Supposed to. No, he didn't know. Well, Deke DeLoach put it on — Johnson put it on the basis that they were invest — they were negotiating the Vietnam peace. The South Vietnamese ambassador [Bui Diem] was very adamant that the Dragon Lady [Anna Chennault] was very close to President Nixon or somebody, or Agnew or somebody, under the circumstances that he had to find what she was saying to them. You know he was a paranoid — he bugged everyone!

KLEINDIENST: I know.

NIXON: And Bobby Kennedy bugged him.

KLEINDIENST: I know.

NIXON: So what the hell? I think a little of this ought to get out, too. Let me — there is this one side note that I am supposed to tell you that I must get to right away. I want you to be sure when you go back to your office today, [convicted labor leader] Jimmy Hoffa announced he was going to run for the Detroit Local. I want you to call Hoffa's lawyer, or somebody to call his lawyer and tell him that if he does that that I will — that you're going to revoke his parole. And also I want you to make a public statement to that effect that I shouldn't [unclear]. I want it —

KLEINDIENST: Today, in talking about that, that John Connally was [unclear] —

NIXON: His parole is to be revoked. It was on the basis he did not engage in any activities and I'd like for you to get out a strong public statement.

KLEINDIENST: [unclear]

NIXON: Do you think — will you do that?

KLEINDIENST: Yeah. Just take him to the [unclear] to the attorney general without any reference to you.

NIXON: That's right.

KLEINDIENST: If he does it —

NIXON: That's right.

KLEINDIENST: — [unclear].

NIXON: You should let him know that he must revoke that and if not — then his parole will be revoked and he's going to go back to jail. Goddamn it! I'm not going to allow that.

KLEINDIENST: It would be a good line.

NIXON: If you would get that out today, I'd appreciate it. Call Ziegler and say [unclear] Ziegler gets this question.

KLEINDIENST: I think that—let me ask you this: suppose I talk to Hoffa's lawyer and tell him what I'm going to do and then he calls me back and says, "Okay, Hoffa isn't going to do it." I don't know whether I ought to make it public.

NIXON: Oh, no. You say, all right, he's to say that publicly or his lawyer has got to publicly get off of this.

KLEINDIENST: And if he does then Hoffa will publicly state that—

NIXON: Get off of this. Yeah, that's all. We're not going to revoke his parole if he doesn't move in it.

KLEINDIENST: Right, but—

NIXON: Hoffa must publicly get out of this damn thing.

KLEINDIENST: But suppose—

NIXON: [unclear]

KLEINDIENST: —Hoffa then says, "I'm not going to run." I don't think then it would help anything if we just say if he does, I'm going to put him back in jail.

NIXON: No, not at all. Not at all. But he must publicly say it or you make a public statement.

KLEINDIENST: Yeah.

NIXON: If he tells you that, then you make a statement to the effect that you have called the lawyer, and you have been assured that he is not going to run.

KLEINDIENST: Right.

NIXON: Then you go on to say that—of course, that would be a violation of parole. Period. But I want to take a very hard line on it. [unclear] with the politics in that union, and also that we are not going to get the impression around here that we're soft on Hoffa, because we're not. [unclear] son of a bitch [unclear].

KLEINDIENST: [unclear]

NIXON: Coming back to this thing—written interrogatories [unclear]. They're not going up there under any circumstances. I really think so. I really think the position should be one, they examine them and that—and then Ervin made a major breakthrough on this. We'll allow this communication in the future, that sort of thing. Under ground rules that are laid down. But we will not—but that I will not [unclear] in public hearings. Public hearings with all the—that sort of [unclear]. We will cooperate with the Congress, but under circumstances of there has to be [unclear]. Both sides, we state—in an intransigent position, we're going to have a constitutional scream-out. On the other hand, as far as the public hearings are concerned, that's something that can't go on. [unclear]

KLEINDIENST: I don't know. [unclear] possibly be in [unclear] got an awfully hardheaded line here.

NIXON: Don't go to the executive session—you know—at this point, under any circumstances. Don't even suggest that. The backup position is the, you know, the—

KLEINDIENST: No, I don't care anymore about that. I wouldn't want us to get that backup position. That would be the last bargaining position we have [unclear] final blow — face-saving, bargaining position [unclear] executive.

NIXON: But that is the final. I'm not going to allow any televised hearing. Do you agree with that?

KLEINDIENST: I think I do. Yeah, I do.

NIXON: That's my view on this. Go just so far and we'll fight the Congress on it. Go to hell with it. There are other — there are worse things than that. We say we've offered this. We've made statements and when we put that record out it's going to look a bit — then he's going to be looking awfully damn unreasonable, too.

KLEINDIENST: That's why —

NIXON: They never did that. You should point out that they didn't do that in the Hiss case.

KLEINDIENST: You know —

NIXON: You study the records in the Hiss case in the Department of Justice. Why don't you just give that a look? I think — and I know exactly what I'm talking about. I did. They didn't. They refused to let anybody come up.

KLEINDIENST: But you covered this. I don't recollect — of course, I read that book several years ago, at least sections of it. But you covered it pretty carefully in that book.

NIXON: [unclear]

KLEINDIENST: I think the public posture that we ought to have right now is we'll wait and see what happens. You know, (a) we have nothing to hide, (b) we're going to cooperate with them, and (c) let's get the damn thing done so that we can go back and do something else.

NIXON: That's right. That's right. That's right.

KLEINDIENST: Uh —

NIXON: Don't make this a political circus and harassment and partisan and the rest. But on the other hand, I want you to hit Baker a little harder on this. Say, "Now, Howard, don't be so damn timid with regard to what they have done. They've done a hell of a lot of things. If, for example, they expand this hearing into this crappy Segretti business — " [to unknown assistant] I'll let you know when I'm ready.

UNKNOWN: Fine, sir.

NIXON: If they have the Segretti business — all right, fine. Then we're going to do all their activities of that sort. I think that's got to be made very clear. I think this hearing should be, frankly, on Watergate. That's very much more — the rest is just shit. It's not — you know what I mean? But if they do go, Howard has got to open the other side up. Don't you agree?

KLEINDIENST: Yeah, I think also a final judgment has to be made soon with respect to this 1968 stuff by Johnson.

NIXON: Yeah.

KLEINDIENST: Knowing that Deke DeLoach was involved in it. He's working for PepsiCo. Don Kendall's a very —

NIXON: Yeah.

KLEINDIENST: — close friend —

NIXON: Yeah.

KLEINDIENST: — of yours and supporter, et cetera, et cetera, et cetera.

NIXON: Yeah.

KLEINDIENST: Because once we get into that, what you're really getting into is criminal conduct, you know? That could lend itself to a criminal prosecution.

NIXON: What — DeLoach? Yeah.

KLEINDIENST: Goddamn [unclear] have done that.

NIXON: That's why DeLoach has gone back on it.

KLEINDIENST: Yeah.

NIXON: I told Gray — I directed him — he was here. I said, "Now you're to call him immediately for a [unclear]. Give him a lie detector test on this." Not because of what I said. The *Star* had the story, see? The *Washington Star* and they went to Johnson and Johnson was — it was about two, three months ago. Just went up his wall and so forth and so on.

KLEINDIENST: The *Star* had this?

NIXON: And we killed it. A reporter at the *Star.* We killed the story from here.

KLEINDIENST: Is that right?

NIXON: Sure. I don't know how it leaked. Somebody got it. We didn't know about it then.

KLEINDIENST: [unclear]

NIXON: No, it had never been printed. Johnson was just beside himself about that. [unclear] let it out. [unclear] I called Haldeman.

KLEINDIENST: [unclear]

NIXON: Listen, more than meets the eye here. [unclear] Bobby and all the rest.

KLEINDIENST: But it's also, I think, a different situation now that Johnson is dead.

NIXON: Yeah.

KLEINDIENST: [unclear]

NIXON: Oh, Christ. You mean [unclear]?

KLEINDIENST: Yeah. Seems to me that we, in consideration of the office of the presidency —

NIXON: Yeah.

KLEINDIENST: — is a little bit different in terms of this —

NIXON: You mean, you should do more for these dead men? Maybe. Well, I'm a dead man. Okay.

KLEINDIENST: Now, as far as [unclear] —

NIXON: Yeah.

KLEINDIENST: — [unclear] and some of those people [unclear] there's a possibility they might not want to — so wrapped up in all of this.

NIXON: Yeah. Let me ask you to do — ask you then to be [unclear] you'll stay on as long as we want you to —

KLEINDIENST: Yes, sir.

NIXON: — here. Second, you'll do the Hoffa thing for us. Right away. Today. That call needs to be made as soon as you get back to the office.

KLEINDIENST: [unclear]

NIXON: Third, you'll talk to Baker as to [unclear] and he will talk to Dean. And I'll tell Dean that he's to talk to you. He's your contact. Nobody else. I don't want you to talk to anybody else over here but Dean. Nobody. Fourth, I think sometime you've got to talk to Mitchell.

KLEINDIENST: I've got to talk to Mitchell? You mean about the Watergate business?

NIXON: Well, either that or you talk to Baker, and Baker's got to talk to him, but —

KLEINDIENST: Yeah.

NIXON: — but —

KLEINDIENST: I don't think I'd want to talk to him.

NIXON: All right.

KLEINDIENST: [unclear]

NIXON: All right, fine. [unclear] —

KLEINDIENST: I don't want to be on the —

NIXON: — Baker. Goddamn it, remember your major problem is Baker and your other major problem is to protect — in my view, is to protect the — which is not, we're not going to protect any wrongdoing. Anybody wrong here and I'm going to kick their ass out of here. As far as the White House staff, I am not concerned, unless they're all double-faced liars, about any of them being involved. On the other hand, I am concerned about the circus. Three of the president's chief assistants up there like criminals. That's what I'm not going to allow and that's just, that's final. Okay?

KLEINDIENST: [unclear]

NIXON: Call — you will — I agree. Call my friend — call Ziegler. Give him some — you say something on this so that he's posted for the [unclear] thing. Fine.

KLEINDIENST: I'll call back over here.

NIXON: Yeah — their stuff. I mean just so that — he may not be asked about it, but you know there's a press conference in the afternoon. But I want you to be the guy —

KLEINDIENST: Do you believe Hoffa intends to make a statement like that?

NIXON: He's already made a statement.

KLEINDIENST: Oh, he has?

NIXON: Already has. He indicated — already issued a statement that he's going to — somebody has issued a statement on his behalf that he's going to run for the president of the Detroit Local. That is a violation of that parole. He should be called. We've heard about it and want to know what the score is. He's either going to have to give an assurance he's not going to run, which you then publicly will say or —

KLEINDIENST: He might want to be testing the constitutionality of that limitation in court.

NIXON: All right, fine. Fine.

KLEINDIENST: [unclear]

NIXON: All right, fine. Then we'll withdraw going into the thing. Fair enough?

KLEINDIENST: Yes, sir. Fine.

NIXON: Good, good. Well, you know one thing, Dick, we sure got our peacenik friends a little calmed down.

KLEINDIENST: Yeah.

NIXON: And haven't those POWs been great?

KLEINDIENST: Yes, they have.

NIXON: It's shaking the country.

KLEINDIENST: It's shaking the country.

NIXON: Yeah.

KLEINDIENST: It really is.

NIXON: People are proud again.

KLEINDIENST: Yeah.

NIXON: Yeah, they're proud. They're carrying their heads high.

KLEINDIENST: You just can't —

NIXON: Yeah.

KLEINDIENST: Know that people told me [unclear] when those fellows came back.

NIXON: Yeah. Good luck. Thank you.

KLEINDIENST: Thank you, sir.

NIXON: You're welcome. You're not a significant drawback [unclear].

KLEINDIENST: [laughs]

The latest closest advisor: John Dean

February 27, 1973, 3:55 p.m.
Richard Nixon and John Dean
OVAL OFFICE

After speaking with Kleindienst, Nixon grew adamant to control the uncontrollable: who was talking to whom in Washington and the halls of the White House. Speaking with a new level of urgency to White House counsel John Dean, Nixon tried to clamp down. He hadn't spoken with Dean in more than four months, even though he continually made reference to him in discussions of Watergate strategies. A native Ohioan, Dean was not an ideological conservative but an ambitious Washington-based lawyer who was named White House counsel in 1970, when he was thirty-one. Speaking with Dean in late February the next year, Nixon reiterated his argument in favor of utilizing executive privilege to protect his aides and especially his communications from investigators. He found Dean far more amenable than Kleindienst on that point. Nixon also discussed in depth the very real problems that he had with various members of the FBI, who he believed were the source of myriad leaks.

• • •

NIXON: Good afternoon, John. How are you?

DEAN: Pretty good.

NIXON: I — this cardinal's [Cardinal-Designate Luigi Raimondi, Vatican delegate to the

United States] not going to interrupt us but I might have [unclear] this afternoon. Did you get your talk with Kleindienst yet?

DEAN: I just had a good talk with him.

NIXON: Yeah, fine. Have you got him positioned properly — the — ?

DEAN: I think he is.

NIXON: [unclear] properly. Has he talked yet to Baker?

DEAN: No, he hasn't. He called Sam Ervin and offered to come visit with both he and Baker. And that was done last week.

NIXON: Mm-hmm.

DEAN: But he thought that timing would be bad to call Baker prior to the joint meeting. So he says, "After I have that joint meeting, I'll start working my relationship with Baker."

NIXON: Well, Baker left with me that he was going to set up a joint meeting. Well, anyway, to try to see what [unclear]. I see. So Kleindienst has talked to — he has talked to Ervin and Ervin said yes [unclear].

DEAN: Ervin has left it dangling and said, "I'll be back in touch with you." I think what disturbs me a little bit about Baker was his move to put his own man in as minority counsel so quickly, without any consultation as he had promised consultation. And I'm told this man [Fred Thompson] may be a disaster himself, the minority counsel.

NIXON: He is? What do you mean to — is he — ?

DEAN: Well he's a — well, I can't knock age. He's thirty years of age. He doesn't know a thing about Washington.

NIXON: Yeah.

DEAN: So, we'll have to —

NIXON: Baker says that he puts the blame on the White House. He says — whatchamacallits his name — Korologos called him and suggested somebody else. That was a great mistake, which I didn't know anything about, but apparently —

DEAN: Well, Baker apparently is quite open in his soliciting: "I want to counsel with you all, and I don't want to move until I've told you what I'm going to do," and then he did just the reverse. So it was curious. One, that he wanted a meeting with you. Secondly, that he suggested Kleindienst as a conduit —

NIXON: That's correct.

DEAN: — and there is hope, I think, that he may try to keep an eye on this thing and not let it get into a total circus up there.

NIXON: Who?

DEAN: Baker. Baker might.

NIXON: Well, that's what he indicated. He indicated, of course, with regard to his situation — his position, though, and with regard to Kleindienst's position, I shook Kleindienst up a bit and I need to know who really is the fellow who's going to get hurt most out of this [unclear] is Mitchell. I said others are going to get hurt, too. But Mitchell is — the real problem is whether or not Mitchell — will get him on perjury.

DEAN: Hmm.

NIXON: I said, now look, perjury's a very damn hard thing to prove too, fortunately. But, if you just keep from popping off. I said, well, I talked to him. I said, "Did you ever talk to Mitchell about this?" Never has.

DEAN: No.

NIXON: He says he has never talked to him. Did you go into the Mexican part of it with Kleindienst or did you get —

DEAN: Well, I —

NIXON: — into any substance at all?

DEAN: I've always braced Kleindienst in the past about, you know, the potential implications of what this whole investigation the bureau conducted — what the U.S. attorney's office was doing —

NIXON: That's right.

DEAN: — what the trial meant —

NIXON: That's right.

DEAN: I think this could come to haunt —

NIXON: That's right.

DEAN: If it gets out of hand, I don't want to get into a lot of specifics.

NIXON: Yeah.

DEAN: I — at this last meeting, I just sat with him and said, "Dick," I said, "I don't think I ought to brief you on everything I know. I don't think — "

NIXON: That's right.

DEAN: " — that's the way to proceed. But if I see you going down the wrong track, I'm going to have to tell you why."

NIXON: Mm-hmm. Good, good. What did he say?

DEAN: He said, "I agree. That's the way it should stand."

NIXON: On the executive privilege one, I worked with — talked to John Ehrlichman a little and decided that the last paragraph, which should be modified so that it covers what I might have to say if I were asked at a press conference, he'll indicate what it — but in a nutshell, rather than simply — flatly say that I think that what we should say is that members of the president's staff will not appear before a formal session of the commission — committee. However, under proper, appropriate circumstances that informal discussions or so forth can be conducted to obtain information and so forth and so on — "appropriate." I want — I'll tell you what we're up against. What here is — Kleindienst has indicated to me — I don't know whether he did to you — that he felt that the backup position here should be an executive session of the committee. And I said, "Well, that's a hell of a difficult thing for the men." I said, "I think that the position should be one of a — that our position should be one of a solution. That you can't get written interrogatories which is unlikely. Of the two committee — the ranking committee members and the counsel, questioning any member of the White House staff, you know, under proper — you know, restrictions — "

DEAN: Mm-hmm.

NIXON: — and so forth and so on. I put that to Baker as well, and Baker probably wants to get—for the same reason that Ervin does, because of the publicity and so forth—wants to haul down the White House staff and—

DEAN: Hmm.

NIXON: —put them in the glare of those lights.

DEAN: Sure.

NIXON: That we cannot have. That we cannot have. On the other hand, we cannot have a stonewall, so that it appears that we're not letting them. And so I think we've got to be in a position to—did you discuss this with Kleindienst, as to what the position would be on that point? That, I think, John, is the important thing that Kleindienst has got to stand goddamn firm on—

DEAN: I did. I talked to Dick about that. I said that, one, there's a statement forthcoming. I don't know the timing on it.

NIXON: Yeah.

DEAN: The president will issue it. I said that it's fortunate the context it's coming out in, because Clark Mollenhoff solicited the statement in a press inquiry that's coming out in unrelated context and not related to Watergate per se.

NIXON: Right, right.

DEAN: And so that'll be out soon and that will define what the outer perimeters are. It also gives—

NIXON: Have Kleindienst say that nobody from the White House staff will testify before a committee.

DEAN: That's right.

NIXON: Of course. That doesn't help much at all.

DEAN: Well, under normal circumstances, if they're—

NIXON: If they were normal.

DEAN: That's the—there's little slide in there. And then what in a practical matter I told them would probably happen would be much like the Flanigan situation where there's an exchange and the issues become very narrow as to the information that's sought.

NIXON: Well, you work with—have you talked to John Ehrlichman? You work at revising that last paragraph.

DEAN: We've done that.

NIXON: Oh, you've already worked with him on that?

DEAN: Mm-hmm.

NIXON: And, well, after I see this Cardinal Raimondi, take me about—I think five—we ought to get rid of him in about fifteen or twenty minutes. You mind bringing it down—you've got it written already?

DEAN: Yes, sir.

NIXON: Then let me take a look at it again.

DEAN: Mm-hmm.

NIXON: And we'll approve the statement. I don't want to put it out right now because I [unclear]. When I decide to do, I'll do it on the press thing.

DEAN: It'd probably be easier not to have those questions in your press conference per se.

NIXON: I would prefer — that's what I want to do — is to have this statement come after the press conference, to say — if they ask anything about it that "I've covered that in a statement that will be issued tomorrow on executive privilege." It's very complicated. So, that's what I had in mind. I'd rather not be questioned on the statement.

DEAN: Mollenhoff himself will debate you right there on the subject.

NIXON: Right. So I'll say I'm covering it.

DEAN: And I did talk to Mollenhoff yesterday, at Rogers's request.

NIXON: — [unclear] want to look in the case.

DEAN: Tell him I want to look in the case and I had an extended discussion with him on the executive privilege question. Of course, he differs somewhat from where we're coming out, but he agrees that certainly the president has the legal authority to do that and he agrees also that it's —

NIXON: Well, in his case, I mean what is he talking about?

DEAN: Well, he says, he thinks that all White House staff should be ready to run up to the Hill and testify and he asked —

NIXON: [unclear]

DEAN: — as to what they're doing and it's a rare exception when the president invokes the privilege. I said, "Clark, that's got to be the other way around. The staff can't operate if they're going to be queried on every bit of communication they had with the president."

NIXON: That's right.

DEAN: Mansfield, himself, Mr. President, has recognized that communications between you and your staff are protected. He said this in a policy statement before they issued this resolution up there on having confirmable individuals agree they'd testify before they are confirmed.

NIXON: Well —

DEAN: I'm —

NIXON: — as for confirmable individuals are concerned, they're all available for testimony though.

DEAN: That's right. It's no problem there.

NIXON: It's no problem there.

DEAN: There's not a giveaway by any means on that.

NIXON: They, of course, will — they — I guess we would not normally claim executive privilege for cabinet officers, would we?

DEAN: No, sir. Only if in, say, the rare instances where we have already, where they're going for information which should be protected. Investigative files, classified material, or say aid programs or something, when we did it in the last — IRS files. Those are the instances in which we've done it.

NIXON: Yeah.

DEAN: And they're quite traditional, and should be expected by the Congress when they go after information like that.

NIXON: I think — went over to Kleindienst, I said just to show you how the worm turns here — what we went through in the Hiss case. There we were, investigating, not espionage by a political — what one political organization against another, but a charge of espionage against the United States of America, which was a hell of a lot more serious. And in that case, the Department of Justice, the White House, the FBI totally stonewalled the committee. The FBI would not furnish any information and here the FBI, I understand, is going to furnish information to this committee.

DEAN: That's —

NIXON: That's according to Gray, right?

DEAN: Right.

NIXON: All right. The Department of Justice refused to give us any information at all and of course the White House used executive privilege and the press was all on their side. You see that was —

DEAN: That's right.

NIXON: — that was a — that's — shoot, whose ox is being gored? Now here you got so-called espionage involving a political organization and so now they want to —

DEAN: Well, you know I've been —

NIXON: — break it down.

DEAN: — in doing some checking —

NIXON: I told Dick this, I said it's just [unclear]. That's what our Democratic friends did when we were trying to get information.

DEAN: Lyndon Johnson was probably the greatest abuser of the FBI, I'm told by people, some of the old hands over there.

NIXON: He used it for everything.

DEAN: He used it as his personal —

NIXON: But didn't he use it against the press?

DEAN: He —

NIXON: That's —

DEAN: — used it against the press. He used it against his own party back in '64 when the Walter Jenkins thing [homosexuality scandal] broke. He had high officials of the FBI out trying to strong-arm a doctor to say that this man had a brain tumor — Walter Jenkins. He also then turned his — the FBI loose on the Goldwater [1964 presidential campaign] staff. This sort of thing is starting to seep —

NIXON: Who knows?

DEAN: — out now.

NIXON: Is it getting out?

DEAN: I'm [unclear].

NIXON: But you, of course, know the incident of his — the famous incident of the bugging of our plane —

DEAN: That's right.

NIXON: — which maybe — they really know is true. And you know, the instances that they talk about the — about our bugging — the FBI stuff, believe me, I know exactly what those were.

• • •

NIXON: And then, of course, the other things involved leaks out of the NSC, where we — they bugged Haig, Lake, or Halperin, I mean. But that was all.

DEAN: That's right.

NIXON: We were as limited as hell. I mean Hoover, good God! We could have used him for everything. He's — but Johnson had just apparently — just used them all the time for this sort of thing.

DEAN: That's what I'm learning. There's more and more of this —

NIXON: Who's — who from the FBI is trying to put out this stuff on us?

DEAN: God, I thought — I wish I knew, Mr. President.

NIXON: You don't believe it's a —

DEAN: I've heard there are several names that are bantered around. I tried, for example, to track the leak.

NIXON: You don't think it's Sullivan?

DEAN: No. I confronted Sullivan, as a matter of fact, right after this. I said, "Bill," I said — I called him into my office. I said, "I want to tell you what *Time* magazine said they have." His reaction was not that of a man who has leaked something.

NIXON: Yeah.

DEAN: And then he helped.

NIXON: [unclear]

DEAN: He told me — he said, "If this ever comes down to the very short strokes," he said, "as far as I'm concerned this was Hoover and Sullivan. No one else. And I'm ready to stand forward and take it at that." I said, "Well, I don't think it's ever going to be that because — "

NIXON: Well, what — why would it be Hoover and Sullivan? Did Hoover order him to do it?

DEAN: Hoover ordered him to do it.

NIXON: In order to —

DEAN: They did this so he could say, "I could cite examples chapter and verse of Hoover telling me to do things like this."

NIXON: Now Sullivan knows that their — it was terribly limited. It was limited.

DEAN: That's right.

• • •

NIXON: And that I must say, I think we did request, though — did we say find out the leaks, and so Hoover goes and bugs people?

DEAN: Well, I think —

NIXON: That's the way to do it.

DEAN: — the way it's postured now, we can stonewall it. Gray can go up there in his confirmation hearings and he's not going to have to bother with it because they'd accused him in the article of being — sitting on top of the bugs —

NIXON: Yeah.

DEAN: It was there once he came in, which is not factual.

NIXON: Well, there weren't any.

DEAN: There were none there when he came in.

NIXON: Well, three years ago that this happened —

DEAN: That's right.

NIXON: — and there hasn't been a goddamn thing since.

DEAN: That's correct.

NIXON: Right.

DEAN: That's correct.

NIXON: Another thing you can say, too, John, is the fact that all this had to do with the war —

DEAN: I know.

NIXON: — and now the war is over.

DEAN: Now —

NIXON: Now Johnson, on the other hand, went bugging his political opponents, and every son of a — everything you can imagine. We've been — that's the problem — we're getting a real bum rap, aren't we?

DEAN: We cert — we are getting a terrible rap —

NIXON: You stop to think of — we got rid of the army bugs. We got, you know, that whole army espionage business — intelligence business, we got. You remember that?

DEAN: That's right.

NIXON: We've limited the FBI things to national security bugs, to very, very certain few — probably too few.

DEAN: We're now [unclear].

NIXON: But somebody's going to get shot one day, and they'll wonder why we didn't bug them, huh?

DEAN: That's right. We are getting a bad rap.

NIXON: Well, for example —

DEAN: The fact is —

NIXON: — as you know, Hoover did bug Martin Luther King.

DEAN: That's right. I was aware of that also.

NIXON: Well, Christ yes. Hoover used to tell us about what his — what a morally depraved son of a bitch he was. And Johnson probably ordered him to do it. Now let's face it.

DEAN: Mm-hmm.

NIXON: So, I don't — well, you can't blame Hoover. I'm sure he didn't do it unless Johnson asked him to. But Johnson was that kind of a man. He used the FBI as his own private intelligence. But God, we've been as careful — I've talked to Hoover any number of times, but we've never ordered anything like that. But he'll come in with his little things.

• • •

DEAN: Johnson —

NIXON: Huh?

DEAN: Johnson used the FBI to cover the New Jersey convention before he dropped out officially. He had all the delegates —

NIXON: He did?

DEAN: That's right, which is kind of fantastic.

NIXON: Sullivan knows this?

DEAN: Mm-hmm. Sullivan is a wealth of knowledge and the more I — you know, sort of generally chat with him about these problems, the more it comes out he's the man that can also document —

NIXON: Why did Hoover have a fight with him? It's a hell of a mistake for Hoover to do that. Sullivan knows too much.

DEAN: That's right.

NIXON: Why didn't Sullivan squawk?

DEAN: I think Sullivan probably is loyal to the —

NIXON: Institution.

DEAN: — the institution and doesn't want —

NIXON: Somebody over there is not — can he help you find out who the hell is not? Isn't it a possibility — ?

DEAN: He advised —

NIXON: — the guy that — *Time* magazine's lawyer, you don't think it's him?

DEAN: He speculates, and the speculation is generally — it's either Sullivan himself, Mark Felt, who is —

NIXON: I know, the lawyer says that.

DEAN: That's right. And the other one is a fellow Tom Bishop who is now departed, who was in charge of their public information and where —

NIXON: Does he know about these things? Hoover didn't tell people like that about these things —

DEAN: No.

NIXON: — did he?

DEAN: For example, the '68 thing. I was trying to determine who might know about that.

NIXON: Yeah —

DEAN: Hoover, apparently —

NIXON: I guess.

DEAN: Hoover apparently told Pat Coyne — Patrick Coyne, who used to be on the NSC staff.

NIXON: I know. I believe — is he still living?

DEAN: I don't know the man.

NIXON: He told Pat Coyne?

DEAN: He told Pat Coyne. Coyne told Rockefeller. Rockefeller relayed this to Kissinger. This was one channel that might have it in a public domain. The other is when Sullivan took the records, or all the documents in connection with this, out of his office, and out of the bureau. He also instructed the Washington field office to destroy all their records, which they did. Hoover, incensed at this — that he couldn't recon-struct — that he didn't have the records and couldn't get them from Sullivan — tried to have the Washington field office reconstruct them, which they couldn't. As a re-sult of that movement and flailing around by Hoover, a lot of people in the agency were aware of what had happened and it was on the grapevine.

NIXON: Oh, that's when it happened then. When Sullivan left, he took the records with him —

DEAN: He took the records with him —

NIXON: And that's the only records there were?

DEAN: — and that's the only records there are.

NIXON: He did it out of — I mean, pissed off at Hoover.

DEAN: No, he was doing it to —

NIXON: Protect —

DEAN: — protect —

NIXON: — the bureau.

DEAN: No, he was doing it to protect the White House and the people over here.

NIXON: Oh, but for Christ's sakes. Hoover, you mean —

DEAN: Hoover never got his hands on the records is what happened. Sullivan had his pissing match with Hoover and then he took them with him at that time.

NIXON: I see.

DEAN: And then he turned them over to Mardian ultimately.

NIXON: I see.

DEAN: And —

NIXON: And so we got them.

DEAN: And then —

NIXON: Where's Sullivan now?

DEAN: Sullivan is back at Justice in the Drug Intelligence [unclear].

NIXON: We owe him something.

DEAN: We do. He wants to go back to the bureau and work on domestic —

NIXON: Why is it that Gray doesn't want him?

DEAN: I think Mark Felt has poisoned Gray on this issue and I think once Gray is —

NIXON: Well, who in the hell — somebody is doing Mark Felt in. You know what, do you believe the *Time* magazine lawyer? Is Felt up to — is he capable of this sort of thing?

DEAN: Well, let me tell you where I — where else I heard that from, was Sandy Smith. I had told — not the lawyer but somebody else told Felt was his source —

NIXON: Yeah.

DEAN: — and this came to Henry Petersen. Henry Petersen's an old hand over there, as you know. And, bless his soul, he's a valuable man to us.

NIXON: Yeah. What did he say?

DEAN: He said that he wouldn't put it past Felt, but the other thing I was talking to Kleindienst about this when I was over there, he said if Felt is the source —

NIXON: Yeah.

DEAN: — and if we get Felt way out of joint we are in serious trouble.

NIXON: Because he knows so much?

DEAN: He knows so much.

NIXON: What's he know?

DEAN: I don't know. I didn't ask for specifics with — he said — one thing he said he could knock —

NIXON: Does he know about the Sullivan stuff?

DEAN: Yes, he knows about that. I called Felt — asked him what he knew about it and he was, for example, very cool when I said, "There's a *Time* magazine story running, Mark, that in '68 — "

NIXON: Yeah.

DEAN: " — or '69 and '70 — "

NIXON: Yes.

DEAN: — and so on and so forth. He said, I — "true or false?" And he said, "True." I said, "How do you know that?" And I said, "I've never heard of that before." He said, "Well, if you talk to Bill Sullivan, he'll tell you all about it." And then he gave me sort of a general — painted a general picture about it. But just cool as a cucumber about it.

NIXON: And what does he say about *Time*? How — is he going to stand up for the denial?

DEAN: He says, "John," he said — I said, "Well, first of all, I don't believe this could happen." I was protecting us, as far as —

NIXON: Yeah.

DEAN: — doubting what he had said. He said, "Well, John, as far as I'm concerned, our phone call is totally off the record. We never had it." So that's a good one to watch, just right there.

NIXON: In other words, you can't blow the whistle on Felt, just like you can't blow the whistle on the son of a bitch out there, the yeoman [Charles Radford] — in the Jack Anderson [Moorer-Radford national security leaks] case, right?

DEAN: That's right, but there will become — there will come a day when Gray's comfortably in there, when other things come to pass, that —

NIXON: Like what?

DEAN: I think that Gray called at some point when, if this sort of thing continues, once he gets through his confirmation, I don't know why he couldn't himself say, "I'm going to take a lie detector test and I'm going to ask everybody in my immediate shop to take one and then we're going to go out and ask some of the other agents to take them."

NIXON: As to leakage.

DEAN: As to leakage, because this only hurts this whole institution.

NIXON: Where do you stand on the—with regard to the—how will we leave it with Kleindienst here? Is there—let me put it this way: you take the responsibility for Kleindienst. I'm going to keep Ehrlichman and Haldeman out of it—out of their—any relationship with Kleindienst. You should have it only. But you've got to watch him and brace him. And on the executive privilege thing, did you tell him what the line is?

DEAN: I have—

NIXON: And where he's to stand?

DEAN: I have told him and I've—I said, "It's going to be important."

NIXON: Didn't he raise the idea of their hurrying the executive session refusal?

DEAN: No, he did not.

NIXON: All right. Be sure he knows what the backup position is, which is two—right? As I understand it, if we would, under proper restrictions, allow two committee members to come down. Is that what you would do?

DEAN: I think we ought to draw the line at written interrogatories. I think the position should be that you are holding nothing back information-wise.

NIXON: That would be sworn.

DEAN: That's right. That would be sworn—you can't be in a position of protecting anybody around here.

NIXON: That's right.

DEAN: The information has to be available. But to go up there and make a circus out of the appearance of people—

NIXON: Right. Good. Well, let me say about Felt, it sounds as if he knows—it sounds as if maybe he's—

DEAN: Kind of watch it like a hawk, Mr. President—

NIXON: Yeah.

DEAN: —and I just got to watch him. He's too close to Pat Gray right now—

NIXON: Yeah.

DEAN: —for our interests.

NIXON: I know it is for mine.

• • •

NIXON: We've just been awful careful. Joe Kraft, of course, should have been bugged. I would think the son of a bitch is practically an agent to the Communists.

DEAN: Well, what you said about Bob and John, too—I think, as before the election, I tried to only bother them or consume any of their time when it was just absolutely essential.

NIXON: Right.

DEAN: And I think that's the way it's been.

[UNKNOWN aide enters.]

NIXON: That's right. That's right.

DEAN: He—

UNKNOWN: [unclear] is here.

NIXON: Fine, fine.

UNKNOWN: Did you buzz?

NIXON: I buzzed twice, that means — for them to come in.

HALDEMAN: Apparently the phones aren't working properly.

NIXON: Oh, fine, sure. Sure, have them come right in.

UNKNOWN: Fine.

DEAN: Well, sir, I'll get that statement on executive privilege.

[UNKNOWN aide leaves.]

NIXON: If you could do your best to — if you could keep me posted on [unclear] that way you need, but particularly with relation to Kleindienst. Okay?

"Put this thing in the funny pages of the history books."
February 28, 1973, 9:12 a.m.
Richard Nixon and John Dean
OVAL OFFICE

By the end of February, Nixon and Dean were speaking on a daily basis to adjust the White House response to the Watergate crisis. On the twenty-eighth, they were candid about the cover-up, naming specific participants, including E. Howard Hunt and, as the president, put it, "the financing transaction." That referred to the funds that Hunt used as hush money for the five men arrested at Democratic headquarters. Nixon, adopting a bunker mentality with Dean, distanced himself even from recent favorites such as Colson. Dean offered no argument with the president's meandering plots and contingencies, agreeing with everything his boss said. Apparently, though, he began to step back from the situation at some point during Nixon's lengthy analysis of the scandal. As Nixon wrapped up the conversation, Dean suggested that even though he was "a little fish," he might be targeted by the Senate committee. Nixon tried to reassure him that he was safe. He wasn't. At almost the same time on that very day, Pat Gray was telling Senator Sam Ervin at his confirmation hearing that Dean had given him an envelope of Watergate-related materials (which he said he later destroyed). He also said that Dean had made requests that amounted to orders for the FBI's investigative files on Watergate. The little fish became a very big name on the last day of February. *

• • •

DEAN: Good morning, sir.

NIXON: Oh, hi. Great. Oh, I wanted to speak with you about what kind of a line to test. Now, I want Kleindienst — this is not a question of trust. You have it clearly understood that you will call him and give him directions and that he will call you — and so forth and so on. I just don't want Dick to go —

DEAN: No. I think —

---

* David E. Rosenbaum, "Reluctant F.B.I. Gave Aide of Nixon Watergate Files," *New York Times,* March 1, 1973, p. 1.

NIXON: —go off, you see, for example, on executive privilege. I don't want him to go off and get the damn thing—get us—

DEAN: Make any deals on this thing—

NIXON: Well, to make a deal—that's the point.

DEAN: Yeah.

NIXON: That Baker, as I said, was [unclear] you know, this and that and the other thing. And you've got to be very firm with these guys or you may not end up with anything. Now, as I said, the only backup position I can possibly see is one of a—is Kleindienst wants to back already [unclear]—but suggested we ought to back them heavily—have them up there in executive session. Well, now you haul them up there in executive session and we still got the problem of a—well, like [unclear] in particular—I'm thinking of Henry [Kissinger] because it's building to him without any question—

DEAN: Sure.

NIXON: —at that point, and that's going to be far more significant. This crap bothers us at the moment, but that's far more significant. And they'll haul him up there and bullyrag him around the damn place and it'll raise holy hell within our—or his relations with Rogers and all the other people. [to unknown assistant] Yeah. Oh, I've sent some notes out—I guess there's a couple of yellow pages—something that I was—from that file on the teachers' thing that I'm not doing today.

UNKNOWN: Yes, sir.

NIXON: Get the yellow pages [unclear]. Might save money for the government.

UNKNOWN: All right, sir.

NIXON: Just send it back to me, please. [to Dean] So you see, I think you better have a good, hard face-to-face talk with him and say, "Look, we've thought this thing over," and you raise the point with him. See, it cannot be executive session because, you know, he's likely to float it out there and they'll grab him.

DEAN: That's right. And as I mentioned yesterday, he is meeting with Sam Ervin and Baker in this joint session and that probably is one of the first things that—

NIXON: Yeah.

DEAN: —that Ervin—

NIXON: The only thing they'll be there to discuss.

DEAN: It'll be—

NIXON: The main thing that will be discussed.

DEAN: That's right.

NIXON: Not only—you see my—the main thing Ervin's going to be, "Now what about executive privilege?" Now, he hasn't had that meeting set yet, though, has he?

DEAN: No, it's not. So there's ample time to have Dick go up—

NIXON: Well, you have a talk with him and say we talked about this and this is where we stand and this is where he is. Now your position—I mean, of course—I know our position is written interrogatories, which they will never—probably accept—but it may give us a position that would be reasonable in the public mind.

DEAN: Correct.

NIXON: If that's what you have in mind.

DEAN: Correct.

NIXON: Now, the other possibility is the one that Ehrlichman, I think, had suggested. You could have — agree that the ranking — the chairman and the ranking member could question under basically the same — under very restricted — a limited area is what we would provide.

DEAN: You mean, coming down here, say?

NIXON: Basically —

DEAN: That's a —

NIXON: — that is the thinking.

DEAN: I think that's a sort of — if we couldn't get written interrogatories. That's still a serious precedent to deal with, though, if they come down here and —

NIXON: Yeah.

DEAN: — start questioning people. I think the issues would have to be so narrowed for even that situation.

NIXON: Yeah.

DEAN: And that's what'll evolve with the —

NIXON: Right.

DEAN: — narrowing of the issues to where what information, say a, a Haldeman might have or an Ehrlichman might have —

NIXON: Yeah.

DEAN: — that the committee needs to be complete in its report or its investigation.

NIXON: Yeah. We will say that you will then — you will [unclear] to written interrogatories under oath — that answer questions.

DEAN: That's — publicly you're not withholding any information and you're not using the shield of the presidency.

NIXON: So, as I say, when you talk to Kleindienst — because I have raised this in previous things with him on the Hiss case — he got — he'd forgotten, and I said, "Well, go back and read the first chapter of *Six Crises*. Tells all about it." But I know very — as I said, I mean, that was espionage against the nation, not against the party. FBI, Hoover himself, who was a friend of mine —

DEAN: Mm-hmm.

NIXON: — even then, said, "I'm sorry. I have been ordered not to cooperate." And they didn't give us one goddamn thing. I conducted that investigation with two stupid little committee investigators. They weren't that stupid. They were tenacious. One had been fired by the FBI. He was a good, decent fellow, but he was a drunk.

DEAN: Mm-hmm.

NIXON: And we got it done. But we broke that thing —

DEAN: Against a wall —

NIXON: — without any help. The FBI then got the evidence which eventually — see, we got Piper [and Marbury, Alger Hiss's law firm], who — we got the Pumpkin Papers, for instance. We got all of that ourselves.

DEAN: Well, you know, I —

NIXON: The FBI did not cooperate. The Justice Department did not cooperate. The administration would not answer questions except, of course, for cabinet officers. I mean, like, [Covington and] Burling [law firm] came down and some of the others [unclear].

DEAN: Funny when the shoe is on the other foot how they look at things, isn't it?

NIXON: They did. Well, and as I said, the *New York Times,* the [*Washington*] *Post,* and all the rest said the administration has an absolute right. They didn't put it in terms of executive privilege. They were just against the investigation. So the real question there is that — now you could say that I, having been through that — we have talked it over and that I feel that I think that was — I have always felt very miffed about that — felt that was wrong. It was espionage against the nation. Now this is another matter. But I think that we ought to cooperate and I'm trying to find an area of cooperation. Here it is: written interrogatories. All right, you see, the Baker theory is that he wants to have a big slam-bang thing for a week and then he thinks interest in the whole thing'll fall off. And he's right about that. And he even — but his point of having the big slam-bang thing for a week is to bring all the big shots up right away. But the big shots you could bring up — you could bring up Stans. They've got to put him on, and they've got to put Mitchell on. But he'd like to get, of course, Haldeman, Ehrlichman, and Colson.

DEAN: I understand that Bob and you have talked about running Stans out as sort of a stalking horse on another post.

NIXON: Well, it's not my idea. It's — I guess [Richard] Moore or somebody mentioned it.

DEAN: I think it was my idea —

NIXON: Oh, you [unclear].

DEAN: — as a matter of fact, and I think it could defuse — could be one defusing factor in the hearings. Stans would like to get his side of the story out. He is not in any serious problem ultimately. It could be rough-and-tumble, but Maury is ready to take it, and it would be a mini-hearing, no doubt about it. But this further detracts from the other committee.

NIXON: It would be a mini-hearing, it's true. Except knowing the press — I'm trying to think out loud a minute — knowing that they, you know, they have — like they have taken — they sold several of these stories on Colson and Haldeman about four times.

DEAN: Oh, I know that.

NIXON: Now, that they can — I just wonder if that doesn't do that? I don't know. Take Stans. They'll get him up [unclear] — somebody's after him about Vesco. [unclear] As I read the — first read the story briefly in the *Post.* And I read, naturally, the first page and I turned to the *Times*— read it. The *Times* had in the second paragraph that the money had been returned.

DEAN: That is correct.

NIXON: The *Post* didn't have it until after you continued to the next section.

DEAN: That's right.

NIXON: The goddamnedest thing I ever saw.

DEAN: Typical.

NIXON: My guess is that as far as that transaction's concerned that it was after — that he got the money after [April] the tenth [1972, after a new, stricter campaign finance law went into effect], but I don't think they pointed out that [Vesco assistant Harry] Sears got it before.

DEAN: Well, it was con — well, for all purposes, the donor —

NIXON: Because I'm sure —

DEAN: Vesco —

NIXON: I'm sure that Stans would never do a thing like that.

DEAN: No —

NIXON: Never. Never. Never.

DEAN: I think we have a good strong case that the donor had relinquished control over the money, and constructive possession of the money was in the hands of the —

NIXON: Harry Sears.

DEAN: — finance committee, and Sears and the like. So that there is no —

NIXON: How did they get my brother in it? Eddie?

DEAN: I'll tell you. You talk of the — that was sheer sandbagging of your brother. Here is what they did. They called him down here in Washington.

NIXON: Who did?

DEAN: It's — let's see —

NIXON: Sears?

DEAN: It was Vesco. It was Vesco and Sears. And said that we want to talk to you about the nature of this transaction because we've had some earlier conversations with —

NIXON: Yeah.

DEAN: — Stans. He really wasn't privy to it —

NIXON: Yeah.

DEAN: — and didn't know much about it. Said, "Sure, I'll come up." And what the long and short of it was they were asking him to find out from Stans whether they wanted cash or check. Stans just responded to your brother and said, "I don't really care. Whatever they want to do," and that's what he relayed back and it's — he wasn't — he didn't even understand why he was there.

NIXON: Sure. [unclear]

DEAN: So — and he's clean as a whistle. There's just no —

NIXON: Oh, I know that. I know that.

DEAN: — just no problem at all.

NIXON: He doesn't know anything about the money side. So you'd sort of lean to having Stans go stalking out there.

DEAN: I think it'd have — I think it would take a lot of the teeth out of the — you know, the stardom of the people they'll try to build up to. If Stans has already gone through a hearing in another committee, obviously they'll use everything they have at that time and it won't be a hell of a lot. It confuses the public. The public is bored with this thing already.

NIXON: Yeah.

DEAN: One of the things I think we did succeed in before the election —

NIXON: Stans is very clean. What I mean is, let's face it on this thing — the way I analyze it, and I have stayed deliberately away from it, but I think I can sense what it is. The way I analyze the thing, Stans would have been horrified at any such thing. And what had happened was that he honestly is outraged. He thinks that what happened is that these pipsqueaks down the line took in some of his hard-earned cash and got into silly business with it.

DEAN: That's right. He —

NIXON: Isn't that what he really thinks?

DEAN: He does, and he is a victim of circumstances, of innuendo, of false charges. He has a darn good chance of winning that libel suit he's got against Larry O'Brien.

NIXON: Has he?

DEAN: He's — that's right.

NIXON: Good. That's why Larry filed a countersuit.

DEAN: That's right.

NIXON: I see Ziegler was disturbed at the news that they subpoenaed newsmen. Did it disturb you?

DEAN: It didn't disturb me at all. No, sir. I talked to Ron at some length about it the other night and I said —

NIXON: Yeah.

DEAN: " — Ron, if it — first of all you can be rest assured that the White House was not — "

NIXON: [unclear]

DEAN: " — involved in that decision." It's not a criminal case. No, it's a civil deposition.

NIXON: It doesn't involve prosecution.

DEAN: No, it's a civil deposition, and — it's not if we haven't reached the newsman's privilege issue yet, and that's way down the road, if for some reason they refuse to testify on some given evidence, what they're trying to establish is the fact that Edward Bennett Williams's law firm passed out an amended complaint that libeled Stans before it was into the court process, so it was not privileged. And the newsmen are the people who can answer that question. Also, they're trying to find out how Larry O'Brien and Edward Bennett Williams made statements to the effect that this lawsuit was not really to — the first lawsuit they had brought against the committee was not really to establish any invasion of privacy, but rather they were harassing the committee.

NIXON: They've made the [unclear]?

DEAN: They made this off the record to several newsmen and we know they did this—that this was a drummed-up lawsuit.

NIXON: So therefore that proves also malice, doesn't it?

DEAN: It makes the abuse of process case that we have against them on a countersuit. And the lawyers made a very conscious and good decision that to proceed with the suit they were going to have to have this information and it doesn't bother me that they subpoenaed nine or ten—

NIXON: Well, it wasn't a hell of a lot of people that are going to give one goddamn about this issue of suppression of the press and so forth. We know that we aren't trying to do it when they all squeal about it. It's amusing to me when they say, when somebody says, "I watched the networks and they weren't—and I thought they were restrained." What the Christ do they want them to do? To go through the '68 syndrome, when they were eight to one against us? They were only three to one this time on the—according to the average. You know, it's really, really, really sickening, you know, to see—

DEAN: Right.

NIXON: —these guys that always—they always figured, "Well, we have the press on our side." Then when we receive a modest amount of support—

DEAN: That's right.

NIXON: Colson, sure, making them move it around, saying [unclear] we don't like this or that, but it didn't affect them.

DEAN: Well, you know Colson's threat of a lawsuit that was printed in [Rowland] Evans and [Robert] Novak['s nationally syndicated column] had a very sobering effect on several of the national magazines. They are now checking before they print a lot of this Watergate junk they print, with the press office trying to get a confirmation, denial, comment, or calling the individual that's involved. And they have said as much as they are doing it because they are afraid someone is going to bring a libel suit on them. So it did have a sobering effect. It will keep them, maybe, honest if we can remind them that they can't print anything. I mean—

NIXON: Well, you of course know that I said at the time of the Hill's case [*Time, Inc. v. Hill*]. Well, it is goddamn near impossible for a public figure to win a libel—

DEAN: Yes, sir. It is.

NIXON: —case anymore.

DEAN: To establish, one, malice, or reckless disregard of—no, they're both very difficult.

NIXON: Yeah. Well, malice is impossible—virtually. This guy up there, "Who, me?" Reckless disregard you can, maybe.

DEAN: Tough. That's a bad decision, Mr. President. It really is. It was a bad decision.

NIXON: [unclear] What the hell happened? What's the name of that—I don't remember the case, but it was a horrible decision.

DEAN: *New York Times* versus Sullivan.

NIXON: And that Sullivan case.

DEAN: [unclear] and it came out of the South on a civil rights—

NIXON: Selma. It was talking about some guy that was—yeah, he was a police chief or something. Anyway, I remember reading it at the time when—that's when we were suing *Life*, you know, for the Hills. When *Life* was guilty as hell. Did they win it? Supreme Court—four to three. There were a couple of people who couldn't—no, five to four—five to three and a half. Basically, the—well, this goes back to executive privilege clearly understood. We must go forward on that. Just so you understand, I think you'd better go over and get in touch with Dick, and say, "You keep it at your level. Don't say the president told you to say so." Well, I guess it's going to be me in the end, but I'd say, "This is the position, Dick, that you need to take." Period. Let's let him get out there and take it. But I don't want them to think they can appeal to me. You can tell him that I took that position with Baker. Baker's a smooth, impressive—"Oh, the president didn't say this or that," he said. "We don't think he'll tell them this." Then he'd say, "All right, they have studied it. They have recommended it and the president has approved it." Right?

DEAN: Now how about—?

NIXON: Is that what you want to say?

DEAN: Yes, sir. I think that's absolutely on all fours. And how about our dealings with Baker? Under normal congressional relations, vis-à-vis Timmons and Baker, should we have Timmons making—dealing with one of the—?

NIXON: Well, he objected to—I mean, something—now that's a curious thing on that. It's hard to know whether this would be a very big gaffe by calling him, urging and trying to influence who would be on his staff. But Jesus Christ! I don't know why he did that if he did. But if he did, I don't know why Baker would resent it. But, nevertheless, he—I don't know how to deal with him, frankly, such as my decision—I gathered the impression that Baker didn't want to talk to anybody but Kleindienst.

DEAN: Okay, I think that's one we'll just have to monitor and that's one we'll have—

NIXON: Fine.

DEAN: —to know an awful lot about if something comes down the road.

NIXON: Well, let's just let Timmons tell Baker that if he wants to talk to—if he wants to get anybody at the White House that I don't want him to talk to Timmons. Of course, Timmons is a party of interest here, too. I don't want him to—

DEAN: That's right.

NIXON: —talk to Haldeman. I don't want him to talk to Ehrlichman—that you're the man and that you're available. But leave it that way, that you're available to talk to him about—for everything. But nobody else. How does that sound to you?

DEAN: I think that sounds good.

NIXON: You tell Timmons that he sees him privately and says that's it. We are not pressing him. We don't care—we're not—because Baker—the woods are full of weak men.

DEAN: I would suspect if we're going to get any insight into what that special committee is going to do, it's going to be through the Gurneys. I don't know about Weicker, where he's—

NIXON: Weicker's a—

DEAN: — going to fall out on this thing.

NIXON: Well, he'll be—

DEAN: Whatever's up—

NIXON: I think Weicker—the line to Weicker is Gray. Now, Gray has got to shape up here and handle himself well, too. Do you think he will?

DEAN: I do. I think Pat is—think Pat is tough. He goes up this morning, as you know. He is ready. He's very comfortable in all of the decisions he has made, and I think he'll be good.

NIXON: But he's close to Weicker. That's what I meant.

DEAN: Yeah, he is.

NIXON: And, so Gray—

DEAN: [unclear] as a [unclear], yes.

NIXON: One rather amusing thing about the Gray thing is that I—and I knew this would come—they constantly say that Gray is a political crony of—and a personal crony of the president's. Did you know that I have never seen him socially?

DEAN: Is that correct? No, I didn't.

NIXON: He's—I think he's been to a couple of White House events, but I have never seen Pat Gray socially.

DEAN: Well, the press has got him meeting you at a social function. And going on from there.

NIXON: When?

DEAN: Back in '47, I think, is something I have read.

NIXON: Maybe Radford had a party or something.

DEAN: Something like that.

NIXON: Something like that. But that's all. Well, that's—I don't know. Gray is somebody that I know only as a—he was Radford's assistant—used to attend NSC meetings.

DEAN: Mm-hmm.

NIXON: So I've met him. He's never been social. Edgar Hoover, on the other hand, I have seen socially at least a hundred times. He and I were very close friends.

DEAN: That's curious, the way the press just—

NIXON: But John—and that's the point. Hoover was my crony and friend. He was as close or closer to me than Johnson, actually, although Johnson used him more. But as for Pat Gray, Christ, I never saw him.

DEAN: While it might have been a lot of blue chips to the late director, I think we would have been a lot better off during this whole Watergate thing if he'd been alive, because he knew how to handle that bureau—

NIXON: Oh—

DEAN: Knew how to keep them in bounds—was a tough cookie.

NIXON: Well, if Hoover ever fought—he would have fought, that's the point. He'd have fired a few people, or he'd have scared them to death. He's got files on everybody, goddamn it.

DEAN: That's right! [laughs]

NIXON: But now, at the present time, the bureau is leaking like a sieve. And Baker and Gray denies it. Just says it's not coming from the bureau. Just who in the hell is it coming from? How in the hell could it be coming from anybody else? It isn't coming from Henry Petersen, is it?

DEAN: No. I just would not —

NIXON: It isn't coming from the depositions, is it?

DEAN: No. It's that, well, they're getting raw data. They're getting the raw, what they call 302 forms.

NIXON: Yeah.

DEAN: Those are the summaries of the interviews.

NIXON: Yeah. Yeah. Well, if you could do — handle it that way, I think that's the best thing to do. Do you ever wonder, really, if Colson, who's got the brass — the balls of a brass monkey, shouldn't bring a suit? Now then understand that I know that Colson — Colson's got a lot of vulnerabilities. You know, in terms of people that he knew, and so forth and so on. It's certainly an issue. But I mean on a narrow issue —

DEAN: Well, Chuck and I talked about this.

NIXON: He could win it.

DEAN: He could possibly win the suit but lose the war for this reason —

NIXON: [unclear]

DEAN: A counterdiscovery in a libel action has no bounds.

NIXON: I get it. Okay.

DEAN: The subject is wide open.

NIXON: [unclear]

DEAN: That's the problem there.

NIXON: That's the district code in the federal court?

DEAN: That's right. They could just come in and depose him on everything he's done at any point in time and that does it.

NIXON: Keep him out of it. Keep him out of it.

DEAN: Right.

NIXON: Why doesn't Stans be the suer? He is the suer, anyway.

DEAN: He's got a good one, and he may well prevail. Way — it may well be the device to force a settlement of all these other suits we've got out there. You know, we've got fourteen million dollars' worth of suits against us, and we've got seven or ten against them.

NIXON: Christ, they all ought to get together and drop them.

DEAN: That's what we're trying to get accomplished.

NIXON: Hell, yes.

DEAN: They're just costing — they're causing everybody problems, and —

NIXON: That's right. That's right. And they've got problems, and we've got them. Now you see this Vesco thing coming on burns my tail, because I raised hell with Haldeman on this and he didn't do anything about it. Well, I guess he couldn't. What in the name of God ever became of our investigation of their financial activities? Jesus Christ, they borrowed, they canceled debts, they borrowed money. What the hell is that?

DEAN: It's still going on, Mr. President. They're look—McGovern's stuff is in such bad shape. That's another unfortunate thing. The GAO comes in to audit us.

NIXON: Yeah.

DEAN: They find all the documents, so they are able to make—

NIXON: That might [unclear] GAO say that.

DEAN: They—well, they have now. But it, you know, gets about that much—

NIXON: Yeah.

DEAN: —coverage in the paper. They can't even figure out what McGovern's done, the books are in such a mess. But you haven't seen them say anything yet. And that's one of those things that, hopefully, we'll—

NIXON: Bring out in the hearings.

DEAN: —bring out as to what a mess this was, and—

NIXON: How are you going to bring it out? You can't bring it out in these hearings.

DEAN: Well, I think—

NIXON: Ervin'll rule it out.

DEAN: I think an independent sort of media type will bring it out. Chuck is going to be of aid when he is out there not connected with the White House.

NIXON: Yeah.

DEAN: Little bits of tidbits can be dropped to Chuck, because Chuck'll still have his channels to—

NIXON: Sure.

DEAN: —push things out.

NIXON: Sure.

DEAN: And also—

NIXON: That's what—in my view, I have use—of course it's hard for him to leave because he loves the action and the rest. But apart from the financial part of it, at his age, and so forth—which everybody has to think of—Colson can be more valuable out than in because, basically, in he just reached the point where he was too visible.

DEAN: He's a lightning rod.

NIXON: And outside, I mean, he can start this and that and tell them, "I'm a private citizen and I'm saying what I goddamn please." Right?

DEAN: That's right. That's absolutely right. I think Chuck can be of great aid in this thing, and I think he'll do it.

NIXON: Now, on the other thing, that is to recap: you will talk to Timmons about the Baker thing. Get that—get him tied down to the extent he can. I doubt if much could be done there. You must talk to Kleindienst, fast, so that Kleindienst knows that it's been decided, and that's it. And he'll say, "Well, they won't take it." [unclear]

That's all right. That's what it is, you know? Go on to the written interrogatory thing. We shall see. Your view would be not to give any further ground on that?

DEAN: I'd say hold — you know, you initially hold the line as far as you go — if it becomes apparent that it's necessary for informational purposes.

NIXON: When the main thing is not to —

DEAN: I mean, the president's not going to hide any information. He's —

NIXON: Huh?

DEAN: You're not going to hide any information.

NIXON: Yeah.

DEAN: Then this can be given in a sworn statement — through an interrogatory. Send your questions down. They'll be answered. We won't hide the information. We won't change the nature of the ability of the president to make decisions, to operate internally and the like —

NIXON: Yeah.

DEAN: — because you have a political circus going.

NIXON: Okay. I understand you — that Mollenhoff still thinks everybody should go up and testify.

DEAN: That's right.

NIXON: But at least you had a talk with him. I do want you to look into the case, though.

DEAN: Yes, sir. I am.

NIXON: If the guy's got a bad rap, his man — goddamn it, we'll get him out.

DEAN: I am doing that. I talked to Clark —

NIXON: Yeah.

DEAN: — yesterday. I talked to him last night again.

NIXON: Yeah. Okay.

DEAN: And I — he's on this as hot and heavy as can be and —

NIXON: Well, does he think he's got a bad rap?

DEAN: He does. He thinks he's got a bad rap. And I, you know —

NIXON: Maybe he has.

DEAN: It's very funny —

NIXON: I know Rule doesn't have a bad rap. That much — which by — when Rule — because when a bureaucrat takes it upon himself to go out and go way beyond the pale in terms of attacking an administration like he did, that can't be tolerated. That — he — you've got to —

DEAN: It's a different —

NIXON: Suppose a congressman or a senator or one of his administrative assistants went out and attacked one of his contributors. What the hell would he do? Fire him. That's right.

DEAN: Right.

NIXON: Now I noticed several of our congressmen and brave Republican senators called upon us to reinstate Rule. Congress is, of course, on its — it can — I guess they are so enormously frustrated that they're irrelevant. Isn't that the point? That's their problem.

DEAN: I think there's a lot of that.

NIXON: It's too bad we — can't take no comfort — we can take very little comfort from this. We have to work. But they become irrelevant because they're so damn irresponsible. Much as we would like that it would be otherwise. Pretty sad lot, isn't it?

DEAN: It is. Yes, sir. I spent some years on the Hill myself and one of the things I always noticed was the inability of the Congress to deal effectively with the Executive Branch because, one, they don't — they've never supplied themselves with adequate staffs, in other words, had adequate information available —

NIXON: Well, now they've got huge staffs, though, compared to what we had, you see.

DEAN: Well, they've got huge staffs — true, as opposed to what they had years ago.

NIXON: [unclear]

DEAN: But they are still —

NIXON: Inadequate.

DEAN: — inadequate to deal effectively —

NIXON: God, don't get into that. Please don't try [unclear].

DEAN: [laughs] No, no, I'm not suggesting it. I keep — I reserve my —

NIXON: Yeah.

DEAN: — my observations for myself. Well, I think this — these hearings are going to be hot, and I think they are going to be tough. I think they are going to be gory in some regards, but I'm also convinced that if everyone pulls their own oar in this thing, in all those we've got with various concerns, that we can make it through these, and minimal people will be hurt. And they may even paint themselves as being such partisans and off base, that they're really damaging the institutions of government themselves, and —

NIXON: I frankly would say that I perhaps rather that they be partisan — that they get to be partisan.

DEAN: I — we're going to hope they —

NIXON: I'd rather have that rather than for them to have the façade of fairness and all the rest, and then come out — because Ervin, in spite of all this business about his being a great constitutional lawyer — Christ, he's got Baker totally buffaloed on that. I mean, Ervin is as partisan as most of our southern gentlemen are. They are great politicians. They're just more clever than our minority. Just more clever.

DEAN: Well, I'm convinced it may be shown that he is merely a puppet for Kennedy in this whole thing.

NIXON: Kennedy?

DEAN: For Kennedy. The fine hand of the Kennedys is behind this whole hearing that's going on — or that is forthcoming. There is no doubt about it. When they considered the resolutions on the floor of the Senate I got the record out to read it. Who asked special permission to have their staff man on the floor? Kennedy —

NIXON: Right.

DEAN: —brings this man [James] Flug out on the floor when they're debating a resolution. He is the only one that did this. It's been Kennedy's push, quietly, his constant investigation, his committee using their subpoenas to get at Kalmbach and all these people —

NIXON: Mm-hmm.

DEAN: —that's kept the quiet and constant pressure on the thing. I think this fellow Sam Dash, who has been selected counsel, is a Kennedy choice. I think it's also something we'll be able to quietly and slowly document. People will print it in the press, and —

NIXON: Mm-hmm.

DEAN: —the partisan cast of this will become much more apparent.

NIXON: Yeah, I guess the Kennedy crowd is just laying in the bushes waiting to make their move. Boy, it's a shocking thing. You know, we talk about Johnson using the FBI. Did your friends tell you whether — what Bobby [Kennedy] did, or whether he knew what they [unclear]?

DEAN: I haven't heard but I wouldn't —

NIXON: Johnson believes that Bobby bugged him.

DEAN: [laughs] That wouldn't surprise me —

NIXON: Bobby was a ruthless little bastard. But the FBI does — they tell you that Sullivan told you that — the [use of the FBI during the 1964 Democratic National Convention in Atlantic City] New Jersey thing? We did use a bug up there just for intelligence work.

DEAN: Intelligence work — just had agents all over [unclear].

NIXON: Frankly, the doctors say that the poor old gent [Walter Jenkins] had a tumor.

DEAN: That's right.

NIXON: The FBI [unclear].

DEAN: Well, he used Abe Fortas and Deke DeLoach backed up by some other people in the bureau that were standing ready to go out and try to talk this doctor into examining Walter Jenkins to say the man had a brain tumor. He was very ill. That's why the erratic behavior. And this doctor wouldn't buy it.

NIXON: The doctor had never examined him before or anything.

DEAN: No.

NIXON: They were trying to set this up though.

DEAN: Oh, yeah. That would've —

NIXON: What other kind of activities?

DEAN: Well, I — you know, as I say, I haven't probed —

NIXON: Sullivan.

DEAN: — Sullivan to the depths on this because he's one I want to treat at arm's length, till we make sure —

NIXON: Right.

DEAN: —he is safe.

NIXON: That's right.

DEAN: But he has a world of information that may be available.

NIXON: But he says that what happened on the bugging thing is — who told what to whom again? The bugging thing?

DEAN: Oh. On the '68 thing, I was trying to track down the leaks.

NIXON: Yeah.

DEAN: He said that the only place he could figure it coming from would be one of a couple of sources he was aware of that had been somewhat discussed publicly. He said that Hoover had told Patrick Coyne about the fact that this was being done. Coyne had told Rockefeller.

NIXON: Yeah, [unclear].

DEAN: Now Rockefeller had told Kissinger. Now, I have never run it any step beyond what Mr. Sullivan said there. Now the other thing is that when the records were unavailable for Hoover — all this and the logs —

NIXON: Yeah.

DEAN: — Hoover tried to reconstruct them by going to the Washington field office and he made a pretty good stir about what he was doing when he was trying to get the record and reconstruct it. And he said that at that time we probably hit the grapevine in the bureau that this had occurred. But there is no evidence of it. The records show at the Department of Justice and the FBI that there's — no such surveillance was ever conducted.

NIXON: Shocking [unclear].

DEAN: Now, about White House staff and reporters and the like, and now the only — the other person that knows — is aware of it, is Mark Felt. And we've talked about Mark Felt, and I guess —

NIXON: What does it do to him, though? Let's face it. You know, suppose that Felt comes out and unwraps the whole thing. What does it do to him?

DEAN: He can't do it. It just —

NIXON: But my point is: who's going to hire him?

DEAN: That's right.

NIXON: Let's face it.

DEAN: He can't. He's —

NIXON: If he — the guy that does that can go out and — you mean he's a — of course, he couldn't do it unless he had a guarantee from somebody like *Time* magazine saying, "Look, we'll give you a job for life." Then what do they do? They put him in a job for life, and everybody would treat him like a pariah. He's in a very dangerous situation. These guys you know — the informers, look what it did to [Whittaker] Chambers. Chambers informed because he didn't give a goddamn.

DEAN: Right.

NIXON: But then one of the most brilliant writers according to Jim [unclear] we've ever seen in this country, and I am not referring to the Communist issue. This greatest single guy in the time of twenty-five or thirty years ago, probably the best writer in this century. They finished him.

DEAN: Mm-hmm. Well, I think I — there's no —

NIXON: Either way, the informer is not wanted in our society. Either way, that's the one thing people do sort of line up against. They —

DEAN: That's right.

NIXON: — they say, "Well, that son of a bitch informed. I don't want him around." We wouldn't want him around, would we?

DEAN: I don't —

NIXON: Hoover to Coyne to N.R. [Nelson Rockefeller] to K [Kissinger]. Right?

DEAN: Right.

NIXON: Good God. Why would Coyne tell Nelson Rockefeller? He was — I've known Coyne for years. I've — not well, but I — he was a great friend of one of my administrative — Bob King, who was a bureau man.

DEAN: Now this is Sullivan's story. I have no —

NIXON: Fine. That's all right.

DEAN: I don't know if it's true, but I don't have any reason to doubt that —

NIXON: Most of this is gospel. Hoover told me, so — and he also told Mitchell, personally, that this had happened. [unclear]

DEAN: Are you talking — I was talking about the '68 incident that just occurred. Not the —

NIXON: I'm talking about the '68 bugging of the plane.

DEAN: Yeah. Oh, I wasn't referring to that now. When this Coyne —

NIXON: Oh, okay.

DEAN: This was the fact that newsmen had been — I, excuse me — I thought he meant the reference to the fact that —

NIXON: Oh.

DEAN: — three years ago the White House had allegedly — the *Time* story.

NIXON: Oh, this is a — that's not the —

DEAN: No. On the '68 incident, all I've been able to find out is what you told me that Hoover had told you, what he'd —

NIXON: Yeah.

DEAN: — told Mitchell.

NIXON: Yeah.

DEAN: He —

NIXON: Mitchell corroborates that, doesn't he?

DEAN: That's right. Then —

NIXON: Sullivan doesn't remember that?

DEAN: [Republican strategist] Kevin Phillips called Pat Buchanan the other day with a tidbit that [former special assistant to Nixon's 1968 presidential campaign] Dick Whelan on —

NIXON: Yeah.

DEAN: — the NSC staff had seen a memorandum between the NSC and the FBI that the FBI had been instructed to put surveillance on Anna Chennault, the South Vietnamese embassy, and —

NIXON: That is a—

DEAN: —the Agnew plane.

NIXON: Agnew.

DEAN: Agnew plane.

NIXON: They put it on our—well, this isn't mine—maybe I'm wrong.

DEAN: Now, and it said—and this note also said that Deke DeLoach was the operative FBI officer on this.

NIXON: I think DeLoach's memory now is very, very hazy in that connection. He doesn't remember anything.

DEAN: Well, I talked to Mitchell about this and Mitchell says that he's talked to De-Loach. DeLoach has in his possession, and he has let Mitchell review them, some of the files on this.

NIXON: But not—

DEAN: But they don't go very far. They don't go very far. This is DeLoach protecting his own hide. The—

NIXON: They are never going to—it's just as well, to be candid with you. Just as well. But, so Hoover told Coyne, and who told Rockefeller—

DEAN: That this—

NIXON: —who told Kissinger that newsmen were being bugged—

DEAN: Yeah.

NIXON: —by us?

DEAN: That's right.

NIXON: Now why would Hoover do that?

DEAN: I don't have the foggiest. This was Sullivan's story as to where the leak might have come from about this current *Time* magazine story, which we are stonewalling totally—

NIXON: Oh, absolutely.

• • •

NIXON: Perfectly legal.

DEAN: Absolutely.

NIXON: [unclear]

DEAN: Well, all these—these are the national security leaks.

NIXON: Sure. And the—and Henry's staff—he insisted on Lake, you see, after working with McGov—for Muskie.

DEAN: Mm-hmm.

NIXON: Incidentally, didn't Muskie do anything bad on there? [unclear] Henry [un-clear]. At least I know—not because I know that—I know that he asked that it be done, and I assumed that it was. Lake and Halperin. They're both bad. But the taps were, too. They never helped us. Just gobs and gobs of material—gossip and bullshitting [unclear].

DEAN: Mm-hmm.

NIXON: The tapping was a very, very unproductive thing. I've always known that. At least—I've never—it's never been useful in any operation I've ever conducted. Well, it is your view that we should try to get out that '68 story then?

DEAN: Well, I think the threat—

NIXON: [unclear]

DEAN: —the threat of the '68 story, when Scott and the others were arguing that the committee up on the Hill broaden its mandate—

NIXON: Yeah.

DEAN: —to include other elections—

NIXON: Yeah.

DEAN: —they were hinting around that something occurred in '68 and '64 that should be looked at.

NIXON: Right. Goldwater thinks he was bugged.

DEAN: That's right. Now I think that threats—

NIXON: Did you think Gold—oh, you—didn't you say that Johnson did bug Goldwater's—?

DEAN: He didn't—well, I—we don't know. I don't know if he bugged him, but—

NIXON: He did intelligence work?

DEAN: —he did intelligence work up one side and down the other—

NIXON: From the FBI?

DEAN: —from the FBI. Just up one side and down the other on Goldwater.

NIXON: Mm-hmm.

DEAN: Now I have not had a chance to talk to the senator, and I've known the senator for twenty years. He is the first man in public life I ever met. Barry Jr. and I were roommates in school together, so I can talk to the man.

NIXON: Sure.

DEAN: I am really going to sit down with him one day and say—

NIXON: I think you should.

DEAN: —say, "What—?"

NIXON: Say, "What the hell do you—?"

DEAN: "—what do you—?"

NIXON: "—do you have any hard evidence?"

DEAN: That's right. Then we can go from there and—

NIXON: Right.

DEAN: —possibly reconstruct some things.

NIXON: Get some stuff written, and so forth. I do think you've got to remember that, as you sure do, this is mainly a public relations thing anyway. What is the situation, incidentally, with regard to the sentencing of our—of the people—the seven? When the hell is that going to occur?

DEAN: That's likely to occur, I would say—could occur as early as late this week. More likely sometime next week.

NIXON: Why has it been delayed so long?

DEAN: Well, they've been in the process of preparing the presentence report. The judge sends out probation officers to find out everybody who knew—

NIXON: Yeah.

DEAN: —these people, and then he'll—

NIXON: He's trying to work on them to break them, is he?

DEAN: Well, there's some of that. They are using the probation officer for more than a normal probation report. They are trying to—

NIXON: Yeah.

DEAN: —do a mini-investigation by the judge himself, which is his only investigative tool here, so they—that they are virtually completed now. They—the U.S. attorney, who handles the assistant U.S. attorney.

NIXON: You know when they talk, though, about a thirty-five-year sentence—now here's something that does not involve—there were no weapons, right? There were no injuries, right? There was no succe—well, success maybe—I don't know. The point is the—that sort of thing is just ridiculous. One of these blacks, you know, goes in here and holds up a store with a goddamn gun and they give him two years and then probation after—

DEAN: And they—

NIXON: —six months.

DEAN: —and they let him out on bond during the time that he is considering his case. These fellows cannot get out—

NIXON: Are they out? Have they been in jail?

DEAN: They're in—well, all but one. Hunt made the bond. Everybody else is in jail. They've got a hundred-thousand-dollar surety bond which means they have to put up actual collateral, but—and none of these people have a hundred thousand dollars. The court of appeals has been sitting for two weeks or better now on a review of the bond issue. They're not even letting these people out to prepare their case for appeal.

• • •

NIXON: You still think Sullivan is basically reliable?

DEAN: I have nothing to judge—

NIXON: No.

DEAN: —that on other—I watched him for a number of years. I watched him when he was working with Tom Huston on domestic intelligence, and his—in his desire to do the right thing. I tried to, you know, stay in touch with Bill and find out what his moods are. Bill was forced on the outside for a long time. He didn't become bitter. He sat back and waited until he could come back in. He didn't try to force or black-mail his way around with knowledge he had. So, I have no signs of anything but a reliable man who thinks a great deal of this administration and of you.

NIXON: You understand the problem we have here is that Gray is going to insist, I am sure, come down hard for Felt as the second man. And that would worry the hell out of me if Felt—I think at the present time it doesn't.

DEAN: It worries me, frankly.

NIXON: But for the future isn't it a problem?

DEAN: I think it is for the future, because only — things can only get more complex over there as we move along. There is no doubt about it.

NIXON: Well, as he gets closer to the next election [unclear]. I don't know Felt, never met him. What's he look like?

DEAN: Well, they call him the white mouse — or the white rat over there. And he's — he has kind of a mouse-looking face with white hair.

• • •

DEAN: Well, I've got to say one thing. There has never been a leak out of my office. There never will —

NIXON: Yeah.

DEAN: — be a leak out of my office.

NIXON: No.

DEAN: I wouldn't begin to know how to leak even. I don't want to learn how you leak.

NIXON: Well, it was a shocking thing. I was reading a book last night on — quite a fascinating little book, not well written, by Malcolm Smith Jr. on Kennedy's thirteen mistakes [unclear] foreign policy practices. They are great mistakes, and one of them had to do with the Bay of Pigs thing. And what had happened there was [former undersecretary of state] Chester Bowles had learned about it, and he deliberately leaked it. Deliberately, because he wanted the operation to fail.

DEAN: Mm-hmm.

NIXON: And admitted it later.

DEAN: Interesting.

NIXON: Admitted it.

DEAN: Interesting.

NIXON: This happens all the time. Well, you can follow these characters to the — to their Gethsemane. I feel for those poor guys in jail. I mean, I don't know — particularly for Hunt. Hunt, with his wife dead. It's a tough thing.

DEAN: Well —

NIXON: We have to do [unclear].

DEAN: — every indication —

NIXON: You will have to do —

DEAN: — that they're hanging in tough right now.

NIXON: What the hell do they expect, though? Do they expect to get clemency within a reasonable time?

DEAN: I think they do. [unclear]

NIXON: What would you say? What would you advise on that?

DEAN: I think it's one of those things we'll have to watch very closely. For example —

NIXON: You couldn't do it, say, in six months?

DEAN: No.

NIXON: No.

DEAN: No. You couldn't. This thing may become so political as a result of these —

NIXON: Yeah.

DEAN: —hearings that it is more—

NIXON: A vendetta?

DEAN: Yeah, it's a vendetta. This judge may go off the deep end in sentencing and make it so absurd that it's clearly an injustice—

NIXON: Yeah.

DEAN: —that they have been heavily—

NIXON: Are they going to appeal—is there any—are any appeals left?

DEAN: Right. Liddy—Liddy and McCord, who sat through the trial, will both be on appeal—

NIXON: Mm-hmm.

DEAN: And there is no telling how long that will last. I think this is one of these things we'll just have to watch.

NIXON: My view is say nothing about the event on the ground that the matter is still in the courts and on appeal.

DEAN: That's right.

NIXON: That's my position. Second, my view is to say nothing about the hearings at this point except that "I trust that they will be conducted in the proper way," and, "I will not comment on the hearings while they are in process." Yeah. And then I—of course if they break through—if they get [unclear]—but you see, it's best not to elevate—and I get Ziegler to do the same—it's best not to elevate that thing here to the White House. Because I don't want the White House gabbing around about the goddamn thing. Now there, of course, you'd say, "But you leave it all to them." [unclear] policy. But the president should not be commenting on this case. Do you agree to that?

DEAN: I agree totally, sir. Absolutely. Now, that doesn't mean that quietly we're not going to be working around the [unclear].

NIXON: All over the city!

DEAN: But, you can rest assured that we're not going to be sitting quietly.

NIXON: I don't know what we can do. The people that are most disturbed about this [unclear] are now the goddamn Republicans. A lot of these congressmen, financial contributors, and so forth are highly moral. The Democrats are just sort of saying, "Oh, Christ, fun and games. Fun and games."

DEAN: Well, hopefully we can—

NIXON: Take that Segretti thing. Ha! Jesus Christ. He was sort of a clownish figure. I don't see how our boys [laughs] could have gone for him. But nevertheless, they did. It was really, shall we say juvenile, the way that was handled. But nevertheless, what the hell did he do? What in the name of God did he do? Shouldn't we get—be trying to get intelligence? Weren't they trying to get intelligence from us?

DEAN: Absolutely.

NIXON: Don't we try to get schedules? Don't you try to disrupt their meetings? Didn't they try to disrupt ours? Christ, they threw rocks, ran demonstrations, and shouted, cut the public address system, they had to tear-gas them in Miami. What the hell was that all about?

DEAN: Well—

NIXON: Did we do that?

DEAN: McGovern had Dick Tuck on his payroll, and Dick Tuck was down in Texas when you went down to the Connally ranch, set up to do a prank down there.

NIXON: That's right.

DEAN: But it never came off—

NIXON: What did Segretti do that came off? Much? I mean—

DEAN: He did some humorous things. He—

NIXON: Yeah.

DEAN: For example, there'd be a fundraising dinner, and he had hired Wayne the Wizard to fly in from the Virgin Islands to perform a magic show, and of course, he hadn't been hired. He sent—

NIXON: Yeah.

DEAN: —he sent invitations to all these black diplomats and—

NIXON: Yeah.

DEAN: —and sent limousines out to have them picked up, and they all showed up and they hadn't been invited. He had four hundred pizzas sent to another—

NIXON: Yeah, sure. Sure.

DEAN: I mean this is—

NIXON: Well, what the hell?

DEAN: —pranks.

NIXON: Tuck do all this sort of thing?

DEAN: And so—

NIXON: They did it to me in '62—in 1960, and the rest. They want to say, "Well, now, that's terrible. Now isn't that terrible?" What the hell?

DEAN: I think we can keep this—the Segretti stuff in perspective because it's not that bad. Chapin's involvement is not that deep. He was a catalyst, and that's about the extent of it.

NIXON: Sure. He knew him and recommended him.

DEAN: That's right.

NIXON: But he didn't run him. He was too busy with us.

DEAN: The one I think they're going to go after with a vengeance, and who I plan to spend a great deal of time with next week, a couple of days as a matter of fact, getting this all in order, is Herb Kalmbach.

NIXON: Yes.

DEAN: Herb has got—they've subpoenaed his records, and he's got records that run all over hell's acre on things for the last few years. You know Herb has been a man who's been moving things around for Maury and keeping things in—

NIXON: Right.

DEAN: —in tow and taking care of little polling inferences.

NIXON: What'll he do about those records? Is he going to give them all to them?

DEAN: Well, he's—they brought his—they've gotten to the banks that had them, and I think what we'll do is we'll—there'll be a logical, natural explanation for every single transaction.

NIXON: Right.

DEAN: It's just a lot of minutiae we've got to go through but we—he's coming in next week and we—I told him we'd sit down and he is preparing everything, getting all of it available, and we're going to sit down with his—with [Kalmbach law partner] Frank DeMarco—and see if we can't get this whole thing—

NIXON: Now, his records—that is, with regards to the campaign. They can't get his records with regard to his private transactions?

DEAN: No, none of the private transactions. Absolutely. That is privileged material.

NIXON: That's right.

DEAN: Anything to do with San Clemente and the like. That is just so far out of bounds that—

NIXON: Yeah. Did they ask for that?

DEAN: No, no, no. No indication of that.

NIXON: Good. Oh, well, even if it is, I mean—

DEAN: Well, it's just none—that's really none of their business.

NIXON: They can't get it. Kalmbach is a decent fellow. He'll make a good witness.

DEAN: I think he will. He's been—

NIXON: He's smart.

DEAN: —he's been tough thus far. He hasn't—you know, he has been taking it. His skin is thick now. Sure it bothered him, and all this press he was getting. The *L.A. Times* has been running stories on him all the time and—

NIXON: Yeah.

DEAN: —and the like. Local stations have been making him more of a personality, and his partners have been nipping at him but Herb's tough now. He is ready and he's going to go through and he's going to—he is hunkered down and he's ready to handle it. So I'm not worried—

NIXON: Yeah.

DEAN: —about Herb at all.

NIXON: Oh, well, it'll be hard for him, because it'll get out about Hunt. It—I suppose the big thing is the financing transaction they'll go after. How did the money get to the Bank of Mexico and so forth and so on.

DEAN: All that stuff. And then—

NIXON: What'll he say?

DEAN: It can all be explained.

NIXON: It can?

DEAN: Yes, indeed. Yes, sir. They're going to be disappointed with a lot of the answers they get—

NIXON: Yeah.

DEAN: — when they actually get the facts, because the *Times* and the *Post* had such fun with innuendo. When they get the facts, they're going to be disappointed.

NIXON: The one point that you ought to — you better get to Baker — I tried to get it through his thick skull. I guess it's — his skull is not thick — but tell Kleindienst — Kleindienst, in talking to Baker and Ervin should emphasize that the way to have a successful hearing and a fair one is to run it like a court. No hearsay. No innuendo. Now you know goddamn well they aren't going to —

DEAN: But that's a hell of a good point.

NIXON: — but don't — no hearsay. Tell them that's the way Nixon ran the Hiss case. Now, as a matter of fact some innuendo came out but there was goddamn little hearsay. We really — we just got them on the facts and just tore them to pieces.

DEAN: Yeah.

NIXON: Say, "No hearsay, no innuendo." And that he — Ervin should sit like a court there. Say, "Now that's hearsay and I don't like it." And tell him that the — and let's have the counsel for our people — he gets up there and says, "I object to that, Mr. Chairman, on the basis that it is hearsay."

DEAN: That's an excellent idea, Mr. President, for somebody to write an article because as this thing gets steamed up, "Will Sam Ervin, constitutional man, be a judge? Will he admit hearsay?" We can probably get some think pieces out to get a little pressure on him to perform that way, or to make it look very partisan when he doesn't, you know? He lets all this in —

NIXON: I'd like to get some articles out that — no hearsay, no innuendo. There'll be no hearsay, no innuendo. This is going to be, shall we say, a model of a congressional hearing. A model. Now that'll disappoint the goddamn press. There's no hearsay, no innuendo, no leaks.

DEAN: Well, there are a lot of precedents. I've been involved in two congressional investigations. One was the [Representative] Adam Clayton Powell [D-NY] investigation [into his legal affairs] when I was working over there as the minority counsel of the House Judiciary. We didn't take hearsay. We made a — we stuck to the facts on that.

NIXON: Mm-hmm.

DEAN: We did an investigation of the Oklahoma judges [Alfred Murrah, Stephen Chandler, and Luther Bohanon]. Again, same sort of thing. We went into executive session when necessary to. I bet — we look around, we'll find respectable investigations that have been conducted up there that could be held up, and some of this should be coming forth to set the —

NIXON: Yeah.

DEAN: — the —

NIXON: Yeah.

DEAN: — stage for these hearings. Well, I'm planning a number of brain sessions to — with some of these media people to —

NIXON: I know. Well, it's very important, and it seems like a terrible waste of your time. [unclear] It's important in the sense that it's — all this business is a battle and they're going to wage the battle. And a lot of this is their enormous frustration about losing the elections, the state of their party, and so forth. And their party has its problems. We think we've got problems. Look at some of theirs. [Democratic National Committee chairman Robert] Strauss is there to pull them all together. He's not doing all that well, you know.

DEAN: Well, I was — you know, we've gone a long road on this thing now. I had thought it was an impossible task to hold together until after the election until things just —

NIXON: Yeah.

DEAN: — started squirting out, but we've made it this far, and I'm convinced we're going to make it the whole road and put this thing in the funny pages of the history books rather than anything serious. We've got to. It's got to be that way.

NIXON: Would it — it'll be somewhat serious, but the main thing, of course, is also the, the isolation of the president from this.

DEAN: Absolutely.

NIXON: Because it's — because that, fortunately, is totally true.

DEAN: I know that, sir.

NIXON: Good God almighty! I mean, of course I'm not dumb, and I will never forget when I heard about this goddamn thing, of course, from Bob. Jesus Christ, what in the hell is this? What's the matter with these people? Are they crazy? I thought they were nuts. You know? That it was a prank. But it wasn't. It was really something. I think that our Democratic friends know that's true, too. They know what the hell —

DEAN: I think they do too.

NIXON: — this was. I mean they know that we then wouldn't be involved in such — they'd think others were capable of it, however. I think — and they are correct. They think Colson would do anything. [laughs] Well, anyway, have a little fun.

DEAN: All right.

NIXON: And now, I will not talk to you again until you have something to report to me.

DEAN: All right, sir.

NIXON: But I think it's very important that you have these talks with our good friend Kleindienst.

DEAN: That'll be done.

NIXON: Give him that [unclear]. We have to work together on this thing. He's the man. I'd build him up, that he's the man who can make the difference. Also point out to him that the fish they're really after — tell him, look, for Christ's sakes, Colson's got brass balls and so forth, but —

DEAN: All right.

NIXON: — I'd really, really be [unclear] here is — let's forget this. Remember, this was not done by the White House. This was done by the Committee to Re-elect, and Mitchell was the chairman, correct?

DEAN: That's correct. And that means that —

NIXON: So, and Mitchell — and Kleindienst owes Mitchell everything. Mitchell wanted him for attorney general, he wanted him for deputy, and here he is. And goddamn it,

Baker's got to realize this, and that if he allows this thing to get out he's going to potentially ruin John Mitchell. He won't. I mean Mitchell won't allow himself to be ruined. He's too clever. He'll put on his big stone face act, but — I hope to Christ he does. The point is that, as you well know, that's the fish they're after.

DEAN: That's right.

NIXON: But the committee is after somebody in the White House. They'd like to get Haldeman or Colson — Ehrlichman. They've got —

DEAN: Or possibly Dean. You know, who — you know, who's — anybody they can. I'm a small fish, but —

NIXON: Anybody at the White House they would. But in your case I think they realize you are the lawyer and they know you didn't have a goddamn thing to do with the campaign.

DEAN: That's right.

NIXON: That's what I think. Well, we'll see.

DEAN: All right, sir.

NIXON: Good luck.

DEAN: Thank you.

Testing the peace

February 28, 1973, 11:28 p.m.
Richard Nixon and Henry Kissinger
WHITE HOUSE TELEPHONE

A month after the Paris Peace Accords were signed, criticisms of its effectiveness — or lack thereof — were rife. Americans particularly resented the failure of the North Vietnamese to release prisoners of war. Kissinger and Nixon looked for ways to force the North Vietnamese to cooperate, employing the hawkish and dour ambassador to South Vietnam, Ellsworth Bunker, to deliver a strong message. In doing so, they bypassed the secretary of state, William Rogers, a man they had long distrusted — along with most of his department. In the privacy of his conversation, Nixon made clear his determination to make the North Vietnamese comply with the peace treaty, even at the expense of the treaty. "What the hell do we care about the agreement?" he exclaimed. "Nothing!" At that juncture, however, each of the signatories was saying much the same thing.

• • •

KISSINGER: Mr. President?

NIXON: Oh, hi, Henry.

KISSINGER: Just wanted you to know we've won.

NIXON: Oh, really?

KISSINGER: Yeah.

NIXON: That's great. Tell me about it.

KISSINGER: Well, they — we called Bunker and told him to demand a meeting of the four-party commission.

NIXON: Yeah.

KISSINGER: They hadn't scheduled it till Friday. They wanted to have an initialing of the — in Paris they wanted to have an initialing of the treaty tomorrow afternoon, and Rogers called and wept all over us that this would be awful if we didn't.

NIXON: Oh, bullshit.

KISSINGER: That is what I said, that your orders were explicit. That you had personally issued them —

NIXON: That's right.

KISSINGER: — and that you —

NIXON: Well, does he seriously think we could sign the treaty with having this thing [unclear]? Nobody could do that.

KISSINGER: Well, he is — he was so focused on his conference that he had forgotten the other game.

NIXON: Shit.

KISSINGER: We then called Bunker. Bunker insisted on a meeting. They held the meeting and their spokesman said the way is now clear to continue the releases. We will not demand anything difficult from the United States' side and it is as good as done.

NIXON: You think that, but he didn't get the names yet?

KISSINGER: No, but he — well, this was at the beginning of the meeting, and they have — the meeting hasn't concluded yet. The meeting just started about fifteen minutes ago.

NIXON: Yeah.

KISSINGER: But when they go into the meeting, and said the way is not clear to continue the releases — all is ready to continue the releases, he said.

NIXON: Yeah. Good, great.

KISSINGER: All the news tickers say —

NIXON: Oh, how did this get out? Bunker put it out or —

KISSINGER: No. Saigon, the North Vietnamese fellow entering the meeting —

NIXON: Oh, he said that?

KISSINGER: He said it on the way in.

NIXON: Oh, great. So what are the news tickers saying, Henry?

KISSINGER: They say, "North Vietnam said today that the way is clear now to resume releases of U.S. prisoners of war." That is the lead on —

NIXON: Yeah. Right.

KISSINGER: — AP. Reuters says the chief delegate, the North Vietnamese spokesman says at last all is ready to continue the releases.

NIXON: [laughs]

KISSINGER: The spokesman was asked whether [North Vietnamese Major] General [Le Quang] Hoa carried into the meeting a list of the next group of one hundred twenty Americans to be freed. We will tell you later today, the colonel said. Well, that's a sure tipoff. The fact that they agreed to a meeting, and they also told us in Paris they want to have a meeting. They wanted us to have a discussion on the economic commission, and [William H.] Sullivan called in and asked what he should do. I said tell them we are not prepared to discuss it until the POWs are released. So they told him it would be settled by noon tomorrow, Paris time.

NIXON: Good, good.

KISSINGER: So I think it is ninety-nine percent done, and if we had been anything other than—

NIXON: We wouldn't get it.

KISSINGER: Never. They would have diddled along—

NIXON: Of course, Henry, you can be sure they were going to keep those people hostage. What had they done up to date? That is the thing that Bill and the rest have got to realize. They have been screwing us all the time. Now they are not going to do a thing, and we will continue to drag our feet on those mines, too.

KISSINGER: Mr. President, if we had let them drag—if we had accepted what they said this morning that they would do it within the sixty days but in four stages, they would have had the four stages all in the last three days. Now your statement which forced them—when you said this morning it was within fifteen days—

NIXON: Yeah, well you put that in.

KISSINGER: But that's—

NIXON: That's right, that's right.

KISSINGER: —and you directing Rogers not to return. That's—

NIXON: That's the point. But you know really it's—for us, believe me, we aren't going to give them one thing if they renege on one part of this deal. Now you know what I mean, this idea of going ahead. What the hell do we care about the agreement? What the Christ do we care? Nothing!

KISSINGER: At the end of March when our prisoners are out—

NIXON: Then—

KISSINGER: —we are in great shape.

NIXON: That's right.

KISSINGER: And we—they thought they could get a little public outcry started, focus it on Thieu—

NIXON: On Thieu. They were trying to do him in, Henry, that was it.

KISSINGER: —and we just reacted very subtly. We sailed the whole minesweeping fleet away, we didn't just have it inactive—

NIXON: [laughs]

KISSINGER: —we moved it a hundred miles offshore.

NIXON: That's a step. Don't think they didn't notice that.

KISSINGER: Oh [laughs], they don't usually cave unless you kick them in the groin.

NIXON: Well, I am delighted. You know it's a—we just have to, as we sail through all these, keep our balance and all the rest.

KISSINGER: You said it this morning when the outcome wasn't clear.

NIXON: We know that we just have to do that.

MARCH

All that the FBI knew about other presidents
March 1, 1973, 9:18 a.m.
Richard Nixon and John Dean
OVAL OFFICE

Patrick Gray's confirmation hearings before the Senate Judiciary Committee quickly developed into a curtain raiser for the Watergate Committee, which was due to convene in May. On February 28, even as the nominee for the FBI directorship sought to distance himself from the White House and its scandal, he was questioned about the investigative files that he'd sent to Dean. Gray tried to insist that the FBI under his aegis was "completely and absolutely nonpolitical," but some on the committee were skeptical. In response, Gray offered to allow any senator the opportunity to see the Watergate files. On hearing that news, Nixon was incensed. In his view, the FBI was an arm of the Executive Branch and therefore of the president — not of the Congress. He made that point in a discussion with Dean the following day. As he did on a seemingly daily basis, he harkened back to his experience in 1948–49 in the Alger Hiss case, when the FBI flatly refused to cooperate with Congress. Nixon plotted with Dean to prove that all presidents had used surveillance and to break that news, he focused on Cartha "Deke" DeLoach, who had been a high-ranking FBI administrator until his retirement in 1970. DeLoach was then working for PepsiCo, under Nixon loyalist Don Kendall, the chief executive officer of the company.

• • •

DEAN: Good morning, Mr. President.

NIXON: Hi, how are you? Well, I was going to ask you about — got along — did you see Kleindienst yet?

DEAN: Yes, I talked with him yesterday and he is going to be very clear in any conversations with Ervin and Baker that first of all, he couldn't begin to speak for the White House. That his own position would be that the White House has a very important principle to protect and that he would assume that basically White House staff would be unavailable and it would have to be a very exceptional set of circumstances before the president would — or he could even counsel the president, to consider —

NIXON: Mm-hmm.

DEAN: And he's going to leave it hanging way out there. For any early conversations which I think will put them on notice that no one is going to be marching right up.

NIXON: Do you think he's [unclear] proper shape?

DEAN: I think he is. He also — I don't know if you've noted what Gray's position was up there yesterday or not?

NIXON: Yeah.

DEAN: Giving the little store away. Dick—

NIXON: [unclear]

DEAN: I don't know. I was very surprised by that.

NIXON: Well, what, you mean like saying—

DEAN: Saying that the FBI records, as far as he was concerned, were available to any senator in the United States Senate.

NIXON: For Christ's sake! He must be out of his mind.

DEAN: Well, that was my reaction. He also said that if they're not satisfied with any material that they're provided, he'll provide agents to come down and brief these people. So Dick Kleindienst last night—

NIXON: Oh, we've got to get to Gray because—

DEAN: He called Gray last night.

NIXON: Why doesn't Kleindienst tell Gray about the Hiss case, for Christ's sakes? That's the standard thing. The FBI—good God! You'll—the Congress will ruin him. The Congress'll ruin him.

DEAN: I think Dick ought to be aware of the Hiss case in some detail as to the position that the government took on this.

NIXON: Well, this isn't detail. It's as simple as hell. The government—and Hoover always felt this—the government never—it wouldn't allow Hoover even to talk to me. That was the Truman position—the truth. No agent of the committee, no counsel of the committee—strictly was not allowed to have any contact with the FBI. They gave no information. They were going to provide leads. They didn't cooperate with—in fact, they were working with Truman, to try to kill the case.

DEAN: Mm-hmm.

NIXON: That's the way it worked. Now goddamn it, that's the line he's got to realize. This is—what was his point, too, about [unclear]? The Republicans, it was rather—it was suggested—he, with reluctance, acceded to a White House request to see the FBI files on Watergate. What the hell's he say? That he gives it to the congressmen for the White House?

DEAN: That's kind of a curious position he's put himself in yesterday.

NIXON: Yeah, but that's what I would think that he would say of course. I did. They were conducting their own investigation.

DEAN: And that was exactly the time—

NIXON: Did he ever say that?

DEAN: He did. He ultimately came out with that. They were pursuing him on whether or not the White House had revealed the FBI reports to Segretti.

NIXON: Segretti.

DEAN: That did not happen, I can assure you—

NIXON: Oh, of course not.

DEAN: —without hesitation. It did not happen. No way.

NIXON: Have you told Ziegler what he's to say today about it?

DEAN: I will—

NIXON: I take it Ziegler should say, very simply — he should say, "Why, of course the White House at the — was conducting its own investigation. The FBI cooperated — a lot of information." Correct?

DEAN: That's correct.

NIXON: But Jesus Christ, if he gets down there and says that any congressman —

DEAN: Well.

NIXON: Any congressman he said?

DEAN: Well, he said any member of the Senate.

NIXON: Of the Senate?

DEAN: Of the Senate.

NIXON: Well, then he goes for the House. He's out of his goddamn mind. The House will insist on the same rights.

DEAN: That's exactly right.

NIXON: You'll have Bella Abzug asking for FBI stuff. What's he going to say? What in the hell is he going to say?

DEAN: He's put himself in a defenseless position. There's no doubt about it. Kleindienst is going to pull him up short on it, say that you didn't clear this position with the attorney general — "This is not my position." As far as I'm willing to go is to give these people a summary of the investigation and if they contest the summary, they can send their counsel down to look at the 302 reports, which are the —

NIXON: Why wasn't he prepared, John, in advance for this? Like a guy over this — Kleindienst should have — like a guy over this —

DEAN: Well, sir —

NIXON: — talked it over with Gray. Jesus Christ! He can't be so — is he a little dumb?

DEAN: Little bullheaded.

NIXON: Yeah, but — what's he trying to — is he trying to pander to these people too much? Is that it?

DEAN: I think that's it. I think he's frightened and a little bit bullheaded on this. I think he knows now that he's made a — that this was a bad slip on his part. And —

NIXON: Yeah.

DEAN: — he knows it this morning, and he's — if he goes back up today he's going to have to say, "I didn't have authority to say that."

NIXON: Yeah.

DEAN: Now that's what I —

NIXON: That's what I should have said, that I was really talking to the committee. Well, anyway.

DEAN: I —

NIXON: Believe me, the FBI cannot make its — the — ask Kleindienst if he is aware of the fact the FBI can't even be available to a committee. It really can't. In fact, this is stretching the son of a bitch far more than we should, to give FBI raw data to a committee of the Congress of the United States. It's not been done.

DEAN: The only situation that I can recall where there's been cooperation between the

FBI and a committee was [Senator John] McClellan's [D-AR] investigative committee [the U.S. Senate Select Committee on Improper Activities in Labor and Management]. The FBI —

NIXON: That's right.

DEAN: The FBI from time to time on organized crime has been of assistance but it's not been overt —

NIXON: Sure.

DEAN: It's been more covert assistance —

NIXON: Yeah, exactly.

DEAN: — to preserve the principle.

NIXON: But in the case of the Hiss case [unclear]. That was a major confrontation and the — Truman said hell, no. The Justice Department said hell, no. That was [Attorney General Thomas Campbell] Clark at that point. No, sir. And Hoover, who was a friend of ours, who was all for what the committee was doing, said no and there was no cooperation whatever. None. Absolutely none. And anyone else says to me are you in this country?

DEAN: That's correct.

NIXON: [unclear] against a party. Now I think that's a hell of a good column for somebody to write or something.

DEAN: I think that's —

NIXON: Let me ask you to do this — write me a memorandum, and for my eyes only, with regard to everything you know about Johnson's use of the FBI for espionage. And then go back — I was reading last night, you know, what Kennedy did on the FBI in this field as you may remember that as a really —

DEAN: No, I don't.

NIXON: You remember when he busted — when [U.S. Steel chairman] Roger Blough tried to raise prices —

DEAN: That's correct. I remember that.

NIXON: And Kennedy sent FBI agents and Bobby Kennedy did it at five o'clock in the morning.

DEAN: That's right.

NIXON: Got newsmen out of bed, et cetera.

DEAN: That's right.

NIXON: Has Ziegler anything — are they aware of that? I mean they talk about harassing newsmen. Have we ever done that? Have we ever had FBI agents go to a newsman to see what happened to their sources?

DEAN: No.

NIXON: Where'd they get that story from?

DEAN: The only thing that ever got distorted in that regard was the [White House request for an FBI investigation of journalist] Dan Schorr incident where he alleged that a full field investigation was put on him and the like.

NIXON: Oh, for Christ's sake!

DEAN: It's all explainable, too.

NIXON: Yeah, well, as a matter of fact that was only — our — of course, as you know, our [unclear] what was happening there. We were trying to get some very — from the FBI on a colder basis, a very — just some background on Schorr. And particularly to see what his connections were with Hanoi.

DEAN: Mm-hmm.

NIXON: It was again part of the — part of that part — don't you see what I mean? The guys don't know anything. They go on a full field investigation on the idea we're going to hire him. That's ridiculous. Even though we hadn't said it — I mean, even though the boys said that was what we were doing. I guess that was their cover. But the idea that they didn't go — they didn't go back for Schorr, though.

DEAN: No.

NIXON: Your FBI agents —

DEAN: Well, they —

NIXON: — in the Kennedy case, they got the — the eight — they got three reporters the hell out of bed and said we want to know where — what is the source of your — it is — you can get it in a little book called *[John F.] Kennedy's Thirteen [Great] Mistakes* by Malcolm Smith Jr. — and the chapter on this — on this policy. It's a fascinating little story. Don't you forget it. But I want, you see, everything Johnson and everything else that you have to sit down some time and dictate what you were telling me the other day —

DEAN: I'll do that.

NIXON: — in terms of what Johnson did. You know, and who — how the reverse of the coin thing and how that came in but how Johnson used it and so forth and so on. I just want to know what the hell we did. Now — and let me see what we can do with it.

DEAN: Mm-hmm.

NIXON: I mean think now. I'll let you know.

DEAN: All right.

NIXON: I think the — this FBI thing, though, it's — we have not used it, frankly, at all. I mean that's the damnedest —

DEAN: I spoke to Kleindienst yesterday.

NIXON: I hope Kleindienst is appalled. It's just unbelievable.

DEAN: It's true. It is, as opposed —

NIXON: That's right.

DEAN: — to what past administrations have done and we have been so kind and so good as far as asking the FBI — in fact, in some instances I thought we should have asked them to do things that —

NIXON: I know, I know.

DEAN: — they are quite capable of doing. Kleindienst also mentioned to me on this '68 bugging of the —

NIXON: Yeah, yeah.

DEAN: That he'd had lunch with DeLoach yesterday —

NIXON: Who lied.

DEAN: — and DeLoach said that — said to Dick — he said that there was no bugging of the president's plane per se, contrary to anything Hoover might have said. And I said, "Well, Dick, how do you read that?" And he said, "Well, one of two things." One, DeLoach knows that he'd be in serious trouble for a potential felony himself if he confessed it. Or two, it didn't happen.

NIXON: Bullshit.

DEAN: So that's — and I said, "Well, how do you read it?" I said I would read it — the man would be — very doubtful if he would confess himself into a felony —

NIXON: That's right.

DEAN: So it's going to be tough to prove. Because DeLoach is the one who probably knows unless we can find through some of the other sources —

NIXON: Yeah.

DEAN: — some of the agents who were involved.

NIXON: Well, you know the point. I think what you've got to do, John, is what I told Gray to do and he hasn't done — is to get right down to the — you've got to get at the little boys who did it.

DEAN: That's right. That's exactly right.

NIXON: I told Gray — I said give them all lie detector tests. He hasn't done that yet. But I said I want — well, you know who does the bugging. Now just go back and see who the hell's done it and put them — and make them all take a lie detector test. That'll shake that bureau right to its roots. That's what I'd do.

DEAN: Well, I think that the timing on that of course would be the —

NIXON: Right after the hearings.

DEAN: Right after the hearings — right after he's sworn in, just go in and start breaking things wide open.

NIXON: That's right. That's right. And I think it will shake loose.

DEAN: Mm-hmm.

NIXON: Just sort of — just bring him in and say, "All right, Deke, we're all taking one. How about you?"

DEAN: Well, Don Kendall could be persuasive in that.

NIXON: Don Kendall can say if he doesn't take one, he gets canned.

DEAN: That's right.

NIXON: Let's find out. I'd like you to tell — you might give Deke — Kendall a call. "You better have a heart-to-heart talk with DeLoach." That "we now have other evidence to corroborate it. We don't want DeLoach to be in a position of having perjured himself because it's going to be investigated." Just get that word out.

DEAN: Mm-hmm. That'll bring him up. Get him a little concerned.

NIXON: [unclear] You could say, "I just don't like it when there's now evidence that he lied to the attorney general." Just put it that way, and "under those circumstances, that there's — there was a case, and if a full field investigation is going to be made shortly" — and that we just want him, just for — because we know he's a friend of

DeLoach's — tell DeLoach he'd better tell the truth or we'll get a perjury rap on him. Fair enough?

DEAN: Mm-hmm. It'll smoke him out if there's something there.

NIXON: It may. It may or may not but at least let him worry.

DEAN: Let him worry.

NIXON: Let people worry a little, you know? That's the thing, you know? Kendall's a blustery kind of a guy. I'd say now — it would just, as if we want you to know as a friend. Don't want to hurt anybody but that — tell him that the boys in the woodwork are talking. The little boys down in the woodwork. Not going to tell you who but it's [unclear], but right after Gray is confirmed that there's a very, very, very big story here. *Newsweek* with a couple of newspaper — oh, hot newspaper reporters on it and DeLoach had better be told he better not continue to lie — hurting himself about that bugging.

DEAN: And there is a hot newspaper reporter. Kevin Phillips is all over this and trying to get it out. I don't know how —

NIXON: See, DeLoach told Mitchell that. Well, he was ordered to do it and then didn't do it. That's what his story to Mitchell was. But that he did do some tapping of telephones — maybe Agnew's phone.

DEAN: Yeah, he's already — he's said — what he told Kleindienst yesterday again. He said that he did trace telephone calls made from Agnew's airplane. We got the toll records of those —

NIXON: Yeah, yeah.

DEAN: — and tracked those down as to where they were going.

NIXON: Yeah.

DEAN: [unclear]

NIXON: Sure.

DEAN: No doubt about it.

NIXON: That's our problem, isn't it?

DEAN: Mm-hmm.

NIXON: Well, just say that there are people in the woodwork —

DEAN: Well, that's —

NIXON: — calling, you know? He won't know whether it's normal bureau channels or not. That there's — they're hot on it. We just want to warn — just warn DeLoach that what he said to the attorney general was not true. That we have — that there's — just say, I guess put it bluntly that what he said to the attorney general was not true and that he better get his story straight with the attorney general, or he'll have some problems. Why not? What do you think?

DEAN: I think it's an excellent idea to let the man worry a little bit.

NIXON: Good God, yes! And he'll worry all those little pipsqueaks'll start talking.

DEAN: Because he might also worry himself into telling us a few more things that would be helpful to us on the other side of the coin.

NIXON: That's right. That's right. Now Kendall is our friend. He's not going to go lurking around. He's going to say that, "Look here, this is only for your own information. This call's never been made [unclear]."

DEAN: Mm-hmm.

NIXON: But, "I think it's important for you to know that this thing's cracking around and he said that he — that if it was not done and he said that the investigation's going forward — the newspapers, they're hot on it. There's some boys down in the woodwork that are cracking and that he'd [DeLoach] better get back."

DEAN: I think it's best to let DeLoach worry a little bit now. He's friendly to Kleindienst. He and Kleindienst have become great friends.

NIXON: Oh, sure.

DEAN: I wouldn't —

NIXON: — trust him.

DEAN: I wouldn't trust him at all. I've always —

NIXON: I never have trusted DeLoach.

DEAN: No?

NIXON: He's a politician.

DEAN: Absolutely. He's out for DeLoach first. He was playing to whoever —

NIXON: He was playing to Johnson, for Christ's sakes — for years.

DEAN: Whoever occupies this office and he thought —

NIXON: Yeah, he probably never thought I was going to win.

DEAN: Mm-hmm.

NIXON: He just played the wrong horse. [unclear] I know. He's basically more a Democrat than a Republican, too, because he's in the Legion. I have known him for years, not well, but I've never had any trust for him. No, the only man we could ever rely on in the FBI was Hoover. The only other guy that really may know was Tolson. What's the matter with Tolson? He's sick.

DEAN: That's right. I understand he isn't well and I've been trying to find out what link we might have to Tolson. Of course, Tolson's brother is with the White House Historical Society. What his relationship with his brother is I don't know, but I just — I've always —

NIXON: I have only — I could talk to him directly but I shouldn't. I may sometime, but no, you never know about a Tolson, whether he's bitter — this or that — he might go out yakking but —

DEAN: Well, at some point, a call on his general health —

NIXON: That's easy.

DEAN: — might not hurt.

NIXON: Me?

DEAN: Yes. If it's — you know, we could check that out first and say that, you know, the surgery —

NIXON: Yeah. Why don't you get a check on him — how he's feeling and so forth?

DEAN: Somebody's got to be seeing him.

NIXON: Check also when his birthday is — that'd be another thing.

DEAN: Right.

NIXON: Knew he'd been under the weather — wanted to wish him well. He's a spunky old bastard.

DEAN: He just might come forward with something. You never know.

NIXON: He knows — you know, Hoover was so — in a — you know, that's the only man Hoover could talk to. They'd go home at night. They always had dinner together. I'm sure Hoover told Tolson every goddamn thing he did because Hoover blabbed a lot. That's where we got that Johnson thing, is that bureau — the way Bobby — the way we have Gray, Jesus Christ! He's done a hell of a bad wicket thing.

DEAN: Tough wicket.

NIXON: Well, the bureau cannot survive, John. It cannot survive. Christ, if Truman was right. That's right.

DEAN: That's right.

NIXON: You're not turning it over to the committee, God almighty. Yet the bureau, the Federal Bureau of Investigation, makes its files available to the members of Congress. What the hell! Some of those congressmen are damn near under Communist discipline. That's the reason Hoover would never do it.

DEAN: Some of them are from the Mafia. No doubt they're backed by the Mafia.

NIXON: Jesus Christ! You could say "only under the strictest regulations of a committee hearing — must be a committee authorized by the Congress of the United States." Individual congressmen, of course, cannot get information. I mean that is not allowed. It must be authorized by the House and Senate investigating committee for a legitimate legislative purpose and all that bullshit. And then under — and then we will furnish a summary and you know that sort of thing, but golly, all these raw files are the most unbelievably crappy things I ever saw.

DEAN: Oh, I know they are. The most spectacular thing is his even saying, "I will make agents who did the investigation, who were on top of this, available." Now these people are full of impressions, innuendo — their own feelings about the case.

NIXON: Yeah, yeah.

DEAN: Whether they were getting cooperation from a witness, whether they weren't —

NIXON: Mm-hmm.

DEAN: There was a considerable amount of bitching, for example, that I sat in on everybody at the White House's interview. Now, I thought that there'd be no other course.

NIXON: Why, of course. Counsel for them, aren't you?

DEAN: That's right.

NIXON: Well, if they want an outside counsel, Jesus, the White House better — they're entitled to counsel.

DEAN: They said that the standard policy of the FBI was that no one was present when they interviewed somebody or they didn't interview them. I said, well, if you want to interview these people, you're going to do it while I'm sitting here, because I think I'm entitled to know, for my own purposes, whether they're —

NIXON: You're conducting your investigation for the president.

DEAN: That's right. That's right.

NIXON: Right?

DEAN: That's correct.

NIXON: That's the line that Gray should take. You're conducting an investigation. You didn't — well, anyway, it's one of those things that's going to go on and on and on and on. I think Gray has demonstrated in his first day's hearing, he's got a — well, you've got to admit it's a weakness of him and the reason I was very hesitant about appointing him. There's too much bravado there. He's a big, strong navy guy, you know? "Everything's great. Boy, let's go. Yeah, yeah, yeah." A guy that has that much outward self-confidence doesn't have much inward self-confidence. That's what I [unclear].

DEAN: Interesting observation.

NIXON: It's like a poker player. You know — the guy that's got the cards. A good poker player, you never know either way — he's got the cards, or whether he doesn't. Christ, you'll never know — never know. But he doesn't have them, he's a little loud — a little loud. He said, "Well, you know, he talks too much," but the good poker player, he's got the cards.

DEAN: I think Gray'll be all right once we get him through these hearings. We —

NIXON: Yeah, he is loyal.

DEAN: No doubt about that.

NIXON: He's a decent man. He'll try but we're going to shake that goddamn FBI up just like Schlesinger's shaking up the other [CIA]. Now the other thing, too, is this that we've got to remember, if — Gray does pander to the Senate too much. We may have to face the fact sometime that he'll have to go. You know what I mean? I have no —

DEAN: Sure.

NIXON: I have no compunctions about that. After all, he's frightened and all that but that would be — that would indicate that we were at least going to put him on — that the FBI was not being adequately managed. You see my point?

DEAN: That's right. It would have to be that way. Otherwise, you're jeopardizing one of the institutions of government that — but I don't see that. I don't see Gray —

NIXON: No.

DEAN: — being in that position, and I think that he wants to be confirmed very badly. He wants to appear —

NIXON: Yeah.

DEAN: — that he has nothing to hide about the Watergate.

NIXON: Right. That's good, too. It's good for him to not want to hide anything because I don't want him to be in a position —

DEAN: He's proud of his Watergate investigation. [laughs]

NIXON: Mm-hmm?

DEAN: I said he's proud of his investigation, and despite the fact he caused us some kind of incredible grief.

NIXON: Yup. I only talked to Gray once since he was confirmed — I mean since we sent his name down there. I called him up on a hijacking case to congratulate the FBI. As I used to call Hoover on such things. Then he raised the point on Watergate with me. I didn't want to have anything about it—well, the White House people were—this was right at the very beginning where—[unclear] recognize the seriousness of—

DEAN: I remember the sequence then. I remember Gray telling me that [unclear].

NIXON: I got ahold of Ehrlichman. I said, "What the hell is this all about?" Ehrlichman, though [unclear].

DEAN: That's right.

NIXON: And I said, "Well, you talk to Gray."

DEAN: And, well, what had happened is we had been leaning on Gray to stay on top of the investigation. And Pat was out making a lot of speeches and we kept telling him, "Pat, you ought to sit on top of this investigation and keep an eye on it."

NIXON: Yup.

DEAN: But he was new in the chair over there and those were, you know, that was a strange office to him. We felt—

NIXON: Yeah, yeah. Interesting, interesting. Well, we should—nobody's perfect. You know, Hoover was the guy, and even at the later times, I mean, sure, there was senility and everything—the little stuff. Say, he did talk too much. He wasn't perfect. Damn it, but he ran a tight ship. Goddamn it! That's the way and the FBI did not leak and it cannot leak. I mean, frankly, I admire that it didn't leak on Johnson and Bobby Kennedy. They shouldn't.

DEAN: That's right. Well, when he said—you know, he said, "Jump," everybody jumped. They might not have liked jumping but they sure did jump.

NIXON: Yes, that's good. You can—

DEAN: I think Pat will—

NIXON: I just want to be sure that Gray was aware of—that those two things—that his testimony is cleared up—that that business about the—

DEAN: I'll get them both straightened out today and I'll get you a—

NIXON: Well, you—let's see. You know, this stuff goes to the private staff. Go over to the bedroom and there's a book in the—on that desk over there—a little book about so thick. You bring it over here to me and [unclear] find this in that book. I'll get that section over to you. Read the Hiss case, the first chapter of *Six Crises*. I think you'll find it very, very interesting.

DEAN: The attorney general just tried to call you. I have no idea what the subject—the subject's unknown. I'll get ahold of Dick and find out what it is.

NIXON: Oh, I've got it on the subject. Tell him I'm in a meeting—

DEAN: I will.

NIXON: —with Golda Meir at the moment and I'd have to step out. If he'd just give us an idea what the subject is, if it's urgent, I can come out.

DEAN: Okay.

NIXON: Put it that way, otherwise I [unclear].

DEAN: All right.

NIXON: Just that, but tell him if it is —

DEAN: I would suspect it's on the Segretti thing — if he's pulled him up short and wants you to know it.

NIXON: All right. Just tell him that I will call him. But if it's urgent, tell him I'll have to step out of a meeting. But I will call him.

DEAN: Good.

NIXON: I will return the call.

DEAN: Good.

NIXON: That I'm in a meeting with Mrs. Meir — just say that.

DEAN: Shall be done.

NIXON: And then let me know.

Tense hours in Washington for Golda Meir

March 1, 1973, 10:05 a.m.
Henry Kissinger and Yitzhak Rabin
OVAL OFFICE

Golda Meir, Israel's fourth prime minister, arrived in Washington late in February to solidify U.S. cooperation, especially in the supply of advanced warplanes. She spent February 28 meeting with administration cabinet members who were so uniformly discouraging that her ambassador to the United States, Yitzhak Rabin, reported that she spoke of packing her bags and skipping her planned meeting with President Nixon the next day. Instead, she and Rabin prepared revised expectations for military and diplomatic aid, an outline that was sent to Kissinger. By the following morning, Rabin had made repeated calls to the White House, but Kissinger was not available. Finally, using the phone in the Oval Office, Kissinger let Rabin know that the outline was acceptable. "After twenty-four hours of undiluted tension," Rabin wrote, "I saw Golda smile again." The summit meeting went off as scheduled, with Kissinger's invisible hand behind every stage.*

• • •

RABIN: Hello?

KISSINGER: Mr. Ambassador.

RABIN: Yes.

KISSINGER: I am with the president, and I've dispatched the matter we dis — our conversations. If the prime minister raises the issue of the interim agreement, the president will then raise the other one and we can proceed in the sense that we discussed. On the planes, I think the prime minister should explain what your request is —

---

* Yitzhak Rabin, *The Rabin Memoirs* (Little, Brown, 1979), pp. 216–18.

RABIN: Yeah.

KISSINGER: — and my impression is that the president will then be prepared to indicate on the production a figure of a hundred, and a sympathetic consideration of the others — of the other figures to be worked out by experts including F-4s and A-4s.

RABIN: All right, and [unclear] after that would work out how to deliver that.

KISSINGER: Right, and I have had a word with Joseph Sisco on that this morning so he is generally — so we can then put it into proper channels.

RABIN: Fine. All right then, see you later.

KISSINGER: Good. See you later.

RABIN: Fine.

Possibly the president's best friend: Bebe Rebozo

March 2, 1973, 8:06 p.m.
Richard Nixon and Bebe Rebozo
WHITE HOUSE TELEPHONE

On March 1 in Khartoum, Sudan, America's newly arrived ambassador, Cleo Noel, and the chargé d'affaires, George C. Moore, were dining at the home of the Saudi ambassador with others from the diplomatic community. Gunmen burst in, kidnapping the two Americans along with eight others. The attackers were from a terrorist arm of the Palestinian Liberation Organization called Black September. Bebe Rebozo, one of Nixon's closest friends, started a conversation on March 2 by joking with the president about the incident. Nixon found nothing amusing about it, however. Rebozo, a businessman from Florida, readily agreed to join the president the following evening at the White House for an evening of entertainment starring Sammy Davis Jr.

• • •

NIXON: Hello?

REBOZO: Mr. President.

NIXON: Bebe, where are you tonight?

REBOZO: Oh, I am at my sister's house down the street. How are you feeling?

NIXON: Just fine. Just fine.

REBOZO: I hope you didn't call to offer me that post at Khartoum.

NIXON: Oh, boy, isn't that too bad. You heard then?

REBOZO: Horrible.

NIXON: Yeah, well —

REBOZO: That is unreal.

NIXON: Of course we couldn't give in to the blackmail.

REBOZO: No way. No.

NIXON: So, I had indicated earlier that we wouldn't.

REBOZO: That all you'd have to do. Just one thing —

NIXON: Well, if we gave in once then they'd kill a — they'd do it everywhere around the world.

REBOZO: Yeah, everybody would be doing it. That's horrendous.

NIXON: Yeah, I was thinking if you've got time why don't you come up tomorrow and come to the Sammy Davis party and then go to Camp David with me for a day?

REBOZO: Sure.

NIXON: Okay.

REBOZO: That would be great.

NIXON: Get on up here and then you could stay at the White House. There is plenty of room. And then I would go to Camp David about Sunday around noon.

REBOZO: Okay.

NIXON: Okay?

REBOZO: Okay.

NIXON: Fine.

REBOZO: What — is the party black tie?

NIXON: Yeah, bring your black tie. You know, otherwise they will think you look like a slob. You know?

REBOZO: [laughs] As an honored guest — black tie?

NIXON: Black tie, and don't bring any mustard.

REBOZO: [laughs] Okay. How are you feeling? All right?

NIXON: Oh, fine. Fine.

REBOZO: You wouldn't believe — I hate to even tell you this but you wouldn't believe the weather we have had all week.

NIXON: Yeah, yeah.

REBOZO: You wouldn't believe it. It's just been gorgeous.

NIXON: Well, that is the way it is. Yeah.

REBOZO: Okay, well —

NIXON: Well, actually you know the — since we are talking, a lot of good things have happened though. The way these POWs have handled themselves.

REBOZO: [unclear]

NIXON: We put it to those bastards and made them come through on that anyway.

REBOZO: You know, I had talked to Walter Annenberg yesterday, and he is just so proud. He is just so proud of that POW return and the way you handled that. He is just bursting at the seams.

NIXON: That's good. That's good.

REBOZO: He really is and properly so.

NIXON: Right.

REBOZO: Well, wonderful.

NIXON: Well, anyway, you can come up and have yourself a good time, you know. Okay.

REBOZO: All right, sir. Bye.

An early instance of Islamic extremist terrorism against the United States
March 2, 1973, 8:28 p.m.
Richard Nixon and Henry Kissinger
WHITE HOUSE TELEPHONE

Hours after Nixon refused to accede to the ransom demands, Noel and Moore were executed by the gunmen. A Belgian diplomat received the same fate. The other hostages, representing Arab countries, were eventually freed.

• • •

KISSINGER: Mr. President?

NIXON: Yeah, Henry.

KISSINGER: Information is just very fragmentary. The major who — the Sudanese major who brought out the information now admits that he didn't see any bodies and now he admits that he — now he claims that the Belgian was alive.

NIXON: But he thinks — he says the Americans are dead.

KISSINGER: Well, that is what he says. But now that — it is even possible, Mr. President, that nobody was killed.

NIXON: Really?

KISSINGER: Well, I wouldn't want to hold that out, but I would have thought that if these Arabs wanted to establish their credibility then why would they kill the Americans, in order to — ?

NIXON: That is what I wondered. Why would they kill us and not the Belgian?

KISSINGER: No, they would do it to increase their credibility —

NIXON: And want us to squeeze the others.

KISSINGER: — towards the remaining hostages.

NIXON: Right.

KISSINGER: To do that it would be better for them to exhibit a body.

NIXON: Yes, and also to keep them alive in order to keep squeezing us.

KISSINGER: Well, if they keep them alive people might think they might — would not kill anybody. I can imagine that they would kill somebody just to show that they can do — to show they are determined. But then it would be, one would think, in their interest to produce the body.

NIXON: In any event, I guess we have got to go ahead. We have already put our statement out and lowered the flags and all the rest and we just let that go, huh?

KISSINGER: I think we should let that go, but I am holding up on the cables a few hours, Mr. President.

NIXON: I see. Yeah, because the cables you mean to —

KISSINGER: To the families.

NIXON: Yes, yes. Yes, my God, we have already ordered the lowering of the flag. Is that a good idea?

KISSINGER: Well, we were given official information from the Sudanese government, Mr. President.

NIXON: Right. So we will go ahead and lower the flag and —

KISSINGER: We were told by the vice president of the Sudan —

• • •

NIXON: Yeah, yeah.

KISSINGER: But this has happened, and he [the vice president of the Sudan] in turn — it now turns out that he was told by a major —

NIXON: Yeah.

KISSINGER: — who had been negotiating.

NIXON: Well, I just pray it isn't true.

KISSINGER: Well, I think the probability is that —

NIXON: They're dead.

KISSINGER: That they are dead, but there is this slight glimmer.

NIXON: Yeah.

KISSINGER: And we will keep you informed, of course.

NIXON: Well, in any event, we are doing exactly the right thing in taking a hard line on it, Henry. We can't give an inch on this.

KISSINGER: Absolutely not, Mr. President.

NIXON: We can't do it. We can't do it. Nobody can.

KISSINGER: There is no — you had — I mean first of all, there wasn't anything —

NIXON: We could do. I know, there was nothing we could do to their ransom demands.

KISSINGER: You would have done — you wouldn't have yielded anyway, but this wasn't a case where you had any choice.

NIXON: Well, they didn't say, "Give us a hundred thousand dollars," they said, "Give us [the assassin of Robert Kennedy, Sirhan] Sirhan," or whatever the hell his name was.

KISSINGER: Sirhan was just one of many requests that —

NIXON: Yeah.

KISSINGER: Specific requests just to get those terrorists out.

NIXON: That's right, and we have no control over that.

KISSINGER: And we have absolutely no —

NIXON: Let's be damn sure though that we get that — all that out in the crap that's being written — said about this. Okay?

KISSINGER: Absolutely. Absolutely, Mr. President.

NIXON: Yep. Okay. Well, incidentally, give some thought to — and put your staff to work on this as to what we may have to do with regard to some sort of insurance policy, or something with regard to ambassadors in critical posts like this. What do you think?

KISSINGER: Well, let me look into this.

NIXON: See what I mean? I just wonder if you can just — we can just, frankly, expect these poor bastards to be over there and just —

KISSINGER: Yeah.

NIXON: Not that that pays for their lives. At least let's show that we are caring about it.

And that we are — and, of course, when a man goes there he's got to know he takes the risk.

KISSINGER: Of course, the Sudan itself was a fairly quiet place. This is a bunch of Arabs —

NIXON: Yeah, but —

KISSINGER: If it had happened in Libya —

NIXON: That kind — that part of the world is always dangerous. Of course, on the other hand, it happened to the Israelis down in Southeast Asia.

KISSINGER: Yeah, in Bangkok, but they got out.

NIXON: I know, but it happened.

KISSINGER: Yeah. The Thais said that the Arabs had been in Thailand too long. They got soft.

NIXON: [laughs] Isn't that something?

KISSINGER: I asked, "How long is that?" They said five days.

NIXON: Yeah, that is the Thai reaction as you might expect.

KISSINGER: Yeah.

NIXON: Well, anyway —

KISSINGER: I'll keep you posted.

NIXON: If there's a — you know, you follow up, and if there's anything I need to know, let me know. If not, we just ride it through —

KISSINGER: Right.

NIXON: — and — but we are going to stand firm. We are not going to give an inch on this business of paying something for them. No way.

KISSINGER: No, we can't.

NIXON: No way. Okay.

KISSINGER: Right.

A route home for American POWs

March 4, 1973, 11:22 a.m.
Richard Nixon and William Rogers
WHITE HOUSE TELEPHONE

In Paris on March 1, Secretary of State Rogers oversaw the completion of a twelve-nation agreement on the return of prisoners of war, in the aftermath of the Vietnam War peace accords. The day before, Nixon had instructed Rogers to refrain from further negotiations on the agreement, unless the North Vietnamese provided the names of POWs who were to be returned, along with a release date. It was a hard line, but it worked, and the "satisfaction" Rogers expressed at the signing was underscored by the list of 106 Americans and one Thai soldier submitted hours before by the North Vietnamese. Within days the POWs were released, representing one contingent of the 591 who would come home between February and April that year.

The terrorist attack in Khartoum continued to trouble Nixon, who discussed it with

Rogers, as they speculated on the punishment that would be meted out to the killers. They were far off the mark. After the attack, the gunmen turned themselves over to Sudanese authorities, who eventually sent them to the PLO for light prison sentences.*

• • •

NIXON: Hello?

ROGERS: Hello, Mr. President.

NIXON: Well, you had a busy week.

ROGERS: Yes, we did. It worked out very well, though. I thought the way you handled that POW thing was excellent.

NIXON: Well, we — it got us in a position, too, Bill, where you see we stood firm, and the like, and your statement over there was the public way. Around here, you know, the — when we pulled the [May 1972] mining [of Haiphong] off, and the rest, the Defense people said they wanted to announce it, and I said, "No, sir." I wouldn't let them say a word. You know, but we just did it.

ROGERS: Sure. Everybody knew it.

NIXON: And everybody knew it, but — I know, but I meant if we had done it and said I am doing this or that, then it was a matter of face for them.

ROGERS: Exactly.

NIXON: It's like the bombing thing.

ROGERS: Exactly.

NIXON: And I went over it all, with Henry and everybody else, and of course he was reflecting the Defense Department point of view, but he completely bought it. I said let's let Bill make the statement over there and we'll state it here, and that will be it. Tell me, Bill, while we are on the subject, how did the congressmen — did they handle themselves all right?

ROGERS: Oh, great.

NIXON: Do you think it will help a little on getting them supporting — well, the fellows over there do support us, don't they, on the aid thing?

ROGERS: Yeah, but well, they are all [unclear]. [Congressman John] McFall [D-CA] of course is the [majority] whip over there [in the U.S. House of Representatives].

NIXON: Yeah.

ROGERS: And oh, I thought it was a great thing.

NIXON: But it will help get them lined up for it later.

ROGERS: That's right.

NIXON: I'd address myself to it again, in my little press conf — I didn't have a night thing, but I did a press conference Thursday and I hit it again.

ROGERS: Yeah.

NIXON: I think we can sell it in the end.

---

* Flora Lewis, "Rogers 'Satisfied': 12 Parties Are to Sign the Accord Today," *New York Times*, March 2, 1973, pp. 1, 3.

ROGERS: Bill Timmons was there, and he was very favorably [unclear] to the thing. I think we can sell it too. My, you know, I have never had any doubt about it.

NIXON: Really?

ROGERS: No, I have never had any doubt about it.

NIXON: Great. Incidentally we had Sammy Davis here last night, and he was just great.

ROGERS: Was he?

NIXON: Absolutely great.

ROGERS: I am sorry I missed it.

NIXON: And he spent the night.

ROGERS: Oh, did he?

NIXON: Yeah. Yeah. Oh, incidentally, I didn't know it, because I thought with the Kennedys and the Rat Packers — this is the first time he had ever performed at the White House, and the first time an American black has ever stayed overnight at the White House.

ROGERS: Is that a fact?

NIXON: So it is sort of like Booker T. Washington, you know.

ROGERS: Isn't that great?

NIXON: I didn't announce it, of course. I didn't say it. I said, "Sammy, I think you," I said, "if you" — he said, "yes, I know." I said, "I don't want to exploit it." He said, "I know." [laughs]

ROGERS: That is very good.

NIXON: But isn't that nice, though?

ROGERS: He is a pretty clever fellow, isn't he?

NIXON: Oh, God, what a performer! He was great. We did it mainly for congressmen. Last night, we had, God, we had about a hundred of them — senators, too. You know, all sorts. I wanted to ask you about one thing. As you know, I am — we are all just — everybody's terribly disturbed about this — what has happened in the Sudan.

ROGERS: Yeah.

NIXON: And, just symbolically, I lowered the White House flag, too, because obviously he is an ambassador from the president as well as the State Department, and so I got it. But anyway, I was wondering what do we provide for the way of compensation in cases of this sort? I mean, is there anything that we do? We are now in a situation where ambassadors, and people around in that part of the world particularly, are in a very hazardous position. You —

ROGERS: I don't know the answer to that. I will find out. I don't — I think of course we have some provision, but I don't think we can get anything special for this kind of —

NIXON: Well, it would seem to me, that for families and so forth, of course that they — it's more than the usual — you know, death on the job, and so forth. But when somebody — here's the point: we have got to tell all our ambassadors, and I don't know quite how to do it, maybe you'll do it or something, I was even thinking that maybe I would sit down with you and the top people in the department and we just talk about it. I think all of them have got to be informed that, in the Foreign Service, that the policy of the United States has to be one of not paying ransom.

ROGERS: Yeah.

NIXON: Mainly because if we ever change that policy we will have a rash of it all over the world. It's bad enough, but on the other hand that nobody has to go. You know what I mean? It is a risky business. That they are —

ROGERS: Well, Mr. President, I don't know if you followed it, but I had a survey made among our Foreign Service people sometime back anticipating this kind of trouble, and they all decided themselves that we should not pay ransom.

NIXON: Yeah.

ROGERS: And we have announced that.

NIXON: Would there be anything worthwhile? You can just think about it. If I were maybe to come over to State maybe on Tuesday or something and just sit down with the group and just say, "Fellows, we just appreciate what you are doing," and all that sort of thing.

ROGERS: I think it would be very good. Very good.

NIXON: And what I was thinking was saying, "I know this is it, and I appreciate the fact that this survey has shown it and we can't begin this but we will want you to know that we will back you up," et cetera. And you could get them together in a large group, or a small group. Would it be something to pay a tribute to the people who had died, and so forth?

ROGERS: It would be a tremendous idea, and I'll be glad to set it up. Did you hear also that the wives have asked that their husbands be buried in Arlington [National] Cemetery? Now, they were both veterans.

NIXON: No problem.

ROGERS: And so were their wives. Interestingly enough, all four, both the two men, and the two women, were veterans.

NIXON: Of course they should be buried there. Of course.

ROGERS: So, what you could do — you could announce that at that day, I think.

NIXON: Yeah.

ROGERS: You could announce —

NIXON: Sure. Sure.

ROGERS: Well, I think —

NIXON: The plane is going to stay there to bring them back I understand.

ROGERS: Yes.

NIXON: [unclear] with the plane. I was going to send the presidential plane, but they said that one was already there so that would be overdoing it.

ROGERS: Yes. I think this is fine.

NIXON: But —

ROGERS: The other thing we were thinking about, you know, the Belgian was killed, too —

NIXON: Yeah.

ROGERS: — and the assessment was made that we stop on the way back and deliver the Belgian — the body —

NIXON: Excellent.

ROGERS: — back to Belgium, to show the international character of this problem.

NIXON: Yeah. Now we don't know about — they are still holding a couple, aren't they? Or —

ROGERS: No, that's all — they have given up now. The assassins have given up, and they are in the hands of the Sudanese government. And the others have been — the Arabs have been released.

NIXON: Now what are the Sudanese government going to do?

ROGERS: Well, that is the problem. I was hoping they would kill them.

NIXON: I wish they — I think they should kill them the minute they see them. That is what they should do.

ROGERS: That's right.

NIXON: Yeah.

ROGERS: But, the Sudanese government handled themselves pretty well. You know, one thing that occurred to me, I have been thinking about it a lot, I think maybe one of the things to do on these things is to cut off all communication with the terrorists. One of the things —

NIXON: Do we communicate with them?

ROGERS: Well, every year, what I am saying is no — cut off the telephone service — cut off — don't — if they drop any notes don't pick them up —

NIXON: Yeah.

ROGERS: Just let them sit there.

NIXON: Yeah.

ROGERS: They have a feeling that they can bargain with the world.

NIXON: Yeah.

ROGERS: And we all get worried about how —

NIXON: Yep.

ROGERS: — how can we bargain with them?

NIXON: You can't bargain with them. Because, like — their suggestion to us was so silly —

ROGERS: That's right.

NIXON: — that like — that's what — you know — when [journalist] Tom Jarriel asked me the question what about [releasing] Sirhan Sirhan, I said, "Well, that is ridiculous." I said, "Of course we can't do that." It's not our business. I agree. Why don't we do that?

ROGERS: Well, we —

NIXON: Why don't we develop — why don't you start developing within the department — you can say that we talked about it, and you are working on it — frankly, a plan to deal with these goddamn things, because we are going to have more. I —

ROGERS: We have — you asked me sometime back, and we have set up a very good task force including a lot of people —

NIXON: Yeah.

ROGERS: — in the government that report regularly, and they have done a pretty good job.

NIXON: Yeah.

ROGERS: But these things happen in such unexpected ways in foreign countries —

NIXON: And you don't know. I see. But you could have certain policies know — well, who would have thought we could go to the Saudi Arabian embassy?

ROGERS: And who would have thought that you would have a fedayeen go to the Saudi Arabian embassy and capture Arabs as well as Americans?

NIXON: And also of all the people to kill, why the Americans?

ROGERS: Well —

NIXON: They want us to squeeze the Jordanians?

ROGERS: That's right, and they were trying also to get some of the fedayeen out of the Jordanian jails. Jordan has got a fedayeen that they were going to execute. Somebody, I think, that was going to try to assassinate the king and they delayed the execution, and one of the things these fellows wanted was the release of this prisoner. It is really unfortunate that Jordan hadn't executed him. The thing to do it seems to me — just be tough.

NIXON: Well, that is right.

ROGERS: You can't dilly-dally with these fellows.

NIXON: And of course there is nothing we can do about being tough on them, except to back up the governments that are tough on them and not back those that aren't.

ROGERS: Sudan is pretty good about it.

NIXON: Yeah.

ROGERS: Pretty good about it.

NIXON: Yeah, well, listen, next it will be them if they don't watch out.

ROGERS: That's right.

NIXON: These people are nuts.

ROGERS: Well, Mr. President, I think that is a great idea, and I will —

NIXON: Well, I was thinking, frankly, the better day for me is Tuesday — rather, Monday. See, I am going to Camp David to do some writing this afternoon, and I could perhaps get back and do it Monday. That might be better, might it not?

ROGERS: It might be.

NIXON: Four o'clock?

ROGERS: It might be, depending on when the bodies get back.

NIXON: Should we wait till they get back? No.

ROGERS: Well, I don't know, it might be better to do it before they get back.

NIXON: I think we should do it, yeah. I tell you what, you get the dope for me and give me a call. I will be leaving here in about fifteen minutes and give me a call as to where the —

ROGERS: All right.

NIXON: As to when they get back.

ROGERS: What I can do, I'll—

NIXON: And then I could come back, or just tell Pete—[White House military aide] Jack Brennan up there, and I could arrange to come back, and come back a little earlier. I could be back around three or four o'clock. But what I had in mind was that, you see, I went over to the Defense Department on the POW thing, and I was trying to think of something to do at State. Of course, God knows, we didn't want this, but I thought I could just go over and talk to the people and say look, I know how you have worked and I know the this and that, and this points it up and we want to thank you and tell you that we back you up, et cetera.

ROGERS: What about, well, let me give some thought to it, and I'll suggest several things and then you can make a choice. For example, we could have a meeting of the Foreign Service Association. We have a lot of them. You could have a talk. We could—what you could do is have a preliminary meeting with some of the top people and then talk to the whole Foreign Service group.

NIXON: Yeah, and then they—remember you could even get them in the—how many would that be in the hall there?

ROGERS: Well, yeah, you could get them in the hall, or you could get them in that eighth-floor room.

NIXON: Right.

ROGERS: You could get four or five hundred of them in there.

NIXON: Yeah. I think hitting four or five hundred is worth doing so that all of them have a feeling that we care.

ROGERS: I do, too.

NIXON: But then hit, so it doesn't just feel like a gimmick we ought to meet with your people first.

ROGERS: That's right. Or we could meet with [Ambassador] Armin Meyer's group [tasked with studying international terrorism] and some of the top, they are the ones that have been working on this problem.

NIXON: Yeah.

ROGERS: They really have been doing a good job, seriously, and they have got the FBI and everybody else, and they have thought of everything in this country you can possibly think of, and they have set up special task forces. They really have done a damn good job, but this was so unexpected. And the one in Haiti [following the death of President François Duvalier in 1971], the same way. How the hell can you guard against that? You know you can—

NIXON: Now wait, we didn't—what did we—

ROGERS: The Haiti one, I ran it—

NIXON: Was that an ambassador?

ROGERS: Yes.

NIXON: Did he get killed?

ROGERS: No, we got him out.

NIXON: Oh, yeah. Now the one before was a U.S., I mean an AID guy. Wasn't that in Brazil or someplace? You remember?

ROGERS: Well, that was Guatemala, wasn't it?

NIXON: No, remember about two years ago, I remember seeing the wife later. You remember?

ROGERS: Oh, yes. Yes. I went out to Ohio to the funeral.

NIXON: Ohio, yes. David [Eisenhower] went out for me. Remember?

ROGERS: That's right. That's right.

NIXON: Now who was that? Wasn't that AID? Or it was Foreign Service?

ROGERS: No, that was AID.

NIXON: AID, but you know it's the same thing.

ROGERS: That's right.

NIXON: But what I mean is, that we — we naturally of course — we have now indicated total backing for our military POWs, which are basically — were hostages.

ROGERS: That's right.

NIXON: I think it is a nice touch to indicate total backing for our others, you know. In a curious kind of way.

ROGERS: Very good. Well, I tell you, I will set it up, and I will give you some choices and you can —

NIXON: Yeah, well, you give me not only choices but a recommendation, too, of what you think. And in the meantime we will — I have some thoughts for some remarks, and that it might be that when I do the full group you'd even let the press cover it.

ROGERS: Oh, sure.

NIXON: You know —

ROGERS: No, I think we should.

NIXON: — so that they — and then I could make a few — what I would do, Bill, is to use it as a basis for saying some good things about the Foreign Service generally. See?

ROGERS: Right.

NIXON: Make about a fifteen-minute talk. That is what I had in mind.

ROGERS: You may have been thinking about how to do this — you know, you and I have talked about this before.

NIXON: And then I could do that, and then I could say I want to talk about the Foreign Service and so forth and so on. That we have been through a great historic year, and now we have got other business, and this, that, and the other thing, and you are going to play a very important part and we want you to da-da-da and then say that I want to talk about this tragedy. This wack —

ROGERS: Well, let me ask one other question. What do you think about it at a meal? A lunch? Would it be better not to, I guess, don't you think?

NIXON: I have no objection. That might mean more.

"This currency thing is working out beautifully."

March 4, 1973, 11:50 a.m.

Richard Nixon and Henry Kissinger

WHITE HOUSE TELEPHONE

By no coincidence, Kissinger called Nixon immediately after the president finished talking to the secretary of state. Kissinger was effectively the nation's top diplomat, a role he guarded carefully. He and Nixon went over the previous conversation, critiquing Rogers together in a more civil tone than they sometimes used for the ostracized secretary of state. They went on to discuss the revolution then under way in the field of currency valuation. Nine European nations, led by Great Britain, were looking for ways to control sharp fluctuations in currencies, precipitated by the devalued dollar in early 1973. The European nations decided to link their various currencies and let them "float," or derive their pricing through daily trading rather than monthly fixing by governmental agencies. Japan and the United States were invited to further conferences related to the crisis.

• • •

NIXON: Hello?

KISSINGER: Mr. President.

NIXON: Hi, Henry. How was the Peking duck?

KISSINGER: Oh, it was very nice, and your telegram was really very well received.

NIXON: Good. Everybody had a good time?

KISSINGER: It is really amazing what a spirit of nostalgia this trip has created.

NIXON: Really? Yeah.

KISSINGER: Well, first of all, there is no other trip where if you said—got them together, say, Moscow or anything else, you wouldn't get—everyone except three people came.

NIXON: Well, I will be darned.

KISSINGER: And they were out of the country.

NIXON: Right.

KISSINGER: And they really spoke of it with a warmth and an affection.

NIXON: Good, good, good.

KISSINGER: You—

NIXON: Did you make some remarks? Did you speak?

KISSINGER: I made some remarks. Yes.

NIXON: Good.

KISSINGER: About half—

NIXON: Right.

KISSINGER: —an account of things they had done there—

NIXON: Mm-hmm. Right.

KISSINGER: —and the other half seriously on what you were trying to do and what it meant for the country that you [unclear].

NIXON: That will trigger them to writing it again.

KISSINGER: That's right. I said it was a moral act of expanding our frontier.

NIXON: Yeah, great.

KISSINGER: The frontiers [unclear].

NIXON: Incidentally, I had an idea that I was — I wanted to get in touch with you earlier about but I just called Bill Rogers about these — this plane over there, and told him that it was all right. They had sent a request that they could drop the Belgian on the way back, which I think is a very good idea. Apparently so it gets an international thing to this. Then I had this thought, and he is looking into it, and he thinks it is a good idea. I have been thinking that we ought to find a way to go over to the State Department sometime. You know, and sort of like we did the Defense Department, and I said that it might be a good idea. Maybe Tuesday, if I could just go over and you know express sympathy and our support of them and so forth.

KISSINGER: That would be nice.

NIXON: And so we will have that in mind. He is going to do some thinking about it and check with some of the others. I had in mind — he said they had made — he had made a survey of all the Foreign Service people, because the point I wanted to get across was that this was a volunteer service and anyone that doesn't think they should take the risk should be — have no need to go. You see what I mean?

KISSINGER: Right.

NIXON: He said they had surveyed them all and that it was unanimous in saying that we should not pay ransom in the event that they were caught or something. You see what I mean?

KISSINGER: Right.

NIXON: So I think it is a good idea, don't you? To sort of show — it would show a little — it is a good way to show support for —

KISSINGER: I think it is a nice gesture. It is a very nice gesture.

NIXON: How is the POW thing? Came off all right?

KISSINGER: It came off all right. The — I have seen some of the movie —

NIXON: Right.

KISSINGER: — some of the clips this morning, and again they made great statements coming off the plane, just like the other group, and they looked so good. I didn't see the other group —

NIXON: Yeah, but they looked good and made good statements.

KISSINGER: Excellent statements, and tomorrow the VC prisoners are coming out. Today it was the Hanoi prisoners, about a hundred and eight of them, and tomorrow thirty-four.

NIXON: Yeah.

KISSINGER: — a hundred and six, and tomorrow thirty-four VC prisoners.

NIXON: They are the ones that have the roughest time.

KISSINGER: Well, I think they may have learned their lesson and they may have put them up to Hanoi.

NIXON: Fed them up a little.

KISSINGER: Yeah. I think that is the reason they are releasing them up there.

NIXON: Ah, yeah.

KISSINGER: I am not sure but —

NIXON: Incidentally, Bill brought up the fact of the POW thing. He said that it was handled just right. [laughs]

KISSINGER: [laughs]

NIXON: No, really, you were exactly right. I didn't remember that, but he said — because I was only hearing these other things. He said, you know, that was just right. I said, "Well, Bill, you know we did some private tough things but we didn't say anything about it."

KISSINGER: Yeah.

NIXON: And I said then that allowed us to be in the public posture of — so they could back off. And he said, "Oh, it was just right." Of course he obviously got a hell of a lot of credit on it. [laughs]

KISSINGER: Well, you know, it gave him a chance to be out there every day.

NIXON: Good, yeah. But it did work out well.

KISSINGER: And now this currency thing is working out beautifully so now —

NIXON: Give me the dope on that.

KISSINGER: We haven't heard from the Europeans yet, because they are probably in a state of shock, but the Japanese — Tanaka sent you a note of extraordinary, great gratitude —

NIXON: He did?

KISSINGER: He is sending a special emissary. He is on the plane either now, or within the next hour, to come over here.

NIXON: Good.

KISSINGER: And I think it shows the Europeans there is a limit — that we can't be pushed.

NIXON: Well, also it shows that — let's face it, Henry, if we and the Japanese got together, that wouldn't be too pleasant for Europe. Would it?

KISSINGER: That is exactly right. That is what it shows them, and it is a way to restore —

NIXON: And incidentally it was a very subtle way to get at the British to — you know, to just to send a sig — we learned through Brandt that, you know, suppose we'd got a wire like that? How would we feel?

KISSINGER: Exactly. No, I think —

NIXON: Did you talk to Cromer?

KISSINGER: No, I sent him a copy. I think they should make the next move.

NIXON: Oh, yes, we should just sit here.

KISSINGER: I don't think we should explain anything, and I think we should sit and let them come to us now.

NIXON: Right. Just sit. I agree. I agree. I agree, and I think we are right though not going, even though Arthur [Burns] feels so strongly about it, on the option of, well, we will, which really — basically is convertibility [of U.S. dollars into gold] again, which puts the responsibility too much on us where, by golly, I am not sure we can deliver anymore.

KISSINGER: If they come back to us, and then it appears as if they want it.

NIXON: Right.

KISSINGER: I can see some advantage in it, too, but the integration part —

NIXON: Yeah, I agree.

KISSINGER: But if we offered it yesterday it would have looked as if we were trying to break up their system —

NIXON: That's right.

KISSINGER: — with a power play. They have now one of two choices: either they are going to go ahead anyway, in which case it gets us greater latitude at the summit —

NIXON: Right.

KISSINGER: — or they are going to come toward us, in which case we have asserted our leadership.

NIXON: Right, right.

KISSINGER: But I think they are going to come towards us. I do not think that Brandt will dare to operate alone, and I think the British, given what they need from us in the nuclear field, aren't going to take us on.

NIXON: Well, the British naturally are trying desperately to get along with the Europeans. But there is a limit, that they have to know that they can't do that without cutting the umbilical cord with us.

KISSINGER: I think it is absolutely essential for the Europeans to know that the party is over. That they cannot pretend on the one hand that the alliance is indivisible in defense, that we have no right to conduct bilateral diplomacy, but they have the right to conduct unilateral economic policy and bilateral diplomacy on their own —

NIXON: That is worded — very well put.

KISSINGER: Which is how Brandt has been doing it.

NIXON: I am going to Camp David and will be working there tomorrow till around four or five o'clock, but I am available any time. So don't hesitate to call if anything comes up.

KISSINGER: Mr. President —

NIXON: You don't anticipate anything tomorrow anyway.

KISSINGER: I will be, in the morning, at the British embassy. They are sending somebody over on that nuclear treaty.

NIXON: Yeah.

KISSINGER: I thought we should have a common decision before Dobrynin comes back.

NIXON: Right, right.

KISSINGER: And also on this nuclear assistance.

NIXON: Right. Fine. Well, you can call me, but when you are there I'd have a heart-to-heart talk with Cromer. He is our friend and I would say, "Now look here, what the hell is going on here?" Don't you think so?

KISSINGER: I will have it.

NIXON: I wouldn't — not to debate — just say — I'd just say that we didn't want to embarrass him, but we thought that it was rather curious that we got this from Brandt. Now we would think that we —

KISSINGER: [unclear]

NIXON: — not that we were trying to limit them, but that we think they should at least inform us maybe.

KISSINGER: And to say that a currency issue will be settled on a basis of European integration. That is one consideration but that is not our principal consideration.

NIXON: Right, right, right, right, right. One other thing I want to do on the schedule thing briefly. Apparently Haldeman tells me that the State Department is giving a big dinner this spring for all the diplomats, and he feels — Haldeman does —

KISSINGER: That's right.

NIXON: — that we ought to put our diplomatic white tie thing off until the fall.

KISSINGER: Well, I just found out about that State Department dinner when I received an invitation.

NIXON: Yeah.

KISSINGER: I think under those circumstances perhaps you should put it into the fall.

NIXON: No. No, there is nothing in it for us to double up.

KISSINGER: No.

NIXON: And you can inform — they can inform the dean — the diplomat — you know, that we are going to have it in the fall, and that's that. It will be a good time to pick up a few crumbs. Okay.

KISSINGER: I ran into Mrs. [Nancy] Maginnes [Kissinger's future second wife]. You were very nice. ›

NIXON: Oh, well, I was glad to talk to her. She is a very attractive and obviously intelligent girl.

KISSINGER: She is a great fan of yours. It meant a lot to her.

NIXON: Well, she's — did she enjoy the dinner?

KISSINGER: Very much, but she's been, of course, she frankly thinks most of the newsmen are too far left for her taste.

NIXON: Interesting what she said about professors, wasn't it?

KISSINGER: I am sure she sat next to somebody she didn't care to be with.

NIXON: [laughs] Okay. Good. All right.

KISSINGER: Bye.

A senator is shot

March 5, 1973, 4:44 p.m.
Richard Nixon and John Stennis
WHITE HOUSE TELEPHONE

On the evening of January 30, Senator John Stennis (D-MS) drove home from the U.S. Capitol and parked in front of his Cleveland Park home. When he exited his car, he was mugged and then shot in the chest and the leg. By early March, his recovery had finally reached a stage where he—the chairman of the Senate Armed Services Committee—could resume some activity. Privately, Nixon commented that while the shooters could receive sentences in the ten- to thirty-year range, the Watergate burglars could receive sentences as high as thirty-five to forty-five years, according to Washington Post *reporting at the time.*

. . .

NIXON: Hello?

STENNIS: Yes, sir, Mr. President.

NIXON: Well, you seem to sound better each time I call you.

STENNIS: Well, thank you, sir. I have turned the corner for more I think.

NIXON: Right.

STENNIS: Everything is coming along all right?

NIXON: Everything is in good shape now—I mean it's coming along on schedule?

STENNIS: It a process as you warned me in the beginning, you know. I hadn't been briefed on how long it might take. It takes time.

NIXON: Well, the main thing is that all those organs are patched up again and then you need a little time to rest a bit and then you will be back on the firing line.

STENNIS: Well, I am anxious to get back of course.

NIXON: Of course.

STENNIS: I hope things are going well with you.

NIXON: We are coming along. We are—things seem to be going about what we'd expect. We were glad to get that second group of POWs back on schedule.

STENNIS: Yes, sir. I am proud for you.

NIXON: We were very tough on them on that—they started to fiddle around, and we didn't say this publicly but as you may have noted we just told them to quit clearing the mines, and quit withdrawing, and we sent up a private message that we were going to continue until they do it and they came through in twenty-four hours.

STENNIS: That's what it took. I knew that was your pattern as soon as you sounded off the first note.

NIXON: That's right.

STENNIS: I knew you would get results, too.

NIXON: The others—they certainly are great when they come back, aren't they though? Their statements are—

STENNIS: Oh, yes. Yes, Lord, I read a full statement today. This young naval pilot, you know—just great.

NIXON: Yeah, yeah.

STENNIS: I hope you get all that compiled and put together in the right way.

NIXON: Yes, we received a letter from Captain [Jeremiah] Denton who was the first one off, you know, on the first flight. I'm going to send you a copy of it. It was really so good.

STENNIS: All right. I'd appreciate it.

NIXON: So good. He sums up everything. Well —

STENNIS: I will be making myself felt a little on the Hill even before I get back out there.

NIXON: Good.

STENNIS: I know where you stand.

NIXON: Right.

STENNIS: Call when you need help.

NIXON: We'll call on you when [unclear].

STENNIS: Thank you for your call.

Segretti, dirty tricks, and a widening field

March 8, 1973, 9:51 a.m.
Richard Nixon and John Dean
OVAL OFFICE

On March 7, Gray told the Senate Judiciary Committee that the FBI had interviewed Nixon's personal lawyer, Herbert Kalmbach of Los Angeles, the previous year. Kalmbach had admitted that the president's appointments secretary, a fellow Angeleno named Dwight Chapin, had asked him to pay a salary in Republican Party funds to a man named Donald Segretti. Chapin and Segretti had been classmates at USC. During 1971–72, Segretti worked for Nixon's reelection campaign, perpetrating schemes that were described in press reports on March 8 as "political sabotage." Nixon was aware that Gray's testimony opened the Watergate scandal far beyond the break-in at the Democratic offices. In something of a panic, he and Dean discussed ways to contain it.

• • •

DEAN: The point is that Dwight Chapin never hired anybody to operate a sabotage — espionage situation. The fact is that he hired somebody to go out and look at the opponents' advancing operations. If this guy saw a chance to be a Dick Tuck–type guy —

NIXON: That's right.

DEAN: — and throw something into their schedule that would screw it up and that was the extent of it and Dwight didn't have any involvement in the day-to-day dealings with this man. So we're working on how to get back and narrow a story that's way out of hand. I think we can handle that.

NIXON: How about Kleindienst — I mean —

DEAN: On Pat Gray?

NIXON: Is Gray doing anything?

DEAN: Pat is going to not honor the innuendo stories in the *Post* this morning. I talked to —

NIXON: [unclear]

DEAN: Pat has closed the store. There's no doubt about that. He did turn around the hearings yesterday.

NIXON: Have you done anything about [unclear]?

DEAN: Yes, sir.

NIXON: The points that I made about [unclear].

DEAN: Yes, sir. Yes, sir, I did. I got questions in yesterday and hopefully we'll get some more in today and if not, when he goes back on the second round we'll have them in. The questions we got in yesterday are questions of course that are not reported — are the investigation by the bureau of the bugging instrument that turned up at the Democratic National Committee in one of their telephones.

NIXON: What did they find, a bug?

DEAN: Well —

NIXON: [unclear]

DEAN: Well, that's what Gray made the point is that one —

NIXON: [unclear]

DEAN: Not a word. Not a word. That's the way it is. That was in the hearings yesterday, but they just won't pick that up. Now the set of questions I've developed are not the kind the press can ignore.

NIXON: Well, they can't ignore — you've got the one on the bugging on the plane.

DEAN: That's right. I — well, I have a whole series of questions that —

NIXON: But be sure that you get the one on the plane —

DEAN: Absolutely, absolutely. And Hruska is programmed to handle that. I was told —

NIXON: [unclear]

DEAN: — that Gurney was not — if it got too hot, Gurney might say, "Well, I got these from the White House," whereas Hruska would never say that. So that is in the works, and it'll come up today or when they go back and return.

On perception, leadership, and the press

March 11, 1973, 10:47 a.m.

Richard Nixon and John Ehrlichman

WHITE HOUSE TELEPHONE

Nixon chose not to go to the annual Gridiron Club dinner in Washington on March 10, but nonetheless he wanted to talk about it with Ehrlichman, who did attend. The Gridiron Club, composed in those days of Washington journalists, most of them bureau chiefs, was famous then and now for hosting an evening of satire every spring. It was at the 1973 dinner that George McGovern, who had lost the previous election by a landslide, delivered the line that "ever since I was a young man, I wanted to run for president in the worst way . . . and I did." In a quiet conversation, conspicuous for its lack of focus on Watergate, Nixon discussed his deeper feelings about the media and the electorate, intertwined as they were and were not. He tried to analyze how such a likable man as McGovern could have been so thoroughly disliked as a presidential candidate.

. . .

EHRLICHMAN: Say, I sat between two of our POWs last night at the Gridiron—

NIXON: Did you really?

EHRLICHMAN: —and they are magnificent. My God—

NIXON: Yeah, aren't they really?

EHRLICHMAN: Oh, what they have—

NIXON: Of course, I have met two as you know, and it just really moves you to tears, doesn't it?

. . .

EHRLICHMAN: He just went through the tortures of the damned. He was down in the South—

NIXON: Yeah.

EHRLICHMAN: —and didn't go through a regular prison camp.

NIXON: If he was with the VC that is the worst thing—worse than death.

EHRLICHMAN: Holds his chin high. My God, he is just magnificent. It's amazing.

NIXON: How they do it, I don't know.

EHRLICHMAN: Now, you just wonder how in the world, because he was in solitary for six years.

NIXON: I was up—I was very pleased on two scores. Bob told me that—first, that McGovern had the good sense to do well, because we want him to stay up there. You know?

EHRLICHMAN: Yeah, sure.

NIXON: But the second point is that, even more that that "Stars"—that John Philip Sousa number—that must have been very moving, wasn't it?

EHRLICHMAN: It really was. And quite something for their—

NIXON: Yeah, and these guys, the Gridiron going perhaps just a bit—you know, it is an interesting thing. I was thinking back to our talk with [*Washington Star* editor] Newby Noyes—

EHRLICHMAN: Mm-hmm.

NIXON: —just a bit back to how it used to be. You know, I know the Gridiron in the old days, in the Eisenhower days. I mean, you know they have that famous song that the Gridiron glows but it never burns, or something like that.

EHRLICHMAN: Mm-hmm. Mm-hmm.

NIXON: But in recent years it has been so vicious that it burns.

EHRLICHMAN: Yeah, yeah.

NIXON: And a lot of the old Gridirons are very sorry about that because it's not fun anymore.

EHRLICHMAN: Matter of fact, two or three of them came up to me, and said, "I don't think we were too hard on you this time."

NIXON: Of course, I don't care about being hard.

EHRLICHMAN: I know but they have it on their mind. You see, it is very interesting the mentality.

NIXON: Yeah, yeah, yep. Well, that's good. I was glad to see, incidentally, that your thing got a good ride. It was the lead story in the *Times,* as you know.

EHRLICHMAN: Yeah.

NIXON: And the dagger in the heart. You know, the phrases, that's what we get. That's what we need, isn't it?

EHRLICHMAN: Right, right. They carried them. The *Post* of course blanked us out.

NIXON: I understand, I understand. And I suppose that is where you wanted it heard because of the damn congressmen, but nevertheless you know how it is. Just keep —

EHRLICHMAN: CBS carried it well.

NIXON: CBS carried it well, and the others noted it, but to have the lead in the *Times* is not insignificant.

EHRLICHMAN: Yeah.

NIXON: An awful lot read it. But the *Post* blanked it out because it's not to their interest.

EHRLICHMAN: That's right, and that will be useful to us.

NIXON: That's right, that sort of thing.

EHRLICHMAN: Two or three months from now —

NIXON: Keep using it.

EHRLICHMAN: — we can cite that. You know, the fact that here was the president taking a position on fifteen bills, and because the *Post* disagreed with it they wouldn't print it.

NIXON: That's right. Use it. Use it today.

EHRLICHMAN: Well, I —

NIXON: If they ask —

EHRLICHMAN: I don't want to give them a chance to repair it. I would like to let it set as a matter of fact.

NIXON: I see, I see.

EHRLICHMAN: So let's let that ride for a little bit, and then we can use it against them.

NIXON: You know it is quite interesting when people wonder whether radio talks are a good forum, when you have something to say.

EHRLICHMAN: Sure.

NIXON: Did you notice how that —

EHRLICHMAN: I am looking at all three papers. I have them out in front of me, and it is just right up there.

NIXON: Yeah.

EHRLICHMAN: It's beautiful. I don't know if you — did you see the Gallup Poll —

NIXON: No, I didn't.

EHRLICHMAN: — in the *Post* today?

NIXON: No, no.

EHRLICHMAN: The most important issues facing — the problems facing the nation today: high cost of living is one, drugs is two, crime and lawlessness is three.

NIXON: Yeah. High cost of living, I noticed *U.S. News* had a piece on that about their disgruntlement about it, but curiously enough not blaming the federal government all that much but blaming the spending and all the rest — some way they seem to feel it. That's the way it goes. Well, let's keep — but on the crime thing, and if you could, whatever you can turn and get a little stuff in on that.

EHRLICHMAN: I think I can ride that today.

NIXON: The idea being that, on all of this, that we have compassion. We want — for example, we want to improve the prisons and correctional institutions, but as you will have noted I struck out about two or three hundred words going on and on about the [Jerome] Jaffe office [the Special Action Office for Drug Abuse Prevention].

EHRLICHMAN: Yeah.

NIXON: We should do the Jaffe office, but we shouldn't talk about it.

EHRLICHMAN: I get you.

NIXON: You know, people, people, people —

EHRLICHMAN: — passion in here — it's got passion for the victims.

NIXON: That's right. Incidentally, let me ask, if this isn't keeping you from your program, let me ask you one other thing. With regard to Noyes, it was very good to talk to him, but the problem, I just wondered at the end — I mean we always of course [unclear] but — I wonder if rather than us being — I mean sure the [unclear] thing and all that he senses. But you know it was very interesting to note if you read through everything he really is saying is that what we call the New Majority that it is basically a bad group of people —

EHRLICHMAN: Mm-hmm.

NIXON: — and that we should not appeal to those bad instincts —

EHRLICHMAN: That's right.

NIXON: — but appeal to the good instincts of the good people. Did I — am I wrong on that?

EHRLICHMAN: No, that is the message. That is the message: that they have base instincts and that the president as the leader of the nation must bring them to overcome their base instincts.

NIXON: Yeah, but the point is, too, as far as the instincts are concerned, then who has the good instincts? Basically the people who either supported McGovern, or who would have if he hadn't have been so nice.

EHRLICHMAN: Yeah, I think that is right. I think that is exactly what he is saying.

NIXON: In other words the old Establishment.

EHRLICHMAN: Yeah.

NIXON: Although — but he is an awful nice guy.

EHRLICHMAN: He is a sweet guy.

NIXON: He really is, and he wants to help —

EHRLICHMAN: [laughs]

NIXON: — and he is right too on the compassion thing. I don't know how you get it across.

EHRLICHMAN: Well —

NIXON: We have tried and tried and — you know, I deliberately stuck a little needle in, which is true, if they ever interviewed the personal staff here at the White House. They hated Kennedy. Johnson, they like him because he gave them gifts but Kennedy just treated them like scum.

EHRLICHMAN: Yeah.

NIXON: He — one of the boys, we get this through other sources, he'd bring in a plate of food and he'd slam the whole plate down on the floor. You know, I mean there was a terrible arrogance, you know —

EHRLICHMAN: Well, Noyes undoubtedly is privy to that as fellows around this town get to be.

NIXON: Yeah, but you know when you talk about the blacks, the personal relationship is terribly important and that is something we don't get across. I don't know why. But — you know what I mean? Well, when I say we don't you know why — hell, the point is the press doesn't use it.

EHRLICHMAN: Well, that's the —

NIXON: What you brought out with regard — I had forgotten, you know, John, it wasn't just New Orleans, but I had at least eight meetings in the Oval Office.

EHRLICHMAN: That's right.

NIXON: And I stood there, and I talked to them, and I worked with them.

EHRLICHMAN: Yep.

NIXON: Now —

EHRLICHMAN: Well, it was very interesting. Now last night [District of Columbia mayor-commissioner] Walter Washington and [National Urban League president] Vernon Jordan made a big show of coming over and talking with me behind the head table —

NIXON: Good.

EHRLICHMAN: — up there in front of the whole, you know, the whole press establishment —

NIXON: Good.

EHRLICHMAN: But I just, that isn't given credence. And it was almost to the exclusion of Hubert Humphrey and the others that were up there.

NIXON: Yeah.

EHRLICHMAN: That is a signal, but it is a signal they don't like and they won't pick up.

NIXON: Yeah. So, well — how do we get — ? Well, good luck on your program.

EHRLICHMAN: Okay.

NIXON: But you see what I mean on the food thing. We have got — we are probably doing everything we can, but we are saying the wrong thing. So we have got to get Butz — that is one of the things — I have got to get Butz off this grin-and-bear-it line too with regard to the consumer.

EHRLICHMAN: He is right about the things he is saying factually, but he is —

NIXON: He's totally right.

EHRLICHMAN: — but it comes through as sort of an avaricious, special-interest kind of an orientation.

NIXON: Well, it comes through as far as the consumer is concerned as grin and bear it and you can't say that. You have got to say look, it's too damn high.

EHRLICHMAN: Yeah.

NIXON: Hamburger is too high, and we are doing something about it. That the president is kicking the ass around here. In other words, put me in the position of kicking the farmer a little. Don't you agree?

EHRLICHMAN: Okay, I'll do that.

NIXON: And kicking the bureaucracy. Okay.

EHRLICHMAN: Yeah.

Phrasing the president's role in Watergate

March 11, 1973, 2:33 p.m.
Richard Nixon and Pat Buchanan
WHITE HOUSE TELEPHONE

Patrick Buchanan was the first advisor hired by Nixon in 1966, at the outset of his successful campaign to gain the White House. Raised in Washington, Buchanan studied journalism and worked as an editorial writer before entering the political world full-time. He offered Nixon a reliable voice of American conservatism, but at the same time Buchanan's mindset was flexible enough to relate with sensitivity to the greater American electorate. He was one of the least antagonistic of the famously rigid corps surrounding Nixon; perhaps for that reason, he didn't become involved with the blatantly unethical "dirty tricks" of Watergate. As a speechwriter and media advisor he did, however, try to counsel the president on the best way to explain the ongoing Watergate investigation to the American people. In early March, Nixon also prepared to announce his support for a federal death penalty, another topic that he discussed with Buchanan. The death penalty had been effectively struck down by the Supreme Court the year before, although individual states — along with the president — were actively seeking ways to address the court's concerns and reinstate it.

. . .

NIXON: Hello?

BUCHANAN: Yes, sir.

NIXON: Well, how did you like the play that soft-line crime statement got?

BUCHANAN: Yeah, terrific line. Have you seen all the morning papers?

NIXON: Yeah, I saw the papers, yeah.

BUCHANAN: It led all the first editions. Mort [Lyndon Allin, editor of Nixon's daily news summary] was telling me that some of the later ones apparently it is the killing of the Bermuda prime minister [Sir Richard Sharples] which might have taken the headlines in the later editions.

NIXON: Who did they kill, [prime minister of the Bahamas Lynden] Pindling?

BUCHANAN: No, not Pindling — it is Bermuda I think.

NIXON: Oh, Bermuda. Bermuda, yeah.

BUCHANAN: Yeah. No, it got terrific play.

NIXON: Not Nassau. Yeah.

BUCHANAN: Terrific play.

NIXON: Yeah. Well, we have got to get across this law enforcement thing and the only way we can do it is to break through with some strong statements on it. Some follow-up with some legislative proposals which I think will come next week with Kleindienst. In other words, we will get a second ride on it about Wednesday or Thursday I think when they have the message go up to the Congress.

BUCHANAN: Well, there is no question that we are on the right side of this thing both substantively and politically. [unclear] —

NIXON: One of the things about it of course is that you know during the campaign, there are many that said, "Don't do this, we will lose the votes" and so forth. But the point is that after the — what really mobilized opinion if it had to be mobilized here, was the killing of that ambassador.

BUCHANAN: Mm-hmm.

NIXON: Because as Rogers was saying to me Friday, he said you can't on the one hand call for the death penalty for the people that killed our prime minister [ambassador] and this chargé [d'affaires] —

BUCHANAN: Mm-hmm.

NIXON: — and then say now let's — let this fellow who killed Bobby Kennedy have life imprisonment. Right?

BUCHANAN: That's right. That's right.

NIXON: Well, this is the line that I think we can — we ought to continue to try to work into our statements and so forth, and for the fact that we will get some opposition to it will make the issue —

BUCHANAN: Did you see the *New York Times* though? They ran a parallel story to yours right on the front page —

NIXON: About the state legislatures.

BUCHANAN: Yeah, the death penalties and the demands that are being made by various governors and the like and how they are getting — the only thing that got a round of applause from some governor was when he mentioned the death penalty.

NIXON: Is that right?

BUCHANAN: Yeah. The only thing he said — I think it was one of those governors. The only thing in his entire speech was when he mentioned the death penalty. So, we are on the right side on this one.

NIXON: Well, some will say we are only appealing, Pat, to our own constituency. But on the other hand what is wrong with that?

BUCHANAN: Well, here is the thing. I think it's, I mean, this is broader than just conservatives and Republicans. There are a hell of a lot of these lower-income Democrats who are one hundred percent in favor of it.

NIXON: Why sure. The people that live in the central cities —

BUCHANAN: Mm-hmm.

NIXON: — are petrified at these people running around, you know? And also I think sticking it to them on the soft-headed judges and the soft-headed probation officers. [laughs] That gets through, too, because they are really the main cause of the problem.

BUCHANAN: Mm-hmm.

NIXON: It is the way they — the judges, you know, on the death — on the handling — when they get these people in, these cop killers and the rest, they just sort of let them out after three or four years of good behavior and they go out and kill again.

BUCHANAN: Mm-hmm.

NIXON: Right? We are going to try to get another press thing for Thursday.

BUCHANAN: Right.

NIXON: And so, we would like something by Tuesday night.

BUCHANAN: Tuesday night, right. I am working on something.

NIXON: You don't have to make it too —

BUCHANAN: Yeah, the last one was too long.

NIXON: Well, it was because we delayed, you know. We had —

BUCHANAN: Yeah.

NIXON: But we have a pretty good idea what the questions will be, and we will just, with regard to the whole business on Watergate and the rest, I am going to take a very hard line on that. I am going to say that I have responded to that, and Ziegler has answered on the others, and I am not going to comment on hearings while they are still in process. You see what I mean?

BUCHANAN: Right.

NIXON: Along that line doesn't matter, don't you agree?

BUCHANAN: Yeah.

NIXON: Otherwise you get into the position —

BUCHANAN: You can't get into all that [unclear] —

NIXON: Well, if I get into responding to what about this charge and what about that charge — well, that is being considered in the Senate committee and I am not going to comment about it while they are in [unclear] process —

BUCHANAN: Mm-hmm.

NIXON: — and then just let them — because it is basically a PR thing really. It's the — what makes the news the minute I say something about it, it just escalates it.

BUCHANAN: Oh, yeah. Oh, yeah.

NIXON: Right.

BUCHANAN: It would stick it right in the headlines if you said something about those — it is going to focus in on the "Did you know that Chapin hired Segretti?"

NIXON: Yeah. That's right. Well, I am just going to say that I am not going to comment on that. It is a matter that is being considered by the committee. Let them look into it. Okay, wilco. Okay, Pat. Thank you.

BUCHANAN: Yes, sir.

"China is bigger than ending the war."

March 12, 1973, 9:30 a.m.
Richard Nixon and Henry Kissinger
OVAL OFFICE

As the Vietnam War trailed off into its tenuous peace, Kissinger was especially anxious to leave it behind and concentrate on the superpowers, mainland China and the USSR, as well as the rising economic power of the region, Japan. He discussed strategies to that end, including visits from Chinese officials and further trips to the Far East by the president. Nicholas Platt, a diplomat on the scene, recalled that many of his colleagues worried that Kissinger was leaving Southeast Asia behind too abruptly. One American diplomat recalled him getting on an elevator in Saigon at that time, muttering, "I've screwed so many people, I ought to open a whorehouse." Coaxing the president through his plans on March 12, he confessed to the same expediency by terming his methods "a cynical approach."*

• • •

KISSINGER: My view is we have to make the Japanese inability to choose work for us. We should suck them into Siberia, we should suck them into Southeast Asia for the reason that the more they frighten others, the better it is for us vis-à-vis China.

NIXON: That's right.

KISSINGER: Again, I wouldn't say this publicly, but we must prevent the Japanese from tying up with any one other country. The great danger is that they'll choose China, and that their resources and Chinese intelligence are going to do to us in Asia what the Common Market may do to us in Europe. That's why it — one reason we have to lean a little bit towards China wherever we can. On the other hand, we should tie the Japanese to us where we can, but one good guarantee — that's why I am not against having the Japanese active in North Vietnam. If they're active in North Vietnam, the Chinese get worried. If they're active in Siberia, the Chinese get worried. If they're active in China, the Russians get worried. It is in our interests to have the Japanese ten percent overextended.

NIXON: That's right.

KISSINGER: Then they'll be — I know that's a cynical approach but that way they are always a little bit off-balance. And since it is impossible to make conceptual deals with the Japanese. Now I think the deal we made with Mao and Zhou is going to last for three to five years. We don't have to maneuver the Chinese through every

---

* Nicholas Platt, *China Boys* (New Academic Publishers, 2010).

little device because they understand that. I don't know whether you've signed these letters [drafts to Mao and Zhou] —

NIXON: No. I want to put some writing on it. I'll have them by tonight.

• • •

NIXON: China is bigger than ending the war. The Russian is bigger than ending the war. The war was going to end. It's a question of how, and the war [unclear]. Now the China and Russia angle — even as big as those things were, we don't look at those as ends in themselves, which many of the jackasses in the press think. They think it's great we've gone to China, we've shaken hands, and everything is going to be hunky-dory. It's not going to be hunky-dory; it's going to be tough titties. So now, now that we have come this far, the real game is how do you build on these great initiatives.

• • •

KISSINGER: I think, incidentally, Mr. President, that after the Russians are here I ought to go for two days to Beijing to brief them.

NIXON: Oh, of course.

KISSINGER: And on that occasion —

NIXON: I understand —

KISSINGER: — tell Zhou Enlai he should come here, and that then you can come back.

NIXON: Where would he go? The UN?

KISSINGER: He can come for the UN and then he comes and visits his liaison mission here.

NIXON: Will we give a dinner?

KISSINGER: Oh, yeah. We'll work — I'm sure that's what's going to happen.

NIXON: Yeah, I think you should tell him that.

"We have passed that point."
March 13, 1973, 12:42 p.m.
Richard Nixon, John Dean, and Bob Haldeman
OVAL OFFICE

After releasing a policy statement regarding Watergate, Nixon used part of the day to prepare for a news conference scheduled for March 15. Watergate would inevitably be the dominant issue, and so in the course of a long talk with Dean, the president covered what he would say. Even more important, he practiced what he would not say in answer to questions from reporters. Nixon and Dean faced the fact that the scandal was broadening, even trading notes on the political and executive crimes that had been committed under Nixon's aegis — trying to launder money arriving from Mexico, for example, or posting an operative in Chappaquiddick, Massachusetts, solely to gather information on Senator Ted Kennedy.

In addition, Dean informed the president that one of his staff members, Gordon Strachan, did indeed know about the break-in at the Democratic Party headquarters before it took place. That destroyed, once and for all, the argument that the White House was innocent of the break-in. So it was that when Dean made a weak suggestion that Nixon simply "let it all hang out" and tell everything he knew, the two of them quickly decided that it was too late. Instead, they looked for a substitute, pouncing on ways that they could sacrifice the FBI to those who wanted to clean out government.

Better yet, Nixon and Dean shared a daydream about utilizing former FBI official William Sullivan to embarrass Democrats, or even putting Sullivan in as head of the bureau. For years, Sullivan ran secret internal security and domestic intelligence campaigns for the FBI and had even been chosen as Hoover's successor before falling out with him and abruptly retiring in October 1971. Nixon and Dean thought they might be able to leverage what Sullivan knew about Presidents Kennedy and Johnson against any future Watergate disclosures. They also hoped Sullivan could restore discipline at the FBI and end leaks to the press.

• • •

HALDEMAN: Say, did you raise the question with the president on Colson as a consultant?

DEAN: No, I didn't.

HALDEMAN: Was that something you [unclear]?

DEAN: It was — the thought was —

NIXON: Hire him as a consultant?

DEAN: Well, it's a consultant without doing any consulting.

NIXON: Yeah.

HALDEMAN: He wanted it [unclear].

DEAN: He wants it for continued protection on —

HALDEMAN: Solely for the purposes of executive privilege protection. So that —

DEAN: One of those things that's kept down in the personnel office, and nothing's done on it.

NIXON: What happens to Chapin?

DEAN: Well, Chapin doesn't have quite the same problems appearing that Colson will.

HALDEMAN: Yeah, but — you have the same problems as Chapin appearing versus Colson.

DEAN: Well —

NIXON: I can't — that would be such an obvious fraud to have both of them as consultants. That won't work. I think he's right. You'd have to leave Chapin —

HALDEMAN: Well, you can't make Chapin a consultant. I — we've already said he's not.

NIXON: Yeah.

DEAN: Yeah.

HALDEMAN: Because we wanted the separation. The question is if he — are you then going to let — as of now, the way they have interpreted executive privilege is that you are not going to let Chapin testify —

NIXON: Anyway.

HALDEMAN: — because it applies to executive privilege but —

NIXON: [unclear]

HALDEMAN: — by the former people in relation to matters while they were here.

DEAN: And the problem area is that Chuck —

HALDEMAN: That same thing would apply to Colson.

DEAN: Well, yes. If Chuck were truly going to be doing nothing from this day on —

HALDEMAN: That's right. He's concerned about what he's doing. Colson's concerned about what he's doing from now on, and he would apply the consulting thing to what — to if he were called regarding actions taken now —

DEAN: That's right.

HALDEMAN: — that relate to Watergate actions.

DEAN: Probably because he will be out stirring up, you know, counter-news attacks and things of this nature and —

NIXON: Jesus Christ! Is he supposed to do that and be consulting with the president on it?

DEAN: No, no. But he's consulting — it's a, you know, wide-open consultantship. It doesn't mean he consults with you.

HALDEMAN: Your idea was just to put this in the drawer, in case you want it [unclear].

DEAN: Put it in the drawer, and then —

NIXON: Not decide it.

HALDEMAN: It would be a consultant without pay.

DEAN: I'd even tell Chuck that, well, just tell Chuck something —

HALDEMAN: Better not tell Chuck. Chuck's [unclear].

DEAN: Is — there is something in the drawer. And just say we —

NIXON: There is no reason to tell Chuck, is there? Why — I would tell him that for — he's not to say anything, frankly.

HALDEMAN: The point would be to date it back last Saturday, so it's continuous.

DEAN: Continuous.

NIXON: That is, his consultant fee stopped, for the present time, but he's still available for purposes of consulting on various problems and the like.

DEAN: Right.

NIXON: Unpaid consultant?

DEAN: Yes. [laughs]

HALDEMAN: We have some of those.

NIXON: Good ones.

HALDEMAN: That's right.

NIXON: Well, what are the latest developments Bob should get something on?

DEAN: Yeah. Uh —

NIXON: Before going into that, I was wondering on that front — that jackassery about some kid who was infiltrating peace groups, which of course is perfectly proper. Christ, I hope they were! I would hope — I would expect we were heavily infiltrated that way, too.

DEAN: The only problem there, Mr. President, is that —

NIXON: Did he get paid?

DEAN: He was paid —

NIXON: By check?

DEAN: He was paid by personal check of another person over there who, in turn, was taking it out of expense money. When the ultimate source of the money — as best, as quickly as we've been able to trace it — was pre–April 7 money. There could be some potential embarrassment for Ken Reitz along the way.

NIXON: Oh. Working for him.

DEAN: So he is. But I think it's a confined situation. Obviously it's something that's going to come up with the Ervin hearings, but it's not another new Liddy-Hunt operation.

NIXON: Well, it's such a shitass thing to think.

DEAN: Oh, it is.

NIXON: For Christ's sake!

DEAN: It is.

NIXON: I mean, what, what happened to the kid? Did he just decide to be a hero?

DEAN: That's right. He apparently chatted about it around school, and the word got out. And he got confronted with it and he knew he'd chatted about it, and so there he was. It's absurd. It really is. He didn't do anything illegal.

NIXON: Of course not. Apparently you haven't been able to do anything on my —

DEAN: But I have, sir —

NIXON: — project of taking the offensive —

DEAN: No, to the contrary.

NIXON: — based on Sullivan.

DEAN: No —

NIXON: Did you kick a few butts around?

DEAN: I have all of the information that we have finished — that we've collected. There is some there, and I've turned it over to Baroody. Baroody is having a speech drafted for Barry Goldwater. And there's enough material there to make a rather sensational speech just by, "Why in the hell isn't somebody looking into what happened to President Nixon when, during his campaign — look at these events. How do you explain these? Where are the answers to these questions?" There's enough of a thread. I've —

NIXON: Double standard.

DEAN: Yeah, and I've pulled all the information —

NIXON: Also, the senator then should also present it to the Ervin Committee and demand that that be included.

DEAN: A letter —

NIXON: He is a senator.

DEAN: What I'm working on now —

NIXON: A senator —

DEAN: — is a letter to Senator Ervin saying, "This has come to my attention, and why shouldn't this be a part of the inquiry?" And he can spring out of '64 and then quickly to '72. And we've got a pretty good speech, Baroody tells me, if we can get out our material.

NIXON: Good.

DEAN: So it's in the mill.

HALDEMAN: Good. [unclear] friends have you got [unclear].

DEAN: That's right.

NIXON: Thank God.

HALDEMAN: Why has there never been [unclear] come up and did it before?

NIXON: Just wasn't enough stuff. They couldn't get anybody to pay any attention. For example, the investigations were supposed to have been taken for the thirty-four-million-odd contributed to McGovern in small — oh, Christ, there's a lot of hanky-panky in there, and the records used on it are just too bad to find out anything.

[HALDEMAN leaves the conversation.]

DEAN: That's one of the problems that he has —

NIXON: That's the problem. And can that be an issue?

DEAN: That will be an issue. That we have — there is a crew working that, also.

NIXON: Do you need any IRS [unclear] stuff?

DEAN: Not at the —

[WAITER enters.]

WAITER: Would you care for some coffee?

DEAN: No, thank you. I'm fine.

[WAITER leaves.]

DEAN: There is no need at this hour for anything from IRS, and we have a couple of sources over there that I can go to. I don't have to fool around with Johnnie Walters or anybody. We can get right in and get what we need.

NIXON: Talk to Elliot Gompers.

DEAN: I've been preparing the answers for the briefing book and I just raised this with Ron. It's my estimation, for what it's worth, that probably this week will draw more Watergate questions than any other week you're likely to see, given the Gray hearings, the new revelations about — they're not new, but they're now substantiated — about Kalmbach and Chapin that have been in the press.

NIXON: To the effect of what? They —

DEAN: That Chapin directed Kalmbach to pay Segretti, the alleged saboteur, somewhere between thirty-five and forty thousand dollars. There is an awful lot of that out in the press now.

NIXON: Yeah.

DEAN: There is also the question of Dean appearing — not appearing — Dean's role. There were more stories in the *Post* this morning that are absolutely inaccurate about my turning information over to the reelection committee for some woman over there — Mrs. Hoback — signed an affidavit, gave it to Birch Bayh, said that I was brought into Mardian's — Bob Mardian's office within forty-eight hours after a private interview I had with the bureau, and confronted with it. How did they know that? Well, it came from internal sources over there, is how they knew it —

NIXON: From what?

DEAN: Internal sources. This girl had told others that she was doing this, and they just told — just quickly filled her to the top when she was out on her own.

NIXON: [unclear]

DEAN: She did. Said we had two or three of those.

NIXON: Why did she do that? Was she mad?

DEAN: She's a registered Democrat.

NIXON: Why did we take her in?

DEAN: I'll — to this day, I do not understand what she was doing. And she was —

NIXON: Who was she working for?

DEAN: She worked in Stans's operation.

NIXON: [unclear] that was a bright move.

DEAN: It wasn't a good move. He had, in fact, that was one of our problems — was the little pocket of women that worked for Maury Stans. No doubt about it, that was — things would have sailed a lot smoother without that pack. Not that they had anything that was devastating.

NIXON: Yeah. Well, now with regard to the questions, and so forth, sure, it would be my opinion, though, not to dodge it just because there are going to be questions.

DEAN: Well, it's going to be — you're probably going to get more questions this week. And the tough questions. And some of them don't have easy answers. For example, did Haldeman know that there was a Don Segretti out there? That question is likely.

NIXON: Did he? I don't know.

DEAN: He had knowledge that there was somebody in the field doing prankster-type activities.

NIXON: Mm-hmm.

DEAN: Uh —

NIXON: So I don't know that. [unclear]

DEAN: So at this — I mean that's the other thing —

NIXON: Yes, but what about my taking — basically, just trying to have to fight this thing at one time. I can fight it later, but it's not going to get any better. I don't think that the way to get into this — did he know or not? I think the thing to say, "This is a matter being considered by a committee and I'm not going to comment upon it while it's being — I don't want to get into the business of taking each charge that comes up in the committee and commenting on it. It is being considered by — and it's being investigated. I'm not going to comment on it."

DEAN: Well, that's exactly the way I drafted these. I have kept them general answers.

NIXON: And I'd just cut them off. No. If I start getting — I think, John, if I start breaking down — it's like on the court thing. The Watergate stuff, I'm not going to comment on it. I know all of these questions. "I am not going to comment on that. That's a matter for the committee to determine." Then I'll repeat the fact that I, as far as the

Watergate matter is concerned, there was no knowledge there. I am not going to comment on anything else. Let the committee find out. What would you say? You don't agree?

DEAN: Well, the bottom line on a draft that — before I came over for [laughs] lunch was, "Well, if you have nothing to hide, Mr. President, here at the White House, why aren't you willing to spread on the record everything you know about it? Why doesn't the Dean report be made public? Why doesn't everyone come out? Why does Ziegler stand out there and bob and weave, and no comment?" That's the bottom line.

NIXON: Well, all right. What do you say to that?

DEAN: Well —

NIXON: You — we are furnishing information. We will do something.

DEAN: I think we — well, of course, we have —

NIXON: We have cooperated.

DEAN: We have cooperated with the FBI in the investigation of the Watergate.

NIXON: That's right.

DEAN: We will cooperate with the investigation of — a proper investigation by the Senate.

NIXON: Right. We will make statements.

DEAN: And, indeed we have nothing to hide.

NIXON: We have furnished information. We have nothing to hide. So we have [unclear] have to handle it.

DEAN: Mm-hmm.

NIXON: What else can we do, really? I mean, we can't — you see, I can't be in the position of basically hunkering down because we got a lot of tough questions on Watergate, and not go out —

DEAN: True.

NIXON: — and talk on other issues because they're going to be — they're embarrassing. It's not going to get better. It's going to get worse. Do you agree?

DEAN: That's — I would agree. I think it's cyclic somewhat. I think after the Gray thing takes one course one way or the other, there'll be a dead period of news on Watergate until the Ervin hearings start again.

NIXON: Yeah.

DEAN: This has obviously sparked the news again.

NIXON: Well, let me just run over the questions again. Now, isn't it best, "What about Mr. Haldeman, Mr. Segretti, and so forth?" "That's a matter which is being considered by a Senate committee. I'm not going to comment on it." That's true, isn't it?

DEAN: That's correct. That's specifically —

NIXON: [unclear]

DEAN: — spelled out in their resolution that they will —

NIXON: I am not going to comment on that one [unclear] being considered by a committee. [unclear] as I have already indicated. I am just not going to comment on it. You already indicated my views on the Watergate thing.

DEAN: Did Mr. Chapin's departure have something to do with his involvement with Segretti?

NIXON: No. The answer's no. And, "But what about Mr. Dean?" My position is the same. "We are going to be — we were — we've been cooperative. We cooperated with the Justice Department — with the FBI completely in trying to — in furnishing information that was relevant in this matter. We will cooperate with the committee under the rules that I have laid out in my statement on executive privilege." Period. Now what else? Let's see.

DEAN: Well, then, you'll get a barrage of questions probably on, "Will you supply — will Mr. Haldeman and Mr. Ehrlichman and Mr. Dean go up to the committee and testify?"

NIXON: No. Absolutely not.

DEAN: "Mr. Colson?"

NIXON: No. No.

DEAN: I think that's —

NIXON: No. Absolutely not. I — no. It isn't a question of — the question is not under what — or somebody — or Ziegler — or somebody had said that we — in our executive privilege statement it was interpreted as being that we would not furnish information. Oh, well. We said we will furnish information, but we're not going to publicly testify. That's the position. But will Dean, and all the rest, will they furnish — you'll furnish information, won't you?

DEAN: Yes. Indeed I will.

NIXON: Yeah. Sure.

DEAN: Well, I think possibly by the time —

NIXON: See, that's what I do. My feeling, John, is that I better hit it now, frankly, as tough as it is. And rather than just let it build up to where we're afraid of these questions and everybody and so forth, and let Ziegler get out there and bob and weave around. I know the easier thing is just to bug out, but I'd rather hit it now.

DEAN: You're right. I was afraid for the sake of debate, because I was having reservations. And —

NIXON: I think so.

DEAN: — it is a bullet biter and you've just got to do it. And because they're not going to go away — the questions. Now the other thing that we talked about in the past, and I still have the same problem, is to have sort of a "Well, here it all is" approach. If we do that —

NIXON: And let it all hang out.

DEAN: And let it all hang out —

NIXON: Yeah.

DEAN: — let's say with the Segretti situation.

NIXON: I guess if we were going to do that, we have passed that point.

DEAN: We have passed that point, plus the fact they're not going to believe the truth. That's the incredible thing.

NIXON: They won't believe the truth. They don't even believe when they convicted seven people.

DEAN: That's right. They will continually try to say that there is [unclear].

NIXON: They'll say, "Haldeman did it." And then they'll say I did it.

DEAN: That's right.

NIXON: I don't think they'll get to that point. They might question his political savvy, but not mine. Not on a matter like that.

DEAN: [laughs] No. Well, the thing on Sullivan, which I have. Sullivan, who as I told you, and — have been prompting him and I said, "Bill, I would like, for my own use, to have a list of some of the horribles that you're aware of." Well, he hasn't responded back to me, but he sent me a note yesterday saying that "John, I am willing at any time to testify to what I know if you want me to." What he has, as we already know, has got a certain degree of — it's a dynamite situation what he's got already: the '68 bugging, the surveillance that Goldwater [unclear].

NIXON: It's not — we [unclear] on the '68 bugging, that it was ordered, but he doesn't know whether it was carried out.

DEAN: That's right. Uh —

NIXON: But at least he will say that.

DEAN: Yes.

NIXON: Tell them, for example, I mean I —

DEAN: I would think —

NIXON: That kind of thing.

DEAN: Well, I've never talked to Bill about this so it must be — I've never really gone into detail, because he's always been very up close about it. But he is now getting to the point if we wanted him to do this, someone — and I don't think the White House should do it — should sit down with him and really take him over cross-examination of what he does know and how strong it is — what he can substantiate.

NIXON: John, who the hell could do it if you don't?

DEAN: Well, that's probably — there's no one. That's the —

NIXON: That's the problem.

DEAN: That's the problem. Now, the other thing is, if we were going to use a tactic like this — let's say in the Gray hearings —

NIXON: [unclear]

DEAN: — where everything is cast that we're the political people and they're not, that Hoover was above reproach, which is just not accurate.

NIXON: Bullshit! Bullshit!

DEAN: Total bullshit. The person who could — would destroy Hoover's image is going to be this man, Bill Sullivan. That's what's at stake there. Also, it's going to tarnish quite severely —

NIXON: Some of the FBI.

DEAN: Some of the FBI. And a former president.

NIXON: Fine.

DEAN: He's going to lay it out, and he — it's just all hell is going to break loose once he does it. It's going to change the atmosphere of the Gray hearings. It's going to change the whole atmosphere of the Watergate hearings.

NIXON: Not much.

DEAN: Now the risk —

NIXON: How will it change, John?

DEAN: How will it change? Because it'll put them in context that a government institute was used in the past for the most flagrant political purposes.

NIXON: How does that help us?

DEAN: How does it help us?

NIXON: I'm being — I'm just being —

DEAN: Yeah, I appreciate what you are doing.

NIXON: Red herring — is that what you mean?

DEAN: Yes. It's a red herring. It's what the public already believes. It's just that people would just, I would say react that — "Oh, Christ! More of that stuff. They're all, you know, they're all bad down there." Because it's a one-way street right now —

NIXON: [unclear]

DEAN: Pardon?

NIXON: Do you think the press would use it? They may not play it.

DEAN: It'd be difficult not to. It'd be difficult not to.

NIXON: Why is it that Sullivan'd be willing to do this?

DEAN: I think the quid pro quo with Sullivan is that he wants someday back in the bureau very badly.

NIXON: That's easy.

DEAN: That's right.

NIXON: Do you think after he did this to the bureau that they'd want him back? "They," if there is a "they."

DEAN: Probably not. But I think that he could also possibly do — what Bill Sullivan's desire in life is to set up a national, or domestic national security intelligence system — a plan, a program. He says we're deficient. We've never been efficient since Hoover lost his guts several years ago. If you recall, he and Tom Huston worked on it. Tom Huston had your instruction to go out and do it. Then the whole thing just crumbled.

NIXON: Do you think Hoover would have cooperated?

DEAN: That's all Sullivan really wants. Even if we just put him off studying it for a couple of years, we could put him out in the CIA or someplace else where he felt —

NIXON: Put him there. We'll do it.

DEAN: I think that's what the answer is. I've never really —

NIXON: No problem with Sullivan. We'll put him — I mean, he's a valuable man. Now, would the FBI then turn on him — piss on him?

DEAN: There would be some effort at that. That's right, they would say he's disgruntled. He was canned by Hoover. He is angry — he's coming back. But that would kind of — I would think a lot of that would be lost in the shuffle of what he is laying out. I don't know if he's given me his best yet. I don't know if he's got more ammunition than what he has already told me. Those were just a couple off-the-cuff remarks.

NIXON: And that's why you said that — why do you think he is now telling you this? Why is he doing this now?

DEAN: Well, the way it came out is, when I — when the *Time* magazine article broke on the fact that it charged that the White House had directed that newsmen and White House staff people be subject to some sort of surveillance for national security reasons, I called, in tracking down what had happened. I called Sullivan and I said, "Bill, you'd better come over and talk to me about that and tell me what you know." I was calling him to really determine if he was a leak. That's one of the reasons. I was curious to know where this might have come from because he was the operative man at the bureau at the time. He's the one who did it. He would not — you know, he came over and he was shocked and distraught, and the like [unclear] his own [unclear] [laughs] frankly, and then — and after going through his explanation of all what had happened, he started volunteering this other thing. He said, "John, what — this is the only thing I can think of during this administration that has any taint of political use but it doesn't really bother me because it was a national security purpose. These people worked — there was sensitive material that was getting out to reporters."

NIXON: You mean what we ordered?

DEAN: That's right.

NIXON: Of course, [unclear] the stuff was involved in the goddamn Vietnam War.

DEAN: That's right.

NIXON: That's what it was.

• • •

DEAN: But he said, "John, what does bother me is that you all have been portrayed as politically abusing — "

NIXON: And we never did.

DEAN: And we never have. He said the Eisenhower administration didn't either. The only —

NIXON: Never.

DEAN: — times that he can recall that there has been a real political use has been during Democratic tenures. I said, "For example, Bill, what are you talking about?" Then he told me this example of the Walter Jenkins affair, when DeLoach —

NIXON: Yeah.

DEAN: — and Fortas, and [unclear].

NIXON: [unclear] The Kennedys used it, let me say, politically on that [investigation into the threat by U.S. Steel to raise] steel [prices] thing.

DEAN: That's right.

NIXON: That was not a national security, was it?

DEAN: No. Now I asked somebody about that and they told me that what happened there is that they were being defensive of Kennedy, and so that the person who would defend Kennedy necessarily was saying that Kennedy had given Hoover orders and Hoover, being typical in his response, tried to get it yesterday as far as the answer for the president. And that's why he sent people out in the middle of the night and the blame really fell on Hoover. And this might be [unclear] over there though, who knows.

NIXON: [unclear]

DEAN: Well, that's right.

NIXON: It's still wrong.

DEAN: That's right. Sure.

NIXON: Good God! Can you imagine if somebody — steel company that had raised hell about — or an automobile company about something? Silly thing. Ruckelshaus does, and we send FBI agents out to arrest? Jesus Christ, now. Does he know about the bugging of Martin Luther King?

DEAN: Yep.

NIXON: I wonder if he'd tell that. That would be good.

DEAN: I think he would tell everything he knows.

NIXON: You do?

DEAN: Mm-hmm. That's why I'm saying he is a trem — he's a bomb. Now the fact is —

NIXON: You really have to keep telling —

DEAN: Well, if that's — the real problem is how it's structured — how can it be done. He sent me this note and I called up and I said, "Bill, I appreciate getting that note very much." I said, "It takes a lot of guts to send a note like that to me." And he said — I said, "It's kind of a pleasure to see a man stand up, blowing a little smoke up him and the like." He said, "Well, John, I mean it. I am perfectly willing to do anything you want. If you want me to go up and testify, I will." I said, "Well, how much — you have just given me some tidbits that you, in our conversation, and I would really like to again repeat: can you put together what you do know? Just for your own use, right now? Just put it together on a pad? Go through all your recollections, and then also tell me how you can substantiate it, and what kind of cross-examination you might be subject to on it if you did testify." So he is doing that. Now, the question I've had is how in the world can we program something like this? The — I just have a feeling that it would be bad for one, Bill Sullivan to quietly appear up on some senator's doorstep, and say, "I've got some information you ought to have." "Well, where did you get it? Where — why are you up here?" "The White House sent me." That would be bad. The other thing is maybe this information could be brought to the attention of the White House, and the White House could say to the — to Eastland, "I think you ought to call an executive session and hear his testimony. This is quite troublesome, the information that has been presented to us. It's so troublesome we can't hold it here and hope to — and rest comfortable."

NIXON: Why — on the other hand doesn't he just present it to Eastland? I mean, why executive session? That doesn't serve —

DEAN: Well, it would, one, because you're trying — the first approach would be not to destroy the bureau, not to tarnish the name. It's going to leak out of there, though, quite obviously. If it doesn't, we'd make sure it did. If Sullivan went up to Eastland cold and just said — or Hruska — I would think they would say, "Go on back down to the Department of Justice where you work, and let's not start all this."

NIXON: Suppose another thing — Patrick Gray says to either Eastland or to Hruska or anybody on that committee, "Who is the tiger on the committee on our side — on the committee — the Judiciary Committee?"

DEAN: Cook's —

NIXON: Cook.

DEAN: Gurney has been good. Gurney was good during the ITT hearings, and he'll study. He'll get prepared. Uh —

NIXON: But would he go after the bureau? Cook, I don't know him.

DEAN: They're not going after the bureau. What they are doing is they're taking the testimony of somebody who is going after the bureau.

NIXON: Yeah. I know that. I'm just thinking of the —

DEAN: Yeah.

NIXON: They ought to look down the road and see what would be the result of what they are doing is — won't they? I would think so. I mean, I'm just trying — how would they go after Johnson? Let's look at the distant future. Look at the — how bad would it hurt the country, John, to have the FBI so terribly discredited? [unclear]

DEAN: Well, I've kicked this around with Dick Moore — these broader questions — and I think it would be damaging to the FBI, but maybe it's time to shake the FBI and rebuild it.

NIXON: [unclear]

DEAN: I'm not so sure the FBI is everything it's cracked up to be. I'm convinced the FBI isn't everything the public thinks it is.

NIXON: No.

DEAN: I know quite well it isn't.

NIXON: [unclear] if you could get [chief of the Washington Metropolitan Police Department] Jerry Wilson in there rather than a political appointee. What is your feeling at the moment about Gray? Can he hang in? Should he? I don't know.

DEAN: Uh —

NIXON: [unclear] of course.

DEAN: I — they're going to vote this — they have an executive session this afternoon to invite me to testify.

NIXON: Sure.

DEAN: There's no question they're going to invite me. I would say based on how I handle the, one, the formal letter that comes out of the committee asking for information, and I programmed that they do get specific. Just what in the hell do they want to know that I've got, and lay it out in the letter that's sent down here asking me to appear so I can be responsive, fully —

NIXON: Respond to the letter.

DEAN: Respond to the letter in full. I think I have — I feel I have nothing to hide as far as the issue they've raised.

NIXON: Would you respond under oath?

DEAN: I think I would be willing to, yes.

NIXON: That's what I'd say because that's what I am preparing in the press thing. I'll say you'll respond under oath in a letter. But you will not appear in a formal session.

DEAN: That sets our precedent [unclear].

NIXON: What if they say, "Would he be willing to be questioned under oath?"

DEAN: That's not what the question is. Yes, I'd be willing to be questioned under oath, but we're not going up.

NIXON: No, no. But here?

DEAN: Oh, I think that would be a hell of a bad precedent.

NIXON: Okay, I just wanted to be sure we don't cross that bridge. I agree. You — but you would respond to written interrogatories.

DEAN: That's right.

NIXON: That's it. Okay.

DEAN: Now after that, if we've been responsive, their argument for holding up Gray's confirmation based on me is — should be gone. Sure, they're going to say it raises more questions than it answers, but if we're — but that can go on forever. We've taken the central points they want answers to — given them the responses. That puts something in Eastland's hand that can say, "All right, it's time to vote." And Eastland says he's got the votes to get Gray through. Now, but what happens on the Senate floor is something else, because [Senator Robert] Byrd is opposing Gray. Byrd's got good control of that southern bloc.

NIXON: Not totally.

DEAN: No?

NIXON: Byrd is running for leader of the whole Senate. A lot of them may desert him on this.

DEAN: But Mansfield, on the other hand, of course, has come out and said that he favors — initially he supported Gray's confirmation.

NIXON: My feeling is that they would like [unclear] I think that they'd like to have an excuse not to do it. Maybe they ought to use not you, but all this crap about this kid [unclear].

DEAN: Well, if they say they have to hold up Gray's confirmation until the Watergate hearings are completed —

NIXON: Oh, that's great.

DEAN: That's the vehicle.

NIXON: The best of both worlds for us, John —

DEAN: That's right.

NIXON: Because Gray, in my opinion, should not be the head of the FBI. Not because of any character or other flaws or thoughtless flaws, but because he is going to be too much like Kleindienst. After going through the hell of the hearing, he will not be a good director as far as we're concerned.

DEAN: I think that's probably true. He'll be a very suspect director. Not that I don't think Pat won't do what we want. I read him a little differently than Dick in that regard. Like he's still keeping in close touch with me. He's calling me. He's given me his private line. We talk at night, just "How do you want me to handle this," so on and so forth. So he still plays — playing in tight, and still being involved. But I think he —

NIXON: But he couldn't do it.

DEAN: But he can't do it. He's under — he's going to be under such surveillance by — his own people watch every move he's making. That'll be the difficult thing for Pat. Not that Pat wouldn't want to still play ball, but he may not be able to.

NIXON: I agree. That's what I meant.

DEAN: Pat has already gotten himself in a situation where he's got this Mark Felt as his number-two man. These other people are surrounding him. If you put a guy like Jerry Wilson in there he could just, you know, wipe this, and say, "Gentlemen, I'm putting my own team in, and I'm going to bring people in I've met around the country who are good office directors — [FBI] SACs out of Chicago" — wherever, and just put his own team together for the headquarters office.

NIXON: So where do you come out?

DEAN: Gray's already been locked into — to major personnel decisions. I wouldn't be surprised to see that occur — that they say that they cannot go forward with Gray's hearings because of Watergate.

NIXON: Where would that be done, John? At what point in the committee, or on the floor, or both?

DEAN: It could happen. It would certainly be voted on first in the committee — in the Judiciary Committee.

NIXON: How do you [unclear]?

DEAN: The question is, then, whether it'll be put on the calendar by the leadership. I assume that that's —

NIXON: The leadership might determine that we will not put it on the calendar until after the Watergate hearings.

DEAN: That's right.

NIXON: Then we could then — Gray could then come in and say, "I will not wait that long."

DEAN: And they'll — when they — you're, "This — you're — this is damaging to the leadership of the FBI, and I will have to withdraw based on this." What would be nice for all would be to get Gray voted out of the committee —

NIXON: Yeah.

DEAN: — with a positive vote, enough to get him out of committee, and then lock him at limbo there.

NIXON: What is Moore's judgment about Sullivan? Does he know?

DEAN: Yeah, he says it's a piece of dynamite. He says it depends, and we both agree, that it — the way it would be done would be a secret — whether it was done. Whether — this isn't the sort of thing we could just leap out and do — have to be very carefully thought through. Have to be — have to decide in advance should the White House not be involved or should we be involved? If we're going to play with it, we are going to probably have to say that we were involved and structure it in a way that there is nothing improper with our involvement.

NIXON: The difficulty with the White House being involved is that if we are involved in pissing on Johnson — that concerns me.

DEAN: That's right.

NIXON: That's why it really ought to be — I mean, if he could just —

DEAN: I suppose the answer is saying — to have him — to say to him —

NIXON: [unclear]

DEAN: You've got — you know, this is something. "What — you've intimated a few things to me. The proper place to take that information is to the Senate Judiciary Committee or to the attorney general possibly." And then have Dick take it to the committee. Or is that too close to the president still?

NIXON: Personally, if he takes it to the committee, it's better if the committee's conducting a hearing on his involvement. Well, wait a minute. He works for the attorney general, doesn't he?

DEAN: That's right. If he takes it to Kleindienst, Kleindienst is going to say, "Bill, just don't do it because you are going to take DeLoach's name down with it, and DeLoach is a friend of ours."

NIXON: Bullshit.

DEAN: Something I have always questioned.

NIXON: Nobody is a friend of ours. Let's face it. Don't worry about that sort of thing.

DEAN: Well, it's something I will — I think I need to kick around with Dick Moore, because —

NIXON: Yeah.

DEAN: But first of all, I've got to — just have to be thought through every inch of the way. It came here —

NIXON: Sure.

DEAN: — late yesterday afternoon.

NIXON: Sure.

DEAN: It was not — Bob said, when I talked to him, he said he was quite excited about it. As Ehrlichman said — gave a very favorable "Mm-hmm." And I said, "Well, I'm not going to rush anything on this. It's — we've a little bomb here that we might want to drop at one — "

NIXON: Yeah.

DEAN: " — point down the road."

NIXON: Yeah. Yeah.

DEAN: Maybe the forum to do it is something totally out of the committee context between the Gray confirmation hearings and the Watergate hearings. Maybe let him go over to *U.S. News,* or who knows what it would be. But we ought to consider every option, now that we've got it, and see if —

NIXON: Rather than doing it in a hearing — doing it in the press. Then that will force the hearing to call him. That's another way to do this. Have him be selected to —

DEAN: Give an interview.

NIXON: — to give an interview. I would do it in *U.S. News,* if you can do it. I would not do it with a wire-service guy or something. A respected damn reporter. Why not go to a jackass like Mollenhoff? No, he's too close to us.

DEAN: Well, that's interesting. Now Mollenhoff is close but, by God, you can't program Mollenhoff to do anything.

NIXON: No.

DEAN: And if —

NIXON: No. And also, we are in a position on Mollenhoff, who's been fighting us some, that maybe Mollenhoff could be a pretty good prospect for this thing. It's the kind of a story he loves — he digs on some. You couldn't tell him, however, [unclear] letting him know — look at the story part. Or Sullivan just goes to talk to him, says, "Look what I have here. You're a hell of a guy, and I just want to tell you a few things."

DEAN: Or can you call Clark and say — can I call Clark and say, "Listen, Clark, a guy has brought me a piece of dynamite I don't even want in the White House"?

NIXON: He will write that, though, won't he?

DEAN: Yeah. Because that'd look like that's a setup deal. Well, Clark Mollenhoff is the first guy to uncover —

NIXON: Yeah.

DEAN: [unclear] anything, and he will say no way.

NIXON: But he's willing to do it.

DEAN: Mm-hmm.

NIXON: That's very important, at least.

DEAN: Mm-hmm.

NIXON: Broadens the scope. Getting to the bottom of the whole thing, don't you feel that that's the need here is to broaden the scope of the damn thing, instead of —

DEAN: The focus is right on us. That's the problem.

NIXON: Yeah. Nothing on the Democrats, and nothing —

DEAN: Nothing.

NIXON: Nothing on what the previous three administrations did.

DEAN: Nothing. It's making —

NIXON: Yeah.

DEAN: Well, it — of course it's still a Washington story. You go out of this city —

NIXON: I know.

DEAN: — and you can't find anybody that even knows what's happening. Although it's increased in the network coverage. That NBC thing last night, which is just a travesty as far as—the very thing Ron was talking about, about shabby journalism. They took the worst edited clips they could, out of context, to respond to things they would say on the lead and they would have a little clip of Ron saying, "Well, I deny that." And he was denying something totally other than what they were talking about in their charge. It was incredible. Someone is going through and putting that all together right now, and Ron ought to be able to have a field day back with that one on NBC. It was just ver—it was very, very dishonest television reporting of a sequence of events. It was out of sequence.

NIXON: Well, you see, John—yeah, I know the situation. Ervin gets up there and, you know, gassing around, he was huffing and puffing about his being a great constitutional lawyer and all. I guess it just makes us wonder about our first decision, doesn't it? [unclear] about sending Gray up. Probably a mistake, but then, we didn't anticipate—

DEAN: Well—

NIXON: Or you think not? Who knows.

DEAN: Who knows. That's right. If you didn't send him up, why didn't you send him up. Because he was—

NIXON: Right. I know. That's what they—

DEAN: That's true.

NIXON: That's what they—you send somebody else somebody will take them on—not doing too well. You know what I mean?

DEAN: Yeah.

NIXON: I won't even announce any [unclear]. I think the problem is, the reason that the Senate was not [unclear] being reasonable was because [unclear] a lot of this stuff hanging out there before the [unclear] has to be brought to the Ervin Committee.

DEAN: Well, we—you know, one thing is that I—the saturation level of the American people on this story is [laughs] depressing. Pretty close, in fact. [laughs] The saturation level in this city is getting pretty high now. They can't take too much more of this stuff.

NIXON: Think not?

DEAN: Nothing really new is coming out.

NIXON: Some kid—they said—I don't think that anybody, incidentally, will care about somebody infiltrating the peace movement that was demonstrating against the president, particularly on the war in Vietnam. Do you think so?

DEAN: No.

NIXON: Anyway, I don't care about that. What happened to this Texas guy [oilman Robert Allen] that took his money [donated to Nixon's Committee to Re-Elect the President] back? Was he—?

DEAN: All hell broke loose for him after. This is Allen.

NIXON: No, no. Allen—yeah.

DEAN: Allen, not [Texas land speculator Walter] Duncan. There were two—

NIXON: Nothing to do [unclear].

DEAN: [unclear]. All hell broke loose for Allen for this reason. He — the money, apparently, originally came out of a subsidiary of one of Allen's corporations down in Mexico. It went to a lawyer in Mexico who put it down as a fee billed to the subsidiary. Then the lawyer, the Mexican lawyer, sent it back into the States, and it came back up here. But, the weakness of it is the Mexican lawyer: one, didn't have a legitimate fee; two, it could be a corporate contribution. So Allen wanted — and Allen had personally put a note up with the corporation to cover it. But Allen is meanwhile having problems with his wife, and a divorce is pending, and tax problems. So he —

NIXON: [unclear] The only problem I saw there was where you put it off — lay it off [unclear] the fact that it was being used for Watergate.

DEAN: That's — I don't know why that went in the letter. I — it wasn't used for the Watergate. That's the interesting thing.

NIXON: It wasn't?

DEAN: No. It was not. What happened is these Mexican checks came in. They were given to Gordon Liddy, who said, "What do we — why don't you get these cashed?" Gordon Liddy, in turn, took them down to this fellow, Barker, in Florida, and said, "Would you cash these Mexican checks?" And so that's how they went through Barker's bank account back in here. They could have been just as easily cashed at the Riggs Bank. There was nothing wrong [laughs] with the checks. Why all that rigmarole? It's just like a lot of other things that happened over there. God knows why it was all done. It was totally unnecessary, and it was money that was not directly involved in the Watergate. It wasn't a wash operation to get money back in to Liddy, and the like.

NIXON: Who is going to be the worst witness up there?

DEAN: Sloan.

NIXON: Unfortunate.

DEAN: Without a doubt. He's —

NIXON: He's scared?

DEAN: He's scared. He's weak. He has a compulsion to cleanse his soul by confession. Now, we're — he's going — we're giving him a lot of stroking, telling him, "You're doing a beautiful job." The funny thing is, this fellow goes down to the courthouse here before Sirica, testifies as honestly as he can testify, and Sirica looks around and calls him a liar. [laughs] He's a sad — Sloan can't win. So Kalmbach has been dealing with Sloan. Sloan [unclear] his job. Kalmbach has done a lot of that. The person that will have the greatest problem with — as a result of Sloan's testimony — is Kalmbach and Stans. So they're working closely with him to make sure that he settles down.

NIXON: Kalmbach will be a good witness.

DEAN: Oh, yes.

NIXON: Knowing what Kalmbach has been through.

DEAN: Kalmbach has borne up very well. In fact, I decided he may be —

NIXON: Kalmbach, of course — this is somewhat embarrassing — he is, they say, lawyer for the president. Well, hell, I don't need a lawyer. He handles that property out there.

DEAN: He's sensitive on that point. He over — he saw a briefing — saw a transcript of a briefing where Ron was saying, "Well, he's really not. That's not the right nomenclature — this 'personal attorney.'" Herb said, "Well, gee whiz. I don't know if Ron knows what all I do." And I said, "Herb — well, don't worry about it."

NIXON: Well, what I meant is that this — I don't care about that, but I meant, it's just the fact that it's played that way, as if he's in — that I am — he's in talking to me all the time. I don't ask him [unclear].

DEAN: I know that.

NIXON: I don't talk to him about anything. I mean, I don't know — I see Herb once a year when he brings the income tax returns.

DEAN: That's right.

NIXON: I'm sure that he handles that San Clemente property and all the rest, but he's — he isn't a lawyer in the sense that most people have a lawyer.

DEAN: No, no. Although he didn't even handle the estate plan, he's done some, you know, dovetailing on it, like —

NIXON: Well, but anyway, we don't want to back off of him.

DEAN: No. Anyway, he's solid. He's solid.

NIXON: He will — how does he tell a story when he gets [unclear]? He's got a pretty hard row to hoe — he and Stans have.

DEAN: He'll be good. He's going over every — Herb is the kind of guy who will check, not once, not twice, on his story, not three times, but probably fifty to a hundred times. Literally. He will go over it. He will know it. There won't be a hole in it. He'll have thought it — he'll do his own Q and A. He'll be — have people cross-examine him from ten ways.

NIXON: Good.

DEAN: He will be ready, as John Mitchell will be ready, as Maury Stans will be ready.

NIXON: Yeah.

DEAN: It's —

NIXON: Mitchell is now studying, is he?

DEAN: He is studying. Sloan will be the worst witness. I think Magruder will be a good witness. This fellow [Herbert] Bart Porter will be a good witness. They've already been through it. They've been through grand jury. They have been through trial. They did well. And then, of course, people around here —

NIXON: I [unclear].

DEAN: — won't be witnesses.

NIXON: They won't be witnesses.

DEAN: Won't be witnesses.

NIXON: Hell, no. They will make statements. That'll be the line which I think we've got to get across to Ziegler, in all of his briefings where he is constantly saying we will furnish information. That is not the question. It is how it's to be furnished, and we will not furnish it in a formal session. That would be to break down the [executive] privilege. Period. Do you agree with that?

DEAN: I agree. I agree. I have always thought that's the bottom line, and I think that's the good thing about what's happening in the Gray hearings right now. If we — they send a letter down with specific questions, I send back written interrogatories, sworn. You know, as a lawyer, that you can handle written interrogatories, where cross-examination is another ball game.

NIXON: I know.

DEAN: They can — you can make a person look like they're inaccurate even if they're trying to tell the truth.

NIXON: "Well, now, really, you sh — you can't mean that." You know, I know — all their face making and all that crap. I know [unclear]. Written interrogatories you can —

DEAN: Can be artfully, accurately answered and give the full information.

NIXON: [unclear] that there will be total and full [unclear]. Well, what about the sentencing? When the hell is he going to sentence?

DEAN: We thought he was going to sentence last Friday.

NIXON: I know. You've said that.

DEAN: No one knows what in the world Sirica is doing. It's getting to be a long time now. It frankly is.

NIXON: [unclear]

DEAN: And no one really has a good estimation of how he will sentence. There's some feeling that he will sentence Liddy the heaviest. Liddy's already in jail. He's in Danbury. He wanted to start serving so he can get good time going. But Hunt he'll probably be very fair with.

NIXON: Why?

DEAN: Pardon?

NIXON: Why? Why Hunt?

DEAN: He likes Hunt. He liked Hunt. He thought Hunt was being open with him and candid, and Hunt gave a statement in open court that he didn't know of any higher-ups involved and Hunt didn't put him through the rigors of trial. And Hunt was a beaten man, the loss of his wife, was ill — they tried to move and have a — him severed from the trial. And Hunt didn't cause a lot of problems. Bittman was cooperative, whereas Liddy played the heavy in the trial. His lawyer raised all the objections and the like, and embarrassed the judge for some in-chambers things he'd said, and —

NIXON: But Liddy's going to appeal the sentence?

DEAN: Liddy is going to appeal the decision — the trial. He will appeal that.

NIXON: That's right — the trial. The trial.

DEAN: Trial — and there's —

NIXON: He was convicted.

DEAN: There is an outside chance that this man has gone, this judge has gone so far in his zeal to be a special prosecutor —

NIXON: Well, some of those statements from the bench —

DEAN: Incredible statements.

NIXON: To me — incredible.

DEAN: Commenting on witnesses' testimony before the jury was just incredible. Incredible. So he may have — there may be a mistrial. I don't — there may be reversible error even. I don't know.

NIXON: What about the Cubans?

DEAN: The Cubans will probably be thought of as hired hands, and nowhere near the sentences of Liddy, I would think. Not all of them — Barker, the lead Cuban, may get more than the others. It's hard to say. I — you know, I just don't have any idea. Sirica's a strange man. He is known as a hanging judge.

NIXON: That's the kind that I want.

DEAN: That's right. [laughs]

NIXON: I understand.

DEAN: That's right. He's tough. He is tough. Now, the other thing, Sirica — there was some indication that Sirica might be putting together a panel. They have this system down there now, based on this informal agreement, where a judge — a sentencing judge convenes a panel of his own to take advice from. If Sirica were being shrewd, he just might get himself a panel and take their recommendations.

NIXON: When will the Ervin thing be hitting the fan most, I mean by that time [unclear]?

DEAN: Well, I would say that the best indication we have now is public hearings will probably start about the first of May. Now, they will — you know, there'll be a big, probably, bang of interest initially. We have no idea how they will proceed yet. We do have sources to find that out other than Baker. Incidentally, Kleindienst was — had called Ervin again — returned the call. Ervin is going to see him this week, with Baker. That's —

NIXON: Public hearings the first of May. Well, that'll be a big show. The public hearings, I wouldn't think, though, I know from experience that, my guess is that — I think they could get through about three weeks of those and then I think it begins to peter out somewhat. Or do you agree?

DEAN: No, I —

NIXON: ITT went longer, but that was a different thing, and it seemed more important.

DEAN: When I told Bob several months ago — I hope they don't think about weekend sessions. He said the way they could have those hearings and do a masterful job on us is to hold one hearing a week on Thursdays — Thursday mornings — they cover it live. That way, you'd get live coverage that day. You'd get the networks that night, the national magazines that week, get the weekend wrap-ups. You could stretch this thing out for nearly —

NIXON: We should insist — our members of the committee, at least, should insist, "Let's get it over with, and go through five-day sessions, and so forth."

DEAN: Yeah. Well, they — you know, they're not that — I don't think they are that —

NIXON: No.

DEAN: — perceptive to figure. [laughs]

NIXON: Well, so be it. This is a — I mean, I noticed in the news summary Buchanan was viewing with alarm the [unclear] the great crisis in the confidence of the presidency, and so forth. [unclear]

DEAN: Well, the best way —

NIXON: How much?

DEAN: Pardon?

NIXON: How much of a crisis? I mean, it'll be in a newspaper — rhetorical — the point is that everything is a crisis. It doesn't have to be a crisis. We've had — screw around with this thing for a while [unclear] it'll be mainly a crisis among the upper intellectual types. The assholes, you know, the —

DEAN: That's right.

NIXON: — soft heads, soft — our own, too — Republicans, Democrats, and the rest. Average people won't think it is much of a crisis unless it affects them. But it'll go on and on and on.

DEAN: Well, I think it'll — you know, I think after the Ervin hearings, they are going to find so much there will be some new revelations. I don't think that the thing will get out of hand. I have no reason to believe it will.

NIXON: Oh, yes, there'll be the revelations in Watergate. They [unclear]? That's the point.

DEAN: Well, they want to find out who —

NIXON: Who — is there a higher-up?

DEAN: Is there a higher-up?

NIXON: They're really — let's face it, after — I think they are really after Haldeman.

DEAN: Haldeman and Mitchell.

NIXON: Mitchell — I mean, Colson is not a big enough name for them. He really isn't. You know, he is a thorn in their side, but Colson's name bothers them none. So they get Colson. They're after Haldeman and after Mitchell. Don't you think so?

DEAN: That's right. Or they'd take Ehrlichman if they could drag him in but they've been unable to drag him in in any way.

NIXON: Ultimately, Haldeman's problem is Chapin, isn't it?

DEAN: Bob's problem is circumstantial.

NIXON: What I meant is, looking at the circumstantial, I don't know that anything — Bob had nothing — didn't know any of those people, like the Hunts and all that bunch. Colson did. But Bob did know Chapin.

DEAN: That's right.

NIXON: Now, what — now however the hell much Chapin knew I'll be goddamn. I don't know.

DEAN: Well, Chapin didn't know anything about the Watergate, and —

NIXON: You don't think so?

DEAN: No. Absolutely not.

NIXON: Did Strachan?

DEAN: Yes.

NIXON: He knew?

DEAN: Yes.

NIXON: About the Watergate?

DEAN: Yes.

NIXON: Well, then, Bob knew. He probably told Bob then. He may not have. He may not have.

DEAN: He was judicious in what he relayed, and — but Strachan is as tough as nails. I —

NIXON: What'll he say? Just go in and say he didn't know?

DEAN: He'll go in and stonewall it and say, "I don't know anything about what you are talking about." He has already done it twice, as you know, in interviews.

NIXON: Yeah. I guess he should, shouldn't he? In the interests of — why, I suppose we can't call that justice, can we? We can't call it [unclear].

DEAN: Well, it —

NIXON: The point is, how do you justify that?

DEAN: It's a personal loyalty with him. He doesn't want it any other way. He didn't have to be told. He didn't have to be asked. It just is something that he found is the way he wanted to handle the situation.

NIXON: But he knew? He knew about Watergate? Strachan did?

DEAN: Mm-hmm.

NIXON: I'll be damned. Well, that's the problem in Bob's case, isn't it? It's not Chapin then, but Strachan. Because Strachan worked for him.

DEAN: Mm-hmm. They would have one hell of a time proving that Strachan had knowledge of it, though.

NIXON: Who knew better? Magruder?

DEAN: Well, Magruder and Liddy.

NIXON: Ah, I see. The other weak link for Bob is Magruder, too. He having hired him and so forth.

DEAN: That's — applies to Mitchell, too.

NIXON: Mitchell — Magruder. Now, where do you see Colson coming into it? Do you think he knew quite a bit? And yet, he could know a great deal about a lot of other things and not a hell of a lot about this, but I don't know.

DEAN: Well, I've never —

NIXON: He sure as hell knows Hunt. That we know. And was very close to him.

DEAN: Chuck has told me that he had no knowledge — specific knowledge of the Watergate incident before it occurred. There have been tidbits that I have raised with Chuck. I have not played any games with him. I said, "Chuck, I have indications — "

NIXON: Don't play games.

DEAN: I don't. I —

NIXON: You've got to be — the lawyer has got to know everything.

DEAN: That's right. And I said, "Chuck, people have said that you were involved in this, involved in that, involved in this." And he said, "I — that's not true," and so on and so forth. I don't — I think that Chuck had knowledge that something was going on over there. A lot of people around here had knowledge that something was going on over there. They didn't have any knowledge of the details of the specifics of the whole thing.

NIXON: You know, that must be an indication, though, of the fact that they had god-damn poor pickings. Because naturally anybody, either Chuck or Bob, was always reporting to me about what was going on. If they ever got any information they would certainly have told me that we got some information, but they never had a goddamn [laughs] thing to report. What was the matter? Did they never get any-thing out of the damn thing?

DEAN: No. I don't think they ever got anything.

NIXON: It was a dry hole, huh?

DEAN: That's right.

NIXON: Jesus Christ.

DEAN: Well, they were just really getting started.

NIXON: Yeah. Yeah. But, Bob one time said something about the fact we got some in-formation about this or that or the other, but I think it was about the [Democratic] convention — what they were planning. I said [unclear]. So I assume that must have been MacGregor — I mean not MacGregor, but Segretti.

DEAN: No.

NIXON: Bob must have known about Segretti.

DEAN: Well, I — Segretti really wasn't involved in the intelligence gathering to speak of at all.

NIXON: Oh, he wasn't?

DEAN: No, he wasn't. He was out just — he was out —

NIXON: Who the hell was gathering intelligence?

DEAN: That was Liddy and his outfit.

NIXON: I see. Apart from Watergate?

DEAN: That's — well, that's right. That was part of their whole — Watergate was part of intelligence gathering, and this —

NIXON: Well, that's a perfectly legitimate thing. I guess that's what it was.

DEAN: What happened is they —

NIXON: What a stupid thing. Pointless. That was the stupid thing.

DEAN: That was incredible. That's right. That's right.

NIXON: I wouldn't want to think that Mitchell would allow — would have allowed this kind of operation to be in the committee.

DEAN: I don't think he knew it was there.

NIXON: You kidding?

DEAN: I don't —

NIXON: You don't think Mitchell knew about this thing?

DEAN: Oh, no, no, no. Don't mis — I don't think he knew that people — I think he knew that Liddy was out intelligence gathering.

NIXON: Well?

DEAN: I don't think he knew that Liddy would use a fellow like McCord, for God's sake, who worked for the Committee [to Re-elect the President]. I can't believe that. You know, that —

NIXON: Hunt? Did Mitchell know Hunt?

DEAN: I don't think Mitchell knew about Hunt either.

NIXON: So Mitchell's thing is to puff the pipe and said, "Gee, I hired this fellow and I told him to gather intelligence, but I" — maybe [unclear].

DEAN: That's right.

NIXON: Magruder says the same thing?

DEAN: Magruder says that, as he did in the trial, he said it was, "Well, of course, my name has been dragged in as the guy who sent Liddy over there," which is an interesting thing. That's a —

NIXON: [unclear]

DEAN: That's right. They said, well, what happened is Magruder asked for a lawyer. He wanted to hire my deputy over there for general counsel and I said, "No way. I can't give him up."

NIXON: Was Liddy your deputy?

DEAN: No, Liddy never worked for me. There was this fellow Fred Fielding, who works for me. And I said, "I can't give him up." He said — Magruder said, "Will you find me a lawyer?" I said, "I will be happy to look around." I checked around the White House. Krogh said, "Liddy might be the man to do it — to go over there. He would be a hell of a good lawyer. He has written some wonderful legal opinions over here for me — "

NIXON: Right.

DEAN: " — and I think he is a good lawyer."

NIXON: Yeah.

DEAN: So I relayed that to Magruder.

NIXON: How the hell does Liddy stand up so well?

DEAN: He's a strange man, Mr. President.

NIXON: Strange or strong, or both?

DEAN: Strange and strong.

NIXON: Good.

DEAN: He — his loyalty, I think, is just beyond the pale. He's just — nothing —

NIXON: He hates the other side, too?

DEAN: Oh, absolutely. He's strong. He really is.

NIXON: What about the hangout thing? [gives a series of instructions to an unknown assistant]

• • •

NIXON: Is it too late to, frankly, go the hangout road? Yes, it is.

DEAN: I think it is. I think — here's the — the hangout road —

NIXON: The hangout road's going to be rejected by — somebody on your staff has rejected it.

DEAN: It was kicked around. Bob and I, and —

NIXON: I know Ehrlichman always felt that it should be hangout. [unclear]

DEAN: Well, I think I convinced him why — that he wouldn't want to hang out either. There is a certain domino situation here. If some things start going, a lot of other things are going to start going, and there are going to be a lot of problems if everything starts falling. So there are dangers, Mr. President. I'd be less than candid if I didn't tell you there are. There's a reason for us not — not everyone going up and testifying.

NIXON: I see. Oh, no, no, no, no, no. I didn't mean go up and have them testifying. I meant —

DEAN: Well, I mean just — they're just starting to hang out and say, "Here's our story — "

NIXON: I mean putting the story out to PR buddies somewhere. "Here's the story, the true story about Watergate." I don't know.

DEAN: They would never believe it.

NIXON: That's the point.

DEAN: The point is — the two things they are working on, on Watergate —

NIXON: Who is "they"? The press?

DEAN: The press —

NIXON: The Democrats?

DEAN: The Democrats, the intellectuals —

NIXON: The Packwoods [recent criticism by Senator Packwood]?

DEAN: Right. Right. "They" would never buy it, as far as, one, White House involvement in the Watergate which I think there is just none — for that incident that occurred over in the Democratic National Committee headquarters. People just — here would — did not know that that was going to be done. I think there are some people who saw the fruits of it, but that's another story. I am talking about the criminal conspiracy to go in there. The other thing is that — the Segretti thing. You hang that out, they wouldn't believe that. They wouldn't believe that Chapin acted on his own to put his old friend [unclear] Segretti in to be a Dick Tuck on somebody else's campaign. They would have to paint it into something more sinister, something more involved — a part of a general plan.

NIXON: Shit, it's not sinister at all. None of it is.

DEAN: No.

NIXON: Segretti's stuff hasn't been a bit sinister.

DEAN: It's quite humorous, as a matter of fact.

NIXON: As a matter of fact, it's just a bunch of crap. It's just a [unclear]. We never knew. Never objected to — you don't object to such damn things. Oh, anyway. On and on and on. No, I tell you this, the last gasp of the, you know — of the — our partisan opponents. They've just got to have something to squeal about.

DEAN: The only thing they have to squeal on.

NIXON: Squeal about that, and perhaps inflation, but that will end. Oh, yeah, they're going to squeal and then they're [unclear]. They're having a hell of a time, you know. They got the hell kicked out of them in the election. They really are. They're going to Watergate around in this town, not so much our opponents, but basically it's the media. I mean, it's the Establishment. The Establishment is dying, and so they've got to show that after some rather significant successes we've had in foreign policy and in the election, they've got to show, "Well, it just is wrong because this is — because of this." In other words, they're trying to use this to smear the whole thing.

DEAN: Well, that's why I — in fact, I keep coming back with this fellow, Sullivan, who could —

NIXON: Who could —

DEAN: — could change the picture.

NIXON: How would it change it though?

DEAN: Well, it —

NIXON: By saying you're another — is that what it is?

DEAN: That's — yeah. But here's another, and it happens to be Democrats. Your — I, you know — I just wish —

NIXON: If you get Kennedy in it, too, I'd be a little more pleased.

DEAN: Well, now, let me tell you something that's — lurks at the bottom of this whole thing.

NIXON: Yeah.

DEAN: If, in going after Segretti, I — Segretti, right — they go after Kalmbach's bank records, you'll recall that sometime back — maybe you, perhaps, didn't know about this, it's quite possible. That right after [Ted Kennedy's role in the death of Mary Jo Kopechne at] Chappaquiddick somebody [Anthony Ulasewicz] was put up there to start observing. Within six hours.

NIXON: Did we?

DEAN: That's right.

NIXON: I didn't know that.

DEAN: That man watched that — he was there for every second of Chappaquiddick, for a year, and almost two years he worked for — he worked for Jack Caulfield, who was originally on John's staff.

NIXON: Oh, I've heard of Caulfield, yeah.

DEAN: He worked for Caulfield originally and then he worked for — when Caulfield worked for John, and then when I came over here I inherited Caulfield and this guy was still on this same thing.

NIXON: Yeah.

DEAN: Well, if they get to those bank records between — it starts on July of '69 through June of '71, and they say, "What are these about? Who is this fellow that's up in New York that you paid?" There comes Chappaquiddick with a vengeance. This guy is a twenty-year detective on the New York State — New York City Police Department.

NIXON: In other words, we—

DEAN: He is ready to disprove and to show that everything from—

NIXON: We don't consider that wrong.

DEAN: Well, if they get to it, it's going to come out and the whole thing is going to turn around on that one. I mean, if Kennedy knew the bear trap he was walking into—

NIXON: How do we know—why don't we get it out anyway?

DEAN: Well, we sort of saved it. [laughs]

NIXON: Does he have any record? Is it any good?

DEAN: He is probably the most knowledgeable man in the country. He can't—you know, there are certain things he runs up against walls when they closed the records down—things he can't get. But he can ask all of the questions and get some—many of the answers. As a twenty-year detective—but we don't want to surface him right now. But if things ever surfaced, this is what they'll get.

NIXON: Now, how will Kalmbach explain that he'd hired this [unclear] in view of Chappaquiddick? Did he—out of what type of funds?

DEAN: We'd have—he had money left over from preconvention—

NIXON: Are they going to investigate those funds, too?

DEAN: They are funds that were quite legal. There's nothing illegal with those funds.

NIXON: How can they investigate them?

DEAN: They can't.

NIXON: Huh?

DEAN: They—the only—the—what they would—happens what would occur, you see, is they would stumble into this in going back to, say, '71 on Kalmbach's bank records. They've already asked for a lot of his bank records in connection with Segretti, as to how he paid Segretti.

NIXON: Are they going to go back as far as Chappaquiddick?

DEAN: Well, yeah, but this fellow worked into '71 on this. He was up there. He talked to everybody in that town. He—you know, he's the one who caused a lot of embarrassment for Kennedy already by saying—he went up there as a newspaperman. "So why aren't you checking this? Why aren't you looking there?" And pointing the press's attention to things. Gosh, the guy did a masterful job. I have never been—had the full report.

NIXON: Coming back to the Sullivan thing, you'd better now go ahead and talk to him. You will now talk to Moore—again to Moore and then what?

DEAN: I'll see if we have something that's viable. And if it's—

NIXON: In other words, have you talked to Sullivan again?

DEAN: Oh, yes. Yes, I plan on it.

NIXON: Why the hell don't you get him in and talk to him? [unclear]

DEAN: Well, he's—I asked him last night and he said, "John, give me a day or so to get my, all my recollections together."

NIXON: Right.

DEAN: And that was yesterday. So I thought I would call him this evening and say, "Bill, I'd just like to know—"

NIXON: You see, the fact that you've talked to him will become known. So maybe the best thing is to say, "I am not concerned here," and you say that he's to turn this over, and you say we will not handle it. Then make—then anyway, it gets to the committee. Aren't they going to say, "The White House turns over information on the FBI"? That's the—I don't know how the Christ to get it down there.

DEAN: Well, that's what I think I can kick around with Dick Moore. He and I do very well just bouncing these things—

NIXON: Yeah.

DEAN: —back and forth and coming up with something that we don't have to be embarrassed about it.

NIXON: I think a newsman—a hell of a break for a newspaper.

DEAN: Oh, yeah.

NIXON: A hell of a story. Maybe the *Star* would just run a hell of a story, I mean a real bust on the FBI. Then, and then the committee member, the man you, for example, on this basis could call Gurney, and say, "Now look, we're onto something very hot here. I can just tell you—I'm not going to tell you anything more. Go after it, forget you ever had this call." Then he goes.

DEAN: Mm-hmm.

NIXON: It seems to me that that's a very effective way to get it out.

DEAN: Mm-hmm. Another thing is, I don't think Sullivan would give up the White House. Sullivan, as I said, could—there's one liability in Sullivan here, is that's his knowledge of the earlier things that occurred—

NIXON: That we did?

DEAN: That we did.

NIXON: Well, now you should tell them. Oh, you mean he wouldn't—he'd say, "I did no political work at all. My work in the—for the Nixon administration was solely in the national security."

DEAN: That's right.

NIXON: And that is totally true.

DEAN: That's right.

NIXON: Okay. Well, good luck.

DEAN: All right, sir.

NIXON: It's never dull, is it?

DEAN: Never.

"I have to respectfully decline the invitation of the committee."

March 14, 1973, 8:55 a.m.

Richard Nixon and John Dean

WHITE HOUSE TELEPHONE

The week leading up to the March 21 "cancer on the presidency" conversation between Richard Nixon and John Dean is arguably the most important week of the Watergate investigation. Nixon's Watergate defense experienced a serious setback as a result of the twin blows of Watergate burglar James McCord's letter to Judge John Sirica that suggested witnesses had perjured themselves and that yet-unscathed higher-ups were involved in the Watergate cover-up. By the end of the week, Nixon's "desk officer" on Watergate — Dean's term for himself — would question his future as the president's counsel. Here, Dean consults with Nixon on how he should respond to the Senate Judiciary Committee's request for him to appear as part of the Gray confirmation hearings.

• • •

NIXON: Hello?

DEAN: Good morning, Mr. President.

NIXON: I thought that before you — before Ziegler went out that maybe you and he would — that you probably ought to come over and let me — and run by your questions and answers today, don't you think so?

DEAN: I think that'd probably be a good — very good idea.

NIXON: Yeah. So, that he's — he may be the [unclear] — have you had the chance to — if — you probably talked to them last night, but you haven't had any chance to [unclear] this morning, huh?

DEAN: No. I — we do have the invitation and response I've been kicking around to Eastland. That's something that, probably, Ron ought to have in hand this morning —

NIXON: Sure.

DEAN: — also before he goes out.

NIXON: Sure.

DEAN: They did not, as you're aware now, ask me any specific questions.

NIXON: Yeah. Well, how it stands then, is about like we anticipated, isn't it? That is — it's an invitation which — do all the Republicans, as — join this as a matter of tactics, or — what is the situation on that? Or do they honestly feel you should be subpoenaed?

DEAN: Well, I think they're in this position. They're afraid to say — and this is probably indicative of what we're going to face all along — "Why shouldn't he come up? Why shouldn't we invite him? What do we need to hide?"

NIXON: Yeah. Yeah.

DEAN: "We don't want to block. We don't want to whitewash."

NIXON: Yeah.

DEAN: And [unclear] —

NIXON: Well, why — you haven't got anybody that would say, "Look, let's find a procedure where he could come up"? Won't any of them step up to that?

DEAN: Well, in the response that I'm — I've drafted, I have not — I wasn't in the meeting where they kicked it around. I thought it best to not be in the meeting this — to hear what, you know, somebody's — a lawyer's not always his own best counsel.

NIXON: Sure.

DEAN: [laughs]

NIXON: Oh, hell, you aren't the one that's —

DEAN: But it's —

NIXON: — that's involved here.

DEAN: No, I know, but I did say in the response that, after the acknowledgment of the letter, "as a matter of the president's personal staff, and consistent with the president's statement of March 12 — "

NIXON: Mm-hmm.

DEAN: " — on the subject of White House testimonial appearances, I have to respectfully decline the invitation of the committee to formally appear and testify. However, as the president has stated, it's the policy of this administration to provide all necessary and relevant information to the Congress. And if members of the president's personal staff can provide such information in a matter that preserves intact the constitutional separation of the branches, such information will be provided. Accordingly — "

NIXON: Rather than, "if members of the staff" — the way I would state that: "and members of the president's staff will provide such that information in ways that" — I think it'd be — I'd state it positively.

DEAN: Right. Then I went on to say, "Accordingly, if the Senate Committee on the Judiciary believes that I can be of assistance in providing relevant information, and wishes to submit questions to me that have a bearing on the nomination of Mr. Gray, I am pleased to respond consistent with the president's statement."

NIXON: You don't want to indicate that you're pleased to respond in a — with a sworn statement. Or do you think — ?

DEAN: Well, I thought why not maintain all options at all times —

NIXON: Right.

DEAN: — here and just — if they come back with a question, if they're — even do that, then swear to them?

NIXON: Mm-hmm. Don't want to say so now?

DEAN: No.

NIXON: Yeah.

DEAN: Because — if — you know, there's a possibility we could set a precedent here —

NIXON: Yeah?

DEAN: — of a non-sworn response to interrogatories.

NIXON: Yeah. Yeah.

DEAN: Just — that's all the better for later precedents.

NIXON: Yeah. Yeah. Which means that — it's — it probably won't work, but nevertheless, then that's all right, too. Then we could come to the other thing if we have to.

DEAN: That's right.

NIXON: If they — because they might come back and say, "Well, you're just going to have a response. What does that mean?" All right, fine, then we'll make it sworn response. "What more do you want, except to badger the witness up there in front of your committee?"

DEAN: That's right.

NIXON: Mm-hmm. Mm-hmm. Okay, after you've had a chance to run it by the others, and so forth — I don't to talk to the — you know, the difficulty here is that I don't want to get Haldeman and Ehrlichman in the thing because they're both parties in interest —

DEAN: Mm-hmm?

NIXON: — but — and you're not. You know — [laughs] — that's — well, that's quite true. You see, because both of them — and I think the best thing is for you to have Ziegler and I to talk about it. And then —

DEAN: All right.

NIXON: — let me make a rather cool decision about it — as to what we ought to do. Don't you agree?

DEAN: I think that'd be a very —

NIXON: Now, you get the views of the others, however. You get all their views and see what they are. Have you — come over whenever you're ready.

DEAN: I shall do, sir.

NIXON: Fine. Bye-bye.

The threat of renewed bombing in Vietnam

March 16, 1973, 7:41 p.m.
Richard Nixon and Henry Kissinger
WHITE HOUSE TELEPHONE

During the day on March 16, President Nixon called an unscheduled news conference to announce that he was strongly considering new attacks by air on North Vietnam. He was responding to reports a few days earlier that the North Vietnamese had moved thirty thousand troops and three hundred tanks toward the border with South Vietnam. Any such repositioning would have been a violation of the Peace Accords, and so Nixon employed what he himself called his "irrationability." Kissinger regarded Nixon's irrationality as one of his "great assets." In the same conversation, the president expressed his utter disrespect for the air force, even consoling himself that if he did order the attacks, the pilots wouldn't hit anything anyway. Although the plan to bomb North Vietnam was largely a bluff, Nixon was prepared to back it up and send a message to the region with a new air campaign against Cambodia.*

        •   •   •

NIXON: Hello?

KISSINGER: Mr. President?

---

* R. W. Apple Jr., "President Warns Hanoi Not to Move Equipment South," *New York Times,* March 16, 1973, p. 1.

NIXON: Henry, anything new today?

KISSINGER: No, it has been fairly quiet. The head of the North Vietnamese, the member of the North Vietnamese Economic Commission, took aside our guy and was bleeding all over him how they were observing the treaty and how we — our intelligence was wrong. And they were not infiltrating. So they are getting nervous.

NIXON: What about our guy? Did he have the gumption to say something?

KISSINGER: Oh, yeah, we had him well coached.

NIXON: Good.

KISSINGER: We had him very well coached. I think just clobbering them for two days next week is going to be very healthy to them.

NIXON: Yeah, because we know they are violating, so what the hell?

KISSINGER: We know they are violating, Mr. President, and they are not going to face us down now.

NIXON: Well, if they want — if they really — I just can't believe they seriously want the economic thing and could blow the whole thing because of a bombing. That's the point.

KISSINGER: They won't blow it.

NIXON: But the point is what the hell the good the bombing does is irrelevant I think perhaps. It isn't going to do much good. The air force never hits a goddamn thing, as you know, except when they put it over Hanoi.

KISSINGER: It will do a little good, but it just raise the price of admission. What it will really do is to show that even while you have prisoners there you are just putting it to them.

NIXON: Yes, I suppose.

KISSINGER: I think that our best hope for preserving this accord is your reputation, Mr. President.

NIXON: Yeah. Yep, interesting thing that Denton told me that when he was talking to them this high-ranking fellow that saw him two or three days before that something that impressed the high-ranking guy was that the prisoners had been so irrational in their conduct. The fact that they — had they been rational they would have caved, but that they were irrational and that was the thing that disturbed them about the president that he was so irrational in the way he conducted himself. So the irrationability, he said, Denton's point was that he said the irrationability really got through to them.

KISSINGER: That is your greatest — one of your great assets with them.

NIXON: And the fact that the — all of your friends in the press — you know, all your old Harvard and other colleagues — constantly talk about irrationability.

KISSINGER: Of course the funny thing is the Chinese all over the world are saying you are the best force for peace. They are the best propagandists we have got.

NIXON: Really?

KISSINGER: Oh, yeah, we are picking up — I don't bother you with it, but we are picking up intelligence all over the world. They are really puffing you up.

NIXON: Because they realize that without us they are nothing.

KISSINGER: Exac — they are in mortal danger.

NIXON: Right.

KISSINGER: And that you are the only one that had the guts to draw the conclusion from it. You know, McGovern or even Humphrey would have bled all over them about understanding and communication —

NIXON: Right.

KISSINGER: — which doesn't mean a damn thing.

NIXON: Right. Mm-hmm.

KISSINGER: And, we are delivering your letters tomorrow morning.

NIXON: Right. To the Chinese?

KISSINGER: Yeah.

NIXON: Right.

KISSINGER: Well, we have until Wednesday, Mr. President. We can always call the other thing off.

NIXON: Let's wait. I mean, we may not call it off. I mean, my point is, we are going to go forward unless they do something.

KISSINGER: Well, that is my very strong advice.

NIXON: Right. Oh, hell yes.

KISSINGER: And that they would have to do something —

NIXON: No, I haven't heard of anything they're going to do yet that sounds like anything but a bunch of damn words which are pretty cheap.

KISSINGER: That is exactly right.

NIXON: And if we can, the only thing that is disturbing to me about it is the ineffectiveness of the air force and the way, you know, except for when we did the Hanoi drill. But goddamn it on the [Ho Chi Minh] Trail, Henry, they never have been worth a damn, as you know. Never been worth a damn.

KISSINGER: They have never had the targets they have now.

NIXON: You don't think so?

KISSINGER: No, they have never —

NIXON: Now, I want a plan this time though that doesn't, you know, give them a lot of warning, and do it all in the daytime and they are gone at night, and we go in and drop a lot of, you know, nothings. Goddamn it! Let's have some surprise. Go back and forth. And then end, and let them think we have gone. Now is Abrams — I mean, well, of course Abrams is in it, and everybody else. But goddamn it, does Moorer got a good plan or not?

KISSINGER: It looks like a good plan to me, because they are going to fake as if they are going into Cambodia. And in the daytime they really have a photo — I have seen the photograph. These trucks are bumper-to-bumper. They are going to get a lot of trucks. You see they do not have to do it at night this time.

NIXON: Yeah.

KISSINGER: They are going to do well, but that is not the real justification. The real justification is to set up a situation where you —

NIXON: They fear it would happen in other places.

KISSINGER: And where that they fear it may happen in the fall.

NIXON: Sure.

KISSINGER: If that is when they want —

NIXON: And that it may happen in other places.

KISSINGER: That's our big point. I will be in Mexico, Mr. President, for the next week.

NIXON: Yeah.

KISSINGER: I am going down there tonight.

NIXON: Yeah.

KISSINGER: But, I will have good communications, and I am easy to reach.

NIXON: Right. Now with regard to the — that's fine you are going to work on the World Report and all that, but the point is that with regard to this whole situation on the North we just keep the heat right on them.

KISSINGER: Right.

NIXON: Everybody is all programmed at State and Defense. There isn't going to be any backwash on this.

KISSINGER: Absolutely not. They are all on board.

NIXON: And the Chinese and the Russians have both been informed so they know.

KISSINGER: They have not been informed what we will do, but they both got very serious warnings.

NIXON: They had a very serious public warning which they will pay attention to.

KISSINGER: That's right.

NIXON: Well, what is your feeling about the bargaining position we have in view of the statements of the Senate caucus, the Democratic Senate caucus? What the hell does it do to us? Does it destroy us, or not quite?

KISSINGER: It doesn't destroy us but it means — here again I think, Mr. President, we have to take them on fairly soon. These bastards made it impossible to negotiate — nearly impossible to negotiate a peace. Now they are making it nearly impossible to preserve a peace. Now they are wrecking us in Europe.

NIXON: They are. That is my point.

KISSINGER: And I think we just have to attack them as being —

NIXON: This isn't just wrecking us in Europe, it is wrecking the chance to negotiate a settlement, a reduction of forces on a mutual basis which would produce —

KISSINGER: You must — of course, they wouldn't dare to put it through two months before Brezhnev comes over here.

NIXON: Well, maybe not.

KISSINGER: We are going to get way ahead of them again but still that doesn't change the moral issue.

NIXON: Yeah, I hope that this gets across. I'd get it across to — good God! Can't some of the columnists or somebody pick this up and knock the shit out of them on this? What is the matter with [Joe] Alsop and the rest? Are they all afraid of this kind of — ?

KISSINGER: Oh, no, Alsop is all right but most of them are pretty stupid.

NIXON: They aren't stupid. They are gutless.

KISSINGER: Gutless.

NIXON: That's right. They know what the Senate is doing. They don't say it.

KISSINGER: Well, except that, I think — essentially, in foreign policy you are likely to win any battle that you really join right now.

NIXON: Maybe. I wouldn't overestimate that though because these people are so partisan now and the mood of the country is so peacenik. You know everything — you know, we got peace, and we are meeting with the Russians and the rest. Why do we have to have all these arms, and why can't we get out of Europe and all the rest. You know?

KISSINGER: Well, it is going to be tough. You would have thought that someone who accomplished what you did would then be left alone for a while.

NIXON: That's my point. They are not leaving us alone. You see, they are making it harder, aren't they?

KISSINGER: Exactly.

NIXON: You get that across to a few people before you leave.

KISSINGER: Right, Mr. President.

NIXON: [Journalists] Dick Wilson, Bill White — call them tonight and tell them goddamn it, they ought to write something. Okay?

KISSINGER: Right, Mr. President.

NIXON: Okay.

"We will win!"

March 16, 1973, 8:14 p.m.
Richard Nixon and John Dean
WHITE HOUSE TELEPHONE

At the end of the week, Dean checked in with Nixon to let him know the latest news. Senators Sam Ervin and Howard Baker had met with Attorney General Richard Kleindienst to work out a mechanism to transmit information from FBI files to the Ervin Committee. Judge Sirica was planning to sentence the Watergate burglars the following week, which would be the talk of the town. Finally, Dean reported that his Watergate investigation concluded that there was "not a scintilla" of evidence that led to the White House. At the same time, he told Nixon that he was hesitant to put that in a written report. "There is a degree of impossibility in writing a sort of let's-hang-it-all-out report without creating problems," Dean said, "that would cause difficulty for some who've already testified." Despite that warning, Dean remained a team player. "We will win!" he said.

• • •

NIXON: Hello?

DEAN: Yes, sir.

NIXON: Any report on the meeting with Kleindienst?

DEAN: There was a report, a good report, a very successful meeting. He laid it out —

NIXON: Who'd he meet with?

DEAN: — exactly what he would do, and he said they didn't balk an inch.

NIXON: Who'd he talk to? Ervin and — ?

DEAN: Ervin, and Baker, and both counsel.

NIXON: Mm-hmm. Mm-hmm.

DEAN: And they bought it. That, one, there would be a summary report, a synopsis report, which would be issued to them only, not for any other members of their committee.

NIXON: Mm-hmm.

DEAN: It would be for investigative purposes only. It could not be put in the record. It could not be displayed publicly in any way. And if they had any questions about that, the synopsis report, then they could come down to the bureau — those four — and look at the raw file they wanted to look at, if they contested something that was in the synopsis.

NIXON: Mm-hmm.

DEAN: That was it. Zero.

NIXON: In other words, this is a report that would be given by Gray?

DEAN: By Gray. Right.

NIXON: Mm-hmm.

DEAN: They put out — in fact, there's a press release that Ervin put out that said they had worked out a satisfactory arrangement with the Department of Justice to receive the necessary information from the FBI in a way that would protect any innocent persons from damage.

NIXON: Mm-hmm. Hmm —

DEAN: And that's the — that went out this afternoon, and —

NIXON: Mm-hmm.

DEAN: — we got a question. Ziegler got a question, and the press office was asked — was the arrangement satisfactory with us? "Absolutely."

NIXON: Mm-hmm.

DEAN: So that — again, that's the spirit of cooperation of turning over information, and —

NIXON: Mm-hmm.

DEAN: — no problem at all.

NIXON: Well, you should go forward, and working with Dick Moore and others, with regard to the matter of getting sort of a general statement that might be prepared — I mean to be given to me after the court sentences. You see?

DEAN: Right, I —

NIXON: I don't know whether we will want to use it or not, but we, in order to know, we've got to see what it could be. You see?

DEAN: I just learned late this afternoon that Sirica is going to, definitely, sentence on Fri — a week from today.

NIXON: Mm-hmm.

DEAN: He plans to give a speech from the bench at that time —

NIXON: Mm-hmm.

DEAN: — that the government is recommending no specific term in years for any of the defendants. Rather, prison sentences for all of them, but not a specified term of years. But the whole thing is up to him —

NIXON: Up to the jury? Then, how — who determines the term of years?

DEAN: Sirica himself will.

NIXON: Oh. Mm-hmm. Then, when will he announce that?

DEAN: That'll be on Friday. At least for the five that pleaded. They may not sentence the two that are on appeal.

NIXON: Mm-hmm. And, so he'll announce the sentences a week from Friday?

DEAN: That's correct. A week from this — today.

NIXON: A week from today. Mm-hmm.

DEAN: I had a long conversation with Dick Moore just this evening. I just arrived home and Dick and I really have been talking all this time about —

NIXON: Sure.

DEAN: — this whole thing, and there is a degree of impossibility in writing a sort of let's-hang-it-all-out report without creating problems that would open up a new grand jury —

NIXON: Mm-hmm.

DEAN: — without creating problems that would cause difficulty for some who've already testified.

NIXON: Mm-hmm.

DEAN: I've caveated some of these to Dick. Dick doesn't have — possess all the knowledge I have.

NIXON: Mm-hmm.

DEAN: Particularly this fellow assigned with Dick.

NIXON: Yeah. [laughs]

DEAN: And, in fact, it might — I told him, I said, "It might be to your attorneys, Dick, [laughs] to write from your basic —"

NIXON: Yeah. Yeah.

DEAN: And, so we've planned to —

NIXON: And then you could look it over. [laughs]

DEAN: Right. We plan to meet tomorrow and see what —

NIXON: Right.

DEAN: — we can frank out, and —

NIXON: Well, that's something is worth, perhaps, doing in terms of the off — well, frankly, what is, what could be helpful if it could be worked out, or just something that where, in the most general terms, the — is virtually saying what I might even say in answer to a press conference question, but in more general terms, that an investigation has been conducted, and we find this, and that, and the other thing. And whack. Just like that. You see what I mean?

DEAN: Mm-hmm.

NIXON: Rather than going into the specifics of who did what to whom. You see what I mean?

DEAN: I do.

NIXON: So that — so that people could say, "Well — "

DEAN: Not a total stonewall.

NIXON: Oh, no, no. And not a total — and not supposed to be a total answer.

DEAN: Right.

NIXON: But, simply saying, "Well, the president has finally said, 'Now that it's over this is it.'" And the — after this is over we can now say that this person — these people were not involved, and et cetera. These were, and — I don't know. But at least think in those terms to see if something could be worked out. In very general terms, I realize the problems of getting too specific, because then — then you do open up the possibility of, "Why didn't you say that? Why didn't you say that?" But you just put it in very general terms, you see?

DEAN: Mm-hmm.

NIXON: I don't know. Do you think that's possible?

DEAN: It's going to be tough, but I think — I think it's a good exercise and a drill that is absolutely essential we do — to go through —

NIXON: Yeah, that's the point. The exercise is important.

DEAN: It sharpens thinking and it, as I — as —

NIXON: Find out what our vulnerabilities are and where we are and so forth and so on.

DEAN: Right. I would — there's [laughs] — maybe there will be sometime when I should possibly report a little fuller than I really have, so you really can appreciate in full some of the vulnerable points and where they lead to.

NIXON: That's right.

DEAN: I don't think that should be a written document right now.

NIXON: Oh, by no means. No, by — I don't want any damn written document about any of that.

DEAN: No.

NIXON: I'm just speaking of a document that is put out.

DEAN: A public document.

NIXON: Yeah.

DEAN: Right.

NIXON: Which you, as sort of a report, perhaps, which we could then deliver to Ervin. You know?

DEAN: That might — it's gonna be tough, but I say it's certainly worth the effort —

NIXON: Yeah. Just sort of a general thing, and very general, very general. You know? Without — by all means, laying off of — don't get into the, "Well, we investigated this. We investigated that. We saw this. We deny this. We support this. And so forth." Lay off of all that. I have in mind a sort of — basically, so that it can be said that something was presented that I have seen, or that — you know what I mean? So that they — so that my reiterated statements from time to time, that, "Well, no one on the White House staff is involved" have some basis, you see.

DEAN: A lot of the — a lot of my conclusions were based on the fact that there was not a scintilla of evidence in the investigation that led anywhere to the White House.

NIXON: Mm-hmm.

DEAN: There's nothing in the FBI file that indicates anybody in the White House was involved.

NIXON: Mm-hmm.

DEAN: There's nothing in what was presented before the grand jury indicating —

NIXON: Mm-hmm.

DEAN: — White House involvement.

NIXON: Well, just saying some of those things could be helpful.

DEAN: That's right.

NIXON: See? It could be helpful —

DEAN: [unclear] —

NIXON: And then we just put it out and then let, let the committee try to prove otherwise.

DEAN: And, I understand that they will not get the grand jury minutes, which is good because the grand jury is even more thorough than the FBI.

NIXON: Mm-hmm.

DEAN: The committee's starting ten paces behind, and Ervin does not, I'm told, have a total disposition for what he's doing. He just doesn't relish it. He wants to find out things. He's —

NIXON: Why not?

DEAN: He's more excited about the confrontation on executive privilege, I think, than he is about what else he might find.

NIXON: We would welcome that, wouldn't we?

DEAN: Oh, he'd love that.

NIXON: Well, so would we.

DEAN: Mm-hmm.

NIXON: I mean, let's have it. Particularly if it's on you — oh, no, he won't have it on you. He'll —

DEAN: No, I don't think he'll [laughs] bite for that —

NIXON: On Chapin, huh?

DEAN: Chapin or Colson.

NIXON: Mm-hmm.

DEAN: I think that the other part of the report that we can probably put out with even greater detail than, say, Watergate is Segretti. And that —

NIXON: That I would like.

DEAN: And that — you see, that would put us in a very forthcoming posture.

NIXON: Mm-hmm.

DEAN: Here's —

NIXON: We could point out that the one case has now been determined by the courts, and that we have nothing to indicate that the White House was involved. Now, second, with regard to Segretti, let's lay all this — let's lay it all out. Here it is.

DEAN: Now, sure, it's a little embarrassing —

NIXON: The problem there —

DEAN: It's nothing evil. It's nothing —

NIXON: Well, it's less embarrassing than what's been charged, and the innuendo.

DEAN: That's right.

NIXON: Of course, I realize the major problem there is the financing, but even that.

DEAN: That's going to have to be answered well before Ervin —

NIXON: That's gonna come out. That's right, so you —

DEAN: — so we might as well leave it out —

NIXON: Yeah. That's right. So, you can think about it. Okay?

DEAN: All right, sir. Well —

NIXON: Fine.

DEAN: We will win! [laughs]

Nixon suggests that Dean prepare a report
March 17, 1973, 1:25 p.m.
Richard Nixon and John Dean
OVAL OFFICE

Nixon's newest idea regarding Watergate was the need for a written report. Describing the break-in, in both planning and execution, the report would be the truth and nothing but the truth. It wouldn't, however, be the whole truth. As Nixon outlined the report for Dean, it was apparent that the text would present conclusions without full documentation. As Dean discussed the proposition, Nixon was particular in determining that Dean didn't know about the break-in before it occurred — though he himself was furtive about his own knowledge of the crime. In fact, when Dean expressed surprise that anyone would bother breaking into the national offices of a political party, saying, "Anybody who's walked around a national committee knows that there's nothing there," Nixon responded by starting to explain just what there was to be gained by such a break-in. He changed topics without finishing. They once again discussed the idea of somehow utilizing former FBI official William Sullivan.

• • •

NIXON: Well, I was wondering what your latest developments were. Do you plan to keep your boys all hopping around?

DEAN: Well, hopefully. Dick Moore and I are going to work on it this afternoon and today.

NIXON: Where do you work?

DEAN: Pardon?

NIXON: Where do you do it — are you staying?

DEAN: Over in [unclear].

NIXON: [unclear]

DEAN: Well, to work over in my office. It's pretty quiet around here today.

NIXON: Anytime that you need to [unclear] it helps, Camp David place is very conducive to that kind of thoughtful work [unclear].

DEAN: I think that might be a good thing. I mentioned that to Mitchell yesterday, that we probably need a good sit-down-kick-this-thing-around session. I would say that as a result of your press conference that the forward momentum that was going and building stopped, and that it fluctuated and again we're in this breathing space. The press this morning is different, for example. It says the — an accord has been reached. The *Post* is even willing to say that as far as the information being provided. It couldn't — I try to find something nasty to say but they realized that it was a cooperative effort. What we have to do is be in a good posture come the opening gun on Ervin's hearings. It's always been to me the most troublesome thing is that if he were going to be nonbiased, if he were going to be nonpartisan, if he were going to be fair and just, and the judge he likes to believe he is, ninety percent of his hearings would be held in executive session —

NIXON: Sure.

DEAN: — rather than —

NIXON: And also the ten percent of them or so [unclear].

DEAN: That's right. That's right. What I've been trying to conceive of is some way that Ervin himself could come to that position. If he did, he would be harming innocent people, but he will be dragging people into things that — it's like really dragging them in, but that's the name of the game in the city and he's going to love to play it.

NIXON: You'd be interested to know that — well, to hark back to the Hiss case. We did that on the Hiss case.

DEAN: You went into executive?

NIXON: The first confrontation, between I — we interviewed — we took — after Chambers went on and called into session, he tried to challenge it.

DEAN: Mm-hmm.

NIXON: Hiss went on and denied it. Then after that, I — executive session with Chambers alone for a couple of hours [unclear] an executive session, Hiss alone. And then the two together in New York in a hotel room.

DEAN: And that was private also, huh?

NIXON: Executive — and then only after the executive, would we go public.

DEAN: Well, that — you know, that would be the fair way for Ervin to play it. And when you're ready to go public —

NIXON: Yeah. Well, anyway, that's a possibility. The thing I guess you've got to figure is to — whether you and Moore, perhaps even individually or [unclear] write the thing collectively — nothing can be done collectively when you're writing a paper, and say that — and sit down and write what I would call a general, a very general statement that maybe I just send to Ervin. I would say, "Senator, you'd be interested to know what the hell we've got here." Here's my point. The — that's one way. The other way would be to put it out. The arg — of course the fact that it's being done, the point that I make is this: we don't want to be in a position of Dean and the White House — you and Dean, et cetera, are acting as the president's counsel to forward him information on the basis of it's confidential. You might just say, "Now I can't say that this is all — everything. But it's everything we know." We can say basically — this would be right after the judge sentences — based on what we [unclear] investigation has been made [unclear] was not involved, or if he was this is all he knows. Chapin — this is what he knows and I'd go into Chapin and Segretti and just lay it all out there. [unclear] and Colson, you know what I mean?

DEAN: Mm-hmm.

NIXON: And — or without going into it you could say no one on the White House staff is involved, so forth and so on. This may be that those kind of [unclear] statements. What I am getting at is that the moment that you get it too specific, then I realize that they're going to say, "Why did you withhold something?" that you could simply say, "Here are the conclusions we have reached based on your evaluation of the information that came to your attention." They got a chance to look at all the other. We want to be as helpful as we can. "Here's what we've concluded and we welcome you to review it."

DEAN: You've raised something that — let me just take one step further. It might be a very interesting approach. If Ervin were to be called down here, and given sworn statements that were given to you, that's after I have prepared my report on Haldeman, Ehrlichman, Colson, Dean, everybody —

NIXON: Right.

DEAN: They stated to the degree of their knowledge — now what would be in there that would be embarrassing politically. And you might put Ervin on the spot — is — because I don't think he would want to embarrass for the sake of embarrassment alone — is that there was knowledge that there was an intelligence operation in place.

NIXON: I say that?

DEAN: But no knowledge that these people were going to do something criminal.

NIXON: That's right.

DEAN: And to the contrary, Mr. President, efforts by the White House to cut off these things that would be illegal.

NIXON: As a matter of fact, as you point out, you could make some self-serving statements all over that I had put — I had given instructions to Mitchell, and I said that he was to pass on to the campaign committee. I did not see them at that point. In other words, there was to be no acting. There was to be no violence. That we expected ours to be — we had to get intelligence on it from the standpoint of security, et cetera —

DEAN: Mm-hmm.

NIXON: — to be prepared. You know? Put that whole thing out. Put out the seamy record of what we expected in San Diego [at the Republican convention], what we expected there and there's what we were trying to get at through intelligence, et cetera. You know what I mean?

DEAN: Mm-hmm.

NIXON: But point out that—you could just say, "Here are some sworn statements signed by [unclear] people that I've gotten from them. I—it was for the record."

DEAN: Mm-hmm.

NIXON: "Want further information? You can ask for it."

DEAN: The interesting thing is in the sequence of the way things occurred. I don't know if anyone has ever taken you through this, but the last involvement to my knowledge of the White House was when I came back from a meeting—

NIXON: [unclear] answer, "I know nothing about Watergate."

DEAN: Right, well—

NIXON: I stayed miles away from it so I didn't know even if there was a White House involvement.

DEAN: Well, there was—you know, there was a preliminary discussion of setting up an intelligence operation—

NIXON: Yeah.

DEAN: —and the last, and the last—

NIXON: [unclear]

DEAN: All right. And the last phase of that—

NIXON: Phase of it was—

DEAN: I came back from a meeting with Mitchell, Magruder, and Liddy and told—after telling them that they couldn't discuss this in front of the attorney general of the United States, came back and told Bob that if there's something like that going on, we've got to stay two miles away from it, ten miles away from it, because it just is not right and we can't have any part of it. Bob said, "I agree" and "We'll have no part of it." That was where I thought it was turned off and the next thing I heard was that—was this—the break-in on June 17, which was—

NIXON: [unclear]

DEAN: —over six months later.

NIXON: You heard discussion of that, but you didn't hear any discussion of bugging, did you, in that—your meetings? Or did you?

DEAN: Yeah, I did. That's what distressed me quite a bit.

NIXON: Oh, you did?

DEAN: Mm-hmm.

NIXON: Who raised it? Liddy?

DEAN: That's right.

NIXON: Liddy at that point said we ought to do some bugging?

DEAN: Right. Mitchell just sat there on his pipe and puffed and said nothing. He didn't agree to it, and I—at the end of the meeting—

NIXON: Well, you won't need to say in your statement about the bugging.

DEAN: No.

NIXON: You could say that they were going to engage in intelligence operations. You said the main thing is that it must be totally legal and that the laws and ethics and so forth and so on. You came back and Bob says, he says [unclear]. You know what I mean?

DEAN: Right.

NIXON: I would think, make — I think you could make self-serving goddamn statements [unclear] and all that. Now —

DEAN: The embarrassment for you would be that the White House knew that there was an intelligence operation going, but —

NIXON: But — why did you mean embarrassed?

DEAN: All right.

NIXON: I think — everybody said it was a naive basis. Who knows? Haldeman knows, right?

DEAN: Right.

NIXON: And of course, but you could be there if you justify it along the basis that —

DEAN: We knew it was to be legal.

NIXON: Not only be legal but that it was totally necessary because of the violence, the demonstrations, the heck — the kind of activities that we knew were threatened against us in our convention and in our campaign and in all of our appearances. We had to have intelligence and about what they were going to do that we could in turn issue instructions to [unclear] to find out what they're doing, and something like that.

DEAN: This is another point on not using the FBI for political purposes either. While we would collect normal demonstration intelligence, we needed specific intelligence as to were there concerted efforts by opposing political people to demonstrate, cause disruption, get these peaceniks whipped up into a frenzy, and the like.

NIXON: That's right.

DEAN: That's not the function of the bureau.

NIXON: You see, I've been thinking I should say, for example, the matter was discussed as to whether or not the bureau should be — it was pointed out that in the 1964 elections, the bureau was used by [unclear].

DEAN: Mm-hmm.

NIXON: Could you get that — the [unclear]?

DEAN: Mm-hmm.

NIXON: You get my point?

DEAN: Mm-hmm.

NIXON: And that's — then Haldeman said under no circumstances, or mention them whatever they are. It all had to be done privately because the bureau may not be involved in a partisan contest. We could not use the bureau in this. You can use them against demonstrations. But for political character, the bureau is never used. Which is true.

DEAN: But I —

NIXON: The Secret Service was used by us, but they—that's their job.

DEAN: But that's their job—

NIXON: They were protecting my life there.

DEAN: But they weren't collecting the same type. They were—

NIXON: Oh, no. They were—

DEAN: Threats and—

NIXON: [unclear]

DEAN: —they were looking to see who was behind it or—

NIXON: What I'm getting at is you have got—you can put off all the self-serving men and they in turn—the main thing is the president has then, you see, that basically clears the president frankly—

DEAN: That's right.

NIXON: [unclear]

DEAN: That's right.

NIXON: [unclear]

DEAN: That's got to be done. That's right.

NIXON: Where it has got to be done. And then—and frankly, they've got to say, "I did this, this, this, and this," and Chapin has to file one, too. Agreed?

DEAN: That's right.

NIXON: And he would say, "I had this and da-da-da-da-da, but I had nothing to do with this—"

DEAN: No.

NIXON: "—or this other thing."

DEAN: It seems to me the way that you would—the way these would be handled publicly—or you want to say or publicly out of—external from the White House—that you might well just give these to Ervin and—directly—and say, "I want you to see—"

NIXON: Right.

DEAN: "—what I know."

NIXON: That's right.

DEAN: "And I think that you know innocent people here, who have committed no crime—"

NIXON: Right.

DEAN: "—but to the contrary have tried to operate in the most proper—"

NIXON: Yeah. That's right.

DEAN: "—way are going to be maligned."

NIXON: That's right.

DEAN: This is the truth.

NIXON: "I want you to know this beforehand. I just want you to know this is all we know—all I know and this is a fact."

DEAN: Mm-hmm.

NIXON: And I hand it to him—and incidentally, I wouldn't have Baker along.

DEAN: No, I would agree with that.

NIXON: You know, it's just a little shot across the bow.

DEAN: Right.

NIXON: What do you think, or [unclear] Baker? You got any further intelligence about his operation?

DEAN: Nothing affirmative that's good at all.

NIXON: Right.

. . .

NIXON: Go ahead.

DEAN: If it might be an affront to Baker, not to bring him in, since he is —

NIXON: Okay, you can bring him in.

DEAN: And try to, you know, get them both on the —

NIXON: We'll try to be spread around. But I'm not going to have a counsel.

DEAN: No, oh Lord, no. I would think at the end there's a lot of appeal just bringing Sam Ervin alone in —

NIXON: [unclear] that's my point. I mean —

DEAN: And a lot of appeal — he is —

NIXON: He is — basically, he is going to be running it. I can just call him down and say I'd informed Baker that —

DEAN: That's the way I think it would be better.

NIXON: That's — I'd say, "Now look, the president wants to be [unclear] put it this way. He's had a talk with you. He wants to have a talk with Ervin."

DEAN: Mm-hmm.

NIXON: Put it that way.

DEAN: Mm-hmm.

NIXON: [unclear] say here it is. I said I want you to know that we cooperated and here's — I've asked for Dean to take sworn affidavits from everybody. They're here. Then he'll say, "Will they appear?" Nope. "Have written interrogatories." Yes, if he wants to go further, but —

DEAN: Mm-hmm.

NIXON: Well, "Suppose I want to come down with my counsel and question them?" No.

DEAN: No. Written interrogatories. We've said every — these are honest, humble men who are going under oath. They're swearing to me this is the extent of their knowledge —

NIXON: And they will what — but on the other hand, we're not saying that — if they have additional questions that come out as a result of this, that you won't answer written interrogatories.

Testing the peace in Vietnam

March 18, 1973, 10:12 a.m.

Richard Nixon and Alexander Haig

On March 17, a ranking Viet Cong general responded to the charges that Nixon had leveled the previous week, regarding the Communists moving men and materiel toward South Vietnam, in violation of the Peace Accords. In denying the accusation, General Tran Van Tra stated that, to the contrary, it was the United States that was violating the Accords by stockpiling munitions in the South. Staying abreast of the situation, Nixon asked Haig for further details on the Viet Cong announcement and, on a related issue, the return of American POWs from Vietnam.

• • •

NIXON: Hello?

HAIG: Good morning, Mr. President.

NIXON: Hi, Al. Any — do you have any new evaluations of the intelligence this morning from where you sit?

HAIG: No, sir. I think there is nothing really significant.

NIXON: What did you think of the North Vietnamese blasting my statement?

HAIG: Yeah —

NIXON: They are very sensitive about that, aren't they?

HAIG: — they are sensitive and I think they obviously paid a great detail of attention to it.

NIXON: You know they are lying, Al. As you know, in that this is all medical supplies and that sort of thing.

HAIG: Right.

NIXON: We know that is incorrect, don't we?

HAIG: Oh, yes —

NIXON: Right.

HAIG: — that is about as phony as it can be.

NIXON: What about the — I mean the ICCS [role in providing oversight of Vietnam peace terms] and so forth — we don't want them into this to check this out, do we?

HAIG: No, I don't think we are going to get anywhere with that. They are turning down one request for inspection violation after another.

NIXON: That is what I had guessed. Somebody asked me — I knew that it was useless. It's just the same kind of a façade that the other one was. Huh?

HAIG: It is, although I am still not convinced that their intention is to do any more than to ride it as far as they —

NIXON: Well, I meant the ICCS thing —

HAIG: Oh, no.

NIXON: As far as instrument it is not particularly effective. As far as policing the agreement we have got to do it. Right?

HAIG: That's right, and we — of course, we are trying to keep this four-party thing intact.

NIXON: Yeah, right. The way it seems to me is that in the light of having gotten their attention though and they are putting the emphasis here that we ought to continue to hold that decision till Wednesday. Don't you think, and not to — ?

HAIG: Oh, absolutely. And even beyond that.

NIXON: Because basically, this thing is — I sort of have, after my talk with you, this same, uneasy feeling about our intelligence. You see the basic thing — I don't have an uneasy feeling about — in terms of say the fact that they are putting in tanks and guns, and that sort of thing. We know the bastards will do that, but let's face it so have we.

HAIG: That's right.

NIXON: You know that they know it. We poured it in, and we poured it in before the cease-fire, and they have got to know that. But the second point is that I am not justifying them because they will cheat and we won't. Now the second point is however that what the intelligence does not tell you. The key point we are discussing is what the hell are their intentions?

HAIG: What they are up to?

NIXON: In other words — what they are up to? They can put in atomic bombs, if they aren't going to use them it doesn't bother me. That is the whole point, isn't it?

HAIG: That's right, sir. I think it is going to be hard in any event to get a handle on —

NIXON: That's right.

HAIG: — their intentions.

NIXON: That's right, but I mean, my point is that's why we cannot make a decision — that is what I am saying, based simply on the fact that they have moved certain quantities and so forth. Because first the intelligence in regard to the movement is not all that accurate, but second because the movement may have several different purposes. Well, in any event, we will have to take a hard look at it.

HAIG: Yeah, I think we should be able to pick up some change in the next week.

NIXON: What is the situation now? Is it the — the last of the prisoners in North Vietnam out now already or are they — ?

HAIG: We have the one batch here. That is cleanup. Now we don't —

NIXON: What do we have left then?

HAIG: I think we have got just about everything out now, except for the Laos problem.

NIXON: I see.

HAIG: And we have — no, I am sorry we have one more batch. This is the third group. We have a fourth group to come out —

NIXON: From Hanoi?

HAIG: Yes, sir.

NIXON: Yeah.

HAIG: And that, in other words, it has been four move —

NIXON: Fourth increment. Yeah, right.

HAIG: We have just now completed the third. The fourth will start at the end of next week. That is why they are looking towards Wednesday, Thursday, and Friday.

NIXON: Right, right, right, right. Okay, well, we will just continue to watch it.

HAIG: Yes, sir. We have got it intensely.

NIXON: Bye.

HAIG: Bye.

"Our friends at least have got to be reassured."
March 20, 1973, 10:47 a.m.
Richard Nixon and Bob Haldeman
OVAL OFFICE

*For weeks, Nixon had been insistent that his aides would testify before the Senate committees only at his discretion. He sometimes allowed that a few minor White House staff members might appear, but he was adamant in denying access to his inner circle, especially Dean, Haldeman, and Ehrlichman. By the middle of March, however, he was aware that the Judiciary Committee, then hearing testimony on the nomination of Patrick Gray to head the FBI, planned to call his close advisors, notably Dean. On March 19, the chairman, Senator Ervin, made his intentions crystal clear, stating that "I'd recommend to the Senate that they send the sergeant-at-arms of the Senate to arrest a White House aide or any other witness who refuses to appear." The following day, Nixon's spokesman, Ron Ziegler, duly termed Ervin's statement "sensationalism," but the fact remained that no one on the president's staff was to be exempted from appearing. That news, so starkly stated, seemed to shock Nixon. He did not intend to capitulate, however. In a talk with Haldeman, they spoke of the need to look for help beyond their inner circle. Nixon's chief of staff, a former advertising executive from J. Walter Thompson, had weathered political storms going back more than a decade at Nixon's side. But this was unlike anything else they had faced together. It was as though Nixon finally realized how dangerously insular his office had become, as he exhorted Haldeman to embrace Republicans in Congress and pull them closer onto the side of the White House.** *

• • •

NIXON: What I think — what it really gets down to, basically, that — I think what needs to be done is that the leadership needs to be briefed on Watergate. Just got — just at least our own friends have got to have a feeling that everything is okay. You understand? Maybe their people will put out a statement. I've worked that out with Dean and they apparently after — according to Dean and Moore, and they've talked to Chapin and Strachan [unclear] just let it go, in other words submit without saying it's a [unclear], you know? I have thought of the possibility —

HALDEMAN: Yeah.

NIXON: But you see, Bob, our own people have got to have some assurance they are not going to get out there on a goddamn limb. They've got to be told and that has not been done —

---

* Carroll Kilpatrick, "White House Assails Ervin Arrest Threat," *Washington Post,* March 20, 1973, p. A1.

HALDEMAN: If they do —

NIXON: — and I am surprised it hasn't.

HALDEMAN: If they do the leadership they ought to, shouldn't they also include the Republican members of the Ervin Committee — so those guys know where we are, too?

NIXON: Right.

HALDEMAN: And that means Weicker, which is a problem. But what the hell? He's going to be investigating it —

NIXON: Sure.

HALDEMAN: — and seems to me we're better off to tell him.

NIXON: True, true. Well, I don't let — but we haven't thought of such things and I guess that's popular what we need to get at, you know. I'm not going to try [unclear].

HALDEMAN: You have to.

NIXON: What I meant, you see — what I'm getting at — at least our friends have got to know. I think the problem is, Bob, that there's probably too much time spent around the White House. Everybody around here — you've talked about the goddamn thing, you know this and that, and I understand all that, but —

HALDEMAN: Well, it was those —

NIXON: — those guys have got — our friends at least have got to be reassured — that's the whole point — on this issue. They read about it. They read the charges and so forth so you've got to reassure them.

HALDEMAN: Yeah, well, this is — that's the point I've raised.

NIXON: Yeah, well, I asked them. They said they couldn't do it.

HALDEMAN: I know it. That's what they tell me.

NIXON: I said we'll put out any kind of a statement and let [unclear]. The point is that we, well, there's only one thing — at least some of them seem to be. Now, what this lacks [unclear] basically is, goddamn it — somebody is in charge. They will come in and say, "All right, now here's the PR plan for your appearance." Now, I haven't been doing it. I've instructed Ziegler and the rest. They haven't been saying much. But, I mean, the point is you can't depend on them to do it. I mean, Timmons is not a guy who can go out — you can't — just won't — can't do it. They aren't going to listen to Timmons as to what points ought to be made.

HALDEMAN: Didn't MacGregor?

NIXON: Huh?

HALDEMAN: Didn't MacGregor when he was [unclear]?

NIXON: You're damn right, it was MacGregor. When I wasn't here, MacGregor's say he didn't see the point to make. Somebody's got to do it, though, see? Ziegler can't [unclear]. Ziegler is good at telling them the questions they're likely to get. But Ziegler does not think enough in terms of "Here is the point we want to get across this day" — huh? You see the point?

HALDEMAN: Yeah.

NIXON: This is the point. Here's where [Herb] Klein would be better than Ziegler with his — all of his fuzzy-mindedness and everything. At least Klein would say — "This is the point you've got to get across today." Ziegler of course is infinitely better in being ready for all the goddamn minefields.

"How it used to be" and "how it will be" in Vietnam
March 20, 1973, 3:10 p.m.
Richard Nixon and Alexander Haig
WHITE HOUSE TELEPHONE

As the border between North and South Vietnam continued to jostle with activity and what one American journalist cynically called "a tolerable level of violence," Nixon spoke about the prospects there with Haig, who was then serving as the vice chief of staff of the army. Nixon also reconsidered his warning that he would unleash a new wave of American bombers if the Communists failed to pull back. He paused to describe his style of brinksmanship, comparing himself with Kissinger and what he termed his security advisor's "psychosis" about following through on threats. As the last American combat soldiers left Vietnam, however, Nixon's rationale for new air attacks weakened, and the prospect of having to involve Congress in his plans only furthered his indecision.*

• • •

NIXON: Hi, Al. I wondered if you had any further thoughts on — in reviewing the intelligence on the things? From what I see, I don't see anything changed from what you told me.

HAIG: No.

NIXON: It doesn't seem to — in fact, if anything, it seems to have tapered off considerably. But I don't know. But maybe the first reports were wrong; maybe the second are wrong. [laughs] What's your view?

HAIG: Well, my view is that there is slightly less reason for quick action. But I think we ought to hold off on that decision another twenty-four hours.

NIXON: Mm-hmm. The problem that I have with it, actually, is this: that I don't know whether the action, at this point — whether the provocation is adequate. That's — you see what I mean? I don't — I never —

HAIG: Right.

NIXON: — never have any damn doubt about action, but you just can't just get up and do something because of a whim, or what appears to be a whim.

HAIG: No, I think we ought to, ought to watch it very carefully. I know that they're intensely trying to look for any changes in the status quo, one way or the other.

NIXON: You mean the intelligence people?

---

* Arnold Abrams, "A Tolerable Level of Violence: Wrestling with Peace in Indochina," *New Leader,* March 19, 1973, p. 10.

HAIG: Yes, yeah. We just haven't gotten anything, and I don't think we really have enough to make a decision here —

NIXON: Yeah. What is — now, I haven't bothered Henry. He's in Mexico, isn't he?

HAIG: Yes, sir.

NIXON: Yeah. And —

HAIG: He's there, and he's — he's watching the thing. I've talked to Scowcroft —

NIXON: Yeah.

HAIG: — and he said that Henry's inclination is to — is to watch it. Although he's still inclined to think we're going to have to do something.

NIXON: Yeah.

HAIG: I just finished forty-five minutes with Ambassador [Tran Kim] Phuong, who —

NIXON: Yeah.

HAIG: — just came back from Saigon.

NIXON: Yeah.

HAIG: And, I was quite encouraged by the discussion. One, he said that, that they're very confident — the South Vietnamese. Two, that the morale of the South Vietnamese military is high and strong. And, three, that he doesn't believe that they have any intentions of seriously upsetting this thing, but that he thinks they're going to just keep pressing in every direction to see what they can get away with.

NIXON: Yeah. I see. The problem I have, Al, actually is that it gets down to the point that I don't want to be influenced in this by the sort of the bravado type of thing, which, you know —

HAIG: That's right.

NIXON: — psychosis, which Henry goes through at times. You know? I mean, having, you know — the idea that, well, we've said we might do something, and now we've got to do something. Well, we don't have to do a goddamn thing, you know. [laughs] You understand what I mean?

HAIG: Yeah.

NIXON: Now, if — so, we mustn't do it simply because — in order to prove that what he has told Dobrynin and others and so forth that we've got to demonstrate. You see, even if, on the other hand, there is an action — I mean, if there's — we've just got to have some pretty solid stuff. But —

HAIG: Well, I don't —

NIXON: And, actually, I don't know. From him — from his sitting down, there, I don't know whether his judgment isn't going to be all that good on it, as on an up-to-date matter.

HAIG: No, I don't, sir. I don't either, and that's one of the odd — oddities of this current moment.

NIXON: Yeah, it is. Isn't it?

HAIG: If he really —

NIXON: Yeah?

HAIG: — feels that something must be done, then he should be back here —

NIXON: Yeah.

HAIG: — when it is done. That I have no question about. But, I would say that — what I would do, sir, is I'd just watch this again.

NIXON: If there's nothing, certainly, then, we'll wait twenty-four hours and —

HAIG: That's right. We have time. We have four or five more days, and it wouldn't make an awful lot of difference if it happens in the midst of the other thing.

NIXON: Mm-hmm.

HAIG: If —

NIXON: Yeah, the whole point is that — yeah, there are other reasons, though, to — we may have to take the, take the good of it at — well, while we can. I — if I really thought — look, here's the other point that we have to have in mind, Al, that — so we say we'd do this in order to indicate that, maybe, we'd do something later. Well, now, there's been enough written, and it's quite on the mark, by even our friends, like an [Joseph] Alsop and others, that — to the effect that, well, after we get everybody out, and after we've withdrawn everything, then you damn near have to get congressional approval to do something.

HAIG: Yes.

NIXON: You — you see that, don't you?

HAIG: Yes.

NIXON: You see, because we have a cease-fire, right?

HAIG: That's right.

NIXON: And for, for them just to up and say, "Now, because of this and that," you say, "For what purpose are you doing it?" Well, you're — for the purpose of [laughs] — you see? I'm — I think we have a — I think we've got a problem there that may not have occurred to Henry. I — it's always occurred to me. I mean —

HAIG: It's a real problem.

NIXON: And, of course, we have, as you know, we've assured Thieu that we would do things. But, do you have any serious doubts in your own mind that we'd really — we would really have to go to their aid, in this case, with — if — let's face it: one of the reasons we were able to do what we were able to do is because they had the prisoners, and we had some troops there. Now, when they're all out, when all the prisoners are out, you're going to have one hell of a time.

HAIG: That's right.

NIXON: I mean, without going to the Congress, right?

HAIG: No, I agree with that, sir —

NIXON: Hitting the North, now — now in the — in the event — in the event there's a massive reinstitution, and so forth, of the — of military actions, that's something else again. But I'm speaking now that the idea that, well, by doing something now, that indicates we might be trigger-happy later. I don't think that argument is quite as strong as Henry has — see, he's thinking as to how it used to be, and not as to how it will be, I think.

HAIG: Well, that's right, although there is something to be said for that logic. That [unclear] —

NIXON: That at that — I know, if we do something now. But my point is: it was more believable before, because we had people there. But, at a time when we don't have anybody there, it's going to be damn tough.

HAIG: Yes. Absolutely.

NIXON: That's the point. I mean, it'd mean — they're smart enough to know that we will have to get some sort of approval. Well, in any event, I haven't decided. We'll take a look at it, and —

HAIG: Yes, sir. I really don't think it's that crucial in terms of timing, because it's not going to be that clean a difference.

NIXON: Well, look, it isn't that clean a difference because it's —

HAIG: I think the whole thing will rest on our ability to justify, through provable violations that are serious in character.

NIXON: Well, the provable violations — what he's basing everything on, at the present time, is the infiltration of equipment, correct?

HAIG: That's right, sir.

NIXON: Now, on that —

HAIG: Individual replacements.

NIXON: What?

HAIG: Phuong told me he didn't think — he thought these are — these were replacements to replace other people that are going to go back home.

NIXON: Well, they aren't even allowed that, I guess, under the thing, are they?

HAIG: No, they're not —

NIXON: Yeah —

HAIG: — but it certainly makes the character of the —

NIXON: Yeah. [laughs]

HAIG: [unclear]

NIXON: It doesn't increase the threat, does it?

HAIG: No.

NIXON: All right. Well, we'll keep in touch. But, it is — I say, it is rather curious that — if Henry feels as strongly about it, that he's there rather than here, too.

HAIG: Well, it's a nice insurance policy, and that's what he's thinking of. Of, you know —

NIXON: You mean an insurance policy in the sense of —

HAIG: No longer [unclear] —

NIXON: — warning them?

HAIG: Yes.

NIXON: Yeah, yeah.

HAIG: It's just that simple, I think.

NIXON: Yeah. But, you — but, you're not convinced that it's worth doing, yet?

HAIG: No, I'm not. If — the indications are it's less of a problem [unclear] —

NIXON: Yeah, than we — than it was last week?

HAIG: That's right.

Further consideration of the viability of renewed bombing in North Vietnam
March 20, 1973, 5:45 p.m.
Richard Nixon and Brent Scowcroft
OVAL OFFICE

*Later in the afternoon, Nixon continued his analysis of Vietnam — and Henry Kissinger — with Major General Brent Scowcroft, who had replaced Haig as Kissinger's deputy. Scowcroft, originally from Utah, graduated from West Point in 1947. He alternated between the military and academic worlds, ultimately receiving a doctorate from Columbia in 1967. Two years later, he joined Kissinger's staff in the Nixon administration. Scowcroft was fascinated by the relationship between Nixon and Kissinger, terming it later as both a "a brilliant partnership" and a "constant rivalry." In the meeting with Nixon about the potential air attack in Vietnam, Scowcroft was meticulous in representing Kissinger, who was traveling in Mexico at the time, even reading verbatim a message from him on the topic of Vietnam.**

• • •

NIXON: I was wondering what the situation is with regard to our — infiltration, and so forth. [unclear] Henry's back [unclear].

SCOWCROFT: Yes, sir.

NIXON: [unclear]

SCOWCROFT: Yes, there has.

NIXON: The point is — the question is: what are the provocations, exactly?

SCOWCROFT: Yes, and I think the reduction is based on the climate season —

NIXON: Right.

SCOWCROFT: — rather than on —

NIXON: Yeah.

SCOWCROFT: — any representations that we have made.

NIXON: Yeah. Yeah.

SCOWCROFT: As near as we can figure out, their infiltration has been, this year, just like it was last year. And that there has been no — in other words, the cease-fire — the agreement, had no effect at all on what they've done. It is, apparently, tapering off.

NIXON: Yeah. What is it — has he — have you had any message from Henry as to what his present feeling about it is? He's there?

SCOWCROFT: Yes. Yes, I have. He is inclined to think that maybe we should delay a day, instead of — I think [unclear] Thursday and Friday — Friday and Saturday. He's afraid, I think, that if we don't do something now, that we'll be in worse shape next fall. And that this is, perhaps, the best time to send them a signal that's unmis-

---

* Alistair Horne, *Kissinger: 1973, the Crucial Year* (Simon & Schuster, 2009), p. 32.

takable. There is a consideration that—about the Laos situation, and Ambassador [George McMurtrie] Godley has pointed out to us that the twenty-third is the date that the new Laotian government is supposed to be formed.

NIXON: That's right.

SCOWCROFT: That—

NIXON: It'd be a pretty good—pretty bad time to hit them then.

SCOWCROFT: That's what he says: that some Laotians want you to encourage a postponement to the twenty-fifth, or the twenty-sixth. There, apparently, may be some acceleration in the last POW release. The PRG have now recommended the—or, proposed the twenty-fifth—

NIXON: Yeah.

SCOWCROFT: —for theirs.

NIXON: The twenty-fifth?

SCOWCROFT: The twenty-fifth. That's Sunday the coming week. Now Henry doesn't really think that a strike would interfere with the POW release.

NIXON: Of course, nobody knows.

SCOWCROFT: I think that the closer the two are together, the more difficult it makes it for them to go ahead with a release. But, I—

NIXON: But, in any event, he's had some second thoughts about the terms, at least as far as the timing.

SCOWCROFT: Yes, he has. Because as a matter of fact, I've got here just a brief paragraph, here. He says, "I believe Godley makes a good point with the possibility of time fouling up the Laotian negotiations. However, none of the considerations advanced last week have really changed," which is true. "I don't believe the North Vietnamese decision on withdrawal will depend on one series of strikes. Another danger is that they will delay release of the POWs. The counterargument is that they would tend to be much more ruthless next fall. The president should be made aware of the Godley argument. We should not, in any case, go before Thursday night. My recommendation, on balance, would be that we go then."

NIXON: That's right.

SCOWCROFT: "The other possibility would be to do it next week, after the POWs are out."

NIXON: Well, except that what Henry's overlooking is the fact that it's—I mean, this makes this one less effective, too. With the use of the—after they are out, the support here for any kind of strike is way down.

SCOWCROFT: It's way down, and I think it also—

NIXON: And it breaks the cease-fire, don't you think?

SCOWCROFT: That's right.

NIXON: Even though it's in Laos.

SCOWCROFT: That's right.

NIXON: The point is, therefore—also, the argument is that if you just—if you hit now, is that the idea being that, well, if you hit now, with the POWs still there, that sort of puts them on notice that, maybe, we might do it again. That's going to evaporate, in my opinion. I mean, we have to be candid about what's really going to happen, due to the fact that the Congress will insist upon an approval of any major strike — I mean, with any strikes — after the withdrawal is complete.

SCOWCROFT: I think I — that's at least right —

NIXON: That's now. But you may be able to do this, depending on how the Congress will vote on the use of American air power. In other words, to help South Vietnam. Cambodia we can get away with for a while. Laos, not after the — if they get a cease-fire there, now. But as far as the use of American air power against North Vietnamese forces coming into the South, unless there is a raw, naked invasion [unclear] it'd be terribly — it would be impossible, really, to get it without a congressional uproar. You see, that's the point of that. The argument that you can make — the arg — it's a very nice argument to say that well, by, by hitting now, we demonstrate that the president is the kind of guy who will use power. Fine. It may demonstrate we'll use it now, but it does not necessarily demonstrate we'll use it later.

SCOWCROFT: No, the circumstances are —

NIXON: That's the problem.

SCOWCROFT: — are very different.

NIXON: And the circumstances will be substantially changed, and that's something we have to consider. So, the real question is whether it's worth doing just by its own sake.

SCOWCROFT: Yes. I, I think that —

NIXON: By its own sake. Not because of the calling card for next November, but by its own sake; whether it's really worth sending these planes over to knock out a few trucks and tanks, or whatever the hell they've got on those roads.

SCOWCROFT: Uh —

NIXON: I know. That's the question.

SCOWCROFT: In terms of its military effect, I don't think it is worth it.

NIXON: That's the point.

SCOWCROFT: You know, we'd —

NIXON: We've hit for years —

SCOWCROFT: — we'd hit them on the road for the first day or two, and —

NIXON: Yeah.

SCOWCROFT: — they would hurt modestly, but —

NIXON: Look, we've done it for years.

SCOWCROFT: — you know, we're talking about a few more days of something to, to make up for what we'd lose in a — what they would lose in a —

NIXON: A strike. Right.

SCOWCROFT: — strike. I feel that if we're going to strike, it really needs to be before the last POW release. So —

NIXON: Yeah, well, I think [unclear] —

SCOWCROFT: I think afterwards, as you say —

NIXON: Afterwards, I think all hell would break loose —

SCOWCROFT: Well, I do too —

NIXON: — here, for the strike. They'd say, "What the Christ are you doing it now for?"

SCOWCROFT: That's right.

NIXON: Well, unless it was tied directly into something in Laos, like —

SCOWCROFT: Well, and that's not likely. We're not likely to have any one incident around which we could coalesce —

NIXON: So —

SCOWCROFT: — support for a strike.

NIXON: — basically, let's face it: this infiltration is not directed against Laos; it's directed against South Vietnam.

SCOWCROFT: That's right. That's right.

NIXON: So, my point is, why do you do it, then? If you do it now, for what purpose? To let them know that, watch out, you're going to lose it again? I guess you can't. I don't know. I don't know whether it's going to be very believable after the rash of stories that are going to come out, without question, after the last American leaves there, the whole feeling of Congress and the country would be, "Now, for Christ's sakes, we're out of Vietnam. Let's don't go back in." [unclear] —

SCOWCROFT: There's no —

NIXON: That's right. And, I just don't — I don't buy that argument. I don't buy that thesis at all, but that's going to be the fact. [unclear] —

SCOWCROFT: There's no question about that.

NIXON: And —

SCOWCROFT: I think —

NIXON: See, Henry's often — always is [unclear] thinks, well, we did it in December, and we're clear. It was quite risky then. And it did work [unclear] difficult things.

SCOWCROFT: Mm-hmm.

NIXON: Well, this time we wouldn't — that we were interested in. To wit: POWs. That was a major difference [unclear]. Then, get a settlement.

SCOWCROFT: Yeah. That's right.

NIXON: But, now, why are we doing it?

SCOWCROFT: Mm-hmm.

NIXON: To guarantee the settlement? Of course, we've told Thieu we'd do it and all that. But, we've also told the American people that we've gotten them ready to defend themselves, and they've got an air force and all the rest, and they say, "Why the hell don't they [the South Vietnamese] do it?"

SCOWCROFT: Well, that, and — though, there's no question about that. I think, on the other side, the argument would be that they obviously are pushing against the agreement. They're testing —

NIXON: That's right.

SCOWCROFT: — to see what they can get away with, to see how far they can go. And, that if we hit them now, we will have registered something with them that —

NIXON: Indicating that, maybe, we can be pushed too far.

SCOWCROFT: That's right. And that, maybe, it would forestall them doing something later on, which they otherwise would do, having decided that they can get away with almost anything, because we didn't react this time.

NIXON: Right. That's the argument.

Sides within an administration and within a scandal

March 20, 1973, 6:00 p.m.
Richard Nixon and Bob Haldeman
OVAL OFFICE

As a busy afternoon turned to evening, Nixon abruptly left his decision on the bombing of North Vietnam and began a discussion of Watergate with Haldeman. Watergate burglar and former CIA director of security James McCord had written a letter to Judge John Sirica strongly suggesting that witnesses had perjured themselves, that the burglars had been paid to stay quiet, and that unnamed higher-ups were involved. Conversations inside the Oval Office could be as defensive as testimony in a hearing, but Haldeman and Nixon were far more candid, discussing the people and crimes of Watergate. Haldeman credited Dean with developing a strategy of containment early in the scandal. Both he and Nixon readily subscribed to it, even as containment evolved into cover-up. The two began to recognize that trap on March 20, as they sorted through the scandal and those it encompassed. At the time, they still hoped the investigation might stop with those closely associated with the break-in—those they called "the Watergate side." It's indicative of the atmosphere in Nixon's administration that Nixon and Haldeman considered themselves utterly separate from them.

• • •

HALDEMAN: Dean's theory is that you aren't necessarily going to get hung. It depends what you define by "hang." There's no question we're going to get smeared.

NIXON: Yeah.

HALDEMAN: There's no question that they're going to keep building the innuendo that will lead into the White House and will be able to come to some proof.

NIXON: Right.

HALDEMAN: What they'll call proof—consider proof on the basis that the line of reasoning they're using now, that Dwight Chapin wouldn't have done anything that I didn't know about.

NIXON: That's right. I understand.

HALDEMAN: Or, it might—that wasn't in my orders and certainly Gordon Strachan did.

NIXON: That's right.

HALDEMAN: That's only partly true. But it's a sustainable assumption—but that part we can live with it and I see all four of them. Now, I'd like to go out and have us go out now and hit—if you take that part of the case and hit mine and admit. Say it's absolutely true. I knew that Chapin was recruiting an old college friend of his to go out and run around doing Dick Tuck stuff — which is absolutely true. I did know. I did not know the guy's name. I did not know the guy. I did not know what he was going to do. I did not know what we were going to pay him. I did know that Chapin was going to authorize some payment to him to cover his expenses and a basic income.

NIXON: Right.

HALDEMAN: That he was going to work full-time on this and was going to try to recruit other college-type guys to do this kind of stuff.

NIXON: Intelligence work [unclear]?

HALDEMAN: Not really intelligence. Because that wasn't what was talked about. See, he wasn't engaged in this — at least I don't think he was engaged in espionage. He was engaged in —

NIXON: Tricks.

HALDEMAN: Yeah, I think some of them got a little — that's a euphemistic term for them — some of them. Because he did get a little far on the tricks. But they talked about — when they talked about doing it — the kind of tricks — that I said, for Christ's sake don't fool around with stuff like — they were going to cut cars, cut tires on press buses. You know, and take the keys out of cars in motorcades and that sort of stuff. I said that's ridiculous. It's childish and doesn't do us any good. So I —

NIXON: [unclear] screw around.

HALDEMAN: What does — do us some good is to have a guy standing around with a sign saying, "McGovern, what about your illegitimate daughter?" or something. I hope we never used that one, but we were ready to —

NIXON: Yeah.

HALDEMAN: Which I just might say if I didn't call them somewhere someday. So I knew they were getting a guy and Chapin did do it with my concurrence and Strachan was a friend of the guy's too. I knew that. That I have no problem with saying.

NIXON: I understand [unclear].

HALDEMAN: And I don't think that hurts you.

NIXON: Yeah.

HALDEMAN: Just say I did that. The problem is can't the truth stop at the truth? Which that does — or does the innuendo go so — come then so hard on top of it that you can't turn it off?

NIXON: And it goes to [unclear] of the truth —

HALDEMAN: It goes to the Watergate or which it seems to me, we ought to be able to turn off. But the problem is the price of turning it off may hurt the people on the Watergate side. At least that's what they tell me. What bothers me is that I still think I'm being had in a sense for being tarred in order to protect some other people.

NIXON: Yeah. Yeah.

HALDEMAN: I think Chapin is being far worse tarred in order to protect other people —

NIXON: Yeah. The people on the Watergate side unfortunately are also our friends.

HALDEMAN: The people on the Watergate side are our friends and there it is far more seriousness. Because there — this one you can say was bad judgment on my part to let Chapin do this or I can say it was bad judgment on Chapin's part to let the guy go as far as he did, or Chapin can say it was bad judgment on Segretti's part —

NIXON: Yeah.

HALDEMAN: — to do some of the things he did.

NIXON: That's right.

HALDEMAN: That's probably right. All the way up to maybe bad judgment on my part. But on Watergate it isn't a question of bad judgment. On Watergate it's a question and there it goes and, ultimately, it seems to me that's what they have got to focus on. And this — who was it that was telling me that what — or convinced they're going to go after is — I guess it's Ziegler. Ziegler's theory is based on what the press guys say — convinced that what they're after is Colson on criminal. They think he's the highest guy they can get on criminal in the White House and Mitchell on the outside. Now, there — the worst — it isn't — the worst you can get to is damn bad out there.

NIXON: It's Mitchell.

HALDEMAN: Because if Mitchell was the authority.

NIXON: He's the attorney general of the United States.

HALDEMAN: As attorney general of the United States, and —

NIXON: The president's campaign manager. That's pretty goddamn bad. That's damn near as bad as it is out here. Do you agree with this?

HALDEMAN: Yeah.

NIXON: Problems —

HALDEMAN: And there, if you have —

NIXON: Protect them to protect them —

HALDEMAN: — then you have to — then you start working your way back down that chain again. And maybe you can't turn it off somewhere and that's what John Dean — where he comes out every time we go around this circle.

NIXON: Yes, sir.

HALDEMAN: Then you get to the thing with Segretti. There is a potential —

NIXON: Segretti?

HALDEMAN: — a criminal violation on Segretti, too.

NIXON: On what? Some mailing? Horseshit, that's so inconsequential.

HALDEMAN: Okay. But then he was Chapin's agent, so does that make Chapin criminally liable? Chapin was my employee so does that make me criminally liable?

NIXON: Is that a felony?

HALDEMAN: No. It's a misdemeanor.

NIXON: That's what I mean.

HALDEMAN: It's a misdemeanor committed without our specific knowledge, so I don't see how we're liable.

NIXON: Listen, campaigns — there's never a campaign that didn't have a mailing disclaimer or —

HALDEMAN: That's right.

NIXON: — [unclear] all they want. There's all sort of [unclear].

HALDEMAN: We had the same thing in '60 — '62 in California. Democrats for Nixon —

NIXON: Yeah, I guess you're right.

HALDEMAN: The Dem — no the Committee to Preserve the — the Committee to Preserve the Democratic Party in California. The thing that crazy woman got us into — Naomi Baxter.

NIXON: Yeah. Yeah. You see the point is that it isn't just Bob [unclear] whatever we're calling it here, but it is a question of — to be frank with you, I — big fish, as we mentioned. Colson I knew was going to be hard to prove. I don't see, I think, unless Colson's lying to Steve — I mean Dean was questioning him. Dean does not believe that Colson — that they [unclear] Colson.

HALDEMAN: I don't either. And as I've told you I've been convinced all along that Colson wasn't — did not know.

NIXON: About this?

HALDEMAN: About the Watergate —

NIXON: I don't think he did, and yet —

HALDEMAN: I don't think he did either.

NIXON: — part of it [unclear] was saying that, of course — this is Magruder's argument. Apparently he's made it, too. Colson was insisting on getting the information but I don't know why. I don't know what — it was all a hoax — why he would be involved. If they were going to have a demonstration in San Diego or not was something I couldn't quite figure out. Know what I mean? But he was in a lot of things. He got interested in too many things.

HALDEMAN: But Mitchell, as you know, was very much involved in the demonstration in San Diego. Remember Mitchell came in very concerned about changing the convention site because he was afraid of inability to control San Diego.

NIXON: Oh, yeah. Well, we got a lot of bad breaks there.

HALDEMAN: Yeah.

NIXON: We got a bad break with the judge, for example —

HALDEMAN: Monumental bad breaks and a string of them one leading to another.

NIXON: This judge, that —

HALDEMAN: Starting with the just incredible thing that one — was *Time* magazine this week started off their thing that one lousy part-time night guard [Frank Wills] at the Watergate who happened to notice the tape on the locks on the doors. If he hadn't seen them the thing probably would have never busted. If you hadn't had Watergate you wouldn't have had Segretti. You wouldn't have had any of that stuff. And then all the stuff on the contributors.

NIXON: Must be for — it isn't they're really after [unclear] the administration and so forth. The people that are yelling about us at us about it are basically the old Establishment, the *Times,* [unclear].

HALDEMAN: Well, let's see.

NIXON: [unclear]

HALDEMAN: The one niche that they—and I don't think they see here where they're going to get but they see there's still an opportunity and they're going to grind away till they either exhaust it or get to something.

NIXON: In a sense, if there was a way to get the hearings over in a hurry, that's it. The theory that Baker had, which of course I rejected, but was [unclear]—give us—get all of them—get us all of them—everybody—have them all up there and have them all testify and he said choke the goddamn thing for the week and after that people will be bored to death. Well, that makes sense provided you could—

HALDEMAN: It doesn't go anywhere.

NIXON: No, provided you can run the risk of having your people go out there and be asked a lot of tough questions by a smart goddamn lawyer. So, my view is probably we would be better advised to stick—the guy that most wants to stick to it is Colson. Obviously, he's—you know, I don't think he wants to be questioned and I can see why because of other involvements [unclear]. So, therefore—

HALDEMAN: He's the only one who doesn't want to be.

NIXON: [unclear] needs to fight for executive privilege. Obviously, no, we're just not going to allow it mainly because we just can't allow that sort of thing to come out. But then what you have to do is to—you've got to fight through the goddamn courts. It's going to take a long time. [unclear] for a long time. The story of cover-up—that's what's involved.

HALDEMAN: Yeah.

NIXON: Right?

HALDEMAN: And that's bad. That's really worse than the—

NIXON: Than the act that [unclear].

HALDEMAN: It isn't really worse—it isn't worse than John Mitchell going to jail for either perjury or complicity.

NIXON: No, no, no. I've balanced that out, too. But you see what they're really after. Hell, take cover-up till hell freezes over. You know what I mean? Because—

HALDEMAN: If that's really where it goes and I guess it is.

NIXON: But John—Bob—you can't figure Magruder did it by himself. That's what—I just don't believe Magruder's that much as a competent operator. [unclear]

HALDEMAN: I'm not sure if that's—I'm not sure.

NIXON: Sounds to me like—see that's the only thing that I think they must really think—the investigator thinks. "Christ, Magruder would a—I mean, a decision like that would be made by Magruder?" Of course, he was the managing manager in effect. Yeah, I think—

HALDEMAN: I think it's now—I think Dean thinks it's possible that it was—

NIXON: —that Magruder may have done on it on his own, because—do you think he was capable?

HALDEMAN: Well, done the specific thing on his own within a broad authority that he misinterpreted—

NIXON: In other words —

HALDEMAN: In other words, Mitchell was clearly aware and fully aware of the Liddy intelligence operation. No question about that.

NIXON: But maybe not of the specific —

HALDEMAN: But maybe not of the specific act, and it would be perfectly —

NIXON: Magruder was aware of the act.

HALDEMAN: Well, he says he wasn't in court. And you can even go to that step and buy it.

NIXON: Yeah.

HALDEMAN: Which is that Liddy was doing it and on — under the broad authority, but then you get down to will Liddy take the heat?

NIXON: Well, let me say this but coming back to the business about trying to get every-body up there and all the rest we've got to remember what could be involved. Let's see the whole view going up, and so forth. [unclear] or maybe not.

HALDEMAN: It wasn't me and I don't think it has to be Dwight, but Dwight I think may have to recant some of these [unclear] or explain them.

NIXON: Yes, that's —

HALDEMAN: Some of what I said earlier.

NIXON: That's right. Well, what I meant then might be an advantage. Let's see. Oh, it's what — I mean, maybe my reasoning is fallacious, if our real concern is Mitchell. Maybe they're going to get him anyway.

HALDEMAN: Well, John, at least the last I got into it in any detail, John Dean didn't think so.

NIXON: That they're going to get Mitchell — that right?

HALDEMAN: See, John Dean's whole approach as I understand it — this is when we went through it out in California for two full days. What came out of is his whole premise — his basic approach to this is one of containment. Keep it in this box and he thinks he can. And that box goes on the theory that Liddy did it without author-ity from above and Liddy's been convicted of doing it. Liddy was the responsible guy at the campaign organization. He's the highest guy that they've got. The other people were employees of Liddy's.

NIXON: Well, that's the way the case stands at the moment. Then, of course, if the judge blasts the hell out of that Friday I suppose he could say he doesn't believe in that — it must go further — didn't get cooperation and so forth.

HALDEMAN: Liddy apparently is a little bit nuts and a masochist and apparently he wants to — looks to the martyrdom of doing this. He kind of likes it. And that's true. Maybe that's where it'll stay. That's Dean's — that's his hope. That's what he's franti-cally trying to keep — not frantically — persistently trying to keep —

NIXON: Liddy'll appeal it —

HALDEMAN: [unclear] strings in —

NIXON: Who are appealing it? McCord? Liddy should beat it. Son of a bitch, they're two of them — McCord. Hunt's not it.

HALDEMAN: Hunt went and pleaded guilty. They all pleaded guilty and —

NIXON: He's appealing.

HALDEMAN: Liddy and McCord didn't plead guilty.

NIXON: Liddy's appealing that —

HALDEMAN: Liddy's appealing but Liddy's not appealing on the merits. He's appealing on the errors. Liddy's going for errors. There you've got another problem. Liddy's a lawyer who thinks he's smarter than the judge and the court, and the court prosecutor, which every lawyer seems to have to convince himself of. Liddy's game is purely, as I understand it, his appeal game is purely on errors.

NIXON: Oh, sure.

HALDEMAN: Then he's apparently got some — at least some possibilities —

NIXON: Sirica?

HALDEMAN: Has some areas of potential challenge of errors.

NIXON: Well, coming back to this, I mean it is the coming free of the White House people.

HALDEMAN: That doesn't impair that other case at all.

NIXON: Magruder and Mitchell, that's my point.

HALDEMAN: Because if containment theory works then I don't see what danger it is in our going up because we don't have anything to say. The people you're protecting by executive privilege — let's face it are — well, Jesus, you've got Ehrlichman. I don't know about Ehrlichman. John knows a hell of a lot.

NIXON: He does know a hell of a lot but not about this case.

HALDEMAN: Doesn't he? Okay.

NIXON: Not about Watergate. He doesn't know a goddamn thing.

HALDEMAN: I don't think he [unclear].

NIXON: He ran the other thing. He ran, you know —

HALDEMAN: Yeah.

NIXON: You know, the stuff about —

HALDEMAN: Well, can they expand to that? If they can what does he do? Sure they can. There are no rules of evidence up there. Their charter is to cover all the campaign activity.

NIXON: They were [unclear]. Fine, fine. But I can't — Ellsberg, I can't.

HALDEMAN: Yeah. Teddy Kennedy.

NIXON: Well, I don't think that's going to be on the market. I think John's in pretty good shape. Now I don't think we could now — however, I don't think we can shift our ground and cave on the idea of privilege thing. But I think we have to find a way to make statements. They will not accept statements until they are free to subpoena. That's the theory I'm working on with them now and Dean and Moore are trying to see what can they say, and then of course everything we say will raise additional questions. But so be it.

HALDEMAN: Well —

NIXON: It's better to have statements —

HALDEMAN: All right, all right. Look, we've agreed to answer written interrogation, right? I — for instance —

NIXON: Yeah.

HALDEMAN: — I have to do that. Chapin has to do that.

NIXON: Everybody.

HALDEMAN: We've all agreed to do that.

NIXON: [unclear]

HALDEMAN: Okay, but why the hell don't we do a — instead of if they submit it, why don't we sit down and do our statement right now?

NIXON: That's what I have suggested.

HALDEMAN: Why doesn't Dean ask me the questions that the committee will ask me? Why don't I write my answers down? Why doesn't Chapin write his? And why don't we give those to the *Washington Star* and let them print the goddamn things in total tomorrow morning?

NIXON: We went over all that.

HALDEMAN: What's wrong with that?

NIXON: I told him — try to see why couldn't each of you make a sworn statement. He and Moore over the weekend decided that it would open too many doors for him.

HALDEMAN: Really?

NIXON: Dean's the expert here. Bob — I think this is —

HALDEMAN: Well damn it, why don't we make them and see? I mean, without putting them out? Why don't we take the step we're doing? We're going to have to apparently anyway and so he says we're going to open too many doors. Aren't they going to open? We've already agreed to do that anyway.

NIXON: Except that they'll — you see his point is, well, anyway let's try it. I don't mind. It's worth trying. His point is that we don't — that they will never take the statements so it's never going to happen. See, that's the other course that's the problem. They're never going to take written statements.

HALDEMAN: You mean they won't accept them at all?

NIXON: Hell no. But that's all right. You see, my point is the way we end up is that if we refuse to go up but they will have a — they will say, "We will not accept that" and then they'll go down and under the law they'll try to subpoena, which we will quash, and we'll have a court test. All right, that's where it stands, so we have to fight that out in the courts and try to make a case with the other witnesses waiting for the court test. Of course, [unclear] and the other way to do it is to — so that rules that out — and you have got no statements at all. Now the problem with that — confronts me with is that it appears that I covered up the White House people. I won't let that statement — so what, that's why I told Dean and the rest, I said, "Why don't you just put out a statement?" Any kind of a statement. Of course, I said make it as general as possible but just so somebody can say that the president — that a statement has been made through the president, upon which he has based his statement to the effect that he has confidence in his staff. See, I mean it looks now that I am just doing that as a thumb-your-nose — screw-off. You see my point?

HALDEMAN: Except that everybody seems to accept the fact that there is a Dean report to the president on the basis of which the president said that.

NIXON: Yeah. Maybe.

HALDEMAN: And we've now established that — as I understand it, that Dean — no, I guess we haven't, but we can't — that it was an oral report, not a written report.

NIXON: Yeah. And that he conducted an investigation and so forth, but that needs — you see, by having a statement prepared — statement or statements prepared which are delivered to the committee, preferably I'd like to have delivery — what I told Dean — make one up, that's what he's working on now, to make a delivery to Eastland. Eastland then puts it out, and the purpose of answering all the recent charges. The most recent charges, not everything —

HALDEMAN: The Dean charges.

NIXON: The Dean charges. And Ziegler said, but "that raises too many questions — new questions," so then John Ehrlichman says that those questions [laughs] are going to be raised anyway.

HALDEMAN: Yeah.

NIXON: That's my point of view that maybe they're going to be raised anyway.

HALDEMAN: I don't understand what Ron means, but maybe he's right. I don't think —

NIXON: I don't think —

HALDEMAN: I've spent more time on this than anybody really and I don't know any questions that aren't already out.

NIXON: But they — I don't quite know either, that's my point. I don't know what the hell other questions —

HALDEMAN: Well, I think if Ron says it'll raise new questions, the burden of proof is on him. What are they?

NIXON: Yeah. I see.

HALDEMAN: I don't — I'm not so sure —

NIXON: He's already [unclear] people [unclear] something to do. Mostly has to do with Segretti and Chapin, that's the thing.

HALDEMAN: Well, I don't understand why we can't run that one out —

NIXON: I personally think that you've got to — you've got a bunch — Segretti and Chapin. We've just got to let that one hang out —

HALDEMAN: Here's the first thing —

NIXON: I really do.

HALDEMAN: I don't — in the first place, the guy that knows the most about the Segretti thing is Segretti.

NIXON: That's right.

HALDEMAN: The guy that knows the next — well, the guy that knows the next most is Chapin, who is protected. The guy that knows the next most after that is Strachan, who's protected. The guy that knows the next most after that is Kalmbach, who's not protected. And the guy that knows the next most is me, who's protected and that's the end of the Segretti story I think.

NIXON: Yeah. So put it out.

HALDEMAN: Okay. The point there is that the guy that knows the most is Segretti. He is not protected.

NIXON: So, he's going to get questioned?

HALDEMAN: So, he's going to get questioned. Now, I've heard Segretti's — Dean has a two-hour tape where he interrogated Segretti and went through the whole damn thing and, maybe I'm stupid, but I listened to the whole tape and for my dough I'd just as soon play it out on the radio tonight on CBS and let the world hear it.

NIXON: That's my feeling.

HALDEMAN: Because what it says to me is not nearly as bad as what I would venture ninety percent of the people in this country think happened.

NIXON: Sure.

HALDEMAN: But it does confirm that Dwight Chapin recruited him, and he gives him the details. He had him to dinner at his house and he had — Gordon Strachan was there. But, what the hell? He went to school with Dwight Chapin.

NIXON: Already, Bob, that's already put out anyway —

HALDEMAN: That's right.

NIXON: That's already been put out.

HALDEMAN: That's right.

NIXON: That he had been recruited. What the hell [unclear]? I disagree.

HALDEMAN: Now Ron's worried because that make — because we denied — we didn't deny it and Ron had covered that.

NIXON: Who denied it? I thought —

HALDEMAN: The press — that Ron — see we denied the Chapin story in the *Post*, but he denied it on the basis that it was based on hearsay —

NIXON: Yeah.

HALDEMAN: — and was fundamentally incorrect.

NIXON: Fundamentally —

HALDEMAN: And it was.

NIXON: Yeah, fundamentally. Yeah.

HALDEMAN: We didn't deny any specifics in it.

NIXON: That, of course — I think what Ron should say is that "fundamentally incorrect." Fundamentally.

HALDEMAN: All we can — let's go back and make the case on that.

NIXON: Say that the *Post* story said this, this, this, and this, and I think that's the way you want to handle that. For example, the *Post* story said this, this, and this. This was incorrect. This is incorrect. This is incorrect. Why? Now what is correct is this, this, this, and this. That's the way you ought to handle that so as to get us off the hook on that. So the press secretary did not lie. Well, my feeling is that taking a — we're not going to [unclear] a plan here. That's all I'm after. The point is, my feeling is that if the facts are going to come out in all this period of time, I would rather have us get them out to the extent we can in a forthcoming way so that [unclear].

HALDEMAN: I don't know if Dean's filled you in on this stuff. I know another thing that worries him. This I'd forgotten about, that it leads to — because he's afraid that Sloan —

NIXON: Sloan?

HALDEMAN: He's afraid that — that you know, he gets Sloan up that — that he's —

NIXON: Yeah.

HALDEMAN: — that he's got to say something because there's another fact that's never come out — they've never tracked down but they could. And again it appears it's terrible —

NIXON: Mm-hmm.

HALDEMAN: — but it isn't at all. And the facts on it are worked out fine. But there was three hundred fifty thousand dollars in cash transferred out of the campaign fund over to a separate holder and it was under Strachan's control. It was, in a sense, trans — in essence, transferred to me. What that was supposed to have been, if you recall, was two million dollars which we, way back, had told Stans we wanted — it was that leftover cash [from the 1970 election] that we wanted set aside.

NIXON: Oh, yeah.

HALDEMAN: Before reporting and all that just so it was there as a reserve fund.

NIXON: Yeah. Yeah.

HALDEMAN: Well, it got boiled down because of reporting problems and everything else to where we only moved three hundred fifty thousand. The three hundred fifty thousand in cash was moved.

NIXON: And that was used for polls?

HALDEMAN: That was the purpose of that was to be for polls and everything else. It was not used for polls or anything else. It wasn't used. And that has been transferred back to the reelection committee. It was transferred after the election. The cash was moved back over —

NIXON: Oh, I see.

HALDEMAN: — to Mardian — not Mardian — LaRue. Fred LaRue and his backup. So, the money was not spent.

NIXON: What's the difference then?

HALDEMAN: Okay. The difference is that establishes, if they want to call it that — you can look at the yellow journalism — a secret fund that Haldeman controlled. You could say, which I guess I did. The question of who controlled it never arose because it was never used. Physically Strachan — actually Strachan did. Then some other guy did. I don't even know who had it — some guy I don't even know put the stuff in a box — in a safe out in Virginia somewhere, I understand. That's where it was held.

NIXON: Well, if they go into all that, there are boxes in every campaign.

HALDEMAN: That worries Dean. That one has never worried me. I — and maybe there's more to it than I — there's something to it than I've found.

NIXON: Sure. Well, that worries me, too. Can you start to [unclear] — I don't know. Of course, none of us really knows what to do here because of —

HALDEMAN: I think each of us filing a statement now that's as complete as we can make it.

NIXON: That's right. That's the way.

HALDEMAN: But that it is not a statement under —

NIXON: Duress.

HALDEMAN: — under questioning that says there is nothing else to say. I wouldn't say it.

NIXON: No.

HALDEMAN: I wouldn't say that this is the whole truth.

NIXON: Yeah.

HALDEMAN: I'd say in relation to the charges —

NIXON: Yeah, very good.

HALDEMAN: — that have been raised —

NIXON: Charges that have been made and then I'll be glad to answer any other questions.

HALDEMAN: Yeah.

NIXON: Yeah. I would say is there any other? I think you've got to abandon the disclaimer at the end.

HALDEMAN: Yeah.

NIXON: Now if other questions are raised I'll be glad to answer them. See what I mean? Sure. Now, that way I don't see how this — and if they raise the other questions, then you answer them.

Dean's off-the-record story of Watergate
March 20, 1973, 7:29 p.m.
Richard Nixon and John Dean
WHITE HOUSE TELEPHONE

The Judiciary Committee's intention to call Dean to testify in Gray's confirmation hearing became a battle even more important than the war. Those within the White House and on the committee had long since realized that Gray's nomination to head the FBI was all but dead, due entirely to the acting director's candor in discussing the Watergate investigation and the aftermath of the break-in. On March 20, in fact, Attorney General Kleindienst starkly ordered Gray to stop discussing Watergate in the hearings. By then it was something of a moot point, though, and his order only roiled committee members, both Democratic and Republican. Even as the chances of a confirmation slipped away, committee members were insistent that Dean testify regarding Gray's comments on Watergate. In fact, they made it an issue more important than Gray's status as a nominee.

• • •

NIXON: Well, you're having rather long days these days, aren't you?

DEAN: Yeah. [laughs]

NIXON: I guess we all have. Yeah.

DEAN: Well, I think they'll continue to be longer.

NIXON: What happened today in the Senate? Anything—

DEAN: Well, I understand that Gray took a little beating up there today. He was—the approach they're working that he's been an abandoned man.

NIXON: Oh boy.

DEAN: Evidenced by the fact that Kleindienst would not let him [coughs]—excuse me—insert things in the record that he desired to insert in the record and it was quite clear that he has been left hanging by—being countermanded by you and your decision.

NIXON: Well, you know in a sense that I didn't countermand him at all, I simply said—

DEAN: No, I know, this is a theme they're playing.

NIXON: Yeah, fine.

DEAN: They're trying to play. And, uh—

NIXON: This is in the committee or on the floor?

DEAN: It's in the committee.

NIXON: Open or executive?

DEAN: This was in open session.

NIXON: Yeah.

DEAN: They are, they subpoenaed three additional witnesses—Tom Bishop, who is a former FBI man who was canned by Gray, who used to run their PR section.

NIXON: Good. That's good.

DEAN: They're trying to pull him in there on sour grapes and—

NIXON: Good. That wouldn't bother me. Does it bother you?

DEAN: No, and it sets a precedent—

NIXON: Mm-hmm.

DEAN: —for this fellow Sullivan going up.

NIXON: Right.

DEAN: Which is interesting.

NIXON: Yeah.

DEAN: Then—

NIXON: Well, the fellow that we could—isn't Gurney a member of that committee?

DEAN: Gurney is.

NIXON: He could just ask for Sullivan.

DEAN: Right.

NIXON: How would that be?

DEAN: That wouldn't be bad at all.

NIXON: You don't have Sullivan's report yet?

DEAN: No, Sullivan told me—he was out of town—he will have it for me tomorrow.

NIXON: Yeah.

DEAN: He will skip a meeting that he has in the morning to make —

NIXON: Just a second. [gives series of instructions to an unknown assistant]

DEAN: — sure he gets it [unclear] and over to me.

· · ·

NIXON: Yeah, go ahead.

DEAN: So he will have it over to me tomorrow, and I said —

NIXON: Right.

DEAN: — I absolutely have to have it tomorrow. There just can't be any further deadline. The time is here to look and see what you've got and he said, "Well, I think I've got good stuff. I think it's supportable, documentable." I said, "Well, Bill, I want to see it just as quickly as possible tomorrow morning."

NIXON: Good.

DEAN: 'Cause it will be over. And the other witness they've now subpoenaed — there are two other witnesses — there's the [Judy] Hoback girl from the reelection committee, who, she was interrogated by committee staff and counsel as a result of her confidential interviews with the FBI — alleging that that had been leaked by me to them and then, of course, that was not —

NIXON: That's not true.

DEAN: — not true. And the other fellow they're calling is a fellow by the name of Thomas Lombard who is trying to establish a link between Dean on that one. Lombard did volunteer work for me in my office and did volunteer work for Liddy and at one time he saw Liddy in my office. Big deal. [unclear] purely campaign. You know.

NIXON: Well, is that what Lombard will testify to, or will he testify to —

DEAN: Well, that's what he'll — he's written a very lengthy letter to the committee asking, declining to testify originally and saying, "This is all I would have to say and it's obviously not relevant. I know nothing of Dean and Liddy's — "

NIXON: Yeah.

DEAN: " — connection — "

NIXON: Yeah, right.

DEAN: " — other than the fact that they — "

NIXON: That's not bad then. Maybe he'll make a pretty good witness.

DEAN: He might. He might. Uh —

NIXON: What about the Hoback girl?

DEAN: The Hoback girl should be broken down. She should come out in tears as a result of the fact that she's virtually lying about what she's saying. And our people will, beyond a —

NIXON: Well, you mean, do our people know what to ask her?

DEAN: Yes, they do. Yes, they do.

NIXON: Mm-hmm.

DEAN: Uh —

NIXON: Why is she doing it? Do we know?

DEAN: She, uh —

NIXON: Disgruntled? Somebody —

DEAN: Disgruntled. She's been fairly disgruntled all along. She's a Democrat that worked over there in the Finance Committee. She professes a personal loyalty to Maury Stans but that is about the extent of it — any extent of her loyalty.

NIXON: Yeah.

DEAN: I never did figure out how she got in there. So, all told — I'm told that today was a bad day for Gray and not much of a, uh —

NIXON: [laughs]

DEAN: — not much of a — but they're taking a whip —

NIXON: Yeah.

DEAN: — out on the floor to see what the [unclear] out there.

NIXON: Yeah.

DEAN: We'll have that tomorrow morning.

NIXON: What's your feeling, though, John, about Gray? Aren't you just as comfortable to let him go down?

DEAN: I don't —

NIXON: Which do you want? I mean, we can put some pressures on, and I just wonder.

DEAN: I don't think it's worth saving, sir. I really don't.

NIXON: Yeah, well, that's my point. Isn't it really a case of if they want to make him the martyr, they're gonna make him the martyr.

DEAN: That's right.

NIXON: Do you agree or not or — ?

DEAN: I would —

NIXON: If you feel differently, let me know.

DEAN: I would agree that they're trying to make him a martyr. I think that Pat Gray's been so damaged by these hearings that he will —

NIXON: Shouldn't be the head of the bureau.

DEAN: — will be difficult for him to be the head of the bureau.

NIXON: That's right.

DEAN: It will be a year, two years for him to recover.

NIXON: That's right.

DEAN: It's like [Congressman] Dick Poff [R-VA] when he decided to withdraw [a Supreme Court nomination in 1971] even from consideration for the court knowing that he would never be an effective justice [during confirmation hearings] for years.

NIXON: That's right. The thing is, too — that Gray though has got to make up his mind on that pretty soon. Don't you think so?

DEAN: I would — you know, I thought I'd be a called [witness] —

NIXON: In fact, I was thinking you ought to do it fairly soon.

DEAN: Mm-hmm.

NIXON: Excuse me, what were you gonna say?

DEAN: I was thinking he might call today, very easily, and say you know, at least make a pro forma gesture to see if someone over there — you know, if you were interested. Now —

NIXON: What's the Kleindienst view of the whole thing now? Is he stayin' a mile away?

DEAN: I'll — haven't talk to Dick tonight, so I don't know —

NIXON: Mm-hmm.

DEAN: — what his reading is on the latest activity.

NIXON: Yeah.

DEAN: It's uh, it might be better to let it just die in —

NIXON: Yeah.

DEAN: — committee and not get it out of there. Apparently, there's — it's tied up at seven to seven now. [unclear] the votes.

NIXON: Oh, it is seven to seven in the committee?

DEAN: That's right. And McClellan and Eastland are hanging, in not knowing which way — not — McClellan and Mathias are hanging in the balance. I suspect we could probably get McClellan's vote and lose Mathias's.

NIXON: It will be eight to eight, huh?

DEAN: Right.

NIXON: [laughs]

DEAN: That ties it up and that will not confirm it from a [unclear].

NIXON: Yeah. Well, if you got it out, yeah. McClellan surprises me. Good God, he knows better than this.

DEAN: He's turned a little funny recently. He's generally, you know, pretty much of a soldier on —

NIXON: What's his trouble, for Christ's sake? He's just got reelected and I helped him.

DEAN: I know it.

NIXON: One hell of a lot.

DEAN: I know it. I know it.

NIXON: Well —

DEAN: Well, [unclear] —

NIXON: Getting old!

DEAN: That's right! [laughs]

NIXON: That's right. Yeah. Well, on that score I don't consider this too bad a day. I think maybe that's the way the dreary thing's gonna roll itself out, isn't it?

DEAN: It's, I think this will be a self-terminating situation. It will just be a no end and —

NIXON: But they didn't bite the bullet with regard to subpoenaing you?

DEAN: No. I don't think there's any chance they're going to do that.

NIXON: That's rather interesting, isn't it? Something ought to be made of that.

DEAN: Unless they get — they're taking more evidence on me, obviously with these other two witnesses. Not that they're going to find something out — it'll just be more —

NIXON: Yeah.

DEAN: — of the same old stuff. I had a conversation with John Ehrlichman this afternoon before he came down to visit you, and I think that one thing we have to continually do and particularly right now, is to examine the broadest implications of this whole thing, and I, you know, maybe thirty minutes, of just my recitation to you of—

NIXON: Mm-hmm.

DEAN: —the facts so that you operate from the same facts that everybody else has.

NIXON: Right.

DEAN: And I don't think—we've never really done that. It's been sort of bits and pieces. Just paint the whole picture for you, the soft spots, the potential problem areas—

NIXON: Mm-hmm.

DEAN: —and the like. So that when you make judgments you'll—

NIXON: Yeah.

DEAN: —have all that out.

NIXON: Would you like to do that? When?

DEAN: I would think if it's not inconvenient for you, sir, I would like to sort of draw all my thoughts together and have a, you know, just make a couple notes to myself so I didn't—

NIXON: Well, could you do it tomorrow?

DEAN: Yes, sir. Yes, sir.

NIXON: Mm-hmm. Then we could probably do it, say, around ten o'clock?

DEAN: That would be fine, sir.

NIXON: How about—you just want to do it alone? Want anybody else there?

DEAN: I think just—

NIXON: It is better with nobody else there, isn't it?

DEAN: Absolutely, I think that's a good way.

NIXON: Anybody else you—they're all parties in interest, virtually.

DEAN: That's right.

NIXON: Right. Fine. The other thing I was going to say is this, that just for your own thinking, I still want to see, though, you know the—you and Dick I guess have still worked on your letter and all that sort of thing?

DEAN: We are and [laughs] we're coming and—the more we work on it the more questions we see that—

NIXON: You don't want to answer.

DEAN: —are creating problems by answering.

NIXON: And so you're coming up then with the idea of just a stonewall then? Is that—

DEAN: That's right.

NIXON: Is that what you come down with?

DEAN: A stonewall with lots of noises that we are always willing to cooperate, but no one's asking us for anything to—

NIXON: And they never will, huh? But, you know, there's no way that you could make even a general statement that I could put—you understand what I'm do—

DEAN: I think we could, uh—

NIXON: See, for example, I was even thinking if you could even talk to the cabinet, the leaders, you know, just you — just orally say, "I have looked into this, and this is that" period, so that people get sort of feel that — you know, your own people gotta be reassured.

DEAN: Mm-hmm.

NIXON: Could you do that?

DEAN: Well, I think I can but I don't think you'd want to make that decision until we have about a —

NIXON: No, I wanna know. I wanna know where all the bodies are first.

DEAN: Right, and then once you decide after that —

NIXON: Yeah.

DEAN: — we can program it any way you want it to.

NIXON: Yeah. Because I think, for example, you could do orally, for example, even if you don't want to make the written statement, you could do orally with, say, the cabinet and the leaders and the rest. You can lay it all out and say, "Look, I" — see I would not be present. You just lay it all out and I just — see what I mean?

DEAN: Mm-hmm.

NIXON: Now that is one thing. The other thing is that in — I do think there is something to be said for this, not maybe this complete answer to this fellow, but maybe just a written statement to me. You know, saying [laughs], "My conclusions are this: bing, bing, bing, bing."

DEAN: Mm-hmm.

NIXON: Even that's a possibility. So what I mean is we need something to answer somebody, answer things with. You know they say that "what are you basing this on," you can say, "Well, I've exam — my counsel has advised me that" — is that possible or not? Or are you —

DEAN: Well, I — you know there's that, and there's always the FBI report which we have probably not relied upon enough, that there's not one scintilla of evidence.

NIXON: I know. But I mean, can't you say that? Or do you want to put it out?

DEAN: Yes, it could be said, and it is something we haven't really emphasized. Pat Gray is the only person that has said it and it has really never gotten picked up.

NIXON: Yeah. How would you do it then? What I meant is isn't that something that you could say? Do you want to publish the FBI report?

DEAN: Oh, no. Oh, no —

NIXON: Then —

DEAN: — because in our, our own —

NIXON: Fine. Right.

DEAN: — structures we're trying to place on it [unclear] —

NIXON: But what — but you could say, "I had this and this is that." What I am getting at is that if apart from a statement to the committee or anything else, if you could just make a statement to me that we can use, you know, for internal purposes and to answer [unclear] and so forth.

DEAN: As we did when you, back in August, made the statement that —

NIXON: That's right.

DEAN: — [unclear] all the things.

NIXON: You've got to have something where —

DEAN: That was a [unclear] —

NIXON: — where it doesn't appear that I'm just doing this, you know, just in a — saying to hell with the Congress and the hell with the people, we're not going to tell you anything because of executive privilege. That they don't understand. But if you say, "No, we are willing to cooperate, and he's made a complete" — you've made a complete statement, you see, but make it very incomplete. See, that's what I mean. I don't want a, quite too much in chapter and verse as you did in your other — your letter. I just want a general —

DEAN: — general [unclear]. Let me, uh —

NIXON: Try just something general.

DEAN: — [unclear] it around.

NIXON: "I have checked into this matter. I can say categorically, based on my investigation, the following: Haldeman is not involved in this, that, and the other thing. Mr. Colson did not do this and Mr. So-and-So did not do this and Mr. Blank did not do this." And da-da-da-da-da, right down the line. See, taking the most glaring things.

DEAN: Mm-hmm.

NIXON: "If there are any further questions, please let me know." See?

DEAN: Mm-hmm. I think we can do that.

NIXON: That's one possibility, and then if you could say that such things — and then use the FBI report to the cabinet and leaders, it might be very salutary. Just — see our own people have gotta have confidence or they are not going to step up and defend us. You see my problem — see our problem there, don't you?

DEAN: And I think at the same time it would be good to brief these people on what executive privilege means, so they can go out and speak about it.

NIXON: That's right.

DEAN: Some of them are floundering, uh —

NIXON: And why it's necessary.

DEAN: I started having somebody in my office today prepare some material that can be put out by the congressional people so they can understand — people who want to defend us have a piece of paper —

NIXON: Sure.

DEAN: — that they know they can talk from as to what it all —

NIXON: Pointing out that we're defending the Constitution, it's the responsibility, the separation of powers, and that we have to do it, distinguishing the [Sherman] Adams case [involving improper gifts he had received] and sort of ignoring Flanigan [laughs].

DEAN: [laughs]

NIXON: Which is one we shouldn't have ever agreed to. But nevertheless — anyway, let's think a little about that, but we'll see you at ten o'clock tomorrow.

DEAN: Yes, sir.

NIXON: Fine.

DEAN: All right, sir.

NIXON: All right, fine.

DEAN: Good night.

NIXON: Take the evening off.

DEAN: [laughs] All right.

A cancer on the presidency

March 21, 1973, 10:12 a.m.

Richard Nixon, Bob Haldeman, and John Dean

OVAL OFFICE

Overnight between March 20 and 21, Dean came to recognize two points: (1) both he and the administration were in the midst of a truly massive crisis, and (2) the president had a shockingly poor grasp of the facts of Watergate. This realization came just four days after Dean emphatically said "We will win!" to Nixon.

Dean was facing an uncertain fate, in terms of testimony and implication in criminal activity. He simultaneously realized that his boss, the man whose lead he followed almost blindly, was making decisions based on a confused or even oblivious understanding of Watergate. Dean resolved that night to take a blunt tone in their meeting on the twenty-first and drive home the realities. Leaving his more usual "yes-man" personality behind, he started his meeting the next morning by telling the president something rather simple: what happened. Just how much of it Nixon already knew has been questioned ever since, but in their conversation that day, Dean left a succinct record of, at the very least, what he knew and when he knew it. Nixon, Haldeman, and Dean all feared that Hunt or one of the Watergate burglars would try to save himself by implicating others, including White House staffers. Nixon pressed the idea of payments in the form of hush money: up to $1 million. Within one day, Hunt had his first payment of $75,000. That constituted obstruction of justice and was the beginning of the end of the Nixon presidency.*

• • •

NIXON: Well, sit down. Sit down.

DEAN: Good morning.

NIXON: Well, what is the Dean summary of the day about?

DEAN: John [Ehrlichman] caught me on the way out and asked me about why Gray was holding back on information — if that was under instructions from us. And, it was and it wasn't. It was instructions proposed by the attorney general, consistent with your press conference statement, that no further raw data was to be turned over to the —

---

* Bob Woodward and Carl Bernstein, "Nixon Debated Paying Blackmail, Clemency," *Washington Post*, May 1, 1974, p. A1.

NIXON: Full committee.

DEAN: — full committee.

NIXON: Right.

DEAN: And that was the extent of it. Then Gray himself is the one who reached the conclusion that no more information be turned over. He'd turned over enough. So this is again Pat Gray making decisions on his own as to how to handle his hearings. He has been totally unwilling all along to take any guidance, any instruction. We don't know what he is going to do. He is not going to talk about it. He won't review it and I don't think—

NIXON: Right.

DEAN: — he does it to harm you in any way, sir.

NIXON: He's just quite stubborn and — he's quite stubborn. Also, he isn't very smart. You know what I mean?

DEAN: He is bullheaded.

NIXON: He is smart in his own way, but —

DEAN: Yeah.

NIXON: — he's got that typical, "Well, by God, this is right and they're not going to do it."

DEAN: That's why he thinks he'll be confirmed, because he thinks he's being his own man. He's being forthright, honest. He is — feels he has turned over too much and so it's a conscious decision that he is harming the bureau by doing this and so he is not going to—

NIXON: I hope to God that we get off— later off though today that this is because the White House told him to do this or that or the other thing. And also, I told Ehrlichman, I don't see why our little boys can't make something out of the fact that, God darn it, this is the only responsible decision you could possibly make. The FBI cannot turn over raw files. Has anybody made that point? I have tried.

DEAN: Sam Ervin has made that point himself.

NIXON: Did he?

DEAN: In fact, in reading the transcript of Gray's hearings, Ervin tried to hold Gray back from doing what he was doing at the time he did it — thought it was very unwise. I don't think that anyone is criticizing —

NIXON: Well, let's say —

DEAN: — your position on it.

NIXON: Let's make the point that the raw files cannot be turned over. Well, I think that point should be made.

DEAN: That—

NIXON: We are standing for the rights of innocent individuals. The American Civil Liberty [Liberties] Union is against it. We're against it. We will — because tradition, and it will continue to be the tradition that all files are — I'd like to turn them all over to somebody. I'd like to get a chance for [unclear] to put it out. What don't you talk to [unclear] and see what his [unclear] on it.

DEAN: How damaging —?

NIXON: Any further word on Sullivan? Is he still — ?

DEAN: Yeah, he's going to be over to see me today — this morning, hopefully sometime. Uh —

NIXON: As soon as you get that, I'll be available to talk to you this afternoon.

DEAN: All right, sir.

NIXON: I will be busy until about one o'clock. After that you can come back. Anytime you are through I would like to see whatever he has. We've got something but I'd like to just see what it is.

DEAN: The reason I thought we ought to talk this morning is because in our conversations, I have the impression that you don't know everything I know —

NIXON: That's right.

DEAN: — and it makes it very difficult for you to make judgments that only you can make —

NIXON: That's right.

DEAN: — on some of these things and I thought that —

NIXON: You've got — in other words, I've got to know why you feel that something —

DEAN: Well, let me —

NIXON: — that we shouldn't unravel something.

DEAN: Let me give you my overall first.

NIXON: In other words, your judgment as to where it stands, and where we go now.

DEAN: I think that there's no doubt about the seriousness of the problem we're — we've got. We have a cancer — within — close to the presidency, that's growing. It's growing daily. It's compounding. It grows geometrically now, because it compounds itself. That'll be clear as I explain, you know, some of the details of why it is. And it basically is because, one, we're being blackmailed, two, people are going to start perjuring themselves very quickly that have not had to perjure themselves to protect other people and the like. And that is just — and there is no assurance —

NIXON: That it won't bust.

DEAN: That that won't bust.

NIXON: True.

DEAN: So let me give you the sort of basic facts, talking first about the Watergate, and then about Segretti, and then about some of the peripheral items that have come up. First of all, on the Watergate: how did it all start? Where did it start? It started with an instruction to me from Bob Haldeman to see if we couldn't set up a perfectly legitimate campaign intelligence operation over at the reelection committee.

NIXON: Mm-hmm.

DEAN: Not being in this business, I turned to somebody who had been in this business — Jack Caulfield, who is — I don't know if you remember Jack or not. He was your original bodyguard before —

NIXON: Yeah.

DEAN: — they had —

NIXON: Yeah.

DEAN: — candidate —

NIXON: Yeah.

DEAN: — protection — an old New York City policeman.

NIXON: Right. I know — I know him.

DEAN: Jack had worked for John [Ehrlichman] and then was transferred to my office. I said, "Jack, come up with a plan that, you know, is a normal infiltration — I mean, you know, buying information from secretaries and all that sort of thing." He did — he put together a plan. It was kicked around and I went to Ehrlichman with it. I went to Mitchell with it, and the consensus was that Caulfield wasn't the man to do this. In retrospect, that might have been a bad call, because he is an incredibly cautious person and wouldn't have put the situation where it is today.

NIXON: Yeah.

DEAN: All right, after rejecting that, they said, "We still need something," so I was told to look around for somebody that could go over to 1701 [Pennsylvania Avenue SE, the address of Nixon's CRP] and do this. That's when I came up with Gordon Liddy, who — they needed a lawyer. Gordon had an intelligence background from his FBI service. I was aware of the fact that he had done some extremely sensitive things for the White House while he'd been at the White House, and he had apparently done them well — going out into Ellsberg's doctor's office —

NIXON: Oh, yeah.

DEAN: — and things like this. He'd worked with leaks. He'd, you know, tracked these things down. And so the report that I got from Krogh was that he was a hell of a good man and not only that a good lawyer, and could set up a proper operation. So we talked to Liddy. Liddy was interested in doing it. Took Liddy over to meet Mitchell. Mitchell thought highly of him because, apparently, Mitchell was partially involved in his coming to the White House to work for Krogh. Liddy had been at Treasury before that. Then Liddy was told to put together his plan — you know, how he would run an intelligence operation. And this was after he was hired over there at the Committee [to Re-elect the President]. Magruder called me in January and said, "I'd like to have you come over and see Liddy's plan."

NIXON: January of '72?

DEAN: January of '72. Like, "You come over to Mitchell's office and sit in on a meeting where Liddy is going to lay his plan out." I said, "Well, I don't really know as I am the man, but if you want me there I will be happy to." So I came over and Liddy laid out a million-dollar plan that was the most incredible thing I have ever laid my eyes on: all in codes, and involved black bag operations, kidnapping, providing prostitutes to weaken the opposition, bugging, mugging teams. It was just an incredible thing.

NIXON: But, uh —

DEAN: And —

NIXON: — that was not, uh —

DEAN: No.

NIXON: — discussed in the —

DEAN: No.

NIXON: — first instance.

DEAN: No, not at all. And —

NIXON: But I [unclear] —

DEAN: Mitchell just virtually sat there puffing and laughing. I could tell because after he — after Liddy left the office I said, "That's the most incredible thing I have ever seen." He said, "I agree." And so then he was told to go back to the drawing boards and come up with something realistic. So there was a second meeting. They asked me to come over to that. I came into the tail end of the meeting. I wasn't there for the first part. I don't know how long the meeting lasted. At this point, they were discussing again bugging, kidnapping, and the like. And at this point I said right in front of everybody, very clearly, I said, "These are not the sort of things, one, that are ever to be discussed in the office of the attorney general of the United States" — where he still was — "and I am personally incensed." I was trying to get Mitchell off the hook, because —

NIXON: I know.

DEAN: — he's a nice person — doesn't like to say no under — when people he's going to have to work with.

NIXON: That's right.

DEAN: So, I let it be known. I said, "You all pack that stuff up and get it the hell out of here because we just — you just can't talk this way in this office and you shouldn't — you should reexamine your whole thinking." Came back —

NIXON: Who else was present? Besides you — ?

DEAN: It was Magruder — Magruder —

NIXON: Magruder.

DEAN: — Mitchell, Liddy, and myself. I came back right after the meeting and told Bob. I said, "Bob, we've got a growing disaster on our hands if they're thinking this way." And I said, "The White House has got to stay out of this and I, frankly, am not going to be involved in it." He said, "I agree, John." And I thought, at that point, the thing was turned off. That's the last I heard of it, when I thought it was turned off, because it was an absurd proposal.

NIXON: Yeah.

DEAN: Liddy — I did have dealings with him afterwards. We never talked about it. Now that would be hard to believe for some people, but we never did. Just the fact of the matter.

NIXON: Well, you were talking about other things.

DEAN: Other things. We had so many other things.

NIXON: He had some legal problems at one time.

DEAN: Now —

NIXON: But you were his advisor, and I understand how you could have some — what, cam — what are they, campaign laws? I knew that was you — you have — Haldeman told me you — that you were heading all of that up for us. Go ahead.

DEAN: Now. So Liddy went back after that and was over, over at 1701, the committee, and I — this is where I come into having put the pieces together after the fact as to what I can put together what happened. Liddy sat over there and tried to come up with another plan that he could sell. One, they were talking — saying to him he was asking for too much money, and I don't think they were discounting the illegal points at this, after — you know, Jeb is not a lawyer. He didn't know whether this was the way the game was played or not, and what it was all about. They came up with, apparently, another plan, but they couldn't get it approved by anybody over there. So Liddy and Hunt apparently came to see Chuck Colson, and Chuck Colson picked up the telephone and called Magruder and said, "You all either fish or cut bait. This is absurd to have these guys over there and not using them, and if you're not going to use them, I may use them." Things of this nature.

NIXON: When was this?

DEAN: This was apparently in February of '72.

NIXON: That could be — did Colson know what they were talking about?

DEAN: I can only assume, because of his close relationship with —

NIXON: Hunt.

DEAN: Hunt. He had a damn good idea of what they were talking about — a damn good idea. He would probably deny it today and probably get away with denying it. But, I still —

NIXON: Unless Hunt —

DEAN: Unless Hunt blows on him —

NIXON: But then Hunt isn't enough. It takes two, doesn't it?

DEAN: Probably. Probably. But Liddy was there also and if Liddy were to blow —

NIXON: Then you've got a problem. I was saying as to the criminal liability in the —

DEAN: Yeah.

NIXON: — White House. Okay.

DEAN: I will go back over that and tell —

NIXON: Was that Colson?

DEAN: — you where I think the soft spots are.

NIXON: Colson — that Colson, you think, was the person who —

DEAN: I think he —

NIXON: — pushed?

DEAN: I think he helped to get the push — get the thing off dime. Now something else occurred, though —

NIXON: Did Colson — had he talked to anybody here?

DEAN: No. I think this was an independent —

NIXON: Did he talk to Haldeman?

DEAN: No, I don't think so. Now, but here's the other — where the next thing comes in the chain. I think that Bob was assuming that they had something that was proper over there, some intelligence-gathering operation that Liddy was operating. And through Strachan, who was his tickler, he started pushing them —

NIXON: Yeah.

DEAN: — to get something — to get some information and they took that as a signal. Magruder took that as a signal to probably go to Mitchell and say, "They are pushing us like crazy for this from the White House." And so Mitchell probably puffed on his pipe and said, "Go ahead," and never really reflected on what it was all about. So, they had some plan that obviously had, I gather, different targets they were going to go after. They were going to infiltrate, and bug, and do all this sort of thing to a lot of these targets. This is knowledge I have after the fact. And, apparently, they had after — they had initially broken in and bugged the Democratic National Committee — they were getting information. The information was coming over here to Strachan. Some of it was given to Haldeman, there is no doubt about it. Uh —

NIXON: Did he know what it was coming from?

DEAN: I don't really know if he would.

NIXON: Not necessarily.

DEAN: Not necessarily. That's not necessarily. Uh —

NIXON: Strachan knew what it was from?

DEAN: Strachan knew what it was from. No doubt about it, and whether Strachan — I have never come to press these people on these points because it —

NIXON: Yeah.

DEAN: — it hurts them to give up that next inch, so I had to piece things together. All right, so Strachan was aware of receiving information, reporting to Bob. At one point Bob even gave instructions to change their capabilities from Muskie to McGovern, and had passed this back through Strachan to Magruder and apparently to Liddy. And Liddy was starting to make arrangements to go in and bug the McGovern operation. They had done prelim —

NIXON: They had never bugged Muskie, though, did they?

DEAN: No, they hadn't, but they had a — they had — they'd —

NIXON: [unclear]

DEAN: — infiltrated it by a — they had —

NIXON: A secretary?

DEAN: — a secretary and a chauffeur. Nothing illegal about that.

NIXON: [unclear]

DEAN: Now, so the information was coming over here and then I finally, after the next point in time where I became aware of anything was on June 17, when I got the word that there had been this break-in at the Democratic National Committee and somebody from the committee had been caught from our committee [CRP] — had been caught in the DNC. And I said, "Oh, my God, that — I can only." You know, if — instantly putting the pieces together.

NIXON: You knew what it was.

DEAN: I knew what it was. So I called Liddy on that Monday morning, and I said, "Gordon," I said, "first, I want to know if anybody in the White House was involved in this." And he said, "No, they weren't." I said, "Well, I want to know how in God's name this happened." And he said, "Well, I was pushed without mercy by Magruder to get in there, get more information — that the information, it was not satisfactory. Magruder said, 'The White House is not happy with what we're getting.'"

NIXON: The White House?

DEAN: The White House. Yeah. Uh —

NIXON: Who do you think was pushing him?

DEAN: Well, I think it was probably Strachan thinking that Bob wanted things, and because I have seen that happen on other occasions where things have been said to be of very prime importance when they really weren't.

NIXON: Why did they want to do it in June I wonder? I am just trying to think as to why then. We'd just finished the Moscow trip. I mean, we were —

DEAN: That's right.

NIXON: The Democrats had just nominated McGovern. I mean, for Christ's sakes! I mean, what the hell were we — I mean I can see doing it earlier but — I mean, now let me say, I can see the pressure, but I don't see why all the pressure would have been around then.

DEAN: I don't know, other than the fact that they might have been looking for information about —

NIXON: The convention.

DEAN: — the conventions.

NIXON: Well, that's right.

DEAN: Because, I understand, also, after the fact, that there was a plan to bug Larry O'Brien's suite down in Florida.

NIXON: Yeah.

DEAN: So Liddy told me that, you know, this is what had happened and this is why it had happened.

NIXON: Liddy told you he was planning — where'd you learn there was such a plan — from whom?

DEAN: Beg your pardon?

NIXON: Where did you learn of the plans to bug Larry O'Brien's suite?

DEAN: From Magruder, after the — long after the fact.

NIXON: Oh, Magruder. He knows?

DEAN: Yeah. Magruder is totally knowledgeable on the whole thing.

NIXON: Yeah.

DEAN: All right, now, we've gone through the trial. We've — I don't know if Mitchell has perjured himself in the grand jury or not. I've never —

NIXON: Who?

DEAN: Mitchell. I don't know how much knowledge he actually had. I know that Magruder has perjured himself in the grand jury. I know that Porter has perjured himself in the grand jury.

NIXON: Porter [unclear].

DEAN: He is one of Magruder's deputies.

NIXON: Yeah.

DEAN: They set up this scenario which they ran by me. They said, "How about this?" I said, "I don't know. I — you know, if this is what you are going to hang on, fine." That they —

NIXON: What did they say before the grand jury?

DEAN: They said — as they said before the trial and the grand jury, that Liddy had come over as a counsel —

NIXON: Yeah.

DEAN: — and we knew he had these capacities to —

NIXON: Yeah.

DEAN: — you know —

NIXON: Yeah.

DEAN: — to do legitimate intelligence. We had no idea what he was doing.

NIXON: Yeah.

DEAN: He was given an authorization of two hundred fifty thousand dollars —

NIXON: Right.

DEAN: — to collect information, because our surrogates were out on the road. They had no protection. We had information that there were going to be demonstrations against them, that we had to have a plan to get information as to what liabilities they were going to be confronted with —

NIXON: Right.

DEAN: — and Liddy was charged with doing this. We had no knowledge that he was going to bug the DNC.

NIXON: Well, the point is that's not true.

DEAN: That's right.

NIXON: Magruder did know that —

DEAN: Magruder specifically instructed him to go back in the DNC.

NIXON: He did?

DEAN: Yes.

NIXON: You know that? Yeah. I see. Okay.

DEAN: I honestly believe that no one over here knew that. I know, as God is my maker, I had no knowledge that they were going to do this.

NIXON: Bob didn't either [unclear]?

DEAN: Uh, but —

NIXON: They know you're not the issue. Bob, now — he wouldn't know.

DEAN: Bob I don't believe specifically knew they were going in there.

NIXON: I don't think so.

DEAN: I don't think he did. I think he knew there was a capacity to do this but he wouldn't — wasn't giving it specific direction.

NIXON: Strachan — did he know?

DEAN: I think Strachan did know.

NIXON: They were going back into the DNC? Hunt never [unclear].

DEAN: All right, so those people are in trouble as a result of the grand jury and the trial. Mitchell, of course, was never called during the trial. Now —

NIXON: Mitchell has given a sworn statement?

DEAN: Yes, sir.

NIXON: To the bureau?

DEAN: To the grand jury —

NIXON: Did he go before the grand jury?

DEAN: He had — we had an arrangement whereby he went down to, with several of the — because it was, you know, the heat of this thing and the implications on the election. We made an arrangement where they could quietly go into the Department of Justice and have one of the assistant U.S. attorneys come over and take their testimony and then read it before the grand jury. Uh —

NIXON: That was [unclear].

DEAN: — although I — that's right, Mitchell was actually called before the grand jury. The grand jury would not settle for less. The jurors wanted him.

NIXON: And he went.

DEAN: And he went.

NIXON: Good.

DEAN: I don't know what he said. I have never seen a transcript of the grand jury. Now, what has happened post–June 17? Well, it was — I was under pretty clear instructions not to really investigate this, that this was something that just could have been disastrous on the election if it had — all hell had broken loose, and I worked on a theory of containment.

NIXON: Sure.

DEAN: To try to hold it right where it was.

NIXON: Right.

DEAN: There is no doubt I — that I was totally aware what the bureau was doing at all times. I was totally aware of what the grand jury was doing.

NIXON: You — I mean —

DEAN: I knew what witnesses were going to be called. I knew what they were going to be asked, and I had to. There just —

NIXON: Why did Petersen play the game so straight with us?

DEAN: Because Petersen is a soldier. He played — he kept me informed. He told me when we had problems, where we had problems, and the like. He believes in you. He believes in this administration. This administration has made him. I don't think he's done anything improper, but he did make sure the investigation was narrowed down to the very, very —

NIXON: Right.

DEAN: — fine —

NIXON: Right.

DEAN: — criminal things, which was a break for us. There is no doubt about it.

NIXON: He honestly feels that he did an adequate job?

DEAN: He—they ran that investigation out to the fullest extent they could follow a lead and that was it.

NIXON: But the point is, where—I suppose he could be criticized for not doing an adequate job. Why didn't he call Haldeman? Why didn't he get a statement from Colson? Oh, they did get Colson.

DEAN: That's right. But see, the thing is based on their FBI interviews. There was no reason to follow up. There were no leads there. Colson said, "I have no knowledge of this" to the FBI. Strachan said, "I have no knowledge of"—you know, they didn't ask Strachan any Watergate questions. They asked him about Segretti. They said, "What's your connection with Liddy?" And he just said, "Well, I, you know, I just met him over there," and they never really pressed him. They didn't—you know, they—look, Strachan appeared as a result of some coaching, he could be the dumbest paper pusher in the bowels of the White House.

NIXON: Right.

DEAN: All right. Now post–June 17: these guys—immediately it is very, very [laughs] interesting. Liddy, for example, the Friday before—on, I guess it was, the fifteenth, sixteenth of June—had been in Henry Petersen's office with another member of my staff on campaign compliance [laughs] problems joking. After the incident, he went—he ran Kleindienst down at Burning Tree Country Club and told [laughs] him that "you've got to get my men out of jail," which was kind of a—Kleindienst said, "Now, you get the hell out of here, kid. Whatever you've got to say, just say to somebody else. Don't bother me," and—but this has never come up.

NIXON: Yeah.

DEAN: Liddy said that, you know, they all got counsel instantly and said that, you know, "We'll ride this thing out." All right, then they started making demands. "We've got to have attorneys' fees. We don't have any money ourselves, and if—you are asking us to take this through the election." All right, so arrangements were made through Mitchell, initiating it in discussions—that I was present—that these guys had to be taken care of. Their attorneys' fees had to be done. Kalmbach was brought in. Kalmbach raised some cash. They we're obv—you know.

NIXON: They put that under the cover of a Cuban committee or something.

DEAN: Yeah, they had a Cuban committee and they had—some of it was given to Hunt's lawyer, who in turn passed it out. This, you know, when Hunt's wife was flying to Chicago with ten thousand. She was actually, I understand after the fact now, was going to pass that money to one of the Cubans—to meet him in Chicago and pass it to somebody there.

NIXON: Why did they [unclear]? Maybe—well, whether it's maybe too late to do anything about it, but I would certainly keep that cover for whatever it's worth.

DEAN: I'll—

NIXON: Keep the committee.

DEAN: After—well, that's—

NIXON: [unclear]

DEAN: — the most troublesome post-thing, because, one, Bob is involved in that. John is involved in that. I am involved in that. Mitchell is involved in that. And that's an obstruction of justice.

NIXON: In other words, the fact that you're taking care of the witnesses.

DEAN: That's right. Uh —

NIXON: How was Bob involved?

DEAN: Well, they ran out of money over there. Bob had three hundred and fifty thousand dollars in a safe over here that was really set aside for polling purposes. And there was no other source of money, so they came over here and said, "You all have got to give us some money."

NIXON: Right.

DEAN: I had to go to Bob and say, "Bob, you know, you've got to have some — they need some money over there." He said, "What for?" And so I had to tell him what it was for because he wasn't about to just send money over there willy-nilly. And John was involved in those discussions, and we decided, you know — that, you know, that there was no price too high to pay to let this thing blow up in front of the election.

NIXON: I think you should handle that one pretty fast.

DEAN: Oh, I think —

NIXON: That issue, I mean.

DEAN: I think we can.

NIXON: So that the three fifty went back to him. All it did was —

DEAN: That's right. I think we can, too.

NIXON: Who else [unclear]?

DEAN: But, now, here — here's what's happening right now.

NIXON: Yeah.

DEAN: What sort of brings matters to the — this is the one that's going to be a continual blackmail operation by Hunt and Liddy and the —

NIXON: Yeah.

DEAN: — Cubans. No doubt about it. And McCord —

NIXON: Yeah.

DEAN: — who is another one involved. McCord has asked for nothing. McCord did ask to meet with somebody, and it was Jack Caulfield, who is his old friend who'd gotten him hired over there. And when Caulfield had him hired, he was a perfectly legitimate security man. And he wanted to know — well, you know, he wanted to talk about commutation and things like that. And as you know Colson has talked to — indirectly to Hunt about commutation. All these things are bad in that they are problems. They are promises. They are commitments. They are the very sort of thing that the Senate is going to be looking for. I don't think they can find them, frankly.

NIXON: Pretty hard.

DEAN: Pretty hard. Damn hard. It's all cash. Uh —

NIXON: Well, I mean, pretty hard as far as the witnesses are concerned.

DEAN: That's right. Now, the blackmail is continuing. Hunt called one of the lawyers from the reelection committee last Friday to meet with him on — over the weekend. The guy came in to me — to see me to get a message directly from Hunt to me for the first time.

NIXON: Is Hunt out on bail?

DEAN: Pardon?

NIXON: Is Hunt on bail?

DEAN: Hunt is on bail. Correct. Hunt now is demanding another seventy-two thousand dollars for his own personal expenses, another fifty thousand dollars to pay his attorneys' fees — a hundred and twenty-some thousand dollars. Wants it — wanted it by the close of business yesterday. Because, he says, "I am going to be sentenced on Friday, and I've got to be able to get my financial affairs in order." I told this fellow [CRP attorney Paul] O'Brien, "You came — all right, you came to the wrong man, fellow. I'm not involved in the money. I don't know a thing about it. Can't help you." Said, "You better scramble around elsewhere." Now, O'Brien is a ball player. He's been — he's carried tremendous water for us. Uh —

NIXON: He isn't Hunt's lawyer, is he?

DEAN: No, he is our lawyer at the reelection committee.

NIXON: I see. Good.

DEAN: So he's safe. There's no problem there. But it raises the whole question of Hunt now has made a direct threat against Ehrlichman as a result of this. This is his blackmail. He says, "I will bring John Ehrlichman down to his knees and put him in jail. I have done enough seamy things for he and Krogh that they'll never survive it."

NIXON: What's that, on Ellsberg?

DEAN: Ellsberg, and apparently some other things. I don't know the full extent of it. Uh —

NIXON: I don't know about anything else.

DEAN: I don't know either, and I [laughs] almost hate to learn some of these —

NIXON: Yeah.

DEAN: — things. So that's that situation. Now, where are the soft points? How many people know about this? Well, let me go one step further in this whole thing. The Cubans that were used in the Watergate were also the same Cubans that Hunt and Liddy used for this California Ellsberg thing — the break-in out there.

NIXON: Yeah.

DEAN: So they are aware of that. How high their knowledge is, is something else. Hunt and Liddy, of course, are totally aware of it and the fact that it was right out of the White House.

NIXON: I don't know what the hell we did that for.

DEAN: I don't either.

NIXON: What in the name of God did that — ?

DEAN: Mr. President, there have been a couple of things around here that I have gotten wind of. There was at one time a desire to do a second-story job on the Brookings Institute where they had the Pentagon Papers. Now I flew to California because I was told that John had instructed it and he said, "I really hadn't. It is a misimpression. That for Christ's sakes, turn it off." And I did. I came back and turned it off. Because you know the — when you — you know, if the risk is minimal and the gain is fantastic, it's something else. But with a low risk and no gain, gee, it's just — it's not worth it. But who knows about this all now? All right, you've got the Cubans' lawyer, a man by the name of [Henry] Rothblatt, who is a no-good, publicity-seeking son of a bitch to be very frank about it. He has had to be turned down and tuned off. He was canned by his own people because they didn't trust him. They were trying to run a different route than he wanted to run. He didn't want them to plead guilty. He wants to represent them before the Senate. So F. Lee Bailey, who was the partner of one of the men representing McCord, got in and cooled Rothblatt down. So F. Lee Bailey's got knowledge. Hunt's lawyer, a man by the name of Bittman, who's an excellent criminal lawyer from the Democratic era of Bobby Kennedy, he's got knowledge. Uh —

NIXON: Do you think that he's got some? How much?

DEAN: Well, everybody — not only all the direct knowledge that Hunt and Liddy have, as well as all the hearsay they have.

NIXON: I [unclear].

DEAN: You've got the two lawyers over at the reelection committee who did an investigation to find out the facts. Slowly, they got the whole picture. They are, I — they're solid, but they're —

NIXON: But they know.

DEAN: But they know. You've got then an awful lot of — all the principals involved know. Hunt — some people's wives know.

NIXON: Sure.

DEAN: There's no doubt about that. Mrs. Hunt was the savviest woman in the world. She had the whole picture together.

NIXON: Did she?

DEAN: Yeah, it — apparently she was the pillar of strength in that family before the death, and —

NIXON: Great sadness. The basis — as a matter of fact there was some discussion over there with somebody about Hunt's problems after his wife died. And I said, of course, commutation could be considered on the basis of his wife, and that is the only discussion I ever had in that light.

DEAN: Right. So that's it. That's the extent of the knowledge. Now, where are the soft spots on this? Well, first of all, there's the problem of the continued blackmail —

NIXON: Right.

DEAN: — which will not only go on now, it'll go on when these people are in prison. And it will compound the obstruction of justice situation. It'll cost money. It's dangerous. Nobody, nothing — people around here are not pros at this sort of thing. This is the sort of thing Mafia people can do: washing money, getting clean money, and things like that we're — we just don't know about those things, because we're not used to, you know — we are not criminals and not used to dealing in that business. It's —

NIXON: That's right.

DEAN: It's a tough thing to know how to do.

NIXON: Maybe we can't even do that.

DEAN: That's right. It's a real problem as to whether we could even do it. Plus there's a real problem in raising money. Mitchell has been working on raising some money. Feeling he's got, you know, he's got one — he's one of the ones with the most to lose. But there's no denying the fact that the White House, and Ehrlichman, Haldeman, Dean are involved in some of the early money decisions.

NIXON: How much money do you need?

DEAN: I would say these people are going to cost a million dollars over the next two years.

NIXON: Could you get that?

DEAN: Mm-hmm.

NIXON: You — on the money, if you need the money, I mean, you could get the money. Let's say —

DEAN: Well, I think that we're going —

NIXON: What I meant is, you could get a million dollars. And you could get it in cash. I know where it could be gotten.

DEAN: Mm-hmm.

NIXON: I mean it's not easy, but it could be done. But the question is who the hell would handle it?

DEAN: That's right. Uh —

NIXON: Any ideas on that?

DEAN: Well, I would think that would be something that Mitchell ought to be charged with.

NIXON: I would think so too.

DEAN: And get some pros to help him.

NIXON: Let me say, there shouldn't be a lot of people running around getting money. We should set up a little —

DEAN: Well, he's got one person doing it who I am not sure is —

NIXON: Who is that?

DEAN: He's got Fred LaRue doing it. Now Fred started out — going out trying to —

NIXON: No.

DEAN: — solicit money from all kinds of people. Now, I learned about that, and I said —

NIXON: No.

DEAN: "My God — "

NIXON: No.

DEAN: " — it's just awful. Don't do it."

NIXON: Yeah.

DEAN: People are going to ask what the money is for. He's working—he's apparently talked to [former ambassador and CRP fundraiser] Tom Pappas.

NIXON: I know.

DEAN: And Pappas has agreed to come up with a sizable amount, I gather, from—

NIXON: Yeah.

DEAN: —Mitchell.

NIXON: Yeah. Well, what do you need then? You need—you don't need a million right away, but you need a million. Is that right?

DEAN: That's right.

NIXON: You need a million in cash, don't you? If you want to put that through, would you put that through—this is thinking out loud here for a moment—would you put that through the Cuban committee?

DEAN: Uh, no.

NIXON: Or would you just do this through a [unclear] that it's going to be—well, it's cash money, and so forth. How, if that ever comes out, are you going to handle it? Is the Cuban committee an obstruction of justice, if they want to help?

DEAN: Well, they've got a pr—they've got priests and—

NIXON: Would you like to put—I mean, would that give a little bit of a cover, for example?

DEAN: That would give some for the Cubans and possibly Hunt.

NIXON: Yeah.

DEAN: Then you've got Liddy, and McCord is not accepting any money. So he is not a bought man right now.

NIXON: Okay.

DEAN: All right. Let me—

NIXON: Go ahead.

DEAN: —continue a little bit here now. The—I—when I say this is a growing cancer, I say it for reasons like this. Bud Krogh, in his testimony before the grand jury, was forced to perjure himself. He is haunted by it. Bud said, "I haven't had a pleasant day on the job."

NIXON: Huh? Said what?

DEAN: He said, "I have not had a pleasant day on my job." He talked, apparently—he said to me, "I told my wife all about this," he said. "The curtain may ring down one of these days, and I may have to face the music, which I'm perfectly willing to do." Uh—

NIXON: What did he perjure himself on, John?

DEAN: His—did he know the Cubans? He did. Uh—

NIXON: He said he didn't?

DEAN: That's right. They didn't press him hard—or that he—

NIXON: He might be able to—I am just trying to think. Perjury is an awful hard rap to prove. He could say that I—well, go ahead.

DEAN: Well, so that's the first—that's one perjury. Now, Mitchell and Magruder are potential perjuries. There is always the possibility of any one of these individuals blowing. Hunt. Liddy. Liddy is in jail right now. He's serving his — trying to get good time right now. I think Liddy is probably, in his own bizarre way, the strongest of all of them. So there's — there is that possibility.

NIXON: Well, your major guy to keep under control is Hunt.

DEAN: That's right.

NIXON: I think. Because he knows —

DEAN: He knows so much.

NIXON: — about a lot of other things.

DEAN: He knows so much. Right. He could sink Chuck Colson. Apparently, he is quite distressed with Colson. He thinks Colson has abandoned him. Colson was to meet with him when he was out there, after — now he had left the White House. He met with him through his lawyer. Hunt raised the question. He wanted money. Colson's lawyer told him that Colson wasn't doing anything with money, and Hunt took offense with that immediately, that Colson had abandoned him. Uh —

NIXON: Don't you — just looking at the immediate problem, don't you have to have — handle Hunt's financial situation —

DEAN: I think that's —

NIXON: — damn soon?

DEAN: — that is — I talked to Mitchell about that last night —

NIXON: Mitchell.

DEAN: — and I told —

NIXON: Might as well. May have the rule you've got to keep the cap on the bottle that much —

DEAN: That's right. That's right.

NIXON: — in order to have any options.

DEAN: That's right.

NIXON: Either that or let it all blow right now.

DEAN: Well, that — you know, that's the question. Uh —

NIXON: Now, go ahead. The others. You've got Hunt —

DEAN: All right, now we've got —

NIXON: — you've got Krogh, and you've got —

DEAN: Now we've got Kalmbach.

NIXON: Yeah, that's a tough one.

DEAN: Kalmbach received —

NIXON: Totally loyal. Do you agree with that?

DEAN: — at the close of the '68 campaign — in January of '69, he got a million seven dollars — a million seven hundred thousand dollars — to be custodian for. That came down from New York. It was placed in safety deposit boxes here. Some other people were on the boxes and ultimately, the money was taken out to California. All right, there is knowledge of the fact that he did start with a million seven. Several people know this. Now since '69, he's spent a good deal of this money and accounting for it is going to be very difficult for Herb. For example, he's spent — oh, close to five hundred thousand dollars on private polling. Now that just opens up a whole new thing. It's not illegal, but it's more of the same sort of thing.

NIXON: I don't think that poses a hell of a problem, does it?

DEAN: No, I don't think so. Uh —

NIXON: Practically everybody does polling.

DEAN: That's right. It's not — there's nothing criminal about it. It was private polls. It was —

NIXON: Nothing —

DEAN: — proper money.

NIXON: The law didn't [unclear] polled all through the years.

DEAN: That's right. He sent four hundred thousand dollars, as he's described it to me, somewhere in the South for another candidate. I assume this was four hundred that went —

NIXON: [George] Wallace.

DEAN: — to Wallace. Right. He has maintained a man who only know by the name of "Tony," who is the fellow who did the Chappaquiddick study and —

NIXON: I heard about that.

DEAN: — other odd jobs like that. Nothing illegal —

NIXON: Yeah.

DEAN: — but closer. I don't know of anything that Herb has done that is illegal other than the fact that he doesn't want to blow the whistle on a lot of people and may find himself in a perjury situation.

NIXON: Well, if he — could because he will be asked about that money?

DEAN: He will. What'll happen is, when they call up there and he, of course, has no immunity, they'll say, "How did you happen — how did you pay Mr. Segretti?" "Well, I had cash on hand." "Well, how much cash did you have on hand?"

NIXON: Right.

DEAN: Where does he go from there? "Where did you get the cash?"

NIXON: Mm-hmm.

DEAN: A full series of questions. His bank records indicate he had cash on hand because some of these were set up in trustee accounts.

NIXON: How would you handle him then John? For example, would you just have him put the whole thing out? I don't think. I mean I don't mind the five hundred thousand dollars and I don't mind the four hundred thousand dollars —

DEAN: No, that —

NIXON: — for activities and so on.

DEAN: — that doesn't bother me either. There's — as I say, Herb's problems are —

NIXON: There's a surplus —

DEAN: — politically embarrassing, but not as — not criminal.

NIXON: Well, they're embarrassing, sure. He just handled matters that were between the campaigns before anything was done. There were surveys, et cetera, et cetera, et cetera, et cetera. There is no need to account for that. No law requires him to account for that.

DEAN: Right. Uh, now —

NIXON: The source of the money — there's no illegality in having a surplus, is there, in cash after — ?

DEAN: No, the money — it has always been argued by Stans — came from preconvention —

NIXON: Preconvention.

DEAN: — for the — and preprimary for the —

NIXON: That's right.

DEAN: — '68 race.

NIXON: That's right.

DEAN: It was just set aside.

NIXON: That's right.

DEAN: That all can be explained. I think that the —

NIXON: All right. How do your other vulnerabilities go together?

DEAN: The other vulnerabilities. We've got a runaway grand jury up in the Southern District [of New York].

NIXON: Yeah, I heard.

DEAN: They're after Mitchell and Stans on some sort of bribe or influence peddling —

NIXON: On Vesco.

DEAN: — with Vesco.

NIXON: Yeah.

DEAN: They're also going to try to drag Ehrlichman into that. Apparently, Ehrlichman had some meetings with Vesco also. Don Nixon Jr. came in to see John a couple of times about the problem.

NIXON: Not about the complaint.

DEAN: That — there's — the fact of the matter is —

NIXON: [unclear] probably wanted about a job.

DEAN: That's right. And, I —

NIXON: We're — is it — Ehrlichman's totally to blame on that.

DEAN: Yeah, well, I think the White House —

NIXON: [unclear] attorney —

DEAN: No one has done anything for —

NIXON: — Vesco. Matter of — not for the prosecutor.

DEAN: No. The —

NIXON: Would Ehrlichman, incidentally, have to appear there?

DEAN: Before that grand jury? Yes. He could very well.

NIXON: We couldn't presume immunity there?

DEAN: Not really. Criminal charge —

NIXON: Criminal charge. Yeah, well [unclear] charges [unclear]. Go ahead.

DEAN: Right. That's a little different. I think that would be dynamite to defend —

NIXON: Yeah.

DEAN: — against that.

NIXON: Also, he distinguishes it. He says, "It's a criminal charge. I'll be glad to go up." Use the Flanigan —

DEAN: Right.

NIXON: — analogy.

DEAN: Right, well that's pretty much the overall picture, and probably the most troublesome thing — well, the Segretti thing. Let's get down to that. I think Bob has indicated to me he told you a lot of it. That he, indeed, did authorize it. He didn't authorize anything like [what was] ultimately involved.

NIXON: Yeah.

DEAN: He was aware of it. He was aware that Chapin and Strachan were looking for somebody.

NIXON: Yeah.

DEAN: Again, this is one that — it is potential that Dwight Chapin could have a felony charge against him in this, because he's —

NIXON: Felony?

DEAN: Felony, because he has to disprove a negative. The negative is that he didn't control and direct Segretti.

NIXON: Would the felony be in perjury again? Or —

DEAN: No, the felony — this — in this instance being a potential use of the — one of the civil rights statutes. For anybody who interferes with a candidate for national office — no, interferes with their campaign in any way.

NIXON: Why isn't that civil rights statute used to pick up any of these clowns that were demonstrating against us then?

DEAN: Well, I have — I've argued that they use that for that very purpose. Uh —

NIXON: Really?

DEAN: Yes, I have. And —

NIXON: We were — those were — that was interfering with the campaign.

DEAN: That's exactly right. It's exactly right, but they —

NIXON: Segretti — when I think — I'm not as concerned about that because it's so bad the way it's been put out on the PR side. Then I think it will eventually end up on the PR side very confused. And it'll look bad when that's attributed, but I don't — I can't see the criminal thing. But I may be wrong.

DEAN: Well, here — what really bothers me is that this — this growing situation. As I say, it is growing because of the continued need to provide support for the —

NIXON: Right.

DEAN: — Watergate people who are going to —

NIXON: Yeah.

DEAN: — hold us up for everything they've got —

NIXON: That's right.

DEAN: — and the need for some people to perjure themselves as they go down the road here. If this thing ever blows, and we're in a cover-up situation, I think it'd be extremely damaging to you and the —

NIXON: Sure. The whole concept of administration justice.

DEAN: That's right —

NIXON: We cannot have —

DEAN: That's what really troubles me. For example, what happens if it starts breaking, and they do find a criminal case against a Haldeman, a Dean, a Mitchell, an Ehrlichman? That is —

NIXON: Well, if it really comes down to that we cannot — maybe we'd have to shed it in order to contain it again.

DEAN: That's right. I'm coming down to the — what I really think is that Bob and John and John Mitchell and I should sit down and spend a day, or however long, to figure out, one, how this can be carved away from you, so it does not damage you or the presidency. Because it just can't. And it's not something — it — you're not involved in it and it's something you shouldn't —

NIXON: That is true.

DEAN: I know, sir. It is. Well, I can just tell from our conversations that, you know, these are things that you have no knowledge of.

NIXON: The absurdity of the whole damn thing.

DEAN: But, it —

NIXON: Bugging and so on. Well, let me say I am keenly aware of the fact that Colson, et al., and so forth, were doing their best to get information and so forth and so on. But they all knew very well they were supposed to comply with the law.

DEAN: That's right.

NIXON: No question.

DEAN: Uh —

NIXON: [unclear] you think — you feel that really the man — the trigger man was Colson on this then?

DEAN: Well, no. He was one of a — he was just in the chain. He was — he helped push the thing.

NIXON: Called [unclear] up and said, "We've got a good plan." I don't know what the Christ he would be doing. Oh, I'll bet you I know why. That was at the time of ITT. He was trying to get something going there because ITT — they were bugging us. I mean they were —

DEAN: Right.

NIXON: — giving us hell.

DEAN: Well, I know he used —

NIXON: Hunt to go out there?

DEAN: Hunt.

NIXON: I knew about that.

DEAN: Yeah.

NIXON: I did know about it. I knew that there was something going on there —

DEAN: Right.

NIXON: — but I didn't know it was Hunt.

DEAN: Right. That's what really troubles me is, you know, one, will this thing not break someday, and —

NIXON: Yeah.

DEAN: Then whole thing —

NIXON: Yeah.

DEAN: — it's a domino situation. You know, they just — I think if it starts crumbling, fingers will be pointing. And —

NIXON: That's right. That's right.

DEAN: — Bob will be accused of things he has never heard of —

NIXON: Yeah.

DEAN: — and then he'll have to disprove it, and it'll just get nasty and it'll be a —

NIXON: Yeah.

DEAN: — real, uh —

NIXON: Yeah.

DEAN: — real bad situation. And the person who will be hurt by it most will be you and —

NIXON: Of course.

DEAN: — the presidency, and I just don't think —

NIXON: First, because I am expected to know this, and I am supposed to check these things and so forth —

DEAN: — that's right.

NIXON: — and so on. But let's come back. Go further. Sure. Yes indeed. But what are your feelings, yourself, John? You know pretty well what they all say. What are your feelings about the options?

DEAN: I am not confident that we can ride through this. I think there are — I think there are soft spots.

NIXON: You used to feel comfortable.

DEAN: Well, I feel — I felt comfortable for this reason. I've noticed of recent — since the publicity has increased on this thing again, with the Gray hearings that everybody is now starting to watch out for their own behind.

NIXON: That's right.

DEAN: Everyone's pulling in. They're getting their own counsel. More counsel are getting —

NIXON: Right.

DEAN: — involved.

NIXON: Right.

DEAN: You know, "How do I protect my ass?"

NIXON: Well, they're scared.

DEAN: They're scared and that's just — you know, that's bad. We were able to hold it for a long time.

NIXON: Yeah, I know.

DEAN: Another thing is, you know, my facility now to deal with the multitude of people I have been dealing with has been hampered because of Gray's blowing me up into the front page.

NIXON: Your cover is broken.

DEAN: That's right and it's with — it was —

NIXON: [unclear] cover. All right. Now. So on. So what you really come down to is — what in the hell will you do? Let's — let us suppose that you and Haldeman and Ehrlichman and Mitchell say, "We can't hold this." What then are you going to say? Are you going to put out a complete disclosure? Isn't that the best plan?

DEAN: Well, one way to do it is to —

NIXON: That'd be my view on it.

DEAN: One way to do it is for you to in — tell the attorney general that you finally — you know, really — this is the first time you are getting all the pieces together. Uh —

NIXON: Ask for another grand jury?

DEAN: Ask for another grand jury. The way it should be done though is a way that — for example, I think that we could avoid criminal liability for countless people and the ones that did get it — it could be minimal.

NIXON: How?

DEAN: Well, I think by just thinking it all through first as to how — you know, some people could be granted immunity —

NIXON: Like Magruder?

DEAN: Yeah. To come forward. But some people are going to have to go to jail. That's the long and short of it, also.

NIXON: Who? Let's talk about that.

DEAN: All right. I think I could, for one.

NIXON: You go to jail?

DEAN: That's right.

NIXON: Oh, hell no! I can't see how you can. But I — no —

DEAN: Well, because —

NIXON: I can't see how. That — let me say I can't see how a legal case could be made against you, John.

DEAN: It'd be tough, but you know —

NIXON: Well —

DEAN: I can see people pointing fingers, you know, to get it out of their own. Put me in the impossible position, disproving too many negatives.

NIXON: Oh, no. Let me say I — not because you're here — but just looking at it from a cold legal standpoint. You are a lawyer. You were a counsel. You were doing what you were doing as a counsel, and you were not doing anything like that. You mean — what would you go to jail on [unclear]?

DEAN: The obstruction of justice.

NIXON: The obstruction of justice?

DEAN: That's the only thing that bothers me.

NIXON: Well, I don't know. I think that one — I think that, I feel, could be cut off at the pass. Maybe the obstruction of justice —

DEAN: It could be a — you know how — one of the — that's why —

NIXON: Sometimes it's well to give them something, and then they don't want the bigger fish then.

DEAN: That's right. I think that with proper coordination with the Department of Justice, Henry Petersen is the only man I know bright enough and knowledgeable enough in the criminal laws and the process that could really tell us how this could be put together so it did the maximum to carve it away with a minimum of damage to individuals involved.

NIXON: Petersen doesn't know —

DEAN: That's what I think.

NIXON: — the whole story?

DEAN: No, I know he doesn't now. I know he doesn't now. I am talking about somebody who I have over the years grown to have enough faith in. It's possible that he'd have to — put him in a very difficult situation as the head of the Criminal Division of the United States Department of Justice, and the oath of office —

NIXON: Tell me — talking about your obstruction of justice role, I don't see it. I can't see it. You're —

DEAN: Well, I've been a con — I have been a conduit for information on taking care of people out there who are guilty of crimes.

NIXON: Oh, you mean like the blackmail.

DEAN: The blackmail. Right.

NIXON: Well, I wonder if that part of it can't be — I wonder if that doesn't — let me put it frankly. I wonder if that doesn't have to be continued? Let me put it this way. Let us suppose that you get the million bucks, and you get the proper way to handle it, and you could hold that side.

DEAN: Mm-hmm.

NIXON: It would seem to me that would be worthwhile. Now we have —

DEAN: Well, that's — yeah, that's —

NIXON: — one problem. You've got a problem here. You have the problem of Hunt and his clemency.

DEAN: That's right. And you're going to have the clemency problem for the others. They all would expect to be out and that may put you in a position that's just —

NIXON: Right.

DEAN: — untenable at some point. You know, the Watergate hearings just over — Hunt now demanding clemency or is he going to blow. And politically it'd be impossible for, you know, you to do it. You know, after everybody —

NIXON: That's right.

DEAN: I am not sure that you will ever be able to deliver on the clemency. It may be just too hot.

NIXON: You can't do it till after the '74 elections, that's for sure. But even then your point is that even then you couldn't do it.

DEAN: That's right. It may further involve you in a way you shouldn't be involved in this.

NIXON: No, it's wrong. That's for sure.

DEAN: Well, whatever — you know, I — there've been some bad judgments made. There've been some necessary judgments made. Uh —

NIXON: Before the election.

DEAN: Before the election and, in a way, the necessary ones — you know, before the election. There — you know, we've — this was —

NIXON: Yeah.

DEAN: — to me there was no way —

NIXON: Yeah.

DEAN: — that, uh —

NIXON: Yeah.

DEAN: But to burden this second administration —

NIXON: We're all in on it.

DEAN: — was something that — it's something that is not going to go away.

NIXON: No, it isn't.

DEAN: It is not going to go away, sir.

NIXON: Not going to go away. It is the idea that — well, that people are going to get tired of it and all that sort of thing —

DEAN: Anything will spark it back into life. It's got to be —

NIXON: Well, it's too much to the partisan interest of others to spark it back into life.

DEAN: And it seems to me the only way that —

NIXON: Who else, though? Let's leave you and — I don't think on the obstruction of justice thing — I think that one we can handle. I don't know why I feel that way, but I —

DEAN: Well, it is possible that I —

NIXON: I think you may be overplaying, but who else do you think has — ?

DEAN: Potential criminal liability?

NIXON: Yeah.

DEAN: I think Ehrlichman does. I think that — I think —

NIXON: Why Ehrlichman? What'd he do?

DEAN: Because of this conspiracy to burglarize the Ellsberg [psychiatrist Dr. Lewis Fielding's] office.

NIXON: You mean that — that is — provided Hunt breaks — ?

DEAN: Well, the funny — let me say something interesting about that. Within the files —

NIXON: Oh, I saw that. The picture [burglars Gordon Liddy and Howard Hunt took of themselves in front of Dr. Fielding's office].

DEAN: Yeah, the picture. That, see — that's not all that buried. And while we can, we've got — I think we've got it buried. There is no telling when it's going to pop up. The Cubans could start this whole thing. When the Ervin Committee starts running down why this mysterious telephone was here at the White House listed in the name of a secretary. One of these, some of these secretaries have a little idea about this and they can be broken down just —

NIXON: Sure.

DEAN: — so fast. That's another thing I missed in the cycle — in the circle. Liddy's secretary, for example, is knowledgeable. Magruder's secretary is knowledgeable.

NIXON: Sure.

DEAN: Uh —

NIXON: So Ehrlichman on the —

DEAN: But what I am coming to you today with is I don't have a plan of how to solve it right now, but I think it's at the juncture that we should begin to think in terms of how to cut the losses, how to minimize the further growth of this thing rather than further compound it by, you know, ultimately paying these guys forever.

NIXON: Yeah.

DEAN: I think we've got to look —

NIXON: But at the moment, don't you agree that you'd better get the Hunt thing? I mean that's worth it at the moment.

DEAN: That's worth buying time on, right.

NIXON: And that's buying time on, I agree.

DEAN: The grand jury is going to reconvene next week after Sirica sentences. But that's why I think that, you know, that John and Bob have met with me. They've never met with Mitchell on this. We've never had a real down-and-out with everybody that has the most to lose. And the most — and it is the most danger for you to have them have criminal liability. I think Bob has a potential criminal liability, frankly. I think — in other words, a lot of these people could be indicted. They might never —

NIXON: Yeah.

DEAN: — might never be convicted, but just the thought of —

NIXON: Suppose —

DEAN: — indictments —

NIXON: Suppose that they are indicted in this. Suppose —

DEAN: I think that would be devastating.

NIXON: Suppose the worst — that Bob is indicted and Ehrlichman is indicted. And, I must say, maybe we just better then try to tough it through. You get my point?

DEAN: That's right. That —

NIXON: If, for example, our — say well let's cut our losses and you say we're going to go down the road. See if we can cut our losses and no more blackmail and all the rest, and the thing blows and they indict Bob and the rest. Jesus, you'd never recover from that, John.

DEAN: That's right.

NIXON: It's better to fight it out instead. You see, that's the other thing — the other thing. It's better just to fight it out and not let people testify, so forth and so on. Now, on the other hand, we realize that we have these weaknesses — that we've got this weakness in terms of blackmail.

DEAN: It's — what — if we — you know, there are two routes, you know. One is to figure out how to cut the losses and minimize the human impact and get you up and out and away from it in any way — in a way that would never come back to haunt you. That is one general alternative. The other is to go down the road — just hunker down, fight it at every corner, every turn, don't let people testify, cover it up is what we're really talking about. Just keep it buried, and just hope that we can do it. Hope that we make good decisions at the right time and keep our heads cool. We make the right moves —

NIXON: And just take the heat.

DEAN: And just take the heat.

NIXON: Now, with the second line of attack. You discussed this, though I do want you to still consider my scheme of having you brief the cabinet, just in very general terms, and the leaders — very general terms — and maybe some very general statement with regards to my investigation. Answer questions, and to basically on the question of what they told you, not what you know.

DEAN: Right.

NIXON: Haldeman is not involved. Ehrlichman —

DEAN: Oh, I can — you know, if we go that route, sir, I can give a show that, you know, there's — we can sell — you know, just about like we were selling Wheaties on our position. There's no —

NIXON: The problem that you have are these minefields down the road. I think the most difficult problem is the — are the guys that are going to jail. I think you're right about that. I agree. Now. And, also the fact that we're not going to be able to give them clemency.

DEAN: That's right. How long will they take — how long will they sit there? I don't know. We don't know what they will be sentenced to. There's always a chance —

NIXON: Thirty years, isn't it? Maximum?

DEAN: It could be. You know, they haven't announced yet, but it —

NIXON: Isn't that what the potential is?

DEAN: It's even higher than that. It's about fifty years, with all the —

NIXON: So ridiculous.

DEAN: Oh, well — you know, what's so incredible is the — these fellows who sh —

NIXON: People break and enter, and so forth, and get two years.

DEAN: Well, the other thing —

NIXON: No weapons. No results. What the hell are they talking about?

DEAN: The individuals who are charged with shooting John Stennis are on the street. They were given — you know, one was put out on his personal recognizance rather than bond. They've got these fellows all stuck with hundred-thousand-dollar bonds. The same judge, Sirica, let one guy who's [laughs] charged with shooting a United States senator out on the street.

NIXON: Sirica did?

DEAN: Yeah. It's just — it's phenomenal.

NIXON: What is the matter with him? I thought he was a hardliner judge.

DEAN: He's a — he is just a peculiar animal, and he set the bond for one of the others — I don't have all the facts, but he set the bond for one of the others — around fifty or sixty thousand dollars. But still, that guy is in — didn't make bond. But, you know, sixty thousand dollars as opposed to a hundred thousand dollars for these guys is phenomenal.

NIXON: When could you have this meeting with these fellows? As I think, that time is of the essence, in my opinion. Could you do it this afternoon?

DEAN: Well, Mitchell isn't here, and —

NIXON: Tomorrow?

DEAN: It might be worth it to have him come down. And now, I think that Bob and John did not want to talk to John about this — John Mitchell. And I don't believe they've had any conversations with him about it.

NIXON: Well, let me get Haldeman in here now.

DEAN: Bob and I have talked about just what we're talking about this morning. I told him I thought that you should have the facts and he agrees. Because we've got some tough calls down the road if we —

NIXON: Let me say, though, that Hunt [unclear] hard line, and that a convicted felon is going to go out and squeal about this [unclear] decision [unclear] turns on that.

DEAN: Well, we can always — you know, on the other side, we can always charge them with blackmailing us, and it's — you know, this is absurd stuff they're saying, and —

NIXON: That's right. You see, even the way you put it out here — of course, if it all came out — it may never — it may not ever — never get there.

[HALDEMAN joins the conversation.]

NIXON: I was talking to John about this whole situation, and I think we — so that we can get away from the bits and pieces that have broken out. He is right in having — in recommending that there be a meeting at the very first possible time. Ehrlichman — and now Ehrlichman's gone on to California but is today — is tomorrow Thursday?

HALDEMAN: He — John doesn't go until Friday.

DEAN: Friday —

NIXON: Well, in any event, could we do it Thursday? This meeting? This meeting — you can't do it today, can you?

DEAN: I don't think so. I was suggesting a meeting with Mitchell —

NIXON: Mitchell, Ehrlichman, yourself, and Bob. That's all. Now, Mitchell has to be there because he is seriously involved and we're trying to keep — we've got to see how we handle it from here on. We are in the process of having to determine which way to go and John has thought it through as well as he can. I don't want Moore there on this occasion.

DEAN: No.

NIXON: You haven't told Moore all of this, have you?

DEAN: Moore's got — by being with me — has more bits and pieces. I've had to give him —

NIXON: Right.

DEAN: — because he is making —

NIXON: Right.

DEAN: — judgments that —

NIXON: Well, the point is, once you get down to the PR — once you decide what you're going to do, then we can let him know, and so forth and so on. But it is the kind of thing — I think what really has to happen is for you to sit down with those three and for you to tell them exactly what you told me.

DEAN: Mm-hmm.

NIXON: It may take him about thirty-five or forty-five minutes. In other words, he knows — John knows about everything and also what all the potential criminal liabilities are. You know, whether it's — what's it like that thing — what, about obstruction — ?

DEAN: Obstruction of justice. Right.

NIXON: So forth and so on. And the — I think that's — then we've got to see what the line is. Whether the line is one of continuing to run a — try to run a total stonewall and take the heat from that, having in mind the fact that there are vulnerable points there. The vulnerable points being that, well, the first vulnerable points would be obvious. In other words, it would be if one of the defendants, particularly Hunt, of course, who is the most vulnerable in my opinion, might blow the whistle. And he — and his price is pretty high, but at least we should buy the time on that, as I pointed out to John. Apparently — who is dealing with Hunt at the moment now that Colson's — ?

DEAN: Well, Mitchell's lawyer and —

NIXON: Colson's lawyer [unclear] —

DEAN: — Colson's lawyer, both.

NIXON: — familiar with him. Hunt has at least got to know before he is sentenced that he's —

HALDEMAN: Who's Colson's lawyer? That Jew in his law firm?

DEAN: Shapiro. Right. Who lied to the, you know, who just — the other day he came up and —

HALDEMAN: Colson's told him everything, hasn't he?

DEAN: Yup, I gather he has. The other thing that bothered me about that is that he's a chatter. He came up to Fred Fielding, of my office, at Colson's going-away party. I didn't go over there. It was over at the Blair House the other night. And he said to Fred, he said, "Well, Chuck has had some mighty serious words with his friend Howard and had some mighty serious messages back." Now, you know, what's a lawyer — how does he know what Fielding knows? Because Fielding knows virtually nothing. [laughs]

NIXON: Well, anyway.

HALDEMAN: That's where your dangers lie is in all these stupid human errors in what has happened.

NIXON: That's very —

DEAN: That's — that —

NIXON: Well, the point is — Bob, let's face it, the secretaries know. The assistants know. There's a lot of the — many of the damn principals may be hard as a rock, but you never know when they're going to crack. But, so — we'll see. First you've got the Hunt problem. That ought to be handled.

DEAN: Yeah.

NIXON: Incidentally, I do not think Colson should sit in this meeting. Do you agree?

DEAN: No. I would agree.

NIXON: Okay. How then — who does sit and talk to Colson? Because somebody has to. Shouldn't we talk to — ?

DEAN: Chuck, uh —

NIXON: Talks too much.

DEAN: I — you know, I like Chuck, [laughs] but I don't want Chuck to know anything that I'm doing, frankly. [laughs]

NIXON: All right.

HALDEMAN: I think that's right. I think you want to be careful not to give Chuck any more knowledge than he's already got.

DEAN: That's right.

NIXON: Sure. Well —

DEAN: I wouldn't want Chuck to even know of the meeting, frankly.

NIXON: Fortunately with Chuck it is very — I talk to him about many, many political things. But I never talk about this sort of thing because he's very harmful. I mean I don't think — he must be damn sure I don't know anything. And I don't. In fact, I'm rather surprised at what you told me today. From what you said, I gathered the impression — and of course your analysis does not for sure indicate that Chuck knew that it was a bugging operation for certain.

DEAN: That's correct. I don't have —

NIXON: On the other hand, that —

DEAN: Chuck denies that —

NIXON: On the other hand, the other side of that is that Hunt had conversations with Chuck, and it may be that Hunt told Chuck that it was bugging, and so forth and so on.

DEAN: Mm-hmm.

NIXON: Is that correct?

DEAN: Mm-hmm. They were very close. They talked too much about too many things.

NIXON: Yeah.

DEAN: They were intimate on this sort of —

HALDEMAN: Well, then Chuck —

NIXON: There's another thing you can't —

HALDEMAN: Chuck has a problem. Chuck loves —

NIXON: Yeah.

HALDEMAN: He loves what he does.

NIXON: Yeah.

HALDEMAN: He likes to talk about it.

NIXON: He also is a name-dropper. Chuck might have gone around and talked to Hunt and said, "Well, I was talking to the president and the president feels we ought to get information about this, or that, or the other thing," and so forth and so on.

DEAN: Well, Liddy is the same way, and —

NIXON: I have talked to — I have talked to — this and that and the other thing. I have never talked to anybody, but I have talked to Chuck and John and the rest and I am sure that Chuck may have — Chuck might have even talked to Hunt along those lines.

HALDEMAN: I would — well, anything could happen. I would doubt that.

DEAN: I would doubt that, too.

HALDEMAN: I don't think he would. Chuck is a name-dropper in one sense, but not in that sense.

NIXON: Well, then do you think — ?

HALDEMAN: I think he very carefully keeps the president out of things —

NIXON: Right.

HALDEMAN: — except when he's doing it — when he's very intentionally bringing the president in for the president's purposes.

NIXON: He had the impression, though, apparently that he was the, as it turns out, really is the trigger man. May have damn well been the trigger man where he just called up and said, "Now look here, Jeb, go ahead and get that information." And I recommend there's got to be a decision on it at that time. This is February.

DEAN: Yes, sir. I figure it was somewhere —

NIXON: It must be the — I — it must have been after —

DEAN: This was the call to Magruder from Colson saying, "Fish or cut bait." Hunt and Liddy were in his office.

HALDEMAN: In Colson's office?

DEAN: In Colson's office. And he called Magruder and said, "Let's fish or cut bait on this operation. Let's get it going."

HALDEMAN: Oh, really?

DEAN: Yeah. This is — Magruder tells me this.

HALDEMAN: Of course, that —

NIXON: Well, on the other hand —

HALDEMAN: Now wait, Magruder testified [unclear].

DEAN: Chuck also told me that Hunt and Liddy were in his office and he made a call.

HALDEMAN: Oh, okay.

DEAN: So it did — it was corroborated [laughs] by the principal.

HALDEMAN: Hunt and Liddy haven't told you that, though?

DEAN: No.

HALDEMAN: You haven't talked to Hunt and Liddy?

DEAN: I talked to Liddy once, right after the incident.

NIXON: That's right, but not — all right. The point is this, that it's now time, though, to — that Mitchell has got to sit down, and know where the hell all this thing stands, too. You see, John is concerned, as you know, Bob, about Ehrlichman, which worries me a great deal because it's a — it — and this is why the Hunt problem is so serious, because it had nothing to do with the campaign.

DEAN: Right, it —

NIXON: Properly it has to do with the Ellsberg thing. I don't know what the hell —

HALDEMAN: But why —

NIXON: Yeah. Why? I don't know.

HALDEMAN: What I was going to say is —

NIXON: What is the answer on that? How do you keep that out? I don't know. Well, we can't keep it out if Hunt — if, you see the point is it is irrelevant. Once it has gotten to this point —

DEAN: You might put it on a national security ground — basis, which it really — it was.

HALDEMAN: It absolutely was.

DEAN: And just say that —

NIXON: Yeah.

DEAN: — that this is not, you know, this was —

NIXON: Let them think it was CIA funds.

DEAN: Uh —

NIXON: No, seriously — national security. We had to get information for national security grounds.

DEAN: Well, then the question is why didn't the CIA do it or why didn't the FBI do it?

NIXON: Because they were — we had to do it — we had to do it on a confidential basis.

HALDEMAN: Because we were checking them.

NIXON: Neither could be trusted.

HALDEMAN: Well, I think —

NIXON: That's the way I view it.

HALDEMAN: — that has never been proven. There was reason to question their —

NIXON: Yeah.

HALDEMAN: — position.

NIXON: You see — really, with the [Kennedy national security advisor McGeorge] Bundy [Bay of Pigs] thing [which involved Howard Hunt and the Cubans] and everything coming out, the whole thing was national security.

DEAN: I think we can probably get by on that.

NIXON: I think on that one, I think you'd simply say this was a national security investigation that was conducted. And the same with the drug field with Krogh. Krogh could say I — if Krogh were to — if he feels that he [unclear], it was a national security matter. That's why —

DEAN: That's the way Bud rests easy, because he's convinced that he was doing it. He said there was treason about the country —

NIXON: Mm-hmm.

DEAN: — and it could have threatened the way the war was handled.

NIXON: Yeah.

DEAN: Uh, and by God —

HALDEMAN: Bud said this?

DEAN: Yes.

NIXON: Well, Bud could say that and say this — it does involve — it was a national security. And I was not in a position to divulge it. Well, anyway, let's don't go beyond that. We're — forget — but I do think now we — I mean, there is a time now when you don't want to talk to Mitchell. He doesn't want to talk and the rest. But John is right. There must be a four-way talk here of the particular ones that we can trust here. We've got to get a decision on it. It's not something that — you see, you've got two ways, basically. There are really only two ways you could go. You either decide the whole goddamn thing is so full of problems with potential criminal liability, which is what concerns me. I don't give a damn about the publicity. We could rock that through if we had to let the whole thing hang out. It would be a lousy story for a month. But I can take it. But the point is I don't want any criminal liability. That's the thing that I am concerned about for members of the White House staff, and I would trust for members of the committee. And that means Magruder.

DEAN: That's right.

NIXON: Let's face it. He's the one that's — I think Magruder is the major guy over there.

DEAN: I think he's got the most serious problem.

NIXON: Yeah.

HALDEMAN: Well, then we talked about yesterday, you've got a question where your cutoff point is. There is a possibility of cutting it at Liddy, where you are now.

NIXON: Yeah.

HALDEMAN: But to accomplish that requires —

NIXON: Requires what?

HALDEMAN: Requires continued perjury by Magruder.

NIXON: Yeah. And it requires total —

DEAN: Commitment —

NIXON: — control — total control over all of the defendants, which in other words [unclear].

DEAN: The basic position —

HALDEMAN: They don't know anything beyond Liddy.

DEAN: Uh, no. Other than the fact that Liddy — they have hearsay —

HALDEMAN: Oh, does he not know about Hunt? Maybe Hunt has it tied into Colson. We don't know that, though, really.

DEAN: No.

NIXON: I think Hunt knows a hell of a lot more.

DEAN: Yeah, I do, too. And, now what McCord —

HALDEMAN: You think he does? I am afraid you're right, but we don't know that.

NIXON: I don't think [laughs] — I think we better assume it. I think Colson —

DEAN: And he's playing hard ball, and he wouldn't play hard—

HALDEMAN: Is he?

DEAN: Yeah. He wouldn't play hard ball unless he were pretty confident that he could cause an awful lot of grief.

HALDEMAN: Right.

DEAN: Yeah.

NIXON: He is playing hard-boiled ball with regard to Ehrlichman, for example, and that sort of thing. He knows what he's got.

HALDEMAN: What's he planning on, money?

DEAN: Yeah, money and—

HALDEMAN: Really?

DEAN: Oh, yeah. He's—

NIXON: It's a hundred and twenty thousand dollars. It's about what—about how much, which is easy. I mean, it's not easy to deliver, but it is easy to get. Now—if that is the case—if it's just that way, then the thing to do is—if the thing all cracks out—if, for example, you say look, we're not going to continue to try to—let's state it frankly—cut our losses. That's just one way you could go—on the assumption that we're—by continuing to cut our losses—we're not going to win. That in the end, we are going to be bled to death. And it's all going to come out anyway, and then you get the worst of both worlds. We are going to lose, and people are going to—

HALDEMAN: And look back at—

NIXON: —and it's going to look like we covered up. So that we can't do. Now, the other line, however, if you take that line that we're not going to continue—to cut our losses, that means then we have to look square in the eye as to what the hell those losses are, and see which people can—so we can avoid criminal liability. Right?

DEAN: That's right.

NIXON: And that means we've got to keep it off of you, which I—which as I say I really think [unclear] the obstruction of justice thing. We've got to keep it off Ehrlichman. We've got to keep it naturally off of Bob, off Chapin, if possible, and Strachan. Right?

DEAN: Mm-hmm.

NIXON: And Mitchell. Right?

DEAN: Mm-hmm.

NIXON: Now—

HALDEMAN: And Magruder, if you can. But that's the one you pretty much have to give up.

NIXON: But Magruder—John's—Dean's point is that if Magruder goes down, he'll pull everybody with him.

HALDEMAN: That's my view.

NIXON: Is it?

HALDEMAN: Yup. I think Jeb—I don't think he wants to. And I think he even would try not to, but I don't think he is able not to.

DEAN: I don't think he is strong enough, when it really—

HALDEMAN: Well, not that —

NIXON: Well, another way to do it then, Bob, is to — and John realizes this — is to continue to try to cut our losses. Now we have to look at that course of action. First, it is going to require approximately a million dollars to take care of the jackasses that are in jail. That could be arranged.

HALDEMAN: Yeah.

NIXON: That could be arranged. But you realize that after we are gone — I mean, assuming these [unclear] are gone, they're going to crack. You know what I mean? And that'll be an unseemly story. Eventually, all the people aren't going to care that much.

DEAN: That's right. It's —

NIXON: People aren't going to care.

DEAN: So much history will pass between then and now.

NIXON: In other words, what we're talking about is no question. But the second thing is, we're not going to be able to deliver on any kind of a clemency thing. You know Colson has gone around on this clemency thing with Hunt and the rest.

DEAN: Hunt is now talking in terms of being out by Christmas.

HALDEMAN: This year?

DEAN: This year. He was told by O'Brien, who is my conveyor of doom back and forth —

HALDEMAN: Yeah.

DEAN: — that, hell, he'd be lucky if he were out a year from now, after the Ervin hearings were, you know, over. He said, "How in the Lord's name could you be commuted that quickly?" He said, "Well, that's my commitment from Colson."

HALDEMAN: By Christmas of this year?

DEAN: Yeah.

HALDEMAN: See that really — that's very believable because Colson —

NIXON: Do you think Colson could have told him?

HALDEMAN: Colson is an — that's your fatal flaw, really, in Chuck, is he is an operator in expediency, and he will pay at the time and where he is —

NIXON: Yeah.

HALDEMAN: — whatever he has to, to accomplish what he's there to do.

DEAN: Right.

HALDEMAN: And that's — I would believe that he has made that commitment if Hunt says he has. I would believe he is capable of saying that.

NIXON: The only thing you could do with him would be to parole him for a period of time because of his family situation. But you couldn't provide clemency.

DEAN: No, I — Kleindienst has now got control of the parole board, and he said that now we can pull paroles off now where we couldn't before. So —

NIXON: Well, parole —

HALDEMAN: Yeah, but Kleindienst always tells you that and then never delivers.

NIXON: Parole, parole.

DEAN: Well, I mean —

NIXON: Let's talk candidly about that. Parole, one, in human terms, and so forth, is something that I think in Hunt's case—you could do Hunt, but you couldn't do the others. You understand?

DEAN: Well, so much depends upon how Sirica sentences. He can sentence in a way that makes parole even impossible.

NIXON: Oh, he can?

DEAN: Sure. He can do all kinds of permanent sentences.

NIXON: On this kind of thing?

DEAN: Yeah. He can be a—just a son of a bitch as far as the whole thing.

HALDEMAN: Of course, can't you appeal on an unjust sentence as well as on an unjust conviction?

DEAN: You've got sixty days to ask the judge to review it. There is no appellate review of sentences.

HALDEMAN: There isn't?

DEAN: Not that I—

NIXON: The judge can review it, yeah.

HALDEMAN: Only the sentencing judge can review—

NIXON: Yeah.

HALDEMAN: —his own sentence?

NIXON: Coming back, though, to this. So you got that—the—hanging over. Now, if—you see, if you let it hang there, the point is you could let all or only part—the point is, your feeling is that we just can't continue to pay the blackmail of these guys?

DEAN: I think that's our greatest jeopardy.

HALDEMAN: Yeah.

NIXON: Now, let me tell you, it's—

DEAN: Because that is—

NIXON: —no problem. We could get the money. There is no problem in that. We can't provide the clemency. The money can be provided. Mitchell could provide the way to deliver it. That could be done. See what I mean?

HALDEMAN: But, Mitchell says he can't, doesn't he?

DEAN: Mitchell says that, well—Mitch—that's—it's—you know, there has been an interesting thing—phenomena all the way along on this—is that there have been a lot of people having to pull oars and not everybody pulls them all at the same time, the same way, because there are developed self-interests.

HALDEMAN: What John is saying is that everybody smiles at Dean and says, "Well, you better get something done about it."

DEAN: That's right.

NIXON: [unclear]

HALDEMAN: And Mitchell is leaving Dean hanging out on a—none of us—well, maybe we're doing the same thing to you.

DEAN: That's right.

HALDEMAN: But I—let me say that I don't see how there's any way that you can have the White House, or anybody presently in the White House, involved in trying to gin out this money.

DEAN: We are already deeply enough in that. That's the problem, Bob.

NIXON: I thought you said you could handle the money?

DEAN: Well, in fact, that — when —

NIXON: Kalmbach?

DEAN: Well, Kalmbach, was a —

HALDEMAN: He's not the one.

DEAN: No, but when they ran out of that money, as you know, they came after the three fifty that was over here.

NIXON: And they used that, right?

DEAN: And I had to explain what it was for before I could get the money.

NIXON: Well, you said —

DEAN: Now, they — now that — they —

HALDEMAN: That was put — that was — in the first place, that was put back to LaRue —

DEAN: That's right.

HALDEMAN: — where it belonged. It wasn't all returned in a lump sum. It was put back in pieces.

DEAN: That's right.

NIXON: And then LaRue used it for this other purpose?

DEAN: That's right.

NIXON: Well, I think they can get that.

HALDEMAN: And the balance was all returned to LaRue.

DEAN: That's right.

HALDEMAN: The problem is we don't have any receipt for that, do we? We have no way of proving that.

NIXON: [unclear]

DEAN: And I think that was because, you know, of self-interest over there. Mitchell would —

HALDEMAN: Mitchell told LaRue not to take it at all.

DEAN: That's right.

HALDEMAN: This is what you told me.

DEAN: That's right. And then you don't give them a receipt.

NIXON: Well, then, but what happened? LaRue took it, and then what?

DEAN: Well, it was sent back to him because we just couldn't continue piecemeal giving, you know? I ask it — every time I asked for it I had to tell Bob I needed some, or something like that —

NIXON: Yeah.

DEAN: — and he had to get Gordon Strachan to go up to his safe and take it out and take it over to LaRue.

NIXON: Yeah.

DEAN: This was just a forever operation.

NIXON: Then what—why didn't they take it all to him?

DEAN: I had to send it over to him.

HALDEMAN: Well, we had been trying to get a way to get that money back out of here anyway.

NIXON: Sure.

HALDEMAN: And what this was supposed to be was loans. This was—

NIXON: Yeah.

HALDEMAN: —immediate cash needs that was going to be replenished. And Mitchell was arguing, "You can't take the three fifty back till it's all replenished." Isn't that right?

DEAN: That's right. Well, you know, we—

HALDEMAN: And then they never replenished it, so we just gave it all back anyway.

NIXON: I have a feeling we could handle this one. Well—

DEAN: Well, first of all, they'd have a hell of a time proving it. That's one thing.

NIXON: Yeah, yeah. I just have a feeling on it. But let's now come back to the money, a million dollars, and so forth and so on. Let me say that I think you could get that in cash, and I know money is hard, but there are ways that could be [unclear]. But the point is what would you do on that? Let's look at the hard facts.

DEAN: I mean, that's been very interesting. That has been, thus far, the most difficult problem.

NIXON: Why?

DEAN: They have been—that's why these fellows have been on or off the reservation all the way along.

NIXON: So the hard place is this. Your feeling at the present time is the hell with the million dollars. In other words, you say to these fellows, "I am sorry. It is all off," and let them talk. Right?

DEAN: Well—

NIXON: That's the way to do it, isn't it?

DEAN: That—

NIXON: If you want to do it clean—

DEAN: Then what—

NIXON: —[unclear] it comes out.

HALDEMAN: See, then when you do it, it's a way you can live with. Because the problem with the blackmail, and that's the thing we kept raising with you when you said there's a money problem—when we need twenty thousand or a hundred thousand or something was yeah, that's what you need today. But what do you need tomorrow and next year and five years from now?

NIXON: How long?

DEAN: Well, that was just to get us through November 7, though.

HALDEMAN: I recognize that's what we had to give—

DEAN: Right.

HALDEMAN: —to November 7. There's no question.

DEAN: Except they could have sold — these fellows could have sold out to the Democrats for a fantastic amount.

NIXON: Yeah, these fellows — but of course you know, these fellows though, as far as that plan was concerned —

HALDEMAN: But what is there?

NIXON: As far as what happened up to this time, our cover there is just going to be the Cuban committee did this for them up through the election.

DEAN: Well, yeah. We can put that together. That isn't, of course, quite the way it happened, but —

NIXON: I know, but it's the way it's going to have to happen.

DEAN: It's going to have to happen. [laughs]

NIXON: That's right. Finally, though, so you let it go. So what happens is then they go out and they'll start blowing the whistle on everybody else. Isn't that what it really gets down to?

DEAN: Mm-hmm.

NIXON: So that would be the clean way. Right?

DEAN: Uh —

NIXON: Is that really your — you really go so far as to recommend that?

DEAN: That — no, I wouldn't. I don't think necessarily that's the cleanest way. One of the — I think that is what we all need to discuss. Is there some way that we can get our story before a grand jury, and so that they can have really investigated the White House on this? I mean, and I must be perfectly honest, I haven't really thought through that alternative. We've been, you know, been so busy —

NIXON: John —

DEAN: — on the other containment situation.

NIXON: John Ehrlichman, of course, has raised the point of another grand jury. I just don't know how you're going to do it. On what basis? I could call for it, but I —

DEAN: That would be, I would think —

NIXON: The president takes the leadership, and says, "Now, in view of all this stripped land and so forth, I understand this, but I think I want another grand jury proceeding and we'll have the White House appear before them." Is that right, John?

DEAN: Mm-hmm.

NIXON: That's the point, you see? That would make the difference. I want everybody in the White House called. And that gives you the — a reason not to have to go up before the [unclear] committee. It puts it in an executive session, in a sense.

HALDEMAN: Right.

NIXON: Right.

DEAN: Uh, well —

HALDEMAN: And there'd be some rules of evidence, aren't there?

DEAN: There are rules of evidence.

NIXON: Both evidence and you have lawyers.

HALDEMAN: So you are in a hell of a lot better position than you are up there.

DEAN: No, you can't have a lawyer before a grand jury.

NIXON: Oh, no. That's right.

DEAN: You can't have a lawyer before a grand jury.

HALDEMAN: Okay, but you do have rules of evidence. You can refuse to talk.

DEAN: You can take the Fifth Amendment.

NIXON: That's right. That's right.

HALDEMAN: You can say you forgot, too, can't you?

DEAN: Sure.

NIXON: That's right.

DEAN: But you can't — you're — very high risk in a perjury situation.

NIXON: That's right. Just be damn sure you say, "I don't — "

HALDEMAN: Yeah —

NIXON: " — remember. I can't recall. I can't give any honest — an answer to that that I can recall." But that's it.

HALDEMAN: You have the same perjury thing on the Hill, don't you?

DEAN: That's right.

NIXON: Oh hell, yes.

HALDEMAN: And they'll be doing things on [unclear] —

NIXON: My point is, though —

HALDEMAN: — which is a hell of a lot worse to deal with.

DEAN: That's right.

NIXON: The grand jury thing has its — in view of this they might — suppose we have a grand jury proceeding. Would that — what would that do to the Ervin thing? Would it go right ahead anyway?

DEAN: Probably.

HALDEMAN: If you do it in executive —

NIXON: But then on that score, though, we have — let me just run by that. You do that on a grand jury, we could then have a much better cause in terms of saying, "Look, this is a grand jury, in which the prosecutor" — how about a special prosecutor? We could use Petersen, or use another one. You see he is probably suspect. Would you call —

DEAN: No —

NIXON: — in another prosecutor?

DEAN: I'd like to have Petersen on our side advising us [laughs], frankly.

NIXON: Frankly, well, Petersen is honest as anybody — not being questioned him, are they?

DEAN: No, no. But he'll get a barrage when these Watergate hearings start.

NIXON: Yes, but he can go up and say that he's been told to go further in the grand jury and go into this and that and the other thing. Call everybody in the White House. I want them to come — I want the — to go to the grand jury.

DEAN: This may result — this may happen even without our calling for it when these —

NIXON: Vesco?

DEAN: No. Well, that's one possibility. But also when these people go back before the grand jury here, they are going to pull all these criminal defendants back in before the grand jury and immunize them.

NIXON: Immunize them — why? Who? Are you going to — on what?

DEAN: The U.S. attorney's office will.

NIXON: To do what?

DEAN: To talk about anything further they want to talk about.

NIXON: Yeah. What do they gain out of it?

DEAN: Nothing.

NIXON: To hell with them.

DEAN: They're going to stonewall it, as it now stands. Except for Hunt. That's why — that's the leverage in his threat.

HALDEMAN: This is Hunt's opportunity.

DEAN: This is Hunt's opportunity.

NIXON: That's why —

HALDEMAN: God, if he can lay this —

NIXON: That's why your — for your immediate thing you've got no choice with Hunt but the hundred and twenty or whatever it is. Right?

DEAN: That's right.

NIXON: Would you agree that that's a buy-time thing? You better damn well get that done — but fast?

DEAN: I think he ought to be given some signal, anyway, to —

NIXON: Yes.

DEAN: Yeah, you know.

NIXON: Well, for Christ's sakes get it in a way that — who's going to talk to him? Colson? He's the one who's supposed to know him.

DEAN: Well, Colson doesn't have any money though. That's the thing. That's been our — one of the real problems. They have been unable to raise any money. A million dollars in cash, or the like, has been just a very difficult problem as we've discussed before. Apparently, Mitchell has talked to Pappas, and I called him last — John asked me to call him last night after our discussion and after you'd met with John to see where that was. And I said, "Have you talked to Pappas?" He was at home, and Martha picked up the phone, so it was all in code. "Did you talk to the Greek?" And he said, "Yes, I have." And I said, "Is the Greek bearing gifts?" He said, "Well, I want to call you tomorrow on that."

NIXON: Well, look, what is it that you need on that — when, now look — well God, I am unfamiliar with the money situation.

DEAN: Well, that, you know, it sounds easy to do, apparently, until everyone is out there doing it and that's where our breakdown has come every time.

NIXON: Well, if you had it, where would you — how would you get it to somebody?

DEAN: Well, I gather LaRue just leaves it in mailboxes and things like that and tells Hunt to go pick it up. Someone phones Hunt and tells him to pick it up. As I say, we're a bunch of amateurs in that business.

HALDEMAN: That was the thing that we thought Mitchell ought to be able to know how to find somebody who could do all that sort of thing, because none of us know how to.

DEAN: That's right. You got to wash money and all that sort. You know, if you get a hundred thousand out of a bank, and it all comes in serialized bills, and —

NIXON: Oh, I understand.

DEAN: And that means you have to go to Vegas with it or a bookmaker in New York City, and I've learned all these things after the fact. It's [laughs] great shape for the next time around! [laughs]

HALDEMAN: Jesus!

NIXON: Well, the main point now is the people who will need the money [unclear]. Well, of course, you've got the surplus from the campaign. That we have to account for. But if there's any other money hanging around —

HALDEMAN: Well, but what about all the — what about the money we moved back out of the — here?

DEAN: Apparently, there's some there. That might be what they can use. I don't know how much is left.

NIXON: Kalmbach must have some, doesn't he?

DEAN: Kalmbach doesn't have a cent.

NIXON: He doesn't?

DEAN: See the new law —

HALDEMAN: No, see that three fifty that we moved out was all we saved. Because they were afraid to — because of this, that's what I mean. That's the trouble. We are so goddamn square that [laughs] we get caught on everything!

NIXON: Well, could I suggest that — this though. Now let me go back around [unclear]. They will then —

HALDEMAN: Be careful.

NIXON: The grand jury thing has appeal. Question is — it at least says that we are co-operating —

DEAN: Well —

NIXON: — with the grand jury.

DEAN: Once we start down any route that involves the criminal justice system —

NIXON: Yeah.

DEAN: — you've got to have full appreciation of there is really no control over that.

NIXON: No, sir.

DEAN: While we did — we had an amazing job of —

NIXON: Yeah, I know.

DEAN: — keeping the thing on the track before —

NIXON: Straight.

DEAN: — while the FBI was out there, all that — and that was only because —

NIXON: Right.

DEAN: — I had a [unclear] on where they were going.

NIXON: [unclear] Right. Right. But you haven't got that now because everybody else is going to have a lawyer. Let's take the new grand jury. The new grand jury would call Magruder again, wouldn't it?

DEAN: But, based on what information it would? For example, what happens if Dean goes in and gives a story, you know, that here is the way it all came about. It was supposed to be a legitimate operation and it obviously got off the track. I heard of these horribles, told Haldeman that we shouldn't be involved in it.

NIXON: Yeah. Right.

DEAN: Then Magruder's going to have to be called in and questioned about all those meetings again, and the like. And it begins to — again he'll begin to change his story as to what he told the grand jury the last time.

NIXON: Well —

DEAN: That way he's in a perjury situation.

HALDEMAN: Except that's the best leverage you've got on Jeb is that he's got to keep his story straight or he's in real trouble.

DEAN: That's right.

HALDEMAN: Unless they get smart and give him immunity. If they immunize Jeb then you have an interesting problem.

NIXON: He wouldn't want —

DEAN: Well, I think we have —

HALDEMAN: [unclear] immunity.

DEAN: — we have control over who gets immunized.

HALDEMAN: Do we?

DEAN: Yeah, I think they wouldn't do that without our —

NIXON: But you see, the grand jury proceeding [unclear] sort of thing, you can go down that road and then — if they had — I'm just thinking of now how the president looks. We would be cooperating. We would be cooperating through a grand jury. Everybody would be behind us. That's the proper way to do this. It should be done through a grand jury, not up there in the klieg lights of the committee or —

DEAN: That's right.

NIXON: Nobody's questioning if it's a grand jury, and so forth. So, and then we would insist on executive privilege before the committee. Flat-out say, "No, we won't do that. We're not going to do it — matter before a grand jury," and that's that. You see —

HALDEMAN: All right, then you go to the next step. Would we then — the grand jury meet in executive session?

DEAN: Yes, sir. They're —

NIXON: Always —

DEAN: — secret sessions. They're secret.

HALDEMAN: Secret session.

NIXON: Secret.

HALDEMAN: All right, then would we agree to release our statement, our grand jury transcripts?

DEAN: That's not for our — we don't have the authority to do that. That's up to the court and the court, thus far, has not released the ones from the last grand jury.

NIXON: They usually are not.

DEAN: It would be highly unusual for a grand jury to come out. What would happen is —

HALDEMAN: But a lot of the stuff from the grand jury came out.

NIXON: Leaks. Well —

DEAN: It came out of the U.S. attorney's office —

NIXON: Yeah.

DEAN: — more than the grand jury. We don't know. Some of the grand jurors may have leaked —

NIXON: Right, right.

DEAN: — it, but they were —

NIXON: Bob, it's not so bad. It's — that's just not the bad — or the worst place. But —

HALDEMAN: Well, what I was — I was going the other way there. I was going to it might be to our interest to get it out.

NIXON: Well, we could easily do that. Leak out certain stuff. We could pretty much control that. We've got much more control there. Now, the other possibility is not to go to the grand jury. Then you've got three things. One, you just say, "The hell with it. We can't raise the money. Sorry, Hunt, you can say what you want." And so Hunt blows the whistle. Right?

DEAN: Right.

NIXON: All right, if that happens then that raises some possibilities of other criminal — because he is likely to say a hell of a lot of things and he's certain to get Magruder on it.

DEAN: It'll get Magruder. It'll start the whole FBI investigation going again.

NIXON: Yeah. So, what else? It'll get Magruder. It could possibly get Colson. He's in that danger.

DEAN: That's right. Could get —

NIXON: Could get Mitchell. Maybe? No.

HALDEMAN: Hunt can't get Mitchell.

DEAN: I don't think Hunt can get Mitchell. Hunt's got a lot of hearsay.

NIXON: Ehrlichman? He could on the other thing except Ehrlichman [unclear].

DEAN: Krogh could go down in smoke.

NIXON: Because Krogh — where could anybody — but on the other hand, Krogh just says he — Krogh says this is a national security matter. Is that what he says? Yeah, he said that.

DEAN: Yeah, but that won't sell, ultimately, in a criminal situation. It may be mitigating on sentences but it won't in the main matter —

HALDEMAN: Well, then that —

NIXON: That's right. Try to look around the track. We have no choice on Hunt but to try to keep him —

DEAN: Right now we have no choice.

NIXON: But my point is, do you ever have any choice on Hunt? That's the point. No matter what we do here now, John —

DEAN: Well, if we —

NIXON: Hunt eventually, if he isn't going to get commuted and so forth, he's going to blow the whistle.

DEAN: What I have been trying to conceive of is how we could lay out everything we know in a way that, you know, we've told the grand jury or somebody else. So that if a Hunt blows —

NIXON: Yeah.

DEAN: — so what's new? You know, it's already been told to a grand jury, and they found no criminal liability, and they investigated it in full. We're sorry, fellow —

NIXON: That's right.

DEAN: We don't — it doesn't —

NIXON: Including Ehrlichman's use of Hunt on the other deal?

DEAN: That's right.

NIXON: You'd throw that out?

DEAN: Well, Hunt will go to jail for that, too, he's got to understand that.

NIXON: That's the point, too. I don't think that — I wouldn't throw that out. I think I would limit it to — I don't think you need to go into every goddamn thing Hunt has done.

DEAN: No.

NIXON: He's done some things in the national security area. Yes. True.

HALDEMAN: We've already said that. Anyway, I mean, we've laid the groundwork for that.

DEAN: Mm-hmm.

NIXON: But here is the point, John. So you go that — let's go to the other extreme. The other angle is to decide, well, if you open up the grand jury, first, it won't do any good. It won't be believed. And then you'll have two things going. The grand jury and you have the other thing. At least the grand jury appeals to me from — the standpoint is the president makes the move. "Since all these charges have been bandied about, and so forth, the best thing to do is to — I have ordered, or I have asked the grand jury to look into any further charges. All charges have been raised." That's the place to do it, and not before a committee of the Congress. Right?

DEAN: Mm-hmm.

NIXON: Then, however, we may say, Mitchell, et al., God, we can't risk that. I mean, all sorts of shit'll break loose there. Then that leaves you to your third thing. The third thing is just to continue to —

DEAN: Hunker down and fight it.

NIXON: All right. If you hunker down and fight it — fight it and what happens?

DEAN: Your —

NIXON: Your view is that that is not really a viable option.

DEAN: It's a very — it's a high risk. A very high risk.

NIXON: A high risk, because your view is that — what will happen out of that is that it's going to come out. Somebody's — Hunt — something's going to break loose —

DEAN: Something is going to break and —

NIXON: When it breaks it'll look like the president —

DEAN: — is covering up.

NIXON: — is — has covered up a huge — this — right?

DEAN: That's correct.

HALDEMAN: But you can't contain the charge.

NIXON: That's not —

DEAN: I just don't —

NIXON: You're —

DEAN: I don't think it's —

NIXON: You now have moved away from the hunker down.

DEAN: Well, I've moved to the point that we've certainly got to make a harder look at the other alternative, which we haven't before.

NIXON: The other alternative appeals.

DEAN: The other alternatives. Right.

NIXON: Three other choices, wouldn't you say? As a matter of fact, your immediate middle ground of grand jury. And then there's finally the other ground of — no, I suppose there's a middle ground —

DEAN: And I would —

NIXON: — or the middle ground of a public statement, but without a grand jury.

DEAN: What we need also, sir —

NIXON: And also —

HALDEMAN: But John's view is if we make the public statement —

NIXON: Yeah.

HALDEMAN: — that we talked — I raised that this morning, the thing we talked about last night.

NIXON: Yeah.

HALDEMAN: If each of us —

NIXON: Yeah.

HALDEMAN: — make moves —

NIXON: Yeah.

HALDEMAN: — he says that will immediately lead to a grand jury.

NIXON: Fine — all right, fine.

HALDEMAN: As soon as we make that statement they'll have to call a grand jury.

NIXON: Then maybe we make the public statement before the grand jury, in order to —

HALDEMAN: So it looks like we are trying to do it over.

DEAN: All right. Say — all right, say here are public statements, and we want —

NIXON: Yeah.

DEAN: — full grand jury investigation —

NIXON: Yeah.

DEAN: — by the U.S. attorney's office.

NIXON: Curious to see whether this statement's then — that's right. That I — but — and that we've said that the reason that we have delayed this is until after the sentencing. You see, the point is — the reason that time is of the essence — we can't play around with this — is that they're going to sentence on Friday. We're going to have to move the goddamn thing pretty fast. See what I mean?

DEAN: That's right.

NIXON: So we've got to act. We really haven't time to move.

DEAN: The other thing is that the attorney general could call Sirica and say that "the government has some major developments that it's considering. Would you hold sentencing for two weeks?" If we set ourself on a course of action.

NIXON: Yep, yep.

DEAN: Say that "the sentencing may be in the wrong perspective right now. I don't know for certain, but I just think there are some things that I am not at liberty to discuss with you, that I want to ask that the court withhold two weeks — sentencing."

HALDEMAN: So then the story is out: "Sirica Delays Sentencing Watergate for — "

DEAN: I think that could be handled in a way between Sirica and Kleindienst that it would not get out.

NIXON: No.

DEAN: Sirica tells me — I mean Kleindienst apparently does have good rapport with Sirica. He's never talked to him since this case has developed —

HALDEMAN: Why not?

DEAN: — but, uh —

NIXON: That's helpful. Kleindienst could say that he's working on something and would like to have a week. I wouldn't take two weeks. I would take a week.

DEAN: I'll tell you the person that I would — you know, I feel that we could use his counsel on this, because he understands the criminal process better than anybody over here does —

NIXON: Petersen?

DEAN: — is Petersen. It's awkward for Petersen. He's the head of the Criminal Division. But to discuss some of these things with him, we may well want to remove him from the head of the Criminal Division and say, that "related to this case, you will have no relation." And give him — on some special assignment over here where he can sit down and say, "Yes, this is an obstruction, but it couldn't be proved," or so on and so forth. We almost need him out of there to take his counsel. That would — I don't think he'd want that but he is the most knowledgeable —

NIXON: How could you get him out?

DEAN: I think an appeal directly to Henry [Petersen] that —

NIXON: Why doesn't the president — could the president call him in as special counsel to the White House for the purpose of conducting an investigation? Represent — you see, in other words rather than having Dean in on it —

DEAN: I have thought of that. I have thought of that.

NIXON: — have him as special counsel to represent to the grand jury and the rest.

DEAN: That is one possibility.

NIXON: Yeah.

HALDEMAN: On the basis that Dean has now become a principal, rather —

NIXON: That's right.

HALDEMAN: — than a special counsel.

DEAN: Mm-hmm.

NIXON: That's right.

DEAN: Mm-hmm.

NIXON: And that he's a —

DEAN: And I could recommend that to you.

NIXON: He could recommend it — you could recommend it, and Petersen would come over and be the — and I'd say, "Now — "

HALDEMAN: Petersen's planning to leave anyway.

NIXON: And I'd say, "Now — "

DEAN: Is he?

NIXON: "I want you to get — we want you to, one," we'd say to Petersen, "We want you to get to the bottom of the goddamn thing. Call another grand jury or anything else." Correct? Well, now you've got to follow up to see whether Kleindienst can get Sirica to put off. Right? If that is — if we — second, you've got to get Mitchell down here. You and Ehrlichman and Mitchell and let's — and by tomorrow.

HALDEMAN: Why don't we do that tonight?

NIXON: I don't think you can get him that soon, can you?

HALDEMAN: John?

NIXON: It would be helpful if you could.

DEAN: I think it would be.

NIXON: You need —

DEAN: Get him to come down this afternoon.

NIXON: It would be very helpful to get it going. And, you know, and then — actually, I'm perfectly willing to meet with the group, or I don't know whether —

HALDEMAN: Do you think you want to?

NIXON: Maybe have Dean report to me at the end as to what are — as to what conclusions, et cetera — is that what you want to do? I think I should stay away from the Mitchell side of it at this point.

DEAN: Mm-hmm.

NIXON: Do you agree?

DEAN: Mm-hmm.

NIXON: And, uh —

DEAN: And I think, unless we see — you know, some sort of a reluctant dragon there —

HALDEMAN: You might try to meet with the rest of us. I'm not sure you'd want to meet with John in a group of us. Okay, let me see if I can get it done.

NIXON: All right. Fine. And my point is that we can — you may well come — I think it is good, frankly, to consider these various options. And then once you decide on the plan — John — and you had the right plan. Let me say I have no doubts about the right plan before the election. And you handled it just right. You contained it. Now after the election we've got to have another plan, because we can't have, for four years, we can't have this thing — you're going to be eaten away. We can't do it.

DEAN: Well, there's been a change in the mood —

HALDEMAN: John's point is exactly right, that the erosion here now is going to you. And that is the thing that we've got to turn off at whatever the cost. We've got to figure out where to turn it off at the lowest cost we can, but at whatever cost it takes.

DEAN: That's what we have to do.

NIXON: Well, the erosion is inevitably going to come here. Apart from anything, you know, people saying that, well, the Watergate isn't a major concern. It isn't. But it would — but it will be. It's bound to be.

DEAN: We cannot let you be tarnished by that situation.

NIXON: Well, I [unclear] also because I — although Ron Ziegler has to go out, they blame the [unclear] the White House [unclear].

DEAN: That's right.

NIXON: We don't — I say that the White House can't do it. Right?

HALDEMAN: Yeah.

DEAN: Yes, sir.

"While Mitchell is here, I should see him."

March 22, 1973, 9:11 a.m.

Richard Nixon and Bob Haldeman

EXECUTIVE OFFICE BUILDING

By March 22, Nixon saw the Watergate scandal with more urgency than before. Dean's no-nonsense account the day before almost certainly contributed to the perspective Nixon exhibited in his discussion with Haldeman, which was more intense than previous ones on the same subject. Nixon recognized that the "second-story job" at Democratic National Committee headquarters could well lead to questions about the slush fund that financed all such shadowy activities. With that, he and Haldeman outlined in remarkable detail the flow of undocumented money. In a combination of new strategies and the same old wishful thinking, they planned ways to protect those working in the White House, even at the expense of close associates, including former attorney general Mitchell — who was then visiting Washington from his home in New York City. The issue on Nixon's mind, all the while, was the degree to which "Mitchell would take some responsibility."

· · ·

NIXON: Here's the thing. I think — this concerns me, Bob. [unclear] cancer growing around the president and that's got to be cut out — somehow. And then, of course, we're trying to figure how we can cut it out. Why you cut it out without hurting and killing a lot of people. [unclear] kill a lot of people.

HALDEMAN: That may be what you have to do.

NIXON: Now — well, I don't know. The point is —

HALDEMAN: Then Dean —

NIXON: [unclear]

HALDEMAN: — his argument is those people are going to be killed anyway —

NIXON: Well, that's the point.

HALDEMAN: — why not kill them with a —

NIXON: Dean —

HALDEMAN: — clean bullet now?

NIXON: Dean goes —

HALDEMAN: And leave the —

NIXON: Dean goes down the line and then the line goes [unclear]. He gets, for example, it appears to me that it's — if you really want to look at the thing, it's — and he's been completely honest. He says that he's involved. He — and I said, "Why the hell — how are you involved?" He said because he was aware of and participated in the obstruction of justice by reason of the fact that he was aware of the fact that they were — they had a fund to take care of these various defendants. I don't know. I don't believe that that is going to be something that is going to set Dean — myself — you know what I mean? That's — well, when Dean ran the fund to — he didn't hand out the money. Others did.

HALDEMAN: We — John and I — worked on that with him. Perhaps he thinks I'm tied into that too because of this. In a sense, it's my fund that he was taking.

NIXON: Yeah. Well — I, that's the kind of thing I'd kind of like to get —

HALDEMAN: What?

NIXON: — out of the way.

HALDEMAN: Okay, but we're very clear on that — except this concern is what they do on the other side. What happened was that — is they needed the money.

NIXON: Right.

HALDEMAN: They were supposed to be getting it themselves from other sources, from other Cubans and all that kind of crap.

NIXON: Right.

HALDEMAN: So they got back to a crunch once in a while when a guy had to have another three thousand dollars or something or he was going to pull the plug —

NIXON: Then, who did it? Dean? That's what worries him.

HALDEMAN: No. Then what happened was, the only — see they knew over there that the only money there was that was usable was this three hundred fifty thousand.

NIXON: Who's they? Who's they?

HALDEMAN: LaRue and Mitchell.

NIXON: Okay.

HALDEMAN: And so, Mitchell said, "You've got to use that money." So, I said, "Turn the whole thing back to 'em. We don't want the money anyway. Give them just enough — I've been looking for a way to get rid of it." I'll admit I was worried about this money. I wanted to get it back into the — where it belonged. So I said give it back to them, and they wouldn't take — Mitchell wouldn't let them take it back, but he did say, "You've got to use some of it." So Dean told Strachan, who was the guy that had the —

NIXON: Yeah.

HALDEMAN: — the physical possession to give X thousand dollars to LaRue. So, Strachan would go and open his safe, take out X thousand dollars, and go trudging over to LaRue's. And this is all after the election. This is in the —

NIXON: After the election?

HALDEMAN: Yeah, on the — yeah, and this in —

NIXON: Oh, after the election.

HALDEMAN: Yeah. And he would go over and give LaRue —

NIXON: Yeah.

HALDEMAN: — you know, X thousand dollars and we can certainly claim that Strachan had no knowledge of what that was for. He was carrying out Dean's instructions — that Dean was carrying out instructions from me, and you've got a provable thing. And my point there was, it's their money, give it back to them, give it all back to them. So we were giving —

NIXON: The way I would — the way I was going to say about it — of course, on the money was [unclear]. First, what was it? The money was money that was collected without regard to the campaign laws at all —

HALDEMAN: That's right.

NIXON: It was in cash. It was for the purpose of taking polls and surveys, and so forth — prior to that — and so forth.

HALDEMAN: That's right.

NIXON: It was not used. After the election it was a surplus.

HALDEMAN: That's right.

NIXON: It was turned back —

HALDEMAN: That's right.

NIXON: — period. Right?

HALDEMAN: That's right.

NIXON: Now, what happened to it after that? Do we have to account for what happened to that money after the election?

HALDEMAN: Well —

NIXON: If it was used to pay campaign bills —

HALDEMAN: Yeah. Somebody has to. We don't have to, but the campaign has to —

NIXON: Somebody has to what — now?

HALDEMAN: The campaign has to account for it.

NIXON: But it wasn't collected in the cam —

HALDEMAN: But they still have to account for — it was cash on hand at the time of the campaign. No, it wasn't, because they got rid of it.

NIXON: Not in the campaign, not in the camp — my point is, I would not treat that — I, that in my view, was —

HALDEMAN: Yeah.

NIXON: — not campaign funds. That was campaign — that was not given for a campaign at all. These were funds that were, shall we say, collected after the 1968 elections and had nothing to do with any campaign law, was not campaign funds, you know, for any purpose. They wanted to know — what did they poll? They polled — what happened to Goldwater, what happened on the meat prices —

HALDEMAN: Yes, sir. Issue — issue polls.

NIXON: Issue polls —

HALDEMAN: And the —

NIXON: — and the rest. The study that you made —

HALDEMAN: — geographic analysis.

NIXON: — and after that they returned it over to the campaign committee.

HALDEMAN: It was a gift to the campaign committee.

NIXON: Well, I don't. I don't know. Anyway, it's a problem, and that's — if Dean sees that it's a problem because the question will be asked. Dean is very good this way. You saw how the next question would be — whack, whack, whack, whack.

HALDEMAN: Well, it's a potential problem. If Dean is inordinately worried about that problem because it does involve him.

NIXON: Yeah.

HALDEMAN: Uh —

NIXON: Yeah.

HALDEMAN: His view, and we — this is what we were talking about — I mentioned to you last night on the phone.

NIXON: Yeah.

HALDEMAN: His view that pulling —

NIXON: The White House —

HALDEMAN: — the wagons around the White House. And Dean's point is, when you get down to it, the White House literally doesn't have any problem prior to the Watergate break-in. And, in other words, there was no White House involvement in the Watergate, he's satisfied. That —

NIXON: Even Colson?

HALDEMAN: He's satisfied with that.

NIXON: He thinks that telephone call — that's the one that worries me.

HALDEMAN: You see that's — yeah.

NIXON: Colson has Liddy and Hunt in his office and calls Magruder and says, "Get off your ass and do something."

HALDEMAN: Well, but he argues that wasn't necessarily —

NIXON: Yeah.

HALDEMAN: — and probably, and maybe —

NIXON: Yeah.

HALDEMAN: — in reality, wasn't knowledge —

NIXON: I guess, but that —

HALDEMAN: — of the operation.

NIXON: I don't know —

HALDEMAN: Now, he did know there was an intelligence apparatus.

NIXON: I recall myself, Bob, that [unclear] the ITT thing. I can imagine Chuck and how he was. Hell, he'd go on for an hour about what he was trying to do like that, and it wasn't like that he was trying to get a counteroffensive. I don't know what he was trying to do.

HALDEMAN: Yeah. That's when he was playing Teddy Kennedy stuff. He was —

NIXON: That's right. Damn most [unclear]. But, well, anyway, I guess that —

HALDEMAN: Dean's point is the only place that the White House is culpable —

NIXON: Yes.

HALDEMAN: — in this thing —

NIXON: Mm-hmm.

HALDEMAN: — in any criminal basis —

NIXON: [unclear]

HALDEMAN: — or any real basis —

NIXON: Yeah.

HALDEMAN: — is in the potential charge of obstruction of justice after the fact — that we have no problem with the crime itself.

NIXON: Right, and on that one he says, "Why don't we just say we turned over the money?"

HALDEMAN: And I don't see why we're even — so the money is used for support stuff for defendants?

NIXON: Yeah.

HALDEMAN: Why is that obstruction of justice anyway?

NIXON: Well, particularly when it's not to sip champagne. I wouldn't say that, I guess maybe —

HALDEMAN: You may not have to get into that at all, see? He's just worried that you might get into it. And if you follow his containment line, the odds —

NIXON: Yeah.

HALDEMAN: — he feels, and I feel strongly on this, are pretty good you won't get into it. He's just worried that there's a little lurking some [unclear] —

NIXON: Possibility [unclear].

HALDEMAN: — because somebody, well, because Hugh Sloan knows that the money was delivered here. That's really where it — what it boils down to.

NIXON: Hugh Sloan knows it.

HALDEMAN: Or if you put Gordon Strachan —

NIXON: Yeah.

HALDEMAN: — up before a grand jury —

NIXON: Yeah.

HALDEMAN: — if they ask the right question — Gordon will never volunteer. He's a lawyer and he's —

NIXON: Yeah. Yeah.

HALDEMAN: — smart —

NIXON: Yeah. Yeah.

HALDEMAN: — and he'll pull —

NIXON: But he must not perjure himself.

HALDEMAN: But, if you get Gordon to a point where they say, "Was there any money?" —

NIXON: Yeah.

HALDEMAN: — somehow —

NIXON: Yeah.

HALDEMAN: — he may — they may get him into where —

NIXON: But this had already been, some had been used yet — is it our money [unclear]?

HALDEMAN: No — well, yeah, but never a fund over here —

NIXON: Yeah.

HALDEMAN: — only that there — that Stans had this fund in his safe, which he did — which, of course, he would have. He had a cash fund in his safe. It was used for various payments and that's where —

NIXON: As far as this is concerned, this is — I'd say constructively that Stans is clean. Now, to go on to — did you ever sign any [unclear]?

HALDEMAN: I don't know. I didn't — I never saw him. I never had a thing to do with the situation.

NIXON: There was nothing in writing involved in it.

HALDEMAN: Well, Strachan may have had to sign a receipt when he took [unclear] —

NIXON: [unclear]

HALDEMAN: Well, what it was, was that money —

NIXON: I know.

HALDEMAN: — that we had left over from '70. Remember we collected all our cash in '70 —

NIXON: [unclear]

HALDEMAN: And we told 'em not to spend all of it if they didn't have to. We ended up, we had a — and it was probably '68 surplus that we used in '70 and carried over.

NIXON: Yeah.

HALDEMAN: It got mixed, of course.

NIXON: Why don't we just say on this money —

HALDEMAN: The money [unclear].

NIXON: Kalmbach's money [unclear] —

HALDEMAN: [unclear] Kalmbach.

NIXON: — was to be used — this was to be used for various candidates but was never used.

HALDEMAN: It was to be used for candidate support and research.

NIXON: For candidate support and research. It was never used, turned over to the committee at the end of the campaign. What they did with it is their problem.

HALDEMAN: That had been collected in years prior to 1971.

NIXON: That's right. Very simple.

HALDEMAN: Which is true, also. At least that was my understanding of that. Now, the problem is that — I think those funds got mixed together and we never got all the money.

NIXON: Yeah.

HALDEMAN: Because they told us we couldn't —

NIXON: Sure.

HALDEMAN: — make a [unclear]. Uh —

NIXON: They didn't use what they thought they did. Anyway, [unclear].

HALDEMAN: Well, it wasn't they thought they needed it. It was their point that under the laws there was no way we could use it — which they were right.

NIXON: Which we never did.

HALDEMAN: There really wasn't. There wasn't even a way we could use what we had.

NIXON: What you mean is that you didn't do a thing with the money, which is good.

HALDEMAN: See, I had the money. I was going to use it to pay for polls [unclear].

NIXON: [unclear] you did the polling through —

HALDEMAN: But they said they had the money to pay for it and they needed places to show where they spend money, so they paid for the bills.

NIXON: I would say that looking at the thing now — Ehrlichman, for example, he gets to him —

HALDEMAN: Not on Watergate.

NIXON: No, but he gets to him on the — if Hunt, with Hunt's —

HALDEMAN: But John doesn't think it does. It gets to Krogh.

NIXON: Well, that bothers me.

HALDEMAN: It — and it clearly does, and it gets to David Young, and David Young is a weaker reed than Krogh.

NIXON: Has Young also lied? They both —

HALDEMAN: Well, they haven't gotten to Young yet, I don't think. I shouldn't say that because I don't know. I don't know.

NIXON: But, what were Young and —

HALDEMAN: It's my impression that they —

NIXON: What were Young and — Krogh didn't, Krogh hit a critical question in his case, apparently, said he didn't know the Cubans. Now how does he get out of that? Has anybody thought of that?

HALDEMAN: Well, Ehrlichman's view on it is — which kind of surprises me — is to be cold-blooded. Yesterday, he said, "When Krogh gets finished with his lying — "

NIXON: He said, "No, I didn't." They said they know Krogh. It's a convicted felon against his word. Well —

HALDEMAN: Plus they may not say anything. You still — the Cubans seem to be the least matter of concern. They're fanatics and they don't seem to really be too concerned about their pulling the plug and their needs are fairly minimal, and Dean confirms again that Liddy is enjoying — Liddy's in jail. He didn't —

NIXON: Yeah.

HALDEMAN: — stay out. He said, "I want to start serving my term," and he's at Danbury and thoroughly enjoying it. He's a little strange.

NIXON: That son of a bitch of a judge gave him thirty-five years.

HALDEMAN: He may enjoy that. As long as he thinks we're going to deal something up for him someday when he — it's, incredibly he's got five kids and all he's concerned about is that there's enough income to take care of his kids and that's being taken care of right now by his father. His lawyer's got something worked out.

NIXON: Goddamn it! The people are in jail! It's only right for people to raise the money for them. I've got to let them do that and that's all there is to it. I think we ought to. There's got to be funds. I'm not being — I don't mean to be blackmailed by Hunt. That goes too far. But we're taking care of these people that are in jail. My God, they did this for — we're sorry for them. We do it out of compassion and I didn't [unclear] the Cuban fund and the people that contribute to it didn't have to report on that damn thing. There's no reporting requirement of any kind whatever. You don't agree? What else should we do?

HALDEMAN: That's why I — it seems to me that there's no real problem on obstruction of justice as far as Dean's concerned. I mean — it doesn't seem to me that we are obstructing justice, for Christ's sake. The people —

NIXON: Yeah.

HALDEMAN: — pled guilty —

NIXON: Yeah.

HALDEMAN: When a guy goes and pleads guilty, are you obstructing justice?

NIXON: When you help his —

HALDEMAN: His argument is when you read the law, that the —

NIXON: Yeah.

HALDEMAN: — that, uh —

NIXON: Yeah, but, Dean didn't do it. Dean, I don't think Dean had anything to do with the obstruction. He didn't deliver the money or — that's the point. I think what really set him off was when Hunt's lawyer was off at this party and said Hunt needs a hundred and twenty thousand dollars. Well, that was a very — that was a shot across the bow. You understand that that would have constituted goddamn blackmail if Dean had gotten the money and never — you see what I mean?

HALDEMAN: Yeah.

NIXON: Let's come to the other. We — when you talk about the wagons around the White House, Bob, what really happens here is that we really have to take a hard look at the situation and realize that we [unclear]. I don't think that we can — has anybody candidly suggested that Magruder was not aware that they were tapping?

HALDEMAN: I don't think so. I don't know, but I have my opin — I have no knowledge. My opinion is that he knew.

NIXON: Yeah.

HALDEMAN: And from the way he talks I'm thoroughly convinced of that. Dean is thoroughly convinced that he knew.

NIXON: All the way through. And it's Magruder's word against the others and he said he didn't.

HALDEMAN: Well, nobody said he did.

NIXON: Well, did he [unclear]?

HALDEMAN: Oh, yeah, but not — they haven't testified [unclear].

NIXON: Speaking now of what Dean tells me — yes, that's what I'm going to do this afternoon, and Dean tells me things have gotten out of control. And he says, well, [unclear] and asked him how Magruder was doing and Dean said Magruder perjured himself. Well, it's pretty rough. I'd say well, with that knowledge can I appoint Magruder to a position in government? That's the problem, you see [unclear].

HALDEMAN: You didn't appoint him to a position in the White House.

NIXON: [unclear] I hired him out. I'd say —

HALDEMAN: That's exactly why we didn't let him get into anything that was a presidential appointment. And you can also argue that we should have told the secretary of commerce. On the other hand, we don't — we can't prove he perjured himself, that's Dean's opinion.

NIXON: [unclear]

HALDEMAN: Well, Magruder, anyway, that's — we went that route for exactly that reason.

NIXON: I know, I know. We didn't.

HALDEMAN: But the other side of that coin is, if you're — unless you decide to throw Magruder to the wolves, you need to keep Magruder on as even a keel as you can. If you decide to throw him to the wolves, [unclear] kind of problem, he's not a guy — he's not a Liddy type. He's exactly the opposite.

NIXON: If you decided to throw him to the wolves, what does that [unclear]? You wouldn't say anything [unclear]. I mean, the point is we say that we have found that Magruder [unclear].

HALDEMAN: No. We don't have anybody who can even testify on Watergate, because we don't have anybody who knows anything about it.

NIXON: Except possibly Colson, and that's just a big possibility — possible. Yet, I don't agree that nobody else would know. Strachan?

HALDEMAN: Well, that's right — I keep forgetting about Strachan. And Gord — what's his name, Dean says Strachan did know.

NIXON: What we do with getting information in sort of a — he may not have known about how we're — you know what I mean? I think Strachan is not that bad if his fish is going to get fried. He's at too low a level.

HALDEMAN: That's the point. Strachan had no authority.

NIXON: He got a tremendous amount of — he just got information, but he didn't issue orders or anything on what he wanted to do.

HALDEMAN: Right. You look at Gordon Strachan. Here's a little, young lawyer, who used to work for John Mitchell in his law firm, and came down to Washington to work in the government, and he's working under a campaign with the attorney general of the United States is in charge of it. Now, how the hell do you expect him to decide whether something that's being done is right or wrong?

NIXON: That's right.

HALDEMAN: I don't know, I don't think — Gordon doesn't, I don't think, doesn't worry Dean much and he doesn't worry — I don't, I would not be concerned about Gordon. He is —

NIXON: A hell of a guy.

HALDEMAN: You never know about anybody. You know, I would have never thought that navy aide would have a nervous breakdown.

NIXON: Didn't you? [unclear] can sure be wrong in picking people that —

HALDEMAN: Gordon is a guy I wouldn't worry about. But, Magruder is a guy I would. Because Magruder is loaded with ego, personal pride, political ambition —

NIXON: He's never going to make it this way.

HALDEMAN: He's had some major success as a young guy. He's, you know, a boy wonder type —

NIXON: Right.

HALDEMAN: — and that kind of guy is —

NIXON: How does John answer the Ellsberg thing? That's the other point I wanted to raise that — John seems to say well —

HALDEMAN: He says, "I didn't know anything about it." He says, "I didn't think they — I — "

NIXON: Talked to Hunt [unclear].

HALDEMAN: No, he didn't. He says he didn't talk to Hunt about it.

NIXON: Krogh did.

HALDEMAN: Krogh did.

NIXON: But what was — what were we doing at that meeting though is the whole point [unclear] about that. I'm rather curious to know myself.

HALDEMAN: Well, you better ask John, because I don't really know. All I know is —

NIXON: All I know is that I think it was part of that whole operation of John and Young, where we were just looking into the whole business of leaks. Henry was in on that. Henry must be aware of some of that. I've got to —

HALDEMAN: What they — the enterprise out of there, which is the key thing that Hunt, you see — what Hunt says is that he'll uncover some of the sleazy work he did for Ehrlichman. He said particularly remind him of the —

NIXON: Yeah.

HALDEMAN: — of the —

NIXON: The Ellsberg affair. That's what Dean told me.

HALDEMAN: All right, and the Ellsberg affair —

NIXON: Yeah, what happened?

HALDEMAN: I'm not sure what happened, but it has something to do with they sent Hunt out, and I guess the Cubans —

NIXON: Yeah.

HALDEMAN: — to break in —

NIXON: To a doctor's office.

HALDEMAN: — to a psychiatrist's office to get a report —

NIXON: Yeah.

HALDEMAN: — on Ellsberg's mental analysis or something, and they bungled [laughs] the break-in — didn't get what they were supposed to get or something, and then they came back and said could they go back again and that request got to Ehrlichman, and he said, "Absolutely not," he says. And they didn't, apparently. That's —

NIXON: Why did they want a report on [unclear]?

HALDEMAN: I don't know, but they had — there was a lot of stuff. They had a lot of interesting stuff on Ellsberg that showed he was, that was — we got some of it.

NIXON: What was the purpose of it though? I mean, to discredit — ?

HALDEMAN: I forgot — yes. [unclear]

NIXON: [unclear]

HALDEMAN: Try and make a spy out of him, and —

NIXON: Oh, I see. Did it make him look as bad after all that national security was involved and so forth?

HALDEMAN: Well —

NIXON: I'm not sure I [unclear].

HALDEMAN: And why were we using private people? Because the question — there was a valid or a real question here as to where the CIA and the FBI fit into it.

NIXON: Also, whether they were leaking —

HALDEMAN: [unclear] because things were leaking from all over.

NIXON: They were leaking from all over and somebody had to find a way —

HALDEMAN: And it had to be done independently.

NIXON: It had to be done independently because of the possibility of leakage.

HALDEMAN: [unclear]

NIXON: Huh?

HALDEMAN: I don't know whether that'll hold up. I am sure that doesn't make it legal —

NIXON: [unclear] now looking again. If you come back, why —

HALDEMAN: That's a long stretched-out [unclear].

NIXON: I'm trying to get down to the end of the point, that the man who knows all this is Hunt —

HALDEMAN: [unclear]

NIXON: So, Hunt becomes rather important.

HALDEMAN: Probably.

NIXON: And Dean's line, Bob, if we want —

HALDEMAN: Dean's point on that one is that —

NIXON: Dean would say that he'd just cut that off [unclear]. That's what you really come down to. Or you, you give him a hundred and twenty thousand dollars or at least give him another contact, you know what I mean? That's a lot of dough. Let's face it, in terms of a pardon or so forth, that if Colson is talking of a pardon by Christmas, you know, right after the fact that the court, that they're convicted, or either before they're sentenced — he's out of his mind. He knows we can't do that.

HALDEMAN: But if Hunt thinks that's what he's been promised —

NIXON: He'll shut up now.

HALDEMAN: He'll, he may shut up now.

NIXON: Yeah, but my point is —

HALDEMAN: But what do you do at Christmastime?

NIXON: Yeah. That's right. And the question is that now it seems to me you'd better find out from Colson what did he promise so that — don't you think so?

HALDEMAN: Yeah.

NIXON: But you've got to go about that before he's sentenced. [unclear] a pardon. Well, what — that would be a —

HALDEMAN: But not if you get the parole board to — a pardon might be, an early pardon — an early parole might not if you get the parole board to —

NIXON: Yeah.

HALDEMAN: — look at the point that the sentence was —

NIXON: Yeah.

HALDEMAN: — way out of proportion to the —

NIXON: Well, the point is that — Dean says — that's why he's thinking of using Petersen. He says that, and Ehrlichman agrees, that the judge has the power to sentence him without parole. That's a rough son of a bitch it seems to me for something like this on the ground that they didn't talk about it, you see. Might make it tough titty, wouldn't it — don't you think, to pardon him? I think it would be perfect [unclear].

HALDEMAN: But the point — the moral of it is that he doesn't — we don't know what Sirica's going to [unclear]. Again, Dean looks at the — what might be the worst. It may not be the worst.

NIXON: [unclear]

HALDEMAN: [laughs] In fact what usually happens is something beyond what you thought was the worst.

NIXON: Well, on the wagons theory, that — what does that mean, I wonder, to put the wagons up around the White House? I mean that — who do you let down the tube? Do you let Magruder down?

HALDEMAN: You don't intentionally. You leave Magruder — what you do is — you see we're doing stuff now. We're keeping quiet and all that —

NIXON: Right.

HALDEMAN: Just try and cov — and putting up this money and everything else. We're trying to keep — when you get right down to it, as Dean says, the only White House guilt — culpability, is in the cover-up.

NIXON: Yeah.

HALDEMAN: And what's the purpose of the cover-up, to protect the White House? No, it protects some individuals at the committee.

NIXON: Mitchell, Magruder.

HALDEMAN: And the question then is how — what individuals — how far up does it go, that you're protecting? And we've already — we're not protecting Liddy, so we [unclear] so we've got to talk to him. The question is can it, if you could — his idea is you separate, you look at the committee as one thing, the White House as another.

NIXON: Right.

HALDEMAN: The White House has no guilt in the Watergate thing.

NIXON: Yeah.

HALDEMAN: So you come up with wagons around the White House, and you just turn it up to — you do whatever you do — issue statements, issue a new statement, well, whatever, to totally cut off the White House from the whole Watergate business. Now, at the same time you do that, it might be — we haven't gotten to this, but it might be you also have to do the Segretti thing and, to a degree, implicate the White House, which is fine.

NIXON: There must be a Dean statement [unclear]. I don't know how you feel about that —

HALDEMAN: Yeah.

NIXON: — or a Moore statement, or a —

HALDEMAN: There has to be something. That's right.

NIXON: Or do you agree?

HALDEMAN: No, I think you do. I think they do.

NIXON: I think we need — I mean, let me say — let me put it — I have a certain balance [unclear] that Dean statement, or a Moore statement, or what have you, sure will [unclear] and so forth, but it's better to have something rather than nothing. You know what I mean?

HALDEMAN: Well, but then the questions that that raises are: they can successfully do that, but can you — are you any better off if the White House is clean but your campaign committee's dirty or if we cut the whole thing off?

NIXON: That's not what I was referring to.

HALDEMAN: In other words, we need [unclear] the campaign committee and [unclear] the White House. First of all, is that believable? It happens to be true, but can it be convincing?

NIXON: Well, that — well, they — what you're —

HALDEMAN: And Dean — if they get as high as Magruder, probably it doesn't hurt too much. If they get to Mitchell —

NIXON: Yeah.

HALDEMAN: He's awfully close to you.

NIXON: Yeah.

HALDEMAN: He's not as close to you as Ehrlichman and, I guess, than Dean and Haldeman now, which [unclear]. Mitchell will find a way out. You have to let them get to him, I think. But Dean's thought, I think — what convinced him to put the wagons around the White House is that it forces Mitchell to take the responsibility rather than allowing Mitchell to hide under the blanket of the White House, which he's been doing, and I think Dean feels that that's — and in a way, it does Colson too, who's out. He feels that Mitchell and Colson can take care of themselves.

NIXON: [unclear]

HALDEMAN: I don't know. But the problem is Magruder can't take care of himself, except with this straight line — his present position —

NIXON: Yep.

HALDEMAN: — and see whether he can make it stick. Now, they may be able to hang him on that —

NIXON: They'll kill him.

HALDEMAN: — but still, it will get to a question. They may be able to indict if they get other people to talk, but can they convict him beyond a reasonable doubt? Maybe not, if he stays with his line they may not be able to convict him. Then Magruder indicted and winning acquittal may be a pretty good route for us to go. We won't know unless we try. And they're — what'll you do if they call us? We can't not go there again. And if I were the prosecutor, well, that decision, it's the Justice Department that prosecutes that so maybe we can control the prosecution and not call 'em.

NIXON: Well —

HALDEMAN: But there again, at least if you call us, we're under rules of evidence and —

NIXON: Right.

HALDEMAN: — and germaneness.

NIXON: You've got lawyers who object — you can go to relevancy there.

HALDEMAN: Yeah, and they can only —

NIXON: Go to relevancy. That's no problem there.

HALDEMAN: So they can't go fishing. And there [the grand jury] there is no problem, unless they get to Strachan and maybe start running that stream.

NIXON: Another thought that has been raised is the idea that [unclear] things going wrong [unclear] a special counselor.

HALDEMAN: I don't know, not being a lawyer, I [unclear] this kind of stuff, but Dean feels very strongly, and John Ehrlichman seems to concur, that it would — that we do need the advice of somebody who knows more about the criminal setup than we do —

NIXON: Yeah.

HALDEMAN: And they —

NIXON: We can't go to Petersen —

HALDEMAN: Well, they both know Petersen's the guy. They wonder if you know what we got into last night after we were in here was the question of whether, I guess it was

Dean, could call Petersen and just say we need advice. "Can I talk to you on a totally confidential basis, outside of school, and it will [unclear]."

NIXON: You wouldn't do that through Kleindienst?

HALDEMAN: No.

NIXON: Kleindienst wouldn't know about it until after you told him? I'm just asking.

HALDEMAN: I don't know. That — the way that we were talking, it's going —

NIXON: Right.

HALDEMAN: — to have to either be —

NIXON: Right. Okay.

HALDEMAN: — just straight bilateral —

NIXON: Right.

HALDEMAN: — Dean to Petersen —

NIXON: Right.

HALDEMAN: — or Dean would just say, "I'm over my head on this — "

NIXON: Yeah.

HALDEMAN: " — and I need counsel on an informal and totally confidential basis. Will you sit down and let me go through this with you? But it'd have to be understood and it might — I recognize that you may be — can't do it because as the head of the Criminal Division it puts you on the other side." It can't be separated. Dean has the feeling that the more Petersen knows, the more helpful he can be, and that he will be.

NIXON: I'm not sure that that's what you can count on.

HALDEMAN: I'm sure you can't count on it, because Petersen's another human being, too.

NIXON: And he's a knowledgeable man. [unclear] you stuck somebody [unclear].

HALDEMAN: But you don't know what his ambitions are and —

NIXON: [unclear] and I just don't know.

HALDEMAN: Well, I know they're all possibilities, but apparently, all the way through this he's been a very solid rock.

NIXON: More so than Kleindienst.

HALDEMAN: The problem you've got with Petersen is that he wants to go out in private practice with Kleindienst.

NIXON: Well, I'd sooner take [unclear].

HALDEMAN: And if you didn't —

NIXON: What are you [unclear] tell Kleindienst too?

HALDEMAN: I don't think that — if you're going to do this — you can't do it without Kleindienst.

NIXON: Right. I think here you've just got to [unclear] get Kleindienst in. [unclear] I'll just call him and say look [unclear].

HALDEMAN: Well, he used to, and I assume that that [unclear] same ones, I think.

NIXON: Does have any report from Sullivan?

HALDEMAN: Yeah, he does.

NIXON: Not very good?

HALDEMAN: Oh, it's got to — it's some — of mostly the same old stuff. It's the Anna Chennault and all — crap, and — well, there's one thing that we could build up that would — that I think we could get built up that would be pretty good which is about the extensive use of the FBI in the 1964 Democratic convention and an attempt to use them in '68. There is also some cover-up on Walter Jenkins, and some instructions by Johnson to the FBI as to what they were to find in their Jenkins investigation and — I don't think we can use that, I mean, it isn't — that isn't —

NIXON: Too nasty?

HALDEMAN: Ah — then there's some Abe Fortas stuff they were involved with. That was intended [unclear] to use Fortas to implicate [unclear]. As precise [unclear] he didn't like but there's a — I think you could blow a hell of a bombshell out of the '64 Democratic convention —

Friends and law partners: Nixon and Mitchell

March 22, 1973, 1:57 p.m.
Richard Nixon, John Dean, Bob Haldeman, John Ehrlichman, and John Mitchell
EXECUTIVE OFFICE BUILDING

In early afternoon, Mitchell visited the Oval Office for a meeting that included Nixon and his three closest advisors. In one of the seminal conversations in the Nixon White House, the president of the United States suggested that Mitchell and those he influenced should "cover up or anything else" in order to block ongoing investigations. Mitchell grew up on Long Island, an athletic young man who worked his way through law school at Fordham University and then joined a law firm specializing in bonds and public finance. He was a success in his profession, liked by those with whom he worked for his genuine courtesy and respect. He could be, however, a cunning and sullen adversary. After meeting Nixon when their firms merged, Mitchell felt that he had found a leader he could support. During the 1960s, Mitchell was openly antagonistic toward the protest movement. He helped to present Nixon in 1968 as the candidate who would return calm to the nation.

Named attorney general at the beginning of Nixon's first term, Mitchell implemented policies that were long on expediency for the police and short on rights for private citizens. For that he was unapologetic. He resigned in mid-1972 in order to head the Committee to Re-elect the President. In fact, the compelling aspect of the conversation he had at the White House on March 22 is how his loyalty continued unabated, helping to sort out solutions to Nixon's many problems with the Justice Department, the FBI, the Senate committees, and the press. At the time, Mitchell was surrounded by four men who had been for weeks — even up to that morning — discussing how to sacrifice him for their own survival.*

• • •

---

* Gerald Caplan, "The Attorney General Reconsidered," *McGeorge Law Review,* 2010, pp. 311–12.

HALDEMAN: Well, John, Howard Baker just had—Hunt had this [unclear] sort of a buddy and Bittman just had lunch with Howard Baker's administrative assistant at the administrative assistant's request.

NIXON: The same one that saw Colson?

HALDEMAN: I don't know that it was the same one, but I would guess. But this fellow wanted to get guidance from Timmons as to what the president was expecting out of the hearings and what he wanted to talk to him about this executive privilege business and where are we going to stand on that. He expressed the personal view that the president couldn't waive executive privilege, which that son of a bitch [unclear] Ervin would accept the written interrogatories, and that they would probably go to the subpoena route [unclear]. But nothing was raised about Baker being concerned that he didn't have contact—nothing on that other report was raised at all. But he did say that Baker was a little pissed off at Kleindienst because he had not met with him at all. He had had one meeting scheduled which they finally were able to set up, but Kleindienst canceled it. And it has not been rescheduled, and so Baker has had no communication with Kleindienst. The day it was scheduled was the day you had your press conference and announced your executive privilege or announced that the president with Dean and nobody would go up which caught Baker unaware. And the disturbing thing is that his understanding is [unclear] the view that Kleindienst would keep him informed of this next time. [unclear]

MITCHELL: Plus the fact they're having a meeting with that committee, as soon as he—

HALDEMAN: Oh, yeah.

MITCHELL: And all Weicker does is [unclear] Moore and Howard [unclear] Justice Department [unclear].

HALDEMAN: Well he's objecting to the agreement that they made with Kleindienst—that Ervin made with Kleindienst—that FBI raw files would be made available to the chairman and the ranking member.

MITCHELL: Yeah, well—

HALDEMAN: Demanding that they be—he's going to demand that they subpoena the attorney general and the director of the FBI to produce all the files, the materials, and so forth.

DEAN: I talked to Kleindienst last night and he raised that. And he said that he worked this out with Weicker, but Weicker was now dissatisfied with the arrangement. So he's going to the chairman and the ranking minority member and the counsel.

NIXON: [unclear] a letter to [unclear].

HALDEMAN: That could be the [unclear].

NIXON: [unclear] Baker's idea. He wanted to talk to Kleindienst about it—didn't want to talk to anybody else. That's the way we left it.

DEAN: [unclear] I think that Kleindienst ought to be aware of the fact that Baker is distressed that he hasn't made any greater effort to see him.

NIXON: Good point. Yeah.

DEAN: I will.

NIXON: Fine [unclear]. Follow through and pick up on that idea. I just want — I think you'd better do it yourself. Don't you?

EHRLICHMAN: Could I suggest that you call Kleindienst? You had the other conversation with him. Could you call him and say you've gotten a rumor that Baker's unhappy? Because [unclear] nobody else can do it.

HALDEMAN: I think he's not really standing on his tippytoes completely.

NIXON: [unclear]

MITCHELL: The nature of the liaison — he's got [unclear].

NIXON: [unclear] communicate back and forth.

EHRLICHMAN: [unclear] will not want to be in position — Baker does not want to be in the position of talking to anybody in the White House.

NIXON: He doesn't want to talk to anybody.

MITCHELL: [unclear] wants to collaborate with us.

NIXON: He doesn't want to talk —

HALDEMAN: But he wants to collaborate — this AA was saying he wants to be helpful, he wants to work things out. He told the president he wanted to do that through the —

NIXON: Yeah.

HALDEMAN: — attorney general.

NIXON: That's right. Said he did want to talk to Kleindienst.

EHRLICHMAN: Does Kleindienst know that?

NIXON: Yes, of course.

HALDEMAN: Well then, call Kleindienst.

UNIDENTIFIED: [unclear] Were you there? [unclear]

MITCHELL: What are they going to collaborate on?

NIXON: [unclear] what?

MITCHELL: Well, now, what are they going to collaborate on?

NIXON: Well, I suppose on such matters — you may recall that Gray wants to — [unclear] wants the FBI. However, [unclear] and so forth having Kleindienst [unclear].

HALDEMAN: Well, again, I know exactly what the trouble is.

NIXON: Oh, okay. [unclear] all done. [unclear] I'm the one that should do it. But you — what Baker was thinking of, says that Kleindienst canceled [unclear] I would think Kleindienst should have done it.

EHRLICHMAN: [unclear] broadcast [unclear].

MITCHELL: Well, that's another thing that [unclear]. For instance — said to Timmons, Baker was expecting all the lawyers to try to get into the confidence of Sam Ervin that [unclear].

HALDEMAN: Yeah, but he shouldn't be too concerned about Baker's public statements in agreement with Ervin with — that established him [unclear].

NIXON: Well, he said that he [unclear] against it. That's what he wants to do. [unclear] Okay. Well, you're going to follow up about two thirty on Gray [unclear]. He's [laughs] a little bit on the stupid side, to be frank with you.

DEAN: The prospects to let himself get sandbagged until then won't happen.

NIXON: You'd better counsel him about it. The problem with him, John, is with Gray, is a certain stubbornness [unclear] talk to Kleindienst. Frankly, I think, too — I think maybe Kleindienst ought to counsel him and talk to him.

DEAN: He has —

NIXON: Did he listen to him?

DEAN: John Ehrlichman talked to Kleindienst last night and said that's where Gray was getting his guidance.

EHRLICHMAN: The whole trouble is that Dick gives him guidance which is very general. Something like this comes up and Gray overreacts — it's almost a spasm reaction. We had, the other day — whether or not, you know, giving them access to the FBI files.

NIXON: Yeah.

EHRLICHMAN: It was the opposite of what Kleindienst told him.

NIXON: I know it.

EHRLICHMAN: And, uh —

NIXON: He shouldn't have even needed guidance on that.

EHRLICHMAN: Of course.

NIXON: Nobody — the director of the FBI should not have even known — should have even known, second nature, that you never turn over raw files to a full committee.

EHRLICHMAN: I talked to Dick Saturday night —

NIXON: Yeah.

EHRLICHMAN: — and he just was beside himself because of that. And he said, "Hell, we covered this," he says, and he was really obsessed on it. And I feel —

NIXON: Well, okay. I'll tell him.

• • •

NIXON: Well, where do we — what words of wisdom do we have from this august body on this point?

EHRLICHMAN: Our brother Mitchell brought us some wisdom on executive privilege which, I believe —

MITCHELL: Technically, Mr. President, I think the only problem [unclear] and I'd prefer you just coming out and stating —

NIXON: That's right.

MITCHELL: — and I would believe that it would be well worthwhile to consider to spoil the picture to the point where under the proper circumstances you can settle with certain former people in the White House and some [unclear] some of the current people at the White House under controlled circumstances should go up and —

• • •

NIXON: We're fairly certain — you could probably hear this afternoon. He [Kleindienst] said he's called Baker about — dozens of times, and Baker, it seems he's out of town making a speech [unclear] and this trip just goes on, and on, and on. But, he'll try. He'll call him right away. He said he talked to Weicker for an hour on the phone [unclear] furnishing the files [unclear]. Well, anyway, he says he talked to him for an hour and a half. When I talked to Kleindienst [unclear]. Maybe it's not Kleindienst, maybe it's Baker.

HALDEMAN: I would guess that there's truth to that, too. I have always said, they're always down here bitching about nobody calling them — nobody giving them anything and all that. They say, "When you catch them, you can't get to them."

EHRLICHMAN: [unclear] catch them [unclear] pass the word to Colson, Webster —

NIXON: That's right.

EHRLICHMAN: — and this —

NIXON: And his — and incidentally, it just looks like he — his administrative assistant called Colson. Now that's what Colson informed me. And I said, "But, what the hell," he said [unclear], but I said —

EHRLICHMAN: Well, that isn't a casual pitch.

NIXON: No.

DEAN: Maybe he's looking for some — Baker's looking for some sort of a link with the White House. Maybe that's what he's —

UNIDENTIFIED: Well —

DEAN: — trying to hint at.

NIXON: It's got to be Kleindienst. Go ahead on executive privilege, I suppose — how would you handle it?

MITCHELL: All I have worked out was —

NIXON: Work out the arrangements.

MITCHELL: — the best formula that we've discussed.

NIXON: Well, I guess under the situation that you — under the statement that we have — we're in a position to [unclear] I think we could — we're in a position to negotiate with the committee as to how — but we are not in a position to have — to cross the bridge in terms of saying that Hunt and Liddy will go down and testify and that members of the White House staff will testify in open, public session, or something like that. But you've got a lot of —

EHRLICHMAN: Formal —

NIXON: — other things —

EHRLICHMAN: Formal is the word.

NIXON: Formally is the word I use. And incidentally, that's what I told Baker, too. I said, "Fine, that's the term."

MITCHELL: On executive —

NIXON: We begin with that proposition — I'd be comfortable there — and see what you can get by with.

MITCHELL: On executive privilege, Mr. President, stay well aware that some have waived it, and the more I think about it [unclear].

NIXON: Yes.

EHRLICHMAN: And it hurts the more you do it, the more you —

MITCHELL: The more it's less [unclear].

NIXON: [unclear] Sherman Adams.

MITCHELL: The point — beyond which you might be able to work it out here.

NIXON: Yeah.

MITCHELL: The point being that this seems to be the only way in which you get involved [unclear].

NIXON: You do.

MITCHELL: I would lay out a formula and negotiate it with Sam Ervin or either through Baker or however else [unclear]. And I would also put together a damn good PR team. [unclear] made available so that the facts can be adduced without putting on a political road show.

EHRLICHMAN: What about this?

MITCHELL: What about the president's team? The team is important.

EHRLICHMAN: Okay, I've written this. I can see that Chapin, for instance, could appear without it in any way being germane to the presidency. So I'm going to decide right now —

HALDEMAN: Baker —

EHRLICHMAN: — that —

NIXON: Not Baker, that'll be a little too —

EHRLICHMAN: Well, whoever you talk to. I've got a report here and I think I see where the danger points are and where they aren't. I'd want to reserve, obviously, as to any question that might be asked.

NIXON: Right.

EHRLICHMAN: I can pinpoint some people now, but it really wouldn't make any difference.

HALDEMAN: John, do you admit there's any danger point? You admit that any one member of the White House staff can testify because it's no danger point for him, but that some other one can't because it's a danger point with him. Then what you're saying is —

EHRLICHMAN: Well, but the first [unclear] —

HALDEMAN: — then you're saying the president was involved.

EHRLICHMAN: I'm saying danger in the sense of that he could — provocative.

MITCHELL: But [unclear] for the sake of going about discussion, in other words that — maybe we think that it's appropriate at this time to formalize John's theory on the Segretti matter and the Watergate matter based on the documentation from the FBI and you may even want to call on the FBI [unclear] in other words based on — can the grand jury — what we know came out of there, the trial [unclear] as far as that's one incident — whatever the record — could have been available to me. This is why the investigation of — we had the memorandum with the backup — you know, obviously the FBI after all [unclear] and so forth couldn't find anything more. It's not expected that you could or [unclear] get out by way of their interrogation [unclear] two memoranda from Dean is important [unclear] appropriate time with it. John did, and say I [unclear] all the public records [unclear].

NIXON: We've tried that though, John.

DEAN: Why won't —

NIXON: We still have grave doubts about it, though.

DEAN: Well, I don't know —

MITCHELL: I did too before, Mr. President. I had severe doubts about it. The — now that the facts have come out as have the FBI reports, and we have had the trial, that you have some documentation [unclear].

DEAN: I think the proof is in the pudding, so to speak — it's how the document is written and until I sit down and write that doc — I've done part B so to speak. I've done the Segretti thing.

NIXON: Mm-hmm.

DEAN: And I am relatively satisfied that we don't have any major problems with that. All right, as I go to part A — the Watergate — I haven't written — I haven't gone through yet — because I — in real whole effort to write such a report, and I really can't say if I can do it where we are. And I think it's certainly something that should be done though.

NIXON: Yeah.

DEAN: And, uh — but we —

MITCHELL: You never know.

DEAN: — you never know until we sit down and try to do it.

NIXON: Now, let me say on the Watergate, that's a case [unclear] Segretti [unclear].

DEAN: We can't be as complete because we don't know. All we know is what — is whether —

NIXON: That's a question [unclear].

EHRLICHMAN: It's a negative setting for us.

NIXON: In setting forth this general conclusion based on [unclear] all these questions. You are — that based on all of your considerations, all of your analysis, and so forth — you have found and very carefully put down that this individual, that individual, that individual, were not involved. We're going [unclear] to have to presume that. Rather than going into every leaked story and other charge, et cetera, et cetera, et cetera, and knock this down — I don't know —

DEAN: Yeah, well, that's why I'd like to — and I don't think I can do it until I sit down this evening and start drafting —

NIXON: Exactly.

HALDEMAN: I think you ought to hole up — now that you — for the weekend and do that.

NIXON: Sure.

HALDEMAN: Let's put an end to your business and get it done.

NIXON: I think you need a — that's right. Why don't you do this? Why don't you go up to Camp David? And —

DEAN: I might do that. I might do that. A place to get away from the phone.

NIXON: Completely away from the phone and so forth. Just go up there and [unclear] I don't know what kind of work this is, but I agree that that's what you could — see what you come up with. You would have in mind and assume that we've got some sort of a document [unclear] and then the next step once you have written it you will have to continue to defend [unclear] action.

EHRLICHMAN: That would be my scenario, that he presents it to you as — at your request. And you then —

NIXON: Publish it.

DEAN: Well, that's —

MITCHELL: That introduces the problem for us [unclear] —

DEAN: — trial.

MITCHELL: — criminal trial and then appeals which may —

EHRLICHMAN: I know that, but I don't care.

DEAN: Well, you ought to be —

HALDEMAN: I don't see why. You're not dealing with the defendants' trial. You're only dealing with the White House involvement. You're not dealing with the campaign.

DEAN: That's where I first [unclear].

NIXON: Well, you can write — you could write it in a way that you say this report does not re — it's not — will not comment upon and so forth and so forth, but, "I — as you directed, Mr. President, and without at all compromising the rights of defendants and so forth, some of which are on appeal, here are the facts with regard to members of the White House staff, et cetera, et cetera, et cetera, which you have asked from me. I have checked the FBI records. I have read the grand jury testimony and this is it — these are my conclusions, chit, chit, chit, chit."

EHRLICHMAN: As a matter of fact you could say, "I will not summarize some of the FBI reports in this document because it is my understanding that you may wish to publish this." Or you can allude to it in that way without saying that flatly. You can say that "I do not summarize all the FBI documents in this report."

DEAN: Or I could say that all of the FBI — it is my understanding that all the FBI reports have been turned over to the Ervin Committee. Another vehicle might —

HALDEMAN: And he has only seen half of them.

DEAN: Yeah.

NIXON: Oh, yeah.

DEAN: Another vehicle might be, take the report I write and give it to Ervin and Baker —

NIXON: Yeah.

DEAN: — under the same terms that they're getting the FBI reports. Say, "Now, this has innuendo in it, little things the press would leak from this and assume things that shouldn't be assumed. But I want you to know everything we know." And publicly state that you've turned over a Dean report to the Ervin Committee. And then begin to say — the next step is, "I think that you can see that various people have various ingredients where they may be of assistance in testifying. But it is not worth their coming up here to be able to repeat really what is here in some forum where they are going to be treated like they are in a circus. But I am also willing, based on this document, to set some ground rules for how we have these people appear before your committee."

EHRLICHMAN: A case in point: the issue of whether or not I had a phone call reporting the burglary.

DEAN: Right.

EHRLICHMAN: Now, that's all I know about the damn thing is that the Secret Service, or some policeman, phoned.

DEAN: But they could go on forever with you on that.

EHRLICHMAN: Exactly.

DEAN: And I think it ought to be things like we've got in this report and this might be, you know — get — give it to Ervin on the confidence that we're not talking about documents being released. We're talking about something that's entirely facts. You could even [unclear] write a [unclear].

NIXON: [unclear] accomplish our purpose if it isn't released.

DEAN: I think it —

NIXON: And I thought the purpose — I thought John's concern [unclear] I guess you'd want him for me to —

DEAN: I do. I —

EHRLICHMAN: My thought is —

NIXON: In other words, rather than fighting it, we're not fighting the committee. We are, of course — but what we're fighting is a public relations battle.

EHRLICHMAN: And I am looking to the future assuming that some corner of this thing comes unstuck at some time you're then in a position to say, "Look, that document I published is the document I relied on, that's the report I relied on and it codified and included all the secret identification of the FBI — "

NIXON: This is all we knew.

HALDEMAN: All the stuff we could find out —

EHRLICHMAN: " — And now, this new development is a surprise to me, and I'm going to fire A, B, C, and D — now."

DEAN: John, let me just raise this. If you take the document publicly, the first thing that happens is the press starts asking Ziegler about it, inspecting the document each day. "Well, why did Ehrlichman receive the call? How did they happen to pick out Ehrlichman?"

NIXON: That's right.

DEAN: "What did he do with the information after he got it?" And so on. Each — every item can be a full day of quizzing.

NIXON: Yeah.

DEAN: They'll just go through the document day after day after day.

MITCHELL: Now what is your concerned judgment as to when and under what circumstances — ?

NIXON: Another thing, however, let me say that while Ziegler could be given all those questions, I would say those are questions — I think Ziegler should cut it off.

MITCHELL: Let it die.

NIXON: This — yeah, fine. I think there should be a cutoff point which [unclear]. If

John just sort of [unclear] "I'm not going to comment on the basic questions that are properly before the committee on the [unclear]."

DEAN: Well, you — you've said you are going to cooperate with a proper investigation.

NIXON: Yeah, but I'm not going to comment on it while it is proper.

DEAN: That's right.

NIXON: As long as it's proper.

DEAN: So why would you — why not put ourselves in a framework where you're way out above it? You're cooperating with this committee. You've turned over the materials —

NIXON: And then no further comment.

DEAN: — and no further comment.

NIXON: You see, I think you could get off with the Ziegler business. I mean, I don't want Ziegler — I was trying to pull Ziegler off of that by my own statement, too. [unclear] cooperate with the committee, give full cooperation, but we're not going to comment while the matter is being considered by the committee —

HALDEMAN: But you don't say —

NIXON: — unless the committee does this and that.

HALDEMAN: — but you don't say that people don't give, don't release, don't publish the Dean report. Only hand it over —

DEAN: — to a proper investigative committee.

NIXON: Well, then if you turn over the — do that, though — then can we get anything out about the Republicans putting out that much of a report? Can we still get out the fact that —

EHRLICHMAN: Well, the president —

NIXON: — there has been a report in which everybody in the White House — which bears out the president's —

HALDEMAN: Ron can make the statement.

DEAN: That's right.

HALDEMAN: That the president —

[Unclear exchange]

NIXON: John wants the statement —

EHRLICHMAN: Another way to do this, and that would be for you to have a meeting with Ervin and Baker.

NIXON: Yeah.

EHRLICHMAN: That would — I told them —

NIXON: Well, we've thought of that — I mean we've thought of that and we've tried it.

EHRLICHMAN: But we didn't have a reason for the meeting. This would be for the purpose of turning over the document and discussing the ground rules. Before you did that you want to have that all agreed in advance as to what the ground rules would be. And you've got quid pro quo here because you could come to Baker and you could come to the committee or to Ervin direct and say, "Look, I'll turn over the Dean report to you provided we can agree on how witnesses will be treated up there." I can even construe —

NIXON: Right.

EHRLICHMAN: — executive privilege.

NIXON: John, for example, if you were — just talking about executive privilege, this really gets down to the specifics in terms of the question what do you do when they say, "What about Colson?" Does he go or not?

MITCHELL: I think that Colson goes.

NIXON: He has to go. Right.

MITCHELL: I think Colson —

HALDEMAN: Everybody goes under John's — including Ehrlichman and me — everybody except John Dean, who doesn't go because he's got the lawyer privilege.

MITCHELL: I think what is happening to you and John and so forth with the committee could be negotiated out of the contents of this report.

NIXON: We should negotiate it — how?

MITCHELL: The president's report will show that your simple thought — your simple involvement was missing in the [unclear].

HALDEMAN: No, it would show more on my book, I'm afraid.

DEAN: But, they'll still — one strong argument —

HALDEMAN: Let us — let us go.

DEAN: Yeah.

HALDEMAN: I don't see any argument against our going if you are going to let anybody go.

DEAN: That's right.

HALDEMAN: Let us go. But, on the condition — you get less trouble with us than you do with some of the others. And if it's not — and, now sure if you get, if you get the big fish up there in front of the television cameras I think that would be tough. I think Strachan going up wouldn't get them nearly as excited as John and me going up.

NIXON: That's Strachan and Chapin.

HALDEMAN: Well, Chapin wouldn't have to appear —

DEAN: Well —

HALDEMAN: — as a focal point, but I think if you could do it in executive session —

EHRLICHMAN: Then I would have a reason to testify.

HALDEMAN: Then why hold us back?

NIXON: The executive session thing has always appealed to me. Now of course, you could say, "Well, in terms of people coming up here, of course you have to adjourn the session, but you got to convin — the committee feels constrained under executive session —

DEAN: We can invite the committee down to the Roosevelt Room or the Blair House.

NIXON: Yeah.

MITCHELL: Oh, hell, you could —

NIXON: Yeah, you could set it at a different venue, that's true. You could put it in a different place. You could say we — which is what I —

MITCHELL: That would be hard to negotiate.

HALDEMAN: Can we maintain informality?

EHRLICHMAN: It will never —

HALDEMAN: It would never fly.

NIXON: Yeah.

HALDEMAN: I don't know why not. Those others go up there.

NIXON: Well, would executive session fly?

EHRLICHMAN: Executive session, I suspect, would at this point, yes, sir — yeah, I really think these guys are concerned about this Mexican standoff that they've got and I think they're —

NIXON: They'll also —

EHRLICHMAN: I think that the — Ervin's crack on television about arresting people crossed the line.

NIXON: Right.

EHRLICHMAN: That would take it quite a bit far.

MITCHELL: In addition to that you have the problem of the long lengthy litigation.

NIXON: It's going to go on for a hell of a long time.

HALDEMAN: Ervin doesn't want that.

DEAN: Let him take it on the counsel then.

HALDEMAN: That's what he doesn't want.

DEAN: I know, but let him — if he —

HALDEMAN: We have offered to do it on Dwight Chapin. That's the easy one for him.

NIXON: Yeah.

HALDEMAN: You got some guy who had no contact with this [unclear].

NIXON: It was quite clear to me that as long as Dean —

HALDEMAN: Won't they test it?

NIXON: No, they didn't test it. We asked them to. We said let's find out. They didn't bite that one very fast, did they, John?

HALDEMAN: Chapin's the guy they'd test it on. You try to hold privilege on Chapin and that's one they'd go to court on. They — they'd —

NIXON: Probably.

HALDEMAN: You might do pretty well, because here's a former employee, a guy who had no policy role, had no —

NIXON: — contact —

HALDEMAN: — major contact with the president and he'd have a hell of a time demonstrating —

MITCHELL: Obviously you'll have to expect a subpoena.

NIXON: Chapin?

MITCHELL: Yeah, because he's no longer employed.

HALDEMAN: Well, because —

NIXON: What I'd —

HALDEMAN: — because with the subpoena, if he's called to testify regarding his employment but not regarding his — any present stuff.

MITCHELL: He doesn't [unclear] legroom. They can get him up there.

EHRLICHMAN: Well, the precedent on this is interesting. I think that his lawyer would advise him to go.

[Unclear exchange]

MITCHELL: They could get him to talk.

NIXON: Do you have any precedent for that? In the case of a present White House employee they couldn't get him up here, right?

MITCHELL: Right.

NIXON: In the case of a past one you could get him up, but then he could — then he would have to go in front of the cameras and say, "I will not because of executive privilege."

MITCHELL: Well, they can get up with him.

EHRLICHMAN: But it's your privilege — you interpose it.

NIXON: I see.

EHRLICHMAN: And first we have the anomaly of Clark Mollenhoff running up and trying to give testimony in a civil service hearing over here now. He's running up saying, "Ask me a question, ask me a question, this is a kangaroo court, and I waive" — the hearing examiner just says, "Sit down and shut up." And what's happening is that the government is asserting the executive privilege.

MITCHELL: No, they are not.

EHRLICHMAN: Well—

MITCHELL: Not executive privilege.

EHRLICHMAN: Yeah, all right —

MITCHELL: In fact you have —

EHRLICHMAN: All right. It's the closest thing to it. But the point is — whose privilege is it to assert? Now, what do you do if it's Chapin? I think — I haven't thought this — this is the reason I called you here to figure out what the scenario is. But I assume what would happen is that immediately the subpoena is issued, that on behalf of the president a letter would go to the committee saying the Executive asserts privilege.

NIXON: Let me ask this. The — this question is for John Ehrlichman and John Dean. Now you were the two who felt the strongest on the executive privilege thing [unclear]. If I am not mistaken, you thought we ought to draw the line where we did. [unclear] Have you changed your mind now?

DEAN: No, sir, I think it's a terrific statement. It's — it puts you just where you should be. It's got enough flexibility in it. It's —

NIXON: But now — what — all that John Mitchell is arguing, then is that now we use flexibility —

DEAN: That's correct.

NIXON: — in order to get off of the cover-up plan.

EHRLICHMAN: And as I told him I am so convinced we're right on the statement that I have never gone beyond that. He argues that we're being hurt badly by the way it's being handled. And I am willing — let's see —

MITCHELL: That's the point.

HALDEMAN: I think that's a valid evaluation. I think [unclear].

MITCHELL: See, that's the only point, the only point —

HALDEMAN: Yeah.

MITCHELL: — where the president —

HALDEMAN: That's where you look like you're covering up right now. That's the only thing — the only active step you've taken to cover up the Watergate all along.

NIXON: That's right.

DEAN: What is?

HALDEMAN: Was that.

NIXON: Even though we've offered to cooperate.

HALDEMAN: To the extent — and on legal grounds, and precedent —

NIXON: That's right.

HALDEMAN: — and tradition, and constitutional grounds and all that stuff, you're just fine. But to the guy sitting at home who watches John Chancellor say that the president is covering this up by re — this historic review blankets the widest exercise of executive privilege in American history and all that. He says, "What the hell's he covering up? If he's got no problem why doesn't he let them go and talk?"

MITCHELL: And it relates to the Watergate. It doesn't relate to Henry Kissinger —

HALDEMAN: That's right.

MITCHELL: — or foreign affairs.

HALDEMAN: That's right. Precedent and all that business — they don't know what you're talking about.

NIXON: Well, maybe then we shouldn't have made the statement.

HALDEMAN: I think we should have because it puts you in a much better position to — they were over here. That's what Ervin wanted. He wanted all of us up there — unlimited, total, wide open. We — the statement in a sense puts us over here. Now you move back to about here and probably you can get away with it.

EHRLICHMAN: Well, you can get away with it in the Watergate context. You see, you said —

HALDEMAN: That's right.

EHRLICHMAN: — executive privilege would work and then you've applied it in the first instance to Gray. You said this fellow can't go.

NIXON: That's right.

EHRLICHMAN: And, I wouldn't change that.

NIXON: I [unclear].

EHRLICHMAN: I can't — anything about that.

NIXON: Great.

EHRLICHMAN: Exactly right.

NIXON: Right.

EHRLICHMAN: At the same time —

MITCHELL: By the way isn't that [unclear].

EHRLICHMAN: [unclear]

NIXON: That's right.

EHRLICHMAN: Uh —

NIXON: [unclear] one-syllable names.

EHRLICHMAN: At the same time, you are in a position to say, "Oh, well, now this, this other case, and what I'm going to do there, consistent with my statement, is so and so, and so and so."

HALDEMAN: Because it very clearly — the questions that the committee properly wants to ask don't have any bearing on these people's relationship to the president. Which they don't. The president had nothing to do with it.

NIXON: I don't know at all. I —

EHRLICHMAN: There again, it's going to be hard to get proof. Well, it'll be hard to — if you — you're right, we're going to need some kind of a PR campaign.

NIXON: Yes, that's true. That's true — what?

EHRLICHMAN: For the average guy.

NIXON: Is thinking about [unclear] Dean —

EHRLICHMAN: This is — the argument will be the president's backed off his rock-solid position on executive privilege and is now letting Chapin and Colson and Haldeman and everybody testify.

NIXON: That the rest of us said that that's perfectly [unclear].

DEAN: It is. I think they're —

EHRLICHMAN: — saying that there are PR problems.

NIXON: But people don't think so, is that right?

EHRLICHMAN: That's right.

DEAN: Sure.

NIXON: In spite of what [unclear].

HALDEMAN: Oh, yeah. They don't think the —

NIXON: I agree. I understand. I understand.

HALDEMAN: They think you clanged down an iron curtain here and you won't let anybody out of here ever. That have ever worked here — scour lady on up. It was my understanding — I thought from you, or maybe it was someone else, that the committee's operating rules do not permit witnesses to have counsel.

DEAN: That's grand jury. I've never heard that about —

HALDEMAN: About the committee?

DEAN: About the committee, no. I can't believe —

NIXON: The committee, on the contrary — committees, ever since the day I was there they always allowed counsel.

MITCHELL: I can't imagine their not having counsel.

NIXON: No, sir. Committees allow counsel.

HALDEMAN: If that's — it seems to me if you're going to do this, that becomes important in that any White House staff member who testifies should not only have private counsel if he wants it — personal counsel — but the president's counsel should be there because you're under a limited waiver of executive privilege and the president's counsel should be there to enforce the limitation and the witness should not have to be in the position of saying, "That's one I can't answer because it is outside the ground." You or Fielding or somebody should be doing that for him.

NIXON: Have you — the executive session thing?

HALDEMAN: They'll bitch about that, too. What are you going to hide? If you're going to let them come up, why do you — why is that secret?

NIXON: Yeah, yeah. How do you handle that PR-wise?

MITCHELL: You don't. One of the hazards [unclear] another Roman holiday like they've had with Kleindienst and Gray. This fact-finding operation — they're to get the facts and not to put another political circus on like they have in the past.

DEAN: And if there were no cameras up there, there would be no reason to have it in executive session because —

HALDEMAN: Well, then they come back and say, "All right, we'll do it in open session, but we'll permit television coverage."

NIXON: Oh, no. They won't do that. That [unclear] their problem because of television. It'll kill them [unclear] executive session written testimony be released. I think that that's the basis of the relation. That is stupid to talk about formal sessions, so that gets away from it. That's a — it is a formal session. Executive session [unclear] release testimony. Correct?

DEAN: That's correct. We have said that no —

HALDEMAN: Point of debate, too. You argue they shouldn't.

MITCHELL: Well, they won't buy it.

EHRLICHMAN: Yeah, but I probably can't get away with it. [unclear] But it's a good thing to start with.

NIXON: Sure.

EHRLICHMAN: You want a bargaining position. I think it's arguable that all they're really interested in this is information, and I think they don't need to release the transcripts, you know.

HALDEMAN: Is there an executive session of a Senate committee — are other senators permitted? They are, aren't they? Any senator has the privilege of committee [unclear]. So Teddy Kennedy could come in and sit there.

NIXON: Sure. He can't ask questions.

HALDEMAN: He can't?

MITCHELL: Not unless you're a member of the parent committee which he is.

HALDEMAN: But this isn't subject —

DEAN: Select — Select Committee.

NIXON: Other members cannot — whether — that should be worked on, too. But I — it normally is the practice that nobody can ask questions except members.

HALDEMAN: Of course, Teddy could still sit there in the audience and then go out to the TV cameras and say, "Look [unclear]."

DEAN: Wouldn't it be wonderful if he would?

NIXON: Probably we're going to have that.

DEAN: I think if he did that, that would be terrific.

HALDEMAN: I was just thinking that, in the membership of the committee, we're in reasonably good shape. The members — the people that you have on the committee are not as bad as most — as some senators who would turn the use of TV afterwards for their own —

NIXON: Not as spectacular — what?

EHRLICHMAN: You know, no way, and [unclear] —

[Unclear exchange]

EHRLICHMAN: Well, I would say [unclear].

NIXON: It's very soon that we're going to be moving on [unclear].

DEAN: Can I point out [unclear]?

NIXON: [unclear]

HALDEMAN: When do they start hearings now?

NIXON: The thing —

DEAN: There's no time set.

HALDEMAN: How would they time that?

NIXON: Well, the top — the hearings won't be — we have plenty of time before the hearings, but what —

EHRLICHMAN: The PR.

NIXON: John's concerned about the PR. We don't have much time.

EHRLICHMAN: Well, but —

NIXON: You don't have much.

DEAN: PR is going to start on this right away with the termination of the Gray hearings for two weeks that'll let some steam out of the —

NIXON: Yeah. Your PR would —

DEAN: Well, it'll have to —

NIXON: The PR would. What I meant is — and anyway the main thing is to do the right thing. Don't rush too fast on the PR but it'll take some time to write something. John's got to have time to write this report. He's got to have a chance to look at — I guess we don't breach — we don't broach or do we broach this whether we have a report or not?

MITCHELL: I think you can broach that.

NIXON: Fine.

MITCHELL: Now —

NIXON: Let me ask you this: on the broaching of that, should we have Kleindienst be the broacher? The point is — who else? I can't.

DEAN: That's right. Well, Kleindienst in his conversations with Ervin and Baker — Ervin indicated that he would like to talk to Kleindienst about the executive privilege question. Maybe it's now time to get that channel reopened again.

MITCHELL: Let me make this suggestion.

HALDEMAN: Write it out so Kleindienst said that both chapter and verse — on this —

NIXON: Without anybody else present.

MITCHELL: For a first step, you're going to have that meeting and we're going to keep John out of that. But you're going to have everybody screaming about executive privilege going on in a committee meeting again. And I think, well, before the committee meeting is held, for somebody to say, "We want to discuss with the chairman of the committee his concept of the appearances of witnesses." And don't discuss it with him until you get all your ducks in a row all laid out. But, at least you advise them that it is a discussion of the subject matter so they don't come out and blast you [unclear].

EHRLICHMAN: Then ask him not to take a committee vote on the subject either until —

HALDEMAN: [unclear] committee locked in, but you can work something, maybe you can work on that.

NIXON: Well, is this the time to — I mean, the point is if the committee — is this the time to [unclear]? That's it. Who's going to talk to him? Who's going to be there? Who do you think should do it?

MITCHELL: Kleindienst talks —

NIXON: Talks to — in other words to Baker and Ervin, basically. That conversation should occur late tomorrow. Why not? If you're going to move in this direction, regardless of the report, we've got to move in this direction [unclear] start the negotiation.

MITCHELL: Well, I think that's too much lead time. In the process before the committee meeting [unclear]. Now what's Wally Johnson's status?

DEAN: That's funny, because I — he is still here — hasn't gone up yet, but he's been announced apparently. I gather he'll be an assistant attorney general. What I was thinking is maybe to preserve my counsel role with Ervin and Baker that I ought to be present with Kleindienst.

NIXON: I agree.

DEAN: And the four of us sit down and talk about executive privilege — we won't get into —

NIXON: Yeah.

DEAN: — any of the substance.

NIXON: Well, the thing about your being at this is that you can keep Kleindienst in step with it.

DEAN: Plus they would appreciate the fact they're dealing with me as counsel. That's another reason I am not —

NIXON: That's right.

DEAN: — you know, when the final wire is drawn —

MITCHELL: Well, it's appropriate for the president's counsel to be present when the discussions take place.

DEAN: That's right.

NIXON: Well, all right. Now let's get down to the [unclear]. How do we want to do this? How do we start there?

DEAN: I would think that possibly Kleindienst ought to call today and let Ervin and Baker know that he would like to meet with them early next week to talk about executive privilege — indicate that I would be present to see if we can find —

NIXON: A formula for —

DEAN: — a formula to resolve —

NIXON: — getting information that they desire.

DEAN: That's right.

HALDEMAN: It's an unpublicized meeting.

DEAN: Unpublicized.

NIXON: I think we'd [unclear] go ahead.

HALDEMAN: [unclear] on top of that. I would say early in the week. You better say Monday so you can get them before the committee meets.

MITCHELL: And naturally cover Watergate first.

NIXON: I don't know how far Ervin's going to go. Ervin's insistence on letting Dean testify — whether he might. We'd have to draw a line there, wouldn't we, John?

MITCHELL: I would agree wholeheartedly that you better not go back on your final statements on the subject.

NIXON: That's right. That's right.

UNIDENTIFIED: Even if there hadn't been statements —

NIXON: That's right. But the point is, we've got to accept the decision of Judge Byrne's [unclear] on the bail. The other thing to do on the Dean thing is say — you'd simply say, "Now, that's out. Dean has — he makes the report. Here's everything Dean knows."

DEAN: Right.

NIXON: That's where — that's why the Dean report is critical.

EHRLICHMAN: I think John, on Monday, could say to Ervin if that question comes up, "I know the president's mind on this. He's adamant about my testifying, as such. At the same time he has always indicated that the fruits of my investigation will be known." And just leave it at that for the moment.

DEAN: One issue that may come up as the hearings go along, if it then becomes a focus, is what did Dean do? As you all know I was all over this thing like a wet blanket. I was everywhere — everywhere they look they are going to find Dean.

NIXON: Sure.

HALDEMAN: That's perfectly proper.

DEAN: But it — I don't think that's bad.

NIXON: I don't know.

EHRLICHMAN: You were supposed to be.

NIXON: You were on it at the first. You were directed by the president to get me all the facts. Second, as White House counsel you were on it for the purpose of representing any people in the Executive Branch who were being questioned on it. So you were there for the purpose of getting information. In other words, that was your job. Correct?

DEAN: That's right.

NIXON: Then you heard — but, but the main point is that you can certainly tell them that Dean had absolutely no operational — the wonderful thing about your position is, I think, as far as they're concerned — Watergate is — your position's one of truly of counsel. It is never as an operator. That's the —

HALDEMAN: You can even, in the private sessions, then maybe volunteer to give them a statement on the whole question of your recommendation of Liddy which is the only possible kind of substantive [unclear] that you could have and in that you can satisfy one of those arguments.

NIXON: That's right.

HALDEMAN: And that you — if you wanted to.

NIXON: At the president's direction you've never done anything — any operational — you were always just as counsel. Well, we've got to keep you out anyway — the Dean thing. I guess we just draw the line, so we give them some of it — not give them all of it. I don't suppose they'd say, John, "No, we don't take him in executive session." Would he go up in public session? What would your feeling on that be?

MITCHELL: I wouldn't let him go.

NIXON: You wouldn't.

MITCHELL: I would not.

NIXON: Why not? You just take the heat of being — all right. How about you wouldn't — but on the other hand you'd let Chapin go. And you'd let Colson go.

HALDEMAN: No, he doesn't.

MITCHELL: No, because —

NIXON: Because they're former White House people.

MITCHELL: You can't keep them out of open sessions. Now, I want to get back to that [unclear] Dean spoke to Chapin. On the basis of that Chapin talked to Segretti last weekend.

DEAN: Well, they can subpoena any of us. There's no doubt about that. They — if they don't serve us here because they can't get in they can serve you at home or somewhere. They can ultimately find you.

EHRLICHMAN: I'm going to move to Camp David.

NIXON: Right.

HALDEMAN: By helicopter. [laughs]

NIXON: Go ahead. [unclear]

DEAN: So, the question is once you're served and you decline, then you've got a contempt situation. Now, I would say that it gets very difficult to believe that they'll go contempt on people who —

NIXON: Present White House staff.

DEAN: Present White House staff.

NIXON: They would on Colson. They could do that, could they?

DEAN: That would be a good test case for them to go on. The other thing is, though, they could subpoena Colson to come up there and Colson could then say, "Well, I decline to testify on the basis that I think this is a privileged communication" — or "privileged activities." And again you get a little fuzzier as to whether or not you —

MITCHELL: I'd rather not answer the question that's asked.

DEAN: That's right.

MITCHELL: See my point.

DEAN: That's right. There it — then it would get much fuzzier as to whether or not they cite him for contempt or not.

NIXON: Suppose the judge tomorrow orders the committee to show its evidence to the grand jury [unclear] then the grand jury reopens the case and questions everybody. Does that change the game plan?

DEAN: I would send them all down.

NIXON: What? Before the committee?

MITCHELL: The president's asked [unclear] this.

DEAN: Now are you saying — ?

NIXON: Suppose the judge opens — tells the grand jury and says, "I don't," says, "I want them to call Haldeman, Ehrlichman, and everybody else they didn't call before." What do you say to that? Then do you still go on this pattern with the Ervin Committee? The point is if a grand jury decides to go into this thing what do you think on that point?

EHRLICHMAN: I think you'd say, "Based on what I know about this case, I can see no reason why I should be concerned about what the grand jury process — "

NIXON: All right.

EHRLICHMAN: That's all.

HALDEMAN: And that would change —

NIXON: Well, they go in — do both. Appear before the grand jury and the committee?

DEAN: Sure.

EHRLICHMAN: You have to bottom your defense — your position on the report.

NIXON: That's right.

EHRLICHMAN: And the report says, "Nobody was involved — "

NIXON: That's right.

EHRLICHMAN: — and you have to stay consistent with that.

MITCHELL: Well, theoretically, I think you will find the grand jury is not about to get out of the [unclear] substance.

NIXON: Right.

HALDEMAN: Thus the danger of a grand jury is they bring indictments on the basis of —

MITCHELL: Which they've studied.

DEAN: Well, there are no rules.

NIXON: The rules of evidence before grand juries are not — pretty fair at this point.

DEAN: That's right.

MITCHELL: When you have something that's reasoned and controlled —

NIXON: Yeah.

DEAN: You have attorneys —

NIXON: Yeah.

MITCHELL: [unclear] the rules of the evidence meet.

NIXON: [unclear]

EHRLICHMAN: Somebody can get one in the form of a letter.

MITCHELL: [unclear] according to [unclear].

HALDEMAN: Well, what would happen? Would Silbert be the prosecutor on this?

DEAN: Unless the court appointed a special prosecutor, which he could do.

NIXON: Yeah. So, we better see tomorrow on that. But — the — so that if that's the case how do we — let's move now on the first one. Now who is to call Kleindienst?

DEAN: I'm involved [unclear].

NIXON: You going to call him and tell him what?

DEAN: I'm going to tell him to call Baker first, and then Ervin, and tell them that you would like to meet with them on Monday to discuss and explore a formula for providing the information they need in a way that does not cause a conflict with the president's general policies on executive privilege.

NIXON: Yet meets their — meets their need for information.

DEAN: Right.

NIXON: Have they requested — they've requested that kind of a talk already, haven't they?

DEAN: Yes.

EHRLICHMAN: And you'll sit down with Dick, Mr. President?

NIXON: Yeah. Yeah. [unclear] you're going to be so busy doing the report there will be no one —

DEAN: Well, I'll work on that over the weekend, and actually it's good because things do slow down a little over the weekend.

HALDEMAN: Also write out a thing for Kleindienst so that —

NIXON: I think you can talk to him. I think you can do most of the talking. Get the main — get to thinking — you can do it. Say you have studied the subject. You also know what my position is.

DEAN: I don't think we ought to read anything in this first session but I think we ought to let him know that we are thinking about —

NIXON: Right.

DEAN: — reaching some sort of —

NIXON: Say, "Now, what is — what would you think here?"

HALDEMAN: Well, just stay loose [unclear].

DEAN: Stay loose.

NIXON: I would say, "Now look, that's what we're going to do. We'll lay out the thing about — with regard to this. We want to see what can be worked out with regard to — we talked about informal sessions. Has Ervin's position been — he insists on formal sessions? Is that his position?

DEAN: Well, we don't know. We've never really [unclear].

MITCHELL: [unclear] gotten into that.

HALDEMAN: His response to your position — that's really what you've got now —

NIXON: Yeah.

HALDEMAN: Ervin's response to the Nixon position and that is, "Written stuff isn't any good. I want the body — you can't ask paper — you can't ask a piece of paper questions." Okay. Now, what we're saying meets that requirement —

NIXON: The written thing was in which?

EHRLICHMAN: That was a Ziegler, I believe.

NIXON: I think so.

EHRLICHMAN: I don't know how it came out. It's not in a statement.

HALDEMAN: No, but it's a general thing. I think —

NIXON: Yeah.

HALDEMAN: — it was in your press conference where you said they will provide written — I think you said it.

NIXON: I may have said it and I don't —

HALDEMAN: In a press conference. And I think Ervin's response was to that.

NIXON: Right.

HALDEMAN: Your statement, if —

NIXON: Could have been.

HALDEMAN: "These people will be happy to provide written answers to questions —"

NIXON: Yeah.

HALDEMAN: "— that — appropriate questions."

NIXON: You think — are you sure it wasn't in the statement — the written statement?

EHRLICHMAN: No.

HALDEMAN: No.

EHRLICHMAN: I think — I am sure we —

NIXON: Right.

EHRLICHMAN: — used formal, informal —

DEAN: It came up the first time is when I responded to —

MITCHELL: That's right. Exactly.

DEAN: — to Eastland. I responded to Eastland's invitation to —

NIXON: You said you would furnish written —

UNIDENTIFIED: Right.

DEAN: Furnish written —

NIXON: I think the — I think that's where you'll find it.

DEAN: And then you — and then it was repeated after that, that we would be happy to supply information and —

NIXON: I think we've been [unclear].

HALDEMAN: But, then Ervin responded — he specifically rejected that only on the grounds that you can't ask questions of a piece of paper.

NIXON: Cross-examine.

HALDEMAN: We need to deal with our questions. So we are giving him that opportunity. He hasn't said that the processes of the Senate require that those questions be answered in [unclear].

NIXON: What is the argument that you give, John, to people who — and why executive session rather than open session?

DEAN: Well, I —

NIXON: You can't really give —

DEAN: I think we'll have —

NIXON: You can't really attack the committee's flamboyance.

DEAN: No, you can't.

NIXON: So, what do you say?

DEAN: I think what I'd do is we'll talk a little about the Constitution, and I'll remind him of the position that he took so vocally in the [Senator Mike] Gravel [D-AK] case [in which Gravel sought to introduce a copy of the Pentagon Papers into the record of the Senate] —

NIXON: That's right.

DEAN: — where he came out and said that legislative aides cannot be called to question for advice they give their senator or congressman. He just went on at great length and cited executive privilege —

NIXON: Then he'll say, "This was not advice to the president." Go ahead.

DEAN: Well, and I'll say that these are men who do advise the president.

NIXON: And that's the principle involved.

DEAN: And we have to draw the line.

NIXON: And to have the principle discussed in open session, and so forth, is the kind of a thing where you've got to — you ought to go off to the bench where the jury doesn't hear it, basically.

DEAN: Well, I —

HALDEMAN: I don't think John or Dick should tip their hands in the Monday meeting as to an offer to appear in executive session and get them onto the executive session wicket. It seems to me —

DEAN: No. No, I agree.

HALDEMAN: — they should only indicate a willingness to listen to ideas as to what would be done —

DEAN: Yeah.

HALDEMAN: — and an open-mindedness to try and work something out.

NIXON: Yeah.

HALDEMAN: Because if you get to that, that's going to become the issue —

NIXON: Yeah.

HALDEMAN: — and it seems to me that's an issue we could win publicly where we may not be able to win it with the —

DEAN: I think —

EHRLICHMAN: How about —

HALDEMAN: — Senate, but you [unclear] —

EHRLICHMAN: What about expressing the president's concern about the protection of his people from a spectacle?

NIXON: That's fine. And also concern about his — about frankly the — having matters that really are a subject of executive privilege debated publicly rather — that's a matter that ought to be debated privately.

DEAN: That's right.

NIXON: Other matters — we have no, and — without, and the fact that it's raised does not indicate guilt. That's part of his argument on Gravel, too. The fact that it's raised does not indicate guilt. That's what we are really talking about here. But having it in public session does indicate that.

DEAN: Well, I will work out a complete negotiating scenario and have thought it through before I go up.

HALDEMAN: Really all your objective in that meeting is simply to indicate to them a willingness to discuss. It's not —

DEAN: That's right.

HALDEMAN: — to lay out a proposal for them —

DEAN: I agree.

HALDEMAN: — to accept or reject.

DEAN: I will —

MITCHELL: John, as part of that — as part of the scenario, you want to hold executive session for the protection of those records.

DEAN: Very true. Uh —

NIXON: There, and it's the record for the future. But that's — that maybe you can tell Ervin — maybe on a mountaintop that this is perhaps a good way to set up a procedure where we could do something in the future and all. You know what I mean?

DEAN: Mm-hmm.

NIXON: Where future cases of this sort are involved. "We're, we're making a lot of history here, Senator. And — "

MITCHELL: And the senator can be a great part of it.

NIXON: No, really. We're making a lot of history. And that's it — we're setting a historic precedent. The president, after all — let's point out that the president — how he bitched about the Hiss case. Which is true — I raised holy hell about it.

DEAN: Ervin away from his staff —

NIXON: Huh?

DEAN: Ervin away from his staff is not very much, and I think he might just give up the store himself right there and lock himself in. I — you know, I've dealt with him for a number of years, and have seen that happen and have reached accord with him on legislation.

HALDEMAN: That's another thing, if you don't offer him anything, you may get an offer —

DEAN: That's —

On the occasion of Richard Nixon's sixtieth birthday, on January 9, 1973, a private dinner was held at the White House for the first family and close friends, including Rose Mary Woods (left) and Bebe Rebozo (second from right).

2600 Virginia Avenue NW, better known as the Watergate building. The break-in at the office of the Democratic National Committee, and the resulting inquiries that linked the White House to it, involved more and more of Nixon's time during the spring of 1973.

All photographs courtesy of the White House Photographic Office Collection, Nixon Presidential Library and Museum, except where otherwise noted.

Former CIA director Richard Helms (left) was appointed ambassador to Iran in 1973. Here he is being given his send-off by Nixon and Henry Kissinger's deputy Brent Scowcroft.

White House spokesman Ron Ziegler first referred to the Watergate break-in as a "third-rate burglary." He and Nixon's former law partner Leonard Garment had the task of fending off the White House press corps during the Watergate investigation.

The Nixons and President Nguyen Van Thieu and his wife at Casa Pacifica in San Clemente, celebrating the cease-fire in Vietnam.

Following the Vietnam cease-fire, Nixon met with several returning POWs, who shared details of their detention, torture, and the conditions inside the "Hanoi Hilton." These POWs included Rear Admiral (and future Alabama senator) Jeremiah Denton, who spent nearly eight years in captivity.

On May 24, 1973, Nixon hosted a White House dinner for six hundred returning POWs and their families, which remains the largest event ever to be held at the White House. Admiral (and former POW) John McCain arrives on crutches with his mother, Roberta McCain.

Senator Bob Dole chaired the Republican National Committee at the time of the Watergate break-in. Nixon replaced him so that Dole could focus on his Senate reelection in Kansas.

Former ambassador to the UN George H. W. Bush replaced Dole as head of the RNC in 1973. Called "Mr. Clean" by Nixon, Bush was careful to distance himself and his staff from the Watergate scandal. Here Bush, along with New York governor Nelson Rockefeller, visits Nixon in the Executive Office Building.

West German chancellor Willy Brandt was a close but uneasy ally of Nixon's. Here he is flanked by (from left) Egon Bahr, Walter Scheel, William Rogers, and Henry Kissinger.

Huang Chen, the first ambassador to the United States from the People's Republic of China, is greeted in the Oval Office by Nixon and the press.

As John Ehrlichman, Nixon's top domestic adviser, spent more and more time dealing with Watergate, Vice President Spiro Agnew found a new role in domestic policy—that is, until Nixon got word in the spring of 1973 that Agnew was being investigated for corruption. Agnew would resign that fall and be replaced by Gerald Ford. Here, with Bob Haldeman (right), Nixon formalizes Agnew's new role.

In May 1973, Nixon reshuffled his inner circle to cope with the departures of Haldeman, Ehrlichman, and John Dean. Former secretary of defense Melvin Laird (left) was brought back as counselor to the president, and Alexander Haig moved from vice chief of staff of the army to become White House chief of staff.

Nixon and Leonid Brezhnev embrace while enjoying the fanfare on the South Grounds during the Soviet leader's official visit to Washington in June 1973.

Nixon hosted a star-studded pool party for Brezhnev at Casa Pacifica as part of Brezhnev's visit. Here he chats with Nixon and Governor Ronald Reagan of California.

Cameras crowded the Oval Office whenever Nixon gave a televised address, but especially so as the Watergate investigation intensified.

President Nixon announced the resignations of Bob Haldeman, John Ehrlichman, and John Dean during a live televised address on the evening of April 30, 1973. The departure of Nixon's inner circle meant he would endure the remainder of his presidency without the help of his closest advisers. He resigned on August 9, 1974.

HALDEMAN: — from him —

DEAN: That's right.

HALDEMAN: — you can't accept. He'll ask you [unclear].

DEAN: That's exactly what he'll do.

NIXON: And if he just takes the adamant — suppose now he just takes the adamant line? Nothing.

HALDEMAN: Sits there and says —

DEAN: I'll say —

HALDEMAN: " — I'll think about that."

DEAN: "That's all right."

NIXON: You could go back —

DEAN: "Doesn't sound like you're interested in information — "

NIXON: Yeah.

DEAN: " — it sounds like you're interested in, in fighting — "

NIXON: Yeah.

DEAN: " — on principle."

NIXON: He says, "Look, we are just going to have public sessions. It's got to be that or else."

EHRLICHMAN: Then, "We've got a lawsuit, Senator, and it is going to be a long one."

UNIDENTIFIED: That's right.

MITCHELL: "How can you expedite your hearings?"

NIXON: Yeah. "If you want your hearings" — and that's the other thing. The other point is, would it not be helpful to get Baker enlisted somewhat in advance? If that could be done by not begging him [unclear]. If we — can we put Kleindienst to that thing?

MITCHELL: On the second step — not on the opening.

NIXON: Well, even on the opening step the problem that I have here, if Baker sits there and just parrots Ervin's adamant thing saying, "Hell, no, there can't be anything except the public sessions," you have nothing to bargain with.

MITCHELL: But, Mr. President, you know how these senators act. Baker will lay the whole thing out on the table.

NIXON: Yeah, I guess you are right.

MITCHELL: Including the contempt. They'll be —

NIXON: Baker, on the other hand — Kleindienst should at least talk to him and say, "Look, Howard, why don't you try to work something out here?" Why couldn't he say that?

HALDEMAN: He could say, "We're going to try — we want to work something out." "Yeah, but then — "

NIXON: "Glad to work something out."

HALDEMAN: " — work with us."

NIXON: Yeah.

HALDEMAN: "We're — "

NIXON: "Now, work — "

HALDEMAN: " — questioning how you — "

NIXON: " — with us, but you can't be [unclear]. Right now, Howard, we're just going for a lawsuit."

HALDEMAN: "Give us a hand and try to open this up." That's — Baker would be fine that much ahead of time.

NIXON: That's right.

HALDEMAN: Be positive this time around.

DEAN: Don't lock yourself in. You hear every —

HALDEMAN: Right.

DEAN: All —

NIXON: Right.

DEAN: So you have another session or so on it.

NIXON: Yeah. The other point is that you be reminded so you get to it. Now, just assume, however, it happens so [unclear] insists that [unclear] you just — then it becomes essential then to put the Dean report out, it seems to me, and say, and then have the lawsuit.

EHRLICHMAN: We can say that if he really — I would say, "Well, okay, then, why don't we now discuss how we frame the legal issue here?" And, "Perhaps we can at least agree on how to frame the legal issues, so that instead of taking three years it will only take a year and a half."

HALDEMAN: Get it settled before this administration leaves [unclear].

DEAN: They know that it's — depending upon who they are going after and the circumstances, that they've got a tough lawsuit ahead of them.

NIXON: Mm-hmm.

DEAN: They've got to hire counsel to —

NIXON: Yeah.

DEAN: It's going to cost money to brief it on their side. They don't have the government repre — you know they don't have the Department of Justice to handle their case. They've got to bring in special counsel who probably knows nothing about executive privilege — has to be educated. Get the Library of Congress clanking away at getting all the precedents out and the like, and — we've got all that. Of course, it's a major operation for them to bring in and they have to —

EHRLICHMAN: The other way —

DEAN: — get a resolution of the Senate to do it.

EHRLICHMAN: Fortunately, Ervin is a constitutional expert.

HALDEMAN: Yeah. He calls himself —

EHRLICHMAN: Self-certified. That's a constitutional expert —

NIXON: Well, anyway —

EHRLICHMAN: While you do that —

NIXON: The — now, we could — have you considered any other poss — have you considered the other — all other possibilities you see here, John? You, you're the one who is supposed to —

DEAN: That's right. I think we —

NIXON: You know the bodies.

DEAN: I think we've had a good go-round on —

NIXON: You think we want to go this route now? And the — let it hang out, so to speak?

DEAN: Well, it isn't really that —

HALDEMAN: It's a limited hangout.

DEAN: It's a limited hangout.

EHRLICHMAN: It's a modified limited hangout.

NIXON: Well, it's only the questions of the thing hanging out publicly or privately.

DEAN: What it's doing, Mr. President, is getting you up above and away from it. And that's the most important thing.

NIXON: Oh, I know. But I suggested that the other day and we all came down on — remember we came down on the negative on it. Now what's changed our mind?

DEAN: The lack of alternatives or a body.

[laughter]

EHRLICHMAN: We went down every alley. [laughs] Let it go over.

NIXON: Well, I feel that this is, that — I feel that at the very minimum we've got to have the statement and let's look at it, whatever the hell it is. If it opens up doors, it opens up doors. You know?

EHRLICHMAN: John says he's sorry he sent those burglars in there, and that helps a lot.

NIXON: That's right.

MITCHELL: You are very welcome, sir.

[LAUGHTER]

HALDEMAN: Just glad the others didn't get caught.

NIXON: Yeah, the ones we sent to Muskie and all the rest — Jackson, and Hubert, and [unclear].

EHRLICHMAN: I get a little chill sitting over there in that part of the table there.

NIXON: Yeah [unclear]. Getting pr — I —

EHRLICHMAN: Yeah.

NIXON: I got to handle my Canadian friend [Prime Minister Pierre Trudeau] right at the moment. Incidentally, you don't plan to have — you weren't planning to have a press briefing [unclear].

EHRLICHMAN: We hadn't planned it. It wouldn't hurt —

NIXON: [unclear] three thirty with John [unclear]. All right.

EHRLICHMAN: He is going to talk to the press tomorrow.

NIXON: Yeah, let's let it go. [unclear]. Suppose you take it — you take care of it now [unclear] and I won't come over there. I — you might, if you get him waltzed around, you let me hear —

EHRLICHMAN: All right.

NIXON: It would be my thought then that I would then break it off at four thirty.

DEAN: All right. Fine.

. . .

[HALDEMAN and EHRLICHMAN leave the conversation.]

MITCHELL: Believe me, it's a lot of work.

NIXON: Oh, great, I may [unclear]. Well, let me tell you, you've done a hell of a job here.

DEAN: [unclear]

NIXON: I didn't mean for you. I thought we had a boy here. No, you, John, carried a very, very heavy load. Both Johns as a matter of fact, but I was going to say John Dean is [unclear] got — put the fires out, almost got the damn thing nailed down till past the election and so forth. We all know what it is. Embarrassing goddamn thing the way it went, and so forth. But, in my view, some of it will come out. We will survive it. That's the way it is. That's the way you've got to look at it.

DEAN: Well, we've got a few miles and months ago, but we're —

NIXON: The point is, get the goddamn thing over with.

DEAN: That's right.

NIXON: That's the thing to do. That's the other thing that I like about this. I'd like to get — but you really would draw the line on — but, I know, we can't make a complete cave and have the people go up there and testify. You would agree on that?

MITCHELL: I agree.

NIXON: You agree on that, John?

DEAN: If we're in the posture of everything short of giving them a public session [unclear] and the whole deal. You're not hiding anything.

NIXON: Yeah. Particularly if we have the Dean statement.

DEAN: And they've been given out.

NIXON: And your view about the Dean statement is to give that to the committee and not make it public, however.

DEAN: That's correct. I think that's —

NIXON: And say it's —

MITCHELL: Give it to the committee for the purpose —

NIXON: — the purpose of their investigation.

MITCHELL: — to limit the number of witnesses —

NIXON: Yeah.

MITCHELL: — which are called up there, instead of a buckshot operation.

NIXON: And say here, and also say, "This may help you in your investigation."

MITCHELL: Right.

NIXON: "This is everything we know, Mr. Senator." That's what I was preparing to say. "This is everything we know. I know nothing more. This is the whole purpose, and that's that. If you need any further information, my — our counsel will furnish it. That is not in here." To the extent that we have it — "this is all we know. Now, in addition to that, you are welcome to have people — but you've got to have" — I think that the best way to have it is in executive session, but incidentally, you say executive session for those out of government as well as in?

MITCHELL: That's right.

NIXON: Chapin and Colson should be called in.

DEAN: Yeah, they're already [unclear].

NIXON: I would think so.

MITCHELL: Sure. Because you have the same problem.

NIXON: You see we ask — but your point — we ask for the privilege, and at least, you know, we — our statement said it applies to former as well as present [unclear].

DEAN: Now, our statement — you leave a lot of flexibility that you normally — for one thing, taking the chance appearing, and — however, informal relationships will always be worked out [unclear].

NIXON: Informal relations.

DEAN: That's right.

MITCHELL: You have the same basis —

NIXON: Well, it might. When I say that the written interrogatory thing is not as clear [unclear] maybe Ervin is making it that way, but I think that's based on what maybe — we said that the — I don't think I said we would only write, in the press conference, written interrogatories.

DEAN: That's right. I don't think —

NIXON: I didn't say that at all.

DEAN: Ervin just jumped to that conclusion as a result of my letter to —

NIXON: I think that's what it was.

DEAN: I think that's what's happened.

NIXON: Not that your letter was wrong — it was right. But, the whole written interrogatory — we didn't discuss other possibilities.

MITCHELL: With respect to your ex-employees, you have the same problem of getting into areas of privileged communications. You certainly can make a good case for keeping them in executive session.

NIXON: That's right.

MITCHELL: [unclear]

NIXON: And in this sense the precedent for working — you can do it in cases in the future — just do it in executive session, and then the privilege can be raised without having, on a legal basis, without having the guilt by the Fifth Amendment, not like pleading the Fifth Amendment —

MITCHELL: Right.

NIXON: The implication always being raised.

MITCHELL: [unclear] and self-protection in that view?

NIXON: What? Yeah.

DEAN: [unclear] Fifth Amendment.

NIXON: That's right. That's what we're going to do here.

MITCHELL: Those — boy, this thing has to be turned around. Got to get you off the lid.

NIXON: Right —

DEAN: All right.

NIXON: All right, fine, Chuck [John].

[DEAN leaves the conversation.]

MITCHELL: Good to see you.

NIXON: How long were you in Florida? Just—

MITCHELL: I was down there overnight. I was four hours on the witness stand testifying for the government in these racket cases involving wiretapping. The goddamn fool judge down there let them go all over the lot and ask me any questions that they wanted to. Just ridiculous. You know, this had—all has to do with the discretionary act of signing a piece of paper that I'm authorized by the statute. There were twenty-seven [unclear] lawyers that questioned me.

NIXON: You know, the—you can say when I [unclear] I was going to say that the—[picks up the phone] can you get me Prime Minister Trudeau in Canada, please? [hangs up] I was going to say that Dean has really been something on this.

MITCHELL: That he has, Mr. President. No question about it, he's a very—

NIXON: Son-of-a-bitching tough thing.

MITCHELL: You've got a very solid guy that's handled some tough things. And, I also want to say these lawyers that you have think very highly of him. I know that John spends his time with certain ones—

NIXON: Dean? Discipline is very high.

MITCHELL: [CRP attorneys Kenneth] Parkinson, [Paul] O'Brien.

NIXON: Yes, Dean says it's great. Well, you know I feel for all the people, you know, I mean everybody that's involved. Hell, all we're doing is the best to their abilities and so forth. [unclear] That's why I can't let you go down. John? It's all right. Come in.

[DEAN joins the conversation.]

DEAN: Uh—

NIXON: Did you find out anything?

DEAN: I was—I went over to Ziegler's office. They have an office over there. Paul O'Brien will be down here in a little while to see you. I'm going over to Ziegler's office and finish this up now.

MITCHELL: Are you coming back?

DEAN: Yes, I'll come back over here then.

MITCHELL: Okay.

NIXON: Yeah. Well, when you come back—he can—is that office open for John now?

DEAN: Yes.

NIXON: Then he can go over there as soon [unclear] this.

[DEAN leaves the conversation.]

NIXON: But, the one thing I don't want to do is to—now let me make this clear. I thought it was a very, very cruel thing as it turned out—although at the time I had to tell [unclear] what happened to [Sherman] Adams. I don't want it to happen with Watergate—the Watergate matter. I think he made a mistake, but he shouldn't have been sacked. He shouldn't have been—and, for that reason, I am perfectly willing to—I don't give a shit what happens. I want you all to stonewall it, let them plead the Fifth Amendment, cover up, or anything else, if it'll save it—save the plan. That's the whole point. On the other hand, I would prefer, as I said to you, that you do it the other way. And I would particularly prefer to do it that other way if it's going to come out that way anyway. And that my view, that — with the number of jackass people that they've got that they can call they're going to — the story they get out through leaks, charges, and so forth, and innuendos, will be a hell of a lot worse than the story they're going to get out by just letting it out there.

MITCHELL: Well —

NIXON: I don't know. But that's, you know, up to this point the whole theory has been containment, as you know, John.

MITCHELL: Yeah.

NIXON: And now we're shifting. As far as I'm concerned, actually from a personal standpoint, if you weren't making a personal sacrifice — it's unfair — Haldeman and Dean. That's what Eisenhower — that's all he cared about. He only cared about — Christ, "Be sure he was clean." Both in the fund thing and the Adams thing. But I don't look at it that way. And I just — that's the thing I am really concerned with. We're going to protect our people, if we can.

MITCHELL: Well, the important thing is to get you up above it for this first operation. And then to see where the chips fall and get through this grand jury thing up here. Then the committee is another question. What we ought to have is a reading as to what is coming out of this committee and we — if we handle the cards as it progresses.

NIXON: Yeah. But anyway, we'll go on. And I think in order — it'll probably turn just as well getting them in the position of — even though it hurts for a little while.

MITCHELL: Yeah.

NIXON: You know what I mean. People say, "Well, the president's [unclear]," and so forth. Nothing is lasting. You know people get so disturbed about [unclear]. Now, when we do move we can do it — we can move in a — in the proper way.

MITCHELL: If you can do it in a controlled way it would help and good, but the other thing you have to remember is that this stuff is going to come out of that committee, whether —

NIXON: That's right.

MITCHELL: And it's going to come out no matter what.

NIXON: As if I — and then it looks like I tried to keep it from coming out.

MITCHELL: That's why it's important that that statement go up to the committee.

• • •

NIXON: Christ. Sure, we'll —

MITCHELL: It's like these Gray hearings. They had it five days running that the files were turned over to John Dean — just five days running the same story.

NIXON: Same story.

MITCHELL: Right.

NIXON: The files should have been turned over.

MITCHELL: Just should have demanded them. You should have demanded all of them.

NIXON: [unclear] what the hell was he doing as counsel to the president without getting them? He was — I told him to conduct an investigation, and he did.

MITCHELL: I know.

NIXON: Well, it's like everything else.

MITCHELL: Anything else for us to —

NIXON: Get on that other thing. If Baker can — Baker is not proving much of a reed up to this point. He's smart enough.

MITCHELL: Howard is smart enough, but we've got to carry him.

NIXON: I think he has —

MITCHELL: I think he has and I've been puzzling over a way to have a liaison with him and —

NIXON: He won't talk on the phone with anybody according to Kleindienst. He thinks his phone is tapped.

MITCHELL: He does?

NIXON: Who's tapping his phone?

MITCHELL: I don't know.

NIXON: Who would he think would tap his phone? I guess maybe that we would.

MITCHELL: I don't doubt that.

NIXON: He must think that Ervin —

MITCHELL: Maybe.

NIXON: Or a newspaper.

MITCHELL: Newspaper, or the Democratic Party, or somebody. There's got to be somebody to liaison with Kleindienst to get in a position where — it's all right from foreknowledge through Kleindienst.

NIXON: You really wonder if you take Wally Johnson and — he's a pretty good boy, isn't he?

MITCHELL: Yeah. Very, very [unclear].

NIXON: You might throw that out to Dean. Dean says he doesn't want to be in such a public position. He talked to the attorney general. It could be Wally Johnson. And he said that —

MITCHELL: Well, he will be in the department —

NIXON: Yeah.

MITCHELL: — talking to the department.

NIXON: [unclear] Mansfield's down there —

MITCHELL: Everything else under control?

NIXON: Yeah, we're all doing fine. I think, though, that as long as everyone and so forth is a [unclear] still [unclear].

MITCHELL: All of Washington — the public interest in this thing, you know.

NIXON: It isn't the national — big national story [unclear] worries the shit out of us here. Watergate [unclear] concerns me.

MITCHELL: Just the *Times*.

NIXON: But the point is that I don't — there's no need for [unclear]. I have nothing but intuition, but hell, I don't know. I, but — again you really have to protect the presidency, too. That's the point.

MITCHELL: Well, this does no violence to the presidency at all, this concept —

NIXON: The whole scenario.

MITCHELL: Yeah.

NIXON: No, it d — that's what I mean. The purpose of this scenario is to clean the presidency. [unclear] what they say, "All right. Here's the report. We're going to cooperate with the committee," and so forth and so on. The main thing is to answer [unclear] and that should be a goddamn satisfactory answer, John.

MITCHELL: It should be.

NIXON: Shouldn't it?

MITCHELL: It answers all of their complaints they've had to date.

NIXON: That's right. They get cross-examination.

MITCHELL: Right. They get everything but the public spectacle.

NIXON: Public spectacle. And the reason we don't have that is because you have to argue —

MITCHELL: They have to argue and —

NIXON: — on a legal matter and you don't want them to be used as a — for unfairly — to have somebody charged.

MITCHELL: It's our fault that you have somebody charged with not answering the committee's questions [unclear] to John. Make sure you put it in — make sure that you put it again in the argument, the clean record, and that's the reason why you have an executive session. Because the record that comes out of it is clean. But in areas of dispute —

NIXON: I'd rather think, though, that all of their yakking about this we often said, John — we've got problems.

MITCHELL: [unclear]

NIXON: Might cost them [unclear]. Think of their problems. They — those bastards are really — it's really something. Where is their leadership?

MITCHELL: They don't have any leadership, and they're leaping on every new issue.

Dean is implicated

March 27, 1973, 11:00 a.m.
Richard Nixon, Bob Haldeman, John Ehrlichman, and Ronald Ziegler
EXECUTIVE OFFICE BUILDING

From March 23 to 27, Nixon spent a long weekend at his home in Key Biscayne, Florida. No tapes were made of his conversations during that eventful span. It was a time of reckoning, though, especially for Dean. First, Gray testified before the Senate Judiciary Committee on March 22 that Dean "probably" lied to the FBI when he told an investigator that he didn't know whether Hunt had an office in the White House. The accusation made an infamous man of Dean. The following day, March 23, Judge Sirica received an unsolicited letter from James McCord, one of those who broke into the Democratic National Committee headquarters. McCord convincingly informed the judge of many ways in which the testimony of witnesses in the Watergate trial had been warped, unleashing new suspicions of the White House. Judge Sirica, who'd had a recent birthday, told one of his clerks a short time later, "This is one of the damnedest birthday presents I've ever gotten. I always told you I felt someone would talk. This is going to break the case."

A few days later, on the twenty-fifth, reporters learned that McCord had been even more specific with Watergate Committee investigators, telling them that Dean, as well as Jeb Magruder, knew about the plans for the Watergate break-in before it occurred. Publicly, Nixon expressed his confidence in Dean, who was even then working on the long-awaited presidential report on Watergate. Privately, Nixon needed to plot a path through a cover-up without Dean. Nixon, Haldeman, Ehrlichman, and press secretary Ronald Ziegler discussed the many figures who might come forward in the wake of McCord: notably Magruder and Martha Mitchell.*

But first, before getting to the latest on Watergate, a different type of crisis was emerging: a standoff at Wounded Knee, South Dakota, between Native Americans and federal officials. Chosen for its significance as the site of the 1890 Wounded Knee massacre, on February 27 followers of the American Indian Movement started a demonstration that would last seventy-one days and result in three killed and fifteen wounded.

• • •

EHRLICHMAN: Hi.

NIXON: Hi. Well, did you get religified over the weekend?

EHRLICHMAN: Yep. Got all pumped up.

NIXON: Great. What's the advice on the Wounded Knee first?

EHRLICHMAN: Well, I had the impression that this thing was drifting and so I got all the players together, and it was. So I've got them working on a plan to a finite conclusion now, one way or the other.

NIXON: Who are they? For us, on our side?

EHRLICHMAN: Ken Cole is chairing the working group.

NIXON: Right.

EHRLICHMAN: And we have Justice and Interior and —

NIXON: Is the marshal [Lloyd Grimm] going to die?

EHRLICHMAN: No. Apparently not. He's serious, but he's not critical.

NIXON: Thank God.

EHRLICHMAN: But the thing's steadily getting worse and worse and worse. The fellow who —

NIXON: The thing to do at the present time — I have a feeling myself — I have watched it drift. I never felt it should get too much, but I think you've [unclear] this kind of

---

* John M. Crewdson, "Gray Testifies That Dean 'Probably' Lied to F.B.I.," *New York Times,* March 23, 1973, p. 1; Donald Farinacci, *When One Stood Alone: John J. Sirica's Battle Against the Watergate Conspiracy* (Author House, 2009), p. 66.

crap too long. Now, Indians have gotten very special treatment. Blacks are a special group —

EHRLICHMAN: Yeah.

NIXON: — and the bad Indians are just like bad blacks. And I think they ought to move tanks, the whole goddamn thing. Put a division in if necessary.

EHRLICHMAN: The army's scared to death of it but —

NIXON: Too bad.

EHRLICHMAN: — I told them I wanted to see —

NIXON: I want a plan.

EHRLICHMAN: — a plan. Spelling out exactly what the military would do. How they would do it. What their estimate of loss of life is and so on.

NIXON: Right.

EHRLICHMAN: Then the whole difficulty here on so many things is they have no PR concept in this thing, and so the government's story is not getting across. The reason why we would send soldiers in is not apparent to anybody. A foundation has to be laid. And so I want a step-by-step as to how we lay the foundation for the use of troops to bring this thing to an all-around conclusion, and so they are in the process of putting those together now.

NIXON: And of course the foundation, if the guy had died that would have been the foundation.

EHRLICHMAN: Well, it was a terrible damn thing, the way they did it to him. And that hasn't gotten out. There is nothing about his family, or what kind of a fellow he is, or any of those kinds of things. So I have got them on that. But he was standing there, and actually Kent Frizzell, who is our assistant attorney general that we are moving over to be solicitor at the Department of Interior, a high-ranking guy, and they are standing way, way off in the distance in an observation point looking down into this village and a sniper picked this marshal off just four feet away from Frizzell. Just the two of them standing there. He could very easily have picked off our assistant attorney general. And it was just one shot. In fact, the guy dropped before the shot was heard. So it was a vicious damn thing.

NIXON: When did this happen?

EHRLICHMAN: Yesterday afternoon.

NIXON: [unclear] out there —

EHRLICHMAN: Well, the Indians have asked for a meeting. Frizzell is in a meeting with them today. Now my sense of this, the reason I called this group together, one of the reasons besides just fear that we didn't have a plan was that we need to have, in my view, some constructive domestic White House activity going on. Now this is a problem, and it isn't constructive in a pure sense, but it would be White House activity if we had a White House person involved in the settlement or the PR of this thing at this point. Pull off some of this poison, and show another aspect of this thing in terms of the White House. So we are going to explore the pros and cons of it. There are a lot of cons to it in the long run and it is a question of whether you want to pay the long-run price for the short-run PR advantage, and that is something I am not prepared to suggest right now, but it is a possibility and would involve somebody like me or Garment, or somebody going up there to neutral ground, talking to Indians on both sides, and in effect delivering an ultimatum in the end and then finding every camera you can get your hands on to put across the PR foundation. It would show the White House in operation in a different setting and different context just like the price thing is —

NIXON: On Thursday, the price thing —

EHRLICHMAN: — is constructive in that business is going on, and things are happening.

NIXON: [unclear] back.

EHRLICHMAN: Yes, you bet.

NIXON: Then you can say so.

EHRLICHMAN: So that is what this is all about, and tomorrow I'm going to work —

NIXON: Well, I am for action on it. Even from the long run.

EHRLICHMAN: Right.

NIXON: Even from the long run, I don't believe you can temporize with this kind of crap. So let — so Indians get shot, that's too goddamn bad. If we lose a couple of Americans that's too bad too.

EHRLICHMAN: Of course that is my concern. Looking at this coming summer, if we fiddle around up there for seven weeks we are just inviting the blacks, or the Chicanos, or somebody to occupy a hotel, or a railroad station, or an airline terminal, or some damn thing with rifles and say, you know, we have these certain demands. It's unanswerable.

NIXON: Should have gone the extra mile.

• • •

EHRLICHMAN: This one — this Watergate thing is potentially very debilitating to morale. But we have to devote a large part of our time to keeping people busy in —

NIXON: I know.

EHRLICHMAN: — affirmative kinds of [unclear].

NIXON: [unclear] because it involves people we know.

EHRLICHMAN: Yeah.

NIXON: It involves, frankly, people who don't [unclear] guilty. This and that.

EHRLICHMAN: Yeah.

NIXON: And also for — you don't want anybody guilty, or — it isn't the question. We know that everybody in this thing did it, whatever they did, with the best of intentions. That's the sad thing about it.

EHRLICHMAN: Sure.

NIXON: I told them all this morning, I don't want people on the staff to divide up and say, "Well, it's this guy that did it, or this guy that did it," or da-da-da-da —

EHRLICHMAN: Yeah.

NIXON: The point is what's done is done. Do the very best we can, and cut our losses and so forth — best you could ever do.

EHRLICHMAN: Did he talk to you about this thing — commission thing?

NIXON: No, I'd like to talk about it, but I don't know what you can do. I don't think, though — I don't think that I — even though it's moving along, that story and so forth. I don't believe that I should go out on national television like tonight or tomorrow and go out on the Watergate Committee and then come on the next day on national television on Vietnam. I don't like the feeling of that. I don't think you get it ready by that time. My view would be to get the Vietnam out of the way and maybe get this right if you could. I think that gives you time.

EHRLICHMAN: The picture of the Congress having an inquiry going on —

NIXON: Yeah.

EHRLICHMAN: And the grand jury having an inquiry going on in the Judicial Branch.

NIXON: Right.

EHRLICHMAN: It seems to me gives you — opening — thinking about it after Bob was talking about it —

NIXON: Step in and say look —

EHRLICHMAN: — step in and say, "There doesn't seem to be anybody except me in the position to resolve this. I have talked with the chief justice of the United States and I have talked with Senator Ervin and Senator Baker and I — after that consultation, have proposed this three-branch — "

NIXON: Well —

EHRLICHMAN: " — board of inquiry."

NIXON: To start with the proposition of Ervin and Baker, where you don't come across right there at the beginning on whether you can get the three men. I'm not sure you can get the three branches, John.

EHRLICHMAN: Well, I'm not sure you could get it either. It —

NIXON: But just suppose you couldn't. Then still think that it is good — possibly a good idea. I mean, but we've got to have somebody other than me that could broker it. The problem you've got to recognize, you see, is that Haldeman can't. You can't. Dean can't. Mainly because — you possibly could, but it's also that I don't want to put out the whole White House. You're the only one who could do it.

EHRLICHMAN: The —

NIXON: I have to do — this is why I told you [unclear], but I might have to use Rogers on the job to be the broker.

EHRLICHMAN: Yeah. Fine. If he can do it, do it.

NIXON: He'd be good [unclear]. I don't know whether you could get a —

[ZIEGLER joins the conversation.]

NIXON: Come in. Oh, hi. How are you?

ZIEGLER: Well, just checking in.

NIXON: Sure, sure. Right.

ZIEGLER: The reason —

NIXON: In position, righ—

ZIEGLER: —we have the patient rehabilitation veto today and the—we hope it's a return shipment to Thieu in South Vietnam, preparations that—

NIXON: Right.

ZIEGLER: —describing—

NIXON: Right.

ZIEGLER: —[unclear] working [unclear].

NIXON: Right.

ZIEGLER: Then tomorrow we should send statistics and so forth. I talked to Dean and to Moore this morning in terms of whether or not we say anything [unclear]—

NIXON: Right, right.

ZIEGLER: —the grand jury stuff, and Dean's feeling is that we should not today.

NIXON: That is my feeling.

ZIEGLER: And Moore's feeling is that we should not today, and I concur in that [unclear].

NIXON: Yeah. My view is today, unless you've got something more to say—

ZIEGLER: That's right.

NIXON: —I would simply say I have nothing to add to what they said yesterday.

ZIEGLER: That's right.

NIXON: I think that would be better [unclear].

ZIEGLER: The, uh—

NIXON: Just get out there and act like your usual cocky, confident self.

ZIEGLER: Then the—if I am asked a question about whether or not Dean would appear before the grand jury, if I'm asked that question—

NIXON: Yeah. It's, uh—

ZIEGLER: How should I handle that? That's where I [unclear]. I could—two options: one would be to say that [unclear]. The other would be to say well [unclear].

NIXON: I'm just saying that if this charge is wrong [unclear] the charge. Well, if you say [unclear] people that have information about it [unclear]. What do you think, John?

EHRLICHMAN: You tell him.

NIXON: Well, it's easier to get out of because it's—that's not a matter [unclear], this point [unclear].

ZIEGLER: I'm inclined to think [unclear]. I'm inclined to think that today my best position is just to say that this was discussed yesterday. I've said all along [unclear].

NIXON: Yeah.

ZIEGLER: We are willing to cooperate [unclear].

NIXON: Couldn't you just say that we've indicated cooperation unless—

ZIEGLER: [unclear]

NIXON: —the forum of the request, or whatever it is—

ZIEGLER: These matters must proceed—this matter must proceed in an orderly and judicious manner and I'm not going to get up here on the podium and listen to that.

NIXON: Right.

EHRLICHMAN: The other thing you might do is say you know a fellow like John Dean is in a very tough spot when somebody levels an accusation against him. He's really in the poorest position to defend himself of anybody in the government.

· · ·

EHRLICHMAN: I don't know whether it would add anything really from our standpoint to say this but the point is here that the poor guy is under disability to step out and defend himself because of his position. Because he is counsel to the president, and that in a —

NIXON: I know.

EHRLICHMAN: — inhibits him from stepping [unclear].

NIXON: I wonder if it is very difficult for John or for Ron to get into that?

EHRLICHMAN: Well, but it is in the setting of — would he appear before a grand jury?

NIXON: That's the thing. Why don't we just say, "Well, that's the matter, that — this is a matter that is not before us." I should point out that he is counsel to the White House — he's the White House counsel, and therefore his appearance before any political group, therefore, is on a different basis from anybody else, which is basically what I, you know, when I flatly said Dean would not appear but that others would. You know, I did say that, of course he —

EHRLICHMAN: It was on a different basis. At the same time —

NIXON: The same time he —

EHRLICHMAN: — a man in any position ought to be given a chance to defend himself —

NIXON: Yeah.

EHRLICHMAN: — against groundless charges.

NIXON: That's it. Mr. Dean certainly wants the opportunity to defend himself against these charges. He would welcome the opportunity and what we have to do is to work out a procedure which will allow him to do so consistent with his unique position of being not just a member of the president's staff, but also the counsel — that is a lawyer — counsel — not lawyer, but the responsibility of the counsel for confidential —

ZIEGLER: Could you apply that to the grand jury?

NIXON: Yeah, yeah.

EHRLICHMAN: The grand jury is one of those occasions where a man in his situation can defend himself.

NIXON: Yeah.

EHRLICHMAN: Clearing himself.

NIXON: Yeah, yes. The grand jury, that — well, actually, if called — look, we're not going to refuse to — for anybody called before the grand jury to go, are we, John?

EHRLICHMAN: Can't imagine it.

NIXON: No, well, he was called — he will be — he will be cooperative, consistent with his responsibilities as counsel. How do we say that?

EHRLICHMAN: That he will be cooperative.

NIXON: He'll fully cooperate.

EHRLICHMAN: You better check that with Dean. I know he's got certain misgivings on this.

ZIEGLER: He did this morning.

NIXON: Yeah. Well, then, don't say that.

EHRLICHMAN: Well, I think you could pose the dilemma without—

NIXON: Yeah.

EHRLICHMAN: —saying flatly what you're going to do.

NIXON: Yeah. We—but maybe you just don't want to [unclear]. You better not try to break into it, John.

ZIEGLER: You get into posing the dilemma.

NIXON: Then you're going to break into questions. I'd simply stonewall them today.

ZIEGLER: I think so.

NIXON: That is not before us at this time. But let me emphasize, he will coop—as the president has indicated, there will be complete cooperation consistent with the responsibilities that everybody has on the separation of powers. Fair enough? And, of course, and consistent with Mr. Dean's responsibilities is—other responsibilities as a counsel. See? How about just saying it that way? Well, John, do you have doubts?

EHRLICHMAN: No. Why don't we—

NIXON: If Ziegler opens—Ziegler has to answer something.

EHRLICHMAN: The only thing that occurred to me is, when I read this stuff yesterday, was that somehow or another we should be introducing the fact that Dean's going to get a chance to clear his name.

NIXON: Yeah.

EHRLICHMAN: But eventually that's going to—there's going to be an opportunity for that in some forum, at some time, in some way. But maybe you get into the business of saying you don't—

NIXON: I don't think this is the day to do it. This is the day [unclear].

EHRLICHMAN: [unclear]

NIXON: Yeah.

ZIEGLER: I think so—

NIXON: Yeah.

ZIEGLER: Give more than a—

NIXON: Say.

ZIEGLER: [unclear] how we approach the whole matter instead of moving [unclear]. The president's expressed confidence [unclear].

NIXON: You can also say that the president is talking [unclear] staff today regarding the Dean situation. I think we should say that—

EHRLICHMAN: There was a meeting here this morning—

NIXON: That's right.

EHRLICHMAN: —involving Deputy—

NIXON: Yeah.

EHRLICHMAN: —Attorney General—

NIXON: Yeah.

EHRLICHMAN: — Undersecretary of Interior —

NIXON: That's right.

EHRLICHMAN: — and others —

NIXON: That's right.

EHRLICHMAN: — on the [unclear] reservation [unclear].

NIXON: Yeah. And that we're — and the [unclear] it doesn't matter if the president is [unclear].

EHRLICHMAN: That the White House is following —

NIXON: The White House is following and we are [unclear] the president's direction. A meeting was held here, the White House is now examining the situation to see what action can be taken to resolve it.

• • •

NIXON: All right. Let it go.

ZIEGLER: [unclear] because if we —

NIXON: Fine, well, we're ready to go something on Wounded Knee.

ZIEGLER: Okay.

NIXON: Let it go. Okay, you go ahead.

EHRLICHMAN: [unclear] Wounded Knee until we have a plan. Just keep out of the stuff today.

ZIEGLER: Okay.

NIXON: Also say that I met with the Japanese — the —

ZIEGLER: Yes, sir. Finance minister.

NIXON: — finance minister.

[ZIEGLER leaves the conversation.]

• • •

EHRLICHMAN: On the FBI, we'll start moving some names to you —

NIXON: I hope you'll look into that guy that Dean mentioned.

EHRLICHMAN: Yeah, I've got [William] Webster.

NIXON: Sounds good.

EHRLICHMAN: We're to get a résumé and some background.

NIXON: A judge with a prosecuting background, claimed that to put him on would be a hell of a good thing.

EHRLICHMAN: Well, uh —

NIXON: I have decided that when we move on it, it must be simultaneous. Gray comes in and says, "I'm sorry we can't put you, you can't," he says, "I can't get confirmed and I don't want to be confirmed in a way that I — that, in which there is any division. There must be unanimous support for whoever is, and support for and trust in the director of the FBI. As a result of the hearings to date, it is obvious that I am not going to get that kind of support in the Senate even though I believe that I may be confirmed. Under the circumstances, I respectfully request you withdraw my name." And send somebody else down. That's a very sound basis. I'm thinking of doing that. I would hope next week right after Thieu.

EHRLICHMAN: Well, what do you think about doing that simultaneous with the appointment of a commissioner? We could —

NIXON: Oh, yeah.

EHRLICHMAN: — it could be written up in the same announcement. Say, "Here's a fine man who's been unfortunately splattered by this thing. It is a case study in how —"

NIXON: Yeah.

EHRLICHMAN: " — bystanders can get splashed with this sort of thing."

NIXON: Right.

EHRLICHMAN: It's now to the point where he can't even —

NIXON: You think, also, John, or at least you thought somewhat of the idea, that we should get Kleindienst out, too, at this point?

EHRLICHMAN: Yeah, yeah.

NIXON: How do we do that?

EHRLICHMAN: Well, I'm going to see him today and Bob's going to talk to him and we will hit him from two directions on this. And —

NIXON: Get Kleindienst to resign?

[HALDEMAN joins the conversation.]

EHRLICHMAN: Oh, no — get him out front. No use of hitting him out of the office. Oh, no. I hadn't — we hadn't talked about that.

HALDEMAN: That's Bill Rogers.

NIXON: Well, I'm sorry, John.

EHRLICHMAN: No. I — we talked this morning about getting him out front. I'm afraid it's —

NIXON: [unclear] of canning him right away. Let's see about that. Maybe we should can him. Well, whatever — what have you got to report? John and I have just started a [unclear].

HALDEMAN: All I have is Dean's report. I did not talk to Mitchell because this may change what we want to do from Mitchell. He had a long conversation again today with Paul O'Brien, who's the guy. He's been — talked with yesterday — you know, this, that, and all that, and he says O'Brien is very distressed with Mitchell. The more he thinks about it the more O'Brien comes down to Mitchell could cut this whole thing off if he would just step forward and cut it off. That the fact of the matter is as far as Gray could determine that Mitchell did sign off on it. And if that's what it —

NIXON: You mean as far as O'Brien is concerned?

HALDEMAN: Yeah.

EHRLICHMAN: You said, "Gray."

NIXON: What's that?

HALDEMAN: I'm sorry. O'Brien, not Gray. As far as O'Brien can determine, Mitchell did sign off on this thing and that's — and Dean believes that to be the case also. He can't — Dean doesn't think he can prove it, and apparently O'Brien can't either, but they both think that that —

NIXON: That's my suspicion.

HALDEMAN: The more O'Brien thinks about it the more it bothers him with all he knows — to see all the people getting whacked around — that he sees getting whacked around — in order to keep the thing from focusing on John Mitchell, when inevitably it's going to end up doing that anyway and all these other people are going to be so badly hurt they're not going to be able to get out from under it. And that's one view. Now to go back on the Magruder situation as O'Brien reports it, having spent several hours with Magruder yesterday afternoon — O'Brien and Parkinson. Jeb believes, or professes to believe, and O'Brien is inclined to think he really does believe, that the whole Liddy plan, the whole supersecurity operation, superintelligence operation was put together by the White House — by Haldeman, Dean, and others.

NIXON: Yeah.

HALDEMAN: Really, Dean — that Dean cooked the whole thing up at Haldeman's instruction — the whole idea of the need for a superintelligence operation. Now there's some semblance of validity to the point that I did talk, not with Dean, but with Mitchell, about the need for intelligence activity and —

NIXON: And that Dean recommended Liddy?

HALDEMAN: Yeah, but not for intelligence. Dean recommended Liddy as the general counsel.

NIXON: Yeah, but you see this is where Magruder might come — well, go ahead. Okay.

HALDEMAN: That Mitchell bought the idea that was cooked up in the White House for a superintelligence operation, and that this was all set and an accomplished fact in December of '71 before Liddy was hired by the committee. But then Liddy was hired by the committee to carry it out and that's why Dean sent Liddy over to the committee. Then there was a hiatus. There were these meetings in Mitchell's office where Liddy unveiled his plan. And the first plan he unveiled nobody bought. They all laughed at it. Because it was so bizarre. So he went back to the drawing board and came back with a second plan and the second plan didn't get bought either. That was at the second meeting and everything just kind of lingered around then. It was sort of hanging fire. Liddy was pushing to get something done. He wanted to get moving on his plans. And at that point he went to Colson and said, "Nobody will approve any of this — you know, we could — we should be getting — "

NIXON: Yeah.

HALDEMAN: " — getting going on it." And Colson then got into the act in pushing to get — which started with the Colson phone call to Magruder saying, "Well, at least listen to these guys." Then the final step was — all of this was rattling around in January. The final step was when Gordon Strachan called Magruder and said Haldeman told him to get this going. "The president wants it done and there's to be no more arguing about it."

NIXON: "This" meaning —

HALDEMAN: — the intelligence activity, the Liddy program. Magruder told Mitchell this, that Strachan had ordered him to get it going on Haldeman's orders on the president's orders and Mitchell signed off on it. He said, "Okay, if they say to do it, go ahead."

NIXON: Was that — this is the bugging?

HALDEMAN: The whole thing including the bugging.

NIXON: Shit.

HALDEMAN: The bugging was implicit in the second plan. I — Dean doesn't seem to be sure whether it was implicit or explicit.

NIXON: Well, anyway —

HALDEMAN: He doesn't think that particular bug was explicit, but that the process of bugging was implicit and — as I didn't realize it, nor did Dean, but it was also in the [Operation] Sandwedge plan [to collect intelligence on the antiwar movement and Democratic rivals] way back — the early plan. That, incidentally, is a potential source of fascinating problems in that it involved [Vernon] "Mike" Acree, who's now the customs commissioner or something [who left his position as assistant commissioner at the IRS to become the head of the Customs Service], Joe Woods [brother of Rose Mary Woods] — a few other people.

NIXON: Nothing happened?

HALDEMAN: It wasn't done — that's right. But there — at some point, according to Magruder, after this was then signed off and put away, Mitch — Magruder — Mitchell called Liddy into the office and read him the riot act on the poor quality of stuff they were getting. That's basically the scenario or the summary of what Magruder told the lawyer. Dean's theory is that both Mitchell and Magruder realize that they now have their ass in a sling and that they're trying to untangle it, not necessarily working together again — at least he doesn't think they are. But in the process of that they are mixing apples and oranges for their own protection. And that they're remembering various things in connection with others [unclear] like Hunt and Liddy [unclear].

• • •

HALDEMAN: He says, for example, Magruder doesn't realize how little Dean told Liddy. He thinks that Dean sent Liddy in. Liddy said — frankly, now as far as Dean screening to Liddy was that — "You as general counsel over there can also take as a side activity the political intelligence question because we do need some input on demonstrators and stuff like that. That they're not doing anything about — " but he never got into any setting up an elaborate intelligence apparatus.

NIXON: Okay.

HALDEMAN: Dean says that as a matter of fact, in contrast to Magruder's opinion, at the first meeting where a Liddy plan was presented everybody at the meeting laughed at the plan on the basis that it was just — it was so bizarre that it was absurd and it would be funny.

NIXON: Yeah.

HALDEMAN: The second meeting, Dean came into the meeting late. He was not there during most of the presentation but when he came in he could see that they were still on the same kind of a thing. And he says in effect, "I got Mitchell off the hook because I said — I took the initiative in saying, 'You know it's an impossible proposal and we can't — we shouldn't even be discussing this in the attorney general's office,'" and all that. Mitchell agreed and then that's when Dean came over and told me that he had just — had seen this wrap-up on it and that they — still it [unclear] was impossible and then we — that they shouldn't be doing it — that we shouldn't be involved in it and we ought to drop the whole thing. Then as Dean said, "I saw a problem there and I thought they had turned it off and in any event I wanted to stay ten miles away from it, and did." He said the problem from then on, starting somewhere in early January, probably, was that Liddy was never really given any guidance after that. Mitchell was in the midst of the IT and T and all that stuff, and didn't focus on it —

NIXON: Martha.

HALDEMAN: — and Magruder was running around with other things and didn't pay much attention, and Liddy was kind of bouncing around loose there —

EHRLICHMAN: Well, now how do you square that with the allocation of money to it? That presumably was the subject in focus by —

HALDEMAN: Somebody else signed off on that.

EHRLICHMAN: Magruder, possibly Mitchell, possibly Stans, certainly [unclear] —

NIXON: But I suppose they could say the allocation of money was just for intelligence operations generally. I think [unclear]. That's what my guess is. That's what Magruder said is true.

EHRLICHMAN: Some was paid to focus on — somebody —

HALDEMAN: Yeah, someone focused and agreed that there had to be some intelligence and that it would take some money and that Liddy should get it.

EHRLICHMAN: And against the background of the two plans being presented and rejected the natural question that would arise is, "Well, what are you going to do with the money? You don't have an approved plan?"

HALDEMAN: Yeah.

EHRLICHMAN: So that doesn't put anything together.

NIXON: Well, it doesn't hang together but it could in the sense that the campaign —

HALDEMAN: Well, what he thinks — he thinks —

NIXON: My guess —

HALDEMAN: — that Mitchell did sign off on it.

NIXON: That's the point. But my guess is Mitchell could just say, "Look, I" — he says, he has this and that and the other thing, "and I said, 'All right, go ahead,'" but there was no buying of this ba-ba-ba —

HALDEMAN: He says if you heard — Dean's opinion is that he thinks Mitchell kind of vacillated.

NIXON: So —

HALDEMAN: Now O'Brien says that Magruder's objective or motive at that moment is a meeting with Mitchell and me. And that what he has told some of the lawyers may well be a shot across the bow to jar that meeting loose. O'Brien doesn't really believe Jeb but he's not sure. O'Brien is shook a little bit himself as he hears all this. But he does see very definitely and holds also to the theory of mixing of apples and oranges. He's convinced that Jeb is pushing together things that don't necessarily fit together in order to help with a conclusion. And again he's very disappointed in Mitchell. He feels that Mitchell is the guy that's letting people down. O'Brien made the suggestion that if you wanted to force some of this to a head, one thing you might consider is that O'Brien and Parkinson, who are getting a little shaky now themselves, are retained by the committee. That is by Frank Dale, who is the, the chairman of the committee.

NIXON: Does it still exist?

HALDEMAN: The — they, did their —

NIXON: They aren't involved in the damn thing, are they? O'Brien and Parkinson?

HALDEMAN: Yes.

NIXON: They ran this all from the beginning?

HALDEMAN: Oh, no.

NIXON: Well, that is what I thought.

HALDEMAN: But they are involved in the post-discovery, post–June 17.

NIXON: They were [unclear]. [Gives instructions to unknown assistant.]

HALDEMAN: O'Brien says, "Everything with the committee," said, "What you might want to consider is the possibility to waive our retainer — waive our privileges and instruct us to report to the president all of the facts as they are known to us as to what really went on at the Committee to Re-elect the President."

NIXON: I've been informed. For me to sit down and talk to them and go through —

HALDEMAN: I don't know that — he doesn't mean necessarily personally talk to you, but he means to talk to Dean or whoever you designate as your man to be working on this. Now — other facts: Hunt is at the grand jury today. [unclear] We don't know how far he is going to go. The danger area for him is on the money, that he was given money. He's reported by O'Brien, who has been talking to his lawyer, Bittman, not to be as desperate today as he was yesterday, but to still be on the brink or at least shaky. What's made him shaky is that he's seen McCord bouncing out there and probably walking out scot-free.

NIXON: Scot-free — a hero.

HALDEMAN: And he doesn't like that. He figures maybe it's my turn. And that he may go —

NIXON: That's the way I would think all of them would feel.

HALDEMAN: And that he may decide to go with as much as is necessary to get himself into that same position, but probably would only go with as much as is necessary. There isn't a feeling on his part of a desire to get people as there is a desire to take care of himself. And that he might be willing to do what he had to do to take care of himself, but he would probably do it on a gradual basis and he may in fact be doing it right now at the grand jury. He feels, in summary, that on both Hunt and Magruder questions we're not really at the crunch that we were last night. He isn't as concerned as he was when he talked to me last night. We are now going with Silbert —

NIXON: Who's that?

HALDEMAN: The U.S. attorney has — is going to Sirica seeking immunity for Liddy so that he can be a witness. Liddy's lawyer will argue against immunity for he does not want it. Dean's judgment is that he'll probably fail. Sirica will grant it given Sirica's clear disposition —

NIXON: Then he gets — if he doesn't talk, then he gets contempt. Is that it?

HALDEMAN: If Liddy is in — if he gets immunity, his intention as of now at least is to refuse to talk and be in contempt. The contempt is civil contempt and it only runs for the duration of the grand jury which is of a limited duration. And as long as he's in jail anyway, it doesn't make a hell of a lot of difference to him.

NIXON: I would almost bet that's what Liddy will do.

HALDEMAN: Well, that's what Dean will also bet. Dean has asked through O'Brien to see Maroulis, or whatever his name is — Liddy's lawyer — for Liddy to provide a private statement saying that Dean knew nothing in advance on the Watergate, which Liddy knows to be the case. To his knowledge, Dean knew nothing about it and Dean would like to have that statement in his pocket and has asked Liddy — Liddy's lawyer to ask Liddy for such a statement, which he feels Liddy will — would want to give him. Raised the question whether Dean actually had no knowledge of what was going on in the intelligence area between the time of the meetings in Mitchell's office, when he said don't do anything, and the time of the Watergate discovery. And I put that direct question to Dean and he said, "Absolutely nothing."

NIXON: I would — the reason I would totally agree with — that I would believe Dean there [unclear] say would be lying to us about that —

EHRLICHMAN: Well, he said —

NIXON: But I would believe for another reason — that he thought it was a stupid goddamn idea.

EHRLICHMAN: There just isn't a scintilla —

NIXON: Yeah.

EHRLICHMAN: — of hint that Dean that knew about this.

NIXON: No —

EHRLICHMAN: Dean was pretty good all through that period of time in sharing things and he was tracking with a number of us on —

NIXON: Well, you know the thing that, the reason I told Bob — and this incidentally also covers Colson — and I don't know whether — I know that most everybody except Bob, and perhaps you, think Colson knew all about it. But I was talking to Colson, remember exclusively about it — and maybe that was the point — exclusively about the issues. You know, how are we going to do this and that and the other thing? Everything from, mainly the [unclear] how do we get the labor thing, how do we get this, how do we get the Catholic school [unclear]?

HALDEMAN: Yeah, the Cath — the aid to Catholic schools on the new, you know — the, Ehrlichman's — I mean, Colson's fight with the parochial.

NIXON: Right. That's what it is — that's what started it. But in all those talks he had plenty of opportunity. He was always saying, "Hey, we've got to do this," but Colson in that entire period, John, I think he would have said that there was, say, "Look, we've gotten some information," but he never said a word. Haldeman, in this whole period, Haldeman, I am sure — Bob and you, he talked to both of you about the campaign. Never a word. I mean now maybe that all of you knew and didn't tell me, but I can't believe that Colson — well [unclear].

HALDEMAN: Maybe Colson is capable of — if he knew anything out of that — of not telling you what we were at least —

NIXON: Well, at least —

HALDEMAN: We were —

NIXON: — nothing of that sort because as a matter of fact, I didn't even know. I didn't know, frankly, that the Ellsberg thing and so forth — electronically thing — you know what I mean?

HALDEMAN: Yeah.

NIXON: You were reporting to me on that.

EHRLICHMAN: I was —

NIXON: And I guess there you deliberately didn't tell me —

EHRLICHMAN: Well, sir, I didn't know what —

NIXON: Dean —

EHRLICHMAN: — Dean and his crowd were up to until afterwards.

NIXON: Right.

EHRLICHMAN: And I told you, afterwards we stopped it — stopped it from happening again.

NIXON: Right.

EHRLICHMAN: In that setting, but —

NIXON: That was in the national security —

EHRLICHMAN: That was in the national security —

NIXON: Leak thing.

EHRLICHMAN: That's right, but the interesting thing about Colson — corroborates what you say — is that when I got a phone call from Secret Service saying there had been this burglary —

NIXON: Yeah.

EHRLICHMAN: — the first guy I called was Colson.

NIXON: Yeah. Of course.

EHRLICHMAN: And his response, as I recall it, was one of total surprise and there was just a — and he could have said then, "Oh, those jerks, I should have, you know, they shouldn't have," or "I knew about it earlier." He could have inferred that he knew about it in a way that would have been meaningful to me but he didn't. He was totally nonplussed —

NIXON: Yeah.

EHRLICHMAN: — the same as the rest of us.

NIXON: Well, the thing is too — that I know that — you know, when they talk about this business of Magruder's saying that Haldeman had ordered it, the president had ordered it to go forward, of all the people who were surprised was, I mean, on the seventeenth of June — I was in Florida — was me!

EHRLICHMAN: Yeah.

NIXON: Why? Were you there?

EHRLICHMAN: No, I was here. [unclear] called me.

NIXON: Who was there?

EHRLICHMAN: Bob was down there. I called Ziegler — in this order I called Colson, Haldeman, and Ziegler —

NIXON: Yeah.

EHRLICHMAN: — and alerted them to this.

NIXON: Yeah. And I read the paper and I said, "What in the name of God is this?"

EHRLICHMAN: Yeah.

NIXON: I just couldn't believe it.

EHRLICHMAN: Yeah.

NIXON: So you know what I mean is that — I mean I believe in playing politics hard but I'm also smart. What I can't understand is how Mitchell would ever approve if somebody signs it off. That's the thing I can't understand here. Well, Magruder I can understand doing things. He is not a very bright fellow. I mean he is bright, but not — he doesn't think through to the end. Jesus Christ! But Mitchell knows the consequences of such.

HALDEMAN: Yeah, but I'll tell you what could have happened very easily there. Mitchell was attorney general. He was using legally and sometimes approaching illegally — and using his very great capacity to wiretap and do other kinds of things every day and you got into a mindset and you get used to that.

NIXON: Could be. Could be.

HALDEMAN: And it doesn't — you don't regard it with the same kind of feeling that —

NIXON: Yeah. Could be. Could be. Well, anyway.

HALDEMAN: Dean says — he says — "I did see Liddy roughly five or six times during that period of January to June and it was always on campaign legal matters." You know?

NIXON: Well, I know, Dean was — remember you always said Dean was — remember you told me — making all these studies of it —

HALDEMAN: Yeah.

NIXON: — and all.

HALDEMAN: Yeah.

NIXON: I believe that.

HALDEMAN: He said at one of those meetings at one time, you know [unclear]. I said to Liddy something about how is it going? He said he started to say, "I'm having a hell of a time getting approval on the intelligence operation." I says — and Dean says, "You know, Gordon, I told you that's something I know nothing about and don't want to know anything about," and he said, "That's right. Okay."

NIXON: Yeah.

EHRLICHMAN: January to June of '72. Right?

HALDEMAN: Now here's another factor. I know he was following up that point. He says, "As a matter of fact, the reason I called Liddy on June 19" — I said, "Now wait a minute. You called Liddy on June 19?" "Yes, and the reason I did is because Kleindienst told me that Liddy had come to see him on the eighteenth at Burning Tree." That was the day after the discovery on Sunday the eighteenth, and the purpose of that was to tell Kleindienst he had to get his men out of jail and all that. Kleindienst said, "I wish that goddamn Liddy would quit talking to me about this stuff." At that time, Liddy told Kleindienst that Mitchell had ordered it.

NIXON: Oh.

HALDEMAN: And you don't know that that's true. All you know is that Liddy was using that as his means for trying to get to the — then the [unclear].

NIXON: You know Mitchell could be telling the truth. Liddy could be, too. But Liddy would just assume he had constructive —

EHRLICHMAN: That's right.

NIXON: — approval. Mitchell could say, "I ordered intelligence. But I never approved this goddamn plan." You've got to figure the lines of defense that everybody's going to take here — that's Mitchell's, right? What's Haldeman's line of defense? Haldeman's line of defense, "I never approved anything of this sort. I just" — you know that — what's Ehrlichman's? Ehrlichman — there's no doubt he knows nothing about it. The earlier thing, yes. We did have an operation for leaks, and so forth. What would you say if they said, "Did you ever do any wiretapping?" What would you say? There is a question on that. Were you aware of any wiretapping?

EHRLICHMAN: Yes.

NIXON: Then you would say, "Yes." Then, "Why did you do it?" You would say it was ordered on a national security basis.

EHRLICHMAN: National security. We had a series of very serious national security leaks.

"I'm too hot to do it now."
   March 27, 1973, 4:20 p.m.
   Bob Haldeman and John Dean
   WHITE HOUSE TELEPHONE

Within days of the "cancer on the presidency" conversation, the fallout was evident. John Dean was quickly becoming a public figure, which meant he could no longer quietly call Department of Justice Criminal Division head Henry Petersen to get the latest scoop on the grand jury's happenings — the schedule of witnesses to be called, the mood of the grand jury, and the current strategy of the prosecution. The Nixon cover-up strategy, and Dean's ability to continue as the Watergate "desk officer," was coming apart. Here, using one of

Nixon's telephones that was taped, Haldeman and Dean discuss ways to overcome their latest setback.

. . .

HALDEMAN: John?

DEAN: Yes, Bob.

HALDEMAN: What is our status on getting a report from grand jury activity now?

DEAN: I was just raising that with Dick Moore — to call — ask him if he would call Henry Petersen.

HALDEMAN: Okay.

DEAN: I used to do that, but I don't think I ought to do it right now.

HALDEMAN: All right, will Petersen talk tomorrow?

DEAN: I'm sure he will.

HALDEMAN: Okay. We're trying to reach Kleindienst now. He's gone to Arizona and we're ordering him back.

DEAN: Good.

HALDEMAN: Ehrlichman is. But we ought to know what happened today. We have to find out what Hunt did.

DEAN: Well, I would — I'll tell you what I was told. After we talked the last time, it was planned that Hunt was going to give a written statement, answer some questions they'd ask him, and take the Fifth on everything else.

HALDEMAN: Well, what is the written statement regarding?

DEAN: Nothing particularly sensitive.

HALDEMAN: And taking the Fifth on everything else, huh?

DEAN: Yeah.

HALDEMAN: Okay.

DEAN: Now, it's going to be hard to get a report out of counsel as to what occurred down there until five or six o'clock or so because they'll have been in court — they had a two o'clock meeting in court — counsel were to be present.

HALDEMAN: Oh. So, the grand jury didn't meet this afternoon?

DEAN: Hmm — yes, they did, but it was after that meeting. All counsel were present in the courtroom, and then Hunt was to go before the grand jury after that situation.

HALDEMAN: Mm-hmm. So, it's going to be going on now?

DEAN: [unclear]

HALDEMAN: Probably. Okay.

DEAN: We have a terrible breakdown in communication with both the committee and now the grand jury. I used to be able to stay plugged in with the grand jury, but I'm too hot to do it now.

HALDEMAN: Mm-hmm.

DEAN: I should call Dick right away and see if he's gotten a report, or —

HALDEMAN: Could Fielding step in and do that? The point being I don't think Dick [Moore]'s fast enough to handle your communication stuff for you.

DEAN: I agree. Let me talk to Fred. Press Henry to know his position — relationship with him. The — here's what the other thing is: he just probably won't know right now what's happened. [unclear] don't report to him hour by hour. He is — has not injected himself into it, so —

HALDEMAN: Mm-hmm.

DEAN: — probably it won't be until this — and you wouldn't get a report from him anyway.

HALDEMAN: Okay. He doesn't expect anything anyhow now.

DEAN: No. Let me tell you another development, though.

HALDEMAN: Okay?

DEAN: F. Lee Bailey called Mitchell. He called him initially to raise that thing that he, apparently — you know, that Mitchell raised down here.

HALDEMAN: That lawyer?

DEAN: That was the — he called on this thing that — you know, he's quiet regarding the gold reserve thing, and all —

HALDEMAN: Oh, yeah.

DEAN: — and then they went on from there and revealed this: that Fensterwald has called F. Lee or Alch — one of the two, I'm not clear on which it was — to ask that they be present in the court when McCord appears on Thursday or Friday. Ask that he, Fensterwald, be present. And —

HALDEMAN: To request that Fensterwald be present?

DEAN: Yeah, along — and join as co-counsel with Bailey's firm. And in the course of the conversation, Fensterwald said to Bailey, "We don't give a damn about McCord. We're after Richard Nixon."

HALDEMAN: Really?

DEAN: Mm-hmm. Now Moore, that's what he's working on right now. He's getting some of the facts back from — some additional information back from — and Mitchell will have F. Lee Bailey step forward. We should have a conference on this.

HALDEMAN: Yeah.

DEAN: Fensterwald put up his bond for one thing.

HALDEMAN: Yeah.

DEAN: And the more I think about Fensterwald, the more I think that could be a [unclear] link to Kennedy. The point was raised that Fensterwald served as the chief counsel to the Administrative Practice and Procedures Subcommittee, which was run by Ed Long, as chairman. Kennedy was the second-ranking member of that committee and then became chairman. I've — it's possible that Fensterwald was even on a while after Kennedy came on. Obviously, they have a relationship.

HALDEMAN: Mm-hmm.

DEAN: It's very, very possible.

HALDEMAN: Okay.

DEAN: Plus the fact that Fensterwald suddenly put up forty thousand dollars for McCord.

HALDEMAN: Okay.

DEAN: Okay?

HALDEMAN: Yup.

DEAN: Good.

HALDEMAN: Thanks.

"Sooner or later you're going to be subpoenaed to that grand jury."

March 29, 1973, 5:35 p.m.

John Ehrlichman and John Dean

WHITE HOUSE TELEPHONE

At the end of March, the Watergate investigation had not yet reached Haldeman or Ehrlichman, but it had reached Dean. The problem was that other witnesses were being called, and they were corroborating Dean's role in the lead-up to the break-in. Leaks from the grand jury were happening almost daily — to Congress, to the White House, and directly to the press. Ehrlichman, using one of Nixon's taped phones, discussed with Dean how to handle some of the difficult questions being raised. The next day, Ehrlichman would take over Dean's duties as Nixon's top advisor on Watergate.

• • •

EHRLICHMAN: John?

DEAN: Yes.

EHRLICHMAN: Returning your call.

DEAN: You're in with the boss right now?

EHRLICHMAN: Well, I just stepped out right now.

DEAN: Oh, okay. What I wanted to bring you up-to-date on is, first of all, how would you handle the question, if called: "Were you aware, either before or after the fact of the meetings in the attorney general's office?"

EHRLICHMAN: Well, you'd have to answer that — well, flat-out, I would think.

DEAN: I mean, how would you answer it?

EHRLICHMAN: Oh, you mean on the basis of hearsay?

DEAN: Yeah.

EHRLICHMAN: Oh, I'd have to say I was aware that there had been some. I had been told of one.

DEAN: Okay. Bob's in the same situation, right?

EHRLICHMAN: Yeah, you told me about one.

DEAN: It's one of these arguments that I should, you know, I'm getting a lot of pressure to go down and do something I'm not capable of doing. And [unclear] as to why it's feasible to even consider it.

EHRLICHMAN: Oh, well, I would never suggest to you that if you went you would anything but say what's true.

DEAN: I understand, I understand. But you understand the consequences of that.

EHRLICHMAN: Well, that was what I was trying to explore with you on the phone earlier.

DEAN: Well, what I was — I was talking to O'Brien about it a little bit further.

EHRLICHMAN: Mm-hmm?

DEAN: And what it'll do is open a — open war pissing match between Magruder, Mitchell, and Dean and the White House. The ultimate solution to this thing is — I mean, to deal with the problems from a post, as well as —

EHRLICHMAN: Mm-hmm?

DEAN: — anything pre- is something that John Mitchell's unwilling to face. He has this lingering hope that he can pull this out.

EHRLICHMAN: Mm-hmm.

DEAN: And it occurred to me — I don't know. Has the president ever talked this over with John?

EHRLICHMAN: Not that I know of.

DEAN: Well, it's a thought. I've mentioned this to Bob, too. That that might be the ultimate solution.

EHRLICHMAN: Well, my thought here is this: that regardless of what, you know, his — Mitchell's feral mind is, is that sooner or later you're going to be subpoenaed to that grand jury. Maybe you don't agree with that?

DEAN: Well, that's what O'Brien is saying — that maybe it won't happen. He's following pretty closely the tidbits that are coming out in the press on McCord.

EHRLICHMAN: Yeah?

DEAN: McCord, apparently, and upon close reading, has said that he understood that Liddy was going to a meeting in Mitchell's office. He would not just say that he was at a meeting.

EHRLICHMAN: Mm-hmm.

DEAN: I think we're reading too much into that press report. We haven't seen any —

EHRLICHMAN: Mm-hmm?

DEAN: — any transcripts or anything of that nature.

EHRLICHMAN: Mm-hmm.

DEAN: The other thing I want to know: did you — were you aware of Weicker's press conference?

EHRLICHMAN: No.

DEAN: Ha! He's supposed to go out and criticize the press for their leaks and [unclear] —

EHRLICHMAN: Yeah. Yeah.

DEAN: On the contrary, he went out and praised them for the beautiful, diligent job they're doing on this whole thing. And that the — the fact of the matter was that the man that ultimately is responsible for this is sitting in the White House today.

EHRLICHMAN: My word! Meaning whom?

DEAN: I don't know. [unclear] —

EHRLICHMAN: They didn't ask him?

DEAN: They didn't. He wouldn't reveal anything but he's done this independent investigation—it's a kind of a McCarthy-type style of thing—

EHRLICHMAN: Well, yeah, because, you know, we had Kleindienst and then Gray get
ahold of him and say, "What evidence do you have?" And he says, "Oh, I was just
talking about the Segretti business."

DEAN: Well, that's his latest.

EHRLICHMAN: Mm-hmm.

DEAN: It's—and it's—apparently it was not—you know, it did not infer Dean. It was
more of a—

EHRLICHMAN: Huh?

DEAN: Fielding, who picked this up from Gurney's men, said it was more like Haldeman.

EHRLICHMAN: Mm-hmm. Well, I think that really the basic question here is a—one
of prophecy as to whether or not you're going to be called or not. But if you are,
then obviously the best position to be in is that you volunteered. If you aren't, then
O'Brien's—

DEAN: That's the thing: if you volunteer it's sort of like you've—well, I can appreciate
the fact you want to go down and cleanse your name sort of [unclear] willing to do
that anytime. But, however, the grand jury has charged me with nothing right now—

EHRLICHMAN: I understand.

DEAN: —[unclear] denied everything.

EHRLICHMAN: Well, obviously, the angle would be one can't expect probity, fairness,
and guarantees of rights before a committee of the Senate that does the kinds of
things this committee's done in the last couple of days. My safe refuge is with the
grand jury.

DEAN: Well, and the thing is I really wonder if now is the time to volunteer that.

EHRLICHMAN: Well, of course, that's the question. That's the basic question. And I
gather you and O'Brien feel that it is not.

DEAN: I think we ought to wait and see how—there's always the chance I won't be
called.

EHRLICHMAN: Yeah, I see.

DEAN: Because they're working on about thirdhand hearsay.

EHRLICHMAN: But if you are then it'll be too late. They just won't care.

DEAN: That's right, but they're—

EHRLICHMAN: The question is whether it's worth the trade.

DEAN: That's right.

EHRLICHMAN: Yeah.

DEAN: The—and if [unclear] go down, then there we go.

EHRLICHMAN: Well, obviously, we're not in the position [laughs] to say you volunteered, unless you are. So, why don't we sleep on it, see where we are in the morning?

DEAN: Okay.

EHRLICHMAN: Okay, good.

DEAN: Bye-bye.

Strong words for North Vietnam
March 30, 1973, 1:09 p.m.
Richard Nixon and Alexander Haig
WHITE HOUSE TELEPHONE

On the evening of March 29, Nixon made his first nationally televised speech to the na-
tion since January 23, when he announced the Vietnam Peace Accords. It was a dramatic
gesture and he used it skillfully, sounding "tough and combative," according to a reporter
for the New York Times. *Nixon expressed his dissatisfaction with North Vietnam's con-*
tinuing mobilization along the border with the South. In terms far stronger than those he'd
used in the middle of the month, he asserted his willingness to begin the bombing again.
Discussing the same decision with Haig the next day, the president seemed frustrated that
"Vietnamization" only meant that the Communists were still his problem. He pounced on
a suggestion that perhaps it was South Vietnam that would initiate the bombing — not a
peaceful prospect, but one that might keep America out of the lingering hostilities.*

• • •

NIXON: As you know, I'm leaving for California soon, and I just read a very ominous memorandum from Henry about his concern about the North Vietnamese buildup, and all that sort of thing and so on.

HAIG: Right, sir.

NIXON: And what's happening in Cambodia. Now you may recall when we made the decision last week not to do the [Ho Chi Minh] Trail, Henry, at that time, was sort of pushing for it but then he backed off some when they had that twenty-third day — oh, you know, in Laos. I still think it was wise that we probably didn't do that. I don't know that we had the provoca — I mean, the — I mean, I don't think we had the public provocation set up obviously. But I don't know. What do you think?

HAIG: I think that last week's timing was not —

NIXON: It wasn't the right time.

HAIG: It wasn't right. It just —

NIXON: Yeah, yeah.

HAIG: It was an awfully tough one and —

NIXON: Yeah.

HAIG: — a tightly balanced one.

NIXON: Right. Everything is that. In any event, that doesn't mean you can't do it. But what is your present evaluation, Al, as to yourself as you look at the whole situation?

HAIG: I'm getting increasingly concerned about Cambodia.

NIXON: Cambodia? But what about the thing — you see, these intelligence reports, you know, the thing you had talked about now, they seem to be going almost overboard in the direction of indicating that everything is going to hell in a hat. I'm not — I

---

* John Herbers, "President Warns Hanoi to Comply with Truce Pact," *New York Times*, March 30, 1973, p. 1.

don't know that it — you know, they've — I — it's just hard for — you know, you've been analyzing them. I don't know. What do you see in the thing —

HAIG: Well, I —

NIXON: — and, incidentally, what the hell is the South doing? Good God, they've got a hell of a big army. I mean, yes, sir, are they — aren't they doing a little fighting themselves?

HAIG: Yes, they are —

NIXON: The number of incidents is actually down some, is it not? Or, not much, but — ?

HAIG: No, the incident rate has been slowly and very mildly decreasing.

NIXON: But only mildly, right. I noticed — that's what I meant. Some, but just very slowly. Yeah.

HAIG: But I think the, the danger is that there are a combination of reasons for it in Cambodia. There have been a series of violations across the board in Laos, South Vietnam, and, of course, no action at all in Cambodia, although we didn't expect that initially. The areas that worry me the most are the broad applications of the overall agreement in Laos, and in South Vietnam, with infiltration, incidents, refusal to investigate. And this — when you combine that with what could be happening in Cambodia, it is reason for some concern. I really — I think it is. But I don't think it's a — it's an immediate thing in the sense of we've got a crisis.

NIXON: Yeah.

HAIG: I think we have an obligation to take a look at every kind of leverage we can —

NIXON: Yeah.

HAIG: — apply to this.

NIXON: You see, the problem we've got, Al, here is on the — that we mustn't get into is the sort of the crisis mentality that like on Cambodia that, well, we'll start to bomb on the — well, we're bombing the hell, there, out of it already, you know.

HAIG: That's right.

NIXON: Good God, I don't know. Are they hitting anything? What is the situation?

HAIG: Well, there are indications that they're hitting it so hard that they're driving a lot of the North Vietnamese into South Vietnam. You know, in that —

NIXON: That's not good.

HAIG: — [unclear] area. Well, no. That's good, I think.

NIXON: It's good to get them out of there.

HAIG: It disrupts them and it keeps them under pressure. And, it takes some of the heat off of Lon Nol.

NIXON: To what extent do you feel that — would you feel right now that we ought to start hitting the — well, I don't mean like today, but maybe next week — start hitting the Panhandle again?

HAIG: I wouldn't discount that. No, I wouldn't, sir. I think the thing that I'm not aware of is what we've said to our customer up there in Hanoi. If we've given him good, strong warnings, I think — well, if we do anything, it's got to be — we've got to make a lot of things evident to him that we're nearing the breaking point.

NIXON: Yeah. Well, of course, I put a very strong warning in that speech last night.

HAIG: That's right.

NIXON: And they can't just ignore that.

HAIG: No.

NIXON: I think — I — strong warnings have gone, I can assure you. Private warnings —

HAIG: Yes.

NIXON: — goddamn strong.

HAIG: Well, then I — I think we should take a very careful look at all of the possible leverage we have. And, we don't have to — it shouldn't be done in a crisis atmosphere, but in a very steely way.

NIXON: See, we got this problem; you have to face it. We've got it growing, building up with the goddamn Congress, now. They all want to stop us doing anything in Cambodia.

HAIG: That's right.

NIXON: Now —

HAIG: We can't do this justified on the Cambodian situation. The only way we'll ever get away with anything, if there's a decision to do it, is in the context of a sacred agreement —

NIXON: Well, the fact — I think we've got to do it not to save Cambodia but because they broke an agreement.

HAIG: Exactly right.

NIXON: Exactly.

HAIG: That's —

NIXON: And that we are keeping an agreement, and that they violated an agreement, and we're therefore continuing ahead. I think as long as it's air operations, that people will generally support it, too.

HAIG: Yes, I do too. I don't think it — there would be a problem with — you know, if we had decided that earlier that if we hit Laos or something. Hell, that's not going to be much of a stir.

NIXON: Yeah, if — except that, before the POWs are out, the one problem, rather symbolically that would have been very bad is that it — before they were out — that you'd lose some planes and have some more.

HAIG: Yeah.

NIXON: You know?

HAIG: And, I think a lot of people will — would say, "Well, you're dumb — "

NIXON: Yeah.

HAIG: " — to have done it that — "

NIXON: That's right.

HAIG: " — that way."

NIXON: But now, again, at this point we can just have to take a damn hard look if these guys are willing to.

HAIG: I think so. I think this — if it were over time to really seriously erode, the price would be incalculable. It just would be very serious. And that we've always played for enough time for other events to — just to —

NIXON: Overrun it, yeah.

HAIG: — pull away from our obligations worldwide. And that's what we've got to have. We've just got to have that.

NIXON: You can't have it collapse, like, immediately.

HAIG: No.

NIXON: That's the point. And, you sure, sure as hell can't have it collapse. Well, as you know, we've been very tough with the Russians, and they claim they're pulling the string, but I don't know. I doubt it.

HAIG: It — there sure isn't an awful [laughs] — much sign of any, anything —

NIXON: Well, it's — and, it — maybe they're pulling the string at the pipeline, but they're — pulling the string, but the pipeline is so full, that it hasn't had any effect yet.

HAIG: Yes. Yeah. Well, I think we should do a very thorough job. Actually, Henry's kicked one off in the WSAG. I'm not confident that it'll be the best thing in the world, but —

NIXON: You mean a, a study?

HAIG: Yes. It's a — he's formed a little interdepartmental group —

NIXON: Yeah, I know.

HAIG: — to solve it.

NIXON: They won't come out. That won't do much. But, anyway, we've got to get something, and we'll have to — we got to line up our, our forces within the government on this, goddamn it.

HAIG: This is right.

NIXON: As we can't have any, any flinching once we —

HAIG: That's —

NIXON: Now one thing that's been mentioned, as probably Henry's talked to you, that I might want you to go out there to Cambodia and take a look.

HAIG: Well, that'd be fine.

NIXON: I don't know what the hell you — but what the hell are you going to find out? I mean, what can we do? They can't —

HAIG: It's just the —

NIXON: They've got to get Lon Nol the hell out of there, some way or other, but you can't overthrow him. But —

HAIG: I don't think we should rush on it in the context of the recent flurry on the Hill. It'll just look like a —

NIXON: Yeah.

HAIG: And it will —

NIXON: I get your point.

HAIG: — increase that syndrome, that we're doing it for Cambodia.

NIXON: Right.

HAIG: We don't want that.

NIXON: You could go out and look at both.

HAIG: That's right.

NIXON: That's what — you might just visit all the areas. That's the way, I think, you're — I mean, if you took a trip, I think you should visit all.

HAIG: That's right. So, it's just —

NIXON: Right.

HAIG: — just an overall assessment.

NIXON: That's right. Fine. Well, certainly, if the DRV continues this kind of asshole stuff, which I — we [laughs] — we're off the hook on the aid thing. That's for damn sure.

HAIG: Oh, yeah.

NIXON: And that's, that's — I don't know if they want it or not. But if they do want it, good God, they are — they aren't going to get it. Not — not as long as they're rolling — doing this. And another thing, too, is that these POWs are now gonna be talking about how they've been lacerated, and —

HAIG: Well, you see, that's right. And that's going to build up a hell of a — you know, among the average American, yesterday's television, and this morning's, is going to raise a hell of a lot of hackles with these monkeys, because this was brutal treatment. And, I don't think you're going to find a lot of people that are going to be patient with — patient with their, now, violating these agreements.

NIXON: If they're in violation, no way.

HAIG: That's right.

NIXON: No way.

HAIG: That's why we have to — that's the theme we have to use, and we have to start drawing attention to it where it's happening. We did that last week. You gave a good shot last night.

NIXON: Mm-hmm.

HAIG: We're looking at every possible military preparatory —

NIXON: Right.

HAIG: — signal —

NIXON: Right.

HAIG: — in character. And that's what we're doing over here right now. We're working on a paper —

NIXON: Right. Right, right. That's — what's Abrams's evaluation? Or is he — about the same as yours?

HAIG: I think so. I think so. He — he's concerned about it. He knows we can't have the thing happen quickly, but he's also — he doesn't panic and doesn't —

NIXON: He also knows — I guess what we got to also realize, Al, is that if Vietnamization meant anything, good God, the South Vietnamese, looking at their situation, ought to be able to do something here. I don't know.

HAIG: They could. There's no question about that. And they're —

NIXON: Hell, they've got —

HAIG: — not going to get upset here in a, in a six-month period. It just couldn't happen. They're —

NIXON: Yeah, Henry was saying that he's — in his memo this morning, I think he's gone a little bit overboard. Here he says that he thinks that there might be even a North — a big Communist offensive in April. Hell, that's, that's three weeks — two weeks away.

HAIG: Well, the intelligence community is — what CIA came in with — they said there could be —

NIXON: Yeah?

HAIG: — an offensive in April.

NIXON: Jesus. I just — I don't —

HAIG: Thieu will probably make that point to you.

NIXON: Yeah, so? So, what does he want us to do, send our forces back in?

HAIG: No, I don't think so.

NIXON: No.

HAIG: No, I don't —

NIXON: He wants us to bomb?

HAIG: I'm not sure that he wants anything other than, maybe, understanding if he takes some action.

NIXON: Yeah.

HAIG: I don't think we'll get any panic from him.

NIXON: Well, as a matter of fact, I don't give a damn if he takes some action. I mean, as far as the cease-fire is concerned now, and — if they're breaking it, he can break it. I mean — and, he could take some rather effective action, couldn't he?

HAIG: Oh, yes. He could take those missiles out of Khe Sanh, and he could put a —

NIXON: With his own air, couldn't he?

HAIG: With his own air. He could put some heavy strikes in around that MR-3 [Military Region 3, which stretched from the northern Mekong Delta to the southern Central Highlands]. In Tay Ninh, they've been constantly taking on this little ARVN unit there, and pounding the hell out of them. They won't let any investigators in and you know, but it's not — none of this is major. It's the compounding of the whole —

NIXON: Yeah.

HAIG: — the whole picture.

NIXON: Cambodia, the real problem there basically is getting a government, Al. Good God, we're putting money in, and we don't have any advisors there. That's —

HAIG: That's right.

NIXON: I don't know.

HAIG: The same strategic considerations that drove us in '70 are — could appear if that country went Communist.

NIXON: Of course. Of course. Well, okay, Al. Thank you.

HAIG: Yes, sir.

NIXON: Bye.

APRIL

A frank talk about war protesters

April 9, 1973, 5:03 p.m.

Richard Nixon, John Flynn, and Brent Scowcroft

OVAL OFFICE

*From April 1 through 8, Nixon was at his home in San Clemente, California. The day of his return, he made time to meet with a veteran pilot who had been a staunch supporter despite being in Hanoi during the entirety of the Nixon presidency. Colonel John Flynn had spent more than five years as a prisoner of war, returning to the United States on March 14, 1973. Originally from Cleveland, Flynn started flying in the National Guard before World War II and then piloted P-51 Mustang fighter planes in the European Theater during 1944–45. He stayed in the air force and was still flying more than twenty years later, when he was assigned as vice commander of a fighter wing operating out of Thailand. After his F-105 Thunderchief was shot down in October 1967, he was captured. He was incarcerated in Hanoi, where he was recognized as senior ranking officer. Flynn is credited with a hands-on style of maintaining order. As soon as possible after returning to the United States and regaining his health, Flynn met with the president, who shared his disdain for the peace movement. With Flynn, Nixon felt free to explain how the antiwar movement had affected the war.**

• • •

NIXON: Well, it's good to see you — as the — for all the obvious reasons. [unclear]

FLYNN: Mr. President, you probably don't remember this but I met you in the Philippines one time —

NIXON: Did you?

FLYNN: Yes, sir. You met me at the elevator and I was a member of the National War College. We were on a trip. We were in Manila, and I think you were there on private business. You were going to the elevator, there was a group of us, three or four, and I know you will not remember this —

NIXON: Tell me the year.

FLYNN: 'Sixty-four — about '64.

NIXON: I would have been on a private trip then.

FLYNN: Yes, sir. You were —

NIXON: Hotel Manila?

FLYNN: Yes, sir, I don't recall the name of the hotel.

---

* VeteranTributes.org, "John P. Flynn"; www.af.mil, "Lieutenant General John P. Flynn."

NIXON: It would have been. It's the only one. Downtown? The old hotel then. Yeah.

FLYNN: Yes, sir. You were kind enough to sit there and chat with us, as we — you took a moment or two with us. Of course, it was a memorable moment for us, meeting the former vice president at the time. We have a mutual friend, a man by the name of Don Hughes — Jim Hughes —

NIXON: You call him Jim?

FLYNN: Yes, sir.

NIXON: He is out in Thailand I think.

FLYNN: Yes, sir. He is with the Thirteenth —

NIXON: I am going to bring him back for the party on the twenty-fourth. The reason we are going to do that is that he was my military aide here. He and Scowcroft were in charge of our liaison office and so forth. So Don used to talk to those poor gals [unclear] and so forth. He was such a comfort to them because of his own record, et cetera, you know.

FLYNN: Yes, sir.

NIXON: So I thought I would have him flown back here for the party.

FLYNN: Mm-hmm.

NIXON: In fact, we're not having — you see we're not going to have any cabinet officers and no other VIPs but I'm just going to have Hughes, and you, of course, and [unclear] fellows here [unclear].

FLYNN: Yes, sir. Oh, that's so very kind of you to do that.

NIXON: I wanted to do it earlier, but I talked to some earlier — [fellow POWs Jeremiah] Denton and [Robinson] Risner, who of course were out earlier — and they both agreed that we should wait until after — about a couple of months until after everybody was back —

FLYNN: Yes, sir.

NIXON: — and so everybody gets a chance to, you know, sort of get their feet back on the ground and so forth — get — their wits collected. So May will be a nice time — the twenty-fourth. It should be pretty out here if it doesn't rain. We are going to have to have it under a big tent because there is so many —

FLYNN: Yes, sir.

NIXON: — you know, the state dining room only seats a hundred and ten.

FLYNN: [laughs]

NIXON: And we — well, the things that I think [unclear]. There were three weeks —

FLYNN: Yes, sir, Mr. President. No —

NIXON: Was it the year — by a chance I heard on one of those trips [unclear] for old times. There was a group, the survivors of the Bataan were celebrating and having a party out there. You remember that — that group was not there?

FLYNN: No, sir.

NIXON: Later?

FLYNN: You told us that you were over there in —

NIXON: That's right.

FLYNN: — just can I — can I just mention it because I had seen all the presidents since the president of the United States —

NIXON: Right. That day?

FLYNN: — that day at the elevator with you.

NIXON: Well that day was something.

FLYNN: But you were still very kind to us.

NIXON: Well, it's one of those days. Were you on your way then to Vietnam?

FLYNN: No, sir. This was —

NIXON: You were with the War College.

FLYNN: — the National War College, and it was one of our typical trips.

• • •

NIXON: Well, you know, you as a senior officer can be enormously proud of what your men went through, what they have done for the morale and the spirit of this country as they return. The nation, as you know, has gone through a very difficult period — it was frankly difficult to survive here in these past four years, perhaps more difficult than the previous four years, because the longer the war goes on the more the people get tired.

FLYNN: Yes, sir.

NIXON: So, each year it has gone on more and more, and I sat in this office — President Johnson, of course, had considerable problems, but they never got to the riot stage — I mean it didn't get to the demonstration stage. [unclear] in October or November why — honestly in October there was about — one march of two hundred fifty thousand around this place, up to three hundred thousand after Cambodia [unclear]. But you know you see those ragtag, they were all ragtag son of a bitches — peaceniks, Quakers — and I'm a Quaker, just — nevertheless. But it was across this country I have [unclear], across this country as I campaigned in 1972, [unclear] and also in all the trips I made around the country it never failed beyond a doubt that I had some demonstrators, and they were vicious, that they — you see, I didn't mind the men, but what concerned me you see little fifteen-year-old girls, you know, a fourteen-year-old went out and dared me, had the finger up, you know, and saying the usual words. And [unclear] but you know that's the kind of thing that makes you wonder what's going to happen to the country. We survived it, I must say, only because — not because the leader class in this country did so very well, because it was rather shameful in its performance — the leaders in the media, the intellectuals, even some of the business people, the Congress with some exceptions — but mainly because out in the country, what are called the common people, God bless them, in some way said well, life is [unclear] see it through the right way. That is what we tried to do, isn't it? And I can't even describe it. I think it was right. I mean I say it was right, but as you know we have a sticky time now. These people up there [unclear] the hearings [unclear] on Laos, on Cambodia [unclear] and the rest. But on the other hand, at least the main thing is that we have solved Vietnam now. The government which is non-Communist — they have the strength to defend themselves, and we ended the long war without basically getting down on our knees and saying just give us our prisoners and we'll get out.

FLYNN: Yes, sir.

NIXON: Had we done that I think your fellows would have been —

FLYNN: We would have been ashamed to come home under those circumstances.

NIXON: Really?

FLYNN: Yes, sir.

NIXON: Had you heard that offer that Congress had voted several times?

FLYNN: Sir. Yes, sir. We had heard that —

NIXON: I told him — I told him "pay attention." That's what they wanted.

FLYNN: Yes, sir. Sir, we understood to a small degree the complexities of the problems here that were facing you. Many of us had studied international affairs and we knew the options and the alternatives facing you. I had my own left-wing and right-wing — very conservative center, and to a very small extent I understood the pressures that you must have been under.

NIXON: You had to make your [unclear].

FLYNN: Yes, sir. And I knew that the problems which faced you were very tough —

NIXON: You know, even if you're right, left, or center most of them wanted to come back right away.

FLYNN: Oh, absolutely, sir. Yes, sir. They wanted it, too.

NIXON: You see, the respect — the point is, it isn't just a question of honor on your sleeve, but the point is that the United States is the only hope that the world now has for a chance for peace with any degree of [unclear]. Now, if the United States [unclear] its credit either amongst its allies or even more importantly among its potential enemies, anytime that is impaired the chances for peace really just goes down.

FLYNN: Yes, sir.

NIXON: That is why we had to see it through. That is why you had to suffer what you had to go through. And that is why it is — it's what the American people [unclear].

FLYNN: Yes, sir. And I want to assure you, Mr. President, that we did not mind that suffering. Our motto — I think you've been told this — is return with honor, and everyone believed in that motto. In fact we —

NIXON: Your motto?

FLYNN: Yes, sir. And we are going to get a plaque with that on it and —

NIXON: Great. You are going to present that on the twenty-fourth?

FLYNN: Yes, sir. We hope it —

NIXON: Great! I would love that.

"Mitchell was the linchpin in this thing."

April 14, 1973, 8:55 a.m.

Richard Nixon, Bob Haldeman, and John Ehrlichman

EXECUTIVE OFFICE BUILDING

After Nixon returned from San Clemente, according to Dean, he adhered to a self-imposed rule against speaking about Watergate with Mitchell, Colson, or Dean, among others. He was distancing himself from those who had grown vulnerable, while using Ehrlichman and Haldeman to plan strategy. The Watergate conversations recorded on April 14 reflect a microcosm of the scandal, which played out with so many shifting alliances on that single Saturday that it is a wonder it didn't make those involved dizzy. It did test the president. In the earliest conversation of the six, when Ehrlichman related that his research had determined at least ten people in the White House knew about the Watergate break-in in advance, Nixon chimed in, "I knew it, I knew it." He immediately tried to pull that comment back, although neither Haldeman nor Ehrlichman was shocked by that point. Their discussion was full of references to criminal activity, in the form of illegal financial transactions, slander, or burglary. The conclusion of their early-morning planning session was to present the White House as having taken control of the investigations and that the president's staff had learned that John Mitchell and Jeb Magruder were behind the Watergate break-in. Nixon would appear as an innocent man and, moreover, a heroic president, rooting out unethical colleagues: Mitchell, head of CRP, and Magruder, his assistant. According to the new plan, Ehrlichman would inform Mitchell of Nixon's stance; Haldeman was to tell Magruder. The plan was that neither would avoid testifying but would instead admit to planning Watergate. In some fashion, Nixon would then make sure they would not serve time for their mistakes.

• • •

NIXON: Let me ask, did you reach any conclusions as to where we are — recommendations?

EHRLICHMAN: No. No conclusions.

NIXON: Problems?

EHRLICHMAN: Dick Wilson, I think, is — has an interesting column this morning.

NIXON: In the *Post*?

EHRLICHMAN: Yeah, it's [unclear] money problem. He's been analyzing this money problem [unclear].

HALDEMAN: [unclear]

EHRLICHMAN: Oh, yeah, last night.

NIXON: Wilson is in the [*Washington Evening*] *Star.*

EHRLICHMAN: Well, then it is twice he made this point.

NIXON: So what?

EHRLICHMAN: [unclear] argues that really the essence of this whole thing is too much money, too easily spent, and so on. And then he [unclear] — that's his great underlying —

NIXON: Yeah. That's what everybody — that's what —

HALDEMAN: No, not everybody. That's a one par —

NIXON: Well, Reston lies.

HALDEMAN: — one group thesis —

NIXON: Yeah.

HALDEMAN: — that Reston —

NIXON: That's right.

HALDEMAN: — Reston has on that side — and why Stans says — he carries it beyond — he says solving Watergate doesn't take care of it, but then there's all the money in —

NIXON: Dick wants the president to speak out on the whole general issue of money and campaign and that sort of —

EHRLICHMAN: Basically that's — generally, but he gets specific on this. He says also [unclear].

NIXON: Is that what you think — go out and make a speech?

EHRLICHMAN: No, I'll tell you what I think. I think that the president's personal involvement in this is important. And I don't —

NIXON: Yeah.

EHRLICHMAN: — I don't think it's a speech.

NIXON: Well, that's the point. I think it's — there're other ways you can get at it. Now, I was thinking of the — before we get into that, though, let's get back — that's something we can get into later. I'd like to get — I'd like to go in, if I could, to what your conversation with Colson was and, in essence. What was his — what did he and the lawyer come to tell you about?

HALDEMAN: Hunt's visit.

EHRLICHMAN: That visit was to tell me that Hunt was going to testify on Monday afternoon.

NIXON: How does he know that?

HALDEMAN: Mm-hmm.

NIXON: How does he get such information?

EHRLICHMAN: Undoubtedly through Bittman.

NIXON: Right.

EHRLICHMAN: Or Bittman through Shapiro.

NIXON: Now why is Hunt testifying? Did he say? Or what —

EHRLICHMAN: He didn't say.

NIXON: — he's testifying about —

EHRLICHMAN: He said — I'll tell you what he said and then I'll tell you what I think the fact is. He said Hunt was testifying because there was no longer any point in being silent. That so many other people were testifying that there was no — he wasn't really keeping any secrets.

NIXON: Yeah. Yeah.

EHRLICHMAN: Couldn't add much. My feeling is that Bittman got very antsy when this grand jury started focusing on the aftermath —

NIXON: And he, of course, was involved in —

EHRLICHMAN: That's it exactly. And then he went to the U.S. attorney and said, "Maybe I can persuade my client to talk."

NIXON: Oh. What does — what do Colson et al. — Colson and Shapiro — think we ought to do under these circumstances? Get busy and nail Wilson [Magruder] and nail Mitchell in a hurry? Is that what he means?

EHRLICHMAN: Yes.

NIXON: How is that going to help?

EHRLICHMAN: Well, they feel that —

NIXON: [unclear] I just want to get the best [unclear].

EHRLICHMAN: — they feel that after Hunt testifies that the whole thing's going to fall in short order.

NIXON: Right.

EHRLICHMAN: That Mitchell and Magruder will involuntarily be indicted.

NIXON: Right.

EHRLICHMAN: Both of them say —

NIXON: Right.

EHRLICHMAN: — that you have lost any possibility of initiative, so — for participation —

NIXON: So, what does Colson say to do?

EHRLICHMAN: He wants you to do several things. He wants you to persuade Liddy to talk.

NIXON: Me?

EHRLICHMAN: Yes, sir. That's his — I didn't bring my notes, but basically —

NIXON: Oh. Last night you didn't mention this, but that's all right.

EHRLICHMAN: Oh, I thought I had.

NIXON: Maybe you did. Maybe you did.

EHRLICHMAN: I didn't — I didn't —

NIXON: [unclear]

EHRLICHMAN: — in any event, he didn't —

NIXON: I would bring — he — let Liddy in and tell him to talk?

EHRLICHMAN: You can't bring him in. He's in jail. But —

NIXON: Oh.

EHRLICHMAN: You would send — you'd send word to him, and of course wanting him to make full disclosure or in some way you would be activist on this score.

NIXON: Yeah.

HALDEMAN: There's no — that isn't — doesn't involve any real problem. As Dean points out Liddy is not talking because he thinks he's supposed not to talk. If he is supposed to talk, he will. All he needs is a signal if you want to turn Liddy up.

NIXON: Yeah, oh — yeah. But the point that —

HALDEMAN: Face it, he believes —

NIXON: — Colson wants is a public signal. Is that right?

HALDEMAN: No, he [unclear].

NIXON: A public signal [unclear] what the hell do you do?

EHRLICHMAN: He wants to be able to be able to say afterward that you cracked the case.

NIXON: Go ahead. What else?

EHRLICHMAN: Well, I forget what else. Do you remember, Bob?

HALDEMAN: Well, that was basically his [unclear].

EHRLICHMAN: Basically it — he feels that the next forty-eight hours are the last chance —

NIXON: Mm-hmm.

EHRLICHMAN: — for the White House to get out in front of this and that once Hunt goes on then that's the ball game.

NIXON: But you've got to be out in front earlier.

EHRLICHMAN: Well —

NIXON: But, I mean — sorry, not earlier, but publicly.

EHRLICHMAN: Either —

NIXON: I —

EHRLICHMAN: — either publicly or with provable, identifiable steps which can be referred to later as having been the proximate cause.

NIXON: He's just not talking because he thinks the president doesn't want him to talk? Is that the point?

EHRLICHMAN: He's — according to them — Mitchell's given him a promise of a pardon through Bittman?

NIXON: Yeah.

EHRLICHMAN: Yeah — according to Colson and Shapiro. And I don't know where they get that.

NIXON: Mitchell has promised Liddy a pardon?

EHRLICHMAN: Yes, sir.

NIXON: Other points that Colson may not have mentioned — I have an uneasy feeling that Magruder story may have been planted.

HALDEMAN: Oh.

NIXON: Or is it true?

HALDEMAN: Apparently there's a third Magruder phone call which I haven't heard that says —

NIXON: Says he did talk to the press?

HALDEMAN: — says he did talk to a reporter on Monday — did not say any of the things he's reported to have said, that — what he — that he said it wasn't an important conversation. He said the same — he gave the reporter the same line.

NIXON: Yeah.

HALDEMAN: That you know — but in listening to Magruder's thing —

NIXON: All right.

HALDEMAN: — I was convinced he wasn't completely telling the truth that he — in what he was saying. As you get into it, I'm convinced that his [unclear] that part was pretty much —

NIXON: Yeah.

HALDEMAN: — prepared.

NIXON: But in coming to this — all these pieces must be put together now. But you come to Magruder — where the hell does Colson get such a thing? Or is Colson a liar or —

EHRLICHMAN: Shapiro says he has a very good press contact who has proved very reliable to him and he says his practice in this town depends on his knowing what's going on. And he's [unclear] press contact. This is one of the — and he's always found it to be —

NIXON: He says that he's talked to Magruder and Magruder said that —

HALDEMAN: Yeah. What they've now told us is we'll never get the transcript. That he —

NIXON: Magruder — think Magruder may have done this?

EHRLICHMAN: I think Magruder may have talked to somebody in the press and that was —

[Unclear exchange]

NIXON: But in the great detail that Colson went into — that he nailed Bob Haldeman — I mean the way Colson did, he says he had Colson in the tube —

EHRLICHMAN: Yeah.

NIXON: — but not in any way that was particularly bad. Right?

EHRLICHMAN: Well, I think like so many things, this got planted as a little seed by Shapiro with Colson and that it grew and —

NIXON: Oh, yeah?

EHRLICHMAN: Mm-hmm. I'd just —

HALDEMAN: I would guess what's happened is he's got this report from — Colson does — from [CRP finance committee member] Danny Hofgren that at the bar in the Bahamas or Bermuda or something and one night said to Hofgren, "Jesus, everybody was involved in this." He didn't use the —

NIXON: Mm-hmm.

EHRLICHMAN: Everybody knew about it.

HALDEMAN: Mitchell, Haldeman, Colson, Dean, the president —

NIXON: Magruder —

HALDEMAN: He specifically said the president.

NIXON: Magruder doesn't believe that, though, does he?

HALDEMAN: No. You know, I've got it — I've got —

NIXON: I just wonder if he believes it. I'm curious because — do you think he believes it, John?

EHRLICHMAN: No. This tape's very convincing and Higby handled it so well that Magruder has closed all those doors now with this tape.

NIXON: What good will that do, John?

EHRLICHMAN: Sure, it beats the socks off him if he ever gets off the reservation.

NIXON: Can you use the tape?

EHRLICHMAN: Well, no. You can use Higby.

HALDEMAN: Why can't you use the tape?

NIXON: Well — it's illegal?

HALDEMAN: No, it's not.

EHRLICHMAN: Yeah.

HALDEMAN: It is not.

NIXON: Unless you tell somebody —

HALDEMAN: No, sir.

EHRLICHMAN: No beeper on it.

HALDEMAN: There is no beeper required. You check the Washington law.

NIXON: Yeah.

HALDEMAN: District of Columbia is under federal law and the federal law does not require disclosure to the other party of the recording of phone conversations. The phone call was made to Magruder's lawyer's office which is also in the District of Columbia so both ends of the conversation were in the District of Columbia and there is no law requiring disclosure.

EHRLICHMAN: Well, that's interesting.

HALDEMAN: It's perfectly legal.

NIXON: Well, anyway —

HALDEMAN: It may be admissible, but it's legal.

NIXON: That's interesting. That's a new one. [unclear] beep every — while then — now and then. I thought it was. However, I never heard anybody beeping — I know they've taken it off.

HALDEMAN: It all depends on where you are. Some — the basic law in most states is that you must disclose to the other party that you're recording the conversation.

NIXON: Yeah. What is the situation — I might — I'll get past this in a hurry — what is the situation, John, in your opinion on what was Colson's and/or Shapiro's motive in building up the Magruder story? Maybe they believe it.

EHRLICHMAN: Their innuendo is that Mitchell has put Magruder up to this.

NIXON: I guess not. Okay. There's the motive. Now, let me come to something else.

HALDEMAN: I don't believe that Magruder's —

NIXON: I don't either. Not at all.

HALDEMAN: I don't believe Mitchell has tried to —

NIXON: Huh?

HALDEMAN: I don't believe Mitchell tried to [unclear] Magruder's faith because he refers to Mitchell and "now that I have decided to talk I am going to tell Mr. Mitchell and he's going to be very unhappy with me because he's told me not to."

NIXON: [unclear] tape, uh —

HALDEMAN: I did.

NIXON: And he's an emotional fellow who's ready to crack.

EHRLICHMAN: I — really, I have no doubt that he's ready to talk.

NIXON: What is he — he hasn't been subpoenaed yet, has he?

EHRLICHMAN: Well, he won't be. But he's already been there.

[Unclear exchange]

EHRLICHMAN: Dean doesn't think they'll give him a chance back unless he comes running at them and just spills it.

HALDEMAN: Because (a) they don't call the suspects and (b) they don't recall a perjury witness.

NIXON: Right. What would you do if you were his lawyer? Wouldn't you advise him to go in and try and purge himself, at least get rid of one charge, doesn't he?

EHRLICHMAN: I'm not sure he's rid of it, but it certainly reduces it when he comes in voluntarily.

NIXON: The way I understand it under the law, John, if he were to come to the —

EHRLICHMAN: But he's hooked.

NIXON: — grand jury.

EHRLICHMAN: Yeah, but he's hooked, see? There's contrary evidence already —

NIXON: Oh, I see.

EHRLICHMAN: — before the grand jury.

NIXON: In other words —

EHRLICHMAN: If he did that —

NIXON: Strachan got in before there was [unclear] evidence.

EHRLICHMAN: Exactly —

HALDEMAN: [unclear]

NIXON: Strachan?

HALDEMAN: No, [unclear] —

NIXON: [unclear]

HALDEMAN: — Magruder.

EHRLICHMAN: And you take the circumstances, now —

NIXON: They better have —

EHRLICHMAN: Yeah. If it's known, for instance, that Hunt is going to come in and testify, then Magruder comes rushing in and says, "I want to tell all," it's — you know —

NIXON: Magruder's stuck on both counts.

EHRLICHMAN: Yeah, but I think he could improve it. I think he really could help to purge himself.

NIXON: [unclear] I've come to the — may I come to the other things that you talked to Colson about? If Hunt going to talk, what is Hunt going to say? Do we have any idea?

EHRLICHMAN: Yes.

NIXON: He says — for example, will he say that Colson promised him clemency?

EHRLICHMAN: No. Apparently not.

NIXON: And you see the only possible involvement of the president in this is that — now apparently, John, either you or Bob — or Dean, somebody told me they said Cols — told Colson not to discuss it with me.

EHRLICHMAN: I did.

NIXON: You did. How did, bar — how did it get to you then, John? How did you know that the matter had to be discussed with Bittman or something like that?

EHRLICHMAN: Well, I —

NIXON: When did this happen?

EHRLICHMAN: I had —

NIXON: I remember a conversation this day, it was about five thirty or six o'clock, that Colson only dropped it in sort of parenthetically. He said, "I had a little problem today" — and we were talking about the defendants — and I said, I sought to reassure him, you know, and so forth. And I said, "Well, that's" — told me about Hunt's wife. He said, "It's a terrible thing," and I said, "Obviously we'll do just, we will take that into consideration." And that was the total of the conversation.

EHRLICHMAN: Well, I had — we had had a couple of conversations in my office —

NIXON: With Colson?

EHRLICHMAN: With, or — I had with Colson. Yeah.

NIXON: Well, how was —

EHRLICHMAN: And I, uh —

NIXON: — who was getting — who was — was Bittman getting to Colson? Was that the point? Who — ?

EHRLICHMAN: No, Hunt had written to Colson.

NIXON: Oh?

EHRLICHMAN: Hunt wrote Colson a very — "I've been abandoned" kind of letter.

NIXON: Yeah. When was this, John?

EHRLICHMAN: I am sorry, I —

NIXON: After the election?

EHRLICHMAN: Oh, yes. Yeah.

NIXON: Oh, and how did Colson — you knew about this letter?

EHRLICHMAN: Colson came in to tell me about it. And he said, "What shall I do?" And I said, "Well, better talk to him — I think somebody'd better talk to him. The guy is obviously very distraught — "

NIXON: Right.

EHRLICHMAN: " — and feeling abandoned."

NIXON: Right. Good advice.

EHRLICHMAN: And he said, "Well, what can I tell him about — clemency or pardon?" And I said, "You can't tell him anything about clemency or a pardon." And I said, "Under no circumstances should this ever be raised with the president."

NIXON: Yeah. Told him not to raise it with me. Well, he raised it, I must say, in a tangential way. Now he denies that, as I understand it, that he said that he'd be out by Christmas. He says —

EHRLICHMAN: I've never talked to Chuck about that. Have you?

HALDEMAN: Yeah.

NIXON: Yeah. What did he say he said? Well, I'll tell you what I — what Dean, or somebody tells me he said he said. He said that he didn't — I — he just talked to — saw Bittman casually, or on the phone or something of that sort.

EHRLICHMAN: Bittman?

NIXON: That was it.

EHRLICHMAN: Oh.

NIXON: And he said to Bittman —

EHRLICHMAN: Oh.

NIXON: — he said, "I," he said, "I — "

EHRLICHMAN: Well, now that —

NIXON: — he said, "I — "

EHRLICHMAN: — a difference.

NIXON: Listen, I have written it. He said, "I know that — I know about Hunt's concern about clemency. I, Chuck Colson, feel terrible about it, because I knew his wife." And he said, "I will go to bat for him and I have reason to believe that my views would be listened to." Well, it's the last part that might in any way remain, although —

EHRLICHMAN: He says he talked to Bittman and that he was very skillful —

NIXON: That's right.

EHRLICHMAN: — in avoiding any commitment. He says Bittman —

NIXON: [unclear]

EHRLICHMAN: — Bittman was pitching 'em, but that he wasn't catching 'em. And —

NIXON: [unclear]

EHRLICHMAN: — he either has a tape of that meeting or a tape of the conversation or some such thing.

HALDEMAN: That's where he lost his thread then. Yes, said you and Dean told him you two promised clemency and that he was smarter than you and didn't.

NIXON: You haven't said you and Dean promised?

HALDEMAN: That Ehrlichman and Dean told him to promise —

NIXON: Shit.

HALDEMAN: — [unclear].

NIXON: Well, anyway, whatever the case might be, let me ask a question —

HALDEMAN: [unclear] a little strange.

NIXON: — does Hunt — well, just so that he — does he indicate that they — that Hunt's going to talk to that subject for example — the promise of clemency?

EHRLICHMAN: He didn't say that. He didn't say that. I didn't ask him.

HALDEMAN: Well, going back to the basis, John, as I recall they don't have anything to indi — we don't know how they know Hunt's going to testify. We assume that Bittman told them —

EHRLICHMAN: Right.

HALDEMAN: (a). (b) We don't — they don't have any indication, based on their knowledge that Hunt's going to testify, of what Hunt is going to testify to, except on the basis of Shapiro's meeting with Hunt —

EHRLICHMAN: The other day.

HALDEMAN: — the other day. And they're assuming that what Hunt told Shapiro is what he will tell the grand jury, but I don't know why they'd have any reason to assume that.

EHRLICHMAN: I don't — Shapiro's general comment was that Hunt would corroborate a lot of McCord's hearsay —

NIXON: Yeah.

EHRLICHMAN: — but that it also would be hearsay.

NIXON: All right. Hunt, however — and this is where Colson comes in, right? Hard — Hunt could testify on Colson's pressure.

HALDEMAN: Yeah. But what they've said he's going to test —

NIXON: Right.

HALDEMAN: — on the cover-up, what he is going to testify —

NIXON: Now wait a minute —

HALDEMAN: [unclear]

NIXON: — I'm talking about something entirely different —

HALDEMAN: [unclear]

NIXON: — you're talking about when Colson —

HALDEMAN: [unclear]

NIXON: — Colson and Liddy were in the office and Colson picked up the phone and called Magruder.

HALDEMAN: That's right. Sure.

NIXON: Now, there — now Colson says that they didn't discuss bugging at that point. Hunt could say, "I went in and I showed this whole plan to Colson and Colson phoned — picked up the phone — "

EHRLICHMAN: That's right.

NIXON: " — and talked to Magruder."

EHRLICHMAN: True.

NIXON: Does Colson realize his vulnerability there?

EHRLICHMAN: Well, of course Colson claims he has no vulnerability, because when Hunt and Liddy came in to talk to him they talked in very general terms.

NIXON: I understand that.

EHRLICHMAN: So, he —

NIXON: I —

EHRLICHMAN: — doesn't acknowledge —

NIXON: I —

EHRLICHMAN: — he doesn't acknowledge that there's any possibility —

NIXON: I understand that, but I'm just simply saying, it's —

EHRLICHMAN: I think he's right.

NIXON: — that Hunt and Liddy could —

EHRLICHMAN: That's true.

NIXON: — could charge that — that's the point. They — if they talk, I would assume they would get into that point with them — any cross-examiner.

EHRLICHMAN: I've asked Colson specifically about that conversation and he maintains that they were talking in general terms about intelligence and when they said intelligence he meant one thing and apparently they meant another.

NIXON: Question — for example, is Hunt preparing to talk on other activities that he engaged in?

EHRLICHMAN: Well, I couldn't derive that —

NIXON: Mm-hmm.

EHRLICHMAN: — [unclear] at all.

NIXON: For the White House and for the — you know?

EHRLICHMAN: I couldn't get that at all.

NIXON: The U.S. attorney, I would assume, would not be pressing [unclear].

EHRLICHMAN: Ordinarily not.

NIXON: [unclear]

EHRLICHMAN: Now, McCord volunteered this [*Las Vegas Sun* publisher and prominent Republican] Hank Greenspun thing [a plot to steal documents that allegedly could be used as blackmail against Democrats] gratuitously apparently, not —

NIXON: Could — can you tell me, is that a serious thing? Did they really try to get into Hank Greenspun's — ?

EHRLICHMAN: I guess they actually got in.

NIXON: What in the name of Christ, though, does Hank Greenspun got with — anything to do with Mitchell or anybody else?

EHRLICHMAN: Nothing. Well, now, Mitchell —

NIXON: [Howard] Hughes?

EHRLICHMAN: Here's — yeah, Hughes. And these two fellows, Colson and Shapiro — Colson threw that out.

NIXON: Hughes on whom?

EHRLICHMAN: Well, you know the Hughes thing is cut into two factions —

NIXON: I don't —

EHRLICHMAN: — (a) and then the —

NIXON: — fighting —

EHRLICHMAN: — and then the other, and they're fighting.

NIXON: Right.

EHRLICHMAN: Bennett — Senator [Wallace Foster] Bennett's son [Robert Bennett], for whom Hunt worked —

NIXON: Oh?

EHRLICHMAN: — represents one of those factions.

NIXON: Yeah. So he ordered the bugging?

EHRLICHMAN: I don't know.

[Unclear exchange]

EHRLICHMAN: They think it's a bag job.

HALDEMAN: They busted his safe to get something out of it.

EHRLICHMAN: Now —

HALDEMAN: Wasn't that it? They flew out, broke his safe, got something out —

EHRLICHMAN: [unclear]

HALDEMAN: — got on the airplane, and flew away.

EHRLICHMAN: Now, as they sat there in my office —

NIXON: There are others —

EHRLICHMAN: What?

NIXON: —other delicate things, too. You've got, apart from my poor damn dumb brother, which unfortunately or fortunately was a long time ago, but more recently, you've got Hubert Humphrey's son works for him and, of course, they're tied in with [Larry] O'Brien, I suppose. But maybe they were trying to get it for that reason.

EHRLICHMAN: I don't know why. The two of them put on a little charade for me in the office just—

NIXON: Shapiro and Colson?

EHRLICHMAN: —as we—yeah, as we talked about this, and it may have been genuine and it may not. But—

NIXON: But they didn't know anything about it?

EHRLICHMAN: —but they—no, they said, one said to the other, "Say, that may have something to do with the New York grand jury," meaning the Vesco grand jury which is a runaway and which is into—

NIXON: You think Colson knew about that?

EHRLICHMAN: I don't know. I don't say he knew about it. I said, he says he doesn't know even who Hank Greenspun is.

NIXON: He should. Everybody knows he's the editor of the *Las Vegas Sun,* for Christ's sakes—

EHRLICHMAN: I'll take him at face value on that one—there isn't any other evidence.

NIXON: You didn't know that either?

EHRLICHMAN: I know very well who he is.

NIXON: All right. Let me just take a minute further and run out the Hunt thing, and then the grand jury. I just want to get all the pieces in my mind—

EHRLICHMAN: Sure.

NIXON: —if I can.

EHRLICHMAN: Sure.

NIXON: Hunt's testimony on payoff, of course, would be very important.

EHRLICHMAN: Right.

NIXON: Is he prepared to testify on that?

EHRLICHMAN: I think so. That's what they say—that he will, and that he will implicate O'Brien and Parkinson. And then, of course—

NIXON: O'Brien and Parkinson?

EHRLICHMAN: The lawyers.

NIXON: Were they the ones that talked to Hunt?

EHRLICHMAN: Well, he says they were and that they handed him the money. He in turn handed it to his wife and she was the go-between for the—

NIXON: Yeah.

EHRLICHMAN: —Cubans.

NIXON: For what purpose? That's the key to it all.

EHRLICHMAN: Well, I think he'll hook—hang 'em up on obstruction of justice.

NIXON: Can Hunt do that?

HALDEMAN: How can he do that? Why would he simply — why doesn't he accomplish his purpose simply by saying they gave the money to handle their legal fees?

EHRLICHMAN: They're — all hang out there apparently.

NIXON: Now this is —

HALDEMAN: I don't think —

NIXON: — this is what Colson tells you guys?

EHRLICHMAN: That's right. I don't —

NIXON: [unclear]

HALDEMAN: — have any other information.

NIXON: That Hunt, then, is going to go. Well, now that raises the problem on — with regard to Kalmbach. He has possible vulnerability as to whether he was aware — in other words, the motive —

EHRLICHMAN: This doesn't add anything to the Kalmbach problem at all.

NIXON: What happened —

HALDEMAN: Dean [unclear] —

NIXON: — what happened on that? Dean called Kalmbach? What did Dean call Kalmbach about?

EHRLICHMAN: And he said, "We have to raise some money in connection with the aftermath," and I don't know how he described it to Herb. Herb said, "How much do you need?" and —

NIXON: It was never discussed then?

EHRLICHMAN: — presumably Dean told him and Herb went to a couple of donors and got some money and sent it back.

HALDEMAN: Dean says very flatly that Kalmbach did not know the purpose for the money and has no problem.

NIXON: Dean does know the purpose, however? Hunt testifies — so basically then Hunt will testify that it was so-called hush money. Right?

EHRLICHMAN: I think so. Now that again, my water can't rise any higher than source.

NIXON: I understand.

EHRLICHMAN: But that's that —

NIXON: What is your — ?

EHRLICHMAN: That's that —

NIXON: What does that serve him — let me ask, just to try to —

EHRLICHMAN: Gen —

NIXON: — I mean, would it serve him?

EHRLICHMAN: The only thing it serves him is to —

NIXON: Would it reduce his sentence?

EHRLICHMAN: — have his sentence remitted, that's all.

HALDEMAN: He'd be serving the same purpose by not saying it was hush money, by saying he gave it to "these guys that I had recruited for this job and I — "

NIXON: I know, of —

HALDEMAN: " — felt badly about their family and," you know, "a great deal about it."

NIXON: That's right. That's what it ought to be and that's got to be the story that — and then —

HALDEMAN: [unclear] his departed wife said we have to [unclear]

NIXON: — that will be the defense of the people, right?

EHRLICHMAN: [unclear] the only defense they have.

NIXON: So on and so forth.

HALDEMAN: But that — that was the line that he had used around here.

NIXON: What?

HALDEMAN: That was the line that they used around here. That we've got to have money for their legal fees and family sup —

NIXON: Support them. Well, I heard something about that at a much later time.

HALDEMAN: Yeah.

NIXON: And, frankly, not knowing much about obstruction of justice, I thought it was perfectly proper.

EHRLICHMAN: Well, it's like the —

NIXON: Would it be perfectly proper?

EHRLICHMAN: — the defense of the —

NIXON: Berrigans [Jesuit priests Philip and Daniel Berrigan, who organized a draft card burning at a Selective Service office in Maryland]?

EHRLICHMAN: — the Chicago Seven.

NIXON: The Chicago Seven [leaders of counterculture riots during the 1968 DNC, including Rennie Davis, David Dellinger, John Froines, Tom Hayden, Abbie Hoffman, Jerry Rubin, and Lee Weiner]?

HALDEMAN: They had a defense fund for everybody.

NIXON: Not only a defense fund, Christ, they take care of the living expenses, too.

UNIDENTIFIED: Was there any — ?

NIXON: Despite what all this crap about just legal fees, they take care of themselves. They raise — you remember the Scottsboro case [nine African-American teenagers accused of raping two women]? Christ. The Communist front raised a million dollars for the Scottsboro people. Nine hundred thousand went into the pockets of the Scotts — Communists.

HALDEMAN: [laughs]

NIXON: So it's common practice.

EHRLICHMAN: Yeah.

NIXON: Nevertheless, that's Hunt then saying about the payoff. All right, Hunt, on other activities — Hunt, then, according to Colson was not — let's get into what did Colson mean about the door of the Oval Office?

EHRLICHMAN: I'll have to get back to you on that, because Shapiro was there and I didn't want to get into it.

NIXON: Right.

• • •

EHRLICHMAN: Dean called and he said, "All right, here's a scenario." He said, "We've all been trying to figure out — "

NIXON: Yeah.

EHRLICHMAN: " — how to make this go." He says, "The president calls Mitchell into his office on Saturday. He says, 'John, you've got to do this and here are the facts: bing, bing, bing, bing.' And that's — you pull this paper out here. 'And you'd better go do this.' And Mitchell stonewalls you. So then, John says, 'I don't know why you're asking me down here. You can't ask a man to do a thing like that. I need my lawyer. I don't know what I'm facing.' He says, 'You just really can't expect me to do this.' So the president says, 'Well, John, I have no alternative.' And with that the president calls the U.S. attorney and says, 'I, the president of the United States of America and leader of the free world, want to go before the grand jury on Monday.'"

NIXON: I won't even comment on that.

HALDEMAN: That's a silly [unclear].

EHRLICHMAN: What I mean is, we're — typical of the thinking of — we're running out every line. So that was twelve thirty this morning. But I —

NIXON: I go before the grand jury — that's —

EHRLICHMAN: I —

NIXON: — that's like putting Bob on national television —

EHRLICHMAN: With Dan Rather.

NIXON: What?

EHRLICHMAN: With Dan Rather.

NIXON: Well, putting it on national television period. When your audience basically is not that big.

EHRLICHMAN: Well, let's take it just as far as you calling Mitchell into the Oval Office, as a — essentially convinced that Mitchell was the linchpin in this thing —

NIXON: Right.

EHRLICHMAN: — and that if he goes down, it can redound to the administration's advantage. If he doesn't then we're —

NIXON: How can it redound to our advantage?

EHRLICHMAN: That —

NIXON: There's others —

EHRLICHMAN: That — you have a report from me based on three weeks' work, that when you got it you immediately acted to call Mitchell in as the provable —

NIXON: I see.

EHRLICHMAN: — wrongdoer —

NIXON: I see.

EHRLICHMAN: — and you say, "My God, I've got a report here. And it's clear from this report that you are guilty as hell. Now, John, for Christ's sake go on in there and do what you should. And let's get this thing cleared up and get it off the country's back and move on." And —

HALDEMAN: Well, plus the given side of it is that that's the only —

NIXON: Even way to —

HALDEMAN: — way to beat 'er down.

NIXON: Well —

HALDEMAN: Now, from John Mitchell's own personal viewpoint — that's the only salvation for John Mitchell. Can you see another way? And, obviously, once you have it, you've — he's got to admit it.

NIXON: He's not gonna make it, anyway.

HALDEMAN: Another factor in that to consider for what it's worth is the point Connally made to me in that conversation we had on this.

NIXON: I ought to talk to Mitchell?

HALDEMAN: I don't know whether he said this to you or not. He made the point that you had to get this laid out and that the only way it could hurt you is if it ultimately went to Mitchell. And that would be the one man you couldn't afford to let get hung on this.

• • •

NIXON: Dean asked — told me about the problem of Hunt's lawyer wanted — had gotten — this was a few weeks ago — needed sixty thousand or forty thousand dollars or something like that. You remember? He asked me about it and I said I don't know where you can get it. I said I would — I mean, I frankly felt he might try to get it but I didn't know where. And then he left it up with Mitchell and Mitchell then said it was taken care of — am I correct? Is my recollection — ?

EHRLICHMAN: Yes, sir. [unclear]

NIXON: Is that approximately correct?

EHRLICHMAN: Yes, you could [unclear].

NIXON: Did he talk to you about that?

EHRLICHMAN: He talked to me about it. I said, "John, I wouldn't have the vaguest notion where to get it."

NIXON: Yeah —

EHRLICHMAN: I saw him later in the day. I saw Mitchell later in the day —

NIXON: Yeah.

EHRLICHMAN: — Wednesday [unclear].

NIXON: What happened?

EHRLICHMAN: And he just said it's taken care of.

HALDEMAN: Mitchell raised the topic. He turned to Dean and said, "What have you done about that other problem?" And Dean said — he kind of looked at us — and then said, "Well, you know, I don't know." And Mitchell said, "Oh, I guess that's been taken care of."

EHRLICHMAN: [unclear] said apparently through LaRue.

NIXON: [unclear]

HALDEMAN: [unclear] LaRue. Were you the one who told me? Who told you? Oh, Dean told us. LaRue. He had, Dean had a long talk with LaRue and LaRue said, "This whole thing is ridiculous now" and said [unclear] said, "Yeah," he said, "if

I were in charge of this now what I would do is I'd get a large bus and I'd put the president at the wheel and I'd throw everybody we've got around here in it and I'd drive up to the Senate and I'd have the president open the door and I'd say, 'You all get out and tell them everything you know and I'll be back to pick you up when you're through.'" He said, "It's all out now and there's nothing we can do about it." And he said, "I can," he said LaRue also said, you know, "I can't figure out how I got into this to begin with, but I — it seems to me all of us have been drawn in here in trying to cover up for John."

NIXON: For Mitchell?

HALDEMAN: Yeah, which is exactly what's happened.

NIXON: LaRue said that?

HALDEMAN: Yes.

NIXON: He's right. [unclear]

HALDEMAN: And if LaRue is called, LaRue is — intends to tell the truth about it.

NIXON: Is he?

HALDEMAN: Yeah. Now, I —

NIXON: Well, what will be his defense —

HALDEMAN: I don't know.

NIXON: — about obstruction?

HALDEMAN: I don't know.

EHRLICHMAN: I don't think he has one.

HALDEMAN: If he doesn't intend —

NIXON: No, well, no. His obstruction will be LaRue'll — that I was helping to get —

EHRLICHMAN: The way Dean talks, LaRue wasn't even thinking about the message.

HALDEMAN: I don't think LaRue cares. I think LaRue's figured that the jig is up.

EHRLICHMAN: [unclear] I — a bit of incidental intelligence that [unclear] dropped yesterday with regard to Mardian. Just a small matter — went out to Phoenix [unclear] elaborate cover story, which he fed to the *New York Times,* which would lay it all back in the White House. [unclear] just gonna know that if they do [unclear] get screwed.

HALDEMAN: Yeah, they've gotten to —

EHRLICHMAN: It will only stand so long as Mitchell stands.

NIXON: Why lay it at the White House?

EHRLICHMAN: That's all that — but I just don't know any other fact and —

NIXON: Well, he could lay it to the White House?

EHRLICHMAN: But bear in, bear in mind Shapiro was giving me this in a whole litany of things that were persuasive and which —

NIXON: Yep, yep.

HALDEMAN: I'm still afraid of Shapiro.

EHRLICHMAN: — what he said to me [unclear] he's a scary guy.

HALDEMAN: I don't believe we can —

NIXON: But what I meant on the Mardian — the point that — let me say, I don't think that Mardian or LaRue or Mitchell or Magruder or anybody wants to hurt the president in this thing.

EHRLICHMAN: [unclear]

HALDEMAN: I'm sure that's right.

NIXON: Do you feel that way?

HALDEMAN: Yes, sir.

NIXON: Colson? How, how about Colson?

HALDEMAN: He — I [unclear] said he'll do everything he can not to hurt the president.

NIXON: Yeah. That has got to be the attitude of everybody because it isn't the man, it's the goddamn office.

HALDEMAN: Sure. Sure.

NIXON: But also it happens to be true. I mean I [unclear] I knew about the son of a bitch.

HALDEMAN: You don't have a — that doesn't apply and they didn't, I think, rationalize to themselves that hurting or getting anybody else could be —

NIXON: That's right.

HALDEMAN: — good for the president rather than bad. And that —

NIXON: In other words —

HALDEMAN: — includes Ehrlichman, Haldeman —

NIXON: Yeah.

HALDEMAN: — Dean —

NIXON: Yeah.

HALDEMAN: — certainly Colson. Colson'd be at the top of that list. Colson first, then Haldeman, then Dean, then Ehrlichman.

NIXON: You see I think a Mardian story to the *Times* will be, frankly, that Colson put the heat on.

HALDEMAN: Well, maybe, but he's gonna last. That could be where you —

NIXON: Maybe Haldeman?

HALDEMAN: Mardian. No, Mardian. I don't think has any personal desire to get me. I think he would — I know he hates Colson.

NIXON: Does he?

HALDEMAN: They all do. And any Mitchell person does, because Mitchell did.

NIXON: You can make — you see, you can make a hell of a circumstantial case on Colson. He's the guy that, you know, he's Dean's buddy, and Liddy he knew well, apparently knew well —

HALDEMAN: Wasn't Dean's buddy.

NIXON: I'm sorry — I meant Hunt's buddy.

HALDEMAN: Yeah, right.

NIXON: Of course, right. But you know, but, I mean, Colson is closer to this group of robbers than anybody else. That's the problem with Colson. Colson's got a very —

HALDEMAN: He has no tie to Liddy.

NIXON: Oh, no, no. Okay.

HALDEMAN: You know, Liddy has talked to him once or twice, but has no string to it. His string is to Hunt.

NIXON: Well, then Hunt —

HALDEMAN: Hunt is the central background figure that —

NIXON: Is Hunt — Hunt takes this money? [unclear] he took it for what? To cover up?

HALDEMAN: Immunity. Bet Bittman's given immunity.

NIXON: They're going to give Hunt immunity?

HALDEMAN: I don't know. I suppose.

EHRLICHMAN: I think that would be their deal.

NIXON: Well, that's the standard — [unclear] give him immunity for additional crimes?

EHRLICHMAN: He's convicted now, you see, so it would be for additional —

HALDEMAN: They haven't sentenced him.

EHRLICHMAN: That's right.

NIXON: So they could give him immunity for the — they could cut his sentence and give him immunity for the cover-up, the hush money — clemency. How do you handle the problem of clemency, John?

EHRLICHMAN: You'd have to stonewall that — it's a cold fact — cold denial [unclear].

HALDEMAN: Well, you don't handle it at all. That's Colson's main point because that's where it comes from.

EHRLICHMAN: That was the line of communication —

NIXON: Colson to Bittman? Well that's the only thing that we have on that, except Mitchell, apparently, had said something about clemency to people.

HALDEMAN: To Liddy.

NIXON: And Mitchell has never disc — has he ever discussed clemency with you, Bob?

HALDEMAN: No.

NIXON: Has he ever discussed it with you?

EHRLICHMAN: No.

NIXON: Needless to say, not with me. The only terms [unclear] we were all here in the room.

HALDEMAN: I think —

EHRLICHMAN: The only time —

HALDEMAN: — he may have said, well, you know, "We've got to take care of these people," and —

NIXON: Yeah. Well, I understand that. But he's never said, "Look, you're gonna get a pardon for these people when this is over." Never used any such language around here, has he, John?

EHRLICHMAN: Not to me.

HALDEMAN: I don't think so.

NIXON: With Dean has he?

EHRLICHMAN: Well, I don't know.

NIXON: That's a question [unclear]. Because Dean's never raised it. In fact, Dean told me an interesting thing. I said, Dean — I said, "John," I said, "where's it all lead?" He said, "Uh." I said, "What's it going to cost? Now you could continue this of course." He said about a million dollars. I said facetiously, "Have you thought of this at all?" [unclear] that's the point. That's the foul-up in the whole Mitchell argument. Unless I could just up and say, "Look, fellows, it's too bad and I could give you executive clemency, like tomorrow. What the hell do you think, Dean — I mean, do you think that — the point is, Hunt and the Cubans are going to sit on their ass in jail for four years and their families not taken care of? That's the point. Now where the hell do you get the money for that?" That's the reason this whole thing falls. I mean, it's that — I mean, that astonishes me about Mitchell and the rest.

EHRLICHMAN: Improbable.

NIXON: Not only improbable, there's no way to get the money, is there? Who was it, Tom Pappas they had to see me?

HALDEMAN: [unclear] about the money.

NIXON: Huh?

HALDEMAN: You didn't talk to him about the money?

NIXON: I don't remember. You told me to see him. In fact, you said that he was helping on the —

HALDEMAN: But, yeah — but you were seeing him and you were seeing a number of contributors.

NIXON: I know and I said hell, "I appreciate the work you're doing for us" and I didn't mention what it was.

HALDEMAN: [unclear]

NIXON: Good old —

HALDEMAN: He was Mitchell's contact.

NIXON: Good old Tom is raising money apparently. He's doing this thing —

HALDEMAN: That's right. I doubt that he is —

NIXON: [unclear] the word never came up, but I said, "I appreciate what you're doing." I do, for — the purpose of helping the poor bastards through the trial, but you can't after that, John. You can't or could you? I guess you could. Attorneys' fees? Could you get a support program for these people for four years?

EHRLICHMAN: I haven't any idea. I have no idea.

NIXON: Well, they've supported other people in jail —

EHRLICHMAN: [unclear]

NIXON: — for years.

EHRLICHMAN: The Berrigans or somebody.

NIXON: Huh?

EHRLICHMAN: I say, I don't know how the Berrigan brothers and some of those —

NIXON: They all have funds.

EHRLICHMAN: — operations. I think those they use —

NIXON: Yes, there are funds [unclear] are developed. I guess that's true.

EHRLICHMAN: So that they —

NIXON: But not to hush up.

EHRLICHMAN: That's right.

NIXON: That's the point. All right. One final thing: Dean. You don't think we have to bite it today?

EHRLICHMAN: Well, I'm not so sure. I'd be inclined to say you are [unclear]. When you say "bite" it's simply a matter of making a decision, in my opinion —

NIXON: Well, I've made a decision. I think he has to go.

EHRLICHMAN: Well, I'm not sure that's the right decision. It's — by framing the issue — I don't mean to imply that —

NIXON: Oh, I see.

EHRLICHMAN: — that's the [unclear].

NIXON: I thought — no, I thought —

EHRLICHMAN: [unclear]

NIXON: When you said you didn't address it, I'm sorry, I thought that was one of the recommendations you had made.

EHRLICHMAN: No, my recommendation is that you recognize that there's a go/no-go decision that has to be —

NIXON: Oh, I see.

EHRLICHMAN: — made right away.

NIXON: Oh, all right, yeah.

EHRLICHMAN: You see, here's your situation as I — look again at the big picture — you now are possessed with a body of facts.

NIXON: That's right.

EHRLICHMAN: And you've got to — you can't just sit here.

NIXON: That's right.

EHRLICHMAN: You've got to act on it.

NIXON: Right.

EHRLICHMAN: You've got to make some decisions and the Dean thing — one of the decisions that you have to make.

• • •

EHRLICHMAN: I'll tell you, I am still heavily persuaded that we affect the grand jury and U.S. attorney's treatment of Dean favorably by keeping him on.

NIXON: Okay.

EHRLICHMAN: And that that's important. Now —

NIXON: Why do you say that? Because they like him?

EHRLICHMAN: No, no. Not at all.

HALDEMAN: Because they can treat him differently as the president's counsel than —

EHRLICHMAN: As the dismissed president's counsel.

HALDEMAN: Exactly.

NIXON: Yeah.

EHRLICHMAN: It's just that it's a very heavy psychological factor.

NIXON: Well, this will be done, because there is another reason too. It isn't like — Dean is not like Mitchell, now let's face it.

HALDEMAN: That's right.

NIXON: Dean is not like Mitchell in the sense that Dean only tried to do what he could to pick up the goddamn pieces and —

HALDEMAN: Certainly.

NIXON: — everybody else around here knew it had to be done.

EHRLICHMAN: Certainly.

NIXON: Let's face it. I'm not blaming anybody else now.

HALDEMAN: I understand.

NIXON: That was his job.

HALDEMAN: I understand.

EHRLICHMAN: I have great trouble in [unclear] that you could be involved in the light of the known involvement that he had —

NIXON: After the — ?

EHRLICHMAN: — in the aftermath.

NIXON: Right, but —

EHRLICHMAN: But —

HALDEMAN: The known involvement in the aftermath was for — what was understood here to be the proper [unclear].

EHRLICHMAN: That's half —

NIXON: The question is motive.

HALDEMAN: That's right.

EHRLICHMAN: That's number one. Number two, there is nothing new about that.

NIXON: That's right.

EHRLICHMAN: As I have developed, in this thing — I'd like you to read this.

NIXON: Yeah.

EHRLICHMAN: There were eight or ten people around here who knew about this — knew it was going on.

NIXON: Yeah.

EHRLICHMAN: Bob knew, I knew, all kinds of people knew.

NIXON: Well, I knew it. I knew it.

EHRLICHMAN: And it was not a question of whether —

NIXON: [unclear] I knew I must say though — I didn't know it, but I must have assumed it though. But you know, fortunately — and I thank you both for arranging it that way and it does show why the isolation of the president isn't a bad position to be in.

EHRLICHMAN: [laughs]

NIXON: But the first time that I knew that they had to have the money was the time when Dean told me that they needed forty thousand dollars. I hadn't been rege — I didn't — I just didn't — I closed my eyes — I couldn't read the goddamn papers on those little envelopes. I didn't know about the envelopes and the [unclear] and all that stuff.

EHRLICHMAN: Well, the —

NIXON: But others did know.

EHRLICHMAN: — the point is that if Dean's — if the wrongdoing which justifies Dean's dismissal is his knowledge that that operation was going on —

NIXON: Yeah.

EHRLICHMAN: — then you can't stop with him. You've got to go through the whole place wholesale.

NIXON: Fire the whole staff?

EHRLICHMAN: That's right. It's a question of motive. It's a question of role, and I don't think Dean's role in the aftermath, at least from the facts that I know now, achieves a level of wrongdoing that requires that you terminate him.

NIXON: No.

EHRLICHMAN: And this other thing —

NIXON: I think you've made a very powerful point to me that, of course, you can be pragmatic and say, "Well, Christ, in fact Dean" and so forth — in other words cut your losses and get rid of him. I mean, give 'em an hors d'oeuvre and maybe they won't come back for the main course. "So out, John Dean." On the other hand, it is true others did know — they did know.

EHRLICHMAN: But more than that, we've made Dean a focal point in the Gray process.

NIXON: Right.

EHRLICHMAN: And he will become a focal point in the Ervin process.

NIXON: Well, we'll have — yes, except if —

HALDEMAN: Yeah, if it goes on.

NIXON: Yeah.

HALDEMAN: And if you dismiss him he'll still be a focal point.

EHRLICHMAN: He'll be a focal point. [unclear]

HALDEMAN: He'll be defrocked with a less — with less protection, that's right.

EHRLICHMAN: And with less incentive.

NIXON: Well, the point that I think — I think Dean — Dean's —

HALDEMAN: What Dean did was all proper —

NIXON: Yeah.

HALDEMAN: — in terms of the higher good.

NIXON: Dean — you've gotta have a talk with Dean. I feel that I should not talk to him.

EHRLICHMAN: I'll have talked to him.

NIXON: But — I mean about motives.

EHRLICHMAN: I have talked to him.

NIXON: What's he say about motives? He says it was hush-up?

EHRLICHMAN: No. He says he knew he had to know that people were trying to bring that result about —

NIXON: Right.

EHRLICHMAN: — and he says, you know, "The way I got into this was I would go to meetings in —"

NIXON: Right.

EHRLICHMAN: "— campaign headquarters, and we'd get through the meeting and

Mitchell and LaRue would say to — I mean, Mardian and LaRue would say to Mitchell, 'Mitchell, you've got to do something about this.'" And Mitchell's stock answer was to turn to John Dean.

HALDEMAN: Say, "What are you gonna do?"

EHRLICHMAN: "What are you going to do?"

NIXON: Jesus Christ.

"He shouldn't throw the burden over here."
April 14, 1973, 2:24 p.m.
Richard Nixon, Bob Haldeman, and John Ehrlichman
OVAL OFFICE

Following his meeting with Mitchell, Ehrlichman appeared in the Oval Office to report on the conversation. Mitchell had not been receptive to Ehrlichman's initial comments and so the conference with the president and Haldeman turned away from the plan to present Nixon as the man who solved the Watergate crime. Instead, the three worked through the pathways of the complex scandal again, in light of Magruder's new intention to testify about White House involvement. The potential for the CRP participants to implicate those at the White House turned the tables on the strategy that the president had outlined in the morning meeting. In fact, as Ehrlichman reported it, Mitchell had in mind to implicate Haldeman for originating the idea of a break-in.

• • •

NIXON: All finished?

EHRLICHMAN: Yes, sir. All finished. He is an innocent man in his heart, and in his mind, and he does not intend to move off that position. He appreciated the message of good feeling between you and him.

NIXON: He got it — that — huh?

EHRLICHMAN: And he appreciated my —

NIXON: Why don't you give me your — how did you get this little chapter and verse?

EHRLICHMAN: Well, I started out by saying that this was a subject that was so difficult for you to talk to him personally about, that you had asked me to do this.

NIXON: And that you had made a study.

EHRLICHMAN: That you had had me doing this. That I had presented you with a set of conclusions that were admittedly hearsay, but that pointed in the direction of his exposure, and Jeb's, and other people. And that you were having me systematically talk to these people because, in the course of this investigation, we had discovered a frame of mind on the part of some people that they should stand mute in order to help the president. And that your sense was that the presidency was not helped by that. And that it was not my purpose to tell anybody what he should do, but only to tell him that as far as your view of the interests of the presidency were concerned, that they were not served by a person standing mute — for that reason alone. Now, there might be plenty of reasons why a person would want to stand mute and put the government on its proof. And that wasn't the question. And obviously be — and then he said, "Well, what you're saying to me is that the president is reserving to me all my options," and I said, "Of course he is, John. The only thing that he doesn't want you to feel is that you don't have the option of going in and talking if you want to do so. That you have completely every option to go in or not to go in." And he said, well, he appreciated that. But he had not been taking the position he had for the reason that he thought he was necessarily helping or hurting the presidency. But he said, "You know, these characters pulled this thing off without my knowledge." He said, "I never saw Liddy for months at a time." And he said, "I didn't know what they were up to." And he said, "Nobody was more surprised than I was. We had this meeting, and — " He lobbed mud balls at the White House at every opportunity. It was very interesting how he dragged it in.

NIXON: Yeah.

EHRLICHMAN: One after the other. For instance, he said, "There were these meetings. These characters came over to my office and Liddy put on this million-dollar presentation which was perfectly ridiculous. Says it comes — the origin of that, of course, was in the White House where Bob Haldeman and I talked about something called the Operation Sandwedge. That was really the grandfather of this whole thing. And, of course, that was never put together because we couldn't get the right people to do it. And they were talking about [Rose Mary Woods's brother] Joe Woods and people of that kind," and so he said, "It never happened."

NIXON: What is Operation Sandwedge?

HALDEMAN: It was something that Jack Caulfield —

NIXON: [unclear] oh, yes.

HALDEMAN: — came up with back in '71, and we needed some intelligence and ought to set up our own [private intelligence agency, like] Intertel.

EHRLICHMAN: So then he went on to say that there were only those meetings. He's still hung up on the only-three-meetings thing. He made it very clear to me that he didn't ever believe there was a fourth meeting. He said that, of course —

HALDEMAN: He wasn't in the fourth meeting, John. There were only three meetings as far as he's concerned.

EHRLICHMAN: No, no. But he didn't refer to three or four. He referred to the meetings themselves. He argues that there was no meeting after the million-dollar meeting. Let me put it that way.

HALDEMAN: Oh, really?

EHRLICHMAN: Right. That's the sense of what he was saying. I didn't press him on it and I tried to play him with kid gloves. In fact, I never asked him to tell me anything.

NIXON: Yeah.

EHRLICHMAN: He just came forward with all this stuff.

NIXON: Right.

EHRLICHMAN: He says that actually Magruder is going to have a problem with all this because Dean talked Magruder into saying the wrong thing to the grand jury, and so Magruder's got a problem.

NIXON: My God, Mitchell was there.

EHRLICHMAN: Yep.

NIXON: Isn't that the meeting they're referring to?

EHRLICHMAN: Yes, sir.

HALDEMAN: Sure.

NIXON: Mitchell was there when Dean talked him into saying the wrong things?

HALDEMAN: That's what he says. That's what Mitchell says.

NIXON: What does Dean say about it?

EHRLICHMAN: Dean says it was Mitchell and Magruder who agreed.

HALDEMAN: Well—

EHRLICHMAN: It must have been the quietest meeting in history because everybody's version is that the other two guys talked.

NIXON: Go ahead. Let's hear the rest of it.

EHRLICHMAN: Well, it goes on like that. His characterization of all this is that he was a very busy man, that he wasn't keeping track of what was going on at the committee, that this was engendered as a result of Hunt and Liddy coming to Colson's office and getting Colson to make a phone call to Magruder, and that he, Mitchell, was just not aware that all that happened until [CRP spokesman] Van Shunway brought Liddy into Mitchell's office sometime in June and that's the first he had knowledge of it. Much later in the conversation—

HALDEMAN: Before the discovery?

EHRLICHMAN: Well, I don't know.

NIXON: [unclear]

EHRLICHMAN: I don't know. He didn't—

NIXON: [unclear]

EHRLICHMAN: You can listen to it. I've got a tape of it.

NIXON: [unclear]

EHRLICHMAN: But in any event, much later, I said that the grand jury felt, or the U.S. attorney felt that they had John wired. And he said, "Well, what possible evidence could they have to feel that way?" And I—

NIXON: John Dean or John Mitchell?

EHRLICHMAN: John Mitchell. And I said, "Well, I understand that one version of the facts is that Magruder brought you a memo with a number of targets on it, and that you checked off the targets that you wanted." And he said, "Why, that—nothing could be further from the truth than that."

NIXON: That was John Dean's version?

HALDEMAN: That's right.

NIXON: That's what he said he said to Mitchell?

EHRLICHMAN: Right. Then—

HALDEMAN: What Mitchell said to me was that he did not. He said, "I checked — I signed off on it."

NIXON: Yeah. Go ahead.

HALDEMAN: I said, "You mean you initialed it?" And he said, "No."

EHRLICHMAN: Then I said they had [unclear] by Hunt and Liddy having a conversation, and Liddy saying to Hunt, "Yes, I know how you don't like this stuff. We have to do it because Mr. Mitchell insists on it." He said, "I never saw Liddy for five months. From February to June, I never laid eyes on him." He said, "I think Liddy is the source of a lot of my problems here. He's using my name, and so forth." So it's very much of a hard-line thing. He said, "If I'm indicted, it is going to be very hard but," he said, "I have to think of my reputation." He said, "I can't let people get away with this kind of thing," and he said, "I am just going to have to defend myself every way I can. Because," he said, "obviously I can't get a fair trial in the city of Washington by any stretch of the imagination. We'll just have to see how that all comes out." He said, "I am sorry to hear that so much of this is going to come to the White House." He said, "Certainly it's not in the president's interest to have all this kind of thing come out." He made a great point of the three hundred fifty thousand dollars. He says that his recollection — and he said, "You want to check this because," he said, "I'm not — I'm very vague on the facts of this." But he said, I told him about Strachan, because Strachan used to work for him. And I told him that Strachan had been — and has to go back and correct from three fifty to three twenty-eight. Well, he said, "That wasn't the only invasion of that money." And I said, "Oh?" And he said, "No, you would have to check with John Dean on this but," he said, "it's my recollection that Dean had Strachan draw other money out of that fund for payment to these defendants." And I said, "Well, that's the first I heard of that. I understood that Strachan had gone to Bob and said what about this fund, and Bob said send it back to the committee and that Strachan had taken it to LaRue as a representative of the committee." He said, "Yes, I think that's the way it all went, but not until some of it had been tapped for the defendants." And I said —

HALDEMAN: I think your defense is it was not known to anybody over here who was going to — whoever received it.

EHRLICHMAN: No, I said, "Was that before the money got to LaRue?" And he said, "Yes, I am sure it was." And I said, "Well, who would know about that because I've never heard that before." And he said, "Well, I think Dean." So —

NIXON: The three [hundred] twenty-eight [thousand dollars] is wrong too then?

EHRLICHMAN: Well, if Mitchell is to be believed, that's right. That's the inference. But you don't know of any other withdrawal, do you, Bob?

HALDEMAN: Well, I told you —

EHRLICHMAN: Yep.

HALDEMAN: — the three [hundred] twenty-eight [thousand dollars] was not returned in one trip.

EHRLICHMAN: But it all went to LaRue?

HALDEMAN: That's what I'm told.

NIXON: In one trip? I mean he did it twice?

HALDEMAN: Yep. Here's the sequence on that. We wanted to get the money back to the committee. The committee wouldn't take it. Mitchell wouldn't let LaRue take it. I said give it all back. LaRue — Mitchell said no. Then they got desperate for money. And being desperate for money, took back — I think it was forty thousand dollars. And that's all they would take. I still said, "Take it all back, not just a segment of it," and made the point that I didn't see what the problem was. If they needed money and we wanted to get rid of money, it seemed to me it was of mutual interest in working it out. And that then was what happened. The balance — if forty thousand [dollars] were taken in one trip then whatever [unclear].

NIXON: Tell Strachan in his testimony on Monday that he better be clear that he didn't give it all in one bunch.

HALDEMAN: Right.

NIXON: Right? Because Strachan has testified apparently that he gave the whole bundle at once.

HALDEMAN: No, sir. He has not.

EHRLICHMAN: No, he wasn't asked that.

NIXON: He wasn't asked?

HALDEMAN: His testimony in that area is not wrong.

NIXON: Good.

EHRLICHMAN: Now, John kept referring to — kept using a phrase, "protecting the rights of people." One of the ways that he used that phrase was in response to my question about what he thought I ought to do with the information that I had collected in the last several weeks.

NIXON: [unclear]

EHRLICHMAN: And he said, "Well, you have to first of all consider the rights of the individual." I said, "Yes. At the same time, here is the president sitting here now with a body of hearsay and not absolute knowledge. My inclination is to give it to Kleindienst." And he thought about that awhile and he said, "Yes, I guess that's the best thing he could do." I said, "Now you should know that Kleindienst just said that if you, in any way, get the crack in this case, that he is going to step aside, regardless of this whole case." And I said, "I understand Henry Petersen also will."

HALDEMAN: Really?

EHRLICHMAN: And, yeah —

HALDEMAN: I think you've got to be kidding.

EHRLICHMAN: — and I said the thing Kleindienst is pushing for is a special prosecutor. John said, "That would be a grave mistake because it would be subversive to the orderly process of justice if every time you have an important case you strive to put together an ad hoc process."

NIXON: Well, how ridiculous — the present prosecutor's going like hell anyway.

EHRLICHMAN: So I said, "At least he thought he should step aside." He got a very wry smile on his face, and he said, "Well, it's great to have friends, isn't it?" He says, "Especially the way that we stuck by them," meaning the ITT business I assume.

NIXON: Because of Kleindienst.

EHRLICHMAN: So that was an interesting little aside. He said, "I would be very grateful if you would all kind of keep me posted."

NIXON: Yeah.

EHRLICHMAN: And I said, "Fine." He knew that we were talking to [Nixon former law partner and informal Watergate legal counsel] Chappie Rose. I told him no decision had been made about a special counsel, but that we were inclined not to appoint a special prosecutor. That you were —

NIXON: He doesn't mind a special counsel?

EHRLICHMAN: And he thinks it's a good idea to have a special counsel. He suggested that maybe the special counsel should be the one to go talk to Kleindienst, rather than somebody from the White House staff. And so that — that was his only reaction to that. I told him again that I thought he ought to be represented, and that Paul O'Brien was now a target of this grand jury and that I thought he really had to think about getting representation. He said he had given it a lot of thought, but that he didn't think that he would want to make a change yet. He thought he would wait and see how O'Brien got along.

HALDEMAN: Which confirms he considers O'Brien to be his attorney?

EHRLICHMAN: Right.

HALDEMAN: That's interesting.

EHRLICHMAN: He asked me how he was involved in — what I had heard about the prosecutor's view of Mitchell's involvement in the obstruction of justice stuff. I said that I really had not been able to find anybody who was an efficient actor, who really went to a defendant and said, "Don't talk," or so and so. And he said, "Well, I really wonder if you ever will, other than their lawyers, because my impression of this is that they were the ones who were worried about their fees and who were really coming to us rather than for any of us going to them to bring about a change in testimony. Matter of fact," he said —

HALDEMAN: [unclear] all along —

EHRLICHMAN: " — the thing that we were talking to Dean about," he said, "I wasn't really worried about what they testified to. I was worried about what they'd say to the press."

HALDEMAN: Exactly when Hunt made the challenge.

EHRLICHMAN: Yep.

HALDEMAN: That — somehow, Dean doesn't see that that way.

EHRLICHMAN: Well, we've got to talk to him some more. He, Mitchell, did not mention Martha at all or — and I didn't raise it. That was just not even in the conversation.

NIXON: Yeah.

EHRLICHMAN: Oh, I told him that the only way that I knew that he was mentioned, insofar as the aftermath was concerned, was that from time to time he would send Dean over saying, "Hey, we need money for this," and he said, "Who told you that?"

HALDEMAN: John Dean.

EHRLICHMAN: And I said, "John, that's common knowledge. And, Dean, among others, has told me that." I said, "Dean has not been subpoenaed. He has not testified and as a matter of fact the way they are proceeding down there it looks like they are losing interest in him."

NIXON: [unclear]

EHRLICHMAN: I — in a sense — well, said this to John because I wanted him to be impressed with the fact that we were not jobbing him.

NIXON: Oh, I get it — the point. Yeah. Yeah.

EHRLICHMAN: We were — Dean [unclear]. That's it.

NIXON: Does he know that Magruder's going to confess?

EHRLICHMAN: I said that in the course of calling to invite people to come talk with me today, and I indicated that there were more than two, that the person who called was told that Dean intended to —

NIXON: Magruder.

EHRLICHMAN: Pardon me — Magruder intended to make a clean breast of it and that was first-party information and very reliable, and that that would tend to begin to unravel this thing from the center in both directions. And he agreed with that. Now he said, "Which version is it that Magruder is going to testify to? Is it the one that he gave Bob and me in Bob's office, or is it some other version?"

HALDEMAN: That's not true.

EHRLICHMAN: I said —

NIXON: What was the version he gave Bob? Was it another version?

EHRLICHMAN: Well, he — let me tell you what Mitchell said. It was another gigging of the White House. He said, "You know, in Bob's office, Magruder said that Haldeman had cooked this whole thing up over here in the White House and — "

NIXON: Had he said that?

EHRLICHMAN: Well, I mean, that's — you know, the sort of —

NIXON: All right.

EHRLICHMAN: And that — and that sort of —

NIXON: Now wait a minute. Your conversation with Mitchell is the one where —

HALDEMAN: I've got the notes somewhere.

NIXON: — where Mitchell [unclear]. It's good you have it, too, but —

EHRLICHMAN: Mitchell's theory —

NIXON: Wait a minute. Whatever his theory is, let me say a footnote —

EHRLICHMAN: Yeah.

NIXON: — one footnote is that his throwing it off on the White House isn't going to help him one damn bit.

EHRLICHMAN: Unless he can peddle the theory that Colson and others were effectively running the committee through Magruder and freezing him out of the operation —

NIXON: Huh.

EHRLICHMAN: — which is kind of the story line he was giving me.

HALDEMAN: Did he include me in the others?

EHRLICHMAN: Yep.

HALDEMAN: That I was freezing him out of the operation?

EHRLICHMAN: That you, in other words — he didn't say this baldly or flatly, but you accumulated a whole bunch of things and it's Colson, Dean, and Bob —

NIXON: Colson and Bob. Bob and Colson.

EHRLICHMAN: — working with Magruder, and that that was sort of the way the lineup went.

NIXON: The fault is the White House's rather than his.

HALDEMAN: He's got an impossible problem with that.

NIXON: Well, I —

HALDEMAN: The poor guy is putting —

NIXON: It's bad if he gets up there and says that. It's a hell of a problem for us.

HALDEMAN: It's a problem for us. No question. But there's no way he can prove it —

EHRLICHMAN: He has a very, very bad tremor.

NIXON: He's always had that.

EHRLICHMAN: Well, I've never noticed —

NIXON: Shakes.

EHRLICHMAN: — it as bad as this.

NIXON: Yeah. Yeah.

HALDEMAN: It's always been bad.

NIXON: You've done your duty today. [unclear]

HALDEMAN: The next question is —

EHRLICHMAN: [unclear]

HALDEMAN: The next question is whether you see Magruder or not and you're now set to see him at four o'clock, and if we're going to cancel him we should do it right now.

EHRLICHMAN: See no purpose in seeing him.

NIXON: Why? Because Magruder's aware of the fact now that we — ?

HALDEMAN: Magruder's already going to do what John's going to tell him to do, so —

NIXON: Yeah.

HALDEMAN: So far we've got it all —

NIXON: Our purpose, of course, [unclear] do it. Our purpose, as I understood it — what I mean, Bob, was to keep a record for the [unclear].

EHRLICHMAN: All right. For that purpose maybe I should. Now, maybe what I should do —

HALDEMAN: Let him tell you what he told me. And then you say, "Good."

EHRLICHMAN: Exactly.

NIXON: I'd like to get what the hell he's — what he's going to say.

EHRLICHMAN: All right. All right.

NIXON: I would particularly like to get what the hell he's going to say about Strachan.

EHRLICHMAN: All right.

NIXON: I mean, I'd say — apparently you could say, "Look, John — look, Jeb, I have to conduct this investigation on the White House. [unclear]." If he says Strachan knew, say, "How do you know he knows?"

EHRLICHMAN: All right.

NIXON: Do you think you should ask him that or do you not want to go digging that?

HALDEMAN: Why not?

EHRLICHMAN: Okay.

NIXON: All right.

EHRLICHMAN: Yeah, once he tell me that he intends to go forward to tell the truth, he has nothing to lose by talking to me.

NIXON: Hell. Well, I know. The point is that I want it to seem you want him to be, without guiding him or leading him, you can at least maybe get that out.

EHRLICHMAN: Right.

HALDEMAN: Well, his lawyer will be there.

EHRLICHMAN: Right.

NIXON: The other thing is what about the — of course, you realize that if he says something about Strachan, then of course that puts an obligation on us to do something about Strachan, doesn't it?

EHRLICHMAN: Well, at least to corroborate it, or investigate it, or go forward on it.

HALDEMAN: You could do it by questioning Strachan?

EHRLICHMAN: Among other things.

HALDEMAN: Here's where it ends up.

EHRLICHMAN: Well, if it ends up that way why then you have a sort of a dogfight. Now, let —

NIXON: Excuse me. Go ahead, sorry.

HALDEMAN: I didn't think Jeb is — let me put it — let me say this: I don't think Jeb wants to hang Strachan. I think Jeb is worried about the fact that in going through this he is going to, he thinks to a degree, implicate Strachan. Now, that's the same kind of thinking as Strachan and Chapin, who were both very concerned about getting me into the Segretti thing. In other words, they see any involvement — any mentioning of the name as being a problem.

NIXON: Yeah.

HALDEMAN: I don't think Jeb sees it or understands the question of whether he really got Strachan in or not. I'm not sure how far he decided he intends to go with Strachan.

EHRLICHMAN: He didn't say. He didn't really make it clear?

HALDEMAN: No. He just said, unfortunately, this whole thing is going to come up and if it comes up —

NIXON: Bob —

HALDEMAN: — but then what's the problem with Gordon? And he said, "Well, I don't know. That depends on what other people say."

NIXON: Other people meaning like a secretary, you mean? Or somebody who typed —

HALDEMAN: Could be.

NIXON: — typed a memorandum?

HALDEMAN: Could be.

NIXON: To a degree, I think I see in Strachan's case — the — well, the other possibility, of course, would be — maybe they're very likely — oh, I think it might be this, Bob, that they're going to ask the question, "Who told you to do this, Jeb — Mr. Magruder?" [unclear]

HALDEMAN: He's flatly denied that Strachan told him to do it. Now, Larry [Higby] did — he brought back that exact story that he —

NIXON: Colson. What about that Colson told you to do it?

EHRLICHMAN: He says that he's going to have to hurt Mitchell.

HALDEMAN: He says, "The one I'm going to hurt is Mitchell, and to some degree John Dean and maybe Gordon."

NIXON: He's obviously talked this through. Isn't it worthwhile for you to find out — ?

HALDEMAN: I think we have to.

NIXON: I think we owe it to ourselves to find out about John Dean, for example — what he now understand — that he thinks [unclear] this is true [unclear] us.

EHRLICHMAN: All right. I think that's right. This is probably a golden opportunity in a way.

NIXON: Right. To find — well, let me put it this way. We've got to find out what the hell he's going to say —

EHRLICHMAN: Yeah.

NIXON: — so that we'll know what to expect, you see —

EHRLICHMAN: Yeah.

NIXON: — rather than have the goddamn thing go on our heads.

EHRLICHMAN: Right.

NIXON: The interesting thing is, did Bob tell you? Are you prepared to say that he says that — Magruder said that they'll indict him and not Mitchell. That's a hard damn theory. Isn't that what you told me? Bob, didn't you tell me that?

HALDEMAN: No. No. He said everybody. No, he said, "Everybody is going to fall on this." He wasn't meaning indictments. He was meaning going to talk.

NIXON: Oh.

HALDEMAN: Himself, LaRue, and so on.

NIXON: Yeah.

HALDEMAN: He said everybody's going to drop except John. And he's going to get out of it. [unclear]

EHRLICHMAN: That's correct. That's correct.

HALDEMAN: He didn't mean that Mitchell wouldn't be indicted. He meant that Mitchell was the only one who was going to continue to hard-line — that everybody else had given up. And that's why he's given up. His point is he's keeping quiet now or lying now serves no purpose because all they're going to do is get him on a perjury count as well as everything else. If he can clean up anything he can live with himself better. He's faced the fact that he's had it.

NIXON: Mm-hmm, so that means LaRue and O'Brien. Is that right?

HALDEMAN: Depends on how far they go.

EHRLICHMAN: That's right.

HALDEMAN: Jeb doesn't know anything much about that.

NIXON: It's under cover. They'll push him. I think he can put up a pretty good fight on the thing, don't you?

HALDEMAN: I would think so. I would be —

NIXON: Even if they indict him, it's going to be a damn hard intricate case to prove. You've got to prove motive there, don't you, John?

EHRLICHMAN: Yes. Dean argues that in a conspiracy such as they're trying to build, they may not have to prove the same kind of animus as to some of the participants, but only that they were in it. I would have to read the cases. I just don't know what the law is.

NIXON: Of course, you've got their defendants the same way, I guess —

HALDEMAN: That's right.

NIXON: — I guess that key witness there is Hunt.

EHRLICHMAN: Well, the defendants — and then it's the defendants' lawyer, Bittman.

NIXON: Hunt and Bittman. They're both — and Hunt will testify tomorrow.

EHRLICHMAN: My guess is that a fellow like Bittman has probably negotiated immunity for himself, and has —

HALDEMAN: Dean strongly feels they wouldn't give it to him.

EHRLICHMAN: Yeah, I know.

NIXON: That they will?

HALDEMAN: Will not.

EHRLICHMAN: But that he's going to tell about a lot of conversations he had with a lot of people.

NIXON: Bittman is?

EHRLICHMAN: Yeah.

NIXON: Do we know that?

EHRLICHMAN: Well, I don't know that, but I know for instance that Bittman had a conversation with Colson that was a Watergate conversation. And I know what Colson says about it — that he was brilliant and adroit, avoided any —

HALDEMAN: And he says Bittman's recollection of it would be exactly the same as Colson's — his recollection of the specific conversation. But he says Bittman may draw conclusions from it.

NIXON: This is the clemency conversation?

HALDEMAN: Yep.

NIXON: And his conclusion would be that he felt the president offered clemency?

HALDEMAN: No. His conclusion is that he, Colson, will have Hunt out by Christmas, because, you know — what kind of pull I [Colson] have here in the White House. I'll be able to work it out. That's what he would imply saying —

NIXON: What — how does Colson handle that?

EHRLICHMAN: He says he's got a tape or a wire — a memo or something that says exactly what he said.

HALDEMAN: It's just a memo. He wrote a memorandum of the conversation immediately after the conversation. Which will — that's all it is — his side of the story.

NIXON: You don't think this, this would lead to an indictment of Colson, do you?

EHRLICHMAN: I haven't any idea. Dean seems to think everybody in the place is going to get indicted this afternoon. Well, I —

HALDEMAN: They're all doing the same thing. What Dean said is just looking at the worst possible side of the coin that you could make a list of everybody who in some way is technically indictable in the cover-up operation. And that list includes, in addition to Mitchell, Haldeman, Ehrlichman, Colson, Dean —

NIXON: Because they all discussed it?

HALDEMAN: — Strachan, Kalmbach, Kalmbach's go-between — Kalmbach's source, LaRue, Mardian, O'Brien, Parkinson —

EHRLICHMAN: Bittman.

HALDEMAN: — Bittman, Hunt, and, you know — so, and just to keep wandering through the impossibles, he said maybe the route for everybody on that list is to take a guilty plea and get immediate — what do you call it, pardon, or — ?

NIXON: Clemency.

HALDEMAN: — clemency.

NIXON: From the president.

HALDEMAN: Mm-hmm. That shows you the somewhat unclear state [laughs] of some of John Dean's analytical thinking.

EHRLICHMAN: No way.

NIXON: It's a shame. There could be clemency in this case, and at the proper time having in mind the extraordinary sentences of Magruder and so forth and so on, but you know damn well —

HALDEMAN: It's got to be down the road —

NIXON: It's ridiculous. They all know that. Colson knew that. I mean, when you talked to Colson and he talked to me.

EHRLICHMAN: The Magruder thing is four o'clock and it's still on.

HALDEMAN: Yeah. I think I have to go confirm it —

EHRLICHMAN: All right.

HALDEMAN: Should I?

EHRLICHMAN: I think so. It's an opportunity. Now the question is whether I ought to get ahold of Kleindienst for, say, five o'clock and get this thing all wrapped up.

[HALDEMAN leaves the conversation.]

NIXON: Have you determined it should be Kleindienst rather than Silbert?

EHRLICHMAN: Yeah. Dean's right about that. I'm sure.

NIXON: I didn't know you'd talked to Dean.

EHRLICHMAN: Well, I did. I asked Dean's advice on this. He said Silbert would ask you to wait a minute. He'd step out of the room. He'd come back to get you and he'd walk you right into the grand jury.

NIXON: Oh.

EHRLICHMAN: And he doesn't dare handle a communication like that personally from the standpoint of the later criticism. He said the better route would be to go to Kleindienst who will probably step aside and refer you to Dean. Then Dean, in turn, would say to Henry Petersen, "They've done this little investigation over at the White House. They've collected a bunch of hearsay. There doesn't seem to be much new, but they've got it there if anybody wants it." Petersen, in turn, would inform Silbert, who would, "Thank God. I got more than I can handle here now. We'll wait and interview that guy later."

NIXON: The purpose in doing this is what?

EHRLICHMAN: The purpose of doing it is to —

NIXON: The White House conducted its investigation and turned it over to the grand jury?

EHRLICHMAN: Turned it over to the Justice Department.

NIXON: Before the indictment?

EHRLICHMAN: Right.

NIXON: How much are you going to tell them?

EHRLICHMAN: I think I'd let them drag it out of me in a way. I don't know, I just really haven't thought that part through.

NIXON: Because they would say, "Why did the White House wait for the Justice Department to do all this?"

EHRLICHMAN: "Did the White House know?" is probably the way this would come. Yes —

NIXON: Yes. And you'd say, "Yes, as a matter of fact — "

EHRLICHMAN: "We had been at work on this for some time. The president — "

NIXON: " — president ordered an independent investigation."

EHRLICHMAN: " — needed it known."

NIXON: I had ordered an independent investigation at the time McCord had something to say. Right.

EHRLICHMAN: All right.

NIXON: At that time, you conducted an investigation.

EHRLICHMAN: And that — "At the time, I was ready to report to you my tentative conclusions. And they were no more than that." You felt that they were sufficiently serious that, well — that you felt that one overriding aspect of the report was that some people evidently were hanging back feeling that they were somehow doing the president a favor. That the president had me personally transmit to them his view that this ought to be a complete open thing. That may or may not have played some part in Jeb Magruder's subsequent disclosures to the grand jury. In any event, rather than for us simply to hold the information that we did have in the White House, we turned it over to the Justice Department for whatever disposition they wanted to make of it.

NIXON: If Mitchell is indicted here, you think he's going to be convicted?

EHRLICHMAN: Yeah, I think so. I can't guarantee it, but I would be amazed once Magruder goes in there.

NIXON: But that's only one man.

EHRLICHMAN: That's plenty.

NIXON: Is it?

EHRLICHMAN: Oh, yes, sir. And, well —

NIXON: [unclear] know criminal law?

EHRLICHMAN: With all the other stuff they've got —

NIXON: All the other stuff they've got?

EHRLICHMAN: They have a way of corroborating —

NIXON: All right. So let's go down the road. Mitchell's indicted. When do you think this is going to happen? With Magruder going in today, it could come sooner.

EHRLICHMAN: Could be, although Dean feels it will not be before May 15 at the earliest. And now with the glut of people coming in it may be later than that. Could be toward the end of —

NIXON: Because they want to make —

EHRLICHMAN: They will want to do it all at once.

• • •

[HALDEMAN joins the conversation.]

HALDEMAN: Would you check Jeb and see if they — why not have him come over and see us here?

EHRLICHMAN: Yes, sir.

NIXON: What is the situation then with Mitchell? Undoubtedly, he will change the venue [unclear].

HALDEMAN: If he [Magruder] could come at three thirty, that would be better here.

EHRLICHMAN: Well, I'd think he'd have maybe a better chance of getting it judged in a different venue [unclear] concerning the witnesses than he would certainly here in Washington who would feel the political heat of letting the Senate go on. I don't know how to calculate that. That's — it's a good question. But, I mean, you'd have to have it in a place like Missoula, Montana.

NIXON: This is a national story.

HALDEMAN: [unclear] Gee, Pascagoula, Mississippi, might be better.

EHRLICHMAN: Yeah, that would be better. Miami would be the place — best place for it.

NIXON: With you here, you men and Dean, and without going as far as we did a month ago, and so forth and so on, he said they will probably indict a pretty big bag.

EHRLICHMAN: Right.

NIXON: Is that right?

HALDEMAN: Could — now he does not think — he does — his opinion is that they will not reach him.

NIXON: Yeah.

HALDEMAN: He does not think he's a target and he doesn't think he will be. He thinks he might be, but he doesn't think he will and if he's not, it doesn't go any — that means it isn't going any further than the White House.

EHRLICHMAN: Well, I'm not so sure you can say —

HALDEMAN: That's right. He said they may be after bigger targets.

EHRLICHMAN: Yeah. Just named defendants.

NIXON: [unclear] like Ehrlichman and Haldeman?

EHRLICHMAN: Like yours truly.

NIXON: Yep.

HALDEMAN: I don't — I think —

EHRLICHMAN: I don't —

HALDEMAN: — he's trying to get attention with that, John. I —

EHRLICHMAN: He got it. [laughs]

HALDEMAN: I don't think he believes it.

NIXON: I don't think, though — I can't see that. John Dean had said we all got to keep our thinking perspective. With John — Kleindienst — a bit tangential — anything — relationship either of you had with the goddamn thing is nothing compared to Dean's because he sat in on the goddamn meetings.

HALDEMAN: That's right.

NIXON: He did participate directly in the thing.

EHRLICHMAN: Oh, I'm certain there's an element of —

HALDEMAN: As — however, and if he can, he's on a somewhat higher level admittedly, but he can establish himself in a similar role to that of Strachan. Say that he was merely a messenger, a conduit, agent —

EHRLICHMAN: Boy, Mitchell —

HALDEMAN: — he's not a principal.

EHRLICHMAN: Mitchell sure doesn't agree with that. He'd be a tough — I assume Mitchell will never testify. That would be my assumption. That —

HALDEMAN: Well, one thing I was thinking of that we didn't talk through but I'm sure you thought through and I have talked to him and told him I was reporting to the president is that the outcome of the Magruder thing is that there will never be any public Magruder testimony.

EHRLICHMAN: That's right.

HALDEMAN: So the question of what Magruder's testimony amounts —

EHRLICHMAN: Well, no —

HALDEMAN: — to is only in terms of what the grand jury is —

EHRLICHMAN: No, that's not right, Bob. Because he will — he'll be indicted. He'll plead guilty. He'll be sentenced.

HALDEMAN: That's right.

EHRLICHMAN: Then he's available.

HALDEMAN: To the committee?

EHRLICHMAN: Well, to the committee or to the court as a witness in somebody else's case.

NIXON: Oh, he is?

EHRLICHMAN: Sure. He'll be brought back in his prison denims, changed into a business suit, and be put on the stand.

NIXON: Oh.

HALDEMAN: Really?

EHRLICHMAN: Sure.

HALDEMAN: Why doesn't he take the Fifth on possible additional self-incrimination?

EHRLICHMAN: They'd give him immunity.

HALDEMAN: Sounds nice for a while, anyway. This stuff wasn't hanging on any of those things anyway.

EHRLICHMAN: No. No.

HALDEMAN: I think we've just got to face the fact that whatever the story is it's going to be out [unclear].

EHRLICHMAN: Well, you'll have the entire story out, plus probably two other stories that two other guys make up.

HALDEMAN: That's right.

EHRLICHMAN: And that anything and everything that's said will be believed.

HALDEMAN: And at least one of which will be enormously damaging to us.

EHRLICHMAN: There would be no way —

HALDEMAN: Not provable, but damaging.

EHRLICHMAN: — no way to deny it.

NIXON: It's terrible when they get such a big bag.

EHRLICHMAN: Yep.

NIXON: What does all this mean with regard to the — our posture here? Would you say let's take the gas? In terms of not cooperating with the committee and so forth. You're not going to — you're now looking at another month of it.

HALDEMAN: I don't think we should take that chance.

NIXON: See if we can in a month or more, I don't want to — Bob, you see the point is I don't want to cooperate with the committee unless I get a resolution of the entire Republican caucus in the Senate. We can't do that. [unclear] based on the [unclear]. Do you not agree? [unclear]

EHRLICHMAN: What should I say to Ervin and Baker on Monday?

NIXON: That's exactly why I am raising this point. [unclear]

EHRLICHMAN: One thing —

HALDEMAN: The lawyer's office, okay —

EHRLICHMAN: I think Magruder and Mitchell and others —

NIXON: If they show up at the Senate —

EHRLICHMAN: — will not be witnesses at the Ervin hearings.

NIXON: You just told me [unclear] that they could be witnesses at that trial.

EHRLICHMAN: Well, they can, but the point is that the — well, all right, after the trial and their sentencing —

NIXON: Yeah, of Mitchell.

EHRLICHMAN: — they could be subpoenaed —

NIXON: Yeah.

EHRLICHMAN: — and they would be delivered up to the committee.

NIXON: But why — you mean until Mitchell is tried, they can't be — ?

EHRLICHMAN: That's right.

NIXON: Why?

EHRLICHMAN: Until they stand trial — well, it would prejudice their rights.

NIXON: Not only they — but he's already given — pled guilty.

EHRLICHMAN: Well, then Magruder could be a witness after he's been sentenced. If he wanted to be and —

NIXON: Wanted to be?

EHRLICHMAN: Now, here's the tricky point. Whether or not Ervin can grant immunity to someone who has been sentenced and is serving a sentence is something that — I don't know whether that would make any difference or not. I have no doubt that a judge can, but I don't know whether the Senate can. I think Ervin's best bet is to suspend as soon as these indictments are announced. I mean, that's — if he were smart, that's what he'd do. And just let this thing tear everything up and then come around afterwards and touch up places that have been missed. Just sort of go around the battlefield and get the coup de grâce.

NIXON: Well, after they get through this kind of indictment there isn't going to be that much gas in the Ervin Committee. I mean, they'll go ahead but I mean they'll say, "Well, now, what the hell? There's old Segretti. Shit, he's too small." [unclear] on the other hand, people —

EHRLICHMAN: He gets the leavings.

NIXON: What?

EHRLICHMAN: He gets the leavings. That's all.

HALDEMAN: They'll delve into it because their whole pitch is that this isn't the Watergate, it's the use of, the misuse of money and all that sort of stuff.

NIXON: I know, but —

HALDEMAN: They're going to run that money game down. Where did it come from?

EHRLICHMAN: Yeah.

HALDEMAN: Where did it go?

EHRLICHMAN: Mitchell said, incidentally —

NIXON: [unclear] million dollars?

HALDEMAN: Well, yeah.

EHRLICHMAN: Mitchell said that we should take great care to establish that three fifty came from the pre-'72 campaign money.

HALDEMAN: Right.

EHRLICHMAN: "Any questions in your mind about that?" And he said, "No, my impression is that this is where it came from," but he said, "Maury Stans and Herb Kalmbach spent a week together trying to tie all these various funds down as to source and that's a big loose end."

NIXON: Well, you better — let's get that one. Well, there was no question about that, was there, Bob?

HALDEMAN: Not in my mind.

EHRLICHMAN: Well, but you see Maury and Herb —

HALDEMAN: The question was that there was — well, a lot more than that the question was how much of it would we set aside. It came down to three fifty.

EHRLICHMAN: Maury —

NIXON: Who brought it over here? Maury?

HALDEMAN: No. Gordon Strachan went over there and got it. Well, either Sloan brought it over here or Strachan went over there. I'm not sure which. Strachan took delivery from Sloan.

NIXON: We heard this one before the campaign started, in other words?

HALDEMAN: It was April 6.

NIXON: April 6?

EHRLICHMAN: That may make a problem.

NIXON: After the day of the —

HALDEMAN: The day before the seventh.

NIXON: It was April 7? But it was the money before.

HALDEMAN: Yeah, it was cash that had been, John [unclear] over from the seventh.

EHRLICHMAN: But John implied that they had bigger problems and that they had to use this money to make up shortages someplace else or some — I don't know. He didn't get into all this, but he said —

HALDEMAN: They never told me that.

EHRLICHMAN: They had problems with making their accountings all come out even, Kalmbach and Stans.

HALDEMAN: Kalmbach assured me all the time that the tack — the cash from '70 was intact, except for some that we knew had been used. But what was intact was — there was supposedly about two million. What was intact was about a million six. And the question — it was way more than three fifty in other words, many times that. And the question was how much of that million six — and they convinced me that you don't want very — you don't want a million six. Or it could have been restored to two million [unclear] but you don't want that because under the new laws and everything. There is no way that you could find to spend it. There isn't that much stuff you can spend it on that wouldn't be traceable. And, so somehow a figure of three fifty was negotiated as being a reasonable figure that might be, you know, would cover what might come up, but wouldn't be impossible and wouldn't put that big a hole in the campaign. So it was — so it was no go. That was money that was not really —

NIXON: Didn't belong to the committee?

HALDEMAN: Belonged to the committee. What happened, really, is that — that we made a contribution to the committee that —

NIXON: Yeah, that's what it was.

HALDEMAN: — the friends of Nixon in '70 —

EHRLICHMAN: Yeah.

HALDEMAN: — made a million three contribution to the committee and kept three fifty of what it had of its carryover funds.

EHRLICHMAN: That's the way to argue that.

HALDEMAN: That's the way it was —

NIXON: [unclear] finish it, if you got time — finish it. It's all there. We'll talk another time. I think, Bob, that —

HALDEMAN: We can't reach Magruder. There's no answer. [unclear] he might be walking over or something. If he arrives here, they'll let us know.

NIXON: We better get the other things out of the way. I think we're going to be — I don't want to be hammered into those hearings. I mean I don't want to — I know the hearings will hammer the hell on us anyway, but I don't want [unclear], but I don't [unclear]. What is involved here — we'll take — I think we'll take a hell of a beating [unclear] what is involved here —

EHRLICHMAN: Mm-hmm.

NIXON: — in the next thirty days, a lot — heat we'll take with regard to why we aren't appearing. Why we are not going to appear before the committee. Now, how do we answer that? We answer that by saying the committee won't agree to our — the proper ground rules? Is that correct?

EHRLICHMAN: We say we don't want to turn it into a circus. We want our testimony received in a judicious and probative way. We are willing to have our people go but only under the right circumstances.

NIXON: Well.

HALDEMAN: You've got to play the Kissinger thing [the question of whether other presidential assistants could be called to testify by Congress once the White House waives executive privilege]. We're releasing the records of your negotiations, don't you?

EHRLICHMAN: Yep.

HALDEMAN: Simply say that this is what we offer.

EHRLICHMAN: Yep.

HALDEMAN: We stand ready to meet this offer whenever the enemy is willing to talk —

EHRLICHMAN: — seriously.

NIXON: Then the question would then arise.

HALDEMAN: Tell them we'll resume the bombing —

NIXON: [laughs] Uh —

EHRLICHMAN: I think it will —

NIXON: Probably not?

EHRLICHMAN: Probably — not in the light of the heat from the grand jury and so on.

HALDEMAN: I still think you can —

NIXON: If we have —

HALDEMAN: Maybe it can't be done, but there ought to be a way to turn the grand jury thing strongly in our way, which is that this proves the rightness of the president's approach of full cooperation with the proper process of justice —

EHRLICHMAN: Yep.

HALDEMAN: — which is bringing people, even at the very highest level, to account.

NIXON: You were cooperating.

EHRLICHMAN: Yeah. I think we should do that.

HALDEMAN: We've been cooperating all along.

EHRLICHMAN: No question about that.

HALDEMAN: And the value of that is [unclear].

NIXON: [unclear] the first man out should not be favored [unclear]. You understand the importance of that and so forth and so on. Then I've got the [unclear] if you can get it to them. Trying to think of — how to use you effectively in this too, John — is a —

EHRLICHMAN: "I have to be unwilling to tell the press what I discovered because of the rights of individuals."

NIXON: Yeah.

EHRLICHMAN: Unless we want to get Mitchell and Magruder off. I could sure as hell give them an ironclad defense.

NIXON: Oh. Oh, I meant the Gray hearing.

HALDEMAN: What's wrong with that?

NIXON: It's time the grand jury has indicted [unclear].

EHRLICHMAN: No, I could prejudice —

NIXON: [unclear]

EHRLICHMAN: I could prejudice their rights in such a way that they could —

NIXON: Oh.

EHRLICHMAN: — never get a fair trial.

NIXON: I guess you're right. You can't do it. See, Bob, that's the problem. You can do [unclear] cooperate with the grand jury [unclear].

EHRLICHMAN: Well, how about if I —

NIXON: It's wrong.

HALDEMAN: What's wrong with prejudicing their rights?

EHRLICHMAN: Well, I don't know. Mm-hmm. How about if I were to do this — ?

HALDEMAN: You get your indictment, but you don't get anybody in jail.

EHRLICHMAN: I could say that I made a report. I could say that I made a deal. I could say that you instructed me to do certain things. One of the things you instructed me to do was talk to Magruder. Another thing you instructed me to do was to talk to the attorney general. And I did all those things.

NIXON: And you did — but not mention.

EHRLICHMAN: And then I wouldn't mention who else. I could say I talked to other people.

NIXON: I — "Did you talk to Mr. Mitchell, Mr. Ehrlichman?"

EHRLICHMAN: I am not going to get into any other names of any people.

HALDEMAN: "Then why did you name Mr. Magruder?"

NIXON: Because he's testifying. That's the only difference. I don't know. You always come up with what not to do to those people.

HALDEMAN: Yeah.

EHRLICHMAN: Yeah, right.

NIXON: Let's come again. Bob — aren't we really sort of in a position where it would be better volunteering in that damn grand jury? I mean, at least pull the wire on something there. I mean, I really think you do. They're making — it seems to me that a hell of a lot of the issue about doing something involves our inability to convey the fact that we're willing to cooperate. That we're willing to waive executive privilege and keep our people silent. Now that's what I'm really trying to do [unclear] — I don't know.

EHRLICHMAN: We will get —

HALDEMAN: I've always heard that that's the right — that that's the point of that kind of argument.

NIXON: Is that [unclear]?

HALDEMAN: [unclear] one-day — one-day-plus story.

NIXON: Yeah.

HALDEMAN: The price for which is weeks of cha —

NIXON: Disaster.

HALDEMAN: Disaster.

EHRLICHMAN: But the thing that's wrong with that is while it's a one-day-plus story, it's also the elimination of ninety days of negative stories.

NIXON: Before you ever get up there. That's the point.

HALDEMAN: And it's setting up ninety days of other negative — more negative stories.

EHRLICHMAN: Well, maybe. Maybe.

NIXON: That's a very good question. The question is how much more negative is there?

EHRLICHMAN: You could have —

NIXON: Then have the senators go out and characterize it and all that crap.

EHRLICHMAN: You could have peace with honor if we could get them to agree, as I believe they will, that executive privilege is reserved till the time of questioning.

HALDEMAN: They've pretty much stipulated that, haven't they?

EHRLICHMAN: That's right.

NIXON: What do you mean reserved till the time — ?

EHRLICHMAN: I mean —

NIXON: Negotiated?

EHRLICHMAN: No.

HALDEMAN: You've got all these privileges regarding the individual question —

EHRLICHMAN: Right.

HALDEMAN: — you only waive privilege as to appearance.

EHRLICHMAN: Right.

HALDEMAN: But you also appear — adhere the merits of each individual question as to whether it relates to privilege or not and ask you what you want question by question. It will be by your representative accompanying the witness. And Connally's happy dream that I go up there charging away at the Senate doesn't work.

NIXON: I think Henry [Petersen] has a good point here, too, and the thought about it is he doesn't want Bob to be the first witness. And if there is an overrule and the cause was empty it makes sense. Although, let me say I do think that we still ought to consider — are we still considering the possibility of getting out the Segretti story?

EHRLICHMAN: Yes. Uh —

NIXON: No way we could do it?

EHRLICHMAN: I think getting out the Haldeman story would be more useful in the light of Magruder and others going down to testify.

NIXON: In other words you'd get that out before they testify?

EHRLICHMAN: If possible.

NIXON: Before they get [unclear].

EHRLICHMAN: Yep, yeah.

HALDEMAN: The best — perfect story to get out would be a White House story.

NIXON: That's right.

EHRLICHMAN: About how we've been working at this.

HALDEMAN: Which meets Henry's objections. Well, it's the Haldeman story, but you can't do it other than the whole thing. It's the —

EHRLICHMAN: You say to Haldeman I have investigated. Packaged up the whole [unclear].

NIXON: What I can do is, basically, just having an Ehrlichman report. We've talked about a Dean report. That would be something — an Ehrlichman report that he makes and here is the situation with regard to the White House involvement. I haven't gone into the committee thing. Now —

HALDEMAN: The current charges on White House involvement primarily are Haldeman charges.

NIXON: That's right.

EHRLICHMAN: Well, I didn't go into White House involvement. I assumed that —

NIXON: No. I —

EHRLICHMAN: — what you needed to know from me, and I mean this would be what I would say, "What the president needed to know was the truth or falsity of charges that were leaking out with regard to — "

NIXON: Yeah.

EHRLICHMAN: " — Committee for the Re-election personnel and any connections to the White House that might exist."

NIXON: Yeah.

EHRLICHMAN: "That was the area of inquiry rather than whether anybody in the White House was involved — "

NIXON: I agree.

EHRLICHMAN: " — in the first place."

NIXON: I've been trying to get you out there in a way that you'd never go into all that stuff across the street —

EHRLICHMAN: I know. I understand. I understand.

NIXON: — other than the fact that you are going to go before the indictments.

EHRLICHMAN: Well, I'd do it before the indictments and say, "Look, we have great confidence in the grand jury process — "

NIXON: That's right.

EHRLICHMAN: " — and I don't want to do anything that is going to in any way impair that process."

NIXON: That's right. A number of people have been called before that grand jury, and I'm not going to —

EHRLICHMAN: The —

HALDEMAN: I'd say everything I've found has been turned over to the Justice Department —

EHRLICHMAN: Exactly.

HALDEMAN: — relating to that —

NIXON: Everything that the grand jury is considering.

EHRLICHMAN: And I doubt seriously that I discovered anything new. What I probably did was simply bring into the White House for the first time a body of information that otherwise was available. Other people — other investigators undoubtedly could do the same thing that I did and maybe a lot better. But we had had no occasion previously to bring all that information before us. "I talked to Kleindienst, so I got what the — what the Justice Department had. I got stuff from all over and we brought it in and we tried to assemble it in a way that was meaningful for the president, and — "

HALDEMAN: Did you review the FBI files?

EHRLICHMAN: No.

HALDEMAN: Why not? That's the original source you said was the most extensive investigation in history. Why the hell didn't you look at it?

EHRLICHMAN: I didn't look at it because I didn't need to look at it. I got a summary.

NIXON: Dean was working on the summary.

EHRLICHMAN: No, and the Justice Department.

NIXON: Yeah, go ahead.

EHRLICHMAN: And, uh —

NIXON: I think that's easy enough [unclear].

HALDEMAN: I do, too.

EHRLICHMAN: I didn't try and duplicate the work of the U.S. attorney. What I tried to do was simply determine for the president's use and for the president's use only whether or not there was substance to charges that we were hearing. And whether or not there was White House involvement with relation to those charges and to determine whether or not the White House ought to be doing anything about its own personnel or about others that it was not doing. We were not trying to determine what the U.S. attorney should do or the grand jury should do or the Justice Department should do. At the same time it [unclear] for us to withhold anything from the Justice Department in the — with the thought that some of this information might not have been previously available to them. So I'm not going to go into it. I'm not going to tell you what I found.

NIXON: Well, but here's the Haldeman story that we found—

EHRLICHMAN: But no, I'm not going to tell you specifically what I found because obviously the purpose of my work was simply for the president to form judgments—as the basis for the president to form judgments with regard to White House personnel and other government personnel and to determine whether or not the White House was actually in any way impeding the progress of the prosecutorial effort, excuse me, by anything that we were inadvertently doing. And so that's not—that's not very fancy and I'd want to think that through and try to—

NIXON: So what I'm trying to get is how you get his story out. That's what I'm [unclear].

EHRLICHMAN: Oh, I see. I'd just put that out—just flat put that out. And do it—hang it on the peg of the Ervin Committee setting a date for their first day of hearings.

NIXON: You mean you'd ask for an early date?

EHRLICHMAN: No. They will—

HALDEMAN: They will announce Wednesday—

EHRLICHMAN: —they will Wednesday announce—

NIXON: Right.

EHRLICHMAN: —their hearing schedule.

NIXON: —and then Haldeman will make his statement—

EHRLICHMAN: Haldeman makes his statement and says, "Well, I have been sitting here waiting for a chance to be heard." We—obvious now that it's going to be umpteen days before—

NIXON: We make an arrangement.

EHRLICHMAN: Well, first of May is the earliest.

HALDEMAN: When they start?

EHRLICHMAN: Yeah. And they—then they're—going to say—

HALDEMAN: And think what—then when they hear McCord and six witnesses—

EHRLICHMAN: Yeah.

HALDEMAN: —before that—before us.

EHRLICHMAN: No, he could say it now looks like it will be several months before I would get a chance to be heard before the Ervin Committee at best, and so I'd like to make a statement at this time going into a number of charges that have been—

NIXON: That have been bandied about—

EHRLICHMAN: Right.

NIXON: Then you—the way I would handle that—I would say, "Now let's take the Segretti matter." No, "First, let's take Watergate." You say, "I had no knowledge, et cetera, et cetera, et cetera, et cetera. Let's take the Segretti thing. Now, here are the facts." Then I would point out to [unclear] point out [unclear] self-incrimination [unclear].

HALDEMAN: No.

EHRLICHMAN: Well, we don't know that.

HALDEMAN: Huh?

NIXON: Okay, John. Then you can go down with Segretti?

HALDEMAN: Well, our view is clearly established, which is totally supported — that Segretti's instructions were that he was to do nothing illegal.

EHRLICHMAN: And, the —

HALDEMAN: And, well, in answer to the question how could you launch a guy out — ?

NIXON: Yeah.

HALDEMAN: — [unclear].

NIXON: Yeah.

HALDEMAN: That's one of the reasons that they that — the — his being a lawyer was —

NIXON: Now, here's what's in that —

HALDEMAN: — looked into.

NIXON: — [unclear] and third, there are charges of money — of money with cash [unclear].

HALDEMAN: I have a whole list of the general charges.

NIXON: Well, the point is on the money thing, I'd lob it in that. I'd say it says here, "The money — yes, there was three hundred fifty thousand dollars left over from the campaign in 1970. It was delivered to the White House."

HALDEMAN: You see, that ties to the same fund that Kalmbach — see, you get a question how could I authorize the expenditure of funds for Segretti?

NIXON: Yeah.

HALDEMAN: Well, I've already established in the Segretti thing that Kalmbach had these funds left over for the campaign and that's what I would assume he would use.

NIXON: Right. Right.

HALDEMAN: He was the custodian in spite of the fact —

NIXON: That these funds were made available for private polling and so forth and so on. "They were used only for — twenty-eight thousand dollars was used for — twenty-two thousand dollars for advertising and the balance of five hundred and three hundred twenty-eight was returned to — "

HALDEMAN: They get very excited about that advertising money. As soon as they find that out they are going to track that down. And that — we had a [unclear].

NIXON: Is it Vietnam?

HALDEMAN: It was "Tell It to Hanoi."

EHRLICHMAN: Hmm.

HALDEMAN: It was a "Tell It to Hanoi" ad countering Vietnam — anti-Vietnam veterans.

NIXON: Was that — [unclear] not political?

HALDEMAN: It wasn't political.

NIXON: That's good.

HALDEMAN: It went to Baroody which was the turn out —

EHRLICHMAN: Bill or another Baroody?

HALDEMAN: No, Sam or Charlie or something.

EHRLICHMAN: Sam.

HALDEMAN: It's not Edgar or somebody. One of the others.

NIXON: That was the "Tell It to Hanoi" ads?

HALDEMAN: Whatever it was, it wasn't — I was scared to death it might be something —

NIXON: Yeah.

HALDEMAN: — a Colson ad, but it wasn't. At least that's what Gordon thinks.

EHRLICHMAN: Mitchell kept lobbing out little tidbits about Colson's operation —

NIXON: Mm-hmm.

EHRLICHMAN: — about sending rioters up to the Capitol steps and other things that he knew about.

NIXON: Well, that was separate from all of Mitchell's stuff though, wasn't it? What Colson did?

EHRLICHMAN: Well, he was saying it's really too bad that all this is coming out because there's so much sordid stuff that would be — that will be imputed to the White House.

NIXON: [unclear] not still sending rioters to the Capitol steps. What do you mean?

HALDEMAN: They weren't rioters, for heaven's sake.

NIXON: Well, they named them counterdemonstrators. Why do you — ?

EHRLICHMAN: Don't tell me, tell it to John Mitchell. [laughs]

HALDEMAN: I don't think anybody, even Chuck Colson, can tell [unclear].

NIXON: The point is that is the [unclear]. My thought with Bob's, though, is true — is not to make the countercharge in his — in this.

EHRLICHMAN: That's right.

NIXON: I think he should save that for the committee. Now do you agree with that, Bob?

HALDEMAN: I don't know. It's weak —

NIXON: I'll even go as far as —

HALDEMAN: It's weak if I don't.

NIXON: Yeah. You've got to say —

HALDEMAN: I think I've got to make it in — I don't mean make it —

NIXON: Put it in general terms, but hold the white paper.

HALDEMAN: I say [unclear].

NIXON: Hold the white paper.

HALDEMAN: Cite some examples and say, "All these were done by the others," but I hold off on the thing that I have requested the committee to look into. And when I'm up there I can say it's a matter of fact — you know, there's a [unclear] said that there —

NIXON: I do feel that we should get this ready and really bounce it and I think that's the day to do it and slap 'er up there, and I'd say —

HALDEMAN: It's ready. Oh, no, it isn't ready but it's close. But it's sure awful long.

NIXON: Will it be all right?

HALDEMAN: I'm not so sure that matters.

NIXON: Perfectly all right to me.

HALDEMAN: [unclear]

EHRLICHMAN: [unclear] the [unclear].

NIXON: And if it says if the committee doesn't — I cannot allow the reputation of the [unclear]. I mean, the effectiveness as an assistant to the president will be seriously damaged — eroded by false charges and so forth and consequently I am making this statement now. I will make this statement under oath. Report that I will make this statement under oath and answer questions under oath when the Ervin Committee finally gets around to hearing me. How's that sound to you, John?

EHRLICHMAN: Sounds pretty good.

NIXON: All right. Now I think I will say — I will point out [unclear] my thoughts. "I do not suggest that — I have only tried to cover in this statement questions of charges that have been made to date. That's what I've said and it has not been, and I am sure that others will be made. And I am prepared to answer those as well."

HALDEMAN: "But I can't possibly anticipate what they — "

NIXON: "I cannot anticipate them. I do not — I cannot anticipate them, but I'd be prepared to answer them." He won't thereby have answered through me questions of Watergate. Now, the only question you have left is, I suppose, sort of the peripheral — in fact, Dean rumbling around here and asking you and Haldeman, "How about getting us some money for Watergate defendants?" Goddamn! I can't believe it. I can't believe they'd put you in the conspiracy if you were asked for that. Maybe they could.

HALDEMAN: I — technically I'm sure they could. Practically, it just seems awfully remote, but maybe that's just wishful thinking.

NIXON: Incidentally, could Strachan be — find it very helpful for him to say what that twenty-two thousand dollars was for before the grand jury? Why not?

EHRLICHMAN: He will have to. I can't imagine that they would —

NIXON: Well, they haven't asked him yet.

EHRLICHMAN: Yeah, but they will. Because —

NIXON: Twenty-two thousand dollars in [unclear].

HALDEMAN: That makes sense.

NIXON: To be sure did you tell him [unclear]? Huh?

HALDEMAN: Yeah.

NIXON: Yeah, let's be sure. Well, you could say [unclear], if it wasn't my [unclear].

EHRLICHMAN: I probably better get up and get set up for Jeb.

HALDEMAN: Let me ask you — does that mean — is there something else for Gordon?

NIXON: Gordon?

HALDEMAN: That I'm supposed to ask Gordon?

EHRLICHMAN: That it was delivered in pieces?

HALDEMAN: Oh, yeah.

NIXON: There was forty thousand dollars on one occasion. Why did he deliver it? Because actually it was a large — that's a large amount of money.

EHRLICHMAN: No, they've already got him on that.

NIXON: Oh, is that correct?

EHRLICHMAN: But it all fit in a suitcase or something and [unclear] of support [unclear].

HALDEMAN: The reason I delivered in pieces was because there was — difficult for them, obviously that — to figure out how to receive back all this cash.

NIXON: Yeah.

HALDEMAN: And they requested that it not be —

NIXON: Requested it in two installments?

HALDEMAN: — all at once.

NIXON: [unclear]

HALDEMAN: Then delivered part of it at the time they asked for it and the balance at the time they asked for it. My interest was delivering all of it as quickly as possible. I don't know what their problem was.

NIXON: Could I just make the suggestion of Magruder? First, get everything you can from him.

HALDEMAN: He's bringing two lawyers with him.

EHRLICHMAN: Naturally. What'll we do?

NIXON: [unclear]

HALDEMAN: Probably one Jewish and one Gentile. [laughs]

NIXON: Well, you know Jeb — I mean, I don't know what we can do about Strachan or about Dean. Right?

HALDEMAN: Right.

NIXON: Just try to get the facts and that's all there is to it.

EHRLICHMAN: I'll get back to you —

NIXON: Be sure you convey my warm sentiments.

EHRLICHMAN: Right.

[EHRLICHMAN leaves the conversation.]

HALDEMAN: I think I ought to get Strachan squared away.

NIXON: Sure.

HALDEMAN: He covers —

NIXON: Well, we'll see what they finally come down to here [unclear]. I frankly think I should say I don't know. But based on what Ehrlichman tells me about the law it's a matter of withholding evidence as far as that was concerned. That was Mitchell's point and the matter of motive doesn't seem to be important.

HALDEMAN: Well, the only sticky wicket on that is Dean. I can't understand because — it is in his interest, too, as well as everyone else's to see the motive for what it was.

NIXON: I guess we're not surprised at Mitchell, are we?

HALDEMAN: No. It's partly true. What he's saying is partly true. I don't think he did put it together.

NIXON: Hmm, he shouldn't throw the burden over here, Bob, on you. Now, frankly Colson I understand, but because Colson certainly put the heat on over there. I don't think John would seriously have believed that you put them up to this thing.

HALDEMAN: I told you I didn't. He knows I didn't. [unclear] No question on that.

NIXON: I should think he knows it. He let it all happen himself. So he'll stonewall it or not?

HALDEMAN: That's what he says.

NIXON: You know, he'll never go to prison. What do you think about that as a possible thing? Does a trial of the former attorney general of the United States bug you? It's goddamn ridiculous —

HALDEMAN: [unclear]

NIXON: He'll have to take the stand at some point. [unclear] hell this has happened now.

HALDEMAN: That's exactly the point. He's got no defense witness that can deny it.

NIXON: You know in one sense, Bob, it's better to [unclear] a couple of these small things but it's much better to hand it to the grand jury. McCord may move on the theory that Mitchell will be sorry and the others, too [unclear] that they have the damn thing and the Ervin Committee gets credit in the Watergate thing?

HALDEMAN: Yep.

NIXON: I don't know. Am I seeing something good develop?

HALDEMAN: No.

NIXON: That really isn't good or am I — ?

HALDEMAN: No, no. That's — that was the thing I was trying to get at this morning. That what that proves is the president's — in my view, is that the president's course was right. The president wasn't covering up. The president was cooperating with the proper place and the proper place has come to the proper result, which is to find out in an orderly manner without tarring innocent people — to find out what's going on.

NIXON: You know the thing I was thinking of saying — I went around — that's always the case of things here in Washington. Mayor Washington kind of stared — was surprised — wondered why you kidded about nine lives.

Magruder's story

April 14, 1973, 5:15 p.m.
Richard Nixon, Bob Haldeman, and John Ehrlichman
EXECUTIVE OFFICE BUILDING

In midafternoon, Magruder called at the White House to speak with Ehrlichman and Haldeman. He wanted to tell them what he had only just told the U.S. attorney. No sooner had he left than they relayed his story to the president, and within minutes Ehrlichman was dialing the attorney general, Richard Kleindienst. The fact that it was a Saturday afternoon and after 5:00 didn't matter. On behalf of the president and the investigation he purported to have directed, Ehrlichman implicated Mitchell and Magruder in criminal activity. Kleindienst, while taken aback at having Watergate land on his lap, made an initial suggestion of employing a special prosecutor to investigate. Nixon and his aides discussed that possibility after the call, with less enthusiasm than before. They congratulated themselves on the fact that with Mitchell and Magruder heading for indictment, the

Watergate hearings would lose their drama. For the moment, the scandal seemed to be almost over. "Indict Mitchell and all the rest," Nixon said, "and there'll be a horrible two weeks." And nothing more, he thought. With that, he dressed for the White House Correspondents' Dinner, where an award was to be given to, as Ehrlichman said in passing, "[Carl] Bernstein and what's his name."

. . .

EHRLICHMAN: Well, he [Magruder] and his two lawyers — who are very bright young guys — came in. So I said, "Evidently, judging by your phone call earlier this is moot." He said, "Yes, we have just come from our informal conference with the U.S. attorney." He proceeded then to voluntarily give me his whole testimony from beginning to end.

HALDEMAN: [unclear] sticky wickets, but no new ones.

EHRLICHMAN: That's right.

NIXON: Your definition of their [unclear].

HALDEMAN: On the other side [unclear]. It's much rougher on Dean.

NIXON: On Dean, he told him to lie?

EHRLICHMAN: No. He's been a participant — an active participant in this thing right from the very beginning.

HALDEMAN: He talks about the case in the most coherent way we've ever had.

EHRLICHMAN: And I must say —

HALDEMAN: We finally will know what happened.

EHRLICHMAN: This has the ring of truth about it. He is a convincing witness. So, you know — but at the same time it has —

HALDEMAN: It also is not in conflict with anything else you've got —

EHRLICHMAN: That's true.

HALDEMAN: — and almost totally corroborates everything else you've got except you go to the end of it this time.

EHRLICHMAN: This all starts back in September of '71, when Dean, Caulfield, and Magruder met and contrived an intelligence effort called Sandwedge. Two months later, Dean had been unable to find the right people to make that thing work. And Dean had approved of Liddy. And two months later Dean, Liddy, and Magruder met. Liddy, after having some contact with Dean and Magruder, is a little vague on [unclear] forward with a million-dollar proposal. Magruder said that Dean said that a million dollars was the right figure. And that's why he picked that figure — budgets, and so the four of them met. They went over it and Mitchell rejected it. A week later, Liddy came back with a budget half as big — the half-million-dollar budget. And that was also rejected —

NIXON: By Mitchell?

EHRLICHMAN: By Mitchell. Dean went on and said, "These kinds of things shouldn't even be run by Mitchell. He's attorney general of the United States. He is sitting over here in his parochial office and he shouldn't even" — Liddy and Magruder then went on to try and develop a satisfactory project proposal.

NIXON: A quarter — ?

EHRLICHMAN: A quarter-million-dollar level. Magruder said he was never satisfied with it. He kept sending Liddy back to the drawing boards. Finally, Colson called, with Liddy and Hunt in his office [unclear] vigorously. Finally, although he — and he felt Mitchell, too, were nervous about it and didn't feel comfortable about it, he said, "Well, all right, I'll start this moving."

NIXON: [unclear] he doesn't say that Colson chewed him out? Specifically about this proposal?

EHRLICHMAN: He said, "Gordon Liddy's projects." He did not say "wiretaps." He used the word "projects." In fact, there was indeed a budget for this quarter-million-dollar proposal. It was in writing. A copy of it was furnished to Gordon Strachan. And it was very specific in terms of the kinds of equipment to be used.

NIXON: It was furnished to Strachan?

EHRLICHMAN: Yes, sir. There was no problem from Strachan. That is he informed Strachan that he was going to go ahead with the so-called Liddy proposal and "I read his nonresponse as okay from higher up. I am not able to say of my own knowledge that there was any knowledge of anyone higher up. In point of fact, the" — he was insisting upon was information on Larry O'Brien. That was the thing he called about and that's the thing that he had been driving at. Around the end of March, Mardian — excuse me — Magruder and LaRue went to Key Biscayne where John Mitchell was.

NIXON: Magruder. LaRue. Right.

EHRLICHMAN: They presented to Mitchell Liddy's final proposal, which [unclear] installed bugs in three places — Watergate —

NIXON: Presented to whom?

EHRLICHMAN: They were in person.

NIXON: Magruder and Mitchell — and LaRue. Presented it to Mitchell?

EHRLICHMAN: Yes, sir.

NIXON: In three places, huh?

EHRLICHMAN: It involved bugging three places — Watergate, McGovern headquarters, and the Fontainebleau. In the conversation, Mitchell orally approved it. Now, it involved other things besides taps and he was not specific. He said, "In all honesty this was a kind of a nondecision. Nobody felt comfortable in this thing but we were sort of bulldozed into it." [unclear] —

NIXON: By Colson?

EHRLICHMAN: That's the inference. [unclear] and Liddy's project, I said, "Well, now, clear up for me just how well informed was Strachan?" He said, "I informed him orally of it. He had the budget."

NIXON: The budget was very specific.

EHRLICHMAN: "[unclear] parts that started to come out of that thing were junk. We got synopses of the [wiretap] log." He said, "I got the only copy. I, Magruder, got the only copy of the synopses." So Mitchell got [unclear] — he thought they were a lot of junk too. [unclear] named Gemstone. The one copy that Magruder had had pictures of the kind of papers that you'd find around a campaign. [unclear] synopses of the pictures to Mitchell. He thought it was so bad he picked up the phone and called Liddy and chewed him out. He called them "shitty." "I told Strachan the synopses were here." He may have come over and read them and as I pressed him on that he got less and less sure of that. He says, "I told him they were there."

HALDEMAN: Strachan now — Strachan says, "I saw three synopses and they were — we had them."

EHRLICHMAN: Now I've got to skip back a ways and then I'll come back to the — to Mitchell.

HALDEMAN: Be sure you make that point to Strachan.

EHRLICHMAN: I think March, about the time of the meeting down in Key Biscayne, Liddy threatened Magruder's life. He said he was transferred to the Stans operation.

NIXON: Yeah.

EHRLICHMAN: LaRue approached Magruder and said, "We need that operation. You ought to take him back because it's dead in the water without him." In fact, from the White House to the headquarters, he says he told the U.S. attorney, convinced him that they needed the operation. Back to the quality of the work, they — what they were getting [from the wiretaps on the DNC] was mostly this fellow [Spencer] Oliver phoning his girlfriends all over the country lining up assignations. And paying money and discussing their Young Leaders Conference. Liddy was badly embarrassed by the chewing out he got. [unclear] again met with him. He said to John Mitchell, "Mr. Mitchell, I'll take care of it." That was all that was said. So the next break-in was entirely on Liddy's own motion. But Magruder says neither Mitchell nor Magruder knew that another break-in was contemplated. I said, "What [unclear] after the firing of Liddy?" Magruder was very nervous about him obviously. He phoned John Dean and asked Dean to talk to Liddy and try and settle him down because he was acting erratic. Who in the White House is involved in this whole thing — the names that I have given you? Dick Howard [staff assistant in Colson's office], some of Colson's people, and a lot of the secretaries in the EOB have various information about a lot of different projects and pickets — all kinds of things that will come pouring out in the process of this whole thing. Well, I said, "Back to the burglary, who else?" He said, "No one else." He said, "The U.S. attorney is hot after Colson. They know he was close to Hunt. The only thing they have him on right now is the phone call to Magruder," so far as Jeb knows. But his attorney then chimed in, and said, "I think the U.S. attorney has a good deal more because the U.S. attorney told the lawyer that Hunt had reperjured himself with respect to Colson," when he was called back in under immunity and testified as to the break-in and the capture of the burglars and the cover-up. Mitchell, LaRue, Mardian, and the lawyers basically — plus Magruder. Dean devised a cover story in concert with these other people and enlisted Bart Porter, who went to the grand jury and perjured himself in concert with the cover story. Dean prepared Magruder and others for the testimony at the grand jury, cross-examining and getting them ready. Likewise, he leaked out information from the grand jury to the people at the Committee for the Re-election. The U.S. attorney knows that he did that. It is illegal to do so.

NIXON: Did he say where he got it?

EHRLICHMAN: He got it from a higher-up. I assume that's Henry Petersen, but I don't know. Okay, with Magruder and Mitchell in the operation of their — of this cover story about these meetings. And they worked out a deal and they canceled one meeting — the million-dollar meeting — and the second meeting, which was the half-million-dollar meeting. They told the grand jury they —

NIXON: He's testified to all this?

EHRLICHMAN: Yes. They talked about election laws. He's just told the U.S. attorney all this. He — destroyed his diary, but he couldn't do that. There's a million and a half dollars in cash that was distributed.

NIXON: Jesus Christ!

EHRLICHMAN: LaRue and Stans know about it. There is quote the famous list unquote of where that money went. I don't know. I am going to have to check my notes with O'Brien. O'Brien may have told me about that. He may have given some idea of where that went. The three fifty is a part of that. Mitchell says to Magruder, "Don't talk."

NIXON: Discouraged him. What about Haldeman?

EHRLICHMAN: Haldeman's very much a target of the U.S. attorney. So far they indicated that they — he was implicated only by association with other people — meaning Strachan presumably. The attorney gave me his private evaluation, that that was a little puffing on the part of the U.S. attorney. He did not think that they had anything. [Robert] Reisner and Powell Moore — Powell Moore is somebody on Timmons's staff who was at the [reelection] committee and who accompanied Liddy on what are called "the Saturday Events." "The Saturday Events" are the events that took place the day after the burglary. Liddy went out to find Kleindienst at Burning Tree and told him to let everybody out of jail on orders from John Mitchell. And LaRue, of course, and Mardian, largely on obstruction. They're developing many counts of obstruction of justice. One of the attorneys then, in winding up, I told him — I gave Jeb your wishes and felicitations and so on and one of the attorneys said, "Well, you know, in all of this there is not a scintilla of evidence that the president was in any way aware of any of these transactions." And he said, "Well, I didn't say that for any purpose except just to express to you an impression I have about the way this thing's going." He said, "Literally tens of dozens of people down there crying to — to be heard by the U.S. attorney." And he said, "This thing is rapidly deteriorating." But he said, "In all of this I don't see any evidence of the involvement of the president." So that was that and I thanked them and sent them on their way. Now I have the attorney general of the United States sitting at home waiting to go to this dinner party and I have the deputy attorney general out of town. But as Bob points out, there isn't anything in my report that isn't pretty well covered and expanded on in what they've just got from Magruder. So, I think what I can do is call the attorney general, tell him what I was going to tell him — tell him that Magruder has just disclosed to me what he has shown to the U.S. attorney and that I really don't have anything to add but that I did want him to be aware of the fact of the work that was done and what I have done today. And —

HALDEMAN: Meetings which you had with Mitchell —

EHRLICHMAN: Yeah.

HALDEMAN: — and Magruder.

EHRLICHMAN: Yeah.

HALDEMAN: The purpose of your meetings was to make the point to them that they should not go on the misguided assumption that that was for the president.

EHRLICHMAN: Right.

HALDEMAN: [unclear] this says that the meetings at Key Biscayne [unclear] existed long after —

NIXON: Tell me this, Bob, what is — what about Strachan? Strachan says he did not know about this.

HALDEMAN: Can I give Strachan a report on this?

NIXON: Sure. Sure. What is your — what was your view about Strachan's perjury?

EHRLICHMAN: I don't know. [unclear] make the headlines.

HALDEMAN: [unclear] he goes to the grand jury Monday morning. That's why it's imperative he be given this information so he doesn't perjure himself.

NIXON: Right.

HALDEMAN: I don't think he's testified on any of this so I don't think he has any perjury problem. What he's got to do is build the defense that —

NIXON: Meets these points.

HALDEMAN: Meets these points and —

NIXON: Could —

HALDEMAN: And he could — he can keep himself as an office boy, which is what he was. A [unclear] boy. If he lied about a thing — he persuaded Gordon to keep Liddy on or something — or Jeb to keep Liddy on — I would think he would argue back that "Jeb said to me, 'Now, what should we do?' and I said, 'Geez, I think we better keep him on. He's getting good stuff.'" [unclear]. I think Gordon knows how to deal with that if you give it to him. But I — see now, I went back to Gordon today on this point [unclear] and he said, "Absolutely, there was no other money." That on the twenty-second the only deal was for a fellow to handle it according to what Howard told him. That's who they sent the money over to.

NIXON: For him [unclear].

EHRLICHMAN: Well, we got Magruder now in this pickle. He's still on the government payroll in the Commerce Department.

NIXON: In Commerce?

EHRLICHMAN: I think it is. I thought he was.

HALDEMAN: As I listen to this the second time around let me tell you what my concerns are. [unclear] when he got down to it he told the truth. And when he is talking to us, at least, he is bringing us into it. He will — for instance, he'll want to elaborate on Sandwedge and say I was involved in it. Now, to the extent that I listened to a presentation I was. But I, at the time, said, "This is something I don't want to be involved in. Something that should not be handled in here. Don't come to me anymore with it," and they didn't. And then he'll say I was also involved in the meetings. That he came to me after that second meeting and said, "They came up with a, you know, the plans — with a preposterous plan." I told him that "it can't be done." They shouldn't even be talking about it in the attorney general's office. I said, "John, get out of it. You stay out of it, too." And he did. He said he would stay out of it from then on, and I suspect he did. They'll tie me in that way by indirection in a sense that, but — the problem is that, I think, his people with him. Maybe that sounds like everybody go down, you know, with the ship but when it comes to this cover-up business — expanding on — yes, he has a feeling — the three fifty. I am not uncomfortable with that, but Dean is uncomfortable.

NIXON: What do you do about Dean? In other words, John —

HALDEMAN: The U.S. attorney's got to [unclear].

NIXON: But Dean has been —

EHRLICHMAN: I think this all has broken since. I think they were probably playing it just right.

NIXON: — playing their game [unclear] Magruder testifies. [unclear]

EHRLICHMAN: I think that's their —

NIXON: Analysis.

EHRLICHMAN: — analysis.

NIXON: Yeah.

EHRLICHMAN: I think they are after Colson, you, me, and [unclear] I say to the highest-level provable objection.

NIXON: Let me say that this — this tends to — with the Ervin Committee overhanging —

HALDEMAN: One of these items each day for months —

EHRLICHMAN: Well, looking at the line — I should call Kleindienst to be sure and catch him before he gets out.

NIXON: Why don't you call him?

EHRLICHMAN: If I can find him.

NIXON: All right.

[EHRLICHMAN calls Attorney General Kleindienst.]

• • •

EHRLICHMAN: He is struggling. I assure that he is.

NIXON: He's closed his eyes to the whole thing.

HALDEMAN: You mean think this was a surprise to him?

EHRLICHMAN: It's a subject of great distress to him, I'll tell you that.

NIXON: Of course he's distressed. Let me ask you, John, about Colson. Everything that has been said here despite the fact that they were not after him it would be consistent with Colson's not knowing the Watergate business.

EHRLICHMAN: Magruder doesn't lay a glove on him.

NIXON: But he said they're hot after him. But where they may have the "hot after him" is on the — what?

EHRLICHMAN: His connection with Hunt. Their premise apparently is, according to their lawyers, that everything Hunt knew Colson knew.

NIXON: But Hunt — then Hunt therefore will — they're going to try to get him to come in and let — lay a glove on Colson now.

HALDEMAN: Colson [unclear]. It will be Colson's role to get himself a defense. [unclear]

EHRLICHMAN: Well, Kleindienst says for reasons I have to be very careful about who I communicate with for the next little while —

NIXON: Okay.

EHRLICHMAN: He wants me to meet with him and Henry Petersen tomorrow. I'm possessed of information establishing the committing of a crime. And I've got to be darn careful about who I talk to.

NIXON: On things that you have done.

EHRLICHMAN: He says that [Joseph] Sneed detached from Watergate — was in a perfect position to act on it but he wishes we'd get a special prosecutor.

NIXON: [unclear]

EHRLICHMAN: He wants to talk about it Monday, and —

NIXON: Do you still think that's a bad idea?

EHRLICHMAN: I think it would be very bad. All these people — prosecutor.

NIXON: I want you to say that to him tomorrow.

EHRLICHMAN: I sure will.

NIXON: That I have just decided against it.

EHRLICHMAN: Well, if you could hear me [unclear] —

NIXON: He thinks it's outrageous — he's considered it. Thought it through. He doesn't want a special prosecutor because then it's a reflection on the people you've got there. They're doing a hell of a job here. As the cases will point out. And we shouldn't throw them out now. Let them continue.

HALDEMAN: Correct?

NIXON: Yeah. I agree.

EHRLICHMAN: Interesting — the interesting fact — the U.S. attorney for the District of Columbia has just had Magruder in the office and can sew up the case —

NIXON: Yeah.

EHRLICHMAN: — [unclear] the attorney general [unclear].

HALDEMAN: He doesn't know anything else.

NIXON: Yeah. If he doesn't resign?

EHRLICHMAN: Well, I don't think —

NIXON: I don't think he has to.

EHRLICHMAN: I don't think he has to though. I think he may want to and if he does want to I think he should.

NIXON: And if he doesn't want to we could put Sneed in the job?

EHRLICHMAN: As acting until you get somebody damn good.

NIXON: You wouldn't keep Sneed — ?

EHRLICHMAN: [unclear] he's [unclear].

NIXON: You'd rather have our friend over at HUD?

HALDEMAN: Somebody like him, yeah. Yeah.

NIXON: Well, we need somebody that's damn good.

EHRLICHMAN: You should have a spokesman.

NIXON: For — particularly not.

EHRLICHMAN: Yeah.

NIXON: [unclear] Ehrlichman to get out the facts that he has made this investigation, that we weren't dragged kicking and screaming into this thing. I don't know.

EHRLICHMAN: Legal problem. I'll talk to Dick tomorrow.

NIXON: Yeah, it may be a legal problem.

EHRLICHMAN: And if a — if there's not a legal problem — be a question on Monday for Ziegler on what Mitchell was doing at the White House. [unclear] he should say he was here talking to me.

NIXON: [unclear] the whole matter [unclear].

EHRLICHMAN: Yeah. [unclear]

NIXON: And he'll say, "Oh, that's been given to the proper authorities." That's what I would say.

HALDEMAN: All he has to say is — why can't you just say — ?

EHRLICHMAN: In due course.

HALDEMAN: Unless you want that authority to say you've been investigating.

NIXON: That's the whole point.

EHRLICHMAN: Given the opportunity, I'm sure it's the occasion.

HALDEMAN: Yeah.

NIXON: With regard to the hearings, shouldn't we at least get this out? First, the hearings when they eventually come are gonna be anticlimactic in my opinion.

EHRLICHMAN: Could be anticlimactic. The networks might just not want them.

NIXON: Because of the fact that the big fish have been indicted.

HALDEMAN: Can't tell.

NIXON: And so forth.

EHRLICHMAN: Or you may have Weicker saying, "The wrong guys got indicted again" and build it up that way. And you could say that —

NIXON: I think I've reached the conclusion, but the two of you and Ziegler will disagree with that conclusion that it's a loser for us to continue trying to say that — I think you've got to say that — I think we ought to [unclear]. What do you think, Bob? Let's be forthcoming on that and get that out fairly soon. [unclear] I'm trying to get some appearance of cooperation. Or — do you agree, Bob, or not?

HALDEMAN: I do, I —

NIXON: Now the question is what do you do about Dean? That may be moot. For that reason I would say — [unclear] is Dean's going to be indicted?

EHRLICHMAN: Magruder does not think Dean with the break-in and the bugging.

NIXON: No, but he says he was there —

EHRLICHMAN: He's in the inception —

NIXON: Yeah.

EHRLICHMAN: But they have —

HALDEMAN: But he's in the inception only up to the rejection of the plan.

EHRLICHMAN: Up to a point. Up to a point. That's right, and he is not a participant in the Liddy-Magruder quarter-million take-it-to-Florida plan.

HALDEMAN: He isn't linked at all to the plan that was carried out.

NIXON: All right then, so they get him in for what? They get him for —

EHRLICHMAN: The aftermath.

NIXON: The aftermath, yeah. He's got a constructive, isn't it?

HALDEMAN: He had a chance.

EHRLICHMAN: He's got a chance.

NIXON: But not much. They say that he believed that he has a constructive —

EHRLICHMAN: Immunity.

NIXON: — immunity there on that.

EHRLICHMAN: But he doesn't have it anymore.

NIXON: No, [unclear] this would tend to bear out the Colson story that Magruder has told us. From here it sounds like the story [unclear].

HALDEMAN: [unclear] but it's in Colson's interest to tell us that Magruder had nailed Dean.

NIXON: That's right.

EHRLICHMAN: It's established that what he told me was substantially what he told the U.S. attorney.

NIXON: I understand.

HALDEMAN: They obviously were interested in giving you all the information [unclear].

NIXON: [unclear]

HALDEMAN: I doubt it. He's completely relaxed. A smile on his face. He wasn't shaking. He wasn't going to fight it the way he's been every time I've seen him. He just said, "I hope this isn't going to be for too long."

NIXON: [unclear] the right thing. We're all — we've all got to do the right thing. Goddamn it! We just cannot have this kind of a business, John. Just cannot be.

HALDEMAN: [unclear] question Magruder. Magruder said the same thing. [unclear]

NIXON: [unclear]

EHRLICHMAN: Yeah.

HALDEMAN: But they are lawyers. They may have this more worked out than we have, too, or something. I —

NIXON: I think Mitchell is beyond belief [unclear] or do you think [unclear]?

EHRLICHMAN: Do you believe Magruder, don't you?

NIXON: [unclear] what I meant is —

EHRLICHMAN: Well, that's true. What it basically comes down to — a question of credibility. Sure, the circumstantials —

NIXON: Does that cut LaRue?

HALDEMAN: LaRue tells the story about McCord —

NIXON: Does he crack Liddy?

EHRLICHMAN: No.

NIXON: Liddy?

EHRLICHMAN: Dean.

HALDEMAN: Well, Liddy can't crack it because Liddy [unclear], according to Jeb.

EHRLICHMAN: Because Mitchell says, "I've seen Liddy doing so and so and so and so." And Liddy says, "Boy, that's crazy. Look here, I saw him on this day, and this day, and this day — "

NIXON: How about Dean? Of course that's the big question. And what about the Haldeman statement? Should it be made now?

EHRLICHMAN: Can't hurt anything.

NIXON: Huh?

EHRLICHMAN: Can't hurt anything.

HALDEMAN: Clearly it would have to be broader on Strachan —

NIXON: The point that I am wondering — you see, I don't know what we could say about [unclear].

HALDEMAN: You think that Strachan did get the thing?

NIXON: Did participate?

EHRLICHMAN: I suspect Strachan is not going to corroborate. "My relationship with the committee was to [unclear] — "

NIXON: Yep. No harm in putting it out. What the hell. You've got to get it out. What do you think, Bob? [unclear]

HALDEMAN: I don't think it does but I'm somewhat, you know, puzzled by it — by — in my own assurance that it's a good idea but I have the feelings of Kissingers and Zieglers that it's a disaster for me to be out front [unclear].

EHRLICHMAN: You're not about to be out front. [unclear]

NIXON: The point is, Bob, that you have [unclear].

HALDEMAN: To be that far out front before this hits. And then this hits. It puts me in the lead with it is what they would argue.

EHRLICHMAN: Enjoying his [Magruder's] newfound freedom he may run around and tell everybody in town. He just launched into this, you know. I didn't ask him.

HALDEMAN: Well, you can understand that. A guy that's had constipation for eight months and all of a sudden is able to take a crap is gonna enjoy it.

NIXON: Why don't you make the deal on Monday for this? It — just so that we keep some honor. And we'll take all the people, any members of the White House staff [unclear] with any privilege, [unclear] any executive privilege waived — reserved to be decided in executive session. How does that sound to you?

EHRLICHMAN: Well, my position would be that they don't get to decide —

NIXON: Oh, I get it.

EHRLICHMAN: — the question of executive privilege. We decide that. Assert it and don't answer.

NIXON: Yeah.

EHRLICHMAN: Let the judge decide.

NIXON: So, you would say that we play by the cover-up though? We —

EHRLICHMAN: We say we are going to send our people up there and we don't care if you have [unclear] or [unclear] in a damn circus tent. You can send them up there and every question is subject to research under objection for executive privilege. We're not guilty and [unclear].

HALDEMAN: What do you do with my knowledge of hearsay? I just throw it all out now?

NIXON: No, you don't do it. Well —

EHRLICHMAN: I have gone into that in great detail with Ervin and he agrees with the concept that we are conduits to the president, that anything that was given to us is privileged.

NIXON: He agrees with you [unclear] given to the president, in other words.

HALDEMAN: If anything is given to me and the [unclear].

NIXON: I would say, "We'll give you Dean in executive session." How does that work out? [unclear] start with Dean. Not at all.

EHRLICHMAN: I did.

NIXON: [unclear] interrogatories. But you see, you get in a position where you can say — they claim executive privilege because of the [unclear] nature of the situation [unclear] of making the substance part public.

EHRLICHMAN: I must say that I think part of the trouble with our agreement —

NIXON: Yes.

HALDEMAN: John Dean may be into this where they can't call him anyway.

NIXON: That's what I'm thinking about, that —

EHRLICHMAN: Yeah. [unclear]

NIXON: You see, I'm just thinking about this one, which appeared to be forthcoming, and I wouldn't let the Dean thing be a big fracas, if necessary. I just think that that's one move you can make now at the present time. I — just go and I think the proponent of the idea that will buy a good headline for a day and invite Dean back for later on. But we're going to get beat around the head and shoulders. Let's face it. We're going to get it until the grand jury indictments, and then till the grand jury [unclear] that would be maybe another two, three weeks. After that, when they do indict then they'll say, "Christ, Mr. President, what the hell are you going to do to that?" We'll beat 'em to the punch. I think we've got to do that. I just feel it's one of those things. [unclear] to announce that I make it tomorrow night. Would you do that?

HALDEMAN: [unclear] to be repudiated by the committee that meets Tuesday.

• • •

NIXON: I think we've got to hit that one and let the — there's another thing I'm thinking of, Bob, is that there's — I'm thinking of the fact that this [unclear] here now may make the hearings a hell of a lot less interesting and also a hell of a lot — they sure as hell can — that's putting my life out there.

[Unclear exchange]

HALDEMAN: I hate to see that stuff keep getting obstructed by Watergate. That isn't the problem we're dealing with today. All this stuff's developing on Watergate. This makes Watergate look a lot worse than it really used to look in a way.

EHRLICHMAN: This does?

NIXON: Oh, I'll say it does because it involves so many people. [unclear] and we got a way [unclear] — stonewall it again? That's our problem.

HALDEMAN: Well, it'll be two weeks before this gets out? Is that — they were saying before that it was going to be May 15, but now if Magruder's in the applesauce. That's — what can they [unclear]?

NIXON: Well —

HALDEMAN: [unclear].

NIXON: [unclear] they want to wind up all the others. If they want to get all the obstructions they've got to hear all these people.

HALDEMAN: Right.

EHRLICHMAN: Not all of them but they've got a — they got [unclear] get a leg up. [unclear] will give 'em a leg up, Hunt they hope will give 'em a leg up. They make their case from the time that they either vote on indictments [unclear]. They may recess the grand jury for a couple of weeks. [unclear] indictments.

NIXON: Where else do you have a — what's the latest we've got on it, Bob? That's my point on the hearings. [unclear] say you're not going to do it because of Dean?

HALDEMAN: If the situation's going to get worse then you maybe have to do something. If this is as bad as it's going to get then, if this is going to change in a different direction maybe you're better off not doing anything. The first alternative will likely be worse. In other words [unclear], if you think you're ready to swing my guess is probably there is an actual danger that the Republican House will meet and pass a resolution calling on the president —

NIXON: That's what I think.

HALDEMAN: — and probably a unanimous resolution.

NIXON: I think it's very close to that right now. I think this would trigger it without question. They would be so horrified about that the White House staff [unclear].

HALDEMAN: Could be. But I guess that's not going to satisfy them. But, this pretty much establishes the Watergate thing and then you say [unclear] like Goldwater — the people that want this done with are going to — you've got to look at the other possible boxes to say, "Well, thank God it all has been cleared up. Now let's forget all this other shit," and some will say, "It's now clear the White House wasn't involved, and thank God they weren't. And it's clear the president wasn't involved and thank God he wasn't. It's a tragedy that that great man, John Mitchell, was."

NIXON: And that so many people at the committee were.

HALDEMAN: And then, everybody will dwell on that.

NIXON: Except that you've got a fair chance that Dean will get a fair chance at the criminal case.

EHRLICHMAN: As you spotlight it as the umbilical cord to get in the White House and the committee and the question will be, "What's at the other end of those umbilical cords?"

NIXON: Then you don't think — ?

HALDEMAN: [unclear]

NIXON: You don't think there's much —

HALDEMAN: The unbelievableness —

NIXON: Dean, no — Dean's high enough.

HALDEMAN: The — now, the unbelievableness of it is being answered by this. "There is somebody higher than Gordon Liddy had to have agreed to spend a quarter of a million dollars — "

NIXON: That's the point.

HALDEMAN: " — to bug the Democratic National Committee." Now you've got that somebody.

NIXON: That's Mitchell.

HALDEMAN: Now that you've got somebody who was — you've got a believable case where you can now say, "Well, so there was some other stuff going on but this was where the problem was."

[Unclear exchange]

NIXON: That's why I'd just like to get Segretti out in our forum. Don't you think so?

HALDEMAN: Yes, you've got to get it out. [unclear] Watergate [unclear] —

NIXON: Haldeman. They'll say Haldeman [unclear].

HALDEMAN: — and let's see what they say.

NIXON: Huh?

HALDEMAN: What they'll say is Haldeman admits guilt. I mean that's pretty clear.

NIXON: I know.

HALDEMAN: It's what I want to do —

NIXON: Yeah.

HALDEMAN: But the Ziegler-Moore-Kissinger view is very strongly that that's what I shouldn't do. I'm the last guy to decide —

NIXON: Yeah.

HALDEMAN: — which is right.

NIXON: Yeah. What do you think, John?

HALDEMAN: John thinks I should.

EHRLICHMAN: I think he should come out.

NIXON: It will come out right after that. Several of the Republicans —

EHRLICHMAN: Now as I say, I haven't heard Henry's—

NIXON: You start with Weicker and other Republicans and right after that and say, "Haldeman should resign because of his involvement in the Segretti matter."

HALDEMAN: Either I do have to resign—

NIXON: Or I defend it.

HALDEMAN: —or you defend it. You can't—I don't think you can ignore it. If I've done that you've either got to then make the judgment that that was sufficient to cause me to resign or it wasn't. That's the first question of the first person. [unclear] it should be answered before [unclear]—

NIXON: [unclear] that Haldeman's gonna resign, you mean?

EHRLICHMAN: Yeah. Ziegler can, the next day, say, "His connection to this was very remote, was very benign." And he—get that out—[unclear] in my view, before it was established that a crime was committed by Segretti.

NIXON: Right. [unclear] I would not be as strong for your getting it out except for his having said "self-incrimination"—the fact that that may leak.

HALDEMAN: You've got a really crunchy decision, which is whether you'd let me to resign or whether you don't. You—that's one you've got to figure out. The problem with that is if I go on the basis of the Segretti matter, you've got to let Dean go on the basis of his implication, which is far worse.

NIXON: Yeah.

HALDEMAN: Strachan's already out of the White House so that's no problem. You can wait a while with Ehrlichman in—you are going to have to let him go.

EHRLICHMAN: He's got sort of a hypothesis that he's developing in our conversation that referring him to Kalmbach was almost as good as actionable.

NIXON: Yeah.

EHRLICHMAN: As a matter of fact, I didn't refer him to Kalmbach. He came to me and said, "May I go to Kalmbach?"

HALDEMAN: He did the same thing to me.

NIXON: Go to Kalmbach for the purpose of?

EHRLICHMAN: For the purpose of getting Herb to raise some money. For the purpose of paying the defendants. For the purpose of keeping them quote on the reservation unquote.

NIXON: Right. With that they could try to tie you and Bob in a conspiracy to obstruct justice.

EHRLICHMAN: That's his theory.

NIXON: He's flailing—questionable.

EHRLICHMAN: Well, I'm not so sure that makes any difference at this point. He's coloring this in order to induce [unclear] that he was a mere conduit.

NIXON: A lesser sentence.

HALDEMAN: Strachan's position is totally tenable and true [unclear] without giving him any help.

NIXON: I know. The way you have to handle that—let's face it, is that—I mean, is there — of course, you've got the whole business of the aftermath as to motive. And there, if you or Bob are asked, what do you say?

EHRLICHMAN: Well, as far as I can reconstruct it and I may be putting it favorably, [unclear] clearly is concerned about what these fellows are going to testify to. The grand jury in secret couldn't hurt, whether they would go out and sell their stories to the *Saturday Evening Post* —

HALDEMAN: *Life* magazine.

NIXON: Sure, sure.

NIXON: That's right. They're not a bit concerned about [unclear].

EHRLICHMAN: So, I was concerned about that particularly Hunt who is a kind of an author type and would be inclined to do that kind of thing.

HALDEMAN: In fact I had no knowledge who was or wasn't guilty or where the thing led.

NIXON: I see. I see.

HALDEMAN: That's exactly right. We weren't protecting anybody.

EHRLICHMAN: I'm even willing to buy that.

HALDEMAN: I know, I said that to John and John didn't agree with me.

NIXON: I wish we could keep Dean away from Magruder. We don't have to get that in [unclear] unless it's a — let me say — let's sleep on what we do with the — my view is, though, I think the odds are that the interest in the committee is less. [unclear] some of the big fish. The second thing is going to be —

HALDEMAN: A lot of people are going to say, "For Christ's sake, you solved the Watergate, now forget it. We've have enough of this."

NIXON: Some of our people should say that. "For Christ's sakes, now what do you want [unclear]?"

HALDEMAN: Just say — the folks out there are getting fed up with it anyway. Just say — just get an answer and get it out of the way. That's what I'm talking about. They don't care.

NIXON: It's really such a crappy thing. And he'll come in, plead self-incrimination and clear him.

EHRLICHMAN: It'll be lively copy when they start bringing in all these people from around the country. What they did or —

NIXON: Who were victims —

EHRLICHMAN: — or witnesses or something.

NIXON: It'd be lively copy, John, but it's sore stuff.

EHRLICHMAN: Yep.

NIXON: It's not going to be [unclear]. Horrible, horrible.

HALDEMAN: [unclear] we've only got eight months to go. [laughs]

NIXON: Well, let me finish my analysis though. [unclear] The — in my opinion, Bob, for the forthcoming thing which I think I tilted against — I think Magruder could be a reason for tilting for — we need any move right now [unclear].

HALDEMAN: I think you've got it if you're going to do it, though, I think you've got to face the likelihood that Magruder or somebody is going to call for my resignation for having hired Segretti.

NIXON: [unclear]

HALDEMAN: I didn't hire Segretti, but [unclear —]

NIXON: It's Strachan.

HALDEMAN: Yeah. [unclear] over a period of time will come back with these. This is the first time. You've got a couple of others who should have been said —

NIXON: We've gotta face that.

HALDEMAN: You might want to tie it to a resignation at the time I do it. On the basis that "well, here is a mistake, and I have no problem with it. But I'm also not going to be in enough trouble in all this stuff now without my sitting here impeding [unclear]."

NIXON: [unclear] ought to resign sometime — don't.

HALDEMAN: I'm not suggesting I'd like to resign.

NIXON: No.

HALDEMAN: To tell you very frankly, I would not like to.

NIXON: No.

HALDEMAN: I'm just completely willing to —

NIXON: I know.

HALDEMAN: — without creating any sticky problems.

NIXON: That's the beauty of our whole staff, and though they would play their role [unclear].

HALDEMAN: I'm free from some other things and I can cut loose, which I do. The problem we get there on the other side is that there's some pluses to it, I think.

NIXON: With an attorney general added in. And a White House counsel, possibly. White House counsel.

HALDEMAN: Pretty big bag, John.

EHRLICHMAN: The biggest.

NIXON: The least. That's the point.

HALDEMAN: Yeah.

NIXON: Historically, people think in perspective but it takes some time.

HALDEMAN: Historically you expect to [unclear] that. [unclear]

NIXON: I see.

HALDEMAN: Well, fire some people, because you cannot —

NIXON: I have given them leave. If they should not fall under indictment [unclear], maybe they can continue their duties.

HALDEMAN: If they intend to plead innocent. [unclear]

NIXON: [unclear] in the United States look, that's about it. Are you gonna plead innocent or guilty? And if you're going to plead guilty — innocent, fine, you are suspended. I'll tell you when you can concentrate on the [unclear].

EHRLICHMAN: Set out the Ervin negotiations and how we get out the investigation and all this.

NIXON: Well, this [unclear], I want to keep Ervin at the [unclear], but I kind of feel myself that [unclear].

EHRLICHMAN: I do, too.

NIXON: We ought to say, and I think—

EHRLICHMAN: With that being the case, and the Dean [unclear]—come in, there's no need to grapple with it.

HALDEMAN: If he breaks off you could make a bargain with the committee.

NIXON: I think—

EHRLICHMAN: Well, I would have to call him.

NIXON: Yes, and what would you say? You could say, "The president has directed—has decided that Bob will appear"?

EHRLICHMAN: Better not say—

HALDEMAN: No.

NIXON: I don't think that's needed tomorrow. I think you ought to meet with Ervin and cut the deal and then even though it isn't much of a compromise you could say, "We have worked out a compromise under which there is an open session," and so forth.

EHRLICHMAN: They won't get you or Dean. Dean goes free.

NIXON: Dean in executive session is the—is very nice [unclear]. Huh?

HALDEMAN: [unclear]

NIXON: How's that sound to you, Bob? [unclear] get a story out which will keep the animals a little cool for a while. [unclear]

EHRLICHMAN: More than that you can date it back to negotiations commencing two weeks ago—

NIXON: Yeah.

EHRLICHMAN: —three weeks ago, whatever it was.

NIXON: Yeah. Yeah.

HALDEMAN: You put it on my statement at the same time?

NIXON: No.

HALDEMAN: You have to do it.

EHRLICHMAN: The next day.

HALDEMAN: The next day—Wednesday.

EHRLICHMAN: Wednesday. You should put my statement out on Wednesday also, or wait until Thursday for my statement. [unclear] we better be right on the heels of the—

NIXON: That's right. I'd put yours out right with it. You're going to have the next day to build it up a little.

HALDEMAN: No, you don't want to build it up.

NIXON: Put it right out. The problem here, let me say, in your case is not Segretti. [unclear] with Segretti stuff and then, the—in your case is Strachan. I mean the [unclear] purpose of keeping it [unclear].

HALDEMAN: [unclear]

NIXON: Oh, yes, [unclear] I know that — testify on that.

EHRLICHMAN: [unclear] would you carry that secret? The question is whether Strachan is indicted or not.

NIXON: If he is indicted?

HALDEMAN: I think I've got to cover myself on the Strachan thing, as you said, in such a way so that if anything does happen it's covered and you can go back to my statement and say I said that he was the guy to contact, that he should not be built up as a central figure, nor should I try to explain his every action. As I can't. Some of his actions were obviously carried out unilaterally.

EHRLICHMAN: I think that's overly objective.

NIXON: I think some of Magruder's stuff could be a bit exaggerated — could be lively. I think it's probably basically true. [unclear] you remember back that far? Think of that for a few days [unclear].

HALDEMAN: You can't be that precise —

NIXON: You can't be that precise. You remember what [unclear] were in — you remember the things that you want to remember, pretty much.

HALDEMAN: Well, especially when you've lived through a whole series of varying — very heated —

NIXON: Magruder's?

HALDEMAN: — [unclear], which he has.

NIXON: Magruder's — you've got to remember now, Magruder isn't going to be as potent a witness — and again as [unclear].

HALDEMAN: Strachan [unclear] a strong witness, too, and they're going to — they are going [unclear] do something.

NIXON: And they will — they have to say, "Who's lying?" "Who's going to lie?" I mean, here's a guy who has a record of lying. He lied this time [unclear]. Are you going to take his word against Strachan who did not lie and came back to the U.S. attorney?

HALDEMAN: We can produce people around here who can give you five different stories than what Magruder's told you —

NIXON: True.

HALDEMAN: — but which one is true?

NIXON: What do you think Mr. Colson is going to be doing to us? You're not going to tell him this, are you?

HALDEMAN: No.

NIXON: I wouldn't think so.

EHRLICHMAN: Colson is undoubtedly sending all kinds of signals to Mr. Hunt —

HALDEMAN: And that Chuck is overkill. I think he's his own worst enemy. He's very likely to [unclear] —

NIXON: [unclear]

EHRLICHMAN: He says that the *New York Times* has a story that he was here for a meeting with me yesterday.

HALDEMAN: He acts like it was the first time he has ever been in the White House and he wants everybody to know. [unclear]

[Unclear exchange]

NIXON: Well, you fellows need a little rest.

HALDEMAN: Rest? Taking us all to that damn dinner [unclear].

EHRLICHMAN: We'll grin at the White House correspondents.

HALDEMAN: That's no rest.

NIXON: Well, then — listen [unclear].

HALDEMAN: That's work.

NIXON: A year from now, it's gonna be different.

EHRLICHMAN: Oh, yes.

HALDEMAN: [unclear] Yes.

NIXON: No, seriously [unclear]. You know what?

EHRLICHMAN: Six months from now.

NIXON: Sooner than you think. Let me tell you, John, the thing about all of this that has concerned me is the dragging the goddamn thing out and dragging it out and being — and having it be the only issue in town. Now the thing to do now is to have the son of a bitch done. Indict Mitchell and all the rest and there'll be a horrible two weeks — a terrible, terrible scandal, worse than Teapot Dome and so forth. And it isn't — doesn't have anything to do with Teapot. It isn't as bad as —

EHRLICHMAN: No.

NIXON: — Adams. I mean good God, there's got to be no venality involved in the damn thing, no thievery or anything of that sort of thing. Nobody got any favors, and — you know what I mean?

HALDEMAN: John [unclear].

EHRLICHMAN: Yeah. That's true.

HALDEMAN: Glad to hear it.

NIXON: The big — the bad part of it is the fact that the attorney general and the obstruction of justice thing, which it appears to be. And yet, they ought to get up fighting, in my view, a fighting position on that. I think they all ought to fight and say this was not an obstruction of justice. We were simply trying to help these defendants. Don't you agree on that or do you think that's my — is that possible? [unclear]

EHRLICHMAN: I agree. I think it's gotta be defended, obviously.

NIXON: Yeah, but —

EHRLICHMAN: Yeah.

NIXON: I know if they could get together on the strategy, it would be pretty good for them.

EHRLICHMAN: Yeah, and I think, undoubtedly that will shake down.

NIXON: I would think that the U.S. attorneys and the rest would see that [unclear].

EHRLICHMAN: Thank you, sir.

HALDEMAN: Yes, sir.

**"If John Dean is believable you have an obstruction
case against Haldeman and Ehrlichman."**

April 15, 1973, 4:00 p.m.
Henry Petersen, Charles Shaffer, and Earl Silbert
WHITE HOUSE TELEPHONE

*In mid-April, John Dean remained counsel to the president even though he was talking
to Watergate prosecutors. Nixon was in a bad spot. If he fired Dean, it might look like he
was being punished for cooperating with investigators. That could transform Dean from
villain to hero in the eyes of the press, and Dean's cooperation could be terrible for Haldeman and Ehrlichman. On the other hand, keeping Dean on the White House staff, with
no real work assigned to him, was also not tenable.*

*In one of the most unusual Watergate conversations ever taped, Henry Petersen used
one of Nixon's taped phones for a conference call — though he was not completely honest about where he was calling from — with Dean's lawyer, Charles Shaffer, and the lead
prosecutor, Assistant U.S. Attorney Earl Silbert. They exchanged the latest prosecution
strategy, which hinged on Dean's version of events being credible.*

• • •

PETERSEN: Hello?

SHAFFER: Yes.

PETERSEN: Is this Charlie?

SHAFFER: Yeah.

PETERSEN: It's Henry Petersen.

SHAFFER: Oh, Henry, just a minute.

PETERSEN: All right.

SILBERT: Hello?

PETERSEN: Earl?

SILBERT: Yeah.

PETERSEN: How are you coming?

SILBERT: We're — Shaffer was in the middle of summarizing his [Dean's] position.

PETERSEN: Mm-hmm.

SILBERT: His position is hardening a little.

PETERSEN: Mm-hmm.

SILBERT: In the sense that if Dean is basically — if John is believable we have an obstruction case against Haldeman and Ehrlichman in that they knew everything that
was going on.

PETERSEN: If John Dean is believable you have an obstruction case against Haldeman
and Ehrlichman?

SILBERT: Well, let me say this to you. They knew everything that was going on. This
was all the plans — like the Magruder plans, and you know they were — like Ehrlichman, his present — again, going through the same stories about, you know,
that Dean said get rid of the — you know, Hunt get out of town. He and Halde-

man are in on the money. I mean Ehrlichman and Haldeman are in on the money. Clearly, I mean, the three hundred fifty thousand dollars comes from Haldeman and he is putting it in and Haldeman told him to get it back over there. And that they knew that the demand for the money was coming in — I mean, the demands were being made, and finally they had to give this money up. It was Haldeman's decision to send it all back to the committee and he told John to do it and that's when John called Strachan. Strachan, you know, did not — Strachan's testimony so far is inconsistent with that — that it was his own idea, Haldeman did not even know the money was there and he just decided to bring it back. He just called up — I mean his story is basically not too believable — that is Strachan's.

PETERSEN: Mm-hmm.

SILBERT: John's is much more credible because he said, "Yeah, I gave it to LaRue because LaRue was given all the money and that is why the money went to LaRue." Whereas, Strachan can say, "Well, you know," he doesn't return it to the finance committee which is normally where it would go back. He returns it to LaRue, and why does he return it to LaRue? Because LaRue is — I mean, Strachan acts like he was a senior campaign official. That doesn't make any sense. Money ought to go back to the person on the finance committee.

PETERSEN: Does he say that Haldeman said that?

SILBERT: Give it to LaRue?

PETERSEN: Yeah.

SILBERT: No. Not that. He said give it back. You know, send it back to the committee and get a receipt. That's what Haldeman said. But there is a — you know, based on the money the — Dean is really giving us only post-[break-in] except for the fact that he advised Haldeman of the first two meetings that took place in the attorney general's office. You know, it's intolerable and he said — well, he said Haldeman agreed and we should have nothing to do with it.

PETERSEN: Nobody stopped them, huh?

SILBERT: Huh?

PETERSEN: But nobody stopped it.

SILBERT: Nobody stopped it.

PETERSEN: Well, how soon — how far are you from winding it up out there?

SILBERT: Pretty quick.

PETERSEN: And then what are you going to do?

SILBERT: I don't know what to do. Got any great ideas? I mean —

PETERSEN: Where are you?

SILBERT: I'm out in Rockville.

PETERSEN: Okay. Why don't you come on by my house on your way in?

SILBERT: I am with Seymour [Glanzer].

PETERSEN: That's fine.

Assessing the new John Dean

April 16, 1973, 9:50 a.m.
Richard Nixon, Bob Haldeman, and John Ehrlichman
OVAL OFFICE

On the evening of April 15, after a long talk with Kleindienst and Petersen, Nixon finally informed Haldeman and Ehrlichman that Dean had placed them at the core of the Watergate scandal. Through his attorney, Charles Shaffer, Dean made it clear to prosecutor Earl Silbert and head of the Department of Justice Criminal Division Henry Petersen that he did not consider it fair that he could be fired and prosecuted yet Haldeman and Ehrlichman would not face similar sanctions. The following morning, when Nixon met with his two aides again, their conversation pertained mostly to Dean, whom the president was to meet at the top of the hour. Nixon's intention was to ask him to sign a letter of resignation. As the reality of Dean's defection sank in, Nixon combed through the events of the Watergate scandal with his two top aides, gauging Dean's ability to do even more harm. With the president and Ehrlichman doing most of the talking, they recalled incidents that once seemed small — the planned bugging of a home in Georgetown, for example, and Hunt's attempt to blackmail Haldeman through Dean. None were as shocking as their common occurrence in the administration, as evidenced by the calm and even mundane discussion Nixon led about them. That Monday, though, no incident was marginal; all were growing dangerous in the hands of Dean, a man no longer loyal to the rest.

• • •

NIXON: John, I want him to — before I see Dean. I tell you what I really want — I want him to sign.

EHRLICHMAN: Did you get those?

NIXON: Yes, I did. I'm going to have him sign. I'm going to ask him which one he wants to sign and just say I want that [unclear] that it seems to me that I should not — I mean I don't want to press anything and I'm not — or should I just have him sign it, whether it's effective today, or not announce it? What's your advice on that? We've got plenty of time. Don't worry about that.

EHRLICHMAN: Well, my — as I made them out it occurred to me that he ought to sign both of them. Then you could use whichever one you wanted or not depending on how circumstances unfold.

NIXON: Okay, that's right. Good.

EHRLICHMAN: And if he won't, you know what to do at that point.

HALDEMAN: And if he — if you go to Petersen and ask you not to —

NIXON: [unclear] I still have — that's right, I have my option to do that. The second point, John, that I want to nail down — what Dean said about other bugs from the White House and so forth and so on. Aren't — isn't — I assume that's the plumbing operation.

EHRLICHMAN: No, no. What he's referring to there —

NIXON: About the FBI.

EHRLICHMAN: — is the FBI bugs on the journalists in the first year.

NIXON: This was not from you? He thought these were private bugs.

EHRLICHMAN: Oh, no. No, no. These —

NIXON: No, he said there were —

EHRLICHMAN: Yeah, well, I —

NIXON: — private bugs —

EHRLICHMAN: These were —

NIXON: — that he knew about.

EHRLICHMAN: These were almost all FBI bugs but not entirely though.

NIXON: What is he referring to if it — what I'm just saying —

EHRLICHMAN: They're all national security.

NIXON: Well, that's what I mean.

EHRLICHMAN: But, I —

NIXON: I was wondering if — what's your advice? If I should not tell him today that anything in that area is national security and privileged.

EHRLICHMAN: I think you should and I think it should cover not only that but the plumbing operation and anything else of which he has knowledge.

NIXON: Yeah.

EHRLICHMAN: Say, "I am impressing that with executive privilege right now."

NIXON: Executive privilege.

EHRLICHMAN: "And I don't want to ever hear — "

NIXON: Yeah.

EHRLICHMAN: " — that you have discussed those matters — "

NIXON: Yeah.

EHRLICHMAN: " — with any third person."

NIXON: I don't know whether he did. He might have.

EHRLICHMAN: Well, you might ask him if he has —

NIXON: Yeah.

EHRLICHMAN: — afterwards, or before. But —

NIXON: But I — see, that didn't occur to me last night. It occurred to me [unclear] in which case I'm going to get him in.

EHRLICHMAN: Now, if you remember that whole operation was because you were afraid there were leaks out of the NSC.

NIXON: That's right. That's right.

EHRLICHMAN: And you were trying to find them.

NIXON: I thought we were — I thought they were through the FBI.

EHRLICHMAN: Well, almost all of them.

NIXON: We were going to do some of them.

EHRLICHMAN: Almost all of them were but there was one in Georgetown at some-body's house that actually never was put on. It wasn't feasible but it was explored and how Dean knows about that I don't know. The FBI files —

NIXON: Query — does Liddy know?

EHRLICHMAN: I can't say. I doubt it. I think that was before his time.

NIXON: The reason that I made the call while in Dean's presence last night was that he said that Liddy's — Liddy was saying — I don't know how he knows this — Liddy had told the bureau or something like that. I said, "John, what should I do?" "Well," he said, "you know, get ahold of his attorney." I said, "Hell, I'm not going to [unclear] his attorney," and he said, "Liddy says he will not talk because of higher authority." I said, "Now look here, higher authorities — it's not the president, it's Mitchell." And I said, "Well," so I called Petersen. I said, "You are to tell Liddy's attorney that — or Liddy, that there's — the president's not asking." Don't you think that's the correct thing to do?

HALDEMAN: That's —

EHRLICHMAN: It can't hurt anything at this point and it certainly is consistent with the things you had me do with Mitchell and Magruder.

NIXON: Such as like what? The —

EHRLICHMAN: To remove any impediment against their testifying by reason of any misplaced loyalty to you.

NIXON: One thing I was — Bob will run over with you [unclear], the subject is very important to just tick it off briefly. Before — one, that if you and he can sit down today and put both your cases down at their worst as to how you think it's going to come out. You know, so that I can look at them and as I say I'm not going to make any goddamn hasty decisions until I see what the hell — how this bounces around. Because Petersen is obviously reacting to the Magruder thing.

[STEVE BULL enters.]

BULL: John Dean is here, Mr. President.

NIXON: [unclear] about five or ten minutes.

[STEVE BULL leaves.]

NIXON: [unclear] building construction [unclear]. Christ! It's obviously disturbed so that — and they're out to demonstrate over there doing this job. The second point is that I would like also a scenario evolved with regard to the president's role. In other words, when the president began to find out about this, what he did — I think it's a pretty good role, John. I'm not sure. It's as good as I can guess because remember I got Dean in, first I said I wanted him to report — sent him to Camp David. He came back and said he couldn't and I want to ask him about that today. And then you — and I want you to get Steve [Bull] your report and everything you did. See what I mean? Also, then third, there is the PR thing as to when we disclose that and how.

EHRLICHMAN: Ziegler has just left my office. He feels we have no more than twelve hours.

NIXON: Right.

EHRLICHMAN: He's got some input from the *Post* and it's his estimate that unless we take the initiative by nine o'clock tonight —

NIXON: Mm-hmm.

EHRLICHMAN: — it will be too late. Now, for that reason, I would suggest that Ziegler sit in a meeting with Petersen and that you and Ziegler persuade Petersen that the announcement has to come from the White House.

NIXON: I'll tell him.

EHRLICHMAN: Otherwise the Justice Department will, of course, try and —

NIXON: Mm-hmm.

EHRLICHMAN: — preempt this whole thing.

NIXON: Yeah.

EHRLICHMAN: But I think it would be a good idea for you to spend —

NIXON: I don't — I think I've got to get Petersen in alone first.

EHRLICHMAN: Sure, sure. I understand.

HALDEMAN: [unclear]

NIXON: [unclear] then I'll pull Ziegler in.

HALDEMAN: Yeah.

EHRLICHMAN: Uh —

NIXON: That's a very good point.

EHRLICHMAN: Now, you may want to listen to Ron for some time ahead of time. He's got this well thought through and well laid out, and I think he's quite dispassionate about it and quite —

HALDEMAN: Well, we'll go over that with him.

EHRLICHMAN: Yeah, we'll do that now while you're gone.

HALDEMAN: There's one point in — before you talk to Dean that I — occurred to me last night that doesn't fit together.

NIXON: Yeah.

HALDEMAN: Maybe it doesn't matter, and that is you said, last night, as I understood it, that Petersen had told you that Liddy has not talked.

NIXON: Yeah.

HALDEMAN: And that they can't get Liddy to talk.

NIXON: Yeah.

HALDEMAN: Dean told us that Liddy had told them everything.

EHRLICHMAN: Told the U.S. attorney everything.

HALDEMAN: There's something screwy —

EHRLICHMAN: Informally.

HALDEMAN: There's something screwy —

NIXON: I know that. I know that, but I —

HALDEMAN: Petersen's either lying to you or Dean's lying to us.

NIXON: I may be — may be a little bold, but what I think is probably closer to the truth is that Dean started this business a few weeks ago with his attorneys —

EHRLICHMAN: Mm-hmm.

NIXON: — and decided to save his ass and his attorneys went in and probably the U.S. attorney gave him a snow job and said that you're — that Liddy has talked.

EHRLICHMAN: Either that or Dean used that story as a cover-up —

NIXON: [unclear]

EHRLICHMAN: — in case anything started to seep out.

NIXON: Did a cover-up?

HALDEMAN: Yeah. Then it would have come from Liddy rather than —

EHRLICHMAN: Yeah, yeah.

HALDEMAN: — from him.

NIXON: How's Ron think it ought to be done? I should do it?

EHRLICHMAN: Ron thinks that it ought to be done from here. That — well, he hasn't said whether you should do it. I mentioned it to him the other day that you thought you should do it here in the press room, if you did it at all.

NIXON: I could do it right here in the Oval Office.

EHRLICHMAN: Yes, but he wants to get out the fact that Dean disserved you — that the Dean report was inadequate. It didn't go far enough. That several weeks ago you reinstituted an examination of the —

NIXON: I began my personal investigation of the case.

EHRLICHMAN: Yeah, and that this culminated in a whole series of actions —

NIXON: Right.

EHRLICHMAN: — over the weekend.

NIXON: Personal investigation of the case in that I spent the weekend working on it. I think that's what we've got to say. The Dean report did not —

HALDEMAN: That this is the week of Mitchell being here Saturday is very important to the circumstances.

NIXON: That's right. But the president asked Ehrlichman to conduct his own investigation.

EHRLICHMAN: Well, now, if I'm going to be splashed on this thing, you're better off not having another discredited Dean.

NIXON: Yeah, well, then somebody's got to do it.

EHRLICHMAN: Well, you can downplay who did it.

HALDEMAN: You can say you did it yourself by talking to all the people —

NIXON: Yeah.

HALDEMAN: — concerned.

NIXON: Yeah.

HALDEMAN: You talked to me and Ehrlichman and everybody else —

NIXON: [unclear] I made my own investigation of the matter.

EHRLICHMAN: I think that's the way.

NIXON: My own investigation of the matter. But I didn't talk to Mitchell, see?

EHRLICHMAN: Well, they say, "Who did?" and you delegated me to do that. I mean that's — but —

NIXON: [unclear] Ehrlichman [unclear] look, your splash though is only on this one goddamn thing.

EHRLICHMAN: Well, I think there's a judgment call here —

NIXON: Yeah.

EHRLICHMAN: —as to whether you want a quote Ehrlichman report unquote—

NIXON: Yeah.

EHRLICHMAN: —out in the media.

NIXON: Yeah.

HALDEMAN: [unclear] because they'll make a big thing about the Dean report—

NIXON: Right.

HALDEMAN: —found out that Dean was guilty and the Ehrlichman report found out that Ehrlichman—

NIXON: Right. No, no. Now query—would you mind telling Moore to see Gray or is that out of the question? I mean he—you can talk to him, can't you? The only point is time is of the essence right now. I—you know, I've got odds and ends here today that I have to—

EHRLICHMAN: I understand.

NIXON: No, I'll do it.

EHRLICHMAN: No, no. I'll take care of it.

NIXON: All right, what you can say is—give him the two by four. Say, "Now, look here, here's the situation." Have you talked to Fielding yet to find out what the situation is?

EHRLICHMAN: No. No. No, as a matter of fact, I've got a problem here. I'm going to have Moore talk to Fielding also—

NIXON: Right.

EHRLICHMAN: —and find out what was in there, because I don't want to know.

NIXON: Right. That's right [unclear] that's great.

EHRLICHMAN: And then Moore can advise you.

NIXON: Okay, and then I don't know what statement—I'd like to have Ron, maybe between now and the time—I've put off my meeting with the guy at one thirty, John.

EHRLICHMAN: Mm-hmm.

NIXON: Petersen—I mean I had to because I couldn't get time to go through—

EHRLICHMAN: Right.

NIXON: —what he wants. [unclear] but that's just well enough because it gives me a chance when I get back to take my breath and take a look at that.

EHRLICHMAN: Right.

NIXON: And be ready for it. But I'm not going to let him put this out that the Justice Department dragged this out of the White House. Your goddamn rights—in fact, I'll—now I can have him do it.

EHRLICHMAN: Well, I'll tell you what you might do is have him standing by you—

NIXON: Yeah.

EHRLICHMAN: —just standing there. You do it, and then you say Petersen here is—

NIXON: Yeah.

EHRLICHMAN: —working with me on this.

NIXON: Yeah. Yesterday I talked to Mr. Kleindienst. He removed himself from my—I mean, because of the people that are involved [unclear] the case. I directed it to

Petersen. I made a decision on Petersen myself. You know, he wanted a special prosecutor.

EHRLICHMAN: Yeah.

NIXON: I said all right, we'll go with Petersen. Say — that's right, Petersen will be with me and Mr. Petersen is in charge of this and so forth and so on. I want Petersen to be able to say what I [unclear] that I made the record with him like nobody's business last night.

EHRLICHMAN: Well, he's got every incentive, so —

NIXON: Right.

EHRLICHMAN: Well, now, in seeing Dean now —

NIXON: Yeah, but the question is —

EHRLICHMAN: — I think the point is that in taking these letters from him, it would be the agreement that neither he nor you would announce it immediately.

NIXON: No.

EHRLICHMAN: So the announcement would be in your discretion —

NIXON: Right.

EHRLICHMAN: — and the decision would be in your discretion as to which way you go.

NIXON: Right.

EHRLICHMAN: But that in view — and you might ask him whether he intends to plead guilty or not.

NIXON: Yeah. Or —

EHRLICHMAN: Or not guilty, because that will weigh —

NIXON: Yeah.

EHRLICHMAN: — in your ultimate decision.

NIXON: That's right. That's right.

HALDEMAN: Then we've got a cop-out.

EHRLICHMAN: Well, then that will come out.

NIXON: That's right. I'm going to find out [unclear]. Well, let me say that if he gets a cop-out he's going to be dead. Which really — that — you can't have him around here with the kind of stuff he's going to cop out about.

HALDEMAN: Oh, no.

EHRLICHMAN: Ask him what you should say publicly about the Dean report.

NIXON: Yeah. He said — he told me — he says there was no Dean report. I don't understand it. I don't think it was an oral report. I said, "Didn't I ask you what its final outcome is?" "Yes." "Didn't you say nobody's involved?" "Yes." I said, "Was anybody involved?" "No."

EHRLICHMAN: I see.

NIXON: Well, I went right down the line —

HALDEMAN: That's all that we've said.

NIXON: — on Ehrlichman, Colson, and Dean. I said, "Did you know?" He said, "No." So at least his line on that is that he didn't know about it before — prior knowledge.

Okay. Only one point that occurs to me that — he did discuss with me the — this need for the funds for Hunt. At least I remember the —

HALDEMAN: Yeah.

NIXON: Did he come in? Who did he discuss that with? I mean, that Hunt needed attorney fees.

HALDEMAN: But on the — certainly [unclear].

EHRLICHMAN: Did he do that to you personally?

HALDEMAN: Yeah.

NIXON: He discussed it and I said I don't know whether you can get it. I mean, I didn't — but what I meant is that it was so —

EHRLICHMAN: Well, you know what I was telling him at the same — at the time —

NIXON: Mm-hmm.

EHRLICHMAN: — was that that should not be a consideration in this thing.

NIXON: Mm-hmm.

EHRLICHMAN: And you know —

NIXON: And then they went back and so Mitchell took care of it — I mean —

EHRLICHMAN: Yeah, but not on account of any jeopardy to me obviously.

NIXON: Dean — huh?

EHRLICHMAN: Not on account of any jeopardy to me. I mean, he did that for his own purposes.

NIXON: Yeah. Mitchell.

EHRLICHMAN: Yeah. Because I was saying, "Look, fellows, if that's the only thing he's doing is blackmailing me, why forget it, you know?"

NIXON: Wait, wait. Hunt sent a message to you? I didn't know about that.

EHRLICHMAN: No, he didn't send it to me. He sent it to Dean about me.

NIXON: I didn't know that.

EHRLICHMAN: Yeah.

NIXON: What did he say? "I'm going to talk about Ehrlichman"? [unclear]

EHRLICHMAN: Yeah.

NIXON: He's referring of course to the things that were done before.

EHRLICHMAN: Sure.

HALDEMAN: He said, "I'm going to pull the plug on all the dirty stuff."

EHRLICHMAN: Yeah.

HALDEMAN: He also said something about that.

EHRLICHMAN: Now, also — you know, in thinking about this —

NIXON: You told him [unclear]. All right, go ahead.

EHRLICHMAN: In thinking about this —

NIXON: But who — but — ?

HALDEMAN: John stonewalled that completely. [unclear] Dean, he doesn't have anything. There is nothing.

EHRLICHMAN: Do you remember when we were planning the Hawaiian trip? The very active discussion we had about Clark MacGregor going out and making a full disclosure on Watergate.

NIXON: Mm-hmm.

EHRLICHMAN: And we had a plan.

NIXON: Right, that I was — I — in on it.

EHRLICHMAN: Well, you were — we discussed with you the possibility. The idea was that you'd be out of town and it wouldn't get on —

NIXON: Right.

EHRLICHMAN: Remember?

NIXON: Mm-hmm.

EHRLICHMAN: And you know who shot that down?

NIXON: Dean?

EHRLICHMAN: Dean and MacGregor.

HALDEMAN: And MacGregor?

EHRLICHMAN: Yeah.

NIXON: Yeah. Why?

EHRLICHMAN: Because they felt that it would be damaging to the campaign.

NIXON: Oh, we all know that's a phony.

EHRLICHMAN: But somewhere, I think I did a memo on that and I'm having it looked for now. But, in any event, we made a kind of a full-court press at that time. Remember, we were at San Clemente and we were going to have MacGregor come out there.

NIXON: Mm-hmm.

EHRLICHMAN: And we had a lot of conversations on the phone and I blasted him and badgered him and urged him. And he dug his heels in and dug his heels in.

HALDEMAN: At least five times during this period, I would get Dean into my office or he'd come in, you know, with his problems and stuff. And we'd go through the whole thing. I spoke to you of this a couple of those times at least. I said, "John, why don't you just put the whole thing out and go with it." He said, "Oh, no, we can't do that." And he can't — he knows —

NIXON: What is the story behind what happened on that, on that fee for representing the last thing for Hunt? Then, I mean, he mentioned it to me and I —

EHRLICHMAN: I know none of the facts. Dean transmitted to me the threat —

NIXON: Yeah.

HALDEMAN: — which he had received personally from Bittman and that —

NIXON: Right, right. Go ahead, go ahead.

EHRLICHMAN: I said to John, "Look, if we're going to live with this — "

NIXON: Right.

EHRLICHMAN: " — all our lives, the hell with it."

NIXON: Right, good. Good — then what?

EHRLICHMAN: So then he went back to Mitchell, apparently. Because the next thing I knew about it we had a meeting in Bob's office about something else and —

NIXON: Mitchell.

EHRLICHMAN: — Mitchell came in and Mitchell said, "I've taken care of it."

NIXON: Okay. Now let's see [unclear]. Well, anyway, we'll get there [unclear] Henry Petersen [unclear]. This scenario [unclear] got to be so [unclear].

EHRLICHMAN: Yes, sir.

HALDEMAN: You bet.

NIXON: And —

EHRLICHMAN: Ron's got to have that information.

NIXON: Well, I may have to just say it myself.

HALDEMAN: Yeah.

NIXON: I conducted this —

EHRLICHMAN: Right.

NIXON: — investigation and so forth.

EHRLICHMAN: [unclear] Petersen standing there right by [unclear].

NIXON: Right, I can say that the Watergate case has been broken.

"I put everybody's feet to the fire because it just had to stop."

April 16, 1973, 10:00 a.m.
Richard Nixon and John Dean
OVAL OFFICE

Dean had visited Nixon at the White House the night of April 15, in order to explain to the president that his testimony and in fact all his recent actions were "motivated out of loyalty to you, the president." On the following morning, when Dean arrived in the Oval Office, Nixon thought that Dean had changed. He was no longer "self-assured and even cocky," as on the previous evening. Instead, he later described him as "tense." The transcript of the conversation reflects that both of them were tense. The two had worked closely together through the heat of the rising scandal, but in the end each one felt betrayed by the other. Nixon was uncomfortable asking Dean to sign a pair of letters for possible use in the very near future, one a resignation and one a request for a leave of absence. Dean was just as determined that Ehrlichman and Haldeman should also be subject to termination. He may have been acting out of spite, as Nixon believed, or only in a stubborn effort to bring the president face-to-face with the facts, as Dean himself contended. While discussing his testimony with the president, Dean finally made the point he'd arrived with: "There is a mythical belief . . . that they don't have a problem," Dean said, referring to Haldeman and Ehrlichman. "And I'm really not sure you're convinced they do. But I'm telling you, they do."

• • •

NIXON: Hi, John, how are you?

DEAN: Good morning. Good morning.

NIXON: Sit down. Sit down. Trying to get my remarks ready to [unclear] the building trades.

DEAN: Oh, I understand.

NIXON: Yes, indeed. Yeah. You know, I was thinking we ought to get the odds and ends [unclear] we talked, and it was confirmed that — you remember we talked about resignations and so forth and so on — that I should have in hand — not to be released —

DEAN: Mm-hmm.

NIXON: But I should have in hand something, or otherwise they'll say, "What the hell did you — after Mr. Dean told you all of this, what did you do?" You see what I mean?

DEAN: Mm-hmm.

NIXON: Now I talked to Petersen about the thing and I said, "Now, what do you want to do about this situation on Dean, and so forth?" And he said, "Well" — he said, "I" — he said, "I would do — I don't want to announce anything now." You know what I mean?

DEAN: Mm-hmm.

NIXON: But what is your feeling on that? See what I mean?

DEAN: Are we talking Dean, or are we talking Dean, Ehrlichman, and Haldeman?

NIXON: Well, I'm talking Dean —

DEAN: Dean.

NIXON: — at this moment.

DEAN: All right.

NIXON: Dean at this moment, because you're going to be — you're going to be doing it. I'll have to handle them also. But the point is — what's your advice that we — you see, the point is we don't have — I just got it — I just typed up a couple — just to have here which I'd be willing to put out. You know —

DEAN: Mm-hmm.

NIXON: — in the event that certain things occurred.

DEAN: I understand.

NIXON: But you see, put the — just putting the — you don't want to put any lies into it, would you? [unclear] What's your advice?

DEAN: I think it'd be the — good to have it on hand.

NIXON: Yeah.

DEAN: I would think, to be very honest with you —

NIXON: Have those others, too.

DEAN: Have those others, also.

NIXON: Yeah, yeah. I will. Well, as a matter of fact, they both suggested it for themselves.

DEAN: Mm-hmm.

[STEVE BULL enters.]

NIXON: So I got that — I am sorry, Steve, I hit the wrong bell.

[STEVE BULL leaves.]

DEAN: [laughs]

NIXON: So I've already done that with them.

DEAN: All right.

NIXON: So, they said, "Look, they're ready anytime you want them." I've got that. Now I want to get your advice on that, too. So what — I would — now what I would think we want to do — we should have it in two different forms here. We should have it — and I would like to discuss with you — the forms. It seems to me that your — the form should be request an immediate indefinite leave of absence. That'd be one thing. And the other, of course, would be just a straight resignation.

DEAN: Mm-hmm.

NIXON: First, what I would suggest is that you sign both. That's what I had in mind. And then we'll talk about after — because you don't know yet what you're going — for example, you could go in and plead guilty. You'd have to resign.

DEAN: That's right.

NIXON: If, on the other hand, you're going in — on a — some other basis, then I think a leave of absence is then —

DEAN: Mm-hmm.

NIXON: — the proper thing to do.

DEAN: I would think so.

NIXON: And that's the way I would discuss it with others, too. But if you have any other thoughts, let me know. I'm not trying to press you on a thing. Just — I just want to be sure, John, you've got the record. That you're — so that I've done everything that I [unclear]. Do you agree?

DEAN: I think it's a good idea. I frankly do.

NIXON: Yeah.

DEAN: But, I think if you do it for one — I think you have problems with others too, Mr. President.

NIXON: I already have done that with others.

DEAN: Yeah. All right. That's what I've been trying to advise you that — you know —

NIXON: But on theirs, both the — pending the — it is all pending their appearance, and so forth. Just as it is in yours. Nothing's going to be said.

DEAN: Mm-hmm.

NIXON: But I've got to have it in hand. You see what I mean? My reason, as I told them — as a matter of fact, after our talk last night, I told them — I said, "We — I've got to have it in hand so that I can move on this if — as Petersen is going to report to me every day." You see?

DEAN: Mm-hmm.

NIXON: I said, "Now, Petersen" — I said, "if you get this stuff confirmed" — I said, "I need to know." And he said, "Well, I" — because I asked him specifically. I said, "What are you going to do?" He says, "Well, LaRue is going to be today." And, I don't know who else. Strachan's going to be today. There are three today I think. I don't know. Who's the third one?

DEAN: I don't know.

NIXON: That's right. You're not supposed to.

DEAN: [laughs]

NIXON: Then — okay.

DEAN: What I would like to do is to draft up for you an alternative letter. Put it in both options and you can just put them in the file.

NIXON: Mm-hmm.

DEAN: Just short and sweet.

NIXON: Mm-hmm. All right. Fine. I had dictated something myself, on my own, which I just — which is [unclear] how this — but you don't have to. If you can give me a better form, fine. I want you to do it either way. Do you want to just prepare something?

DEAN: I'd like to prepare something.

NIXON: Good. All right. Fine. Why don't you take this? And take those, just as an —

DEAN: Sure.

NIXON: — idea. And have something that — I've got to see Petersen at one thirty.

DEAN: All right.

NIXON: Understand, I don't want it — put anything out, because I don't want to jeopardize your position at all. You've got a right to — just as everybody else has, to — let's say you've been — you've carried a hell of a load here and I — but I just feel that since what you said last night that we've got to do on this and with Haldeman and Ehrlichman. I have leave of absences from them. Which, however, I will not use until I get the word from Petersen on corroboration —

DEAN: All right.

NIXON: — which he advised himself. I talked to him after I talked to you. Left about eleven forty-five. I told the son of a bitch — he doesn't know how hard we work around here.

DEAN: And you will have something within a couple of hours.

NIXON: Well, I —

DEAN: You think just put it in the file?

NIXON: I won't be back. I won't be back. Yeah. You can — you draft what you want me to — in other words —

DEAN: And if you don't like what I draft, tell me and I will change it in any way —

NIXON: Oh, sure. Sure.

DEAN: — that you want.

NIXON: But I can't make a decision —

DEAN: Yes, sir.

NIXON: — of course, you see — and also, it may depend — well, put it this way. Put it this way, you draft what you — what you want. And we can — if I have any concerns about it, I'll give you a ring. You can be around, and so forth.

DEAN: Mm-hmm.

NIXON: And — but you would agree you should — but nothing should be put out now. Right?

DEAN: I would agree. I was thinking about that.

NIXON: You see, we've got the problem — today the thing may break. You know, with Magruder and so forth. And I'm — you know what I mean. That's what I wanted to run over with you, briefly, as to — you know, to get your feeling again as to how we handle it — how we — you know, you were saying the president should stay one step ahead of this thing. Well, we've got — the point is, the only problem is what the hell can I say publicly? Now, here's what we've done.

DEAN: Well, you see —

NIXON: I called in — I got in Kleindienst. We've — I've been working on it all week —

DEAN: Right.

NIXON: — actually, I mean I got — as soon as I got the Magruder thing, then I got in Kleindienst, and then at four o'clock we got in — sold Petersen. Kleindienst withdrew and assigned Petersen. I said, "All right, Henry, I don't want to talk to Kleindienst anymore about this case. I'm just going to talk to you."

DEAN: Mm-hmm.

NIXON: "You're in charge. You follow through and you're going through to get to the bottom of this thing and I am going to let the chips fall where they may." And we covered that all the way down the line. Now, I have to follow him to a certain extent on the prosecution side. On the other hand, on the PR side, I sure as hell am not going to let the Justice Department step out there —

DEAN: Right.

NIXON: — and say, "Look, we dragged the White House in here." I've got to step out and do it, John.

DEAN: That's right.

NIXON: Don't you agree?

DEAN: That's right.

NIXON: But yet, I don't want to walk out and say, "I — look, John Dean's resignation has been accepted." Jesus Christ, that isn't fair.

DEAN: Nor would it be fair to say Ehrlichman and Haldeman's have.

NIXON: Yeah. What —

DEAN: You know, I've already examined —

NIXON: [unclear] because you see they haven't been charged yet. As soon as they're charged [unclear]. But see he's — but in your case, is you haven't been charged with anything yet —

DEAN: No, I have not.

NIXON: That's my problem, see, with it. All I wanted is to have on — the only reason I'm doing this is to — because of you — what you said about some — what you said about them. And that's why I'm getting it from them, too.

DEAN: Well, it's a — there's a chance — well, there's a chance that today when LaRue goes down that Haldeman and Ehrlichman's names are going to be right down there before the grand jury.

NIXON: Right. Well, the name will be in, but the point is you don't just throw somebody out because of a name in court.

DEAN: I understand.

NIXON: You understand. Would you — you could also, if you would — here's — and I would like for you to prepare this in a letter that you would have for Ehrlichman and Haldeman. Would you do that too?

DEAN: Yes, sir.

NIXON: And then I'll give them the form and let them work out their — something that's appropriate. Would you prepare that for me, then?

DEAN: Yes, I will.

NIXON: But they told me last night, orally, just as you did, that —

DEAN: They stand ready.

NIXON: Cover the record. They said, "Look, we will leave in a minute. We'll leave today. You can do whatever you want." And I said, "What the hell? We're going to have to wait until we get some evidence." You know what I mean?

DEAN: Mm-hmm.

NIXON: Which I think you agree with.

DEAN: I — that's what — I do, and the question is timing, and —

NIXON: Yeah. Now, let's get Dean's advice as to how we handle this now — from now on. What is your — what's your advice?

DEAN: Well, I would say you should have the letters in hand and then —

NIXON: Right.

DEAN: — based on what you learn from Petersen, you can make a judgment as to timing. I think you're still five steps ahead of what will ever emerge publicly. I don't think they —

NIXON: They think in twelve hours it may break. Somebody told me the news — the *Post*'s, according to Ziegler — has got something now on this. Magruder talking around and everything. I don't know.

DEAN: Well, I know what — some of the things Magruder said. He said that the prosecutors had asked him a number of questions about Ehrlichman and Haldeman. So there's no doubt that that's going to be out on the —

NIXON: Yeah.

DEAN: — the street fast also.

NIXON: Well, then we ought to move on that, too.

DEAN: Mm-hmm.

NIXON: That's my point. You see —

DEAN: It's unfortunate that I — you know, I'm hoping that the ultimate resolution of this thing is that no one has any problems. And that's possible —

NIXON: Legally.

DEAN: — legally.

NIXON: That's right. Which I hope is your case, too. In other words, when I say no one, nobody at the White House staff — not you, not Colson, not Ehrlichman, not Haldeman. Because goddamn it! Let me summarize this specific point again because I need to, you know, they — we know there was no — on the Dean report. Ziegler has always said it was oral.

DEAN: That's right.

NIXON: Right. But you remember when you came in, I asked you the specific question: "Is anybody on the White House staff involved?" You told me, "No."

DEAN: That's right. And I have no knowledge —

NIXON: You still believe that?

DEAN: Yes, sir. I do.

NIXON: Yeah. But you did tell me that in the aftermath there were serious problems.

DEAN: That's right.

NIXON: Right. And I said, "Well, let's see what they are." Right?

DEAN: And now you're beginning to see what they are. They're potential — technical — obstruction of justice problems.

NIXON: Sure. But not necessarily — well, I talked to Petersen last night and he made exactly the same point. He says the obstruction was morally wrong. No, not morally — he said it may not have been morally wrong, and it may not be legally wrong, but he said from the standpoint of the presidency, you can't have it. That's what his point was. So he seems to think that this — that the obstruction of justice thing is a goddamn hard thing to prove —

DEAN: That's right.

NIXON: — to prove in court, which I think should be some comfort to you.

DEAN: Well, my lawyer tells me that, you know, "legally you're in damn good shape."

NIXON: Is that right?

DEAN: That's right.

NIXON: Because you're not —

DEAN: That's right. It's a —

NIXON: You were simply helping the defendants get their fees and their —

DEAN: Well —

NIXON: Huh? What does he say?

DEAN: In that position, I'm merely a conduit. It's very technical, very technical. I am a conduit to other people. That is the problem.

NIXON: Mm-hmm. What was the situation, John? This — the only time I ever heard any discussion of this supporting of the defendants — and I must say I guess I should have assumed somebody was helping them. I must have assumed it, but — and I must say people were good in a way — I was busy — was when you mentioned to me something about the — I mean, I think the last time we talked about Hunt having a problem.

DEAN: Well, that's —

NIXON: But that — and that was — then we — but that was handled at — by Mitchell. Was that true or what the hell happened?

DEAN: That's the last time we had a request was the —

NIXON: How did it work out? Did you — ?

DEAN: — the Monday before sentencing.

NIXON: He hit you with a —

DEAN: No.

NIXON: — at a dinner or something?

DEAN: No, no. O'Brien, who was one of the lawyers who was representing the reelection committee was asked by Hunt to meet with him. He came to me after the meeting and said that "Hunt asked the following message be passed to you." And I said, "Why me?" He said, "I asked Hunt the same question."

NIXON: To you, Dean? Or to me, the president?

DEAN: Asked of me —

NIXON: Oh.

DEAN: Dean.

NIXON: Oh, yeah.

DEAN: It's the first time I'd ever heard anything like this. And I said —

NIXON: He had never asked —

DEAN: No.

NIXON: — you before?

DEAN: No. Uh —

NIXON: Let me tell you. What did you report to me on it, though? I — it was rather fragmentary, as I recall it. You said —

DEAN: Right.

NIXON: — Hunt had a problem, and —

DEAN: Very fragmentary. I was, I —

NIXON: Yeah, but that's not the thing. I said, "What, John — what's it going to cost to do this?" That's when I sent you to Camp — and said, "Well, for God's sake, let's see where this thing comes out."

DEAN: That's right.

NIXON: And you said it'd cost a million dollars.

DEAN: I said, "It," you know, "it conceivably could, and the way this —" I said, "If we don't cut this thing —"

NIXON: Exactly.

DEAN: Uh, anyway —

NIXON: But that's the only conversation we had. Where — how was that handled? Who the hell handled that money?

DEAN: Well, let me tell you the rest — what Hunt said. He said, "You tell Dean that I need seventy-two thousand dollars for my personal expenses, fifty thousand dollars for my legal fees."

NIXON: Mm-hmm.

DEAN: "If I don't get it, I'm going to have some things to say about the seamy things I did at the White House for John Ehrlichman."

NIXON: Mm-hmm.

DEAN: All right. I took that to Ehrlichman. Ehrlichman said, "Have you talked to Mitchell about it?" I said, "No, I have not." He said, "Well, will you talk to Mitchell?" I said, "Yes, I will." I talked to Mitchell. I just passed it along to him. And then there was a meeting down here a few days later in Bob's office with Bob and Ehrlichman and Mitchell and myself. And, Ehrlichman said at that time — he said, "Well, is that problem with Hunt straightened out?" He said it to me and I said, "Well, ask the man who may know — Mitchell." And Mitchell said, "I think that problem is solved."

NIXON: That's all?

DEAN: That's all he said.

NIXON: Right. That's good. In other words, that was done at the Mitchell level?

DEAN: That's right.

NIXON: But you had knowledge. Haldeman had a lot of knowledge, and Ehrlichman had knowledge.

DEAN: Right.

NIXON: And I suppose I did — I mean I am planning to assume some culpability on that [unclear].

DEAN: I don't think so.

NIXON: Why not? I plan to be as tough on myself as I am on the other thing, though. I must say I didn't really give it a thought at the time because I didn't know —

DEAN: No one gave it a thought.

NIXON: You did. You did.

DEAN: No one —

NIXON: You didn't tell me this about Ehrlichman, for example. When you came in on that day —

DEAN: I know.

NIXON: You simply said, "Hunt needs this money." And you were using it as an example of the problems ahead.

DEAN: I have tried all along to make sure that anything I passed to you myself didn't cause you any personal problems.

NIXON: John, let me ask you this. Let us suppose if this thing breaks and they ask you, John Dean, "Now, John, you were the president's counsel. Did you report things to the president? What did you report to the president?"

DEAN: I would refuse to answer any questions as to anything —

NIXON: No, no, no, no, no. I think you should — let me ask you this —

DEAN: — unless you waive —

NIXON: Let me say, on this point — I would not waive. You could say, "I reported to the president." That "the president called me in." I mean, "The president has authorized me to say he called me in and asked me — "

DEAN: Mm-hmm.

NIXON: Make that before, that when the event first occurred, you conducted an investigation and passed to the president the message, no White House personnel, according to your investigation, was involved. You did do that, didn't you?

DEAN: I did that through Ehrlichman and Haldeman.

NIXON: That's it. You did do that.

DEAN: If I'm under oath, now I'm going to have to say I did that through Ehrlichman and Haldeman.

NIXON: No. But I know you did that. I didn't see you.

DEAN: That's right.

NIXON: Remember I didn't see you until after the election.

DEAN: That's right.

NIXON: But you see — all right. Now, but then you say, and then after the election the president, when the McCord thing broke, called you in. I think that's when it was, wasn't it?

DEAN: No, uh —

NIXON: After the McCord thing.

DEAN: No. It was before the McCord thing because you remember you told me after the Friday morning that McCord's letter —

NIXON: Mm-hmm.

DEAN: You said, "You predicted this — that it was going to happen." Because I had in about the week, or two weeks —

NIXON: How did it — why did I get you in there? What triggered me getting you in?

DEAN: Well, we just started talking about this thing and —

NIXON: But I called you in — you and Moore together, didn't I?

DEAN: Well —

NIXON: For a Dean report.

DEAN: On a Wednesday morning —

NIXON: Because — what was — well, I know what was involved. What was involved was the damn executive privilege and all that crap.

DEAN: That's right. It was — the Gray things were popping, but on the —

NIXON: Yeah.

DEAN: — the Wednesday morning before I asked —

NIXON: We had three conversations to my recollection.

DEAN: Oh, sir, I think we had more than that, but of course we'd have a record of that through —

NIXON: Yeah.

DEAN: — those people. I think we had more than that. But the one report where I finally — I called Bob —

NIXON: [unclear] this office. Good.

DEAN: Yeah. I called Bob and I said, "Bob" — I said, "I don't think the president has all the facts."

NIXON: That's right. And then you came and sat in this chair and that's the first time that I realized the thing.

DEAN: That's right.

NIXON: And what — and now the question is, "Well, Mr. Dean, why didn't you tell the president before?" And your answer there is — ?

DEAN: I didn't know. That is absolutely correct.

NIXON: That's what you told me last time. You see, I don't want you, John, to be in a position — and frankly I don't want the president to be in a position where one of his trusted people had information that he did keep — kept from him. So I just want —

DEAN: I did not know.

NIXON: Fine. You did not know. "How did you find out then?" they'll ask. Okay. But you — that's your — but you can handle that.

DEAN: That's right.

NIXON: But I did ask you and I think you should say the president has authorized you to say this. "I won't reveal the conversation with the president, but he's — and he asked me this question. I told him this and he — that nobody in the White House was involved. And then, in addition to that I — to the best of my ability kept" — I guess. Or what do you think you ought to handle with the presidential things?

DEAN: Well —

NIXON: Maybe you better —

DEAN: I think, the less said about —

NIXON: All right. Fine.

DEAN: I think that's privileged, and I think [unclear].

NIXON: Except that if you do this —

DEAN: I think you say anything you want to say about it.

NIXON: Right. But I have to say it. Well, let me tell you, I am going to handle that properly and I just want to be sure that it jibes with the facts. I can say that you did tell me that nobody in the White House was involved and I can say that you then came in, at your request, and said, "I think the president needs to hear more about this case."

DEAN: That's right.

NIXON: And it was at that time that I started my investigation.

DEAN: That's right.

NIXON: Correct?

DEAN: That was the Wednesday before they were sentenced. Now I can get that date. I don't have it off the top —

NIXON: Would you do me this? Get your chronology of that Wednesday you came in and told me. That would be helpful for me to have.

DEAN: That's what I had in mind —

NIXON: You see, I want to —

DEAN: [unclear]

NIXON: You see, I — that's when I became interested. I was — I became frankly interested in the case and I said, "Now goddamn it! I want to find out the score." And I set in motion Ehrlichman, Mitchell, and a few of — not Mitchell, but others. Okay.

DEAN: Sure.

NIXON: One other thing. And the privilege thing, I think nothing, so that you could be sure that — you know, nothing is privileged that involves wrongdoing —

DEAN: That's correct.

NIXON: — on your part or wrongdoing on the part of anybody else. I'm telling you that now and I want you to — when you testify, if you do, to say that the president has told you that. Would you do that?

DEAN: Yes, sir.

NIXON: Would you agree with that?

DEAN: I do.

NIXON: Fine. However, let me say that with regard to what we call the electronic stuff they heard — in what I have now have found is in the leak area — national security area — that I consider privileged.

DEAN: I do, too.

NIXON: And I think you should say, for example, on that — but what I meant is I would — I think in the case of the [1969 wiretap on journalist Joe] Kraft stuff, what the FBI did — they were both, I find — I've checked it back. There were some done through private sources [through John Caulfield]. Most of it was done through the bureau after we got going.

DEAN: That's right.

NIXON: Hoover didn't want to do Kraft. But what it involved, John, apparently was this — there were leaks in the NSC. They were in Kraft and other columns. We were trying to plug the leaks.

DEAN: Right.

NIXON: And we had that — so we checked it out. Finally, we turned it over to Hoover. Then when the hullabaloo developed, we didn't — we just stopped it altogether.

DEAN: I understand.

NIXON: And that includes [unclear]. But in my view I consider that privileged.

DEAN: I have no intention of raising that in any —

NIXON: Have you informed your lawyers about that?

DEAN: No.

NIXON: I think you should not. Understand, not because of cutting anything, except that I do think it's privileged. But it's up to you. I mean, I —

DEAN: No. I think it is privileged, also.

NIXON: Yeah. It's important to know — and this was necessary to use. We had Hoover do a bit, and in control — as Lyndon Johnson [unclear] better. Now, your guess as to when — well, I'll ask Petersen today. When will you be called? Perhaps Tuesday, Wednesday, or —

DEAN: I would think sometime this week.

NIXON: You don't think the thing is likely to break today then, huh?

DEAN: No, I don't.

NIXON: I wonder what Ziegler's got. He must have — he seems to think that something's going to bust. He hasn't been in to see me. I'll have to get him in later. But, well, I'll have him make — I'll ask Petersen.

DEAN: Mm-hmm.

NIXON: Petersen. But don't you agree with me?

DEAN: I don't think—

NIXON: That the president should make the first announcement and not the Justice Department?

DEAN: Yes, I do.

NIXON: [unclear]

DEAN: [unclear] on his own staff.

NIXON: Huh?

DEAN: On his own staff.

NIXON: Oh, hell. I'm going to make the announcement with regard to Magruder, too. Goddamn it! It's our campaign. I'm not going to have the Justice Department—

DEAN: Oh, I see what you mean.

NIXON: We triggered this whole thing. You know what I mean?

DEAN: That's right.

NIXON: Don't you agree?

DEAN: Well, if — when the —

NIXON: You helped the trigger.

DEAN: When history is written, you'll — and you put the pieces back together, you'll see why it happened. It's because I triggered it. I put everybody's feet to the fire because it just had to stop.

NIXON: That's right. And you put—

DEAN: And I still continue to feel that—

NIXON: That's right. You put Magruder's feet to the fire.

DEAN: Yes, I did.

NIXON: Where did you see Magruder?

DEAN: I didn't. I sent — in fact, I refused to see him. That was one of the problems.

NIXON: Oh. And that's why he—

DEAN: I started — I talked to him. I met with him in one of these outer offices out here at a meeting.

NIXON: What got Magruder to talk?

DEAN: Uh—

NIXON: I would like to take the credit.

DEAN: Because, well, [laughs] he knew that—

NIXON: I thought — I was hoping that you had seen him, because—

DEAN: There was — well, he was told, one, that, you know, there was going to be no chance—

NIXON: You remember, though, when you made the statement about just making a note here about drawing the wagons up around the White House. Based on — basically, you thought the primary [unclear]. This was talking about pre—

DEAN: Pre—

NIXON: —knowledge. Was all in the committee. Right?

DEAN: That's right. Where it is.

NIXON: That's right. But on Magruder — come again. What's the deal there?

DEAN: The situation there is that he and Mitchell were continuing to talk — continuing to talk about proceeding along the same course they'd been proceeding to — to lock in their story. But my story did not fit with their story. And I just told them I refused to change — to alter my testimony — other than to repeat it just as I knew it.

NIXON: When?

DEAN: This had to do with a number of meetings in the Department of Justice.

NIXON: Incidentally, I heard this [unclear], but I remember. You told me this. Everybody tells me that you said — Dean said, "I will not go to the — I am not going down there and lie," because you said your hand will shake and your emotion — remember you told me that?

DEAN: Yeah. No way I could. I'm incapable of it.

NIXON: Fine. Thank God, John. Don't ever do it, John. I want you to tell the truth. That's the thing that you're going to — I have told everybody around here — said, "Goddamn it! Tell the truth." Because all they do, John, is compound it.

DEAN: That's right.

NIXON: That son of a bitch Hiss would be free today if he hadn't lied about his espionage. He could have just said — he didn't even have to. He could've just said, "I — look, I knew Chambers. And, yes, as a young man I was involved with some Communist activities but I broke it off many years ago." And Chambers would have dropped it.

DEAN: Well —

NIXON: But the son of a bitch lied, and he goes to jail for the lie rather than the crime.

DEAN: Uh —

NIXON: So believe me, don't ever lie with these bastards.

DEAN: The truth always emerges.

NIXON: We know that.

DEAN: It always does.

NIXON: Also, there is a question of right and wrong, too.

DEAN: That's right.

NIXON: What is right and what is wrong.

DEAN: That's right.

NIXON: Perhaps there are gray areas, but you're right to get it out now I'm sure. On Liddy, I wanted to be sure that I — that you recall — on our conversation, I — you asked me to do something. I've left it with Petersen now. He said he'd handle it. That's the proper place —

DEAN: That's right.

NIXON: You see, when Liddy says he can't talk unless he hears from higher authority — I am not his higher authority.

DEAN: No.

NIXON: It's Mitchell.

DEAN: Well, but I think he's looking for the ultimate —

NIXON: What do you think he's thinking about?

DEAN: I think he's thinking about the president.

NIXON: Clemency?

DEAN: He thinks — he has the impression that you and Mitchell probably talk on the telephone daily about this.

NIXON: You know we've never talked about it.

DEAN: I understand that.

NIXON: I have never talked to Mitchell about this. Oh, except about when — whether we go — the executive privilege thing.

DEAN: Right.

NIXON: He came in and said, "Everybody should testify in executive session." Mitchell said that — except you. Which I think would be — listen, I think, incidentally, about executive privilege —

DEAN: I think, Mr. President, the Ervin hearings —

NIXON: The later —

DEAN: — are going to fizzle.

NIXON: What?

DEAN: I think when the — when Petersen finishes his —

NIXON: You don't think we should hold to executive privilege anyway, do you, John, now?

DEAN: To hold an executive privilege?

NIXON: Yeah. What's your advice on that? What should I do?

DEAN: I think if you — if there are indictments down there in that courtroom, none of the individuals should go up and testify. I think the Watergate is just going to be totally carved out of the Ervin hearings.

NIXON: Yeah. That's the Watergate, right? Then the other stuff is not that important — Segretti and all that?

DEAN: Segretti, yeah.

NIXON: Mm-hmm.

DEAN: That stuff is not that important. They'll probably — they can have a lot of fun with it but it's not very meaningful.

NIXON: So you think Liddy thought that I was calling Mitchell. [unclear] Good God almighty! Well, we covered that last [unclear].

DEAN: That's right.

NIXON: You were there.

DEAN: That's resolved — think —

NIXON: Is that enough?

DEAN: That's right. Petersen — if it doesn't —

NIXON: You tell me now if it isn't enough.

DEAN: No, I think it's enough.

NIXON: I'm going to expect you to — after all, you're still the counsel around here. [laughs] No, but I'm serious. You've got to advise me and that's the same with Haldeman and Ehrlichman. As long as you are around here, we've got to have it out.

DEAN: Well, I want to lay one thing out.

NIXON: Mm-hmm.

DEAN: I think there is a mythical belief — I've not talked to Bob or John about this — that they don't have a problem, Mr. President. And I'm really not sure you're convinced they do. But I'm telling you, they do.

NIXON: A problem?

DEAN: Yeah.

NIXON: There's no question about it.

DEAN: No question.

NIXON: They are —

DEAN: I just wanted —

NIXON: Yeah. Petersen made the point. I said, "Tell me what the facts are." And he says, "The problem is — the problem here is that they're going to get splashed." And he said, "When they get splashed, you've got a problem, Mr. President." Now, but then he goes on to say, as far as the legal [unclear] is concerned, I mean he covers all three of you here —

DEAN: Mm-hmm.

NIXON: — he said, "It's a very difficult case to prove." Do you agree with that?

DEAN: That's right.

NIXON: You see, that's the point. And I would hope it works. I mean I'm speaking now in personal terms. I —

DEAN: It's a technical case and it's a tough case.

NIXON: "It's a tough one to prove." What's he mean by that? I —

DEAN: Apparently, my lawyer said, "Now, I've won cases on this with tougher facts than you've got, I'll assure you."

NIXON: Yeah.

DEAN: It would not be a —

NIXON: See, that's their real vulnerability — together.

DEAN: It would be —

NIXON: Both Ehrlichman and Haldeman are in on the obstruction. And that's the point.

DEAN: That's right. I think it'd be a very good idea if they had counsel.

NIXON: I told them — yeah, last night — to get lawyers. So I'm one step ahead of you there. Now, do you — is there anything else you think I should do? You don't think I should — shit, I'm not going to let the Justice Department break this case, John.

DEAN: I understand. You've got to break it. You are breaking it, in a sense.

NIXON: Well, goddamn it! That's what we've done.

DEAN: That's right.

NIXON: I could have told you to go to Camp David and concoct a story, couldn't I?

DEAN: That's right.

NIXON: And you've never heard that said, have you?

DEAN: No, sir.

NIXON: In fact, I think I know [unclear]. But on the other hand, it was your job to tell me, wasn't it?

DEAN: Mm-hmm.

NIXON: And you have. Basically, what you've done — no, you've told me the truth, though. You've told me the truth. It was your job to work for the White House, the president, the White House staff, and they were not involved in the pre-thing. But then you thought about the post-thing. You thought about it and that's why you decided to — as you said, "Cut it out."

DEAN: That's why I said —

NIXON: You broke it, right?

DEAN: — the cancer is growing because —

NIXON: Right.

DEAN: — to keep this whole thing in.

NIXON: Look, one thing I want to be sure is in here — when you testify, I don't want you to be in a position, so — and I don't want the president to be in a position that his counsel did not level with him. See my point?

DEAN: No, sir. There's no point that I have not leveled with you, as you know.

NIXON: No, what I meant is, when they say, "Well, now, Mr. Dean," I am speaking now —

DEAN: They will not ask [unclear].

NIXON: [unclear] "Why didn't you tell the president? Did you know about this? Why didn't you tell the president?"

DEAN: That's a PR situation, Mr. President. The U.S. attorneys are not going to ask me questions as —

NIXON: I see.

DEAN: — to what I said to the president or what I didn't.

NIXON: Well, I favor — I frankly think — I would hope you could help on the PR there by —

DEAN: Be expecting to help on it —

NIXON: I would like for you to say, and you're free to talk about it. You're to say, "I told the president about this. I told the president first there was no involvement in the White House. Afterwards, I told the president that I — and the president said, "Look, I want to get to the bottom of this thing, period." See what I'm driving at? Not just the White House — you continued your investigation, and so forth. The president went ahead, investigated in his own way, which I have done.

DEAN: Mm-hmm.

NIXON: Believe me. I put a little pressure on —

DEAN: Mm-hmm.

NIXON: — Magruder and a few of these clowns. And, "As a result of the president's action, this thing has been broken."

DEAN: That's right.

NIXON: Because also I put pressure on the Justice Department. I told Kleindienst, "Goddamn it! That —"

DEAN: No, I think you're in front right now and I — and you can rest assured everything I do will keep you as far as —

NIXON: No, I don't want that, understand? When I say, "Don't lie," don't lie about me either.

DEAN: No, I won't, sir. You're — I'm not going —

NIXON: Because I think I've done the right thing. But I want you to do it. I want you to do — if you feel I've done the right thing I want — I think the country is entitled to know it. Because we're talking about the presidency here.

DEAN: This thing has changed so dramatically, the whole situation, since I gave you the picture —

NIXON: Since you sat in that chair.

DEAN: In that chair over there and gave you what I thought were the circumstances, the potential problems, and the like. You have done nothing but try to get to the bottom of this thing and —

NIXON: I think so.

DEAN: — and, uh —

NIXON: Well, I said, "Write a report." But my purpose was to write a report — as I said, I want the Segretti matter — put the Segretti stuff in. Put everything else in. Whether the White House — what was the White House involvement?. You know? What do you say? How about one last thing — Colson? You don't think that they're going to get him into this, huh?

DEAN: I think he has some technical problems — post- also. I don't know if he has any — if — to the best of my knowledge, he has no — had no advance knowledge of the thing.

NIXON: Right. I suppose the key there is Hunt, you know? The — he was so close to Hunt. I just want to know about it just for my own benefit. I — as I told you last night, I don't want —

DEAN: Chuck has —

NIXON: — to be in a position —

DEAN: Chuck has —

NIXON: "What about Chuck Colson?" I want —

DEAN: Chuck has sworn up and down to me —

NIXON: I'm going to say to you, John Dean. "Was Colson involved?"

DEAN: I have no information that he was at all.

NIXON: Post-?

DEAN: Technical problems.

NIXON: Those two things you mentioned last night.

DEAN: That and — let's face it, there's other technical problems, but you know —

NIXON: Mm-hmm. Yeah.

DEAN: — it's all the obstruction is technical stuff that mounts up.

NIXON: Yeah. Well, you take, for example, the clemency stuff. That's solely Mitchell, apparently, and Colson's talk with Bittman where he says, "I'll do everything I can, because as a friend — "

DEAN: No, that was with Ehrlichman.

NIXON: Huh?

DEAN: That was Ehrlichman.

NIXON: Ehrlichman with who?

DEAN: Ehrlichman and Colson and I sat up there, and Colson presented his story to Ehrlichman —

NIXON: I know.

DEAN: — regarding it, and then John gave Chuck very clear instructions on going back and telling him that it — you know, "Give him the inference he's got clemency but don't give him any commitment."

NIXON: No commitment?

DEAN: Right.

NIXON: Now that's all right. But first, if an individual — if it's no commitment, I've got a right to sit here — take a fellow like Hunt or a Cuban whose wife is sick and something. That's what clemency's about.

DEAN: That's right.

NIXON: Correct?

DEAN: That's right.

NIXON: But John specifically said, "No commitment," did he? He —

DEAN: Yeah.

NIXON: No commitment. Then Colson then went on to, apparently —

DEAN: I don't know how Colson delivered it —

NIXON: — apparently to Bittman —

DEAN: — for —

NIXON: Bittman. Is that your understanding?

DEAN: Yes, but I don't know what his, you know, specific —

NIXON: Where did this business of the Christmas thing get out, John? What the hell was that?

DEAN: Well, that's a —

NIXON: That must have been Mitchell, huh?

DEAN: No, that was Chuck, again. I think that —

NIXON: That they all — that they'd all be out by Christmas?

DEAN: No, I think he said something to the effect that Christmas is the time that clemency generally occurs.

NIXON: Oh, yeah. Well, that doesn't — I don't think that is going to hurt him.

DEAN: No.

NIXON: Do you?

DEAN: No.

NIXON: Clemency, he says — one [unclear] he's a friend of Hunt's. I'm just trying to put the best face on it. If it's the wrong — if it is, I've got to know.

DEAN: Well, one of the things I think you have to be very careful — and this is why Petersen will be very good — is if you take a set of facts and let the prosecutors who have no — they'll be making no PR judgments.

NIXON: Yeah.

DEAN: But they'll give you the raw facts as they relate to the law and it's later you've got to decide, you know, what public face will be put on it. In other words, they'll — if their —

NIXON: Oh, I understand.

DEAN: It's going to come out in court, you know.

NIXON: You can help on that, John.

DEAN: Yes, sir.

NIXON: You know that —

DEAN: Wherever I may be, I'll be available to help on that.

NIXON: Well, I hope you're right. You think you testify when? Well, Petersen will decide that, I guess.

DEAN: Yeah.

NIXON: Do you want me to say anything to him about it?

DEAN: No.

NIXON: [unclear] that [unclear] lawyers.

DEAN: Well, I think my lawyers and the U.S. attorney's office ought to continue to work in —

NIXON: Yeah, I'm having him report to me daily now —

DEAN: Right.

NIXON: — which I judge that I should do. And, so all that I'll say is — I'm going to tell him that we had a talk today and I went over again the various materials.

DEAN: What would be the best thing in the world is if they decide that they've got nothing but technical cases against people at the White House and they chuck them all out. That's not impossible.

NIXON: Should I help?

DEAN: No, sir.

NIXON: [laughs] That's what they ought to hear.

DEAN: That's right.

NIXON: It'd be a tough case for them to prove, John.

DEAN: Well, they may decide not — I did not do it and then nothing — none of these things are even released. It could very well happen.

NIXON: Well, that's what I want. I mean, I — understand, the reason I have to have that is in case there's a break tonight. I don't want to have to call John Dean in and say, "Look, John, can I have it?" It looks like I was — what the Christ am I doing? I've got to know because I do have some knowledge that there might be vulnerability. All that I am saying with this, as you know, is that I have heard things from the U.S. attorney, and from John Dean, and from my own people, that indicate there could be a technical violation — that there could be obstru — under the circumstances, I feel that it's my duty to have your resignation in hand. Of course, the president always has a resignation.

DEAN: Well, uh —

NIXON: How does that sound to you?

DEAN: That's right. The thing is — the phrasing in the letter is important.

NIXON: All right.

DEAN: You don't cause anybody, you know, problems with a fair trial. So that's why I'd like to —

NIXON: Good, John. Well, that's right. I mean, that's — understand, those are my dictations. I just [unclear].

DEAN: I understand.

NIXON: Only it's a form for you. And you work it out and work it out so that it would be one that could apply to you and then work out the — and to Ehrlichman, Haldeman, anybody else.

DEAN: Mm-hmm.

NIXON: Just a form that I can give anybody. Strachan — no, he's not going.

DEAN: Yes, he's gone — USIA.

NIXON: Well, that doesn't come to me, does it?

DEAN: Well, the whole Executive Branch, is —

NIXON: No, well — no, I mean —

DEAN: No, it wouldn't come —

NIXON: — his resignation can be submitted to [USIA director James] Keogh.

DEAN: That's right, Keogh.

NIXON: Well, I'll get his resignation. And I'll tell — I don't mean about — I'll tell those guys that he —

DEAN: I would have — I don't think you ought to tell Strachan. I think —

NIXON: No, no, no, no, no. Tell Keogh he ought to ask for the resignation.

DEAN: I think Bob ought to do that, though.

NIXON: Bob Haldeman?

DEAN: Mm-hmm.

NIXON: Good. I'll tell him. I'll tell Bob then to get them. That'll be Strachan and Magruder coming up. That'll be it.

DEAN: All right, sir.

NIXON: All right. That's your advice. Also, if you do have any random thoughts on how many more we could do on the presentation of this thing — sit over in your office and think of it, I mean, as to how to handle the —

DEAN: Well, I want you to —

NIXON: So that the president is in front. You know what I mean?

DEAN: I want to give you some notes on that that I think will help.

NIXON: Would you do that?

DEAN: Yes, sir. I will.

NIXON: The record. Here's what I've done. Here's what I've done, and what you think the president ought to do and when. You see what I mean? And then if we have to use these things — I pray to God we don't, because you guys don't deserve it. You don't deserve it.

DEAN: Well, at least the important thing is that it not damage you.

NIXON: No — well, I know. Maybe — it isn't me personally. It's this place.

DEAN: Well it's —

NIXON: The office and the campaign office as well.

NIXON: All right. Remember, be back —

DEAN: All right, sir.

NIXON: I would — I'd just hang tightly.

DEAN: I couldn't be —

NIXON: Hang tightly.

DEAN: — I couldn't be more objective, Mr. President. And, you know, I just have — don't think I've lost my objectivity in this thing at all.

NIXON: What?

DEAN: I said — don't think I've lost my objectivity at all in this —

NIXON: Right.

DEAN: — even though I'm right at the peak on it. All right, sir.

NIXON: Good enough.

The need for a statement from the president

April 17, 1973, 9:47 a.m.

Richard Nixon and Bob Haldeman

OVAL OFFICE

On April 17, the president was scheduled to host an important guest, Giulio Andreotti, the prime minister of Italy. Regarded as the most powerful politician in his country for more than two decades, Andreotti was nonetheless referred to as nothing more than "the Italian" by the president. Haldeman met with Nixon in the morning, mostly to pressure him into making his statement on Watergate before the end of the day. Nixon had delayed as long as possible, waiting to learn more about Dean's negotiations for immunity. In his statement, Nixon planned to draw a line that would tacitly blame Dean for some part of the Watergate activity and, more than that, for the cover-up of the previous ten months. The statement was to be, in effect, the end of Dean at the White House, and on that basis Haldeman and Nixon discussed their former colleague. Nixon also tried to prepare Haldeman and, by association, Ehrlichman for the fact that with Dean about to level charges on them publicly, their own futures were in doubt. He admonished Haldeman to think about it, not just for the "national good . . . the president and all that crap," but to keep their downward spiral from dragging out indefinitely.

. . .

HALDEMAN: I don't know if you saw the *L.A. Times* has a story.

NIXON: About?

HALDEMAN: The White House has got to —

NIXON: Yes. Yeah.

HALDEMAN: — move, and the thought came that if we're going to move today, we probably ought to meet earlier, so that we're ready to move by three o'clock —

NIXON: Fine.

HALDEMAN: — three thirty or something.

NIXON: Okay. If you get together, I think we have to move today.

HALDEMAN: Well, if we look like we — we ought to move on something, if we've got anything —

NIXON: Yeah.

HALDEMAN: — just to get out front in some way.

NIXON: Well, you might have to give them a full report today the way it's breaking so fast. Let me say that the problem you've got here is that — I had a long talk with Rogers, and so forth, of course he was much more rational than Len [Garment] is. Len's supposedly quite a pro, but on the other hand, I — you've got the problem of being — you and John being sort of nibbled to death over a period of time —

HALDEMAN: Yep.

NIXON: — and by not moving having a situation where, frankly, your chances of your being — I mean of your being publicly attacked, and also even the steam of the prosecution is greater. You know what I mean? It's a curious thing, but that's — but I'm afraid that's the way it operates. We — you know, every day there's some other damn little thing that somebody talks around with, you see, so everything can be explained and try to defend and all that sort of thing. But I'm not prepared to make that judgment and I want you to talk to John about it.

HALDEMAN: Yeah. Okay.

NIXON: Get a line on what the prosecutors, Petersen [unclear] — Petersen [unclear] Ehrlichman was informed by Dean of a meeting that Dean had with Liddy on the nineteenth of June. Well, actually, this was — that was done when he was in California in January but — irrelevant, it was later anyway. That kind of thing just keeps banging around. You know, that prosecution gets out the damn stuff? Did John talk with you about it?

HALDEMAN: Yeah, he mentioned it, and —

NIXON: Yeah.

HALDEMAN: — Dean did tell us that story up in Ehrlichman's office last week or two weeks ago.

NIXON: But not to go through this?

HALDEMAN: I don't think so.

NIXON: Yeah.

HALDEMAN: I think I mentioned it to you, remember? I described the story to you in some detail when he walked down Seventeenth Street —

NIXON: No. This was all after we had started our own investigation.

HALDEMAN: Oh, yeah.

NIXON: I mean, it wasn't back then. It wouldn't indicate that we knew about all this, and so forth. Another thing [unclear].

HALDEMAN: And also [unclear] John Dean [unclear].

NIXON: John, and you get — sit down and do some hard thinking about what kind of strategy you are going to have with the money. You know what I mean?

HALDEMAN: Yeah.

NIXON: That's got to be something perhaps better than say, well, either one of the defendants can talk to the press and I don't. What in the hell the strategy is I think you ought to talk about that. But I'm a little concerned about the last bite or two — the one twenty-seven. I don't know who talked about that one but to Hunt's lawyer.

HALDEMAN: Oh.

NIXON: Who's — who was the one that made that original —

HALDEMAN: Dean. Bittman dealing directly to Dean on that.

NIXON: Right. Right. Then Dean came in and asked us — and what happened?

HALDEMAN: We said we didn't know what to do about it, and we said that's — you know, that's something that obviously Mitchell should be taking care of.

NIXON: Yeah. Well, in any case, taking care of.

HALDEMAN: And then they —

NIXON: But —

HALDEMAN: — indicated in the meeting with us —

NIXON: Yeah.

HALDEMAN: — the next day [unclear].

NIXON: [unclear] On the other hand, that, of course, indicates knowledge and so forth.

HALDEMAN: That's right.

NIXON: Look, they're going to call Kalmbach so I want to be sure. I've been trying to find out from Dean what the hell he is going to say he told Kalmbach. What did Kalmbach say that Dean told him? They wanted money for this support purpose?

HALDEMAN: I don't know. John is talking to Kalmbach.

NIXON: Well, be sure that Kalmbach is at least aware of this. LaRue has talked very freely. He's a broken man. And the other thing is that this destruction of the evidence thing is troublesome, of course. John tells me, too — and basically the culprit is Pat Gray. Has Colson talked — know about that? That's why Colson — why they're calling Colson because Colson was in the room when it was handed to Gray.

HALDEMAN: No, he wasn't. Well, apparently he wasn't.

NIXON: He says he wasn't?

HALDEMAN: Colson thought there was a meeting before that, where they talked about the deep-sixing and all that supposedly—

NIXON: He was in that meeting?

HALDEMAN: —which Colson was supposed to have been in.

NIXON: Right. Right. Right.

HALDEMAN: Colson doesn't remember being in it, but Colson flatly says that he had—that he—there was never anything where he was where there was a discussion—

NIXON: Yeah.

HALDEMAN: —of Hunt getting out of the country.

NIXON: All right.

HALDEMAN: [White House staff secretary Bruce] Kehrli says the same thing. He was also supposed to be at that same meeting. In fact, Ehrlichman has checked everybody who was at that meeting and nobody recalls that being said except Dean. And we now have the point that Dean is the one who called Liddy and told him to telephone Hunt to get out of the country and then called him later and said not to.

NIXON: Get this—get—I'd like a positive—if you could, could you get a positive story on Monday. I think, Bob, though, we have to think. I must say that I haven't—that we've got to think about a positive move and I think it's got to be today.

HALDEMAN: I agree.

NIXON: I think it should be at three today. The important thing, which I don't know, is I hope the story doesn't break today, but—

HALDEMAN: Even if it does, you can get into cycle with it.

NIXON: Yeah. Well, I don't want to be answering it.

HALDEMAN: No.

• • •

NIXON: I want a thing done today and you and John have got to think, frankly, in terms—let me say, not—don't just think in terms as a national good for the, well, the president and all that crap [unclear]. But also you got to think in terms of having this goddamn thing continue to be dragged out bit by bit on answers that are dragged out bit by bit. Anyway, I suppose—but the point is that Dean's incentive with the U.S. attorney—incentive with everybody else will be this and that. You get my point?

HALDEMAN: Yep.

NIXON: I'm sure you and John have talked about it. You see, what's happened here, the prosecution has been pretty clever. They got Magruder. Well, Magruder just caved, but it had to come. It had to come, Bob. There was no way it wasn't going to come.

HALDEMAN: Right. There have been some [unclear]. I think it had to and should.

NIXON: That's right. The other point is, the other element of this question now is Hunt. And as far as Dean is concerned, he's basically the one that surprises me and disappoints me to an extent, because he really is trying to save his neck and doing so easy. He's not—to hear him tell it when I talked to him, he's not telling things that are, you know [unclear].

HALDEMAN: That's not really true though. He is —

NIXON: I know, I know, I know. He tells me one thing and tells the others other things. That's when I get mad. But, Dean is trying to tell them enough to get immunity. That's frankly what it is, Bob.

HALDEMAN: That's the real problem we've got. It had to break and it should break —

NIXON: That's a hell of a problem to break.

HALDEMAN: — but what you've got is people within it, as you said right at the beginning —

NIXON: Thanks a lot.

HALDEMAN: — with Petersen, they've got an incentive to exaggerate. So, they've been told the more they give them the better they'll come out.

NIXON: Yeah, well, I got to go. I'll be ready by one.

HALDEMAN: Okay.

A final huddle

April 17, 1973, 12:35 p.m.
Richard Nixon, Bob Haldeman, John Ehrlichman, and Ron Ziegler
OVAL OFFICE

Nixon used much of the afternoon for a final huddle to discuss his planned statement to the press. He had to make sense of the different inputs — some of them conflicting — that he had gotten from Haldeman, Ehrlichman, and even Colson. And then there was also the problem of what Dean's next move might be. The tone of their discussion suggested the inevitability that Nixon's inner circle would soon leave the White House staff. On the one hand, that would put some distance between Nixon and the investigation that was now consuming more of his time than ever before. But it would also mean that by being separated from those who could best advise him, he had less control of his own fate.

• • •

NIXON: Where did we come out?

EHRLICHMAN: Well, we got two things. We got a press plan —

NIXON: Yeah.

EHRLICHMAN: — but it rests upon some decisions —

NIXON: Right.

EHRLICHMAN: — that you have to make on sort of an action plan.

NIXON: Right, all right.

EHRLICHMAN: And I just finished an hour with Colson who came over very concerned and said that he had to see you. That the message that he had for you that he had to and wanted to explain at length is why Dean had to be dealt with summarily. His partner has a tie-in with the U.S. attorney's office and they seem to know what's going on there. Very simply put, I think his argument will be that the city of Washington generally knows that Dean had little or no access to you. That Haldeman, Colson, and Ehrlichman had a lot of access to you.

NIXON: True. That's quite right.

EHRLICHMAN: That—

NIXON: Dean was just a messenger.

EHRLICHMAN: —knowledge imputed to us is knowledge imputed to you, and if Dean is critical and testifies that he imputed great quantities of knowledge to—or passed great quantities of knowledge to us, and is allowed to get away with that—

NIXON: Yeah.

EHRLICHMAN: —that will seriously impair the presidency ultimately. Because it will be very easy to argue that all you have to do is read Dean's testimony, look at the previous relationships, and there she goes! So he says the key to this is that Dean should not get immunity. Now that's what he wants to tell you.

NIXON: Well, he told me that, and I couldn't agree more.

EHRLICHMAN: Now he says you have total and complete control over whether Dean gets immunity—

NIXON: Yeah.

EHRLICHMAN: —through Petersen.

NIXON: I don't think so.

EHRLICHMAN: Now that's what he says, and he would be glad to come in and tell you how to do it, why, and all that stuff.

NIXON: I don't want Colson to come in here because—

EHRLICHMAN: Right.

NIXON: I just feel that way. I feel uneasy about that—his ties and everything in there. I mean, they—I realize that Dean is the candidate. Dean—of course, let's look at what he has—his threats and so forth about [unclear] don't want him to go popping off about everything else that has taken place—that he's done in the government. You know, and the bugging of the—

EHRLICHMAN: Well, the question—

NIXON: Whether they—

EHRLICHMAN: —the question is, I suppose, which way he is liable to do it most—

NIXON: Well, first of all, if he gets immunity, he's likely to be—I mean he'll pay just as little price as he can.

EHRLICHMAN: Well, the price is the—the price that he paid, the—that the quid pro quo for the immunity is to reach one of the three of us or all of us.

NIXON: Or all of us, so [unclear]—just mentioned [unclear] just said Colson will not come down to Washington.

EHRLICHMAN: And the president at—and Colson argues that if he is not given immunity, then he has even more incentive to go light upon his own malefactions, and he will have to clam up and he will have to defend himself.

NIXON: Now, when he talked to me I said, "Now I understand you, John." I said, "I understand the tactic—you know, of all three resigning." And I said, "All offered to resign." I told him that—you understand. I told him that you and John had offered to resign and so he's aware of that.

HALDEMAN: Well, have they told him that the price of his immunity is that if we resign they'll give him immunity? Do they feel that makes their case? Or does he have to give them evidence?

NIXON: I don't know.

HALDEMAN: He's going to have a tough time with that.

NIXON: [unclear] get him over here.

EHRLICHMAN: Well, to go on —

NIXON: All right.

EHRLICHMAN: — now, my action plan —

NIXON: What would your plan be?

EHRLICHMAN: My action plan would involve —

NIXON: Yeah.

EHRLICHMAN: — either suspension or firing of Dean in the course of an explanation — a historical explanation of your reliance on the Dean report — its apparent unreliability.

NIXON: But going out, you see, I — the Garment guy — got him in today. Garment says [unclear] his — you've got to get it out. It's all going to come out anyway. He points out that LaRue, Strachan, et cetera, et cetera, et cetera — and that's, of course, with the U.S. attorneys. I mean, what — that's what Petersen's view is, of course.

EHRLICHMAN: What's that? The Garment deal?

NIXON: That it is all going to come out. It's all coming out and Haldeman and Ehrlichman are going to resign. He told me that on Sunday. He's told me and I asked him again yesterday. I said, "Now, look at this — pretty goddamn flimsy, you know." He said, "Yes, I'm not talking about legal exposure. I'm just talking about the fact that as this stuff comes out they're going to be eaten to pieces — eaten alive. The president — eventually the clamor is going to be something you cannot stand." I said, "Better for them to get leave or something of that sort now?" And he said, "This is the government, and I — rather than to sit there and act later as a result of this tidbit and that tidbit and so forth — 'He lied and I don't lie,' and so forth. Haldeman against Dean and Haldeman against this. And Ehrlichman against Dean and Colson — you know, and all that. Who the hell's lying?" He said, "Definitely they'll say, 'For Christ's sake, Mr. President, can't you let these fellas — ?'" Now that's my point. That's what he said.

EHRLICHMAN: I understand.

NIXON: That's an argument that'll be made.

EHRLICHMAN: Yep.

NIXON: He said that to Rogers last night, and that's — that of course is Garment's argument.

EHRLICHMAN: Mm-hmm.

NIXON: And I guess Rose [Mary Woods] agrees. It's got to be Rose, or whatever. My problem at the present time is I just don't want to have to talk to each of those — these sideline people individually, because — I don't know. I think some — Garment came in and was talking about the [Ron] Ostrow story in the [*Los Angeles*] *Times*. Petersen told me about it last night. He said Ostrow had called. And I told him I — "that it must have leaked out of your place." He said, "No. It didn't." Could it've leaked out of here? Could it have been Garment?

HALDEMAN: Could have been, but it doesn't — it isn't at all likely.

NIXON: Yeah.

HALDEMAN: It's a Justice problem.

NIXON: But you see what you say about Dean? I said — too much, all three. That — he supports the Garment plan. He's talked to Garment and Garment has talked to Dean.

EHRLICHMAN: Dean has talked to everybody in this place.

NIXON: I told him not to talk to him anymore. But, you see, Dean — look, let's see — what the hell — what's he got? What the hell's he have with regard to the president? He came and talked to me, as you recall, about the need for one hundred twenty thousand dollars for clemencies and the rest.

EHRLICHMAN: I know. I — you told me that the other day. I didn't know that before.

HALDEMAN: But so what?

NIXON: What?

HALDEMAN: So what?

NIXON: I said, "How" — I said, "What in the world?" I mean, "John," I said, "John, you can't continue on this short notice. What's it cost if you do it for four years?" He said, "A million." I sort of laughed and said, "Well, I guess you could get that."

EHRLICHMAN: Now is he holding that over your head? Saying —

NIXON: No, no, no, no, no. I didn't — I don't think Dean would go so far as to get into any conversation he had with the president — even Dean I don't think.

HALDEMAN: Well, he can't. He's got — you have both executive privilege in conversation with him and —

NIXON: Executive privilege. Period.

HALDEMAN: And this is in relation to the [unclear].

NIXON: Let's just call it executive privilege. Period.

HALDEMAN: Well, [unclear].

NIXON: But on the other hand you've got to figure that Dean could put out something with somebody else.

HALDEMAN: But you're not —

NIXON: That's the only thing I can think of that he's told me, but I — I've not gotten him in yet to ask about this thing he said about you — Liddy told you —

EHRLICHMAN: Oh, well —

NIXON: — told Petersen and Petersen said [unclear].

EHRLICHMAN: There'll be one of those a day, I'm sure, from now on.

NIXON: Well, that's the point. The point is can we survive it? Let's face it.

EHRLICHMAN: Well —

NIXON: Can Haldeman and Ehrlichman survive it? The point that I [unclear] —

EHRLICHMAN: Look —

NIXON: Let me say this. I know your attitude is a hell of a lot different from John Dean. I know that as far as you're concerned you'll go out and throw yourselves on a goddamn sword. I'm aware of that. And I am trying to think the thing through with that in mind because goddamn it, you're the two most valuable members on the staff. I know that. The problem is you're the two most loyal and the two most honest. We don't have to go into that crap. You know how I feel about that. It's not crap, it's the truth. The problem we got here is this. I do not want to be in a position where the goddamn public clamor makes, as it did with Eisenhower with Adams, makes it necessary for me to call — to have Bob come in one day and Bob says, "Look, Mr. President, because of the public — da, da, da, da, da, da — I'm going to leave." Now that's the real problem I've got on this goddamn thing, and I don't think that kicking Dean's ass out of here is going to do it. Understand, I'm not ruling out kicking his ass out. But I think you got to figure — what the hell does Dean know? That he did do — what kind of blackmail does he have? You see, then everything apparently that I don't know what all he does have —

EHRLICHMAN: Let me make a suggestion.

NIXON: All right.

EHRLICHMAN: You've got Dean coming in saying to you, "I've talked to the U.S. attorney and I've told him a lot of things that I did wrong."

NIXON: Right. Right.

EHRLICHMAN: So you put him on leave. He isn't charged with anything yet, but he's said that to you.

NIXON: He said — I asked him that and he said, "I'll go on leave with Haldeman and Ehrlichman."

EHRLICHMAN: Well, he's not in any position to bargain with you on that. Now, when the time comes that I'm charged with anything wrong —

NIXON: Well, you — John, you have been by a U.S. attorney and by —

EHRLICHMAN: All right, all right.

NIXON: — Petersen to me. Petersen is not charging you legally.

EHRLICHMAN: Well, that's what I mean. See, I mean — I understand the difference.

HALDEMAN: They have charged Dean legally.

EHRLICHMAN: That's right.

HALDEMAN: That's the difference.

EHRLICHMAN: You see, legally Dean has broken the law on the face of his —

NIXON: Yeah.

EHRLICHMAN: — admission to you.

NIXON: Petersen has said to me — he says that there is — that because of this evidence that has come in here that Haldeman and Ehrlichman should take a leave. Now I'm faced with that damn hard fact. Now, based on that —

EHRLICHMAN: Well, that takes me to my next step, which is my continuing misgivings about Petersen. And I'm sorry to be put in the position of having to raise this question in the light of his having said that about me because it's makes it a very doubtful kind of a statement, but—

NIXON: How do I feel about Petersen?

EHRLICHMAN: I don't know, but just from a personal, selfish standpoint, I would a whole lot rather that the case were in the control of somebody who would call them right down the middle than some guy that I know has egg on his face from his previous working with Dean. And I know that out of Dean's mouth. Now—

HALDEMAN: If you have any doubt about that and want it from an unbiased source, call Dick Moore and ask him because there is no question that Petersen is up to his ass with Dean in violation of the law. And you have knowledge of that now, too.

EHRLICHMAN: Now, I just cannot sit by quietly. If I take a leave and I go out of here, I am going to very vigorously defend myself. And one of the first things I am going to do is sink Petersen.

HALDEMAN: The first thing is Dean. The second is Petersen.

EHRLICHMAN: Well, Dean sunk himself as far as I'm concerned. But I will not have Petersen left in a position to make the prosecutorial decisions. Because I just—as sure as I'm sitting here I promise you that he will indict me.

NIXON: Oh, will he?

EHRLICHMAN: Yes, sir. He will, whether there's any evidence or not. He will indict me because it is very much to his interest to do so.

NIXON: Goddamn it! Why did we put him in charge of the case?

EHRLICHMAN: Well, I wish he hadn't. I thought it was an ad interim thing until—you know, on the basis of your conversation with Kleindienst.

NIXON: Kleindienst had to step aside and he did.

EHRLICHMAN: Well—

NIXON: So Petersen [unclear]—

EHRLICHMAN: Okay. But—

NIXON: —special counsel. Remember? We talked about that.

EHRLICHMAN: I just want to say to you in the strongest kind of terms that I will have no choice in this matter.

NIXON: That's right.

EHRLICHMAN: And I'll do it by fair means or foul.

NIXON: I hope so.

HALDEMAN: Well, no, because that's going to hurt, too.

EHRLICHMAN: Well—

HALDEMAN: And that's just going to [unclear].

EHRLICHMAN: Hell, Bob—

HALDEMAN: I didn't get that. Hell. I'm not arguing that you shouldn't do it. I'm arguing that we should try to avoid getting to the push.

EHRLICHMAN: Oh, I'd love to avoid it.

HALDEMAN: [unclear] if we have to do it—

EHRLICHMAN: I'd love to avoid it.

HALDEMAN: — because — that's just one more dagger in the whole goddamn thing —

EHRLICHMAN: I know. I know.

HALDEMAN: — which is a dagger that shouldn't have to be stuck.

NIXON: All right. Get me the action plan. Go down the line.

EHRLICHMAN: Well, step —

NIXON: Now, can I ask you to do one point — as I said, this silly business of this — what in the name of God is going to be said by Dean — let me ask you for one minute — about that packet of papers? How's that end up — that Gray's a liar? Is that what it adds up to on that?

EHRLICHMAN: He's either a liar or he's an obstructer — one or the other.

HALDEMAN: Or both.

EHRLICHMAN: Or both.

NIXON: Because something given to him —

EHRLICHMAN: No question about that.

NIXON: You saw?

EHRLICHMAN: Yes, sir. I did. I was standing right there.

NIXON: Who gave it to him?

EHRLICHMAN: John Dean handed it to him in my presence in my office.

NIXON: What did John say? "This is a politically sensitive"?

EHRLICHMAN: That "here the — here's this material from Hunt's safe."

NIXON: And he said it was politically sensitive?

EHRLICHMAN: No, sir. Not in my — not that I can recall. He just said, "Here — "

NIXON: But I heard the words "hot political stuff."

EHRLICHMAN: I told you about a previous conversation where it was described to me in those terms.

NIXON: By Dean.

EHRLICHMAN: I think so. I think so.

HALDEMAN: That's precisely what Dean's told me after the fact — that's what happened.

NIXON: Mm-hmm. See you get that in — say don't give immunity. Colson thinks that I can order him not to give immunity, huh?

EHRLICHMAN: Right.

NIXON: And tell him. Then he would say, "Well, what are you going to do about Haldeman and Ehrlichman?"

EHRLICHMAN: Well, [unclear].

NIXON: What could I say?

EHRLICHMAN: What you have to —

HALDEMAN: He doesn't have to say that.

EHRLICHMAN: — say is nobody —

NIXON: Yes, he does.

EHRLICHMAN: I think what you have to say is nobody in this White House —

NIXON: Dean isn't going to say it. I mean, Petersen's the guy that can give immunity.

HALDEMAN: Well, tell him not to give us immunity either.

NIXON: How? That's the problem now. He doesn't want it.

HALDEMAN: Well, see, it's none of his business whether you suspend us or not. That's your decision.

NIXON: I know it is. I know it is. But the point is — let me put it candidly. If I do not suspend you, he will probably give him immunity. That's the problem I think if I — we're looking right down that barrel. If you do take a leave, I think he will — it's very — it's possible — well, it's possible that even if you do leave that he would still give Dean immunity.

EHRLICHMAN: I agree.

NIXON: Because Dean is the guy that he's got to use for the purpose of making cases.

HALDEMAN: Yes, but even Ehrlichman, which he already admits he doesn't have a case on Petersen, thought he had significance.

NIXON: Well, we got in too deep. He says that legally, yes he does. In the case of Haldeman, it'll — I discuss — the Strachan things have been determined from a lot to do with what Strachan says and what Kalmbach says. You know, it's the three hundred fifty thing and that sort of thing.

HALDEMAN: Kalmbach has no relation to me on that.

EHRLICHMAN: That —

NIXON: Have you thought when you say — before it gets too difficult — the tangential thing out of the way — have you given any thought to what the line ought to be — I don't mean a lie but the line on raising the money for these defendants? Because both of you were aware that was going on. You see, the raising of money — you were aware of it, right?

EHRLICHMAN: Yes, sir.

NIXON: And you were aware. You see, you can't go in and say, "I didn't know what in hell he wanted the three hundred fifty for." You could say —

HALDEMAN: No, I've given a great deal of thought. I've got what I've written down.

EHRLICHMAN: Yeah.

NIXON: Well, I wonder. I'm not — look, I'm concerned about the legal thing, Bob, and so forth. What — you say that our purpose was to keep them from talking to the press?

EHRLICHMAN: Well, that was my purpose. I — and before I get too far out on that I want to talk to an attorney and find out what the law is, which I have not yet done.

NIXON: Right.

HALDEMAN: Which is what I want to do, too. This is —

NIXON: That's right.

HALDEMAN: — only a draft.

NIXON: That's right. Well, good. The only point is I think it's not only that but you see that involves all of our people. That's what I really feel. It involves Kalmbach —

EHRLICHMAN: Well —

NIXON: — and as to what the hell Kalmbach was told.

EHRLICHMAN: Mr. President, when the —

NIXON: I just want to [unclear].

EHRLICHMAN: —truth and fact of this is known, that building next door is full of people who knew that money was being raised for these people.

NIXON: EOB?

EHRLICHMAN: Yes, sir.

NIXON: Yep.

EHRLICHMAN: Just full of them.

NIXON: Many who knew, but there were not so many actors. In other words, there's a difference between actors and novices.

EHRLICHMAN: Okay. Well, apparently not because I'm not an actor —

HALDEMAN: Neither am I. The question there is the testimony, I suppose.

NIXON: I said I'm not trying to make any case —

EHRLICHMAN: No, but I just want you to think —

NIXON: I'm not stating a case.

EHRLICHMAN: I want you to think very critically about the difference here between knowledge of the general transactions going on on the one hand —

NIXON: Yeah.

EHRLICHMAN: —and being an affirmative actor on the other because that's the difference between Dean and me.

NIXON: That's right.

EHRLICHMAN: Now, on this business of whether Dean should have immunity, I think you have to ask yourself really the basic question whether anybody in the White House who does wrong ought to get immunity no matter how many other people he implicates. The —

NIXON: Strachan included?

EHRLICHMAN: Anybody, anybody. I just question whether in the orderly administration of justice it looks right for anybody in the White House to get immunity.

NIXON: I could call Petersen in and basically I'm trying to identify that myself. I've got to get this public statement out by three o'clock. Is that right?

EHRLICHMAN: Right.

HALDEMAN: But if we're not — well, yes, but you don't have to —

EHRLICHMAN: Now, but look —

NIXON: Well, Garment says we have to. He says [unclear] —

HALDEMAN: Well, but Garment said it yesterday, the day before, and the week before that. Garment just panics —

NIXON: You mean he panics?

HALDEMAN: —every time a cloud goes over. So —

NIXON: Well, understand, I'm not panicking myself. But they tell me that there seems to be a considerable feeling that —

EHRLICHMAN: Well, I agree with you, but I think what we should do —

NIXON: [unclear] LaRue's been called, Strachan's been called, and Dean's — Dean might

put up a story for the *Times*. You never know. You know, named Haldeman and
Ehrlichman —

EHRLICHMAN: Yeah, but you see it's typical.

NIXON: That's right.

EHRLICHMAN: Dean's position now —

NIXON: [unclear]

EHRLICHMAN: Now — if Dean is treated different from us, he will go out and say, "I'm
a scapegoat for higher-ups."

HALDEMAN: That figures because he knows Ostrow, because Ostrow is the guy that
covers Justice.

NIXON: I see. And Petersen told me that. He told about conversations with — that the
wife of Jurgen apparently has sat at some table with a [unclear] libber and the rest.
And the top guy, Rosenblatt [Rothblatt], or something like that, at the *Post* was talking to somebody else on that staff [unclear]. He feels that the president ought to get
out in front, and we've got a hell of a lot more than we're — we've just held it back.
Now, they may be bluffing. I would doubt that they are at this point.

HALDEMAN: I think they probably have more, but I would guess what they have more
of is in the committee. I don't think they've got much more in the White House
unless — I don't know what it could be unless they've got Colson's stuff. That would
be the only area —

NIXON: Colson's activities?

HALDEMAN: Yeah, that's the only area where you have any jeopardy in the White House.

NIXON: I doubt — let me say with regard to Colson, John, I think it's very — you could
say that I'm way ahead of them on that. That I've got the message on that and that
he feels that Dean — but believe me, I've been thinking about that all day yesterday
as to whether Dean should be given immunity.

EHRLICHMAN: Well, the thing that specifically —

NIXON: The point is — I know that it can happen, but I can call Petersen in and say
he cannot be given immunity, that nobody on the White House staff can be given
immunity. And I — whether he'll carry that order out is that — that's going to be
an indicator that — that's the — Dean has evidence to hold. And then what do I say
about Dean? Do I tell him that he goes?

EHRLICHMAN: Well, see, the thing that precipitated Colson's coming over here is that —

NIXON: He was [unclear].

EHRLICHMAN: — and he found that — no, he found that Dean is still here. You see,
Dick Howard called Chuck —

NIXON: I know.

EHRLICHMAN: — and went through that business of the FBI men sending him into the
arms of Dean.

NIXON: That's right. That's right.

EHRLICHMAN: So Colson called and says, "You've got an asp at your bosom over there."

NIXON: That's right.

EHRLICHMAN: And so today he checked again apparently with Howard and discovered Dean is still here and he called and said, "I've got to see you." And he came in and he said, "You guys are just out of your minds," and said, "I want to see the president." And he was just fit to be tied about it, so —

NIXON: Colson was?

EHRLICHMAN: Yeah, because he thinks — having being [unclear] —

NIXON: But you see if I say, "Dean, why don't you leave today?" why, he'd go out and say, "Well, the president's covering up for Ehrlichman and Haldeman." All right. There you are. Because he knows what I know. That's what he said he would say. I tried to put the — I mean, I'm trying to look and see where, John — what the hell we are really up against. You said no — first it was Liddy who was the scapegoat, now John Dean is.

HALDEMAN: Well, the answer to that is that the president, if he says it publicly, is that the president is not covering up for anybody, and will not tolerate any cover-up.

NIXON: But the way he's put it — the way he's put it to me — why, very cute, very cute, as I have said, "I'd like for you to give me some resignations." I said, "I'd like to rewrite it so it doesn't [unclear]." He rewrote it in a way that says, "In view of what you have told me that Haldeman and Ehrlichman are willing to resign," and so forth — you know what I mean, da-da-da-da-da. "I, too, will resign." In other words, he basically conditioned it on the other — which of course is what led me to the conclusion that that's exactly what I thought that his attorneys told him to do. If he can get Haldeman and Ehrlichman, that some way gets him in the mix. That's what you have here.

EHRLICHMAN: Yeah, because then that will be argued back to the U.S. attorney, "Well, you see, the president thought enough of Dean's charges to let these guys go." And I understand —

NIXON: Well, I — I was trying to indicate to him that both of you had indicated a willingness to — in the event, that — you know what I mean.

EHRLICHMAN: And I said — and here's a guy that comes in and in effect confesses to you the commission of crimes.

NIXON: And charges you.

EHRLICHMAN: And charges us.

NIXON: That's right. And I said, "Now wait, these charges" — I said, "these charges are not" — and you see he also has an alibi in the U.S. attorney —

EHRLICHMAN: Small wonders.

NIXON: He was asked that — the assistant attorney general has said that the president should act —

EHRLICHMAN: Well, you see my point and —

NIXON: Yeah.

EHRLICHMAN: — and you'd have to obviously, call us when —

NIXON: Yeah.

EHRLICHMAN: — as you —

NIXON: Go ahead. Go ahead on the action plan that you did — first?

EHRLICHMAN: Well, it would involve the suspension because it would involve a recounting of how you happened to get into the personal investigation of this by reason of Dean's being unable to reduce his report — his full report to writing for you. And that rang a bell then, and you personally turned to and have spent a great deal of your time in the last several weeks on this, and have seen dramatic progress in the grand jury in the last several days. That would be step one. Now in addition to that you would say the Ervin Committee has come up with a good set of ground rules which do provide us with —

NIXON: Well, did you work that out?

EHRLICHMAN: Well, maybe you'd say this — I think you're going to find that they are going to go on television under oath pretty much regardless, but the ground rules give you a toehold. They do provide for executive session.

NIXON: Is executive session considered executive privilege?

EHRLICHMAN: And they will consider executive privilege —

NIXON: And they will consider executive privilege — right. And otherwise they will go on television. They will go into open hearings.

EHRLICHMAN: Yes.

NIXON: [unclear]

EHRLICHMAN: But there again executive privilege is reserved.

NIXON: Where executive privilege can be reserved, fine.

EHRLICHMAN: Yeah.

HALDEMAN: At this point, the way we're in the soup now we lose nothing by going up there.

NIXON: That's right.

HALDEMAN: I think we may gain a lot.

NIXON: That's right. I couldn't agree more. So, if you can prepare me with at least that much, I'll agree — that I can say that today.

HALDEMAN: Well, that's a hell of a bombshell just right there.

NIXON: Yes, it is. But that's our knowledge of it, John. What's the rest of it?

EHRLICHMAN: That's it. That's all I have for today. But it gets you into the case — gets you leading it. It notices the progress and the grand jury as related to your efforts and it doesn't say what they are.

NIXON: Well, the point is, though — that the story today is that John Dean then is suspended, but — and then John Dean is going to be out there blasting the shit out of — saying the president has indicated that Haldeman and Ehrlichman, too, might go. I didn't say that.

HALDEMAN: All right. Let me suggest a different process, which is that you instruct, that you don't —

NIXON: The U.S. attorney.

HALDEMAN: — that you don't suspend John Dean, but that you instruct John Dean that he is not to come to work anymore. He is to stay — he is in effect suspended, but not publicly suspended.

NIXON: That's right. He'll say, "What about Haldeman and Ehrlichman?"

HALDEMAN: I would suggest to you that you do the same with us. And I was going to suggest that I was going to request that action —

NIXON: Well, but the White House —

HALDEMAN: — anyway, for this reason —

NIXON: Sure.

HALDEMAN: — I, at least, am speaking for myself. John's got to speak for himself. I have now concluded that my course is I must put out my story.

NIXON: Right.

HALDEMAN: I must put it out in total and in my words —

NIXON: Yeah.

HALDEMAN: — before I go to this — now —

NIXON: Before you go to [unclear]?

HALDEMAN: — no, well, I don't know about the grand jury.

NIXON: Before you go to the committee?

HALDEMAN: Before I go to the Senate committee, because if I'm going to have to put it out there anyway —

NIXON: I know. Be careful you get to the Senate committee. I don't think the committee hearings will ever go forward.

HALDEMAN: I do. I don't think there is any chance of their not going forward.

NIXON: Well, maybe not.

HALDEMAN: You think because of the legal case will make?

NIXON: Well, that's what Rogers — he says whatever it's [unclear].

HALDEMAN: Okay. That's great if they don't. Then maybe I never tell my story. But my view is that at some point in time I'm going to have to tell it.

NIXON: But you — the way I would do it, I would reserve, Bob, the right to tell that story until you felt you did have to go to the committee. You see what I mean? Or, unless you got —

HALDEMAN: — till a partial [unclear] —

NIXON: — to a point where you were nibbled to death.

HALDEMAN: That's right. Or until a partial charge comes up. For instance, if the grand jury leaks —

NIXON: Yeah.

HALDEMAN: — or the Justice people leak the Strachan stuff —

NIXON: That's right.

HALDEMAN: — then I have — then that forces my hand.

NIXON: Do you agree with this, John, on Bob?

EHRLICHMAN: Well, subject to an attorney's advice.

HALDEMAN: Well, now, that's the next point I was going to say. I will not make this statement until I have cleared —

NIXON: Yeah.

HALDEMAN: — and worked it out.

NIXON: Well, it sounds — Bill [Rogers] says he doesn't have anything to do to [unclear].

HALDEMAN: Well, we've got some leads we're going to start on today, so —

NIXON: Great.

HALDEMAN: — we've got that, but I want — my interest is served and I will also argue that the better off I come out of this, the better off you come out of it vis-à-vis me. In other words, anything I do to my interest is to your interest.

NIXON: Let me ask you this, John — it could be — shall I try [unclear]?

EHRLICHMAN: What's that?

NIXON: You said that you ought to — you ought not to come for a while. On what basis? In other words, I don't — we do this on an oral basis.

HALDEMAN: What I'm doing now is requesting you on an oral basis —

NIXON: Yeah.

HALDEMAN: — to not expect me to carry out any duties for a while —

NIXON: Yeah.

HALDEMAN: — because —

NIXON: Because you've got to work on this.

HALDEMAN: — I must perfect this and get it ready.

NIXON: Where will you do it — at home? You wouldn't do it at the office here?

HALDEMAN: I can do it wherever you want me to.

NIXON: Well —

HALDEMAN: Well, I think it'd be a mis — I think I ought to do it in the office, but I don't —

NIXON: All right.

HALDEMAN: I don't think —

EHRLICHMAN: If Dean wants it public [unclear].

NIXON: I [unclear] Dean backs out of here [unclear].

EHRLICHMAN: All right. Let me suggest that if Dean says, "What about Haldeman and Ehrlichman?" you just say, "John, I'm talking to you about you."

NIXON: All right.

EHRLICHMAN: "Now, I'll take care of them in my own way. I'm not going to have you bargaining with me."

HALDEMAN: I don't think you can —

EHRLICHMAN: Well —

HALDEMAN: — let yourself get into that.

EHRLICHMAN: — I don't know how much of a bind we're in.

HALDEMAN: [unclear] I'm saying I don't think the president can be in the position of making a deal with John Dean on anything.

EHRLICHMAN: Yeah. "I'll go if they go." Supposing I said, "I won't go unless Henry Kissinger goes!" Yeah, it's ridiculous. Here — let me speak to this. I have pretty much unplugged myself of my day-to-day stuff —

NIXON: Sure, that's all right.

EHRLICHMAN: — because this — with this kind of thing going on you just can't think about anything else.

NIXON: Oh, of course, it's been a little hard for me to, also.

EHRLICHMAN: Sure. Now, I have a need to get into all kinds of records —

NIXON: Yeah.

EHRLICHMAN: — and my date books —

NIXON: Right.

EHRLICHMAN: — and these are volumes and volumes of correspondence —

NIXON: Right. Right.

EHRLICHMAN: — and stuff. If I couldn't come into the office, I probably couldn't prepare a defense.

NIXON: What about Dean coming in? Why not him? Why bite the bullet on Dean coming into the office and the rest? I don't think — I think because I've told him he's to have nothing more to do with this case.

EHRLICHMAN: Well, he's sure not following out your orders, if that's the case —

NIXON: You see what I mean?

EHRLICHMAN: Now, you'd have another problem —

NIXON: Yeah.

EHRLICHMAN: — and I don't know what's been going on in the last week or so, but I imagine he's carted stuff out of here by the bale.

NIXON: Oh, well that's a [unclear] against him.

EHRLICHMAN: I just don't know.

HALDEMAN: You don't know that.

EHRLICHMAN: I certainly —

HALDEMAN: If you suspend him or tell him to leave in any way, you're also going to move in to get — take care of his files.

NIXON: Could I say this, John? That I would say that "Haldeman and Ehrlichman have both requested the opportunity to be relieved of their duties — I mean their main duties, so that they can —"

HALDEMAN: Concentrate on this.

NIXON: " — concentrate on this matter and prepare for their appearance before the grand jury." Could I say that?

EHRLICHMAN: Sure. It's true.

NIXON: Then I'd say, "John, I want to relieve you of all your duties so that you can concentrate on your appearance before the grand jury."

EHRLICHMAN: Well —

NIXON: Now, wait a minute. Wait a minute.

EHRLICHMAN: Sure, I don't — if that's —

HALDEMAN: Well, the trap you're falling into there —

NIXON: [unclear]

HALDEMAN: — is that you're admitting to Dean that you regard the allegations that he has raised against us as of the same validity as his own criminal admission to you.

EHRLICHMAN: Maybe you do, and if that's the case then that's what you should say.

NIXON: No, no, no, no, no, no, no, no.

EHRLICHMAN: If it is —

NIXON: I know. I don't — what we — there are two different levels.

EHRLICHMAN: All right. Then that's the way it ought to be put.

NIXON: That's right.

EHRLICHMAN: He's brought in a bunch of silly garbage about me which doesn't add up to a nickel's worth of a lawsuit. He's come in and told you that he's been involved in all kinds of stuff. It seems to me a very different qualitative kind of problem. Here again I hate to argue my case here.

NIXON: Whether it's —

EHRLICHMAN: I just —

NIXON: Whether it's —

EHRLICHMAN: I just — very awkward.

NIXON: [unclear]

EHRLICHMAN: I — well —

NIXON: [unclear] goddamn it. [unclear]

EHRLICHMAN: No, I shouldn't. I ought to —

NIXON: [unclear] the problem I've got here is whether I can try myself —

EHRLICHMAN: Well —

NIXON: — I can [unclear] this business about the — when I said, "Look, John" — I said, "both Haldeman and Ehrlichman have offered to resign."

EHRLICHMAN: Well, I offered to resign at your total and sole discretion. You don't have to have a reason.

NIXON: That's right, and he said, "They have all — both said that." And I said, "I will certainly have better consideration."

EHRLICHMAN: And now there's another matter.

NIXON: Yeah.

EHRLICHMAN: If this is awkward for you, hell, the best thing you could do is get rid of me —

NIXON: Yeah.

EHRLICHMAN: — you know, once and for all.

NIXON: Yep.

EHRLICHMAN: But if it is anything short of that —

NIXON: Yeah.

EHRLICHMAN: — then it seems to me that you have to take into account the qualitative differences.

NIXON: Yep.

EHRLICHMAN: And if you don't want to make a formal suspension of Dean, then the thing to say to him is, "I want you to stay away from the office."

NIXON: Yeah.

EHRLICHMAN: "Just don't come around because I know everything that happens in this building is being funneled directly to the U.S. attorney through you, or I have reason to think that, and I cannot have that situation." Now that's the way I'd put it. I don't know what —

NIXON: I agree.

EHRLICHMAN: — previous commitment to him is, but he's not being fired, he's not being suspended.

NIXON: Right. Right. Right.

EHRLICHMAN: He's being directed to stay away from the office.

NIXON: [unclear] you tell him. Because of the fact that you are talking to a U.S. attorney. I don't know. If I could put it that way to him, I might be able to make some hay.

EHRLICHMAN: Now, if —

NIXON: Bring the U.S. attorney in. And I'll say don't give him immunity.

EHRLICHMAN: From a public policy stance —

NIXON: Yep.

EHRLICHMAN: Is this — ? Well —

NIXON: And I would say he wouldn't try to because I'll tell you what Petersen did tell me, which does say it — it says — when he said — I said, "What about Dean?" And he said, "Well, we haven't made a deal with him yet."

EHRLICHMAN: Mm-hmm.

NIXON: I think I told you about this —

EHRLICHMAN: Yep.

NIXON: I said, "Why didn't you make a deal?" And he said, "Well" — he said — and I — "because he didn't want us to use the word immunity." And I said, "What do you mean you let him off?" "Well," he said, "that's what you do, Mr. President." I said, "Well" — I said, "you're sending him to the Senate to lie, isn't he?" We've had some real good talks —

EHRLICHMAN: Yeah.

NIXON: — pretty [unclear]. And I sat down — I mentioned this to Rogers. Rogers just shook his head and said, "Jesus Christ." He said, "I escape them [unclear]." And I said, "All right."

EHRLICHMAN: Well —

NIXON: Now, wait a minute. Then Petersen, he said, "We've got to have corroborative testimony." So you see what I mean?

EHRLICHMAN: Yep.

NIXON: Before we could get — let me put it this way. He realizes that before he could get — does try to give Dean immunity — he's got to have corroborative testimony on the value of Dean's evidence and that's what he's trying to get at the present time. That's why he was calling Strachan, Colson, Kalmbach, et al. The purpose of it being, John, to get corroborative evidence that would say, well, Dean's evidence is so valuable insofar as other people are concerned, that we can — therefore, give him immunity. Now I'm not a criminal lawyer, but does that make any sense?

EHRLICHMAN: I don't know. I don't know.

NIXON: But you see what his tactic is?

EHRLICHMAN: Yes.

NIXON: So he isn't going to do it simply on the basis — he isn't giving Dean immunity simply on the basis of what Dean has already said.

EHRLICHMAN: I understand. My fear here is that —

NIXON: Dean getting immunity?

EHRLICHMAN: Dean getting immunity or anybody in the White House getting immunity.

NIXON: Yeah.

EHRLICHMAN: It is in itself treatable as a cover-up. And obviously if we are put in a position of defending ourselves —

NIXON: Right. Right.

EHRLICHMAN: — the things that I'm going to have to say about Dean —

NIXON: Go ahead.

EHRLICHMAN: — are that basically Dean was the sole proprietor of this project —

NIXON: Mm-hmm.

EHRLICHMAN: — and that he reported to the president. He reported to me only incidentally, and that [unclear].

NIXON: Reported to the president?

EHRLICHMAN: Yes, sir. I would have to say that because —

NIXON: When?

EHRLICHMAN: Well, I don't know when but the point is —

NIXON: The problem that you've got there is that — Dean does have a point there which you've got to realize. He didn't see me when he came out to California. He didn't see me until the day you said, "I think you ought to talk to John Dean."

EHRLICHMAN: Yep.

NIXON: I think that was in March.

EHRLICHMAN: All right.

NIXON: And he's going to say that.

EHRLICHMAN: But the point is that basically he was in charge of this project.

NIXON: He'll say he reports to the president through other people.

EHRLICHMAN: Well, okay. Then you see what you've got there is an imputation. He says then as that kind of a foundation, "I told Ehrlichman that Liddy did it." What he is saying is that "I told the president, through Ehrlichman, that Liddy did it."

HALDEMAN: Which means that it was privileged knowledge as far as Ehrlichman was concerned and there was nothing that you were required to do about it anyway.

EHRLICHMAN: That's right. But see I get into a very funny defensive position then vis-à-vis you and vis-à-vis him and it's very damn awkward. And I haven't thought it clear through. I don't know where we come out.

NIXON: Yeah. Yeah. You see Dean's little game here — as I know, Dean doesn't [unclear] that stands up for — one of the reasons this staff — and it's so goddamn good. I mean, basically, of course he didn't report to me. I was a little busy, and I didn't think you—all of you would [unclear] tells you but "let's let Dean handle that and keep this the hell out of the president's office. If we want the president, we can get him for other reasons, too."

EHRLICHMAN: Well, I was busy—

NIXON: But he did.

EHRLICHMAN: Well, the case I'm going to make—

NIXON: Well, of course, he would then say, "Who the hell did he report to?"

EHRLICHMAN: Well, he—in many cases, to no one. He just went ahead and did things.

HALDEMAN: That's right.

• • •

NIXON: Remember I said, "How much is it going to cost to keep these three guys?" He said, "A million dollars." I just shook my head.

HALDEMAN: Then we got into the question if there's blackmail here then we're into a thing that's—

NIXON: All right.

HALDEMAN: —just ridiculous and he said—he raised the point. Now my feeling on that point—remember that—Jesus, you can't say it's a million dollars. It may be ten million dollars.

NIXON: That's right.

HALDEMAN: Once we get into that.

NIXON: That's right. That's right.

HALDEMAN: And that we—

NIXON: Ought to—

HALDEMAN: —that we ought not to be in this and then we left it—you know, we can't do anything about it anyway. We don't have any money, and it isn't a question to be directed here. This is something—relates to Mitchell's problem. Ehrlichman has no problem with the thing with Hunt. And Ehrlichman said, "Christ, if you're going to get into blackmail, the hell with it."

NIXON: Good. The word "blackmail"—thank God you were in there when it happened. But you remember the conversation?

HALDEMAN: Yes, sir.

NIXON: I didn't tell him to go get the money, did I?

HALDEMAN: No.

NIXON: No—you didn't either, did you?

HALDEMAN: Absolutely not. I said, "You've got to talk to Mitchell. This is something you got to work out with Mitchell, not here. There's nothing we can do about it here."

NIXON: I think we've got a pretty good record on that one, John, at least.

HALDEMAN: But there's a couple of complications he can throw in there [unclear] which would be of concern. But I just can't conceive that a guy—he may—I can see him using it as a threat. I cannot see him sinking low enough to use that. I just—although I must admit the guy has really turned into an unbelievable disaster for us.

NIXON: Yes.

HALDEMAN: But I can't — people don't — he's not un-American and anti-Nixon. I'll tell you what he did — I'll tell you during that period —

NIXON: Yeah.

HALDEMAN: — he busted his ass trying to work this out and it wore him to a frazzle and I think it probably wore him past the point of rationality. I think he may now be in a mental state that's causing him to do things that when he sobers up, he's going to be very disturbed about with himself.

NIXON: Also, he's probably got a very clever new lawyer — named Shaffer. I think that's part of the problem.

HALDEMAN: Could very well be.

NIXON: [unclear]

HALDEMAN: Could very well be. But John I can't believe is a basically dishonorable guy. I think there's no question John is a strong self-promoter, self-motivated guy for his own good, but —

NIXON: Yet in that conversation, I — we were — I was very — I said, "Well, for Christ's sake, but — "

HALDEMAN: You explored in that conversation the possibility of whether such kinds of money could be raised. You said, "Well, Christ, we ought to be able to raise money like that."

NIXON: That's right.

HALDEMAN: "How much money is involved?" and he said, "Well, it could be a million dollars over the next year."

NIXON: [unclear]

HALDEMAN: And I jumped and said, "That's ridiculous. You can't say a million. Maybe you say a million — it may be two or ten, and — "

NIXON: But then we got into the blackmail.

HALDEMAN: You said, "Once you start down the path with blackmail, and it's constant escalation, and — "

NIXON: Yeah, yeah. That's my only —

HALDEMAN: [unclear]

NIXON: — conversation with regard to that.

HALDEMAN: They could jump and then say to us, "Well, that was morally wrong." What you should have said is, "Blackmail is wrong," not that it's too costly.

NIXON: Oh. Well, at that point that we got into [unclear] we went into the investigation.

HALDEMAN: [unclear] that's right.

NIXON: You see my point? We were then in the business of the — this was one of Dean's — when he was — was it after that we sent him to Camp David?

EHRLICHMAN: You sent him to Camp David on about the twenty —

NIXON: I would like to know with regard to that conversation, Bob. I just wanted to know.

EHRLICHMAN: It took place about the twenty-third. That is his trip to Camp David, about the twenty-third of March.

HALDEMAN: When was that Hunt threat?

EHRLICHMAN: I haven't any idea. I have no idea.

NIXON: Get that worked out, please.

HALDEMAN: I don't know. Better check on it.

NIXON: Well, the date — oh, hell.

EHRLICHMAN: Well, you'll know the date of your meeting here.

NIXON: Well, anyway you can't [unclear] you could simply say — I suppose then we should have cut it off — shut it off — because later on you met in your office and — I mean, and Mitchell said, "That was taken care of."

EHRLICHMAN: The next day.

HALDEMAN: That's right.

UNIDENTIFIED: The same day.

HALDEMAN: Maybe I can find the date by that.

NIXON: Yeah, and Dean — Dean was there and said, "What about this money for Hunt?" Wasn't Dean there?

HALDEMAN: No. What happened was Ehrlichman and Dean and Mitchell and I were in the office — my office — and we were discussing other matters. And in the process of it, Mitchell said, "Let me raise one point," and he turned to Dean. He said, "Let me raise another point. Have you taken care of the" — the other problem — "Hunt's problem?" Something like that. I don't know how he referred to it. But we all knew instantly what he was — what he meant and Dean kind of looked a little flustered and said, "Well, no. I mean, I don't know where that is" or something. And Mitchell said, "Well, I guess it's taken care of." And so we assumed from that that Mitchell had taken care of it, and there was no further squeak out of it. So I now do assume Mitchell took care of it so —

NIXON: Yeah, the problem I have there is I said [unclear].

HALDEMAN: — Mitchell — that LaRue, as I understand it, LaRue was Mitchell's agent, but —

NIXON: Yeah, as I understand it — what I meant is I'm just trying to seek out whether — I'm just seeing where Dean's lines of attack are.

HALDEMAN: And you're saying, "Did I know about that?" I did. Yeah, there's no question.

NIXON: Say, "Yes, there was talk about it and so forth, and Mitchell took care of it." But that you had — but on the other hand, you make the case as to [unclear].

HALDEMAN: You can't testify to that. It's presidential —

NIXON: In this office. But not in the other office — not in your office.

HALDEMAN: Okay. But in the other office the question of —

NIXON: That's right.

HALDEMAN: — and the specifics never arose. And there again Dean is the agent on it. Dean's coming in saying, "What should I do?" Dean's the agent on all of this. That's where my money goes. All the input to me about the three hundred fifty came from Dean, and all the output came from Dean. That's the only time I —

NIXON: Then Dean was the one that said, "Look, Bob, we need three hundred fifty for — or need the rest of the money."

HALDEMAN: No, they didn't even come that way. Dean said, "They need money for the defendants — "

NIXON: Right.

HALDEMAN: — "for their fees."

NIXON: Right.

HALDEMAN: And that's the — was always put that way. That's the way it was always discussed.

NIXON: Right. That's why I want that line in the thing. I think that's most important you can work on. Get a lawyer. [unclear] —

HALDEMAN: And I said —

NIXON: — lawyer.

HALDEMAN: And I said to Dean at that time, "Well, look, you've got a situation here. We've got the three hundred — I thought it was three hundred fifty — it was three hundred twenty-eight in cash that we needed to get turned back to the committee."

NIXON: Right.

HALDEMAN: "Apparently they had a need for money so we have a coincidence of needs here. Now you ought to be able to work out some way to get them to take the cash and that will take care of our needs and apparently help meet their needs."

NIXON: Right, right.

HALDEMAN: Then he went back to Mitchell and Mitchell wouldn't do it. And then they agreed to take forty thousand of it, which they did. And shortly thereafter they agreed to take the rest, which they did.

NIXON: Do you think — did you check with [unclear] before the election and some afterwards?

HALDEMAN: It was not before the election, no.

NIXON: That was a story that somebody had. Dean said it was before — forty before and he says —

HALDEMAN: Strachan said it was in late November — thirtieth or twenty-ninth or something like that.

NIXON: Right.

"For God's sakes . . . we have got to keep the grand jury from leaking."

April 18, 1973, 2:50 p.m.

Richard Nixon and Henry Petersen

WHITE HOUSE TELEPHONE

At 4:30 in the afternoon of April 17, Nixon delivered his remarks on Watergate in a hastily arranged press conference. First he announced that members of his administration would testify before the Watergate Committee and that he did not expect any of them to be granted immunity. Second, he explained that he had come into information on March

21 that persuaded him to initiate his own investigation of Watergate and that "major developments" would be forthcoming. At the mention of that date, those in the know realized that he was referring to Dean and would lay the blame for his own purported innocence of Watergate on his counsel. Those who were not in the know analyzed the statement endlessly. "This political city, which has waited for him so long," wrote James Reston of the New York Times, "is jumping with excitement and jumping to conclusions."

With Dean, Haldeman, and Ehrlichman now too damaged to get the inside scoop on the grand jury from the Department of Justice, to whom could Nixon turn? He had to do it himself. For about a month, from mid-April to mid-May, Nixon's taping system recorded hours of meetings and phone calls with Henry Petersen, exactly for that purpose. It was an awkward arrangement in that Petersen technically reported to Nixon through the attorney general, so it was unclear how much Nixon should know about the prosecution's strategy — and how much he should not. The regular updates included discussions of subjects such as which witnesses were being called, places where testimony conflicted, and even whether John Dean would receive immunity.

• • •

NIXON: Hello?

PETERSEN: Hello, Mr. President.

NIXON: Well, what's — anything I need to know today?

PETERSEN: No, sir. There are no significant developments.

NIXON: Right. All right.

PETERSEN: Strachan is coming in. Fred Vincent, former assistant attorney general under Johnson, is representing him.

NIXON: Representing who?

PETERSEN: Strachan, I think it is. He's going to come in.

NIXON: Strachan? Strachan. Oh, Gordon Strachan — yeah, yeah.

PETERSEN: But there have been no developments, they are still negotiating. We have a problem with the grand jury. The only copy of the grand jury transcripts have been locked up in the prosecutor's office. We've got the FBI checking out the reporter on the grounds that they have leaked it. The judge called us in about it this morning about it.

NIXON: Sirica did?

PETERSEN: Yes. And —

NIXON: What, you mean part of it was leaking?

PETERSEN: He was concerned about leaking —

NIXON: Yeah. [laughs]

PETERSEN: — and of course Anderson's been printing some of it. We've changed reporters. We haven't even been bringing it over here for security reasons.

NIXON: Yeah, for God's sakes that's — even then, we have got to keep the grand jury from leaking but —

PETERSEN: Well, you know, I don't want to go too far on it either because I don't want to get into a diversionary battle with Jack Anderson.

NIXON: Exactly. Oh, hell no. I wouldn't pay that much attention to it. I wouldn't — I agree, I agree. No, what I meant is just do the best to control it —

PETERSEN: We will indeed.

NIXON: — because we know it's just wrong. Now, I've instr — we're handling it over here, I trust, all right, because I just told Ziegler to — he won't comment on anything because it might affect the rights of either the prosecution or the rights of innocent people or the rights of defendants.

PETERSEN: Well, we aren't taking any calls at all while we're here.

NIXON: So that is all we are saying.

PETERSEN: We can't talk to them about it.

NIXON: Fine.

PETERSEN: I was kind of pleased with the response your statement got.

NIXON: I think it was probably the right thing to say.

PETERSEN: Yeah.

NIXON: What have you got — you still got the — you haven't made any — you haven't finished the thing with Magruder yet then, huh?

PETERSEN: No, we haven't finished the thing with Magruder.

NIXON: Dean the same, huh?

PETERSEN: Dean's — well, we have just backed off on him for a while. His lawyers want time to think.

NIXON: Yeah, I have — deliberately, Henry — I have left Dean in a position where I said it's — look, he's going to be treated like everybody else —

PETERSEN: Yeah.

NIXON: — because it isn't fair, I mean, for him to be at all — you know what I mean. Like when we talked about resignation and so forth, if I don't — since he's made some charges, or — well, it isn't that since he has at least had some private discussions but they haven't been in the grand jury form so I have to respect those.

PETERSEN: I think that is right.

NIXON: So that was your suggestion, at least, that we should not do anything on Dean at this point?

PETERSEN: I think that is right. I think you just ought to let him sit.

NIXON: All I have is *ex parte* — all I have is just information, basically —

PETERSEN: That's right.

NIXON: — from you and from him. But it is information which —

PETERSEN: I think that we have to —

NIXON: — the gravity of which I just can't judge till I see whether it is corroborated.

PETERSEN: Well, we have to treat that as private in any event.

NIXON: Private, don't I? Yeah, and for that reason if I were to move, we'd do it. So, I think we are in the right position and then — fine. Okay, then I won't expect any more from you today. I won't bother you, huh?

PETERSEN: No. I am just —

NIXON: Good.

PETERSEN: I am a little concerned about Senator Ervin's committee. They have just — under the agreement that Kleindienst worked out with Senator Ervin —

NIXON: Yeah.

PETERSEN: — have called the bureau and asked to see the interview statements of Magruder, Porter, Strachan, and LaRue.

NIXON: Oh, my God.

PETERSEN: And I feel like I am sitting on a powder keg there but I don't feel like I can dare go to Senator Ervin until I get a definite commitment from Magruder.

NIXON: Yeah, yeah. Magruder — well, what else — what's waiting besides the committee — oh, what is waiting besides the committee with him? That's — oh —

PETERSEN: Well —

NIXON: — the DC jail?

PETERSEN: — that's right, and whether or not the judge is going to clap him in right away, and whether or not the committee is going to put the pressure on him.

NIXON: In other words, you think that the — you haven't yet tried to talk to Ervin?

PETERSEN: No, sir. And I don't want to until I can tie him down —

NIXON: Until you've got him tied. Yeah, I get it.

PETERSEN: Well, you've got — you know, I've got to be able to come out and say I'm coming out with something public in terms of a charge.

NIXON: Yeah, I see.

PETERSEN: You know, in order to have a valid basis for the rest those holed up.

NIXON: Right, right, right. I see. Okay. Well, in any event I am glad that you thought the statement went well. I worked on it to be sure that it didn't compromise anybody one way or another and as you noticed I put the immunity thing — that leaves the ball in your court, but —

PETERSEN: [laughs] I noticed. I'm not sure!

NIXON: But on the other hand, I had to express the view, because basically people are going to ask me, well, what about Mitchell — what about, you know, a lot of people — and I just can't be in that position.

PETERSEN: I agree wholeheartedly.

NIXON: Lower people are different, but you know —

PETERSEN: Yeah.

NIXON: — upper people — Christ, they might think I am protecting Gray.

PETERSEN: I agree.

NIXON: [laughs] Okay.

PETERSEN: All right, Mr. President.

NIXON: Fine.

PETERSEN: Thanks.

Nixon's prerogative in blacking out incidents of national security

April 19, 1973, 10:12 a.m.

Richard Nixon and Henry Petersen
OVAL OFFICE

In what had become a daily occurrence, Nixon and Petersen had a meeting, which Nixon steered toward the impact of national security on certain parts of the investigation. In his view, that was a wide field and included efforts to identify leaks in departments or areas even distantly related to national security programs. Nixon managed to include in the conversation his contention that bugging was common in the Johnson administration, including surveillance of the Nixon campaign plane. With the Gray nomination for FBI director having fallen apart in the Senate, Nixon also let Petersen know that he'd be cleaning house at the bureau, and he intimated that Petersen was a leading choice for director. That being an inappropriate offer, even as an intimation, Petersen backed away from the subject.

• • •

PETERSEN: Morning, Mr. President.

NIXON: Why don't you come back in before we get you back in the courtroom? I wanted to tell you this — which I think probably should be [unclear] with regard to Mitchell and the national security element.

PETERSEN: Yes sir, I need to know.

NIXON: Well, the problem basically is this. This is the Ellsberg case. You remember our late, dear departed friend Edgar Hoover. You may recall he did not want to get into the Ellsberg case — in other words, a personal reason. It involved [Louis] Marx. He was one of his closest friends. Marx. Not the Marx Brothers, but the toy makers.

PETERSEN: Mm-hmm.

NIXON: Marx's daughter [Patricia] is married to Ellsberg and Hoover just kicked and churned and said, "I'm just not going to investigate this thing. I can't do it." I mean, well, this is at least what we got through Mitchell. Under the circumstances then an investigation was undertaken with a very, very small group at the White House. That's where the Hunt group — nothing in terms of break-ins or anything was approved. But seeing what these crazy bastards have done since and seeing what — now the investigation also and this is the hopeful thing as far as the prosecution — it didn't do a damn bit of good. I mean all they got — they got — most of this appeared in the papers, that Ellsberg has psychiatric problems, that Ellsberg was a — which he could have learned from Henry Kissinger. He was one of his students at one time — quite a, apparently he liked —

PETERSEN: Well, by the time I told [unclear] group —

NIXON: Well, the point that I make is this. None of it is a win for the prosecution. Then, after that finally Hoover got into it. Now, when Hoover got into it, he should know he wiretapped.

PETERSEN: Oh.

NIXON: He did. There's no question about that. I don't know who he wiretapped. But I mean that national security taps were used at that time and then as you know with the hullabaloo that all arose out there we knocked off all of those taps except for the bag jobs [unclear] —

PETERSEN: [unclear]

NIXON: — I am quite aware of the fact that we do a lot of [unclear] things in this field.

PETERSEN: Yes, sir. Yes, sir. And I don't know —

NIXON: I just want you to know. I just — want you to know that my purpose —

PETERSEN: Yes, sir. We could hardly be called illegal in this field —

NIXON: My purpose in the Hunt thing in calling you is simply to say it is — it was a national security investigation. It is not related in any way to the Watergate thing.

PETERSEN: Correct.

NIXON: And that the purpose of it was —

PETERSEN: Well, is there any other? You know, I can't stay away from that which I don't know.

NIXON: Certainly. You mean did Hunt do anything else?

PETERSEN: Is there any other national security stuff that we could —

NIXON: Yes.

PETERSEN: — inadvertently get into through Hunt?

NIXON: Yes, you could get into other things. For example, Hunt — nothing involved in bugging, apparently — but tried, for example, on one occasion, he was — it was basically the whole Ellsberg period. You know, this place was leaking like a sieve. And you remember Kissinger's national security people.

PETERSEN: Yes, sir. I do.

NIXON: We had a horrible time and frankly the country was in jeopardy because I — it was imperative that our situation with foreign governments and a lot of others that I'd get Hoover in and say, "Goddamn it, we've got to" — well, Mitchell got him in and I got him in once myself. You know how Hoover was. We all know, but he hated to get into anything involving the press.

· · ·

NIXON: I know that when I first came into office he used to send that stuff over here by the cartload. He used to love that sort of thing. That we discontinued also. We discontinued that.

PETERSEN: Well, I should say, Mr. President, just coincidentally that since they transferred the Internal Security Division to me —

NIXON: You ever done any?

PETERSEN: Yes. And I — but I also —

NIXON: I don't know —

PETERSEN: The authority runs from you to the attorney general.

NIXON: That's right.

PETERSEN: The way some of it is being exercised is only an application.

NIXON: What?

PETERSEN: The way some of it is being exercised is only an application.

NIXON: Right now?

PETERSEN: Yes, sir. And I just set up —

NIXON: Let me be clear.

PETERSEN: I just —

NIXON: I don't want the goddamn thing done, you know, because — you understand? I understand it's been knocked off. I don't want —

PETERSEN: [unclear]

NIXON: — I don't want to use — I don't want to use it for national security. I understand you're going after gangsters or other things like that. It just isn't worth it. You don't get —

PETERSEN: No. I am just talking about the nat — the stuff in the country. I am talking about either foreign intelligence stuff — I am holding some of them up because they're —

NIXON: [unclear]

PETERSEN: — deputy somebody over at the State Department and we are tightening up the procedure. That's all.

NIXON: The president approves, you see —

PETERSEN: I understand.

• • •

NIXON: Now, you have also heard about Joe Kraft.

PETERSEN: Yes, sir.

NIXON: You read that column. That was a Hoover bug, I think — I just got this from Mitchell. But what it involved were leaks of national security documents that were — got into Kraft's columns and so forth and so on. Nothing came of it as a result except I think fired somebody over here. Now that — now that's —

PETERSEN: Well —

NIXON: I just wanted you to know that they're — a definite — but it is minuscule compared to what Johnson was doing. You know what I mean. As you know, it was very heavy in those days — very, very heavy. Just ask Bill Sullivan. He's sent a memorandum to me and it's pretty shocking. He went after some people at the Democratic Committee and also bugged our plane during the [1968] campaign [unclear] go anywhere.

PETERSEN: I understand that.

NIXON: Now, my point is that that doesn't justify anything now. But in the case of the Hunt thing you should know that when he was at the White House and he was working in the field of drugs, he worked on this particular activity and Liddy worked with him as I understand. I think Liddy did, too. This I have found but frankly I really didn't know this myself until this case came out. I said, "What in the name of God is Hunt doing?" I understand now what he was doing and I would have approved it — yet I would have approved it at the time because we had nothing that we could get out of Hoover. Hoover did conduct the investigation after that and did a hell of a good job. Hoover did recommend the inv — the prosecution though on Ellsberg which I think is probably a mistake. I don't know if he will make it or not.

PETERSEN: I don't know either.

NIXON: I hope so. But my point is —

PETERSEN: Incidentally —

NIXON: —I want you to understand that I have never used the words "national security" as far as Watergate is concerned or any of that crap — you just burn their asses. Like when I called you the other day [unclear] I am not going to let any stone unturned and that is what you and I have got to understand. But on national security only two places, Henry, where it's very important in terms of privilege that you — that you have to act — one, any conversations with the president are obviously privileged. There shouldn't —

PETERSEN: Yes, sir. I understand that. No, sir.

NIXON: —be any question about that. And that should be something that everybody should do — should have in mind. And any convers — and anything in the national security area, but you can ask — we don't have anybody around here now that you have Dean on the carpet — you've got Ehrlichman's and Haldeman's attention on the carpet. So just ask me if it's a national security area. But I do think in this view — if Hunt was involved in the Ellsberg case, and he was involved in what — they called it the plumbing operation. And basically it was leaks from the National Security Council which appeared in the columns. That's all. And it involved only — and did not involve any — it did not involve any, as I understand, electronic eavesdropping, but it involved a hell of an investigation — one hell of a lot.

PETERSEN: I indicated to you —

NIXON: That's as much as I know about it at this time.

PETERSEN: —I indicated to you the other day —

NIXON: I don't know whether Dean — Dean may be quite familiar with this because he was very much — you know what I mean. He was sort of in charge of this kind of activity and he may be familiar with it and he may not be, but I have tried to get this sorted out. I have just had them check on it over here — I said now what did they do and what is there as far as I am concerned. I don't mind anything coming out, but I don't want anything coming out on the Ellsberg thing.

PETERSEN: Right.

NIXON: We had to do it. I don't want anything coming out on what we were doing with NSC. I don't want anything coming out — what we were doing for the others — it's slop over Hoover, and it isn't going to look very good with Hoover.

PETERSEN: [unclear]

NIXON: I don't — the bureau hurt any more because of that. I just — I am hoping for the day when the man I have in mind for that job gets away from what he is presently doing so I can put him in. We've got to get a man in there and fast. And I am going to clean everybody out of the bureau at the second level. Everybody.

PETERSEN: Well, that's — he needs —

NIXON: [unclear] as you know, you deal with [unclear] a job [unclear].

PETERSEN: It's not a job anybody should run for, Mr. President.

NIXON: What's that?

PETERSEN: It's not a job anybody should ask for or run for. The responsibilities are almost as great as your office.

NIXON: You should know that I felt — that you were — you came highly commended. [unclear] Mitchell said, "Henry Petersen is the best guy for the job."

PETERSEN: Even in this present difficulty I am flattered.

NIXON: Well, it's a hell of a thing — a very important thing. But that's all that I wanted you to know. Now the — otherwise on Hunt, get behind the [unclear].

PETERSEN: Mr. President, the other day I indicated we had a problem with leaks, as you know we do.

NIXON: It was shocking to me to see Strachan's testimony — not his latest testimony — where the U.S. attorney —

PETERSEN: Well, I think we are going to have to do something —

NIXON: Verbatim. Verbatim. And I — I don't know — doesn't that have some effect on the legality of this thing?

PETERSEN, Yes, sir.

Seeking support from Jewish leaders

April 19, 1973, 11:13 a.m.
Richard Nixon, Henry Kissinger, Leonard Garment, William Timmons, and
various Jewish leaders (Max M. Fisher, Jacob Stein, Richard Maass, Charlotte
Jacobson, Al E. Arent, Rabbi Israel Miller, Herman Weisman, David M. Blumburg,
Rabbi Arthur Hertzberg, Paul Zuckerman, Mel Dubinsky, Philip Hoffman,
William Wexler, Albert Spiegel, Jerry Goodman, and Yehuda Hellman)
Cabinet Room

During the spring of 1973, Nixon and Kissinger proposed granting most favored nation (MFN) status to the Soviet Union for purposes of removing restrictions related to trade. The proposal was an outgrowth of Nixon's visit to Moscow the previous year, when both sides pledged to improve trade ties. However, Senator Henry Jackson inserted an amendment, supported by seventy-six senators, that would link passage of the MFN proposal to the elimination of a tax placed on Russian Jews emigrating to Israel. Nixon needed the support of the Jewish community to overcome veto-proof majorities in Congress. Nixon and Kissinger presented a Soviet proposal that they hoped would break the deadlock.

• • •

KISSINGER: It's in everybody's interest to make clear that this is from the Soviet leadership and not from one individual. Now let me read the communication which we received from Moscow. And it's in the form of an unsigned, written oral note. "Applications of Soviet citizens who wish to leave the USSR for permanent residence in other countries are considered. And decisions concerning such applications are made on an individual basis taking account of concrete circumstances. As a rule, these requests are granted," which is an interesting statement. "For example, with regard to persons who, in 1972, expressed a desire to go to Israel, permission was received by ninety-five point five percent of those who applied. A similar approach will be maintained in the future." Then they added, "Many of you know that more than two thousand persons who received permission to leave for Israel in 1972 did not, in fact, make use of that permission." I do not know if that is true. "As regards the refunding of state educational expenses by Soviet citizens leaving for permanent residence abroad —"

NIXON: That's the — that's the tax —

UNKNOWN: The head tax.

NIXON: Right.

KISSINGER: "— the decree of the Presidium of the USSR's Supreme Soviet of August 3, 1972, and the decision taken in accordance with it by the USSR Council of Ministers, provides that Soviet citizens who receive permission to emigrate can be exempted fully from refunding the expenses mentioned above. Accordingly, Soviet authorities, in considering the applications of Soviet citizens wishing to emigrate, have the right to decide that only state duties normal in such cases be collected from such persons. The authorities are now exercising this right. Consequently, only such normal and insignificant duties, which were also collected before the decree of August 3, 1972, are being collected, and will be collected, from those persons who are leaving the Soviet Union for permanent residence in other countries." In other words, they are saying that they will not collect the head tax. When we received this, I transmitted it, of course, to the president and he asked me to put a number of supplementary questions to Dobrynin. First, he said, is this an official communication, or just a personal expression? Second, how do we know that this is not just now — when they say it's not being collected or will be collected — how do we know this doesn't have a time limit on it? Thirdly, he said, does this mean the law is being repealed? And fourthly, he asked, can we communicate this to other people? We received a —

NIXON: These were questions that Henry and I worked out in my office —

KISSINGER: That's right.

NIXON: — and I think they are the right questions to ask. So we asked this senator yesterday and we got a fairly rough time. I mean, I had the feeling at the end that I was sort of soft on communism!

[LAUGHTER]

• • •

KISSINGER: Then we received another oral note from them on April 10 which —

NIXON: That was the time that I got in touch with Stans and suggested we have a meeting, and we just turned Baker on to it now.

KISSINGER: Because we —

NIXON: We have to see the leaders first.

KISSINGER: Here is what the second oral note said. It said, "That in reply to certain supplementary questions, the Soviet government provides the following information: (a) the above statement—that is to say the one on March 30—should be regarded as an official Soviet statement. Two, the phrase—or (b) the phrase in that statement—'that only such normal duties which were also collected before the decree of August 3, 1972, are being collected, and will be collected'—has no time limit attached to it, and any interpretation implying the existence of a time limit does not correspond to the position of the Soviet government."

NIXON: The reason this is important is that Scoop Jackson raised the point, he said, well, there's no—there's—well, he raised the point suppose we give them that and then a month after that crack—there it goes again. It's a real problem. But there it is, and that—but the point that I make there—I interpret that, Henry—would be that if they would then—then reimpose it, they're breaking their word. And then, of course, that gives me the provocation to do a few things they may not want.

KISSINGER: It's absolutely clear in our communications to them that we will consider the abrogation of this undertaking as inconsistent. May I finish the other—

• • •

KISSINGER: "(c) The exemption from the requirement to refund state educational expenses is being granted on the basis of the terms of the decree of August 3, 1972, itself, and on the subsequent decision taken in accordance with that the decree by the USSR Council of Ministers. In the Soviet view, this situation obviates the need for repealing the decree of August 3." [Kissinger is then asked to repeat this portion and reads it again.] In other words, the decree makes it possible for them to suspend the requirement to refund state educational expenses. So it's a face-saving—Mr. President, it's a face-saving formula of saying they're not going to repeal the law, but they said the exemption from the requirement to refund state educational expenses is being granted on the basis of the law.

• • •

NIXON: What they are saying is that their law of August is still in force—in force—but that the law expressly provides for exemption, and their action in providing for exemption here is consistent with the law. The law remains, but actually under that law we get an exemption. And that's it. That's really what you're getting here, and I think that's the face saver.

[Unclear exchange]

NIXON: In fact, the law is a dead letter in effect besides the [unclear]. The law, as far as this group is concerned, is a dead letter. That's what it means. That's all it means.

KISSINGER: And number "(d)" then is just a technical point: "The president is free to transmit the contents of the official Soviet statement, as well as of these additional explanatory points, to the Congress."

UNKNOWN: [unclear]

KISSINGER: To the Congress. So, this is—therefore, has a high degree of formality attached to it. These are the communications which, in our judgment, effectively restore the situation to what it was on August 1, 1972, so that then — now our problem is this: do we use the MFN legislation, which has — we've already used effectively to get the head tax repealed — to attach additional riders to it and therefore sabotage the whole context of the negotiations into which this was built, including Soviet restraint in the Middle East? Or do we go back to what was the original approach: namely steady presidential pressure, in his channel, on the Soviet government to help improve the situation as it was on August 1, 1972, which we're not declaring to be satisfactory? This is the issue which we now face, and this is why we have made such a strong case.

• • •

NIXON: If the Jackson amendment is passed, you know, with a straight-out declaration that makes the Soviet back down before the whole world on this thing that it would seriously jeopardize the possibility of going forward with the meetings we're going to have.

"The U.S. attorney would have a hell of a time concluding you were in the conspiracy."
April 19, 1973, 1:03 p.m.
Richard Nixon and John Ehrlichman
OVAL OFFICE

Nixon and Ehrlichman were worried. What was Dean's next move? He did not seem to be getting very far in discussions related to immunity, in part because there were so many conflicts in testimony to sort out among those who had testified. What Nixon and Ehrlichman feared was that Dean could be motivated to offer details to the prosecutors that expanded the scope of their investigation, which Nixon sometimes referred to as going into "national security" matters. These were details that were very bad for Haldeman and Ehrlichman, but not especially bad for Dean, including the previous break-in at Daniel Ellsberg's psychiatrist's office, Howard Hunt's work for the White House, and money paid to the Watergate burglars. If Dean's testimony held up on these new subjects, that might be enough to get immunity from prosecution and also vault the Watergate investigation to even higher levels in the White House.

• • •

EHRLICHMAN: Mr. President.
NIXON: John, how are you?
EHRLICHMAN: Fine, sir.
NIXON: The — did you see that piece?
EHRLICHMAN: Yes, I did.
NIXON: I told Ron that obviously the secretary — I've run down the background.
EHRLICHMAN: Yes, good.
NIXON: [unclear] I guess Dean has really been shot across the bow there [unclear] he's the scapegoat.
EHRLICHMAN: Yeah.

NIXON: Yeah.

EHRLICHMAN: Have they made a deal with him of any kind?

NIXON: No, sir. No, sir. Not yet. So — discuss that one through.

EHRLICHMAN: All right. [unclear]

NIXON: But you know on the other hand what the — I just don't know what the hell Dean can talk about. He knows a hell of a lot, but —

EHRLICHMAN: Well, we're going over that now.

NIXON: I see.

EHRLICHMAN: Taking time to kind of spin it all out, but it's pretty hard to —

NIXON: Yeah.

EHRLICHMAN: — but it's pretty hard to see how —

NIXON: I understand he's still on the White House staff, where there's a problem as to whether —

EHRLICHMAN: Yeah.

NIXON: We're going to bite that bullet [unclear].

EHRLICHMAN: Yeah, well, I'm sure if he were not, he would not have been as restrained as that.

NIXON: Yeah, I think it's best to keep him here.

EHRLICHMAN: Yeah.

NIXON: I had Ron call him and check and say that "we're going to say that there's not going to be any statement." We're trying to get the truth and my question [unclear] whether or not [unclear] the lawyers [unclear].

EHRLICHMAN: Well, they're going to go right over there this afternoon.

NIXON: They are? Fine, and —

EHRLICHMAN: [unclear]

NIXON: That's what I went through [unclear]. I told him about Hunt and the NSC thing — and the investigation — I mean, our investigation — why we had to do it, and how we're going to do the other thing and so forth and so on. [unclear] the Department of Justice [unclear]. He said, "What else did Hunt do?" [unclear] We need to know. And I said, "I think he did — he was working in other fields regarding leaks to this matter."

EHRLICHMAN: Right.

NIXON: And I said, unless — but I don't want anything involving eavesdropping, which was carried on. Is that correct?

EHRLICHMAN: Yes, as far as I know.

NIXON: Yes, fine. But Dean — was Dean in charge of this?

EHRLICHMAN: No, no.

NIXON: This was ours, okay. But Dean must know about it — is that right?

EHRLICHMAN: I think he must.

NIXON: He was concerned about the grand jury. He was very concerned.

EHRLICHMAN: Good.

NIXON: I said I was a little mystified. He said it's just terrible. He didn't know what to do.

EHRLICHMAN: Our attorneys think that may be fatally defective.

NIXON: Fatally defective —

EHRLICHMAN: May be an illegal grand jury.

NIXON: Well, don't you think you'll get another grand jury?

EHRLICHMAN: I suppose they could, but it may just — it just may screw up this whole process.

NIXON: Would you do that? This grand jury is for anybody —

EHRLICHMAN: The prosecutors have a tough decision whether to go forward with these cases — these new cases with this grand jury or go right out and reprocess everybody through another one.

NIXON: I asked Bob Haldeman — I said, "Look, suppose I use him as an example, such as to postpone [unclear]. Would it affect our [unclear] much stress on that?" [unclear] I put it to him — I said, "Dean inferred to me that if Haldeman and Ehrlichman left, that would be you," meaning if Petersen could grant immunity. He said that's not true. He said it would have no effect on the immunity [unclear] of the corroboration. I suppose Dean's theory — I suppose that is basically he carried out the orders of others. I said, "Does that put — what effect does that have?" He says only in litigation — now you can't — an agent committing a crime — so, you can't do that — so Dean rebutted the situation. What he's going to get — he's going to get total immunity, or whether he's — and I suppose the way I look at it, all we've got to consider is — we really got this thing [unclear]. With the facts coming out anyway whether giving him total immunity is going to make him act better. Your view is to have him hold it over us for the rest of our lives anyway — that your point?

EHRLICHMAN: That would be my fear. These fellows don't seem to think Dean can get immunity at this point, but they're going to go down and talk to Glanzer and see what's going on.

NIXON: Good. The second point with regard to the cases — the case — are you [unclear] don't have that much of a case — the deep-six thing and they said that [unclear]. "Bob," I said, "it looks to me like they gave the contents to Gray. Gray [unclear] it out." And I said, "Who delivered it to Gray?" He said, "Ehrlichman and Dean."

EHRLICHMAN: That's arguable. I was there.

NIXON: All right, fine. That's all. But I said, "Did either of those things occur?" And I said I didn't raise the point — did it all occur before [unclear].

EHRLICHMAN: Right. Right.

NIXON: The other thing is, I suppose — how else do you get Ehrlichman in on the conspiracy thing, you know? Well, he simply says that perhaps the only way you could possibly would be that Dean going to Ehrlichman with regard to the need for funds for the defendants. Now he did go to you at one point, didn't he?

EHRLICHMAN: Right.

NIXON: And including, of course, this last time — did he about this last —

EHRLICHMAN: Bittman? Yes, I expect he lied.

NIXON: What did you do with the earlier point?

EHRLICHMAN: The early one I told him it was all right to call Kalmbach.

NIXON: Now, how do we — there I suppose that's a defense vulnerability.

EHRLICHMAN: These fellows say they're not completely finished. We're right in the middle of this right now, but their tentative view is that we have to look at it as you're doing, from two standpoints, the illegal and the apparently doubtful.

NIXON: Let's get the illegal first.

EHRLICHMAN: Okay. Well, they say there's nothing illegal about that.

NIXON: Why not?

EHRLICHMAN: Because I wasn't an actor. See, the reason he had to come to me in order to call Kalmbach is that Kalmbach didn't want to work for Stans anymore. And we used a pretext with Maury that Kalmbach was going to be under Bob and my aegis from now on to do special projects, and so he couldn't be a fundraiser anymore.

NIXON: I see.

EHRLICHMAN: And that was effective the sixth of April.

NIXON: Right.

EHRLICHMAN: And so Mitchell and Stans had been told that the only way they could use him is if we okayed it. And that was to protect Herb [Kalmbach] from having all kinds of demands made on his time by the committee.

NIXON: So he came to you and asked you to do it.

EHRLICHMAN: Dean said, "Would you — ?"

NIXON: No — nothing but illegal in that case but what about the conspiracy thing there? They [unclear]. That's why I was digging — that we've got him as far as the conspiracy.

EHRLICHMAN: Well, that's arguable. These fellows seem to think that there's a legitimate defense in that that doesn't elevate — that doesn't get up to the level of being an actor in a conspiracy.

NIXON: That's all involved in the case. The case on Bob is harder. He said that basically it gets down to a conflict in testimony which they cannot resolve between Strachan and Magruder into letting — into thinking of asking you to take a lie detector test. I said I don't like that but maybe we have to do that, I don't know — not going to get into that. Strachan, in effect, says that Haldeman did not receive the specifics — the budget, you know, and I don't know what Haldeman says on that or not. I think he says he can be either, and that Haldeman did not receive Watergate stuff that was recognizable as such. Magruder, he says, said Haldeman received the budget. I don't know that Magruder has gone so far as to say he received the specifics.

EHRLICHMAN: [unclear] synopsis.

NIXON: Got it?

EHRLICHMAN: Yeah.

NIXON: [unclear], huh?

EHRLICHMAN: He does.

NIXON: Magruder said that?

EHRLICHMAN: Yeah, he said that to me.

NIXON: But, and the — of the budget?

EHRLICHMAN: Yes.

NIXON: But did it indicate that bugging was involved?

EHRLICHMAN: That Strachan got it. He says he doesn't know if Bob got it.

NIXON: Then Strachan may have committed perjury.

EHRLICHMAN: No, Strachan devoutly, sincerely, and with every fiber of his being says he never got it. And he would remember if he ever got a budget that said anything like that — he'd know.

NIXON: And Magruder says that he received the budget here.

EHRLICHMAN: They sent it over.

NIXON: Right, and Magruder's also saying that the information —

EHRLICHMAN: The transcript of the synopsis —

NIXON: Yeah, the synopsis.

EHRLICHMAN: I see.

NIXON: The other thing is that Haldeman's apparently ordering or anticipating the order to rehire Liddy.

EHRLICHMAN: No.

NIXON: I don't know. He didn't mention this, but very important [unclear]. They are far from having this case nailed down.

EHRLICHMAN: Did he say anything about timing?

NIXON: No, nothing this weekend. They haven't made their deal with Magruder yet.

EHRLICHMAN: So, he's not going in this week.

NIXON: No, sir. Well, he said — I said, "Look, I might take off for Easter." He said, "Yeah," so apparently —

EHRLICHMAN: Will they recess the jury for Easter? Well, anyway, he won't go before Monday. Is that what your reading is?

NIXON: [unclear] no, I got time. Yeah. And of course Haldeman ordered the three fifty to be paid, knowing that it would be paid to the defendants. Now Haldeman agrees on that, does he?

EHRLICHMAN: No, we've gone into that in elaborate detail with the lawyers this morning.

NIXON: What do they say on that?

EHRLICHMAN: John Wilson says, "There's nothing illegal about what you did, Mr. Haldeman. The president has to decide whether the appearance of it regarding — "

NIXON: [unclear] I hope there isn't anything on it.

EHRLICHMAN: He said not, because of Bob's state of mind at the time.

NIXON: Bob was not intending to try to keep the —

EHRLICHMAN: He was attempting only to get rid of money that he had that didn't belong to him. And what the recipient did with it, he didn't have any control, intent, design —

NIXON: Yeah, but if he knew —

EHRLICHMAN: — or contemplation.

NIXON: [unclear] if he knew.

EHRLICHMAN: Well, what he — he's told Wilson everything he knows — what he knew then —

NIXON: Yeah, when Bob handed the money over Bob knew that it was going to the defendants.

EHRLICHMAN: Not of a certainty. Not of a certainty, he did not. And that's something Wilson bored in on very hard this morning. He said, "Now, Mr. Haldeman, in effect would you have been surprised to learn that instead of using that money for the defendants, they had used it to pay printing bills?" And Bob says, "Well, I didn't have that strong a conviction about what they were going to use it for. I knew they needed money over there." But he said, "No, it wouldn't have surprised me." So then Wilson bored in on him two or three different ways. This old boy is good. He's quite something. When we got all done, he said, "Well," he said, "I know the questions in the president's mind," and he said, "I want to reserve — get it all done today." But he said, "You must bear in mind the difference between a criminal act —"

NIXON: Yeah, and what else did he say?

EHRLICHMAN: " — and the problems presented to the president by the mere appearance."

NIXON: Yeah, which basically — incidentally that I — it isn't that I trust this fellow Petersen — in a way, he's trying to do his best. He's just all tormented.

EHRLICHMAN: Sure.

NIXON: He loves Mitchell.

EHRLICHMAN: Sure.

NIXON: He loves the White House.

EHRLICHMAN: Yeah.

NIXON: But you know, that's the way it is.

EHRLICHMAN: I understand. Well, it's heartbreaking.

NIXON: Apparently he liked Dean, too.

EHRLICHMAN: Yes, I know he did.

NIXON: Now, the only thing that I — that comes to the back of my mind is that you got to — is that last conversation with Dean about that one hundred and twenty —

EHRLICHMAN: With Bittman?

NIXON: With somebody. Did Dean come in and tell us about that — told me about that?

EHRLICHMAN: About Hunt demanding it?

NIXON: That Bittman said that Hunt needed one hundred twenty thousand dollars for attorneys' fees, et cetera.

EHRLICHMAN: Right, right.

NIXON: And the way Dean's going to tell it or he's going to blow the whistle, right?

EHRLICHMAN: Yeah, now blow the whistle on the national security operation. That was the threat.

NIXON: Was it?

EHRLICHMAN: Yes, sir. And you'll remember our response to that was you cannot defend blackmail in that kind of a situation.

NIXON: That's right.

EHRLICHMAN: And that's all that is, is pure blackmail.

NIXON: Mm-hmm.

EHRLICHMAN: And we said, "No dice." And I could be just as flat-out on that as that's the honest-to-God truth.

NIXON: Now let me just put one other question to you that can be very — I know it's very painful for you to think of this and it is for me too. But anyway — but — I think it would be helpful if you had this [unclear] when you talk the rest of the day — this and that — bother you the rest of the day. I think the separation problem has to be considered. I want you to look at it very coldly now in terms of Bob and the president. We have an atmosphere — Mr. So-and-So — look at this thing in terms of your — about how you were involved in terms of whether it's going to be — and how you were involved in what Dean may say. I don't know what the son of a bitch is going to say. I don't know what you do with a Dean though — he's obviously very upset. He's just lashing out. Goddamn it, I don't know what we've been told. I just don't know, John. Frankly, I'm at a loss. We were all talking frankly, that's why the counsel was sworn.

EHRLICHMAN: Well, as I said —

NIXON: That goddamn Dean.

EHRLICHMAN: As I said this morning, I think you can very truthfully and logically and properly say that —

NIXON: I was trying to bury — I was trying — I was really trying to probe his thought processes. I went down every road we possibly could —

EHRLICHMAN: Exactly right.

NIXON: — and see where we were.

EHRLICHMAN: And it paid off. You see, you're the one who then came back and said, "I've got to have that all written down. Send that man to Camp David if necessary and have him take as much time as necessary and let's get it all down." That's when he was uncovered.

NIXON: I suppose that really isn't true.

EHRLICHMAN: Well —

NIXON: Not that he was uncovered. It was simply the fact that he said, "By God, this thing is such a cancer and so forth that I can't write it and there's no way we make a statement." And I said to you, John, "You better get into it." Take —

EHRLICHMAN: Yes, but I happen to be —

NIXON: Well —

EHRLICHMAN: This may be some measure of hindsight, but I really don't think it is because my very conscious, contemporary reaction when Dean came back and didn't have anything for us was, whoops, there's something more here because Dean could have constructed some kind of an artful evasion if he hadn't been so pervasively involved —

NIXON: [unclear]

EHRLICHMAN: — for the campaign committee or the White House, or whoever he wanted to protect. But the thing that occurred to me when Bob told me what Dean said that he couldn't write it, I just had a mental image of the guy sitting there with big piles of paper saying, "I've just written a confession, and I would be nuts to deliver this to anybody."

NIXON: Well, that's what we have to say.

EHRLICHMAN: Well, I think that's very, very probable.

NIXON: [unclear]

EHRLICHMAN: Yup.

NIXON: Dean's got Shaffer and the rest. I don't know that he can't be — we may be able to exert privilege on Dean before the grand jury but we can't before the press. I still —

EHRLICHMAN: You can at the trial. And you certainly can in the press.

NIXON: [unclear]

EHRLICHMAN: I'd send a fellow around to talk to Dean if this is a problem. Just say, "Look here, you are going to be liable — separately liable — for breach of confidentiality and — "

NIXON: Is that a case?

EHRLICHMAN: Well, I think you ought to get Petersen to advise you on this, but there certainly is a statutory protection, and I think you could invoke it.

NIXON: [unclear] breach of confidentiality of a conversation with the president?

EHRLICHMAN: Well, no, not as such, but on various national security bases. I'm just not that familiar with the statutes. I don't know what all you have in the way of statutory protection, but you remember that our CIA case —

NIXON: Yeah.

EHRLICHMAN: — where the guy was enjoined by the court —

NIXON: Yeah.

EHRLICHMAN: — we fell back on that body of law.

NIXON: Incidentally, the other point he says that Dean obviously knows all of these — and that's why he says Bittman is gravely concerned about the matter of the one twenty because that gets him involved.

EHRLICHMAN: Sure.

NIXON: So, we may not — just Dean may talk about this but Bittman is not likely to. I would say, "What the hell is in it for Bittman to say that we asked for that?" I just ask you, does that involve the lawyer?

EHRLICHMAN: Boy, puts him in the soup. Puts him in the soup, sure.

NIXON: That he came and said, "I want a hundred and twenty for — "

EHRLICHMAN: You bet.

NIXON: "— or otherwise you're going to blow the whistle or something."

EHRLICHMAN: Yeah. Yeah, you're right.

NIXON: So here you've got a —

EHRLICHMAN: Well, this is good information. It'll be helpful — this fits right into our conversation in there. I will talk — I'll tell you what I think I would do —

NIXON: Yeah.

EHRLICHMAN: — if you don't mind. I will take John Wilson aside and talk to him about this separation business.

NIXON: Right. That's right.

EHRLICHMAN: He's very wise and very —

NIXON: I don't know how and we've got to get his judgment on it ultimately now — but Bob said this morning [unclear]. We have to do this one ourselves. We generally are hurting ourselves in this case. I guess we just haven't been hard enough, have we? In a sense, though, let's face it, John Mitchell lurks in the back here. Isn't that what it really gets down to? But God almighty, we weren't protecting the White House now, right?

EHRLICHMAN: That's correct.

NIXON: We weren't protecting that. We're protecting John Mitchell.

EHRLICHMAN: Yes, sir.

NIXON: All the way through.

EHRLICHMAN: In the first instance we were protecting your reelection in a sense. We didn't know what from.

NIXON: That's right.

EHRLICHMAN: Afterwards, though, this cover-up business was pure Mitchell.

NIXON: Sure, now. Bob says that, you know, you're going to look bad if he goes.

EHRLICHMAN: Well, there are two ways of looking at that, obviously —

NIXON: Yeah, but the point is there is that strong argument that people are making that somebody is the president, who — no, I suppose I [unclear]. Let's look at it this way. Let's suppose I don't know [unclear] it. The Dean argument will be that he told me all these things about Haldeman and that I didn't move on it. Correct?

EHRLICHMAN: Sure, and that Dean's being made a scapegoat.

NIXON: He's been made a scapegoat. And then, so all this about Haldeman comes out. Haldeman would probably have to go, wouldn't he? To be quite candid.

EHRLICHMAN: Yeah, because actually they'd drag him out.

NIXON: Yeah.

EHRLICHMAN: You know.

NIXON: With this much in his case.

EHRLICHMAN: It could be played a lot of different ways and back and forth.

NIXON: You've got —

EHRLICHMAN: You've given me some stuff here —

NIXON: Yeah.

EHRLICHMAN: — as a worry for him that we didn't have before that may add to this.

NIXON: Like what?

EHRLICHMAN: Oh, this business about the dispute between Strachan and Magruder.

NIXON: Yeah.

EHRLICHMAN: I think what I'll do — Bob and I talked about this at breakfast. It was his idea —

NIXON: Yeah. What I was thinking was that Bob goes in the way of simply — "I'm going out to fight this battle — I will use my—"

EHRLICHMAN: Yeah.

NIXON: "—my situation has been made untenable and I will fight this battle," and so forth and so on.

EHRLICHMAN: You know what he said?

NIXON: Yeah.

EHRLICHMAN: He said, "I'm going to get *Six Crises* and I'm going to read the chapter about the fund." And he said, "That's going to be my guide."

NIXON: Separability is there, but then you've got to think back as to what the hell Dean is up to with regard to you.

EHRLICHMAN: Yeah, and that's what we were doing when you called. We were going into everything and anything that I could remember that had anything to do with this.

NIXON: Let me come down to the final point. As I look at it at the present time, looking at this evidence, the U.S. attorney would have a hell of a time concluding you were in the conspiracy that — nonindictable [unclear].

EHRLICHMAN: Well, see, they're going over there when they get finished with this.

NIXON: I see, fine. Looking at this evidence I think there is a very strong possibility that Haldeman will be [unclear].

EHRLICHMAN: Yeah.

NIXON: Do you agree with that?

EHRLICHMAN: Well, they seem to think so.

NIXON: They think so?

EHRLICHMAN: Yeah. Yeah.

NIXON: Looking at this evidence, too — however, I think there is a very little possibility that you would be, if you would ever be indicted — that you would be criminally indicted.

EHRLICHMAN: Well, now, they say, though, that the prosecutor like this Glanzer — Gleazer — or whatever his name is, will sometimes indict somebody that he doesn't expect to get a conviction on.

NIXON: Yeah.

EHRLICHMAN: Just to get a big name into the case.

NIXON: Well, he's going to have enough big names, I think, this time.

EHRLICHMAN: Well, that's another thing that they're going to probe.

NIXON: That's right.

EHRLICHMAN: But they said to look after that. Don't take much comfort from the fact that —

NIXON: Well, if you're indicted, that's it.

EHRLICHMAN: Yeah.

NIXON: You will leave the White House — let me put it this way. I do not see you getting convicted.

EHRLICHMAN: Well, I don't either.

NIXON: The second point on Bob — on the conspiracy, is there a chance he'd be convicted? Do they think so?

EHRLICHMAN: Well, they say so far not from what they've heard. They think not — that it is not actionable in the ultimate sense. But, they're being very guarded, obviously, because we're just now giving them the facts and they haven't tested what we're telling them.

NIXON: The way they'd have to do it is to start to build a web that Bob was involved in all this —

EHRLICHMAN: Sure.

NIXON: He rehired Liddy, who received the budget. He received the information —

EHRLICHMAN: Yeah.

NIXON: — and he ordered the three hundred and fifty Gs. That's really the case on Bob, in a nutshell, isn't it?

EHRLICHMAN: It would be a whole elaborate — as you say, a web of no one fact of which would do it.

NIXON: But I think even there, Bob, with a good attorney can beat it.

EHRLICHMAN: Well, I think we've got the best in the town in there.

NIXON: Well, that's all I ask.

EHRLICHMAN: Thank you. That was very helpful.

NIXON: If it's at all useful, let me say I feel that I've — when you've finished with your lawyers and so forth, maybe you and Bob would like drop over to talk a little later.

EHRLICHMAN: All right, fine.

NIXON: You know, when you've got something like this on your mind, you would just as soon talk about it. It's very helpful.

EHRLICHMAN: Thank you.

NIXON: The other thing, too, that I'm trying desperately to keep — the problem is, of course, John, as you know everybody — Henry has come in last night and talked to me about it. I mean it's — they bring up things that I had thought over umpteen times. I don't need to talk to Garment. I don't need to talk to Henry. I don't need to talk to [William] Safire. Ziegler — his work [unclear]. But don't you agree?

EHRLICHMAN: Ron is great. Ron's just been terrific in this.

NIXON: Ron is really innocent. Talk about separability. Okay, give them the judgment.

The fate of Haldeman and Ehrlichman
April 19, 1973, 5:15 p.m.
Richard Nixon and John Ehrlichman
EXECUTIVE OFFICE BUILDING

The talk of the capital on April 19 was the report in the Washington Post *that Dean and Mitchell would be accused by Magruder of planning the Watergate break-in and arranging hush money for the perpetrators. Indictments would follow, according to the article. Ehrlichman arrived at the Oval Office late in the afternoon with new hope for survival, and he made a point of arranging for his lawyers to see Nixon that very day. After the president agreed, Ehrlichman made a strong case for him to keep Haldeman on staff, despite — and even because of — the mounting pressure to fire him. "I have to go back to my Siamese twin analogy," Ehrlichman said. "You cut those Siamese twins apart and somebody dies." To outsiders, Haldeman and Ehrlichman seemed like the twins of Watergate. Inside the Oval Office, though, the "Siamese twins" were Nixon and Haldeman.*

• • •

EHRLICHMAN: I am just coming out of the shower bath. I get kinda woolly. Figured I'd go and just get wet.

NIXON: Good. Your counsel's over at the lawyers'?

EHRLICHMAN: They're there right now.

NIXON: Yeah.

EHRLICHMAN: They have an appointment with Glanzer and Silbert.

NIXON: I thought that it'd be useful to talk to Dick Moore.

EHRLICHMAN: Oh, good.

NIXON: So, we'll see what the hell he recalls.

EHRLICHMAN: Yeah, good. Because I haven't talked to — could I borrow a piece of your paper a minute?

NIXON: Take the whole pad.

EHRLICHMAN: I haven't really talked to Dick.

NIXON: Yeah. Well, I need his report, you know, since they're gonna call him and so forth.

EHRLICHMAN: What else did he recall?

NIXON: He recalled the La Costa [Country Club] meeting.

EHRLICHMAN: Mm-hmm. I hope he recalls it better than I do.

NIXON: Well, his recollection [unclear] — he says Dean at that says, "By the way, the defendants need money, and it's urgent." I told him, [unclear] I said, "Well, you're [unclear] back on this [unclear]." [unclear] says, Bob or John says, "Can't LaRue go underground and raise it?" [unclear] it was three [unclear]. John says [unclear], "Can't Mitchell get it from Rockefeller if you give him half a million dollars?" [unclear] his recollection of the La Costa meeting. [unclear] that of course is [unclear] what you recall too, as I re — as I said.

EHRLICHMAN: Well, I don't recall the Rockefeller.

NIXON: Well, the Rockefeller — look, he won't recall it either, then.

EHRLICHMAN: But, I mean — I just literally don't. In fact —

NIXON: [unclear] discussion with LaRue perhaps you don't [unclear] and so forth. But [unclear] you should be aware of the fact that LaRue and Liddy [unclear] —

EHRLICHMAN: Day to day [unclear].

NIXON: Dick is one guy that ran the program who I think that —

EHRLICHMAN: No, I'll tell you what that — he came and I got that [unclear].

NIXON: Yeah, well, I thought you'd be aware.

EHRLICHMAN: Yeah. That's important. That's important —

NIXON: To see what —

EHRLICHMAN: — what isn't. Does he talk at all about the purpose of that meeting? Because I think that's also important.

NIXON: Oh, yes. Yes. He said for two days he talked about the hearings and programming the hearings and [unclear] and getting a statement from [unclear] work up a statement.

[MANOLO SANCHEZ enters to serve refreshments.]

EHRLICHMAN: Oh, thank you, Manolo.

[SANCHEZ leaves.]

NIXON: You see [unclear] in other words. Oh, yes, he remembered it all. He said this was only the — presentence is out in two days. But this was a [unclear] sign, an agreement I'm [unclear] that I raise it with him. I said, "No. Then, the hell with Dean." But I couldn't talk about it then. I said, "You listen to what" [unclear], personally, I suppose [unclear] Colson about this business [unclear] Kalmbach or something like that. I think that that was where it came to you.

EHRLICHMAN: Came to Haldeman. True?

NIXON: I said, "Can't be [unclear] Kalmbach to raise money for the defendants when we're faced with that." Right?

EHRLICHMAN: Right. No question about that.

NIXON: La Costa after the trial is [unclear] —

EHRLICHMAN: La Costa is just — that's that rainy weekend in February.

NIXON: [unclear] Yeah.

EHRLICHMAN: February 20 or somewhere along in there.

NIXON: Well, this is after — before sentencing?

EHRLICHMAN: They hadn't sentenced them yet as a matter of fact.

NIXON: My — Dean — the other thing is that Moore recollected something about this Bittman conversation, too. He says that Dean told him that Hunt needed money before he gets sentenced. Also he told Dean, "Look, this is blackmail." So that's how that came in. So when Dean came in to see me, and raised the subject [unclear] blackmail to see if I could find [unclear] that Bob was involved in, you know. I guess you weren't in the [unclear] Bob, Dean, and Mitchell. Right? And Bob told me the story that he said that Dean asked, "What about that money?" and Mitchell asked —

EHRLICHMAN: The meeting in Haldeman's office where almost in an aside —

NIXON: Yeah.

EHRLICHMAN: — Dean said to Mitchell, "What about that other matter?"

NIXON: Yeah.

EHRLICHMAN: And Mitchell said, "It's taken care of—"

NIXON: Yeah.

EHRLICHMAN: "—and [unclear]."

NIXON: I assume—

EHRLICHMAN: [unclear]

NIXON: I assume what happened here on that is that Dean's not getting the money here, so he called Mitchell as quick as he could.

EHRLICHMAN: Evidently. Evidently.

NIXON: Dean's whole theme of course, which I've already reported to you [unclear].

EHRLICHMAN: Yeah.

NIXON: That's the only thing you'll have got, John.

EHRLICHMAN: Okay.

NIXON: Those things—don't think that [unclear] if it comes to a—the question of Dean's [unclear] perjury or not, [unclear] very, very hazy about that.

EHRLICHMAN: Yes, how did you leave it with him? Did you—?

NIXON: I'm not talking to him.

EHRLICHMAN: Oh, you aren't—okay. Well, I—if I could suggest a point of view on La Costa—

NIXON: Yeah.

EHRLICHMAN: —it is that our inability to do what you asked us to do at La Costa, which was—

NIXON: Yeah.

EHRLICHMAN: —to draft a public statement which could be—

NIXON: Right.

EHRLICHMAN: —put out as such—

NIXON: Yeah.

EHRLICHMAN: —led in quick succession to—

NIXON: Yeah.

EHRLICHMAN: —your long talks.

NIXON: Listen—

EHRLICHMAN: Dean reported back to you, but it was a fruitless weekend—

NIXON: That's right. That's right.

EHRLICHMAN: —and—

NIXON: The fact that he [unclear] to see me. Right.

EHRLICHMAN: That's right.

NIXON: Yeah.

EHRLICHMAN: And it was a fruitless weekend. Dean kept saying, "You can't say that. You can't say that," and so forth. And that led to your talks with Dean, and that led to Dean going to Camp David.

NIXON: Right.

EHRLICHMAN: And then that eventually led to cracking him.

NIXON: That's right. That's right.

EHRLICHMAN: So it all started in the fact that —

NIXON: That's right.

EHRLICHMAN: — the four of us could not put together —

NIXON: Even this, let me say that this conversation about this money and so forth. You've got to find out who's [unclear].

EHRLICHMAN: Yeah, that's this particular [unclear].

NIXON: That's one of the things that led us to conclude that we had to move off this [unclear]. You know, [unclear] money. There isn't any question, I suppose, that — in the way the whole thing is presented [unclear] possibly concerned with the [unclear] knowledge of — at least knowledge, certain knowledge of that, in Bob's case, a case of the three fifty participation — in the three fifty [unclear] to the [unclear] tell you about that [unclear] again but there were a few things the law —

EHRLICHMAN: Well —

NIXON: [unclear]

EHRLICHMAN: This is where we left it with him. We felt that if you're agreeable —

NIXON: Mm-hmm.

EHRLICHMAN: — the best way to do this would be for them to go over there, talk with the prosecutors and come back.

NIXON: Right.

EHRLICHMAN: Report to us, and then, if you are available, for you to talk to Mr. Wilson confidentially alone.

NIXON: All right.

EHRLICHMAN: He very much has your interest at heart —

NIXON: Right.

EHRLICHMAN: — and he's trying to approach this from your standpoint —

NIXON: Right.

EHRLICHMAN: — rather than from ours, really. And you'll see that.

NIXON: Yeah.

EHRLICHMAN: So, Bob and I agreed privately —

NIXON: Right.

EHRLICHMAN: — that that would be a very desirable thing from your standpoint —

NIXON: Right.

EHRLICHMAN: — to have his counsel.

NIXON: In other words he could if he ever needed somebody to —

EHRLICHMAN: He has forty years of experience in this business.

NIXON: He's for us.

EHRLICHMAN: He's totally loyal — just totally in fact avidly loyal.

NIXON: Right.

EHRLICHMAN: And so rather than to have the two of us strain what he thinks —

NIXON: Let me ask you this — when is he going to see them [unclear]?

EHRLICHMAN: He's there right now. He's there right now. He expects to be here by six o'clock.

NIXON: Could he see me tonight?

EHRLICHMAN: Yes, sir. He'll come back — see you tonight if you don't — you get back from the boat [USS *Sequoia,* the presidential yacht].

NIXON: [unclear]

EHRLICHMAN: He'll come back and — when he can be available to you. [unclear] [laughs] You wouldn't know what to do. The younger of the two is a very steady trial man with a lot of experience.

NIXON: You're both talking to these people?

EHRLICHMAN: Yes, sir. They both know [unclear].

NIXON: You get back and I hope you discuss this and I will discuss it with them, too. You get back with Dean if you can [unclear] around here. [unclear] this on Moore too, and I know it's — I know it sounds unbelievable, but I just wonder about this.

EHRLICHMAN: Let me tell you about that.

NIXON: They don't believe it?

EHRLICHMAN: They say it's a dream world, but that just can't be.

NIXON: I don't agree.

EHRLICHMAN: But no, do —

NIXON: I don't —

EHRLICHMAN: I think you ought to hear their view —

NIXON: Yeah.

EHRLICHMAN: — if it's appropriate — their goal —

NIXON: Dean's going to do it, as damned as anybody.

EHRLICHMAN: They think that he has every incentive to and that there's no way to remove that incentive.

NIXON: Right.

EHRLICHMAN: That's their feeling.

NIXON: So if he goes to jail, he's got a little less incentive to kick the president. Is that it?

EHRLICHMAN: I think that would be [unclear].

NIXON: Can anybody [unclear] keep him from [unclear] from kicking?

EHRLICHMAN: Unless they turn up something different down there. They say that they know Glanzer extremely well.

NIXON: Yeah.

EHRLICHMAN: And they know Silbert well —

NIXON: Right.

EHRLICHMAN: — and they know their boss and —

NIXON: So they'll find out.

EHRLICHMAN: So they'll find out — I think quite a lot.

NIXON: If Petersen has any indication, of course — the —

EHRLICHMAN: Now, they do not have a high opinion of him professionally.

NIXON: No, but I'd have to tell you that if he's any indication of Glanzer and Silbert — [gives instruction to aide] send that to the out box please [unclear] girl [unclear] — yeah, I know. I know. But, I meant that you've got to remember that Petersen, if this reflects the U.S. attorney, came in with Kleindienst and said they, you know, came on with the resignation deal.

EHRLICHMAN: Yeah, yeah.

NIXON: It's their view of the Haldeman [unclear]. We're not going to be panicked by any [unclear].

EHRLICHMAN: That's right.

NIXON: Since you're going to talk to him in person —

EHRLICHMAN: That was [unclear]. They were to be there at four thirty so it's an hour already.

NIXON: — possibly [unclear], correct? [unclear]

EHRLICHMAN: He'll probably want to go on — back to their office if we haven't soaked up all day today here. But I'll arrange for them to come back and see you privately.

NIXON: You have told them about the La Costa — did you recall that the [unclear] of money had come up at La Costa at all or — ?

EHRLICHMAN: I hadn't —

NIXON: I hadn't — that's a new element to me.

EHRLICHMAN: I had touched on it — no, what I told them was that at various times and intervals [unclear].

NIXON: [unclear]

EHRLICHMAN: [unclear] if I didn't have a present recollection, I still —

NIXON: Yeah.

EHRLICHMAN: — you know, I don't have a recollection of that.

NIXON: [unclear] time and intervals.

EHRLICHMAN: That this subject came up in Dean's conversation —

NIXON: Mm-hmm.

EHRLICHMAN: — and that he would ask me for advice —

NIXON: Yeah.

EHRLICHMAN: — he would ask me what to do and almost invariably —

NIXON: I know.

EHRLICHMAN: — I had no response for him.

NIXON: I understand.

EHRLICHMAN: I was helpless in that situation. The one time that I did respond was when he specifically asked if they could use Kalmbach.

NIXON: Yeah.

EHRLICHMAN: And that's the only time.

NIXON: Yeah.

EHRLICHMAN: I've never been able, other than the Bittman thing where I said, "Hell, no" —

NIXON: Yeah.

EHRLICHMAN: — I've just never been able to help him. And so it doesn't surprise me if I said, you know, "Get somebody else to help you, John."

NIXON: Yeah, yeah. Why doesn't LaRue help, so that we could —

EHRLICHMAN: Or Rockefeller or Mitchell or —

NIXON: Dean — Dean, that —

EHRLICHMAN: That doesn't, you know that doesn't nonplus me.

NIXON: Yeah, LaRue [unclear] grounds of course, that that was realized [unclear].

EHRLICHMAN: John was getting increasingly desperate as time went on.

NIXON: Dean.

EHRLICHMAN: Yeah.

NIXON: Trying to keep the lid on.

EHRLICHMAN: Trying to keep the lid on.

NIXON: Which was his job.

EHRLICHMAN: And, I never could help him.

NIXON: [unclear]

EHRLICHMAN: That's right.

NIXON: What's the guy say then about that again? Now he said that — about that being obstruction. He said that isn't on the [unclear].

EHRLICHMAN: Yesterday the — that's right.

NIXON: [unclear]

EHRLICHMAN: He said that the circumstances will be difficult to explain.

NIXON: Yeah.

EHRLICHMAN: No question about that. But he said a great deal rests upon whether Bob intended, believed, and desired — or desired —

NIXON: Yeah.

EHRLICHMAN: — that the funds be used for a specific purpose when he sent 'em back over there.

NIXON: [unclear] now how did Bob fit into the conversation?

EHRLICHMAN: Oh. They just thought that was silly. I went through this whole business of deep six and the guy leaving the country and the Kalmbach episode and all that, and they said, "Well, what do we get for the crimes?" So I said, "You just heard one." And he said, "Well, there's nothing there. It's ridiculous."

NIXON: They don't consider that as being part of a conspiracy [unclear].

EHRLICHMAN: They do not.

NIXON: Why?

EHRLICHMAN: They do not.

NIXON: Because you didn't do anything.

EHRLICHMAN: Because I didn't do anything. And they said, "Why was Kalmbach subservient to you?" And I explained that. And he said, "Well it all fits together." And they just didn't have any trouble with it. Now they may get an earful over there this afternoon. It's the prosecutors' job.

NIXON: Sure, they'll scare 'em to death.

EHRLICHMAN: And so they may have something good when they get back. I've suspected all along that we were being lulled as far as I'm concerned.

NIXON: Yeah.

EHRLICHMAN: And that Dean had unloaded a good deal more than that. And so I'm going to be interested to see what they come back with.

NIXON: To the extent the prosecutors will tell them [unclear] of the two, Dean and Magruder — Magruder's [unclear]. Dean says Magruder is a pathological liar.

EHRLICHMAN: That's true, Magruder's been all over the place in this case.

NIXON: [unclear] Bob I would have thought it was a lie [unclear] hurt Bob.

EHRLICHMAN: Oh, it wasn't. I'm sure it was not intentionally because when I asked him if anybody in the White House had been involved —

NIXON: And you talked to him after you'd already talked to [unclear].

EHRLICHMAN: That's correct. But he said he was telling me everything that I had told you.

NIXON: What did he say?

EHRLICHMAN: He said that he could not in any way implicate Bob, that Strachan, yes — Dean, yes — but not Bob.

NIXON: Strachan, how? By — did he know about — ?

EHRLICHMAN: You see Magruder's testimony is that he sent budgets to Strachan that showed that the thing was going to be done. And then he sent —

NIXON: Strachan denied that —

EHRLICHMAN: — synopses and Strachan —

NIXON: — denies that.

EHRLICHMAN: — denies the budget, admits the synopses.

NIXON: Right.

EHRLICHMAN: And, as a matter of fact, Magruder doesn't even go so far as to say he sent the synopses. He just says, "I told him that they were available. He could come see." But he steadfastly maintains through all of that that he is — that he has no evidence that Haldeman saw any of that stuff. Now —

NIXON: We'll know a little more, I mean, after we have a talk tonight [unclear] to how much the [unclear].

EHRLICHMAN: I think so.

NIXON: I mean that we're at a situation where I think it's just going to be too difficult to wield.

EHRLICHMAN: Yes.

NIXON: Don't let me reach it. I mean I don't — understand, I don't reach it until I — I don't — I'm not going to reach it with anybody else.

EHRLICHMAN: I've tried to — I've tried reasoning this out from the standpoint of your well-being —

NIXON: Exactly.

EHRLICHMAN: — and it seems to me I have to go back to my Siamese twin analogy. You cut those Siamese twins apart and somebody dies.

NIXON: That's right.

EHRLICHMAN: And —

NIXON: Both die.

EHRLICHMAN: Maybe. You are so terribly close in the perception of the press.

NIXON: Yeah.

EHRLICHMAN: Perception of the —

NIXON: I agree with that. But, you also have this situation involved in keeping all this [unclear]. In other words, I couldn't agree more. I believe in fighting like hell and so forth. Trying to keep —

EHRLICHMAN: Well, it isn't really a question of demonstrating loyalty or anything like that.

NIXON: No, no. I believe in trying to keep it if it can be done.

EHRLICHMAN: Yeah, well, I think we have to analyze this, and I think if you kept it, you would have to go out and say, "I have carefully reviewed the evidence which the U.S. attorney and the assistant attorney general have brought me on the subject, [unclear] announced to so and so, [unclear] had to weigh on the one hand this — the validity and seriousness of the charge versus the value to me of the individual — "

NIXON: Yeah.

EHRLICHMAN: " — and the integrity of the office is an overriding consideration." In the — you could do this either way whether he stays or goes.

NIXON: That's right.

EHRLICHMAN: If you say, "Weighing this I've come to the conclusion that — "

NIXON: [unclear]

EHRLICHMAN: It's not clear-cut either way.

NIXON: That's right.

EHRLICHMAN: "I must do so and so."

NIXON: Right.

EHRLICHMAN: But, I think you have to make a public explanation either way.

NIXON: That's right. Yeah. A public explanation is believed. And [unclear] it might be the other, but if we make a public explanation, we're [unclear] the facts. That's all there is to it.

EHRLICHMAN: However, Weicker will.

NIXON: Hmm.

EHRLICHMAN: You know Weicker will.

NIXON: Yeah. Let me say that in that case, doing it that way, [unclear] every intention, I mean I wish we could do it that way, but doing it that way we — we'd say all of these things happened [unclear].

EHRLICHMAN: Yeah.

NIXON: Or I could say I've asked for a week or maybe Haldeman could go out and tell them that.

EHRLICHMAN: Either that or we're going to have to have a statement or synopsis or something. I don't know —

NIXON: Right.

EHRLICHMAN: — how you do that.

NIXON: Here are the facts and people I will [unclear].

EHRLICHMAN: People may disagree with you. It's a judgment call. But this is the way I have to call it. [unclear] If you don't do it that way, then all [unclear] ugly inferences arise. Either way, if you keep him, ugly inferences arise that you're covering up. If you let him go, then the inferences arise that you're disloyal or he's venal or [unclear] that sort of thing. So you've got to go to the [unclear].

NIXON: It seems to be true that both [unclear] and [unclear] yours [unclear] get my —

EHRLICHMAN: It's not too early for you? You won't be back that early, will ya?

NIXON: [unclear] sharp.

EHRLICHMAN: He's very reliable. He's very sharp.

NIXON: You can't [unclear] the options on a thing like resignations.

EHRLICHMAN: Yes. Yes, indeed, we sure have. And —

NIXON: Oh, good. Good. Why [unclear] this point?

EHRLICHMAN: They're very preliminary, but they both try to look at it from your standpoint. That Bob leaving would hurt you more than help you.

NIXON: What's their reason?

EHRLICHMAN: On the fact pattern. In other words that it would look like you were overreacting, number one. That the facts known were not sufficient to justify it so there must be other facts hidden that you're not expressing.

NIXON: Oh, I see.

EHRLICHMAN: And that —

NIXON: In your case doubly so.

EHRLICHMAN: That would be the [unclear] extension [unclear].

NIXON: All right. Second point —

EHRLICHMAN: That's a very tentative conclusion.

NIXON: That's before they go down [unclear].

EHRLICHMAN: [unclear] so you shouldn't rest [unclear] on that.

NIXON: The second point is, well, I don't know.

EHRLICHMAN: Well, [unclear] the second point is [unclear].

NIXON: Well, thank you very much. All right, now let's come down to the hard place. [unclear] that, what did they say? Anything about there is an indictment — that your name is co — an unindicted co-conspirator?

EHRLICHMAN: Well, of course, that's got them on their ear. They just don't even understand what that is. This is something that they can't understand. It's one of the reasons they went down there. Just to find out what that's all about.

NIXON: All right.

EHRLICHMAN: Because they say that's just not proper procedure, and of course they're also just on their ear about the fact that the reporters' notes got out and they say that that is Glanzer. That's a typical prosecutor's trick to give [journalist Jack] Anderson those reporters' notes on Strachan's interrogation.

NIXON: I just — I told Petersen today, I said that came right out of the U.S. attorney's office. Yeah, I said, "Don't give me that stuff that the report — that you changed the report [unclear]."

EHRLICHMAN: Old Wilson said, "Listen, I've been around this town for thirty-five years," and he said that, practicing law here, and he said, "That's the U.S. attorney. That's the only place that could ever [unclear]."

NIXON: It's a terrible thing to do to somebody. What does it do, John? [unclear]

EHRLICHMAN: In a proceeding, of course, what it really does — it just cuts the hell out of Haldeman. It's a vicious cut and it's Glanzer softening him up is what it amounts to.

NIXON: Because —

EHRLICHMAN: Well, they're going to check. They don't know. They don't know.

NIXON: Be very hard to prove that that's what — well, the fact that it came out, apart from who did it —

EHRLICHMAN: Sure.

NIXON: Is [unclear] which the grand jury [unclear].

EHRLICHMAN: They said that there's some story going on the wire about somebody taking eight boxes of political papers out of the White House the day after the burglary.

NIXON: Political papers.

EHRLICHMAN: Yeah, some lawyer is going down and [unclear] court for an order absolving him and his client of contempt by reason of their taking eight boxes of materials out of the White House on the eighteenth of June and holding them until just before the election and then returning them to the Committee for the Re-election. And so they secreted them during that period of time.

NIXON: Apparently —

EHRLICHMAN: [unclear] no idea. No idea at all —

NIXON: Did Colson tell them the truth?

EHRLICHMAN: I assume so, but I haven't the foggiest notion.

NIXON: No.

EHRLICHMAN: Now, he's coming over to see me. He's over there now.

NIXON: Who — Colson?

EHRLICHMAN: Yeah, and I'll find out.

NIXON: But the material is still —

EHRLICHMAN: In the custody of the Committee to Re-elect.

NIXON: Oh, it's not destroyed, so what the hell?

EHRLICHMAN: I don't know even what the significance of it is. He said somebody had some guilty knowledge of the fact the truck came here to [unclear].

NIXON: And the lawyer — the individual who did it?

EHRLICHMAN: And his lawyer.

NIXON: Was charged with it?

EHRLICHMAN: No, no — have petitioned the court for absolution to keep his skirts clean by coming forward and making a clean breast of things, I guess. I — it's all very muddy and obscure to me, but —

NIXON: Shit. [unclear]

EHRLICHMAN: Yup.

NIXON: You still think I should go to Florida?

EHRLICHMAN: [laughs] Well, I don't think there's much point in you sitting here. You can always come back.

NIXON: Yeah.

EHRLICHMAN: You sit here and these things just keep grinding away — something like that every twenty minutes. And —

NIXON: Sure.

EHRLICHMAN: — if you didn't hear that — why — it wouldn't make any difference and you'd be a lot better off for it.

NIXON: That's right.

EHRLICHMAN: So, yeah, I think —

NIXON: Another matter, John, that's right.

EHRLICHMAN: I think you're just better off down there, and everybody can keep you informed, and —

NIXON: [laughs] I hope not.

EHRLICHMAN: Well, I mean you know —

NIXON: Yeah.

EHRLICHMAN: If some big deal comes up, Ron will follow this very closely, and he'll interrupt you if it's something that comes up that has to have your attention.

NIXON: Eight boxes of —

EHRLICHMAN: Political material — whatever that is.

NIXON: Went over to the Committee to Re-elect?

EHRLICHMAN: Eventually. But it stayed hidden for months. [unclear] Apparently [unclear] hadn't had his name in the paper for a while so he reported that his safe had been broken into this morning. Like a movie star.

"This thing is so frigging bizarre."
April 19, 1973, 9:37 p.m.
Richard Nixon and Bob Haldeman
WHITE HOUSE TELEPHONE

Early in the evening of April 19, Nixon met with the lawyers representing Haldeman and Ehrlichman. One was Wilson, the other was Frank Strickler — two of the toughest, even gruffest attorneys around. For over an hour they worked on Nixon, arguing that for him to fire their clients would be equivalent to labeling them as guilty. Not only did Wilson and Strickler implore Nixon to retain Haldeman and Ehrlichman, they wanted him to make a public statement of faith and support for both of them. No sooner had they left than Nixon received word that someone representing Dean had contacted the Washing-

ton Post *to say that Dean would not become the "scapegoat" of Watergate. Furthermore, his testimony would implicate Haldeman and other ranking White House officials at the core of the scandal. Haldeman was the only one mentioned by name. In a telephone call with the president that night, Haldeman discussed the advice of the two lawyers for Nixon to stand by his aides. Haldeman broke with them. "I don't think," he said, "that you as president should now endorse anybody." They also analyzed Dean's announcement. Nixon was headed to Florida for the Easter weekend, while Haldeman tried to decide what he would do for the holiday.*

• • •

NIXON: Bob?

HALDEMAN: Yes, sir.

NIXON: Oh, hi. I talked to the two boys here.

HALDEMAN: Couple of characters, aren't they?

NIXON: They really are, but it was very useful — very interesting. I say, they didn't — they only had a half-hour with the U.S. attorneys —

HALDEMAN: Yeah.

NIXON: — and I said stand firm.

HALDEMAN: Ha-ha. They had a —

NIXON: Yeah.

HALDEMAN: — short session. Apparently they had — those guys had a busy day. They had Hunt in there and all this [unclear] breaking on the —

NIXON: Yeah. What is that? Have you ever found out what the hell it is?

HALDEMAN: No. Just that, I haven't found out and I don't know if anyone knows or not. Nobody seems to have any idea what it is. Ehrlichman had some [unclear] on it that it was offered to Silbert at some point and he didn't want it, which has put him in a very awkward position which is — he is on — he's denouncing the whole story as preposterous.

NIXON: He's denouncing it.

HALDEMAN: Silbert is, yeah.

NIXON: What is this? Eight cases of stuff that was carried out of the White House. Is that what it is?

HALDEMAN: That's what they say. Out of Hunt's, it was the contents of Hunt's desk.

NIXON: Eight cases?

HALDEMAN: [laughs] Six cases I guess.

NIXON: Oh, that's what it is.

HALDEMAN: Six cartons of —

NIXON: And carried to where, to an apartment?

HALDEMAN: It was taken to someplace where it was stored somewhere by this guy's client. This guy's a lawyer who's telling the story. He says his client stored it for the summer and then returned it to the Committee to Re-elect just before the election.

NIXON: [unclear] don't have then.

HALDEMAN: Which is a weird story.

NIXON: They have it now then. They have the material?

HALDEMAN: Well, they don't. I don't know where the material is. What this guy is doing apparently as all this stuff is coming out this guy's scared he's going to get hung on an obstruction of justice thing and so he's going in and filing notice that he knew about this —

NIXON: Who is the guy, Bob? Is he somebody that worked for the committee or —

HALDEMAN: It's a lawyer. I don't know who his client is.

NIXON: That's what I meant. Who's the client?

HALDEMAN: I don't know. I have no idea who his client is. He won't say. That's very strange.

NIXON: Colson doesn't really know?

HALDEMAN: I don't know. I haven't — John Ehrlichman talked to Colson about it so he may have more of a reading on it.

NIXON: Well, just another one of those things.

HALDEMAN: [unclear] run all the way through with John. We have another one that the *Post* going to tell the story tomorrow.

NIXON: Yeah.

HALDEMAN: This is an associate of John Dean's who is seeking to make John Dean's version of this whole thing public so that Dean, in his testimony before the grand jury, will implicate people above and below himself and will state that Haldeman engineered a cover-up to hide the involvement of presidential aides in the [unclear] operation, and that one close associate said that Dean is prepared to tell whatever role he might have played in the Watergate case came as a result of orders from superiors in the White House, despite the allegations Dean had no advance knowledge of the bugging, that the truth is long and broad and it goes up and down, higher and lower, and that they can't make a case that this was just Mitchell and Dean. Dean will welcome the opportunity to tell his side to the grand jury. He's not going to go down in flames for the activities of others. The *Post* called the White House for comment on that —

NIXON: Oh, boy.

HALDEMAN: — tried to reach me, I guess, for comment. [unclear]

NIXON: Yeah.

HALDEMAN: And [unclear] this guy, that he called, he tried to reach Dean and finally got through to him and he's having his calls screened by Fielding and he's hiding in a hotel somewhere. Dean called him back —

NIXON: Yeah.

HALDEMAN: — and Ron gave him the story and Dean said his first comment was, "Oh, fuck." And then he said, "I have a pretty good suspicion who it is and he's got things scrambled. I never mentioned Haldeman. I just said higher up and [unclear] apparently." And he said — then Ron said well, "Why don't you call the *Post* and [unclear] — "

NIXON: Yeah.

HALDEMAN: " — the story's not true before they run it." Dean said, "Well, Ron, there's some fact and some fiction in it and [unclear] call them and deny it." And he said why — Dean then said to Ron, "Why don't you call the *Post* and say that they can't run the story unless Dean confirms it and Dean hasn't confirmed it." Ron said, "That's ridiculous, John, and you know it. They won't hold on that. Ron suggested that Dean have Fielding call the *Post* and handle it. And Dean said, "Well, I, maybe I can do that. I want you to know I'm not playing games. This is a fishing-type story and they're just trying to smoke something out." Later Dean called Ron back, just a minute ago as a matter of fact, and he said, "I can't call the *Post*, but why don't you, Ron? Call the guy from the *Post* and say that you have talked with me and that at no time did I say that Haldeman was in [unclear].

NIXON: Well, so [unclear].

HALDEMAN: So Ron's going to try that but —

NIXON: Yeah.

HALDEMAN: — he's afraid that Dean cleverly waited till nine thirty to tell him that so that it would be too late to change the story.

NIXON: [unclear] this is a look, Bob. These are the things — we sort of expect this, don't we?

HALDEMAN: Sure.

NIXON: The Dean thing. And we just stand firm on it. That's all, don't you agree? What the hell else can you do?

HALDEMAN: I don't think we want to [unclear], more of it lying down than we have to.

NIXON: I agree, I agree. Except I don't know what the hell to do with Dean. That's the problem, isn't that it?

HALDEMAN: Dean's obviously got other people playing his game now that are tougher than he intends to be.

NIXON: His lawyer probably, huh?

HALDEMAN: I would say his lawyer, yeah.

NIXON: His associates up and down, huh. Was he referring to Ehrlichman and you and who the, who's down?

HALDEMAN: Well, Colson —

NIXON: Colson, of course.

HALDEMAN: Or it could be people over at the committee, or you know, LaRue and Mitchell —

NIXON: Mitchell, right.

HALDEMAN: All sorts of people.

NIXON: Your fellows, I asked them their judgment and they said that [unclear] for whatever it's worth, I mean they don't buy the Garment theory. You know?

HALDEMAN: You mean on our taking any action now?

NIXON: On might — yes, on —

HALDEMAN: On you taking any action now.

NIXON: — on resigning. They said, well, we just have to — of course with all this you have to remember they said that they didn't see that it would. They just — it would be an admission of guilt. That's what they'd say.

HALDEMAN: Well, I think they're right.

NIXON: That's the point. So we're going to have to fight it out.

HALDEMAN: An admission of guilt [unclear] as long as everywhere else really screws things up.

NIXON: But the point is that what you do is to let them run their story and then — their stories and so forth and so on, but then we have to play it as they say, day by day, and the U.S. attorney is confronted with a tough choice, whether he's gonna indict or put you on a list of nonindictable people.

HALDEMAN: Or nothing at all, which is what they think he's going to do.

NIXON: At this moment, yes.

HALDEMAN: Yeah.

NIXON: They don't think he's got corroboration but if he doesn't, why that's fine, and —

HALDEMAN: They probably told you they find this whole procedure highly —

NIXON: Yes.

HALDEMAN: — irregular.

NIXON: Yeah, they do, but they say it's done. It's irregular but it's done.

HALDEMAN: Yeah.

NIXON: Ah —

HALDEMAN: That guy's really an interesting guy.

NIXON: Yeah, he sure is. I like 'em both.

HALDEMAN: I do, too.

NIXON: But they both say they have — I don't think they've seen these stories, but I mean they aren't going to be affected by stories that come out. I told 'em, I said, "You're gonna have a hell of a lot of stories here. It's gonna be blasting off." And I think you gotta expect more of it, don't you?

HALDEMAN: Yeah.

NIXON: Yeah. We just batten down the hatches and take it. Isn't that right?

HALDEMAN: I'm not sure how [unclear]. We've gotta get the legal part perfected —

NIXON: Yeah.

HALDEMAN: — and then we've gotta move on the public.

NIXON: On the PR.

HALDEMAN: We can't just hunker down and take it for —

NIXON: I agree, I agree. They, of course, ruled. I didn't talk to them about — what do they think about your making a statement or something or that sort of thing. They —

HALDEMAN: They're worried about it, but they — see, they're not close to it —

NIXON: Yeah.

HALDEMAN: — at this point —

NIXON: That's right.

HALDEMAN: I think there's, you know, we can —

NIXON: Right.

HALDEMAN: — probably convince them that that's not a bad idea.

NIXON: Right.

HALDEMAN: They've gone over my statement. I've given it to 'em.

NIXON: Yeah, right. Right.

HALDEMAN: They have a lot of — they don't have much trouble with it, except in a couple areas —

NIXON: Right, right.

HALDEMAN: — and —

NIXON: Incidentally, are you and John going to Florida?

HALDEMAN: I don't know. We were planning to.

NIXON: Yeah.

HALDEMAN: But the thing with them, we're trying to figure now whether we should or not. It may be that we ought not to be gone this weekend.

NIXON: Ought to work with your attorney?

HALDEMAN: Yeah, yeah.

NIXON: Probably so, probably so, but do what you want. You know, you're certainly welcome.

HALDEMAN: Yeah, well, that's very nice.

NIXON: Nice, hell, it's just whatever you want. You know you're —

HALDEMAN: It — we were concerned about appearance if we don't go, or if I don't, but I don't really think that matters much, especially —

NIXON: No.

HALDEMAN: — because it's Easter.

NIXON: It's Easter. You're going to stay with your family.

HALDEMAN: No, I hadn't thought about it. And we can just say you're going down to spend Easter with your family and we're spending Easter with our families.

NIXON: That's right. It's a family deal, sure.

HALDEMAN: If we don't go, what we might do if it's okay is go up to Camp David —

NIXON: Right, right.

HALDEMAN: — for a day or two.

NIXON: Very excellent idea.

HALDEMAN: We've got reporters camping on the door here now —

NIXON: Oh, Christ, yes! Go up to Camp David, Bob.

HALDEMAN: Well, we'll see, but —

NIXON: Incidentally, and I — the cabinet tomorrow, be sure to be there.

HALDEMAN: Yes, sir. Don't worry.

NIXON: Don't worry. We're gonna be right there and a lot of [unclear]. I'll just state it out front, you know, my own conviction. Don't you think I should to the cabinet?

HALDEMAN: Yeah, but don't give your own conviction about you're gonna follow this through, but don't support anybody. Don't say you'll stand by us or anything.

NIXON: Well, why not? I mean that —

HALDEMAN: I just don't think you should. Look, there are so many weird bounces in this. If one of us gets a bad bounce at some point and has to do something then you don't want egg on your face.

NIXON: Right. [unclear] I say then, that we've [unclear] investigating this whole thing. That I —

HALDEMAN: And that "I'm not going to mention any names."

NIXON: Any names.

HALDEMAN: "Because as I said publicly I will say privately to you. There is going to be no cover-up in this."

NIXON: Right.

HALDEMAN: And —

NIXON: And that there's never —

HALDEMAN: "This is gonna — that our record on this investigation is gonna prove that we've done everything we could in the proper fashion."

NIXON: Right. That's what you say.

HALDEMAN: Affecting both the need to prosecute and the need to protect.

NIXON: Right. You'd prefer it and rather than to say that I stand by Ehrlichman and Haldeman and that sort of thing that's what I would [unclear].

HALDEMAN: Because, see, the thing is nobody yet has [unclear] a word about, really about Ehrlichman and they're now all saying that there is no evidence on me.

NIXON: Until this story that's a — Dean, though.

HALDEMAN: Well, yeah, that's right. And that's Dean and that, it may not go out.

NIXON: The *Post* would use it, don't you think?

HALDEMAN: I don't know, they may not. Tell me what, there's a —

NIXON: It's a dangerous thing.

HALDEMAN: — [unclear] being played here. There's a lot of rough games being played here and it's —

NIXON: They may be afraid of the libel?

HALDEMAN: We come out better playing a strong game than we do a weak game, all the way along, but I don't think in that —

NIXON: Yeah.

HALDEMAN: — that you as president should now endorse anybody.

NIXON: [unclear] I guess you're right.

HALDEMAN: Because, in the first place, if you say I —

NIXON: First of all, first —

HALDEMAN: [unclear] Haldeman and [unclear] Ehrlichman —

NIXON: What do I say about Mitchell?

HALDEMAN: Then you — well, what do you say about Mitchell, what do you say about Dean?

NIXON: That's right.

HALDEMAN: There's a lot more suspicion on Dean now. Are you gonna say you stand by me, but not by — ?

NIXON: That's right, that's right. And if I say that, then Dean says, what the hell, why don't I stand by him?

HALDEMAN: You could say, "I'm not gonna mention any names, but I would caution any of you to come to any conclusions about any individuals—"

NIXON: Yeah, that's right.

HALDEMAN: "—because there are a lot of those charges in here as well as some valid ones—"

NIXON: That's right. That's right.

HALDEMAN: "—and until they are properly sorted out, it would be very wise for everybody to keep his mouth shut—"

NIXON: Right.

HALDEMAN: "—and his mind open."

NIXON: Right. That's good, Bob. That's good. Well, that's—this thing about this stuff and Hunt stuff that was carted up. I don't know what now—

HALDEMAN: [unclear] it's incredible. This thing is so frigging bizarre that it's beyond—

NIXON: Yeah, but you say Silbert, what does he say about it? I didn't hear that.

HALDEMAN: Well, Ehrlichman has some story, I guess he got from Colson, saying that it was, this material was offered to Silbert at some point. They said they'd give it to him and he said he didn't want it, and that puts him in a very sticky wicket now that it's known that it exists. So he has said this story that this lawyer had it—that this lawyer's client had it for all through the summer—it's preposterous. It's kind of a stupid thing for him to say. There's no point in his saying anything. He overreacted, I guess, to this and lawyers may have told you when they talked with Silbert today, they said he was very uptight—

NIXON: Mm-hmm.

HALDEMAN: —and very formal, and—

NIXON: Yeah.

HALDEMAN: —and obviously [unclear] harassed. They don't know Silbert very well though, they know—

NIXON: But Silbert, yeah, they've only met him once. Does [unclear] the law—the lawyer says that he offered it to Silbert? Is that the story?

HALDEMAN: No, [unclear] Colson says, so Colson obviously must know something about this and I think John—I didn't get the full fill on this because John came in at the end of the meeting [unclear] and [unclear] in and—

NIXON: Mm-hmm. Colson—that it was offered to Silbert and—

HALDEMAN: Yeah.

NIXON: —it was contents of his safe?

HALDEMAN: [unclear]

NIXON: His office.

HALDEMAN: [unclear] his office [unclear] safe obviously because his safe they didn't get in so—and it doesn't, they said that things from his desk—

NIXON: Yeah.

HALDEMAN: —from Hunt's desk. It was the next morning. See, that could be Colson, who was worried about the safe, as I recall —

NIXON: Yeah.

HALDEMAN: —too, who may have told somebody, you know, "For heaven's sake get over there and do something."

NIXON: Yeah.

HALDEMAN: Well —

NIXON: Anyway —

HALDEMAN: We gotta be careful not to draw conclusions.

NIXON: That's right.

HALDEMAN: You just really don't know.

NIXON: We don't know. That's right.

HALDEMAN: And it would be awful unfair to somebody by —

NIXON: That's right. I couldn't agree more.

HALDEMAN: — by skipping something.

NIXON: That's what — we're not going to do that. Well, it's certainly — the difficult one here to figure out is Dean, isn't it?

HALDEMAN: Yes, sir.

NIXON: Goddamn him. He's — I don't know what —

HALDEMAN: He's totally distorted in his own mind now and he —

NIXON: Yeah.

HALDEMAN: — consequently, I guess, very dangerous —

NIXON: Yeah.

HALDEMAN: — but, sort of pathetic at the same time.

NIXON: Yeah, trying to save himself.

HALDEMAN: He's lost his moorings and his, you know —

NIXON: [unclear] saying anything.

HALDEMAN: — swinging out in all kinds of ways.

NIXON: That's right. Okay.

HALDEMAN: We'll just have to see.

NIXON: That's right. Thank you.

HALDEMAN: Okay.

"God, it's complex."

April 20, 1973, 8:15 a.m.
Richard Nixon and Bob Haldeman
OVAL OFFICE

The cascading bad news continued. Former secretary of the treasury John Connally was now a target of the investigation of what would later be termed the "milk fund," questionable donations to Nixon's presidential campaign from the Associated Milk Producers, Inc., a conglomerate of 20 dairy cooperatives. Rather than getting in front of the news, as Nixon desperately hoped, he was falling further and further behind. The accusations were now multiplying so quickly that Nixon and Haldeman struggled to reconstruct their schedules — whom they met with, when, and the subjects discussed.

• • •

NIXON: I don't know whether we can do anything about getting the grand jury process speeded up.

HALDEMAN: It's a strange thing. I — it's hard to figure what they're doing. I guess they're so —

NIXON: Well, they got [unclear] Mitchell today.

HALDEMAN: Yeah, they're so inundated with all this sidebar stuff that, you know, they lob in these six pieces of [laughs] material.

NIXON: Look, I see this morning — it says the lawyer says that it had Watergate bugging stuff —

HALDEMAN: Yeah.

NIXON: — in it. So —

HALDEMAN: Yeah.

NIXON: The other guy on the staff wanted the legal, and apparently it was delivered before he was charged, so it was an obstruction of justice. Did he stick it out? I was just curious as to how the hell it got out of here.

HALDEMAN: If that applies, the lawyer cautioned John on that. They have that one case on John Connally that they —

NIXON: Yeah.

HALDEMAN: — except that he said there's — God, it's complex.

NIXON: Yeah. I know that but let me say that on that, or as far as we know, Bob, nobody here knew anything about it. I never heard about it. Have you heard anything about Haldeman's crap-out?

HALDEMAN: No, sir.

NIXON: Did you think Colson swears he ain't heard about — ?

HALDEMAN: I don't know [unclear] sums up.

NIXON: Well, Dean's story is predictable.

HALDEMAN: Well, I'm not really sure what Dean's story is. It — well, yeah, for sure that he is saying there were higher-ups and lower-downs also involved. He's determined he's not going to be alone.

NIXON: Right.

HALDEMAN: And the *Post* modified the story because they ran a — see, originally they were saying Haldeman engineered the cover-up operation.

NIXON: They can't say that.

HALDEMAN: Now they said Haldeman and others in the White House were involved in the cover-up, which at least is not quite as —

NIXON: That's right.

HALDEMAN: — as —

NIXON: That's the point about the lawyers [unclear]. They've been accused of trying to go into that one with quite a summary and they said, well, it's a question of the intent to turn over the truth [unclear] you object?

HALDEMAN: Well, if it's a question of intent then there's no problem.

NIXON: If you had knowledge, of course, you might admit it, but you [unclear]. They said they needed money. You said, "All right, turn it over to LaRue." [unclear] Strachan [unclear] wouldn't you say Strachan?

HALDEMAN: Strachan, yeah. Strachan, I would guess, had less knowledge than I did. I mean, I think he —

NIXON: What about the money? Did he turn it over?

HALDEMAN: He turned it over, but I don't think he had any knowledge of why he was turning it —

NIXON: Let me ask you about one conversation. The only thing that troubles me about this is my own recollection of a conversation with Dean [unclear] that last — that what — where you were with him when he said that Bittman had stated that he needed money for Dean's attorneys' fees at forty thousand dollars.

HALDEMAN: I think — I can't figure out when that was and I can't find any notes on it.

NIXON: Were you in the room with them?

HALDEMAN: I thought I was, but the meeting that you had for — and according to your log — that you had where I was in the room with Dean, it was an hour — I mean a hundred-and-ten-minute — two-hour meeting —

NIXON: Yeah.

HALDEMAN: — with Dean. But it was in the morning.

NIXON: Well —

HALDEMAN: I don't know why, but I distinctly have the feeling that the meeting that I remember was in the evening and I remember discussing —

NIXON: But you do remember talking about that, with the —

HALDEMAN: Yeah.

NIXON: — that with the — with the thing?

HALDEMAN: Yeah, I do.

NIXON: Now, I was there. Do you remember where the million dollars, where I said how long would it take to — take it?

HALDEMAN: I remember it was general discussion — you know, kind of running out the string.

NIXON: Yeah.

HALDEMAN: [unclear]

NIXON: But did Dean as well say that I said, "Well, let's go get the money"?

HALDEMAN: Oh, no. I don't think so.

NIXON: Yeah, because basically, I was very — as I told you, I was prepared to be of assistance. I said, "Christ, turn over any of the cash we got." You know what I mean?

HALDEMAN: [unclear]

NIXON: I wasn't thinking of cover-up. I was just thinking in the moment — trying to hold the line. We've got our own ducks to roll.

HALDEMAN: Well, you may have said something about — you know — well — you know, when he said they had to have the money. You may have said something about — well, that we ought to be able to get —

NIXON: Yeah.

HALDEMAN: — we ought to be able to get the money, but —

NIXON: Right.

HALDEMAN: — but then we got into the thing with running out the string.

NIXON: But —

HALDEMAN: You know, the —

NIXON: Yeah.

HALDEMAN: [unclear]

NIXON: Basically what the issue is was whether we could get the money quite [unclear]. We didn't — you, Dean, and what — how did it eventually get back to Mitchell so that he did that?

HALDEMAN: I don't know.

NIXON: Well, Bob, you were in the room and Mitchell was there.

HALDEMAN: But I — Mitchell wasn't there.

NIXON: No, but when it was discussed in your office. Do you remember that?

HALDEMAN: In my office? The only thing that was discussed we were in general meeting on the others — not that point. And Mitchell had an interrupted point and then Dean [unclear]. Mitchell had a whole list of things.

NIXON: Yeah.

HALDEMAN: [unclear] covered [unclear] long even there.

NIXON: Yeah.

HALDEMAN: We got a chance, but didn't relate to the general subject — basics of it. He said to Dean, I'm not sure of the words, but in effect, what have you done about the —

NIXON: Yeah.

HALDEMAN: — the Hunt thing —

NIXON: Yeah.

HALDEMAN: — or that other problem?

NIXON: Yeah, right.

HALDEMAN: Something that — it was clear to all of us that — what he was talking about. But it was not spelled out in any detail. "What have you done about it?" And Dean looked kind of puzzled and he said, "Well, I don't know." Then he just kind of, like that, and Mitchell said, "Oh, I guess it's taken care of." And we just — nobody asked any more questions, or —

NIXON: Yeah.

HALDEMAN: — gave any more answers. That was the extent of it and we assumed from that thing that Mitchell had it under control, whatever he's supposed —

NIXON: See in effect Dean imparted knowledge to me among others that the — Bittman had, you know, wanted the money. Did I — ?

HALDEMAN: That's right.

NIXON: Two places where others, if they had knowledge, one when Colson came in and said, "Well, Hunt wanted clemency. That one there's no problem because I handled it right." In this case.

HALDEMAN: That was —

NIXON: You remember?

HALDEMAN: — that was in January, I guess, apparently because —

NIXON: Oh, no. No, shortly after the campaign. You know, that's what he said before Christmas, but whatever it was —

HALDEMAN: But on this one I don't see that you have any problem at all. In the first place, at that time you were in the investigation of the case. You were probing, you know, all directions with everybody you could get —

NIXON: That's correct.

HALDEMAN: — and everything you could get, with no obligation to move in at any fixed time — only an obligation to work this thing out. The other factor in that is that was clearly — distinctly as the threat was relayed — related to national security. Because Hunt specifically said he needed this or he was going to spill beans on —

NIXON: [unclear]

HALDEMAN: — the seamy stuff he did for Ehrlichman, and that, as you instantly knew, anything he did for Ehrlichman was involved in the national security project over here.

NIXON: And we couldn't pay blackmail for that.

HALDEMAN: And we didn't.

NIXON: Well, we're talking —

HALDEMAN: You didn't —

NIXON: — we're talking about, I guess — I don't know. I don't know how much we should be talking about any of this.

HALDEMAN: I don't think Dean's going to do that. I don't think it's going to come out at all. It's privileged conversation, that's for sure.

NIXON: That's for sure. But the reason, you see, that I —

HALDEMAN: Whatever was done, it was done by Mitchell. He lobbed it down here.

NIXON: Right. The reason I want to let you know that [unclear] what happened with Bittman — got ahold of Dean [unclear] the reason that strategy didn't work. The reason I want you to know — the reason I had to treat Dean — you know, as Ehrlichman — you know, in the meantime wanted me to fire him on Monday because of his resignation. You've got to remember that he has sat here and talked at great length to me about this damn case and he wanted a reason. You know he was desperate to see what he could do. You don't agree?

HALDEMAN: No, you were investigating him then. You were trying to get out of him at that point — the first place, at that point you had no reason to believe him. Because, you now have found he was lying on various things so what you had you couldn't act on what he told you. You could merely receive what he told you to determine and then check that out against other things.

NIXON: Well, we say he was lying about — in our fairness to him we have to say [unclear] for us that he was doing it. Because I had told him on several occasions, "You've sure done a hell of a job here." You know, "Good job."

HALDEMAN: Well—

NIXON: I wasn't speaking to the job he'd done on the — on raising money. I was thinking of the way he handled all—

HALDEMAN: That's right. Which we thought he had — but now you point out that there was — that he was playing a double game apparently.

NIXON: I think probably [unclear]. On the money raising I guess we didn't know he was doing that. Yes, I guess we did know it.

HALDEMAN: Oh, no. We knew he was doing something.

NIXON: We knew he was pressing on — you mean like, for example, the activation of Kalmbach — which is he produced you in that, right?

HALDEMAN: No question about that. We told the lawyers and they have no trouble with it.

NIXON: They — what, they just said, "That's all right. You didn't do anything."

HALDEMAN: That's right.

NIXON: Could they be asked permission? They said okay. Well, the lawyers said we're going to have to think about it over the weekend. I think it's just great you, John, and families — I want you all to move to Camp David and use it.

HALDEMAN: Well, it's very nice.

NIXON: Use the nice one.

HALDEMAN: I don't know whether that'll — I think we just have to see what we need. The first thing is to —

NIXON: Get out of your house if you can.

HALDEMAN: Yeah, well, this goddamn press had me straddled there last night.

NIXON: Oh, shit. I don't see what—

HALDEMAN: They do it every morning. But the — that's no problem — that—

NIXON: Yeah, sure.

HALDEMAN: [unclear]

NIXON: Well, be free to go, Bob.

HALDEMAN: The main thing — what — I'm trying to go at this in an orderly way, because we've been kind of dashing around —

NIXON: Yeah.

HALDEMAN: — and we've got to get —

NIXON: Right.

HALDEMAN: — we've got to perfect and solidify our legal base —

NIXON: Right.

HALDEMAN: — and then I hope to get that done fast.

NIXON: Yeah.

HALDEMAN: I mean — and work with these guys to get it done —

NIXON: Good.

HALDEMAN: — so we know exactly where we are — what our problems are — what our strengths are.

NIXON: Take them with you to Camp David.

HALDEMAN: Only thing I say — come up [unclear].

NIXON: No, take him up.

HALDEMAN: But, we'll [unclear]. Once that is settled, then I want to turn to trying to —

NIXON: To the public relations.

HALDEMAN: — work a public plan out and work out all these kinks and look down the road because I think we can —

NIXON: Do better.

HALDEMAN: — deal with that effectively, too. And I —

NIXON: Can I ask you one thing? Could you do something to [unclear] let's get a line on this money thing — in terms of saying goddamn it it's all right.

HALDEMAN: But we have to —

NIXON: You've got to say that. You've got to say, "Yes, money was raised for the [unclear] worked for the committee and they worked. They were in trouble and they were entitled to legal counsel [unclear] assistance." That's what the purpose of it was.

HALDEMAN: But that's why we've got to get the legal claims. The lawyers [unclear] and they've got to figure out where there's any legal problems with them. Just raise the question [unclear].

NIXON: I'd rather be on the offensive on that. Say, if you can — you could say, "Yes, money was raised." Obviously the money was raised so why did they put it on the doorstep? Well, that's the way it was given to Mrs. Hunt. That was the way she handled it — raised the cash for that purpose.

HALDEMAN: Well, you've got to separate — in the first place, we — as far as I know, we were involved in the raising of very little money. Because all we were involved in the raising of was okaying Kalmbach. And I think that was not very much money, I don't know.

NIXON: Yeah.

HALDEMAN: Uh —

NIXON: Except —

HALDEMAN: The other thing, as we were — I was involved in the moving of the three fifty —

NIXON: That's right.

HALDEMAN: — which was, in my view, and under advice of counsel — worked out in order to put money where it belonged. Now I sure as hell knew, and I can't argue that —

NIXON: That they needed money.

HALDEMAN: — that they needed money. That was a way to persuade them to take this money. Work out a way of handling the receipt of this money. What they did with it, I haven't any idea.

NIXON: I'm glad Mitchell at least is having the good sense to come clean to the extent of the fact you had knowledge — the three you saw in *Time* this morning.

HALDEMAN: No.

NIXON: Well, he admitted—he did have three meetings.

HALDEMAN: Oh, really?

NIXON: He's going to testify today—but that he had turned it off—

HALDEMAN: Well, that's true.

NIXON: —and rejected the plan. I think you may have two consummate lawyers here, Dean and Magruder.

HALDEMAN: Well—

NIXON: Magruder I'm sure.

HALDEMAN: Well, except it's not your thing [unclear] because Magruder states that press sources can still be botched up. Magruder still has that story of going down to Key Biscayne.

NIXON: Yeah.

HALDEMAN: Now, there were two meetings and Mitchell knows Dean—

NIXON: And Magruder [unclear].

HALDEMAN: See, that's why Mitchell sent Liddy [unclear] because Liddy [unclear] Magruder, who was at the third meeting. The third meeting being Key Biscayne—

NIXON: How does Mitchell keep quiet?

HALDEMAN: —Dean wasn't at. And I think, apparently—see, they had Liddy over there yesterday—

NIXON: Mm-hmm.

HALDEMAN: —and he wouldn't talk.

NIXON: Is that right?

HALDEMAN: In spite of your signal.

NIXON: I did my job.

HALDEMAN: You're supposed to. [laughs]

NIXON: And that's why Dean wanted me to get him to talk. I did my job. The U.S. attorneys know. I'm glad I did.

HALDEMAN: I'm glad you did, too. Well, we'll just step—

NIXON: Sure.

HALDEMAN: Well, I really—we need to get the money back. Get out ahead of it. Get a line on it. And we need to get—I hope I can get out ahead on the whole thing. I don't know if they'll let me. Work out a way to get out [unclear]. I'd like to—with all this stuff that's busting. Now, I'd like to sort of just bust the whole thing loose. Lay it out and then see what happens.

NIXON: Say that by—you say that the president's suggesting that you would be perfectly willing—in other words, the idea that now the case [unclear] could knock off. This time give the reasons for this time because of this and that. Now here are the facts.

HALDEMAN: That—I've got to say that I—these are the facts as I know them regarding my situation. I—see, I used to be worried about having to be told to testify about hearsay. I'm no longer worried about that because I now find the hearsay I was given, some of it was clearly not true. In other words, even the people I was relying about weren't telling the truth.

NIXON: I'm not talking about that.

HALDEMAN: So, I don't know — I was — all I say is I don't know what the facts are — and a lot of it [unclear] whether I have to talk or not. I — there's no question about the presidential communications.

NIXON: Do you feel that clearly is designed to — ?

HALDEMAN: [unclear] said he didn't [unclear].

NIXON: Do you feel that — I think still provides for your employer, don't you?

HALDEMAN: Absolutely.

NIXON: That's the story every day, isn't it?

HALDEMAN: Yeah, but that's — there's going to be a story every day and there's no point in reading —

NIXON: Well, [unclear] but —

HALDEMAN: I know, but it —

NIXON: You say anything about [unclear].

HALDEMAN: It's there. I was just talking to Timmons who — you know, we've got a good crew around here [unclear]. Well, we — I understand you want to help.

NIXON: Except for [unclear], they all want to help.

Burgeoning

April 20, 1973, 11:07 a.m.
Richard Nixon and Bob Haldeman
OVAL OFFICE

By mid-April, the Watergate scandal had turned into scandals, plural. Among the emerging issues was the use of at least one undercover agent by the Republican National Committee to infiltrate protest groups on college campuses. The evidence of such "dirty tricks" was enough to lead to problems for the RNC executive who oversaw the program. Ken Reitz, manager of the committee's youth campaign, was thirty-two years old and already a veteran of successful campaigns on behalf of Republicans. When Magruder began to describe to investigators how money was paid for spying on college campuses, Reitz fired his assistant, the person directly in charge of the program. The problems didn't end there, though. George H. W. Bush, who had been chair of the RNC since January 18, cut all ties with Reitz — who would be out of a job and out of Washington before April 25. The evidence against Reitz was the money that had been paid out, according to Magruder's remarks. Nixon and Haldeman discussed the Reitz affair and then the trail of money, focusing on where else it might lead.

• • •

NIXON: I had a talk with Bush. He wants to be just as helpful as he can but, boy, he's a workhorse.

HALDEMAN: Really?

NIXON: Yeah. Well, you know [unclear] said — and you know and then something about Reitz. He says Reitz — he let him go because Magruder told Reitz that Magruder had talked about Reitz's involvement in what was called the dirty tricks department, which I don't know apparently about — what it is and I said, "What the hell is that?" And [unclear]. He said, "Well, it was something about some demonstration in front of the White House here," or some damn thing, which he charges are illegal.

HALDEMAN: For God's sake — that was something — they had a guy — let's see, come over and join the demonstration group over here to tell them — to listen to what they were doing and report back.

NIXON: Yeah. You're right. So, I — so George says he's rewritten —

HALDEMAN: At least that's what the story is.

NIXON: He's got a lawyer.

HALDEMAN: Reitz has?

NIXON: Yeah.

HALDEMAN: Good Lord.

NIXON: And, he's got [unclear] involved [unclear] fifteen or sixteen in the White House.

HALDEMAN: In the White House?

NIXON: Either past or present.

HALDEMAN: In the dirty tricks thing?

NIXON: Everything.

HALDEMAN: Reitz says that?

NIXON: This is something *Newsweek* would want to keep track. He said, "How much would they have?"

HALDEMAN: Oh. [unclear] well, if you take past or present, that would be good. [unclear] sounds like probably true.

NIXON: Anyway, that's what they say.

HALDEMAN: I would doubt that — say, how you could — well, unless they're stretching out people that haven't any real — any direct tie in [unclear].

NIXON: And [unclear] the — of course, burgeoning. I don't know — kind of hard to figure out, isn't it, Bob? Very hard —

HALDEMAN: Well, yeah, it's burgeoning — burgeoning in other directions.

NIXON: What the hell is there putting Magruder into the — ? I know what's going on — that sort of thing I can't figure out. Can you?

HALDEMAN: Magruder's lashing out on the thing you know. I think the damn thing is here —

NIXON: That's right.

HALDEMAN: So what he's — what's happening is that he's trying for a better deal than they're giving him and they're trying to get more information out of him. They've already given him a better deal. Looking at their past [unclear].

NIXON: Magruder.

HALDEMAN: What this is — Magruder has given them something that will nail that down and we'll knock off [unclear].

NIXON: Magruder's coming close. See, he told Reitz what he had done [unclear]. Magruder's basically telling everything.

HALDEMAN: But Reitz better be careful. Magruder's told a lot of people what he's done that he hasn't done. And that's — this is a part of a process where people are panicking because somebody said something that isn't — that hasn't happened. Now, Magruder — you cannot — see, this is the problem here. We tend to look at each individual shop as having some — having validity under the circumstances. That's the *Washington Post* story today or yesterday or the Magruder story that he told one person or that he told another but they don't check. So something is wrong with some of them. You can't take all of them because they don't come together. And maybe you can't take any of them. The truth of the matter is you have to take some but the question is which and who knows which?

NIXON: Yeah.

HALDEMAN: And that is still a real problem. People look at you and say, "Well, you know, come clean and tell us what really happened." Who knows?

NIXON: I tried to explain to George that moment he said [unclear]. I said, "But George, you know every campaign there's going to be activities of demonstrations, counter-demonstrations, and that sort of thing and I suppose that Reitz is involved in that, but I don't know that." I said, "Was he involved in Watergate?" and he said, "Well, I don't think so." You know, George is [unclear].

HALDEMAN: Well, I can imagine that they had the youth crew working in all kinds of various — you know, demonstrations, infiltrating other demonstrations, anti-demonstrations to find out what was going on.

NIXON: George called it the dirty tricks department they were in.

HALDEMAN: That would be.

NIXON: Really — in the dirty tricks department?

HALDEMAN: [laughs]

NIXON: But Magruder —

HALDEMAN: If they had one it wasn't very damn good because that was one of our problems is you could never get anything — any action in their area.

NIXON: Magruder — I said, "George" — I said, "Give me the truth. Have I done the right thing here?" And he said, "Oh, yes. It's like everything else. It's right for twenty-four hours and they say, 'Try to do something more.'" [laughs] Right?

HALDEMAN: Well, yeah, but I guess you could — well, you know, and that's that —

NIXON: [unclear]

HALDEMAN: — no matter what bright thing you do —

NIXON: He's reflecting I think, Bob, the concern of the people on the Hill as you said. He goes up there —

HALDEMAN: Of course, this is just what we said when we say it could just be — if you could just release your people to speak at the Senate, that'll take care of it. So you release your people to speak to the Senate and they say, "What else will you do?" Then you say you've busted the case and you shifted the people over and the truth is going to come out. And now you have — first, you nail them — it would appear public pressure — nailing the attorney general —

NIXON: That's right.

HALDEMAN: — campaign manager. One of the columns this morning made the point that they're not gonna settle for scapegoats. You can't get away with trying to blame this on Magruder and Dean, which I think is probably true. And then they said so you have to move it up to Haldeman and then totally ignore Mitchell. And because you have to move to someone who was high enough to have had the responsibility, but the dilemma that you have — the president answers — if you move to Haldeman, then there's no way the president escapes responsibility.

NIXON: That's right.

HALDEMAN: The other point is that on the Watergate, you can't move the [unclear]. On the other thing, you can only very remotely remove him.

NIXON: Structures?

HALDEMAN: Yeah. And even there, making the worst possible case of adding every-thing up and believing it, of all the worst things that could be said you make a very remote case of knowledge and of one overt act that was in itself indirect three times removed. And that's why we've got to with for the lawyers on this. So that's a good question in taking it at its very worst and saying that every adverse witness testi-mony is accepted and acceptable, and believed — where would we come out? And even there, they say you don't come out where it matters.

NIXON: Well, you know I think — how I feel the [unclear].

HALDEMAN: If you talk about Mitchell, you do come out. There's no —

NIXON: The Mitchell thing is going to be clear as hell. He's going to be indicted. I don't think —

HALDEMAN: See, that's not really accepted yet. The thing we don't realize is that we read these stories knowing more than the people who read them know. And the people now, I think —

NIXON: Think it's going to be Haldeman?

HALDEMAN: No, I don't think they know. I don't — but I don't think they're — I don't think they believe what they're reading. And even the analysts I don't think believe what they're reading. I think a lot of people just can't accept the possibility in their own minds that John Mitchell was involved. I don't think they can accept the pos-sibility I was either. I think that they —

NIXON: They might.

HALDEMAN: But then on the other side —

NIXON: The enemies?

HALDEMAN: The enemies would like to. But then on the other side, they have to say somebody must have been. And we damn well better find out who because it won't suffice that we knew that —

NIXON: Haldeman and Ehrlichman and Dean did it —

HALDEMAN: — that some low-level types did it.

NIXON: I mean Magruder.

HALDEMAN: Magruder and Dean. Well, unless you can make a rock-bottom case on that but now I don't think you can. There are too many people that know that the truth is otherwise.

NIXON: Why'd the grand jury know? They're getting into the strangest issues. The dirty tricks department is more than I can figure out.

HALDEMAN: I would guess that why they are is that they're — well, it's the same thing you talked about when you talked with them on Sunday [unclear] thing you concluded which is that they are scared to death to let the Ervin Committee uncover anything that they haven't already uncovered, because that will then move to legislative action or at least higher. "Why in the hell didn't you discover this?"

NIXON: I don't believe I'll ask Petersen — you've got to reach your lawyers. I don't think I'm going to ask Petersen about what Hunt talked about and so forth. I'm afraid it wouldn't do any good.

HALDEMAN: Yeah.

NIXON: What do you agree?

HALDEMAN: I think so. I don't think you ought to ask anything on it. I — you get these day-to-day developments. There's nothing you can do about it. I think we've got to look at it in a little bit broader picture. You can't help but get sticklered by each one of them, but then each one gets revised or changed or overwritten by something else.

NIXON: Yeah. The only problem is the Hunt thing. Go over again and these damn national security taps.

HALDEMAN: They [unclear].

NIXON: Huh?

HALDEMAN: If they know.

NIXON: How can we avoid it, Bob?

HALDEMAN: That — he can just avoid talking about it if he wants to. We don't know what — so far —

NIXON: I told them not to question him about it. That — I'm sure they're into it.

HALDEMAN: Well, if they go into it — well, if they go into it at the grand jury, then it'll be out as a grand jury leak. That's why I can't understand — the lawyers don't seem to get very excited about it. I guess so maybe it's not exciting. It seems to me that that is more than the thing where you just sit and say, "Oh, it must have been the court reporters."

NIXON: Sure.

HALDEMAN: And if it is the court reporters, they ought to indict the court reporters right now. And there ought to be — it seems to me that's as big a scandal as the Watergate is, but nobody seems to think so.

NIXON: [laughs] I guess they figure that when it's the truth getting out to the columnists that are trying to do us in and so forth.

HALDEMAN: But what happens to the process of justice? What's the point of a grand jury when Bill Rogers [unclear] about the whole — you know, that you're entitled to be indicted before you are charged. And ordinary —

NIXON: Yeah.

HALDEMAN: — people are —

NIXON: What the hell — ?

HALDEMAN: — even more so.

NIXON: I want to say that we really get the chance over the weekend. Go over [unclear] it seems to me [unclear] — it's a grateful point. As you say, it's the PR of the presidential posture of the goddamn thing. We've already talked about that. The presidential posture — you think we're in the right posture at the moment?

HALDEMAN: I sure do.

NIXON: Something now — their line I suppose is they have to get something higher. We can't — no scapegoats, so it's got to be Haldeman —

HALDEMAN: No.

NIXON: — or it's got to be Mitchell. What else?

HALDEMAN: It's got to be someone. Obviously, they're going to keep trying on all of this. It's a quicker target. Of course, that's what they make of it. Somebody has to make the legal thing work and then the public point.

NIXON: Right.

HALDEMAN: Somehow it's a question of really putting that out and seeing where it comes out.

NIXON: Wonder when — will Dean start trashing Ehrlichman?

HALDEMAN: I had a feeling that he did but he didn't name names. So that he — what he said was you know there's people higher up — people from lower down —

NIXON: He's a puppet man.

HALDEMAN: — and then the guy that put it out assumed it was Haldeman and said it. Because John — what Ron says — John was surprised, startled, and chagrined that the name was named because he says he didn't name any — he didn't name my name. And I think he's playing both that the guy misunderstood him — he told him to get the story out, said it was higher-ups involved in this. And that that's his cover on it which we expected it would be. He was doing what he was told. Now the question is who will we say told him? And then can you get away with saying that we told him? I assume he'll say both of us did. He may just say I did. Got a tough one there because he had much more communication with John than he did with me.

NIXON: That's correct.

HALDEMAN: He had no communication with you so there's no way he can hang you into it.

NIXON: That's right.

HALDEMAN: Come after the part that you were investigating. That's why I think you're covered. Even on the — well, the Hunt — but that's — you're covered under national security grounds on that.

NIXON: Well, I don't know. But the recollection — my recollection — frankly, I did make notes on that conversation. I don't think we'd want to —

HALDEMAN: Apparently I didn't either because I can't find any.

NIXON: May be just as well. But, the point was it was also discussed in terms of blackmail because it was the same conversation.

HALDEMAN: I think so.

NIXON: Well, I remember specifically my saying, "How much would it cost?" "A million dollars." He said "a million dollars." "I guess we can get that."

HALDEMAN: But then I said about that — but then I said, "We've started down that track," and you agreed that — you know, you won't get anywhere. That doesn't accomplish anything. The fact that you said a million or ten million or —

NIXON: Right. And Dean agreed.

HALDEMAN: — the fact still remains —

NIXON: Dean [unclear].

HALDEMAN: — that's privileged conversation —

NIXON: That's right.

HALDEMAN: — he can't use. He can try and use it publicly and then you — we want it some other way.

NIXON: Well, there was no action taken as far as we're concerned. That's the one thing. Right?

HALDEMAN: None.

NIXON: I don't know, either. Did he call Mitchell then or who did call him — John Ehrlichman?

HALDEMAN: I don't know. I don't have any idea. I don't know that anybody did.

NIXON: You don't think John did?

HALDEMAN: John Ehrlichman?

NIXON: Call Mitchell or Moore?

HALDEMAN: No, because John Ehrlichman wasn't the least bit concerned about it.

NIXON: About the leak?

HALDEMAN: He said come and [unclear] it out.

NIXON: Is that right? Let them leak.

HALDEMAN: Almost complete [unclear].

NIXON: That's fine. If we have a leak, just let the grand jury —

HALDEMAN: We just know they were leaking.

NIXON: Well, so — get in and see them and —

HALDEMAN: See what the boys think this morning —

NIXON: Well, my view is, I'd like to perhaps have a short talk after you've met — for forty-five minutes — perhaps we could meet — you and John could come in and we'd have a little —

HALDEMAN: Okay.

NIXON: — [unclear] maybe ten after?

HALDEMAN: Sure.

NIXON: Particularly if you could discuss the question of how we view the public — the public [unclear] thing and how we stand on the — what we know is the crescendo that's going to be built up —

HALDEMAN: Yeah.

NIXON: — perhaps on you — and, perhaps on John, too. In other words, we got to really have a — we've got to have both on the illegal, but we've got to have a public stance there. And I just don't think Ziegler could go out without an expression of confidence in you and John. That's what I'm concerned about.

HALDEMAN: I think he's got to.

NIXON: Huh?

HALDEMAN: I think he's got to. I think he can express confid — well, I want to talk to him. I don't think you should express confidence in anyone.

NIXON: We'll see you. Fine.

"We are treating them the same and nobody is off."
April 25, 1973, 8:56 a.m.
Richard Nixon and Henry Petersen
WHITE HOUSE TELEPHONE

In another update from Henry Petersen, the head of the Criminal Division notified Nixon that Jeb Magruder had resigned, thereby avoiding any potential conflict with executive privilege — he was now a former member of the administration. While it was too late to save him, Nixon wanted to make sure that Haldeman and Ehrlichman would be treated fairly by the prosecutors, which also meant making sure Dean did not think they were being privileged over him. Nixon also continued to express concern regarding leaks from the grand jury that ended up in the press.

• • •

NIXON: Hello?

PETERSEN: Mr. President.

NIXON: Yeah, I just wanted so you could get your schedule, that would about five thirty be all right with you today?

PETERSEN: Indeed so.

NIXON: That will get you time to finish up your work and I will finish mine. Why don't you just drop over to that — why don't you come — just let me see what they are having here in the Oval. Just — why don't you just drop over, Henry, to the Oval Office? Just come in — where do you come in?

PETERSEN: I just went in the West Gate there.

NIXON: You can come in the West Gate?

PETERSEN: Yes.

NIXON: Fine. Fine.

PETERSEN: Yep.

NIXON: Fine. I just wanted to keep me out of the line of fire— [laughs]

PETERSEN: [laughs]

NIXON: —there's a few people. Fine. Fine.

PETERSEN: Okay. I'll see you at five thirty.

NIXON: Yeah. Another thing I wanted to ask you for my own guidance—I noticed something in the paper this morning about these continuing leaks, you know, which I know which must distress you—

PETERSEN: Yes, sir. They do.

NIXON: —it's a major story. And it occurred to me that the least you should do to make your record—you know, it is very easy to make—change the court reporters, but the least you should do is take the three members of the prosecuting team and put them to the lie detector test. Now I do that with members of my staff and I am therefore directing you do that to them. All right?

PETERSEN: Mr. President, I would like to talk to you more about that this evening.

NIXON: Do you think you know who did it?

PETERSEN: No, sir. But I would like to talk to you more about that this evening before we get into that.

NIXON: Well, the only problem I am concerned about here is with the way that the leaks are coming out, I mean it gives the impression that we really aren't getting at it. You see what I mean? I just want you to be s—

PETERSEN: I understand but I think we ought to discuss that more.

NIXON: All right.

PETERSEN: I think there is terrible significance to that.

NIXON: Yeah, you are afraid to do that then, huh?

PETERSEN: I am reluctant. I think we ought to—

NIXON: Well, the only thing is I remember our mutual friend Edgar [laughs] used to put his people to one.

PETERSEN: Well, you know that—

NIXON: That was pretty rough, huh?

PETERSEN: They have changed considerably. They have an altogether different policy.

NIXON: Yeah, well, I don't want to embarrass anybody except that I just want, Henry, with [unclear] and all these other people—

PETERSEN: I understand.

NIXON: —jumping on, I just don't want the feeling that you, as the director of this thing, I want you to be—you've gone the extra mile, you know, on stopping it. It seems to be coming out all over the place, doesn't it?

PETERSEN: It does indeed. It does indeed.

NIXON: [laughs] You know, I don't ask you what goes on, but I can read it in Jack Anderson's column.

PETERSEN: Well, that is right. That's terrible. You know—

NIXON: Right. I know it.

PETERSEN: I would have — indeed I learn more out of the newspapers on some of this.

NIXON: That's right. Right. One other thing — well, I do need to know if I — without getting into what is it — I understand you had the Wolf — and you had the name of the individual. Is he a member of the White House staff? If so, I need to know.

PETERSEN: No, sir. He is not. He is an individual named Shepherd. [laughs] As soon as I heard, that was the first thing I asked. Was he the reputed from Alexandria, Virginia, who we think has a reputation as a con man? He is coming in the grand jury tomorrow.

NIXON: Shepherd, Shepherd. Well, that's — you understand why I had to ask, because if he was I would have to fire him.

PETERSEN: Yes, sir.

NIXON: Now, another point I need to ask, too, because I — Ziegler got a question about this yesterday with regard to Magruder, as you know. We still don't have him — we still have him as an employee. You know what I mean? Now —

PETERSEN: I am not sure you are up-to-date on that, Mr. President. His resignation was accepted by the secretary of commerce.

NIXON: Oh, he has resigned?

PETERSEN: To take effect on Friday.

NIXON: Friday of this week?

PETERSEN: Yes, sir.

NIXON: Okay.

PETERSEN: It's not publicly known, but you recall I told you he offered his resignation.

NIXON: Yeah, and I remember you said that we didn't want to — all right, I will not tell anybody. But well, now what if Ziegler is asked that? What do you want him to say?

PETERSEN: I would just refer them to the secretary of commerce.

NIXON: Well, then what do you want — secretary of commerce will call Ziegler and ask him what to say? In other words do you want him to be split out?

PETERSEN: The secretary of commerce should simply say that "Mr. Magruder offered his resignation and I accepted it."

NIXON: Yeah.

PETERSEN: Nothing more.

NIXON: In other words there is no problem to you to have it known that Magruder has accepted — has resigned.

PETERSEN: Not in the context that Magruder offered his resignation. No.

NIXON: Mm-hmm. Mm-hmm. Okay. You see, what I am getting at here — I just — Ziegler has said that I better be sure that if he is asked that he wants to know whether or not — you see, we are taking a line on Dean, for example, as well as Haldeman, Ehrlichman, is that we are not — we are treating them the same and nobody is off. So with Magruder I figure we can't do that.

PETERSEN: Well, I think the basic difference of course is that Magruder offered his —

NIXON: Yeah.

PETERSEN: I don't know if the others did or did not but Magruder offered his and the secretary accepted it.

NIXON: Yeah, yeah. Except — I get your point. And as far as Dean is concerned, nothing new on that? Well, we will talk at five thirty about that.

PETERSEN: Yes, sir.

NIXON: Fine. Thank you.

PETERSEN: Very good.

NIXON: Thank you.

New defense against Dean

April 25, 1973, 11:06 a.m.
Richard Nixon, Bob Haldeman, and John Ehrlichman
EXECUTIVE OFFICE BUILDING

As Nixon returned to Washington after his Easter break in Florida, the rumors that his top aides would resign were so overheated that the new speculation pertained to their successors: John Connally was mentioned, as was Melvin Laird. If Haldeman and Ehrlichman were at the precipice of disaster, though, they wanted to let the president know that he was not far behind. To that end, they met with Nixon on the morning of April 25 and discussed impeachment for the first time. The two aides pressed hard to make the president realize that their fates were intertwined with his. Their conviction was that Dean was the only person in a position to level the serious charges of complicity and cover-up. Haldeman, making reference to the tapes of conversations between Dean and the president, suggested that they could be used for defense. The point on which they all agreed was that Dean couldn't prove what he'd said, but the president could.

• • •

HALDEMAN: A quick run-through on what Connally says, as he — as I'm sure Ron's told you. This'll be —

NIXON: Yeah.

HALDEMAN: — be some of what Ron has said. I think that it may even put it differently.

NIXON: Sure.

HALDEMAN: He says, "I think the general situation seems extremely bad, that little by little more and more becomes involved — that every day there's something new. All the press talks about is this stuff now."

NIXON: There may not be —

HALDEMAN: "It now implicates the president in many minds and it must be brought to some resolution soon." It appears to Connally, as a reader of the newspapers, knowing nothing about the facts that Mitchell is undeniably involved, that Dean is probably equally involved, that Magruder is probably equally involved, and that Haldeman and Ehrlichman had more knowledge than anyone thought they had.

NIXON: Right.

HALDEMAN: He says, "You and John have got to take a good look at your hole card — analyze how much you knew and how much you're involved on the periphery to the — even if you didn't know."

NIXON: Right.

HALDEMAN: He thinks my judgment and others familiar with the case is better than anyone else's. The question I've got to face is am I guilty of knowing about something that, if not illegal, was at least unethical. You've got to work on the basic assumption that whatever the facts are they'll come out. Because everybody now is out to save his own skin. And a lot of people are out to nail other people.

NIXON: I think that's quite true. Do you agree, John? Everybody's in business for themselves.

EHRLICHMAN: Sure.

HALDEMAN: Most everybody, yeah.

NIXON: Including Colson.

HALDEMAN: And then he says —

NIXON: Except for you two. [laughs]

HALDEMAN: Also, well — we've got a Nixon position, too —

NIXON: Right.

HALDEMAN: He also says, "You've got to assume that everything that comes out will be cast by the press in the worst possible light."

NIXON: Right. Right.

HALDEMAN: "So, you've got to look at things from two standpoints, the president's and yours." He thinks that the president should at least consider, aside from Ehrlichman and Haldeman, looking at the whole thing, trying to make a new start, ending this somehow and making the point. He said, "It's clear that everybody who clearly is involved and knowingly is involved must get out and get out now," and that specifically, he means, and by that he specifically means Dean. He said, "The president ought to look for other things to do as follows: like going to Congress and recommending a ten-year term for the FBI director and nominating a big man, moving Kleindienst out of the Justice Department, and — "

NIXON: Right.

HALDEMAN: " — giving them a new attorney general — "

NIXON: That's right.

HALDEMAN: " — and meanwhile, then," he said, "if you and John leave, I don't think the president realizes the problem he has in how he handles that [unclear]." He said, "If it's inevitable that you're going to have to leave at some point in this you should get out as soon as you can and prove your innocence. And you should get out on the basis of your loyalty to the president." He said, "I would not, by any means, discard the idea of taking a leave of absence. I had not originally thought of that as viable, but it might well be." The thing that worries him, he says, "is the money payoff to the defense, which he feels is at least as big as the bugging, right now, maybe bigger."

NIXON: Bigger?

HALDEMAN: Yes. And he said, "What you have to do is consider with your — with the president and with your lawyers, first of all, the wiretap area, secondly the money payoff, and both of those you've got to look at first from the question of legal vulnerability and second the question of moral, ethics, publicity, and PR vulnerability." He said, "That's where it appears to me your vulnerability comes. And that —"

NIXON: The second is the thing that I'm [unclear].

HALDEMAN: Right. Right. And he says, "That, in turn, depends upon what people say, whether it's true or not. It does not depend on the facts."

NIXON: You mean, like, what Hunt says —

HALDEMAN: Yeah.

NIXON: — what McCord says, what the loose cannon Dean says —

HALDEMAN: That's right.

NIXON: — and what LaRue says.

HALDEMAN: That's right. And he said, "There's a clear danger here with all these people rattled that somebody's going to decide to lie some more. Just as obviously people have already lied. And to lie to try to do — it's conceivable, to lie to try to tie you into something you had no knowledge of. Somebody could come out, quietly come out and say, 'I reported to Haldeman every evening on the wiretaps.'"

NIXON: Well. Now you can't prove it on that. On that I would say it isn't — I think, what is more likely to land on the money side, perhaps on the face of the — that in view of the later things that happened, not at the time you were there, but at the time in other words, the time the three — the three twenty-two went over and at the time that John talked to Kalmbach at that time, certainly the humanitarian — they were employed at the committee and so forth, I think makes a great deal of sense. The later time, the so-called La Costa conversation, and the troublesome conversation that Dean had where he reported that Bittman had told [unclear].

HALDEMAN: [unclear] He makes the point, though, that that position depends on what people say and whether you have a chance to answer —

NIXON: Yeah.

HALDEMAN: — which you may or may not have. He said, "You gotta face the fact the press is determined to destroy the president. He said, "One of the first things that will happen if you resign is that everyone will assume that you're more deeply involved than you are."

NIXON: Correct.

HALDEMAN: For that reason, a leave of absence becomes in his mind a possibly more viable alternative. He says, "But, if you're ever directly involved by anybody in either the wiretapping or the papers, then your — you've got a real problem whether it's true or not." Then, he says, "Under the circumstances the president could say, 'I'm convinced that Haldeman and Ehrlichman are not directly involved.'" He said, "You've got to do a very careful statement with the lawyers." [unclear]

NIXON: All right — just say that "I have been indeed assured by" — another rather interesting thing from the legal standpoint, John, is that the lawyers — they are writing me a memorandum to the effect —

HALDEMAN: Yeah.

NIXON: — "we have studied all this and they are not involved," and I said, "I have this from their lawyers, da-da-da-da." Not bad. It's a pretty good option. I mean, I think that's something we should consider in any event.

HALDEMAN: [unclear] —

NIXON: Yeah.

HALDEMAN: — that you could say that, and then say, "But notwithstanding their innocence as this is stated, they have asked for a leave of absence until this is cleared up. And I've granted it."

NIXON: There must be no [unclear].

HALDEMAN: Well —

NIXON: As John, you see, indicated to me in earlier conversation, that he didn't go with a leave of absence.

HALDEMAN: He said that to me, too. He said he had not thought a leave of absence was viable —

NIXON: He told Ziegler flat-out no.

HALDEMAN: Well, he said that — that he hadn't thought it was viable. But then he got back to him, and he said, "The other thing to do — you should not rule this out — is to do nothing, in other words." And he said, "The problem with that — that's the strongest position to take and basically the best position, but it's also the highest risk, because if you do that and then somebody successfully lays anything at your door you will have destroyed the president." That is the problem he feels with that area. Now, he says, "If you know they can't successfully lay anything at your door, then that's clearly the route to take."

NIXON: Now, on "successfully at your door," did he say there that he approached both areas, both legal and inference — ?

HALDEMAN: Yes.

NIXON: You see what I mean —

HALDEMAN: Yes.

NIXON: — as far as laying something successfully at your door. That's been done in your case already, and John's maybe in the future.

HALDEMAN: Not really. I mean he doesn't think that.

NIXON: Well, then I — not legally, but the inference, the inference thing, I — what I —

HALDEMAN: Okay. He says he "has a lingering fear about the stories of the feud between Ehrlichman and Mitchell and that they've sworn vengeance on each other, or something," because he said they —

NIXON: What about that? Is that — I wonder if there isn't something to that — not on your part but Mitchell's.

EHRLICHMAN: Not on mine, I know —

NIXON: But you remember Mitchell, John —

EHRLICHMAN: [unclear] in the [Joe] Alsop piece [where Alsop based a column on comments Mitchell made at a party] — it is [unclear]. Alsop printed a sort of a tattle-tale the other day. What happened, and I mentioned this to you at the time, Mitchell got drunk at a party and fell on me in the presence of [*Washington Post* publisher] Kay Graham and Alsop [unclear] —

NIXON: Where was this? When?

EHRLICHMAN: Well, this was when he was attorney general.

NIXON: Oh.

EHRLICHMAN: And — came down on me very hard at that time.

NIXON: About what, John?

HALDEMAN: He was "too liberal."

EHRLICHMAN: I was "too liberal" and I was misadvising you and I had to get out of the White House and on and on and on.

HALDEMAN: This is typical John talk.

EHRLICHMAN: Alsop never forgot that.

NIXON: Yeah, yeah.

EHRLICHMAN: And so —

NIXON: Also, I remember, too, I mean, John, in that connection something Bob told me. Remember, Bob said you talked to Mitchell about what we should do and Bob this, "Haldeman," no, I mean, "Ehrlichman and Colson must go."

HALDEMAN: Yeah.

EHRLICHMAN: Well, then Alsop put together the fact that I was the one who talked to Mitchell down here a week ago Saturday —

NIXON: That's right.

EHRLICHMAN: — and that the whole conversation — and he made a story on that.

NIXON: Sure. Okay, but go ahead on that — that's a side issue.

HALDEMAN: Okay, his point there is, though, he says Mitchell's already lied and you don't know what he'll do next and that worry — he sees that as a late [unclear].

NIXON: We all agree with that — is that Mitchell is — Mitchell has lied once.

EHRLICHMAN: At least. [laughs]

HALDEMAN: There's no way of disagreeing with that because he's told conflicting stories so one of them has to be a lie. He said he wasn't at a meeting, he said he was at a meeting, both of them under oath —

NIXON: Oh?

HALDEMAN: — or at least we're told that.

NIXON: Yeah. [unclear] How does he feel [unclear]?

HALDEMAN: I don't know. That's a curious thing. Nobody seems to get very upset about it.

EHRLICHMAN: Is Petersen telling you anything about Mitchell's problems in New York with that grand jury [in the Vesco case]?

NIXON: Not yet.

EHRLICHMAN: I understand they're very close to indicting him for perjury.

HALDEMAN: John says tomorrow, as we take you over this, you should operate on the basic approach that first you have to go back to the fundamental issues. On the legal issue that you're involved legally, get out now. On the moral PR issue, you've got to assume that they probably can nail you on something —

NIXON: Yeah.

HALDEMAN: — in some way, but you don't know that. You've got to assume that if you are accused, people will believe the accusation. The tendency will be to believe it —

NIXON: The question is whether you can disprove it.

HALDEMAN: The question's whether you can undo it —

NIXON: Yeah.

HALDEMAN: — and you've got to go on the basis that whatever the facts are, they'll come out — that you've got to be prepared for the possible deliberate charge against an innocent person even if it's a lie.

NIXON: That's right.

HALDEMAN: You've got to be prepared that anyone who touched the money or knew the purposes of the money were to buy off witnesses —

EHRLICHMAN: To defend.

HALDEMAN: — obstruct justice, will be guilty in the public mind and that the worst possible picture will be painted of anybody and everybody. "Now," he says, "if you move out, if you resign, two assumptions will immediately be made by the public, and these will be total in your view. One, you're guilty, and two, the president knew about it."

NIXON: Sure.

HALDEMAN: "So, that will not — that act will not relieve the president of any immediate problem that he now has."

NIXON: Absolutely right.

HALDEMAN: The only possible thing it does is preclude the possibility of adding to that problem, as new revelations come out if you know that they are going to come out. He says, "It won't hurt you in the long haul to resign because ultimately the truth will be known, and either you are in or you are out and whatever that is will be known, whether you're in the White House or whether you're not." But, on the short-term basis, is — there's an enormous increase in vulnerability for you if I get out, especially against the deliberate lying. He expands on that a little bit more later. "So, then," he says, "so it gets back to what can Mitchell or Dean put on you?" He said, "One thing I — you better remember, you could ride out PR vulnerabilities, but you cannot ride out legal culpability because legal culpability you have."

NIXON: Now, by that, he means, any kind of an indictment [unclear].

HALDEMAN: Well, not indictment — indictment that isn't on a valid charge, that is where I have to plead guilty, or where I wouldn't be able to successfully defend myself.

EHRLICHMAN: Right.

HALDEMAN: He says, "You've got to make some decisions. And I appreciate the president's feeling that you should. And you ought to decide now what to do. You ought to stick with it and not go back and relook at it unless the facts materially change and then you ought to — you have to relook at it." He said, "The president has told me that he is convinced that you've done nothing illegal. I have to say, Bob," he said, "that it is my feeling that if that is what the president believes, then he has the duty to stand by you. Then," he said, "don't resign just because you think that solves the problem, because it doesn't. It aggravates the problem. Once you're out, the enemies — both the press and the political — have a wide-open shot at the president, and they have a wide-open shot at you, especially the people who want to lie." He said, "The fundamental question is whether the president survives in a viable fashion." Then that brought him back and he says, "I don't know, maybe you shouldn't even take a leave. You've just got to go on the best guess as to what all the people involved here are going to do." He said, "If you're innocent and clearly innocent, then don't move a peg. But face the fact that they can still make you look bad even though you are innocent. Then it comes back to the basic question of fundamental innocence. You've got to look at this on the legal basis, the PR basis, your personal jeopardy, and the president's position. You've got to analyze all those factors." He says, "I have to believe that if a man is innocent, he should stand his ground. He should not move. But the problem of advising on this is that I don't know the facts, so I have to deal with the law of probabilities." He said, "The worst problem is you don't know the facts, so you have to deal with the law of probability."

NIXON: We may know the facts. But we don't know what's gonna come out yet.

EHRLICHMAN: [unclear] all right, let me say we have a pretty good —

HALDEMAN: Well, I think we've got — if we know the facts I think we ought to assume they'll come out.

NIXON: That's my point. Go on.

HALDEMAN: So then, he says, "Go back to the fundamentals. Get your lawyer's advice." Then he goes through [unclear] you of all people who will decide the right thing [unclear].

NIXON: Sure.

HALDEMAN: Then he said, "That my final advice to you is," he said, "Nellie's just come in and she's sitting here on the bed and she says to give you her love and to tell you that she's standing by you — "

NIXON: Right.

HALDEMAN: " — and she doesn't believe any of this," and he said, "Don't ever take a needless risk. Don't make any move unless you know it has to be made. It's not enough to say that you can obviate your association with the president PR-wise by taking a leave or for — by resigning. No matter what you do, the president will be affected."

NIXON: No question.

HALDEMAN: "And your moving out will definitely be an adverse move to both you and the president in the short run. So, what you've got to weigh is that adversity worth whatever you gain by it." Now, that's quite a bit different because he spelled it out in a lot more detail —

NIXON: That he's thought it through more.

HALDEMAN: — than where it came out with Ron and —

NIXON: [unclear] you know usually like on this [unclear] business comes out and he says —

HALDEMAN: That's right.

NIXON: — part of me thinks about it and says, "Well, maybe you've got to think it through."

HALDEMAN: Now, I sure don't want to fault Ron on his every —

NIXON: No, no, no. Ron reported to me exactly what he'd said.

HALDEMAN: [unclear] And —

NIXON: And [unclear].

HALDEMAN: [unclear] says to me I think he — I think that's what is — he said. What Rogers said to me was — he said, "Bob, I can't decide this because I don't know the facts, and I keep saying every time Ron calls me and I even said it to the president when I talked to him, that he's got to decide." He said, "I believe that your case is going to be especially tough, and there is a problem of how you can do your job with this stuff hanging there — "

NIXON: That's the point he later —

HALDEMAN: — and he said, "The way I lean upon this is that you should take a leave of absence until it's cleared up."

NIXON: Well, did he get leave of absence?

HALDEMAN: Yes, sir, he raised it. That's why I raised it with Connally.

NIXON: See, he was the leave of absence man, [unclear] basically the [unclear] of Connally — the two best judgments we've got here. [unclear] leave of absence thing on the basis of fairness [unclear].

HALDEMAN: Rogers then said — he said, "I don't know anything about John. I just [unclear]," but he said, "I keep — on all of this — I keep coming back to where I was, and I'd called him saying I wanted to talk to him, and he said he didn't want to talk with me." [unclear] He said I did — he was concerned about his position.

NIXON: Yes.

HALDEMAN: He said, "I can't be in the position of being an arbiter between you and the president."

NIXON: Oh, yeah. Yeah.

HALDEMAN: "I'm not asking that, Bill, I'm asking about — all I had in mind was asking your advice. Because I'm concerned that the decision is being made on the wrong basis or for the wrong reasons."

NIXON: Right.

HALDEMAN: "If that's the case, I want to be sure that all the opposing views — "

NIXON: Right.

HALDEMAN: " — to that decision, regardless of how they affect me, are weighed and I see you, Rogers, as being — "

NIXON: Sure.

HALDEMAN: " — the most likely guy to make that possible, because nobody else can talk to the president about this — "

NIXON: That's right.

HALDEMAN: " — and the president is in one hell of a position because normally in these things — "

NIXON: I have somebody I can talk to — you'd do it or John would.

HALDEMAN: " — [unclear] involved in it. John was an advocate in some areas, that I never was really, like on foreign policy things or anything else."

NIXON: Sure.

HALDEMAN: You had somebody here who could argue the opposite of whatever was coming up. Bill said, "I must not be in the position of making a decision." I'm not asking you that. He said, "Talk to the president. He wants to talk to you — "

NIXON: Good.

HALDEMAN: — and he said, "It's important that you talk it through with him. [unclear] basis." Then he said, "If, after you've talked with the president, you still feel that the approach is wrong or that the understanding's wrong or anything else from the standpoint of the presidency, then I'd be happy to talk with you about it and hear what your problem is [unclear] — "

NIXON: Sure.

HALDEMAN: " — come out with."

NIXON: Yeah. Well, they're both right — being good lawyers in saying, "Look, we can't make a judgment on it without all the facts."

HALDEMAN: Without the facts.

NIXON: And that's really the basic thing that we've got to talk about here today.

HALDEMAN: I think it is, because —

NIXON: We've got to look a — what I'd like to do, basically, is to look at the facts which I discussed, of course, with the lawyers — the legal matter first. The facts on the [unclear] question of let us suppose [unclear], the grand jury [unclear] let me get through here just a minute, say one or two things that cannot wait. The lawyers with me again lean on Petersen, direct him to get this goddamn thing closed up. And I said, "I will." I said, "Can I tell Petersen with regard to Bob and John making [unclear] they've been wanting their counsel to — they've been wanting to tell their story to the prosecution, you know — and to the grand jury."

HALDEMAN: They did that last week.

EHRLICHMAN: Yeah.

NIXON: Not really. They said, "We're ready any time." But the point is they left it with the fact that they would be in touch with them. They did it a little differently. They — what they're really getting at, Bob, is to take a more affirmative stance on that, in other words come in publicly.

HALDEMAN: Yeah.

EHRLICHMAN: They hit us on this yesterday —

NIXON: Publicly.

EHRLICHMAN: — and we said, "Wait."

NIXON: Okay.

HALDEMAN: Our lawyers went in and did it publicly.

NIXON: Yeah, well, no problem. I'm not suggesting — after we kicked it around. You see because they were trying to — it's really not fair to have lawyers trying to pick up a PR problem here. But they kicked it around. I said, "Well, if you wrote a letter to this sort — put it out." I said, "We'd have no objection." We've got to determine the PR. I said, "Now, the other thing is, with regard to Bob and John — if you're not — if you take a leave of absence or tough it out, either way, it is necessary to do something — most everybody agrees with that." Now by doing something, I mean for your sakes and perhaps also for the presidency. Let me say in terms of your sakes first because otherwise you allow the crescendo of leaks and *ex parte* statements and so forth just beating the shit out of you [unclear] without your taking a strong affirmative position that, "by God, we want to be heard — we want to be cleared, and we're innocent." In other words, I just think it has to be said. Also, from the standpoint of the president, the president's got to be in a position that he has talked to his top assistants and they want to be heard. They want to be, as early as possible — they want to be cleared, and so forth, and so on. Now — but anyway, we'll talk about that. That's a tactic which I think would come into play — in fact, in any event, whatever we do, whatever you do — whatever you do you cannot just sit and wait, you and John, until the grand jury finally does its deadly process, leaks come out of there, and the whole damn thing appears in Anderson's column and then in addition to that every son of a bitch puts out statements to the effect that, like the *Post*, [unclear] "the president was told in December about the —" Let me say, I talked to Colson many times, as you know. No such conversation ever took place. He would — he would have talked with — did he ever say that to you, John? Bob, did he ever say it to you? He might not have said it to John, but did he ever say it to you?

HALDEMAN: No. [unclear] You know what he said to me is, "You've got to hunker down, don't let anybody out, maintain executive privilege on everybody — "

NIXON: Yeah.

HALDEMAN: " — because — "

NIXON: [unclear] I thought maybe I'd lost my goddamn mind —

HALDEMAN: Colson's line has been the solidest of anybody here, and the most consistent of anybody here —

NIXON: Yeah, yeah.

HALDEMAN: [unclear] total stonewall —

EHRLICHMAN: Until the last two weeks.

HALDEMAN: That's right.

NIXON: Well, what the heck —

HALDEMAN: I mean, just total almost to the point of pathological —

EHRLICHMAN: Yeah.

HALDEMAN: — you know, he would panic anytime there was any thought of any disclosure of anything.

NIXON: Yeah, he said, "Don't do it, don't do this — "

HALDEMAN: "Don't give up privilege — don't go to" [unclear].

NIXON: — ba-ba-ba-ba-ba-ba.

EHRLICHMAN: He's changed his PR advisors recently [unclear]. On this business of prosecutor, did they tell you about panic at the prosecutor's office right now?

NIXON: Well, yes.

EHRLICHMAN: [unclear] you know —

NIXON: The panic because of the leaks.

EHRLICHMAN: Kleindienst apparently has landed on them and has charged them in line with your comment to Kleindienst — has charged the prosecutor with being responsible for the leaks. The judges —

NIXON: My comments to Kleindienst were made incidentally not last Friday but the Sunday that he came in —

EHRLICHMAN: I see. Well —

NIXON: That's a —

HALDEMAN: They were also made at the cabinet meeting.

EHRLICHMAN: He made some at the cabinet meeting.

HALDEMAN: See, you said at the cabinet meeting, you said, "Those leaks are coming from the prosecution." Kleindienst said, "They're coming from the grand jury." You turned around and snapped at him and said, "Dick, let's not be ridiculous, grand jurors don't keep things of testimony."

NIXON: Oh, good.

HALDEMAN: You really zapped him and —

EHRLICHMAN: Well, the upshot of this now —

NIXON: [unclear]

HALDEMAN: [unclear] carried that that yesterday.

NIXON: Well, isn't that news as well?

EHRLICHMAN: Sure.

HALDEMAN: I think it's great.

EHRLICHMAN: The upshot of it is though that Glanzer and Silbert are on the verge of nervous breakdown.

NIXON: Well I —

HALDEMAN: And plus, you see, they are being hit by this refusing, this lawyer of that guy with the six cases of stuff —

NIXON: Yeah.

HALDEMAN: — says that Glanz — that Silbert was engaged in a massive cover-up and wouldn't accept this evidence.

EHRLICHMAN: — then the fifteen —

NIXON: Oh, incidentally, I asked for your — I asked — I said, "I've got to know one thing." I called Petersen this morning and made a date for five thirty this afternoon [unclear] right time to get him. And I said, "Now," I said, "I don't want anything about what happened at grand jury. But I know this [witness Peter H.] Wolf was there [and revealed to the grand jury the name of a CRP employee who allegedly received the results of the Watergate wiretap reports]. I've got to know. It's reported in the press — you've got the name of the person who got it. Who was it? Was it a member of the White House staff?" He said, "No." I said, "Well, who was it?" He said — then he volunteered, "A fellow by the name of Shepherd."

HALDEMAN: Who?

NIXON: I don't know him. Shepherd. I said, "Who is he?" And then he used the term, "He's going to come before the grand jury tomorrow." He said, "He's sort of a con man."

EHRLICHMAN: Con man?

NIXON: Yes, understand — I know nothing about this except that it smacks — well, it smacks basically of Hunt —

EHRLICHMAN: Yeah.

NIXON: — wanting to clean his office out — getting it to Shepherd. Hunt is the kind of a guy —

EHRLICHMAN: Is it Shepherd like a fellow who takes care of sheep? Shepherd? We have a fellow on the staff here named Shepard.

HALDEMAN: We do?

EHRLICHMAN: Yeah. On the Domestic Council staff.

HALDEMAN: Oh, your guy? Yeah.

EHRLICHMAN: Big tall kid.

HALDEMAN: He's a lawyer, too, isn't he?

EHRLICHMAN: Yeah.

NIXON: I asked him. He said he lived in Alexandria.

EHRLICHMAN: Yeah.

HALDEMAN: Does Geoff live in Alexandria?

EHRLICHMAN: Yeah.

HALDEMAN: [unclear] Well, maybe he does now. [unclear]

NIXON: Has he been here all the time? [unclear]

EHRLICHMAN: He's been here — he was a White House Fellow and then we kept him on. He's been here a long time.

NIXON: Did he work in Colson's office? Or — ?

EHRLICHMAN: No, he worked — he handled Justice Department affairs for us.

HALDEMAN: Oops. Krogh's office? With Hunt?

EHRLICHMAN: No, no.

HALDEMAN: [unclear] that Plumber business?

EHRLICHMAN: No, he never had anything to do with that.

HALDEMAN: Better check that.

EHRLICHMAN: Right. I will.

[EHRLICHMAN leaves the conversation to call Geoff Shepard.]

• • •

EHRLICHMAN: He said there used to be a George Shepherd in OEP but he doesn't know of any other Shepherds around here. He said he's clean.

NIXON: Well, OEP is not [unclear] —

EHRLICHMAN: No, I mean he, Geoff Shepard, says he's clean. Doesn't know Peter Wolf. Never heard of him.

NIXON: Right. That's enough. All right, fine. Go ahead, John, on your stuff. [unclear]

EHRLICHMAN: Oh, well, I was just going to say that all the judges of the District Court convened and they landed on the prosecutor, apparently the grand jury leaks — while you were gone.

HALDEMAN: And told the grand jury to investigate the grand jury.

EHRLICHMAN: So the prosecutor's now catching it from three sides, and when our fellows dropped in to see Glanzer last night, they were down at the courthouse taking depositions. They stopped by to see if they could pick up any tidbits, and Glanzer was just up on the chandelier, and obviously [unclear] —

NIXON: Yeah. Well, obviously they're concerned about that. Incidentally, I heard before you just came here [unclear] before we get into that. Let's come now to [unclear] solutions therefore. However [unclear] more incentive [unclear]. Do you favor it?

EHRLICHMAN: Sure.

NIXON: That's the problem. That's the —

EHRLICHMAN: Sure. No question.

NIXON: [unclear] look down the road [unclear] and second [unclear]. Let them present their case. We'll keep them all [unclear] we're not [unclear] enough time [unclear] anxious, willing — and I am making no offer and I insist that you — that I've got to have my people. I want my people [unclear] by then. How about that?

EHRLICHMAN: And then you want a report —

NIXON: And "I want a report from you, Henry." I want you to do it. You call [unclear] questions if necessary. But I've got to have this for my own [unclear] where I am. [unclear] and third, [unclear] you ask him to put down for me, which I don't know whether he can do this [unclear] or not, but I ask him [unclear] got information [unclear]. Well, he's already, I said — based on what you have today, [unclear] "What is your case, potentially, against these men?"

EHRLICHMAN: Likewise, I would think he'd want it against Dean, to know whether there's an indictment upcoming or what the —

NIXON: Well, that's right. Let's talk about the Dean problem. The Dean problem is a goddamn tough one [unclear] because, I heard about his conversation [unclear] another one of his threatens [unclear] counsel which is not granted with that understanding [unclear] the president gets caught in obstruction of justice. Now what in the name of Christ he means by that, I don't know. I mean, unless he probably means that I'm trying to keep Petersen from [unclear].

EHRLICHMAN: Petersen reported to me round about your phone call from Camp David.

NIXON: Immunity?

EHRLICHMAN: No. About not getting into national security stuff.

NIXON: I'll ask him.

EHRLICHMAN: Could have been very direct. In other words, if you order Petersen not to take that testimony he may have started to give it [unclear] and Petersen said, "I've been ordered not to give that information — "

NIXON: Not on national security, no.

EHRLICHMAN: He may be —

NIXON: Is that obstruction of justice?

EHRLICHMAN: No. But what Dean is obviously doing here [unclear] a — he's trying to construct a big dam cluttered by — in my opinion — I think he's being very —

NIXON: Well, I told Dean, too, I said, "Now, John, anything with me is privileged, and anything with national security is privileged." I told him that.

EHRLICHMAN: Let's — I think that's really sort of an open question in all this —

NIXON: Yeah.

EHRLICHMAN: — and if I can say it, I'll go back and forth with Ron and so on [unclear] in thinking about this, I keep coming back to Dean because there are things that don't add up otherwise —

NIXON: Right.

EHRLICHMAN: — in this whole thing.

NIXON: That's right.

EHRLICHMAN: And, I don't know if you feel you can do this, but I think the three of us know one another well enough, that — we've been through enough together — but [unclear] necessary that we have your very candid —

NIXON: Assessment?

EHRLICHMAN: — assessment of the threat to you. Obviously, neither one of us want to do anything to harm you in any way. We want to avoid harming you.

NIXON: The threat to me because of Dean?

EHRLICHMAN: Yes, sir.

NIXON: All right.

EHRLICHMAN: Now, let me, let me just spin something out for you as a —

NIXON: Right.

EHRLICHMAN: — as a — probably a far-out point, and then work back from it.

NIXON: Right.

EHRLICHMAN: I think it's entirely conceivable that if Dean is totally out of control and if matters are not handled adroitly that you could get a resolution of impeachment —

NIXON: That's right.

EHRLICHMAN: — in the Senate.

NIXON: That's right.

EHRLICHMAN: I don't know if you've thought of this or not, but I got thinking about it last night — on the ground that you committed a crime.

NIXON: Right.

EHRLICHMAN: And that there is no other legal process available to the United States people other than —

NIXON: Right.

EHRLICHMAN: — other than impeachment. Otherwise, you have immunity from prosecution.

NIXON: Right.

EHRLICHMAN: So I think we have to think about that. We have to [unclear] —

NIXON: Right.

EHRLICHMAN: — and see about — see what the point is. Is it a crime, if any? And how serious it is, and whether Dean is a threat and what we do about it. My own analysis is that what he has falls far short of any commission of a crime by you so far as I know.

NIXON: Yeah.

EHRLICHMAN: I don't know what you may have talked about with him in those ten or twelve hours you and he spent there in the months of February and March.

NIXON: Right.

EHRLICHMAN: But you get down to a point where you've got John Dean prancing in there and saying, "The president said this and the president said that," and having somebody in your behalf come back and say, "No, the president didn't say that, and that's ridiculous." And so you get a kind of credibility thing unless — like he seems to be doing, he's very busy dredging up corroborating evidence and looking for documentation or taking statements from people based on leads that may have developed from those conversations. And I think really the only way that I know to make a judgment on this is for you to listen to your tapes and see what actually was said then, or maybe for Bob to do it, or somebody. See what was said there. And then analyze how big a threat that is.

NIXON: Right.

EHRLICHMAN: If it didn't come out of those meetings, then I think it's manageable.

NIXON: Right.

EHRLICHMAN: Because it then does not come out of your mouth, it comes by reason of the actions of — or something that one of us said or did, and it can be handled. But if you're really confronted with that kind of a dilemma, or that kind of crisis in this thing, I think before any other steps are taken — any precipitous steps [unclear] on us for that matter, you'd better damn sure know —

NIXON: That's right.

EHRLICHMAN: — what your hole card is.

NIXON: I agree.

EHRLICHMAN: Beyond that, hell, I'm not afraid of Dean —

NIXON: I know.

EHRLICHMAN: — and what he might say about me, for instance. I think it can be handled. I don't think Bob has anything to fear from Dean, basically then — particularly based on what the attorneys tell us. He has an almost unlimited capacity to dredge up anecdotes from a dim and murky past and we're just going to have to handle it one by one. You mentioned the La Costa plan. I don't know — our fellows probably didn't tell you this but Dick Moore's attorney called on him — on John Wilson, and indicated that Dick Moore just doesn't have any memory at all about La Costa. He can barely remember even being out there.

NIXON: Dick Moore told me —

EHRLICHMAN: I understand.

NIXON: — he said there was something —

EHRLICHMAN: I understand.

NIXON: — maybe his memory's become dim.

EHRLICHMAN: His memory is, apparently, feeble beyond measure, because his attorney has explained to him what his exposure is —

NIXON: That's right.

EHRLICHMAN: — and Dick is scared shitless, apparently.

HALDEMAN: To the point where he has contacted Silbert to ascertain that he will not be indicted prior to his daughter's wedding so that he can go to his daughter's wedding.

EHRLICHMAN: Now that was his proposal — his attorney to do that.

HALDEMAN: Okay. He wanted his attorney to go and find out.

NIXON: Is Dick thinking he could be indicted for that?

EHRLICHMAN: Yeah, yeah. Not for — not for that conversation —

HALDEMAN: [unclear] wrong —

EHRLICHMAN: — if Dick has been cheek and jowl with Dean all through this process. And far more than either of us — far more.

NIXON: Well, let me suggest this, Bob — you've got the conversations apparently [unclear] if you need to get them.

HALDEMAN: Yeah.

NIXON: [unclear] can get them. You've got to know [unclear] calendar.

HALDEMAN: Yeah.

NIXON: Now, let me say — [unclear] I think I remember — I would remember except, you see, there's always a possibility that Dean may have discussed with me as to [unclear] — I know the Bittman conversation, however.

HALDEMAN: Yeah.

NIXON: I know, however, that in that conversation, the question was raised of blackmail.

HALDEMAN: Yeah.

NIXON: I know, however, that in that conversation I also raised the question how much is it going to — would it cost —

HALDEMAN: Yeah.

NIXON: — to continue down this road? "A million dollars." And I said facetiously, "Well, I guess we can get a million dollars." It was then that we started my whole investigation. Now, I don't know — how does that one sound to you?

EHRLICHMAN: Well, that sounds tough and —

NIXON: Yeah.

EHRLICHMAN: — yet, it's manageable. [unclear]

NIXON: Yeah. Point out that that was the thing that triggered it.

EHRLICHMAN: If we know, obviously, knowledge is —

NIXON: Yeah.

EHRLICHMAN: — is terribly important here.

NIXON: Absolutely.

EHRLICHMAN: And this guy is using this to leverage you. Either he is using this or he's using something else. I don't know what the something else would be. He certainly can't use the Hunt escapade on the coast because that was totally outside of your knowledge and it doesn't reach you.

NIXON: [unclear] it reaches people [unclear].

EHRLICHMAN: Oh, well, yeah, but that isn't our problem here as I see it.

NIXON: Yeah.

EHRLICHMAN: He's got to have a lever that works on you —

NIXON: Right.

EHRLICHMAN: — and, so it's got to involve your personal cognizance in this thing, so —

NIXON: I asked Petersen whether — I talked to Dean, and Dean said before he pled, he would like to talk to me and Petersen said no, so I'll find out from Petersen what Dean's story is.

EHRLICHMAN: Well, I think Dean is —

HALDEMAN: Did Dean go to the grand jury today?

NIXON: I don't know. No, not yet. They haven't made a deal yet.

EHRLICHMAN: Is he thinking of making a deal — Silbert and Dean?

NIXON: I guess. Well, a deal, no. His attorneys are still at arm's length on Dean testifying, that's to use his terms.

EHRLICHMAN: All I'm saying is that before you decide, I think we have to look at the ultimate problem here —

NIXON: Yeah.

EHRLICHMAN: — and I must say that that may not totally resolve the ultimate problem. I'm trying to think of where your problems are in this. I don't think we can brush them off by just saying, that the problems of being able to govern, or the problems of —

NIXON: No.

EHRLICHMAN: — the press onslaught —

NIXON: No.

EHRLICHMAN: — or anything of that kind. I think there's an ultimate problem here —

NIXON: That's right.

EHRLICHMAN: — and there're going to be a lot of —

NIXON: Whether I was involved in obstruction of justice.

EHRLICHMAN: — or in the bugging, or in — you know, any of these episodes and there are going to be a hundred and fifty-eight reporters in this town digging away at the individuals involved in this case —

NIXON: Yeah.

EHRLICHMAN: — for the next year, next two years, trying to get some guy to crack.

NIXON: So, we get them — so we get at least the situation. As far as we know, La Costa I never heard about — you remember, you didn't talk to me about it and I didn't see Dean. Bob, let's listen to these conversations, and what the hell, Dean — Dean could have discussed that. I don't remember specifically, you know, but he could have discussed the fact — well, we've got the problem, when he made his — what he calls his "cancer on the heart of the presidency" speech, which he may — which was Moore's phrase. He could have discussed there the problem of these — of defendants and — you know what I mean?

HALDEMAN: Yeah.

NIXON: The payoffs and all that sort of thing. I was there for [unclear] — whether I said anything that led him to believe that we should pay them off —

HALDEMAN: Let's —

NIXON: — I don't think so.

EHRLICHMAN: Let's not worry about it. It's either there or it isn't.

NIXON: That's right.

EHRLICHMAN: We'll see what's there —

NIXON: And if it is?

EHRLICHMAN: — and listen to it.

NIXON: If it is? Then we have to play in terms of I was having to find out what his implication was.

EHRLICHMAN: I think then it becomes very important how you couch your decision on Dean —

NIXON: That's right.

EHRLICHMAN: And you can go one of several ways depending on what the problem is and you can co-opt it. You can preempt this pretty much, I think, by the way you do it. That's really a separate subject from what happens here. And it seems to me —

NIXON: Did he come up and talk to you about the Bittman conversation?

EHRLICHMAN: Yes.

NIXON: How did he present it to you? After he talked to me?

EHRLICHMAN: No, I don't think so. I think this was before he talked to you, but I'm not sure.

HALDEMAN: You don't know because, we don't — we can't still — I still can't fix when he talked to you on it.

NIXON: Yeah.

EHRLICHMAN: He talked to me around the twentieth.

NIXON: Was that, Bob, after we talked? You don't think you were in the room now, do you, when he talked to me?

HALDEMAN: Yeah, I remember the conversation.

NIXON: You do?

HALDEMAN: Yeah, but I think it was — see, I keep — I remember —

NIXON: Is your memory about like I stated?

HALDEMAN: Yes.

NIXON: Did we say, "Let's go out and get the money"?

HALDEMAN: Yeah, I don't remember the specifics. I just remember the —

NIXON: Was there any — do you remember my saying, "Look, we've got to get the money. Can't you find somebody to get the money?"

HALDEMAN: You didn't — I don't remember your saying, "We've got to get it." I remember you saying, "Can't some — we ought to be able to raise that kind of money, or — "

NIXON: "A million dollars."

HALDEMAN: " — there ought to be that kind of money available."

NIXON: "Yeah, a million dollars."

HALDEMAN: Something like that, yeah.

NIXON: That's right.

EHRLICHMAN: But you didn't say to do it, or that you would — or anything like that. Other than that, I don't recall, but I can't fix going through the logs and everything. I can't fix when that conversation was, this —

NIXON: Well, you've got to find out. And then if we find that to be the case, if there's anything that I said at that point, I mean, you can understand, John, I could have talked with him about it. We were talking at the time [unclear] whole goddamn thing, of course. We talked about it.

EHRLICHMAN: Well —

NIXON: My point is that if we find that out, if we have to couch, we have to remember what our — what the line is and the line has got to be, "I was conducting an investigation and finding out what — where this thing went."

HALDEMAN: Well, I'm sure that's the case because the timing has to be in the frame of March 19, 20, 21.

NIXON: Yeah.

EHRLICHMAN: Let me —

HALDEMAN: That's when you were getting into the investigation.

EHRLICHMAN: Let me ask you a question about my conversation with him.

NIXON: Yeah.

EHRLICHMAN: He came — first of all, his version of the conversation, as I understand it is — and we have this pegged pretty well because of the conversations I've had and played this back. His conversation with me was — he came and told me about Bittman making this demand on behalf of Hunt. And I simply referred him back to Mitchell. Now, that's not quite accurate. I can —

NIXON: You say that is what he has said?

EHRLICHMAN: That's what he has said.

NIXON: How do you know?

EHRLICHMAN: Well, because he told Bob this in a long conversation which would — is in effect his bill of particulars.

NIXON: But when did he — ?

HALDEMAN: It's rather interesting. I have a very — I didn't realize I had it. I have quite a voluminous set of notes that Dean reports to me on things in general in this investigation period when he was up at Camp David obviously spinning out his web —

NIXON: Yeah.

EHRLICHMAN: — and he tried out bits and pieces, that — not bits and pieces — he tried [unclear] —

NIXON: Did he bring me into the conversation about Bittman? He did not.

EHRLICHMAN: No.

NIXON: Did he raise the [unclear] with you?

EHRLICHMAN: No.

NIXON: [unclear] you were there.

EHRLICHMAN: And in point of fact, sure I was — unless I'm dreaming —

HALDEMAN: [unclear] or something. [laughs]

EHRLICHMAN: In point of fact, what did happen was that he and I had a conversation and I raised the point of this being an endless set of demands —

NIXON: Yeah.

EHRLICHMAN: — and said that for my part, I would rather test the privilege on national security, which I knew was involved.

NIXON: Yeah. Oh, that reminds me of one thing. Dean said that the — basically, the Bittman thing was — he said that was blackmail. He said no, that was not blackmailing the presidency — that was blackmailing Ehrlichman.

EHRLICHMAN: Mm-hmm.

HALDEMAN: And that's the way he presented it to me, in fact. You know, there's a point here that's never been raised in all the discoveries. This triggers my memory on it. Dean at one point was very intrigued with using blackmail as a defense.

NIXON: Yeah.

EHRLICHMAN: On the whole cover-up operation.

NIXON: He told me that. Early on.

HALDEMAN: That that was the thing we could develop a case that it was — that that was a legal defense. We weren't obstructing justice. We were victims of blackmail.

NIXON: Which I —

HALDEMAN: It never made any sense. It's not a [unclear] spelling out — spinning out —

NIXON: Well —

EHRLICHMAN: What I did as soon as he presented this to me was to check my files and talk with Krogh and talk with Dave Young to see what the — to refresh my recollections so when the whole chain of circumstances had been. I became convinced in that review that the matter was not as serious as I had sort of carried around in my thought that it was in terms of culpability. But more than that, that it was a legitimate national security subject and that we are to stonewall it, but there was no sense in starting to buckle in to this kind of a demand. So that was my second response to Dean. He then apparently went back to Mitchell and we had only an oblique — kind of glancing reference to it in the Mitchell, Dean, Haldeman, Ehrlichman meeting of the following day, which would have been about the twenty-second or -third, where Dean says to John something like, "What's the status of that matter?" — or John raised it with him and they went back and forth, and Mitchell finally said, "Well, I think it's taken care of." Now that —

NIXON: Dean raised it?

EHRLICHMAN: Well, Dean or Mitchell raised it in that case.

HALDEMAN: I have. I may be wrong. But maybe I've just convinced myself that —

NIXON: Mitchell —

HALDEMAN: I have a very strong recollection on that, that it was in an oblique reference about the middle — there was a lull in the discussion and Mitchell turned to Dean, said, "What have you done about the Hunt matter or about that problem we had yesterday?" or some — I'm not sure how he had identified it. He said, "What have you done about the problem?" I was fascinated with this because I was watching the son of a bitch at work and trying to figure out what the hell he was doing himself. "So what have you done about that problem?" Dean looked a little confused and said, "Well nothing." And Mitchell said, "Well, I think — I guess it's — I guess it's taken care of" and it was that fast. I mean, it was —

NIXON: You reported that to me.

HALDEMAN: — like a total of about three or four sentences —

NIXON: Yeah.

HALDEMAN: — out of a three- or four-hour meeting.

NIXON: Yeah.

HALDEMAN: And I have a strong feeling that's all that was —

NIXON: Well, look. It's very important that you go back and just — that you get the tapes of everything we had with Dean and see what the hell has been discussed. I can assure you that we may have covered the waterfront of some of those things, because basically he raised lots of questions and that I think — you know what I mean — I have no recollection, John — no recollection of — except the obstruction of justice thing he raised. I said, "What is the obstruction of justice — have we run into the legal — ?" I said, "Is it obstruction of justice to help the defendants?" No, if that's the purpose. But it is obstruction of justice if it's to keep them quiet. And I said, "Well, the question of intent." "Yes." We went into that apparently, and so forth and so on. Go ahead.

EHRLICHMAN: How to just — to just tie this down. Bob and I have been, of course, rigorously going through every scrap of paper we have trying to reconstruct. I am forcibly struck with the realization that I began to understand this case, what Dean's involvement was and what Mitchell and Magruder's involvement was only in the month of March this year. And that this all began surfacing about the time that Dean realized that he had his tit in a crack and began constructing his theory of the case and then began unloading on us, item by item and bit by bit —

HALDEMAN: And brainwashing us. [unclear] —

EHRLICHMAN: — and — yeah.

HALDEMAN: — I mean, over and over he'd work you over, every time he'd get you, he'd work on a line like, "I knew that he had told me after the meeting that we'd — they'd canceled the intelligence operations." He must have told me that thirty times.

NIXON: He said what — Dean?

EHRLICHMAN: That he had reported to me after the second meeting with Mitchell and all that they had gone through another shot at a ridiculous intelligence operation. That —

NIXON: That he informed you.

EHRLICHMAN: — that he and Mitchell had turned it down. And that he felt that there was no profit in pursuing that any further and that he'd like to — pull out of it completely and didn't I agree? And he says, "I agree," and he had no further contact with any intelligence planning from then on. Now, I suspect that Mitchell says and some of the other evidence says that he was in the third meeting. That he may have been involved in another meeting after that. He was using all this with me to try and get me as a corroborating witness that he wasn't. Now, so now I don't know what I believe.

NIXON: Yeah. Okay. Let me suggest this — that before I meet with Petersen I want you to listen to those things.

HALDEMAN: I can't do it. It's twelve hours of tapes. I may be able to focus in on it — I could focus on Bittman. We know when that is.

[Unclear exchange]

NIXON: I'd like to get it all. Well —

HALDEMAN: Well, I think I know which meeting it was.

NIXON: Yeah. Yeah. Can you do that?

HALDEMAN: I think I can get — I think I can zero in on that one and find this. I can work out from that two ways and come up with it pretty fast I think.

NIXON: [unclear] that's what he's really saying — to [Larry] Higby, wasn't it?

EHRLICHMAN: I assume so. I — that's the only thing I can think of.

HALDEMAN: It's a danger of assuming that because —

EHRLICHMAN: Yeah.

HALDEMAN: — you could be wrong. The thing that impressed Higby most out of that conversation was that Dean was totally cold — totally, not much different from the old John Dean. And he said, "Larry, I have nothing to fear here, I fear no man in this world."

NIXON: Because he has every man involved.

HALDEMAN: Larry said afterward he acted as if he were in [unclear].

EHRLICHMAN: Dean is terribly afraid, and this has come up two or three times. He's terribly afraid of his inability to carry on the line. He's afraid that —

NIXON: Slight hand shake.

HALDEMAN: Yes, he told me that earlier when there's this question that popped up with

Mitchell and Dean. [unclear] Goddamn! You know, the son of a—they've got to take into their minds, somehow, the assumption that Dean may be lying and try to break him, too. They can't just use Dean as a witness on other people. They've also got to look at Dean as a principal.

NIXON: Yeah.

EHRLICHMAN: Part of the reason that we've got to get down there and talk to this U.S. attorney—

NIXON: Yeah. How do you face this? We're quite cold. You're not—what Dean can say about you, it would be your word against Dean. Where they're concerned is [unclear] Dean saying something about the president. Opportunity [unclear] to the present day—damn cold on that point. [unclear] work on that principle. So we can all be [unclear] sure, Mr. President, and all that sort of thing. Obstruction. I don't know [unclear]—you bartering for more trouble for him and probably not with Dean. You have an individual here who's out to do various things—

HALDEMAN: You've got the other side of it though. If it comes down to Dean versus the president—Dean won't be believed either.

NIXON: Well—

HALDEMAN: And—

NIXON: Well—

HALDEMAN: And well—

NIXON: That's a terrible charge though.

HALDEMAN: It—

NIXON: You don't know what he has [unclear]. But, if you think [unclear].

HALDEMAN: Yes, sir.

NIXON: And I'll ask him where the [unclear].

HALDEMAN: Yes, sir.

[Unclear exchange]

NIXON: If we could leave that for a moment—

HALDEMAN: Let's just stay with it for a second.

NIXON: Or—well, I mean, let me say—yeah, I'm going to stay with it, but I made the point. The point that I'm also making though is that before I meet with Petersen tonight, I want to know what the damn tapes are. Now, the earlier tapes I am sure dealt almost exclusively with, with executive privilege or that sort of thing.

HALDEMAN: Sure. Yeah, but your meeting with Dean and Moore was on the subject of how to deal with the Ervin Committee that time.

NIXON: That's right.

HALDEMAN: That's how it all started. At least the way—

NIXON: That's right. The Dean report—

HALDEMAN: [unclear]

NIXON: —and all that sort of stuff and so forth and so on. But, at a later point, you see, Dean may have decided in his own mind, "Well, I've got to get the president involved—"

HALDEMAN: No.

NIXON: " — and that's probably why he told me about it."

HALDEMAN: One day on an afternoon —

NIXON: You don't think so?

HALDEMAN: Well, I think — on an afternoon you told him apparently by phone — you didn't see him from what I could gather because he apparently talked to me afterwards. You said, "John, I want you to come in here tomorrow morning at nine o'clock — or whatever it was — and I want you to give me the entire story, everything, all the facts, because I don't have all the specifics." Dean called me and said, "The president wants me to do this. I should, I — get into everything?" I said, "Yes, sir. That's a privileged communication."

NIXON: But you don't know the date of that.

HALDEMAN: Yes, I do.

NIXON: When was that?

HALDEMAN: I think it was the twentieth. I can check but I don't have it right here. But I have it. The reason you called him, one of the reasons — and I told Dean at that time, "Give him everything" and then the next morning you met with Ehrlichman for an hour and then Dean came in. Met with Dean for about two hours, the last forty minutes of which you had me in.

NIXON: Probably to talk about this.

HALDEMAN: I think so. That must have been the time that we talked about this because I recollect it as being an afternoon. But that afternoon you met with Ehrlichman and Dean and with me, but it was in this office — not over there and I know the meeting that I remember was in the Oval Office.

NIXON: [unclear]

HALDEMAN: This one was about our concern of —

EHRLICHMAN: The reason you called Dean and asked for this information was you were on our backs, very hard, to get a statement out.

NIXON: Yeah.

EHRLICHMAN: And we kept telling you we couldn't — that we kept running into blind alleys and there doesn't seem any way to crack this. And finally we suggested to you that you talk to Dean. Because Dean was saying to us, rolling his eyes and saying, "You don't want to know that," or "I don't want to get into that with you." And we could never crack this. And so we decided that one way to satisfy you on this would be for you to hear from Dean in a privileged conversation what the facts were. Now we decided that without ourselves knowing what the facts were.

NIXON: You know the date of that. Well, as soon as we can —

HALDEMAN: These things work — I can find out.

NIXON: Well, it's very important that — see, I didn't —

EHRLICHMAN: See, this came out of La Costa. La Costa was for two reasons. One was to talk about what we do about the Ervin problem. The other was that all through my notes of the preceding month, you're saying, "Damn it, we've got to get a statement out. We've got to get something out that will satisfy [unclear]. Remember the [unclear] letter. We gotta get something out that we can show [unclear]."

NIXON: Well, I have a fairly good, I think, record during that whole period — March 21 till about [unclear] —

EHRLICHMAN: This goes back —

NIXON: — I told Ziegler today to say, "Why didn't he do it before March 21?" He said, "Well, on March 21 he personally began his own investigation. Before that he had relied on others, and now he personally" — which I don't —

EHRLICHMAN: March 21 is the morning you met with Dean. There must be twelve or fifteen different places in my notes and conversations with you over the preceding six months where you are banging away on the necessity of getting this to happen.

HALDEMAN: I have it, too. If I — you know, time after time.

EHRLICHMAN: And we kept coming back to you and saying —

NIXON: [unclear]

EHRLICHMAN: — we can't.

HALDEMAN: We will. We'll say — we'll get that.

EHRLICHMAN: But we kept coming back to you with a dry hole. We sat for five hours in La Costa and came up with three sentences. Now why was that? Well, it — for the reason I've just suggested.

[Unclear exchange]

NIXON: I think my recollection of the Bittman conversations is about correct then.

HALDEMAN: I do, too.

NIXON: I — you know what I mean? For blackmail — I didn't. I simply — the only thing that I — it's unfortunate to — I said, "Well, John, what would it cost to keep — for four years?" "A million dollars." "Well, I guess we could get that kind of money." You remember how I said it.

HALDEMAN: But then we turned it off. I mean this was —

NIXON: Oh, I said get that then. Then I think that somebody said that, "My God — you just — you can't do that." You know what I mean?

HALDEMAN: Well, let's not worry about it. Let me listen to it [unclear] —

EHRLICHMAN: The point here is to try and disarm him. He may — I'm morally certain he does not know that he is on tape. And —

NIXON: I wonder if he has a tape himself.

EHRLICHMAN: That might be. That might be, and —

NIXON: Is it possible that he carries a tape? Does he do that, do you know of?

EHRLICHMAN: I don't know that he does that. But if he ever did —

NIXON: I would doubt that he would do that [unclear].

HALDEMAN: Not at that that point, I mean. Later he might have. Larry [Higby] said he carried something in with him [unclear] a tape recorder in his office [unclear].

NIXON: Well, he carries with him — when he came with me, he didn't have a briefcase. But can he carry it in his hip or something?

HALDEMAN: [unclear] but it's tough.

NIXON: It is?

EHRLICHMAN: Yeah. Those things almost always go haywire.

HALDEMAN: Then he can't use that tape anyway. It's a privileged conversation.

EHRLICHMAN: [unclear] tape of a privileged conversation —

NIXON: [laughs] "Privileged conversation" has all going out the window here.

EHRLICHMAN: That's the point. If privilege were of any use here, why — you know, we wouldn't have a problem. But I think that what he's doing here —

NIXON: Trying to blackmail me.

EHRLICHMAN: — is trying to manipulate the president on the basis that no confession of a crime is privileged and if the president's guilty of a crime, and that by golly he'd better get immunity in this thing or that's what's going to happen.

HALDEMAN: Okay. Let's assume the worst then which is that that's exactly what it is. Then you don't have only one route. You say immunity is the price or whatever that we'd have to pay. That we — my argument would be that that's the worst thing you can do because that then puts you in as a permanent hostage for the rest of your life to John Dean and if you look beyond that to Henry Petersen, and beyond that probably to Silbert and Glanzer and to the court reporter and others.

EHRLICHMAN: Two — the lawyers in Rockville.

HALDEMAN: Yeah, Dean's lawyers, et cetera. If you, if — as soon as you let them go that way then you are admitting the problem. And it seems to me that your only route — really your only real route is to destroy Dean rather than to — rather than to preserve him perhaps which is what that does.

NIXON: Yeah.

EHRLICHMAN: I think it's too soon to know. Obviously this road goes two directions.

NIXON: Yep.

HALDEMAN: And when we see what the — what you have why then we'll know much more clearly or you'll know what you have.

NIXON: How could you? Let's just take — possibly —

HALDEMAN: All right.

NIXON: How could you destroy him?

EHRLICHMAN: We call Petersen in and just say Dean apparently had a conversation with Higby yesterday. [unclear] I had a conversation with Dean — whenever the last time it was that you had a conversation with Dean where he asked us to sign those letters and maybe it was on another occasion. Say, "Henry, I do not have any overt, concrete, satisfactory documentary evidence that I'm being blackmailed here but that is the distinct impression that Mr. Dean gives me. I want to tell you that this president is not subject to blackmail, and I want this turned on Dean. I want you to lay a trap for him. I want you to determine whether or not he is attempting to blackmail me and indirectly you. And I want the full weight of the law to fall on him if that's what he's up to." Now, you may not — you may not catch him —

NIXON: Yeah.

EHRLICHMAN: — Petersen may not want to do it. There may be all kinds of things, but at least the important thing —

NIXON: Well, Petersen [unclear] what do you say about him?

EHRLICHMAN: Yeah, he turned the thing around in the opposite direction —

HALDEMAN: That's the other thing —

EHRLICHMAN: [unclear]

HALDEMAN: He's probably blackmailing Petersen.

EHRLICHMAN: I'm confident he is.

NIXON: Yeah, I think he is on this business of information —

HALDEMAN: [unclear] Petersen who are allies with the president as a fellow black-mailee. It might put [unclear] too.

EHRLICHMAN: All I'm suggesting is that there is another direction to go and it's stronger I think than — from the standpoint of the president — than the immunity thing, which —

NIXON: Well, I can't. I don't know. I guess you're right. You go the immunity route —

HALDEMAN: It's one more cover-up.

NIXON: Yeah. It's another cover-up. I'm trying to cover up because — trying to silence Dean. And frankly, if I said something was wrong then I deserve to be impeached.

EHRLICHMAN: Well, look at it this way, if you did, and you try to live it out, that way —

NIXON: That's right.

EHRLICHMAN: You talk about you got to get this cloud over and you got to start moving on to new directions and doing your job. You sure as hell can't do it that way.

NIXON: Well, but face it, basically, if I said some stupid thing [unclear]. I'm not — I'm quite candid about it. I mean, I'm not a Christian Scientist.

EHRLICHMAN: [laughs]

NIXON: No, seriously, John, I mean if I — if Dean — if I was most [unclear] president. It would be allowed [unclear] even my counsel [unclear]. Jesus Christ, I thought at least we could talk to our people. I mean, you all recommended it. I talked to [unclear] Dean and everybody. [unclear] just had him in.

HALDEMAN: Well, see that's the other way to destroy Dean — is not only by Petersen trapping him but by the president, if we had the argument here that the president's got to go out and do something — which is an argument that seems to be strongly made by everyone — that you can get out and take the following steps. You can talk — that's — the obvious answer is always the president goes out on TV, talks to the people. Well, let's say at some point you have to do that. Okay? You hit them that you're their leader, or you present yourself as their leader in time of crisis even when it's your own crisis. And that they've got to understand and share the agony that you've been going through. That you can and must suspend — take the resignation of John Dean. You can't operate the presidency by threat. You don't say this — but this is what you've got to do. You have to remove the threat in order to do it and you say that that's what you've done. This is a man who's disserved you. The American people — you've got to go on the assumption that the American people want to believe in their president. I think that's absolutely true. And they want you to say it isn't true, and when you say it they're going to be — they're going to say, "I'm glad he said it." But you're going to have to hang somewhere [unclear]. You've got to accept ultimate blame for what happened.

NIXON: [unclear] of course.

HALDEMAN: Which moves — removes you from the actual guilt of the, you know, the —

NIXON: Well, I —

HALDEMAN: — individual act.

NIXON: — I already have that.

HALDEMAN: And go through all you've accomplished — you've got to go on accomplishing that. Order Petersen to get this thing brought to Justice and indicate that some of your closest aides have come under attack and that you have been informed that they're not guilty but they are responsible for what's done. And, so — but if anything comes out, then they've had it. [unclear] But you can't use a gimmick to cover up which I think our going out early maybe does. Maybe you then got to take the offensive in saying as to where this does show there has been something wrong in American politics. This campaign has been subject to the most microscopic scrutiny — the only microscopic scrutiny that any presidential campaign's ever been subjected to and it doesn't stand up well. You're sad to see — by that — any more than any other campaign would and that doesn't make it good. That makes it bad. Because bad — you're going to lead a crusade as a retiring president in changing the American political campaign structure. So I think you've got to play some — that kind of game somehow.

NIXON: Sure.

HALDEMAN: Because there's just too much other stuff coming out. It isn't the Watergate. It's this guy — all this financing shit. And the appearances of problems in that way, and the things that we did — that we admit we did. The Segretti business and the having hecklers at rallies and the — you know, all that kind of stuff. I think we've got to say that we did it because we had to in self-defense. We don't apologize for it, but looking at it now, now that finally someone's looking at a campaign, it ain't right.

EHRLICHMAN: There's an angle in there, too. That part of this is a product of our whole media structure.

NIXON: Yeah.

EHRLICHMAN: And that campaigns today didn't just spring full bloom from foreheads of campaign managers. They are the product of the condition [unclear] so to speak.

NIXON: Well, of course, finding out without trying to say, well, "They did it, we did it," that [unclear], for example on the letters — the wires generated at the May bombing. We generate wires all the time. We try to — but so does the other side. Just as a common practice it — that I think can be defended although I don't know who was the asshole over there [unclear] who said we never [unclear] somebody in the reelection committee.

HALDEMAN: [unclear] *Post* story. [unclear]

EHRLICHMAN: They're turning to all that now.

HALDEMAN: You've got to assume that they're turning to the Colson stuff. That story is the first to come of all of that coming out, I think, because it's —

NIXON: Yeah.

HALDEMAN: — part of that. We're going to be faced with that.

EHRLICHMAN: They have, apparently, the key to that in my other notes on my talk with O'Brien — O'Brien gave me the rundown on these various expenditures and it would look like they had [unclear] —

HALDEMAN: — spent a lot of money.

EHRLICHMAN: — [unclear] there's a lot of money.

HALDEMAN: They're going to [unclear] out one by one.

EHRLICHMAN: Yeah. And you could make it — you could make a big story on each one. Bringing the Cubans up here to be counterdemonstrators and all that sort of stuff. It's bound to come [unclear].

NIXON: Some of that stuff I think we can survive.

HALDEMAN: I do, too.

EHRLICHMAN: Sure, but it'll be a —

HALDEMAN: But it's just all more credit.

NIXON: Mm-hmm. [unclear] —

HALDEMAN: The only thing you can't survive is presidential culpability. And that, I don't think there is.

NIXON: Well, basically — let me put it this way. You shouldn't survive if the president was culpable out there. But in this instance —

EHRLICHMAN: But you're not.

NIXON: — apparently [unclear] being forced. [unclear] suggests from unreliable sources and so forth and so on.

HALDEMAN: You didn't even know about those.

NIXON: I never saw any.

HALDEMAN: No, sir.

NIXON: It never came to my desk.

HALDEMAN: That's right.

NIXON: So I know nothing about anything of that sort.

HALDEMAN: There's no way to make that case at all or even implied.

NIXON: As far as afterwards is concerned, the only conversation I remember in the summer even — the only conversation in the summer involving — with John, I walked on the beach, and he said, "Eventually the problem of these people — " Maybe you had already made the call to Kalmbach, at that point. You didn't tell me you —

EHRLICHMAN: No, I don't believe so. I think it was later that month or the following month. We can't pin it down very closely.

NIXON: But anyway, but you said, "You know, I think the problem of these defendants is going to be bigger than there are higher-ups in it." Right?

EHRLICHMAN: Right.

NIXON: We didn't — even then though we didn't talk about Mitchell being in, did we?

EHRLICHMAN: Didn't know it. I —

NIXON: Or Magruder.

EHRLICHMAN: I had — we still don't know it. I still don't know it. But at that time, all I had was a lingering suspicion. As a matter of fact, it wasn't until the end of the month, I hope you remember the details of our walk, but you kept saying to me, "Is Colson in this?" And I kept saying, "I don't know." And —

HALDEMAN: At that time you thought he was.

EHRLICHMAN: I thought he was.

NIXON: Yeah.

EHRLICHMAN: And I would be very guarded about this whole thing because I thought Chuck was up to his ass in this thing. That was in July. That was a month after.

NIXON: All right. Then the — I think — lay it all out as far as the clemency thing.

HALDEMAN: Yeah.

NIXON: The clemency plan was raised by Chuck with me. But it was handled totally responsibly. That I remember. It was right in this room.

HALDEMAN: Well —

NIXON: [unclear] and he said, "What about clemency for Hunt, because of his wife?" I said, "Chuck, I feel sorry for the fellow," and so forth and so on. That, of course, would have to be considered. But that's all I said. And I don't think Colson was going to get his tit in a wringer on that one.

HALDEMAN: No. He's very solid about that. He says that area —

NIXON: That is the only time clemency was ever discussed with him. I — do you recall any others?

EHRLICHMAN: I do not.

NIXON: Then that — there's no discussion of that — I recall, clemency — with Dean.

HALDEMAN: What about with Mitchell?

NIXON: Mitchell never raised the subject. I didn't talk to Mitchell about this matter. Do you realize that?

EHRLICHMAN: Yeah. That's why —

NIXON: I —

HALDEMAN: Look at [unclear] these press stories put out.

NIXON: I never talked to Mitchell, period!

HALDEMAN: One of the stories now says that "Mitchell visited the president — had to know about what was going on or something because he met daily with John Mitchell." [unclear]

NIXON: You could get that out —

HALDEMAN: [unclear] —

NIXON: I —

HALDEMAN: [unclear] with John Mitchell.

NIXON: And I never met with him alone. We can all [unclear] in those meetings in the Oval Office. That, frankly, is —

HALDEMAN: [unclear]

NIXON: — is, uh —

HALDEMAN: No, they were talking about back in January, that you were meeting daily with John Mitchell —

NIXON: January?

HALDEMAN: — setting up the campaign plans. So you had to know about the intelligence plan.

NIXON: Never, never, never. That was — perhaps you ought to go back over and see him. It might be worthwhile to see how often did I meet with Mitchell.

HALDEMAN: I am.

NIXON: How often was it?

HALDEMAN: Well, I haven't gone back to that period because I was working on the other period. That's easy to do. It was virtually, you know —

NIXON: I don't remember that. Why I didn't discuss the campaign with Mitchell. I was — honestly, frankly — working on other things.

HALDEMAN: Sure as hell were.

NIXON: I wanted to stay out of that. I left it to other people. See? So there's that. Then the other thing. You know the other thing is basically this last conversation with Dean. But let's take that at its very worst now — its very worst. That has to be played flat-out that at that time I had a grave suspicion of Dean and I had to find out what the story was.

EHRLICHMAN: You were then in about your tenth hour of conversation with him that night or something —

NIXON: That's right.

HALDEMAN: And if you were thinking something was fishy, why can't we get something now? Goddamn it, somebody's got to tell me what the facts are on this.

NIXON: When did I bring you into the matter?

EHRLICHMAN: Thirtieth. A week later.

NIXON: A week later.

EHRLICHMAN: Now —

HALDEMAN: [unclear] here is the week that Dean spent up at Camp David under orders from you to get the thing written out.

EHRLICHMAN: Exactly. See, he gave you some stuff.

NIXON: Yeah.

EHRLICHMAN: He came right out of those meetings with you and you sent him to Camp David for six days.

NIXON: No. He went to Camp David —

EHRLICHMAN: He was only supposed to take two days.

NIXON: There was a reason he went to Camp David as I recall. Somebody had charged him with —

EHRLICHMAN: That's right. Gray.

HALDEMAN: Pat Gray said he'd lied.

NIXON: Something like that — the television was out.

EHRLICHMAN: That was on [unclear] —

NIXON: Told John, "Get up to Camp David to try to — "

HALDEMAN: Right.

NIXON: " — write this damn story out."

HALDEMAN: Exactly.

EHRLICHMAN: And that occurred right about the time that you were talking to Dean all through this thing. And that also shook everybody's confidence in Dean a little bit — the way that whole thing was handled. And so you sent him up there to put this thing down on paper. At the end of two days, he said he didn't have it done. We were then on the coast as I recall —

NIXON: Well, I didn't see him in that [unclear].

EHRLICHMAN: You were out of town. You were out of town all through that —

HALDEMAN: You never saw him again. Until, you know, just the recent stuff.

EHRLICHMAN: But anyway, he came down from the mountain —

HALDEMAN: — and you didn't see him.

EHRLICHMAN: — on the sixth day and reported that there were no tablets, [laughs] that he didn't write it down.

NIXON: Wait a minute. Where were we then?

EHRLICHMAN: Well, we had come back to town.

NIXON: Were we in Florida?

EHRLICHMAN: We were — San Clemente.

HALDEMAN: But we only stayed a couple days. Remember that was the San Clemente trip you cut short.

EHRLICHMAN: No, no, no —

NIXON: Well, that was February — the San Clemente trip cut short.

EHRLICHMAN: — [unclear] short in February. Well, this was the last swing to San Clemente. But we came back on the twenty-eighth.

NIXON: [unclear] to talk with Dean and [unclear]?

HALDEMAN: No.

EHRLICHMAN: He said [unclear] — I've got this all laid out. Why don't I get it? It's important.

NIXON: Let's get it.

[EHRLICHMAN retrieves his calendar.]

[HALDEMAN retrieves tapes of Nixon and Dean.]

• • •

EHRLICHMAN: John Dean saw the president for forty-five minutes on Monday.

NIXON: Monday what?

EHRLICHMAN: Monday the nineteenth.

HALDEMAN: But that isn't the one.

EHRLICHMAN: Sixty minutes on Tuesday the twentieth.

HALDEMAN: That isn't it.

NIXON: Well, yes —

EHRLICHMAN: A hundred and five minutes on Wednesday the twenty-first.

HALDEMAN: It's more than that. It's a hundred and ten in the morning. [unclear] here at midday here in the EOB with Mitchell and then he met later in the day here with you and me.

NIXON: Well, I don't care about all those meetings. You see what I mean? I just want the ones that I alone had with him. I don't —

EHRLICHMAN: And there were a lot of meetings the previous week.

HALDEMAN: We can —

NIXON: I know. You apparently made no notes then, Bob, of your meeting with Dean and me with regard to the Bittman conversation?

HALDEMAN: It's very surprising.

NIXON: But, incidentally, Dean made no notes either.

HALDEMAN: Is that what he says?

NIXON: He never made notes when he was in my office that I recall. He never made notes; that's why I wondered if he had a recorder. I wonder if it's possible he carried a recorder.

HALDEMAN: It is possible. But it's highly unlikely.

EHRLICHMAN: Dean went to Camp David the twenty-third. He was there until the twenty-eighth. We were in town the whole time. You didn't go to San Clemente until the thirtieth.

NIXON: Well, I was in town that week working on a speech.

EHRLICHMAN: Oh, yeah. And —

NIXON: I called him three or four times while he was up there, at least.

EHRLICHMAN: Yeah, yeah. He was there all —

NIXON: "You, are you doing?"

EHRLICHMAN: — weekend until the middle of the week. And then it was — he came back the twenty-eighth. The twenty-ninth is a variable. The thirtieth is when you asked me to take over.

HALDEMAN: You didn't see him —

NIXON: The reason I asked you to take over was he was so easily — what'd I say?

EHRLICHMAN: You said, "Dean is up to his ass, ears, elbows — something — in this, and he simply cannot be permitted —"

NIXON: Was it because he had charges of — in his conduct of the FBI and all of this?

EHRLICHMAN: No. You didn't even elaborate that one. You just said that you had the feeling — you brought this right out of right field. This was not a subject we were discussing. You raised it, and you said to me, "Dean is in this so deeply that I just can't have him continue. You're going to have to get in."

HALDEMAN: It was — I think at that point it was a combination of factors. There was this problem with the FBI and the Pat Gray business and your dissatisfaction that we weren't getting anything out of the [unclear], and Dean was being hammered at that point. I was reporting to you on that [unclear] about his own problems. And he was — we were into at that point — we were into the start, I think, of the problem of Dean versus Mitchell on whether there was a meeting or not.

NIXON: Yeah.

HALDEMAN: Preplanning meeting of the Watergate. I mean the problem — if Dean —

NIXON: Well, one thing I did test him on was whether in his testimony did —

HALDEMAN: — hit the grand jury, would —

NIXON: — would impeach Mitchell.

HALDEMAN: That's right.

NIXON: Well, that was discussed.

HALDEMAN: That's right.

NIXON: Moore apparently had been — I discussed that —

HALDEMAN: That's right.

NIXON: — but I didn't tell 'em to change a goddamn thing.

HALDEMAN: Absolutely.

EHRLICHMAN: And neither did I. All of that night, Dean was — looking to me for support on — I can't lie. I kept saying he didn't — "Nobody's saying you should lie." He said, "Mitchell is saying I should lie."

NIXON: Well then [unclear] John Mitchell [unclear] be sure to [unclear].

EHRLICHMAN: It may be you would say there would be — if you're going to move on that, you've got to be sure, you know? It's got to be done.

NIXON: That's what I should have said, but I — you know what I mean?

HALDEMAN: No, I think you did.

NIXON: Huh?

HALDEMAN: I think you did. I don't think —

NIXON: Dean at that point was talking about — when did he make his, "Draw up the wagons around the White House"?

HALDEMAN: In the afternoon of the twenty-first, after the meeting here as we walked out. And it was — that was when he said it on the steps going down this building, after Dean, Ehrlichman, and I had met with you in here late afternoon.

NIXON: That was when we had the executive privilege meeting on the — or Mitchell, too?

HALDEMAN: He — no, Mitchell had met with us in here earlier, midday.

NIXON: Oh, then Dean-Ehr — what was that conversation about?

HALDEMAN: It was about the Ervin Committee.

NIXON: Yeah?

HALDEMAN: And then Dean on the way out — I'd probably got into other things. I've got some notes on that. Then Dean on the way out said, you know, "I keep thinking we should draw the wagons up around the White House so there's nobody in here who has any problem. The problems are outside. We can draw it up here and hold tight." Well, what I now know is that the only one in here with any problem was him. And that was one route, he was — he was looking for routes. Go backwards and you can see. One route he was looking at was, "Give me immunity and let me go to the grand jury." Pushed that one hard for a while. Then he was doing the "Gather up the wagons around the White House and there's none of us that have any problems — let those guys go down." And then he went to the — then he — none of those were working. And then he started in on the blackmail route of his attack — started with the [unclear].

NIXON: Bittman?

HALDEMAN: Well, Bittman — no, that wasn't blackmail at that time. That was the problem he was trying to figure out how to deal with it.

NIXON: But we described it —

HALDEMAN: [unclear]

NIXON: — as blackmail — at that time.

HALDEMAN: I think so. And, he, at some point he got into the — using blackmail as a defense theory but I don't know where that went.

EHRLICHMAN: Let me read you just two excerpts from my notes that may — [unclear] February 27, we'll go back. That was about the time that you began to meet first with Dean at any length and that was twenty-five minutes on that day. And here are the notes that I took from what you said to me. "I disapprove the executive privilege statement. It does not solve the nonappearance situation. Try to state the standard case and review the statement — quote until later. Phone Kleindienst and Dean and tell them to get into the game quickly with regard to the Ervin Committee. Haldeman and Ehrlichman should stay out of this. The president should see Dean at once. Ehrlichman should immediately take over the congressional sales strategy in the Domestic Council and cabinet people — that was on the other problems." Then skipping to March 20, the day before your — here probably. You had a meeting with Bush and I sat in. Bush raised the problem of the Watergate case building, urged that Dean be available to testify before the Ervin Committee. And then you said, "I suggest that the general John Dean statement on the Watergate matter be prepared that Bush can send out along with assurances of cooperation. This will also serve to assist Ziegler. This would be the preferred method — write it out, so we can give copies to the congressional leaders, et cetera." I mean it appears a dozen times.

HALDEMAN: You are really worried about that [unclear].

EHRLICHMAN: "Dispose of many of the pending questions, with regard to Chapin, Dean, et cetera. Deal with the Watergate matter — campaign. Also, we should issue a statement by Maury Stans referring to the campaign fund question. Answer the Kalmbach and other issues that have been raised. Dean should in effect prepare a brief on this. Things to be hit in the statement including the fact that the president wants the chips to fall where they may. That there was no White House investigation because the FBI was so thoroughly investigating the other matters. That there was a White House investigation by Dean." What it showed: "Why not put it down? The president must insist that the facts not be hidden. Dean should brief the cabinet on Watergate and answer questions. He should also brief the leaders." [unclear] the twentieth.

HALDEMAN: Except it was also on the twentieth that you told Dean you wanted him to come out on the twenty-first of February and tell you the whole story. You see, you were sort of getting on top. You were saying, "I want this statement." Then you're saying, "By God, I've got to know what this is." Then you — then we, I think, said, "You've got to know because we're — we don't. We can't write this. He won't tell us."

NIXON: Well, Dean's story that [unclear] as I recall was the "cancer in the heart of the presidency" speech as he calls it now. Let me tell you the problem. The problem is that in the aftermath the money was raised and so forth and so on. The Bittman thing came in. [unclear] met with Mitchell the next day.

HALDEMAN: I think it might have come before that.

EHRLICHMAN: It didn't come much before that. It was only kickin' around here a couple of days. I don't know.

NIXON: When did th — when did he talk to you about Bittman?

EHRLICHMAN: I believe he talked to me on the twentieth in the morning.

NIXON: [unclear] talk to you? That could have been [unclear]. Did I see him the twentieth?

EHRLICHMAN: Might have been. I don't have any notes.

HALDEMAN: See, he wouldn't have to, because it was the Bittman thing and was a direct threat to Ehrlichman. [unclear] done to Ehrlichman.

NIXON: Yeah, yeah. My point is though that I —

HALDEMAN: [unclear]

NIXON: Your recollection of any part of the meeting you were in — why you're going to get the tape — you'll find out what? That I did not tell Dean to go out and raise the money. Did I ever do anything like that? John? Bob?

HALDEMAN: Not that I know of.

EHRLICHMAN: The Bush [unclear] says, so to speak —

NIXON: Yeah.

EHRLICHMAN: — [unclear] is the foundation for your having the long session with Dean the next day.

NIXON: Yeah, yeah.

EHRLICHMAN: The point is what did —

NIXON: Whether or not I suggested that to Dean, well, we've got to get the money. I may have said that. I may have said that. And if I did, what the hell's the defense to that, John?

EHRLICHMAN: I don't know. It would depend on how it came out. It may be that it was — you could — you can say, "I was on an investigation kick. It was entrapment. I intended to find out how far this guy was in this. I wanted to see what his response would be. The fact that he didn't respond to me by saying, 'Mr. President, I couldn't do a thing like that' told me volumes about this and I probably couldn't have worked any other way."

NIXON: That's right.

EHRLICHMAN: The point is that, too — that day, that very day you must've instructed him to "write this down." Two days later —

NIXON: I, probably — more likely to have said — look, I think I'm more likely to have said, "John, this is a Mitchell problem," or something like that. But, it's —

EHRLICHMAN: That's what he was keeping from everybody.

HALDEMAN: The problem you've got if you follow this route now is how do you explain the coddling of Dean up to now?

NIXON: Well, the — we haven't got — the point is that Dean, well, basically because Petersen has told him — told me, too.

EHRLICHMAN: [unclear] counsel.

NIXON: Petersen has said, "We're trying to get Dean to testify or to plead." Therefore, like I said, I've asked him. I said, "Should I ask for his resignation?" He said, "No." Now, that's — I think we've got a pretty good case there. [unclear]

HALDEMAN: Then why didn't you follow his advice and get our resignation?

NIXON: What?

HALDEMAN: Apparently he told you he wanted you to get our resignation.

NIXON: Yes, he did. He did. He and Kleindienst both did. They said, "They ought to resign." And I said, "No," et cetera, et cetera.

HALDEMAN: That's rather incredible, to want us to resign and want you to keep him.

NIXON: No, but you see if —

HALDEMAN: I remember — it was tied to the immunizing him and getting the [unclear].

NIXON: The context for the whole deal probably was the immunizing. That and getting your resignations.

HALDEMAN: So he has some view that if he can come down in our company he comes down better than if he comes down alone.

EHRLICHMAN: Oh, yes. The press is getting more and more immobile.

NIXON: Like what?

EHRLICHMAN: In other words, I'm saying that John Dean will testify to the grand jury that [unclear].

NIXON: [unclear] description. Like what?

EHRLICHMAN: Haldeman set up a plan for obstruction of justice when he was just a little fellow who carried it out.

NIXON: Haldeman said that — for obstruction of justice?

HALDEMAN: That's one.

EHRLICHMAN: Yeah. And there was another one [unclear] that you and I would be implicated by Dean and his testimony before the grand jury. It's quite specific.

NIXON: Is that right? These things move fast. Good thing I'm going to see Petersen today. Probably it's a good thing I hadn't seen him before. [unclear]

EHRLICHMAN: And Dean's evidently come up with some new stuff. Because that was his intimation to Higby —

NIXON: On [unclear]?

EHRLICHMAN: On us. You remember he said that he — the president knew some but not entirely all —

HALDEMAN: Of what he was going to say.

EHRLICHMAN: — of what he was going to say.

NIXON: The president himself knew what he was going to say?

HALDEMAN: Most but not all of what he was going to say at the grand jury. He said, "I'm going to tell nothing — I'm just going to tell the truth. The president knows most but not all of what I'm going to say."

NIXON: I think, for sure, you can be sure before the grand jury. They will never ever ask him about a conversation with the president. [unclear] I know that. Well, when I say they — Petersen says that's privileged. I mean, nobody questions that.

HALDEMAN: I think that's right. That's — it has to stay that way until they decide they're making a case against [unclear] — presidential — well, that's only when you go to — because they can't make the case against the president. That's the execution [unclear].

NIXON: Impeachment? Is that being talked about now?

EHRLICHMAN: No, I tell you this is a figment of my imagination. This whole — the whole subject —

NIXON: No figment.

EHRLICHMAN: — but I sat and looked at the wall last night for an hour and tried to think this thing through. And that's where I keep coming out. And that's the ultimate — the ultimate play here.

NIXON: Well, let's take it at its worst which [unclear] an hour or two.

. . .

NIXON: I didn't know this before that Dean and Magruder are supposed to be mortal enemies — now each is trying to do the other in.

HALDEMAN: That's not surprising.

EHRLICHMAN: It isn't that. And Magruder of course in talking to me, being responsible for having contrived the story and —

NIXON: That Dean told him to say? Is that right?

EHRLICHMAN: Constructed the cover story, coached him on how —

NIXON: This is after he had talked to the U.S. attorney.

HALDEMAN: Yeah.

EHRLICHMAN: Yeah, but Magruder told me that before in the meeting I had with Magruder and Mitchell that day.

NIXON: What did he say?

HALDEMAN: He said the same thing Dean had told him to say. He said, "Dean can't go out and undercut my story because the reason I gave my story was Dean told me to. I could have easily said there were the two meetings." It wouldn't have made any difference to my case, but Dean told me not to because they wanted to keep Dean's name out of it. Mitchell was present when that happened and Mitchell admits he was present when that happened. [unclear] meeting in [Department of Justice

Criminal Division attorney Benton] Becker's office. You know, it's all detailed on that.

NIXON: Well, Dean has certainly — well, Magruder has told that story.

HALDEMAN: That if you recall is the kind of thing that I was worried about at the time we were talking about going up to testify and all and saying I have information that I don't have to testify to. I don't know if it's true but I know what was told.

NIXON: Yeah.

HALDEMAN: But if it is hearsay in that sense then it's hearsay on principle. [unclear] testify to that because of being put in a position of incriminating Mitchell. I didn't think I was incriminating —

NIXON: John, just think of the Bittman thing. I don't know. You were there, Bob. Do you remember my saying to Dean, "Well, look, for Christ's sakes, take care of him? Be sure the son of a bitch doesn't talk."

HALDEMAN: Nothing like that.

EHRLICHMAN: I think, actually, you've got a good point here, on — this suborning of perjury thing's a pretty good example of the kind of ignorance we were living in over here with regard to what Dean was doing. Now, it's also true, over in the money department, in the payoff of the defendants, the hush-up money.

NIXON: How's that?

EHRLICHMAN: That we were basically in the dark as to what Dean was doing, except when he would come to us on a specific instance as he did when he needed us to get Kalmbach. I have a hunch that if we hadn't had to lock on Kalmbach the way we did, he'd have just short-circuited us out and gone direct to Kalmbach and done it that way. But he discovered that Kalmbach would not take orders from him.

NIXON: But he — Dean — wanted the money for hush — here again.

HALDEMAN: I don't know that.

EHRLICHMAN: At that time, which was in July and August —

NIXON: [unclear] Mitchell.

EHRLICHMAN: I think not. I think they had monumental attorneys' problems and that they were legitimately concerned about how to hire counsel for these guys and that —

HALDEMAN: [unclear] Then how to retain them because after they got counsel, counsel was walking on.

EHRLICHMAN: See, they got very high-powered guys like F. Lee Bailey's office, and others. And they must have had big money problems.

HALDEMAN: Well, we know that. Some lawyer that was one of their — was Hunt's lawyer, somebody —

EHRLICHMAN: Ran into our attorney on the street.

HALDEMAN: Ran into our attorney on the street and said, "The son of a bitch still owes me a hundred thousand dollars" or something.

NIXON: Hunt does?

HALDEMAN: Yeah.

EHRLICHMAN: He'd been promised cash payment in full, and received twenty-five hundred dollars. So, I think at the time Herb got into this, that —

NIXON: It was in your view — it was your concern it was attorneys' fees — the rest were the same —

EHRLICHMAN: Absolutely.

NIXON: — at the time you paid the three fifty — or ordered the three fifty.

EHRLICHMAN: Well, when you get an even more compelling case on the three fifty because it certainly can be, I think, successfully argued that there was no motive at all —

NIXON: After the election.

EHRLICHMAN: — in the White House.

HALDEMAN: What happened to these defendants after the election. I couldn't care less what happened if they got burned. I didn't know — I didn't know what was going on there or, you know, who was where. In fact [unclear] —

NIXON: Well, somebody [unclear] story on it. One story kicking around that was forty — forty was the election and some afterwards. Is that correct or not?

HALDEMAN: That's very [unclear] because I don't know. I'm told that it was all after the election but that there were two chunks, that there were a chunk of forty and then another chunk.

NIXON: You see they put [unclear] — Petersen told me — this is for your information only, not about the [unclear]. But he did tell me that Magruder did a lie detector test. Strachan did not pass and Magruder did. Tell Strachan but don't tell Magruder that they believe Magruder and don't believe Strachan. I said, "Well, what the hell is it about?" I said, well, "At what point?" "Well, it's about Strachan's having furnished the budget and tape." No, not that — about Magruder had furnished it to Strachan. I said, "Well, what about Haldeman?" Well, on that, the lie detector — well, it wasn't as clear on that — so I got a little something out of that.

EHRLICHMAN: So that's the question of whether Magruder had sent a budget over here. That said there were bugs being [unclear].

NIXON: That's right. And — two questions: one — whether Magruder sent it — whether Strachan — and what Strachan [unclear]. Strachan's in a hell of a spot. He's got to face perjury or tell the truth.

EHRLICHMAN: Well, they can't — I mean, they're going to prove it at some point. They can't get by on just Magruder because Magruder's going to be a convicted perjurer by that time. So, Strachan's — and the lie detector probably isn't admissible.

NIXON: Oh, no, no, no, no. He claimed that that [unclear]. That's right.

EHRLICHMAN: So, they still gotta make a case on Strachan.

HALDEMAN: That's amazing that they'd use that. I thought they didn't use lie detectors.

NIXON: Well, they do it sometimes and he said, "We just came to the point where there's a question of who is lying and they didn't force him." "You will? Will you take it?" Magruder said, "Sure." Strachan, of course, said, "Sure." I think Strachan is probably more likely to be telling the truth than Magruder. I think Magruder basically is a facile liar.

HALDEMAN: Yeah.

NIXON: Magruder can pass any lie detector test and Strachan will be — figure goddamn that's a sensitive question and probably the thing would jiggle up and down. That's another reason the lie detector goes down.

HALDEMAN: You see Strachan could be at — in telling the truth, thinking that's going to be — this is going to be harmful and get the jiggle [unclear] but —

EHRLICHMAN: Well, I listened to them both and —

NIXON: Did you talk to Strachan?

EHRLICHMAN: Yes, sir. I talked with both on the subject, and I think Strachan's more believable on the explanation which is, "If I had ever seen anything like that, I'm sure I would have remembered it." And that's a — you know, I mean he's very categorical in his denial. At the same time he just may have some recollection of having seen it, you know? And I wouldn't be in a position to know. But I had to decide in my own mind who was telling the truth on that and I came down on Strachan's side. [unclear] conflict [unclear] Bittman business —

NIXON: [unclear] you mean there. I — we were informed that the attorney fees had been taken care of. Here —

HALDEMAN: Good.

NIXON: Was I present —

HALDEMAN: No.

NIXON: — when — at any time did Dean ever tell me that?

HALDEMAN: I don't know. It's possible that came up in a meeting here that afternoon.

NIXON: Yeah.

HALDEMAN: I don't recall it at all. But it pushed the question. I would say that's possible. But —

EHRLICHMAN: It does ring a little bell with me. Was I here?

HALDEMAN: Yes.

EHRLICHMAN: I — yeah, and somebody said Mitchell says that's all taken care of.

NIXON: That would still be consistent with the president trying to get at the goddamn thing.

EHRLICHMAN: [unclear] right, right.

NIXON: Or is it?

EHRLICHMAN: Yeah, I don't — I can't say that happened. I'll check on it.

NIXON: What would you fellows answer, for example, if they ask you a question whether or not about — and Dean testifies that there was a discussion of — Bittman had to get paid off?

EHRLICHMAN: Okay, but before you make trouble on that let's see what the tapes do.

NIXON: Well, what the tapes say — but I mean apart from the tapes there's another conversation I was not present at. What the hell do you say [unclear] Mitchell would deny?

EHRLICHMAN: "For those three weeks I didn't really understand what the president was up to." See, the first thing he did he took me off Ervin — I'm speaking now — took me off the Ervin matter, said Dean's going to handle this. And then he did a very unusual thing. He began seeing a lot of Dean which he didn't usually do, and I didn't know what was up. I didn't know what they were talking about. I couldn't get a hint. However, anything the president was saying to me about what he was up to with Dean I just knew he had gotten into this because he'd been pushing for a statement and couldn't get one. The next thing I knew he'd sent Dean up to Camp David and then on the thirtieth he announced to me that Dean was in this thing so deep that he had to take him out. So it was obvious then, in the — hindsight, that the president had been up to something this whole time. Now I can think back and think of bits and pieces and I can see he was playing a poker game —

NIXON: Well, what about the questions or charges Dean had made that Mitchell indicated at that time [unclear] taken care of? [unclear]

EHRLICHMAN: Well, I'd just say you were being pretty inscrutable with Dean all through that period of time.

NIXON: Right.

EHRLICHMAN: [unclear] you had something [unclear] and on the thirtieth, I discovered where it was.

HALDEMAN: Now you might be interested in this — the phone conversation that John Dean called me, or I called him, on March 26 — which was while he was up on the mountain and we had obviously discussed [unclear]. The question was raised that John — that we ought to make an offer for John Dean to go to the grand jury. And he said, "Check with Dean and see if he has any problems and if we do — do that." [unclear] Dean said there would be no problem. Then he wanted to tell me about some of the things he had been working on — brought me up-to-date. He had just talked with Jeb Magruder about the [unclear] business — all that. Then he obviously got into his notes that he was working on and reconstructing the situation 'cause he says, "The main problem area that we're faced with is the blackmail situation. I was aware," this is Dean talking, "I was aware that Mitchell and others were being blackmailed by those involved and I sought to ignore it, so I am vague on the specifics. First time I was aware of it was when Mitchell told me that the defendants wanted help regarding money for bond. This was relayed from Mrs. Hunt to Bittman, to Parkinson, to Mitchell and LaRue, and they — the defendants were threatening to cause general havoc if they were not helped. Parkinson said he did not want to be involved further in this so Bittman used O'Brien. O'Brien is unhappy with his role in this, too. O'Brien reported the threats to Mitchell and LaRue and Dean, and Dean passed on some of it to some people in the White House." [unclear] Mitchell had to —

NIXON: Yeah, now that would mean —

HALDEMAN: Here are the specifics on it. "After Mitchell had the original draft, he told Dean to tell Haldeman and Ehrlichman that we needed to use Kalmbach money to raise — use Kalmbach to raise money, and he should get Haldeman and Ehrlichman to authorize this. Kalmbach raised the money and delivered it per instructions to LaRue, about seventy thousand dollars. The next time there was a threat to the committee there was no money available. Stans and LaRue were aware that the three hundred fifty thousand for the White House for polling. The White House had not met — had not spent this money and wanted to return it. Only Strachan with Haldeman approval could spend the money. There was one problem — about twenty-two thousand of it had already been spent, and I don't know the purpose." This is Dean. "The problem was how to return the funds without a big deal in the press. So the funds just sat in Strachan's safe. Mitchell asked Dean to ask Haldeman for some of this money, assured that it could be replenished. Dean called Haldeman and said there was a bad situation here growing worse. LaRue or O'Brien said it was a crisis. Haldeman said to have Strachan get the money but to clear it as soon as possible. Haldeman said to get all the money out of here and get a receipt for it. Strachan did get the money out but got no receipt. I am not aware of the extent of the threats to the committee." Those were two examples. He was not aware how far threats to the committee went "but there were two blackmail threats to the White House. One, Mrs. Hunt to Colson's secretary made a veiled threat and Colson didn't know what it was about, and referred it to Dean. Dean advised Colson to take no more calls from Mrs. Hunt and reported the incident to O'Brien. The second was when O'Brien told Dean that Hunt insisted on a meeting and that he send a message to Dean regarding a need for seventy-two plus fifty and that if it was not received he would reconsider his options and disclose the seamy things he did for Ehrlichman and Krogh. Dean advised Haldeman and Ehrlichman of this threat. Ehrlichman requested that Dean discuss this with Mitchell and Colson. Dean discussed it with Mitchell but not Colson. Mitchell said in a later meeting there was no problem." There are Dean's notes. "I am not in a position to fully evaluate the situation on blackmail. That all concerned made the point of dire threats to the White House and when people are being blackmailed they imagine the worst." That's all of this on blackmail. Now, he says, "Regarding clemency, O'Brien told Dean that Bittman was asked by Hunt to meet with Colson. Ehrlichman said Colson should meet with Bittman and he did. Colson said it was essential that Hunt be given assurance — "

NIXON: Colson said.

HALDEMAN: Yeah, " — and Ehrlichman agreed. Colson told Bittman that he could make no commitment but as a friend he would assist. He referred to Christmas as the time when clemency actions were usually taken and Hunt was satisfied with this."

NIXON: The only thing that does is to tie — try to say that Ehrlichman [unclear].

EHRLICHMAN: Well, I recall Dean — I had two meetings, Dean, Colson, and me, in which this problem was discussed and it was decided — I had urged that Colson talk with Bittman —

NIXON: Right.

EHRLICHMAN: — because Hunt was obviously very distraught and that Colson not talk with Hunt —

NIXON: Right.

EHRLICHMAN: —and that Colson be extremely circumspect about what he said to Bittman and we discussed clemency and Colson's recollection and mine both are that I was very categorical in saying you cannot in any way infer the possibility of clemency. Now this was late in the game. This was in January or February so there was already a lot of talk in the papers about hush money and I was very concerned that any inference could be raised in this meeting that would in any way come back to you. That's the reason for stressing it as I did. Colson had to meet with Bittman—says he'd reduced the meeting to memoranda which I've never seen, but he says that he did not in any way induce Hunt's cooperation.

NIXON: What if Colson were asked if he ever discussed it with the president?

EHRLICHMAN: He tells me he did not.

NIXON: He's got to stick to that, I guess.

HALDEMAN: That's what he—remember you had me check with him when we were down—

NIXON: Yeah.

HALDEMAN: —in Key Biscayne for a few hours that afternoon.

EHRLICHMAN: If I'm ever asked, I will say that I told Colson flatly never to discuss it with the president.

NIXON: Correct. Colson did discuss it but it was—I must say that conversation I'm not afraid of because anybody would have a right to say—he didn't say, "I have to this or that or the other thing." He simply said Hunt's in a hell of a shape—

HALDEMAN: Colson has every intention of and it's to his overriding interest to do so to say that any conversation he ever had with the president on any subject he will not discuss with anyone.

NIXON: Yeah, that's right. Well, I guess I don't want it to appear, though, that he's covering up for somebody now.

HALDEMAN: Yeah, but he'll say that on a consistent basis, so if it isn't—in relation to this or anything else, it's policy—

NIXON: He should also—I even think you have to go further—I would say this is the subject you never bring—I don't want to say discuss any conversation but I can assure you that [unclear]—

EHRLICHMAN: Except that Chuck was in a bad frame of mind for Hunt at this time.

NIXON: Because of himself?

EHRLICHMAN: Well, because of his wife and his kids—

NIXON: Chuck's.

EHRLICHMAN: —over the whole thing and Colson was making a case for his going and talking to Hunt—for seeing Hunt—and he really had on his mind he might do that.

NIXON: Let's look at Hunt now. Hunt now realizes that no clemency's hanging out there. He sure knows that, doesn't he? Huh?

HALDEMAN: No.

NIXON: He must figure that. How could he get clemency after all this that's going around here now. I figure though that Hunt might at this time — who else would take care of, for example — nobody's going to take care of Hunt's kids now, is there?

EHRLICHMAN: Well, he doesn't need it now. See, he got an awful lot of money. His wife was heavily insured. So it may not have to save —

NIXON: Maybe not Hunt. What about Bittman — what's he gonna say?

EHRLICHMAN: Well, Bittman's in incredible jeopardy. [unclear] Colson gave the proposition.

NIXON: When you get Bittman, [unclear], I suppose.

HALDEMAN: Yeah. I would guess so. I would [unclear].

NIXON: [unclear] Bittman would say that Colson said he had talked to the president and the president promised clemency [unclear].

EHRLICHMAN: [unclear] to me he's well prepared to handle that.

NIXON: I think we have a strong witness there hopefully.

• • •

EHRLICHMAN: You got Dean, whom I bet Petersen will tell you is going to be indicted.

NIXON: Either that or he gets immunity.

EHRLICHMAN: Well, what — even there he can't be given immunity for suborning perjury. That doesn't reach us. He's going to have to take a fall on that by himself and I think Dean — I don't know what Petersen will tell you, but I suspect he'll tell you that he's going to be indicted on some basis and he'll get case immunity on things where he implicates other people. But that's something to ask Petersen about. But let's assume that's he going to be indicted. Then I think you could say, "I've been advised by the assistant attorney general that John Dean is — the U.S. attorney has indicated sufficient involvement — that I have no choice but to — that's the situation. There's a class of cases where people in the White House have been openly and notoriously charged with implications. I answered that determination by people in the judicial process. I'm not going to prejudge that situation, but I am going to insist that people in that situation take a leave of absence at least." And so that's the second — until it's cleared up or firmed up by act of the grand jury. So that's the second classic case. Then — "there's a third group of people in the White House who have not been publicly charged with anything. But from my investigation — my understanding of the facts — have some direct or indirect involvement into the subject matter of the case. I know who they are. They know who they are and my decision on them is to have them in place for the time being. With the expectation that in the course and development of the prosecution in this case, they — a firm body of facts will become available to me on which I can make a decision." Now that's the end of it. Generalized — it's a generalized kind of thing. We made a list this morning to try and see who were in the same boat as I am personally in this. That is not charged with anything, with no evidence before the grand jury yet, with an incipient problem, and there are seventeen of us. In the same identical situation.

NIXON: Really?

HALDEMAN: That's principals — not looking at secretaries or [unclear].

NIXON: Like who? Name them.

HALDEMAN: You put me in the second category. I'm publicly charged. Okay. Higby would be in your category. Baroody is conceivably in that category, although I really don't think so.

NIXON: I doubt that.

HALDEMAN: Dick Moore is either in mine or yours. I don't know which. Dick Howard [unclear] clearly in that. Powell Moore, who works in Baroody's office, is clearly in that. Bruce Kehrli is a remote possibility in the sense that he was there to open the safe. I think that's the only [unclear]. John Dean is in the first category. Fred Fielding would be in your category, and everybody in Dean's office. Ehrlichman is in that category. Noel Cook is in that category. He's involved with Colson. Bill Timmons is in that category, and Wally Johnson.

NIXON: How are they involved?

HALDEMAN: Timmons was alleged at one point to have received the bugging output and I think does have some involvement in the convention problems which this focused around at that time. Wally Johnson was very much involved, and so was Timmons, in the meetings that went on that could be considered by Dean — cover-up.

NIXON: Meeting about what?

HALDEMAN: How to deal with the Watergate problem at various points of time.

NIXON: Right. Right.

HALDEMAN: And Wally — Timmons I would say was more direct. Then you get the whole problem with the press office. Ziegler — he was publicly accused of lying —

EHRLICHMAN: And who has had a lot of private transactions with Dean through this whole time with Dean and me in an effort to get Ziegler positioned —

NIXON: Yeah.

EHRLICHMAN: — and is probably chargeable by Dean with notice of some of the things that I am charged with.

HALDEMAN: Gerry Warren falls under the same problem as Ziegler.

NIXON: Like for example, Ziegler —

EHRLICHMAN: Well, I've got in the calendar half a dozen meetings with Dean, Ehrlichman, and Ziegler. It would be the kind of situation where the McCord letter is about to come out and Dean would have had inside information as to what it was. And so we would sit down and talk about the press handling this. The Segretti matter, Ziegler had all kinds of inside information on Segretti which Dean got from his investigation.

NIXON: Right, right, right.

HALDEMAN: Gerry Warren sort of falls into the same thing. Ken Clawson is in there, both in that area and in the Colson area during the campaign when he was — I am sure he was heavily involved in the Colson-type activities, as was Bill Rhatican [unclear] Colson [unclear] and the Ziegler office.

NIXON: We're now mixed. We're now including not only Watergate —

HALDEMAN: Including —

NIXON: Segretti.

HALDEMAN: No, this isn't Segretti-type stuff. This is —

NIXON: All Watergate?

HALDEMAN: No, it's not Watergate either.

EHRLICHMAN: Bringing the Cubans up to rough up the demonstrators.

NIXON: Campaign activities. I got that.

HALDEMAN: Right, right.

NIXON: Ervin Committee.

HALDEMAN: Ervin Committee at least, but it's coming out now so it's going to be press before Ervin Committee.

EHRLICHMAN: My [unclear] —

HALDEMAN: And probably, will get in some way logged into the grand jury business because of the money.

NIXON: [unclear]

EHRLICHMAN: Yeah, for instance — like Howard gets involved in the money. Now if the premise is that someone is going to be a problem to the functioning of the presidency —

NIXON: Right. We've got to clean out a hell of a lot.

EHRLICHMAN: — then, you've got — there isn't any good place to stop without going all the way because if we're off the scene and we both take up farming in Iowa —

NIXON: Yeah.

EHRLICHMAN: — then Bill Rhatican someday becomes just as big a problem to you as I might be if I were here. Because they haven't got me to focus on.

HALDEMAN: If they can't tell you who's not it never becomes a big problem because they can't tie that into the president.

EHRLICHMAN: Well, they'll test it. I think rather than to be specific about an individual or individuals, you really have to par it off for yourself as kind of a generic classification, and decide what you're going to do about those people. You can do one of two things. You can say, "I've checked this and it now goes down eighteen deep and they're all gone tomorrow morning." Or you can say, "There're shades and gradations on this thing but judicial process is under way. And I'm going to let the remedy fit the crime, so to speak."

· · ·

EHRLICHMAN: I have a real practical problem with a resignation, which shouldn't really weigh in your consideration.

NIXON: It's how do you live?

EHRLICHMAN: That's exactly it.

NIXON: I understand that.

EHRLICHMAN: I say it shouldn't weigh as a factor —

NIXON: That is a factor.

EHRLICHMAN: Well, it is a factor only in this sense — that I then have to get a job. I have to go to work —

NIXON: How the hell can you?

EHRLICHMAN: Practicing law. I can. I mean that is not the problem. I can — I know immediately where I go to get a relatively good-paying job. You wouldn't be terribly happy with it, but I would be terribly happy with it. But I would be in a kind of any-port-in-the-storm situation at that point. You're with me on that?

NIXON: Yeah.

EHRLICHMAN: To say again I wouldn't want to be.

NIXON: Let me ask you this, to be quite candid. Is there any way you can use cash?

EHRLICHMAN: I don't think so. I don't think so.

NIXON: As I said, there are a few — not much [unclear] as much I think as two hundred there's available to the '74 campaign already.

HALDEMAN: That compounds the problem. That really does.

NIXON: That's what I think. Okay. I just want you to know that.

EHRLICHMAN: Everybody —

NIXON: Well, I got another way. I agree.

EHRLICHMAN: [laughs] Well, that has the disadvantages and none of the advantages of staying here. You know, I mean that it decidedly links us in a way that I don't think you can afford. The lead thing is sufficiently ambiguous, I think, that you avoid some of the problems of if we were in a direct relationship. No, as I say [unclear] it isn't a question —

NIXON: The more I think of the resignation thing, in light of this — well, it's the option that [unclear] down on. Oh, incidentally, let me tell you, too — Ziegler saw Harlow this morning. He had breakfast with him. Harlow is coming down on the resignation side. I mean —

EHRLICHMAN: Oh [unclear] has to be —

NIXON: Yeah. But the difficulty with the resignation thing is just that it condemns you. Nothing will clean up the problem. The idea, as I told your lawyers, [unclear] legs are gangrene. Who the hell can — ?

HALDEMAN: Continuing the analogy, that would be a gangrene in the legs. I'm not sure cutting off both arms —

NIXON: Yeah — cures it.

The dirty trick in a doctor's office
April 25, 1973, 6:57 p.m.
Richard Nixon and Bob Haldeman
WHITE HOUSE TELEPHONE

During the afternoon, Kleindienst urgently requested a conference with Nixon. The topic was not Watergate, at least not in the strict definition of the term. Instead, it pertained to the Pentagon Papers, an extensive military report critical of the Vietnam War that had been released without permission by Daniel Ellsberg in 1969. At the time, the White House was infuriated. During late April 1973, Ellsberg and an accomplice were on trial in Los Angeles, charged with espionage and other crimes for their part in disseminating the Pentagon Papers. Nixon had previously been informed that John Dean had given the Justice Department information about the Ellsberg case. He said that a group called the "Plumbers" (so named because they plugged "leaks") had broken into the office of Ellsberg's psychiatrist in 1971, in order to steal records on Ellsberg's mental health. It was one of the lowest of dirty tricks, but it produced nothing of the slightest use.

For days after being informed about the crime, Nixon argued with both Petersen and Kleindienst that anything connected with Ellsberg and the Pentagon Papers should be considered a matter of national security. Finally, on April 25, Kleindienst told the president that Dean's information would not be withheld on security concerns. The Justice Department would submit paperwork to the trial judge, William Matthew Byrne, indicating that the break-in had been perpetrated by some of the same co-conspirators arrested at the Watergate office of the DNC. Both trails led to Ehrlichman.

• • •

NIXON: Oh, Bob, you got home?

HALDEMAN: Yeah.

NIXON: Oh, fine. You rushing off?

HALDEMAN: No, no, not at all.

NIXON: No, I'll just take a second. Were you able to hear any of the rest of that?

HALDEMAN: No, I didn't. I'm trying to get a different machine that I can —

NIXON: Right.

HALDEMAN: — hear better on. Go back to it.

NIXON: Just a second. I had a good talk with Petersen and told him that, you know, about the need to expedite the grand jury. I told him I wanted it — a paper from him with regard to you and John. He said he'd have it by Friday afternoon.

HALDEMAN: Hmm.

NIXON: And I —

HALDEMAN: Yeah.

NIXON: — mean, he said, "I'd like to pull my thoughts together" and so forth and he said, "We just don't have it yet." I said that I wanted to be sure that you and John had an opportunity at the earliest time to meet with the prosecuting team. You know?

HALDEMAN: Yeah.

NIXON: And he said, "Have your counsel" — and I haven't talked to John, you can pass it on to him —

HALDEMAN: Okay.

NIXON: — and your counsel, "and request it and that'll be done." I said the other thing I wanted you to have the opportunity to appear before the grand jury, I mean so that there'd be no question of, you know —

HALDEMAN: Yeah.

NIXON: — of waiting. He said, "Well, we might have to have them twice then." I said,

"That's all right." I said the main thing is I want them — I mean I really think your getting up there is important.

HALDEMAN: Yeah.

NIXON: Soon.

HALDEMAN: Yeah.

NIXON: You agree?

HALDEMAN: Yeah.

NIXON: Also it's a positive move we can make.

HALDEMAN: Yeah.

NIXON: And it's at our initiative. You see?

HALDEMAN: Yeah.

NIXON: And that's that.

HALDEMAN: Okay. Good.

NIXON: And now, with regard to the piece of paper I gave you on Ehrlichman, they have sent that you know out to the —

HALDEMAN: Yeah.

NIXON: — prosecutor. They had to do that for this reason, that Dean basically, that was basically a little blackmail by him, on them, you see.

HALDEMAN: Yeah.

NIXON: Which they said if we didn't put it out — I mean if they didn't then they'd say why did you withhold it from the Ellsberg case, you see.

HALDEMAN: Yeah.

NIXON: So — but that is likely — it could come out I mean. Byrne may ask for — divulge the source. It will be Dean and Dean will have to testify. If he does, then that piece of thing, that Watergate buggers involved in the Ellsberg thing — it will not blow the Ellsberg case, you know, in his opinion, due to the fact that it wasn't used. On the other hand, the fact of it will come out. But I think that that was gonna come out anyway. Don't you feel so?

HALDEMAN: Probably. Probably. Yeah, and I think we gotta assume any of that stuff is.

NIXON: Yeah. But the point is —

HALDEMAN: I'm not sure that's bad if it does.

NIXON: Well, [laughs] Watergate —

HALDEMAN: In among other things.

NIXON: Huh?

HALDEMAN: Well, it adds confusion to the whole thing.

NIXON: Yeah. The Watergate buggers try to knock over Ellsberg's psychiatrist.

HALDEMAN: Yeah.

NIXON: Right. Well, in any event, that was about it. So if you could call in to John — he wasn't home. If you tell the White House operator that you —

HALDEMAN: Right.

NIXON: You call John. You talk to him and fill him in. You sent him the piece of paper, did you — did you get it to him?

HALDEMAN: I covered it with him, yeah.

NIXON: Yeah.

HALDEMAN: I'll give it to him in the morning.

NIXON: Mm-hmm. He understood the significance of it, of course.

HALDEMAN: Yeah.

NIXON: Yeah. Did he see any other option?

HALDEMAN: No. He — no. His only concern was that it was getting fairly broad distribution.

NIXON: Well, I know.

HALDEMAN: But —

NIXON: It's gonna get more broad distribution because they're gonna —

HALDEMAN: Yeah.

NIXON: — they, you see — what else could I tell Kleindienst, forget it? Get my point?

HALDEMAN: Yeah.

NIXON: I just couldn't do that.

HALDEMAN: Yeah.

NIXON: And, you know, I could say, "Look, this is national security, and you cannot turn it over to them because Dean," another [unclear].

HALDEMAN: That's obstruction of justice.

NIXON: Yeah. Exactly.

HALDEMAN: Yeah.

NIXON: The other point that it, I went — I leveled with Petersen on all the conversations that we had and I said, "Now I want you to know this" and I said, "We'll not be blackmailed on it. We didn't do anything about it but that's when I started my investigation." And that's our line there, I think. The more I —

HALDEMAN: Yeah.

NIXON: — the more I think of that, you know, I know that I'm in no illusions on it and incidentally I think that should just be between you and me.

HALDEMAN: Okay.

NIXON: Or, I think at this point I don't think we ought to spread that to John and have him worry about it and the rest.

HALDEMAN: Okay.

NIXON: Unless you want to.

HALDEMAN: You mean the contents?

NIXON: Yeah.

HALDEMAN: No. I didn't intend to.

NIXON: I think, let's just — so that we can know that, in other words, as far as the conversation it's one that I had and that you had and —

HALDEMAN: Yeah.

NIXON: — and we'll just see what — if Dean wants to play that then we'll play it for whatever it's worth. Petersen —

HALDEMAN: Did it bother Petersen?

NIXON: Oh, well, everything bothers him.

HALDEMAN: [laughs]

NIXON: But he said that Dean, he says, has always indicated, he says he'll never — he says he'll deal — he won't lie for that goddamn Ehrlichman but he will of course defend the president da-da-da-da-da and I said, "Well, we'll see." But I said —

HALDEMAN: Out to get John apparently, huh?

NIXON: Well, I think he's out to save himself but he'll — he's gonna play every card that he can, and — a desperate man he may want to bring the president down, too. But in this case then, Bob, there's no other choice — it's to fight like hell. This is an evil man, you know. He knows that this was a legitimate thing to be doing; he was deeply in it. And incidentally he's likely to be called as a witness in the Ellsberg case, too. I mean in the Vesco case because —

HALDEMAN: Dean is?

NIXON: Yeah, because apparently he made a telephone call, it is alleged, in order to quash an indictment on the — allegedly against Vesco, so —

HALDEMAN: Good Lord!

NIXON: — is that the name — Vesco? Yeah.

HALDEMAN: Yeah.

NIXON: Yeah, so [unclear] me on that damn thing, too.

HALDEMAN: My God! Does Petersen still feel you can't make any move on Dean?

NIXON: Not at this point.

HALDEMAN: Yeah.

NIXON: Well, because he's — they're still trying to — he's gonna try to make Dean's lawyers come to him. You know? And —

HALDEMAN: And he's right.

NIXON: He's right. In other words, but let me say, there can't be any move made on you and — you and/or Bob — or John, until the Dean thing's resolved and I made that damn clear to Petersen. I said I wasn't gonna, that I can't — I said, "You realize that if you — if I have these fellows resign I'm in effect saying, 'I judge them guilty,'" and I said no — any other way of [unclear]. I said if I do that, I said I have to do it — the right to do it with them and Dean and so forth and so on. You know, I went through the whole drill and told him that — I sort of gave him the impression that I wasn't going to do a damn thing, that I wanted to look over his papers.

HALDEMAN: Yep.

NIXON: You see what I mean?

HALDEMAN: Yep.

NIXON: My own belief at this point is that, for yours and John's information, that we've just got to stand goddamn firm today, tomorrow, Friday, the weekend, you know what I mean?

HALDEMAN: Yeah.

NIXON: And if the Ellsberg thing blows, I'd just as soon, you know, just as —

HALDEMAN: Get it all out now.

NIXON: I wouldn't just as soon but I think it's going to come anyway. Whatever John Dean knows is gonna come out, Bob.

HALDEMAN: That's right. That's right.

NIXON: But, incidentally, you know, I always wondered about that taping equipment but I'm damn glad we have it, aren't you?

HALDEMAN: Yes, sir, I think it's just one thing I went through today. It was very helpful.

NIXON: Yes. It's helpful because while it has some things in there that —

HALDEMAN: Well, you —

NIXON: — we prefer we wouldn't have said, but on the other hand we also have some things in there that we know we've — that I've said that weren't, that were pretty good, I mean.

HALDEMAN: That's right.

NIXON: "This is wrong" and "blackmail" and "How much is this gonna cost?" and so forth and so on. Then, on the other hand, I said, well, "Let's — we could get that, but how would you handle it?" But that, of course, those are all leading questions. I don't know how you analyze it but I don't know.

HALDEMAN: I really don't think it would be, if it all gets — if that comes out, it's another hard thing to explain but I think it's explainable.

NIXON: Right.

HALDEMAN: And if — that I just think Dean's — well, I can't imagine that he'll do that.

NIXON: Yeah. Except as he sees it —

HALDEMAN: Did Petersen know what Dean's big bomb thing was?

NIXON: No, he didn't.

HALDEMAN: Wasn't he supposed to get some big threat from Dean or something?

NIXON: Well, he won't get that, Bob, until he meets with Dean and —

HALDEMAN: Yeah.

NIXON: — and it hasn't occurred, I said. He doesn't know when that'll occur.

HALDEMAN: I see.

NIXON: I said, "Well" — so, he doesn't know. I said, "Well, I just wanted to be sure. Maybe it's this" — I said, he thinks maybe it's some conversations he had with Dean. That may be, but I think it's this, don't you?

HALDEMAN: I would. I don't know. I don't really.

NIXON: Maybe. Well, what the hell else could it be then, Bob? I mean, and if he's got a big bomb — if he's gonna throw — yeah, I think it's this, I would say that he's gonna say, well, the president was — he told the president about the, you know, that they're gonna pay these people off and so forth, and that John Mitchell and — I think he — the other thing is that John Mitchell is in the presence of Haldeman and Ehrlichman, said that it had been taken care of, or words to that effect.

HALDEMAN: Mm-hmm.

NIXON: Is that right, is that, is — I suppose he could say that, right?

HALDEMAN: Yeah.

NIXON: And then it's his word against the rest of you, right?

HALDEMAN: Yeah. That's why you just — I don't see how we — there's no way you really can stay with Dean on this, I don't.

NIXON: No way. No, no, no. No way. You want to try to — you see the only problem is that to handle it in such a way that he doesn't become a totally implacable enemy.

HALDEMAN: That's right.

NIXON: Totally implacable and I think for that reason handling it the way I have, at least may —

HALDEMAN: That's right.

NIXON: — may help in that respect. I, at least, have treated him decently. In fact, more decently than he deserves.

HALDEMAN: Yeah.

NIXON: On the other hand, he may become totally intractable. If he does, you're gonna have one hell of a pissing contest.

HALDEMAN: Yeah.

NIXON: And, on the other hand —

HALDEMAN: If you do, I — that's, you just — you gotta win it.

NIXON: What else can you do? Yeah, really. What else can you do? And you know when you think of this, all this kind of thing, you know, when John talks about — I was just thinking a little bit more about the impeachment thing, that I don't see the Senate or any senators starting an impeachment of the president based on the word of John Dean.

HALDEMAN: That's right.

NIXON: That's all it is, you know, and I mean, John Dean says that this and that and the other thing happened.

HALDEMAN: And there's no way he can support it. I mean there's no way to make a case.

NIXON: Well, except he could be — recorded his conversations, you know — back, made a memorandum, told his lawyers immediately thereafter and so forth and so on.

HALDEMAN: Yeah.

NIXON: But, even there, I mean, here is —

HALDEMAN: Still his word, unless he's got a tape recording. Still his word unless he has a tape recording.

NIXON: Mm-hmm.

HALDEMAN: And even with the tape recording I think you could make the case the other way.

NIXON: Mm-hmm. I don't know, a tape recording is — I can't believe that he could have walked in there with a tape recorder that day, because that day, I mean I'm not trying to be wishful thinking, that particular day he wasn't really out to get the president, I don't think.

HALDEMAN: That's right, no, sir, he wasn't. He was the exact, going just the other way.

NIXON: Trying to help?

HALDEMAN: That's right, and I just can't conceive that he would have done that, because I was going to [unclear].

NIXON: Unless he tape-records every — does he tape-record everything that he comes in?

HALDEMAN: No. No.

NIXON: Does he — you're sure of that?

HALDEMAN: No, I'm not sure of it, but I am convinced — never had any reason to believe that he did.

NIXON: Mm-hmm. Mm-hmm.

HALDEMAN: And the way you know he dresses, just casual enough in his clothing and all, that I can't imagine you'd — he'd have a tape recorder. It's bulky and you gotta get it in your —

NIXON: Yeah.

HALDEMAN: — pocket somewhere and all that. It isn't all that easy to do.

NIXON: Right, right, right. Well, in any event that's that. That's that. And he — so we don't want to borrow trouble. I mean we got enough without borrowing any, don't we?

HALDEMAN: Yeah, yeah.

NIXON: And, let me say that this is April 25. We can figure that this is the day we start up. Seriously —

HALDEMAN: I think that's right. I think —

NIXON: I don't mean — I don't think I'm being Pollyanna-ish about it. I think that if Kleindienst with that damn thing, all right, my God, there it is. Put it out. And I wouldn't hear your lawyers — we'd be saying, I mean we can't go on this damn business of resignation. Now it isn't gonna work! That's right, it just isn't gonna work right now. The leave of absence thing, I don't know, with regard to you, do you really think that that really buys us anything?

HALDEMAN: I don't know. It —

NIXON: Well, we'll consider it. You'll have to, we'll have to think about it, in terms of one other thing Steve [Bull] told me today that he thought there was a chance that I would not — maybe we could, I could get out of doing that damn finance dinner on May 9. He said that the tick — that they hadn't had — the program wasn't going as well as they expected and so forth and so on, is there a chance — ?

HALDEMAN: I don't know. I —

NIXON: The New Majority dinner so called —

HALDEMAN: Yeah, it's probably —

NIXON: — and so forth. That's the thing I should avoid like the plague if I could but —

HALDEMAN: Except that appearance, I would think, if you don't do it, they'll make a big thing out of they couldn't sell any tickets because of the Watergate and the president —

NIXON: I see.

HALDEMAN: — wouldn't come.

NIXON: I see.

HALDEMAN: That's my view now. I've — I'm not so sure, I'm not sure of what the situation —

NIXON: They say they're not selling too many tickets someway or other but, I've heard that at least, but you know we heard other things from Bush that they'd sold 'em well.

HALDEMAN: Yeah.

NIXON: But if it's there I could do it. Another thing I could do is, rather than — that is really just give a reception at the White House and shake hands for a couple hours.

HALDEMAN: Mm-hmm.

NIXON: You know what I mean? As — you know, rather than going out and having to make a speech —

HALDEMAN: Yeah, the problem is the people that go to that dinner, your lobbyists and all that stuff.

NIXON: Right. That's right. That's all right, but I'd hell of a lot rather be shaking their hands, Bob, than, than to —

HALDEMAN: Yeah.

NIXON: — than to go out and be making a political speech that day, you know. What's a political speech without mentioning Watergate?

HALDEMAN: Yeah.

NIXON: I think that's an option at least.

HALDEMAN: Yeah.

NIXON: Mm-hmm. I plan to go to Mississippi Friday, you still for that, are you?

HALDEMAN: Yes, sir, absolutely.

NIXON: Yeah.

HALDEMAN: By all means.

NIXON: And —

HALDEMAN: That's all good, that one.

NIXON: Right. You know, when you really stop to think of it, in terms of this whole thing, the line basically of everybody, you know, Connally, Rogers, et al., which of course varies — I mean [Bryce] Harlow, the [unclear] resignation line and so forth is one that is so terribly attractive in terms for a couple of days. [laughs]

HALDEMAN: That's right.

NIXON: I mean, you know what I mean? This, well, now the president's finally started off with a new team but then for Christ's sakes. Something else blows, huh?

HALDEMAN: That's right.

NIXON: On the other hand, the other line is to say, all right, the grand jury's going to hear it and they're gonna see it through. I mean to that point. That's a tenable line also, isn't it?

HALDEMAN: Yeah.

NIXON: Of course the problem with that I suppose is that —

HALDEMAN: Well [unclear] the stuff —

NIXON: — the problem with that is that — what you could say is that rather than the president cleaning his house, the grand jury did. But in the sense, in the sense if you want to argue that we can say no, the president said that's the way to do it. You see my point?

HALDEMAN: Yeah. And that is the point. That you're — the confidence in our institutions and —

NIXON: Mm-hmm.

HALDEMAN: You know, the way things are supposed to be done.

NIXON: That's right. We're presenting all the things. That's why the appearance before the grand jury, the —

HALDEMAN: Yeah.

NIXON: — the going down there, and at my suggestion and so forth and so on, that's — that line you and John might work out in the morning.

HALDEMAN: All right.

NIXON: All right, you tell him not to have John return the call — you fill him in. Okay?

HALDEMAN: Right.

NIXON: Bye.

HALDEMAN: Okay.

"I've got to clear the goddamn air."
April 26, 1973, 3:59 p.m.
Richard Nixon, Bob Haldeman
EXECUTIVE OFFICE BUILDING

Nixon had a conversation with Haldeman lasting five hours, starting late in the afternoon of April 26, entirely on the subject of Watergate. Both men knew that the taping system in Nixon's offices might leave dangerous evidence; they'd talked about that subject a few weeks before (on April 9). Both were keenly aware they were being taped that afternoon; in fact, much of the first part of the discussion consisted of Haldeman's account of previous tapes. Yet without any compunction at all, they delved into scenarios and outright lies to cover their actions of the previous year, particularly regarding the authorization of hush money and interactions with Dean.

In the midst of formulating his stories, Nixon worked the telephone while Haldeman listened in, speaking to Kleindienst, Petersen, and Ehrlichman, in turn. He received two pieces of news that raised the stakes of the Watergate scandal, taking it far from the original office break-in. First, Petersen let the president know that Judge Byrne was seriously considering the legal impact of new information about the burglary at the office of Ellsberg's psychiatrist. Second, Ehrlichman told the president that the New York Times was about to break the story that Gray had destroyed the files given to him after meeting with Ehrlichman and Dean. Nixon's initial response was that Gray needed to resign. He had the same theme on his mind for Ehrlichman, by that point, and also discussed Haldeman's departure with a mix of firmness and fantasy. Even if Haldeman left under the cloud of Watergate, Nixon suggested, he could come back in some other job. Not even Haldeman could pretend that was going to happen.

. . .

NIXON: Bob, how are you doing?

HALDEMAN: Okay.

NIXON: Had a long day, haven't you?

HALDEMAN: I got the — here's your letters. [unclear] wrote one on each of us — separate ones.

NIXON: Good.

HALDEMAN: And as he said, they are legal letters, not PR letters, but he said they thought they had to be. That's right.

NIXON: Okay.

. . .

NIXON: Colson, at least in this instance — it's — well, Colson basically, nobody else. Let's face it, with all that he's done.

HALDEMAN: Yeah, he is. But I, really —

NIXON: [unclear]

HALDEMAN: — wish he'd quit trying to help.

NIXON: Yeah, but I mean he's a loyalist in one sense that here he's trying to help to nail Dean. He'd better watch out. Dean will try to nail him.

HALDEMAN: Yeah, well, and Dean will lash back. Now, Dean will read this and figure out — he has to assume that it either came from Colson or Ehrlichman or both. Because it nails Dean, builds Colson, and to a degree builds Ehrlichman.

NIXON: What it says about Ehrlichman is true, is it not?

HALDEMAN: I guess so.

NIXON: That Ehrlichman —

HALDEMAN: Ehrlichman didn't really confront Dean with charges though.

NIXON: No.

HALDEMAN: What Ehrlichman did is say — yeah, he sort of did because he said, "Here's the way the thing stacks up." I don't think he confronted him with him having advance knowledge because Ehrlichman still doesn't think he did have advance —

NIXON: That's right. Well, Dean —

HALDEMAN: In fact, these charges are not right. Did Dean have advance knowledge? No. Dean ordered Hunt out of the country — now that's true, but then he rescinded the order.

NIXON: That's right.

HALDEMAN: Dean's trying to hang that order on Ehrlichman.

NIXON: That's right.

HALDEMAN: Because Ehrlichman's trying to hang it on Dean. And Dean had authorized payments to the defense to keep their mouths shut. Well, I don't think John ever tried to nail Ehrlichman on that.

NIXON: Well, I don't know that Dean tried to do that.

HALDEMAN: [unclear]

NIXON: Dean can say very well, "No, I didn't do that for that purpose."

HALDEMAN: He may have a real problem with that though because — in that he apparently is dealing directly with the lawyers, which I didn't know.

NIXON: Dean? That's what going on.

HALDEMAN: [unclear] LaRue.

NIXON: Oh.

HALDEMAN: The fact that some [unclear].

NIXON: Well, LaRue's going to have to tell everything. He's going to have to plead guilty in order, that's for sure. Whoever dealt with him is gonna come out.

HALDEMAN: Well, I don't know. I assume that Dean dealt — well, I'm sure he had conversations with him and I assume he dealt with him.

NIXON: You didn't have to talk to LaRue? Did Ehrlichman?

HALDEMAN: I don't believe so.

NIXON: Needless to say I —

HALDEMAN: Did you notice I now — I sure as hell don't think [unclear]?

NIXON: LaRue didn't call you and say that we need money for the defendants?

HALDEMAN: [unclear] because it wasn't —

NIXON: But on that point, Bob, you've got to simply say your story still is "I was helping for humanitarian reasons." That's what your counsel says, don't they?

HALDEMAN: Legal fees.

NIXON: Huh?

HALDEMAN: He says "legal fees" — concerned about their [unclear]. But I'm sure [unclear].

NIXON: How about the fifty — about the three fifty, was that [unclear]?

HALDEMAN: Sure. Well, no, the three fifty, I — the three fifty came up in a separate context from their need for money at first which was the question what do we do with this money. And I said, "It should be turned over to the committee."

NIXON: But who asked you that?

HALDEMAN: Strachan.

NIXON: Strachan. Right.

HALDEMAN: We — I'd forgotten we had the money.

NIXON: Strachan —

HALDEMAN: Strachan was through closing on his files here and getting ready to leave.

NIXON: Right.

HALDEMAN: And he said, "What do I do with the three fifty?" And I said, "Good Lord, I'd forgotten we had it. That should go over to the committee. Get it over there quickly. We don't want to be sitting around here holding cash." And I said to him — he says — and this fits together, I told him to talk to Dean and work out a way of getting it over there. And he assumed that by that I was saying work out the legal arrangements because we —

NIXON: Right.

HALDEMAN: —got to get that taken care of. And so he did. And Dean didn't get it moved over. And then Dean—the next I know is Dean is saying to me, "We need money—daily money for the defendants." And I say, "Well, what about the three fifty thing? Don't they have that?" He said, "No, we haven't been able to get it over there." And I say, "Well, we got two needs that both fit. We want to get rid of the money and they need money—"

NIXON: Right.

HALDEMAN: "—at the committee. So why don't we try and work that out?"

NIXON: Right.

HALDEMAN: Dean indicates in the middle of this—and that's where there's a discrepancy and I've been checking this—that's one of the facts that I've had the lawyers try to work out—is this point that you say Petersen says that Dean says that forty thousand got [unclear] before the election.

NIXON: That was just dropped in someplace. Peter—Dean told me that.

HALDEMAN: I—well, it's not true. I checked that fact and no money—the date—all that money was held over in Arlington in a safe deposit box until November 28, and on November 28 it was turned over to Strachan.

NIXON: But your thought was—

HALDEMAN: Now, there's a problem there because Strachan is not sure, he says, what he did with the bag of money when it was turned over to him. Whether he put it in his safe here or whether he gave it to John Dean. And he says he may have given it to Dean.

NIXON: Well, you mean about the—is he speaking of all the three hundred, rather than LaRue. Is that what he said?

HALDEMAN: Oh, no. Ultimately, he knows he gave it to LaRue. He may have, when he first got it, given it to Dean on the grounds that I had told him, "Work out with Dean a way of getting it over there." So the money came, he said to Dean, "Here's the money to get over there." And then Dean—he's not sure whether he put it immediately in the safe or whether he gave it to Dean and Dean held it for a while and then gave it back to him to put in the safe. Now there's a potential which is spin out here. I have no reason to believe it's the case but I have no reason to believe it is not. Which is that he did give it to Dean and that Dean used it in piecemeal chunks—took money out of it to use for the payments to LaRue.

NIXON: Yeah. Gave it to him when? This would be when?

HALDEMAN: After November 28, because he didn't have it till—

NIXON: Why didn't he have it before November 28?

HALDEMAN: Because it—the subject never came up. It was sitting over in the safe deposit box.

NIXON: That's your best recollection of the money?

HALDEMAN: I don't have any recollections. I had nothing to do—

NIXON: Strachan.

HALDEMAN: That's what I'm told.

NIXON: Strachan told you.

HALDEMAN: I'm told independently by Strachan and by Butterfield. You see, Strachan couldn't get it out of the box. Only Butterfield could get it out.

NIXON: Right.

HALDEMAN: Or Butterfield's friend whose box it was. But the root of the money out of the box had to meet Butterfield's friend to Butterfield. And Butterfield says that there was one withdrawal in May—he said twenty-two thousand.

NIXON: All right.

HALDEMAN: And there was no other withdrawal until the total thing was taken out on November 28. He's the one that supplies that date. Strachan says he doesn't know what the date was, but he says it was after the election.

NIXON: Butterfield's memory would be goddamn clear because he [unclear]—

HALDEMAN: Because Butterfield's so prim and precise.

NIXON: So that would make it here the question of forty thousand before.

HALDEMAN: Before the election.

NIXON: Just don't—on that one, let me say, I just have no—I'm not sure of anything on that at all. Because he stated that some before and some after, but Dean may be wrong.

HALDEMAN: Well, there's another thing that's logged in here that I wasn't aware of, which is that Dean apparently made the point that either Strachan or Higby, at one point, that he would have to mortgage his house in order to get money to keep this thing going. It would indicate that Dean was up to his ass in personal efforts to supply this money and that as he got super-desperate—would come back to whatever source he could get. Well, going back to this meeting—

NIXON: Wait a second. [unclear] mortgage his house?

HALDEMAN: He made that comment. I don't know whether that was a facetious comment or a—

NIXON: But he told Higby?

HALDEMAN: I'm not sure which. But, he said—Dean said when they ran out of Kalmbach money—I played this part back and made more notes on it. Incidentally, I played the earlier part back and made more notes but they don't really add anything—

NIXON: Right.

. . .

HALDEMAN: That's something, incidentally, that is still a mystery to me. I don't why we care if the Cubans talk. Unless it's about the national security stuff—about the other jobs we did.

NIXON: That's right.

HALDEMAN: Because—

NIXON: Well, that's what—where the conversation differs, because it is about—it was about Hunt saying "the seamy things" that we did. That's why we discussed it at length.

HALDEMAN: But that had to do with what he did at the White House though — not what he did in —

NIXON: Right.

HALDEMAN: — in this case.

NIXON: That's right. Not obstruction of justice.

HALDEMAN: No, because if it was obstruction of justice, it was obstruction of justice on a charge not yet filed, which is not obstruction of justice. The charge that he had burglarized [the office of] Ellsberg['s psychiatrist, Dr. Lewis Fielding].

NIXON: But even then, we didn't [unclear]. Dean says, "Well, I called Pappas and I told him about your other trump card." He naturally [unclear] lawyers all this obviously — called Pappas.

HALDEMAN: Well, the other thing is see, you're dealing with the facts here. You're looking at —

NIXON: Yeah.

HALDEMAN: — actual things that were said. Dean will be dealing with how he wants to construe those facts and that may not come out exactly the same way. And Dean may be telling his lawyers and may be even thinking in his own mind a lot worse than what really happened. He may think the president instructed him to do this sort of thing and said we have to work this plan out — all this sort of thing — which is not [unclear]. You didn't. You just explored [unclear]. And if we get to the thing somewhere —

NIXON: Where he puts this to you?

HALDEMAN: — where he puts it to us. I think then we may have to pull out this tape recording and let him do it. Somebody like the chief justice or somebody, you know, and just —

NIXON: It's better if you give your recollection. That's the important part. And then afterwards, Ehrlichman said, "We will not — there's no dice [unclear]. We're not going to do anything." Right — on that?

HALDEMAN: Yeah, I guess.

NIXON: So he said, you did get —

HALDEMAN: Oh, yeah. Ehrlichman to me — what I heard on that from Ehrlichman's viewpoint was screw him.

NIXON: Yeah.

HALDEMAN: Which surprised me, to be perfectly frank, because I thought Ehrlichman would be concerned about it and he wasn't. He really coldcocked it to the extent that it surprised me very much and he checked with Krogh, who — see this refreshes me now. Dean thinks this thing here about Krogh being in terrible — you know, really trouble. And Ehrlichman says, "I talked to Krogh and he doesn't think he's going to be in trouble at all." And it's not — Dean was making Krogh as being trembling with agony — crazy and all sorts of things. Couldn't live with himself — hadn't slept a night.

NIXON: Is this true, or what is the case with Krogh?

HALDEMAN: Well, Ehrlichman says Krogh has no problem. He said it then, he says it now. He talked with Krogh. Krogh's had two hours with them.

NIXON: Grand jury?

HALDEMAN: No. I guess with the Senate committee. [unclear] Baker said.

NIXON: His stuff doesn't involve the campaign, does it? Does it involve the Watergate?

HALDEMAN: It involves national security [unclear]. Anything he had to do with these people is totally unrelated to the campaign.

NIXON: I think part of it — I understand —

HALDEMAN: John?

NIXON: Yeah. Right.

HALDEMAN: And that's true.

NIXON: Absolutely true and we have it goddamn right. We're going to stick hard on that.

The destruction of Hunt's files

April 26, 1973, 7:12 p.m.
Richard Nixon and Henry Petersen
WHITE HOUSE TELEPHONE

Nixon was nearing the decision to gut his inner circle, which would effectively be a decision to turn Haldeman, Ehrlichman, and Dean over to the prosecutors. Meanwhile, the most shocking news of the day was that Pat Gray testified to destroying files from Howard Hunt's safe that Dean and Ehrlichman had given to him. They allegedly had nothing to do with Watergate but instead touched on national security concerns. It was a startling admission, a significant oversight for the acting director of the FBI that would doom his appointment to be permanent director.

• • •

NIXON: Hello?

PETERSEN: Mr. President?

NIXON: Yeah, I wondered if you had had your talk with —

PETERSEN: We just started. We are in the [unclear] office now.

NIXON: Let me say — let me say this, the one thing that is — the more I think about this — that is totally devastating, because I have checked my notes on what Dean has told everybody here. I have also on this matter, and Ehrlichman is putting out his own statement. Pat Gray, Henry, was not told to destroy this. He must not say that. That is going —

PETERSEN: Well, we are just going over that now.

NIXON: — you see that is going to compound it, particularly in view of the fact that he had two conversations where he didn't even remember getting it. You see, it's the only thing — you see, if he really — you have to put it to him very personally. I don't want to do it myself, if necessary, but I will. He can't do that because I would have to say he lied on that myself.

PETERSEN: Well, you know, up to this point he is going to say, "No comment." You know, and we have just begun the conversation —

NIXON: Fine.

PETERSEN: — and we just raised —

NIXON: Let me just say —

PETERSEN: — the question of whether or not he was told to destroy them.

NIXON: He must not. All that does —

PETERSEN: Right.

NIXON: You understand?

PETERSEN: I understand.

NIXON: It doesn't help him anymore, and it hurts terribly here. You know what I am saying?

PETERSEN: We are not talking about what is going to be said. We are just trying to listen to the story in detail. Now I just want to say one more thing.

NIXON: Yeah.

PETERSEN: You know, it is going to look terrible if Gray goes —

NIXON: As a result of this.

PETERSEN: And nobody else has.

NIXON: I understand. What do you do about Dean then? Where does that one stand?

PETERSEN: Well, I don't know. You know, we may be coming to a situation where we can't hold any longer. But, you know, if we feel like we have to continue to hold on the others, maybe we ought to on this one, too.

NIXON: On Gray? Well, I am not suggesting that Gray would go as a — we don't have to do that in the first thing, not based on this one story.

PETERSEN: Yeah.

NIXON: That was your suggestion. I am going to think about it.

PETERSEN: All right. Okay.

NIXON: I agree. I agree, because he's got a right to his day in court, too.

PETERSEN: Aye, aye, sir.

NIXON: And we don't have — and another thing, I don't have a substitute.

PETERSEN: Yeah.

NIXON: Not yet. Okay.

PETERSEN: Very good. All right.

A link between Ellsberg and Watergate

April 27, 1973, 4:31 p.m.
Richard Nixon and Henry Petersen
WHITE HOUSE TELEPHONE

The trial of Daniel Ellsberg for leaking the Pentagon Papers to the press was in its seventy-ninth day. The prosecution introduced evidence against Ellsberg that Judge Byrne said had to be shared with the defense. The prosecution resisted. Byrne was so infuriated that he sent the jury home, temporarily stopping the trial in its tracks.

While not yet public, the evidence would eventually demonstrate the link between the Ellsberg trial and Watergate, a link that would eventually help him walk free from the courthouse in Los Angeles. The link was that the break-in at Ellsberg's psychiatrist's office in Beverly Hills was conducted by some of the same burglars who conducted the Watergate break-in. There was even photographic evidence to prove it, developed on a CIA-owned camera on loan to Gordon Liddy and Howard Hunt.

Moreover, one of the government wiretaps that picked up an Ellsberg telephone call was one of the illegal seventeen wiretaps that Nixon authorized in 1969, installed by Bill Sullivan and the FBI. When fully disclosed, the prosecution's case against Ellsberg would crumble, and the label "Watergate" would take on yet another added dimension.

· · ·

NIXON: Hello?

PETERSEN: Mr. President?

NIXON: Yes. Hello, Henry. How are you?

PETERSEN: I just wanted to call you and give you a report on that —

NIXON: Yeah.

PETERSEN: — Danny Ellsberg case.

NIXON: Yeah.

PETERSEN: Judge Bryne had opened it up last night and then [unclear] was inclined to the view that disclosure to him was sufficient, and then apparently overnight he changed his opinion.

NIXON: Right.

PETERSEN: And read a memorandum from Silbert to me in open court, indicated that the defendants were entitled to a hearing on it [the fact that a government-sponsored break-in of Ellsberg's psychiatrist's office had occurred], requested the disclosure of the source which I have authorized, and asked for all the information that the government has. We don't have anything, you know.

NIXON: No.

PETERSEN: But —

NIXON: You mean there was nothing — there was no material, was there?

PETERSEN: Well, that's right.

NIXON: As far as we know.

PETERSEN: I've asked the bureau to interview —

NIXON: You remember our telephone call that night. And I told you, I understand when I say all I can tell you is what people tell me, Henry. [laughs] And these days I don't know what the hell to believe!

PETERSEN: Well, you know —

NIXON: Maybe they burned it!

PETERSEN: [unclear] interview Dean.

NIXON: What did he say?

PETERSEN: Well, we haven't — I said we are going to have the bureau interview Dean —

NIXON: Yeah, right.

PETERSEN: — and Ehrlichman and see if they know anything about it.

NIXON: Right.

PETERSEN: And in effect, we are going to try and locate the psychiatrist — Ellsberg's psychiatrist — and see whether or not there was a report of a burglary, or what have you.

NIXON: Yeah. Right, right, right.

PETERSEN: And do the best we can.

NIXON: Right, right. Thank God you didn't get anything. You never knew of anything you ever got?

PETERSEN: No, sir. We can't find any trace of it here.

NIXON: Yeah. I didn't know a damn thing about it either. Fine, fine. Well, things have moved fast today.

PETERSEN: Indeed so.

NIXON: Right, and I think he [Magruder] had to resign though. It is a sad, sad thing, though. Jesus Christ!

PETERSEN: He called and told me because you know your officials were just so upset —

NIXON: I know.

PETERSEN: — and of course, in my judgment —

NIXON: A fine man.

PETERSEN: — a [unclear] victim.

NIXON: [unclear] victim. There are quite a few in this.

PETERSEN: Mr. President, you asked me for something —

NIXON: A piece of paper, if I could get it.

PETERSEN: — I don't think I can produce. I'll tell you why. Most of the information — is not —

NIXON: Is not corroborated. Yeah.

PETERSEN: Except that which I have given you in writing —

NIXON: Yeah.

PETERSEN: — is all grand jury.

NIXON: Oh, I see. I get it. Well, I can't have it then. That's right. That's right. Well, under the circumstances then we will just have to leave me in the spot for — where I've just got to, you know, look at matters. You see the problem I have. I am trying to get —

PETERSEN: I understand.

NIXON: — conduct my own investigation, and yet — I don't want the grand jury stuff. That's for darn sure.

PETERSEN: That's right, and now that's what — it's a direct conflict.

NIXON: Yeah. Yeah. I get your point. All right, all right, I understand. I understand, and that is the way we've got it and we will just leave it there. Oh, I do understand — do

I understand that they are going to finally see Haldeman and Ehrlichman? Or have they worked anything out?

PETERSEN: [unclear] for the third [of May].

NIXON: Gosh, I wish they could get earlier — God darn it, can't you do it Monday?

PETERSEN: Well, you know we tried to work that out. This is actually going to work out with John Wilson —

NIXON: I see.

PETERSEN: — and our fellows. And we are going to try to get — we want to get Magruder in to the grand jury in the early part of the week.

NIXON: Yeah. Now where does the Dean thing stand?

PETERSEN: Well, you know — no place. He's been served with a forthwith subpoena to appear in New York on the Vesco thing —

NIXON: Yes.

PETERSEN: — and he will do that, I assume. Whether he takes the Fifth Amendment is yet to be determined.

NIXON: Yeah.

PETERSEN: Our negotiations with him are, you know, just no place.

NIXON: Well, what — ?

PETERSEN: We are not getting any further.

NIXON: What — ?

PETERSEN: I would have to say at this point, Mr. President, that you cannot jeopardize our position with Dean by anything that you might do now. There is no basis for me to ask you to withhold any longer so far as he is concerned.

NIXON: I see. Well, I just don't know what to do on that one, do we?

PETERSEN: No, sir.

NIXON: Because he is in effect saying that he goes provided the other guys go, and so forth, and that is not a proper way to do — I mean, nobody can tell me that —

PETERSEN: Well —

NIXON: You know what I mean. The others can say they will go if he goes. [laughs]

PETERSEN: Well, you know —

NIXON: You say everybody should go.

PETERSEN: Yes, sir, I do. You know, I think the longer you wait the worse it gets.

NIXON: Right, right. All right, okay. Thank you very much.

PETERSEN: You are welcome, sir.

NIXON: Thank you. Bye.

Nixon disperses the inner circle

April 28, 1973, 6:33 p.m.
Richard Nixon and John Ehrlichman
CAMP DAVID TELEPHONE

Ehrlichman, who had once suggested that Gray, during difficult questioning in the Senate, should be left to "twist slowly, slowly, in the wind," was doing just that in one of his last conversations with Nixon on April 28. The day before, Gray had resigned as FBI acting director, the first of the major terminations to result from the Watergate scandal. And one day before that, Magruder had left his job as assistant secretary of commerce. Nixon knew that more dismissals were coming, as he prepared to give a speech to the nation on the subject of Watergate on April 30.

One purpose of the speech, so he said, was to announce the departure of Haldeman and Ehrlichman, although even in their last days on the White House staff they weren't certain how they'd leave or even if they would. The president continually seemed to change his mind on that point. On the twenty-eighth, as Ehrlichman faced the end of his employment, he implored the president for a private meeting, probably to campaign one last time for his job. It was all to no avail. Nixon also had to deal with the problem of John Dean, who appeared to be out of options in seeking immunity from prosecutors. In fact, he would receive only limited immunity from the Ervin Committee.

On April 30, Nixon addressed the nation. Even while praising Haldeman and Ehrlichman, he announced he had accepted their resignations. With no comment at all, he said that he had also accepted Dean's resignation. And finally, he added that Kleindienst was resigning, not for any misdeeds, but because their friendship presented a conflict in his duty to investigate Watergate, as attorney general.

· · ·

NIXON: Hello?

EHRLICHMAN: Yes, sir.

NIXON: Hi, John.

EHRLICHMAN: How are you?

NIXON: How are you? I had a long talk with Bill Rogers today and he made a suggestion that I think puts the Dean thing in a context that I will — maybe — appeal to you. What he says is this: he says that the way the cases should be separated is, basically — and he pointed out that in the Eisenhower administration they had a rule that anyone who was called before the grand jury and testified freely, of course, retained his position. Anybody who testified and pled the Fifth Amendment, or claimed immunity, of course was — resigned. And he thought that the way to present it to Dean was to say, "Mr. Ehrlichman, Mr. Haldeman are going to take leave and testify freely about this matter. You can do likewise if you want to testify freely. If you want to take immunity we want your resignation." In other words, so it really amounts — it's going to be a resignation because he isn't going to go in and testify freely.

EHRLICHMAN: Well, he is all over the papers today saying that he is.

NIXON: He is going to testify freely?

EHRLICHMAN: Yes, sir.

NIXON: Without immunity?

EHRLICHMAN: Yeah. That's what he is saying.

NIXON: Well, I know — I wonder. All right, that is going to be a different game then. But we shall have to see. I saw that the morning paper indicated that but that he said he would testify freely before the grand jury and the —

EHRLICHMAN: Without immunity.

NIXON: Without immunity.

EHRLICHMAN: Now what that means is that the jig is up. He wasn't able to make his deal. And he is trying to put the best face on it that he can.

NIXON: Well, then, he is — what does that mean that he would do then? He is going to try to bluff it through?

EHRLICHMAN: I assume so.

NIXON: And try to say that he didn't suborn perjury and he didn't — ?

EHRLICHMAN: Well, I don't know. I don't know how —

NIXON: You see, he's got a few problems, doesn't he?

EHRLICHMAN: Well, he's got a lot of problems. And I don't know how you reconcile it, but I think you have to anticipate that he would stare Garment down on that one.

NIXON: Stare to — what?

EHRLICHMAN: I say — if Garment were sent to tell him that, or whoever it was, why he'll be prepared to stare them down.

NIXON: But, if he's prepared to do — that's the point then. If he's going to testify freely, it's one thing — I mean, our point all along, as I thought — as I understood, was to avoid giving him immunity so he could do more. Isn't that true?

EHRLICHMAN: Well, that's certainly true.

NIXON: Yeah.

EHRLICHMAN: One of the objectives. But, I just — anybody who knows anything about the case, just can't — simply can't understand why he is being accorded the courtesies of the office.

NIXON: Yeah.

EHRLICHMAN: And —

NIXON: Yeah, well, let me just say that I'll — then I'll have to think of something else then. All right. I'll think of something by that time. What time will you and Bob be up here do you think?

EHRLICHMAN: Well, at your convenience. We just arbitrarily picked eleven o'clock if that is —

NIXON: That's good.

EHRLICHMAN: — if that is a good time for you.

NIXON: That's good. I would like to meet then, and then I can get on with my talk and so forth. I'll have to get to work.

EHRLICHMAN: Sometime during the time that we're there I would very much appreciate having a few minutes alone with you.

NIXON: Sure.

EHRLICHMAN: I know that we are sort of coupled like Siamese twins in this — Bob and I — but I —

NIXON: I understand.

EHRLICHMAN: — do have a couple of things I would like to —

NIXON: I understand, Bob — John. Fine. Of course, you can — a few moments alone there. Let me ask one thing. Ron said that the interest today is sort of — is moving toward the California — and the Plumbers operation. Is that right?

EHRLICHMAN: Well, I don't know. I haven't been following it.

NIXON: Yeah, yeah. On that one, I mean — have you — well, we can talk about that tomorrow. Do you have any thoughts about it at the moment?

EHRLICHMAN: No, I really don't. I assume that could run quite far.

NIXON: Yeah. It is a question of a — basically, I suppose the question is of who was in charge. Was Dean in charge?

EHRLICHMAN: No. I was, and Krogh and Young of course ran the operation.

NIXON: And the purpose was to look out for leaks.

EHRLICHMAN: Sure.

NIXON: But from what I understood — from what we have heard to date, as far as so-called electronic surveillance is concerned, none of that — maybe was contemplated — but none was tried, as far as we know, from the White House. It was from the FBI. Is that proximately correct?

EHRLICHMAN: That is correct.

NIXON: That is correct?

EHRLICHMAN: As far as I know. That's right.

NIXON: As far as this operation in California, do you know when he [Hunt] left?

EHRLICHMAN: No. I don't.

NIXON: In other words, after he — after it happened, and you learned about it did you have Liddy and him in? And talk to them about it?

EHRLICHMAN: No. No, indeed.

NIXON: How did — ?

EHRLICHMAN: I never saw him again.

NIXON: How then did it get turned off, in effect?

EHRLICHMAN: I talked to either Krogh or Young.

NIXON: Yes. And did they inform you of the fact that they had done it?

EHRLICHMAN: Yes.

NIXON: And they, what — in a word, what happened? They had done it. They had acquired nothing, or they —

EHRLICHMAN: Right. They got nothing.

NIXON: It failed, in other words?

EHRLICHMAN: Right.

NIXON: And they wanted to go back again?

EHRLICHMAN: Right.

NIXON: And you negatived it?

EHRLICHMAN: Right.

NIXON: Right. And — well, it's a solid position, I think. Isn't it? I mean —

EHRLICHMAN: Well, it's what actually happened.

NIXON: No. What I meant is, I know that's what happened. What I meant is, I am just trying to put, in terms of saying, that as far as your operation, your part of it was concerned, you — that this was something that you never authorized.

EHRLICHMAN: That's right.

NIXON: You learned that they tried something like this. You said, "That is absolutely out, and you are not to do it."

EHRLICHMAN: Right.

NIXON: That's right. That's right. Yeah, well, I — let me say in terms of — I realize that the cases are different, and we should talk about it. And we'll — you got any thoughts? Good God! I have been doing a lot of praying about this, as you know.

EHRLICHMAN: I can imagine! And so have I. [laughs]

NIXON: Of course you have, John. Had a good talk with Rogers and he feels strongly that Kleindienst must go soon.

EHRLICHMAN: Will he step in there?

NIXON: No, but I have another thought that is quite intriguing. I'll tell you about it. If it works out I'll know within a couple of hours. It is one that I think you will like if it works. He won't, for reasons that I think are good. Mainly the fact that he is so goddamn close to me. You know what I mean? In terms of, in a sense — he is, in a public sense, despite all of that — but nevertheless, whatever the reason is, he isn't going to do it. But I have another name, John, that has not occurred to any of you. It occurred to me late last night and I just busted it on him today and we've been calling the chief justice and a few others today on it, and it may be something that'll work. I'll know within a couple of hours. As a matter of fact, if I get an affirmative on it, I will call you back and let you know if you'd like to know.

EHRLICHMAN: Thank you. I think that is very healthy to make that change.

NIXON: Now, on that, let me ask you this. In terms of my talk, it was not my thought to mention you or Bob in the talk —

EHRLICHMAN: I would agree.

NIXON: — and I don't want to talk any about that. It was not my thought — however, on the AG thing I would have to — it was my thought, probably, to do that Wednesday, but — or — of course, if I could get Kleindienst lined up and so forth I could bust that in the talk. Just for purposes of my thinking which do you think would be better?

EHRLICHMAN: I would put it in the talk. The more motion you can show in the talk the better.

NIXON: Mm-hmm. "That I have some today that I'm going to send to the Senate tomorrow. I am going to nominate so-and-so to be so-and-so." Something like that?

EHRLICHMAN: Yeah. Yep.

NIXON: Well, just pray that Rogers has success in the telephone calls he will make in about a half an hour. He is on his way by helicopter back again. Fine. Fine. Did you have a good talk with your lawyers?

EHRLICHMAN: Yes. We have drawn two letters, one each which we think are —

NIXON: Yours are different now I guess.

EHRLICHMAN: Oh, yes. Yes indeed.

NIXON: Right.

EHRLICHMAN: And a draft statement —

NIXON: By me?

EHRLICHMAN: By you from Ziegler which is about a paragraph long. No, actually about two paragraphs long.

NIXON: Referring to one or both?

EHRLICHMAN: Referring to both.

NIXON: Not referring to them separately?

EHRLICHMAN: No, but I mean it's both —

NIXON: I think that is correct. Rather than letters back. Rather than letters back. I see. I see. Well, we will look it over and see where it is. This is the product of you and —

EHRLICHMAN: Yeah. We've been at work all day on them. They are pretty well honed. I think you'll find —

NIXON: Yeah. You see your case is totally differentiated in a very important way. You had nothing to do with the campaign.

EHRLICHMAN: That's it.

NIXON: That's the point that I make. You had nothing to do at all with this whole damn period before June 19. You had nothing to do with the so — well, except for the call to Kalmbach you had nothing to do with the —

EHRLICHMAN: That was after, you see?

NIXON: No, no, no. But I mean you had nothing to do with the so-called cover-up that —

EHRLICHMAN: No. That's it.

NIXON: — but at that point, you don't — certainly nobody would have considered that a cover-up. Right?

EHRLICHMAN: Right.

NIXON: Is that the position?

EHRLICHMAN: That's it exactly.

NIXON: Yeah, with regard to the papers, I am just looking at yours, in terms of its — your lawyer and so forth. What you — did you turn it over to — as your statement with regard to Gray — you had no reason to think that the stupid bastard was going to burn the stuff.

EHRLICHMAN: None whatever.

NIXON: Incidentally, do you know who knows the contents? Fielding or whoever it is?

EHRLICHMAN: I believe it's Fielding.

NIXON: Yeah. Yeah. Yeah. I wonder if the stuff in the Plumbers operation comes from those papers, if they know — or if Fielding or somebody knows — ?

EHRLICHMAN: I would doubt it but I don't know.

NIXON: But let me ask you — but where would anybody know about that? But John, if — would that be — Dean wouldn't know, would he? He wasn't in that, was he?

EHRLICHMAN: No. He might know of it though. He well might know of it.

NIXON: Know of it from Krogh?

EHRLICHMAN: Well, you know — yeah. Everyone confided in him. Just —

NIXON: Yep!

EHRLICHMAN: — for example, on advice and so on. That's what is so damn treacherous about all of this.

NIXON: Mm-hmm. That's right. That's right. I see.

EHRLICHMAN: No, you know, at one point Dean told me that Henry Petersen was aware of that whole business.

NIXON: Well, I told — you remember when you were at Camp David? I told Petersen about it.

EHRLICHMAN: Yeah.

NIXON: Didn't I tell him?

EHRLICHMAN: He has known about it for months.

NIXON: Oh, he has?

EHRLICHMAN: Oh, yes.

NIXON: Remember what I said to him? I said, "You cannot go into national security operations."

EHRLICHMAN: Yeah.

NIXON: Is that his own position, or not? I think it is.

EHRLICHMAN: I think it is.

NIXON: Well, I don't know. Tell me if I am wrong. It is — unless it is illegal operations — isn't that correct?

EHRLICHMAN: Well, even then. I mean because your FBI —

NIXON: Yeah, if it's the FBI. I mean — but my point is the FBI can do it legally but if illegal operations by a White House person are not authorized by law, and the president would not be authorizing a White House staffer to do something illegal, would he?

EHRLICHMAN: I am not sure that the FBI can legally do it. I think they just do it.

NIXON: I think a certain number of national security taps, for example, are allowed.

MAY

The United States and China: the "critical problem of our age"
May 3, 1973, 9:48 a.m.
Richard Nixon and David Bruce
OVAL OFFICE

The month of April hollowed out the Nixon presidency, sweeping away dominant person-
alities, as well as some measure of Nixon's own passion for the office. His gusto returned,
however, whenever he discussed foreign relations and especially the relationships of the
world's superpowers. In a masterful overview, he described his strategy for China and to
some extent the USSR, India, and Japan in a conversation with David Bruce. Within a
few weeks Bruce would leave to lead the U.S. Liaison Office in Beijing. Nixon's expecta-
tions were complex, even on the personal level. Although he was increasingly dependent
on Rogers, the secretary of state, for advice pertaining to the Watergate investigations,
he continued to give him low status in matters of diplomacy. The State Department was
relegated to matters of "this is how we grow figs," as Nixon termed common consular work.
Kissinger was still in place to handle major issues with Beijing. Nixon envisioned that
Bruce, a remarkably sociable man, could make friends with Chinese officials and learn
who was likely to take over the government in the near future, after the era of Mao and
Zhou Enlai ended. Unfortunately, the Chinese forbade fraternization with foreign diplo-
mats, and so Bruce's charms were wasted in what was to become a very lonely posting,
much different from his experience as an ambassador in European capitals.*

• • •

NIXON: Well, the great thing for you, as you know, substantively, probably not a great
   deal will happen for a while.

BRUCE: Yes.

NIXON: But the most important thing about this is the symbolism. I mean, symbolism
   sometimes is not important, but now it is enormously important.

BRUCE: The fact that —

NIXON: The fact that you are there. Let me tell you one thing that I particularly would
   like is that I know that the social world is a total pain in the rump, but to the extent
   that you can, if you could get around and have your colleagues get around and give
   us an evaluation of the people on the way up who are there now.

BRUCE: Yes. Yes.

NIXON: You've got to understand, Mao will soon be leaving; Zhou Enlai is in his seven-

---

* Nancy Bernkopf Tucker, *China Confidential: American Diplomats and Sino-American Relations,*
1945–1996 (Columbia University Press, 2001), pp. 292–93.

ties but he's as vigorous as can be — terrific. You're going to really like him, you'll like them both. Zhou Enlai is an amazing man. But on the other hand, except for some men in their thirties — late thirties and forties — I don't see much coming up. And I think, you know, you can do that. Look around, see who the power is. That's one thing that would be very important for us to know. Isn't it?

BRUCE: Well, I think it is, yes. Because if they have sort of a collegial [unclear] —

NIXON: The Russians have quite a few in their shop that you know might come along.

BRUCE: Yes.

NIXON: And you know, an interesting thing, the Russians too [unclear], so pretty soon we know in four or five years there's going to be change there. But there will be a change in China. And the world changes. Well, there's that. Then, of course, the just, you know, your sense of the country, its people. I mean, I'm really, really more interested in that than I am in the routine cables, "Well, today we did this, or that, or the other thing. We signed an agreement." You know, "This is how we grow figs."

BRUCE: Exactly. [laughs]

NIXON: Huh?

BRUCE: Yes.

NIXON: Don't you agree?

BRUCE: I do agree.

NIXON: We're trying to see what this great — I mean, we've got to get along with this one-fourth of all people in the world. The ablest people in the world in my opinion — potentially. We've got to get along with them. It's no problem for the next five years, or the next twenty years, but it's the critical problem of our age.

BRUCE: Yes, I think it is.

NIXON: The other thing is, if you could, constantly of course, whenever you're talking, they're very subtle — and they're not like the Russians, who, of course, slobber at flattery and all that sort of thing. But you should let them know how — two things: one, from a personal standpoint how much I appreciated the welcome while we were there. Second, we look forward to sometime returning. Third, I would very much hope that Zhou Enlai will see his way clear to come here to the UN.

BRUCE: Yes.

NIXON: Or something. I would like to entertain him here, and it can be worked out in a proper way. And fourth, and I think this is the most important, that I look upon the Chinese-American relationship as really the key to peace in the world. Always have in the back of your mind without playing it too obviously, the fact that the only thing that makes the Russian game go is the Chinese game. Always have in the back of your mind that if you say anything pro-Russian is not in our interest. Always have in the back of your mind the fact that the Russians are their deadly enemies.

BRUCE: Yes.

NIXON: And they know it, and we know it. And that we will stand by them.

BRUCE: Yes.

NIXON: And that's the commitment that I have made.

BRUCE: Right, sir.

NIXON: I have.

BRUCE: Yes.

NIXON: How we do it, I don't know. But that's what keeps — because, David, what is probably in our time maybe that big collision could occur. And collisions even between enemies these days will involve all nations of the world, they're that big. So we want to avoid that too. But my point is the Chinese must be reassured they have one heck of a friend here. They hate the Indians, as you know.

BRUCE: Yes.

NIXON: Well, they don't hate them as much as they have contempt for them. They think that India is becoming a, you know, a sort of a satellite of Russia. And of course the Japanese, they have a fear and respect for them as well. So with the Japanese, sort of say the right thing in terms of we want to get along with Japan and the rest. And it's very important that we have our, that we maintain our, in other words the shield there, because otherwise Japan goes into business for itself and that's not in their interest. And the other point that they're terribly interested in, looking at the world scene, another point, apart from the fact they'll go through the usual jazz as to [unclear] all countries and all that — revolutions in mind. That's fine. What they do in Africa I don't care anymore. But Europe — they don't want us to get out of Europe. Because they realize as long as the Russians have a tie down in Europe, that — you see what I mean?

BRUCE: Oh, I do.

NIXON: So some of our well-intentioned congressmen go over there and reassure them, "Oh, look, we're going to get out of Asia. We're going to get out of Japan, we're trying to reduce our forces in Europe." Well, that for the Chinese scares them to death.

BRUCE: Well, I was struck by the conversations that you've had, and how they came back to the necessity about preserving forces in Europe. They were very pro-NATO for their own reasons. It was interesting.

NIXON: Absolutely.

BRUCE: Well, I've got all those points in mind. Those conversations that you had there I've read. I must say they really are quite not only [unclear] but fascinating to read.

NIXON: Yeah. You're one of the few in the country who's read them.

BRUCE: I'd forgotten — but I do think they're absolutely fascinating.

NIXON: Yeah. A lot of history was made there.

BRUCE: It was indeed. I think probably the most significant history, diplomatic history, of our time. No question about it. And I don't see anything which could really ruin it in the time being. Without any hesitation I can tell you I always thought the preservation of good relations should have sort of ordinary courtesies and whatnot in the beginning, it'll probably be all business, but you try and get to know as many people as possible. [unclear]

NIXON: Let them think that we are strong, respected, and we're not going to be pushed around by the Russians or anybody else. Mideast — we have no answer there, as you know.

BRUCE: I know.

NIXON: They haven't either. But I think the great irony is that today the United States of all nations is China's most important friend. [laughs]

[Unclear exchange]

NIXON: Romania? Tanzania? Albania? [unclear]

BRUCE: [unclear] That's pretty good stuff.

NIXON: My point is, with that in mind — would you like a little coffee?

BRUCE: No, I wouldn't like some. I just had some.

NIXON: Oh, fine. I'll have a little, just a cup.

BRUCE: But this is a most fascinating development, I think.

NIXON: It sure is.

BRUCE: We must replace the policies that have become so embedded almost in the American consciousness that nobody in particular complained about it, and nobody intended to do anything about it.

NIXON: Look, for twenty years, do you know, we were sort of — now look, I'm supposed to be the number-one Red-baiter in the country. I have earned that reputation for what you know very well. Had we just continued the policy of just a silent confrontation and almost non-communication with the PRC —

BRUCE: Yes.

NIXON: — in the end we would reap a nuclear war. No question.

BRUCE: Yes. Yes.

NIXON: We just had to break through.

BRUCE: Yeah.

NIXON: Also, as I said, it was so important to the Russian game.

BRUCE: Terribly important.

NIXON: Yeah.

BRUCE: Terribly important.

NIXON: Yeah.

BRUCE: It must have [unclear]. How hard does one explain to the Chinese that we want to preserve a relationship that has great importance to us, a meaningful relationship with Russia? The Chinese are undoubtedly our favorites between the two. But —

NIXON: The Russians are saying — "Now look, this is very important — that Nixon is having another meeting with Brezhnev." There's going to be a lot of agreements that come out of that meeting. The important thing there to remember is that Russia and the United States are superpowers. That our interests do rub together in the Mideast and in Europe, particularly. That their rubbing together is a danger that is almost unbelievably great, and that under these circumstances that we feel what we have to do is try to limit that danger as much as we can through communication. But, on the other hand, we do not consider putting it quite bluntly as between the two — we consider the Soviet, because of its power and of its long history of expansionism, we consider it more of a danger that we have to deal with than we do China, which has a longer history of, frankly, defense. Now, I think a little of that is well worth saying.

In other words — and also I'd be very blunt about it. Just say you've had a long talk with the president and there's no illusions — our systems are different — both the Chinese and the Russians. They're better Communists than the Russians are today. But we want to get back to national interests. And the president considers — he's a man of the Pacific — he considers that China and America have a hell of a lot more in common than Russia and America, and that is the God's truth.

BRUCE: Yes, that's true.

NIXON: And that therefore, looking at the historical process, I want to work toward that direction. And I think that's what we have to do. But the Chinese-American relationship can be the great linchpin of peace in the world.

BRUCE: Well, I'll tell you that after you've talked to Brezhnev, the Chinese will be filled in rather completely.

NIXON: Totally. I've instructed, I'll have — of course we'll be in touch with you, but we'll probably have Kissinger go over again. Incidentally, I want to tell you one thing. Normally on these visits when he goes, this is very important, he has sometimes met alone with their leaders — so far. But in this instance, I want you to feel, David, that you are basically not the State Department's ambassador, you are the president's, and I want you to be in on everything. You see what I mean? You've got to remember that we cannot — there's parts of these games that we don't want to go to the bureaucracy. It's no lack of confidence in Bill or any of the others. But you know how it is. So will you have this in mind, please?

BRUCE: I will, Mr. President. I certainly will. Because the security of the State Department, in my mind, is nonexistent.

NIXON: It's nonexistent. [unclear]

BRUCE: No, it's absolutely impossible.

NIXON: That's right.

BRUCE: No, I think that I understand that part of the [unclear]. And I think the back channel can be used [unclear].

NIXON: Well, I want to use the back channel. And also, when Henry gets over there to do the briefings, I think it's very important that you be with him.

BRUCE: Well, I would like that.

NIXON: So that you can, you know, get the feel of the thing too.

BRUCE: Yes, I think it would be on that occasion, good. He offered when they came to Paris in connection with the Vietnam peace talks taking me to secret meetings. And I was very indisposed to do it. I think it was my great mistake. I never would have been able to —

NIXON: Oh, yes. When you were there?

BRUCE: Yes. But I think in China it's probably a different thing.

NIXON: Well, in China it's [unclear] I know I have — I'll see that it's done.

BRUCE: All right, sir. I've only got one other thing, which I have not talked to the ambassador but I [unclear] because they are behind the times with what's going on. This Cambodia thing, I wonder if it's possible to settle.

NIXON: God, I don't know. I wish it were. We're willing to settle anyway—China and them.

"Soccer is very different from American football."

May 8, 1973, 12:34 p.m.
Richard Nixon, Edson Arantes "Pelé" do Nascimento, and Rosemeri dos Reis Cholbi
OVAL OFFICE

In a twist on Ping-Pong diplomacy, Brazilian soccer great Pelé and his wife visited President Nixon for an exchange of greetings and gifts. Pelé discussed the sport's rising popularity in the United States, and Nixon responded that the greatest American players were at Howard University in Washington, DC. Pelé discussed his interest in initiating cultural exchanges between Latin America and the United States.

• • •

NIXON: You are the greatest in the world.
PELÉ: [Hands Nixon a newspaper clipping from São Paolo while photographers take photos]
NIXON: Do you speak any Spanish?
PELÉ: No, Portuguese. It is all the same.
NIXON: He always wins.
CHOLBI: Yes.
NIXON: The national champions of soccer in the United States are here in Washington, at Howard University. Here is a clipping of my visit with Pelé to São Paolo in 1967.
PELÉ: Soccer is very different from American football.
NIXON: Do I know that! The main thing is to use your head.
PELÉ: Here is a film of soccer which I would like to present. I know you are busy.
NIXON: Sports films I watch.
PELÉ: It shows the worldwide soccer and the training that is required.
NIXON: You have no sons, but maybe your grandsons will want to learn from it. [Nixon hands out pens.]
PELÉ: Soccer is played more and more around the world and in the United States. My aim is to send soccer technicians to the U.S. and have your basketball technicians come to Latin America.
NIXON: That is a great enterprise and I wish you well.

Kissinger's trip to Moscow

May 11, 1973, 10:15 a.m.
Richard Nixon and Henry Kissinger
OVAL OFFICE

On May 10, Kissinger returned from a trip to Moscow, where he had met with Leonid Brezhnev, ostensibly about the plans for a June visit by the Soviet leader to the United

States. During the course of four official meetings and a boar-hunting trip, Kissinger also discussed matters that included the possibility of reaching an agreement on MIRV missile systems, as well as relations with China. The high-level mission meant a lot to Kissinger at that juncture, with the White House in turmoil and his position within it under pressure, at least in his perception. In an off-the-record conversation, atop a hunting blind, Brezhnev had expressed his concern that Senator Henry Jackson's legislation on the emigration of Jews from the USSR would do more harm than good. Kissinger and then Nixon were not hard to convince on that point.

• • •

KISSINGER: Now, we have a massive problem with the Chiefs and [William] Clements, who's stupid but well meaning on SALT.

NIXON: Ah, yes.

KISSINGER: And I'm not going to bother you with the technical details, but they are digging in on almost everything. The point is, the Russians will turn down almost anything, and we —

NIXON: I know.

KISSINGER: — just the — the issue is they want to nail the Russians now to agree to equal numbers on both sides before they will talk about MIRVs. Now, the MIRV proposal they are making is so unilaterally advantageous to us. Namely, that we should stop deployment of our land-based missiles, MIRVs, of which we have already completed nine-tenths of our program. If they don't put any MIRVs on their land-based missiles, there's no chance that it will ever be accepted, but if we can make it and get them to turn it down — but, if they did accept it, it would be spectacularly advantageous to us because we — our program would be nearly complete —

NIXON: Mm-hmm.

KISSINGER: — and they would never start theirs.

NIXON: That's right. Right. Right. All right, what do you want me to do? To get the Chiefs —

KISSINGER: I —

NIXON: — in and what else?

KISSINGER: No, no —

NIXON: And tell them —

KISSINGER: No, no —

NIXON: By God, then, I will —

KISSINGER: I —

NIXON: — because I've had enough with these goddamn Chiefs.

KISSINGER: I'll draft a memo for your signature today to send over to them.

NIXON: All right, let me say: make it tough. Say that I have — you know, I have thought this thing through. This is a decision, and I expect it to be loyally and scrupulously adhered to, and I'm placing personal responsibility on everyone who gets the memorandum to see that there is no undercutting, and no playing members of the Congress, or with the press —

KISSINGER: Right.

NIXON: — on this matter. How's that sound to you?

KISSINGER: That's excellent.

NIXON: Put the words in to that effect. Okay?

• • •

KISSINGER: On China, I'm getting worried. I'm beginning to think that they [the Soviet Union] want to attack China. [unclear, Brezhnev?] took me hunting. He — you hunt there from a tower. You sit in a tower and shoot these poor bastards as they come by to feed. They put out the food. Well, when night fell, and he had killed about three boars and God knows what else — and that's when it was dark — he unpacked a picnic dinner and said, "Look, I want to talk to you privately — nobody else, no notes." And he said, "Look, you will be our partners, you and we are going to run the world — "

NIXON: Who'd he use as translator on that?

KISSINGER: [Viktor] Sukhodrev. And he said, "The president and I are the only ones who can handle things." He said, "We have to prevent the Chinese from having a nuclear program at all costs." I've got to get that information to the Chinese, and we've got to play a mean game here —

NIXON: I know.

KISSINGER: — because I don't think we can let the Russians jump the Chinese.

NIXON: No.

KISSINGER: I think the change in the world balance of power would be —

NIXON: [unclear]

KISSINGER: — too unbelievable.

NIXON: We all know that.

KISSINGER: And, uh — so he [unclear] on politics, he said, "Anything you want," he said, "the Republicans have to be back in in '76." He said, "Anything we — "

NIXON: He didn't give you the crap on Watergate [unclear] been exposed to here?

KISSINGER: The only thing on Watergate that Dobrynin said —

NIXON: Don't let it get you down, Henry —

KISSINGER: No. And, now, Dobrynin, the basic — the only thing Dobrynin is complaining about is the amateurishness of the guys who did it. He said, "Why did you do it out of the White House?"

NIXON: [unclear]

KISSINGER: But, I'm just telling you what Dobry — that's the only —

NIXON: Well —

KISSINGER: — the only concern the Russians have is they hate the Democrats. I mean, you should hear Brezhnev on Jackson. It's not to be believed.

NIXON: Good.

KISSINGER: And he says they want you [unclear] —

NIXON: Oh — did they get into the business of — of the — that doggone exit visa, and that other thing?

KISSINGER: Yeah.

NIXON: I worked with the senators [unclear] —

[Unclear exchange]

KISSINGER: — promised it wouldn't be reintroduced. I gave them a list of those forty-two people who are being kept.

NIXON: Yeah?

KISSINGER: And they promised —

NIXON: And if we look at all we can do [unclear]. "Just don't let it" — I keep threatening the senators that if they continue to insist on [the] Jackson [amendment], it'll blow the whole thing. Now, you know it won't, but my point is —

KISSINGER: Oh, it will. Who knows?

NIXON: What I meant is, it won't because we're going to get Jackson modified.

KISSINGER: Yeah.

NIXON: Jackson's got to be modified in a way that they could be given [unclear]. I have threatened the hell out of the senators.

KISSINGER: Yeah.

NIXON: But, did he mention — is there anything they know about that?

KISSINGER: Well, he said that if the Jackson amendment goes through, no Jew is going to leave the Soviet Union again.

NIXON: That's right.

KISSINGER: He — he said to me —

NIXON: That's the point I've been making.

KISSINGER: Well, you can't repeat this, but he said — he took me aside privately, he said, "Do you know what your people are doing?" He said, "The Jews are already the privileged group — in a way, a privileged group. They live in cities, they're the only group that can have an exit visa. No one else receives an exit visa, and if you people keep humiliating us you're going to create the worst anti-Semitism ever in the Soviet Union." And I believe that it's true.

NIXON: We can — we're going to work on the Jackson amendment. I'm working my tail on it, Henry.

A mysterious set of documents

May 16, 1973, 2:51 p.m.
Richard Nixon and J. Fred Buzhardt
WHITE HOUSE TELEPHONE

On May 14, 1973, John Dean turned over a secret cache of intelligence records to Judge John Sirica, effectively a shot across the Nixon White House bow. The intelligence community panicked, scrambling to determine exactly which documents were included, as well as to make sure they would not become public or even fall into the hands of congressional investigators. Among the documents were the White House copy of the Huston Plan, a program of surveillance and illicit activities aimed at American citizens, and related cor-

respondence. The CIA, NSA, and DIA worked intensely to make sure the records, which included details of government domestic intelligence, electronic eavesdropping, and even break-ins, were not linked to the Watergate wiretapping and break-in. In the end, they cut a deal with Sirica, and the records have remained in the custody of the District Court for the District of Columbia ever since.

• • •

NIXON: Did you finish your meeting with Chuck [Colson]?

BUZHARDT: Yes, sir.

NIXON: Are you free now?

BUZHARDT: Yes, sir. We are now going over these documents, Mr. President —

NIXON: I see.

BUZHARDT: — that we have —

NIXON: Oh, yeah.

BUZHARDT: — and we would like to get in a report to you. I would like a little while longer.

NIXON: Yeah. Take your time.

BUZHARDT: All right. Thank you, sir.

NIXON: But they are the type that you described?

BUZHARDT: They are the type, but they do present problems nevertheless.

NIXON: Well. Okay.

BUZHARDT: All right, sir.

White House espionage and its attempted use of the CIA

May 16, 1973, 4:55 p.m.
Richard Nixon and Alexander Haig
OVAL OFFICE

Within days of losing four key advisors, Nixon faced two new issues in the Watergate investigation. First, the existence of the Huston Plan was now public. It was, at least in part, a reaction to the protest movement. Unchecked by any legal mechanism, the plan was serious enough as an infringement of civil rights, but it also opened the door to political espionage. A second problem to emerge during the first week of May was that of White House pressure on the CIA to suppress the Watergate investigation. The deputy director of central intelligence, General Vernon Walters, testified before the Senate Armed Services Committee that Dean had requested help in paying hush money and that Haldeman and Ehrlichman had sought the CIA's help in stopping an FBI investigation into political funds laundered through a Mexican bank. He also submitted a written statement to clarify his position. Walters, a native of New York City, had been raised in France and England. He rose quickly in the ranks of the army and served as an aide to President Dwight Eisenhower, in part because he was entirely fluent in several languages. A Nixon loyalist, Walters was at first mildly sympathetic to the request for help with the FBI, though his boss at the time, Richard Helms, squelched any such idea. Ultimately, Walters didn't *cooperate with either request and testified to that effect before Congress. Nixon discussed the new problems with his new chief of staff, Alexander Haig, and a special advisor, Fred Buzhardt.**

. . .

NIXON: I remember this [Huston] Plan, and I think [unclear] put it out, you see rather than — I think there's one — [unclear] damn good man — a little bit of a tendency to, you know [unclear] let's go out and, for example, this thing on Walters. I am not too sure we have to give on that. What do you think? I don't know. We may have to.

HAIG: I would never give on it. There is no reason for it yet. Our problem right now is to get the facts and I bet a million dollars they are (a) nothing was ever done. A summary [unclear] by the NSA by [unclear] totally political. (b) Huston — have you talked to Fred since he talked to you?

NIXON: No. Has he talked to you? Did he talk to you?

HAIG: Yes.

NIXON: What did he say? I just talked —

HAIG: Huston, first of all, he said he says to make it clear that you rescinded the approval.

NIXON: I made the order for the rescission.

HAIG: Well, he says that he recalls [unclear] when they broke in: "My God, what have [unclear]?"

NIXON: [unclear] Oh, that's right. The plan wasn't working. That's why I rescinded it or something like that. This may be more of a flap than an opportunity here. Goddamn it, Al, we can't react so — you know what I mean, it's a nightmare.

HAIG: I know that.

NIXON: I don't think [unclear] would come up on that, that we still have on. But don't tie it into Krogh, and don't tie it into the buggers, and don't tie it into the [unclear]. That is a terrible mistake, and makes it look like a giant conspiracy. I feel that I've just got to say that Krogh did this and that was a mistake, and the buggers did this.

. . .

[FRED BUZHARDT joins the conversation.]

NIXON: I think Dean planned it all. When I say I think that, something in the back of my mind tells me that. I don't know —

HAIG: Be careful —

NIXON: He's never told me this. He never admitted it to me.

HAIG: Well, it wasn't his plan anyway. [unclear] thinks one of these young activists planned it and said here's what we're really [unclear] at that point.

NIXON: But as far as Huston was concerned, he doesn't remember anything being done with the damn plan?

---

* Marjorie Hunters, "Dean Tied to Plea to C.I.A. to Help Watergate Group," *New York Times*, May 16, 1973, p. A1.

HAIG: Yes.

NIXON: That is what I thought. I never — [unclear] check my memory a little bit. Al is right on [Tom Charles] Huston. Huston got pissed off and left. He said that nothing was ever done under this goddamn thing.

BUZHARDT: I talked —

NIXON: He said [unclear] is a lie.

BUZHARDT: I talked —

NIXON: And he [unclear] it. And Al says that Huston recalls that I rescinded it and I think that is right. I don't remember it but I think what happened was it just wasn't working or something like that. I don't remember — something came across — but look like hell — we may find something in the file.

BUZHARDT: Let me give you where we are right now. Huston says that his best recollection is that it was recalled. I am going to search his files. He may have a copy. He thinks not but I have sent him home to look.

NIXON: Is he here in Washington?

BUZHARDT: No, sir. He is in Indianapolis.

NIXON: He took his files with him?

BUZHARDT: He did take his files with him.

NIXON: Well, [unclear] Jesus Christ.

BUZHARDT: Next, he said that in August of 1970 John Dean came into the White House. He was moved to Dean's office and Dean took over his responsibility with respect to this type of activity.

NIXON: Oh, that's how Dean got in it.

BUZHARDT: He said at the same time Mardian came in as assistant attorney general for internal security. And he was aware that Dean and Mardian formed an interagency committee [on intelligence]. He doesn't know anything about what they did. His recollection is that he had sent out a memorandum saying the decision is reversed in implementing the plan.

NIXON: That who had sent out the memorandum?

BUZHARDT: He originally said he thinks that he had sent out a memo implementing the plan. Telling that your decision —

NIXON: Huston did?

BUZHARDT: Huston did.

NIXON: Yeah.

BUZHARDT: He said he thinks he probably sent out a memorandum telling — recalling that document.

NIXON: After —

BUZHARDT: After —

NIXON: — Dean came in?

BUZHARDT: — he said that he thought Mitchell — no, before Dean came on board — he said that Hoover went to Mitchell, Mitchell came to you, and you turned it off.

NIXON: I don't recall except for that I know that Mitchell did that — that Hoover didn't like it worth a damn and wasn't working on it. And—but you know what I mean, for God's sakes you see how it is on these things.

BUZHARDT: Right.

NIXON: I just had one meeting and I don't recall anything else.

BUZHARDT: That was the initial meeting.

NIXON: Mitchell was following my goddamn advisors!

BUZHARDT: Yeah. That was the initial meeting apparently.

NIXON: That's right—in this room! [unclear]

BUZHARDT: Just to put together the plan.

NIXON: As a matter of fact, they all wanted a meeting—

BUZHARDT: Yeah.

NIXON: —at that point. Helms, Gayler, and Hoover were all—

BUZHARDT: Worked up.

NIXON: —working together and I said get them one room, and I said now goddamn it, get together and Hoover is in charge. Hoover wanted that. And that's what they came up with.

BUZHARDT: Now I talked to NSA. I talked to both Sam Phillips and Lou Tordella. Lou Tordella says that to the best of his memory he had it orally that the plan had been approved and that he never remembered getting a memo on any of it. He remembers no turn-off. Now Lou Tordella, I told him to pull together every scrap of paper he had related—

NIXON: All right.

BUZHARDT: —and to come in here and tell me what procedures he did under the authority of this thing. He is on his way in and should be here shortly. I got ahold of DIA—Defense Department's very recent director Bennett—

NIXON: [unclear]

BUZHARDT: —and he says, "So far as I know we didn't do a damn thing." He knows they didn't do anything. I mean he swears to me. He has talked to his people. He said there may have been a memorandum here—we have no receipt for it. But he's got memos still working—searching the files to see if there was a memorandum turning it off or turning it on—that matter—to see any records they have regarding it. I have not met managed to reach Schlesinger yet. He is out of pocket. Mardian was out for an hour. They couldn't reach him. I left word for him to call back. That is where we are at the moment.

NIXON: Mardian's the chief.

BUZHARDT: Mardian's the [unclear] because we can talk to Dean—

NIXON: That's right.

BUZHARDT: —as to what they did.

NIXON: Huston was the [unclear] and I know he didn't do—did he know of anything while he was here?

BUZHARDT: He says nothing was done while he was here. See, he left just after the approval of the thing. He moved to Dean's office and out he went. And he said Dean took it over. He left in frustration at Hoover. He was just furious.

NIXON: But he wrote the memorandum.

BUZHARDT: He wrote the memorandum.

NIXON: Then maybe Dean did something then.

BUZHARDT: Maybe Dean did do something. If anything was done it was done between Dean and Mardian. There was some activity, Mr. President. I know they had a committee. I know they produced intelligence reports — whether they got it from the [unclear] — whether they did anything extra I don't know. I suspect quite frankly that we'll find there's a fair likelihood that the Ellsberg thing was justified on this. I know Bob Mardian quite well.

NIXON: Yeah, I know —

BUZHARDT: Bob was extremely aggressive. It may be that that's what he'll hang his hat on if he was involved. He may not have been but we will find out when we get him. In the meanwhile we've got the others looking to see if there are any documents — turning it on, turning it off, or whatnot to look into.

NIXON: Well, I will lay a little bet on that that Ellsberg was not justified on that. They may try it on it.

BUZHARDT: I say they may try to justify it —

NIXON: Because I'll tell you what — I think this is [unclear]. The Ellsberg thing was something we set up. Let me know tell you — I don't [unclear] here, and Al knows what happened. We set up in the White House an independent group under Bud Krogh to cover the problems of leaks involved at the time of the goddamn Pentagon Papers. Right? Remember we called it — they called it — I don't remember — remember they called it the Plumbers operation. That was independent. It was not connected with these things at all [unclear]. Not at all. They had no connection whatever — in addition to those.

BUZHARDT: Right.

NIXON: And may I say that I think that back to our earlier conversation. I think we should treat them separately. Treat them separately. I think this idea of saying that could have been this, and maybe the reason that we had to check the Watergate buggers was because of this. Then — aha! I don't think so. I think that you are going to find that this thing was either dead, because it appears in limbo, or it was one of those things that was never implemented. Now here is my theory of the case at this point, which of course is a little different than what we thought it was at first. I think you can prepare a contingency as I think they may think they have got more than they have got. Well, they may think, well maybe Dean knows, but Dean is going to have to —

HAIG: This is what we are talking about.

NIXON: What?

HAIG: This is what Dean's defense is —

BUZHARDT: That's right.

HAIG: — the son of a bitch is — that's why he created that document —

BUZHARDT: That is why I say that they're — that's why I say they're probably going to try —

NIXON: Yeah.

BUZHARDT: — to hang the whole business on this. That is how they are going to try to get — I am not saying it will work —

NIXON: Well, so Dean's defense will be what? The whole Watergate thing was the result of this? That's [unclear] — I'm just trying to think.

BUZHARDT: I can conceive he will try to hang the whole thing on that. Yep!

NIXON: It won't work.

HAIG: That he would say — of course it would work — [unclear] a man who's got his hand in the cookie jar and is about to get fried. [unclear]

BUZHARDT: That's right. That's the paper I can only figure he could [unclear].

NIXON: Okay. Well, let me say what I think, Fred. I'd like for you to think of it in totally separate terms.

BUZHARDT: All right.

NIXON: I don't want to get Ellsberg involved. Let's leave that where he belongs. Let Ellsberg be where it was. I mean I'm sorry for Krogh and hope that California law isn't too tough on Danbury, Connecticut. Have you found out yet?

BUZHARDT: No, sir. I'll have the answer [unclear].

NIXON: Goddamn let's hope it's a misdemeanor.

BUZHARDT: I hope so.

NIXON: It should be. Incidentally are you in touch with Krogh?

BUZHARDT: I have not. I haven't talked to Bud.

HAIG: I haven't talked to him either.

NIXON: Someday when you call him just tell him that I think he's a hell of a guy, would you?

HAIG: All right, sir.

NIXON: Good. Okay, as far as this thing and as far as [unclear]. As far as this thing is itself is concerned, I wouldn't anticipate that [unclear] in effect that we're going to get all our bowels in an uproar because something like this is going to — maybe come out. Let's see, in — remember, this is a classified document. Let's remember that. My view is if they start leaking the goddamn document, and then we go on the attack of the leak of classified documents — in other words, make the case about — again about the Pentagon [Papers] — here's a classified document. But then here is my third point — most important point is this: if we found that very little if nothing was done with the goddamn thing, or if we happen to find that it happened to have been rescinded, you can kill it. I doubt anything was done with this at all. I just think it was a nonstarter.

HAIG: Well —

NIXON: I'm not trying to say — but that's — my recollection of the thing, Al, was that we were all around here — I remember when you [unclear] and you said Huston left because he was pissed off. And I do remember. He was, you know, he was an arrogant —

BUZHARDT: Yes.

NIXON: — an activist kind of a guy, and he got pissed off — just took off — said it didn't work. Now I don't know where — somebody else did something. I would doubt it. I would doubt it.

BUZHARDT: I would doubt if they had any illegal entries.

NIXON: That's my point.

BUZHARDT: Now I am very sure that NSA brought [unclear].

NIXON: What did the NSA — will they — what kind of action did they do — do they do?

BUZHARDT: Well, they picked up communication stuff. They don't actually tap things. There is no tapping of the [unclear].

NIXON: Anything that NSA did is totally defensible.

BUZHARDT: I think it is defensible but they moved into a broader category with respect to domestic affairs.

NIXON: Right. Right. Meaning picking up by —

BUZHARDT: [unclear]

NIXON: — electronic surveillance?

BUZHARDT: Targeting — yes, sir. Targeting U.S. citizens' conversations that were on international circuits.

NIXON: Doing so because of their concern about their being involved in violence?

BUZHARDT: Yes, sir.

NIXON: Is that right?

BUZHARDT: Yes, sir. Now, I will get a complete rundown —

NIXON: Fight them like hell on that issue.

BUZHARDT: What?

NIXON: Fight them like hell on that issue. Well, that's interesting. I would not move too quickly on this.

BUZHARDT: Well, we want to move quickly to get as many facts as we can. That's the only way we can move what we're doing —

NIXON: No, what we're doing, really — this is just the way — what I meant is I am thinking of our PR strategy here. This is one —

BUZHARDT: Let me tell you. They bought a little time.

NIXON: What?

BUZHARDT: They bought a little time. The intelligence agencies consigning to intercede on the basis of the sensitivity of the document with the Ervin Committee — to lock the document up. So he is going to take the mainstay and they are going to try to convince him tomorrow of the high sensitivity and the damage that could be done — to try to hold this document —

NIXON: Who is going to do it?

BUZHARDT: — get it turned back. It is going to be done by CIA and NSA.

NIXON: Are going to see who? Ervin?

BUZHARDT: They are going to see [Senator] Symington. If Symington is convinced he is going will try to get Ervin to give the document back. I don't frankly think it will work, but in the meanwhile it buys us time while they are considering the question. We have nothing to lose. It might buy us some time.

NIXON: What are [unclear]?

BUZHARDT: It has bought us some time so far.

NIXON: You mean Ervin. But Ervin is likely to say [unclear].

BUZHARDT: I think that is a likely result but in the meanwhile he has at least told me —

NIXON: You see, the thing that is good about this is that it is so broad based. Do you understand — what I meant is they don't like to get caught with their hands in the cookie jar but basically the worst kind of a thing is frankly the Plumbers operation.

BUZHARDT: Yes.

NIXON: It looks like well, a few goddamn clowns hired a bunch of people here. But here you have the CIA, the NSA, the DIA, the FBI all working together on something —

BUZHARDT: — and Internal Revenue.

NIXON: Huh?

BUZHARDT: And Internal Revenue.

NIXON: They did it too?

BUZHARDT: Yes.

NIXON: There you are. All working on something like this. Well, goddamn it! Now when they all get together on a paper for the president of the United States that something is pretty goddamn important, isn't it? That is what is involved here. It involved groups that were engaging in violence, disruption — unbelievable hell around this place. The trouble is that we didn't do much to it.

"A certain domestic intelligence plan"
May 16, 1973, 4:57 p.m.
J. Fred Buzhardt and Robert Mardian
WHITE HOUSE TELEPHONE

After J. Edgar Hoover tried to put an end to the Huston Plan in 1970, a new avenue of intelligence gathering emerged. An entity called the Intelligence Evaluation Committee was formed as a means of using surveillance capabilities already in place to respond to White House initiatives. In the aftermath of Dean's revelations about the Huston Plan, the extent of the Intelligence Evaluation Committee's work also became an issue, especially since the body was more or less a sequel to the Interagency Committee on Intelligence, the Hoover-chaired group that created the Huston Plan.

In an Oval Office conversation that did not include Nixon, Fred Buzhardt called Robert Mardian to find out what the committee actually did. Buzhardt, a South Carolina lawyer, had been a fervent supporter of Strom Thurmond and had worked for him in Congress during the 1960s. He had a focused mind and an almost heroic dedication to the Republican Party. While Buzhardt was working as counsel at the Defense Department in *early May, Nixon tapped him to become special counsel for Watergate. Mardian had been out of government for a year. A native of Pasadena, California, he was working success-fully as a lawyer in the banking industry when he was swept up in Republican politics, ultimately serving as an assistant attorney general under John Mitchell. He left that post to work for CRP as chief counsel. A professed supporter of law and order, Mardian was an outspoken opponent of the protest movement, even when it operated within the law. He was living in Arizona when Buzhardt reached him to discuss the Intelligence Evaluation Committee.**

• • •

BUZHARDT: Hello?

MARDIAN: Hello, Fred. How are you?

BUZHARDT: Bob, how the hell are you?

MARDIAN: Fine, thanks.

BUZHARDT: It's been a long time.

MARDIAN: It has. What's your new job?

BUZHARDT: I am special counsel to the president.

MARDIAN: Good.

BUZHARDT: On guess what?

MARDIAN: [laughs]

BUZHARDT: Bob, there were some documents that were released by the court today —

MARDIAN: Yeah.

BUZHARDT: — which consisted of a certain domestic intelligence plan —

MARDIAN: A what?

BUZHARDT: A certain domestic intelligence plan — that's dated the summer of 1970. Are you reading me?

MARDIAN: Yeah.

BUZHARDT: Okay. Now this was handled here by a fellow named Huston until about August of '70 at which time Dean came aboard and took over the responsibility.

MARDIAN: Right.

BUZHARDT: Sometime along about that time you came aboard and formed a commit-tee — Interagency [Committee on Intelligence].

MARDIAN: Yes.

BUZHARDT: Now, we — you know, the [Ervin] committee has the documents inciden-tally —

MARDIAN: Yeah.

BUZHARDT: Now there are certain things we need to know quite urgently.

MARDIAN: Yeah.

BUZHARDT: On the committee you ran, Bob, was it an analysis group, solely and sim-ply, or were there any activities?

MARDIAN: No activities whatsoever.

---

* Michael A. Genovese, *The Watergate Crisis* (Greenwood Press, 1999), p. 12.

BUZHARDT: No collections?

MARDIAN: What?

BUZHARDT: No collections?

MARDIAN: No. The only activity was an attempt to — I understood this was at the direction of Ehrlichman — the president actually, that's what they told me — and the only purpose was to — originally, it was set up in the White House, then it was moved over to [Department of Justice] Internal Security because everybody — the various members of the intelligence group were concerned about everybody seeing them coming in and going out together when they had meetings.

BUZHARDT: Right.

MARDIAN: The sole purpose was to attempt to bring the intelligence, to coordinate the activities of the various law enforcement intelligence agencies within the government.

BUZHARDT: All right, now —

MARDIAN: Now what they were doing — see, now as I say, it started — it was a White House operation —

BUZHARDT: [unclear] my shop.

MARDIAN: — and what they would do would be to respond to requests. There's a charter — there's a — I don't call it a charter, but an agreement as to what they would do. What their scope would be.

BUZHARDT: When did this come into being, Bob?

MARDIAN: Oh, I would guess January or February of 1971 and it was a friend of — a judge, a former justice of the Washington Supreme Court was supposed to be the working director of it [the Intelligence Evaluation Committee].

BUZHARDT: Did he ever show up?

MARDIAN: Oh, yeah, and he was just there on — served as a special assistant to the attorney general. We put him on the payroll there. That was Ehrlichman's idea. He was Ehrlichman's neighbor and subsequently when he got appointed back on the court — he went back on the — I think the Federal District Court. Bernie Wells, who was in my shop —

BUZHARDT: Yeah.

MARDIAN: — was put in charge of it, and he is still in charge of it.

BUZHARDT: Yeah.

MARDIAN: But there is nothing — all it is, all it was, was an attempt to get the various agencies to work together. It included National Security Agency —

BUZHARDT: Yeah.

MARDIAN: — your shop, Defense Intelligence Agency, although I guess they never admitted they had anybody working on it over there. But there was a — as I recall —

BUZHARDT: I know the guy that was liaison.

MARDIAN: Yeah. Well, that is all they had was liaisons.

BUZHARDT: Okay, let me ask you —

MARDIAN: It was a problem that the White House wanted staffed out, if CIA had input on it, it had a foreign aspect, it would contribute what information it had. If the FBI had input on it they would give it input —

BUZHARDT: All right. Let me ask you this, Bob. I have got to know some specifics here. To your knowledge, and I need to know this on the square, were any surreptitious entries made specifically for this purpose?

MARDIAN: Absolutely not. Hell no!

BUZHARDT: Okay.

MARDIAN: Well, if it were — that's — no, it couldn't have been. Bernie Wells was running it, for Christ's sake. It was — all they were doing were making assessments.

BUZHARDT: Okay.

MARDIAN: To my knowledge that's all they ever did.

BUZHARDT: Only assessments.

MARDIAN: That's all. There would be a request for information concerning whatever it was that the White House wanted — an assessment was made and copies went to the constituent liaison agencies —

BUZHARDT: Right.

MARDIAN: — as well as the White House and that's all.

BUZHARDT: Okay.

MARDIAN: But that's all they did was to make assessments. They weren't operating anything.

BUZHARDT: All right. Who was your point of contact over here? Did you work with Dean at all on it?

MARDIAN: Actually I didn't really have much to do with it except to put, to help put the group together.

BUZHARDT: Yeah.

MARDIAN: The contact was direct from Dean's office, as I recall, to Bernie Wells.

BUZHARDT: Yeah.

MARDIAN: And copies of the work product, as I say, went to each of the constituent departments and agencies. But look, I forget what the hell assessments they made but there was nothing of any consequence and there certainly weren't any covert operations that I was aware of. I am sure there weren't. Bernie Wells wouldn't have gone into anything like that —

BUZHARDT: At this time —

MARDIAN: In fact, they never did work together too well, Fred, because, well, you can imagine trying to get a bunch of people like that all — they are all holding their own information. This was simply an attempt to establish liaison between them with respect to particular problems that the White House had.

BUZHARDT: Okay. To the best of your knowledge, I know the problem while Hoover was there — I am sure there weren't any. But thereafter you know of no entries made by the bureau?

MARDIAN: Hell, no. No siree. Here again, not as a result of that operation. What the hell did they come up with as far as in these papers to indicate what this group were doing?

BUZHARDT: Well, I don't want to talk too specific over the phone. But —

MARDIAN: I would suggest you get in touch with Bernie Wells. You know Bernie.

BUZHARDT: Yeah, I will talk to Bernie.

MARDIAN: I'd get Bernie, and Jesus Christ — Fred, if there is anything amiss over there I would sure appreciate you calling me and letting me know.

BUZHARDT: I don't believe there is, Bob. I am just trying to verify that there isn't.

MARDIAN: I am sure there wasn't.

BUZHARDT: I am trying to verify a negative — you know how hard that is.

MARDIAN: Well, you talk to Bernie and he will level with you.

BUZHARDT: But I have got to know. You know? We can't say no —

MARDIAN: Is there some inference that there was?

BUZHARDT: I suspect there is going to be a claim there was.

MARDIAN: Well, that's a lot of crap.

BUZHARDT: Okay.

MARDIAN: Well, to my knowledge. Unless — I am never surprised by anything like that —

BUZHARDT: Right. Okay.

MARDIAN: — but I just can't imagine Bernie. In fact, after the Watergate thing came out and Liddy was arrested, Bernie Wells told — I heard from Bernie Wells, or Jim McGraff that worked over there, that this asshole was over there and said hell, the only way to break — this was during the *Time* and *Post* case, or the Pentagon Papers case — there is only one way to do that and that was to bug the *New York Times*.

BUZHARDT: Oh, God.

MARDIAN: They thought he was joking and never reported it to me.

BUZHARDT: Yeah. Okay. Thanks a lot, Bob. I've got to run.

MARDIAN: I am just telling you that Bernie [unclear] on that basis.

BUZHARDT: I'll go back.

MARDIAN: Will you call me back and let me know?

BUZHARDT: Yeah, I will.

MARDIAN: I'd appreciate it.

BUZHARDT: Okay.

MARDIAN: Thank you.

The Intelligence Evaluation Committee as a cover

May 16, 1973, 5:39 p.m.

Richard Nixon and J. Fred Buzhardt

OVAL OFFICE

As special counsel for Watergate, Buzhardt hit the ground running, determined to research the president's position on a number of issues related to Watergate. As in the call to Mardian, he tried to pull bad news from those who had been involved in related activities. Unlike his predecessors in advising the president on the scandal, Buzhardt wasn't interested in coercing selective memory from those who had been involved. Soon after Buzhardt hung up with Mardian, he and the president discussed the Intelligence Evaluation Committee and what Nixon should say about it to the American people. They further worked on a theory that Dean would try to explain away all of his Watergate-related activities by claiming they came under the aegis of the committee.

. . .

NIXON: Mardian been reached yet?

BUZHARDT: They found him. I was dealing with the Sullivan call and I was going to get him next.

NIXON: Fine. My feeling is that I guess you have got to check with — I guess Mardian can tell you. I think, Fred, the damn thing was rescinded. That is the [unclear]. I think [unclear] or something, you know what I mean? I cannot recall, but there is something there. Huston seemed to think so — is looking, is that correct?

BUZHARDT: That is correct. Also, the DIA can help. Somebody there thinks it was rescinded.

NIXON: They think it was.

BUZHARDT: They are now looking. I've got them looking.

NIXON: If they can find one piece of paper and —

BUZHARDT: We are in business.

NIXON: Yeah. Where else? What about the CIA?

BUZHARDT: CIA — I haven't gotten [James] Schlesinger yet. He's somewhere they can't reach him, which is unusual.

NIXON: Maybe Walters can try and help.

BUZHARDT: That's true, but Walters didn't know anything about this.

NIXON: Neither did Schlesinger.

BUZHARDT: Schlesinger knows nothing about it but he can find the right people to inquire. We might be a little bit better. Since Walters is a witness —

NIXON: I agree. I agree. I agree. Walters is a witness.

BUZHARDT: Since Walters is a witness —

NIXON: Walters is a witness.

BUZHARDT: — I think we shouldn't pick anybody we know is going to be a witness.

NIXON: I am going to take Al and investigate something [unclear] out of this house for a little while. So I — and we'll call you within — well, you've got to go, don't you?

BUZHARDT: No, I'll be here. I'll be here.

NIXON: But I'll try to call you back. But I'll tell you, if we can detain this one, we can handle this. I think this — I have a recollection that the goddamn thing is — look, I know it isn't an operation. It hadn't been in operation in two years!

BUZHARDT: I am sure —

NIXON: I just don't know how went out of business. That is my point.

BUZHARDT: I am sure it hasn't been operating legitimately in quite a while. I feel that is true.

NIXON: Without — as an operation as a group. It hasn't been operated with the — it had an original authorization and then the question is —

BUZHARDT: It was terminated, but we can't find a record of the termination. That would be our best bet — to find the record of the termination.

NIXON: But if we can't we'll still say it was terminated.

BUZHARDT: We will still have to say it was terminated.

NIXON: It was terminated.

BUZHARDT: Right.

NIXON: And all the agencies will then say that — just have to back it up.

BUZHARDT: That's right. That is the recollection of DIA. They are looking for the papers. I believe we will find the papers, Mr. President.

NIXON: DIA says they think it was terminated.

BUZHARDT: They think it was terminated. They think that the — and they told me independently from Huston that they think the approval was recalled and that's what Huston said. He thought we recalled the approval he gave it. Now we're going to check this thoroughly with NSA and the reason it is important is because, as you remember, that was the most aggressive group to go forward.

NIXON: NSA?

BUZHARDT: NSA and I suspect they are the only ones that did do it.

NIXON: You haven't been able to reach them, huh?

BUZHARDT: They are on their way in here now. Traffic hour — it takes a while to get from Fort Meade in here. But they will be here shortly.

NIXON: Why you've got to tell me.

BUZHARDT: So, I am going to find out.

NIXON: Stir it up — find anything — I am just confident that I never heard of them doing anything on this. But you know what I mean.

BUZHARDT: Well, whatever their operations are there's no problem with them.

NIXON: NSA, DIA — so forth and so on.

BUZHARDT: DIA — they did absolutely nothing.

NIXON: NSA probably did some electronic work. Goddamn it! We'll defend that —

BUZHARDT: We can defend that.

NIXON: — until hell freezes over.

BUZHARDT: We'll defend that.

NIXON: The problem with the memorandum is what it says in regard to the break-in.

BUZHARDT: That is the only problem.

NIXON: Because it says "break-in."

BUZHARDT: A "surreptitious entry." What — in the accompanying memorandum it says this is a forced burglary. That's our problem.

NIXON: The copy of the memorandum is from me?

BUZHARDT: From Huston to Haldeman.

NIXON: Well, for Christ's sake. It's his characterization of the thing, but the way he will have to answer that is to say that his characterization of a surreptitious entry meant electronic. He —

BUZHARDT: It is made clear, Mr. President, in the memorandum. That is what is spelled out.

NIXON: Huh?

BUZHARDT: This one is spelled out in the memorandum.

• • •

BUZHARDT: [unclear] domestic disturbances —

NIXON: All right.

BUZHARDT: — and with respect to the selected internal security targets to find out much the same thing. What they are doing — what —

NIXON: This would be the Weathermen — things like that?

BUZHARDT: They name them — the Weathermen, the SDS —

NIXON: Good.

BUZHARDT: — the Black Panthers, and all of the organizations are described, their capabilities are given, all it's laid out.

NIXON: Yeah, and they're to find out there —

BUZHARDT: That's right. What they're up to.

NIXON: Well, my own view though I still think, Fred, is to play them as separable instances. I know that the Krogh incident is separate. I know it is, wasn't it? Is Krogh — ?

BUZHARDT: Oh, yeah. The record so indicates.

NIXON: — he operated from here with my total approval. My approval didn't include the burglary. But my point — it was stupid, but nevertheless Krogh is a great guy and operated here. I was totally aware of it — as was everybody in this shop. But when you get, for example, to the break-in of the Chilean embassy [on May 13, 1972, but never linked to the White House], that thing was a part of the burglars' plan as a cover!

BUZHARDT: That's true.

NIXON: Those assholes are trying to have a cover for a CIA cover, I don't know. I think Dean concocted that —

BUZHARDT: I think that he concocted and it may come out that he concocted more than what we now know about, Mr. President.

NIXON: There's strong signs —

BUZHARDT: All indications are now that the thing got badly askew and by his statement, this document I can only assume he wasn't aware of evidence of the turnoff of this thing, or the withdrawal of approval —

NIXON: If there was one.

BUZHARDT: — if there was one, and that he thought that he had a cover —

NIXON: A cover for everything that he had done.

BUZHARDT: — for everything that he had done in the form of a document that would give him the cover of presidential approval. I can't help but feel, you know —

NIXON: But I don't think he's in for that. Because I don't — what it involves is [unclear] Watergate and the [unclear]. He says — go ahead —

BUZHARDT: — [unclear], Mr. President.

NIXON: It'd be better for me.

BUZHARDT: I really think what happened is probably —

NIXON: Because he would say that the Watergate thing was approved because of this? If this was [unclear]?

BUZHARDT: I anticipate they might. He, because you know, we've heard the stories how the reason — we've read in the paper that McCord had said the reason they were going in was to find out their connections with the dissident groups and the demonstrators. Now if Dean is using this as a cover, particularly if we can find a memorandum of withdrawal or something of this, it cuts him off at the water. I suspect, looking at the date — see Dean didn't get this document back till the summer or spring of '72. He probably didn't recognize the utility of it in terms of his activities until much later.

NIXON: Well, [unclear]. He didn't even know the document existed.

BUZHARDT: He probably knew it existed but he didn't have this copy of it probably.

NIXON: When? To when?

BUZHARDT: Until '72. I don't know. You see it is not clear how much of the material was sent to him by Sol Lindenbaum.

NIXON: But when did that come to him? In March of '72?

BUZHARDT: In March of '72. He probably didn't even think of this document as a cover until long after the incident occurred and the heat got on him. I suspect he really didn't think of it as a cover perhaps until the week that he really made the break. When he was looking desperately for something to cover with.

NIXON: Yeah, but if he [unclear]. This fellow sent this over to Dean in March of '72.

BUZHARDT: He sent over a memorandum that said, "I am enclosing documents." I don't know how many of those documents were enclosed, how many of these documents were actually enclosed with Lindenbaum's memorandum. But I suspect that sometime around the time he went to Camp David he was desperate. He looked in the files and found this document, thought he needed a cover, and took it on the outside. And from there on in he found a smug out.

NIXON: Let me say, however, this document did not authorize any nongovernmental activity at all.

BUZHARDT: No, sir.

NIXON: Now that is where he has no cover for that. This didn't authorize any nongovernmental activity at all, as bad as it is. Goddamn it! I bet you it had been knocked off though. I bet it was knocked off in the summer of that year. It was about two or three months only — can't Huston even remember that?

BUZHARDT: He thinks it was.

NIXON: Huh?

BUZHARDT: I told him —

NIXON: Did he volunteer it?

BUZHARDT: Yes, sir. He volunteered it.

NIXON: But can he — is there anybody else we can check with? We don't have —

BUZHARDT: He is looking at his own files. I think we will find it in one of the agencies. One of the agencies probably —

NIXON: You've got to — my God, that's one time I have to find something.

BUZHARDT: We're going to look.

NIXON: [unclear] if we do, we could cut these boys right off at the pass.

BUZHARDT: Then we can really lay it in the woods.

NIXON: Lay it in the woods, and cut them off at the pass. Okay. We'll call you when we get back.

BUZHARDT: All right, sir.

The Huston Plan: its firm beginning and nebulous end
May 17, 1973, 8:44 a.m.
Richard Nixon and J. Fred Buzhardt
OVAL OFFICE

Buzhardt and Nixon continued to examine the effect of the Huston Plan, even as reports circulated that the White House had done the unthinkable in American society: spying without limit on law-abiding citizens. An article in the Washington Post *that morning described "an elaborate, continuous campaign of illegal and quasi-legal undercover operations conducted by the Nixon administration since 1969." When the Watergate Committee hearings convened only hours later, Ervin took a longer view, stating at the very outset that "the questions that have been raised in the wake of the June 17 break-in strike at the very undergirding of our democracy." On that same morning, Nixon and Buzhardt talked through the dates relevant to the Huston Plan. One of those whose name was pulled into the discussion was James Schlesinger, the acting director of the CIA. Raised in Chicago, Schlesinger was educated at Harvard, culminating with a PhD, an economist with a special knowledge of nuclear power. Schlesinger chaired the Atomic Energy Commission in the Nixon administration until February 1973, when Helms was forced out as CIA director over his refusal to squelch the FBI's investigation into Watergate. Schlesinger, with no particular credentials in espionage, took his place. A hawkish man, Schlesinger was loyal to Nixon. One of Buzhardt's jobs was to establish just how loyal.*

• • •

NIXON: I was thinking a little about our program here and how we get this thing handled. I mentioned one thing to [unclear] have that in mind. It seems to me that as soon as you get your facts — I trust you will get them early at least —

BUZHARDT: Right.

NIXON: — as soon as you get everything nailed down — or some of it nailed down — that you should alert on a very quiet basis our friends like, for example — and the people we have to count on. By that I mean Petersen, Schlesinger, and Ruckelshaus should know —

BUZHARDT: Right.

NIXON: — what happened here. Now maybe they already know, but how — can you do that?

BUZHARDT: I can do that. Yes, I can talk to Henry [Petersen] and Bill [Ruckelshaus]. Jim Schlesinger already knows.

NIXON: Yeah, how — what does he know?

BUZHARDT: He knows that it was not — never went forward.

NIXON: Yeah, I want him to know. I want him to have utter confidence, you see, so that —

BUZHARDT: I have taken time out to talk to him. I went to see him Sunday afternoon. He had some misgivings, and I had a long talk with him and explained, I think, the Walters memorandum — sit him on down, personally called Henry, made the appointment, reassured him all the way through.

NIXON: You called Henry about this —

BUZHARDT: No, Jim was a little worried about the —

NIXON: Walters.

BUZHARDT: — Walters thing and so I —

NIXON: Worried about presidential involvement?

BUZHARDT: Yes, so I went over and —

NIXON: Yeah.

BUZHARDT: — personally had a talk with him. Jim and I are kind of longtime friends.

NIXON: I just wanted Jim to know that by God, I am totally [unclear] the Walters thing, whatever it may have been. [unclear] CIA [unclear].

BUZHARDT: I explained that to him.

• • •

NIXON: 'Sixty-eight?

BUZHARDT: 'Sixty-eight they made an effort. They had a meeting here about reinstituting.

NIXON: This is not involve the bureau. [unclear]

BUZHARDT: Yes, it did involve the bureau.

NIXON: Right. Right. And NSA also?

BUZHARDT: NSA. [Secretary of Defense] Clark Clifford presided at the meeting.

NIXON: And they decided not to do it?

BUZHARDT: He didn't make a decision.

NIXON: Right.

BUZHARDT: He held that one —

NIXON: Right.

BUZHARDT: — he was going to think about it some more —

• • •

BUZHARDT: — and they raised the question again in '70 when they could get some-body's attention. They had discussions with Hoover meanwhile.

NIXON: They raised that one [unclear]. Well, Dean's meeting which is — from which the Dean — or the forty-three-page memorandum emanated, the policy shift — em-anated as a result of a battle between the various agencies after the Cambodia thing as to what the hell they should do in this area. Is that correct?

BUZHARDT: It wasn't a battle at that point, Mr. President. There had been a number of meetings between the agencies. There was concern.

NIXON: Yeah.

BUZHARDT: In the initial instance, Hoover did not really express his objections. He had a two-and-a-half-hour meeting apparently with Noel Gayler and Lou Tordella. Just the three of them.

NIXON: Yeah.

BUZHARDT: Over there. As it was explained to me, they got a lecture on communism and he got a lecture on why they needed these entries.

NIXON: Right.

BUZHARDT: He appeared to be convinced.

NIXON: Right.

BUZHARDT: So they then had the meeting when it was all discussed. Here. Supposedly.

NIXON: That was the meeting here.

BUZHARDT: That they needed additional intelligence coverage.

NIXON: That's right. Everybody discussed it.

BUZHARDT: They were told, "All right, go develop a plan. Tell me what these limita-tions are. Look at them all — "

. . .

BUZHARDT: At that point, no specifics were apparently discussed, Mr. President.

NIXON: I see.

BUZHARDT: They just talked about constraints. They were then sent back, with the re-sults of that meeting to have an interagency group to sit down and thoroughly work this thing out — what it was they were supposed to do.

NIXON: Right, right.

BUZHARDT: That the result of that was the forty-three-page plan [the Huston Plan].

NIXON: Who is your — who is your witness that tells you this — this is Sullivan?

BUZHARDT: Tordella —

NIXON: Tordella?

BUZHARDT: — is the best witness.

NIXON: He's still — he's at NSA?

BUZHARDT: Yes. He has been deputy director out there since the place was formed.

NIXON: Is he an honest man?

BUZHARDT: Very honest.

NIXON: Right.

BUZHARDT: Very honest.

NIXON: Okay, then what happened? They developed a forty-three —

BUZHARDT: Then they developed a forty-three-page plan. It was signed by the four of them: Helms, Hoover, Gayler, and Bennett.

NIXON: Right.

BUZHARDT: All four of them signed it. All the recommendations were unanimous.

NIXON: Except —

BUZHARDT: Nope. No excepts. It was unanimous when it came to you.

NIXON: Right. And I approved it.

BUZHARDT: You approved it.

NIXON: The policy paper.

BUZHARDT: The policy paper. Then — and this place is kind of murky. You didn't approve it immediately.

NIXON: I didn't?

BUZHARDT: Not when it was submitted. There was a period of two or three months in there, about when a decision was discussed. Hoover, at some point, raised the objection. Now it's — this is where we are getting the notes on — to get pinned down on the dates. Because when the approval and the subsequent disapproval came was not immediately following submission of the plan. It was some later date.

NIXON: But — I understand I approved the plan. I was thinking about it last night — one day — I wouldn't to [unclear] two days later and I —

BUZHARDT: Right. We are still looking to get the specifics —

NIXON: Yeah. No, what I meant is about — this representation was made to me. I approved the plan. Did I sign it or something?

BUZHARDT: No, sir — didn't. I say you approved the plan.

NIXON: I approved the policy.

BUZHARDT: One of the — well, it was a policy. There were no specifics in that.

NIXON: So the plan later [unclear].

BUZHARDT: The Haldeman note back to Huston, telling him to go ahead —

NIXON: Haldeman wrote a note?

BUZHARDT: He wrote a memo to Huston.

NIXON: Saying what? Go ahead?

BUZHARDT: Saying the president has approved the plan.

NIXON: Now this was the forty-three-page plan?

BUZHARDT: Yes, and to go ahead. But to do it with the procedures they had discussed, or to that effect instead of you signing off on the plan.

NIXON: Oh, I see.

BUZHARDT: At the end of the plan they had a page for you to sign on each one.

NIXON: Right, right. Okay. Go ahead.

BUZHARDT: Now we need to pin down — we still don't have pinned down the precise dates on — subsequently, at some point in the process, Hoover had agreed to it, and then —

NIXON: Tolson.

BUZHARDT: Tolson got to him. He changed his mind. Now on one copy of this plan, somewhere, we are going to try and find it, Hoover wrote footnotes. This is indicated by the memorandum we have — we don't have the actual footnotes — to which he took exceptions to a number things that were in there. There are a lot of exceptions.

NIXON: Wiretapping and break-ins?

BUZHARDT: Yes. Those were the two key things.

NIXON: That's right.

BUZHARDT: Then at — when that came back he took it to Mitchell, or came here to see you. Now we don't know whether he went through Mitchell and Mitchell came, or whether he came. And, as a result, according to the word that I get, or was told the word was passed that the decision had been suspended. The go was recalled. The decision was held in abeyance.

NIXON: The what?

BUZHARDT: The decision was — the go was held in abeyance.

NIXON: Sure, the go. The go, yeah.

BUZHARDT: It did not come out as an absolute no. It was just a suspension of your earlier decision to go.

NIXON: Which meant that things were to go forward as they had previously, but nothing new.

BUZHARDT: That's right. Nothing new.

NIXON: Now that was implemented, however, by Sullivan, as we know.

BUZHARDT: Yes.

NIXON: Sullivan —

BUZHARDT: Sullivan was the one that passed the word. Sullivan — we are going to try to get him down here to get his notes — he's up in New England.

NIXON: But he remembers that?

BUZHARDT: Yes.

NIXON: He told you that on the phone?

BUZHARDT: Sullivan — well, we know from Tordella also.

NIXON: Sullivan. All right.

BUZHARDT: Little leery of Sullivan's memory.

NIXON: Huh?

BUZHARDT: I am a little leery of Sullivan's memory.

NIXON: So am I. But Tordella says — Tordella says — what does he say?

BUZHARDT: Tordella specifically remembers —

NIXON: That —

BUZHARDT: — Sullivan calling him and telling him it was "go." Calling him back very shortly thereafter and telling him —

NIXON: No.

BUZHARDT: — "no go." And he's looking for his notes now.

NIXON: All right. Now you haven't found anyone who knows the principals?

BUZHARDT: No, sir.

NIXON: What about the CIA?

BUZHARDT: They're checking, but they don't — they don't think that anyone out there did anything. They are checking now to make sure. They are going down into the bowels of the place. I am sure that had to have come —

NIXON: I am not — I was wondering not simply whether they did something, but whether they ever got the word from Sullivan. Besides Tordella, do you have anyone that get the word from Sullivan? That there were —

BUZHARDT: We know — the word came independently to me from DIA that some of the people knew that the plan was no go —

NIXON: Yeah.

BUZHARDT: — that it never did go. But they have not located who called, who got the call yet.

NIXON: Right.

BUZHARDT: I suspect it was Bennett. But Bennett is in Korea and I have not been able to reach him.

NIXON: Right.

BUZHARDT: I think it was probably the deputy director because he was a participant.

NIXON: Right.

BUZHARDT: So this is —

NIXON: He's a what — general?

BUZHARDT: Yes sir. He's four stars now. He's commanded —

NIXON: I'd just ask him. I'd do it on the phone.

BUZHARDT: I'll call him and ask him. Now, this morning's *Washington Post* — they've already placed the business. You know, you can see it all —

NIXON: Right.

BUZHARDT: — that the two *Washington Post* reporters have — interestingly, they say that the series of burglaries, they say that this was a whole pattern. There were many of them, yet undisclosed —

NIXON: Yeah.

BUZHARDT: — you know, what we anticipated. Wide-scale wiretappings, but they allege that these were not done by the agencies, but done by separate front groups and special groups working out of the White House. That's the word this morning, Mr. President.

NIXON: Well, it's worse when it's true.

BUZHARDT: Well, I doubt if it's true. You know, outside of this one group, and all the evidence indicated that they really didn't do any others. You know, Hunt was telling everything. I went back and read his testimony this morning. He swore under oath and laid it all out, but he said no, they did no others.

NIXON: They did no wiretapping and no burglaries and all that stuff.

BUZHARDT: No wiretaps and no burglaries, except the one of them — the psychiatrist. Krogh's affidavit says he knew of no other —

NIXON: That's right.

BUZHARDT: — of these activities.

NIXON: I mean, I know of no other group.

BUZHARDT: I know of no other group.

NIXON: I know another group, whatever —

BUZHARDT: I have never heard of another group. Of course, we hadn't heard of this one either, but I — somebody would have a rumble of it surely. Whether they used a front group such as the Cubans — now our problem is that they used Cubans in this and obviously the Cubans could have done a lot of things on their own. You know, if they play this every time a Cuban is involved in a burglary, even if they are just there to steal money —

NIXON: Well, but maybe —

BUZHARDT: — so we are going to — it's — what I'm saying is we're going to have to work very hard because it's difficult to recuse a negative — prove a negative.

NIXON: The main point though that I, Fred, to work on today is — to knock the Dean papers out of the goddamn water.

BUZHARDT: Right.

NIXON: Because the Dean papers would indicate that it was a government-wide, official thing done, and it was not.

BUZHARDT: Right.

NIXON: You have no evidence of any government agency doing anything as a result of this paper.

BUZHARDT: None whatever.

NIXON: None whatever.

BUZHARDT: No, sir.

NIXON: Now, you have a Sullivan on that and you have Mardian.

BUZHARDT: Yes, sir.

NIXON: And you have Tordella?

BUZHARDT: Tordella on that. [De] Poix on that at DIA.

NIXON: You got him.

BUZHARDT: Yes, sir. He says absolutely nothing —

NIXON: Right, right, right.

BUZHARDT: — and I know pretty well on DIA because I monitored that one very closely.

NIXON: Now, CIA didn't — they're so damn terrible.

• • •

NIXON: On this one though, Fred, we can blow them out of the water —

BUZHARDT: We can.

NIXON: — if we move at our pace.

BUZHARDT: I want to get affidavits on all these people.

NIXON: Mm-hmm.

BUZHARDT: Get them in concrete.

NIXON: That's right. Now I think Tordella will give you an affidavit, won't he?

BUZHARDT: I don't think there is any doubt. I can get affidavits across the board.

NIXON: If you get Tordella, you get Sullivan, and say that there will be nothing in [unclear]. All right. We'd hope to get Gayler an affidavit.

BUZHARDT: I hope to get Gayler's, and Bennett's, and their successor people — whoever worked in this area. I will get one from —

NIXON: What about — ?

BUZHARDT: — Bernie Wells who ran the committee.

NIXON: Ran the committee, but ran the committee after all this.

BUZHARDT: After all this.

NIXON: And his committee was what? What was his committee?

BUZHARDT: That was the coordinating committee [Intelligence Evaluation Committee] of the intelligence community to try to get them to work together. And he puts it just bluntly — he said however much we talked about being able to analyze the intelligence, the truth of the matter was that Hoover cut off liaisons to all the agencies. No agent would meet with the other agencies. So we had this group —

NIXON: The reason we had this darn meeting in here, as I now remember, is every agency was bitching about Hoover and they said we've got to get Hoover to cooperate.

BUZHARDT: That's right.

NIXON: That's what it was.

BUZHARDT: This was the whole fracas.

NIXON: And Hoover didn't even want to meet in the same room with Helms.

BUZHARDT: That's true.

NIXON: So I think what happened was he went back and thought about it a bit and a couple of months later apparently Tolson said it. When they got the go signal, and then he said you got a go signal and two days later a no signal. Is that right?

BUZHARDT: That's Tordella's recollection and he is looking now for his notes.

NIXON: He'll have them, won't he?

BUZHARDT: I am quite sure he will, coming from where he does. I don't know — I wouldn't be surprised if they tape the conversations going in and out of there. I don't think they would admit it, but —

NIXON: No, they shouldn't.

BUZHARDT: Even to me, but —

NIXON: Well, [unclear] sure, I think Hoover tapes all his conversations.

BUZHARDT: I think it is a common practice in town.

NIXON: Sure. But they never have to admit it. They never have to use it. And shouldn't. [unclear]

BUZHARDT: Yes, sir.

NIXON: I am sure everything in here is taped. I never used it.

BUZHARDT: Yes.

NIXON: I just — I guess they probably do it. You know what I mean?

BUZHARDT: Yes.

NIXON: Johnson set it up years — no, Kennedy did. They tell me. They tell me. I don't know. But I'll never use it.

BUZHARDT: Yeah.

NIXON: Well, anyway, if you can get this one nailed today.

BUZHARDT: Right. We are going to work diligently on getting it.

NIXON: Can you get a plane and get Sullivan flown down —

BUZHARDT: We'll get him flown down.

NIXON: — and get an affidavit from him? He is the key in the sense that it was turned off.

BUZHARDT: I think so. I think we need to bring Huston back, too.

NIXON: Yes. He's in California?

BUZHARDT: He is in Minneapolis.

NIXON: Minneapolis. You bring Huston back, and Huston comes back with all those terrible memories so that he —

BUZHARDT: He told me it didn't go.

NIXON: Huh?

BUZHARDT: He told me that it didn't go.

NIXON: And that is why you're —

BUZHARDT: The decision went against him, and that's why — he said, you know, "I was really keyed up and I left." He didn't say precisely that was the reason —

NIXON: I know.

BUZHARDT: — but he said, "I was really teed off and I left."

NIXON: If you know Tom Huston that sounds like him. I only met him about three or four times but he was an explosive —

BUZHARDT: I think I met him when —

NIXON: — right wing —

BUZHARDT: — he was a college freshman, Mr. President.

NIXON: He was smart as hell. Smart and ruthless. Well, and a decent man. But he just wanted to do something.

BUZHARDT: Naturally.

NIXON: But Huston should have a memorandum because he was here at the White House.

BUZHARDT: He looked last night. He hasn't found the memorandum in his files. He said he would not have taken anything that was classified with him.

NIXON: Yeah. But he could come here and find out where his files were.

BUZHARDT: Yes.

NIXON: This would have been classified possibly. Might have been.

BUZHARDT: It might have been. Depending on what he put in it. I suspect he didn't write a memorandum. Maybe he called Hoover — I mean called Sullivan.

NIXON: Sullivan. He would have — Hoover would never have been called on this. And Huston said it did not go.

BUZHARDT: Yes.

NIXON: All right, so independently, I'm just — understand. I'm just trying to get the facts.

BUZHARDT: Yes, sir.

NIXON: No matter how we want the facts to appear, if the facts are wrong screw it. I mean, [unclear] is wrong anyway. Goddamn it, we want the truth. Independently, you've heard a tip from Huston that the [unclear] as planned — whatever that damn thing he talked about was that he talked about — did not go. Independently, Sullivan told you that he made calls —

BUZHARDT: He did not tell us —

NIXON: — indicating that it did not go. And independently, Tordella said he got a call that it did not go.

BUZHARDT: Yes.

NIXON: Is there anybody else you should have? There's nobody else really.

BUZHARDT: No, we have people in the Defense Intelligence Agency who know it did not go, but they don't know who received the word.

NIXON: No, but they didn't — when you say they know it, they heard that it did not go at the time?

BUZHARDT: That's right. General [Richard] Stilwell was there with staff at the time —

NIXON: Yeah.

BUZHARDT: — and he said it did not — it never went. They got the word. He doesn't remember from precisely where.

NIXON: God. They must have made notes on that.

BUZHARDT: Whoever did the talking should have made notes.

NIXON: [unclear]

BUZHARDT: They are trying to find out.

NIXON: But, based on what we have up to this point. It seems to me that you are in a position to have — to give [unclear] talking points —

BUZHARDT: Yes.

NIXON: — so that he can — I mean [unclear] no link. No link.

BUZHARDT: Yes, sir.

NIXON: My view is don't — what I meant is simply say that — I mean put in the whole story that in 19 — da-da-da-da — that there has been an issue within government going back to '67. It was discussed in '67. It was discussed again in 1968. In 1967, it was brought to the president's attention. There was a unanimous recommendation for the policy. The president approved the policy. For two months — no, after two months —

BUZHARDT: We will run down the exact dates.

NIXON: After two months, the president approved the policy — was conveyed by Huston — I mean Haldeman. Let's put it that way. The approval was conveyed by Haldeman to —

BUZHARDT: Huston.

NIXON: Huston. And Huston conveyed it to the agencies. Two days later, as a result of — I would then say then let's give the bureau a brownie point, as a result of the objections of the FBI — that's really what it was, wasn't it?

BUZHARDT: It was. As to reconsideration.

NIXON: Yeah.

BUZHARDT: Because Hoover — because see he signed it originally.

NIXON: Yeah, and the result —

BUZHARDT: Changed their minds.

NIXON: And as a result eventually — and Mr. Hoover asked for reconsideration, and the policy was then —

BUZHARDT: The approval was withdrawn.

NIXON: The approval was — withdrawn.

BUZHARDT: Withdrawn.

NIXON: Approval withdrawn. And then the bottom line — no activities were undertaken under this policy. Not in accordance with law. Correct?

BUZHARDT: Right.

NIXON: No activities were undertaken under this policy. The point being that it basically, Fred, turns out to be, if you look at it, a study paper. What I mean by a policy paper that is developed in the government by the [unclear] where you go through and agonize and you come up with a paper and somebody signs it and then somebody bitched about it and then the goddamn thing doesn't go through.

BUZHARDT: Yes, sir.

NIXON: And then nothing ever happens. Is that about a fair and accurate [unclear]?

BUZHARDT: That's right. I would say almost the majority of papers we generate go that way.

NIXON: Right. Now, [unclear] handle that depends on how it is handled —

BUZHARDT: How it develops.

NIXON: —by others. But if you could get that kind of a paper to, for example — Schlesinger should have that. It seems to me, I don't know, or do you think the best thing for you to do is get Schlesinger?

BUZHARDT: I think I can talk to Jim. I don't think you should hand your paper around.

NIXON: Right. Okay.

BUZHARDT: Until the time comes to use it.

NIXON: Otherwise it will leak.

BUZHARDT: That's true.

NIXON: Fine. You just tell Jim, "Jim, there is no worry. No sweat on this. Because it was a thing where," and point out that the activation — it was true — was in NSA —

BUZHARDT: That's true.

NIXON: It was — the activation.

BUZHARDT: No question.

NIXON: And that the result of Hoover's objections — it was approved and then disapproved. We want him to know that that is the situation. And that's that.

BUZHARDT: Right.

"Reassure John though that I am taking total responsibility on this."

May 20, 1973, 12:26 p.m.

Richard Nixon and Bob Haldeman

CAMP DAVID TELEPHONE

Although Haldeman was no longer a part of the administration, Nixon still spoke with him by telephone and sometimes saw him in person. On May 20 he called him to discuss the content of a formal statement that he planned to release on the subject of Watergate. While going over some of the points pertinent to the Huston Plan, Nixon insisted that he would protect Haldeman and Ehrlichman from indictment or the need to testify regarding some Watergate activities. It was a grand gesture, yet Haldeman didn't seem impressed. The president was going to claim that some of the meetings and even the break-ins were critical to national security. Haldeman had heard that line of defense before, many times. Nonetheless, he still spoke with Nixon, which is more than Ehrlichman was willing to do, except on rare occasions.

• • •

HALDEMAN: Hello?

NIXON: Hi, Bob?

HALDEMAN: Morning.

NIXON: How was your church today? You didn't get followed?

HALDEMAN: No, they got me at home before I went.

NIXON: I'll be goddamned. [laughs] What did they get you there about?

HALDEMAN: They just wanted to ask about the CIA stuff, and the — I don't know, whatever was in the news. I don't pay much attention to questions because I don't answer them, which is —

NIXON: Right. That's good.

HALDEMAN: — the same thing — I did get a chance — they raised — I made my usual pitch about, you know, that I am cooperating fully and that I know that when the truth is known there, this is going —

NIXON: Good.

HALDEMAN: — to get this all cleared up. And then they said something about, "Well, did the president know anything about the Helms meeting?" or something like that. I said, as I said before — "I am not going to comment on any specific questions. I can tell you flatly and categorically that the president had absolutely no knowledge or involvement in any kind of cover-up or anything else related to the Watergate in any way, shape, or form."

NIXON: Good.

HALDEMAN: And I said, "I am sure that that will become totally clear, too — "

NIXON: Right.

HALDEMAN: " — as the facts are known."

NIXON: The general statements are the best to make.

HALDEMAN: And I just left it at that. I am not going to get into —

NIXON: That's right.

HALDEMAN: — the specifics at this point.

NIXON: Well, we will get into that. Look, I didn't want to — I don't want to hold you if you were just going to have lunch or something. You got about a couple of minutes?

HALDEMAN: Sure.

NIXON: I can go over three or four things and nail them down?

HALDEMAN: Sure.

NIXON: For what we are planning to do, first, with regard to the — I am planning, probably, to meet with the leaders, including bipartisan leaders, including the Armed Services Committee, and I am going to put out all of the national security kind of stuff — which, incidentally, is going to be very helpful, not so far from your standpoint but from John's standpoint, because I am going to take the — say that I ordered the Plumbers operation, that I ordered the meeting. I am going to say that I directed that you and John meet with Helms and Walters for the purpose of seeing whether the CIA was involved, and so forth and so on. I think this is a good idea. Don't you think so?

HALDEMAN: Absolutely. I think it is essential.

NIXON: Yeah. Well, you see the point is that —

HALDEMAN: That way you can clear your —

NIXON: It's the truth and also —

HALDEMAN: Clear it then.

NIXON: And we put the issue out where it belongs. That you are goddamn right we had a meeting and so forth.

HALDEMAN: Right.

NIXON: And so forth. The — you see, the only difficulty — well, the difficulty with the so-called Helms — I mean the memor — Walters's memcons [memoranda of conversation] is —

HALDEMAN: Yeah.

NIXON: — an indication that — that is the follow-up of Dean's —

HALDEMAN: Right.

NIXON: — you see, where he went and asked for cover. Because the implication there would be that you and John and of course then the president. That we set up this whole goddamn thing for the purpose of getting the CIA to put a cover on this and so forth. Which is not the truth.

HALDEMAN: Right.

NIXON: And John flatly will testify to that effect, or has, I assume.

HALDEMAN: Yep.

NIXON: I just want to be sure, you know, that we don't put anything into this statement that is not —

HALDEMAN: Right.

NIXON: — is going to be at all —

HALDEMAN: Right.

NIXON: — contrary to what he says. But that you and John talked about it, you had your meeting, but the purpose of the meeting was the four things that you mentioned.

HALDEMAN: That's right.

NIXON: Right. We'll get that in, but I think that is a very good thing to do and we are working on that today.

HALDEMAN: Good.

NIXON: I am going to slap it to them hard and tell them why we did it.

HALDEMAN: Well, that is the only answer on this now is to —

NIXON: Go on the offensive.

HALDEMAN: — do it exactly that way.

NIXON: That's right.

HALDEMAN: Because it is right.

NIXON: And the whole Plumbers operation I am going to take that. Also, I want you — I, deliberately, am only calling you, because I don't want to talk to John —

HALDEMAN: Plus he is out of town. He is out in California.

NIXON: — and obviously I don't want to talk to Colson but I want to talk to you because I think you can follow through better than anybody else. Tell John he need have no question. I will take sole — complete responsibility for putting a national security cover on this. Also, see I called Petersen on the eighteenth at John's suggestion and told him, "Look, you can question Hunt about anything about Watergate but you must not get into national security matters." And I have told Petersen that since.

HALDEMAN: Yeah.

NIXON: So — and that will stand up. If — I mean, because as Petersen says, well, "The important thing is that we did get the information out there before the trial was over."

HALDEMAN: Yeah.

NIXON: Also, he says the important thing is, as you told me on the phone, none of the information obtained in this so-called operation ever got to the prosecution.

HALDEMAN: Right.

NIXON: Which is what John will also remember.

HALDEMAN: Yep.

NIXON: But those recollections —

HALDEMAN: Well, that is all solid I am sure.

NIXON: Yep. Second point, on the famous Dean papers, you'll be pleased to know, that we have got that nailed down on all four corners. [laughs]

HALDEMAN: Good.

NIXON: The order — the "go" order was issued by you. I mean, to — and carried out by Huston on one day, and then twenty-four — forty-eight hours later a "no" order was issued.

HALDEMAN: Mm-hmm.

NIXON: And everybody — and we have affidavits on that, and some have notes on it that they had the "no" order. The other point is that nothing whatever was done by any of the agencies involved.

HALDEMAN: That is what I thought.

NIXON: You know, what I mean is there were no break-ins. There were no — so forth and so on, even though that sort of thing was in the damn paper. But the main point is, as that — as far as we are concerned — you see, what happened here was that this thing, this paper took two months for them to write.

HALDEMAN: Yeah, I remember that.

NIXON: And then it came in to me and I had, you know, I said all right, fine, let's go forward on it, you see. Let's go forward. Then Hoover objected on two counts. And I, my recollection is that Mitchell probably called me, but I am not going to say that, because I don't know what the hell Mitchell would say.

HALDEMAN: Yeah. I wouldn't. Yeah.

NIXON: I don't want to get him in it. But I am just going to say that because of his objections we therefore put a "no" order. But that sounds pretty good. Doesn't it? I mean it is the truth.

HALDEMAN: Yeah.

NIXON: But you have nothing that —

HALDEMAN: I recall nothing that would in any way not go along —

NIXON: Yeah.

HALDEMAN: — with that, because — as I told Haig when he first told me about it — the only thing I could remember about it was that, everything I recall, was that nothing had been done.

NIXON: That's correct.

HALDEMAN: I forgot why, but I knew Hoover —

NIXON: Well, we have had Buzhardt check the damn thing from *A* to *Z* and nothing was done. That we know. As far as we know. Now, of course some asshole may have done something we don't know about.

HALDEMAN: But you are going to cover that though?

NIXON: Oh, hell yes.

HALDEMAN: That's great. Because then you'll be out ahead on —

NIXON: Yeah, and we're going to put out the whole damn statement, too.

HALDEMAN: Good.

NIXON: Now, it's a rough one. I mean, not rough on us so much but it's rough in terms of these agencies recommending everything from surreptitious entries to bugging to everything else. But the point is —

HALDEMAN: But it was signed by all of them.

NIXON: They all recommended it.

HALDEMAN: Yeah.

NIXON: It was unanimous.

HALDEMAN: Well, that is good because that shows the tenor of the times —

NIXON: That's right.

HALDEMAN: — and that needs to be done.

NIXON: It needs to be done, Bob. Also I will point out the Plumbers thing — why we did it. That we had massive leaks and that I had given — they had given orders to all departments to do everything that they could, and at the White House we developed a capability to do what we could there.

HALDEMAN: Yep.

NIXON: And that everything that we did there was on that. Now on that point, just a couple of things to nail down. I want to be sure — because I don't want to do a damn thing that would be at all harmful, or inconsistent with what you or John may have recalled, and therefore have testified to. I have no recollection of John ever telling me about the unsuccessful break-in, or whatever it was, until after — I mean until we got into the March period.

HALDEMAN: The psychiatrist?

NIXON: Yes, and I don't know what his recollection is. Do you know?

HALDEMAN: That's what I recall too, but I can check it with him.

NIXON: Just — well, if he is — the point is that he once said that he thought that I knew, and I don't remember. I have no recollection of his coming in and saying, "Look, Krogh's — or the group did this." My — you know what I mean. See, John says that, you know, Krogh stood up like a man and took the blame for it —

HALDEMAN: Yeah.

NIXON: — and said that Ehrlichman had done it, but I don't remember, Bob — John ever telling me that "look, there was an unsuccessful break into a psychiatrist's office and you should know it." Will you nail that one down for me?

HALDEMAN: Sure.

NIXON: Because I don't want to say it unless it is true.

HALDEMAN: Yep.

NIXON: You know what I mean?

HALDEMAN: Yep.

NIXON: If I had to know, I had to know. But I — what I meant is, I don't [laughs] —

HALDEMAN: Right.

NIXON: — I don't want John to get up and testify to the effect, "Well, I told the president something and then —"

HALDEMAN: Yeah. Okay.

NIXON: I don't think he would, because I don't think he did tell me, my point is.

HALDEMAN: Yep.

NIXON: But he's never discussed that with you? You have never been specific on that.

HALDEMAN: The only thing I can remember on it was simply that, you know, he didn't know.

NIXON: No, I did —

HALDEMAN: He did at some point, because he knew about that picture [of Liddy and Hunt posing in front of Dr. Fielding's office].

NIXON: Yeah, that was in March though, but —

HALDEMAN: Oh, was it? Okay.

NIXON: I mean, we heard about this damned picture, you know, and we heard about it from Dean.

HALDEMAN: Yeah. Yeah, because I didn't know about that. You must have been told about that sometime when I wasn't there. Because that came as a surprise to me later when — no one told me about it and I raised it, and you said yeah, you had heard about that.

NIXON: Heard about the picture? When did — ?

HALDEMAN: Heard about it from John or somebody I think, or maybe from Justice.

NIXON: When did you raise that with me?

HALDEMAN: That would have been probably in April.

NIXON: I see. Well, get that nailed for me. You get the facts, and I don't want it to go through too many hands here. If you could do it — and I could do it. The third point is that be sure to reassure John though that I am taking total responsibility on this. So that he can — see he has, very properly I think, told the grand jury that he will not testify with regard to national security matters. I have told Petersen that, too, on the Hunt thing. And I am saying that — you know what I mean. I am not backing off that one goddamn inch —

HALDEMAN: Yeah.

NIXON: — and I shouldn't. Don't you agree?

HALDEMAN: Yep.

NIXON: That's right. The third point is that — you have already told me, but I just want to be sure. That there is nothing that you have said, or anything — I was not told about the three fifty transaction until March is my recollection. And if you have testified to something else, I, of course —

. . .

HALDEMAN: I think at some point in March when this was coming —

NIXON: Yeah.

HALDEMAN: When Dean had told you about our — the concern that —

NIXON: He said, "Bob's got a problem, and that's the three fifty."

HALDEMAN: Yeah, and I think I told you then.

NIXON: Yeah, yeah.

HALDEMAN: That yes, I can see why he would feel that.

NIXON: Yeah.

HALDEMAN: Because there was this question.

NIXON: Yeah, but they may have been after the twenty-first. They may have been part of the March 21 thing. It may have been earlier in March, but I —

HALDEMAN: It was in that period.

NIXON: But it was in that period.

HALDEMAN: I think it was probably later.

NIXON: But, whatever — or it might have even been March 21. The other point is the — that I need some recollection on the part of John, is on this issue of clemency. I have said, you know, that I — and Ziegler has said that I never authorized anyone to offer clemency. Now that is a flat statement and that is true. I never did. The question is that they said well, whether or not anyone ever discussed it with me. The only recollection I have of any discussion was — which John reminded me of — was on the beach in June or July just before we went over to there, and it was only for a minute. He said, "Looking down the road one of the problems that we are going to have is that I imagine" — he said, "I would imagine these fellows will want clemency." And I said, "Well, we will have to face that when we come to it," or words to that effect. I need to know whether he has — is going — has —

HALDEMAN: Yeah.

NIXON: — all I need to know is this: whether I just want him to —

HALDEMAN: Because that's a correct recollection.

NIXON: Here's — no, the main point is this. Dean had made this preposterous statement to the effect that they had talked about clemency, and that John Ehrlichman had walked into the Oval Office and then came back and said that you can offer clemency but don't be too specific. The president says so.

HALDEMAN: John totally denies that.

NIXON: Does he deny that?

HALDEMAN: Yes.

NIXON: Well, the point is — the other point is whether or not we discussed it and so forth.

HALDEMAN: Yep.

NIXON: As far as the meeting with Colson, as I told you about that because that came in when he just mentioned it again tangentially — he said about Hunt. Only Hunt. He didn't mention the others, but Hunt — and Hunt's wife having been killed in an accident. And I said, well, that was a factor that certainly could be considered, you know, but that would have to be considered, you know, at the time — but this was not the time. Colson now, I think, backs that a hundred percent. I don't know. You don't know either?

HALDEMAN: I don't know.

NIXON: Well, don't you bother with that. I'll handle that.

HALDEMAN: I can't because —

NIXON: No, no, no.

HALDEMAN: — I have to stay clear of him.

NIXON: No, no, no. Stay clear of that. Fine.

HALDEMAN: But I think you are right.

NIXON: Yeah.

• • •

NIXON: I am going to lay it all out there.

HALDEMAN: Well, I think that will —

NIXON: On the national security thing, I am going to defend the bugging. I am going to defend the bugging. I am going to defend the Plumbers. I am going to defend — not only am I going to defend it I am going to say why we did it. And I am going to say why we tried to keep it out of the Watergate —

HALDEMAN: Yep.

NIXON: — and that was that.

HALDEMAN: Yep.

NIXON: But these other questions are questions on Watergate that, you know —

HALDEMAN: Henry [Kissinger] has got to have a positive attitude on all this, too.

NIXON: Henry?

HALDEMAN: Yeah.

NIXON: Oh, he will!

HALDEMAN: And they're are trying to make him out as being so deeply concerned about the morality of this and all that, and that is a lot of baloney. And he has got to get off of that and get on to the thing —

NIXON: Well, Haig is —

HALDEMAN: — that was the question of leaking the stuff out.

NIXON: Haig is being — going to be very tough with him when he gets back.

HALDEMAN: Yeah.

NIXON: If Henry wants to be — to talk about morality, I mean, we have him nailed six ways to one.

HALDEMAN: Right.

NIXON: Because, you remember, Bob —

HALDEMAN: Oh, yeah.

NIXON: — who the hell was pushing for this stuff?

HALDEMAN: Absolutely.

NIXON: Who was squealing the most about the leaks? You know, about these NSSMs, the mems — the NSSMs and so forth. I didn't give a shit about the NSSMs.

HALDEMAN: But he was right.

NIXON: I know. I know he was right.

HALDEMAN: He was right about squealing about them.

NIXON: I know. What I meant is though that he can't say now that whether or not it was moral or immoral to bug these goddamn people. How else are you going to get the leaks? And that is what we were trying to do —

HALDEMAN: Yep.

"They threw their arms around me, kissed me, had pictures taken. It was the damnedest thing I ever saw."
May 25, 1973, 12:58 a.m.
Richard Nixon and Alexander Haig
WHITE HOUSE TELEPHONE

The evening of May 24, 1973, saw the largest dinner ever held at the White House, before or since: a welcome-home celebration for six hundred Vietnam War prisoners of war and their families. It was so large that a special tent had to be erected on the South Lawn. After the festivities finally wound down in the wee hours of the next morning, Chief of Staff Al Haig called Nixon to tell him, "I don't think the White House has ever had a greater evening, sir. I just think it was outstanding."

• • •

NIXON: Hello, Al.

HAIG: Yes, sir, Mr. President.

NIXON: Oh, well — you saw the show?

HAIG: I don't think the White House has ever had a greater evening, sir. I just think it was outstanding.

NIXON: Ziegler wouldn't see this, but my daughters did. They said that they have never seen the press so furious and frustrated. See, you know what I did? I went around tabletops and shook hands with these people and so forth, and my God they were just moved beyond belief, you know? And how did you like when they said — when I said, "By God, I was so proud of those guys that went in with those B-52s [during the Christmas 1972 bombing]."

HAIG: Well, I tell you, sir. I don't think the White House ever had a night like it had tonight.

NIXON: Do you think it will do any good?

HAIG: These guys, of course they know exactly what it was that did it. Everyone I talked to said that the December bombing is what got them home.

NIXON: Yeah.

HAIG: Every one of them. Of course, having seen the [unclear] news, the demonstrations. My God, the press is just — they really are just reeling from it.

NIXON: Well, what's Henry [Kissinger] doing [unclear]?

HAIG: He was very moved. I walked back with him from the [unclear] and he said he has never been so moved in his life. He said these were the greatest people, and he — he wants to fight. He said, "Boy, I tell you it is time to take all these monkeys on." He is a very good fellow, sir. I think he said something tonight —

NIXON: If he — he doesn't know it though. If I take them on, it will be a fight to the death. It will probably kill me, but by God if I do I am going to kick their ass around the block. I really am, because we cannot allow this crap about Watergate and all the cover-up and the rest destroy the greatest foreign policy this country has ever had. And good God, wasn't Jimmy Stewart nice? And ol' John Wayne, you know? He says just, "Thank you, boss. Not just for something, but for everything."

HAIG: Well, it just — I just — I tell you I was so proud tonight. It made everything, all the fighting we have done worthwhile to see what it accomplished. And by God, sir, it just makes you want to stand up and take these monkeys on, as we are doing, and we're going to wipe them out.

NIXON: Well, of all this crap, good God, you know, what they are really trying to do is tell the — I was telling [unclear] and Julie [Nixon Eisenhower] — I can now see it so clear — the Democrats are basically just trying to destroy the president because they realize that that will destroy the Republican Party, and they don't give a damn about what happens in the world. You know, the thing about my speech today, which Henry wouldn't understand because he thinks in more sophisticated ways, but I was really saying, "Look, fellows, we got where we are by being strong and respected and now there is the chance, the greatest chance in the world, to go forth and do more. Now goddamn it, let's do it!" That is what the goddamn *New York Times* and the *Washington Post* ought to be writing.

HAIG: Exactly.

NIXON: Yeah.

HAIG: Well, they never will, but it doesn't make any difference because they are not with the country and the country isn't with them. You saw the country out there tonight with those fine young men.

NIXON: Well, I am not sure. There is a part of the country that is grateful to me to bring them back.

HAIG: Well, just [unclear] —

NIXON: Well, you should have seen the women, and of course I met all the men. My God, I table-hopped because I wanted to be sure that the people didn't feel they were out — my God, Negro girls and others. Good God, they threw their arms around me, kissed me, had pictures taken. It was the damnedest thing I ever saw.

HAIG: I think it is the greatest night the White House has ever had. I really do.

NIXON: They tell me though that the press girls — you know, [UPI journalist] Helen Thomas they said was utterly furious.

HAIG: Yeah. [laughs]

NIXON: So what do you do about that?

HAIG: No, well, I am not so sure. They were down to their knees with their long faces, they just can't cope with it. What they saw there was real, true —

NIXON: But coming right down to it, Al, you look at it and all this crap they're taking, and the Congress being Democratic and the Republicans being weak and all the rest. Wouldn't it really be better for the country to just check out and —

HAIG: [laughs]

NIXON: — and — no, seriously, I mean that because I — you see, I am not at my best. I have got to be at my best and that means fighting this damn battle, fighting it all out. And I can't fight the damn battle, you know, with people coming in with their little tidbits, and their rumors, and all that crap, and "Did the president," you know, "make a deal?" You know, "to pay off this one or that" and the other thing?

HAIG: I tell you, sir, if you ever even conceived of leaving [unclear], think about what it would have done to those people who were there tonight.

NIXON: Yeah, but they are such a small group, Al.

HAIG: No, sir, they are not. Not at all. I saw two groups, one at noon today, last night, and I tell you it is just not so. They are all with us, and they are with you. It would be the greatest shock the country ever had.

"This is a great moment to have this guy in here."

May 30, 1973, 9:15 a.m.

Richard Nixon, Huang Zhen, Chi Chao-chu (interpreter), and Henry Kissinger

OVAL OFFICE

Like Nixon's selection of a senior official — David Bruce — for the assignment to Beijing, Huang Zhen was no ordinary ambassador assigned to Washington. Huang was the senior overseas Chinese diplomat, the first PRC ambassador to Paris, and a former deputy foreign affairs minister. His loyalty to Chairman Mao went back to the Long March in the 1930s, and he was among the original cadre of officials who helped to form the People's Republic of China in 1949. Huang was also the first PRC official to step foot into the Oval Office, here in a conversation in which Nixon reassured him that the upcoming agreement between the United States and the Soviet Union would not be detrimental to China. Nixon also emphasized the importance of working toward a supplementary Southeast Asian peace agreement that included Cambodia and Laos.

• • •

KISSINGER: There are two things — two points you might make, [unclear].

NIXON: Oh, yes.

KISSINGER: Cambodia.

NIXON: Two: Soviets.

KISSINGER: Two: Saying that you want to give him an understanding which repeats what I've already said, that we will do nothing —

NIXON: That would be detrimental to their interests. Yep.

KISSINGER: Right. And I offered to them yesterday that you're willing to formalize that. They'll make a consultation between you [unclear].

NIXON: Well, I'll write a letter.

KISSINGER: I know, but then — that you — an agreement that we will not do anything with a third country directed at — involving their —

NIXON: [unclear] He'll know. He's been through it. I suppose he's very [unclear]. This is a great moment to have this guy in here.

KISSINGER: I hope you have a press picture.

NIXON: Don't worry! I ordered it. But the Chinese journalist thing was a good thing, too, you know?

KISSINGER: It played well in —

NIXON: [unclear] a little history thing like that. Everything with China touches a sensitive nerve. You know, the idea of saying, "Well, I might be there in the spring," and that "this is the most significant thing we've done," and all that. I believe that it was! People will think [unclear]. You know, you're worried — you're concerned about the press meddling on you on this [Watergate]. Listen, they won't even remember who the hell did the bugging. Incidentally, a study is now being made in the Justice Department. We're going to find — I'm going to — I've decided that we have to publicly prove [Mc]George Bundy is a liar.

KISSINGER: Good.

NIXON: And—

KISSINGER: Good.

NIXON: Edgar Hoover told me that he bugged twice as much for Bobby Kennedy as he did for Johnson or for me.

KISSINGER: That's what I was told.

NIXON: Hell yes!

KISSINGER: I was here when—

NIXON: Joe Alsop told me that—told me that!

KISSINGER: And I was here when Hoover told you that! Now this fellow [Huang Zhen] is a member of the Central Committee, the only ambassador to be—

NIXON: Yeah.

• • •

[HUANG ZHEN, CHI CHAO-CHU, RONALD ZIEGLER, and members of the press join the conversation.]

NIXON: Come on in. Hello! Come on in. Well, good morning! How are you, my friend?

HUANG [through interpreter]: The ambassador is very much happy to be able to meet Mr. President in the White House today and he would express his respect for you and this special honor.

NIXON: Why don't we have pictures of the two of us over here? We'll send a copy of this to [unclear]. Just sit here for the press pictures. You don't have to look up. Right there.

[ZIEGLER gives instructions to members of the press, who take numerous photographs.]

[Unclear exchange]

NIXON: We were very appreciative of the welcome you gave to Ambassador Bruce. The crew worked all night. Ambassador Bruce is more accomplished than any ambassador in the history of America. Before he left, he said he thought that this [the assignment to Beijing] was the whole peak of his career.

HUANG: Well, we are all grateful from all of our [unclear]. And for [unclear] you have provided for our group [unclear]. And the possibility [unclear] some of our work [unclear].

PRESS: Thank you.

NIXON [to the press]: I wish you could stay a while, but we have to talk a little about substantive matters for the next [unclear]! [laughs] You're all welcome.

[ZIEGLER and members of the press leave the conversation.]

[Unclear exchange]

NIXON: I said yesterday to the press from China that I hoped to go again, in the spring. I didn't say—while I was president—you could say—which spring? But I would love to go back.

HUANG: This is very good news indeed. In fact, our [unclear].

[Refreshments are served.]

HUANG: As the ambassador told Dr. Kissinger yesterday, we would like to thank Mr.

President for your very frank reception for press delegation. When we talked with them, they told us [unclear] and to also [unclear]. And the ambassador might avail himself [unclear] to make to Mr. President, the greetings of Chairman Mao Zedong, his wife, Madame Jiang Qing, our Premier Zhou Enlai, his wife, Madame Deng Yingchao, to you personally and Mrs. Nixon.

NIXON: Would you extend my best wishes from Mrs. Nixon and me to them?

HUANG: And also, the ambassador also says the chairman and the premier have both read your letter to them dated the fifteenth of March.

NIXON: After Kissinger's visit?

HUANG: That's right.

NIXON: Well, since we have such a short time, and also since I know that we — that you are a member of the Central Committee — that you direct — with regard to some messages I would like for you to pass directly to, on substance, to the chairman and, of course, to Premier Zhou Enlai. First, Dr. Kissinger had some very sensitive talks with Chairman Mao and Premier Zhou Enlai with regard to U.S. relations, particularly insofar as those relations might involve the actions of a third party. The statements that Dr. Kissinger made, and that I confirmed in my letter, are statements that were not made off the cuff. They represent a considered position that this government, at least as far as I represent it — that they represent a commitment on our part regarding this policy. If Premier Zhou, and Chairman Mao, approve, I would welcome the opportunity for the ambassador, Dr. Kissinger, and myself to work towards a more formal understanding on these points. However, I wish to emphasize that a formal understanding is not necessary in terms of the commitment. The commitment is made. The ambassador does not know me well, but most people who do know me well know that, really, when I make a personal commitment it is solid. Let me put it in terms of U.S. self-interest. I believe the self-interest of the United States requires good relations between the government of the People's Republic and the government of the United States. I also believe the self-interest of the United States requires the People's Republic remain an independent, strong nation, without having its sovereignty in any way threatened by its neighbors. It will be a cornerstone of U.S. foreign policy, as long as I am in this office, to see that actions are taken which will help to guarantee that a strong, independent PRC — which I would like to say that those actions are being taken because of the good personal relations that I have with Chairman Mao and Premier Zhou Enlai. But let me be quite candid. Those actions are taken because I believe they serve the interests of the United States. I also believe they serve the interests of the PRC. And that's why we're together. Now, there is a meeting coming up with Brezhnev. It's a very important meeting. We're going to try to get a limitation on nuclear arms. We'll be working towards other matters. When I say a limitation — just an extension of what we had previously is very hard. There will be —

KISSINGER: The [unclear] Russian here so that he could greet Brezhnev! [laughs]

[Unclear exchange]

NIXON: The important thing that I want the ambassador to convey to Chairman Mao and Premier Zhou Enlai is this: we're going to have eight days of conversations. We will make some agreements about trade and some other important matters. But I can make a commitment that nothing will be agreed to between the United States and — at this point nothing will be agreed to — that is [to unknown assistant who enters: "I'll let you know when I'm ready — I will be delayed — I'll let you know when I'm ready"] — that in any way — that in any way would be detrimental to the PRC. I want to — I asked Dr. Kissinger to talk directly to the ambassador to fill him in on these talks. He is — I do not need to impress upon the ambassador the need for confidentiality. We have found, incidentally —

KISSINGER: [unclear]

NIXON: We find that in terms of our friends in the PRC, Henry, that they're the best people we know at keeping a secret. The other point I wish to relate to the ambassador relates to the talks we have had with Le Duc Tho on the Southeast Asia situation. The peace agreement removes a major irritant in our relations, something we — that Premier Zhou Enlai and I had to talk about a great deal in Beijing, February last year. There is one outstanding problem, as the ambassador knows. That is Cambodia. I cannot emphasize too strongly the importance that we place on trying to get a peace agreement or a cease-fire in Cambodia such as we hope to have in Laos. Here, China plays a very important role. It would be a tragedy of our time, and it would be a tragedy in this new year of our relationship if we allow the Cambodian situation to be the cause of a flare-up of hostilities throughout Indochina. Let me emphasize for the ambassador, we are not committed to any one man in Cambodia, in any form of government, to any one government. What we want is a government that will bring peace to that troubled country. But it cannot be peace if it comes at the point of a gun. On either side. There are warring elements there that must learn to live together. They must be, basically, a coalition. Then, over a period of time, the people of Cambodia will determine which part of the coalition is the best for their future. In the meantime, I would greatly appreciate it if the ambassador would convey to — show that Dr. Kissinger and I — Dr. Kissinger [unclear] should have the highest priority attempting to implement a — or not implement, unfortunately — to work out a — some sort of peace agreement in Cambodia. I have talked too much, but I had these things on my mind. And I knew that the ambassador was quite aware of the issues, but if he [unclear] these messages I would appreciate it. And on our part, the ambassador can be sure that anytime he has anything that he needs to pass to me — no need to come in. He can give it to Dr. Kissinger — the secret channel — at that direction, however — anything that is really confidential, rather than putting it on diplomatic channels —

KISSINGER: [unclear]

NIXON: — diplomatic channels.

HUANG: I am very grateful to you, Mr. President, for seeing me at this present time. I will do right away what the president has asked me to do. At the same time, the ambassador will give a report of the messages the president has just said, for Chairman Mao and Premier Zhou Enlai. In my work, I look forward to the support and help from you, Mr. President, and the support and help of Dr. Kissinger. [unclear]

NIXON: Well, I will say that when we — I would say that when we finish this meeting [unclear] with Brezhnev, when I talk to the ambassador again I will give him a personal report — again, for his convenience.

JUNE–JULY

The Dean accusation

June 3, 1973, 12:35 p.m.
Richard Nixon and Bob Haldeman
CAMP DAVID TELEPHONE

In the long statement that Nixon released on May 23, he wrote with perfect clarity that "I took no part in, nor was I aware of, any subsequent efforts that may have been made to cover up Watergate." On June 3, the headline on page 1 of the Washington Post *offered a stark contradiction: "Dean Alleges Nixon Knew of Cover-Up Plan." With that, Carl Bernstein and Bob Woodward revealed the fact that Dean had told investigators that Nixon, in conjunction with Haldeman and Ehrlichman, had discussed cover-up schemes during at least thirty-five conversations that included Dean in early 1973. Dean was especially specific in citing Haldeman's role. "Senate and Justice Department sources reported that although initially skeptical of Dean's version of events," wrote Bernstein and Woodward, ". . . the prosecutors now take the former presidential counsel's account seriously." Nixon had become the loser in the battle of credibility. He read the newspaper reports of Dean's disclosure and telephoned Haldeman to go over it in some detail, while making plans for future strategy. Talking to Haldeman was easy for Nixon, but it didn't do him any good in learning why he was, by then, trailing behind his former counsel and trying in vain to lead from behind.*

• • •

NIXON: Hi, Bob.

HALDEMAN: Yes, sir.

NIXON: Goddamn! I always seem to bother you on a Sunday right at church.

HALDEMAN: Not at all.

NIXON: If you don't mind. Yeah. Fine. Look, we're just — I flew up to Camp David and just trying to be sure that the facts are all straight on a couple of things. The boys are still looking over the latest thing that, you know, the —

HALDEMAN: Yeah.

NIXON: — Dean's just lobbing.

HALDEMAN: Yeah.

NIXON: Their, incidentally, their — Buzhardt's analysis is that this is part — that simply — that it did not come from the U.S. attorney, or the committee, but from Dean's lawyer.

HALDEMAN: That's mine too.

NIXON: They think that what it is, is part of his public campaign —

HALDEMAN: Right.

NIXON: — to build immunity. They feel this is not the time to take him on personally because that will have the Left, the libs, all put their arms around him. You know.

HALDEMAN: Right. I agree.

NIXON: He's the big hero. How's that sound to you?

HALDEMAN: Great.

NIXON: On the other hand, they put out a sharp denial, of course, of —

HALDEMAN: I think it was too sharp.

NIXON: You do, huh?

HALDEMAN: Yep. I think it was —

NIXON: Overreacting?

HALDEMAN: Over — yeah. It's overblown rhetoric and it doesn't — it also doesn't fit with — and it lends incredibility to the evenhanded treatment of Dean. I think he's got to have that run in the same story, or the adjacent column to his story, that he goes into his files and take his notes out, and all that, and it makes it seem kind of absurd. But —

NIXON: Well, I'll —

HALDEMAN: — I just think they ought to slow down a little. I don't think it has done any harm, but —

NIXON: — I just can't keep on top of all of it. You know?

HALDEMAN: Oh, sure.

NIXON: I didn't even know they put it out. But I hope you'll just pass your judgment on to me on this thing. Because I want to work through you on it. I think it is perfectly plausible, you know, that I have to work on transition things and so forth and so on.

HALDEMAN: Yeah.

NIXON: But, in any event that is that. Let me just check, be sure on a couple of facts that — in terms of the — and it may be the deal that he'll — that he may be misleading his lawyers a bit. But Dick Kleindienst, you know, told me — remember that I told you that when I had told him that I had only seen Dean once — or twice — or you know —

HALDEMAN: Yeah.

NIXON: — during the period actually twice as it turned out — picture that — tell me — he says Dean told me he was practically in your office every day. See what I mean?

HALDEMAN: Yeah, yeah.

NIXON: Now this says, apparently this — Dean says that in January, February, March, April, that he saw me thirty or forty times. Well, the times are irrelevant. Maybe it is eighteen, but the point is our files show, Bob, that the first time I saw him was February — not the twenty-seventh but February 28, with Dick Moore. See?

HALDEMAN: Mm-hmm. Yeah.

NIXON: Yeah. I thought it was the twenty-seventh but they went back and checked.

HALDEMAN: I think it is the twenty-seventh.

NIXON: Well, it doesn't make any difference.

HALDEMAN: No.

NIXON: We are not going to put any statement out. The point is that it was the twenty-seventh or twenty-eighth whatever it was.

HALDEMAN: Well, he says that. That he didn't see you at all before January.

NIXON: But this is February 28.

HALDEMAN: I know it, but he makes the point that he didn't see you at all until this year. And that then starting in this year he saw you from January through April — saw you some thirty-five or forty times.

NIXON: Right.

HALDEMAN: Or had that many conversations with you.

NIXON: Sure. Sure.

HALDEMAN: With the phone calls that may not be too inaccurate.

NIXON: Oh, sure, and as a matter of fact, we aren't going to quarrel about that. I mean we are not going to quarrel about the number of times.

HALDEMAN: Yeah.

NIXON: That sort of thing. Don't you agree?

HALDEMAN: Yeah. Now, what you should know, and John Ehrlichman is trying to get to —

NIXON: Buzhardt?

HALDEMAN: Ziegler — no, Buzhardt won't talk to us.

NIXON: No, but he is talking to your lawyers.

HALDEMAN: Yeah.

NIXON: Well, I think that will be —

HALDEMAN: Right — no, I am not questioning that. But Ehrlichman was trying to get with Ziegler to tell him of an interview that he had with ABC this morning, and which he did a superb job of spelling out the nature of —

NIXON: The fact that Ehrlichman had an interview with ABC?

HALDEMAN: Yeah.

NIXON: Good. I didn't want to ask you to do it.

HALDEMAN: Well, I did, too, but I didn't go into the deal that John did. And I think —

NIXON: Well, did they ask about this conversation — this Dean thing?

HALDEMAN: Oh, yeah. That is what they were there for. They were on my doorstep this morning.

NIXON: I figured they would be.

HALDEMAN: So, what I said was that I — see, I have a consistent position that I want to stay with, and I — it is helpful most of the time, although once in a while it gets in the way.

NIXON: [laughs] That's all right.

HALDEMAN: What I said was that "I will not comment on any specific story, or any hearsay, or any allegations that have come up." So, "I am not going to comment on the story today. I will say, however, categorically, that the president had no part in any way, shape, or form, in any cover-up with the Watergate affair."

NIXON: That's the stuff. Yeah.

HALDEMAN: And I said, "I also will say, as I have said, and I said that before. And that I also repeat what I have also said before, which is that I had no part in any way, shape, or form in any cover-up in the Watergate affair. Now beyond that I am not going to comment on charges that are lobbed up day by day. I am simply going to say that's the truth. And as the truth becomes known that will be confirmed."

NIXON: Good.

HALDEMAN: "And I have full confidence that that will be the case. And I have no concern about any of these charges that are being lobbed up." He said, "Well, that in effect is denying Dean's charges." And I said, "Let me emphasize I am not responding to any individual charges. I am telling you what the truth is" and I left it at that.

NIXON: Right. Good.

HALDEMAN: Now John went substantially beyond that in a long interview and made the point that Dean's communication with the president came about at John's — at Ehrlichman's and my suggestion. That as this thing was spinning out it would — the president ought to now talk directly with Dean because, you know, there appeared to be more there than what was meeting the eye. And that the president did, and the reason he did was to find out what was going on. Find out the facts in the thing, and he builds a very plausible thing — plausible because it was true.

NIXON: Did he nail the date down, or try to?

HALDEMAN: I think he probably did. Yeah.

NIXON: It doesn't make too much difference.

HALDEMAN: I think he did.

NIXON: Actually, if I can interrupt a minute — you know, Bob, from February 28 until about the fourteenth when I had a — you know, I had two press conferences. Believe me, we weren't talking about the goddamn Watergate statement. We were talking about executive privilege, and the Ervin Committee, and Pat Gray, and his being a liar and that sort of stuff. You know what I mean?

HALDEMAN: Yeah.

NIXON: Then we picked up the other stuff. Go ahead, John [Bob].

HALDEMAN: Well, he makes the point that as you got into this and got more facts and that you did have these discussions with Dean to try and get caught up. Then we went into our cycle of sending him up to write his report and all that. But, I think John's — I am not characterizing it very well, because he gave me a quick run, but —

NIXON: I will let Ziegler [unclear].

HALDEMAN: I was very impressed with what John said — he covered with ABC. And I think it is something that Ron will want to get a transcript of it, because ABC won't carry the whole thing. But maybe they can give him a tape of it.

NIXON: Good. Ron, the reason you can't get him is they are in this meeting, you know. They are meeting down there right now and trying to get, you know —

HALDEMAN: Right.

NIXON: They are all trying. As a matter of fact, Bob, they aren't — nobody's, you know, getting panicky, and so forth, but this isn't something people expect.

HALDEMAN: That's right.

NIXON: And, I think part of the reason for their maybe going with it this week is that they were disturbed about what had happened the last ten days or so. You know they haven't been making too much headway.

HALDEMAN: That's right.

NIXON: Or — I don't know whether you agree.

HALDEMAN: No, I think that is absolutely right.

NIXON: I think they began to see some problems and had to lob something else up there. So they are going very hard now with their star witness. When I say "they" are, I mean the press.

HALDEMAN: Yeah, I agree.

NIXON: Dean also —

HALDEMAN: I agree with Buzhardt's theory that this is not from the prosecutors.

NIXON: You do, huh?

HALDEMAN: This is Dean's play. Because it fits a pattern. He does this every weekend.

NIXON: Yeah.

HALDEMAN: He has a new escalator each weekend.

NIXON: Must have some kind of lawyer with him, don't you think? Well, no, he is capable of it.

HALDEMAN: That is what they say. No, I am told that this guy that he has got is very clever, and very unscrupulous.

NIXON: What you are [unclear] you though — you and John are doing the right thing. And it just, you know the thing — when we were up there in the library that night, and I was sort of depressed a bit. Goddamn it, Bob, you and John and I are telling the truth.

HALDEMAN: That is the whole point.

NIXON: We are telling the truth. So when people say do this or that, goddamn it we're telling the truth. I mean, there are things which are hard to explain, like that CIA thing, but it happens to be the truth. The three fifty happens to be the truth. The Kalmbach thing happens to be the truth. The fact that — the fact too that neither you nor John told me about either the, you know, the three fifty or the Kalmbach thing happens to be the truth, because at that time people forget. Goddamn it! I was in the middle of a campaign. I was running a war, and doing a hell of a lot of other things —

HALDEMAN: There was no reason to tell you about it. It was not significant. It wasn't a big deal that we were involved in. It was a —

NIXON: Well, as a matter of fact John did, I think. He approved it routinely, the Kalmbach thing you know. And Kalmbach never spoke to me. Well, I didn't see him. I had no reason to. But that's that.

HALDEMAN: That's —

NIXON: Oh, incidentally, one more thing that I think our files are wrong on says that we saw him on the twenty-first, and it says on the twenty-second that I saw him again with you and at least — part of it, I mean — and then you and Ehrlichman, and Mitchell. My recollection was that we didn't see Mitchell on the twenty-second. Do you remember?

HALDEMAN: I think we did.

NIXON: But was that the —

HALDEMAN: Oh, no, wait. The twenty-second?

NIXON: The twenty-first and the twenty-second. The twenty-second was the day I thought we went to Florida.

HALDEMAN: Wait just a second. Let me get a piece of paper here.

NIXON: Yeah.

HALDEMAN: The twenty-second was the day we went to Florida.

NIXON: It was? I don't know when I would have — could have seen —

HALDEMAN: But, now —

NIXON: Wasn't that the day you and John and Dean met with Mitchell? I guess you had to meet —

HALDEMAN: Yeah, but so did you.

NIXON: Met with all of you?

HALDEMAN: Yep. In the Oval Office. We came over. After — you had us meet with him and then you said you would meet with us afterwards. And the original plan for that meeting was not for Dean to be there, but then he was there. And it was at that meeting we talked about —

NIXON: That is what I was wondering. What did we talk about?

HALDEMAN: Well, we talked about —

NIXON: Because by that time we knew about the damn Bittman thing but I don't think we talked about it. We didn't talk about it as I recall. Or we might have.

HALDEMAN: No, no. We didn't. That was undone by then. Or, you know —

NIXON: You had already had that committed. Dean would have to casual reference to Mitchell.

HALDEMAN: In the morning meeting.

NIXON: I see.

HALDEMAN: Or early afternoon, or whatever it was. We were with you at two o'clock, or one forty-five.

NIXON: Right.

HALDEMAN: We met with you for two hours. It was a fairly long meeting.

NIXON: Well, what the hell did we discuss for two hours?

HALDEMAN: Well, we talked about how to deal with the double — Ervin Committee and the Watergate business. And whether — and then that is where we decided we ought to get a paper out by John Dean.

NIXON: Oh, I see. The Dean report.

HALDEMAN: That's right.

NIXON: Mitchell was there?

HALDEMAN: That's right, and then we also got into at that meeting the whole business of Pat Gray. That was the day, or — yeah, that was the day that Pat Gray said that Dean had lied.

NIXON: Yeah.

HALDEMAN: And so we got into that discussion and you picked up the phone and called Kleindienst about something during that meeting. About that you wanted him to work — oh, that you wanted him to work with the Ervin Committee.

NIXON: Oh, yes.

HALDEMAN: And, you know, that he — because then we had had those feelers about who was going to, you know, Howard Baker was saying that his administrative assistant who would work with —

NIXON: Yeah, that's right. Now it comes back.

HALDEMAN: So we covered a whole lot of stuff at that meeting.

NIXON: Yeah.

HALDEMAN: But it was all [unclear] trying to get the goddamn report done.

NIXON: The thing about all of this was an attempt on our part to get the facts.

HALDEMAN: Well, there is no question about that.

NIXON: Except that Dean's, where he normally — incidentally, it wasn't a concession at all, but — except for the twenty-first thing where he mentioned his fear about the Bittman thing. You know? He never, you know — he'd lob out, "Well, Krogh's got a problem, and I think he" — the three fifty thing. I think March 21 was the first time he mentioned the three fifty.

HALDEMAN: I think that is right. He mentioned that problem, and he mentioned Ehrlichman's Plumbers' leak problem.

NIXON: Did he mention it then?

HALDEMAN: I think so.

NIXON: I am not sure. Well he might have — might not have. But nevertheless, the whole fact of the matter is he didn't mention the problems he had. You know of — that he is the one that offered the clemency. That he was the one that suborned the perjury of Magruder. You know. Those were the things —

HALDEMAN: Right. [laughs]

NIXON: Those things — even then, he [unclear] — he didn't raise all those. Well, anyway.

HALDEMAN: He sure didn't.

NIXON: In fact, he never did — never told me those things. Even on April 15 he didn't. I don't think he has told the U.S. attorney those things either.

HALDEMAN: Well, what I would like to do, and I have got to find a place to do it, and I have got to get into my notes again. [laughs] Figure out a way of doing that.

NIXON: Memorize them — I know.

HALDEMAN: I guess so, but what I want to do now is write a chronology. Which I can do.

NIXON: I wish you would.

HALDEMAN: Of what you did, and what I did, and what Dean did.

NIXON: Right.

HALDEMAN: And the story, you see, holds up awfully well of Dean — your coming into an intensive period of trying to get this stuff worked out with Dean, and then finding that it didn't work, and then cutting him off, and then turning Ehrlichman loose on him.

NIXON: When did I turn Ehrlichman loose?

HALDEMAN: March 30.

NIXON: March 30?

HALDEMAN: Yep.

NIXON: After my — well, right after we arrived in California.

HALDEMAN: Yep. It was en route to California. It was on the plane that he gave you that —

NIXON: Why did I turn him loose? I can't recall why I did it.

HALDEMAN: I think mainly because we weren't getting the Dean thing. See that was — Dean had just come, met up at Camp David, and come back down, and we weren't getting any answers. And you weren't finding out that we were still — the thing was still wallowing around in conflicting stuff and not knowing what the story was.

NIXON: Right. So that was on the way to the — California, and I said, "Now, John, you take over."

HALDEMAN: Yeah, you may have said it before we went. Then he — remember, he wrote up a note for you to sign to him that would — you give him attorney-client privilege.

NIXON: Oh, yeah.

HALDEMAN: Because at that point we were worried about, you know, if he got into investigating that he would be protected.

NIXON: Yeah, I signed a note to him, didn't I?

HALDEMAN: And you signed some note saying, "I direct you to take over this investigation." And you dated it by hand, he says. And I think the date was March 30.

NIXON: You doing that chronology would be very helpful. Let me tell you something, the reason I don't want to do one, Bob, myself —

HALDEMAN: You shouldn't.

NIXON: I don't want to write a memorandum out because —

HALDEMAN: Good Lord, no!

NIXON: Don't you agree?

HALDEMAN: Yes, sir.

NIXON: I mean, for example, I don't want to say that I was not aware of the three fifty until such and such. I wasn't aware, you know the things like that.

HALDEMAN: I wouldn't do it.

NIXON: If you wouldn't mind, you know, because you remember, before we got our statement out I called you and we nailed down everything.

HALDEMAN: Well, that's the plus of your having eliminated executive privilege —

NIXON: Yeah.

HALDEMAN: — is that I can go, now, through these things and I have got to figure out how to do it. I think I want to do it publicly.

NIXON: Well, that is the other thing. Dean and our enemies are playing all of their stuff publicly, John — I mean Bob. And playing it publicly. I'm inclined to think it's time for us to start playing it publicly.

HALDEMAN: Well, I think it may be, and I can do it. I can do on a — two ways. One, I can go back on my deposition, but that isn't going to get run. I think the way to do it, probably, is to go to Bob Woodward at the *Washington Post* and say, "Bob, I will give you an interview if you will print the whole thing. And I will tell you my — I will tell you the story."

NIXON: Yeah, at the present time, as you are well aware of, they are really not after you or John. We have always —

HALDEMAN: Oh, hell no.

NIXON: They are after the president.

HALDEMAN: There is no question about that.

NIXON: And they are not after John Mitchell, the poor fellow. I mean —

HALDEMAN: And that is who they ought to be after, of course. And they ignore him.

NIXON: That is — isn't that interesting? They —

HALDEMAN: The reason they ignore it is that they know he is got, and they know that getting him isn't going to get you. And they don't want — they are concerned about letting it lie at John Mitchell.

NIXON: They are afraid it will stop there.

HALDEMAN: Which is where it does stop. With Mitchell and John Dean.

NIXON: Well, it stops with Mitchell, Magruder, and John Dean.

HALDEMAN: See, an interesting point I have got to get to somebody at some point publicly, and I'll do it. As soon as I get a question that links it to me I can do it on television — is that they keep saying all this cover-up, and they keep overlooking the fact that to this day that there is no allegation by anybody in this case that anyone at the White House was involved in the planning or execution of the Watergate break-in — with the remote possibility of Dean — remote possible exception of Dean. But beyond Dean there is — nobody has alleged that anybody at the White House — in other words the Dean report that they got so upset about in August is still, even though Ron says is inoperative, it is not inoperative. It is still operative. It is still — that is the fact as we know it today.

NIXON: That's correct.

HALDEMAN: And that seems to get overlooked. And that is what gets overlooked at the McClellan [Ervin] Committee. Where they started lobbing, well, Ehrlichman and I must have done the Watergate. Therefore we wanted to cover it up.

NIXON: Yeah.

HALDEMAN: You have got to go back to a motivation thing here. We didn't have anything to cover up.

NIXON: That's correct. Not a goddamn thing.

HALDEMAN: John Dean may have or may not have. I do not know.

NIXON: Exactly.

HALDEMAN: Because I still don't know. From all he has told me he didn't have.

NIXON: Yeah, he says he didn't know they were going to go forward with it. That was his line throughout.

HALDEMAN: That's right.

NIXON: You know, and drawing the wagons up around the White House. When did he say that?

HALDEMAN: On the twenty-second.

NIXON: Is that when he said that?

HALDEMAN: Twenty-second — no, make that the twenty-first. The afternoon of the twenty-first.

NIXON: Oh, he said, "Draw the wagons up"? That was even after the conversation we had.

HALDEMAN: Yep.

NIXON: Oh, he met later with you and John?

HALDEMAN: And you. We met over at the EOB that afternoon for forty minutes.

NIXON: Later, I see.

HALDEMAN: At five thirty.

NIXON: I see.

HALDEMAN: And it was after that meeting. I have notes on that.

NIXON: And he went over and said [unclear].

HALDEMAN: And that's when he pulled the "wagons around the White House" line.

NIXON: Yeah.

HALDEMAN: He said that if we do that nobody will sink. We are all okay. Now it turns out that that was a self-serving thing because he was trying to hang himself onto us, knowing that we were clear, and bring himself in. Now he may still be clear, I don't know.

NIXON: Well, he is not clear on one — his real Achilles' heel is on the meeting with Mitchell and Magruder. Where Magruder will, I am sure, testify that he was told to perjure himself. See, on that one I think he is a dead and goner.

HALDEMAN: Yeah.

NIXON: But that is something —

HALDEMAN: He did meet with you on the twenty-seventh.

NIXON: The twenty-seventh?

HALDEMAN: Of February.

NIXON: Well, that is fine.

HALDEMAN: That was his first meeting. It was that —

NIXON: That was with Moore then. That was with Moore.

HALDEMAN: Nope. Moore wasn't in that one. Moore came a little later. You met with him for half an hour on the twenty-seventh at four o'clock and for an hour on the morning of the twenty-eighth.

NIXON: With Moore. Moore was there sometime.

HALDEMAN: Neither of those was with Moore. Then you met with him quite a few times on the first. There was about half an hour in the morning.

NIXON: That was about my press conference.

HALDEMAN: Another ten minutes and then another ten minutes.

NIXON: Right. See, I was preparing for the second —

HALDEMAN: That's right. That's exactly right. And then you have the press conference on the second.

NIXON: Right.

HALDEMAN: And then you didn't meet Dean that day at all.

NIXON: Yeah.

HALDEMAN: Or the following day, or that weekend at all but then you got into March, you met with him for a couple of minutes on the sixth in the morning. And again on the seventh for half an hour in the morning.

NIXON: These are just quick —

HALDEMAN: I mean they are not the long —

NIXON: Just checking in on what's going on I guess.

HALDEMAN: Then I don't see where the Moore thing started. The Moore meetings started on the fourteenth.

NIXON: Who? Fourteenth? Oh, that is when I was preparing for the press conference and he came in after the press conference, he and Moore together came in after the press conference. I think that was it. Well, anyway, you can see I can't try to get my recollection, Bob, in this goddamn —

HALDEMAN: You shouldn't. Let me go back through it, but let me just stay with the facts.

NIXON: That's right.

HALDEMAN: You know, so we don't get caught up on something that — but I am going to try to do a thing.

NIXON: And you think an interview in the paper is better than something on TV, huh?

HALDEMAN: I can do both, and I think — but I do in the sense I think we need a public record on it.

NIXON: Yeah. Basically, let's face it, you are not going to get a decent public record out of the Ervin Committee.

HALDEMAN: Oh, no.

NIXON: You'll never get a good public record of course out of the grand jury because that's nothing. I mean that will be months before —

HALDEMAN: The other place I can will be my deposition for the Democratic National Committee.

NIXON: Yeah.

HALDEMAN: Because that does become public and I have already done that, but you see our lawyers have taken the position that anything relating to events after June 17 is irrelevant.

NIXON: Yeah.

HALDEMAN: Because their suit is for damages for — as a result of the break-in.

NIXON: Yep. Yeah, yeah.

HALDEMAN: If we can drop that irrelevance then I could give all this in my deposition. I could get a second — I have already had three rounds, so I could get a fourth round on my deposition.

NIXON: Right.

HALDEMAN: And get that in and make that public, but you can't be sure what they will print of that. Where if I go to the *Post* directly, or the *Times, Newsweek,* I can pick anybody I want.

NIXON: Do you think Woodward is better than the *Times?* You know?

HALDEMAN: Well, he knows more about it. The *Times* might be more fair.

NIXON: That is the point. The *Post* is so biased on this thing —

HALDEMAN: Yeah, they are.

NIXON: You wonder how they would handle it, Bob. I mean, they could take — they could ignore all your defenses — "We didn't know," so forth and so on.

HALDEMAN: Well, they — well, I wouldn't do it except on a deal, and they have offered this — and, of course, AP has, too. I could do it with the AP for that matter, but nobody would print it. You see, if you do it with the *Post* you know it is printed.

NIXON: Sure.

HALDEMAN: I can do it with somebody though. On the deal with — that many have offered, that they will carry the entire thing. Of any length, anything I want to say.

NIXON: Yeah. Incidentally, you are very well advised though — don't make it too long.

HALDEMAN: That's right.

NIXON: Categorical imperative — that is the thing here.

HALDEMAN: Yep. Well, especially on TV, that's — I am convinced of that.

NIXON: Oh, the TV. Yeah, you murdered them.

HALDEMAN: Like this thing I did this morning, if they carry any of it they have to carry it all.

NIXON: Incidentally, John did a hell of a job last week, too. As I said, I mean when I raised the [former deputy director of the CIA Robert] Cushman thing, I was only raising it because I was so pissed off at Cushman.

HALDEMAN: Yeah.

NIXON: You know what I mean?

HALDEMAN: Well, Cushman and Walters both are sort of reverting to type on the military rather than the public interest.

NIXON: Just — well, frankly they know better. They are sort of protecting their own ass and letting everybody else be hurt. Aren't they?

HALDEMAN: Yep.

NIXON: Well, I shall not forget.

HALDEMAN: And in the process they aren't really protecting their own ass either.

NIXON: No — they look bad, don't they? So it was on the twenty-second then that we told Dean to write the damn report.

HALDEMAN: Yep, on the twenty-second we left for Key Biscayne. And he went up to Camp David. And then I had those — you spent that whole weekend at Key Biscayne really probing into —

NIXON: Did I?

HALDEMAN: — new questions kept coming to your mind. That was that weekend where I was over at your house that one day for six hours calling people.

NIXON: Were you?

HALDEMAN: Yeah.

NIXON: What kind of people were you calling?

HALDEMAN: Geez, everybody. Colson, Rogers, Mitchell, Dean, Moore, and it was —

NIXON: What were you calling them about?

HALDEMAN: Partly factual, to get specifics like the Colson phone call. Remember? Dean had told us about the Colson phone call to Magruder. He was trying to tie Colson in. So I called Colson to check that out. And we were talking to Rogers about whether we should — there was the debate then as to whether to offer everybody to the grand jury, or whether — what to do —

NIXON: Oh, yeah.

HALDEMAN: And that was the week that McCord came out with his letter to the judge.

NIXON: Yeah.

HALDEMAN: And it was a big weekend of revelations — or, not really revelations but of new insights.

NIXON: That's right.

HALDEMAN: And those created questions that were asked. And you had lots of notes of questions that had occurred to you, and you were grinding away on them. I would go out — remember, I would go out into the living room and make phone calls and report to you. And you would have a new batch of stuff —

NIXON: God!

HALDEMAN: — and then I would go back out to the room and make a call or batch of calls, and give you a rundown on that.

NIXON: That is when all the rumors were flying around.

HALDEMAN: That's right, and that is what I would like to get out. I would like to get out what was flying at that point.

NIXON: And I was trying to get the facts.

HALDEMAN: And that through it all, they were all contradictory and they still are. And this baloney about why you don't tell people the truth is ridiculous. You don't know it!

NIXON: Yeah.

HALDEMAN: And you still don't — least I don't know. If you do, you have it by divine revelation, not by any concrete evidence.

NIXON: I don't. I have suspicions.

HALDEMAN: Well, sure you have suspicions, and so do I. But you or I, or anybody else, aren't entitled to announce our suspicions?

NIXON: I am not going to tell anybody about suspicions. I am not going to announce any in the press.

HALDEMAN: That's right. What could be more irresponsible than for the president of the United States to say, "I suspect this is what happened"?

NIXON: Well, anyway, the — I will be talking to Ziegler around two o'clock when they break this meeting.

HALDEMAN: Well, tell him to call John about the interview.

NIXON: I will, and I will tell him to call you too.

HALDEMAN: All right. No need to call me.

NIXON: Well, I mean — the only thing I can suggest — if you could do this chronology for me, John — Bob, I would appreciate it, because I don't want to do it.

HALDEMAN: Right. Well, I am going to do that. I am going to go in tomorrow morning and work in the files tomorrow. On an in-and-out basis, I am going to have to memorize and go out and write and come back in, but I can do that, and —

NIXON: It is interesting. Apparently in this story Dean's other source says that Dean doesn't have any documentary evidence. I wonder why he says that. He doesn't of course.

HALDEMAN: Well, they probably asked him, and he — well, it is interesting though, did you see that they lobbed out that he had tape recordings?

NIXON: No.

HALDEMAN: That is buried in one of the stories, that one of his sources lobbed out that everybody was making tape recordings of phone calls, and that Dean did, too. I don't think that is true.

NIXON: Let me say this — tape recordings that he had, I don't believe that — he didn't have any at Camp David, Bob. When you called him here, when I called him at Camp David, you know. You know what I mean? I don't know how the hell he could tape-record Camp David. Do you?

HALDEMAN: No, he'd have — well, yeah, you can easily because I have a little thing you just plug onto the phone and just stick it on your tape recorder and it records the conversation.

NIXON: Well, so be it.

HALDEMAN: Just a little suction cup on the telephone — you can do it.

NIXON: So he does have them? What the hell's the difference?

HALDEMAN: That doesn't bother me. They hurt him worse than anybody. At least his conversations with me do. And he didn't have very many with you, I don't think.

NIXON: On the phone?

HALDEMAN: Any phone conversations — he must have had some.

NIXON: I must have called him on — I probably called him while we were in Florida. Don't you imagine?

HALDEMAN: He is claiming that the Easter phone call — he makes the claim that said in that phone call you were just kidding about that we could raise a million dollars if needed.

NIXON: We never even discussed it.

HALDEMAN: He may have a recording of that that has something in it that they are trying to make something out of that. We can set that one to rest on the basis of investigations. I mean, hell, at that point you were trying to find out in the first place if there was the —

NIXON: Now let me tell you that in the Easter call, I remember that very well. That was a very brief call, and we didn't discuss damn anything of that sort at all.

HALDEMAN: Okay.

NIXON: He talked about his — wanted to — how he was going to plead, and all that sort of thing. And wanted to see — and of course we couldn't do that.

HALDEMAN: Yeah.

NIXON: But on the million dollars, is this the first time he raised that, or has he raised that previously?

HALDEMAN: This weekend's story is the first time it has come up.

NIXON: Yeah. What does it say in effect?

HALDEMAN: It says that you asked at some point — I think he puts it at the March 21 meeting — that you asked how much money would be needed beyond the four hundred sixty-five thousand that had already been paid —

NIXON: [unclear]

HALDEMAN: — to defendants. And he said a million dollars, and that you had said, "Well, we can raise that."

NIXON: I did.

HALDEMAN: But that isn't the point.

NIXON: No, that's right. The whole point is that I did, but we — but Bob, you remember when you were in the conversation. Fortunately, you — we said that there were three points that were made. I said, first, you could raise the million dollars, but then you would have the problem of clemency. We can't give clemency, you know. And I, also — you recall, I at one point, thank God, said that it is wrong. Is that correct?

HALDEMAN: Yep. Yep. That is correct.

NIXON: Because the whole purpose of that account —

HALDEMAN: You were drawing in and out, and that is what has to be made clear.

NIXON: The whole purpose of that conversation was to show how insane, or foolish this whole business of trying to pay off the people who did it.

HALDEMAN: That's right.

NIXON: I mean the clemency thing, for example. Actually I made one unfortunate statement, or said you couldn't even consider clemency — the way I put it, as I recall, until after the '74 elections. I don't know what your recollection is on it, but what I was really meaning to say that you —

HALDEMAN: I don't recall that, but that is perfectly possible. I think so.

NIXON: You could just simply say that you just couldn't consider clemency at this time.

That is really the whole point, and therefore the whole business of paying the defendants —

HALDEMAN: In any event, that was on March 21. All offers of clemency and all that stuff were in January, according to what —

NIXON: Yeah.

HALDEMAN: — McCord and all those people have testified. So what difference does it make what was discussed in March? I think what happened is Dean, or somebody, offered clemency way back early and was trying to get it ratified.

NIXON: Yep.

HALDEMAN: In March.

NIXON: Well, we didn't ratify it.

HALDEMAN: The fly was already in the soup.

NIXON: We never ratified it. I never ratified it.

HALDEMAN: Nope.

NIXON: You were there when we talked about it. You couldn't even consider it. That is what you would naturally say.

HALDEMAN: Yep. That's right.

NIXON: Well, I am glad that he has lobbed out the million dollars thing, because you know I was a bit concerned about his conversation. Mainly because we were talking to a trusted confidant, and basically because why the hell — why would I ask the question about how much would it take? "Well, we could get a million dollars. Well, we could get a million dollars." So what in the hell, does that mean that we were going to do it? You know, and that sort of thing.

HALDEMAN: At that point, you were making the point that it isn't a question of money, it is a question of what was being done, first of all, whether it was right or wrong. And there was still a question, at least in my mind, at that point, of whether we were talking about money for lawyer fees and support, or whether or not it was a —

NIXON: Hush-up.

HALDEMAN: — hush-up money. There was only a semi-factor of blackmail or hush-up in it —

NIXON: Except in the Bittman thing.

HALDEMAN: That's right, and that was not related to the Watergate.

NIXON: True.

HALDEMAN: So.

NIXON: Well, that is interesting. He says in the Easter call that I mentioned the million dollars. We didn't discuss it.

HALDEMAN: No. No, he says that your point of being able to raise the money that you were just kidding or something like that.

NIXON: On Easter?

HALDEMAN: Mm-hmm.

NIXON: Hell, no! No, we didn't discuss that. We were — I know what I said on that occasion.

HALDEMAN: Okay. Well, whether it works or not —

NIXON: That is something we will have to remember. But you — we can knock — it is kind of a game they are playing. We will have to knock them out of the box but at the right time.

HALDEMAN: Yep. But we can lay our groundwork now.

NIXON: Right.

HALDEMAN: Our factual base.

NIXON: I will have him call you around two o'clock.

HALDEMAN: Okay.

"I've just spent nine hours on this crap."

June 4, 1973, 10:05 a.m.
Richard Nixon, Steve Bull, and Alexander Haig
EXECUTIVE OFFICE BUILDING

It is safe to say that June 4 was not Steve Bull's favorite day at work. Having taken over earlier in the year from Alexander Butterfield as personal assistant to President Nixon, Bull immediately inherited an incredible responsibility, unparalleled in the modern presidency: safeguarding Nixon's secret taping system. Still more than a month before Butterfield's public disclosure of the system to the Ervin Committee during sworn testimony, June 4 also marked the only occasion when Nixon spent the day reviewing his tapes. It is a difficult recording to follow, but it was even more difficult for Nixon. He was facing his massive inventory of tapes for the first time, and he seemed to forget where taping occurred, which days he met with certain people, and even which tapes he had already listened to. Nixon's tapes did not collect the tidy record of his presidency that he had originally hoped they would.

• • •

NIXON: [Plays a tape from February 28, 1973.]

　　DEAN: " — the others were arguing that the committee up on the Hill broaden its mandate to include other elections." [Speaks into telephone.] Bull, please — Steve. Hello? Thank you.

[BULL joins the conversation.]

NIXON: I finished this one.

BULL: Well, that's it. I just finished calibrating this one here.

NIXON: What's this?

BULL: This is the next day, and —

NIXON: The twenty-seventh — yeah.

BULL: Yes, sir. And that will mean [unclear].

NIXON: You mean you didn't have this office done?

BULL: On the twenty-seventh [unclear].

NIXON: [unclear] We do have this office done, haven't we?

BULL: Yes, sir.

NIXON: Then why wouldn't we have that?

BULL: I'm not sure. It may have been an equipment failure. It was a twenty-five-minute meeting [unclear].

NIXON: Well, you got to go down and get some [unclear].

BULL: There are three meetings.

NIXON: Yeah.

BULL: [unclear]

NIXON: Well, we didn't [unclear].

BULL: That's what I mean. And that's the thing I wanted to impress on [unclear]. I'm not sure whether he understands the sensitivity.

NIXON: [unclear] or anybody else. Nobody should know.

BULL: [unclear] no one besides yourself —

NIXON: You.

BULL: Me, Haldeman, Butterfield. [unclear]

NIXON: [unclear]

BULL: It's happened once or twice before. They're activated by different means.

NIXON: I see. Well, [unclear].

BULL: All right, sir. Mr. President, if you do want to hear any of the others —

NIXON: Yeah.

BULL: — here's what their numbers are. I'll be around. This first one goes from one eighty-six to three eighty-five [unclear].

NIXON: Right.

BULL: The second one, if you'll run it ahead to six twenty-five —

NIXON: I agree. I know.

BULL: And then they're really — you only got three digits here —

NIXON: Yeah. Yeah.

BULL: — and if you go past a thousand you start rewi — you know, and start again at zero. So actually this final meeting is one o'clock to one ten. [unclear] there are a couple of telephone calls. There's a call made that day to [unclear]. We have the calls. We have the telephone calls. [unclear] there is one that [unclear] your conversation with Dean [unclear].

NIXON: [unclear] we have the calls. They're on here?

BULL: No, sir. They're on a separate reel. [unclear]

NIXON: Get lost, Steve.

BULL: All right, sir.

NIXON: [Plays a tape.] [Speaks into telephone.] General Haig, please. Hello? Thought I'd take a break for a minute or two. Could you come over? Thank you. Bye. [Hangs up telephone.]

[HAIG joins the conversation.]

NIXON: Come in. Hello. Okay.

HAIG: I think we got [White House secretary] Nell [Yates] coming around again now.

NIXON: You have?

HAIG: I going to use him as [unclear] for a price. Magruder and Buzhardt—

NIXON: Yeah.

HAIG: —and [unclear].

NIXON: Right.

HAIG: [unclear] You know, a second thing is I talked to Elliot [Richardson] about the wiretaps.

NIXON: Yeah.

HAIG: He has found in a Justice Department file confirmation that newspaper people, political figures, were tapped. During the Kennedy period. Kennedy removed all of 1961's wiretaps from the Justice Department. We think they're still in the FBI. The FBI—

NIXON: We don't [unclear] about our individuals, yet? We haven't found any there, in there, as yet, have we?

HAIG: No. But the FBI is working on — we have right now confirmation that the character of the past — in the past — is no different than the character now. That includes newspaper people—

NIXON: [unclear] were newsmen tapped during the Kennedy period?

HAIG: They were. We had in that kind of a [unclear] case confirmed in Justice.

NIXON: [unclear]

HAIG: We don't know who it is, and he's—

NIXON: I know he—

HAIG: —he's carrying the names.

NIXON: I know.

HAIG: He's going to be over tonight.

NIXON: Brandon? Brandon's been tapped for years. That's what Hoover told me.

HAIG: Now the names — he'll be over here tonight. [unclear] of this preliminary check. They're going on with work in each case. I told them—

NIXON: Right.

HAIG: —that as soon as that's finished [unclear] I sent [unclear] down, and he's working on it attentively. But I had a meeting this morning with [unclear] and Len [Garment].

NIXON: Yeah.

HAIG: We all think that we should — we want to get something—

NIXON: Hold it till you get it.

HAIG: —quickly. Well, we think we ought to get something out quickly.

NIXON: Yeah. It's — you mean — oh, I see your point.

HAIG: We — I've got a [unclear] now which it'd be well to get this story—

NIXON: Yeah.

HAIG: —out.

NIXON: Get our story on.

HAIG: And we're thinking the filler game plan will look—

NIXON: Good. It's a good counterattack right now.

HAIG: Right.

NIXON: Right.

HAIG: Uh—

NIXON: The— well, I think highly— but I thought you had urged we should wait [unclear].

HAIG: Well, I wanted to be sure—

NIXON: There were newsmen. Yeah.

HAIG: There were newsmen and government officials.

NIXON: We could just say, "Newsmen were included."

HAIG: That's right.

NIXON: We don't need to— nobody's going to counteract that.

HAIG: Yeah. We're working out the game plan to have— maybe Scott come out of the leadership meeting tomorrow. That could—

NIXON: Right.

HAIG: —come back with a complete pressing. We knew this went and in the past, and—

NIXON: And we had, and I—

HAIG: —the preliminary results confirm.

NIXON: Yeah. Well, why don't we do this? The leadership meeting tomorrow— I can say, "Senator Scott asked me privately whether or not there were any other [unclear]. I've got the figures, gentlemen, and here they are. And newsmen were tapped."

HAIG: [unclear] located, Mr. President.

NIXON: You have?

HAIG: Yes, sir, if you'd like me to set it up for you [unclear].

NIXON: Oh, well, I'm— well, I've— yeah, but I'm— I haven't finished this. I've done the first half-hour. Got two more, ten minutes on this one and I think there's nothing in them but I assume that— but— why don't you just stand by? Or I'll buzz you when I'm ready. [unclear]

HAIG: Okay.

NIXON: Good.

HAIG: So, it's— I— we're going to have some good stuff in—

NIXON: Yeah.

HAIG: — this weekend. This is— we'll get that out tomorrow. And that will enable Jerry [Gerald Ford] to stand up on Wednesday and clobber McCloskey and— because he's been getting scoops on wiretaps. [unclear] Christ, he could stand up and just crucify him.

NIXON: Right.

HAIG: Now another thing that's come up is Herb [Kalmbach] wants to announce his resignation Tuesday. I told him to hold up. With the idea if he did it Tuesday, and we had some reorganization, including Ron—

NIXON: Yeah.

HAIG: — on Wednesday.

NIXON: Yeah.

HAIG: I was very fussy by it. So he's going to do whatever best suits our purpose.

NIXON: Sure.

HAIG: I'm seeing two FBI guys this afternoon as potential FBI directors so that we — it looks as though we've done a thorough job.

NIXON: Right.

HAIG: Richardson wants very much to get Ruckelshaus over there as deputy attorney general. I don't think so. He's not a good team —

NIXON: He's not our man.

HAIG: Yeah. It's not a good team.

NIXON: Want me to take a minute to tell you what's on this crap?

HAIG: Yes. Yes, sir.

NIXON: You haven't got Buzhardt yet, have you?

HAIG: Well, Buzhardt's standing by over the — the trouble is there's six file cases down there of Dean's stuff. He's going through the first two that Dean's been into, because they look like they'd be the ones that we should be looking at.

NIXON: Yeah. Yeah.

HAIG: And he's working on it full-time.

NIXON: It's good that Dean asked him to —

HAIG: Oh, God!

NIXON: — get his own file out of there, because the fact that [unclear]. See, that's the thing I was really concerned about.

HAIG: Well, we all were, and that's —

NIXON: Yeah.

HAIG: — a godsend.

NIXON: Let me just get the — go over this so you can, you know, reassure you a little on it. [unclear] you know. I think about it. This is the meeting of the twenty-eighth, an hour-and-ten meeting — an hour-and-ten-minute meeting. It'll also tell you why I don't want others doing it, and why we cannot — why, you know — you — I'm feeling [unclear] this report. Why we — I re — without regard to Watergate, according to [unclear] just hang fire [unclear]. But, first, it was about — it started with executive privilege. We discussed — Dean says, "You're not withholding any information on there, you know — on that line. We had a press conference and I got you a history for every bit of information that we're going to cooperate with." And then Dean had an idea to run Stans up first to pursue as a stalking horse, as he put it. He said he can sandbag them. That's the word, then went on to say he thought that the public was bored on the Watergate back there. He said Stans is a victim of circumstance. He said — he went on to say, "The White House is not involved."

HAIG: Great.

NIXON: This is a [unclear]. To quote Dean, "The White House is not involved." I've got that, and I'm writing to them. He talked about Colson. Colson expected a lawsuit but, you know, he said that, "well, that has a sobering effect," because it would show their position [unclear]. It's — talked to him about Colson. [unclear] but that was all right. Then the question as to how to deal with Baker, because you see I just — and I don't know. The question was whether Timmons could do it. And I told him that Dean would be available to talk to him, that he'd be number one, so let's [unclear] everything centered in one person. Well, we talked about Gray. He said that — Dean was talking about — he said, well, he's comfortable with his testimony, and so forth — that kind of thing. And I said, "Well, I would be very close to [unclear]." And I told him that I had never seen Gray socially. That I know Hoover much better, and I've not been — President Johnson, who's been more — then we let — went back to Colson. I would have vulnerability for — regarding another area. You and Dean and I [unclear] who he's talking about Colson's various things, but not [unclear] that case. He says he could win the suit but lose the war. This is Dean talking. But he said on the other hand, it'd be a good idea. And then the question of all the lawsuits [unclear]. Fourteen million dollars' worth were brought [unclear] on our side. Seventeen on their side. I said, "Well, all those suits should be settled. We should drop." He said, "I agree totally." So that was that. Then he wondered how the Democrats could borrow money and so forth and not report it. So he said, "McGovern's files were in terrible shape." I said, "Well, let's get that brought out in the hearing." And then he said, "Well, maybe the media can bring it out. Maybe that's something that Colson — told him to go over and make sure you get a word with Kleindienst, because Kleindienst was also talking to the committee about whether we should interrupt the questioning and on whether we should have interrogatories. And Dean said, "The president isn't going to hide any information." He said, "That's the line that we should — that's the truth [unclear] should say." He said, "The hearings are tough," and so forth and so on. "Everyone can still pull their same oar." "Frankly," said he, "they've pulled them." And I said, it was [unclear] he said, "[unclear] pardon. Look, they're going to be that [unclear] they're going to be [unclear]." Then he went — then he said, "Ervin's a puppet for Kennedy."

HAIG: He said that?

NIXON: "The fine hand of Kennedy is in this whole thing. Kennedy's men were on the floor during the debate. Dash is a Kennedy man, which we're trying to document that. That story should [unclear] sometime." This is Dean talking. Then I said, "Johnson believed Bobby bugged him." I did. He said, "Abe Fortas was the guy who was in charge of that sort of thing. He was a big Kennedy man." He told me a [unclear] story where a doctor in the FBI, [unclear] to the FBI — set it up so that a doctor would examine Jenkins and say that he was having brain problems. A brain tumor. The FBI refused to approve the story.

HAIG: No, I hadn't heard the story.

NIXON: Well, Hoover wouldn't play it. I missed a point. Then we got into the '68 bugging. We didn't have any bugging, you know. And then he went into this very interesting thing with regard to this thing: Hoover told Pat Coyne. Pat Coyne told

Nelson Rockefeller. And Nelson Rockefeller told Kissinger that newsmen were bugged — whether by us, or by others, I don't know. Or [unclear] but anyway that's the — that thing came out. But it gives you an idea of the kind of thing we were talking about.

HAIG: Yes, sir. It does.

NIXON: And the grapevine of the bureau is that they did it. Records, however, show no evidence. [unclear] should be fired.

HAIG: Should be fired.

NIXON: [unclear] and I told him that Hoover told me — told Mitchell that I had been bugged [unclear]. [unclear] it's in a memorandum, where the Agnew plane out of Chicago had been bugged. DeLoach was then going to go through Mitchell [unclear]. *Time* magazine [unclear].

HAIG: No.

NIXON: No. Then we talked about getting out the '68 story. Getting out the president's story. Goldwater had been [unclear] Goldwater [unclear]. Then for the first time, we got into Watergate, at that point. He said that the — that they were using probation officers [unclear]. Dean [unclear] in a very flagrant way said [unclear]. And then I said, "Thirty-five-year sentence" — then went into something, "no weapons, and no injuries and so forth. And this is just a very flagrant thing." I said, "For example, if a black held up a store with a gun, he'd get perhaps two years." And Dean kind of — "Yeah, he'd get two years, and he'd get a suspended sentence."

HAIG: That's a [unclear].

NIXON: And then, he said — then he told me these fellows can't even get out on bail. He said the point would come that — then we got into the court. About what [unclear]. And I said, "When is that son of a bitch [U.S. Court of Appeals for the District of Columbia Circuit judge David] Bazelon going to get out of there?" [unclear] See, we tried to get a bill to get Bazelon out so that we can — and he said, "Well, I think he's going to wait us out." And I said, "Well, we've got to get a list — a kind of a list of the best people in the country for judges: Circuit Court, District Court, and Supreme Court. We've got to do that in a hurry."

HAIG: Did he agree?

NIXON: [unclear] on to the Supreme Court. And here's the kind of thing that you would not want [unclear] the press [unclear] out. We talked about a black. Mar — he pointed out that [Thurgood] Marshall was in bad health. I said, "Well, I didn't know whether that was confirmed or not." And I said, "In my view," I said, "if there's a good fellow, a black — who's that fellow, Brown, who's the head of the Equal Economic Opportunity." But I said, "Maybe [Deputy Solicitor General] Jewel Lafontant is the best." I said, "There you kill two birds with one stone. You've got a black and a woman." And he said, "Brilliant. She's great. She'd be fine." Right. [unclear] but that's the kind of talk we had.

HAIG: Yeah, but [unclear] you can't make it public.

NIXON: Well, we can't — but he might.

HAIG: [unclear]

NIXON: But I — is that going to be bad? What the hell difference does that make? That is irrelevant to this whole investigation. And I said, "The people in the Senate can't possibly vote against Jewel." He says, "Absolutely." [unclear] I told him to talk to Kleindienst about this whole problem [unclear]. He sympathized. I said, "How would you like Teddy Kennedy to propose the judges?" [unclear] I said, "I want you to know that appointments are not going to go on the basis of — they're saying that you need a Jewish seat." And I said, "Now look, there's no Jewish seat on that court." I said, "There are Jews all around this White House." I said, "You've got Arthur Burns. You've got Henry Kissinger. You've got [unclear]." And I said, "What we have to do, we've got to re — realize we've got to appoint some [unclear]. They may not be quite up to what we think is the standard, but we've got to get them and pull them up." I said, "That's the way our system works." I said, "Republicans are worse than the Democrats in this respect, because they're snobbish. And here's Nixon telling him, 'We've got to spread the base. And [unclear].'"

HAIG: [unclear] absolutely. [unclear]

NIXON: [unclear]

HAIG: [unclear] but there isn't any difference.

NIXON: No, but I mean, I'm trying to point out now that in this [unclear] you — you'll know the damn truth [unclear] reference to Watergate [unclear]. That may be something that's a plus. But goddamn it, my recollection is correct. Now we go into Sullivan. He said he watched him work with Huston. "He's a good man, reliable, et cetera." He said Felt was known as the "white rat" at the FBI. And the question, I think he raised, is — is he Jewish? And Dean said, "He could be." [unclear] I said, "We have that here at the White House." So he says, "Huh?"

HAIG: [laughs] Exactly right.

NIXON: And Dean says, "Well, there will never be a leak from me, because I don't know how to leak. I couldn't possibly leak." The question that we got people in jail. I said, "I feel for these guys in jail, particularly for Hunt. His wife has been killed, and so forth." Dean said, "Well, they're all hanging in tough." I said, "What are they doing, looking for clemency?" He said, "Yes." And I said, "We couldn't do it." [unclear] said, "Well, maybe it will get so absurd, so political, and so forth, that we could do something later on." And it was dropped. That was the only talk about clemency, and my remark was "[unclear] clemency, and let's keep it clean." Then we got into this disruption of — by the Democrats. And he pointed out that McGovern had Dick Tuck on his payroll. He tried to do a couple of [unclear] didn't come off. And then I said, "What the hell did Segretti do?" And Dean says, "He did some funny things, but nothing really serious." And he said, "We could keep — " and he said, "Chapin is not involved, except tangentially." He said, "They're going after Herb Kalmbach with a vengeance. But," he said, "Herb is a strong man who makes — has a logical explanation for everything." And I said, "Look, they are going to bring in his representation of the president at San Clemente, my private [unclear]. Nobody's asking for that."

But the important thing to note here is not about Kalmbach afterward, but before. You see, Kalmbach raised money before, because I have said—but the thing that concerns me is that—the fact that I read this in some [unclear] the money was sent through a bank in Mexico—or through Mexico. [unclear] Watergate thing. And Dean said, "That can all be explained." But he didn't mention the fact that [unclear] and so forth, up to this point, that afterwards Kalmbach raised money, which is the point that I—he even indicated [unclear] to put that in a box.

HAIG: Yes, sir.

NIXON: It's not—I said, "Get Baker—what we ought to do is get Baker and the others to come out to run this hearing like a court. No hearsay." He said, "Excellent idea. Make it a model of [unclear]." [unclear] and Dean said, talking about the past—he says, "Well, I—it's been a long way, but I'm convinced that [unclear] but I'm convinced we're going to make it." That could be an implication that we—that—just, no [unclear] he didn't even suggest cover-up. We talked about the hearings, and I—and they are just—and I said, "John, you [unclear] that the president has told the truth." And Dean emphatically said, "I know. I know." I said, "When I heard about this, I thought they were all crazy. I thought they were nuts." He said, "I know." Then he said at one point, "You know, they don't—they'll be after Colson and Ehrlichman—Haldeman and Ehrlichman. They might even be after Dean." This is—at that point, I said, "No, they can't be after you—why?" That was all. On the first, the next day, the question was whether Kleindienst would [unclear] Baker [unclear]. Gray, Dean said, had given a story in his testimony that he wanted so terribly to be confirmed. And when he said records would be available to any senator—FBI records. Then I went into the business about the Hiss case, how they wouldn't even let us have anything, let alone records—raw files is what he meant. Then Dean emphatically says, "I never gave the FBI records to Segretti. I never showed him an FBI record." And I said, "Yes, John." I said, "You were conducting an investigation for the White House." He said, "That's right. And I was entitled to sit in those investigations." [unclear] talked about Gray and I said, "It looks to me like he's going to be done. He's trying to pamper the senators." "That's right," Dean says. "He's bullheaded." Then I said to him, "We've got to just show you the kind of colorful language, [unclear] that we—about how this FBI thing—hell, it's the worst [unclear]. The FBI cannot turn raw files over to the Senate or anywhere else!" Then I asked him for a memorandum with regard to how the Democrats had used the FBI. One little thing—the [FBI investigation of journalist] Dan Schorr [unclear]. And I said, "We all know about that." I said, "Let's understand." But there was no bugging involved. That was simply—a study had been made [unclear]. But as you know, that was one where [unclear]. Dan Schorr—we never intended to hire him, and he knew it, and everybody else knew it. What happened was we just asked for a name check on the son of a bitch, due to the fact that he was [unclear]. It was a national security matter. But that's an old story, and it isn't much really. We have been so kind, and so good—as using the FBI is concerned compared with previous administrations. We then talked about DeLoach. DeLoach had had lunch after seeing Kleindienst. And he said, Klein — DeLoach said, "There had been no bugging under President Kennedy, they say," and I told Gray — and then I told Dean that I had told Gray when he came in — when I said the same thing about the [unclear] and I urged him to give all the FBI people lie detector tests. And then Dean said, "Yes, but that should be after the hearings." And I said, "I agree. But the goddamn place has got to be cleaned out. You got to have this be believed [unclear]. And I'd also tell DeLoach that we have other evidence." [unclear] and I also came to him to tell Kendall that so that DeLoach would be put on notice that we have had some information on that [unclear]. I never trusted DeLoach, myself, because he's a politician [unclear]. I pointed out [unclear] the difficulty with all [unclear] FBI [unclear] the bureau can't survive [unclear] came back with us then about sitting in on the investigation [unclear]. Then Gray bitched about his sitting in on the investigation. Said, "John, nobody ever sat in on an FBI investigation before." Dean insisted because he was conducting an investigation for the president. [unclear] no question about it. Commented on Gray, and I said, "The trouble with Gray — he has outward self-confidence but not inward self-confidence." And I gave an analogy [unclear]. Dean said, "Well, then Gray will be okay." I said, "Well, what we have to do is to clean out the FBI like Schlesinger was doing with the CIA. We've got to get the dead wood out," or words to that — then we talked about Gray's investigation of Watergate. That he was proud of his investigation, and Dean said, "Though he caused us some grief." What he meant by that I don't know. Then I recounted to him that I had talked to Gray once. [unclear] "Yes, I've heard about that." He said, "The difficulty with Gray is that he was around the country making speeches rather than sitting on top of the investigation." A little finger comes in there. What Dean was trying to do was to get Gray — not — get my point?

HAIG: Yeah.

NIXON: [unclear] and I gave him a copy of my book *Six Crises* to read the chapter on Hiss. That's two days of it.

HAIG: [unclear]

NIXON: All day tomorrow. You never know when another of these conversations — but, you know, I ordered it! Christ, you know, you pick up the paper and it says, "Dean says that the president" — this, now these are — but this is an hour, almost — an hour and forty-five minutes of conversation, Al.

HAIG: And they're the ones that really think there's been anything. They wanted their man.

NIXON: I don't know. You mean at the beginning? [unclear]

HAIG: [unclear] I got to tell Steve to get the telephone. If you have a call — so that we're sure he didn't have someone there. [unclear] well, this is a good thing to do.

NIXON: I know.

HAIG: [unclear].

NIXON: Yeah.

HAIG: [unclear] do you have a question?

NIXON: Well, they put out the [unclear]. They had McCloskey [unclear] too, and then they put out [unclear]. I hope the fellows on the Hill are not panicking because of that thing [unclear] over the weekend.

HAIG: I don't have any signs of panic this morning. That's why I'll tell you — we're over the hump. Hell, if this had been three weeks ago you'd be in — our phones would be buzzing every minute.

NIXON: Would they?

HAIG: Yes, sir. But, the — our — we're getting close to the time when we won't really want it dismantled. We're not there yet. Hell, we're getting close to it.

NIXON: Yeah. Well, I ought to go through this crap.

HAIG: [unclear]

NIXON: Here, first of all, he's demolished in the sense that from the first of January he has not —

HAIG: [unclear]

NIXON: Now, this is through February. Well, I've got one other half-hour — I don't know what the hell is on it.

HAIG: You see it's so good because nobody in Congress likes him. You know — you don't know whether he —

NIXON: Goddamn it, how?

HAIG: Some kind of remark that the son of a bitch could twist out of context. [unclear] no [unclear] no general with —

NIXON: What?

HAIG: The worst trouble he could do, even if he's reasonably accurate — now, if he's going into a full-fledged perjury job of the greatest magnitude, then we can take the son of a bitch on.

NIXON: That's right. Well, as I told you, we do know we have one problem: it's that damn conversation of March 21 due to the fact that [unclear]. But I think we can handle that.

HAIG: I think we can. That's — yeah, we can handle it.

NIXON: Bob — he'll get up there and say that — Bob will say, "I was there. The president said — "

HAIG: That's exactly right.

NIXON: So, we'll see what else is in the goddamn —

HAIG: [unclear] for your own — really your own peace of mind. You —

NIXON: Yeah.

HAIG: You just can't recall [unclear].

NIXON: As you know, we're up against ruthless people.

HAIG: Well, we're going to be in great shape now, because we're going to prepare. [unclear] really put the screws on him for that. That guy left here at one o'clock last night. Worked on them at home. Started again this morning. Got Buzhardt in on it [unclear] what the hell's he doing.

NIXON: You taking this issue here — now take clemency, that's well handled, isn't it?

HAIG: Textbook.

NIXON: Yeah. And it's well handled in that March 21 thing. I put it in the context of that, I said you couldn't even consider clemency — clemency until after the '74 election — is the way I put it. But, what the hell? In two years — bastards are in jail that long. I said I didn't — can't even consider it.

HAIG: Yeah, you see, it probably wouldn't hurt — I mean, it's conceivable now when we get working with Buzhardt you go down the line here. It may be that [unclear]. Well, that's — you know, that's the judgment I wouldn't make now —

NIXON: I won't. It's very important [unclear]. However, not even Buzhardt knows.

HAIG: Well, you know, Buzhardt knows this because you told him, in your office. [unclear] but he knew it also because when you were checking on wiretaps, on the Johnson years — with the Secret Service, it came out. Those bellyaches who'd been handling it for Johnson, as a matter of fact — so he knows it. But, I tell you, he's the only one who knows.

NIXON: All right. No further. He shouldn't tell anyone. I'd rather — I don't want it put out that somebody is — been saying they're going to get the president's records and it's got —

HAIG: Oh.

NIXON: Let's just assume we goofed. If you get back to Buzhardt you tell him you had national security stuff.

HAIG: That's right. That's right.

NIXON: This is hard work.

HAIG: Yes.

NIXON: But I've got to do it. Got to do it. And it's best for me to do it, too.

HAIG: Only you. Only you.

NIXON: Thank you a lot, Al. Oh, what about Buzhardt's stuff? [unclear]

HAIG: [unclear]

NIXON: Al, we can put out the story to the effect that he has [unclear] that he has [unclear], chronologies, telephone recordings, and all that sort of thing.

HAIG: Why do you honestly — ?

NIXON: I wonder if that's Hunt.

HAIG: That's [unclear].

. . .

NIXON: [Speaks into telephone.] Hello? Hi. Fine. Yeah. Great. Great. Marvelous. Great accomplishment. I've just spent nine hours on this crap. I've got to go to bed. The whole damn meetings are a fraud [unclear]. I didn't realize it, but it was a damn fraud. Yeah. They didn't find it in the files but I've listened to stuff, and you know, looking back I can see where he may have been involved. I wasn't involved. Yeah. Well, I've listened to stuff [unclear] and I missed more telephone calls. One from — two from Camp David — two from Florida we don't have recorded. But they can't be that important. Well, that should be answered. Yeah. That's right. But, no, no, no, no — this is — tell me how the Laird thing went, Al. Where'd you see him? Great. [unclear] You be there, too. You've got to be there. [unclear] The main thing is to announce you're going to be with us. He had a tremendous night. Marvelous. Great. Tell him he's [unclear] with us. Everybody's — great, great, great. How's he feel about it? Is he in good spirits? [unclear] After our [unclear] yesterday [unclear]. That's going to shatter Dean. Right. Right. Al, you've done a great job, believe me. Getting Mel to [unclear]. You'll get a hell of a load off me if you get Mel, Bryce [Harlow] — the three of you will be — you'll run the shop. You're the chief of staff. [unclear] the other guys go out [unclear] you know, kiss the ass of a few — but you don't have to [unclear]. Don't you think so? Bryce feel pleased? I'll see you [unclear]. Yeah. I don't [unclear]. [unclear] indicates that he's going to leave and still consult with us on energy. You must say that. [unclear] must not. Just say that I — he's leaving but it must not because he — you can say, "Look, John, we've got to have you on salary for something much bigger later." Good. [unclear] just deny that fact [unclear]. He's — but that's his problem. Goddamn [unclear] problem. Tell him that I think that his staying [unclear] very important because [unclear]. [unclear] back to Harvard, he's not going — I'm sorry about [unclear]. I knew he was out — would be out of sorts, but he just takes more time than I can give him right now. The main point is that he is the man [unclear] job [unclear]. But the main thing is that I don't want him to travel abroad. [unclear] as my representative. Now Henry doesn't want that. There's no problem about conflict of interest and all that crap. He can travel abroad, you know [unclear]. He's afraid I wouldn't be close enough to Mel. Good God, I would bring Mel abroad. What is it? He's concerned about Mel coming at all? Right. Yeah, well — he knows damn well [unclear]. Absolutely. Absolutely. That's great, Al. We have an eight thirty meeting? Right, well, I tell you I've been through the damnedest experience today. Eight hours of listening to the damn tapes and telephone calls. We don't have some — I made two through Key Biscayne, on the twenty-third, and I made two from Camp — one from Camp David. We don't have them. [unclear] but I tell you, there's nothing in, nothing in these calls. It could. It could. It could on the twenty-third, perhaps, after we talked on the twenty-first, but after that I was investigating. That's right. But, my God! You know, we've really gone through — yeah, and Buzhardt, too, though he [unclear]. Isn't that great? [unclear], huh! Okay, we've got Richardson confirmed so he said Petersen could. Okay. Fine. See you tomorrow eight thirty. [Hangs up phone.]

BULL: Those two outstanding days, sir — the fourteenth between Moore, and — there were four of us sitting in. Then again on the twentieth Ziegler and I were in here [unclear].

NIXON: Get the best reports you can get.

BULL: Yes, sir. Yes, certainly will.

NIXON: These telephone calls — you just don't have [unclear]. You sure you don't?

BULL: We don't have them unfortunately, sir.

NIXON: Just don't have them, right? How long did I do this today?

BULL: I bet you did this about nine, an average — had to be about nine hours, maybe more, sir.

NIXON: No, no. Not that much. Maybe eight [point] five — maybe six.

BULL: I haven't totaled it all up but you've gone through many meetings — all these telephone calls.

"I put the earphones on, you see."
June 4, 1973, 10:05 p.m.
Richard Nixon and Bob Haldeman
WHITE HOUSE TELEPHONE

Now more than a month since Bob Haldeman left the White House, his departure caused more than simply a staff reshuffle. Nixon realized just how much he depended on him, especially since no one else kept such detailed notes of Oval Office meetings or conversations. Haldeman kept a dictated diary and detailed notes on yellow pads, and he rode herd over the paper mill that flowed in and out of the Oval Office each day. Nixon's notes were, in essence, recorded on his tapes, which is why he had no choice but to dive deep into them to reconstruct his memory and his schedule. Even then, he still asked Haldeman to remind him of when certain meetings and events occurred.

• • •

NIXON: Hello? Have you got a minute?

HALDEMAN: Sure.

NIXON: I thought you should know that starting at nine thirty this morning, I have been working until just now. I listened to every tape.

HALDEMAN: Good Lord!

NIXON: You know, the thing that you did and boy I know the agony that you went through. I put the earphones on, you see.

HALDEMAN: Did you? That's the way to do it.

NIXON: And I listened to every damn thing, and Bob, this son of a bitch [John Dean] is bluffing.

HALDEMAN: Well, sure.

NIXON: Also, we sent Buzhardt over this — and this is just for your private information.

HALDEMAN: Yeah.

NIXON: He went through the files and not a goddamn memcon in the files.

HALDEMAN: Really?

NIXON: None. Period. He didn't make any.

HALDEMAN: I didn't see how there could be any that would matter because you do not have anything unless he made 'em up.

NIXON: Yeah. Well, he could make memcons of conversations, you see, but he didn't have those either.

HALDEMAN: Yeah.

NIXON: Unless he took them out.

HALDEMAN: I'll be darned.

NIXON: And we don't think so. The other thing is that throughout this thing you should be interested to note, he doesn't mention the three fifty until the twenty-first —

HALDEMAN: I didn't think so.

NIXON: — and he didn't mention Ehrlichman's deal with Kalmbach till the twenty-first.

HALDEMAN: I didn't think so. I thought —

NIXON: And also —

HALDEMAN: — that came through on the twenty-first. [unclear]

NIXON: And also — that was new — and also, he did mention the Krogh thing on about the seventeenth.

HALDEMAN: Oh, really.

NIXON: Yeah, but that's all right. You know he mentioned that —

HALDEMAN: Yeah.

NIXON: — that was there and so forth, but only in passing as if it weren't a big thing or so forth.

HALDEMAN: Well, he must have mentioned that at some earlier point, the doctor's office break-in.

NIXON: That's what I mean.

HALDEMAN: Yeah. Because it became sort of apparent in the — at the later point that he hadn't mentioned that earlier.

NIXON: Yeah. But that's it. I thought you should also know that —

HALDEMAN: Boy, that's great.

NIXON: — he said throughout this conversation that "nobody in the White House is involved." He said that —

HALDEMAN: Yeah.

NIXON: — "Ehrlichman isn't, Haldeman isn't," you know he kept — he said that on at least four occasions in this thing.

HALDEMAN: Yeah.

NIXON: I hit him straight on, you know, at that point.

HALDEMAN: Yeah.

NIXON: He said, "Nope, they're not."

HALDEMAN: Well, that's what he —

NIXON: The only —

HALDEMAN: — told me all along.

NIXON: The only thing that he has in there, which he did hit about the seventeenth, or maybe the fourteenth, was that Strachan might be —

HALDEMAN: Yeah.

NIXON: — involved in terms of getting material.

HALDEMAN: Yep.

NIXON: Only that.

HALDEMAN: Yep.

NIXON: But you know, what the hell was that — what the hell to make out of that? I didn't know what — that was true or not.

HALDEMAN: And that was a might. And there's still doubt about that.

NIXON: Mm-hmm.

HALDEMAN: Well, there still is.

NIXON: That's only his — he didn't indicate that Strachan knew about it in advance.

HALDEMAN: Right.

NIXON: He only indicated that he had some, as he put it, the fruits of the investigation.

HALDEMAN: Well, there's a question about that.

NIXON: But, and be that as it may, I want you to be sure to tell John.

HALDEMAN: Well, that's gre —

NIXON: Both you and he — he just throughout until the twenty-first, didn't say one damn word that — indicated that either of — he mentioned that Ehrlichman's involved with something about the Chappaquiddick thing. And I, and there's nothing wrong with that.

HALDEMAN: Mm-hmm.

NIXON: You know the Chappaquiddick thing?

HALDEMAN: Well, that was with that Tony or something, huh?

NIXON: Huh?

HALDEMAN: With that guy Tony?

NIXON: Yeah.

HALDEMAN: Yeah.

NIXON: And so what the hell is that, that we — that an investigation was conducted? He says that's a problem for Ehrlichman, he said. That's a problem.

HALDEMAN: Those are all, what he's talking about there, are —

NIXON: Have nothing to do with Watergate.

HALDEMAN: Political embarrassment or public embarrassment, but not problems of any legal —

NIXON: Nope. Nope.

HALDEMAN: — culpability.

NIXON: But, I thought you'd be interested, pleased to know, that I went through this agony for eight hours, nine hours today. I did nothing else. Just damn near broke me down. But you know how tough it is to listen to that stuff.

HALDEMAN: Oh, it is. It's nerve-racking and then, of course, I was trying to make notes, which, and you probably were too.

NIXON: I made notes all the way through.

HALDEMAN: It makes it even worse.

NIXON: The only thing I missed, that I hope you will do — I did not make — I did not pick the twenty-first conversation because I figured you ought to be the witness on that.

HALDEMAN: Yeah.

NIXON: I did not make notes on the twenty-second conversation, figuring that you, Ehrlichman, and — were there, you know —

HALDEMAN: Yeah.

NIXON: — and that you would make notes on that.

HALDEMAN: Yeah.

NIXON: So, you'll have to cover that if you will, and, and give us — give me a little, you know, just for my own information, what the hell he said on those occasions. Twen — you got it? On the twenty-second. And the telephone calls from Key Biscayne I don't have because they don't have those recorded. I called him twice from Key Biscayne and —

HALDEMAN: Yeah. But, that —

NIXON: But I think it was about McCord, but I don't know.

HALDEMAN: I think it probably was because — or it could have been on a lot of other que — sort of question things. But they were all on — they weren't on this subject at all.

NIXON: It could have been about Bittman. You know, I could have mentioned that to him.

HALDEMAN: That's possible, yeah.

NIXON: And — but, suppose we did. You know, I said, "Well, listen, I understand Bittman's taken care of or something." That's a question of evidence, right?

HALDEMAN: Yeah, but that isn't likely. I can't imagine that you would have —

NIXON: I might have — no, I might have mentioned that because I was concerned about it you know. About whether Bittman had —

HALDEMAN: Yeah.

NIXON: — was gonna blow. Not because of Watergate, because he was going to blow on —

HALDEMAN: On the other project.

NIXON: Yes, that's right. But except for those two conversations from Key Biscayne on the twenty-third, I've got it all now, and there ain't nothing there, believe me.

HALDEMAN: Well —

NIXON: As far as — basically, if you'd be interested to know, on the twenty-seventh, the twenty-eighth, which I have the first and all the other conversations we had, Bob, they were about, every, usually, about executive privilege, Gray —

HALDEMAN: Yeah.

NIXON: — getting Sullivan to get us some dope on the bugging.

HALDEMAN: Yeah.

NIXON: Things of that sort.

HALDEMAN: Yeah.

NIXON: But there's not a goddamn — he didn't ever mention the cover-up. Never.

HALDEMAN: Well, I didn't think so, and on the basis of the twenty-first, you have to assume that he hadn't because, as I told you, it was so clear that this was new stuff.

NIXON: Yeah.

HALDEMAN: That — I didn't see how he could have mentioned it earlier.

NIXON: I'm going to have Moore make memos with regard to what he talked to him about on the twentieth. I don't know what the hell he did talk to him about, but I had a conversation with him on the twentieth that had nothing to do with all this.

HALDEMAN: Did you listen to those too?

NIXON: Hell yes.

HALDEMAN: Good Lord.

NIXON: I mentioned it so — I listened to everything there was, that we had available. But the stuff in the EOB doesn't come through. So I haven't got that pretty well [unclear].

HALDEMAN: Oh, really.

NIXON: No.

HALDEMAN: It doesn't —

NIXON: No.

HALDEMAN: — pick up.

NIXON: It's not clear. But, nevertheless, the point is that those conversations are always ones where you or John are both — were present, see.

HALDEMAN: Yeah.

NIXON: So you're the witnesses on that.

HALDEMAN: Well, there were only a couple of them.

NIXON: Yeah, well, the Mitchell one and another one, apparently there was one — I didn't realize this, on the afternoon of the twenty-first. Did you — ?

HALDEMAN: That's right.

NIXON: What the hell was that all about?

HALDEMAN: At five thirty, that was the one afterwards that he said bring — pull the wagons up around the White House.

NIXON: Yeah.

HALDEMAN: It was —

NIXON: Did he mention all this Bittman stuff?

HALDEMAN: No, uh-uh.

NIXON: Mm-hmm.

HALDEMAN: Not at all. Not at all.

NIXON: Shows you maybe whe — the Bittman thing is something that concerns us more than him.

HALDEMAN: Yep.

NIXON: Mm-hmm. But the point is that this whole jazz, to the effect that, or — from January throughout we had thirty-five meetings and telephone calls in which it — we discussed the cover-up, Bob, is totally false.

HALDEMAN: Well, that's, I know that.

NIXON: Totally false.

HALDEMAN: And I was sure of that from going through the log yesterday.

NIXON: And I wasn't sure, you know, until I heard it.

HALDEMAN: Even — and then it just — it's awfully good that you did. All right, what're you going to do with that now, other than know it?

NIXON: Well.

HALDEMAN: Can't do anything.

NIXON: I can't do a thing except —

HALDEMAN: Except that you [unclear].

NIXON: — reassure our own people and to know that we know what the hell the facts are.

HALDEMAN: Yeah.

NIXON: And we're going to let him go out his string a little further now. You know what I mean?

HALDEMAN: Yeah, right.

NIXON: Let's see what he does. I — don't you agree? Or do you?

HALDEMAN: Sure, sure. Because that — see, that just discredits him all the more.

NIXON: Yeah.

HALDEMAN: And you get that story out of the thirty-five meetings to — on the cover-up, that is just clearly not true. And if it's —

NIXON: The only possibility is that he —

HALDEMAN: You can prove it.

NIXON: He might have a telephone call from Key Biscayne on the twenty-third. That's the only thing I can figure.

HALDEMAN: That, that's after the investigation and —

NIXON: Mm-hmm.

HALDEMAN: — when you're into it, you're about to pull him off of it or you know, you've got him going on. I can —

NIXON: But you were talking to him then. Weren't you, Bob?

HALDEMAN: Darn right.

NIXON: What the hell was he talking about on the twenty-third?

HALDEMAN: I've got a lot of details on that.

NIXON: What'd he talk about?

HALDEMAN: Oh, all kinds of stuff. The McCord thing, and his — you know, just trying to sort it all out.

NIXON: Did he go into the Bittman thing with you on those — on that occasion?

HALDEMAN: No. Uh-uh. No, it never came up again.

NIXON: Mm-hmm.

HALDEMAN: Except, you know, as a later — he referred to it as one of the examples of blackmail. That was on the twenty-sixth. He gave me a long spell-out on the twenty-sixth of a lot of his theories on things, which was after he'd been up there for a while and it was clear then.

NIXON: If you could give me, for my own private information, just your own — just send it to me, you know "eyes only," of your recollections of the twenty-second and the afternoon of the twenty-first, it would be helpful.

HALDEMAN: All right. There isn't very much, but I can.

NIXON: Huh?

HALDEMAN: There's not much. I can't —

NIXON: Just your recollection of what the hell it was.

HALDEMAN: Okay.

NIXON: Anything that's really relevant to all this thing.

HALDEMAN: Okay.

NIXON: But you and John should be pleased to know that there wasn't any god — there wasn't a damn thing except for the Strachan thing. He mentioned that. He did mention that on the thirteenth or fourteenth.

HALDEMAN: Mm-hmm.

NIXON: About Strachan, he said was, you know, "possibly vulnerable," as he put it.

HALDEMAN: Yeah.

NIXON: And that might make you possibly vuln — and I said, "John, does that mean Haldeman knows?" He said, "No." You know.

HALDEMAN: Yeah.

NIXON: Flat-out.

HALDEMAN: Yeah.

NIXON: In fact, through the twenty-first, he said you were not — you and John were not involved except in this tangential way, you know — John on this basis. As a matter of fact, the whole thing is — one that shows that the fellow was not, if anything, leveling with us about what the hell —

HALDEMAN: That's a point.

NIXON: I mean, except he's — let's — that he did mention the break-in on the seventeenth. He mentioned that. But that's when I first heard of it, and I jumped out of the chair, virtually, and said, "What the hell is that all about?" That's the first time I heard about the break-in, you know.

HALDEMAN: What do you mean, the doc — the psychiatrist?

NIXON: Yes.

HALDEMAN: Yeah.

NIXON: But, that's all right. We covered that in our statement. I didn't say twenty-first. I said in March I learned about it. See?

HALDEMAN: Yeah.

NIXON: Okay.

HALDEMAN: Well, that's very interesting. I see your friend Cox is all excited now that he's —

NIXON: What, what's he saying now?

HALDEMAN: [unclear]

NIXON: I heard that he's taking on Ervin.

HALDEMAN: Well, he took on Ervin on the — he had a press conference and called on Ervin to hold up for ninety days.

NIXON: Mm-hmm.

HALDEMAN: And Ervin and all the other senators told him to go to hell.

NIXON: Mm-hmm.

HALDEMAN: But they also — apparently the White House was asked if you had a log that showed whether you had these meetings with Dean and they said that that would not be put out. You know, that's —

NIXON: Well.

HALDEMAN: — president's papers or something. And the — Cox leaked out and said that he would of course get those papers. He'd been promised access to all papers and that he would expect to have access to all papers and there would be no —

NIXON: We've got to stand firm on that. Don't you think?

HALDEMAN: So — I think so, except —

NIXON: We could put the log out.

HALDEMAN: Yeah, I'm not sure you'd have to. Well, I don't know though.

NIXON: I don't want to put these pap — I don't want to put the papers out though, basically because there's, you know, there's some very frank talk in there about what I think of the Supreme Court and a hell of a lot of other things. I don't want it out.

HALDEMAN: Oh, yeah. You can't do that.

NIXON: What would you do?

HALDEMAN: Well, it seems to me that — well, of course they did see — they say they won't release the log. I don't think you do want to release your log, because that releases your private meetings and all that. I think what they've done is right, which is they said they confirmed that you had met with Dean —

NIXON: Mm-hmm.

HALDEMAN: — a number of times during the —

NIXON: That's right.

HALDEMAN: — this period. Let's see, one of the things Dean makes the point is, you know, that the meeting started January 1 —

NIXON: [unclear]

HALDEMAN: — which is significant in that they didn't start till February 27.

NIXON: Mm-hmm.

HALDEMAN: And —

NIXON: Might put that out, huh?

HALDEMAN: I just wonder if maybe it shouldn't be better characterized that there were a series of meetings starting on the twenty-seventh, regarding executive privilege and —

NIXON: Right.

HALDEMAN: — the questions of dealing with the Senate hearings and [unclear] —

NIXON: And no cover-up was ever discussed.

HALDEMAN: — relating to your press conferences. And there was absolutely no discussion of cover-up.

NIXON: That's right.

HALDEMAN: At any time.

NIXON: Right.

HALDEMAN: In any of those until — I think you could say until the meeting of the twenty-first, because you said in your —

NIXON: Yeah.

HALDEMAN: — first speech that on the twenty-first you received new information.

NIXON: I wondered if you would mind giving Ron a call and telling him that. Would you mind doing that?

HALDEMAN: Okay.

NIXON: Fine, fine. But I, boy, if I never had a harder day in my life, you know, I've —

HALDEMAN: [laughs]

NIXON: You could do it, a younger guy. But I can see how — that you went through the agony on that twenty-first thing. Jesus, listening to this crap is unbelievably tough. But it was worth it. And as I said, Buzhardt spent the whole day in his [Dean's] files, just for your information. Didn't find one single damn memcon.

HALDEMAN: Mm-hmm.

NIXON: Unless he's taken them out.

HALDEMAN: Well, he may have.

NIXON: And Buzhardt thinks he doesn't think he made any because he checked other things that he's worked on. He has no memcons on that.

HALDEMAN: Yeah. Well, I didn't think he did.

NIXON: Yeah.

HALDEMAN: [I] told you; he says he made a chronology at the end of each day.

NIXON: Ah —

HALDEMAN: But I think that's a lot of BS, just like all the rest of that —

NIXON: He didn't find it. I mean, they didn't find any chronology in there.

HALDEMAN: And if he did, there wouldn't be anything in it.

NIXON: I —

HALDEMAN: So, you know — I, what difference does it make if he does — did? In fact it disserves his purpose to say he did make one, because it would —

NIXON: Yeah.

HALDEMAN: — disprove his point.

NIXON: Some way or other I think his lawyer is the one that's moving —

HALDEMAN: [unclear]

NIXON: — out here. I don't think Dean, strangely enough, is —

HALDEMAN: I think you're right.

NIXON: I think his lawyer is out really sla — I mean making flamboyant charges and so forth and they won't stand up.

HALDEMAN: Yep.

NIXON: But let's let him get out on a little limb, a little bit more.

HALDEMAN: Yep.

NIXON: If you would call Ziegler on this other point and say we ought to get that out, would you?

HALDEMAN: Okay.

NIXON: Thanks, Bob.

HALDEMAN: Yes, sir.

A Beijing invitation

June 4, 1973, 11:16 p.m.
Richard Nixon and Henry Kissinger
WHITE HOUSE TELEPHONE

Even as Watergate rained down around Nixon, he still had moments in which to muse about international affairs. In fact, it was as he was listening to his tapes that afternoon that the Chinese liaison officer in Washington, Huang Zhen, passed a personal invitation for Nixon to visit Beijing from Chairman Mao to Kissinger. The president was tantalized by the idea of having a replay of his February 1972 visit to China, "the week that changed the world." But Nixon's domestic political situation was worlds different by this time. He would eventually make a follow-up visit to China, but it would not be until he was a former president.

• • •

NIXON: With regard to Mao['s invitation for Nixon to visit China again], you know, that is quite significant, don't you think?

KISSINGER: Oh, I think that's of enormous significance, Mr. President.

NIXON: The other thing I was going to say, though, that —

KISSINGER: Because it means that they think that they are going to deal with you for the foreseeable future.

NIXON: Right. The other thing is do you think that we should get in — well, we can't do it before you leave — but if you could get a message to the ambassador here that we think it's very important for Zhou Enlai to come to the UN. Or do you want to wait till August to do that?

KISSINGER: I've already done that, Mr. President.

NIXON: You have?

KISSINGER: I did that —

NIXON: You see —

KISSINGER: I took the liberty of doing that in response —

NIXON: You see, it's going to look rather strange if I go running to China if he doesn't come here.

KISSINGER: No, I've already done that.

NIXON: How'd you do it?

KISSINGER: I had already extended an invitation at your suggestion a few months ago.

NIXON: Yeah, I know, but recently?

KISSINGER: I repeated it and I said we can do it in one of two ways: either go to the UN, or better yet just come to Washington on a personal visit.

NIXON: No, what he should do is come to the UN and then drop down here and we'll give him a nice dinner, you know, without the head of state thing, but it will be everything except the drill.

KISSINGER: Right. Well, I told him we could handle it either way. And —

NIXON: And he's going to forward that to them, huh?

KISSINGER: And he said — well, he didn't turn it down. You know, in the past they said they could never do it as long as the ROC was —

NIXON: Yeah, I know. I know. Yeah.

KISSINGER: He said, well, he's very busy and he'll look at his calendar.

NIXON: Well, in view of the Mao thing, you see, the Mao thing has to be significant, because if it came from Zhou Enlai that would be one thing, but coming from Mao —

KISSINGER: It came from both. It was a joint invitation.

NIXON: Right.

KISSINGER: And I don't know whether you noticed, Mr. President, when he came that he said to you, "Mr. and Mrs. Mao."

NIXON: Yeah! Yeah, I know.

KISSINGER: Well, that was very significant considering her role in the Cultural Revolution.

NIXON: Yeah, and as a member of the Central Committee.

KISSINGER: Yes, and of the Politburo.

NIXON: Politburo, I meant. Yeah. Yeah.

KISSINGER: So I thought it was an extremely significant event.

NIXON: Yeah.

KISSINGER: And also that they answered you within three days. I mean, you only saw him last Wednesday.

NIXON: Right. Right.

KISSINGER: And they also gave us a rather good message on Cambodia.

NIXON: Oh, did they?

KISSINGER: Yes, but we mustn't refer to that in any sense.

NIXON: Oh, no, no, no. Because they can't get caught at it, I know.

"Mr. Hoover, like many strong men, left no one to run it."

June 6, 1973, 10:05 a.m.
Richard Nixon and Clarence Kelley
OVAL OFFICE

With the withdrawal of Pat Gray's name midway through the confirmation process, the FBI had lacked a permanent director for more than a year following J. Edgar Hoover's death on May 2, 1972, after forty-eight years at the helm. Gray's chances for nomination were fatally flawed; he was considered too close to Nixon, and his conduct during the FBI's Watergate investigation had come under question. Gray resigned from the FBI on April 27, leaving William Ruckelshaus as acting director until a permanent director could be found.

Nixon needed a new candidate. Clarence Kelley, sixty-one, was the police chief of Kansas City. His nonpolitical background and extensive law enforcement experience helped even Nixon's greatest critics breathe a sigh of relief that the FBI could soon get back to normal. "*This agency is so much on the ropes at the present,*" *a Justice Department official said. "They will be happy with most anybody.*"*

. . .

NIXON: Well, as you are, of course, probably aware, I would like to nominate you as director of the bureau.

KELLEY: Thank you, sir.

NIXON: I would like to say that in doing so we have considered twenty-seven people seriously, of course there have been a hundred people's names suggested. After looking it all over, I think you are the man for a variety of reasons. One, you were with the bureau. Secondly, fortunately you also have a law degree — not that that should mean anything. There are so many flipping lawyers that that is probably a liability rather than an asset. Third, and this is news that impressed me, you have a distinguished record in the law enforcement field. You are strong and tough and yet "progressive." I use that word in quotes, not progressive like [unclear]. The other thing about you that is very important is that, by all accounts, that you are a serious administrator. We have to talk very candidly about the bureau. You know, Mr. Hoover, like many strong men, left no one to run it. Clyde Tolson might have, but Tolson was [unclear]. That's why these taps — Hoover took perfectly legitimate national security taps, half of which Kennedy and Johnson created — were removed from the FBI files by Sullivan, who did the tapping, and brought them to the Justice Department rather than the White House because he said that he was afraid that Hoover might use them as blackmail. So, I don't know what in the world [unclear]. Why is that? To think that an officer of the bureau would suggest that Edgar Hoover would blackmail the attorney general or the president of the United States is just unbelievable. I don't believe it today. I think it is a variable strength of his, going back to his days in the [unclear] going back, in his case, to his time as a young congressman. And I didn't know Pat Gray despite all the talk around town here. I met him a couple of times, purely social occasions, but he was a fine man. But down through the bureau now, in Washington, in the bureaucracy is enormous fighting for power, jealously, hatreds — all things that Hoover kept suppressed through frankly fear, and respect — just popped off as soon as he left. And, at the present point — I mean, I don't suppose you, as a former bureau man, would ever dream that the bureau would leave anything. What the [unclear].

KELLEY: [unclear]

NIXON: It is just hard to believe. I didn't know [unclear] either. What is needed at the bureau is not just a figurehead — you'll be a fine figurehead because of your background and so forth — but what is needed is a fearless administrator with the spirit of a young J. Edgar, and I would strongly recommend that you consider taking virtually the whole top echelon and transferring them to the field or retiring them

---

* John Herbers, "Nixon Names Kelley for F.B.I.; Senate Confirmation Expected," *New York Times,* June 8, 1973, A1.

and finding people that you can bring up. Now this can't be done overnight. But you must get your team in there and get them in fast. I am not ordering you to do this, you understand, but I am telling you this based on my — well, the analysis I have had — everybody that has studied justice — the bureau desperately needs this.

"Henry's having a hell of a time, huh?"

June 12, 1973, 11:17 a.m.
Richard Nixon and Brent Scowcroft
OVAL OFFICE

Despite the signing of the Paris Peace Accords back in January, instability in Southeast Asia continued, in large part because of flaws in the original terms of peace and a lack of enforcement of its provisions. Conflict continued in neighboring Laos and Cambodia. The United States accused North Vietnam of violations, and the North directed blame at the South. Both sides were guilty of moving men and weapons and of "land grabbing" in contravention of the terms of peace. Henry Kissinger left for Paris for an emergency negotiating session with Le Duc Tho and South Vietnamese foreign minister Tran Van Lam to address the situation, and it was not going well. Here, Kissinger's deputy, Brent Scowcroft, updates Nixon on the status of the negotiations.

• • •

NIXON: Well, I guess Henry's having a hell of a time, huh?

SCOWCROFT: He's having a hell of a time.

NIXON: Yeah. Has he — has it broken up yet, or — ?

SCOWCROFT: No, they're still meeting. They're still meeting. So —

NIXON: What are they meeting about?

SCOWCROFT: Well, the, the GVN came in with, with two propositions.

NIXON: Yeah, I heard.

SCOWCROFT: One was to insert the article from the agreement about elections into the communiqué.

NIXON: I know.

SCOWCROFT: And, the other one was a complaint about the, the terminology of zones of control.

NIXON: Yeah.

SCOWCROFT: Joining zones of control.

NIXON: Yeah.

SCOWCROFT: That, I think, they'd fall off on. My guess is that what, what Henry's working on is to try to get a statement on elections inserted into the communiqué, in hopes that the GVN would then buy it. It's fairly innocuous. You know, we've — I've quoted — the communiqué, now, does contain other quotations [unclear].

NIXON: Sure.

SCOWCROFT: But, of course, elections is one that the DRV is, is sensitive about right now.

NIXON: Well, there's not going to be any elections. They know that.

SCOWCROFT: Of course — of course not.

NIXON: So why even say it?

SCOWCROFT: Well —

NIXON: Why do they object? We could easily put it in ways that it could be handled, simply. We could say this communiqué, in no way — it, it abrogates any of the subjects that are covered in the previous communiqué, and not mentioned in this one. Now, that's it —

SCOWCROFT: And — and, as a matter of fact, it does contain language like that. And, of course, both sides are equal on the idea. I called Ambassador Phuong again today, and I said, "You know, look: whether it's in, or whether it isn't in, the agreement is still completely valid — "

NIXON: And the president will say so.

SCOWCROFT: " — and" — that's right —

NIXON: Why don't you just — ?

SCOWCROFT: " — and we have given them those — "

NIXON: Yeah. All right, why don't you tell him — or, call him on the phone and tell him that you've talked to me, and that I will make a public statement to the effect that the article with regard to elections is, is in —

SCOWCROFT: [unclear] —

NIXON: — or something like that. And I will say it in a public statement that I — that the president, himself, will say that the article with regard to that is in.

SCOWCROFT: [unclear] —

NIXON: I will write to President Thieu a letter to that effect, too. And I'll tell him that — tell him they've got to get this thing done.

SCOWCROFT: Well, it, it, it really mystifies me why they're hung up on these two points, neither one of which means anything in comparison to what —

NIXON: I know [unclear] the reason for this in their relations, and not ours. Well, it's in ours because we don't want them to fall, but you know very well that there has got to be — the Congress will go up the wall —

SCOWCROFT: No question.

NIXON: — and they'll play right into the hands of our enemies if Hanoi is able to blame South Vietnam for failing to agree to strengthen the agreement on everything, like MIA, and everything else like that.

SCOWCROFT: That's right.

NIXON: And good heavens! And the Congress doesn't want to give them aid anyway — either side.

SCOWCROFT: That's right.

NIXON: Either side.

SCOWCROFT: That's right.

NIXON: And we're going to have a terrible fight. And if he thinks for one minute that he's just going to sit there and get it, he's out of his mind. So, they're, they're looking down, they're looking down the gun barrel right now.

SCOWCROFT: There's, there's no question on it. And — and we know, for example, that Ambassador Phuong has reported quite accurately —

NIXON: Yeah.

SCOWCROFT: — the conversation with you, and the ones that we've had —

NIXON: Yeah, yeah. How come — ?

SCOWCROFT: I think it's just hard to figure out what's in their minds.

NIXON: Yeah.

SCOWCROFT: They just seem to be —

NIXON: Would it be helpful — I don't know; maybe it isn't helpful. If you want, though, you can tell the ambassador that the president will make a statement to that effect, or the White House will make a statement to that effect. Or do you think it's worthwhile?

SCOWCROFT: Well, I'll —

NIXON: Don't do [unclear] this goddamn thing.

SCOWCROFT: Let me — let me see what — where we are. I suspect, you know, that, that by the time he could get back there —

NIXON: Yeah, yeah, yeah.

SCOWCROFT: — with a message and get turned around in Paris —

NIXON: Yeah, yeah, yeah.

SCOWCROFT: — it's probably going to be —

NIXON: Too late.

SCOWCROFT: — over one way or another. But, I'll, I'll hold that, and if it looks like, if it looks like that's — that will turn the trick, then we can do it. But, it's — but it's either, it's either — that's what Henry's working on now, or, or trying to figure out some formula for a two-party document that we could agree to without [unclear], but, I, I don't think that —

NIXON: They couldn't agree with [unclear] —

SCOWCROFT: I don't think so. And, and, and that's —

NIXON: [unclear] —

SCOWCROFT: — that's of no real value to us, anyway, because —

NIXON: No.

SCOWCROFT: — because it's the other two parties that, that have to commit themselves.

NIXON: Well, suppose we don't get it. Then we go back to one of the previous agreements, huh?

SCOWCROFT: That's right. That's right.

NIXON: It just says that we were unable to reach agreement; we'll continue to work on it.

SCOWCROFT: That's right, that's right. I think —

NIXON: It'll be a, it'll be a — all the sophisticates will say you've made a terrible, terrible thing. It isn't terrible. No, no, no — I mean, it is — it's too bad among certain areas, but as far as the public interest in this is concerned, believe me, it is zilch.

SCOWCROFT: Okay.

NIXON: They don't — clearly don't want to hear about the war. They don't want to hear about Paris. [unclear] They want that we've got the POWs back, and our troops out of there, and [unclear] over. Good heavens. They think, "Thank God." You know, let's face it.

SCOWCROFT: Oh, there's no question about that.

NIXON: So, we, we don't need to be as desperately concerned as we were in January — December and January.

SCOWCROFT: Oh, oh, it's an entirely different —

NIXON: I'd much like to get it done, but if we don't get it done, we don't. Then, we go on to meet with Brezhnev.

SCOWCROFT: That's — I, I think the chief problem if, if we don't get it done is, is going to be with the Congress, and it's going to be — there's going to be growing opposition to South Vietnam, and [unclear] to our doing what we can to help them.

NIXON: All over Southeast Asia. It isn't just Cambodia.

SCOWCROFT: Of course.

NIXON: South Vietnam, Laos, Thailand, everything. The Congress wants to get out, alone.

SCOWCROFT: They want to get out, and this will be another argument to get out: "We've tried, and we can't do any more. Let's just get out and cut our losses." I think that, that will be the impact.

NIXON: So, in the end they would have won the battle that we've fought for four years to keep that in play. In other words, their battle all along has been to sink the whole thing, get out, and let it go down the drain.

SCOWCROFT: Well, then, of course, that would be the tragedy if this —

NIXON: That's right.

SCOWCROFT: — this —

NIXON: Tragedy.

SCOWCROFT: — contributes to it on such —

NIXON: Hmm. On the other hand, I think that [unclear]. The GVN's going to survive for a while, don't you think so?

SCOWCROFT: Oh, yes, sir.

NIXON: They should —

SCOWCROFT: Effectively, sir, they're — they're quite strong. I think their army has now quite a good deal of esprit. I think they —

NIXON: Yeah.

SCOWCROFT: — they think they can handle it. And I think they're in pretty good shape for now. But, over the long term, if we can't shore them up, it's — it's hard to be really optimistic.

NIXON: I know. They've always known that. On the other hand, we've been — we've gone the extra mile.

SCOWCROFT: Oh, there's no question about that, no question on that. And, this communiqué, how much it would help, it's, it's difficult to say. But — so, I think there's still an outside chance that we might get something there. They wouldn't still be meeting if it would really help us. And, as I say [unclear] —

NIXON: It's, now, about four thirty in Paris — five hours' difference, you say?

SCOWCROFT: It's five hours' difference. So, it's —

NIXON: Four twenty-five.

SCOWCROFT: Four twenty-five. So, there's no question that they're, they're grappling with, with the substance, and I guess it — my guess is, it's on this one point on that — which is of no significance, one way or another, really.

NIXON: Yeah, with either one.

SCOWCROFT: It just doesn't matter whether it's in, or whether it's —

NIXON: Well, the zones of control, I understand. They think that's a partition. [laughs] It couldn't — of course, it's a partition. Wasn't it?

SCOWCROFT: Well, they're, they're so confused on that. It is a, it is a partition — but it's, in fact, a partition, right now. They came out, last month, and started pressing for defining "zones of control."

NIXON: The GVN did?

SCOWCROFT: They did. And — so, then, we, we said, "Fine, that's, that's a good idea." And now, now, they're afraid of legitimizing the split of the country in — into two parts. But, it's very carefully caveated in the communiqué. The two parties have to agree on who controls what, and that, they'll never be able to do. They've agreed on where they'll station these two-party teams; it doesn't have to be along the zones of control. So, it, it really does not tie them down anymore. It's a psychological problem.

NIXON: Yeah.

SCOWCROFT: And I can understand the concern on, on that point.

NIXON: Sure —

SCOWCROFT: By — by comparison to what they're risking.

NIXON: They'd better take a hard look at the American psychology, at the moment, which is a, basically, a new isolationist bug-out psychology — not only with them, but for Europe.

SCOWCROFT: Exactly.

NIXON: That's our problem we have —

SCOWCROFT: Exactly.

NIXON: These enormous cuts in defense that they're talking about is — I mean, there is a feeling of withdrawal in this country, which, except for us, would lead us to a disastrous policy of weakening ourselves, and of isolationism that — and, frankly, giving the Russians a free hand to do it —

[Unclear exchange]

SCOWCROFT: That's right. I don't think there's any —

NIXON: We're fighting a desperate battle —

SCOWCROFT: And if — if it weren't — as you say, if it weren't for your strength, we'd already be way down the road.

NIXON: Yeah. Yeah.

SCOWCROFT: And I think it would just be a disaster.

NIXON: Yeah.

SCOWCROFT: But how do you convince the GVN?

NIXON: Well, we've tried to. I couldn't have said it more bluntly to the ambassador.

SCOWCROFT: You couldn't have.

Another truce in Vietnam

June 14, 1973, 9:34 a.m.

Richard Nixon, Henry Kissinger, and Alexander Haig

OVAL OFFICE

Kissinger returned to Washington two days later, having made a breakthrough in the negotiations. He, Tran Van Lam, and Le Duc Tho issued a joint communiqué on June 13 agreeing once again to adhere to the Paris Peace Accords. Nixon congratulated his national security advisor on the breakthrough.

• • •

NIXON: Hello, Henry.

KISSINGER: Hi, Mr. President. Thank you for your cable.

NIXON: [laughs] You got it, did you?

KISSINGER: It was received —

NIXON: I also cabled the White House. It's not quite as —

KISSINGER: Oh, marvelous — and [Assistant Secretary of State William H.] Sullivan.

NIXON: I sent a wire to him, but that's [unclear]. But I — but yours, I thought, you could pass on to the staff.

KISSINGER: Yes.

NIXON: But, Al, this, of all — I told Al last night, of all the things you've done, was the toughest, because you had no cards. I mean, you went to this thing with a broken flush. And the other thing, you were looking, and, and you were looking at a — basically at four aces. And you knew damn well he had four aces. And, by golly, you, you pulled it off. I don't know how you did it.

HAIG: That's right.

KISSINGER: Well, I must —

NIXON: All I did was write the most nasty cables to Thieu that he's received since [unclear] —

KISSINGER: Well, but, Mr. President —

NIXON: But, boy, we — I, I — I'm sure you don't mind, that after Scowcroft brought him in, I gussied him up a little. [unclear] you were there when the ambassador [unclear]. I hated doing it because he's a nice guy. [laughs] He went out of here shaking like a leaf. I told him, I said, "Look, if we don't get this, our leaders are going to say [unclear] won't have any aid [unclear]."

KISSINGER: No, I think you, again, put yourself on the line, and that put it over in Saigon. But, they were in a suicidal mood in Saigon.

"A double, extra-good omen"

June 18, 1973, 11:31 a.m.
Richard Nixon, Leonid Brezhnev, and Viktor Sukhodrev (interpreter)
OVAL OFFICE

Amid crisis, for a fleeting moment Nixon was back on top again — his old self, the master of international affairs. The front pages of the nation's newspapers were dedicated to the summit between the world's two most powerful leaders. In fact, Leonid Brezhnev was just the third Soviet leader ever to set foot on American soil. Even the Watergate hearings were postponed for the occasion.

Nixon didn't just roll out the red carpet; he rolled out every red carpet he could find. He feted Brezhnev at Camp David, the Cabinet Room, and in one-on-one meetings in the Oval Office, and he even threw him a star-studded pool party at his home, Casa Pacifica, in San Clemente, California. Here, the anti-Communist and the anti-imperialist appear more like old friends than archenemies. As there was no note taker present, the White House tapes constitute the only known record of this meeting.

• • •

BREZHNEV: But we have an omen in Russia that when it rains as you are leaving on a trip it's a good sign. And it was raining by chance at the airport. It happened. But that, too — but that, too, is according to the Russian folk tradition a good omen. And especially since it was raining both in Moscow and in Washington, that makes it a double, extra-good omen.

NIXON: Mm-hmm.

BREZHNEV: Mr. President, because of the ceremonies and all the protocol, I didn't get a chance to say, and I want to do this right from the start, to extend to you the very good, the best wishes, greetings, and good feelings of all my comrades, all my associates who saw me off at Moscow airport. It's okay if I may talk?

NIXON: Oh, absolutely.

SUKHODREV: [unclear] Is that okay? I'll try it.

NIXON: Try it. Okay.

SUKHODREV: Good.

BREZHNEV: You see, I have a cigarette box there. It has a special timing mechanism and I can't — I won't be able to open it for an hour.

NIXON: Oh, how's it open?

BREZHNEV: See, the mechanism, the timing mechanism is now working and I won't be able to open that for another hour. In one hour it will unlock itself.

NIXON: [laughs] That's a way to discipline yourself!

BREZHNEV: That's right! Mr. President, on a personal level [unclear] I need to just say that as I was being seen off at the airport in Moscow, and all my colleagues and my comrades were there, and I had a few words with them, and, well, I just said, "I thank you all for your trust that you vested in me for this visit for my talks with President Nixon, and I only hope that you will support me in all that we do together with the president of the United States." And all of my colleagues who were there at the airport said they were absolutely confident that these new talks, at summit level, between the Soviet Union and the United States, would yield new and truly historic results. And with those words, with that sendoff, I climbed the steps up to the plane and flew off to Washington. That was really a word-for-word — that was a word-for-word description of what went on at the airport, and how the world may be changed. And, also, last Thursday, when we had our regular meeting of our leadership, the Politburo of the party, where we had a free discussion, a long discussion about Soviet-American relations, about all that has been achieved already, and all that we want to achieve in the future, and the prospects that we are aiming at, there was complete unanimity of views as regards the basic principles of the development of our relations and of the main questions on which we have achieved already a preliminary agreement and on those that we still have to discuss. Of course, there are certain matters that I have not raised in that forum before having had a chance to ask for your advice, consult with you on. With all this hope, purely, personally, and at this meeting permit me to say that I have certainly come to this country with very good feelings, with good intentions, and with high hopes for these forthcoming negotiations. Although doubtless certain problems are complex, and they may be difficult of solution for both yourself and myself, but I always believe that there are no — there are no situations out of which a way cannot be found, and there are no problems for which a solution cannot be found. And if I might just make two personal points before we go over to official discussions —

NIXON: Mm-hmm.

BREZHNEV: When you called it — the first thought I had [unclear] certain doubts about the San Clemente visit —

NIXON: Sure.

BREZHNEV: — and that's why I came to you, to contact you through the ambassador, but then when I learned that, Mr. Nixon, that you were very anxious for me to be there and go there. I am now — and I immediately responded. And I am — let me say that I am now really happy that I have revised my initial decision and I — and it was a personal decision on my part, and I do believe now, especially when I know that you — the symbolic — the symbolism that you put into the name of that house in San Clemente —

NIXON: House of Peace.

BREZHNEV: House of Peace [unclear]. Exactly, and I do believe — I'm, as I say, I'm happy that I am going there, and I do believe that that symbolism will turn into reality. And that is something that I [unclear] —

NIXON: [unclear]

BREZHNEV: And the second point is a family — is a family one. Everything seemed to be going very well and I had hoped to come here with some of the members of my family, but, well, you see, my wife was not well anyway. She got a little worse and she was put to bed. And for a short time I hoped, but, anyway, that's the way it happened. And then, I also wanted to bring my son along, but then he has his own kid. Now, the trouble is that his — my grandson, his son that is, is finishing his high school this year.

NIXON: Uh-huh.

BREZHNEV: And so he's got his examinations, his graduation examination, and then his entrance examination to Moscow University. And so you know how parents are. I mean in our country, especially, they insist on going, [unclear] to the school [unclear] or to the university, and they insist on pacing the corridors, waiting for the results of the examinations. I keep saying that you can't help them, anyway, but that's what they do. So, well, those are the circumstances that prevented me from bringing any of the members of my family along.

NIXON: That's okay.

BREZHNEV: So, there was really nothing I could do about it. But I — but I will say that Tricia [Nixon Cox] [unclear] and made a very big impression on my children, and they still remember every minute of their meeting and the way they went along together. Well, I assured them that I will let them come to Washington to be able to spend some time with Tricia, the other of your — younger — and your other children. I will come. My son, my daughter, and my daughter-in-law wrote a collective letter and asked that it be given to Tricia, so I don't want to give it to anybody else. I want you, as a father, to give it to Tricia.

NIXON: Well, I would like, Mr. Brezhnev, to extend from me, and from Tricia and Julie, an invitation for the members of his family to come here as our special guests. [That] we would like, and we appreciate the very warm welcome that was given to Tricia and her husband when she was in Moscow. We look forward to having them here as our personal guests. Thank you. And at any time. Any time.

BREZHNEV: Thank you. Maybe sometime in the fall.

NIXON: Sure.

BREZHNEV: It is advised —

NIXON: Tell him the weather is good. It's good anytime.

BREZHNEV: They'll be happy to hear that.

NIXON: Right. Also, I want to say before the others come in is that I very much appreciated the personal remarks that Mr. Brezhnev has made. [unclear] We both — we must recognize, the two of us, that I for three and a half more years in this office and the general secretary, I hope, for that long or longer, we head the two most powerful nations and, while we will naturally in negotiations have some differences, it is essential that those two nations, where possible, work together. And the key really is in the relationship between Mr. Brezhnev and myself. If we decide to work together, we can change the world. That's what — that's my attitude as we enter these talks. Thank you. [unclear] [laughter] I know it's all right.

BREZHNEV: Well, thank you very much. And, in fact, I did indeed have two opportunities fairly recently to speak of you, Mr. President. Once was during my meeting with a group of American senators, and I was speaking really from my heart — and, incidentally, let me proceed here to say that when I did meet the senators, I was struck by the fact that they all, all of them regardless of party affiliation, evinced sincere — what I felt to be a sincere respect for you, Mr. President. And there was no attempt in any way to kind of, to sort of needle you through — in their — in the way they talked about you or in their general attitude. And in fact, after the — after the meeting, Senator [Vance] Hartke [D-IN], who led the delegation, he came up to me separately, and he said that he had never had, just at the beginning of that conversation, and he had never before had such hopes for a better atmosphere in relations between our two countries as he now has after the foundation made jointly by the president and by myself. Now, he spoke really so highly, I was moved, I was deeply touched. Say, is he a Republican or a Democrat?

NIXON: Democrat. Very partisan. [laughs]

BREZHNEV: [laughs] [unclear]. But, you know, Mr. President, if he spoke that highly of you always, well, I'd live for nothing better. [unclear] And I was just recalling that I was asked once, during my meeting with President Pompidou at Zaslavl, one of the correspondents there, and I met some of them at the airport, they were asking me about my forthcoming trip to the United States and whether that was still on. I said — at that time I said, "Of course it is, certainly." And then in Bonn, out walking with Chancellor Brandt, there was also — we came across a group of correspondents and one of them asked me, "Is your trip to the United States still on?" I said, "Well," I said, "what are you expecting? A great big earthquake in the United States that will prevent me from going and meeting with the president?" [unclear] And of course I would go, and, well, that made a big hit with them.

NIXON: Mm-hmm.

BREZHNEV: So, and — well, for the first time, as I say, that I spoke to a group of Americans about my paying my respect for you was with this group of senators, and I really spoke from my heart. And the second time was during my interview with the biggest group of American correspondents that I've ever received. There were eleven of them.

NIXON: Mm-hmm.

BREZHNEV: And I — in fact, I can — I spent a lot of time with them. I can send you a full transcript of my discussion and my interview with them. And in that conversation I — twice in different sorts of settings and different circumstances I mentioned and emphasized what I see as the role and the significance of President Nixon and his policies in the — in changing relationships and improving relationships between the Soviet Union and the United States. But you know, come to think of it, twelve or so years ago one former very — formerly very prominent Soviet diplomat and statesman told me that "now you" — and I was then — "you are just a sort of a newly initiated statesman. You're an up-and-coming statesman," he said to me —

NIXON: Yes.

BREZHNEV: — at that time, and —

NIXON: Absolutely.

BREZHNEV: — and he said, "Now, and I want to give you some advice." He told me,

"Now, you're new in politics but believe me that personal, good relationships, even in grand politics, are at times the most important thing for progress at any time." And, you know, I remember those words and I, personally, I agree with them. And I do believe that personal confidence and loyalty to even a gentleman's agreement without setting down anything on paper are the best thing for any relationships at any time. And it's with that hope that I come here, and in that spirit I want to shake your hand.

NIXON: Uh-huh.

BREZHNEV: Now, I believe that our personal relationships and the respect which I certainly harbor, very sincerest regard for you and I know it's reciprocal, can be confirmed by two events and that is: your arrival to Moscow last year, and mine in Washington this year. This is not in any way to remember the bad past or to empha-size anything out of the present, but, simply, I'm giving an answer in substance and what is, I think, is realistic. Yesterday, I had a very pleasant conversation with Dr. Kissinger and I guess he must have told you at least about it in general terms, but I want to say now — I said this to him yesterday, and I do want to say it now — that it is certainly my very earnest desire that you should pay another visit to the Soviet Union sometime next year, in 1974. I think that would be very good —

NIXON: For the election?

SUKHODREV: Yeah, pretty much.

BREZHNEV: [unclear]

NIXON: You'll come back in '75 here.

SUKHODREV: That's what he's talking about now —

NIXON: Oh, go ahead. Please go on —

BREZHNEV: Let me say here that this is not something I just say in a personal — only in a personal capacity. At the last meeting of the Politburo, I suggested — made the suggestion that I should make an official visit to — I should extend an official invita-tion to you to come to the Soviet Union in 1974. That suggestion received unani-mous support by the entire Politburo, so it's both a personal and a unanimously supported decision, and a considered decision by our leadership. And then, you see, I think that new meeting between us would give a new impulse to what has already been done and it would be fully in accord with the arrangement — the agreement, actually, that we entered into last year that these meetings should be a regular, an-nual event. So, today, I'm here with you in the United States, and I shall be hoping that you will accept our invitation to visit us in 1974, and then, if we get an invita-tion, we can come back to the United States in '75.

NIXON: Thank you. That's right.

BREZHNEV: And then, in 1976, you come and pay us another visit. And that will, I'm sure, that this series of meetings of this sort will give continued — will give new and continuous impulses to the development of a real, lasting relationship between our two countries. Now, of course, I don't have with me any brief or any official or formal proposals as to the problems we could take up for discussion next year or the agreements that we could sign next year, but this is something that we could someday at a point have a general discussion about, exchange views, consult one another, but I believe that our experience, the experience of preparing for last year's meeting, and of preparing for this one, shows that we can do some very fruitful work, preparatory work together, and then, if we do that prior to the visit, there is — there can be more, time can be spent on seeing, traveling more through the country. You could go down south, see something in the Caucasus, for instance, some other part of the country. And, in short, we can prepare all of the business part of the trip so well, in advance, as to leave the minimal time for formal discussions and the settlement of various problems. So — but we certainly seek to ensure that the next visit is at least as important as — each next visit is at least as important as each preceding one. But we can talk about that a little later.

NIXON: Well, I want to say before the others come in that I have the same feeling of respect for and a very personal basis, for the general secretary, and of friendship on a personal basis. He's a very — as I have told people in this office, I've indicated this: he is a strong man, and he represents a very strong country. And my greatest desire is to have this personal relationship, so that our two very strong countries can be a force that's working together, rather than like that. If they work together, then the whole world benefits. If they work like that, the whole world is greatly endangered. And Mr. Brezhnev and I have the key, and I think that our personal relationship will unlock the door for the continuing relationship between our two countries, which will contribute to peace in the world.

BREZHNEV: Oh, thank you. And I should like in that connection to say that I, for one, take pride in the fact that my country is a very big and powerful one, that it's got, has many millions — two-hundred-fifty-million-strong population. It's got the vast mineral resources, and agricultural and industrial potential. And all this is something that heartens us. It cannot fail to do so. But, on the other hand, I have never said that I regret the fact that the United States is also a big, important, a very powerful and a very strong, economically strong, country. And as, in fact, I told the last plenary meeting of our Central Committee, the ruling body of the — for our party and of the country, that the United States is worthy of the greatest respect as a major, as a big world power. And I spoke of the role that our two countries can play in strengthening world peace and in working together on a basis of cooperation. Now, there are some people who keep throwing in this idea of there being two superpowers in the world who are out to dictate their, as they say, dictate their will, to foist their will upon others, and so forth. Now, but, are we to blame for being big? Are we to blame for being strong? What can we do about it? That is the way it is. I mean, what do these people want us to do, become countries? I am praising those who have made their nations strong. What are we to be? What are we to do? To turn ourselves into some kind of Guinea, or a country like that? And, surely, the main thing is the fact that we have — we are strong, but we don't intend to use that strength against either one another or against any other third parties. Now—and there are—and people—except there are some people who keep reproaching us that we—that that is exactly what we allegedly want to do. But those—I think that is a deliberate attempt to spoil relations thrown in by certain people on the side. Now—but, and doubtless, neither the United States nor the Soviet Union can turn themselves into a Luxembourg where the entire army is made up of seventy-eight policemen. Well, so far I'm taking a kind of tolerant, patient attitude towards those who propagate that theory, the superpower theory, but I think that sometime later I will make a big, serious speech and deal with that theory, I mean the so-called superpower theory, and really strike out against it, so as to crush that theory. And in that speech I'd certainly emphasize the constructive role that our two countries can make. And, finally, that we should take up for discussion and endeavor to solve not only various current problems, but, also, we should endeavor to look far ahead, because if we can look ahead we can really create a basis of stable relationships and peace. And, as they say, if you don't look ahead, you will inevitably lag behind and fall back, and I want us both to look forward together to a peaceful—a more peaceful, and a stronger future. [unclear]

NIXON: [unclear] Well, I think the key is personal friendship plus respect for each other's peoples. Those two added together mean a constructive and positive relationship. And we have that.

BREZHNEV: Now, as regards the schedule and the general protocol of our meetings, I'm happy to go along with any suggestions that you might make, with all those that you have made already, and any that you might make—wish to make in the future with regard to any minor changes or adaptations, or alterations, or anything—

NIXON: I realize that—

BREZHNEV: Anything you suggest, I'm happy to go along with. I like the gaiety of Camp David.

NIXON: We'll have a good meeting up there.

BREZHNEV: It's quiet, peaceful.

NIXON: And you'll like San Clemente, too. That's very quiet. All you hear there is the ocean waves. You'll like that.

BREZHNEV: The same goes for me. I like them—I like hearing the sound of the sea.

NIXON: Well, should we invite—would you like to invite Gromyko? [unclear]

BREZHNEV: As—as you wish, Mr. President—

NIXON: Yeah?

BREZHNEV: —as protocol dictates [unclear] protocol [unclear].

NIXON: Right. I think the—I think that we should have Gromyko, Rogers, and Kissinger, and [unclear] Soviet Union, sort of—we can have a sort of, as we did in Moscow, a plenary session.

BREZHNEV: Well, yeah, for this sort of plenary meeting I'd like to have Gromyko in, certainly, and it's natural if our two other ministers, Patolichev and Bugayev, just for the first one.

NIXON: Would you like them, too, today? We were going to have — I thought that to-morrow we'd have an economic meeting. [unclear] today —

BREZHNEV: And then — I fully agree — and then, the — our — we have most of our other meeting times, I guess, could be held in [unclear].

NIXON: That's right. That's right.

BREZHNEV: If you will take Gromyko on our side, and —

NIXON: Yeah.

BREZHNEV: — or — and some of them might be just personal.

NIXON: Yeah, that's right. I'd like to have that, too. We can talk on the plane, we can talk at Camp David. That's all right.

BREZHNEV: Now, I wanted to consult you on this —

NIXON: Sure.

BREZHNEV: — on the question of the prevention of nuclear war, this plenary session we say that "well, so" — we call it the first question, so we have — we say something like, "Well, we have reached an understanding on this first question of ours," and then [unclear]. Things like that now.

NIXON: Going into it?

BREZHNEV: So as to prevent any leaks to the press in advance. [unclear] Right from the start.

NIXON: We don't want anything said about that, no.

BREZHNEV: And — well, Mr. President, what's your — do you have any ideas as to how we should conduct this first —

NIXON: I think we [unclear] —

BREZHNEV: — [unclear] session, how do we start out?

NIXON: What I would suggest is that I will ask — that Mr. Brezhnev being the guest — I will ask him to talk first, and he can talk generally about our relations. [unclear] And I will respond. By that time it'll probably be about — we'll run a little over, but [unclear] —

BREZHNEV: That'll be fine. I'll use the lunch break to have a little nap —

NIXON: Good.

BREZHNEV: — because I'm still a little weak.

NIXON: That's good that [unclear].

BREZHNEV: [unclear] our time difference.

NIXON: That's very important.

BREZHNEV: Because if we take Moscow time, tonight's dinner will end at something like five a.m. [laughs]

NIXON: Well, we'll break him of that. I would suggest —

BREZHNEV: I'm now happy to go on with any of you —

NIXON: — we meet now for maybe forty-five minutes.

"We should think big . . . we should think long term."

June 19, 1973, 4:45 p.m.

Richard Nixon, William Rogers, Henry Kissinger, George Shultz, John Connally, Peter Flanigan, Hal Sonnenfeldt, and Soviet delegation (Leonid Brezhnev, Andrei Gromyko, Anatoly Dobrynin, Nikolai Patolichev, Andrei Aleksandrov, and Viktor Sukhodrev)

OVAL OFFICE

In an honor that would be unusual even for the closest American ally, Nixon hosted a mock cabinet meeting with the visiting Soviet delegation. As he noted, the only other occasion he did this during his presidency was when he hosted British prime minister Harold Wilson, in 1969. Brezhnev loved the attention. The meeting was more than symbolic, focusing on ways to expand U.S.-Soviet economic cooperation and bilateral trade.

• • •

BREZHNEV [through interpreter]: Mr. President, I had a very pleasant meeting with very influential Americans, Senator Fulbright, and some other notable congress — senators and congressmen and members of the Foreign Relations Committee. And I [unclear] and am aware of the great importance of bodies such as the Congress because in my own country I was for more than four and a half years I myself was president of the [unclear] Supreme Soviet. And I am still a member of the — of that body, so I am deeply aware of the importance of the bodies of the Supreme Soviet in our country and the Congress of the United States. And well, we — I try to — now, this is particularly true at a time when we are endeavoring to resolve major questions bearing on our relations and during my address I expressed my gratitude to you, Mr. President, for all the work you have done to enable this meeting a reality. And I thank Senator Fulbright for arranging my meeting today with him and his colleagues. It was — the discussion went on in a friendly atmosphere, and I, in my statement and my remarks, I [unclear] upon many issues, basic problems, in a broad way. I referred to our relationship in general. I stressed the importance of last year's meeting, and I stressed the responsibility that rests upon us, and also I stressed the fact that — I tried — I stressed the fact that our line, is being in respect to relations between the Soviet Union and the United States, is — enjoys the support of our people, and point out that as far as I know, that most of the senators seem to be supporting the president and he is surely supported by the majority of the American people, who expressed their support for him by voting to keep him in office for a second term. Then — I then turned to the substance of our relationships, and spoke about the [unclear] ties between our two countries. And then finally there, on their initiative, I spoke about the so-called question of [unclear] official government statistics on that problem. Generally speaking my impression was I was well received by the senators. They thanked me for a frank exposé of my thinking, if that is what it is. In fact, that is what I did. I put it to them in a frank and sincere way, and so I can say, summing it up, that I am satisfied with the way the meeting went, though it was a bit tiring, a bit hot in the room, too. And I spent more than three and a half hours with them. So, we all — they all said they thought that yesterday's — the meeting yesterday that started the official [unclear] was an important event. Well, I told them that I was having a [unclear] meeting with you, Mr. President, and they looked forward to still more important decisions which [unclear] would be welcomed by the senators and the American people generally, and so I would say that they had a pleasant, a very good impression. One of the senators asked me about my attitude towards the Jackson amendment. And he asked whether — something to the effect that whether that amendment could be beneficial to the development of our relations. As I told one of the senators, well, any amendment can have a counter-amendment attached to it. And one of the senators there said, "Well, that may be the way things go. We may introduce an amendment to the amendment."

UNIDENTIFIED AMERICAN: Well, that is just one of the jokes we have.

BREZHNEV: I trust you will get a fuller report on the —

UNIDENTIFIED AMERICAN: It is important that you debrief me on the substance —

UNIDENTIFIED AMERICAN: I think it was a useful joke.

NIXON: Well, I greatly appreciate the time the general secretary has spent with the senators, and I am sure that it will be helpful in getting our support for our legislative program. Stopping such things as the Jackson amendment, and getting [unclear]. I regret that they kept him such a long time. And we hope he gets time to get to bed earlier tonight.

BREZHNEV: Thank you, Mr. President. You know, I have over the years — that tiredness is always — something that always accompanies any visit such as this one. It couldn't have been easy for you last year to adapt yourself to our — the time difference either.

NIXON: Well, I want to say, first to welcome all of our [unclear] to this cabinet table. The only other time that I can recall, since I have been president, that we have had visitors at the cabinet table was when Prime Minister Wilson was here, in our first year. The subject that the general secretary and I have agreed we should discuss today is one on which there is total agreement with regard to goals. And the question is how to achieve the goals. The general secretary has often said he told me last year, and again this year, that our economic systems are complementary. And we should think big and not small with regard to increasing economic relations. And that we should think long term and not short term.

BREZHNEV: I certainly reaffirm that, Mr. President — that is the way I put it to the senators today.

NIXON: Now, as we know, that Secretary Shultz and Mr. Patolichev have been discussing these matters. The problems we have, have to do with how we can take an economy like ours which has many private and independent businesses and work out arrangements where this economy can dovetail where it serves our mutual interest with an economy like yours which is basically a government-controlled economy. I have asked Mr. Connally to come today for two reasons. One, he is a former member of our cabinet. Second, he now is in what we call the private sector. And he is very familiar with the problem of how private companies can — will have in attempting to make arrangements with the Soviet Union, or investment trade. I think we can look back over the last year and be pleased with the increase in trade, but also looking to the future the possibilities are much greater than we achieved during the last year. The problem we have, however, is to find the ways that many American companies would like to invest in the Soviet Union, more trade and so forth, and ways they can do so. And it's here that Secretary Shultz works — has been working with Mr. Patolichev with some success and I am sure that [unclear]. As I told the general secretary yesterday, the attitude on the government's side will be positive where the questions come up. Yet, as practical men, we know that there are many practical problems to be worked out.

UNIDENTIFIED: That is true.

BREZHNEV: Well, I believe that we have things that we can sell each other and we certainly have spheres for — areas where we go — mutually advantageous cooperation. The problem is to find the adequate forms of such cooperation. As regards the political trends we have in our — a very broad positive program which will be fully approved by the last leaders' meeting of the Central Committee in our party. And I am quite sure that the members of the Central Committee of the party present here, and they include Ministers Gromyko and Patolichev, Ambassador Dobrynin, and Mr. Aleksandrov and Mr. Sukhodrev that can all confirm that this plan is a very — has been approved. And I have to add also that we have given instructions to our [unclear] agencies and planning bodies to depart from all traditions, old and outdated traditions, and to make an effort to find new ways for cooperation without any discrimination and on a broad and long-term basis. Now in my [unclear] meeting with the group of American senators in Moscow I raised the question of gas. Now, that is not an area in which we are insisting on. We're not —

UNIDENTIFIED: Gas?

BREZHNEV: Gas. We are not trying to impose anything on you in that regard, but gas is indeed today a product, it is a primary commodity, with which one can do wonders. They can make things out of gas today that were inconceivable just a mere twenty years ago. And I told them, and I wish to repeat, that we have in our country vast deposits of gas, and as I said then we could, the Soviet Union could offer the United States one trillion cubic meters of gas, and it would be of course not for me, but for the businessmen — for the various economic organizations in the Soviet Union and for the businessmen of the United States to calculate and to see how this — that question can be resolved, what arrangements could be made. But there is one very important area for cooperation in the economic field, and if for instance, the business circle of the United States wanted to take something like twenty-two or twenty-five billion cubic meters of gas a year, that would mean that we entered into an arrangement that would last for some forty years. So, I would be well in favor of Secretary Shultz and Mr. Connally looking into this matter and discussing it with Mr. Patolichev, for instance. So, there are obviously also other areas in which we can reach certain useful agreements. Of course, there would also be some trade in consumer goods, but I guess that would be less in volume and significance than these long-standing, long-term, and large-scale arrangements. So there is a meeting to think it over very carefully. Perhaps it would help matters if we speeded up the equivalent in Moscow of the U.S. trade center, so [unclear] businessmen could come over and engage in economic discussions on the subjects. I can certainly assure you that we will give our full cooperation to the building of that trade center in Moscow. And we could — in the meantime, we could also, I think, perhaps we could set up some works groups, one to deal with the problems with power, another to deal with problems of cooperation in the field of various mineral resources, a third one to deal with problems, possible joint projects which could — and the [unclear] of which could run for a period of some forty years or so, in the field of trade and techno-logical cooperation. And we could sort out problems of repayment. We could buy, repay the investments made, or the credits extended let's say over a period of ten, or five, or twenty years as our people agree. So it will all then be a matter of pure arith-metic. Now at this time it is not for me to make any specific — to set out a specific program, or to list any specific deals or contracts that we could negotiate. But I do, in general, fully agree with your opinion as you set it out just now. So as I say, that if Secretary Shultz and Mr. Connally think something up of a constructive nature with Mr. Patolichev we would certainly welcome it, not only I, but the entire leader-ship in our country. [unclear] so if we are, and it does seem that we are [unclear] as regards to the basic goals it remains for us to think over how this — we can imple-ment this — we can reach these goals. And we need to have the experience — the necessary experience, surely it was not the easiest of — it was not a possible thing to reach free business during your first visit to the Soviet Union, and yet we managed to do so. And to arrive at important decisions, on very — on questions of very major significance. We managed to agree on the basis for the development of the economic relationships between our countries. I agree with you that this past year has given us cause for gratification. Our trade has increased from two hundred to seven hun-dred million dollars in the past year, and we have already used seventy to eighty percent of the credit you extended to us. That means we will be repaying that credit with interest and that will be to the advantage to America — to the United States. Now, we are now certain the negotiations are now under way on cooperation in the aviation deal, certain negotiations with Boeing Aircraft Corporation, and there is — some talks are going on as regards the sale of Soviet-built [unclear] forty aircraft to be — with the interior decorations and finishings to be provided by the American side, so that too will be a large-scale transaction. Then there has been some progress in the deal of chemical — in the field of the construction of plants for the production of artificial chemical fertilizer. And in return for which the Soviet Union will sell the U.S. some money. Now, of course, there are some areas where I guess we won't be able to sell certain products — certain of our products in the United States. I don't think we could sell you our automobile, because the American automobile industry is more advanced than ours, but I do think if we really get down to business and really start to think things over we can find tens — we can find dozens of subjects of areas where economic cooperation could be arranged. And well, perhaps, Mr. President, on our side, I would suggest Mr. Patolichev might add something on that general subject of economic ties.

NIXON: Good.

PATOLICHEV [through interpreter]: Let me just add to that, all these very important problems will require certain support in the form of credits which we shall naturally repay with interest, but today most of the major companies of the world are proceeding from the need to negotiate large-scale — to think big, in the [unclear] times. For instance, the Japanese business circles are making a very vigorous — are working quite vigorously on negotiations for a deal whereby they would use — help develop the [unclear] coal pockets for use in Japan. We gave our consent to that. Then there was another version — whereby another version — for the Japanese to cooperate with the United States in developing the [unclear] oil deposits and we agreed to that possibility as well. In another area, in the field of metallurgy, the [unclear] company in the Federal Republic of Germany suggested building a new type of metallurgical plant, and one that bypasses the blast furnace stage to — and produces [unclear] directly from the ore. We have negotiated a contract for building a plant on the basis — of course metal deposits, that will be a very highly productive plant, and we are counting on repaying the investments in the form of the finished product to be sent to whatever country the West German company indicates. I was recently told there was an American company which also wanted to cooperate with us in that field and which had offered to build an even bigger plant of that same kind. So I am saying all this not to suggest some kind of deal but merely to give an example — but merely to give an example that today most business circles of most countries of the world are thinking in the way we are thinking. And so we must try and find some new forms of business by cooperation and that will lead to the strengthening of mutually advantageous ties between [unclear]. That, of course, is a fact that the development of that kind of cooperation can be achieved more swiftly and on a durable basis if the whole thing gets the wholehearted support of the president on the American side and our support on our side. With your permission, Mr. President, and yours, General Secretary, may I say that we have a joint Soviet-American commission on trade matters.

"This must be dealt with with great privacy."
July 12, 1973, 5:09 p.m.
Richard Nixon, Alexander Haig, Ronald Ziegler, and Walter Tkach
OVAL OFFICE

In the final month of the taping system, Nixon spent a substantial amount of time at his homes in Florida and California, traveling on Air Force One, or hosting the Soviet delegation at Camp David, all locations not recorded. By the second week of July, he had run himself ragged. The daily press coverage of Watergate was so substantial that some days

Nixon's morning news summary must have felt like the entire newspaper. "This will really accomplish what the bastards want, Al. They've killed me," Nixon complained to his chief of staff. "The only time the press corps will ever be happy is when they write my obituary." In one of the only released conversations to feature his personal physician, Walter Tkach, Nixon is advised to go to the hospital. But first, he is updated on the latest Watergate news and the fallout from John Mitchell's testimony before the Ervin Committee.

. . .

NIXON: Let me say that I am going to go out there and check and if the damn thing [chest x-ray] shows anything—significant evidence of—I am just going to go to Walter Reed and sit on my ass for a week.

HAIG: I think that's—

NIXON: At least four or five days.

HAIG: I think that is good thing.

NIXON: And I will meet with people out there. People can come out to see me, and then I would do the—that would give us a chance to go deep enough, and I will do us a paper. Because we ought to do that anyway.

HAIG: That's right.

NIXON: As a matter of fact, I just wanted to mention one thing to you, Al, that I am sure it occurred, people like to be asked to help when they offer to help. Curtis says, "Look, there are nine people that will do it for you, you know." Timmons probably didn't think of this because he doesn't think too much of things. I mean he is great if you tell him what to do, but I suppose he is not creative but he is so much better in other areas. Why the hell don't we just ask Curtis, those fine senators, to stand up on this [possible Ervin subpoena of White House] papers deal—stand up to Goldwater and the rest? Do you think we can do that or not?

HAIG: Sure, without a shade of difficulty.

NIXON: I think they would do it. Just say the president has got to stand here. We want your support. Can you muster some other support? Or should we do that? We should not be—the thing I am concerned about right now, Al, is being defensive about all this, wringing our hands, worrying about it and so forth. I know how people are. It is like every decision we ever made. They look back, like Cambodia, and May 8 [bombing of Hanoi and mining of Haiphong], and [the] December 18 ["Christmas bombing" of North Vietnam]. But my point is you must not do it. If you make a tough decision you have got to go through and plow through and take the heat. Now if they want to give us heat, fine, let the goddamn committee—they unanimously come out and want the papers. Okay, find they want the papers. They aren't going to get the papers.

HAIG: I—

NIXON: The Un-American Activities Committee unanimously in 1953 asked Harry Truman to appear under subpoena. He didn't.

HAIG: No. I just read the riot act to him—

NIXON: Did you?

HAIG: — and there was no question about it. No question, and the only guy who was squeaming a little bit was Mel; the others are fine. Bryce is always one hundred percent. He said, "I just want to take them outside — "

NIXON: How did you explain it? Didn't you explain it to him? How you — how do you take one paper — first, I can't let Dash go through my papers.

HAIG: Oh, no. No.

NIXON: Second, if we go through the papers we are going to be charged with selecting only those things that are not incriminating. So we lose that way. Third, if we go through the papers, the difficulty is how in the name of God are we going to be able to tell what we can give and not give? I don't know. I just don't know.

HAIG: There isn't any way. Incidentally, Dick Moore —

NIXON: Tell me about that.

HAIG: He got up there and read a statement that was just — that was the best thing ever.

NIXON: Was it really?

HAIG: He just killed Dean. Absolutely crucified him.

NIXON: How did he do it?

HAIG: Well, when he was through with his discussion, he said, "Now Mr. Dean refers to discussions between me and Timmons and our discussion on this had to come — he brought to the president's attention. He said in my continuing discussions with this man, on no occasion was there any inkling that he believed nor did I believe that the president of the United States had any knowledge whatsoever of the events."

NIXON: That's what he came in on March 21!

HAIG: He just laid into him. My God!

NIXON: Great.

HAIG: Really just —

NIXON: That is why Dean took him on. See, Dean knows that he knows the truth.

HAIG: So I — Dean is absolutely clobbered. He is discredited beyond —

NIXON: Also, and I think Rose [Mary Woods] was telling me that well, in a meeting on the [March] twentieth that he — it was he, not Dean, that said, "Have you told the president?"

HAIG: [laughs]

NIXON: Good God! Now goddamn it, if it looks like Dean being the actor — he being the good guy inside here and getting this thing out. Bullshit. Goddamn it! Why didn't he say so? In my conversations, as you know, [unclear] there were six occasions where I said, "Is anyone in the White House involved?" He said no, but there are also, I think, five occasions where I said, "John, why not let it all hang out?" First, he said, "Well, they wouldn't believe it." Second, when I said, "Why don't you go down and testify," [he said,] "That would raise problems." You know, all that he was giving was excuses. I never knew why the hell he was giving excuses, because I didn't dream the hell that he was deep in it himself!

HAIG: [unclear] of a jerk.

NIXON: But anyway that's that.

HAIG: Well—

NIXON: On the paper thing I don't know. I want Buzhardt also to check the court date. I am not so goddamn sure that we are going to have to cave to Cox when he comes in, do you? It's going to be awful rough.

HAIG: Oh, no, I am not either.

NIXON: On Cox, we just may have to fire the son of a bitch. You know?

HAIG: I — well, we're —

NIXON: Incidentally, it is good to have those two on. That is why today — they knew what Moore was going to say. Why, Ervin let the letter out today. Understand?

HAIG: That's right.

NIXON: Did Ziegler handle it properly?

HAIG: Beautifully. Beautifully.

NIXON: What did he say?

HAIG: (a) That yes, there had been a letter. (b) That there had been a telephone discussion. (c) That you had agreed to sometime —

NIXON: Meetings — meet with the chairman.

HAIG: — at the chairman's request. The chairman requested this, and this was of course, the indication of the courtesy response.

NIXON: Good.

HAIG: (d) That there was absolutely no change in the position —

NIXON: That's right.

HAIG: — of the president. That letter [unclear] to the committee chairman on the sixth, and it's important because the way that bastard will fight it was the way I thought he would, that he suddenly had gotten a compromise and [unclear] it. So, Ron is also giving it to the wire guys before TV because that is the way they interpret it. They were in [unclear] compromise. [unclear]

NIXON: So he is saying—

HAIG: So he is saying—

NIXON: I — you heard what I said to him. What in the hell can his response be? Maybe there isn't any reason for us to meet.

HAIG: But this is very significant. It means that the moves made today were moves of weakness, and not strength by the committee, because if they were moves of strength, your toughness would have been what they emphasized.

NIXON: But they didn't though?

HAIG: They didn't, and we cannot lose sight of it. That is what our boys — little boys in here are losing sight of. Goddamn it! You are getting stronger, you are going to stay strong, and get stronger every day, and by God they better stop wringing their hands —

NIXON: Oh, I am not going to be weak. I haven't been up to this point, but I must say I have had some bad advice during this period — maybe it wasn't bad. Maybe we didn't have any choice, but screw them now. We are going to — they have misused the judicial process, and whether it is little Elliot Richardson, or anyone else it is going to be "no go," boys. Barry Goldwater is going to get a kick in the ass. I won't see him.

HAIG: I told Bryce to give him a call and say goddamn it, we don't expect him to be leading the charge for the opposition.

NIXON: That's right.

HAIG: So [unclear] any of that crap.

NIXON: Well, there may be some of that, but if he does he breaks his pick. Now understand, he breaks his pick. [unclear] doesn't stand it is a matter of party principle. Now—

HAIG: Well, Ron came back to me after that earlier meeting, before I saw you, and said, "Jesus Christ, Al," he says. "He has been playing right into their hands. Thank God that you pulled that back."

NIXON: What meeting?

HAIG: "Well," I said, "you know, that I told him that there wouldn't be any meeting with Laird. That Laird would not meet with Gurney. For Christ's sake! He said the way the press has played — is going to play this if we don't get it tamped down — you're going to have to get that strong statement — is a compromise — that the president has caved."

NIXON: I see.

HAIG: Like hell he's caved.

NIXON: You sure — you're confident that Ron got that across? If not, I'll put it out —

HAIG: Ron's statement came out very strong, a brief Warren statement and Ron had the wire guys in and he is saying, "Goddamn it, this is a courtesy meeting at the request of the chairman. Of course the president will meet him — meet that — "

NIXON: There was no change in his position.

HAIG: No change.

NIXON: Did he emphasize that to the chairman?

HAIG: The fact is it is almost too strong, but I am glad. He said there will be no change.

NIXON: Good. Fine.

HAIG: [laughs]

NIXON: Fine. Leave it right there.

HAIG: That's where it is.

NIXON: I hope they play it that way. I must get Ron in — you got a minute?

HAIG: Sure.

NIXON: I want to get him in right now to be sure he hits that hard.

• • •

NIXON: See, I am never sick. As you all would expect, I haven't missed a day in four and a half years.

HAIG: It's been remarkable.

NIXON: Not a day, not an appointment, nothing. I've been sick a few times, [unclear] a lot of other things like everybody else, but I don't [unclear] me now. But I don't think you can fool—

HAIG: No.

NIXON: — around with this crap [pneumonia].

HAIG: You can't fool with it.

NIXON: They tell me it is very debilitating — well, I don't take it that seriously. It could [unclear].

HAIG: You can't fool around. I think if this x-ray shows what I am sure it is going to —

NIXON: Well, it may or may not. These guys [unclear] around.

HAIG: No, even if it doesn't you ought to think about it.

NIXON: Let me say that even if it doesn't, I could use maybe a couple — three days.

HAIG: Right.

NIXON: But then [unclear].

HAIG: No, I don't think that's in order.

NIXON: Hell no. Let me ask you to do this, and incidentally I'll — then we'll have the economic climb the day I come out of the hospital. That's not bad either. I just — as a matter of fact I tell you what I can do. I can do the radio from there. That's not a bad idea, you know? Walter Reed hospital, suffering from viral pneumonia, president reads a radio address to the nation on phase four. What the hell? Don't tell anybody. Christ, they'll go up the wall. But that's not bad.

HAIG: I don't think it is bad. I think it might be just exactly what we need.

NIXON: The Bhutto dinner is coming up, but believe me I am not —

HAIG: You wouldn't be missing anything there.

NIXON: [unclear] have the vice president step in and have him call on me there? Right.

HAIG: Perfectly good way to — I am not even sure you want anyone calling on you there —

NIXON: May be.

HAIG: — because you have a case of this viral pneumonia, and by God the thing is to get well.

NIXON: Right. Well, you can prove you're doing — you're signing documents or some damn thing. But I don't know, if you start having people call, I wonder if that is a good idea. Well, it's not — the committee won't find it. And I'm afraid they will. You mean you don't think you'd have people call [unclear] out there.

[ZIEGLER joins the conversation.]

HAIG: [unclear] until you are feeling one hundred percent I wouldn't take any calls.

NIXON: Oh, Ron, I wanted to be sure [unclear] that you have totally understood the position because if any senator ever had laid down [unclear] Ervin today. Now, I think you ought to give Ron the feel also of the leak stuff and so forth so we can run that in some columns. You know what I mean?

HAIG: That's right.

NIXON: That's what I said. Let it ride. Ride it on everything we share in their committee. Your staff leaks. You can't let anybody do [unclear] put out a top-secret document in a public thing. I said this — I want that — let's get that out and get it out fast. You go over your notes and give Ron everything that you can't do.

• • •

NIXON: Have you told Ron about the potential problem we may have here?

HAIG: I started to, and then I told him I would be in here.

NIXON: You are not to tell anybody but in about twenty minutes I have to go out for an x-ray. I have been with the doctors most of the night. And the preliminary diagnosis is viral pneumonia. [unclear] they do the electrocardiogram and —

ZIEGLER: This must be dealt with with great privacy, Al. I don't know where you are going to get the x-ray, and I do not want to know. If the president —

NIXON: It's all right. It is a naval installation right there.

ZIEGLER: Yeah, it's right down the street. I've been there.

NIXON: Yeah.

ZIEGLER: But I'll tell you, if the president of the United States is seen going into the naval x-ray thing, and some little technician leaks that out of there, or that gets leaked out, that can do very funny crazy things to the world.

NIXON: [unclear] understand that as soon as I finish this x-ray I will know.

ZIEGLER: Understand.

NIXON: And just say he had to go for a problem. I either have viral pneumonia or I don't.

ZIEGLER: Yes, sir.

NIXON: And you are to make an announcement. You understand? We are not going to be —

HAIG: You see what we are saying here, Ron, at this juncture is it bad for the president to be ill? I don't think so.

NIXON: [unclear] I can't afford to get sick. I also can't afford to get sicker. Well, if that is what it is, why — get Tkach for me.

HAIG: Yes, sir.

ZIEGLER: A couple of observations I would make. First of all, the most important thing is that you can't afford to get sick. Secondly we cannot — we do not want to announce the x-ray obviously so we've got to handle this very clearly.

NIXON: If it comes out.

ZIEGLER: If it comes out.

NIXON: Absolutely. It would be very —

ZIEGLER: It would be wrong for us to —

NIXON: No, no, no —

ZIEGLER: That's why —

NIXON: No, we go — you are to announce, yes? He had some — the president had some —

ZIEGLER: Yeah.

NIXON: — which is basically true — has a virus and they just checked it now and it was clear, or he had a virus — he has viral pneumonia, and he's going to go to the hospital. It is going to be one story or the other. Fair enough?

ZIEGLER: Well, I don't think it has to be. If you don't have viral pneumonia, I think we should not announce the x-ray. That is why I think the x-ray should be done in great privacy.

NIXON: That's [unclear].

ZIEGLER: Do you see? Because if — well, I don't want to burden you with it —

NIXON: Yeah, I understand.

ZIEGLER: My view is keep the x-ray private. If he has viral pneumonia we say that he has been diagnosed and that we still mention nothing about the x-ray. We just say that he will be spending three times, three days, or whatever it is recuperating at Bethesda [Naval Hospital] I guess — wherever. If it is not diagnosed that way, we keep that private.

HAIG: That's the way we are conceiving it.

ZIEGLER: Because if we announce the fact that he's been there, or he is going —

NIXON: Let's assume that you don't and it will still get out.

ZIEGLER: Yeah, that's probably right.

[TKACH joins the conversation.]

NIXON: Come in. Come in. Whoever it is, come on in.

ZIEGLER: Help me think this through — something — we won't do anything unless —

NIXON: What time are we going over to that place?

TKACH: A quarter to six, sir.

NIXON: Should we go now? In other words, or what time do we go to the place?

TKACH: We have got it all set for six thirty, but we can change it. We can go for — they're waiting.

ZIEGLER: You don't understand —

NIXON: My point is, can the — how secure is it?

TKACH: It is about as secure as it can be.

NIXON: What I meant is, it is about as secure as the people that take the x-rays?

TKACH: Nobody knows that you are coming except one man. The others know that there is a man coming.

ZIEGLER: Yeah, but —

TKACH: Now there will be people that see you, there will be people that see the president.

ZIEGLER: Yeah, but my point is, Walt —

NIXON: Stop.

ZIEGLER: — should we take him over here to this naval box, this x-ray thing? Where — ?

NIXON: There ain't no other place to go.

ZIEGLER: We have all had x-rays there, and I —

NIXON: You can't bring the machine here.

TKACH: No, sir —

ZIEGLER: You don't want to walk —

TKACH: — because it will not give us the detail that we want.

ZIEGLER: My point is that you don't want to walk him through that bottom part where people are all clustered around waiting —

TKACH: Well, see it is about six thirty in the [unclear].

ZIEGLER: But is there a way that we can work it out so that you don't have the wife of the PIO officer of Fort Benning sitting there who would—?

TKACH: There is a way—we do not have to go through that main entrance part. It has already been canvassed and planned and we do not have to go through that main part, is correct. But somebody will see us when you come.

NIXON: Let me ask you—your current preliminary diagnosis is that, assuming this is nothing [unclear]?

TKACH: Well, I know it is still [unclear], Mr. President.

NIXON: Well, I know, but still—

TKACH: [unclear]

NIXON: Huh?

TKACH: [unclear] was there.

NIXON: Why the hell are we taking the x-ray then?

TKACH: Because we want to see how extensive it is.

• • •

NIXON: Well, let me tell you what I have decided. I have decided that if it is anything that has any consequences of seriousness that I am not going to try to go through [unclear] of covering it.

TKACH: Right, sir.

NIXON: So what I want to do, if it is that—I guess I don't want to do it tonight, or do I? No, I should go tonight. What do you think?

TKACH: As far as announcing it?

NIXON: No, going to the hospital. I have decided that I am not going to stick around the damn White House.

TKACH: Right, sir. I mean that if it is serious enough that you can't—

NIXON: If it is viral, if it is even a mild case of viral pneumonia, I'm going to the hospital.

TKACH: Right. We discussed that—the possibility—because this would be the safest thing to do.

NIXON: That is what I would like to do. I would like—incidentally, if we can find—to go to Walter Reed rather than the other place. You don't like that?

TKACH: No, I'll tell you why.

NIXON: Our guys there tell us [unclear].

TKACH: No—[unclear] not. There is a lot of construction work out there, and the whole goddamn place is a mess.

ZIEGLER: Bethesda, that's a very [unclear]—

TKACH: Well [unclear]. It's the best—

NIXON: My point is that if you find something tonight, your view is that we should go tonight.

TKACH: Yes. Yes, sir.

ZIEGLER: You realize what we are dealing with here. I agree with the president. If we—

NIXON: If you don't announce viral pneumonia they will think I have had a heart attack or a stroke.

ZIEGLER: Plus the fact that you do not want to go immediately from that x-ray center.

NIXON: Oh.

ZIEGLER: I mean you come back here, and then we make the announcement, and then we — you know what happens. You've got press centers out at the hospital, and the whole thing. I mean this is the —

NIXON: Screw them!

ZIEGLER: I know. I mean this is the — if the president of the United States goes to the hospital with — well, mild —

NIXON: Do you think this is a mistake?

ZIEGLER: No, sir. I am not saying this as a negative. I am just pointing out that this —

NIXON: I don't think —

TKACH: Another aspect of this too — if the president goes to the hospital it's going to be a national [unclear].

ZIEGLER: No.

TKACH: It always has been.

NIXON: Well, it has been. But most presidents have gone to the hospital with either a stroke, diabetes, or a heart attack.

TKACH: Well —

NIXON: Viral pneumonia is not considered a [unclear].

TKACH: That's right. Actually, President Johnson, I understand as I recall, did go to the hospital with a bad cold once. It was almost a flu — this physician that put him in. Turns out it was a good thing, because he had something up here.

ZIEGLER: The question is not how we handle it publicly. It is a medical decision. I just want to say that — I don't want to burden the president with this, but when we — when he goes — we announce it — we will not benefit by anything —

NIXON: Don't cover it up.

ZIEGLER: Clearly making it — knowing what it is. Don't you agree, Al?

HAIG: Totally.

ZIEGLER: You will have to give the briefings. And Doug will have to —

NIXON: Not bowel movements —

ZIEGLER: No, no, no.

NIXON: None of that crap.

ZIEGLER: No, he never does.

TKACH: These are things I stop. These are things —

NIXON: Temperature may be better — is that what the hell you would say? Prognosis is good, and so forth —

TKACH: Right.

NIXON: — happens to be a precautionary nature.

TKACH: What we do is the best thing of all. We sit down and write a short statement, and read it and that is all, and sorry, gentlemen, that's all there is to it.

NIXON: Well, my view is that you better start making it ready—

TKACH: All right, sir.

NIXON: —because I have decided myself if I am in the residence.

TKACH: Let's think of another alternative. If the x-ray shows minimal or nothing, you still have some congestion in your lungs [unclear]. You have a low-grade fever. You could still go to Camp David. It would be perfectly safe.

NIXON: No. Well, but that's fine. If it is viral pneumonia, get the hell to the hospital. That's my view. Camp David with a low-grade fever is not too good an idea either. I mean I would be better off to stay here, and not be exposed to the weather and everything up there. You know there are different problems—also not for damn work.

ZIEGLER: I just think everyone would feel better if it is anything like that for the president to be in the hospital under good constant care, away from—

NIXON: If you have a low-grade fever, you can be sure—it has got to be described as a high-grade problem.

TKACH: Well, you started out at a hundred and one. You have to start it off at a hundred and one before you call for help.

NIXON: What I mean—no, no, no. Not just the fever. If you don't have viral pneumonia specifically then what the hell else do you call it?

TKACH: Well, you guys could say that we have [unclear] a piece of collapsed—part of your lung is collapsed.

NIXON: Supposedly the lung is not collapsed.

TKACH: Nothing is found at all on the x-ray?

NIXON: Nothing is found except for the fact that I just don't feel well. I've got the flu or something.

TKACH: All right.

NIXON: I just happen to be suffering from an acute virus.

TKACH: This is what happens.

ZIEGLER: With a high fever, a hundred and two is a high fever.

NIXON: Say with an acute virus.

TKACH: As Al knows [unclear] in California.

NIXON: I think you can go to the hospital with an acute virus.

ZIEGLER: And a hundred and two fever.

HAIG: Absolutely, and I think that being in the White House with an acute virus where you can't see anybody is not a good position to be in. You are better off—people feel better when you are under care.

NIXON: In the hospital for purely precautionary reasons.

• • •

NIXON: This entire meeting falls into the other [unclear]. But in the event that it is something that I am going to feel—I'm not to be perfect—I don't feel very well—

TKACH: Okay, let's take you to—

NIXON: [unclear] perfect frankly—

TKACH: Let's just go to the hospital.

NIXON: I should get to the goddamn hospital and lie around there. Now one thing that if I go that I do want though. I want either — if I go, I don't want those Corps men — I don't mind those Corps men, but I want Manolo out there —

TKACH: Right, sir.

NIXON: — so I can push a button or something so he can come.

TKACH: Right, sir. Well, I am going down a subject — it will be an exercise in a waste of time, because of the — you are sick.

NIXON: Oh, what?

TKACH: We could just go to Bethesda from here — the naval hospital.

NIXON: No, but you want to take the picture [unclear].

TKACH: Well, they can take it [unclear].

ZIEGLER: Walt —

TKACH: All right.

NIXON: No, it's better —

ZIEGLER: You make — whatever medical decision you make is, I don't want to — but it would be far better to get a diagnosis so we have got to know where we are because once you announce this —

NIXON: That's right.

ZIEGLER: — we have got to announce it. [unclear]

NIXON: If it is not viral pneumonia, we should say it is a very serious virus. Right?

ZIEGLER: That's right.

NIXON: Suffering from a virus infection.

ZIEGLER: With a high fever.

NIXON: And say a high fever — well, it was only a hundred and one.

ZIEGLER: Well.

NIXON: You can fudge that a little, can't you?

ZIEGLER: We will work that out.

TKACH: Actually, I took —

[Unclear exchange]

TKACH: — the last time I took it.

HAIG: That is plenty high.

ZIEGLER: Well, we will work that out. We will be accurate — just about.

NIXON: No, I took it myself.

ZIEGLER: I understand. But you see, Walt, if the president goes directly to Bethesda and we are unable to say why because you can't validate.

TKACH: All right, I see your point.

ZIEGLER: Then it can escalate anywhere from a heart attack to —

NIXON: A stroke.

ZIEGLER: — to anything.

TKACH: I see. I see.

ZIEGLER: That is why you have got to go privately —

HAIG: X-ray first just the way we discussed.

NIXON: But you can't work it out sooner? They wouldn't be ready? Or it is all set for six thirty?

TKACH: Right, sir. And I will go with you.

NIXON: In any event, if it is just a virus, my inclination is to go. I don't know, thinking of the PR aspects, Ron, people don't go to a hospital for a virus. They stay at home, don't they?

TKACH: Yes, they do, sir. They go to the hospital for a virus.

NIXON: Really?

TKACH: Yes, sir.

ZIEGLER: Particularly a president.

NIXON: What do you think, Al?

HAIG: Well, I think the description on it — it has to be — there can't be any question about that in terms of the description. And that we have to settle before the president goes.

ZIEGLER: Yeah, that —

HAIG: Sounds like a hospital situation.

NIXON: It has got to be one that the people are convinced that he ought to go to the hospital.

TKACH: Right, sir.

ZIEGLER: And you have got to say — quite frankly, we have to get the diagnosis before we think of this — even talk. But let's say it is diagnosed as — hopefully it will be — as a virus. The president does feel bad. He feels weak. He has a high fever. "This afternoon the president was diagnosed by his physician to have a high-grade virus and he's running a high fever. As a result — "

NIXON: [unclear]

ZIEGLER: "As a result, the president obviously feels tired," which he does. "The doctor suggested that he check into Bethesda Naval Hospital today."

NIXON: This will really accomplish what the bastards want, Al. They've killed me. Get rid of the old son of a bitch — people don't want him anyway. We've heard that. The only time the press room will ever be happy is when they write my obituary — only time.

The only time the White House Press Corps will clap

July 12, 1973, 8:41 p.m.
Richard Nixon and Rose Mary Woods
WHITE HOUSE TELEPHONE

Watergate-related coverage on the front page of the New York Times *on July 13 contained no fewer than six different stories, a photograph, an image of a letter from Senator Ervin, and a three-row banner headline about Nixon's proposal to meet with Ervin regarding White House cooperation with his Watergate Committee. Buried on the lower half was a notice that Nixon had entered Bethesda Naval Hospital after running a 101- to 102-de-*

gree fever and being diagnosed with viral pneumonia. What the public didn't know was that after Nixon departed the White House that evening, his taping system was deactivated by Chief of Staff Al Haig and would never record another conversation again. Nixon used the final recorded minutes to let close aides know he had decided to go to the hospital so that they would not be caught off guard when Ronald Ziegler alerted the press corps to Nixon's condition.

Taping in the Nixon White House ended just as inconspicuously as it had begun 3,700 hours earlier, in February 1971.

· · ·

NIXON: Hello?

WOODS: Hi.

NIXON: Oh, because of the — I didn't want you to read it in the papers. We had the x-ray and they did find that it was viral pneumonia. So I have to go to the hospital for perhaps a week — five days — maybe a week, and we think we'll get over it by that time. I think I may beat it by a little, if everything works out. So I just want you to —

WOODS: I think the main thing is you should try and get some rest.

NIXON: [laughs]

WOODS: If you want anything just —

NIXON: I rest all the time!

WOODS: Oh sure, sure.

NIXON: Yeah. God, being in the hospital drives me nuts.

WOODS: I know, it is very difficult. So if you want anything, you want us to bring out FYIs or if you want me to come out there and do anything let me know.

NIXON: Okay, hon, thank you.

WOODS: And good luck.

NIXON: Oh, it's going to be fine. Don't worry.

WOODS: I know it is, but you will be a lot better tomorrow, but try to rest.

NIXON: I told Ziegler to make the announcement because I said it's the only time in his career he will hear the press corps clap.

WOODS: Oh, those bastards. They won't clap.

1973–1974 TIMELINE OF KEY EVENTS

January 8, 1973: *U.S. v. Liddy et al.,* the trial of the five burglars arrested at the Watergate offices of the Democratic National Committee, as well as two accomplices, begins. Howard Hunt would plead guilty on January 11. Bernard Barker, Frank Sturgis, Eugenio Martinez, and Virgilio Gonzalez plead guilty on January 15.

January 20, 1973: Richard M. Nixon is inaugurated president of the United States at the U.S. Capitol in Washington, DC, and begins his second term of office.

January 22, 1973: The Supreme Court rules in *Roe v. Wade,* 410 U.S. 113 (1973), that the constitutional right to privacy "is broad enough to encompass a woman's decision whether or not to terminate her pregnancy."

January 23, 1973: Nixon announces that an agreement has been reached to end American combat in Vietnam, which also marks the end of the military draft and a transition to an all-volunteer military.

January 27, 1973: The peace treaty ending the Vietnam War is signed in Paris; it requires that all American POWs be returned.

January 30, 1973: Watergate burglars James McCord and G. Gordon Liddy are convicted of conspiracy, burglary, and wiretapping. Several key questions go unanswered, such as who ordered the burglary and what the burglars were looking for.

February 7, 1973: The U.S. Senate creates the Senate Select Committee on Presidential Campaign Activities with Senate Resolution 60, more popularly known as the Ervin Committee for its chairman, Senator Sam Ervin (D-NC).

February 12, 1973: The first group of Vietnam POWs returns to the United States.

February 28, 1973: Hearings begin for the confirmation of L. Patrick Gray as director of the FBI. Gray had been serving as acting director since J. Edgar Hoover's death the previous May.

March 17, 1973: Watergate burglar — and former CIA director of security — James McCord writes a letter to Judge Sirica suggesting that some with knowledge of the Watergate break-in had perjured themselves, and that higher-ups were involved, a claim that leads investigators to focus on the White House.

March 21, 1973: Nixon, Bob Haldeman, and Counsel to the President John W. Dean III discuss the Watergate break-in and the subsequent cover-up. Dean tells the president that the cover-up is "a cancer on the presidency" that must be excised or his presidency will be in danger.

April 6, 1973: While remaining counsel to the president, John Dean begins cooperating with Watergate investigators.

April 17, 1973: Nixon announces that members of the White House staff are to testify before the Senate Watergate Committee, a breakthrough in White House cooperation with the investigation.

April 23, 1973: The White House issues a statement denying that Nixon had prior knowledge of the Watergate break-in.

April 27, 1973: L. Patrick Gray resigns after the revelation that he destroyed files from Howard Hunt on the orders of the White House. William Ruckelshaus is appointed as his replacement.

April 30, 1973: Nixon accepts the resignations of his two closest White House aides, H. R. "Bob" Haldeman and Assistant to the President for Domestic Affairs John D. Ehrlichman, as well as Attorney General Richard Kleindienst and John Dean. Nixon publicly accepts responsibility for Watergate.

May 1, 1973: The U.S. Senate votes in favor of a resolution calling for the appointment of a Watergate special prosecutor.

May 17, 1973: The Ervin Committee begins televised hearings.

May 25, 1973: Archibald Cox is sworn in as the Watergate special prosecutor.

June 3, 1973: John Dean tells prosecutors that he discussed the Watergate cover-up with Nixon at least thirty-five times.

July 1, 1973: The United States Drug Enforcement Administration (DEA) is founded.

July 7, 1973: Nixon informs the Ervin Committee that he will not testify and will not permit access to presidential records.

July 12, 1973: The last presidential conversation is recorded on the secret taping system. Chief of Staff Alexander M. Haig Jr. orders the cessation of all taping, but only after 3,700 hours have been recorded.

July 13, 1973: During a private interview with investigators from the Ervin Committee, Alexander P. Butterfield, administrator of the Federal Aviation Administration and a former White House aide, reveals the existence of the secret White House taping system in advance of his public testimony.

July 16, 1973: During his testimony at the televised hearings of the Ervin Committee, Butterfield is questioned about the White House taping system and gives details of how the system worked.

July 23, 1973: The Ervin Committee and the special prosecutor subpoena the first White House tapes and presidential records as part of their investigation. Two days later, Nixon states that he will refuse to cooperate with the subpoena on the basis of executive privilege and separation of powers.

July 31, 1973: U.S. Representative Robert F. Drinan (D-MA) introduces an impeachment resolution in Congress.

August 9, 1973: The Ervin Committee files suit against Nixon for failing to comply with the subpoena.

September 22, 1973: Henry A. Kissinger is sworn in as secretary of state.

October 6–24, 1973: An Arab-Israeli war, later known as the Yom Kippur War, commences when a coalition of Arab nations led by Egypt and Syria attacks Israel.

October 10, 1973: Vice President Spiro T. Agnew resigns as a result of corruption charges unrelated to Watergate. The charges stem from activities going back to when he was county executive of Baltimore County, Maryland.

October 12, 1973: Nixon nominates House Minority Leader Gerald R. Ford to replace Spiro T. Agnew as vice president.

October 19, 1973: In a compromise offered by the White House, Senator John Stennis would be permitted to listen to the White House tapes and prepare a summary for the Ervin Committee and the special prosecutor.

October 20, 1973: Cox refuses Nixon's compromise. Attorney General Elliot Richardson and Deputy Attorney General William Ruckelshaus resign rather than fire the Watergate special prosecutor, as ordered by President Nixon. However, Acting Attorney General Robert Bork agrees to fire Cox. These events would become known as the "Saturday Night Massacre."

October 23, 1973: Nixon agrees to comply with the subpoena for his tapes.

October 24, 1973: Nixon vetoes the War Powers Resolution, which is passed by Congress over his veto. The intent of the War Powers Resolution is to make the president more accountable to the Congress during wartime.

November 1, 1973: Leon Jaworski is named Watergate special prosecutor.

November 17, 1973: Nixon famously says to a gathering of Associated Press managing editors, "People have got to know whether or not their president is a crook. Well, I'm not a crook."

November 21, 1973: The Ervin Committee discovers an eighteen-and-a-half-minute erasure on one of the subpoenaed tapes, which becomes known as the "eighteen-and-a-half-minute gap." White House secretary Rose Mary Woods admits responsibility for a portion of the erasure.

December 6, 1973: Gerald R. Ford becomes vice president.

January 2, 1974: Nixon signs the Emergency Highway Energy Conservation Act, which establishes a national fifty-five-mile-per-hour speed limit.

February 6, 1974: The House of Representatives votes to proceed with its presidential impeachment probe, to be conducted by the Judiciary Committee.

March 1, 1974: Nixon is named as an unindicted co-conspirator.

April 16, 1974: Jaworski issues a subpoena for sixty-four White House tapes.

April 29, 1974: Nixon announces that he will publish 1,200 pages of edited transcripts of taped conversations subpoenaed by the Watergate special prosecutor and the House Judiciary Committee in the hope that Congress will not subpoena any additional tapes. He submits them to the House Judiciary Committee the next day.

May 7, 1974: Nixon signs the Federal Energy Administration Act of 1974, which represents the first energy policy in the history of the United States.

May 9, 1974: Impeachment hearings begin in the House Judiciary Committee.

July 24, 1974: The Supreme Court rules in *U.S. v. Nixon* that President Nixon must hand over subpoenaed tapes to John Sirica, U.S. District Court chief judge, in a major revision of executive privilege.

July 27–30, 1974: The House Judiciary Committee adopts three articles of impeachment against President Nixon, which charge Nixon with obstruction of justice, abuse of powers, and failure to comply with subpoenas.

August 8, 1974: In a television broadcast, Nixon announces to the nation that he will resign, effective the next day.

August 9, 1974: Nixon departs the South Lawn of the White House at 10:00 a.m. on *Marine One* for the last time. He flies to Andrews Air Force Base, Maryland. From there, he flies to El Toro Marine Corps Air Station, California, aboard the *Spirit of '76*, the name he gave *Air Force One* to commemorate the forthcoming bicentennial celebration.

September 8, 1974: Nixon accepts a pardon from President Gerald R. Ford "for all offenses against the United States which he, Richard Nixon, has committed or may have committed or taken part in during the period from January 20, 1969 through August 9, 1974." While Nixon would never admit any wrongdoing, many in the public conclude that accepting a pardon suggests that he is in fact guilty of something.

ACKNOWLEDGMENTS

Our books have benefited greatly from the many archivists who have generously shared their time and input. Special recognition is due to Jon Fletcher at the Richard Nixon Presidential Library for his patience in helping us to find the best photographs. Of all of the exceptional people at the National Archives — too many to name — we are especially thankful for Fred Graboske, Maarja Krusten, James Mathis, Cary McStay, Jay Olin, David Paynter, Rod Ross, and the Special Access/FOIA staff at NARA. Over the years, experts at the Historian's Office of the Department of State have served as an invaluable sounding board. In particular, Richard Moss and Anand Toprani did much formative work, which ended up spread across numerous *Foreign Relations of the United States* volumes.

The field of Nixon studies is currently in its most productive phase. Just a sampling of those who have contributed to this debate in recent years includes Jonathan Aitken, Roham Alvandi, Pierre Asselin, Gary Bass, Carl Bernstein, Conrad Black, Nigel Bowles, Pat Buchanan, William Burr, Len Colodny, Robert Dallek, John Dean, Jack Farrell, Mark Feldstein, Niall Ferguson, J. Brooks Flippen, Jeffrey Frank, Daniel Frick, Don Fulsom, Irwin Gellman, David Greenberg, Jussi Hanhimäki, George Herring, Jeff Himmelman, Joan Hoff, Max Holland, Alistair Horne, Ken Hughes, Walter Isaacson, Marvin Kalb, Laura Kalman, Barbara Keys, Jeffrey Kimball, Henry Kissinger, Stanley Kutler, Mark Lawrence, Ray Locker, Fredrik Logevall, Margaret MacMillan, Allen Matusow, Kevin McMahon, Richard Moss, Lien-Hang Nguyen, Keith Olson, Rick Perlstein, John Prados, Andrew Preston, Lubna Qureshi, Stephen Randolph, Brian Robertson, James Rosen, Thomas Schwartz, Geoff Shepard, Melvin Small, Jeremi Suri, Evan Thomas, Anand Toprani, Tim Weiner, Jules Witcover, and Bob Woodward.

We also benefited from those who reviewed or provided feedback on *The Nixon Tapes: 1971–1972,* including Peter Baker, Nigel Bowles, Jack Farrell, John Lewis Gaddis, David Greenberg, David Kennedy, Ray Locker, Martin Nolan, James Rosen, Mark Strassmann, Evan Thomas, Del Wilber, and Judy Woodruff. In addition, over the years we gained many insights from those personally associated with Richard Nixon at one time or another: Marje Acker, Dick Allen, Bob Bostock, Jack Brennan, Pat Buchanan, Steve Bull, George H. W. Bush, Dwight Chapin, Dick Cheney, Chuck Colson, Tricia and Ed (and Christopher) Cox, John Dean, David and Julie Nixon Eisenhower, Frank Gannon, Billy Graham, Al Haig, Steve Hess, Lee Huebner, Henry Kissinger, Gordon Liddy, Fred Malek, K. T. McFarland, Ed Nixon, Ray Price, Sandy Quinn, Nancy Reagan, Don Rumsfeld, Bill Safire, Geoff Shepard, George Shultz, John Taylor, Ron Walker, and David Young.

At Texas A&M University–Central Texas, thanks are due to Marc Nigliazzo, Peg Gray-Vickrey, Russ Porter, Jerry Jones, Allen Redmon, and Michael Cotten. At Houghton Mifflin Harcourt our editor, Bruce Nichols (and his team), was superb. He heroically edited the manuscript to a manageable size, which was no small task. Two of our friends and colleagues — Julie Fenster and Virginia Northington — helped us in a myriad of indispensable ways. Lisa Bankoff of ICM was a huge booster of this project from the start. Ditto for Lora Wildenthal and Allen Matusow of Rice University. We are grateful to all.

INDEX OF SUBJECTS

INDEX OF NAMES